R. Stadie

MULTISENSORY
TEACHING of
Basic Language Skills

3RD EDITION

twins–twins
transfusion
syndrome

bring in EF
info from
wkshp

MULTISENSORY
TEACHING of
Basic Language Skills

3RD EDITION

edited by

Judith R. Birsh, Ed.D.

·P·A·U·L·H·
BROOKES
PUBLISHING C°®

Baltimore • London • Sydney

Paul H. Brookes Publishing Co.
Post Office Box 10624
Baltimore, Maryland 21285-0624
USA

www.brookespublishing.com

Paul H. Brookes Publishing Co. is a registered trademark of
Paul H. Brookes Publishing Co., Inc.

Typeset by Auburn Associates, Inc., Baltimore, Maryland.
Manufactured in the United States of America by
Sheridan Books, Inc., Chelsea, Michigan.

The individuals and situations described in this book are based on the authors' and volume editor's experiences. In all instances, names have been changed; in some instances, identifying details have also been altered to further protect confidentiality.

A companion activity book, *Multisensory Teaching of Basic Language Skills Activity Book, Revised Edition* (ISBN 978-1-59857-209-4), by Suzanne Carreker and Judith R. Birsh, is also available from Paul H. Brookes Publishing Co. (1-800-638-3775; 1-410-337-9580). For more information on the *Multisensory Teaching of Basic Language Skills* materials, go to www.brookespublishing.com

Library of Congress Cataloging-in-Publication Data
Multisensory teaching of basic language skills / edited by Judith R. Birsh.—3rd ed.
    p.   cm.
    Includes index.
    ISBN-13: 978-1-59857-093-9 (hardcover)
    ISBN-10: 1-59857-093-5 (hardcover)
    1. Dyslexic children—Education—United States.   2. Dyslexics—Education—United States.
    3. Language arts—United States.   I. Birsh, Judith R.   II. Title.
    LC4708.85.M85   2011
    371.91'44—dc22   2011011793

British Library Cataloguing in Publication data are available from the British Library.

2015   2014   2013   2012   2011

10   9   8   7   6   5   4   3   2   1

Contents

About the Editor vii

Contributors viii

Foreword   *Sally E. Shaywitz* xiv

Preface xvi

Acknowledgments xxix

1   Connecting Research and Practice
    Judith R. Birsh 1

2   Multisensory Structured Language Education
    Mary L. Farrell and Gordon F. Sherman 25

3   Development of Oral Language and Its Relationship to Literacy
    Lydia H. Soifer 49

4   The History and Structure of Written English
    Marcia K. Henry 93

5   Teaching Phonemic Awareness
    Joanna K. Uhry 113

6   Alphabet Knowledge: Letter Recognition, Naming, and Sequencing
    Kay A. Allen, with Graham F. Neuhaus and Marilyn Beckwith 145

7   Teaching Handwriting
    Beverly J. Wolf 179

8   Teaching Reading: Accurate Decoding
    Suzanne Carreker 207

9   Teaching Spelling
    Suzanne Carreker 251

10   Fluency in Learning to Read: Conceptions, Misconceptions, Learning
    Disabilities, and Instructional Moves
    Katherine Garnett 293

11   Word Learning and Vocabulary Instruction
    Nancy E. Hennessy 321

12   Strategies to Improve Reading Comprehension in the Multisensory
    Classroom
    Eileen S. Marzola 365

13   Composition: Evidence-Based Instruction
    Judith C. Hochman 405

14   Assessment
       Margaret Jo Shepherd and Eileen S. Marzola 427

15   Planning Multisensory Structured Language Lessons and the
       Classroom Environment ✓
       Judith R. Birsh and Jean Schedler 459

16   Instruction for Older Students with a Word-Level Reading Disability
       Barbara A. Wilson 487

17   Adolescent Literacy: Addressing the Needs of Students in Grades 4–12
       Joan Sedita 517

18   Learning Strategies and Study Skills: The SkORE System
       Claire Nissenbaum and Anthony Henley 549

19   Working with High-Functioning Adults with Dyslexia and Other
       Academic Challenges
       Susan H. Blumenthal 587

20   Language and Literacy Development Among English Language Learners
       Elsa Cárdenas-Hagan 605

21   Multisensory Mathematics Instruction
       Margaret B. Stern 631

22   Technology that Supports Literacy Instruction and Learning
       Linda Hecker and Ellen Urquhart Engstrom 657

23   Rights of Individuals with Dyslexia and Other Disabilities
       Jo Anne Simon and Michele Kule-Korgood 685

Appendix A: Glossary
Marilyn Martin 699

Appendix B: Materials and Sources
Marilyn Martin 721

Index 769

About the Editor

Judith R. Birsh, Ed.D., Certified Academic Language Therapist (CALT), Qualified Instructor (QI), 333 West End Avenue 6B, New York, New York 10023

Dr. Birsh's enduring belief that well-prepared, informed teachers are the major influence on effective instruction in the field of reading and dyslexia had its beginning in 1960, when she met her first student who, although 18 years old, read poorly. The quest to find answers to this puzzle led her to a master's degree in remedial reading and a doctorate in reading and language at Teachers College, Columbia University. After training with Aylett R. Cox in Dallas, Texas, she became a Certified Academic Language Therapist and Qualified Instructor, founding and directing the multisensory teaching of basic language skills courses at Teachers College in the Department of Curriculum and Teaching, Program in Learning Disabilities. Since her retirement in 2000, Dr. Birsh has maintained her commitment to teacher preparation by giving professional development workshops, consulting with private and public schools, writing articles, and working with students with dyslexia. In 2008, she received the Luke Waites Academic Language Therapy Association Award of Service and the Margaret Byrd Rawson Lifetime Achievement Award from The International Dyslexia Association.

Contributors

Kay A. Allen, M.Ed., Adjunct Instructor for Adult Literacy, Neuhaus Education Center, 4433 Bissonnet Street, Bellaire, Texas 77401. Ms. Allen is a Qualified Instructor and a Certified Academic Language Therapist in private practice. She served as Executive Director of Neuhaus Education Center from 2000 to 2007 and is a board member of the International Multisensory Structured Language Education Council (IMSLEC). She is coauthor of *Multisensory Reading and Spelling* (Neuhaus Education Center, 1993).

Marilyn Beckwith, Associate Director (Retired), Neuhaus Education Center, 4433 Bissonnet Street, Bellaire, Texas 77401. Ms. Beckwith has had a 40-year interest in the relationship of spoken language to written language, which resulted in her using multisensory structured techniques to teach basic language skills to both dyslexic and nondyslexic individuals. This interest also resulted in her following related research made possible by advancing technology, which confirms the principles taught to teachers at the Neuhaus Education Center.

Susan H. Blumenthal, Ed.D., Licensed Clinical Psychologist, Private Practice; Founder, The Learning Difficulties Program, Institute for Contemporary Psychotherapy, New York, New York. Dr. Blumenthal specializes in psychoeducational evaluations and cognitive remediation for adults and adolescents with learning difficulties and academic work output problems. She started an innovative program at the Institute for Contemporary Psychotherapy to train psychotherapists to work with adult patients with learning disabilities. In addition, she has trained teachers at Teachers College, Columbia University; Hunter College; and Manhattanville College.

Elsa Cárdenas-Hagan, Ed.D., Director, Valley Speech Language and Learning Center, 535 Stovall Road, Brownsville, Texas 78520. Dr. Cárdenas-Hagan is a bilingual speech-language pathologist and a Certified Academic Language Therapist. She holds a doctoral degree in curriculum and instruction. She works with the Texas Institute for Measurement Evaluation and Statistics at the University of Houston. Dr. Cárdenas-Hagan is the author of *Esperanza (HOPE)*, a Spanish language program designed to assist students who struggle with learning to read. Her research interests include the development of early reading assessments and reading interventions for Spanish-speaking English language learners. She serves as a board member of The International Dyslexia Association.

Suzanne Carreker, Ph.D., CALT-QI, Director of Teacher Development and Vice President of Research and Program Development, Neuhaus Education Center, 4433 Bissonnet Street, Bellaire, Texas 77401. Dr. Carreker works at the Neuhaus Education Center, a nonprofit organization in Houston, Texas, that has offered professional development in evidence-based reading methods to more than 60,000 teachers since its inception in 1980. Dr. Carreker, a past president of The Houston Branch of The International Dyslexia Association (HBIDA) and a current vice president of the national IDA board, is a frequent speaker at regional and national conferences and has authored a number of multisensory curricula and journal articles. She was the recipient of the 2009 HBIDA Nancy LaFevers Community Service Award for her contributions to students with dyslexia and other related learning differences in the Houston community.

Ellen Urquhart Engstrom, M.A., Director of Teacher Training, Groves Academy, 3200 Highway 100 South, St. Louis Park, Minnesota 55416. Ms. Engstrom is Director of Teacher Training at Groves Academy, a K–12 independent school for students with learning disabilities and attention deficits in Minneapolis, Minnesota. Before joining the staff at Groves Academy in October 2010, Ms. Engstrom was a lead education specialist in the Landmark College Institute for Research and Training in Putney, Vermont, where she gave multiple workshops and courses for educators on integrating assistive technology into the curriculum. She has a long-standing interest in language and reading disorders, as well as the assistive technologies that support students with language-based learning difficulties.

Mary L. Farrell, Ph.D., Professor, Peter Sammartino School of Education, Fairleigh Dickinson University (FDU), 1000 River Road, Teaneck, New Jersey 07666. Dr. Farrell earned her Ph.D. at Teachers College, Columbia University. She directs the FDU Center for Dyslexia Studies, through which FDU's International Multisensory Structured Language Education Council–accredited Orton Gillingham teacher training program is provided. Dr. Farrell is also University Director of the Regional Center for College Students with Learning Disabilities, a comprehensive support program.

Katherine Garnett, Professor, Department of Special Education, Hunter College, City University of New York, 695 Park Avenue, New York, New York 10065. Ms. Garnett founded Hunter College's learning disabilities graduate program in 1980. A year later, she launched the HC Learning Lab, nationally recognized in 1996 as an "Exemplary LD Program." Ms. Garnett also developed the special education training for The Edison Schools, as that experiment grew from 4 to 120 sites nationwide. She has spearheaded grant programs; authored articles, chapters, and monographs; served on editorial boards; and served as longtime editor of *The DLD Times.*

Linda Hecker, M.Ed., Lead Education Specialist, Landmark College Institute for Research and Training, Post Office Box 820, Putney, Vermont 05346. Ms. Hecker has served many roles at Landmark College since its founding in 1985. She frequently presents workshops, seminars, and graduate courses for educators and parents and is the author of numerous articles and book chapters.

Anthony Henley, Psy.D., 481 Carlisle Drive, Suite 112, Herndon, Virginia 20170. Dr. Henley is a clinical psychologist in the Washington, D.C., area whose practice focuses on learning and attention disorders. He has worked for more than 20 years as a learning disabilities specialist providing remediation, evaluation, and consultation services, and he has presented locally and nationally on the diagnosis and remediation of learning disabilities.

Nancy E. Hennessy, M.Ed., Educational Consultant, The Consulting Network, 1008 Martins Point Road, Kitty Hawk, North Carolina 27949. Ms. Hennessy is Past President of The International Dyslexia Association. She is an experienced teacher, diagnostician, and administrator. While working in public schools, she provided leadership in the development of innovative programming for students with special needs, statewide revision of special education code in New Jersey, and an award-winning professional development initiative. She has delivered keynote addresses, workshops, and training to educators nationally and internationally. Her publications include articles and chapters on the dyslexic experience, study strategies, and mentoring. She recently coauthored the second edition of Module 6 of *LETRS, Digging for Meaning: Teaching Text Comprehension* (with Louisa C. Moats; Sopris West, 2009).

She is a national trainer for *Language Essentials for Teachers of Reading and Spelling (LETRS)* and an adjunct instructor with Fairleigh Dickinson University.

Marcia K. Henry, Ph.D., Professor Emeritus, Special Education, San José State University, Post Office Box 368, La Pointe, Wisconsin 54850. Dr. Henry received her doctorate in educational psychology from Stanford University. She was a Fulbright Lecturer/Research Scholar at the University of Trondheim, Norway, in 1991. Dr. Henry served as President of The International Dyslexia Association from 1992 to 1996. She now provides professional development for schools and organizations across the country.

Judith C. Hochman, Ed.D., Founder and Senior Faculty Member, Windward Teacher Training Institute, 40 West Red Oak Lane, White Plains, New York 10604. Dr. Hochman is Former Head of the Windward School in White Plains, New York, an independent school for students with learning disabilities. She was also Superintendent of Schools for the Greenburgh-Graham Union Free School District in Hasting, New York. She has been a teacher and administrator and is presently a consultant in both general and special education settings.

Marilyn Martin, M.Ed., has been a learning specialist in private practice since 1991 and has worked with students of all ages with dyslexia, attention-deficit/hyperactivity disorder, and nonverbal learning disabilities. She is also the author of *Helping Children with Nonverbal Learning Disabilities Flourish* (Jessica Kingsley, 2007).

Michele Kule-Korgood, J.D., is an attorney in private practice, with an office located in Forest Hills, New York. Her practice focuses almost exclusively on representing parents of children with disabilities in obtaining appropriate special education services. Ms. Kule-Korgood has more than 15 years of experience in special education law and has represented families who are challenging the recommendations made by school districts in more than 1,000 matters. Her experience as a former special education teacher gives her unique insight into the complex issues surrounding these matters. She is an active member of the New York State Bar Association's Committee on Issues Affecting People with Disabilities and sits on the board of the Center for Learning Differences and the Council of Parent Attorneys and Advocates. She is a frequent speaker at conferences regarding the rights of students with disabilities to secure an appropriate education. Ms. Kule-Korgood earned her juris doctor degree from Hofstra University Law School and, prior to that, obtained a bachelor of science degree in special education and a bachelor of arts degree in psychology from Boston University.

Eileen S. Marzola, Ed.D., Marzola Educational Services, New York, New York. Dr. Marzola is an independent educational consultant who received her doctorate in special education (with a focus on learning disabilities) from Teachers College, Columbia University. She taught for more than 35 years at every level from kindergarten through graduate school and conducted numerous staff development trainings for those interested in improving instructional strategies for struggling learners. Dr. Marzola has been a keynote speaker and presented papers at many national and international conferences and published articles in professional journals including *Journal of Reading Instruction, The Journal of Learning Disabilities,* and *Journal of Reading, Writing, and Learning Disabilities International.* Dr. Marzola was honored by the New York State Federation of the Council for Exceptional Children with the New York State Teacher of the Year Award. She is Past President of the New York Branch of The International Dyslexia Association and serves on their board of directors.

Graham F. Neuhaus, Ph.D., Faculty, Department of Social Sciences, University of Houston–Downtown, 1 Main Street, Houston, Texas 77002. Dr. Neuhaus is a faculty member of the Psychology Department of the University of Houston–Downtown, where she teaches, mentors students, and conducts research in the area of automaticity and reading fluency.

Claire Nissenbaum, M.A., Emeritus Director, Atlantic Seaboard Dyslexia Education Center, Rockville, Maryland 20850. Ms. Nissenbaum is Founder and Emeritus Director of the Atlantic Seaboard Dyslexia Education Center (retired September 2009) and Founding Board Member of the International Multisensory Structured Language Education Council (IMSLEC). Ms. Nissenbaum has been a specialist for more than 35 years. She is a member of the Professional Advisory Board of the Masonic Children's Learning Centers and received the Siena School (Maryland) Award for Significant and Lasting Contributions to the Education of Children and Adults with Learning Disabilities (2009). She has also received the Etoile DuBard Award from IMSLEC for Excellence in Education (2009).

Jean Schedler, Ph.D., Educational Consultant, Schedler Educational Consulting, 23 Borens Shore Road, Elkton, Maryland 21921. Dr. Schedler is an educational consultant in private practice, working with schools to ensure sustainability of reading instruction and intervention at all tiers of implementation, using a systems design approach. She evaluates and designs individualized education programs, conducts academic evaluations, provides teacher training and mentoring, and is a fellow of the Academy of Orton-Gillingham Practitioners and Educators. Her clinical and research interests are in implementing reading comprehension intervention programs in middle and high school settings.

Joan Sedita, M.Ed., Founding Partner, Keys to Literacy, 319 Newburyport Turnpike, Suite 205, Rowley, Massachusetts 01969. Ms. Sedita is Founding Partner of Keys to Literacy (http://www .keystoliteracy.com), which specializes in professional development for adolescent literacy. She worked at the Landmark School for students with learning disabilities from 1975 to 1998. She was the lead trainer in Massachusetts for Reading First and a national *LETRS* trainer and author. At Keys to Literacy, she develops professional development programs that focus on content literacy instruction, as well as literacy planning models for Grades K–12. Ms. Sedita received her bachelor of arts degree from Boston College and her master of education degree in reading from Harvard University.

Margaret Jo Shepherd, Ed.D., Professor Emeritus of Education, Teachers College, Columbia University, 525 West 120th Street, New York, New York 10027. Dr. Shepherd was cofounder of the program in learning disabilities and the Special Education Child Study Center at Teachers College, Columbia University. Unlike most programs preparing teachers for students with specific learning disabilities, the Teachers College program included a required course in multisensory language instruction. Since retiring from the Teachers College faculty in 1998, Dr. Shepherd has developed a graduate program preparing special education teachers at Cairo University and new primary school textbooks for government schools in Afghanistan. She also helped create an in-service program for teachers in rural schools in Afghanistan. She is currently working with Teachers College team on a teacher education project in Pakistan.

Gordon F. Sherman, Ph.D., Executive Director, Newgrange School and Education Center, 407 Nassau Street, Princeton, New Jersey 08540. Before joining the Newgrange School and Education Center, Dr. Sherman was Director of the Dyslexia Research Laboratory at Beth Israel Deaconess Medical Center and a faculty member in neurology (neuroscience) at Harvard

Medical School. He received his doctorate in developmental psychobiology from the University of Connecticut. Dr. Sherman is a former president of The International Dyslexia Association (IDA) and a recipient of two of its most prestigious honors, the Samuel T. Orton Award and the Norman Geschwind Memorial Lecture Award. He also was inducted into IDA's Sylvia O. Richardson Hall of Honor. Dr. Sherman speaks nationally and internationally to parents, teachers, and scientists about cerebrodiversity, learning differences, and brain development.

Jo Anne Simon, J.D., Adjunct Professor, Fordham University School of Law, 356 Fulton Street, Brooklyn, New York 11201. Ms. Simon is an attorney in private practice in Brooklyn, New York, concentrating on disability rights litigation and consultation in higher education and high-stakes testing. A former disability services provider, teacher of the deaf, and sign-language interpreter, she was lead counsel to the plaintiff in *Bartlett v. New York State Board of Law Examiners* through all phases of litigation. In 2008, she testified before the U.S. Senate regarding the impact of the Americans with Disabilities Act (ADA) Amendments Act (PL 110-325) on education and standardized testing. She is currently President of The International Dyslexia Association–New York and a member of the Professional Advisory Board of the Learning Disabilities Association of America. She regularly advises faculty and administrators regarding issues pertaining to higher education and the transition of students with disabilities from high school to postsecondary education.

Lydia H. Soifer, Ph.D., Language and Speech Pathologist and Director, The Soifer Center for Learning and Child Development, 333 Old Tarrytown Road, White Plains, New York 10603. Dr. Soifer is Assistant Clinical Professor of Pediatrics at Albert Einstein College of Medicine of Yeshiva University and is a faculty member of the Early Intervention Training Institute of the Rose F. Kennedy Center for Research in Mental Retardation and Human Development. As a parent educator, teacher trainer, and staff developer in both public and private schools, Dr. Soifer's focuses have been the developmental needs of children regarding their learning, behavior, and communication and the nature of language functioning in academic performance and success. She regularly offers a course in language as it relates to learning and oral language as it relates to literacy, vocabulary development, and language assessment procedures.

Margaret B. Stern, M.Ed., was a math consultant to The Gateway School, where Structural Arithmetic was further developed. She is coauthor with Catherine Stern of *Children Discover Arithmetic* (HarperCollins, 1971) and the *Structural Arithmetic Teacher Guides and Workbooks* (Random House, 1965–1966). She is the 1989 recipient of the Orton Dyslexia Society Award and the 1998 recipient of the Bank Street College of Education Award for Outstanding Accomplishment in the Field of Education.

Joanna K. Uhry, Ed.D., Professor of Literacy Education, Graduate School of Education, Fordham University, 113 West 60th Street, New York, New York 10023. Dr. Uhry teaches teachers about beginning reading and about dyslexia. She is the coordinator of Fordham University's Ph.D. Program in Language, Literacy, and Learning and carries out research on the underlying cognitive processes used by young children learning to read and write. Earlier experiences include teaching reading as an elementary teacher; directing a clinic for assessment and tutoring for children with learning disabilities at Teachers College, Columbia University; and directing the Ennis William Cosby Graduate Certificate Program, a professional development program at Fordham University for teachers in high-needs, early childhood urban classrooms.

Barbara A. Wilson, M.S.Ed., Cofounder and President, Wilson Language Training, 47 Old Webster Road, Oxford, Massachusetts 01540. Ms. Wilson has developed comprehensive professional development programs to prepare educators and practitioners to diagnostically teach reading and spelling, especially to older students experiencing difficulty; these models are included as part of college and university master's degree programs. Ms. Wilson has served as a consultant for several adult and adolescent literacy research initiatives and was invited to speak at the White House on middle and high school literacy. She is the author of four multisensory structured language programs based on the principles of Orton-Gillingham: the Wilson Reading System, Wilson Fundations, Wilson Just Words, and Wilson Fluency.

Beverly J. Wolf, M.Ed., Slingerland Consultant, is a master teacher in the Slingerland Approach, working with children and adults with language disabilities and their teachers for more than 30 years. She has served on the local and national boards of The International Dyslexia Association (IDA) and serves on the IDA Council of Advisors. Ms. Wolf is the author of articles and books about dyslexia and creative activities for the classroom and language-related guides for classroom teachers; she is a frequent speaker on those subjects. She is coauthor, with Virginia W. Berninger, of *Teaching Students with Dyslexia and Dysgraphia: Lessons from Teaching and Science* and *Helping Students with Dyslexia and Dysgraphia Make Connections: Differentiated Instruction Lesson Plans in Reading and Writing* (both from Paul H. Brookes Publishing Co., 2009).

Foreword

This new, third edition of *Multisensory Teaching of Basic Language Skills,* edited by Judith R. Birsh, continues to be a treat—a gift—for anyone interested in teaching reading. I am pleased to share the good news that it has been enhanced still further, if that is possible, and represents an important and welcome update. I have no doubt that this third edition will be the go-to book, a handy and helpful reference, for teachers and tutors engaged in literacy instruction across the developmental spectrum, from preschoolers to adolescents and continuing to high-functioning adults who are dyslexic. The wide-ranging breadth of topics covered is impressive and extremely helpful. This edition includes not only chapters focused on the specific components of an evidence-based approach to teaching reading but also additional chapters that ensure that all aspects of successful reading instruction are provided to the readers. Topics include oral language; assessment; planning multisensory structured lessons; learning strategies and study skills; working with high-functioning adults; literacy instruction for English language learners; multisensory mathematics instruction; technology; and the legal rights of individuals with disabilities, including dyslexia. It is clear from the range of topics carefully chosen that this book has been the result of a labor of love of an experienced, knowledgeable, and pragmatic educator who cares deeply about education, who understands the fundamental nature and challenges of teaching reading, and who is passionate about bringing the highest levels of scientifically based literacy instruction to all children (and adults) who are struggling to learn to read.

As the consummate educator she is, Judith Birsh ensures that literacy instructors and all those who care about struggling readers not only know the basics of teaching reading but also have well-rounded, in-depth knowledge of all the important areas necessary to provide the best and most effective research-based instruction to the whole child. The educator who accesses this volume will not only know what to do and how to do it in teaching children and adults to read, but critically, these teachers will know *why* they are carrying out each step— the underlying theory and historical evolution of thinking updated to the present in each area—explained in clear terms. This third edition will empower teachers, helping them to understand the basis and rationale for what is recommended so that they are not just given "recipes" detailing what to do but are provided with the knowledge that will allow them to judge and determine what is best for each learner in their class. The volume is both scholarly and practical, presenting scientific evidence and forthrightly discussing controversies where they exist. Although education policies change over the years, the material presented in this book is so capably discussed and is so scientifically grounded that even if education policies are modified in the future, this book will continue to stand as an excellent and trustworthy resource about the art and science of teaching reading. For example, response to intervention (RTI) is all the vogue now, and helpful examples of how to incorporate lessons into an RTI framework are found throughout the book. However, should RTI go out of favor in the coming years, the basic knowledge presented here will continue to be sound and relevant no matter what the education policy framework.

I am confident the reader will find, as I did, the new chapters in this third edition extremely appealing. For example, this new edition is enhanced by Katherine Garnett's superb chapter on fluency, a critical but often-overlooked component of reading that is now the focus of both intense scientific inquiry and growing practical clinical concern, especially as the lack of fluency increasingly affects struggling readers as they mature. Garnett fully embraces and explains every key facet of fluency: 1) clearly defining *fluency*, 2) providing revealing data on the high prevalence of the lack of fluency, 3) explaining fluency's developmental progression, 4) elucidating the complex interactions between reading fluency and myriad other influences on reading that work "in concert to produce a full orchestra— skilled proficient reading" (p. 294), and 5) wisely emphasizing that fluency is not an end in itself but rather a key facet of the process of learning to read. Building on this solid foundation, Garnett then provides a highly practical and useful discussion of the essentials of teaching fluency, including the best way to improve fluency (i.e., differentiating approaches at early and then more advanced reading levels), how to integrate fluency instruction with other elements of instruction, and very specific methods along with examples of each of these approaches. The reader will come away with a new, more nuanced understanding of the role of fluency in reading and the methods for improving fluency in all kinds of readers.

Although I have selected Garnett's chapter to explicitly focus on, the chapters in this book meet such a high standard that, given more space, I could have easily written admiringly about Eileen S. Marzola's extremely well-written and comprehensive chapter on strategies to improve reading comprehension in the multisensory classroom; Joan Sedita's chapter on adolescent literacy; Barbara A. Wilson's chapter on instruction for older students with a word-level reading disability; Suzanne Carreker's chapter on teaching reading; Jo Anne Simon and Michele Kule-Korgood's chapter on the rights of individuals with dyslexia and other disabilities under the law; and other high-quality chapters written by distinguished educators.

Teachers will be better informed and more effective at teaching reading, and their students will fare incomparably better for their teachers having read this book. Given the breadth and depth of the topics covered and the attention to clarity and to providing a contemporary understanding of the issues involved, the audience for this book extends beyond educators to other professionals, including administrators, speech-language pathologists, and health care professionals. This book can also serve as a reference source for parents and advocates who want access to the highest levels of understanding of the nature of the problems of struggling readers and scientifically based approaches to their treatment. The extraordinary combination of hard facts about reading and teaching struggling readers and a soft heart for those children and adults who engage in the struggle make this a very special volume that possesses both scientific credibility and human understanding and compassion. It gives me great pleasure to be able to strongly recommend *Multisensory Teaching of Basic Language Skills, Third Edition,* edited by Judith R. Birsh. I learned from reading this volume, and I know all those interested in teaching reading will benefit from reading it as well.

Sally E. Shaywitz, M.D.
Audrey G. Ratner Professor in Learning Development
Yale University School of Medicine
Co-Director, Yale Center for Dyslexia & Creativity
Author, Overcoming Dyslexia

Preface

Reading is reading, or is it? Just a short time ago, it would have been hard to imagine the numerous platforms for reading, writing, and listening to the written word that have emerged recently. However, the reader and writer have to communicate through the words in order to receive or deliver the message. Language is still the medium that has to be mastered for whatever form literacy assumes. Accuracy gets you where you want to go, and fluency gets you there faster.

It is with great optimism and dedication that I present the updated third edition of this textbook in the hopes that such a vital resource will encourage many preservice and in-service teachers and their instructors to explore and discover the richness of the study of the disciplines underlying literacy. Armed with knowledge and practice methods, teachers and other professionals will be able to deliver reading instruction to a wide spectrum of students such as those with dyslexia and other struggling readers who need explicit, direct, systematic, intensive, multisensory lessons, as well as students who confidently soar using the breadth and depth of this information as an added benefit.

The conversation has changed about reading instruction and learning difficulties, along with ways of communicating and obtaining information since the last edition of this book in 2005. At the head of the education reform agenda is the promotion of data-based decision making of response to intervention (RTI) with the possibility of helping to address reading difficulties early and identifying dyslexia and related learning disorders. No longer is the IQ discrepancy model of identifying reading disability the sine qua non. The emphasis on differentiated instruction has risen to prominence as a must for all good teachers to apply in their classrooms. We now know, based on data from assessments of reading skills, at least 15%–20% of the school-age population is in need of explicit, systematic evidence-based standard treatment protocols. The responsibility often falls on teachers in general education classrooms, where one half of students with disabilities exist. What today's classrooms call for are well-prepared, consistently supported, and clinically experienced teachers (Fuchs, Fuchs, & Stecker, 2010).

The goal of the third edition, like the second edition, is to bring to its readers an updated and expanded version that will continue to provide an explanation of multisensory structured language education (MSLE). By keeping track of new scientific evidence about our understanding of language learning disabilities, its biological and environmental bases, and studies on responsiveness to remediation from the fields of cognitive psychology, education, and neuroscience, this new edition provides the foundation for teacher knowledge about the components of informed, language-based reading instruction and effective teaching strategies.

NEW EDITION

One of the major purposes of this new edition is to promote high-quality preparation of teachers for their day-to-day work with students so they can use informed and effective instruction. All of the chapters have been updated with the latest research related to their topics and the strategies for instruction within them. They are aimed at personnel who operate at the highest and most intensive levels of need, recognizing that there are students who will succeed only if this kind of instruction, supported by in-depth knowledge of what to teach and how to teach it, is available regardless of whether they are in elementary, middle, or high school. With these needs in mind, I am pleased to announce the introduction of two new chapters to expand the usefulness of the text-book and to meet the demands for a broader approach to teacher preparation and professional development for a wider range of ages. The first is Chapter 10 on fluency, by Katherine Garnett, a topic that has drawn well-deserved attention because it relates to every aspect of literacy development as students strive to become good readers and writers. The second is Chapter 17, by Joan Sedita, which addresses the emerging field of adolescent literacy and the challenges it brings for students in Grades 4–12. In addition, Nancy E. Hennessy has rewritten the chapter on vocabulary development and instruction (Chapter 11).

Another new feature is welcoming two chapters into the book that were on a companion web site to the second edition. Chapter 22, "Technology that Supports Literacy Instruction and Learning," by Linda Hecker and Ellen Urquhart Engstrom, and Chapter 23, "Rights of Individuals with Dyslexia and Other Disabilities," by Jo Anne Simon and Michele Kule-Korgood, have now joined the other chapters in this volume. Another change has to do with the order of the chapters. It seemed to make sense that handwriting be closer to alphabet knowledge and reading since it comes early in literacy learning. Keeping the language content chapters close in order at the beginning of the book improves the flow of content information. The planning and assessment chapters follow them. Instruction directed at older students is in the next group of three chapters. The last group of chapters takes up executive function and study skills, biliteracy instruction, multisensory mathematics, assistive technology, and the rights of individuals with dyslexia under the law. These all have implications that teachers need to keep in mind as they work with students in their classrooms.

Suzanne Carreker has updated the *Multisensory Teaching of Basic Language Skills Activity Book* (by Carreker & Birsh; Paul H. Brookes Publishing Co., 2011) to include new activities that are tied directly to the chapters in this book as well as to Aaron, Joshi, and Quatroche (2008). With these varied exercises, teachers can reinforce their new knowledge as they get ready to use this language-rich content and practice their new skills with confidence. Together, the textbook and the activity book can help guide teachers by presenting numerous models of evidence-based practices to use in the complicated task of literacy instruction across the grade levels.

HISTORY OF THE BOOK

The idea for the first edition evolved from a gathering of teacher educators beginning in 1990. The Committee on Teacher Education Initiatives of The International Dyslexia Association, 60 people representing a wide range of MSLE programs that prepared teachers to work with students with dyslexia, met yearly to create an accrediting body for organizations that prepare specialists in the education of individuals with dyslexia. Their aim was to set high professional standards for teachers, clinicians, and teacher education programs in the field of specific language disability or dyslexia already existing in college and university setting, hospitals, and other organizations that have MSLE preparation as their function and encourage the growth of new ones. By 1995, the group incorporated as the International Multisensory Structured Language Education Council (IMSLEC). It is presently accrediting programs to ensure that individuals who need effective intervention and their families are indeed receiving help from well-prepared professionals who have been held to exemplary standards of teaching.

Today, IMSLEC accredits programs. Graduates of those programs may apply to The Alliance for Accreditation and Certification to take the National Alliance Registration Exam at either the therapy or teaching level. If successful, they will become either Certified Academic Language Therapists (CALT) or Associate Academic Language Teachers (AALT) and members of the Academic Language Therapy Association, whose members provide quality professional services for students with dyslexia and/or related disorders. Another organization that accredits programs and certifies individuals is the Academy of Orton-Gillingham Practitioners and Educators. (See the section for Chapter 2 in Appendix B for contact information for these organizations.)

During those early collaborative forums of expert teacher trainers and therapists, it became clear that there was a great need for a comprehensive textbook for MSLE instruction that would gather together in one place resources based on research in reading and learning disabilities. In particular, the first edition was designed to reflect the group members' long years of professional experience in the classroom and in one-to-one and small-group practice. It brought together research and clinical experience from the second half of the 20th century, a time rich in innovation in teaching written language skills to children and adults with dyslexia, the most prevalent learning disability. We are truly indebted to the struggling readers who forced us to deconstruct the act of reading to shed light on how to teach those who struggle to grasp even the essential connection of letters and sounds at the outset. Still tuned to the same rich background of experience and dedication, the third edition builds on those priorities with contributions from classroom and clinical experience and ongoing research.

SUMMARY OF CHAPTERS

Each chapter begins with a conceptual framework based on updated research in that specific topic, followed by content knowledge and explicit how-to guidance for teaching the content. The text as a whole contains the essence of informed literacy instruction and is suitable for use as a core text in college and university courses, as a handbook for teacher practitioners, as a source for parents and allied professionals, and as a guide to the field of dyslexia studies. It is a highly useful resource for schools of education, professional development personnel, and teacher training organizations because it offers in-depth treatment of all aspects of written language instruction: references, illustrations, and examples of hands-on procedures; an updated glossary of key terms; and an extensive updated appendix of materials and resources for more information. Terms defined in the glossary are set in boldface on first occurrence in the text. Throughout the book, phonic symbols (e.g., /b/, /ă/, /th/) are used to refer to sounds, except when International Phonetic Alphabet symbols (e.g., /æ/, /θ/) appear in a figure reprinted from another source. This was done because teachers and reading specialists are more familiar with phonic symbols and use them with their students.

Chapter 1, "Connecting Research and Practice," by Judith R. Birsh, stresses the primacy of maintaining a strong focus on research-based practices. The research pertaining to prevention and intervention for reading difficulties is reviewed with the purpose of highlighting the specific information and approaches to instruction set forth in the subsequent chapters. Four major concerns from research are explored so that readers may have at hand ways to think about and apply relevant theory and substantiated practices: 1) What is scientifically based reading research and why is it important?

2) What has scientifically based reading research explained about the components of reading? 3) How has scientifically based reading research advanced our understanding of dyslexia? and 4) How can teachers deliver evidence-based reading instruction with fidelity of implementation so that students learn to read with accuracy, fluency, and comprehension? This chapter provides readers with a working definition of dyslexia (Lyon, Shaywitz, & Shaywitz, 2003) and its relationship to teachers' knowledge of language and evidence-based reading instruction. The implications for teacher preparation and professional development are discussed, with suggestions for major changes in how teachers access intensive preparation to work successfully with students struggling with reading and related issues.

In Chapter 2, "Multisensory Structured Language Education," Mary L. Farrell and Gordon F. Sherman explore why expert teachers have, for generations, been committed to structured language approaches despite the lack of scientific research validation and explanation. They delve into current findings regarding the nature of reading development, the efficacy of certain reading instruction practices, and the multisensory organization of the brain to explain why clinicians and teachers have embraced and effectively used multisensory teaching techniques since the earliest teaching guides were written. The chapter defines MSLE, discusses the role of multisensory strategies in effective instruction of language skills and how it has been implemented in the past, identifies the instructional practices that are consistently supported by research, and reviews recent findings from neuroscience.

In Chapter 3, "Development of Oral Language and Its Relationship to Literacy," Lydia H. Soifer observes that language is perceived and used by humans on many levels and for many purposes, including reading. She helps teachers understand language and its relationship to literacy from a developmental and pedagogical point of view and compares the differences and the similarities between oral and written language to heighten teachers' awareness so they can help their students learn. This chapter describes the inextricable role of language in learning to decode and comprehend, which begins long before children receive reading instruction. Soifer provides an insight into each component of the language system, including patterns of typical and disordered development and their analogous relationships to the higher-level language skills of reading and writing. Oral and written language are viewed as a continuum, and the varying influences of oral language knowledge and use on the development of early decoding processes and subsequent comprehension processes are noted.

In Chapter 4, "The History and Structure of Written English," Marcia K. Henry sets us up to understand the origins of words in the English language, thus freeing teachers from thinking English is just an arbitrary compilation of unrelated fragments of language. Gillingham and Stillman (1997), whose work is the foundation of MSLE, deemed it essential that both teachers and students be aware of the history of the English language so that they could grasp reading and spelling concepts more easily and with greater understanding. Keeping with that tradition, Henry proposes that instruction in phonics alone is not sufficient. Once students have learned the basics of letter-sound correspondences, syllable types, and syllable division patterns, they will need to acquire facility with English words of Anglo-Saxon, Latin, and Greek origin. The historical forces that influenced written English also provide a framework for MSLE teaching of decoding and spelling curriculum based on word origin and word structure. Teachers who understand the origins of words can enhance their presentation of reading instruction, improve their assessment skills, communicate clearly about the features of the language, and convey useful strategies to their students. Henry outlines events in the development of English and then describes the letter–sound correspondences, syllable patterns, and morpheme patterns unique to English words of Anglo-Saxon, Latin, and Greek origin. This chapter also presents sample lessons centered on words from these origin languages.

In "Teaching Phonemic Awareness" (Chapter 5), Joanna K. Uhry emphasizes the importance of phonemic awareness in the early stages of reading acquisition. She explains four important points: 1) What is phonemic awareness and how does it serve as a foundation for early word reading? 2) How do weaknesses in phonological processing disrupt the acquisition of word reading? 3) What should be included in an effective instructional plan for phonemic awareness? and 4) How do we assess to see if the plan is working? At the outset, she carefully defines *ph-* terms that are often confused: *phonics, phonemic awareness*, and *phonology*. She explains how phonemic awareness is a critical predictor of how easily children will acquire reading, how early instruction turns children into more successful readers, and how children with dyslexia have great difficulty with phonemic awareness and other phonological processing skills. Therefore, children with dyslexia need to receive explicit, direct phonemic awareness instruction before and while they are learning to read; otherwise, their attempts may be extremely frustrating. Uhry reviews research on the benefits and effectiveness of phonemic awareness instruction. She also describes RTI using kindergarten children as the example because this is the point at which early identification and prevention is most effective in catching children up to peers in this important foundation to early reading. In addition, several programs are described that may be useful with all children but that are critical to the reading success of children at risk for reading failure.

In Chapter 6, "Alphabet Knowledge: Letter Recognition, Naming, and Sequencing," Kay A. Allen (with Graham F. Neuhaus and Marilyn Beckwith) adds new evidence on the significance of automatic letter identification and naming. Beginning readers who can begin recognizing familiar letter sequences as units have taken an essential step in automatic word recognition. It is difficult for both teachers and struggling readers to believe that "skillful readers visually process virtually every individual letter of every word as they read, and this is true whether they are reading isolated words or meaningful, connected text" (Adams, 1990, p. 18). However, Allen et al. provide us with evidence of the importance of automatic letter recognition as the starting point of successful reading. They advocate for multisensory, structured, sequential teaching of letter recognition and naming. The second section of this chapter describes letter knowledge development in students with and without dyslexia. It presents principles of effective classroom teaching, as well as the instruction, guided practice, and review that *all* students, especially those with dyslexia, require. Important concepts to be applied to reading later, such as *before* and *after, accent, initial, medial,* and *final,* are developed using games and manipulatives. Alphabetizing and dictionary strategies are also demonstrated.

In Chapter 7, "Teaching Handwriting," Beverly J. Wolf highlights the importance of handwriting instruction in early education and in remediation. Wolf gives the rationale for including both print and cursive handwriting as a vital component of multisensory instruction of literacy skills and a component skill for developing a student's functional writing system. Wolf contends that, as necessary communication and educational skills, handwriting, spelling, and composition are highly intertwined. In addition, handwriting is important in developing the orthographic skills for reading. In this chapter, Wolf provides a brief history of handwriting instruction and discusses some of the syndromes related to difficulties with handwriting. Following that are reports of research evidence of the efficacy of direct teaching of handwriting to dyslexic students. An important section of the chapter introduces the general principles and specific information on how to teach print and cursive handwriting using a multisensory framework that integrates handwriting instruction with reading and spelling and ends with a brief discussion of keyboarding and assistive technology alternatives.

In Chapter 8, "Teaching Reading: Accurate Decoding," Suzanne Carreker takes great care to point out that what teachers know and do not know about the fundamentals of literacy directly affects how their students will perform in reading related skills. She states at the beginning, "The goal of this chapter is to inform teachers who provide literacy instruction about the underlying theories and principles, terminology, concepts, and practice of effective decoding instruction." This is the most fundamental chapter in the book. It is the fulcrum on which everything leading up to it and everything following it is balanced. Carreker first stresses the role of accurate and automatic decoding in supporting fluency, which leads to efficient comprehension and reading success. Each element of what needs to be taught in a well-organized decoding curriculum is clearly outlined and laid out in detail: sound–symbol correspondences, structural analysis (six syllable types and affixes), syllable division, accent, instant word recognition, and irregular words with an emphasis on fluency and comprehension. Decoding instruction requires a direct, multisensory presentation of each element (i.e., vowels and consonants) using guided discovery teaching, which is clearly outlined. Carreker also details the necessary steps in teaching decoding to readers with dyslexia which, in the end, helps most other students, too. Readers will find this chapter a rich resource as they begin teaching and one to return to in order to confirm the significance of what needs to be taught.

Although spelling needs the same sustained attention to systematic, explicit, instruction as reading, this is often not the case in many classrooms. In Chapter 9, "Teaching Spelling," Suzanne Carreker explains that learning to spell is not a simple byproduct of learning to read and is not learned by memorization. The role it plays is linked to reading instruction and enhances reading proficiency by heightening awareness of phonemes and orthographic patterns and helps students with pronunciations of words and their meanings. Spelling, however, is far more difficult to learn than reading. In this chapter, Carreker carefully describes the difficulties inherent in translating the spoken words into written symbols in a language like English, although 85% regular for spelling. She points out that, much like reading, the complex linguistic demands of spelling draw on simultaneous integration of syntactic, phonological, morphological, semantic, and orthographic knowledge to reach proficiency. She also explains how spelling develops, the differences between good and poor spellers, and the often-intractable poor spellers with dyslexia who have phonological and memory problems. Carreker emphasizes the active role teachers must assume in teaching the phonological awareness and production of speech sounds that support spelling as well as morphology and word origins. The chapter clarifies ways to teach regular, rule-governed, and irregular words in a suggested order of presentation with examples of multisensory, guided discovery procedures for ease of learning.

The new Chapter 10, "Fluency and Learning to Read: Conceptions, Misconceptions, Learning Disabilities, and Instructional Moves," brings a new voice into the book. Katherine Garnett approaches fluency in all aspects of literacy as an evolving concept. The chapter explores how there are a variety of extant definitions of *fluency*. There are also questions about when to work on it. Garnett also examines the outcomes of students with reading and learning disabilities when given fluency instruction. Readers will find her descriptions of what constitutes fluency fascinating. The connections between accuracy, fluency, and comprehension are discussed in depth. Garnett is careful to include cautions with her wide variety of instructional methods for fluency practice. What comes next is a storehouse of information in the relatively new field of research in fluency, accompanied by interesting clinical case studies and examples of practical applications of teachers working with students who have difficulty attaining fluency.

Chapter 11, "Word Learning and Vocabulary Instruction," also brings a new voice into the third edition. Nancy E. Hennessy's chapter delves deeply into the specific topics of vocabulary and its relationship to reading proficiency; how we acquire vocabulary; the individual differences among students in their vocabulary acquisition and use; the design and delivery of effective instruction; and finally, using technology to enhance vocabulary. Throughout the chapter, Hennessy stresses the interconnectedness of vocabulary with other linguistic components of reading such as phonemic awareness, word identification, comprehension, word background knowledge, and syntax, all doing their part in promoting meaning. Her emphasis on the critical role that adults play in early vocabulary development will intrigue readers and make them want to use the suggested activities with young children themselves for vocabulary growth and enrichment. For students with long-standing reading difficulties and English language learners, it is imperative that they have access to the necessary intensity of instruction, practice, and application of new words and word-learning strategies that she describes at length. Her goals for vocabulary instruction embrace not only comprehension but also the development and access to a lexicon that allows students to not only listen and read with comprehension but also to also express understanding and thinking orally and in writing.

In Chapter 12, "Strategies to Improve Comprehension in the Multisensory Classroom," Eileen S. Marzola points out that since the last edition of this book appeared, the focus on comprehension instruction has broadened and intensified dramatically in this country. She acknowledges the explosion of interest in improving students' comprehension of texts, offering tantalizing guides to improving reading instruction as well as some challenging questions for further study. While the primary factors affecting a skilled reader's comprehension of text have not changed, there are three new factors have appeared to affect comprehension. The first is the growth of RTI as a framework for evaluating the effectiveness of strategies used with struggling students, forcing educators to determine best practices to monitor progress in comprehension. The second is the comprehension challenges facing English language learners, and the third is the growing call to apply comprehension skills judiciously to the Internet, thus invigorating discussion among researchers and practitioners. Marzola offers a brief history of how comprehension instruction has changed since the 1960s. She then presents a developmental framework for comprehension followed by a review of research-supported strategies as well as other promising methods designed to improve this essential reading skill within a multisensory learning environment. Many examples of how to put these strategies into practice, with accompanying graphics and lesson prompts, will help teachers adapt these strategies for their classrooms.

In Chapter 13, "Composition: Evidence-Based Instruction," Judith C. Hochman brings vast experience matched with a review of the research in writing development and instruction to the third edition of this book. She provides the rationale for her clear guidelines and goals for instruction to improve writing and addresses what exactly to teach to foster this growth among students who struggle to express themselves. Hochman enumerates many factors that play an important role in hindering writing, in-

cluding learning and language problems, difficulties with decoding, spelling, word retrieval, and syntax, often exacerbated by a limited vocabulary and limited background
knowledge. Direct, systematic instruction in expository writing is emphasized, with
participation from content-area teachers at all grade levels. This chapter describes strategies for writing sentences, paragraphs, and compositions because, according to Hochman, sentence activities are the foundation for revising and editing skills, which are
crucial in developing competency in writing. There are activities for paragraph writing,
using topic sentences, and supporting details with attention to grammar and usage. For
various kinds of longer expository compositions, three useful outline forms are described, with preliminary activities and directions on carrying out these sequenced steps
in writing. The chapter suggests techniques for revising and editing and lists many questions that teachers can use to help students focus on ways to improve and correct their
compositions.

Contributors Margaret Jo Shepherd and Eileen S. Marzola have come back together
in this edition to revise Chapter 14, "Assessment." Since the second edition, there has
been much rethinking about testing and assessment and their role in driving instruction and the accountability for positive outcomes from instruction. Shepherd and Marzola devote a major part of the chapter to RTI. It is the *pulse* of the chapter because they
say it is designed to enable efficient, frequent, and continuous monitoring of learning
during reading instruction. They also review instruments for identifying students who
are at risk for reading and other learning disabilities and several procedures, in addition
to RTI, for monitoring progress during all phases of reading instruction. There is background concerning federal laws that relate to assessment and identifying learning disabilities and dyslexia. Assessment of progress leads to information of great value to
teachers, parents, and students themselves. The classification of tests into the categories
of formal, informal, as well as norm-referenced, criterion-referenced and curriculum-
based measurements is explained. The importance of early screening of all students for
early identification and prevention of reading difficulties is emphasized with a thorough discussion of tools for screening and monitoring progress through Grade 3. In
terms of assessment of progress or learning of specific skills, Shepherd and Marzola discuss options for collecting formative and summative data. The chapter concludes with
an explanation of the critical aspects of a full evaluation for dyslexia.

Judith R. Birsh and Jean Schedler have revised Chapter 15, "Planning Multisensory
Structured Language Lessons and the Classroom Environment," so that it reflects the
strong interest in finding interventions based on RTI that work with students who are
struggling in the general education classroom. Their commitment to planning MSLE remediation for students with dyslexia and related difficulties is still a major focus for
the chapter. Birsh and Schedler show how to plan and organize lessons that contain all
of the elements for building literacy described in detail in the previous chapters, coupled with ongoing monitoring of progress and sensitivity to differentiating instruction
to meet the needs of individual students. Here is where research on what to teach, clinical experience, and intensive teacher preparation come together. The chapter begins
with a brief history of the development of the multisensory structured lesson plan,
based on the work of the pioneers Anna Gillingham and Bessie Stillman in the 1930s
and 1940s. Next, planning multsensory structured language lessons shows how to bring
together the language concepts with how to teach them according to research-based
principles of learning and instruction. Then, research that supports systematic instruction is considered as it applies to carrying out instruction based on MSLE. Following
that, they describe how both teachers and students benefit from this kind of precisely

planned lessons. There are sample lesson plans to demonstrate how all of the levels of language can be combined into an integrated whole. Two other concerns are explored that impact the lives of students. One is the classroom environment in which instruction takes place, and the other is the adequacy of the preparation of the teachers assigned to do the instruction. Lesson plans cannot stand alone; the classroom environment is also important to consider, such as attention to the space for teaching, including space for students, teachers, and materials; teachers' organization of that space and the learning environment; plus encouraging good student behavior through strong, caring teacher–student connections. All of this depends on rigorous teacher preparation.

Although the title of Chapter 16, "Instruction for Older Students with a Word-Level Reading Disability," might lead you to think this is just about basic skills, Barbara A. Wilson uses the need for word-level instruction as a starting point when working with older students. Recent research cited by Wilson substantiates the necessity of word-reading interventions beyond Grade 3, motivated by its effects on higher level skills. A typical adolescent poor reader often guesses at or misreads multisyllable words. The serious consequences of so many high school graduates, primarily in urban school settings, lacking basic literacy skills has led her to develop a much-needed system of intervention beginning with phonics and moving on to fluency, vocabulary, and comprehension of complex texts aimed at struggling students from fourth grade through adolescence. Many of these older students are identified late as having difficulties and need MSLE that targets what they failed to learn earlier. Wilson also acknowledges the discomfort on the part of both teachers and students who need to overcome reluctance to begin working with basic skills in a direct but sensitive way. She provides a carefully sequenced guide for intensive, systematic instruction that is based on both an assessment plan and comprehensive action plan and includes how to teach accuracy and automaticity of single-word reading; application of fluency with both controlled and decoable text; and the all-important development of vocabulary, background knowledge; and comprehension. There are many examples for teachers to use at each step. Two important issues emerge from this chapter: It is never too late to improve the literacy skills of the older student, and teachers need to be skilled and proficient with multisensory structured language teaching methods to be able to present the systematic language instruction with confidence. Teachers also benefit from substantial targeted professional development and ongoing administrative support.

With the spotlight squarely on the problems of older readers, in new Chapter 17, "Adolescent Literacy: Addressing the Needs of Students in Grades 4–12," Joan Sedita presents a review of the new field of adolescent literacy. She ponders what it means for success in education, work, citizenship, and our personal lives in the 21st century when students lack literacy skills. This chapter discusses literacy as it specifically relates to students in Grades 4–12 and how it has evolved as a separate issue from early literacy development. While the research base is nascent, a growing body of work is developing about how students in these grades learn to increase their reading and writing skills, why some struggle, and what effective instruction looks like. Sedita defines adolescent literacy, summarizes evidence from major research reports concerning adolescent literacy instruction and interventions, and presents a multicomponent model for literacy planning at the intermediate, middle, and high school grades. Because of increasing demands for more sophisticated reading and writing skills as children move through the upper grades, Sedita has devised a literacy planning framework that addresses instruction at two levels: instruction for all students embedded in all subject areas that focuses on vocabulary, comprehension, and content writing and for students with dyslexia and related learning difficulties, which is supplemental and intensive instruction delivered in an intervention setting that focuses on decoding, fluency, and language structure as well as vocabulary, comprehension, and content writing.

In the revision of Chapter 18, "Learning Strategies and Study Skills: The SkORE System," we welcome the contributions of Anthony Henley on executive function; he has joined Claire Nissenbaum in presenting a fuller picture of helping students learn how to study. The chapter focuses on the techniques for helping students to organize themselves and manage their time efficiently, along with specific learning strategies and practical study skills to be adapted immediately and applied to content subjects. Nissenbaum and Henley describe the typical difficulties of dyslexic adolescents and the effect of these difficulties on learning and academic success. With respect to study skills, the most relevant executive function issues are time management; organization, including problems with recognizing and creating structure; prioritizing; self-monitoring; and the ability to change strategies, when necessary. When working with these students, teachers can learn how to use carefully described materials in ways to enhance the teaching of study skills and specified learning strategies. The preliminary step of this study skills training consists of Quick Tricks and Advanced Quick Tricks to help improve the student's relationship with his or her teachers in the content areas. The first main phase of the training focuses on preparing to read a passage of text. The second phase addresses how to clear up high-frequency spelling and mechanics errors and to give the student strategies for completing work and dealing with long texts in emergencies. The third phase attends to critical thinking and developing higher order language skills used in writing summaries and creating outlines. Nissenbaum and Henley conclude that the part that executive function deficits play in this type of work and on the academic achievement of students is profound. This is an area that teachers need to be sensitive to in students who are working hard to learn study skills.

Many high-functioning adults with dyslexia seek to move on in their academic work or their careers yet suffer from chronic feelings of inadequacy, stress, and low self-esteem regarding their ability to learn new information, read, or write. For these individuals, a history of difficulty in the early grades and uneven functioning throughout school are common experiences. In Chapter 19, "Working with High-Functioning Adults with Dylexia and Other Academic Challenges," Susan H. Blumenthal outlines how remedial specialists can work with these individuals on a one-to-one basis, starting with an assessment that includes tests and a writing sample called Educational Memories that recounts school memories. This written passage provides a rich source of diagnostic information and a way for a remedial specialist to get to know the individual. Along with case histories, this chapter presents excerpts from adults' writing samples that illustrate the painful experiences and feelings arising from early schooling that have had an impact to this day. Blumenthal explains the areas in which high-functioning dyslexic adults often need help and names goals of remediation: helping each individual perceive him- or herself as a person who can learn, teaching the individual to be aware of his or her thinking process, and reducing learning-related anxiety. The chapter gives pointers on how to achieve these goals.

Chapter 20, "Language and Literacy Development Among English Language Learners" by Elsa Cárdenas-Hagan, describes a model for MSLE instruction in Spanish based on research in a Texas–Mexico border community for students whose first language is Spanish. The first section of this chapter reviews the changing demographics in the United States and the need for understanding how to best to instruct Spanish speakers who are the largest language minority group in the country. The RTI model and its im-plication for English language learners are discussed. For the purpose of extending the knowledge base of most teachers, Cárdenas-Hagan reviews briefly the structure of the Spanish language, its phonology, morphology, and syntax. Using a multisensory teach-ing approach, she explains introducing literacy development in the students' own na-tive language. Then comes the transfer of language and literacy skills from the native language to the second language using a well-designed, evidence-based instructional approach. Many of the linguistic elements of Spanish and English overlap, and these commonalities can be emphasized in this instructional model. Cárdenas-Hagan offers many examples of similarities in phonology, semantics, morphology, and syntax to ease the transition. The aim is to have students literate—reading, writing and spelling—in both languages by third grade. The final section describes how to serve adolescent English language learners and the future directions for research. What this chapter of-fers is an understanding of language and literacy development within and across Span-ish and English in order to provide effective instruction.

The difficulties students with dyslexia have with language concepts and associa-tions, memory, and sustained attention also affect these students' grasp of mathemat-ical concepts. In Chapter 21, "Multisensory Mathematics Instruction," Margaret B. Stern explains an MSLE teaching approach that helps children discover mathematical con-cepts and relationships through student and teacher manipulation of multisensory materials such as blocks, numbered tiles, and trays of various sizes. Current neuro-psychological and educational research points to spatial understanding as central to mathematical understanding. It has been found that mathematical mental representa-tion, akin to mental imagery, develops from direct sensory experience with three-dimensional, moveable, and comparable things in actual space. Notably, Stern describes students' exploration of the materials and the many things that the students can do with numbers. After developing a language of mathematics as students naturally ex-press their thoughts about their discoveries, the next step is to record the ideas with math symbols. Then, students learn number patterns related to addition and subtrac-tion facts. They also learn how to record math facts as equations. The chapter explains the use of numerous games and activities from which students can gain confidence in such concepts as place value, zero, and the meaning and structure of two-digit numer-als. Next, students learn the concept of regrouping for addition and subtraction. The chapter then suggests a sequence for teaching the multiplication tables. Division, in-cluding division with a remainder and word problems, is addressed in the final section of the chapter.

Chapter 22, "Technology that Supports Literacy Instruction and Learning" by Linda Hecker and Ellen Urquhart Engstrom, has been welcomed between the covers of the third edition from its former companion web site to the second edition. Hecker and Engstrom begin their new version with a discussion of universal design for learning and instruction as a theoretical framework that addresses the challenge of making learn-ing more accessible to diverse groups of students. Because of its ability to lower or even eliminate the barriers to academic achievement for so many students, assistive tech-nology (AT) fits well into a universal design framework. AT has reached an unprece-dented level of sophistication since this chapter was originally published and is now being used with students for reading comprehension and fluency, study skills such as note taking, organization, research, and writing. For students with language-based learning disabilities, there are standard features in computer operating systems, such as text readers and voice recognition capabilities, that provide support and access to students who struggle with reading and writing. There are digitized books with supports for students who have trouble decoding or comprehending. Listening to text while reading; responding to prompts while being asked to question, predict, or summarize text; hyperlinks to definitions; and background information are just a few examples of universal supports readily available and integrated into standard school curriculum. The use of AT in conjunction with learning strategies and remedial reading instruction is particularly effective. The use of AT can also be integral to the RTI model for quickly identifying students who are struggling and responding to them with appropriate interventions. Hecker and Engstrom review the current research on AT, as well as discuss the state-of-the-art technology tools for supporting reading, writing, and study skills for students. They provide resources for professionals to keep up with the ever-evolving research and development of AT. How to match AT to student needs is at the heart of improving student performance. Hecker and Engstrom present various frameworks, resources for selections, and effective ways of using AT.

The other chapter to be welcomed between the covers of the third edition from its former companion web site to the second edition is Chapter 23, "Rights of Individuals with Dyslexia and Other Disabilities" by attorneys Jo Anne Simon and Michele Kule-Korgood. This chapter is focused on changes in the law that affect individuals with learning disabilities. Simon and Kule-Korgood present basic information about special education law focusing on federal legislation and its impact on special education. They bring in landmark cases that led to changes in how children who have disabilities are served. They describe procedural safeguards within the laws. The Individuals with Disabilities Education Act (IDEA) of 1990 (PL 101-476) and its amendments and who is eligible for funding for special education are discussed, along with two other important civil rights laws that protect children with disabilities. How children are identified, referred, evaluated, and receive services under their individualized education programs (IEPs) under the law are also explained. Simon and Kule-Korgood track the latest amendments and reauthorizations to federal laws by the U.S. Congress that directly affect how children with learning disabilities are educated and their rights. Each reauthorization of IDEA and Section 504 of the Rehabilitation Act of 1973 (PL 93-112) brings new opportunities for amendments to these laws, with expansions or contractions of these rights. For educators in need of further information, they have provided a list of resources on the rights of students with disabilities.

APPENDIXES

Marilyn Martin has added new information and organized both Appendix A (Glossary) and Appendix B (Materials and Sources), which appear at the end of the book. The glossary terms are printed in boldface at first occurrence in the chapters. Appendix B offers readers extended and updated resources on

- Training programs, professional development sources, and professional organizations

- Reference articles and books

- Curricula, teaching guides, and activities

- Sources for teaching materials, including manipulatives, for use with students

- Publishing companies and distributors

- Professional journals

- Web sites and hyperlinks to information

- Software and AT

- DVDs

CLOSING THOUGHTS

The content and principles of multisensory language instruction embedded in the chapters of this book form a solid foundation of knowledge in the critical areas of oral language development, phonology and phonemic awareness, letter knowledge, handwriting, phonics, fluency, vocabulary, comprehension, spelling, and writing skills. As with the earlier editions, users can turn to this text time and again at each step of the way toward becoming expert practitioners. Obviously, all of the information cannot be integrated at once. Multiple readings and intensive practical applications in the everyday work of planning and teaching bring deeper understanding of the multilayered content and theory. With the help of one's own students, much of the complexity becomes clear when successful instructional outcomes occur. Like listening to a great symphony or poem several times, each encounter brings fresh insights and new understanding.

REFERENCES

Aaron, P.G., Joshi, R.M., & Quatroche, D. (2008). *Becoming a professional reading teacher: What to teach, how to teach, why it matters.* Baltimore: Paul H. Brookes Publishing Co.

Adams, M.J. (1990). *Beginning to read: Thinking and learning about print.* Cambridge, MA: The MIT Press.

Carreker, S., & Birsh, J.B. (2011). *Multisensory teaching of basic language skills activity book* (2nd ed.). Baltimore: Paul H. Brookes Publishing Co.

Fuchs, D., Fuchs, L.S., & Stecker, P. (2010). The "blurring" of special education in a new continuum of general education placements and services. *Exceptional Children, 76*(3), 301–323.

Gillingham, A., & Stillman, B.W. (1997). *Remedial training for children with specific disability in reading, spelling and penmanship* (8th ed.). Cambridge, MA: Educators Publishing Service.

Individuals with Disabilities Education Act (IDEA) of 1990, PL 101-476, 20 U.S.C. §§ 1400 *et seq.*

Lyon, G.R., Shaywitz, S.E., & Shaywitz, B.A. (2003). A definition of dyslexia. *Annals of Dyslexia, 53*, 1–14.

Rehabilitation Act of 1973, PL 93-112, 29 U.S.C. §§ 701 *et seq.*

Acknowledgments

I would like to thank Sarah Shepke, Senior Acquisitions Editor at Paul H. Brookes Publishing Co., for her gentle prodding and wise advice as I worked on the revisions for this third edition. No question ever went unanswered. Mika Sam Smith, Production Manager, and Janet Krejci, Production Editor, also deserve special praise for their uncompromising pursuit of skillful layout, accuracy, and clarity to help readers understand the content and find the information they are seeking. It is with the deepest admiration and respect that I offer special thanks to Janet Wehner, Senior Project Manager, who held us all to high standards through her patience, skill, diplomacy, and clear insight into the needs of both authors and readers.

First of all, I would like to acknowledge contributors who joined together for only the first edition of this book as a trial run because they believed in the need for such a resource for future teachers: Dorothy Flanagan, Anne M. Glass, Joan Knight, Shary Maskel, Cecily Selling, Lynn Stempel-Mathey, and Margaret Taylor Smith. Contributors from the second edition, whose influence also hovers over this third edition even though they are no longer among its authors, need acknowledgment as well: Joanne F. Carlisle, Holly Baker Hill, Lauren A. Katz, Betty S. Levinson, and Louisa C. Moats.

I deeply appreciate the dedication and collaboration of all the contributors who worked diligently to revise and expand their chapters to reflect new research and new ideas in literacy instruction. I would like to welcome the new authors who willingly coordinated their topics with the existing chapters, thus adding needed information to the book in a seamless way. Suzanne Carreker, too, has devoted her expertise to adding challenging new practice materials to the revised edition of the companion workbook, *Multisensory Teaching of Basic Language Skills Activity Book,* based on revisions to this edition.

Thanks go to all of the readers whose suggestions and criticisms helped refine the content of this volume. Ideas came from many teacher educators and professional development providers, among them: Holly Baker Hill, Harry Burg, and Elaine Cheesman. They gave helpful suggestions on how to improve the organization of the book and make it more useful. I would also like to thank Regina Boulware-Gooden for stepping in to help when asked for her expertise. I particularly appreciate the encouragement I have been given from the many teachers and teacher educators who hold the book as their beacon for instruction in all of the literacy skills.

My gratitude goes to William, my first student in 1959, whose reading difficulties took me on a journey to identify and understand dyslexia. With the help of colleagues and mentors at meetings of the International Dyslexia Association, I learned about mutisensory instruction and the neuroscientific underpinnings of dyslexia and all aspects of remediation and gained a foothold that has carried me through my career in literacy.

And, finally, a broad acknowledgment of all the people across the country, too numerous to mention in person, who are devoting themselves to improving the outcome of reading instruction: teachers, teacher educators, principals, administrators, and parents; researchers, including psychologists, neuropsychologists, pediatricians, and speech-language specialists; and law makers. The work of all these constituencies is reflected in this volume.

With love and gratitude to my children,
Andrew, Philip, and Joanne Hope, and to their children,
Alexander, Abigail, Mark, Neena, Charlotte, and Nikolai

1

Connecting Research and Practice

JUDITH R. BIRSH

In the midst of many cultural treasures,
reading is by far the finest gem.

—Stanislas Dehaene (2009)

Teachers rarely remember how they learned to read, unless they met with difficulty. Some remember they learned by looking at the words and the pictures and putting them together early in first grade. Yet, understanding the complex linguistic tasks involved is crucial to their ability to succeed as exemplary teachers of literacy. To many, reading seems a natural act, whereas it is anything but natural. Oral language is hard wired into our brains, but written language has to be acquired through instruction. Being in charge of the details within words, sentences, and paragraphs comes about from exposure to expert teachers who have the knowledge and skills to deliver top-notch instruction from elementary school through high school. To be ready for such high-level tasks, teachers need to undergo extensive preparation in the disciplines inherent in literacy: language development, **phonology** and **phonemic awareness, alphabet** knowledge, handwriting, decoding, spelling, **fluency, vocabulary, comprehension,** composition, testing and **assessment,** lesson planning, and behavior management, along with **study skills,** history of the English language, use of technology, and the needs of older struggling readers.

The spotlight on literacy is intense due to several developments. One major concern is the movement toward data analysis and research to improve instruction. For example, following the No Child Left Behind Act of 2001 (PL 107-110) legislation and the subsequent Reading First initiative have come 1) **response to intervention (RTI)** as a way of assessing risk of failure, benchmarking progress, and providing **differentiated instruction** to students struggling with literacy; 2) the creation of the Common Core State Standards Initiative: Preparing America's Students for College and Career (Council of Chief State School Officers & National Governors Association Center for Best Practices, 2010); and the adoption of The International Dyslexia Association's (IDA; 2010) set of *Knowledge and Practice Standards for Teachers of Reading.* Using research-based information, each "movement" is an attempt to bring high-level content and best practices to schools to improve the delivery of instruction equally and to uphold high standards for administrators, teachers, parents, and students. Along with these efforts are organizations formed to change states' licensure for teaching reading and attempts to change how teachers are prepared in schools of education and through professional development in alternative pathways.

Teachers with a wide range of experience and a strong foundation of knowledge enhanced by scientifically based reading research from which to make judgments about what to teach, how to teach it, when to teach it, and to whom, ensure a successful outcome when working with all students but especially with students at risk of failing to learn to read or with those who have already fallen behind (Aaron, Joshi, & Quatroche, 2008; McCardle, Chhabra, & Kapinus, 2008). When a child struggles with written language, none of the myriad layers of language processing can be taken for granted. Differentiated instruction is language based—intensive, systematic, direct, and comprehensive. Each individual is different and brings unique cognitive and **linguistic** strengths and weaknesses to the task. Therefore, teachers who work at prevention, intervention, or remediation require a foundation based on scientific evidence and need to be informed about the complex nature of instruction in reading and related skills. Fortunately, since the early 1980s, a broad range of individuals have made major contributions to research on the component processes of learning to read, reading disabilities, and **models** of effective instruction.

This keen interest in the newly acknowledged science of reading has involved general and special educators, psychologists, linguists, neuroscientists, geneticists, speech-language specialists, parents, and children with and without reading difficulties. What has changed in reading instruction is that it is no longer based on opinion but is being informed by science in an orderly progression of research data that shows what works. This volume's main focus is scientifically based instruction in reading and related literacy skills. In this chapter, four major concerns from research are explored so that teachers have ways to think about and apply relevant theory and substantiated practices.

1. What is scientifically based reading research and why is it important?

2. What has scientifically based reading research explained about the components of reading?

3. How has scientifically based reading research advanced our understanding of **dyslexia?**

4. How can teachers deliver evidence-based reading instruction with fidelity of implementation so that students learn to read with accuracy, fluency, and comprehension?

DEFINITION AND IMPORTANCE OF SCIENTIFICALLY BASED RESEARCH

Scientifically based research, also referred to as **evidence-based research,** gathers evidence to answer questions and bring new knowledge to a field of study so that effective practices can be determined and implemented. Scientific research is a process.

A scientist develops a theory and uses it to formulate hypotheses. A study is designed to evaluate the hypotheses. The methods used in the study depend on the hypotheses, and these methods result in findings. The scientist then integrates what is found from this particular study into the body of knowledge that has accumulated around the research question. As such, scientific research is a cumulative process that builds on understandings derived from systematic evaluations of questions, models, and theories (Fletcher & Francis, 2004). Lyon and Chhabra (2004) underscored that good evidence is derived from a study that asks clear questions that can be answered empirically, selects and implements valid research methods, and accurately analyzes and interprets data.

Using **randomized controlled trials** is a critical factor in establishing strong evidence for what works (causation) in **experimental** research. This means that individuals in an intervention study are randomly assigned to experimental and control groups. With randomized controlled trials, all variables are held constant (e.g., gender, age, demographics, skill levels) except the one variable that is hypothesized to cause a change. This allows the researcher to show a causal relationship between the intervention and the **outcomes;** in other words, the intervention caused a change, thus establishing what does and does not work. **Quasi-experimental research** attempts to determine cause and effect without strict randomized controlled trials and is valid but less reliable. The **meta-analysis** done by the National Reading Panel (NRP; National Institute of Child Health and Human Development [NICHD], 2000) reviewed both experimental and quasi-experimental studies of instructional practices, procedures, and techniques in real classrooms. The NRP's criteria closely followed accepted practices for evaluating research literature found in other scientific disciplines such as medicine and in behavioral and social research (Keller-Allen, 2004).

Peer review and the **convergence of evidence** should also be considered. Peer review stipulates that the results of an intervention study be scrutinized and evaluated by a group of independent researchers with expertise and credentials in that field of study before the results are publicly reported in a journal article. Another avenue of critical review is through presentations and papers that are scrutinized by fellow scientists to bring objectivity and reliability into the process of educational research (Fletcher & Francis, 2004). Convergence of evidence derives from the identical replication of a study in a similar population by other researchers because the outcomes from a single study are not sufficient to generalize across all populations. Other caveats for educational research are to be clear about the specific intervention, monitor it, and then use valid and reliable outcome measures (Reyna, 2004).

There are two kinds of educational research methodology: qualitative and quantitative. **Qualitative research** involves observing individuals and settings and relies on observation and description of events in the immediate context. **Ethnographic observation** is an example of qualitative research in which researchers observe, listen, and ask questions to collect descriptive data in order to understand the content, context, and dynamics of an instructional setting. Qualitative research can be scientific if it follows the principles of scientific inquiry. It is difficult to say what works or does not work (causation) in qualitative research; however, this kind of research affords a picture of what is happening and a description of the context.

Quantitative research uses large numbers of individuals to generalize findings to similar settings using statistical analyses. Quantitative research must use experimental or quasi-experimental design methods to gather data. The debate over whether quantitative or qualitative research is better obscures the principle that it is not the method of observation (qualitative versus quantitative) that qualifies a study as providing rigorous evidence; it is the design that follows scientific inquiry that qualifies a study as rigorous. For example, it is essential to have enough individuals in well-matched groups in a study so that statistical significance between groups can be established. A new broadened definition of the What Works Clearinghouse's "gold standard" of research design is beginning to emerge. Regression-discontinuity (Schochet et al., 2010), which uses a cut-off point instead of random assignment in making comparison groups, and the use of single-case studies (Kratochwill et al., 2010) are now being considered along with randomized controlled trials. This expansion to include both experimental and descriptive research paradigms will be interesting to follow for their effect on the outcomes of interventions in reading. The What Works Clearinghouse, a section of the federal Institute of Education Sciences, reviews experimental research on program impact. The U.S. Department of Education, Institute of Education Sciences (2008), is a resource that further explains evidence-based research and provides educational practitioners with tools to distinguish practices supported by rigorous evidence from those that are not. To find out what works in education, see the What Works Clearinghouse web site (http://ies.ed.gov/ncee/wwc/), and see the Florida Center for Reading Research web site (http://www.fcrr.org) for excellent reviews of programs.

The National Reading Panel

In 1997, the U.S. Congress asked the director of the NICHD, in consultation with the Secretary of Education, to convene a national panel to assess the status of research-based knowledge, including the effectiveness of various approaches for teaching children to read (NICHD, 2000).

Thus, unlike previous inquiries, the NRP set about analyzing experimental and quasi-experimental research literature, using rigorous research standards, to determine specifically how "critical reading skills are most effectively taught and what instructional methods, materials, and approaches are most beneficial for students of varying abilities" (NICHD, 2000, p. 1-1). The NRP intensively reviewed the following topics:

- Phonemic awareness

- **Phonics** instruction

- Fluency

- Comprehension

- Teacher education and reading instruction

- Computer technology and reading instruction

The findings from the meta-analyses (i.e., longitudinal studies, cognitive and linguistic studies, studies in neurobiology) by the subgroups in this list of topics reviewed by the 14 members of the NRP (NICHD, 2000) revealed consensus among effective educators on what works in reading instruction. As a result of the review of the literature, the panel arrived at some very strong conclusions (Pressley, 2002) and identified the following five critical components that are essential for teaching young children to read:

1. Phonemic awareness

2. Phonics

3. Vocabulary development

4. **Reading fluency,** including oral reading skills

5. Reading comprehension strategies

Research by itself cannot improve practice. The importance of converging scientific evidence in reading research and its relationship to practice, however, has begun to gain new prominence in the thinking of not only teacher educators and teachers but also among government officials on the federal, state, and local levels charged with educational reform; business people; and parents and caregivers of young children. The report of the most recent National Assessment of Educational Progress (NAEP) indicated that fourth-grade reading scores were unchanged from 2007, with 67% of students performing at or above *basic* level and 33% performing at or above *proficient*. Eighth-grade reading scores showed 75% of students performed at or above *basic* level and 32% at or above *proficient*. Achievement gaps still persist, however, with no significant changes among racial/ethnic groups, gender, or types of schools (National Center for Education Statistics, 2009). The tests measured knowledge of literary and informational reading comprehension. We must adopt more effective instructional practices and policies to close the reading gap and to solve the problem of pervasive, persistent reading failure. Through the ongoing, dynamic process of scientifically based reading research, the causes of reading failure and the practices that help children learn to read, including those children most at risk, are being identified. Snow (2004) emphasized that knowing which practices work to produce specific results in the critical areas of reading instruction could help many teachers use methods and approaches in their daily work that are consonant with research-based evidence and could thus help significantly more children learn to read proficiently.

SCIENTIFICALLY BASED RESEARCH EXPLAINS THE COMPONENTS OF READING

While researchers were studying learning disabilities such as dyslexia, they learned how reading develops in readers who have impairments and who do not have impairments. This led to data on more than 42,000 readers participating in NICHD-sponsored studies of both poor and skilled readers. These findings have straightforward, practical implications for teachers of typically developing readers and those students with dyslexia and other related co-occurring problems (Lyon, 2004).

There is a broad scientific consensus based on empirical evidence on what is needed to become a good reader. Two important sources for this agreement are the National Research Council report (Snow, Burns, & Griffin, 1998) and the NRP report (NICHD, 2000). This consensus on the high-priority skills that children must acquire as they learn to read is based on clear evidence.

How the five essential components of reading instruction are taught based on accumulated scientific evidence subsequently became the essential ingredients of Reading First grants as part of the No Child Left Behind Act to improve reading instruction for kindergarten through third-grade students throughout the United States. These are sometimes referred to as the *building blocks for reading* (Partnership for Reading, 2003). Most educators agree that no one single reading component is sufficient in itself. Students need to acquire all of the combined essential components in a balanced, comprehensive reading program to become successful readers. The chapters in this book give detailed analyses of the research and provide the reader with in-depth discussions of approaches for developing and implementing instruction in each of these component areas. Let's consider the conclusions of the NRP on essential reading skills instruction.

Phonemic Awareness

Phonemic awareness is "the ability to notice, think about and work with the individual sounds in words" (Partnership for Reading, 2003, p. 2). The NRP meta-analysis confirmed that phonemic awareness, along with knowing the names and shapes of both lower- and uppercase letters, is a key component "that contributes significantly to the effectiveness of beginning reading and spelling instruction" (NICHD, 2000, p. 2-43). Phonemic awareness plays a vital role in learning to read because it helps children connect spoken language to written language. It helps expose the underlying sounds in language that consequently relate to the alphabetic symbols on the printed page. Phonemic awareness has a causal relationship with literacy achievement, and understanding it in kindergarten is the single best predictor of later reading and spelling achievement in first and second grade. In kindergarten, phonemic awareness predicts growth in word-reading ability (Torgesen, Wagner, & Rashotte, 1994). Children at risk because of early speech-language impairments and those with dyslexia perform more poorly on tests of phonemic awareness than typically developing children. When children do not have good word-identification skills, they fall behind in reading, and without appropriate intervention, they have only a 1 in 8 chance of catching up to grade level (Juel, 1988). Without the ability to think about and manipulate the individual sounds in words, beginning and remedial readers risk falling behind or never catching up to their peers.

Isolating and manipulating sounds in words using oral segmenting and **blending** activities helps children learn the **alphabetic principle** as they are learning to read and spell. Learning letter names and shapes is an important adjunct to these skills. Although phonemic awareness is a means to understanding and using letters and sounds for reading and writing, it is not an end in itself (see NICHD, 2000, p. 2-43). Phonemic awareness stands as one of the major components of a comprehensive program of instruction when taught in small groups and in moderate amounts. Children differ in their need for instruction, but phonemic awareness benefits everyone, especially those with little experience with detecting and manipulating speech sounds (see Chapter 5).

Phonics

Systematic and explicit instruction in *phonics,* the relationship between letters or letter **combinations** in written language (**graphemes**) and the approximately 44 sounds in English spoken language (**phonemes**), has proven effective for improving children's reading (Adams, 1990; NICHD, 2000; Partnership for Reading, 2003). It is best introduced early in kindergarten and first grade, which leads to accurately recognizing familiar words and decoding unfamiliar words. Teaching phonics is beneficial for children from all socioeconomic groups, especially when it is accompanied by memory aids such as **key words** for sounds, pictures, and articulatory gestures (McCardle et al., 2008).

Eden and Moats pointed out the reciprocal relationship between phonemic awareness and reading in that "learning how letters represent sounds (phonology) and seeing words in print (**orthography**) helps novice readers to attend to speech sounds" (2002, p. 1082). Phonics, deemed valuable and essential, should be integrated with other types of reading instruction in a comprehensive program that includes all of the reading components listed earlier in this chapter. The NRP (NICHD, 2000) found solid support for using systematic phonics rather than an unsystematic approach or no phonics at all because systematic phonics provided a more significant contribution to children's growth in reading. It has a great impact on children in kindergarten and first grade, with the greatest effects shown with beginning readers who are at risk and of low socioeconomic status (Keller-Allen, 2004). However, **effect sizes** among children from low- and middle-income homes for the outcomes of phonics instruction did not differ, leading Ehri, Nunes, Stahl, and Willows to conclude that "phonics instruction contributes to higher performance in reading in both low and middle class students"

(2001, p. 418). It is clear that systematic phonics has its greatest effect in the early grades; that is, in kindergarten and first grade for all beginning readers, children at risk, and children diagnosed with reading disabilities. Phonics instruction at any age, however, facilitates learning to read.

Another important finding of the NRP meta-analysis was that positive results were produced whether through one-to-one tutoring, in small-group instruction, or in whole-class programs (Ehri et al., 2001). Furthermore, systematic phonics can be taught through **synthetic** phonics, **analytic** phonics, phonics through spelling, analogy phonics, and **embedded phonics** (see Ehri, 2004, for descriptions of these methods). Pressley (2002) agreed that phonics instruction calls for more than a one-size-fits-all approach. Many variations are possible as long as the program is both extensive and systematic. One added benefit of systematic phonics instruction is its impact on beginning readers' comprehension. Subsequent to the NRP report, researchers have found that phonics does indeed have benefits for struggling readers who are older when taught systematically (Connor, Morrison, & Underwood, 2007). In many ways, Jeanne Chall (1967) said it best when she said we need both phonics and meaning-focused activities in balanced reading programs (see Chapter 8).

Fluency

Beginning readers need to be fluent in letter naming, knowledge of sounds, and phonemic awareness activities. *Fluency*, however, is most often referred to as "the ability to read a text accurately and quickly, recognize words, [and] gain meaning from text" (Partnership for Reading, 2003, p. 22). This is a key concept, with well-documented converging evidence supporting the connection between fluency and reading comprehension (Snow et al., 1998). Without the advantage of fluency, children remain slow and laborious readers. Meaningful improvements in reading fluency are well documented when a range of well-described instructional approaches are used (see Chapter 10). Major approaches to teaching fluency include **guided oral reading** procedures that include repeated oral reading, with modeling by the instructor, in which students receive feedback from peers, parents, or teachers. Guided oral reading and encouraging students to read are effective in improving fluency and overall reading achievement (see NICHD, 2000). Gaps in fluency remain in older students, however, in both those with extremely low word-level reading skills and those with good, compensated word accuracy skills.

Vocabulary

Knowing word meanings is a major contributor to students' ability to communicate and comprehend text. The NRP analyses confirmed that there is a strong relationship between vocabulary learning and comprehension gains (NICHD, 2000). Although the database of studies on vocabulary instruction and measurement that qualified for the NRP review was small, the panel did find some trends in the data that have implications for instruction:

- Vocabulary should be taught both directly and indirectly.

- Repetition and multiple exposures to vocabulary items are important.

- Learning in rich contexts is valuable for vocabulary learning.

- Vocabulary tasks should be restructured when necessary.

- Vocabulary learning should entail active engagement in learning tasks.

- Computer technology can be used to help teach vocabulary.

- Vocabulary can be acquired through **incidental learning**.

- How vocabulary is assessed and evaluated can have a differential effect on instruction.

- Dependence on a single vocabulary instruction method will not result in optimal learning.

See Chapter 11 for research and teaching activities for vocabulary.

Comprehension

Comprehension is making sense of what we read and depends on good word **recognition,** fluency, vocabulary, world knowledge, and verbal reasoning. Good instruction calls for attention to comprehension when children listen to books read aloud and as soon as they begin reading text. Since the 1980s, research on comprehension instruction has supported using specific **cognitive strategies,** either individually or in concert, to help readers understand and remember what they read (NICHD, 2000). Direct instruction of these cognitive strategies in the classroom leads to active involvement of the readers and helps readers across the range of ability. Chapter 12 presents many research-supported strategies as well as other promising methods designed to improve this essential reading skill within a multisensory learning environment.

Metacognition is thinking about thinking. Good readers think about what they are reading in complex ways. The research suggests that students will improve in their ability to comprehend text through modeling and metacognitive instruction by the teacher. Effective strategies include question answering and generation, summarization, graphic and semantic organizers such as story maps, **comprehension monitoring,** and **cooperative learning.** Many opportunities for discussion and writing enhance comprehension. The evidence reviewed by the NRP led the panel to conclude that instruction that provides a "variety of reading comprehension strategies leads to increased learning of the strategies, to specific transfer of learning, to increased memory and understanding of new passages, and in some cases, general improvements in comprehension" (NICHD, 2000, p. 4-52).

Other Factors Critical to Reading

The research cited in this chapter has focused mainly on reading development and reading instruction from kindergarten to third grade. It has prominently addressed phonemic awareness, phonics, and reading **decodable texts.** More research needs to be done in the areas of fluency, vocabulary, and comprehension, especially as they relate to older age groups and other special populations such as **English language learners** (McCardle & Chhabra, 2004). Along with these five broad areas of skills that are needed to learn to read, scientifically based reading research has identified other critical factors needed for children to become good readers (see Table 1.1).

SCIENTIFICALLY BASED READING RESEARCH HAS ADVANCED OUR UNDERSTANDING OF DYSLEXIA

Understanding dyslexia is one way to have a sophisticated understanding of the reading process. Following is the definition of *dyslexia* adopted in 2003 by The International Dyslexia Association (IDA) in collaboration with the NICHD.

Table 1.1.   Consensus from scientifically based research on learning to read and write

Oral language—Long before children begin to read, they need solid oral language and literacy experiences at home and in preschool that will support them later in acquiring abstract linguistic skills necessary for reading. These include language play such as saying rhymes; listening to, discussing, and examining books; developing oral vocabulary and verbal reasoning; and learning the purposes of reading along with large and fine motor writing activities. Exposure to reading aloud and oral language play fosters development of sounds and symbols and a language about reading. Oral language is the foundation of comprehension and helps the reader use decoding strategies.

Phonemic awareness—Reading development depends on acquiring phonemic awareness and other phonological processes. Phonemic awareness is the ability to understand the sound structure in spoken words. To learn to read, however, children also must be able to pay attention to the sequence of sounds or phonemes in words and to manipulate them. This is difficult because of the coarticulation of the separate sounds in spoken words. Children learn to do this by engaging in intensive oral play activities of sufficient duration, such as identifying and making rhymes, counting and working with syllables in words, segmenting initial and final phonemes, hearing and blending sounds, analyzing initial and final sounds of words, and segmenting words fully before learning to read and during beginning reading. This training facilitates and predicts later reading and spelling achievement.

Alphabet knowledge—It is essential that children learn the alphabet and be able to say the names of the letters, recognize letter shapes, and write the letters. They need to know the difference between upper- and lowercase letters. These skills are powerful predictors of reading success.

Phonics—Along with instruction on letter names, children need well-designed and focused phonics instruction to learn predictable letter–sound correspondences. Fast and accurate decoding of familiar and unfamiliar words and spelling rest on the alphabetic principle: how the written spellings of words systematically represent the phonemes in the spoken words. The efficacy of the code emphasis approach is supported by decades of research. It requires explicit, systematic, and sequential instruction for at least 25% of students; without this instruction, students are likely to fail.

Fluency—Fluency and comprehension depend on accuracy and speed of word recognition. Slow decoders are poor at comprehension due to reduced attentional and memory resources. Adequate oral reading fluency rates with connected texts leads to better comprehension. There are reading fluency goals for first through eighth grade supported by research (Hasbrouck & Tindal, 2006). Overall, it is important to note that fluency needs to be addressed in each of the components of reading instruction.

Vocabulary development—Vocabulary facilitates phonological awareness and word recognition in students and is important for reading comprehension. The predictive value for vocabulary in later reading comprehension and the relationship between kindergarten and first-grade word knowledge and elementary, middle, and secondary reading performance have been documented. Vocabulary growth benefits from repeated exposure to word meanings and use in context and from studying morphology with direct, explicit instruction across the curriculum. Wide reading mitigates against reduced exposure to rich vocabulary, which is often the experience of struggling readers.

Comprehension—Comprehension depends on accurate, fluent decoding skills and efficient, active comprehension strategies, including monitoring for understanding while reading. Comprehension also depends on activating relevant background knowledge and is related strongly to oral language comprehension and vocabulary growth. Along with explicit vocabulary instruction and understanding sentence structure, teachers should model and use direct teaching of metacognitive strategies such as questioning, predicting, making inferences, clarifying misunderstandings, and summarizing, and using graphic organizers while reading should be included in comprehension instruction. Written expression reinforces students' comprehension skills.

Spelling—English orthography is 87% reliable. When children are familiar with the spelling regularities of English, their reading and spelling are strengthened. Opportunities to apply the predictable and logical rules and spelling patterns that match the reading patterns being learned give children a double immersion in the information. Spelling is an essential and interconnected complement to reading instruction as it enhances reading proficiency by reinforcing sounds and letter patterns (Adams, 1990). Explicit instruction in the sounds of the language and exposure to consistent and frequent letter patterns and spelling rules lead to successful spelling outcomes.

Handwriting—Manuscript and cursive handwriting is a vital component of multisensory instruction of literacy skills and a component skill for developing a functional writing system (Berninger & Wolf, 2009). Formal, multisensory handwriting instruction reinforces students' knowledge of letter shapes and letter formation while connecting them to letter names and sounds in beginning reading. Later, both legibility and fluency aid students in the quality of their compositions, improve spelling, and help in proofreading and notetaking. Motor skills in handwriting can be improved with practice. Instruction in accurate keyboarding is an appropriate use of technology with students.

(continued)

Table 1.1.   *(continued)*

Written expression—Three areas need to be addressed in written expression: the purpose and structure of sentences, including grammar, word choice, and sentence expansion; step-by-step building of paragraphs and compositions with the emphasis on developing ideas for expository text; and revising and editing compositions. Direct, explicit instruction is needed in grammar, punctuation, and capitalization, using multisensory methods differentiated for students' unique abilities and weaknesses. Teaching writing should contain oral language practice activities preliminary to paper-and-pencil tasks. Working on complex ideas for sentence generation has an effect on reading comprehension.

Well-prepared teachers able to implement research-based instruction—Well-prepared, knowledgeable, and accomplished teachers who can screen students for potential problems, analyze their work, monitor progress, set goals and plan efficiently, provide opportunities for constructive feedback, and review and practice while continuing to learn about effective practices are the mainstay of children's success in learning to read and write.

Dyslexia is a specific learning disability that is neurobiological in origin. It is characterized by difficulties with accurate and/or fluent word recognition and by poor spelling and decoding abilities. These difficulties typically result from a deficit in the phonological component of language that is often unexpected in relation to other cognitive abilities and the provision of effective classroom instruction. Secondary consequences may include problems in reading comprehension and reduced reading experience that can impede growth of vocabulary and background knowledge. (Lyon, Shaywitz, & Shaywitz, 2003, p. 2)

Dyslexia is a **specific learning disability** because it is associated with specific cognitive deficits in basic reading skills (Lyon et al., 2003). It affects 80% of those identified with learning disabilities and is one of the most common learning problems in children and adults (Lerner, 1989). Dyslexia is estimated to occur in approximately 5%–17% of the population in the United States (Shaywitz, 1998), where up to 67% of all fourth graders and 75% of all eighth graders score at or above *basic* level in reading on the NAEP assessment (National Center for Education Statistics, 2009). Among these children not showing even partial **mastery** of grade-level skills in reading, there is a disproportionate representation of those who are poor, from racial minorities, and nonnative speakers of English. Large numbers of children from every social class, race, and ethnic group, however, have significant difficulties with reading. Children most at risk for reading failure have limited exposure to the English language; have little understanding of phonemic awareness, letter knowledge, **print awareness,** and the purposes of reading; and lack oral language and vocabulary skills. Children raised in poverty, children with speech and hearing impairments, and children whose parents' or caregivers' reading levels are low are also at risk for reading failure.

"Children with **reading disability** differ from one another *and* from other readers along a continuum" (Lyon, 1996, p. 64), with reading disability representing the lower tail of a normal distribution of reading ability (Shaywitz, 2003). It is typical that a person with dyslexia will have some but not all of the problems that are described next because of individual differences and access to early remediation. The clinical diagnosis of dyslexia with its long-term outcomes is a language-based **learning disability** and is the most widespread form of learning disability. Some common signs of dyslexia are difficulties in learning to speak; problems organizing written and spoken language; difficulty learning the letter names and their sounds; inaccurate decoding; slow, laborious reading lacking fluency due to using compensatory systems; conspicuous problems with spelling and writing; difficulty learning a foreign language; having a hard time memorizing number facts; and difficulty with math operations. Dyslexia varies in severity, and the prognosis depends on the severity of the disability, each individual's specific patterns of strengths and weaknesses, and the appropriateness and intensity of intervention.

Dyslexia is not caused by a lack of motivation to learn to read, sensory impairment, inadequate instruction, a lack of environmental opportunities, or low intelligence.

Reading is widespread throughout the brain, with many different regions used in reading. The present working definition, based on empirical support, emphasizes that dyslexia is neurobiological in origin because the neural systems in the brain that process the sounds of language and are critical to reading are involved (see Figure 1.1). Dyslexia is manifested by a disruption in these language systems, which leads to **phonological** weaknesses. The phonological weakness occurs "at the lowest level of the language system" and, in turn, impairs decoding (Shaywitz, 2003). In fact, there are two neural systems for reading: one for word analysis in the parieto-temporal region and the other for automatic, rapid responses localized in the occipito-temporal area that is used by skilled readers for rapid word recognition. Low **phonological processing** skills are the result of left hemisphere posterior processing anomalies typical of children with dyslexia.

This means that individuals with dyslexia have difficulty gaining access to and manipulating the sound structure (phonemes) of spoken language. Such a deficit prevents easy and early access to **letter–sound correspondences** and decoding strategies that foster accurate and fluent word decoding and recognition. A vast majority of individuals with dyslexia have a phonological core deficit (Morris et al., 1998; Ramus et al., 2003). Phonological abilities include awareness of the sounds of words in sentences, awareness of **syllables** in words, and awareness of phonemes in words or syllables (see Chapter 5). Approximately 17%–20% of school-age children are affected to some degree by deficits in phonemic awareness (Lyon, 1999). The result is that individuals with dyslexia have difficulty recognizing both real and **pseudowords,** which leads to over-reliance on context and guessing and prevents building words in memory instead of using the alphabetic principle to **decode** words. Readers with dyslexia may also have difficulties with processes underlying the rapid, precise retrieval of visually presented linguistic information. Measures of letter, digit, and color naming are predictors of later reading fluency (Wolf, Bowers, & Biddle, 2000).

Difficulties with accurate and/or fluent word recognition mean that poor readers lack the ability to read quickly, accurately, and with good understanding (Partnership for Reading, 2003) and thus do not get to the meaning of the text, avoid reading, and fail to develop the necessary vocabulary and **background knowledge** for comprehension.

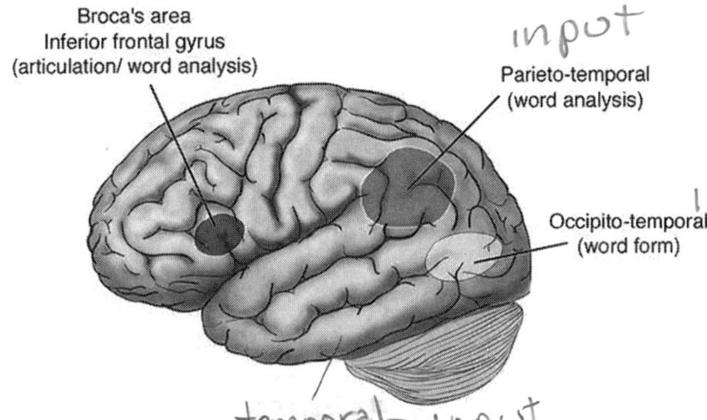

Broca's area
Inferior frontal gyrus
(articulation/ word analysis)

Parieto-temporal
(word analysis)

Occipito-temporal
(word form)

Figure 1.1.   The brain system has three important neural pathways: 1) an anterior system in the left inferior frontal region (Broca's area) for articulation and slower word analysis; 2) a parieto-temporal region for step-by-step analytic word reading; and 3) an occipito-temporal word-form area for skilled, rapid reading. (From OVERCOMING DYSLEXIA [p. 78] by Sally Shaywitz, M.D., copyright © 2003 by Sally Shaywitz, M.D. Used by permission of Alfred A. Knopf, a division of Random House, Inc.)

Poor spelling is a hallmark of dyslexia because of its intimate connection to reading. Educators can identify students with phoneme and word-recognition weaknesses early by administering screening tools for phonemic awareness and other prereading skills validated by research and promptly applying appropriate intervention in kindergarten and first grade before failure sets in, creating a pattern later on of compromised text-reading fluency, deficient vocabulary acquisition, and difficulty with reading comprehension (Eden & Moats, 2002).

Another aspect of the biological origin of dyslexia is that it runs in families. It is common for a child with dyslexia to have parents and siblings who also have dyslexia. Having a parent with dyslexia means that between one quarter and one half of the children will have dyslexia too (Shaywitz, 2003). According to Olson (2004), genetic influences on reading disability are just as important as shared environmental ones. Both are dependent on the quality of instruction available because improper instruction and lack of reading might affect brain processes. A number of different genes play a part in individual differences in phonemic awareness, word reading, and related skills. Deficits in phonemic awareness and reading of pseudowords are heritable. Evidence from research on identical and fraternal twins, funded by NICHD and conducted at the Colorado Learning Disabilities Research Center, has shown that these genetic constraints can be remediated so that children read normally after engaging in intensive practice with an early emphasis on phonological skills and more time in later grades spent reading for accuracy and fluency to promote continued growth. Olson (2004) suggested that there may be a genetic influence on learning rates for reading and related skills. Children with a family history of dyslexia should be monitored for early signs of oral language problems and attention given to prereading language play at home and the opportunity for effective beginning reading instruction at school.

Data from the Connecticut Longitudinal Study, funded by the NICHD, underscored that early identification along with intensive, scientifically based instruction can bring poor readers up to grade level. Unless these readers receive intensive help early on, the gap between good and poor readers stays the same, although both groups progress over time. Children facing reading difficulties at the beginning of school remain poor readers (see Figure 1.2). As noted by Lyon, a reading disability "reflects a persistent deficit rather than a developmental lag" and "longitudinal studies show that of those children who have a [reading disability] in the third grade, approximately 74% continue to read significantly below grade level in the ninth grade" (1996, p. 64). They are unlikely to catch up without informed teaching. Compounding that dire circumstance is the fact that students who receive help often receive it for a short period of time, inconsistently, and from untrained teachers using methods that lack a scientific base (Shaywitz, 2003).

Dyslexia is recognized in the definition as difficulty in learning to read that is unexpected in relation to other cognitive abilities and the provision of effective classroom instruction. The **discrepancy model** in which decoding and word-recognition deficits need to be lower than IQ in order to be considered dyslexic is still recognized. In identifying dyslexia, an alternative is the need to compare reading age with chronological age or, in the case of adults, career attainment level. New to the definition is the idea that effective classroom instruction to meet the range of needs children bring to school may be factored in to recognize dyslexia and to tease out reading failure from inadequate instruction, poor preschool preparation, and lack of response to quality instruction. In addition, there are secondary consequences such as weaknesses in vocabulary development and reading comprehension due to less developed accuracy and fluency and a smaller store of background knowledge to support comprehension. Much of this

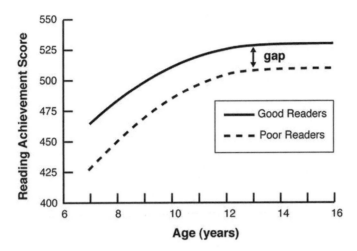

Figure 1.2. Trajectory of reading skills over time in readers with and without dyslexia. The *y* axis indicates Rasch scores (*W* scores) from the Reading subtest of the *Woodcock-Johnson–Revised Tests of Achievement* (Woodcock & Johnson, 1989). Both readers with and without dyslexia improved their reading scores as they get older, but the gap between the two groups remains. Thus, dyslexia is a deficit and not a developmental lag. (From *Multisensory Teaching of Basic Language Skills, Second Edition* [p. 12]. Originally adapted from *Frames of Reference for the Assessment of Learning Disabilities: New Views of Measurement Issues* [p. 40] edited by G. Reid Lyon, Ph.D., copyright © 1994 by Paul H. Brookes Publishing Co., Inc.)

is due to reduced reading experience. Deficits in attention, problems in short verbal memory, and difficulty with word retrieval and mathematics have also been identified in students with dyslexia. These deficits can affect listening and reading comprehension. Students with dyslexia who spell poorly often have difficulty with the motor aspects of writing. Poor pencil grip and messy handwriting persist. Expression of ideas clearly in both written and oral form is slow to develop. According to Ramus et al. (2003), it is not clear why sensory and motor disorders are often associated with phonological deficits.

Parents and teachers, therefore, should be aware of the manifestations of dyslexia in early childhood, such as difficulty learning to talk and incorrectly pronouncing words. Following directions, retrieving names of things such as letters of the alphabet, **sequencing,** and/or forming letters or numbers also can be areas of poor functioning. Characteristics that may accompany dyslexia include time management and organization problems, lack of social awareness, difficulty with attention (e.g., **attention-deficit/hyperactivity disorder**), poor spatial sense, and difficulty with motor skills.

Between 12% and 24% of those with dyslexia also have attention disorders (Shaywitz, 2003). Reading disabilities and attention disorders, however, are distinct (Lyon, 1996; Shaywitz, 2003). Although they are separate from learning disabilities, attention disorders and organization difficulties frequently co-occur with language-based reading disability. The severity of a reading disability may be compounded by attention disorders (Lyon, 1996). The IDA's web site (http://www.interdys.org) is a good resource that explains these symptoms and offers timely and research-based information. See Chapter 14 for hallmarks of good reading assessment.

Perhaps what puzzles teachers and parents the most is that students who fail to learn how letters represent speech sounds and how sounds are represented by the letters in words often are good thinkers and are talented in other areas. Because dyslexia is domain specific, other cognitive abilities such as reasoning, comprehension, vocabulary, **syntax,** and general IQ typically are unaffected (Shaywitz & Shaywitz, 2004). In fact, although IQ and reading in the typical reader influence each other over time, IQ and reading are not linked in the reader who has dyslexia (Ferrer, Shaywitz, Holahan, Marchione, & Shaywitz, 2010). People with dyslexia may excel in the arts, law, politics, architecture, science, medicine, business, and sports, for example. Data from the representative sample of children tested in the Connecticut Longitudinal Study showed that although boys are identified as having dyslexia four times more often than girls, there are as many females as males with dyslexia.

Boys are more often referred for special services due to behavior that signals problems, whereas girls in need of help are less likely to be identified (Shaywitz, 2003). There are accurate and reliable screening and identification procedures available that are linked to prevention programs. Early identification and intervention are essential to successful treatment of children who are at risk for reading failure. There has been a shift in the approach of identifying a specific reading disability. According to Lyon, "Definitions that measure the discrepancy between IQ and achievement do not adequately identify learning disabilities, particularly in the area of beginning reading skills" (1996, p. 64).

There is growing evidence in support of an alternative approach. Fletcher, Coulter, Reschly, and Vaughn stated, "Our most pressing challenge is conveying urgency about preventing disabilities through early screening and effective instruction, and for those who do not respond sufficiently, providing effective special education interventions that change achievement and social/behavioral outcomes" (2004, p. 312). The claim that using RTI as identification criteria can lead to targeting intervention first and assessment second; using formal progress monitoring with data on student response for accountability and planning; and building bridges between general and **special education** (Fletcher et al., 2004) has no evidence yet to support it.

As mentioned previously, dyslexia persists across the life span and is not a developmental lag. This is most clearly seen in the manifestations of dyslexia among adults (Brozgold, 2002). As in children, it exists across a continuum, with varying indications depending on the individual. Adults with dyslexia show decreased reading efficiency (i.e., slower reading rate and lower accuracy) relative to individuals without dyslexia despite good intelligence, education, and career attainment. Their **phonetic** decoding is impaired relative to their reading comprehension, which may be better because they rely on context cues and know about the subject that they are reading. When tested, their decoding of pseudowords is impaired. Other language-based difficulties can be observed, such as mispronouncing words and names and word-retrieval difficulty. Written composition is problematic because writing calls on integrating so many language skills. Spelling is likely to be persistently weak. Unless the text is of particular interest, the individual may have ongoing difficulty retaining information that he or she reads. A diagnosis of dyslexia in adults can have significant therapeutic and practical value because it confirms and validates the individual's strengths and weaknesses and leads to interventions and **accommodations,** especially extended time on tests, which can improve academic skills, vocational functioning, and self-esteem (Brozgold, 2002).

TEACHERS CAN DELIVER EVIDENCE-BASED READING INSTRUCTION TO ALL STUDENTS

Consensus on effective teacher preparation has been widely accepted by scholarly panels, scientific investigators, and noted professional organizations as indicated previously. Being able to teach the elements of language structure well to diverse groups of students in need of such instruction is paramount.

Effective Instruction Improves Reading and Changes the Brain

Although dyslexia affects individuals over the life span and cannot be cured, reading skills can be increased with the right early intervention and prevention programs. Researchers have drawn attention to the interactions between the neurobiological and environmental factors in students with reading disabilities using functional magnetic resonance imaging (fMRI). Specifically, when children with reading disabilities were given intensive, systematic code-based reading interventions, they demonstrated increased activation in the left occipito-temporal brain region and also made significant gains in reading fluency and comprehension 1 year after the intervention had ended. Shaywitz et al. (2004) reported that this outcome provides evidence of plasticity of neural systems for reading and demonstrates that a scientifically based reading intervention brings about significant and durable changes in brain organization so that the brain facilitates the development of those fast-paced neural systems that underlie skilled reading.

Using a scientifically based reading intervention with children who were poor readers who participated in a fMRI study, researchers showed that the intensive, phonologically based intervention made "significant and durable changes in brain organization so that brain activation patterns resemble those of typical readers" of the neural system for reading (Shaywitz et al., 2004, p. 931). The children's reading fluency improved. NICHD-supported research also has found that older individuals with dyslexia can improve with intervention that focuses on remediation of reading and writing skills and other areas of weakness. Sometimes, it is a matter of learning how to learn (see Chapter 19). As children get older, however, "the intensity and duration of reading interventions must increase exponentially" (Lyon, 1999) to achieve the same improvement possible with younger children. In fact, adolescent students will attain grade-level standards only with "instruction sufficiently powerful to accelerate reading development dramatically so that students make more than one year's progress during one year of school" (Torgesen et al., 2007, p. 5). Effective programs must involve intensive instruction using a systematic, structured language approach. It is crucial that the programs be consistent and of sufficient duration for individuals to make progress in improving reading and related skills (Shaywitz, 2003). **Modifications** and accommodations, although not a substitute for remediation, along with robust use of technology to support learning, can pave the way for many poor readers to gain information, expand their world knowledge, and be successful at school or work. They can improve their decoding and comprehension skills at any age but often remain slow readers. Accommodations that build on the strengths of older students and adults with dyslexia can help them to lead successful lives.

Content and Delivery of Reading Instruction Is Critical

It is clear from the consensus of scientifically based reading research that the nature of the educational intervention for individuals with reading disabilities and dyslexia is critical. Characterizing reading and writing as language is central to every aspect of intervention for individuals with language-based learning disabilities. Knowing language development and disabilities is essential for those who do assessments and interpret them, are trained to deliver instruction, and design and carry out programs at all levels (Dickman, Hennessy, Moats, Rooney, & Tomey, 2002).

The Relationship Between Teacher Preparation and Student Achievement

As teachers learn about underlying concepts and instructional strategies in the components of reading accompanied by comprehensive instruction and practice, they begin to incorporate these ideas into their everyday work and student achievement improves (Moats & Foorman, 2003). Evidence shows that student achievement and teacher preparation and domain-specific knowledge are correlated (Darling-Hammond, 2000; Moats & Foorman, 2003; NICHD, 2000).

There is also mounting evidence that teachers are being underprepared in schools of education by not designating the science of reading, the five basic components of reading, and, most important, knowledge of language structure as essential information (Spear-Swerling, Brucker, & Alfano, 2005; Walsh, Glaser, & Wilcox, 2006). Spear-Swerling et al. pointed out that the most experienced and well-trained teachers do not promote student growth unless they use this knowledge and translate it into classroom practice. In a survey, teacher educators were asked how important it was for public school teachers to "teach phonics and phonemic awareness when teaching literacy in the early grades." Only 44% thought it was "absolutely essential" (Farkas & Duffett, 2010). Too often, content knowledge and depth of training are lacking in the most basic areas of preparation for reading instruction. For example, Cheesman (2004) found that the beginning certified teachers she surveyed lacked the ability to differentiate between phonemic awareness and phonics and the ability to segment written words by phonemes. This raises questions about the quality of preservice teacher education and the availability of quality professional development and mentoring for beginning certified teachers. Other studies have found that teachers cannot count speech sounds in words. From a study done by Piasta, Connor, Fishman, and Morrison (2009), it is clear that not only was teacher knowledge about language and literacy concepts, including elements of explicit decoding instruction, important but so were the actual classroom practices that accompanied this specialized knowledge that produced student gains in first-grade word-reading growth. It is well to keep in mind the synergy of having both expert teaching practice and the knowledge to call on when responding to student errors (Moats, 1999). Through better preservice and professional development and mentoring, teachers can be sufficiently prepared to deliver effective reading instruction that teaches listening, speaking, reading, and writing using explicit, systematic, cumulative, and multisensory methods based on scientific research to students at risk or who are dyslexic.

Because of well-documented insufficient preparation of classroom teachers and specialists in teaching students who are struggling with reading, the IDA saw the need to adopt and promote standards for "1) content knowledge necessary to teach reading and writing to students with dyslexia or related disorders who are at risk for reading difficulty; 2) practices of effective instruction; and 3) ethical conduct expected of professional educators and clinicians" (2010, p. 3). The IDA *Knowledge and Practice Standards* call for teacher educators to base their courses on the following standards:

- Foundation concepts about oral and written language learning

- Knowledge of dyslexia and other learning disorders

- Interpretation and administration of assessments for planning instruction

- Structured language teaching

> Phonology
> Phonics and word study
> Fluent, automatic reading of text
> Vocabulary
> Text comprehension
> Handwriting, spelling, and written expression
> Ethical standards for the profession

These standards are also appropriate for classroom teachers, who are responsible for recognizing and preventing reading difficulties. The knowledge and practice criteria outlined in detail in this book are aligned with these standards to assist teachers and their instructors in the complex endeavor to become the experts their students deserve.

Elements of Effective Instruction

To minimize reading failure, classroom reading approaches must include systematic, explicit instruction in phonemic awareness (orally identifying and manipulating syllables and speech sounds); particular attention to letter–sound knowledge (phonics); spelling integrated with reading; fluency (developing speed and **automaticity** in accurate letter, word, and text reading); vocabulary building; and text comprehension strategies. If such classroom programs prove to be insufficient for students with dyslexia, then students will need to have a **multisensory structured language education (MSLE)** program, one that incorporates systematic, cumulative, explicit, and sequential approaches taught by teachers trained to instruct language structure at the levels of sounds, syllables, meaningful parts of words, sentence structure, and paragraph and discourse organization (Eden & Moats, 2002). Some commercial programs that fit this description are Alphabetic Phonics, Slingerland, Project Read, LANGUAGE!, the Sonday System, Orton-Gillingham, Wilson Language, the Spalding Method, Lindamood-Bell, Take Flight, and Preventing Academic Failure (see Appendix B for more information about MSLE programs). Instruction in all of these programs is multisensory and engages the learner in visual, auditory, and **kinesthetic** responses and feedback with deliberate and intensive practice in reading and spelling controlled for what has been taught. Teachers use structured lesson planning and ongoing monitoring of progress to organize instruction and chart the growth in skills.

Figure 1.3 shows the content (the structure of the English language) allied with the principles of instruction inherent in all multisensory structured language programs. All are consonant with the IDA *Knowledge and Practice Standards*. To better understand the terms, there is an explanation in Table 1.2.

Importance of Intensity of Instruction

From 25 years of prevention and intervention research targeting the five major components of reading, Torgesen (2004) concluded that explicitness and intensity of instruction are the key ingredients in teaching this knowledge and these skills to students who are struggling greatly with reading. By that he meant, "Explicit instruction is instruction that does not leave anything to chance and does not make assumptions about skills and knowledge that children will acquire on their own" (p. 363).

Content: Structure of the English language	Principles of instruction				
	Simultaneous multisensory VAKT	Systematic and cumulative	Direct instruction	Diagnostic teaching to automaticity	Synthetic/ analytic instruction
Phonology and phonological awareness	✓	✓	✓	✓	✓
Sound–symbol association: visual to auditory, auditory to visual, blending and segmenting	✓	✓	✓	✓	✓
Syllables: types and patterns for division	✓	✓	✓	✓	✓
Morphology: base words, roots, affixes	✓	✓	✓	✓	✓
Syntax: grammar, sentence variation, and mechanics of language	✓	✓	✓	✓	✓
Semantics: meaning	✓	✓	✓	✓	✓

Figure 1.3. Multisensory structured language programs: Content and principles of instruction. (*Key*: VAKT, visual, auditory, kinesthetic, tactile.) (Adapted from: IMSLEC Directory: MSL Training Courses and Graduates [2010]. Dallas, TX: The International Multisensory Structured Language Education Council, page 11.)

In contrast to leaving things to chance or assuming that students are absorbing the necessary concepts to decode new words or comprehend text, explicit instruction calls on teachers to make clear connections between letters and sounds and their consistent, systematic relationships; teach individual word meanings and word-learning strategies; provide modeling for fluent reading and have students engage in repeated oral reading; and learn how to use explicit, carefully sequenced instruction in comprehension strategies. Research has shown that more favorable outcomes are associated with systematic phonics instruction than with an approach emphasizing implicit phonics (Lyon, 1996; NICHD, 2000).

Furthermore, Torgesen (2004) reinforced the importance of explicit instruction for remediation and intervention by including the need for intensity, which is wholly different from general education classroom experiences. Through small-group instruction of 1:1 and 1:3 with intensity guided by students' rate of progress (Vaughn & Linan-Thompson, 2003), students with reading problems have a better chance of closing the grade gap with their peers in reading accuracy and reading comprehension than in large-group configurations. To make gains, students need to engage in highly structured, sequential activities and be closely monitored in ways not possible in the general education classroom, forming direct connections between the known and the new, with time for explicit practice of what is being learned to build automaticity and fluency. In addition, there should be a sequential order in the curriculum for instruction and practice. Teachers in the general education classroom can also apply these practices with students struggling with reading by incorporating these teaching approaches and rethinking their grouping of students. The instructional practices and curriculum content in the following chapters fit this model of intervention and remediation. It is en-

Table 1.2. Definition of terms

Content of structured language teaching

Phonology and phonological awareness—Phonology is the study of sounds and how they work within their environment. A phoneme is the smallest unit of sound in a given language that can be recognized as being distinct from other sounds. Phonological awareness is understanding the internal linguistic structure of words. An important aspect of phonological awareness is the ability to segment words into their component phonemes [phonemic awareness].

Sound–symbol association—This is knowing the various sounds in the English language and their correspondence to the letter and combinations of letters that represent those sounds. Sound–symbol association must be taught (and mastered) in two directions: visual to auditory and auditory to visual. In addition, students must master blending sounds and letters into words as well as segmenting whole words into the individual sounds.

Syllable instruction—A syllable is a unit of oral or written language with one vowel sound. Instruction must include teaching the six basic types of syllables in the English language: closed, open, vowel-consonant-*e, r*-controlled, vowel pair [or vowel team], and final stable syllable. Syllable division rules must be directly taught in relation to the word structure.

Morphology—Morphology is the study of how morphemes are combined to form words. A morpheme is the smallest unit of meaning in the language. The curriculum must include the study of base words, roots, and affixes.

Syntax—Syntax is the set of principles that dictate the sequence and function of words in a sentence in order to convey meaning. This includes grammar, sentence variation, and the mechanics of language.

Semantics—Semantics is that aspect of language concerned with meaning. The curriculum (from the beginning) must include instruction in comprehending written language.

Principles of instruction

Simultaneous, multisensory (VAKT)—Teaching is done using all learning pathways in the brain (visual, auditory, kinesthetic, tactile) simultaneously in order to enhance memory and learning.

Systematic and cumulative—Multisensory language instruction requires that the organization of material follow the logical order of the language. The sequence must begin with the easiest and most basic elements and progress methodically to more difficult material. Each step must also be based on those [elements] already learned. Concepts taught must be systematically reviewed to strengthen memory.

Direct instruction—The inferential learning of any concept cannot be taken for granted. Multisensory language instruction requires the direct teaching of all concepts with [continual] student–teacher interaction.

Diagnostic teaching to automaticity—The teacher must be adept at prescriptive or individualized teaching. The teaching plan is based on careful and [continual] assessment of the individual's needs. The content presented must be mastered to the degree of automaticity.

Synthetic and analytic instruction—Multisensory structured language programs include both synthetic and analytic instruction. Synthetic instruction presents the parts of the language and then teaches how the parts work together to form a whole. Analytic instruction presents the whole and teaches how this can be broken down into its component parts.

From McIntyre, C.W., & Pickering, J.S. (1995). *Clinical studies of multisensory structured language education for students with dyslexia and related disorders* (p. xii). Poughkeepsie, NY: Hamco; adapted by permission.

couraging to realize that the research evidence has arrived at a consensus on the critical element of instruction and how it is to be delivered.

Reading disability has far-reaching consequences, which is why we must be prepared to intervene early and intensively until the reader is on target for success. It is important for pre- and in-service teachers to be prepared to work directly with children with reading, writing, and spelling disabilities who also may have other co-occurring difficulties, such as difficulties with arithmetic calculation. Without question, both general and special education teachers need the tools to identify students with language-based learning disabilities to intervene with explicit instructional procedures and to continue to sustain their students with intensive support for as long as they need it.

CONCLUSION: IMPACT OF RESEARCH ON PRACTICE

There have been more than 45,000 participants in the NICHD-funded research programs in reading development, reading disorders, and reading instruction. Both children and adults have participated, including more than 22,500 good readers at the 50th percentile and above and about 22,500 struggling readers below the 25th percentile (Lyon, 2004). We have learned from these studies and others how children read, why some children have difficulties, how we can prevent difficulties from being ingrained, and how to provide intervention when readers continue to struggle.

The beginnings of reading emerge from substantial and significant oral language experiences from birth onward. The importance of providing oral language and literacy experiences from birth onward, including reading to children, playing with language through rhyming and games, and encouraging writing activities is well documented. These activities encourage vocabulary development and enhance verbal reasoning, semantic, and syntactic abilities. The importance of early assessment and intervention for reading problems is borne out by the findings that show that reading problems identified in Grade 3 and beyond require considerable intervention because children do not just outgrow reading problems. In fact, 74% of children identified as having a reading disability in Grade 3 still had a reading disability in Grade 9, according to a study by Francis, Shaywitz, Stuebing, Shaywitz, and Fletcher (1996).

The risk factors for dyslexia can be seen in kindergarten and first grade—trouble with letter–sound knowledge, **phonological awareness,** and oral language development. The earliest clue to dyslexia is "a weakness in getting to the sounds of words" (Shaywitz, 2003, p. 93). Lyon noted that "the best predictor of reading ability from kindergarten and first-grade performance is phoneme **segmentation** ability" (1996, p. 64). It is best to assess all children and intervene first in the classroom, with explicit instruction in phonemic awareness, phonics, and comprehension with an emphasis on fluency in all these competencies. The instruction should be guided by a carefully constructed sequenced curriculum that is designed to be explicit about language structure and leaves nothing to chance. The texts chosen for practice need to be controlled and later decodable so that children are taught to mastery. Developing phonemic awareness is necessary but not the sole component of learning to read. From the beginning, reading instruction must include attention to phonics principles for accurate and rapid decoding and active use of comprehension strategies.

"The ability to read and comprehend is dependent on rapid and automatic recognition and decoding of single words. Slow and inaccurate decoding are the best predictors of deficits in reading comprehension" (Lyon, 1996, p. 64). Additional factors impeding reading comprehension include vocabulary deficits, lack of background knowledge for understanding text information, deficient understanding of semantic and syntactic structures, insufficient knowledge of writing conventions for different purposes, lack of verbal reasoning, and inability to remember and/or retrieve verbal information. There are now proven strategies to maximize reading comprehension and develop background knowledge and vocabulary through reciprocal teaching and monitoring feedback.

Educators can make changes by intervening early with instruction that changes the way the brain learns. Much has happened to disseminate the new science of reading. For example, neurobiological investigations show that there are differences in the parietal-temporal and occipital-temporal brain regions among people with dyslexia from those without dyslexia. Although these differences affect the ability to read, neural systems for reading are malleable and highly responsive to effective reading instruction. In their research using fMRI to study the effects of a systematic phonics-based intervention with 6- to 9-year-old children, Shaywitz et al. (2004) found evidence of plasticity of neural systems for reading. The changes in the brain made these readers comparable with good readers. The children were still making gains in reading fluency and comprehension 1 year later after the intervention ended.

Shaywitz et al.'s conclusion was that providing "evidence-based reading intervention at an early age improves reading fluency and facilitates the development of those neural systems that underlie skilled reading. Teaching matters and can change the brain" (2004, p. 931). Many states are using research to guide their policy in reading education. With high-level preservice preparation and professional development efforts that pay strict attention to this evidence, the impact of science should bring about changes at the school level. This book is dedicated to that goal and to teachers in the classroom.

There is still serious underpreparation among teachers regarding the theory and contents of language instruction. Teachers need to have multiple layers of expertise on how children acquire reading, the relationship between language development and reading development, the characteristics of disabilities, and the basic tenets of reading instruction methodologies. There needs to be serious reform in colleges of education and professional development programs.

The time has come to merge the evidence from the science of reading, the knowledge gained from research on what works in the classroom, with serious and sustained preservice training and ongoing professional development so that teachers can better carry out the complex demands of reading instruction. Efforts are underway in many colleges and universities and private training organizations to rethink and explore new ways of delivering coursework, online and in the classroom, in conjunction with innovative ways of gaining practical, hands-on experience with validated practices (Moats, 2003). The way to proceed has been explicitly described by many guides who understand what expert teachers should know and be able to do (Brady & Moats, 1997; Clark & Uhry, 1995; Learning First Alliance, 2000; NICHD, 2000; Snow et al., 1998).

Teachers have to know how reading develops from prereading to reading for information and enjoyment. Detecting reading difficulties early and providing appropriate intervention in time to keep children from failing is critical. A thorough knowledge of the structure of language and how to teach it layer by layer helps teachers to monitor their students' progress and gives them the tools to pace lessons and move their students along based on consistent monitoring of progress (Moats, 1999; Moats & Brady, 1997). This ensures that special educators, who work with the students with the most serious problems, and general educators, who must reach a range of students with diverse needs on a daily basis, receive the best professional development based on what scientifically based reading research shows is effective. Good instruction can prevent a lifetime of difficulties: A good beginning has no end.

REFERENCES

Aaron, P.G., Joshi, R.M., & Quatroche, D. (2008). *Becoming a professional reading teacher.* Baltimore: Paul H. Brookes Publishing Co.

Adams, M.J. (1990). *Beginning to read: Thinking and learning about print.* Cambridge, MA: The MIT Press.

Berninger, V.W., & Wolf, B.J. (2009). *Teaching students with dyslexia and dysgraphia: Lessons from teaching and science.* Baltimore: Paul H. Brookes Publishing Co.

Brady, S., & Moats, L.C. (1997). *Informed instruction for reading success: Foundations for teacher preparation.* Baltimore: International Dyslexia Association.

Brozgold, A.Z. (2002, March 22). *The diagnosis of dyslexia in adults.* Paper presented at the 29th Annual Conference on Dyslexia and Related Learning Disabilities, New York Branch of the International Dyslexia Association.

Chall, J. (1967). *Learning to read: The great debate.* New York: McGraw-Hill.

Cheesman, E.A. (2004). *Teacher education in phonemic awareness.* Unpublished doctoral dissertation, University of Connecticut.

Clark, D.B., & Uhry, J.K. (1995). *Dyslexia: Theory and practice of remedial instruction.* Timonium, MD: York Press.

Connor, C.M., Morrison, F.J., & Underwood, P. (2007). A second chance in second grade? The cumulative impact of first and second grade reading instruction on students' letter–word reading skills. *Scientific Studies of Reading, 11*(3), 199–233.

Council of Chief State School Officers (CCSSO) & National Governors Association Center for Best Practices (NGA Center). (2010). *Common core state standards for English language arts and literacy in history/ social studies, science and technical subjects.* Retrieved January 13, 2011, from http://www.corestandards.org/the-standards

Darling-Hammond, L. (2000). *Teacher quality and student achievement: A review of state policy evidence.* Retrieved October 12, 2004, from http://epaa.asu.edu/epaa/v8n1/

Dehaene, S. (2009). *Reading in the brain: The science and evolution of a human invention.* New York: Viking Penguin.

Dickman, G.E., Hennessy, N.L., Moats, L.C., Rooney, K.J., & Tomey, H.A. (2002). *The nature of learning disabilities: Response to OSEP Summit on Learning Disabilities.* Baltimore: International Dyslexia Association.

Eden, G.F., & Moats, L.C. (2002). The role of neuroscience in the remediation of students with dyslexia. *Nature Neuroscience, 5*(Suppl.), 1080–1084.

Ehri, L.C. (2004). Teaching phonemic awareness and phonics: An explanation of the National Reading Panel meta-analyses. In P. McCardle & V. Chhabra (Eds.), *The voice of evidence in reading research* (pp. 153–186). Baltimore: Paul H. Brookes Publishing Co.

Ehri, L.C., Nunes, S.R., Stahl, S.A., & Willows, D.M. (2001). Systematic phonics instruction helps students learn to read: Evidence from the National Reading Panel's meta-analysis. *Review of Educational Research, 71*(3), 393–447.

Farkas, S., & Duffett, A. (2010). *Cracks in the ivory tower: The views of education professors circa 2010.* Washington, DC: Thomas B. Fordham Institute.

Ferrer,, E., Shaywitz, B.A., Holahan, J.M., Marchione, K., & Shaywitz, S.E. (2010). Uncoupling of reading and IQ over time: Empirical evidence of a definition of dyslexia. *Psychological Science, 21*(1), 93–101.

Fletcher, J.M., Coulter, W.A., Reschly, D.J., & Vaughn, S. (2004). Alternative approaches to the definition and identification of learning disabilities: Some questions and answers. *Annals of Dyslexia, 54*(2), 304–331.

Fletcher, J.M., & Francis, D.J. (2004). Scientifically based educational research: Questions, designs, and methods. In P. McCardle & V. Chhabra (Eds.), *The voice of evidence in reading research* (pp. 59–80). Baltimore: Paul H. Brookes Publishing Co.

Francis, D.J., Shaywitz, S.E., Stuebing, K.K., Shaywitz, B.A., & Fletcher, J.M. (1996). Developmental lag versus deficit models of reading disability: A longitudinal, individual growth curve analysis. *Journal of Educational Psychology, 88*(1), 3–17.

Hasbrouck, J., & Tindal, G.A. (2006). Oral reading fluency norms: A valuable assessment tool for reading teachers. *The Reading Teacher, 59*(7), 636–644.

International Dyslexia Association. (2010). *Knowledge and practice standards for teachers of reading.* Baltimore: Author.

International Multisensory Structured Language Education Council. (2010). *IMSLEC directory: MSL training courses and graduates.* Dallas, TX: Author.

Juel, C. (1988). Learning to read and write: A longitudinal study of 54 children from first to fourth grades. *Journal of Educational Psychology, 80,* 437–447.

Keller-Allen, C. (2004). *The National Reading Panel: The accuracy of concerns about the report.* Unpublished manuscript.

Kratochwill, T.R., Hitchcock, J., Horner, R.H., Levin, J.R., Odom, S.L., Rindskopf, D.M., et al. (2010). *Single-case designs technical documentation.* Retrieved November 15, 2010, from http://ies.ed.gov/ncee/wwc/pdf/wwc_scd.pdf

Learning First Alliance. (2000). *Every child reading: A professional development guide.* Washington, DC: Author.

Lerner, J. (1989). Educational interventions in learning disabilities. *Journal of the American Academy of Child and Adolescent Psychiatry, 28,* 326–331.

Lyon, G.R. (1996, Spring). Learning disabilities. *The Future of Children, 6*(4), 54–76.

Lyon, G.R. (1999). The NICHD research program in reading development, reading disorders, and reading instruction: A summary of research findings. In *Keys to successful learning: A national summit on research in learning disabilities.* New York: National Center for Learning Disabilities.

Lyon, G.R. (2004). *The NICHD research program in reading development, reading disorders, and treading instruction initiated: 1965.* Paper presented at the 31st annual conference of the New York Branch of the International Dyslexia Association.

Lyon, G.R., & Chhabra, V. (2004). The science of reading research. *Educational Leadership, 61*(6), 13–17.

Lyon, G.R., Shaywitz, S.E., & Shaywitz, B.A. (2003). A definition of dyslexia. *Annals of Dyslexia, 53,* 1–14.

McCardle, P., & Chhabra, V. (Eds.). (2004). *The voice of evidence in reading research.* Baltimore: Paul H. Brookes Publishing Co.

McCardle, P., Chhabra, V., & Kapinus, B. (2008). *Reading research in action: A teacher's guide for student success.* Baltimore: Paul H. Brookes Publishing Co.

McIntyre, C.W., & Pickering, J.S. (1995). *Clinical studies of multisensory structured language education for students with dyslexia and related disorders.* Salem, OR: International Mulitsensory Structured Language Education Council.

Moats, L.C. (1999). *Teaching reading is rocket science: What expert teachers of reading should know and be able to do* (No. 372). Washington, DC: American Federation of Teachers.

Moats, L.C. (2003). *Language essentials for teachers of reading and spelling (LETRS).* Longmont, CO: Sopris West Educational Services.

Moats, L.C., & Brady, S. (1997). *Informed instruction for reading success: Foundations for teacher preparation.* Baltimore: International Dyslexia Association.

Moats, L.C., & Foorman, B.R. (2003). Measuring teachers' content knowledge of language and reading. *Annals of Dyslexia, 53,* 23–45.

Morris, R.D., Stuebing, K.K., Fletcher, J.M., Shaywitz, S.E., Lyon, G.R., Shankweiler, D.P., et al. (1998). Subtypes of reading disability: Variability around a phonological core. *Journal of Educational Psychology, 90,* 347–373.

National Center for Education Statistics. (2009). *The nation's report card: Reading 2009.* Washington, DC: U.S. Department of Education.

National Institute of Child Health and Human Development. (2000). *Report of the National Reading Panel: Reports of the subgroups. Teaching children to read: An evidence-based assessment of the scientific research literature on reading and its implications for reading instruction* (NIH Publication No. 00-4754). Washington, DC: Government Printing Office.

No Child Left Behind Act of 2001, PL 107-110, 115 Stat. 1425, 20 U.S.C. §§ 6301 *et seq.*

Olson, R.K. (2004). Environment and genes. *Scientific Studies of Reading, 8*(2), 111–124.

Partnership for Reading. (2003, June). *Put reading first: The research building blocks for teaching chil-dren to read. Kindergarten through grade 3* (2nd ed.). Washington, DC: Author.

Piasta, S.B., Connor, C.M., Fishman, B.J., & Morrison, F.J. (2009). Teachers' knowledge of literary concepts, classroom practices, and student reading growth. *Scientific Studies of Reading, 13*(3), 224–248.

Pressley, M. (2002). *Reading instruction that works* (2nd ed.). New York: The Guilford Press.

Ramus, F., Rosen, S., Dakin, S.C., Day, B.L., Castellote, J.M., White, S., et al. (2003). Theories of developmental dyslexia: Insights from a multiple case study of dyslexic adults. *Brain, 126,* 841–865.

Reyna, V.F. (2004). Why scientific research?: The importance of evidence in changing educational practice. In P. McCardle & V. Chhabra (Eds.), *The voice of evidence in reading research* (pp. 47–58). Baltimore: Paul H. Brookes Publishing Co.

Schochet, P., Cook, T., Deke, J., Imbens, G., Lockwood, J.R., Porter, J., et al. (2010). *Standards for regression discontinuity designs.* Retrieved from http://ies.ed.gov/ncee/wwc/pdf/wwc_rd.pdf

Shaywitz, S.E. (1998). Current concepts: Dyslexia. *New England Journal of Medicine, 338*(5), 307–312.

Shaywitz, S. (2003). *Overcoming dyslexia: A new and complete science-based program for reading problems at any level.* New York: Alfred A. Knopf.

Shaywitz, S.E., & Shaywitz, B.A. (2004). Neurobiologic basis for reading and reading disability. In P. McCardle & V. Chhabra (Eds.), *The voice of evidence in reading research* (pp. 417–442). Baltimore: Paul H. Brookes Publishing Co.

Shaywitz, B.A., Shaywitz, S.E., Blachman, B.A., Pugh, K.R., Fulbright, R.K., Skudlarski, et al. (2004). Development of left occipitotemporal systems for skilled reading in children after a phonologically-based intervention. *Biological Psychiatry, 55*(9), 926–933.

Snow, C.E. (2004). Foreword. In P. McCardle & V. Chhabra (Eds.), *The voice of evidence in reading research* (pp. xix-xxv). Baltimore: Paul H. Brookes Publishing Co.

Snow, C.E., Burns, M.S., & Griffin, P. (Eds.). (1998). *Preventing reading difficulties in young children.* Washington, DC: National Academies Press.

Spear-Swerling, L., Brucker, P., & Alfano, M. (2005). Teachers' literacy-related knowledge and self-perception in relation to preparation and experience. *Annals of Dyslexia, 55,* 266–293.

Torgesen, J.K. (2004). Lessons learned from research on interventions for students who experience difficulty learning to read. In P. McCardle & V. Chhabra (Eds.), *The voice of evidence in reading research* (pp. 355–382). Baltimore: Paul H. Brookes Publishing Co.

Torgesen, J.K., Houston, D.D., Rissman, L.M., Decker, S.M., Roberts, G., Vaughn, S., et al.

(2007). *Academic literacy instruction for adolescents: A guidance document from the Center on Instruction.* Portsmouth, NH: RNC Research Corporation, Center on Instruction.

Torgesen, J.K., Wagner, R.K., & Rashotte, C.A. (1994). Longitudinal studies of phonological processing and reading. *Journal of Learning Disabilities, 27,* 276–286.

U.S. Department of Education, Institute of Education Sciences. (2008). *WWC procedures and standards handbook: Version 2.0.* Available at http://ies.ed.gov/ncee/wwc/references/idocviewer/Doc.aspx?docId=19&tocId=6:

Vaughn, S., & Linan-Thompson, S. (2003). Group size and time allotted to intervention: Effects for students with reading difficulties. In B.R. Foorman (Ed.), *Preventing and remediating reading difficulties: Bringing science to scale* (pp. 299–324). Timonium, MD: York Press.

Walsh, K., Glaser, D., & Wilcox, D.D. (2006). *What education schools aren't teaching about reading and what elementary teachers aren't learning.* Washington, DC: National Council on Teacher Quality.

Wolf, M., Bowers, P., & Biddle, K. (2000). Naming-speed processes, timing, and reading: A conceptual review. *Journal of Learning Disabilities, 33,* 322–324.

Woodcock, R.W., & Johnson, M.B. (1989). *The Woodcock-Johnson–Revised Tests of Achievement.* Itasca, IL: Riverside.

2

Multisensory Structured Language Education

MARY L. FARRELL AND GORDON F. SHERMAN

Multisensory structured language education (MSLE) is commonly endorsed and practiced by teachers of students with a wide range of learning difficulties. Although clinicians and teachers have embraced and effectively used multisensory teaching techniques since the earliest teaching guides were written (e.g., Fernald, 1943; Gillingham & Stillman, 1960; Montessori, 1912; Strauss & Lehtinen, 1947), these techniques have seldom been well defined, and clinical wisdom has been waiting for scientific research validation and explanation. We are closer to understanding why expert teachers have been committed to structured language approaches because of current findings regarding the nature of reading development, the efficacy of certain reading instruction practices, and the **multisensory** organization of the brain.

This chapter defines MSLE, discusses the role of **multisensory strategies** in effective instruction of language skills, describes how these strategies have been implemented in the past, identifies the instructional practices that are consistently supported by research, and reviews recent findings from neuroscience.

WHAT IS MSLE?

The term *multisensory* is often used to describe strategies that involve learners in activities that include the use of two or more sensory modalities simultaneously to take in or express information. The term *multisensory* in this volume pertains to teaching strategies to guide students in linking eye, ear, voice, and hand to bolster learning in the carefully sequenced teaching of language structure. For example, in learning letter–sound associations, the student is visually reinforced by looking at the letter; auditory reinforcement is derived from listening to and hearing the sound identified with the letter.

Portions of this chapter were written by Louisa C. Moats for the second edition of this book. Gordon Sherman wishes to thank Carolyn Cowen for her contributions to this chapter.

Kinesthetic reinforcement stems from the student feeling the articulatory muscle movement associated with saying the letter sound, and **tactile** reinforcement occurs through writing the letter on a roughened surface and feeling the associated sensations. In other parts of a typical structured language lesson, teachers and students develop paragraph structure with **graphic organizers,** or students learn the identity of phonemes by feeling and seeing the position of the mouth, lips, and tongue (see Figure 2.1).

Multisensory Teaching Strategies

Although practitioners emphasize the use of multisensory strategies as pivotal for student success, these strategies are not always well understood. In a study reporting on the specific nature of the multisensory strategies taught in MSLE teacher training programs, directors of 30 programs were asked to identify the specific sensory **modality** used in multisensory strategies in each section of MSLE lessons as taught in their programs (e.g., phonology, **sound–symbol association,** syllables, **morphology,** syntax, semantics) (Farrell, Pickering, North, & Schavio, 2004). A survey item was written for each **strategy** within each sensory modality, within each instructional section (see Appendix 2.1). Program directors were then asked to rate the frequency with which their teachers are trained to employ the sensory strategy represented in each of the survey items according to the following scale: 0 (*never*), 1 (*occasionally*), 2 (*as needed*

Figure 2.1.   A multisensory sound–symbol activity.

for certain students), 3 (*systematically used for certain students*), 4 (*systematically used for all students*), and 5 (*other*).

The table in Appendix 2.1 presents the percentage of recommended use for each sensory strategy within each instructional section. Columns 2 (as needed for certain students), 3 (systematically used for certain students), and 4 (systematically used for all students) have been highlighted and aggregated. Items for which the sum of percentages is 75% or greater have been flagged (*). An analysis of the table indicates that approximately 60% of the sensory strategies have been identified as ones that teachers are trained to use with at least 75% of their students.

Content of MSLE Instruction

Multisensory instruction is one important dimension of the practices and approaches useful with students who have problems with language learning, including reading and writing. Most programs that follow the **Orton-Gillingham approach** for teaching language-related academic skills (see Clark & Uhry, 1995) have also emphasized that the core content for instruction is the carefully sequenced teaching of the structure and use of sounds, syllables, words, sentences, and written discourse. Orton-Gillingham–based approaches, such as *The Language Tool Kit, Alphabetic Phonics, Project Read, LAN-GUAGE!*, the *Sonday System, Wilson Language Training, Slingerland Approach,* and the *Spalding Method*, emphasize the necessity for explicit language teaching to be systematic, cumulative, direct, and sequential. According to clinical consensus, it is the combination of these principles that facilitates a student's ability to learn and recall information (see the training guidelines of the members of the Alliance for Accreditation and Certification of Structured Language Education, 2003).

History of MSLE

The idea that learning experienced through all senses is helpful in reinforcing memory has a long history in pedagogy. Educational psychologists of the late 19th century promoted the theory that all senses, including kinesthetic, are involved in learning. The second volume of James's (1890) *The Principles of Psychology* discussed Binet's theory that all perceptions, in particular those of sight and touch, involve movements of the eyes and limbs and because such movement is essential in seeing an object, it must be equally essential in forming a visual image of the object. This theory was illustrated through descriptions of typically developing individuals who used tracing to bolster visual memory. Consistent with this theory were observations that the loss of acquired reading ability as a result of impaired visual memory in adults with brain injury could be bypassed through the use of a kinesthetic modality (tracing letters).

> Individuals thus [injured] succeed in reading by an ingenious roundabout way which they often discover themselves: it is enough that they should trace the letters with their finger to understand their sense. The motor image gives the key to the problem. If the patient can read, so to speak, with his fingers, it is because in tracing the letters he gives himself a certain number of muscular impressions which are those of writing. In one word, the patient reads by writing. (James, 1890, p. 62)

The late 19th-century medical literature also contained discussions about using bypass strategies in individuals who had lost their ability to read because of cerebral dysfunction (Berlin, 1887; Dejerine, 1892; Morgan, 1896). Hinshelwood (1917) was the first physician to advocate a specific instructional approach for written language disorders in children identified as "word blind." On the supposition that reading failure was due to underdevelopment or injury of the brain, Hinshelwood recommended instruction using an alphabetic method in a manner that would appeal to as many "cerebral centers" as possible.

Orton (1925, 1928) was the first to report in the American medical literature on **word blindness**. Like Hinshelwood (1917), he advocated using all sensory pathways to reinforce weak memory patterns. Orton (1928) called for education methods based on simultaneous association of visual, auditory, and kinesthetic fields (e.g., having a person sound the visually presented word and establish consistent **directionality** by following the letters with the fingers during sound synthesis of syllables and words). He stressed the unity of the language system and its sensorimotor connections and stated that listening, speaking, reading, and writing were interrelated functions of language that must be taught in tandem.

Prominent early educational approaches strongly associated with multisensory instruction were those developed by educators such as Montessori (1912), Fernald and Keller (1921), and Strauss and Lehtinen (1947), whose methods for teaching reading, based on their writings, are summarized in Table 2.1. A review of their methods reveals the multisensory nature of their instruction and, in particular, the strong role that the tactile/kinesthetic component plays in the learning process. Their rationales for tactile and kinesthetic teaching strategies reflected their belief in the tenacity of muscle memory (Montessori, 1912) or the belief that children with nonspecific, developmental neurological impairments would profit from compensatory or bypass techniques used effectively with children with brain injury (Fernald, 1943; Strauss & Lehtinen, 1947). Fernald also asserted the need for tactile experience in word learning and reported that learning rate increased when finger tracing, as compared with a stylus or pencil, was used. She quoted the work of Husband (1928) and Miles (1928) on maze learning to support her assertion.

The educators listed in Table 2.1 attributed the educational growth of students to using tactile/kinesthetic methods. Each method also emphasized systematic, sequential, and organized teaching of language components. Montessori (1912) and Strauss and Lehtinen (1947) emphasized direct teaching of phonics. Fernald's (1943) technique differed from the others in that whole words or whole syllables were taught, rather than individual sound–symbol relationships.

Given the multiple factors that may have accounted for these practitioners' successes, including the intensity of their small-group and individual interventions, their case study reports and anecdotal claims cannot be taken as absolute proof of the efficacy of multisensory instruction. Strauss and Lehtinen (1947) acknowledged that the effect attributed to multisensory teaching could possibly be a consequence of augmented attention rather than of tactile/kinesthetic learning per se.

While the medical and psychological literature of the time influenced the use of multisensory strategies in methods developed to serve children struggling to learn to read, using multisensory strategies also has a long history with students in the general education population. Hunt (1964) reported that motor response was considered extremely important in learning in the early 20th century. Fernald (1943) described how the kinesthetic aspect of multisensory learning, primarily used for reinforcing word recognition through writing, was incorporated into the approaches of many leading practitioners of the time, including Dearborn (1929); Gates (1927); Hegge, Sears, and Kirk (1932); and Monroe (1932).

Bryant (1979) reported that until the 1970s, special education teachers firmly believed in the value of kinesthetic reinforcement and cited a number of well-known

Table 2.1.   Overview of early 20th-century multisensory programs

Montessori (1912)

Population: Children 3–7 years old from the tenements of Rome

Cause of disability: Economic and cultural deprivation

Method

1. Daily practice with pencil is given in nonwriting activities to develop muscles for holding and using pencil.

2. The child is prepared to write through daily use of light sandpaper. Vowels are taught, then consonants are begun.
   - The teacher presents two vowel cards and says sounds. The child traces the letters repeatedly, eventually with eyes closed.
   - The child is asked to give the teacher cards corresponding to two sounds the teacher pronounces. If the child does not recognize letters by looking, then he or she traces them.
   - The teacher asks the child to give sounds for letters that the teacher presents.
   - When the child knows some vowels and consonants, the teacher dictates familiar words that the child "spells" by selecting cardboard letters from a set containing only letters he or she knows.

3. After about 1 month (for 5-year-olds), the child spontaneously begins to write (i.e., he or she uses a pencil for composing words).

4. When the child knows all of the sounds, he or she reads slips of paper with names of objects that are well known or present.

Length of training: Two weeks is the average time for learning to read and write. The child begins reading phrases that permit the teacher and child to communicate; they play games in which the child reads directions alone and then implements them.

Curriculum control: Although Montessori reported no control for difficulty of words, there is strict control of graphemes written and read through preparatory stages. The child then reads only familiar words after learning all of the sounds.

Phonics: Within the writing program, presentation of graphemes is sequential and cumulative.

Kinesthetic component: "There develops, contemporaneously, three sensations when the teacher shows the letter to the child and has him trace it: the visual sensation, the tactile sensation, and the muscular sensation. In this way the image of the graphic sign is fixed in a much shorter space of time than when it was, according to ordinary methods, acquired only through the visual image. It will be found that the muscular memory is in the young child the most tenacious and, at the same time, the most ready. Indeed, he sometimes recognizes the letters by touching them, when he cannot do so by looking at them. These images are, besides all this, contemporaneously associated with the alphabetical sound" (Montessori, 1912, p. 277).

Strauss and Lehtinen (1947)

Population: Children with brain injury (i.e., organic impairment resulting in neuromotor disturbances in perception, thinking, and/or emotional behavior)

Cause of disability: Disturbances caused by accidental damage to the brain before, during, or after birth

Method

1. Readiness exercises "emphasize perception and integration of wholes; visual discrimination of forms, letters, and words; organization of space; [and] constructing a figure against a background" (Strauss & Lehtinen, 1947, p. 176) as well as "ear training" (p. 177).

2. The child learns to discriminate and reproduce sounds and to blend orally. Next, the child learns to associate visual symbols and writing with sounds. The child learns to articulate sound(s) while writing single letters and then pairs. The child attends to auditory components and visual words, makes words on cards or paper with a stamping set, copies them with crayons emphasizing significant features with color, writes them on the blackboard, and builds them with letter cards.

3. Before the child reads a story, he or she will have learned approximately 10 words in the story as single words, simple sentences, or phrases. The words are later presented in varying contexts or exercises to check comprehension. The child is not expected to conform to absolute standards of accuracy while reading words.

4. The child composes a short story to be dictated to the teacher. The stories are then written or typed with a primer typewriter to be read again.

(continued)

Table 2.1.   *(continued)*

Length of training: Not specified

Curriculum control: "The child's study of phonics is systematically enlarged. He prepares study materials for himself in the form of lists, cards, sliding devices, booklets, etc. using the phonograms [graphemes] which he encounters in his reading lesson. The work is extrinsic, i.e., the phonic study is supplemental to the reading lesson but closely correlated with it" (Strauss & Lehtinen, 1947, p. 180).

Phonics: No phonics training given

Kinesthetic component: "The reading instruction emphasizes accurate perception of words and very early attempts to make the relationship between visual and auditory perception a functioning one. In as many ways as possible, his attention should be drawn to the components of a word, both visual and auditory. He should build words from copy, making them on cards or paper with a stamping set; he should copy them with crayons, emphasizing significant features with color, write them on the blackboard, and build them with letter cards" (Strauss & Lehtinen, 1947, p. 179).

Fernald and Keller (1921)

Population: Nonreaders (i.e., children of typical intelligence who failed to read after individual instruction by other recognized methods in Fernald's clinic)

Cause of disability: "Certain variations" (Fernald, 1943, p. 164) in the integrated brain functioning of the same region in which lesions are found in acquired alexia

Method

1. A word that the child requests is written in large script. The child repeatedly traces the word with index and middle fingers, saying it over to him- or herself until he or she can write it from memory. The word is erased, and the child writes it, saying the syllables to him- or herself while writing. If word is incorrect, then the process is repeated until the word can be written without the script copy. After a few words are learned, the child is asked to read the word in manuscript print as well as in cursive and then in print only. If the word is incorrect, then it is retaught as in the first presentation.

2. The child starts writing stories initially on subjects of interest to him or her and then, as the child's skill increases, on projects in various school subjects. The child asks for any word he or she does not know how to write, and it is taught as described before he or she uses it. After the story is finished, the child files new words under the proper letters in his or her word file.

Length of training: Average tracing period is about 2 months, with a range of 1–8 months. After a period of tracing, the child develops the ability to learn any new word by simply looking at it in script, copying it, and saying each part of the word while writing it.

Curriculum control: Because the child usually is able to recognize words after having written them, this provides a reading vocabulary that usually makes it unnecessary to simplify the content of the first reading.

Phonics: The sound of each letter is never given separately, yet the child is instructed to segment the word into syllables while writing.

Kinesthetic component: "Individuals who have failed to learn to read by visual and auditory methods show a spurt of learning as soon as the kinesthetic method is used. The end product is a skill equal to that of individuals who learn by ordinary methods" (Fernald, 1943, p. 168). Fernald and Keller (1921) reported that the learning rate is much more rapid when using tracing with finger contact than when using a stylus or a pencil.

names in the fields of reading and learning disabilities who stressed the importance of multisensory approaches (Ayres, 1972; Cruickshank, Betzen, Ratzeburg, & Tannhauser, 1961; Dearborn, 1940; Frostig, 1965; Gates, 1935; Hegge, Kirk, & Kirk, 1940; Johnson, 1966; Kephart, 1960; Money, 1966; Monroe, 1932; Strauss & Lehtinen, 1947; Wepman, 1964). She also reported that textbooks used to train teachers of students with learning disabilities typically recommended using multisensory techniques for word-recognition instruction and other domains of symbolic and conceptual learning.

Bryant (1979), however, was unable to find any scientific evidence to support the then-current theories for why multisensory instruction was needed for students with learning disabilities (e.g., the theory of deficient **cross-modal integration**). She noted that the popularity of both generic and reading-specific multisensory practices was attributable primarily to reports of success rather than to empirical evidence supporting either the theory or the practice of multisensory teaching. Bryant's review as well as subsequent reviews of the research literature in learning disabilities (e.g., Clark, 1988; Lyon & Moats, 1988; Moats & Lyon, 1993; Torgesen, 1991) failed to find research evidence to support the rationale for multisensory strategies. Bryant herself compared visual-auditory-kinesthetic word-study techniques with visual-auditory word-study techniques and reported that young readers responded equally well to both. She concluded that other principles of good instruction, including enhancing student attention, providing feedback and modeling, avoiding overloading the student, giving sufficient practice, and providing effective reinforcement, accounted for student success.

Although many of the programs incorporating these strategies have been effective according to clinical reports, the specific contribution of the multisensory component to the overall success of those programs has not yet been thoroughly documented or explained through rigorous manipulation of instructional conditions and subsequent measurement of outcomes. Yet, research in cognition demonstrating the need for active learner engagement, scientific evidence of the efficacy of phonics instruction, and insights from neuroscience (see the section on the multisensory nature of the brain) lend support for the rationale, content, and overall approach of MSLE programs.

CURRENT RESEARCH

Empirical evidence for the specific importance of the multisensory component to the success of MSLE teaching may be explored in studies of cognition as well as studies on the efficacy of phonics instruction. Theoretical support for the added benefit of the multisensory component may be sought in studies of neuroscience.

Studies of Cognition

Even before much was known about the nature of linguistic processing in reading disability, there was substantial evidence that successful instructional practices with students who had learning disabilities included deliberate provision of reinforcement and conscious employment of responsive, strategic learning (Lyon & Moats, 1988; Swanson, 1999; Wong, 1991). As cognitive psychologists have demonstrated, learning is an active, constructive process in which new information is linked with established schemata (Wittrock, 1992). The brain transforms new information in accordance with stored information that it has activated during the learning process. **Active learning** is that which causes the learner to mentally search for connections between new and existing information. That is, instruction that includes teaching metacognition—the deliberate rearrangement, regrouping, or modal transfer of information and the conscious choice of and evaluation of the strategies used to accomplish a task—is more effective than rote or passive memorization approaches in almost every domain of learning. Students who must do something as they learn attend better to the details of a stimulus and are likely to remember more. For example, students who create their own **mnemonic strategies** tend to learn from those more readily than students who are provided with a mnemonic strategy. Students who think aloud while working remember more and make fewer errors.

Adams, Treiman, and Pressley (1998) completed an extensive review of the research literature on reading comprehension instruction. They concluded that the active (vocal) modeling and rehearsal of basic comprehension functions such as summarizing, questioning, and predicting during an interaction among a teacher and group of students was much more effective in improving comprehension than was structured seat work or independent silent reading. The high rate of active response on the part of students, the combination of reading and **verbalization** of ideas, and the emphasis on deliberate employment of learning strategies characterized instructional conditions that resulted in retention and generalization of reading comprehension skills.

Studies of the Efficacy of Phonics Instruction

Traditionally, methods for teaching reading in an **alphabetic language**, beginning with the methods used by teachers in ancient Greece, have included direct teaching of the links between sounds and symbols (Matthews, 1966). Even before the work of the National Reading Panel (NRP; National Institute of Child Health and Human Development [NICHD], 2000), several comprehensive reviews concluded that direct, systematic teaching of phonics for beginning and remedial readers, along with practice in text reading and instruction in various comprehension skills, was a necessary component of effective instruction if all students were to be successful (Adams, 1990; Anderson, Hiebert, Scott, & Wilkinson, 1985; Chall, 1967, 1983). The studies reflected a variety of research methodologies, including small, well-controlled laboratory experiments and large-scale, multiple-classroom research. None of the major, comprehensive evaluations of research in reading instructional methods ever concluded that phonics was unnecessary or unimportant in elementary instruction. It has always been the case that children who have received direct instruction in speech–print correspondences learn to read words, spell, and define vocabulary better than children who do not receive such instruction, especially if they are defined as at risk for failure, even though educators have eschewed those research findings with regularity (Moats, 2000; Snow, Burns, & Griffin, 1998).

Research has explained why phonics instruction is necessary and effective for children learning to read and spell an alphabetic orthography. Skilled reading requires accurate processing of the internal details of words—their phonological, **morphological,** and orthographic features (see Adams et al., 1998; Rayner, Foorman, Perfetti, Pesetsky, & Seidenberg, 2001; Share & Stanovich, 1995; Vellutino et al., 1996, for reviews). Beginning readers must be aware or must learn that words are made up of individual speech sounds (phonemes). They must be able to represent in their minds the linguistic structure of words they are learning to read, primarily at the phoneme level (Ehri et al., 2001), and at other levels of language structure as well, especially morphology or the meaningful parts of words (Henry, 2010). Although it appears that good readers guess at words or that they read whole words as units, good readers in fact process virtually every letter of the words they read and are able, on demand, to translate print to speech rapidly and efficiently. The fluency of this translation process permits a good reader to attend to the meaning of what is read. Therefore, it is logical that effective instruction with poor readers would seek to increase their awareness of phonemes and other linguistic units and that the speech-to-print translation process would become a focus of teaching until the children read fluently enough to focus on comprehension.

Indeed, a wide range of studies has shown that poor readers are marked by weaknesses in **phoneme awareness**, slow and inefficient decoding skills, inaccurate spelling, and related language-processing difficulties. Poor readers' problems are linguistic in nature and are related to inaccurate and inefficient linguistic coding at basic levels of word and subword processes. Comprehension is impaired when readers cannot decode print accurately; too much mental energy is being used to recode the message, and too little is available for making meaning. Effective instruction addresses these issues as directly and systematically as possible (Blachman, Schatschneider, Fletcher, & Clonan, 2003; Lyon, Fletcher, & Barnes, 2003; Torgesen et al., 2001; Vellutino et al., 1996).

Neuroscience Offers Insights into Reading and Multisensory Processing

The efficacy of structured, systematic, explicit teaching of all language-based skills is no longer questioned by leading researchers (Lyon, Fletcher, Fuchs, & Chhabra, 2005), but evidence is still needed to explain the popularity of multisensory activities in language learning. Empirical support for the power of multisensory techniques remains illusive in studies of reading instruction (Bryant, 1979; Clark, 1988; Lyon & Moats, 1988; Torgesen, 1991). Nevertheless, theoretical support for the added benefit of multisensory techniques can be sought from neuroscience studies

Imaging the Reading Brain: Window into Structure and Function

Neuroscience research is advancing our understanding of reading and reading disabilities and elevating our knowledge of the multisensory nature of the brain. In particular, **neuroimaging** research is providing insights into the reading brain, whereas another body of work is generating findings about the brain's holistic multisensory design. Both are promising avenues of research for investigating the contribution of the multisensory component to the effectiveness of MSLE. Modern imaging techniques are revealing new insights into the structure and function of human brains.

Structural neuroimaging (MRI) allows us to examine the brain's physical characteristics. **Functional neuroimaging** (fMRI), in which images are constructed showing brain activity while individuals perform specific activities, provides a glimpse of how the brain is organized for complex cognitive tasks such as reading. These powerful imaging technologies explore the inner workings and architecture of living brains and have changed the landscape of neuroscience. A report by Vul, Harris, Winkielman, and Pashler (2009), however, suggested that incorrect statistical assumptions may bias the results of some fMRI studies, a cautionary note worth keeping in mind. Poldrack and Mumford (2009) provided a number of recommendations (e.g., use larger sample sizes, use controls for multiple comparisons, use appropriate statistical methods).

Normal Reading

Multiple brain areas and complex connections among those areas are activated during typical reading. The brain does not store information in localized compartments but rather establishes highly specialized and widely distributed multisensory networks. At the risk of oversimplifying a complex process, messages from print are processed first in the visual (occipital) cortex, then in the **left angular gyrus**, which is linked to the left hemisphere's speech-processing centers. The left angular gyrus is the primary location for translating visual-orthographic information into phonological representations (linking symbol to sound). The nearby language association areas connect meaning to those phonological codes. Other connections also link the visual association cortex to speech-processing areas. (Figure 1.1 in Chapter 1 shows the areas of the brain that are involved in reading.)

The neural connections for reading are so specialized that the type of word being read—for example, a noun or an adjective—affects the exact areas that are activated for processing. Processing proceeds simultaneously and interactively, even though specific modules or neural connections are highly specialized for processing specific jobs (Rumsey, 1996).

Reading Disabilities

Understanding language-based learning disabilities, their biological bases, and their responsiveness to treatment has been enhanced by information obtained using modern neuroimaging techniques (Eden & Moats, 2002; Lyon, Shaywitz, & Shaywitz, 2003; Shaywitz, 2003). During reading, children with poor phonological processing skills show reduced cerebral blood flow in the left frontal and temporal cortices (where incoming language is coded and interpreted) and reduced activation of language areas normally involved in reading. Dyslexic readers also may rely more on the right cerebral hemisphere (Shaywitz & Shaywitz, 2004).

An fMRI study in dyslexic children looking at both dyslexia and reading ability suggested that underactivation of the left parietal cortex (involved in mapping phonology onto orthography) and in the fusiform cortex on both sides (the left side is usually involved in orthographic coding) reflect functional difficulties related to the person's dyslexia (Hoeft et al., 2007). The hyperactivation seen in the left inferior and left middle frontal cortices and in certain subcortical structures, such as the caudate nucleus and thalamus, however, was not related to dyslexia, but instead was related to low reading levels. This study suggested that atypical activation patterns in some cortical structures (parietal and fusiform areas) may continue to characterize dyslexic adults, even when they have learned to read reasonably well.

Neuroanatomical Differences

A number of imaging studies documenting anatomical differences in dyslexia converge with the seminal neuropathological studies that found neuronal migration differences, including polymicrogyria (a severe type of neuronal migration abnormality), in the cerebral cortex of people with dyslexia (e.g., Galaburda et al., 1985). A neuroanatomical study also discovered perisylvian (lateral surface of the brain) polymicrogyria in several individuals from three families that had developmental language disorders and/or reading impairments (Oliveira et al., 2008).

Other examples of neuroanatomical differences in people with dyslexia include a reduction in gray matter volume in the left parietal cortex of dyslexic children (Hoeft et al., 2007) and in the right supramarginal gyrus and also bilaterally in the fusiform gyrus of adolescents (Kronbichler et al., 2008).

Kronbichler et al. (2008) also found decreased gray matter on both sides of the anterior cerebellum. Although researchers have suggested for years that the cerebellum played a key role in dyslexia (Nicolson & Fawcett, 1999), only recently has this view been generally accepted. Pernet, Poline, Demonet, and Rousselet (2009) dramatically concluded that the right cerebellum was the best biomarker for dyslexia based on their findings of greater variability in the volume of the right cerebellar declive (the vermal lobule caudal to the primary fissure) and right lentiform nucleus (a subcortical structure that is part of the basal ganglia). They suggested that lower gray matter volume in the right cerebellar declive (which is involved in motor sequence learning) leads to a lack of automatization (critical for efficient reading) in the right lentiform nucleus. Strikingly, the cerebellar difference turned out to be the best predictor for poor performance in both phonological and lexicon-related tasks.

Brain-Based Intervention Studies

Several studies on the effect of intensive, systematic, structured language instruction on children with reading disabilities have shown that functional brain patterns may become more normalized as a consequence of instruction (Berninger et al., 2003; Blachman et al., 2003; Meyler, Keller, Cherkassky, Garbieli, & Just, 2008; Shaywitz, 2003; Simos et al., 2002). Increased activation of left hemisphere parietal-temporal and occipital-temporal regions was seen in response to structured language teaching methods. This indicated that after instruction with these methods, these brain areas might be better able to handle the complicated task of automatic word recognition. Also, functional connectivity differences in children with dyslexia in comparison with controls were eliminated after a 3-week treatment program consisting of explicit instruction in the alphabetic principle and linguistic awareness training (Richards & Berninger, 2008).

Thus, one possibility is that individuals with dyslexia with weak phonological processing must establish stronger and/or alternative circuits for word recognition to compensate for disruption of the circuitry normally relied on for reading. Also, it is possible that activation of sensorimotor pathways through the use of remedial instruction strategies involving the fingertips, hand, arm, whole body, and/or vocal speech apparatus during symbolic learning can make circuits necessary for word recognition more easily established and accessed. The neurobiological mechanisms by which brain changes may be influenced by multisensory instruction are largely unknown, although there are hints from understanding the multisensory nature of the organization of the human brain.

The Multisensory Brain: A Powerful Design

For years, students of neuroscience were taught that the neocortex is subdivided into three functional areas: sensory, motor, and association. As it turns out, this traditional view of cerebral cortex organization is wrong. Another view based on more recent research—that processing is unimodal involving an arrangement of interacting specialized cortical areas with minimal architecture dedicated to multisensory integration—also is wrong (Kaas & Collins, 2004).

Scientists are discovering that the brain is far more multisensory than once thought. The clinical wisdom of MSLE practitioners has long capitalized on the multisensory design of the brain. Now science is discovering that the brain's multisensory processing capabilities are more elaborate and less compartmentalized than previously understood. Old models of cerebral cortex organization with neatly compartmentalized regions specializing in specific modalities are giving way to a greater appreciation of the holistic multisensory nature of the brain. Here are 10 multisensory revelations (for in-depth discussion see Calvert, Spence, & Stein, 2004):

1. Multisensory processing of sensory inputs is a fundamental rule of brain structure and function. We constantly use information from all of our senses. Even experiences that appear specific to one sense (e.g., vision) are modulated by activity in other senses (Calvert et al., 2004).

2. The brain's multisensory design facilitates attention, perception, and learning. Reaction times are faster to multisensory stimuli (Wallace, 2004).

3. Multisensory brain regions that respond to two or more sensory modalities (e.g., vision, auditory, tactile, olfactory) may exist in the human brain from infancy.

4. We are not always aware of multisensory interactions. For example, there is activity in the visual cortex during tactile perception (Macaluso & Driver, 2004), and speech comprehension increases when a speaker is seen as well as heard (Calvert & Lewis, 2004).

5. Multisensory inputs merge (sensory convergence) onto single neurons or onto adjacent neurons within a cortical region (Schroeder & Foxe, 2004).

6. Individual sensory inputs converge from their sensory-specific areas to shared multimodal control areas, resulting in multisensory integration by sensory convergence (Macaluso & Driver, 2004).

7. Multisensory integration includes parallel stages of convergence at early and late stages of information processing in what historically were considered primary sensory areas as well as in previously identified multisensory areas (Calvert et al., 2004).

8. Multisensory neurons may be specifically designed and activated by using tools such as pens, pencils, and keyboards.

9. Voluntary motor responses link (bind) with their intended and expected perceptual effects, leading to synchronization of distant brain areas so that noise in the system is reduced and communication is improved, resulting in the "collective enhancement of precision" (Tabareau & Slotine, 2010).

10. Speech perception is the product of multisensory networks stimulated by auditory (voice) and visual (movement of the lips and mouth) inputs resulting in rich interpersonal interactions. This may have implications for understanding Asperger syndrome, in which there may be a deficiency in the organization of multisensory connections—possibly in mirror neuron circuits—that play a role in empathy and understanding the emotions felt by another person.

The human brain is a multisensory organ—with multiplicities of cross-modal convergence at the single neuron level to the cortical region level and from early to late stages of processing. The seminal work of Norman Geschwind (1965) established relationships between the brain's structure and function. The fundamentals of these relationships have not been challenged, but emerging research does show that the interrelated elements and connectional patterns necessary for integrated multisensory processing are stunningly complex and intertwined. Harnessing this powerful and encompassing cerebral design and its learning capacity should be a goal in education, particularly for children challenged by certain learning tasks (e.g., students with dyslexia).

Implications for Research and Practice: A Two-Way Street

What does all this mean for educators, particularly those incorporating multisensory teaching into evidence-based reading interventions for children with reading disabilities? What have we learned from the powerful imaging technologies, and what have we discovered about the brain's holistic multisensory design to support the efficacy of multisensory strategies? Has neuroscience validated the multisensory component of MSLE? Not quite.

A basis of support is emerging, but neuroscience has not yet provided a definitive answer—a point underscored by the Santiago Declaration (2007; http://www .santiagodeclaration.org). Overreaching interpretation of the application of neuroscience research to practice led an international group of distinguished neuroscientists and cognitive psychologists at a conference in Santiago, Chile, to issue a declaration stating, "Neuroscientific research, at this stage in its development, does not offer scientific guidelines for policy, practice, or parenting."

In an era of increasing focus on translation research, this cautionary message is noteworthy. Translational research is emerging as an important trend. For several years, the National Institutes of Health (NIH) have issued funding opportunities for community-based participatory research—scientific inquiry that researchers and communities, such as networks of schools, conduct jointly. Nevertheless, the Santiago Declaration asserted that important principles of consensus about child development and early learning are "based primarily on findings from social and behavioral research, not on brain research." That said, the declaration concludes, "Current research offers a promissory note, however, for the future."

The bottom line is that exciting breakthroughs in neuroscience have not yet translated into equally exciting breakthroughs in education. Indeed, brain-based pedagogy (and its various publications, trainings, and products) is more about marketing than science. Regarding the potential value of multisensory strategies in MSLE, neuroscience has provided intriguing glimpses into the likely power of these strategies, but it has not yet provided empirical evidence supporting their contribution to evidence-based instruction.

The same holds true for the imaging studies, which correlate with behavior studies on reading disabilities and effective reading instruction but are mute on the question of the contributing value of the multisensory component. As discussed previously in this chapter, consensus reports (NICHD, 2000; Snow et al., 1998) and subsequent education intervention research (see Fletcher, Lyon, Fuchs, & Barnes, 2007) have contributed a wealth of knowledge about reading, reading disabilities, and the essential components and principles of effective reading instruction. Neuroimaging findings are consistent with the solid base of evidence that supports intensive, systematic, and cumulative methods and approaches focused explicitly on teaching the structure of language. MSLE approaches typically share the content components and teaching principles that characterize evidence-based reading instruction—with the notable exception of the multisensory tenet, for which there is scant supporting evidence (see Fletcher et al., 2007).

As disheartening as this dearth of empirical support from neuroscience and behavioral research may be for practitioners seeking scientific validation for multisensory teaching principles, it is important to keep in mind that this lack of evidence reflects not only a lack of rigorous research comparing evidence-based reading instruction with and without the multisensory component but also the challenges inherent in such research. One study did find that a multisensory articulatory component was not necessary to effective intervention (Wise, Ring, & Olson, 1999), but much more research needs to be conducted to rule in or out the efficacy of multisensory strategies in academic skill instruction and to understand the intricacies of multisensory processing and the possibilities in harnessing these capabilities for academic learning.

Since the early 1990s, three cardinal principles have emerged from scientific research to shape education policies and professional standards and practices, particularly as they relate to reading and reading disabilities. First, instruction should be scientifically based (NICHD, 2000). Second, "training in motor, visual, neural, or cognitive processes without academic content does not lead to better academic outcomes" (Fletcher et al., 2007, p. 130). Third, reading disabilities can be prevented in many young children (optimal approach with best return) and alleviated at any age (Lyon et al., 2001). All three principles are pillars in evidence-based reform and are elevating standards of knowledge and practice among educators working with children with reading disabilities or at risk for reading failure (see The International Dyslexia Association [IDA], 2010). All three also factor into any discussion about the efficacy of the multisensory component in MSLE approaches.

The second and third principles are entirely consistent with the tenets of MSLE. A caveat is in order regarding the first principle, however. Scientifically based instructional practices have proven value, but it does not follow that instructional practices lacking scientific evidence necessarily have no value. Carl Sagan's controversial quote— "absence of evidence is not evidence of absence"—applies. "In other words, lack of scientific evidence supporting the efficacy of the multisensory strategies in MSLE reflects lack of scientific study, the absence of which does not refute the value of these strategies" (Cowen, personal communication). It does, however, reflect the inherent difficulties in such study. Given the brain's dynamic and holistic multisensory nature, the challenges in attempting to isolate and manipulate multisensory inputs and outputs in the context of evidence-based reading instruction cannot be overstated.

Decades of support from generations of knowledgeable practitioners certainly offer some basis for assigning value to the multisensory ingredient in MSLE approaches, particularly for children with reading disabilities. Yet,

> In this era of evidence-based education, citing clinical support and testimony will not suffice, even when authoritative and compelling. Lack of scientific evidence can be misconstrued, particularly as education policy makers, leaders, and teachers struggle to implement federal regulations while juggling formidable competing priorities. In this pressure-cooker climate, unsubstantiated practices risk being overlooked or viewed as low priorities, if not dismissed outright. (Cowen, 2004)

The irony is that the community of practitioners, schools, programs, and organizations that practice and promote the principles of MSLE helped lay the groundwork for research in reading and dyslexia, which in turn helped pave the way for evidence-based education policies. As the emerging translational research trend gathers momentum, however, MSLE educators may once again have a vital role to play. A grass roots coalition has helped raise funds to establish the Multisensory Research Grant Program (administered by the IDA; http://www.interdys.org) to stimulate research investigating the multisensory component in MSLE.

Just as research can inform instruction, educators' insights can inform research.

> Translating research to practice—a Holy Grail in education for decades—mostly has been an ivory-tower-to-troops-in-the-trenches-campaign. True, scientific research has yielded a wealth of exciting information about the brain, reading, reading disabilities, and essential elements of reading instruction. Important strides have been made with this top-down approach. But even the most promising behavioral research findings sometimes disappoint in their application to complex, real-school environments. (Cowen, 2009, p. 4)

And, for the most part, neuroscience is not quite ready to offer scientific guidelines to educators. Even with all that is known, researchers do not have all the answers, and formidable challenges remain in implementing and scaling the answers they do have.

A new approach, one that partners educators and researchers tasked with generating translational research (practice-based research to achieve evidence-based practice), might lead to answers that help bridge the clinic to classroom chasm and facilitate scalable scientifically based practices (Sherman & Cowen, 2009). Clinical observations can be wellsprings for hypotheses. At the very least, knowledgeable practitioners' insights might lead researchers to important questions such as, "What is the contribution of the multisensory component to evidence-based instruction?"

Neuroscience is advancing the understanding of reading and reading disabilities and elevating knowledge of the multisensory nature of the brain. A basis of support for the multisensory strategies in MSLE might emerge in the continuing application of powerful imaging technologies to further illuminate the structure and function of the brain. Support also might emerge in the unfolding discoveries about the brain's powerfully holistic multisensory design. Even with all the advances science and its technologies offer, fundamental points might be being missed. It would be a mistake to dismiss the potential value of multisensory strategies in MSLE before the research has been done.

SUMMARY

Multisensory teaching links listening, speaking, reading, and writing. The simultaneous deployment of **visual, auditory, kinesthetic, and tactile** sensory modalities (**VAKT**) used in multisensory instruction has traditionally been a staple of remedial and preventive intervention for students with learning disabilities and/or dyslexia. Multisensory methods support the connection of oral language with visual language symbols and can involve using touch and movement to facilitate conceptual learning in all academic areas. The appeal of multisensory instruction endures even though it has been poorly defined and is not well validated in existing intervention studies.

As noted in this chapter, MSLE techniques have been cited and recommended by experts in learning disorders before and throughout the 20th century. Although respected instructional programs incorporate similar instructional principles, research has contributed more to the definition and explication of the nature of dyslexia and learning disorders than it has contributed to supporting the use of MSLE.

It is ironic that research-based conceptions of reading and language-based learning disabilities may provide a better theoretical rationale to explain why MSLE works than are provided by the theories of the methods originators. Poor and novice readers at risk for reading and spelling difficulties are usually lacking in phonological skill and often have related problems with **short-term memory** of verbal information and rapid retrieval of verbal information. In addition, at least one third of children with language-based learning disabilities also have coexisting attention disorders. Research has demonstrated unequivocally that such learners benefit when the structure of spoken and written language, beginning with phonemes, is represented for them explicitly, sequentially, directly, and systematically in the context of balanced and comprehensive reading instruction. Multisensory experiences with linguistic units such as single phonemes, letters, **morphemes,** words, and sentences may in fact activate more circuitry during language learning than unisensory experiences.

Conceptions of memory organization, neural activation patterns in language processing, and the importance of metacognition are consistent with the efficacy of multisensory techniques. New neural networks, which in the human brain are highly specialized for certain processing functions, are established through repeated activation. A more complete and explicit registration of linguistic information (phonological and other) is likely to occur in the learner's **working memory** when attention to linguistic detail is enhanced through multisensory involvement. Those transient associative memories are more likely to be stored in connection with existing information in the language processor if other movement or sensory events occur with them. Most likely, it is not simply the multimodal nature of such practice that explains its power but the mediating effect of various sensory and motor experiences on attention and recall.

Knowledgeable clinicians have been hoping for a scientific explanation for accepted instructional practices for years, and much progress has been made. Eventually, cognitive psychology, educational psychology, and the neurosciences may provide even more definitive support for specific techniques of teaching and refinements of practice. Research is slowly but surely addressing the question of what to do, for which types of children, when, how much, for how long, and in which environments. Although neuroscience, cognitive psychology, educational psychology, and educational intervention research pave the way toward an even better understanding of reading development and reading remediation, the practices detailed in this book rest on both clinical experience and good science.

REFERENCES

Adams, M.J. (1990). *Beginning to read: Thinking and learning about print.* Cambridge, MA: The MIT Press.

Adams, M.J., Treiman, R., & Pressley, M. (1998). Reading, writing, and literacy. In I. Sigel & A. Renninger (Eds.), *Handbook of child psychology: Vol. 4. Child psychology in practice* (5th ed., pp. 275–355). New York: Wiley.

Alliance for Accreditation and Certification of Structured Language Education. (2003). *Alliance directory: A list of accredited training courses and certified individuals* [CD-ROM]. Baltimore: International Dyslexia Association.

Anderson, R.C., Hiebert, E.H., Scott, J.A., & Wilkinson, I.A.G. (1985). *Becoming a nation of readers: The report of the Commission on Reading.* Washington, DC: U.S. Department of Education, The National Institute of Education.

Ayres, J. (1972). Improving academic scores through sensory integration. *Journal of Learning Disabilities, 5*(6), 338–343.

Berlin, R. (1887). *Eine besondere art der wortblindheit: Dyslexia* [A special kind of word blindness: Dyslexia]. Wiesbaden, Germany: J.F. Bergmann.

Berninger, V.W., Nagy, W.E., Carlisle, J., Thomson, J., Hoffer, D., Abbott, S., et al. (2003). Effective treatment for children with dyslexia in grades 4–6: Behavioral and brain evidence. In B.R. Foorman (Ed.), *Preventing and remediating reading difficulties: Bringing science to scale* (pp. 381–417). Timonium, MD: York Press.

Blachman, B.A., Schatschneider, C., Fletcher, J.M., & Clonan, S.M. (2003). Early reading intervention: A classroom prevention study and a remediation study. In B.R. Foorman (Ed.), *Preventing and remediating reading difficulties: Bringing science*

to scale (pp. 253–271). Timonium, MD: York Press.

Bryant, S. (1979). *Relative effectiveness of visual-auditory vs. visual-auditory-kinesthetic-tactile procedures for teaching sight words and letter sounds to young disabled readers.* Unpublished doctoral dissertation, Teachers College, Columbia University, New York.

Calvert, G.A., & Lewis, J.W. (2004). Hemodynamic studies of audiovisual interactions. In G. Calvert, C. Spence, & G.C. Stein (Eds.), *The handbook of multisensory processes* (pp. 483–502). Cambridge, MA: The MIT Press.

Calvert, G., Spence, C., & Stein, G.C. (Eds.). (2004). *The handbook of multisensory processes.* Cambridge, MA: The MIT Press.

Chall, J.S. (1967). *Learning to read: The great debate.* New York: McGraw-Hill.

Chall, J.S. (1983). *Stages of reading development.* New York: McGraw-Hill.

Clark, D.B. (1988). *Dyslexia: Theory and practice of remedial instruction.* Timonium, MD: York Press.

Clark, D.B., & Uhry, J. (1995). *Dyslexia: Theory and practice of remedial instruction* (2nd ed.). Timonium, MD: York Press.

Cowen, C.D. (2004). *International Dyslexia Association's multisensory research grant program initiative: A bold and challenging initiative.* Retrieved February 8, 2010, from http://www.interdys.org /ResearchMSIGrantProgramandDonors.htm

Cowen, C.D. (2009). *Independent LD schools: Catalysts for change and valuable research partners.* Retrieved February 8, 2010, from http://leadership summit.ning.com

Cruickshank, W.M., Betzen, F.A., Ratzeburg, F.H., & Tannhauser, M.T. (1961). *A teaching method for* brain-injured and hyperactive children: A demonstration-pilot study. Syracuse, NY: Syracuse University Press.

Dearborn, W.F. (1929). Unpublished paper presented at the Ninth International Congress of Psychology, Yale University, New Haven, CT.

Dearborn, W.F. (1940). On the possible relations of visual fatigue to reading disabilities. School and Society, 52, 532–536.

Dejerine, J. (1892, February 27). Contribution a l'étude anatomo-pathologigue et clinique des différentes variétés de cécité verbale [Contribution to the anatomo-pathological and clinical studies of different types of word blindness]. Mémoriale Société Biologigue, 61.

Eden, G.F., & Moats, L.C. (2002). The role of neuroscience in the remediation of students with dyslexia. Nature Neuroscience, 5, 1080–1084.

Ehri, L.C., Nunes, S.R., Willows, D.M., Schuster, B.V., Yaghoub-Zadeh, Z., & Shanahan, T. (2001). Phonemic awareness instruction helps children learn to read: Evidence from the National Reading Panel's meta-analysis. Reading Research Quarterly, 36, 250–287.

Farrell, M., Pickering, J., North, N., & Schavio, C. (2004, Fall). What is multisensory instruction? The IMSLEC Record, 8(3).

Fernald, G.M. (1943). Remedial techniques in basic school subjects. New York: McGraw-Hill.

Fernald, G.M., & Keller, H. (1921). The effect of kinesthetic factors in development of word recognition in the case of non-readers. Journal of Educational Research, 4, 355–377.

Fletcher, J.M., Lyon, G.R., Fuchs, L.S., & Barnes, M.A. (2007). Learning disabilities: From identification to intervention. New York: The Guilford Press.

Frostig, M. (1965). Corrective reading in the classroom. The Reading Teacher, 18, 573–580.

Galaburda, A.M., Sherman, G.F., Rosen, G.D., Aboitiz, F., & Geschwind, N. (1985). Developmental dyslexia: Four consecutive cases with cortical anomalies. Annals of Neurology, 18, 222–233.

Gates, A.I. (1927). Studies of phonetic training in beginning reading. Journal of Educational Psychology, 18, 217–226.

Gates, A. (1935). The improvement of reading: A program of diagnostic and remedial methods. New York: Macmillan.

Geschwind, N. (1965). Disconnexion syndromes in animals and man: I–II. Brain, 88, 237–294, 585–644.

Gillingham, A., & Stillman, B. (1960). Remedial training for children with specific disability in reading, spelling, and penmanship (6th ed.). Cambridge, MA: Educators Publishing Service.

Hegge, T.G., Kirk, S.A., & Kirk, W.D. (1940). Remedial reading drills. Ann Arbor, MI: George Wahr.

Hegge, T.G., Sears, R., & Kirk, S.A. (1932). Reading cases in an institution for mentally retarded problem children. Proceedings and Addresses of the Fifty-Sixth Annual Session of the American Association for the Study of the Feebleminded, 15, 149–212.

Henry, M.K. (2010). Unlocking literacy: Effective decoding and spelling instruction (2nd ed.). Baltimore: Paul H. Brookes Publishing Co.

Hinshelwood, J. (1917). Congenital word blindness. London: H.K. Lewis.

Hoeft, F., Meyler, A., Hernandez, A., Juel, C., Taylor-Hill, H., Martindale, J.L., et al. (2007) Functional and morphometric brain dissociation between dyslexia and reading ability. Proceedings of the National Academy Sciences USA, 104, 4234–4239.

Hunt, J.M. (1964). Introduction: Revisiting Montessori. In M. Montessori (Ed.), The Montessori method (A.E. George, Trans.). New York: Schocken Books.

Husband, R.W. (1928). Human learning on a four-section elevated finger maze. Journal of General Psychology, 1, 15–28.

International Dyslexia Association. (2010). Knowledge and practice standards for teachers of reading. Retrieved from http://www.interdys.org/standards.htm

James, W. (1890). The principles of psychology (Vol. 2). New York: Henry Holt & Co.

Johnson, M. (1966). Tracing and kinesthetic techniques. In J. Money (Ed.), The disabled reader: Education of the dyslexic child (pp. 147–160). Baltimore: The Johns Hopkins University Press.

Kaas, J.H., & Collins, C.E. (2004). The resurrection of multisensory cortex in primates: Connection patterns that integrate modalities. In G. Calvert, C. Spence, & G.C. Stein (Eds.), The handbook of multisensory processes (pp. 285–293). Cambridge, MA: The MIT Press.

Kephart, N.C. (1960). The slow learner in the classroom. Columbus, OH: Charles E. Merrill.

Kronbichler, M., Wimmer, H., Staffen, W., Hutzler, F., Mair, A., & Ladurner, G. (2008). Developmental dyslexia: Gray matter abnormalities in the occipitotemporal cortex. Human Brain Mapping, 29, 613–625.

Lyon, G.R., Fletcher, J.M., & Barnes, M.C. (2003). Learning disabilities. In E.J. Mash & R.A. Barkley (Eds.), Child psychopathology (2nd ed., pp. 520–586). New York: Guilford Press.

Lyon, G.R., Fletcher, J.M., Fuchs, L.S., & Chhabra, V. (2005). Learning disabilities. In E. Mash & R. Barkley (Eds.), Treatment of childhood disorders (3rd ed., pp. 512–594). New York: Guilford Press.

Lyon, G.R., Fletcher, J.M., Shaywitz, S.E., Shaywitz, B.A., Torgesen, J.K., Wood, F.B., et al. (2001). Rethinking learning disabilities. In C.E. Finn, Jr., R.A. Rotherham, & C.R. Hokansom, Jr. (Eds.), Rethinking special education for a new century (pp. 259–287). Washington, DC: Thomas B. Fordham Foundation and Progressive Policy Institute.

Lyon, G.R., & Moats, L.C. (1988). Critical issues in the instruction of the learning disabled. *Journal of Consulting and Clinical Psychology, 56,* 830–835.

Lyon, G.R., Shaywitz, S.E., & Shaywitz, B.A. (2003). A definition of dyslexia. *Annals of Dyslexia, 53,* 1–14.

Macaluso, E., & Driver, J. (2004) Functional imaging evidence for multisensory spatial representation and cross-modal attentional interactions in the human brain. In G. Calvert, C. Spence, & G.C. Stein (Eds.), *The handbook of multisensory processes* (pp. 529–548) Cambridge, MA: The MIT Press.

Matthews, M.M. (1966). *Teaching to read: Historically considered.* Chicago: University of Chicago Press.

Meyler, A., Keller, T.A., Cherkassky, V.L., Gabrieli, J.D., & Just, M.A. (2008). Modifying the brain activation of poor readers during sentence comprehension with extended remedial instruction: A longitudinal study of neuroplasticity. *Neuropsychologia, 46,* 2580–2592.

Miles, W. (1928). The high finger relief maze for human learning. *Journal of General Psychology, 1,* 3–14.

Moats, L.C. (2000). *Whole language lives on: The illusion of "balance" in reading instruction.* Washington, DC: Thomas B. Fordham Foundation.

Moats, L., & Lyon, G.R. (1993). Learning disabilities in the United States: Advocacy, science, and the future of the field. *Journal of Learning Disabilities, 26,* 282–294.

Money, J. (Ed.). (1966). *The disabled reader: Education of the dyslexic child.* Baltimore: The Johns Hopkins University Press.

Monroe, M. (1932). *Children who cannot read.* Chicago: University of Chicago Press.

Montessori, M. (1912). *The Montessori method.* New York: Frederick Stokes.

Morgan, W.P. (1896, November 7). Word blindness. *British Medical Journal, 2,* 1378.

National Institute of Child Health and Human Development. (2000). *Report of the National Reading Panel. Teaching children to read: An evidence-based assessment of the scientific research literature on reading and its implications for reading instruction: Reports of the subgroups* (NIH Publication No. 00-4754). Washington, DC: U.S. Government Printing Office. Available at http://www.national readingpanel.org

Nicolson, R.I., & Fawcett, A.J. (1999). Developmental dyslexia: The role of the cerebellum. *Dyslexia: An International Journal of Research and Practice, 5,* 155–177.

Oliveira, E.P., Hage, S.R., Guimarães, C.A., Brandão-Almeida, I., Lopes-Cendes, I., Guerreiro, C.A., et al. (2008). Characterization of language and reading skills in familial polymicrogyria. *Brain Development, 30,* 254–260.

Orton, S.T. (1925). "Word-blindness" in school children. *Archives of Neurology and Psychiatry, 14,* 581–615.

Orton, S.T. (1928). Specific reading disability—strephosymbolia. *JAMA: Journal of the American Medical Association, 90,* 1095–1099.

Pernet, C.R., Poline, J.B., Demonet, J.F., & Rousselet, G.A. (2009). Brain classification reveals the right cerebellum as the best biomarker of dyslexia. *BMC Neuroscience, 10,* 67–86.

Poldrack, R.A., & Mumford, J.A. (2009). Independence in ROI analysis: Where is the voodoo? *Social Cognitive Affective Neuroscience, 4,* 208–213.

Rayner, K., Foorman, B., Perfetti, C., Pesetsky, D., & Seidenberg, M.S. (2001). How psychological science informs the teaching of reading. *Psychological Science in the Public Interest, 2*(2), 31–74.

Richards, T.L., & Berninger, V.W. (2008) Abnormal fMRI connectivity in children with dyslexia during a phoneme task: Before but not after treatment. *Journal of Neurolinguistics, 21,* 294–304.

Rumsey, J.M. (1996). Neuroimaging in developmental dyslexia: A review and conceptualization. In G.R. Lyon & J.M. Rumsey (Eds.), *Neuroimaging: A window to the neurological foundations of learning and behavior in children* (pp. 57–77). Baltimore: Paul H. Brookes Publishing Co.

Schroeder, C.E., & Foxe, J.J. (2004). Multisensory convergence in early cortical processing. In G. Calvert, C. Spence, & G.C. Stein (Eds.), *The handbook of multisensory processes* (pp. 295–309). Cambridge: The MIT Press.

Share, D., & Stanovich, K.E. (1995). Cognitive processes in early reading development: Accommodating individual differences into a mode of acquisition. *Issues in Education: Contributions from Educational Psychology, 1,* 1–57.

Shaywitz, S. (2003). *Overcoming dyslexia: A new and complete science-based program for reading problems at any level.* New York: Alfred A. Knopf.

Shaywitz, S.E., & Shaywitz, B.A. (2004). Neurobiologic basis for reading and reading disability. In P. McCardle & V. Chhabra (Eds.), *The voice of evidence in reading research* (pp. 417–442). Baltimore: Paul H. Brookes Publishing Co.

Sherman, G.F., & Cowen, C.D. (2009). A road less traveled: From dyslexia research lab to school front lines. How bridging the researcher-educator chasm, applying lessons of cerebrodiversity, and exploring talent can advance understanding of dyslexia. In K. Pugh & P. McCardle (Eds.), *How children learn to read: Current issues and new directions in the integration of cognition, neurobiology, and genetics of reading and dyslexia research and practice* (pp. 43–64). New York: Psychology Press.

Simos, P.G., Fletcher, J.M., Bergman, E., Breier, J.I., Foorman, B.R., Castillo, E.M., et al. (2002). Dyslexia-specific brain activation profile becomes normal following successful remedial training. *Neurology, 58,* 1203–1213.

Snow, C.E., Burns, M.S., & Griffin, P. (Eds.). (1998). *Preventing reading difficulties in children.* Washington, DC: National Academies Press.

Strauss, A., & Lehtinen, L.E. (1947). *Psychopathology and education of the brain-injured child.* New York: Grune & Stratton.

Swanson, H.L. (1999). Reading research for students with LD: A meta-analysis of intervention outcomes. *Journal of Learning Disabilities, 32,* 504–532.

Tabareau, N., & Slotine, J.J. (2010). How synchronization protects from noise. *PLoS Computational Biology, 6,* e1000637.

Torgesen, J. (1991). Learning disabilities: Historical and conceptual issues. In B. Wong (Ed.), *Learning about learning disabilities* (pp. 3–37). San Diego: Academic Press.

Torgesen, J., Alexander, A.W., Wagner, R., Rashotte, C.A., Voeller, K., Conway, T., et al. (2001). Intensive remedial instruction for children with severe reading disabilities: Immediate and long-term outcomes from two instructional approaches. *Journal of Learning Disabilities, 34,* 33–58.

Vellutino, F.R., Scanlon, D.M., Sipay, E.R., Small, S.G., Pratt, A., Chen, R., et al. (1996). Cognitive profiles of difficult to remediate and readily remediated poor readers: Early intervention as a vehicle to distinguish between cognitive and experiential deficits as basic causes of specific reading disability. *Journal of Educational Psychology, 88,* 601–638.

Vul, E., Harris, C., Winkielman, P., & Pashler, H. (2009) Puzzlingly high correlations in fMRI studies of emotion, personality, and social cognition. *Perspectives on Psychological Science, 4,* 274–290.

Wallace, M.T. (2004). The development of multisensory integration. In G. Calvert, C. Spence, & G.C. Stein (Eds.), *The handbook of multisensory processes* (pp. 625–642). Cambridge: The MIT Press.

Wepman, J.M. (1964). The perceptual basis for learning. In H. Robinson (Ed.), *Meeting individual differences in reading.* Chicago: University of Chicago Press.

Wise, B.W., Ring, J., & Olson, R.K. (1999). Training phonological awareness with and without explicit attention to articulation. *Journal of Experimental Child Psychology, 72,* 271–304.

Wittrock, M.C. (1992). Generative learning processes of the brain. *Educational Psychologist, 27,* 531–541.

Wong, B.Y.L. (1991). Assessment of metacognitive research in learning disabilities: Theory, research, and practice. In H.L. Swanson (Ed.), *Handbook on the assessment of learning disabilities: Theory, research, and practice* (pp. 265–283). Austin, TX: PRO-ED.

Percentage of Respondents Using Multisensory Strategies Along a Continuum of Usage

Modality	Strategy	% Usage by score[a]					
		0	1	2	3	4	5
	Phonology						
Visual	Look at mouth of teacher to discriminate mouth positions (e.g., vowel versus consonant)	5.26	0	5.26	21.05	68.42	0*
Visual	Look at mouth in mirror to discriminate mouth positions	15.79	0	15.79	21.05	47.37	0*
Visual	Look at pictures or other graphic representations to discriminate mouth positions	36.84	5.26	21.05	5.26	31.58	0
Auditory	Listen (hear) to discriminate individual sounds	0	0	0	0	100	0*
Auditory	Discriminate voiced and unvoiced sounds	0	5.26	5.26	5.26	84.21	0*
Auditory	Discriminate number of sounds in spoken words	0	0	0	0	100	0*
Auditory	Identify location of each sound in spoken word	0	5.26	0	5.26	89.47	0*
Kinesthetic	Feel movement of articulatory muscles when phonemes are spoken	0	0	10.53	15.79	68.42	2.63*
Kinesthetic	Tap out individual sounds in spoken words	0	5.26	10.53	15.79	63.16	2.63*
Tactile	Feel placement of articulators and verbalize the placement when phonemes are spoken	0	5.26	15.79	26.32	52.63	0*
Tactile	Feel presence or absence of voicing airflow	0	5.26	5.26	21.05	68.42	0*
	Sound–symbol association						
Visual	Look at mouth of teacher to discriminate mouth positions	0	0	10.53	15.79	73.68	0*
Visual	Look at letter or letter combinations	0	0	0	0	100	0*
Visual	Discriminate letters	0	0	5.26	89.47	0	5.26*
Visual	Look at a card with letter(s) and key word or picture	15.79	0	10.53	5.26	68.42	0*
Auditory	Listen to (hear) the sound and identify its name with symbol	10.53	0	5.26	0	84.21	0*
Auditory	Listen to (hear) the sound and identify it with its symbol	0	0	0	0	100	0*
Auditory	Say key word and sound(s) or letter name identified with symbol	10.53	5.26	10.53	5.26	68.42	0*
Auditory	Discriminate sounds	0	0	0	0	94.74	5.26*

From Farrell, M., Pickering, J., North, N., & Schavio, C. (2004, Fall). What is multisensory instruction? *The IMSLEC Record, 8*(3); adapted by permission.

[a]*Key: 0, never; 1, occasionally; 2, as needed for certain children; 3, systematically used for certain children; 4, systematically used for all children; 5, other.*

*Sum of percentages is 75% or greater.

Modality	Strategy	% Usage by score[a]					
		0	1	2	3	4	5
Kinesthetic	Feel articulatory muscle movement when phonemes are spoken	0	0	10.53	15.79	68.42	5.26*
Kinesthetic	Use sky writing	5.26	5.26	10.53	15.79	63.16	0*
Kinesthetic	Write letter on roughened surface with fingertip	5.26	5.26	15.79	15.79	57.9	0*
	Syllables						
Visual	Look at mouth of teacher to discriminate syllable division	26.32	10.53	10.53	10.53	36.84	5.26
Visual	Look at printed words to identify vowel sounds and number of syllables	0	0	0	0	94.74	5.26*
Visual	Look at syllable division markers (e.g., slashes, blank spaces) to determine number of syllables	5.26	0	0	5.26	84.21	5.26*
Auditory	Listen for (hear) syllables in spoken words	0	0	5.26	0	89.47	5.26*
Auditory	Discriminate number of syllables in spoken words	0	0	5.26	0	89.47	5.26*
Auditory	Segment spoken words into syllables	0	0	0	0	94.74	5.26*
Auditory	Blend syllables into a word	0	0	0	0	94.74	5.26*
Kinesthetic	Feel movement of articulatory muscles when syllables are spoken	0	0	15.79	5.26	68.42	10.53*
Kinesthetic	Pat or tap out syllables	0	5.26	5.26	0	84.21	5.26*
Kinesthetic	Build syllables with letter cards	15.79	5.26	15.79	10.53	47.37	5.26
Kinesthetic	Build words with syllable cards	36.84	0	5.26	10.53	42.11	5.26
Kinesthetic	Segment words into syllables	0	0	0	0	94.74	5.26*
Kinesthetic	Use syllable markers to break word into syllables	0	0	0	5.26	89.47	5.26*
Tactile	Feel placement of articulators and verbalize the placement when syllables are spoken	15.79	5.26	26.32	10.53	31.58	10.53
Tactile	Pat or tap out syllables	0	5.26	5.26	0	78.95	10.53*
Tactile	Build words with syllable cards	26.32	0	10.53	10.53	36.84	15.79
	Morphology						
Visual	Look at mouth of teacher to discriminate word parts	21.05	0	15.79	21.05	31.58	10.53
Visual	Look at bases and roots and affixes	0	0	0	10.53	89.47	0*
Visual	Identify prefixes, base words, and suffixes in printed words	0	0	0	10.53	89.47	0*
Auditory	Listen for (hear) bases and roots, affixes	0	0	10.53	5.26	84.21	0*
Auditory	Identify prefixes, base words, and suffixes in spoken words	0	0	5.26	5.26	89.47	0*
Kinesthetic	Feel movement of the articulatory muscles when morphemes are spoken	21.05	5.26	36.84	0	26.32	10.53
Kinesthetic	Segment words into prefixes, base words, and suffixes	0	0	0	10.53	89.47	0*
Kinesthetic	Build words with base and/or root and affix cards	5.26	0	10.53	21.05	57.9	5.26
Tactile	Feel placement of articulators and verbalize the placement when morphemes are spoken	21.05	5.26	31.58	5.26	15.79	21.05

(continued)

(continued)

Modality	Strategy	% Usage by score[a]					
		0	1	2	3	4	5
Tactile	Segment words into prefixes, base words, and suffixes	0	0	0	10.53	84.21	5.26*
Tactile	Build words with base and/or root and affix cards	5.26	0	10.53	21.05	52.63	10.53*
	Syntax						
Visual	Look at mouth of teacher (e.g., to dis-criminate word parts)	31.58	5.26	21.05	0	26.32	15.79
Visual	Look at sentences to identify sentence parts (e.g., subject/verb, parts of speech)	0	0	10.53	5.26	84.21	0*
Visual	Look at diagrammed sentences to label parts of speech	15.79	5.26	15.79	5.26	57.9	0*
Visual	Look at graphic or symbol to identify part of speech	15.79	5.26	5.26	5.26	63.16	5.26
Auditory	Listen to sentences	0	0	0	0	94.74	5.26*
Auditory	Say and read sentences	0	0	0	0	94.74	5.26*
Auditory	Explain diagrammed sentences	15.79	5.26	10.53	15.79	52.63	0*
Kinesthetic	Feel movement of the articulatory muscles	26.32	5.26	15.79	0	31.58	21.05
Kinesthetic	Diagram sentences	15.79	5.26	5.26	15.79	52.63	5.26
Kinesthetic	Build sentences with word cards	15.79	0	15.79	10.53	47.37	10.53
Kinesthetic	Use graphics or symbols to signify parts of speech	15.79	5.26	5.26	0	68.42	5.26
Kinesthetic	Manipulate cards to represent parts of speech	21.05	5.26	5.26	10.53	52.63	5.26
Kinesthetic	Write sentences	0	0	0	0	100	0
Kinesthetic	Write sentences from dictation	0	0	10.53	5.26	84.21	0*
Tactile	Feel placement of articulators and verbalize the placement	26.32	5.26	21.05	0	26.32	21.05
Tactile	Diagram sentences	15.79	5.26	5.26	15.79	52.63	5.26
Tactile	Build sentences with word cards	15.79	0	15.79	10.53	47.37	10.53
Tactile	Use graphics or symbols to signify parts of speech in sentences	15.79	5.26	5.26	0	68.42	5.26
Tactile	Manipulate cards to represent parts of speech in sentences	15.79	5.26	15.79	5.26	52.63	5.26
Tactile	Write sentences	0	0	0	0	94.74	5.26*
Tactile	Write sentences from dictation	0	0	10.53	5.26	78.95	5.26*
	Semantics						
Visual	Look at mouth of teacher to discri-minate easily confused words, (e.g., *from* and *form*)	15.79	0	31.58	15.79	36.84	0*
Visual	Look at word	0	0	5.26	0	94.74	0*
Visual	Look at graphic or symbol to repre-sent meaning	10.53	5.26	15.79	5.26	57.9	5.26
Auditory	Say words and/or definitions	0	0	0	5.26	94.74	0*
Auditory	Listen to sentences and explain meaning	5.26	0	0	5.26	89.47	0*
Auditory	Use words in oral sentences that demonstrate meaning	0	0	0	5.26	94.74	0*
Auditory	Read sentences and explain meaning	0	0	0	0	100	0*
Auditory	Paraphrase sentences accurately	0	0	5.26	5.26	89.47	0*
Auditory	Paraphrase paragraphs accurately	0	0	5.26	10.53	84.21	0*

Modality	Strategy	% Usage by score[a]					
		0	1	2	3	4	5
Kinesthetic	Feel movement of articulatory muscles	31.58	0	21.05	0	26.32	21.05
Kinesthetic	Draw graphics to represent meaning	0	21.05	21.05	15.79	36.84	5.26
Kinesthetic	Act out meaning (pantomime)	5.26	15.79	31.58	15.79	42.11	10.53*
Tactile	Feel placement of articulators and verbalize the placement	31.58	0	0	0	31.58	15.79
Tactile	Draw graphics to represent meaning	0	26.32	26.32	10.53	26.32	10.53

3

Development of Oral Language and Its Relationship to Literacy

LYDIA H. SOIFER

Imagine the elegant intricacies of Beethoven's "Ode to Joy" or Mozart's "Serenade in G Major" (*Eine Kleine Nachtmusik*) played captivatingly by an artist. It is as beguiling to the experienced listener as to the naïve ear. Now imagine pages of musical notation, an array of dots and lines splayed across a page, interrupted by assorted squiggles and swirls. If you can read music, then you may sense the beauty in your mind's ear, much the way Beethoven did. Can't read music? Then what remains is a morass of dots, lines, squiggles, and swirls. The same is true with language, an amazing latticework of interrelated complexities in which the oral (spoken) and aural (heard) in combination with memory, sensory, and motor function; environment; and culture form the basis from which literacy evolves. The challenge of teaching about language is that the language itself is the vehicle for learning. Thus, in large part, the very thing that you are attempting to learn about consciously in this chapter is exactly what you are experiencing spontaneously as you comprehend or generate language. Learning about language is a **metalinguistic** task in which language is analyzed and considered as an entity and behavior. When a person speaks or listens, reads or writes, and effectively communicates or understands a particular purpose or intention, the language system has performed efficiently.

Mattingly suggested that there was something "devious" (1972, p. 133) about the relationship between the processes of speaking and listening and the process of reading. Listening and reading both are linguistic processes but are not really as parallel or analogous as many people assume. The differences are in the form of information being presented (complex auditory signals versus more static visual symbols) in the linguistic content (additional information available from the intonational and speech patterns that can be perceived in listening versus the many possible pieces of phonological information contained in one symbol) and in the relationship of the form to the content (enormous variation in what can be produced by voice versus alphabets with limited information carried by any single symbol). Listening and speaking are automatic and natural ways of perceiving and using language, acquired as part of a developmental process. In contrast, the written form of a language must generally be taught, and not all individuals are able to learn it with ease. In addition, not all spoken languages have a written form.

There is agreement that reading is a language-based skill (Catts & Kamhi, 1986; Liberman, 1983; Perfetti & Lesgold, 1977; Snyder, 1980; Vellutino, 1979) and that the relationship between oral language and reading is reciprocal (Kamhi & Catts, 1989; Stanovich, 1986; Wallach & Miller, 1988), with each influencing the other at different points in development (Menyuk & Chesnick, 1997; Snyder & Downey, 1991, 1997).

Oral and written language, although intimately and intricately related, are not the same. Teachers need to be aware of the similarities and differences (Moats, 1994; Moats & Lyon, 1996) so that they can facilitate students' language learning and academic success (Bashir & Scavuzzo, 1992). This chapter helps foster an awareness of the inextricable role of language in learning to decode and comprehend. The processes of language learning (on which reading is based) begin before children receive reading instruction. This chapter provides an insight into each component of the language system, including patterns of typical and disordered development and their analogous relationships to the higher level language skills of reading and writing. In this chapter, oral and written language are viewed as a continuum, and the varying influences of oral language knowledge and use in developing early decoding processes and subsequent comprehension processes are considered. Furthermore, this chapter offers a discussion of the oral–written language connection and the different levels of language processing to enhance teachers' ability to be informed observers and, as a result, to be more effective in planning instruction.

LANGUAGE: A DYNAMIC, RULE-GOVERNED PROCESS

Learning to talk appears easy but, in fact, is enormously complex. The marvel is that most children learn to talk so well and so quickly (Hart & Risley, 1999). The enormity of the task is confounded because most children are not taught to use language, but rather discover the rules that govern language in the context of social interaction as they strive to understand and convey meaning.

What is language? Bloom and Lahey offered a superb definition of *language*: "Language is a code whereby ideas about the world are represented through a conventional system of arbitrary signals for communication" (1978, p. 4). The key concepts to consider are communication, ideas, code, system, and conventional. The purpose of language is communication. We use language for a variety of purposes in vastly different ways according to our needs, the needs of the listener, and the circumstances surrounding us. Language enables us to express an array of ideas. We have ideas about objects, events, and relationships. Our ability to express those ideas through language is different from the objects, events, or relationships themselves. Think about the page you are reading and the words you have available to represent your ideas about the page, what is on it, what you are doing with it, and your relationship to it. Each is different from the page itself, the writing on it, the act of reading, and how you are relating to the page by viewing it or touching it. In this way, language is a code, a means of representing one thing with another in a predictable and organized system. There are many different codes, from maps, to Morse code, to words spelled in a book. Sounds may be combined into words, words into sentences, and sentences into conversation.

The rule-governed predictability of the system enables us to understand it and learn how to use it. Consider the following:

'Twas brillig, and the slithy toves
Did gyre and gimble in the wabe:
All mimsy were the borogoves,
And the mome raths outgrabe.
(Carroll, 1865/1960, p. 134)

If asked, one could identify the parts of speech, such as noun (*toves, raths*), verb (*gyre, gimble*), adjective (*outgrabe*), or adverb (*brillig*); the subject, predicate, and object; have a reasonable idea of how to pronounce these novel words; and answer comprehension questions ("Were the borogoves mimsy?"). All of these tasks are possible because Carroll used the predictable, rule-governed nature of the sounds and grammar of English to create "Jabberwocky."

The code of language is also conventional. It consists of a socially based, tacitly agreed-on set of symbols and rules that govern their permissible combinations. The conventions of language allow users to share their ideas. Linguistic competence is a person's implicit knowledge about the rules of the language. Possessed of linguistic competence, a child or an adult has the knowledge to be a competent language user. In general, unless called on to do so specifically, a language user need not state the rules of language explicitly. The ability to generate an infinite number of sentences and understand varying forms of language across a plenitude of environments demonstrates knowledge of the rules.

THE ORAL–WRITTEN LANGUAGE CONNECTION

Literacy is much like a great pyramid. It is built on a broad foundation that is linguistic, sociological, cognitive, and pedagogic. Literacy evolves from well-developed oral language abilities; exposure to written language that gives rise to a child's notions of how print works and what it can do, called **emergent literacy** (Sulzby & Teale, 1991; Van Kleeck, 1990); a level of cognitive maturation that allows for metalinguistic awareness that permits a child to view language as an entity, something to be considered and analyzed; and a reasonable quality of instruction that can provide varying degrees of facilitation and support.

Language is the vehicle that drives curriculum. Although one may study aspects of the language in discrete ways (e.g., phonics, grammar, vocabulary), even then the very language being studied is the one that is employed to learn. In no instance does this resonate with greater truth than in acquiring literacy skills—reading and writing. "Learning to read and write is part of, not separate from, learning to speak and comprehend language" (Wallach & Butler, 1994, p. 11). Despite **whole language** arguments to the contrary, however, "learning to read is not the same as learning to speak" (Wallach, 1990, p. 64).

Indeed, Van Kleeck (1990) allowed that the foundations of literacy are created at birth and are interrelated with the evolution and fullness of a child's oral language because reading is a language-based skill dependent on a set of well-developed oral language abilities. Language learning and literacy learning are actually reciprocal. That is to say the relationship between the two is dynamic and changes over time with each influencing the other at different developmental stages (Kamhi & Catts, 1989; Sawyer, 1991). Nonetheless, there are considerable differences between language learning and literacy learning (Scott, 1994) because reading is not just speech written down (Liberman, Shankweiler, Camp, Blachman, & Werfelman, 1990).

Understanding oral language requires a well-integrated knowledge of the form, content, and use of the language. Recognizing word patterns, word structure, and sentence forms; knowing the meanings of words, how words relate to one another, and how they are influenced by their position in the sentence; and interpreting the intent of the speaker with the context and in relationship to one's own knowledge base enable a listener to understand. Understanding written text requires the same linguistic knowledge that is necessary for understanding spoken language. The analogy of hearing spoken language to decoding print serves quite well: "I heard what you said, but I don't know what you mean" is similar to the phenomenon of asking a child to tell about what he or she has just read and being met with a look of noncomprehension that implies, "I know that I read [decoded] it, but I don't know what it means!" As described throughout this chapter, deficits in oral language, syntax, morphology, **semantics** (word meaning and relationships), **pragmatics,** and narrative structure have a negative affect on reading comprehension.

In addition to oral language skills, emergent literacy is a foundation for literacy development (see Van Kleeck, 1990, for an extended discussion of emergent literacy). Emergent literacy is an outgrowth of **"literacy socialization"** (Snow & Dickinson, 1991). When children are exposed to print by being read to, whether from books, signs, instructions, or birthday cards, they begin to develop a sense that the marks on the page, box, or card are related to the words being said (Linder, 1999). They also begin to develop an awareness of how books are manipulated, literally which way is up and in which direction the text flows and the pages turn. Children who have been exposed to print in early caregiver–child interactions also benefit from the positive emotional connection between reading and nurturing experiences. Provided with literacy socialization experiences and, as a result, the emergent literacy skills that precede learning to decode, children who have been read to as preschoolers unquestionably find the process of learning to read an easier experience (Dickinson & McCabe, 1991; Wolf & Dickinson, 1993).

Children raised in low-income families who are in child care up to 13 hours each day while their parents are working have far less exposure to enriched language, play experiences designed for cognitive stimulation, and literacy experiences. In child care settings in homes, fewer than half had at least 10 books appropriate for each age group cared for within that home. Furthermore, fewer than half the home care providers read even one book to children within any 13-hour day. Play activities that comprised approximately one third of the day were directed at reading or being read to less than 10% of the time (Layzer & Goodson, 2006). The affect on oral language development, socialization skills, and early literacy cannot be underestimated given the present-day expectations for preschool and kindergarten.

Metalinguistic ability, as discussed later in this chapter, permits a child to focus on language from a distance; to view language as an object of consideration; and to reflect on its discrete, particular aspects and characteristics. It is metalinguistically that children recognize word boundaries; make letter–sound correspondences; consider which printed sequences of letters represent which words and meanings; and analyze, blend, and reconstruct words. Little, if anything, in the oral language experience prepares children to view words as discrete units (e.g., *sit*) to isolate the parts of each unit (e.g., *s-i-t*) in order to reformulate and orally produce them (e.g., "sit"). Certainly, phonological awareness activities are dependent on metalinguistic skills. Beyond the task of decoding, conscious use of linguistic knowledge strongly influences reading comprehension. Oral language development, however, does not require these metalinguistic abilities. The speech stream is continuous with boundaries that are not discrete, and the context is immediate and supported environmentally by the situation in which the talking is occurring. In oral language development, reflection on linguistic knowledge is not part of the process until a fair degree of cognitive maturity and linguistic sophistication has been attained.

Literacy is also built on good teaching. Moats and Lyon (1996) strongly urged changes in teacher education related to reading instruction to place a greater emphasis on knowledge of language structure. They cited disturbing findings in a survey of 103 teachers in which fewer than one third were proficient in the basic knowledge of language structure, such as identifying an inflected ending (-*ed* in *instructed*) or the number of phonemes in words such as *ox, precious,* or *thank.* Teaching children to read requires teaching them language at a higher and more conscious level. Successful teaching, particularly of those children who bring linguistic, experiential, cognitive, or environmental vulnerabilities to the task, requires a powerful, integrated knowledge of the language that is being taught.

ORAL–WRITTEN LANGUAGE DIFFERENCES

There is no doubt that reading is a language-based skill, yet there are numerous and obvious differences between oral and written language. These differences have been considered from a variety of different vantage points, either as parallels or continua (Horowitz & Samuels, 1987; Kamhi & Catts, 1989; Rubin, 1987; Scott, 1994; Wallach, 1990; Westby, 1985). In the course of human development, literacy is recent (Wolf & Dickinson, 1993). Learning to read and write does not come naturally to everyone, and these skills are not a requirement in every society. Writing, as anyone who has ever struggled with a blank page or experienced writer's block well knows, requires a much greater effort than producing oral language. Rubin highlighted his difficulty when he wrote that "no one is a native speaker of writing" (1987, p. 3). Human beings are socialized to communicate, and they have a biological predisposition to oral language that enables societal groups to have and pass on oral language systems. Reading and writing are acquired deliberately, rather than spontaneously and more naturally. The differences are in the aspects of production, influences of context, grammar, and vocabulary and in the degree of explicitness.

Oral language is transient and ephemeral. It exists only at the moment when it is spoken. It can be repeated or clarified, but that occurs at the request of the listener. Written language is permanent and more enduring than oral language, except when the latter is recorded. Print allows the reader multiple opportunities for exposure and decision-making authority regarding the rate and depth of analysis with which the text is read. In oral language, the rate of presentation is at the discretion of the speaker. In oral language, temporal sequencing is crucial, whereas in print, spatial sequencing is important. Print can be revisited more readily. A word, sentence, or paragraph can be reread or rewritten. It is a different experience to have someone attempt to repeat, exactly, the sentence just uttered.

Most oral language occurs face to face. Reciprocity exists between the speaker and listener. Interpersonal context and situational support exist in the form of vocal, facial, and physical gestures. When people are engaged in conversation or discussion, less needs to be explicitly stated and sentence structures can be more fragmentary. Vocabulary and syntax can be more familiar and less sophisticated. To appreciate the lack of explicitness, as well as the fragmentary, familiar, and contextually and physically supported nature of oral language, request a transcript of a television talk show that you have watched. While watching and listening to the discussion, you probably had little difficulty understanding the ebb and flow, intent, and effect of the exchanges among the participants. Reading the transcript of the same exchange will provide an immediate insight into the significant differences in the explicitness of a written text and the literate, grammatically dense nature of written language versus oral language that has been written down. In oral language, cohesion between sentences and ideas can be established grammatically or paralinguistically through physical signals such as the shrug of a shoulder or a pregnant pause. In a written text, the cohesive devices and transitional **markers** that bind ideas or shift focus must be conveyed concretely and explicitly through a careful choice of words. The conventions of punctuating written language that are communicated orally through intonational gestures must be taught specifically; however, written text does provide other cues to organization and meaning through the structure of paragraphs and using boldface, italics, underlining, and other **typography**.

Although written language contains the intent to communicate with another or others or to interpret another person's message, the experience is generally more solitary and involves only the reader and the book, page, or computer screen. The interaction between writer and reader is limited and is decontextualized—separated by time and distance. It is necessary for the communicator to be more explicit and succinct in print.

Written language relies on the **lexicon** to create the melody and meaning provided by the **intonation, stress, pause,** and **juncture** patterns of spoken language as well as the vocal characteristics of the speaker. An anxious tone, a sinister laugh, or a lascivious lilt can be heard, recognized, and interpreted without being explicitly stated by the speaker as such. What is said and meant can be potently influenced by how it is said, and thus the message and intent of the speaker and the response of the listener may vary. The most literate of writers attain a level of mastery that enables them to arrange, adapt, maneuver, integrate, and entwine words and sentences in ways that communicate so effectively that it seems as though these writers are talking to the reader. With that level of written language mastery, it is possible to write the same thing in many ways, ranging from the most informal to the most deliberately formal tone.

After considering the oral–written continuum, it is important to look at writing itself. Writing is the most sophisticated, complex, and formal aspect of language. Even the most well-read and literate individuals may not have equivalent skill in expressing thoughts on paper. Writing is a dynamic interaction among cognitive and linguistic factors, motor skills, and emotional considerations. The most sophisticated language act, writing involves the simultaneous convergence of cognitive factors (abstracting, generating, and ordering ideas), linguistic factors (arriving at semantic [word meaning and choice] and syntactic [grammar] production appropriate to the nature of what is being written, such as a thank-you note versus an expository paragraph), narrative considerations (structuring information for varied purposes), **graphomotor** skills (recalling, planning, and executing complex motor acts), visual ability (recalling sequences of letters with phonetic rules for spelling), and temporal factors (writing legibly and appropriately under specific time constraints) while controlling for the emotional factors involved in risk, exposure, and evaluation of the final product. It is readily apparent why many children (and adults) might prefer to speak rather than to write. The teaching of writing can be an art form (see Chapter 7).

THE COMPONENTS OF LANGUAGE

Bloom and Lahey (1978) conceptualized three major interactive components of language: form, content, and use (see Figure 3.1). Each component is governed by a complex set of rules that together compose language.

Language Form

Language form consists of the observable features of language. It includes the rules for combining sounds (phonology), structuring words (morphology), and ordering words in sentences (syntax). These features and their development and the relationship of disorders in these elements of language form are described in the following sections.

Phonology

Phonology is the sound system of a language. It comprises **suprasegmental** aspects (intonation, stress, loudness, pitch level, juncture, and speaking rate) and **segmental** aspects (**vowels, consonants,** and phonemes).

The suprasegmental aspects of phonology provide the melody of speech. They are related to speech because they are produced by the vocal tract but are concerned with larger units of production: syllables, words, phrases, and sentences. They are significant in the ability to communicate emotions and attitudes. These suprasegmental features help us recognize different sentence types—declarative (e.g., Joshua eats pizza.), interrogative (e.g., Does Russell like ice cream?), or imperative (e.g., Sit down now!). Awareness of phrase structure helps us understand where a comma might be placed in a sentence. These aspects also permit us to say the same sentence and communicate markedly different meanings. Varied aspects of the suprasegmental features of language are used in talking to different people of different ages and status. Consider the number of ways to say "Don't be silly" to an infant, a spouse, or an employer. At a conversational level, the suprasegmental characteristics of language also may be used to convey sarcasm, to tease, and to mock.

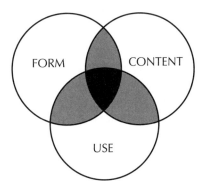

Figure 3.1. Venn diagram illustrating language form, content, and use. (From Bloom, L., & Lahey, M. [1978]. *Language development and language disorders* [p. 22]. Published by Allyn & Bacon; Boston, MA. Copyright © 1978 by Pearson Education. Reprinted by permission of the publisher.)

The suprasegmental aspects of phonology are influential in reading. When reading aloud, fluent readers read with full intonation, communicating an understanding of the intent of the author. Early readers or those who struggle to decode may read each word individually, then, having derived meaning, reread with appropriate inflection.

Inefficient readers may pause with a downward intonation at the end of a printed line of words rather than at the end of the sentence. Thus, the suprasegmental features of language play an essential role in comprehension.

Vowels and consonants compose the segmental features of language. Each language has a set of vowels, consonants, or phonemes that may be combined to form words. A *phoneme* is the smallest linguistic unit of sound that can change meaning in a word. Consider the word family of *bat*. Changing any of the phonemes could produce a variety of new words (e.g., *sat, bit, ban*).

Standard English orthography has only 26 letters with which to represent the approximately 44 phonemes of English. More striking still, there are only 5 vowel letters available to represent the approximately 15 vowel sounds. Knowledge of phonemes and their role in language and reading is essential for teachers. Long before children are able to recognize, read, and write the letters that represent the sounds of English, they must begin to master the elaborate task of making those speech sounds correctly so that they are able to clearly produce the sounds of the language. Children learn each of those 44 sounds and their possible variations by being exposed to them, hearing others speak, and storing information about the qualities that make up each sound. It is an unconscious and intricate task.

Speech production is the complex coordination of respiration (breathing), phonation (the vibration of the vocal folds), resonation (the quality of voice affected by the shape and density of the neck and cavities of the head), and **articulation** (the rapid, alternating movements of the jaw, tongue, lips, teeth, and soft palate). When we speak, the flow of speech is generally uninterrupted. Speech is produced in breath groups ("Whenneryagoin?") rather than in individual words ("When are you going?"). Yet, early readers decode word by word and, at times, sound by sound. Liberman noted that "if speech were like spelling, learning to read would be trivially easy" (as cited in Brady & Shankweiler, 1991, p. xv). Awareness that the flow of coarticulated, overlapping phonemes can be segmented into sounds, syllables, and words is a precursor to cracking the code of language in print (see Chapter 5). Although speech and reading are clearly related, they are not equal.

Oral language, of which speech is the observable form, is learned naturally. Reading is not (Liberman & Liberman, 1990). A bounty of literature, however, emphasized the role of phonological awareness (the ability to attend to and recognize the sound structure of language) in acquiring early reading (Adams, 1990; Blachman, 1989, 1991; Blachman, Ball, Black, & Tangel, 2000; Stanovich, 1987; Wagner & Torgesen, 1987).

The speech sound segments, vowels and consonants, may vary in their productions (**allophones**) and are guided by a set of rules for their production and placement in words. From the earliest moments of life, infants are acquiring information about the sounds of their language (Eimas, Siqueland, Jusczyk, & Vigorito, 1971). Through continuous exposure, babies acquire the set of acoustic features that define the sounds of their language. Over time, the speakers of a given language come to recognize the possible variations in phoneme production while still recognizing the specific phoneme. For example, the phoneme /p/ is a **voiceless** stop plosive (i.e., there is no vocal fold vibration, it is not produced in a long stream as /s/ is, and it produces a puff of air). Yet, the production of /p/ varies by the amount of **aspiration** (puff of air) produced according to where it appears in a word. Pronounce *pot* and *spot* aloud to feel the different amount of aspiration. Nonetheless, speakers of English recognize these variations as the phoneme /p/. Moreover, any of the plosive sounds (i.e., /p/, /b/, /t/, /d/, /k/, and /g/) when said in isolation or as a segmented phoneme must be produced with an accompanying vowel sound, the **schwa** (/ə/), typically produced as "uh." This is particularly relevant for teachers; as Liberman noted, "The word is 'bag,' not 'buh-a-guh'" (as cited in Brady & Shankweiler, 1991, p. xv). The distortion can be so great that some children are unable to recombine the sounds into the word *bag*. Combining /b/ and /ĕ/ in a smooth, connected production eliminates the /ə/. In addition, by not producing the /g/ with an overemphasis, the /ə/ is once again reduced, thus allowing the word being analyzed and synthesized to sound more like its real-world production. This enables the young reader to use language knowledge of the word to recognize it as a phonological/phonemic phenomenon.

Other phonetic distinctions may be made by limitations of the vocal tract. These distinctions may become important for spelling, particularly for children with vulnerabilities in phonological awareness. Plurals, possessives, and the third-person singular marking of the verb all are accomplished by the addition of -*s* (or -*es* for certain plurals) when being spelled. The sounds produced, however, may be /z/ or /s/. This is determined by the nature of the preceding phoneme. **Coarticulation** with a **voiced** consonant (one produced with the vocal folds closed) or a vowel will create /z/ or /ĭz/. Say *hugs, kisses,* and *hits* aloud to hear and feel the distinctions. A similar pattern emerges for creating the regular past tense, typically created in print as -*ed*. In speech, however, it may be produced as /d/, /t/, or /ĭd/, as in *hugged, kissed,* or *lifted*.

Vowels and consonants, which combine to form syllable structures, are separated into distinct classes by the nature of their production. A vowel is typically "formed as sound energy from the vibrating folds escapes through a relatively open vocal tract of a particular shape" (Bernthal & Bankson, 1998, p. 12).

The tongue, jaw, and lips serve to create the shape of the vocal tract. Because the jaw and tongue work together, vowels are classified by identifying the position of the tongue during articulation (front, mid, or back; high or low) and the lips (rounded or unrounded). Vowels may also be tense or lax. **Tense vowels** (e.g., /ē/ in *bee*) are longer in duration; **lax vowels** (e.g., /ĭ/ in *bin*) are shorter in duration. Figure 3.2 demonstrates the position in the mouth of each vowel's production. Table 3.1 shows the spellings of different vowels. Moats's (2010) view of sound production in its relationship to spelling gives an accompanying image of the appearance of vowels (see Figure 3.3).

Consonants are created by either a complete or a partial constriction of the air stream along the vocal tract. The closure is affected by the position of the lips and the placement of the tongue in relation to the teeth and its position in the mouth. Consonants are classified as **stops** (e.g., /t/, /k/), **nasals** (e.g., /n/, /m/, /ng/), **fricatives** (e.g., /f/, /z/), **affricates** (/ch/, /j/), **glides** (e.g., /w/, /y/), or **liquids** (/l/, /r/).

Table 3.2 provides a clear view of where consonants are produced in the vocal tract. In addition, consonants may be described as voiced (caused by vibrations of the vocals folds when closed) or voiceless (open vocal folds). Several sets of phonemes, called **voiced-voiceless cognates,** are produced in the same place in the mouth, in the same manner, but vary only in the voicing characteristic. They are /p/ and /b/, /f/ and /v/, /t/ and /d/, /s/ and /z/, /k/ and /g/, /th/ (*think*) and /th/ (*this*), /sh/ and /zh/, and /ch/ and /j/. (The distinction between a voiceless and voiced phoneme can be felt as well as heard by placing the fingers gently against the throat. Start to say /s/, then without altering the position of the tongue and jaw, say /z/.) In addition, the environment in

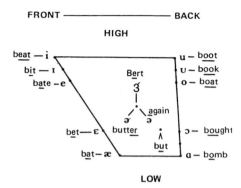

Figure 3.2. Vowel chart. (From Bernthal, J.E., & Bankson, N.W. [1998]. *Articulation and phonological disorders* [4th ed., p. 16]. Published by Allyn & Bacon; Boston, MA. Reprinted by permission of the publisher.)

which a consonant or vowel exists (i.e., the other phonemes near it) may vary the production of that consonant or vowel.

The relationship of vowel, consonant, and syllable production and **discrimination** and phonological awareness leading to more effective reading and spelling is significant. In addition to rules for the production and perception of phonemes, there are rules that apply to how phonemes may be combined into meaningful words. These rules allow some sounds to appear in certain positions in a word but not in others. For example, in English, /ng/ may appear in the **middle** or at the end of a word but never

Table 3.1. American English vowels

Phonetic symbol	Phonic symbol	Spellings
/i/	ē	beet
/ɪ/	ĭ	bit
/e/	ā	bait
/ɛ/	ĕ	bet
/æ/	ă	bat
/ɑj/	ī	bite
/ɑ/	ŏ	bottle
/ʌ/	ŭ	butt
/ɔ/	aw	bought
/o/	ō	boat
/ʊ/	o͝o	put
/u/	ū	boot
/ə/	ə	between
/ɔj/	oi, oy	boy
/æw/	ou, ow	bough

From Moats, L.C. (2010). *Speech to print: Language essentials for teachers* (2nd ed., p. 41). Baltimore: Paul H. Brookes Publishing Co.; reprinted by permission.

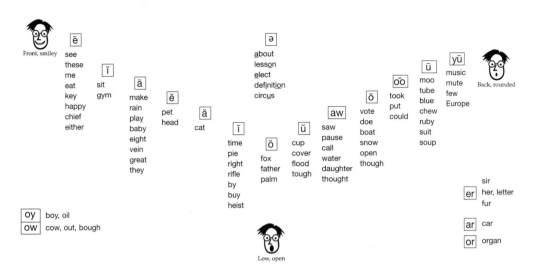

Figure 3.3.   Vowels (phonic symbols) by mouth position. (From Moats, L.C. [2010]. *Speech to print: Language essentials for teachers* [2nd ed., p. 96]. Baltimore: Paul H. Brookes Publishing Co.; adapted by permission.)

at the beginning. Furthermore, certain combinations of sounds are restricted so that /ts/ may occur at the end of a word but not at the beginning. This set of **phonological rules** has implications for early reading and spelling as children learn to segment the flow of speech and recognize and represent it in print.

Table 3.2.   American English consonants (phonic symbols)

Class of consonant	Lips	Lips/ teeth	Tongue between teeth	Tongue behind teeth	Roof of mouth	Back of mouth	Throat
Stop							
voiceless	/p/			/t/		/k/	
voiced	/b/			/d/		/g/	
Nasal	/m/			/n/		/ng/	
Fricative							
voiceless		/f/	/th/	/s/	/sh/		
voiced		/v/	/th/	/z/	/zh/		
Affricate							
voiceless					/ch/		
voiced					/j/		
Glide							
voiceless						/wh/	/h/
voiced					/y/	/w/	
Liquid			/l/	/r/			

From Moats, L.C. (2010). *Speech to print: Language essentials for teachers* (2nd ed., p. 34). Baltimore: Paul H. Brookes Publishing Co.; reprinted by permission.

Phonological Development   Traditionally, speech sound development was thought to occur through unit-by-unit learning of each phoneme in a developmental sequence. In fact, phonological development is integrally related to the language system as a whole. Phonological development progresses with physical maturation, the mastery of sound features and phonological processes that reflect the linking of sounds to words and meaning, and the growth of syntactic and semantic rule knowledge and ability. Children employ phonological or natural processes to master adult-level speech productions.

Typically, children produce their first recognizable words by 12–18 months of age. The ability of toddlers to make themselves fully understood (without available **context clues**) is often limited by inadequate production of sounds. However, 3-year-olds are generally intelligible and by age 4 have suppressed or eliminated the remaining phonological processes that hinder their intelligibility (Hodson, 1994) Typically developing children are able to produce speech sounds adequately by age 4 and require additional time (until age 7) for complete mastery, including the elimination of lisps and the production of **multisyllabic** words (see Table 3.3).

Relationship of Phonological Disorders to Literacy   When preparing to teach early reading skills, teachers should be aware of two areas of consideration: intelligibility of speech production and its relationship to phonological awareness. Children who have problems with speech sound production at the time they are being introduced to reading instruction or who have a history of such difficulties have been shown to be less adept at tasks of phonological awareness than their typically developing peers (Webster & Plante, 1992). Webster and Plante explained that "productive phonological impairment may hinder performance in phonological awareness because it precludes efficient phonological coding in working memory" (p. 176). In the same vein, Fowler (1991) suggested that articulation ability may be an important prerequisite for acquiring an awareness of phoneme structures.

Consider the dilemma of a child who does not have a stable speech production system. Certain speech production problems may be caused by neurological oral-motor dysfunction, including weaknesses of the musculature necessary for making the coordinated movements to produce speech (**dysarthria**). Other speech problems

Table 3.3. Phonemic acquisition—age at which 75% of children tested correctly articulated consonant sounds

Age	Sounds
2.0	/m/, /n/, /h/, /p/, /n/, /r/ (*ring*)
2.4	f, j, k, d
2.8	w, b, t
3.0	g, s
3.4	r, l
3.8	/sh/ (*shy*), /ch/ (*chin*)
4.0	/<u>th</u>/ (*father*), /zh/ (*measure*)
4.01	/j/ (*jar*), /th/ (*thin*), v, z

From Prather, E., Hedrick, D., & Kern, C. (1975). Articulation development in children aged two to four years. *Journal of Speech and Hearing Disorders, 40;* adapted by permission.

may be caused by sensorimotor disruptions in which the signals to the muscles necessary for speech production are not consistently or efficiently received (**dyspraxia**). When children encounter a new word, they must be able to store it in phonological short-term (working) memory as part of the process of creating a phonological representation for it. Children who have speech articulation difficulties, however, are at a disadvantage:

> What they are able to say may not match what they have heard. In the phonological awareness tasks of rhyme, segmentation, and blending and in spelling tasks, being able to rehearse a word with proper production plays a contributing role in the successful completion of those tasks. Thus, for some children, speech disorders are a hidden contributor to the apparent phonological processing and spelling difficulties. (Stackhouse & Wells, 1997)

Children with reading disabilities have been found to make more speech production errors than their typical peers (Catts, 1986; Snowling, 1981). There are similar findings documented for college students with dyslexia (Catts, 1989). The college students with dyslexia had greater difficulty in repeating complex phrases rapidly and made significantly more errors than their typical peers. It is hypothesized that children and adults with reading difficulties have greater challenges in encoding phonological information and in planning (for articulation) of complex sequences of sounds (Catts, 1989).

Phonological processing difficulties may manifest differently across the developmental continuum. They may stem from a variety of causes and vary in severity (Spear-Swerling & Sternberg, 1994). In the preschool years, developing oral language may be related to slower vocabulary growth (Catts, Hu, Larrivee, & Swank, 1994), and children may be less sensitive to rhyme, **alliteration,** and **nonsense words** (Fey, Catts, & Larrivee, 1995). During the elementary school years, children with phonological processing difficulties may be weaker in using segmentation strategies to analyze phonemic structure and slower in word recognition, secondary to having reduced awareness of the relationship between phonemes and the alphabet (Catts, 1989; Ehri, 1989). If a child persists in having significant speech production difficulties, then spelling ability may be affected (Clark-Klein & Hodson, 1995). Reduced rate of vocabulary acquisition and difficulty acquiring words with **multiple meanings** and **figurative language** as well as word-retrieval difficulties may become obvious (Catts et al., 1994; Milosky, 1994; Snyder & Godley, 1992). Comprehension problems may begin to emerge both orally and in print (Catts, 1996; Snyder & Downey, 1991).

Montgomery (2002) offered an intriguing approach to the problem of processing deficits in children with language impairments by examining the nature of **lexical** processing in children with regard to both temporal processing and more generalized processing capacity deficits. He presented a compelling argument for the effect of the processing capacity limitations identified in children with language impairments as an explanation for their performance difficulties in temporal processing tasks, in which resource allocation is a significant component. Further research and documentation are necessary before a full evaluation of this controversial conceptualization and approach can be made.

Phonological awareness abilities are critical to the development of early reading (see Chapter 5). The evidence is so strong that commercial materials have appeared with increasing regularity to aid educators in identifying weaknesses in phonological awareness abilities (Robertson & Salter, 1997) and developing these skills (Adams, Foorman, Lundberg, & Beeler, 1998; Catts & Vartiainen, 1997). The main point of the research is not only that phonological skills underlie early reading but also that they can be taught. Catts (1997) developed a checklist to aid in the early identification of language-based reading difficulties. The value of the checklist is twofold. First, its structure identifies six significant areas of observation for the teacher: speech sound awareness, word retrieval, verbal memory, speech production and perception, comprehension, and expressive language. Second, when used in collaboration with a speech-language pathologist, it can be of enormous value in targeting students who may be vulnerable to reading difficulty and pinpointing their particular areas of need (see Figure 3.4).

Phonology is too often simplified to its superficial relationship to speech or phonics instruction. In reality, it has far-reaching significance for the rate of language acquisition (Paul & Jennings, 1992), vocabulary size (Stoel-Gammon, 1991), working memory (Adams & Gathercole, 1995), word retrieval (Katz, 1986; McGregor, 1994), and phonological awareness skills (segmentation, **sound deletion,** blending, and counting), which are believed to underlie early literacy (Catts, 1993). Expressive phonological disorders have negative effects on early literacy (Bird & Bishop, 1992; Bird, Bishop, & Freeman, 1995) and spelling (Moats, 1995). The relationship between speech and print is anchored by an understanding of phonology and phonological processes. Making this connection is a vital step for children in developing literacy. For teachers, understanding this connection brings power of knowledge to teaching.

Teachers are faced with a daunting challenge in our increasingly multicultural society as the expectations of the No Child Left Behind Act of 2001 (PL 107-110) mandate universal literacy. As researchers work to understand the impact on literacy acquisition of variations in the language and cultural literacy of African American (Craig, Connor, & Washington, 2003; Laing & Kamhi, 2003) and **Hispanic** children (Gottardo, 2002; Hammer, Miccio, & Wagstaff, 2003), teachers must support the learning needs of culturally and linguistically diverse populations. A particular challenge facing teachers is the impact of variation in vowel and consonant production in the oral language of populations of linguistically diverse speakers. The relationship between phonology and decoding is affected at a fundamental level by these variations. For teachers to be fully effective in meeting the needs of struggling readers of cultural and linguistic backgrounds different than their own, they must know the structure of the linguistic knowledge that the children bring to school (Labov, 2003). Research is being devoted to the specific needs of Spanish-speaking English language learners (ELLs), who make up the largest population of children who require literacy instruction. Several findings are of importance to teachers. It is crucial to differentiate between language impairment, which would be apparent in both languages and bilingualism. Language impairment and bilingualism represent a different status for the learner. (August et al., 2006). Establishing the level of language ability in the first language is essential as well. Children who have not been exposed to English prior to school entry must be given additional time to learn English—2–3 years for conversational purposes and 5–7 years for academic functioning. Furthermore, children who have been exposed to both languages will have different knowledge and abilities than monolingual learners (Hammer & Miccio, 2006). In a study of Spanish-speaking preschool children who were acquiring English, Lopez and Greenfield (2004) established that English phonological awareness skills were predicted by English oral proficiency, Spanish oral proficiency, and Spanish phonological awareness skills. The role of oral language proficiency as a foundation for literacy development for ELLs parallels the essential role of oral language for monolingual learners. Thus, intervention designed to prevent reading difficulties among students acquiring English must carefully attend to oral language development with an emphasis on vocabulary and phonological awareness (August & Shanahan, 2006; Vaughn, Mathes, Linan-Thompson, & Francis, 2005). Indeed, the task is daunting but not insurmountable for creative, devoted educators (see Chapter 20).

Early Identification of Language-Based Reading Disabilities: A Checklist

Child's name: _____   Birthday: _____

Date completed: _____   Age: _____

This checklist is designed to identify children who are at risk for language-based reading disabilities. It is intended for use with children at the end of kindergarten or beginning of first grade. Each of the descriptors listed below should be carefully considered and those that characterize the child's behavior/history should be checked. A child receiving a large number of checks should be referred for a more in-depth evaluation.

Speech sound awareness
_____ Doesn't understand and enjoy rhymes
_____ Doesn't easily recognize that words begin with the same sound
_____ Has difficulty counting the syllables in spoken words
_____ Has problem clapping hands or tapping feet in rhythm with songs and/or rhymes
_____ Demonstrates problems learning sound–letter correspondences

Word retrieval
_____ Has difficulty retrieving a specific word (e.g., calls a sheep a "goat" or says, "you know, a woolly animal")
_____ Shows poor memory for classmates' names
_____ Speech is hesitant, filled with pauses or vocalizations (e.g., "um," "you know")
_____ Frequently uses words lacking specificity (e.g., "stuff," "thing," "what you call it")
_____ Has a problem remembering/retrieving verbal sequences (e.g., days of the week, alphabet)

Verbal memory
_____ Has difficulty remembering instructions or directions
_____ Shows problems learning names of people or places
_____ Has difficulty remembering the words to songs or poems
_____ Has problems learning a second language

Speech production/perception
_____ Has problems saying common words with difficult sound patterns (e.g., *animal, cinnamon, specific*)
_____ Mishears and subsequently mispronounces words or names
_____ Confuses a similar sounding word with another word (e.g., saying, "The Entire State Building is in New York")
_____ Combines sound patterns of similar words (e.g., saying "escavator" for *escalator*)
_____ Shows frequent slips of the tongue (e.g., saying "brue blush" for *blue brush*)
_____ Has difficulty with tongue twisters (e.g., *she sells seashells*)

Comprehension
_____ Only responds to part of a multiple element request or instruction
_____ Requests multiple repetitions of instructions/directions with little improvement in comprehension
_____ Relies too much on context to understand what is said
_____ Has difficulty understanding questions
_____ Fails to understand age-appropriate stories
_____ Has difficulty making inferences, predicting outcomes, drawing conclusions
_____ Lacks understanding of spatial terms such as *left/right, front/back*

Expressive language
_____ Talks in short sentences
_____ Makes errors in grammar (e.g., "he goed to the store" or "me want that")
_____ Lacks variety in vocabulary (e.g., uses "good" to mean *happy, kind, polite*)
_____ Has difficulty giving directions or explanations (e.g., may show multiple revisions or dead ends)
_____ Relates stories or events in a disorganized or incomplete manner
_____ May have much to say, but provides little specific detail
_____ Has difficulty with the rules of conversation, such as turn taking, staying on topic, indicating when he/she does not understand

_____
(continued)

Figure 3.4. Checklist for early identification of language-based reading disabilities. (From Catts, H.W. [1997]. Appendix A: Early identification of language-based reading disabilities. A checklist. *Language, Speech, and Hearing Services in Schools, 28,* 88–89; reprinted by permission. Some descriptors have been taken from *Language for learning: A checklist for language difficulties,* Melbourne, Australia: OZ Student.)

Figure 3.4. *(continued)*

> ***Other important factors***
> _____ Has a prior history of problems in language comprehension and/or production
> _____ Has a family history of spoken or written language problems
> _____ Has limited exposure to literacy in the home
> _____ Lacks interest in books and shared reading activities
> _____ Does not engage readily in pretend play
> ***Comments***
> _____
> _____
> _____

Morphology

Language form, one of three major components of language (Bloom & Lahey, 1978), also includes a set of rules for forming words. *Morphology* is the study of word formation, or how *morphemes* (the smallest units of meaning in language) combine to form words. Morphemes (unlike phonemes) are endowed with meaning. Words are made up of one or more morphemes. A morpheme that can stand alone, such as *smile, book,* or *cute,* is called an **unbound morpheme** (or **free morpheme**). Another group of morphemes, called bound morphemes, must be attached to other morphemes. **Bound morphemes** are typically the **affixes** of a language, such as *un-* and *-ing* for the word *unsmiling, -s* in the plural *books,* and *-est* in the superlative *cutest.* Unbound morphemes have lexical (word) meaning of their own. They are the content words of the language: nouns, main verbs, adjectives, and adverbs. Other morphemes, called *function words* or *grammatical morphemes,* such as prepositions, articles, **conjunctions,** and auxiliary verbs, serve grammatical functions in a sentence by creating the connection between lexical morphemes. Bound morphemes may be either inflectional or derivational. **Inflectional morphemes** modify tense (*-ed* in *played*), possession (*-'s* in *Vicki's*), or number (*-s* in *dollars*). Acquiring inflectional morphemes is a hallmark of early language development and reflects a child's increasing analysis of the structure and meaning of words. **Derivational morphemes** change one part of speech to another; for example, the verb *argue* plus *-ment* becomes the noun *argument,* and the adjective *happy* plus *-ness* becomes the noun *happiness.*

The resulting changes in spelling are another indication of the underlying complexity of the relationship between speech and print. Morphemic structure allows the language user to extend and modify meaning. Young language learners making their way through the dense forest of sounds, words, and meanings learn to mark the differences in tense, number, or possession by attending to the ends of words. Older children learn to recognize the relationships among words (e.g., *nation, national, nationality, nationalism, nationalistic*). Indeed, **prefixes** and **suffixes,** which are most commonly derived from Greek and Latin, permit a learner to extend lexical knowledge (White, Power, & White, 1989; see Chapter 4).

A further intrigue exists in the **morphophonemic relationship**—change in pronunciation caused by change in the morphological structure in a word, such as the changes that occur when the following words are said aloud: *sign, signature; medicine,* *medical.* Although phonemically such pronunciation changes may seem irregular, from a morphological view many of these changes are predictable.

Morphological Development   In the earliest stages of language development, morphological development is measured by acquiring the first 14 morphemes that emerge in children's language (Brown, 1973). As morphemes may either be words (unbound) or affixes (bound), the first 14 morphemes range from the present progressive marker *-ing,* to the use of the irregular third-person singular verb form *has,* to the contracted copula (*to be*) such as *-'m* in *I'm going.* These acquisitions generally occur between the ages of 2 or 2½ years and 4 years. Brown identified this initial phase of acquisition as occurring across five stages of development that span the period of approximately 1½–5½ years of age. During early language development, children acquire pronouns, articles, and adjective and noun suffixes. At a certain point in early development, morphological and syntactic development merge when *no* and *not* become part of the evolution of negative sentence structures.

Later morphological development involves acquiring comparatives (*-er*) and superlatives (*-est*), irregular forms (*children*), and advanced prefixes and suffixes (*un-, dis-, -ness, -ment*), including those that mark noun (*-er* in *baker*) and adverb **derivation** (*-ly* in *slowly*). Spelling and pronunciation are affected by the structure of more advanced morphological development (e.g., *child/children, happy/happiness*). Wiig and Semel provided a sequence of acquisition of morphological or word formation rules:

> 1) Regular noun plurals, 2) noun-verb agreement for singular and plural forms of irregular nouns and verbs in the present tense, 3) regular noun possessives in the singular and plural form, 4) irregular noun plurals, 5) irregular noun possessives, 6) regular past tense verbs, 7) irregular past tense verbs, 8) adjectival inflections for the comparative and superlative forms, 9) noun and adverb derivation, 10) prefixing. (1980, p. 50)

Morphology plays an essential role in language development and growth. From their earliest role in the emergence of grammar as a child passes beyond the single-word stage to the adolescent's urgent need to master Greek and Latin **roots** and affixes in preparation for the SAT, morphological knowledge and mastery contribute to vocabulary growth, spelling, comprehension, and the richness of a student's written language. Across the school years, morphological knowledge is crucial to developing literacy. From early decoding to increasingly frequent exposure to lengthier, more complex words in the middle and high school years, students' morphological knowledge is an essential component of successful decoding, comprehension, spelling, and writing.

Green (2009) aptly summarized the importance of morphological awareness in developing literacy skills crucial to academic success, word decoding, fluency, comprehension, and spelling. Morphological awareness can facilitate a young reader's approach to decoding while improving linguistic comprehension and fluency. Siegel (2008) gave the example of the long, and therefore potentially intimidating, word *sleeplessness*: if the word is recognized as three morphemes, *sleep, -less, -ness,* then it becomes less of a challenge to a reader. Similarly, when direct instruction of roots and affixes is available, readers are facilitated in pronunciation (e.g., *-tion* is pronounced *shun*) as well as in fluency. Knowledge of morphemic and **structural analysis** also enhances both vocabulary and comprehension skills. Teachers could readily improve students' awareness of word structure and word meaning and provide a metacognitive tool by teaching, creating, and displaying a derivational morphology chart that summarizes common suffixes (e.g., people nouns end in *-er, -or, -cian, -ist*; thing nouns end in *-tion, -sion*; nouns can be made by adding *-ment, -ity*; verbs are created by adding *-ize, -ify*). Thus, systematically teaching children about word structure (roots and affixes) provides them with both structural and strategic knowledge to be used for word reading (Carlisle, 2000; Carlisle & Stone, 2005), vocabulary growth (Baumann et al., 2002; Nagy & Anderson, 1984; Nagy & Scott, 2000), reading fluency (Bashir & Hook, 2009; Snow, Griffin, & Burns, 2005; Troia, 2004), comprehension (Katz, 2004; Nagy, Berninger, & Abbott, 2006), and spelling (Apel, Masterson, & Hart, 2004; Green et al., 2003). Morphological knowledge is influential in recognizing spelling changes as a result of morphological additions as well as facilitating recall and access to words. Facilitating access reduces the burden on working memory.

Morphological awareness becomes even more crucial in later elementary and middle school when textbooks are introduced and used. A majority of words encountered in informational text are **derivative** in nature (e.g., *constitute, constitution, constitutional, constitutionally*). Morphological awareness empowers a reader to analyze the internal and derivative structure of unfamiliar words by analogy to words already within his or her repertoire.

Carlisle (1988), in her studies of fourth-, sixth-, and eighth-grade students, demonstrated that children know more about derivational morphology than they use in their spelling. She recommended direct instruction of words that undergo both phonological and orthographic changes (e.g., *deep/depth*) as opposed to those that undergo only phonological change (e.g., *equal/equality*). Further indications for the merit of direct instruction appear across the literature from the benefits to early, first-grade readers (Wolter, Wood, & D'zatko, 2009) to fifth- and eighth-grade students (McCutchen, Logan, & Biangardi-Orpe, 2009). Moreover, late elementary and middle school students were studied, and their performance on measures of explicit morphological production was a significant predictor of both word identification and reading comprehension.

Relationship of Morphological Disorders to Literacy   Children with language learning disabilities often present with impairments in reading as their primary academic problem. The rate of morphological acquisition is slower for these children than for their typically developing peers. Although morphological acquisition has not been widely studied, several investigations have pointed to the relationship between morphological awareness and literacy. Mahoney and Mann (1992) found positive correlations between second graders' ability to appreciate phonologically and morphologically based puns and their reading ability. Ruben, Patterson, and Kantor (1991) reported a relationship between morphological knowledge and spelling ability in typically developing second graders, children with learning disabilities, and adults with literacy problems. Ruben and colleagues demonstrated that the morphemic errors made in writing reflected impairments in both the implicit and explicit levels of morphological knowledge. What was most striking, however, was their evidence that these impairments do not resolve simply by maturation and increased exposure to written language. Furthermore, underlying phonological weakness may contribute to the difficulty poor readers have with certain morphological relationships. Fowler and Liberman (1995) found that poor readers have greater difficulty in producing morphological forms that involve a phonological change (e.g., *courage/courageous*) than they do when there is no phonological change (e.g., *danger/dangerous*).

Morphology is relevant to both reading and spelling for several reasons. Among those reasons concerning English morphology, Elbro and Arnbak (1996, p. 212) identified the following:

- The role morphology plays in orthography
- The value of morphemes as indicators of meaning

- The economical nature of storing words in written lexicon as morphemes rather than as wholes (because of the relative unpredictability of sound to letter accuracy)

- Morpheme analysis and recognition as a reading strategy may provide a more direct route to the lexicon of the spoken word; certain reading and spelling errors are morphologically based (e.g., *procedure/proceed*)

Morphological awareness has been shown to be a strong indicator of reading comprehension (Carlisle, 1995), and morphological awareness training has been shown to have a positive effect on comprehension (Elbro & Arnbak, 1996). Children with dyslexia have weaker morphological awareness ability than their typical reading peers (Casalis, Cole, & Sopo, 2004; Elbro & Arnbak, 1996; Siegel, 2008). Morphological awareness training with students with dyslexia (Arnbak & Elbro, 2000) and other reading disabilities (Berninger et al., 2003; Katz & Carlisle, 2009) has been effective in improving decoding, comprehension, and spelling skills across age and grade levels (Kirk & Gillon, 2009).

Morphological awareness, however, is not seen as fully independent from phonological awareness (Fowler & Liberman, 1995). Phonological awareness skills are essential in early literacy acquisition before word structure becomes increasingly complex. Then, in concert with phonological knowledge, awareness of morphological structure and meaning plays an increasingly important role in decoding, comprehension, vocabulary, and spelling. Although researchers continue to determine the specific nature and interrelatedness of the systems of language that influence reading, teachers must remain conscious of the constant reciprocity among language components.

Syntax

Syntax is a third aspect of language form. Syntax is the system of rules that directs the comprehension and production of sentences. Syntax (sometimes referred to as *grammar*) specifies the order of words and the organization of words within a variety of sentence types. Syntactic rules allow the user to combine words into meaningful sentences and to alter the form of a sentence (e.g., *"The boy is walking"* may be transposed into *"Is the boy walking?"*) Despite a finite set of sentence types, an infinite number of sentences can be generated. In addition, syntactic knowledge allows a language user to decide whether sentences are grammatical.

Syntactic Development   Typically developing children acquire the rudiments of syntax early in the language acquisition process. As they progress beyond the basic form of noun phrase and verb phrase, children master the variety of sentence types common in preschool language: negative, interrogative, and imperative forms. Subsequently, they begin to develop the earliest complex sentence structures of coordination, demonstrated by the use of *and* ("Joshua went to grandma's house *and* had a good time"); complementation, indicated by using a clause structure that modifies the verb ("Tell me *what he is eating"*); and relativization, in which a clause restricts or modifies the meaning of another portion of the sentence ("The boy *who ate the cake* has a tummy ache"). Use of early complex sentence structures generally emerges at approximately 3 years of age and is mastered by age 5 or 6. Complex sentence development continues through the school years. Embedding of clauses, either parallel ("She gave him a toy *that he did not like"*) or nonparallel ("He called the man *who walked away"*); using **gerunds** (verbs with *-ing* that function as nouns; e.g., *"Cooking* is fun"); and using passive structures ("The cookie *was* eaten by the boy") continue to emerge across the school years with mastery of some forms as late as 11 years old. Other, more mature grammatical structures also evolve with the mastery of new forms such as more sophisticated conjunctions (e.g., *although, nonetheless*), mass nouns and their quantifiers (*"How much* water do you want?" rather than *"How many* water do you want?"*), and using reflexive pronouns (e.g., *himself, herself*). The mature language user can use sentence complexity to convey numerous relationships among actions, ideas, and locations.

As summarized by Scott (2004), several factors contribute to sentence complexity and, therefore, to the ability to comprehend complex sentences. First is the meaning relationship of words within a sentence, especially nouns and verbs. The passive structure is typically more challenging for children to process when it is in the reversible form ("The duck was chased by the goose") rather than in the nonreversible form ("The cake was baked by the girl"). Support for understanding the nonreversible form is obvious in that cakes do not bake girls. In addition, the nature of verbs themselves can influence syntactic structure. Certain verbs, for example *sit,* only require an agent that is someone to sit. Other verbs, however, have more complex syntactic requirements and need both an agent (someone to perform the action of putting), an object (something to put), and a location (a place to put it). Beyond the semantic–syntactic relationship (meaning to word order) are two other aspects of syntactic complexity. Sentence length, a common measure of children's language that increases with age, influences comprehension, particularly as the subject is distant from the verb as a result of dependent clauses ("Alex, a determined young man of Cuban descent who tolerated cold winters in the north so that he could reach his ultimate goal of a college education, returned to Miami for a week"), thus placing increasing demand on the listener or reader. Sentences with pronoun referents that are not transparent or where relationships are ambiguous pose a challenge ("Emma hugged Marsha before *she* closed the door;" "Ellie laughed at the bookstore"). Clearly not all sentences are equally easy to process whether spoke or written.

Changes in the sophistication of noun and verb phrases and the development of nominal, adverbial, and relative clauses contribute to the growth in complexity of syntax. Sentence complexity continues to grow through the high school years and into adulthood, with increased maturation reflecting the development and influence of written language skills. Using expository text is the norm during the period of middle elementary school through high school. With syntax as the "vehicle even *workhorse* of meaning" (Scott, 2009, p. 185), the complexity of informational text, both for content and the syntax used to convey it, emerges as a crucial component of reading comprehension for students. Sentences written in informational text are typically longer and therefore denser than those in **narrative** text. Chaney (1992) suggested the value of good syntactic knowledge in reading comprehension and reported that readers with better awareness of grammatical structure have better paragraph comprehension, possibly because they are able to use strong grammatical knowledge to monitor comprehension.

The ability to deconstruct sentences for comprehension or to construct them either orally or in writing to convey meaning is dependent on knowledge of syntactic rules. Understanding the meaning of sentences requires knowledge of syntactic rules, word meaning, and the relationships between and among the words. It is possible to understand sentence grammar separate from meaning ("Jabberwocky") and appreciate meaning in the context of inadequate grammar ("It don't mean nothing"). In addition, to some extent, syntactic interpretation relies on the ability to maintain sentences in working memory (Adams & Gathercole, 1995) and to exploit phonological memory (Montgomery, 1996).

Whereas phonological knowledge and skills are relevant to early decoding, morphological and syntactic knowledge are significant to fluency and comprehension in later reading development. Beyond the initial stages of reading, most typically in second grade (Chall, 1983), increased fluency and comprehension become the focus of reading instruction. Knowledge of syntax enables readers to make predictions from among a set of possibilities about what type of word or words must be coming next. This can be easily demonstrated using the **cloze technique (fill-in-the-blank technique)**, which is common to research designs in the study of syntax: *Sam gave Ida the _____.* Knowledge of syntactic structure helps an individual to predict the likelihood of either an adjective or a noun or both coming next. This predictive ability aids in automaticity. As a clinician and teacher trainer, I have taught many the practice of "grammatical parsing" to aid in developing fluency with appropriate level decodable text. By teaching children to recognize phrase structure in part by their responses to a set of *wh-* questions, fluency is increased as syntactic structure is exposed. ("After hearing/the dog growl/the boy/who was frightened/screamed for his mother"). Embedded in this practice is the increased transparency of word combinations based on semantic–syntactic relationships.

Relationship of Syntactic Disorders to Literacy   For children who have difficulty with expressive or receptive syntax, the effect on reading may not become obvious until later in elementary school when the emphasis shifts from decoding to comprehension. Moreover, comprehension difficulties may not emerge until the density of text increases beyond the reader's syntactic knowledge limits. As with all aspects of language, there is a continuum that reflects both a developmental sequence and degree of complexity (from single words to complex sentences). A parallel continuum involves the degree of severity and pervasiveness (one particular aspect or all aspects) of the language difficulty.

Studies of early syntactic delay were predictive of subsequent reading disability (Scarborough, 1990, 2001), as were studies of children identified more globally as having language impairments in which disordered syntax was a characteristic (Aram & Hall, 1989). Moreover, there is ample documentation of the persistence of early identified language impairment, including syntax-specific deficits (Nippold, Mansfield, Billow, & Tomblin, 2008; Scott & Windsor, 2000) into adolescence with academic consequences (Conte-Ramsden & Durkin, 2008; Johnson, et al., 1999; Nippold, Mansfield, Billow, & Tomblin, 2009). Other research has shown that children with reading difficulties have sentence comprehension problems as well. In particular, children and adolescents have difficulty interpreting later occurring complex structures such as those that contain **embedded** or **relative clauses** (Byrne, 1981; Morice & Slaghuis, 1985; Stein, Cairns, & Zurif, 1984). For children with a history of oral language impairment, longitudinal studies document the evolution of reading disability (Catts, Adlof, & Ellis Weismer, 2006; Catts, Adlof, Hogan, & Ellis Weismer, 2005; Scarborough, 2001). The oral–written language continuum is manifested in comprehension deficits as well. Reliance on semantic (meaning) strategies and limitations in working memory that would enable the child to retain the sentence for a sufficient period of time to analyze are possible contributing factors to difficulty in sentence comprehension. Many measures of sentence comprehension are confounded by precisely this working memory factor.

Lahey and Bloom (1994) offered that sentence comprehension is far more complex than issues of working memory limitations would imply. As always, they considered a more encompassing view of sentence comprehension that includes working memory capacity, the ability to automatically retrieve the language knowledge needed to construct in mind what the sentence (and its parts) is representing, the nature of the material being processed (in or out of a context familiar to the child), and the availability and strength of any context cues. Sentence comprehension is not a simple process for anyone, but for a child with learning and language difficulties, it is an even greater task. Cain and Oakhill (2007) reviewed available research and identified the relationship between reading comprehension and syntactic awareness tasks. What remains unclear is the specific nature of the relationship between syntactic comprehension problems and reading disability, although there is sufficient evidence to suggest that they coexist. Direct instruction in the writing of complex sentences via sentence combining techniques (Eisenberg, 2006) has been suggested by Scott (2009) as one means of improving sentence level comprehension. Manipulating short, kernel sentences with a variety of clausal forms (e.g., adverbial, relative) allows for a range of complex sentence structures. Such activities are part of a written language program (Hochman, 2009) that uses content area material in an integrated reading comprehension/written language program (see Chapter 13).

Comprehension of spoken syntax is supported by the discourse (conversational) structure of the interaction as well as by the **paralinguistic** and **situational** cues. Far fewer cues are available to the reader, and, as such, failure to accurately analyze sentence structure can result in deficient comprehension. In addition to the differences in interpreting sentences that are spoken versus those that are written, genre (narrative versus expository) influences comprehension as well (Scott, 2004, 2005).

The elements of language form (phonology, morphology, and syntax) have clear relationships to one another as one aspect of the foundation on which literacy is built. Early reading ability is strongly connected to phonological knowledge, as is the later development of spelling. Morphological knowledge adds to the skills required for spelling and comprehension. Later reading development, fluency, and comprehension have their roots in morphology and syntax while continuing to rely on efficient phonological processing.

Language Content

Language content, often referred to as *semantics,* is the meaning component of language. Language content reflects our world knowledge and what we know about objects, events, and relationships. The study of semantics is concerned with the meanings of words and the relationship between and among words as they are used to represent knowledge of the world. As explained by Lahey (1988), language content involves both the endless number of particular topics that can be discussed and the general categories of objects, actions, and relationships. Thus, all children of different cultures or experiences talk about content in terms of the objects, events, and relationships of their world, but the topics within each of these categories are different. Children raised in Mexico City or in Brooklyn will talk about food (object), eating (action), and possession (relationship) but are likely to ask for different foods.

Language content involves not only individual word meanings, as in analyzing a child's vocabulary, but also understanding the meaning features that compose a word; how a word may (or may not) be used in a phrase, a sentence, or discourse; and the literal and figurative meanings of words. Words are composed of clusters of meaning features that allow us to define words and to differentiate among them. Most often our knowledge of these features is unconscious. Try, for example, to define the word *walk*. Although all of us know what it means, and most are able to demonstrate it, defining *walk* is quite difficult. Furthermore, when asked, "What does *draft* mean?" one could potentially supply six different responses ranging from conscription (being drafted into the military) to an alcoholic beverage (an ice-cold draft beer). Thus, determining whether a person knows a word extends beyond checking his or her ability to point to a picture of it or even to use it in a sentence. Moreover, knowledge of the world and the words used to represent that knowledge grows continuously across the life span. Over time, a person may come to associate varied meanings with each word because of increased exposure to assorted usage or varied personal experience. With exposure to print, a person may read about places, events, or people not directly experienced but may acquire new knowledge as well as the lexicon (vocabulary) that represents the experience. In addition, there are rules that govern how words may be used in combination.

Consider, for example, "The bachelor's wife is beautiful." Although superficially the sentence is grammatically acceptable, the relationship between *bachelor* and *wife* raises a serious question as to the meaning of the sentence. Furthermore, the varying roles that words may play in a sentence can result in ambiguity that requires the language user to consider not only word meaning but also context. Consider the sentence, "Visiting relatives can be a nuisance." The meaning varies depending on the grammatical role ascribed to *visiting* as either a gerund or an adjective. These rules for using words in combination begin to develop quite early in a child's language acquisition process and form part of the basis for later semantic knowledge.

Word meaning may be literal or figurative. Part of the richness of language is in the imagery that it can create to express the more emotional and ethereal aspects of the human experience. Whether one has *had a ball* (had a good time at a party or possessed a baseball at some time) or *opened a can of worms* (went fishing or unintentionally caused a problem), the semantic knowledge and use are reflected in the way in which meaning is colored.

Meaning in language is conveyed through using words and their combinations. Language content is the knowledge of the vast array of objects, events, and relationships and the way they are represented.

Semantic Development

People talk or write to communicate meaning just as they listen or read to determine meaning. The process of learning to assign meaning begins in infancy during the preverbal stages of development. Meaning can be represented in a word, in a sentence, or across sentences, as well as in nonlinguistic ways.

Each of us has a lexicon, a mental dictionary within our semantic memory. Individual word meanings as well as how words may be used are found in the lexicon. In early development, children may ascribe a word to represent a variety of objects or events or relationships. Thus, in the single-word stage of language development, *cup* pronounced as "kuh" may mean a request for a drink or a request that a fallen cup be returned to the tray of the highchair. In early stages of language acquisition, word meaning may be overextended so that, for example, any four-legged furry animal is called "cat." Obviously, children and adults do not use words in the same way. Although a child may use a word taken from adult lexicon (e.g., *cat*), the meaning may be different as reflected in the overextensions of meaning that children make. Fortunately, word meanings are consistently refined over time so that speakers of the same language share common definitions for words.

In the early single-word stages of language development, children have already begun to code meaning for the words they use. They will use a word to indicate a variety of semantic categories such as existence (indicated by looking at, naming, touching, or referring to an object that exists in their world), nonexistence or disappearance (an object expected to be seen does not appear; "bye-bye"), or recurrence (the reappearance of an object or the recurrence of an event; "more").

As children progress to the two-word stage of language development, new semantic relations emerge, both individually and in combination. Between 18 and 36 months of age, children steadily acquire an increasing number of meaning relations that they can represent, such as agent-action ("Russell kiss") or attribute-entity ("big book").

With continued development, children begin to acquire vocabulary at a rapid rate. From the toddler years through first grade, children acquire new words at a pace of approximately 9 words per day. The vocabulary of a 6-year-old may be as large as 14,000 words (Carey, 1978). It is a massive task and remarkable feat to acquire sufficient information from interacting with the world (with little direct instruction) to developing a lexicon of nouns, verbs, adjective, adverbs, and prepositions, as well as the words to represent a huge array of concepts such as time, space, and causality.

Learning a word is a long-term developmental process. It includes determining that a set of sounds are a word; learning the word's meaning components, privileges, and restrictions on its use; and learning its syntactic properties (parts of speech, how it may be used in a sentence) and the conceptual foundations on which that word is based. Not only must children develop word meanings, but they also must learn contextual meaning. In the preschool years, words and sentence meaning expand. Later, children must learn to discern meaning from context (both linguistic and nonlinguistic) as well as to use later developing, more sophisticated cohesive devices to connect sentences into discourse.

Cohesive devices (Halliday & Hasan, 1976) include using pronouns or definite articles that refer to someone or something previously mentioned. This process is called **anaphora** (e.g., "Marsha was hungry. *She* went out to get lunch"). Another cohesive device, **ellipsis,** is the deletion of information available in a portion of the discourse immediately preceding (e.g., "Can you ice skate? I can"). Still another cohesive device, called **lexical cohesion,** involves the use of **synonyms** that refer to previously identified referents (e.g., "The *puppy* excitedly chased his tail. Our new *pet* was very entertaining").

In addition to relational meanings and contextual meaning, children must master the nonlinguistic aspects of meaning. **Deictic terms** are words that shift in meaning depending on how the nonlinguistic context changes. The meanings of words such as *I, you, here,* and *tomorrow* depend on who is speaking, where the participants are, and when the words are spoken.

Children acquire meaning of words and sentences and meaning across sentences in discourse. They must master a vast amount of information about the semantic and syntactic roles of words and about contextual and nonlinguistic aspects of meaning. It is amazing that much of this is accomplished in the preschool years. Later semantic development is concerned with continued refinement of previous content knowledge as well as with ongoing growth in vocabulary and in the mastery of **nonliteral language** such as **metaphors,** idioms, proverbs, and humor.

The power of word knowledge is seen most clearly in its impact on listening and reading comprehension, as well as writing. The strong connection between vocabulary knowledge, both breadth and depth of word meanings, and reading comprehension has a long history in research. The logic of the relationship between lexical knowledge and reading is intuitive; you will understand what you read if you know the meaning of the words. Vocabulary growth is a function of exposure, reading and problem-solving ability, and good instruction. Effective vocabulary instruction involves the creation of word-rich classroom environments, independence in word learning, development of authentic instructional strategies, and the use of realistic assessments (Blachowicz & Fisher, 2002). As children become literate, the opportunities for growth in semantic knowledge grow considerably. After children learn to read, reading becomes a vehicle for learning (see Chapter 11).

Relationship of Semantic Disorders to Literacy

There is more to reading than decoding (determining the pronunciation of words by noting the positions of vowels and consonants). The proof of a skilled, fluent reader may be the ability to read a professional manual filled with unfamiliar technical jargon. Being able to decode the words may very well be insufficient to provide the intended meaning or comprehension of the text. Once the reader has gained access to the words through decoding, the meaning of the words and sentences must be analyzed and synthesized for comprehension to occur. Comprehension in reading then is dependent on semantic, syntactic, and world knowledge. Consider *diadochokinesis,* a word unfamiliar to most. A strong decoder can syllabicate and decode the word syllable by syllable, a likely approach given the length of the word, but may not be able to guess the meaning (rapid alternating movements such as those associated with speech articulation).

Gough and Tunmer (1986) referenced two sets of skills in reading: decoding and linguistic comprehension. Reading is not a unitary action, nor is the use of oral language. Rather, both activities reflect a complex integration of skills. When looking at different groups identified as having reading disorders, dyslexia, language disorders, or specific language impairment, it is important to consider the criteria that are selected to define the group and which skills are under investigation before generalizing the implications of research findings.

During a consideration of semantic deficits in vocabulary and word knowledge, word retrieval, and the relationship to syntax and sentence comprehension, it is necessary to be concerned with the dynamic relationship of form, content, and use. Specifically, weak phonological coding may be related to establishing poorer networks of word meanings as well as poorer access to those words. Thus, facility or difficulty in one aspect of language as it relates to reading does not preclude the same ease or difficulty in the other aspects of reading. Some good decoders have poor comprehension, just as in the early stages of reading mastery, and poorer decoders may have adequate comprehension. Swank (1997) demonstrated that in addition to phonological coding, meaning and grammar are important to the decoding abilities of kindergarten and first-grade readers. Similarly, Snowling and Nation (1997) wrote that syntactic and semantic information derived from sentences allowed children to alter their inaccurate pronunciation of decoded **target words** so that the words made sense in the context of the sentence. In older children with reading difficulties, semantic deficits may be the result of what Vellutino, Scanlon, and Spearing referred to as having "accrued" (1995, p. 76) as a consequence of prolonged decoding difficulty in which poor readers are denied access to semantic information about word meaning and use. Early in their school careers, children learn to read, and for the remainder of their academic years, read to learn (Chall, 1983). Nippold suggested a "symbiotic" (1988, p. 29) relationship between literacy and learning during the later school years.

By fourth grade, reading becomes the primary means of acquiring new vocabulary. When children have inherent language deficits, semantic functions may be restricted, thus influencing learning to read as well as later reading to learn. Semantic deficits may manifest at different times in the reading process, dependent in part on the kind of reading instruction a child receives. Emphasizing phonics in a highly structured sound–symbol system in which word identification is stressed may allow comprehension difficulties based on semantic deficits to go unnoticed for longer periods of time. When text-based approaches to early reading are stressed, semantic deficits are more likely to be exposed earlier in the process of learning to read.

Semantic competence involves a high degree of organization among the concepts that are being accumulated in the semantic system. Semantic networks must be formed to provide the structure for the concepts that a child is learning. Children who are weaker at concept formation are likely to have less robust vocabulary and weaker semantic networks. Lack of exposure to concepts or difficulties in concept formation or in the organization of the concepts may result in less effective reading comprehension. So, children with ongoing oral language difficulties remain at higher risk for reading comprehension difficulties if their oral language deficits result in depressed semantic knowledge.

Children with reading deficits have been shown to have difficulties in vocabulary, word categorization, and word retrieval. Many children with reading impairments have more difficulty than same-age peers in providing accurate definitions for words. Hoskins (1983) reported that children with reading impairments were more likely to offer descriptions and examples of words they were asked to define rather than to provide more formal, specific definitions. This is a frequently observed clinical behavior. It reflects one level of general comprehension of word meaning and use (e.g., "I know how to use it, but I can't really tell you what it means"). For teachers who are concerned about the reading comprehension abilities of their students, defining versus describing is a skill to watch for.

Categorization abilities, another semantic skill reflecting a knowledge base, is also frequently deficient in children with reading difficulties. Children with reading and other learning disabilities often demonstrate restricted word meanings as well as weakly developed associations among words and classes of words. Limitations in reading comprehension may result from restricted word meanings that reduce the reader's ability to interpret sentences; reduced vocabulary knowledge so that less familiar, multisyllabic words are more difficult to decode; and poorly developed semantic networks between word meanings and categories.

Other than word meaning itself, it is necessary to consider several other important aspects of semantics. Understanding a word also requires knowledge of synonyms, **antonyms,** and multiple meanings of a word. At higher levels of abstraction, semantic knowledge includes appreciating and using humor, slang, idioms, **similes,** and metaphors (Roth & Spekman, 1989). World knowledge also plays a considerable role in how semantics functions in reading comprehension. Lack of world knowledge means that a decoding error is more likely to remain uncorrected when reading on an unfamiliar topic. Lack of an adequate knowledge base to judge the content that is being read may result in comprehension errors as well.

Word retrieval problems are another frequently observed semantic deficit that affects literacy. Word retrieval problems may be described as a person's difficulty in gaining access to a specific, intended word from his or her vocabulary. So, despite knowledge of the word, there is a disruption in recovering or retrieving the phonetic structure (sound pattern) of the word to express it in spontaneous production. Common behaviors of people with word retrieval difficulties are delay in retrieving the word; substitution of other, similar words; circumlocutions (descriptions of aspects of the word, as when a person says, "You know, the place where you swim," but means *pool*); the use of gestures or demonstration to represent the word; and the substitution of nonspecific words (e.g., *thing, stuff, the place*) for the specific word. Children with reading disabilities have been shown to have a slower rate of naming, more frequent naming errors, and longer delays before responding (Denckla & Rudel, 1976; German, 1982; Wiig, Semel, & Nystrom, 1982; see Chapter 5).

Children with word-retrieval difficulties may read less fluently, with many hesitations and rephrasings. A child may look at a word and offer a definition but may be unable to say the specific word. Given the frequent substitution of similar or related words, comprehension may not be seriously effected; however, the dilemma may be in demonstrating comprehension when specific words are not readily accessible.

Finally, as children become more adequate decoders, they read for meaning across sentences and through extended text rather than from individual words. At this juncture, semantic knowledge must become integrated with syntactic knowledge and the more pragmatic, or discourse-related, aspects of language that include a knowledge of narrative structure and the ability to determine the writer's intent.

Language Use

Language use is frequently referred to as *pragmatics*. Pragmatics involves a set of rules that dictate communicative behavior in three main areas: reasons for which we communicate, called *communicative functions* or *intentions;* different codes or styles of communication necessary in a particular context; and conversation or discourse. Each person speaks for a variety of purposes with an assortment of intentions. These intentions refer to the speaker's goals in talking. For example, one may speak to greet, inquire, answer, request a behavior or information, negotiate, or teach, among many other possibilities.

Success in communicating intentions depends on several factors. A speaker must choose the appropriate code or style from among the variety of ways in which something can be said. To make that decision, a speaker must consider the context and the listener's needs. The words and sentences that are chosen to formulate the thought depend on the ages, knowledge bases, and relative status of speaker and listener. Imagine using the greeting, "Hi, sweetie!" uniformly when greeting your 3-year-old, your pharmacist, and your boss. Similarly, the words chosen depend on what is occurring or what is present at the time the words are spoken. Two people standing on a train platform at 7 a.m. on a weekday would find it appropriate to hear, "Here it comes." The same utterance while standing in line at the supermarket might be met with a quizzical, "What?"

Finally, pragmatics involves rules of conversation or discourse. To communicate effectively, a speaker must be able to start a conversation, enter a conversation in process, and appropriately remain in a conversation. Moreover, competent communicators must be able to take turns within a conversation, recognize the need for clarification and provide it, change the subject appropriately, listen and respond meaningfully, and tell a coherent and cohesive story (narrative). The minutiae of competent conversation and narrative are an extensive area of study because of their significance in the social and academic lives of children (Applebee, 1978; Brinton & Fujiki, 1989; Dore, 1978; Halliday, 1975; Prutting & Kirschner, 1987; Rees, 1978).

Mastering the social uses of language is an ongoing process for young language learners. In school, classroom discourse patterns and a literate level of talking and understanding represent a level of language use that is critical for academic success.

The difference between everyday discourse and the language of the classroom and expository writing is dramatic. Although a child may have adequate linguistic ability for everyday conversational interactions, the same child may not have achieved a level of language use that is necessary to comprehend the language of instruction, which requires understanding more sophisticated vocabulary, words with multiple meanings, figurative usages, more varied and complex sentence structures, the distinction between what the sentence is saying and what it is intended to have the listener do, and the higher (less direct in interpretation) levels of understanding. Such vulnerability can be easily overlooked and is seriously deleterious to a child's learning ability.

Pragmatic Development

The earliest observations of communicative development can be made during the period between birth and approximately 10 months of age. This stage of preverbal communication is the first of three periods identified by Bates, Camaioni, and Volterra (1975). In this earliest period, the child is not aware of the communicative effect of his or her behavior. Although a child might point or reach toward an object of interest, he or she does not do this to elicit an adult's attention or action. In the next stage of communicative development, the one-word stage, between 10 and 15 months old, a child more definitely intends to communicate with the adults around him or her. Although these attempted communications may not involve speech, they are clearly recognized by both the infant and the adult as having intent. These attempts may be gestural and/or gestural and vocal (as differentiated from verbal attempts alone). Once an infant begins to use words to communicate, he or she is at the multiword stage, the third stage of this early period of communicative development. The infant's previous intentions were conveyed by gesture and vocalization. Now, more conventional word forms begin to serve similar purposes. As the use of words accomplishes goals for an infant or a toddler, the child begins to monitor and learn from the listener's reactions. The infant begins to see the effects of his or her utterances; as such, social interaction provides the context for learning about communication.

Roth and Spekman (1984) identified three sets of categories of intentional behavior for children in preverbal, one-word, and multiword stages that reflect a developmental process.

1. Intentional behavior from preverbal attention seeking, requesting, greeting, protesting or rejecting, responding/acknowledging, and informing

2. A more advanced stage in which words are added and allow for the refinement of the original intentions and the addition of naming and commenting

3. Multiword utterance stages in which intention is more varied and refined and may now express rules and opinions

The last set is foundational for using language in a more adultlike manner for regulating and controlling conversational interactions.

As these multiword toddlers become preschoolers, they begin to learn more complex ways of using language for social purposes. Their conversational skills grow, as do their discourse skills, such as telling stories, describing with greater clarity, and recounting personal experiences. As children's language skills grow, language can be used for an increasing number of school-related skills, such as instructing or reasoning. As they progress toward the school years, children begin to use their pragmatic skills for an ever-growing number of purposes at a higher, more refined level. Now, language used to plan and organize must help to construct narratives of greater density and longer sequences of events. An increasing number of communicative intentions, more sophisticated conversational skills, and improved narrative (storytelling skills) all mark the development of language use in preschoolers.

Conversational skills develop further during the school years. In the preschool years, conversation between children and adults is often supported by the adult. If a pre-schooler has not effectively communicated his or her intent, and a clarification is requested, then the child will typically repeat what he or she has just said. By the early elementary school years, however, a student will not only repeat but also will elaborate in an attempt to be more clear for the listener. By the middle elementary school years, a student cannot only elaborate but also explain, provide additional background information, and monitor the listener's comprehension in an ongoing way (Brinton, Fujiki, Loeb, & Winkler, 1986). Conversation among school-age children also involves the mastery of slang. In addition, children speak to each other in sentence structures that are more complex, elaborate, and varied than they do when speaking to adults. This is consistent with parents' observations of the difference in the way children talk at home versus how they communicate among friends (Owens, 1996). Certainly, among teenagers, using language for social purposes becomes more crucial. Also important is the ability to effectively shift from one conversational style (social) to another (academic) to meet the higher expectations of teachers for a fully literate style of language use (Larson & McKinley, 1995).

The school-age years bring with them another level of maturation and an increased demand on children's pragmatic abilities. During the school years, several important changes take place in pragmatic development and use. The number of communicative functions must expand. Children have to use their language skills but must do so with increased levels of appropriateness and often more indirectly. The demands on narrative production increase steadily. Preschoolers' simple storytelling of one or two facts or events grows to become the requirements of show and tell as well as book reports and essays. Children who have heard stories read and told throughout their lives come to these school-based narrative tasks better equipped than peers with fewer literacy experiences (Linder, 1999). There is a structure and pattern to the ways stories are constructed (Stein & Glenn, 1979). When children have been exposed to this pattern frequently because they have been read to on a regular basis, they come to school with a tacit knowledge of the structure of stories that becomes more available to them as it is required in the school environment.

The language of the classroom is different from the everyday language that is used for social interaction. In school, there is a greater degree of formality. The choice of words is often more abstract and unfamiliar; sentence structures are more complex; the interactions are planned and controlled; the topics, which are also controlled, are often related to texts; the rate of speech is faster; and, above all, the language of the classroom is decontextualized (Nelson, 1986). When language is decontextualized, there are few contextual clues that children can use to understand the language of the classroom. As communicators, people are supported by context in cues such as facial expressions, gestures, intonational patterns, and the presence of the object being discussed.

Unlike conversation, instructional discourse provides less meaning and support from context. Understanding is more fully dependent on the words. The purposes of language in the classroom are more instructive, regulatory, and acknowledging and are far less individualized and supportive than in conversation. There is a communicative imbalance that is particular to the classroom. Teachers control topics and turns. They ask questions to which they already know the answers (and judge the responses) and create an environment with the language of authority. Britton (1979) wrote that in a conversation the partners are participants who have a generally equal role in the course and direction of the conversation. He described another style of conversation in which one partner is dominant and the other is more of a "spectator" (1979, p. 192). Spectators, he noted, "use language to digest experience" (p. 192). Indeed, when considering classroom discourse, students most frequently play the role of spectators.

The differences between social and instructional discourse can be highlighted by comparing a request for information and its aftermath in a social context and in a classroom environment. A special form of instructional dialogue exists within classrooms (Cazden, 1988; Nelson, 1985), referred to as the initiation-response-evaluation interaction pattern that consists of teacher initiation, student response, and teacher evaluation. Thus, in a classroom one might hear the following:

Teacher: [Initiating] What is the capital of California?

Student: [Responding] Sacramento.

Teacher: [Evaluating] That's right. Very good.

In a social environment, a similar exchange would end somewhat differently:

Speaker 1:   What is the capital of California?

Speaker 2:   Sacramento.

Speaker 1:   Thanks.

In the classroom, the question is a test, although it is phrased as a request for information. In an everyday interaction, the request for information is a genuine request. (See Table 3.4 for a discussion of the differences between oral language and literate [classroom] language.)

Relationship of Pragmatic Disorders to Literacy

The emphasis on the relationship between language and reading has grown stronger (Catts, 1996; Catts & Kamhi, 1986; Greene, 1996). For certain children whose oral language skills are age appropriate when they enter school, early literacy acquisition and accommodation to school discourse may not be negatively affected. Yet, as the demands of the curriculum escalate, these same children may not have developed enough linguistically to meet expectations. Skills that were adequate in early grades when the emphasis was on decoding and when instruction was more experiential in nature are now insufficient as reading to learn becomes the expected mode (Chall, 1983). Moreover, as the curriculum expands, topics become less familiar; new vocabulary and more complex sentences, paragraphs, and texts must be analyzed and interpreted; more reading and writing are expected; and the cognitive demands become more abstract.

Reading comprehension is an enormously complex integration of high-level linguistic ability and problem-solving skills. Approaching reading with the intent to understand and gain information and with the expectation that the text will make sense are the behaviors of good readers. They recognize that the goal of reading is to comprehend, and to that end they monitor their own comprehension. Poor readers, by contrast, will often perceive the purpose of reading as sounding out and saying the words aloud. The expectation or intent to understand what has been decoded is sharply re-

Table 3.4. Oral/literate language differences

Oral language	Literate language
Function	
Talking to regulate social interaction—requesting, commanding, protesting, seeking interaction	Talking to reflect on the past and future—predicting, projecting into thoughts and feelings of others, reasoning, imagining
Questions generally asked by speakers to gain information they do not have	Pseudoquestions asked to get the listener to perform for the speaker who knows the answers
Used to share understanding of the concrete and practical	Used to learn and teach
Symmetrical communication—everyone has an equal right to participate in the conversation; participants collaborate on the discourse	Asymmetrical communication—one person has the floor and is responsible for organizing the entire discourse
Content	
Talk is about the here and now—the concrete	Talk is about the there and then—the past and future; the abstract
Topic-associative organization; chaining of ideas or anecdotes	Topic-centered organization; explicit, linear description of single event
Meaning is in the context (shared information or the environment)	Meaning is in the text
Structure	
Use of pronouns, slang, and jargon; expressions known only to the in-group	Use of explicit, specific vocabulary
Familiar words	Unfamiliar words
Repetitive syntax and ideas	Minimal or no repetition of syntax and ideas
Cohesion based on intonation	Cohesion based on formal linguistic markers (*because, therefore,* and *so forth*)

From Westby, C. (1995). Culture and literacy: Frameworks for understanding. *Topics in Language Disorders, 16*(1), 59; reprinted by permission.

duced or is not a concern of poorer readers (Bos & Filip, 1982; Brown, 1982; Myers & Paris, 1978; Owings, Peterson, Bransford, Morris, & Stein, 1980; see Chapter 12).

An essential higher-order linguistic ability in text comprehension is the aspect of language use called *discourse,* which includes both conversational and narrative ability. Numerous higher-order language and cognitive skills are necessary for text comprehension, including the following (as identified by Roth & Spekman, 1989): understanding the relationship between words and word parts, grasping sentence cohesion (i.e., the relationship between two sentences or parts of a sentence as signaled by cohesive devices), identifying words based on context or familiarity, determining vocabulary meaning based on context (including multiple meaning words and figurative language), understanding at different levels from literal to inferential (identifying main ideas, summarizing, predicting, and determining character traits and emotions), determining the communicative intent of the author, identifying and retaining relevant information, and using knowledge of narrative structure.

Knowledge of narrative structure and determining the author's intent can play crucial roles in comprehension when syntax (sentence structure) and semantics (meaning aspects) are otherwise intact. Recognizing narrative structure and the intention of the writer is part of the active construction of comprehension that extends beyond the interpretations of the grammatical and meaning components of a piece of writing.

The ability to appreciate and use narrative structure in comprehension (and oral and/or written production) has been studied in children with reading problems. Using story grammars that describe the internal structure (both the components of the story and the rules for the order and relationship among the story components) of a story has been the most common way of analyzing narratives (Mandler & Johnson, 1977; Stein & Glenn, 1979).

Stein and Glenn's (1979) story grammar consists of a setting category and a system for ordering episodes within the story. This system is easily recognizable to those with the tacit knowledge of narrative structure and familiarity with literature. They are as follows: setting statements (*Marsha looked out across the expanse of land that she knew could now be hers*), initiating events (*The matching numbers were so unexpected*), internal responses (*Marsha remained numbed by the news*), plans for obtaining a goal (*Marsha started a telephone list. There was little time to waste*), attempts at achieving the goal (*Call after call, Marsha reported the news*), direct consequences of the attempts to reach the goal (*Everyone had been reached. They would arrive within 2 days*), and reactions that describe the emotional response (*With a grin on her face, she dropped into her favorite chair, exhausted and exhilarated!*).

Children with language and reading disabilities have less appreciation for narrative structure as defined by story grammar. Poorer understanding of temporal and causal relationships, limited detail, mistaken information, shorter retellings, and difficulty with inferential questions were also observed in children with language disorders (Gerber, 1993; Roth, 1986). Westby (1989) reported that children with language disorders tell shorter stories with fewer complete episodes, use a more restricted vocabulary, and have less well-organized stories than their peers who use language more typically.

In addition to knowing and using narrative structure, understanding the intent of the writer (or speaker, in oral discourse) is another pragmatically based aspect of comprehension. This involves appreciating information that is not presented explicitly. This grasp of suggested or implied information, called presupposition, is necessary for the message being communicated to be understood (Bates, 1976; Rees, 1978).

In order to be a successful communicator, it is necessary to have sufficient language flexibility to adjust what is being said according to the needs of the listener. That may mean altering word choice, sentence structure, gestures, and paralinguistic features such as intonation patterns based on a variety of characteristics including age, relative status (of speaker and listener), intellectual level, and awareness of the listener's prior knowledge of the topic. Sociolinguist Dell Hymes (1972) offered a definition of pragmatics as "knowing what to say to whom, how and under what circumstances." A listener must monitor his or her comprehension and request clarification if necessary.

The parallels of pragmatics of oral language or discourse to reading are strong. Written language can be used for a variety of purposes with different intentions. In writing, one can request, create, solicit, inform, educate, entertain, describe, and persuade, among a lengthy list of other purposes. For the reader, the mandate is to discern the communicative intent of the author in nonfiction and of the author and characters in fiction. When children have vulnerabilities in determining a speaker's intent in oral discourse, they are clearly at risk for failing to make these determinations from print. So much emphasis is placed on the decoding process in the early school years that the functional and communicative intents of writing are often neglected (Creaghead, 1986). Children who are weaker in understanding implied meaning in conversation (e.g., the sarcasm in "Nice haircut" said with a sneer) may struggle later on when they are expected to interpret humor, sarcasm, figurative language (idioms), metaphors, and other less explicitly stated intended meanings. Moreover, in reading, the physical and environmental cues on which speakers and listeners depend, such as an arched eyebrow, a falsetto voice, or the gape of onlookers, are absent or may be reflected in more abstract ways (should the author choose to do so) as italics or punctuation (! ; ? " "). In conversation, the speaker may recognize a furrowed brow as confusion and attempt to clarify before asked to do so. No such author-given support is available to the reader. I have lost track of the number of times I have needed to help students recognize the need to actively construct their comprehension because Edgar Allan Poe, O. Henry, or Guy de Maupassant is unavailable to explain himself! Conversely, children can be motivated to consider the needs of their reader (typically a teacher) when writing an assignment via a reminder that the teacher is unlikely to call them at home and ask, "Just what did you mean in the second paragraph on page 3?" It is crucial for teachers to recognize and remember that when children have vulnerabilities in discourse, they are at risk for comprehension difficulties with conversation and narrative despite having decoding skills. Active participation in the process of comprehending what is read involves a complex amalgam of skills among which language use or pragmatics is a subtle and often unrecognized vulnerability. When a child has adequate social language skills, the more hidden pragmatic weakness that can negatively effect comprehension may be overlooked easily. Direct instruction in narrative structure via story grammars and in identifying and interpreting the communicative intentions of the author can markedly improve a student's level of reading comprehension.

Metalinguistic Development

At the most developed level of language use, beyond the basic pragmatic skills required for conversation and narrative, is another tier of language competence called *metalinguistic abilities* (Miller, 1990). Metalinguistic abilities permit a child to view language as an entity, something to talk and think about. Metalinguistic skills enable a child to use language to talk about language. In preschoolers, language is viewed primarily as a means of communication, not as an object of consideration. During the school-age years, however, children become increasingly able to reflect on language and make conscious decisions about their own language and how it works. This is different from having tacit, underlying knowledge that allows the generation of sentences with specific words that are appropriate to a situation. Metalinguistic skills are essential to successful school learning because they influence a number of school-based tasks and are particularly important to developing early decoding ability. Bunce (1993) identified the diverse nature of the metalinguistic skills required for literacy acquisition, comprehension, and successful school learning. At a phonological level, a child must be able to segment a word into its sounds and determine whether two words have the same sound. Another metalinguistic task is to determine whether two sentences have equal meaning or to identify a sentence by its syntactic form (e.g., declarative, interrogative). Recognizing multiple meanings, summarizing, and analyzing information are metalinguistic tasks as well.

Wallach and Miller (1988) established a sequence in the development of metalinguistic skills that evolves from 1½ to 10 years of age and older. In the earliest stages, children learn to recognize some printed symbols, such as fast-food signs or the first letter of their name. By the beginning of the later stages of metalinguistic awareness, between 5 and 8 years of age, children's metalinguistic knowledge becomes an essential part of learning to read. Among these skills are those associated with phonological awareness, such as rhyming, segmentation, and **phoneme deletion**. It is widely agreed that phonological awareness makes a major contribution to early decoding ability. Well-developed metalinguistic skills are as crucial to early reading ability as they ultimately are to classroom success in understanding the discourse patterns of the classroom and the ongoing need to analyze the language being used to teach the language that must be learned.

When children have weaker skills in language comprehension and use, they are at risk for academic difficulty at many levels. For some children, the shift from contextualized, social, familiar, adult-supported language to the decontextualized, pedagogic, novel, adult-directed, evaluative, metalinguistic language of the classroom is overwhelming. Such language difficulties can be virtually invisible in a child whose speech is clear and whose demeanor is undemanding. A common misperception is that these children lack motivation or interest; rather, their skills are not on the same level as the language and communication demands of the classroom. Language is a part of every aspect of the school day, and what appears to be inattention or lack of motivation may, in fact, be a lack of comprehension of the level of language presented and the rules of classroom discourse.

WORKING MEMORY, EXECUTIVE FUNCTION, LANGUAGE, AND LITERACY

Each day in school, a child is likely to hear the question, "What was that about?" after having read a passage. Teachers readily assume that a child will read with the intent to understand. Not all children do. Not all children can. It has been well established that reading is a language-based skill. Language is the mediator for most thinking and reasoning. As long ago as 1962, Vygotsky noted that "speech and language plays a central role in the development of self-control, self-direction, problem-solving and task performance." Moreover, language is the mediating force for an integrated set of cognitive capacities and abilities that involve storage, organization, retention, access, and manipulation of information. These capacities, working memory and executive functions, are essential to literacy development and particularly crucial to reading comprehension and writing.

Working memory is the capacity (as differentiated from ability) to hold information in mind for short periods of time while *manipulating* it. Working memory is essential to all aspects of learning and, therefore, academic performance; effectively, it is a mental workspace (Gathercole & Alloway, 2008) where new information is temporarily stored while old information is retrieved and processed. Working memory is crucial to effective executive function. Executive functions, which are metacognitive in nature, are the management functions of your mind that are invoked when the challenge of a novel task is presented. Executive functions plan and make decisions in order to recognize, approach, analyze, plan, sustain involvement, tolerate obstacles, strategize, and solve a problem along with the ability to regulate behavior, both actual and emotional ("stop, think, plan, [revise if necessary], do") (Baddeley, 2006; Denckla, 1996; Meltzer, 2007). Having sufficient working memory capacity is crucial because the "mental workspace" must be adequate for all the simultaneous mental activity. Of note, working memory is not vulnerable to socioeconomic factors (Engel, Santos, & Gathercole, 2008), whereas environmental factors have been demonstrated to have an influence on other aspects of cognitive development (e.g., language; Hart & Risley, 1999).

Richards (2003) catalogued several readily recognizable functions of working memory for a student: 1) holding an idea in mind while developing, elaborating, clarifying, or using it; 2) recalling from **long-term memory** while holding some information in short-term memory; 3) holding together the components of a task in memory while completing the task; 4) keeping together a series of new pieces of information so that they remain meaningful; 5) holding a long-term plan in mind while thinking about a short-range goal. There are numerous realizations of these functions in the day-to-day activities of a classroom: 1) remembering all the components of a multistep direction; completing the steps in a multipart math problem; 2) retrieving the information necessary to answer a question while remembering the question (the failure of which can result in the often heard, "I forgot" or "Never mind"); 3) the demands of written language "mechanics" while composing; 4) decoding and blending the syllables in a multisyllabic word; 5) rushing through a task and producing "careless" errors in the attempt to finish it before "forgetting" what was required.

Working memory is vital to language and literacy development as well as classroom learning. Limitations in working memory affect multiple aspects of language learning (Baddeley, Gathercole, & Papagno, 1998); for example, lexical and morphological (Ellis Weismer, 1996), vocabulary (Gathercole, Service, Hitch, Adams, & Martin, 1999), and comprehending complex sentences (Montgomery & Evans, 2009). The impact of limited working memory capacity (phonological and verbal) is significant in all aspects of literacy development and phonological processing, which includes phonological awareness (Kamhi & Pollack, 2005), decoding (DeJong, 2006), fluency (Swanson & O'Connor, 2009), comprehension (Cain, 2006; Cain, Oakhill, & Bryant, 2004; Cain, Oakhill, & Lemmon, 2004; Just & Carpenter, 1992; Seigneuric & Ehrlich, 2005; Seigneuric, Ehrlich, Oakhill, & Yuill, 2000; Swanson, Howard, & Saez, 2006), and writing (Kellogg, 1996; Swanson & Berninger, 1996; Swanson & Siegel, 2001). As such, the impact on classroom functioning of limited working memory capacity is far reaching and includes mathematics learning (Alloway, 2006; Bull & Espy, 2006).

The executive functions are similarly crucial to all aspects of academic learning. Teachers can appreciate the manner in which executive controls are in effect throughout the school day, particularly in reading comprehension. In order to appreciate what is being read, a student must have basic language and literacy skills, which are necessary but not sufficient to successfully comprehend. Readers must "construct" meaning from any form of text. In order to accomplish that, one must have the capacity to plan ("I am going to read this because..."), prioritize ("Do I need that information?"), activate prior knowledge ("What do I already know about this topic?"), hold and manipulate the information in mind (working memory), invoke strategies ("What can I do because I don't know what that word means?"), and self-monitor ("Did that make sense?"). A teacher wants to avoid the experience of asking a child to read a passage, inquiring as to its meaning, being informed that the young reader has no notion of what has just been read, and hearing in response to your incredulous question, "Well then, why did you just read that?", the innocent but very concerning response, "Because you told me to."

Gaskins, Satlow, and Pressley (2007) identified seven executive principles that help define the relationship between reading comprehension and executive function. These principles can be explicitly taught to readers to build skills for successful engagement with text. For effective readers, such principles are a given. For those for whom reading remains a struggle, either decoding, comprehending, or both, their importance is less obvious. The seven principles underlying the reading comprehension—executive control relationship are as follows:

1. Reading must make sense.

2. Understanding is the result of planning.

3. Prioritizing leads to maximizing time and effort.

4. Gaining access to background information helps organize new information.

5. Self-checking enhances goal achievement.

6. Having a flexible mindset provides opportunities for increased understanding.

7. Understanding is improved by self-assessing.

Teaching the skills and strategies that support these principles can be done as part of the curriculum. Indeed, the curriculum itself becomes the vehicle for learning the components of executive function and the strategies that are their concrete realization.

CLOSING THOUGHTS

Consider once more the marvelous melodies and harmonies of *Eine Kleine Nachtmusik*. There are but seven notes in the Western musical scale, yet the combinations and permutations are endless. In a similar vein, a language system has a set of components that are conceptualized as form, content, and use. Within each of these components are an infinite number of combinations and variations that function alongside rules and regularities, permitting the language user, young or old, to communicate. No child is like every other child. Genetics, personality, experience, emotion, developmental patterns, intellect, neurology, perception, memory, and **linguistics** intertwine so that the whole is greater than the sum of its parts. Still, there are certain regularities in language development that teachers must know to enrich the understanding of how language influences a child's ability to learn. Simultaneously, the variability from one child to another must be kept in mind so that teachers focus on the child and not only on the task. At times, the child's knowledge and ability as well as the task itself influence performance and learning.

Throughout this chapter, four strands of research have been woven together: language and speech-language pathology, learning disabilities, reading, and education. In-depth knowledge of oral language development and language related to learning and reading comes from the discipline of speech-language pathology. Understanding the many aspects of learning and flexibility in skill and strategy development emerges from studying learning disabilities. Reading research and instruction provide an intense consideration of all aspects of the enormous task of "breaking the code" and then encoding to complete the reading process. Educational theory and practice offer a wide array of techniques for encouraging and facilitating learning. For teachers, an awareness and integration of this information offers the opportunity for greater power in teaching.

Language is omnipresent in education. It is an immutable aspect of literacy, a treasured gift that many, but not all of us, share. Teachers have a greater opportunity to share the gift by understanding and appreciating the role that language plays in learning and literacy and by thinking about the needs of one child at a time.

REFERENCES

Adams, A., & Gathercole, S. (1995). Phonological working memory and speech production in preschool children. *Journal of Speech and Hearing Research, 38,* 403–414.

Adams, M. (1990). *Beginning to read: Thinking and learning about print.* Cambridge, MA: The MIT Press.

Adams, M.J., Foorman, B.R., Lundberg, I., & Beeler, T. (1998). *Phonemic awareness in young children: A classroom curriculum.* Baltimore: Paul H. Brookes Publishing Co.

Alloway, T. (2006). How does working memory work in the classroom? *Educational Research and Reviews, 1*(4), 134–139.

Apel, K., Masterson, J., & Hart, P. (2004). Integration of language components in spelling. In E. Silliman & L. Wilkinson (Eds.), *Language and literacy in schools* (pp. 292–315). New York: Guilford Press.

Applebee, A. (1978). *The children's concept of story.* Chicago: University of Chicago Press.

Aram, D., & Hall, N. (1989). Longitudinal follow-up of children with preschool communication disorders. *School Psychology Review, 18,* 487–501.

Arnbak, E., & Elbro, C. (2000). The effects of morphological awareness training on the reading and spelling skills of young dyslexics. *Scandinavian Journal of Educational Research, 44,* 229–251.

August, D., & Shanahan, T. (2006). *Developing literacy in second language learners: A report on the National Literacy Panel on Language Minority Children and Youth.* Mahwah, NJ: Lawrence Erlbaum Associates.

August, D., Snow, C., Carlo, M., Proctor, C., Rolla de San Francisco, A., Duursma, E., et al. (2006). Literacy development in elementary school second-language learners. *Topics in Language Disorder, 26*(4), 351–364.

Baddeley, A. (2006). Working memory: An overview. In S. Pickering (Ed.), *Working memory in education* (pp. 3–33). Burlington, MA: Academic Press.

Baddeley, A., Gathercole, S., & Papagno, C. (1998). The phonological loop as a language learning device. *Psychological Review, 105,* 158–173.

Bashir, A., & Hook, P. (2009). Fluency: A key link between word identification and comprehension. *Language, Speech, and Hearing Services in Schools, 40,* 196–200.

Bashir, A., & Scavuzzo, A. (1992). Children with language disorders: Natural history and academic success. *Journal of Learning Disabilities, 25,* 53–65.

Bates, E. (1976). Pragmatics and sociolinguistics in child language. In D. Morehead & A. Morehead (Eds.), *Normal and deficient child language* (pp. 411–463). Baltimore: University Park Press.

Bates, E., Camaioni, L., & Volterra, V. (1975). The acquisition of performatives prior to speech. *Merrill-Palmer Quarterly, 21,* 205–226.

Baumann, J., Edwards, E., Font, G., Tereshinski, C., Kame'enui, E., & Olejnik, S. (2002). Teaching morphemic and contextual analysis to fifth-grade students. *Reading Research Quarterly, 37*(2), 150–176.

Berninger, V., Nagy, W., Carlisle, J., Thomson, J., Hoffer, D., Abbott, S., et al. (2003). Effective treatment for children with dyslexia in grades 4-6: Behavioral and brain evidence. In B. Foorman (Ed.), *Preventing and remediating reading difficulties: Bringing science to scale* (pp. 381–417). Timonium, MD: York Press.

Bernthal, J.E., & Bankson, N.W. (1998). *Articulation and phonological disorders* (4th ed.). Boston: Allyn & Bacon.

Bird, J., & Bishop, D. (1992). Perception and awareness of phonemes in phonologically impaired children. *European Journal of Disorders of Communication, 27,* 289–311.

Bird, J., Bishop, D., & Freeman, N. (1995). Phonological awareness and literacy development in children with expressive phonological impairments. *Journal of Speech and Hearing Research, 38,* 446–462.

Blachman, B. (1989). Phonological awareness and word recognition: Assessment and intervention. In A.G. Kamhi & H.W. Catts (Eds.), *Reading disabilities: A developmental language perspective* (pp. 138–158). New York: Little, Brown.

Blachman, B. (1991). Early intervention for children's reading problems: Clinical applications of the research in phonological awareness. *Topics in Language Disorders, 12*(1), 51–65.

Blachman, B.A., Ball, E.W., Black, R., & Tangel, D.M. (2000). *Road to the code: A phonological awareness program for young children.* Baltimore: Paul H. Brookes Publishing Co.

Blachowicz, C., & Fisher, P.J. (2002). *Teaching vocabulary in all classrooms* (2nd ed.). Upper Saddle River, NJ: Pearson Education.

Bloom, L., & Lahey, M. (1978). *Language development and language disorders.* Boston: Allyn & Bacon.

Bos, C., & Filip, D. (1982). Comprehension monitoring skills in learning disabled and average readers. *Topics in Learning and Learning Disabilities, 2,* 79–85.

Brady, S., & Shankweiler, D. (Eds.). (1991). *Phonological processes in literacy: A tribute to Isabelle Y. Liberman.* Mahwah, NJ: Lawrence Erlbaum Associates.

Brinton, B., & Fujiki, M. (1989). *Conversational management with language impaired children: Pragmatic assessment and intervention.* Rockville, MD: Aspen Publishers.

Brinton, B., Fujiki, M., Loeb, D., & Winkler, E. (1986). Development of conversational repair strategies in response to requests for clarification. *Journal of Speech and Hearing Research, 39,* 75–82.

Britton, J. (1979). Learning to use language in two modes. In N. Smith & M. Franklin (Eds.), *Symbolic functioning in childhood* (pp. 185–198). Mahwah, NJ: Lawrence Erlbaum Associates.

Brown, A. (1982). Learning how to learn from reading. In J. Langer & M. Smith-Burke (Eds.), *Reader meets author: Bridging the gap* (pp. 26–54). Newark, DE: International Reading Association.

Brown, R. (1973). *A first language: The early stages.* Cambridge, MA: Harvard University Press.

Bull, R., & Espy, K. (2006). Working memory, executive functioning and children's mathematics.

In S. Pickering (Ed.), *Working memory in education*. Burlington, MA: Academic Press.

Bunce, B.H. (1993). Language of the classroom. In A. Gerber (Ed.), *Language related learning disabilities: Their nature and treatment* (pp. 135–159). Baltimore: Paul H. Brookes Publishing Co.

Byrne, B. (1981). Deficient syntactic control in poor readers: Is a weak phonetic memory code responsible? *Applied Psycholinguistics, 3,* 201–212.

Cain, K. (2006). Children's reading comprehension: The role of working memory in normal and impaired development. In S. Pickering (Ed.), *Working memory in education* (pp. 61–91). Burlington, MA: Academic Press.

Cain, K., & Oakhill, J. (2007). Reading comprehension difficulties: Causes, correlates and consequences. In K. Cain and J. Oakhill (Eds.), *Children's comprehension problems in oral and written language: A cognitive perspective* (pp. 41–74). New York: Guilford Press.

Cain, K., Oakhill, J., & Bryant, P. (2004). Children's reading comprehension ability: Concurrent prediction by working memory, verbal ability, and component skills. *Journal of Educational Psychology, 96,* 31–42.

Cain, K., Oakhill, J., & Lemmon, K. (2004). Individual differences in the inference of word meaning from context: The influence of reading comprehension, vocabulary knowledge, and memory capacity. *Journal of Educational Psychology, 96*(4), 671–681.

Carey, A. (1978). The child as word learner. In M. Halle, J. Bresnan, & G. Miller (Eds.), *Linguistic theory and psychological reality* (pp. 264–293). Cambridge, MA: The MIT Press.

Carlisle, J. (1988). Knowledge of derivational morphology in spelling ability in fourth, sixth and eighth graders. *Applied Psycholinguistics, 9,* 247–266.

Carlisle, J. (1995). Morphological awareness and early reading achievement. In L.B. Feldman (Ed.), *Morphological aspects of language processing* (pp. 189–210). Mahwah, NJ: Lawrence Erlbaum Associates.

Carlisle, J. (2000). Awareness of the structure and meaning of morphologically complex words: Impact on reading. *Reading and Writing: An Interdisciplinary Journal, 12*(3), 169–190.

Carlisle, J., & Stone, C. (2005). Exploring the role of morphemes in word reading. *Reading Research Quarterly, 40*(4), 428–449.

Carroll, L. (1960). *Alice's adventures in wonderland and through the looking glass.* New York: The New American Library. (Original work published 1865)

Casalis, S., Cole, P., & Sopo, D. (2004). Morphological awareness in developmental dyslexia. *Annals of Dyslexia, 54,* 114–138.

Catts, H. (1986). Speech production/phonological deficits in reading disordered children. *Journal of Learning Disabilities, 19,* 504–508.

Catts, H.W. (1989). Phonological processing deficits and reading disabilities. In A.G. Kamhi & H.W. Catts (Eds.), *Reading disabilities: A developmental language perspective* (pp. 101–132). New York: Little, Brown.

Catts, H. (1993). The relationship between speech and language impairments and reading disabilities. *Journal of Speech and Hearing Research, 36*(5), 948–958.

Catts, H. (1996). Defining dyslexia as a developmental language disorder: An expanded view. *Topics in Language Disorders, 16*(2), 14–25.

Catts, H. (1997). The early identification of language-based reading disabilities. *Language, Speech, and Hearing Services in Schools, 28,* 86–89.

Catts, H., Adlof, S., & Ellis Weismer, S. (2006). Language deficits in poor comprehenders: A case for the simple view of reading. *Journal of Speech, Language, Hearing Research, 49*(2), 278–293.

Catts, H., Adlof, S., Hogan, T., & Ellis Weismer, S. (2005) Are specific language impairment and dyslexia distinct disorders? *Journal of Speech, Language, and Hearing Research, 48*(6), 1378–1396.

Catts, H.W., Hu, C.F., Larrivee, L., & Swank, L. (1994). Early identification of reading disabilities in children with speech-language impairments. In S.F. Warren & J. Reichle (Series Eds.) & R.V. Watkins & M.L. Rice (Eds.), *Communication and language intervention series: Specific language impairment in children* (Vol. 4, pp. 145–160). Baltimore: Paul H. Brookes Publishing Co.

Catts, H.W., & Kamhi, A. (1986). The linguistic basis of reading disorders: Implications for the speech-language pathologist. *Language, Speech, and Hearing Services in Schools, 17,* 329–341.

Catts, H.W., & Vartiainen, T. (1997). *Sounds abound.* East Moline, IL: LinguiSystems.

Cazden, C. (1988). *Classroom discourse: The language of teaching and learning.* Portsmouth, NH: Heinemann.

Chall, J. (1983). *Stages of reading development.* New York: McGraw-Hill.

Chaney, C. (1992). Language development, metalinguistic skills, and print awareness in 3 year old children. *Applied Psycholinguistics, 13,* 485–514.

Clark-Klein, S., & Hodson, B. (1995). A phonologically based analysis of misspellings by third graders with disordered-phonology histories. *Journal of Speech and Hearing Research, 38,* 839–849.

Conte-Ramsden, G., & Durkin, K. (2008). Language and independence in adolescents with and without a history of specific language impairment (SLI). *Journal of Speech, Language, and Hearing Research, 51*(1), 70–83.

Craig, H., Connor, C., & Washington, J. (2003). Early positive predictors of later reading comprehension for African-American students: A preliminary investigation. *Language, Speech, and Hearing Services in Schools, 34,* 31–43.

Creaghead, N. (1986). Comprehension of meaning in written language. *Topics in Language Disorders, 6*(4), 73–82.

DeJong, P. (2006). Understanding normal and impaired reading: A working memory perspective. In S. Pickering (Ed.), *Working memory and education* (pp. 33–60). Burlington, MA: Academic Press.

Denckla, M.B. (1996). A theory and model of executive function: A neuropsychological perspective. In G.R. Lyon & N.A. Krasnegor (Eds.), *Attention, memory and executive function* (pp. 263–278). Baltimore: Paul H. Brookes Publishing Co.

Denckla, M., & Rudel, R. (1976). Rapid "automatized" naming (RAN): Dyslexia differentiated from other learning disabilities. *Neuropsychologia, 14,* 471–479.

Dickinson, D., & McCabe, A. (1991). The acquisition and development of language: A social interactionist account of language and literacy development. In J. Kavanagh (Ed.), *The language continuum: From infancy to literacy* (pp. 1–40). Timonium, MD: York Press.

Dore, J. (1978). Requestive systems in nursery school conversations: Analysis of talk in its social context. In R. Campbell & P. Smith (Eds.), *Recent advances in the psychology of language: Language development and mother–child interaction* (pp. 271–292). New York: Plenum.

Ehri, L. (1989). Movement into word reading and spelling: How spelling contributes to reading. In J. Mason (Ed.), *Reading and writing connections* (pp. 65–81). Boston: Allyn & Bacon.

Eimas, P., Siqueland, E., Jusczyk, P., & Vigorito, J. (1971). Speech perception in infants. *Science, 171,* 303–306.

Eisenberg, S. (2006). Grammar: How can I say that better? In T. Ukrainetz (Ed.), *Contextualized language intervention* (pp.145–194). Eau Claire, WI: Thinking Publications.

Elbro, C., & Arnbak, A. (1996). The role of morpheme recognition and morphological awareness in dyslexia. *Annals of Dyslexia, 46,* 209–240.

Ellis Weismer, S. (1996). Capacity limitations in working memory: The impact on lexical and morphological learning by children with language impairment. *Topics in Language Disorders, 17,* 33–44.

Engel, P., Santos, F., & Gathercole, S. (2008). Are working memory measures free of socioeconomic influence? *Journal of Speech, Language, and Hearing Research, 51,* 1580–1587.

Fey, M.E., Catts, H.W., & Larrivee, L.S. (1995). Preparing preschoolers for the academic and social challenges of school. In S.F. Warren & J. Reichle (Series Eds.) & M.E. Fey, J. Windsor, & S.F. Warren (Vol. Eds.), *Communication and language intervention series: Vol. 5. Language intervention: Preschool through elementary years* (pp. 3–37). Baltimore: Paul H. Brookes Publishing Co.

Fowler, A. (1991). How early phonological development might set the stage for phoneme awareness. In S. Brady & D. Shankweiler (Eds.), *Phonological processes in literacy: A tribute to Isabelle Y. Liberman* (pp. 97–117). Mahwah, NJ: Lawrence Erlbaum Associates.

Fowler, A., & Liberman, I. (1995). Morphological awareness as related to early reading and spelling ability. In L. Feldman (Ed.), *Morphological aspects of language processing* (pp. 157–188). Mahwah, NJ: Lawrence Erlbaum Associates.

Gaskins, I., Satlow, E., & Pressley, M. (2007). Executive control of reading comprehension in the elementary school. In L. Meltzer (Ed.), *Executive function in education: From theory to practice* (pp. 194–215). New York: The Guilford Press.

Gathercole, S., & Alloway, T. (2008). *Working memory and learning: A practical guide for teachers.* Los Angeles: SAGE.

Gathercole, S., Service, E., Hitch, G., Adams, A., & Martin, A. (1999). Phonological short term memory and vocabulary development: Further evidence on the nature of the relationship. *Applied Cognitive Psychology, 13,* 65–77.

Gerber, A. (1993). *Language-related learning disabilities: Their nature and treatment.* Baltimore: Paul H. Brookes Publishing Co.

German, D. (1982). Word-finding substitution in children with learning disabilities. *Language, Speech, and Hearing Services in Schools, 13,* 223–230.

Gottardo, A. (2002). The relationship between language and reading skills in bilingual Spanish–English speakers. *Topics in Language Disorders, 22*(5), 46–70.

Gough, P., & Tunmer, W. (1986). Decoding reading and reading disability. *Remedial and Special Education, 7,* 6–10.

Green, L. (2009). Morphology and literacy: Getting our heads in the game. *Language, Speech, and Hearing Services in Schools, 40*(3), 283–285.

Green, L., McCutchen, D., Schwiebert, C., Quinlan, T., Eva-Wood, A., & Juelis, J. (2003). Morphological development in children's writing. *Journal of Educational Psychology, 95*(4), 752–761.

Greene, J. (1996). Psycholinguistic assessment: The clinical base for identification of dyslexia. *Topics in Language Disorders, 16*(2), 45–2.

Halliday, M.A.K. (1975). *Learning how to mean: Explorations in the development of language.* London: Edward Arnold.

Halliday, M.A.K., & Hasan, R. (1976). *Cohesion in English.* London: Longman Group.

Hammer, C., & Miccio, A. (2006). Early language and reading development of bilingual preschoolers from low-income families. *Topics in Language Disorders, 26*(4), 322–337.

Hammer, C., Miccio, A., & Wagstaff, D. (2003). Home literacy experiences and their relationship to bilingual preschoolers' developing English literacy abilities: An initial investigation. *Language, Speech, and Hearing Services in Schools, 34,* 20–30.

Hart, B., & Risley, T.R. (1999). *The social world of children learning to talk.* Baltimore: Paul H. Brookes Publishing Co.

Hochman, J. (2009). *Teaching basic writing skills: Strategies for effective expository writing instruction.* Longmont, CO: Sopris West Educational Services.

Hodson, B. (1994). Helping individuals become intelligible, literate and articulate: The role of phonology. *Topics in Language Disorders, 14*(2), 1–16.

Horowitz, R., & Samuels, J. (1987). Comprehending oral and written language: Critical contrasts for literacy and schooling. In R. Horowitz & J. Samuels (Eds.), *Comprehending oral and written language* (pp. 1–52). San Diego: Academic Press.

Hoskins, B. (1983). Semantics. In C. Wren (Ed.), *Language learning disabilities* (pp. 85–111). New York: Aspen Publishers.

Hymes, D. (1972). On communicative competence. In J.B. Pride & J. Holmes (Eds.), *Sociolinguistics* (pp. 269–293). London: Penguin Books.

Johnson, C., Beitchman, J., Young, A., Escobar, M., Atkinson, L., Wilson, B., et al. (1999). Fourteen-year follow-up study of children with and without speech-language impairments: Speech/language stability and outcomes. *Journal of Speech, Language, and Hearing Research, 42*(3), 74–76.

Just, M., & Carpenter, A. (1992). A capacity theory of comprehension: Individual differences in working memory. *Psychological Review, 99,* 122–149.

Kamhi, A.G., & Catts, H.W. (1989). Language and reading: Convergences, divergences and development. In A.G. Kamhi & H.W. Catts (Eds.), *Reading disabilities: A developmental language perspective* (pp. 1–34). New York: Little, Brown.

Kamhi, A.G., & Pollack, K.E. (2005). *Phonological disorders in children: Clinical decision making in assessment and intervention.* Baltimore: Paul H. Brookes Publishing Co.

Katz, L. (2004). An investigation of the relationship of morphological awareness to reading comprehension in fourth and sixth graders. (Doctoral dissertation, University of Michigan, 2004). *Dissertation Abstracts International, 65,* 2138.

Katz, L., & Carlisle, J. (2009). Teaching students with reading difficulties to be close readers: A feasibility study. *Language, Speech, and Hearing Services in Schools, 40*(3), 325–340.

Katz, R. (1986). Phonological deficiencies in children with reading disability: Evidence from an object-naming task. *Cognition, 22,* 225–257.

Kellogg, R. (1996). A model of working memory in writing. In C. Levy & S. Randell (Eds.), *The science of writing* (pp. 57–71). Mahwah, NJ: Lawrence Erlbaum Associates.

Kirk, C., & Gillon, G. (2009). Integrated morphological awareness intervention as a tool for improving literacy. *Language, Speech, and Hearing Services in Schools, 40*(3), 341–351.

Labov, W. (2003). When ordinary children fail to read. *Reading Research Quarterly, 38,* 128–131.

Lahey, M. (1988). *Language disorders and language development.* New York: Wiley.

Lahey, M., & Bloom, L. (1994). Variability and language learning disabilities. In G. Wallach & K. Butler (Eds.), *Language learning disabilities in school-age children and adolescents: Some principles and applications* (pp. 354–372). Boston: Allyn & Bacon.

Laing, S., & Kamhi, A. (2003). Alternative assessment of language and literacy in culturally and linguistically diverse populations. *Language, Speech, and Hearing Services in Schools, 34,* 44–55.

Larson, V., & McKinley, N. (1995). *Language disorders in older students, preadolescents and adolescents.* Eau Claire, WI: Thinking Publications.

Layzer, J., & Goodson, B. (2006). *Care in the home: A description of family child care and the experiences of the families and children who use it. National Study of Child Care for Low Income Families.* Washington, DC: U.S. Department of Health and Human Services Administration for Children and Families.

Liberman, I. (1983). A language-oriented view of reading and its disabilities. In H. Myklebust (Ed.), *Progress in learning disabilities* (Vol. 5, pp. 81–102). New York: Grune & Stratton.

Liberman, I., & Liberman, A. (1990). Whole language vs. code emphasis: Underlying assumptions and their implications for reading instruction. *Annals of Dyslexia, 40,* 51–76.

Liberman, I., Shankweiler, D., Camp, L., Blachman, G., & Werfelman, M. (1990). Steps toward literacy. In P. Levinson & C. Sloan (Eds.), *Auditory processing and language: Clinical and research perspectives* (pp. 189–215). New York: Grune & Stratton.

Linder, T.W. (1999). *Read, play, and learn!: Storybook activities for young children. Teacher's guide.* Baltimore: Paul H. Brookes Publishing Co.

Lopez, L., & Greenfield, D. (2004). The cross-language transfer of phonological skills of Hispanic Head Start children. *Bilingual Research Journal, 28,* 1–18.

Mahoney, D., & Mann, V. (1992). Using children's humor to clarify the relationship between linguistic awareness and early reading ability. *Cognition, 45,* 163–186.

Mandler, J., & Johnson, N. (1977). Remembrance of things parsed: Story structure and recall. *Cognitive Psychology, 9,* 111–151.

Mattingly, I. (1972). Reading, the linguistic process and linguistic awareness. In J. Kavanagh & I. Mattingly (Eds.), *Language by ear and by eye: The rela-*

tionship between speech and reading (pp. 133–144). Cambridge, MA: The MIT Press.

McCutchen, D., Logan, B., & Biangardi-Orpe, U. (2009). Making meaning: Children's sensitivity to morphological information during word reading. *Reading Research Quarterly, 44*(4), 360–376.

McGregor, K. (1994). Use of phonological information in word finding treatment of children. *Journal of Speech and Hearing Research, 37,* 1381–1393.

Meltzer, L. (2007). *Executive function in education: From theory to practice.* New York: Guilford Press.

Menyuk, P., & Chesnick, M. (1997). Metalinguistic skills, oral language knowledge and reading. *Topics in Language Disorders, 17*(3), 75–87.

Miller, L. (1990). The roles of language and learning in the development of literacy. *Topics in Language Disorders, 10,* 1–24.

Milosky, L. (1994). Nonliteral language abilities: Seeing the forest for the trees. In G. Wallach & K. Butler (Eds.), *Language learning disabilities in school-aged children and adolescents: Some principles and applications* (pp. 275–303). Boston: Allyn & Bacon.

Moats, L.C. (1994). Honing the concepts of listening and speaking: A prerequisite to the valid measurement of language behavior in children. In G.R. Lyon (Ed.), *Frames of reference for the assessment of learning disabilities: New views on measurement issues* (pp. 229–241). Baltimore: Paul H. Brookes Publishing Co.

Moats, L.C. (1995). *Spelling: Development, disability, and instruction.* Timonium, MD: York Press.

Moats, L.C. (2010). *Speech to print: Language essentials for teachers* (2nd ed.). Baltimore: Paul H. Brookes Publishing Co.

Moats, L.C., & Lyon, G.R. (1996). Wanted: Teachers with a knowledge of language. *Topics in Language Disorders, 16*(2), 73–86.

Montgomery, J. (1996). Sentence comprehension and working memory in children with specific language impairment. *Topics in Language Disorders, 17*(1), 19–32.

Montgomery, J. (2002). Examining the nature of lexical processing in children with specific language impairment: Temporal processing or processing capacity deficit? *Applied Psycholinguistics, 23,* 447–470.

Montgomery, J., & Evans, J. (2009). Complex sentence comprehension and working memory in children with specific language impairment. *Journal of Speech, Language, and Hearing Research, 52*(2), 269–288.

Morice, R., & Slaghuis, W. (1985). Language performance and reading ability at 8 years of age. *Applied Psycholinguistics, 6,* 141–160.

Myers, M., & Paris, S. (1978). Children's metacognitive knowledge about reading. *Journal of Educational Psychology, 70,* 680–690.

Nagy, W., & Anderson, R. (1984). How many words are there in printed school English? *Reading Research Quarterly, 19,* 304–329.

Nagy, W., Berninger, V., & Abbott, R. (2006). Contributions of morphology beyond phonology to literacy outcomes of upper elementary and middle-school students. *Journal of Educational Psychology, 98*(1), 134–147.

Nagy, W., & Scott, C. (2000). Vocabulary processes. In M. Kamil, P. Mosenthal, P. Pearson, & R. Barr (Eds.), *Handbook of reading research* (Vol. 3, pp. 269–284). Mahwah, NJ: Lawrence Erlbaum Associates.

Nelson, N.W. (1985). Teacher talk and child listening: Fostering a better match. In C. Simon (Ed.), *Communication skills and classroom success: Assessment of language-learning disabled students* (pp. 65–102). San Diego: College-Hill Press.

Nelson, N.W. (1986). Individualized processing in classroom settings. *Topics in Language Disorders, 6*(2), 13–27.

Nippold, M. (1988). The literate lexicon. In M. Nippold (Ed.), *Later language development: Ages nine through nineteen* (pp. 29–47). San Diego: College-Hill Press.

Nippold, M., Mansfield, T., Billow, J., & Tomblin, J. (2008). Expository discourse in adolescents with language impairment: Examining syntactic development. *American Journal of Speech-Language Pathology, 17*(4), 356–366.

Nippold, M., Mansfield, T., Billow, J., & Tomblin, J. (2009). Syntactic development in adolescents with a history of language impairments: A follow-up study. *American Journal of Speech-Language Pathology, 18*(3), 241–251.

No Child Left Behind Act of 2001, PL 107-110, 115 Stat. 1425, 20 U.S.C. §§ 6301 *et seq.*

Owens, R. (1996). *Language development: An introduction* (3rd ed.). New York: Merrill/Macmillan.

Owings, R., Peterson, G., Bransford, J., Morris, C., & Stein, B. (1980). Spontaneous monitoring and regulation of learning: A comparison of successful and less successful fifth graders. *Journal of Educational Psychology, 72,* 250–256.

Paul, R., & Jennings, P. (1992). Phonological behavior in toddlers with slow expressive language development. *Journal of Speech and Hearing Research, 35,* 99–107.

Perfetti, C., & Lesgold, A. (1977). Discourse comprehension and sources of individual differences. In M. Just & P. Carpenter (Eds.), *Cognitive processes in comprehension* (pp. 141–184). Mahwah, NJ: Lawrence Erlbaum Associates.

Prather, E., Hedrick, D., & Kern, C. (1975). Articulation development in children aged two to four years. *Journal of Speech and Hearing Disorders, 40,* 179–191.

Prutting, C., & Kirschner, D. (1987). A clinical appraisal of the pragmatic aspects of language. *Journal of Speech and Hearing Disorders, 52,* 105–119.

Rees, N. (1978). Pragmatics of language: Applications to normal and disordered language development. In R. Schiefelbusch (Ed.), *Bases of language intervention* (pp. 191–268). Baltimore: University Park Press.

Richards, G. (2003). *The source for learning and memory strategies*. East Moline, IL: LinguiSystems.

Robertson, C., & Salter, W. (1997). *The phonological awareness test*. East Moline, IL: LinguiSystems.

Roth, F. (1986). Oral narratives of learning disabled students. *Topics in Language Disorders, 7*(1), 21–30.

Roth, F., & Spekman, N. (1984). Assessing the pragmatic abilities of children: Part I. Organizational framework and assessment parameters. *Journal of Speech and Hearing Disorders, 49*, 2–11.

Roth, F., & Spekman, N. (1989). Higher order language processes and reading disabilities. In A.G. Kamhi & H.W. Catts (Eds.), *Reading disabilities: A developmental language perspective* (pp. 159–98). New York: Little, Brown.

Ruben, H., Patterson, P., & Kantor, M. (1991). Morphological development and writing ability in children and adults. *Language, Speech, and Hearing Services in Schools, 22*, 228–235.

Rubin, D. (1987). Divergence and convergence between oral and written communication. *Topics in Language Disorders, 7*(4), 1–18.

Sawyer, D. (1991). Whole language in context: Insights into the great debate. *Topics in Language Disorders, 11*(3), 1–13.

Scarborough, H. (1990). Very early language deficits in dyslexic children. *Child Development, 61*, 1728–743.

Scarborough, H. (2001). Connecting early language and literacy to later reading (dis)abilities: Evidence, theory and practice. In S. Neuman & D. Dickinson (Eds.), *Handbook of early literacy research* (pp. 97–110). New York: Guilford Press.

Scott, C. (1994). A discourse continuum for school-aged students: Impact of modality and genre. In G. Wallach & K. Butler (Eds.), *Language learning disabilities in school aged children and adolescents: Some principles and applications* (pp. 219–-52). Boston: Allyn & Bacon.

Scott, C. (2004). Syntactic contributions to literacy learning. In A. Stone, E. Silliman, B. Ehren, & K. Apel (Eds.), *Handbook of language and literacy: Development and disorder* (pp. 340–362). New York: Guilford Press.

Scott, C. (2005). Learning to write. In H. Catts & A. Kamhi (Eds.), *Language and reading disabilities* (2nd ed., pp. 233–273). Boston: Pearson.

Scott, C. (2009). A case for the sentence in reading comprehension. *Language, Speech, and Hearing Services in Schools, 40*(2), 185–191.

Scott, C., & Windsor, J. (2000). General language performance measures in spoken and written narrative and expository discourse of school age children with language learning disabilities. *Journal of Speech, Language, and Hearing Research, 43*(2), 329–339.

Seigneuric, A., & Ehrlich, M. (2005). Contributions of working memory capacity to children's reading comprehension: A longitudinal investigation. *Reading and Writing, 18*, 617–656.

Seigneuric, A., Ehrlich, M., Oakhill, J., & Yuill, N. (2000). Working memory resources and children's reading comprehension. *Reading and Writing: An Interdisciplinary Journal, 13*, 81–103.

Siegel, L. (2008). Morphological awareness skills of English language learners and children with dyslexia. *Topics in Language Disorders, 28*(1), 15–27.

Snow, C., & Dickinson, D. (1991). Skills that aren't basic in a new conception of literacy. In A. Purves & E. Jennings (Eds.), *Literate systems and individual lives: Perspectives on literacy and schooling* (pp. 179–192). Albany: SUNY Press.

Snow, C., Griffin, P., & Burns, S. (Eds.). (2005). *Knowledge to support the teaching of reading: Preparing teachers for a changing world*. San Francisco: Jossey-Bass.

Snowling, M. (1981). Phonemic deficits in developmental dyslexia. *Psychological Research, 43*, 219–234.

Snowling, M., & Nation, K. (1997). Language phonology and learning to read. In M. Snowling & C. Hulme (Eds.), *Dyslexia: Biology, cognition and remediation* (pp. 153–166). San Diego: Singular Publishing Group.

Snyder, L. (1980). Have we prepared the language disordered child for school? *Topics in Language Disorders, 1*(1), 29–45.

Snyder, L., & Downey, D. (1991). The language of reading relationship in normal and reading disabled children. *Journal of Speech and Hearing Research, 34*, 129–140.

Snyder, L., & Downey, D. (1997). Developmental differences in the relationship between oral language deficits and reading. *Topics in Language Disorders, 17*(3), 27–40.

Snyder L., & Godley, D. (1992). Assessment of word finding in children and adolescents. *Topics in Language Disorders, 12*(1), 15–32.

Spear-Swerling, L., & Sternberg, R. (1994). The road not taken: An integrative theoretical model of reading disability. *Journal of Learning Disabilities, 27*, 91–103.

Stackhouse, J., & Wells, B. (1997). How do speech and language problems affect literacy development? In M. Snowling & C. Hulme (Eds.), *Dyslexia: Biology, cognition and intervention* (pp. 182–211). San Diego: Singular Publishing Group.

Stanovich, K. (1986). Matthew effects in reading: Some consequences of individual differences in the acquisition of literacy. *Reading Research Quarterly, 21*, 360–407.

Stanovich, K. (Ed.). (1987). Introduction: Children's reading and the development of phonological awareness [Special issue]. *Merrill-Palmer Quarterly, 33*(3).

Stein, C., Cairns, H., & Zurif, E. (1984). Sentence comprehension limitation related to syntactic deficits in reading disabled children. *Applied Psychology, 5,* 305–322.

Stein, N., & Glenn, C. (1979). An analysis of story comprehension in elementary school children. In R. Freedle (Ed.), *New directions in discourse processing* (pp. 53–120). Greenwich, CT: Ablex.

Stoel-Gammon, C. (1991). Normal and disordered phonology in two year olds. *Topics in Language Disorders, 11*(4), 21–32.

Sulzby, E., & Teale, W. (1991). Emergent literacy. In R. Barr, M. Kamil, P. Mosenthal, & P.D. Pearson (Eds.), *Handbook of reading research* (Vol. 2, pp. 727–757). New York: Longman.

Swank, L. (1997). Linguistic influences in the emergence of written word decoding in first grade. *American Journal of Speech-Language Pathology, 6*(4), 62–66.

Swanson, H., & Berninger, V. (1996). Individual differences in children's working memory and writing skill. *Journal of Educational Psychology, 63,* 358–385.

Swanson, H., Howard, C., & Saez, L. (2006). Do different components of working memory underlie different subgroups of reading disabilities? *Journal of Learning Disabilities, 39,* 252–269.

Swanson, H., & O'Connor, R. (2009). The role of working memory and fluency practice on the reading comprehension of students who are dysfluent readers. *Journal of Learning Disabilities, 47*(6), 548–575.

Swanson, H., & Siegel, L. (2001). Learning disabilities as a working memory deficit. *Issues in Education: Contributions from Educational Psychology, 7,* 1–48.

Troia, G. (2004). Building word recognition skills through empirically validated instructional practices: Collaborative efforts of speech-language pathologists and teachers. In E. Silliman & L. Wilkinson (Eds.), *Language and literacy learning in schools* (pp. 98–129). New York: Guilford Press.

Van Kleeck, A. (1990). Emergent literacy: Learning about print before learning to read. *Topics in Language Disorders, 10*(2), 25–45.

Vaughn, S., Mathes, P., Linan-Thompson, S., & Francis, D. (2005). Teaching English language learners at risk for reading disabilities to read: Putting research into practice. *Learning Disabilities Research and Practice, 20,* 58–67.

Vellutino, F. (1979). *Dyslexia: Theory and research.* Cambridge, MA: The MIT Press.

Vellutino, F., Scanlon, D., & Spearing, D. (1995). Semantic and phonological coding in poor and normal readers. *Journal of Experimental Child Psychology, 59,* 76–123.

Vygotsky, L. (1962). *Thought and language.* Cambridge, MA: The MIT Press.

Wagner, R., & Torgesen, J. (1987). The nature of phonological processing and its causal roles in the equation of reading skills. *Psychological Bulletin, 101,* 192–212.

Wallach, G. (1990). Magic buries Celtics: Looking for broader interpretations of language learning in literacy. *Topics in Language Disorders, 10*(2), 63–80.

Wallach, G., & Butler, K. (1994). Creating communication, literacy and academic success. In G. Wallach & K. Butler (Eds.), *Language learning disabilities in school-age children and adolescents: Some principals and applications* (pp. 2–26). Boston: Allyn & Bacon.

Wallach, G., & Miller, L. (1988). *Language intervention and academic success.* New York: Little, Brown.

Webster, P., & Plante, A. (1992). Effects of phonological impairment on word, syllable and phoneme segmentation and reading. *Language, Speech, and Hearing Services in Schools, 23,* 176–182.

Westby, C. (1985). Learning to talk—talking to learn: Oral literate language differences. In C. Simon (Ed.), *Communication skills and classroom success: Therapy methodologies for language learning disabled students* (pp. 181–213). San Diego: College-Hill Press.

Westby, C. (1989). Assessing and remediating text comprehension problems. In A.G. Kamhi & H.W. Catts (Eds.), *Reading disabilities: A developmental language perspective* (pp. 199–260). New York: Little, Brown.

Westby, C. (1995). Culture and literacy: Frameworks for understanding. *Topics in Language Disorders, 16*(1), 50–66.

White, T., Power, M., & White, S. (1989). Morphological analysis: Implications for teaching and understanding of vocabulary growth. *Reading Research Quarterly, 24,* 283–304.

Wiig, E., & Semel, E. (1980). *Language assessment and intervention for the learning disabled.* Columbus, OH: Charles E. Merrill.

Wiig, E., Semel, E., & Nystrom, L. (1982). Comparison of rapid naming abilities in language learning disabled and academically achieving eight year olds. *Language, Speech, and Hearing Services in Schools, 12,* 11–23.

Wolf, M., & Dickinson, D. (1993). From oral to written language: Transitions in the school years. In J. Gleason (Ed.), *The development of language.* Columbus, OH: Charles E. Merrill.

Wolter, J., Wood, A., & D'zatko, K. (2009). The influence of morphological awareness on the literacy development of first-grade children. *Language, Speech, and Hearing Services in Schools, 40*(3), 286–298.

4

The History and Structure of Written English

MARCIA K. HENRY

T his chapter presents a short history of written English and introduces the structure of English orthography—the English spelling system. English is a dynamic
language, and numerous historical forces shaped the development of written English. The historical perspective is of primary importance to studying word formation
in English. As Nist (1966) and Venezky (1970) asserted, English orthography begins to
make sense when understood from an historical perspective.

An understanding of the historical forces that influenced written English, along
with a grasp of the structure of the English spelling system, provides teachers and their
students with a logical basis for the study of English. Students who recognize letter–
sound correspondences, syllable patterns, and morpheme patterns in words of **Anglo-
Saxon,** Latin, and Greek origin have the strategies necessary to read and spell unfamiliar words. Students begin by learning phonics, basic orthographic (spelling) patterns
and their related sounds, and **syllable types** and **syllable division patterns**.

The English spelling system is said to be opaque (or deep or nontransparent) in
contrast to transparent orthography (or shallow), such as Finnish and Italian. In transparent orthographies, letters and their pronunciations have almost one-to-one correspondence. In English, however, many words do not carry this relationship. Yet, many
psycholinguists believe that English is more transparent than traditionally thought.
Hanna, Hodges, and Hanna concluded that the results of their studies of the consistency in English graphemic representation of speech sounds "indicated that our written code is not so inconsistent that analysis of phoneme–grapheme correspondences
cannot provide the basis for teaching spelling" (1971, p. 76). They found that roughly
80% of the phonemes contained in the traditional spelling vocabulary of elementary
school children used the alphabetic principle in their letter representations. Pinker

noted, "Indeed, for about eighty-four percent of English words, spelling is completely predictable from regular rules" (1994, p. 190).

Students move on from phonics to learn the morphemes, or meaning units, in English. These include Anglo-Saxon **compound words** and affixes (the prefixes and suffixes added to **base words**); Latin roots, prefixes, and suffixes; and Greek **combining forms**. The importance of teaching more than basic phonics cannot be stressed enough. Brown (1947) found that 80% of English words borrowed from other languages came from Latin and Greek. Therefore, teaching relatively few Latin and Greek roots provides students with the key to unlocking hundreds of thousands of words.

HISTORY AND ENGLISH ORTHOGRAPHY

Among the important languages of the world, English is one of the youngest. The original inhabitants of the British Isles, the Celts, spoke a different language in the **Indo-European** family. They were conquered by Julius Caesar in 54 C.E. (Common Era).

The Britons continued to speak Celtic, whereas the Romans spoke Latin. The Romans departed and returned almost a century later and stayed for nearly 400 years. Table 4.1 highlights important events contributing to the changes in written English over the centuries.

During the 5th century C.E., Germanic groups—the Jutes, Saxons, and Angles—began to settle in different parts of England. They did not speak the Celtic language and did not practice the Celtic religion (Balmuth, 2009). Rather, Anglo-Saxon became the dominant language and the vocabulary revolved around the people, objects, and events of daily life. The Roman alphabet, which the Romans had adapted from Greek via Etruscan, was reintroduced to the British Island by Christian missionaries at this time.

Five major factors shaped the English language during the period of Old English between 450 and 1150 C.E.: Teutonic invasion and settlement; the Christianizing of Britain; the creation of a national English culture; Danish–English warfare, political adjustment, and cultural assimilation; and the decline of Old English as a result of the Norman Conquest (Nist, 1966). During this time, Germanic, Celtic, Latin, Greek, Anglo-Saxon, Scandinavian, and French words entered Old English. At the end of the period, "that language was no longer the basically Teutonic and highly inflected Old English but the hybrid-becoming, Romance-importing, and inflection-dropping Middle English" (Nist, 1966, p. 107).

The period of Middle English (1150–1500) heralded great changes in the native tongue of Britain. Early Middle English (1150–1307) sounded much like present-day German. Claiborne estimated that after the Norman Conquest "more than ten thousand French words passed into the English vocabulary, of which 75 percent are still in use" (1983, p. 112). Anglo-French compounds (e.g., *gentlewomen, gentlemen; faithful, faithfulness*) appeared during this period.

A renewed Latin influence penetrated the language during the period of Mature Middle English (1307–1422) in the 14th and 15th centuries. Chaucer wrote *The Canterbury Tales* in the late 1300s. This was the time of the Renaissance, which brought a wave of cultural advancement. Hanna et al. observed,

> The Latin vocabulary was felt to be more stable and polished and more capable of conveying both abstract and humanistic ideas than was a fledgling language such as English. Further, Latin was something of a lingua franca that leaped across geographical and political boundaries. (1971, p. 47)

Table 4.1. Events related to periods in the development of the English language

Period	Year(s)	Event
Pre-English	54 B.C.E.	The ancient Britons (or Celts) defend their land from Julius Caesar and are defeated.
	50 C.E.	Roman Emperor Claudius I colonizes Britain; Celtic and Latin languages co-exist.
	450 C.E.	Romans leave Britain; the Teutonic tribes (the Jutes, Angles, and Saxons) invade.
	600	England divides into seven kingdoms; Northumbria emerges as the dominant Christian kingdom affiliated with the Roman Catholic Church.
Old English	800	The Danes (or Norsemen or Vikings) invade England and are defeated by King Alfred in 878.
	900	Old English reaches its literary peak under the West Saxon kings.
	1000	The Danes successfully invade Britain, yet the Anglo-Saxon language continues its dominant role.
	1066	William the Conqueror, Duke of Normandy, invades Britain; Norman French becomes the official language of state while English remains the language of the people.
Middle English	1350	Edward III takes control; English again becomes the official language of state.
	1400	Geoffrey Chaucer dies, leaving his classic *Canterbury Tales.*
	1420	Henry V becomes the first English king to write in Middle English.
	1475	The Renaissance reaches England. English borrows from Latin and Greek languages. William Caxton begins printing in English.
Modern English	1600	Queen Elizabeth I and William Shakespeare write in Modern English.
	1755	Samuel Johnson compiles the first comprehensive dictionary of English.
	1828	Noah Webster compiles a dictionary of American English.
	1857–1928	The Oxford English Dictionary is developed and published in parts; it is published in full in 1928.

From HENDERSON. *HENDERSON TEACHING SPELLING 2E.* © 1990 Wadsworth, a part of Cengage Learning, Inc. Reproduced by permission. www.cengage.com/permissions

Many of the words used in English today are borrowed from the Latin of this period, including *index, library, medicine,* and *instant.* During the time of Mature Middle English, Latin affixes entered the language in great numbers. Prefixes (e.g., *ad-, pro-*) and suffixes (e.g., *-ent, -ion, -al*) were added to word roots to form words such as *adjacent, prosecution,* and *rational* (Claiborne, 1983).

The written word grew in importance during the period of Late Middle English (1422–1489). English pressman William Caxton introduced the printing press to England and printed books using the English spoken in London by the well-to-do. Many spelling conventions were set into place at this time. Also, words from Greek and Romance languages enriched English enormously during the English Renaissance. The Romance languages include Latin-based languages (e.g., Portuguese, Spanish, French, Italian, Romanian).

During the periods of Late Middle English and Early Modern English, the sound patterns, especially the vowel sounds, of the language underwent changes. Nist commented that

> The changes in the pronunciation from the Mature Middle English of Chaucer to the Early Modern English of Shakespeare, insofar as these tense vowels were concerned, were so

dramatic that Jespersen [1971] has named their phonemic displacement the Great Vowel Shift. (1966, p. 221)

The vowel shift resulted in certain vowel sounds being articulated in new positions and ensured a sharp separation between phonology and spelling. For example, in Chaucer's time, the vowel sound in *bide* was pronounced like /ē/ in *bee,* but in Shakespeare's time, it shifted to /ā/ as in *bay.* This shift caused problems for spellers "because stabilized spellings now came to represent different sounds" (Hanna et al., 1971, p. 49).

Changes continued through the periods of Authoritarian English (1650–1800) and Mature Modern English (1800–1920) to reach the pronunciation of today. The period from 1920 to the present has been called World Power American English as English becomes the global language for much of the Internet and international trade. New words continue to form. In the mid- to late 2000s, words related to the real estate and financial crises brought us the new words *subprime* and *bailout.* In addition, new immigrants to the United States bring greater linguistic diversity.

English, then, is a **polyglot,** and the Anglo-Saxon, Latin (Romance), and Greek languages all played a role in establishing the words as they are spoken and written today (Balmuth, 2009; Hanna et al., 1971; Nist, 1966). Claiborne noted,

> The truth is that if borrowing foreign words could destroy a language, English would be dead (borrowed from Old Norse), deceased (from French), defunct (from Latin) and kaput (from German). When it comes to borrowing, English excels (from Latin), surpasses (from French) and eclipses (from Greek) any other tongue, past or present. (1983, p. 4)

FRAMEWORK FOR CURRICULUM AND INSTRUCTION

One framework for teaching a decoding and spelling curriculum is based on word origin and word structure (Henry, 1988a, 1988b, 2010b). The three origin languages most influential to English are Anglo-Saxon, Latin, and Greek. Teachers who understand the historical origins of words enhance their presentation of reading instruction. The major structural categories are letter–sound correspondences, syllables, and morphemes. By teaching all of the components of this framework, teachers can ensure that their students will learn the primary patterns found in English words. Teachers are encouraged to use a multisensory approach for teaching each component so that students will simultaneously link the visual symbol with its corresponding sound and form the pattern accurately (see Chapter 2).

Teaching phonics offers a strategy for decoding and spelling that works when the letter–sound correspondence system carries all of the demands of word analysis. When students do not recognize syllabic and morphological patterns, however, they are constrained from using **clues** to identify long, unfamiliar words. Unfortunately, most decoding instruction largely neglects the instruction of syllable and morpheme patterns, perhaps because these techniques are only useful for the longer words found in literature and subject-matter text beyond second or third grade, at which point decoding instruction becomes virtually nonexistent in most schools.

Students in fourth grade and beyond are expected to read numerous multisyllabic words. Those who know how to use rules for **syllable division** exhibit strategies for word analysis beyond the use of letter–sound correspondences. Students who recognize meaningful morpheme patterns incorporate still another word analysis strategy. Yet, many students in upper elementary school, secondary school, and adult literacy programs lack the strategies necessary to read and spell longer words. By learning basic syllable and morpheme patterns, these students will be able to analyze numerous multisyllabic words of Latin and Greek origin.

Figure 4.1 represents the categories in the word origin and word structure framework. Each entry in the matrix corresponds to words of Anglo-Saxon, Latin, or Greek origin that are related to letter–sound correspondences, syllables, or morphemes. In the following sections, the major components of the framework are discussed.

ANGLO-SAXON LAYER OF LANGUAGE

Words of Anglo-Saxon origin are characterized as the common, everyday, down-to-earth words that are used frequently in ordinary situations. Nist provided a clever example of Anglo-Saxon words:

> English remains preeminently Anglo-Saxon at its core: in the suprasegmentals of its stress, pitch, and juncture patterns and in its vocabulary. No matter whether a man is American, British, Canadian, Australian, New Zealander, or South African, he still *loves his mother, father, brother, sister, wife, son and daughter; lifts his hand to his head, his cup to his mouth, his eye to heaven and his heart to God; hates his foes, likes his friends, kisses his kin and buries his dead; draws his breath, eats his bread, drinks his water, stands his watch, wipes his sweat, feels his sorrow, weeps his tears and sheds his blood; and all these things he thinks about and calls both good and bad.* (1966, p. 9)

As the Nist passage shows, most words of Anglo-Saxon origin consist of one syllable and represent everyday objects, activities, and events. Although consonant letters are fairly regular (i.e., each letter corresponds to one sound), vowels are more problematic.

	Letter–sound correspondences	Syllables	Morphemes
Anglo-Saxon	Consonants *bid, step, that* Vowels *mad/made, barn, boat*	Closed: *bat* Open: *baby* VCE: *made* Vowel digraph: *boat* Consonant-*le: tumble* *r*-controlled: *barn*	Compounds *hardware* *shipyard* Affixes *read, reread, rereading* *bid, forbid, forbidden*
Latin	Same as Anglo-Saxon but few vowel digraphs Use of schwa /ə/: *direction* *spatial* *excellent*	Closed: *spect* VCE: *scribe* *r*-controlled: *port, form*	Affixes *construction* *erupting* *conductor*
Greek	*ph* for /f/ *phonograph* *ch* for /k/ *chorus* *y* for /ĭ/ *sympathy*	Closed: *graph* Open: *photo* Unstable digraph: *create*	Compounds *microscope* *chloroplast* *physiology*

Figure 4.1. Word origin and word structure matrix. (*Source:* Henry, 1988b. Matrix from Henry, M.K. [2010]. *Unlocking literacy: Effective decoding and spelling instruction.* Baltimore: Paul H. Brookes Publishing Co; adapted by permission.)

Words that are learned early on in school are often irregular and may cause difficulty for students with specific reading disabilities. Students must memorize the spellings of these "weird" or "outlaw" words, such as *rough, does, only, eye, laugh, blood,* and *said,* because the vowels do not carry the normal short (lax) or long (tense) sound associated with these spellings.

Letter–Sound Correspondences

Letter–sound correspondences are the relationships between the consonant and vowel letters (graphemes) and their corresponding sounds (phonemes). Anglo-Saxon letter–sound correspondences are the first symbol–sound relationships taught to children learning to read and spell. Consonant letters (e.g., *b, c, d, f, m, p, t*) represent the speech sounds produced by a partial or complete obstruction of the air stream. The consonant pairs *gn-, kn-,* and *wr-* are Anglo-Saxon forms. Vowel letters (i.e., *a, e, i, o, u,* and sometimes *y* and *w*) represent the sounds that are created by the relatively free passage of breath through the larynx and oral cavity.

Liberman and her colleagues (Liberman, 1973; Liberman & Liberman, 1990; Liberman & Shankweiler, 1985, 1991; Liberman, Shankweiler, Fischer, & Carter, 1974) noted that children's phonological awareness, or understanding of the role that sounds play in the English language, is extremely important in learning to read. Before learning letter–sound correspondences, often called *phonics,* children benefit from training in phonological awareness. Phonological awareness is an awareness of all levels of the speech sound system, including rhymes, stress patterns, syllables, and phonemes. Students practice rhyming, segmentation, and blending (see Chapter 5) before learning letter names and letter formation (see Chapter 6). *Phonemic awareness,* which is only one component of phonological awareness, is the awareness that speech is made up of discrete sounds and the ability to manipulate sounds into words.

Balmuth (2009), as well as Adams (1990), Chall (1983), Chall and Popp (1996), Ehri (2005), and Richardson (1989), provided insights on the importance of phonics in education since the 19th century. When learning phonics, students must link the graphemes and phonemes of English. Tables 4.2 and 4.3 represent the primary graphemes that spell or correspond to each of the approximately 44 phonemes of English. Teachers generally use dictionary markings (phonic symbols) as guides to pronunciation. Linguists and specialists in speech-language disorders tend to use symbols from the International Phonetic Alphabet. Both ways of marking pronunciation are shown in Tables 4.2 and 4.3. (See Moats, 1995, 2010, as well as Chapter 3 in this book, for further information on **phonetics,** identifying and describing speech sounds, and articulating specific sounds.)

Graphemes are organized either in consonant or vowel patterns. Single-letter consonant spellings seldom vary; each letter stands for a specific sound. The letters *c* and *g,* however, have more than one possible pronunciation: a hard and soft sound. The letter *c* usually has the sound of /k/ as in *carrot* but becomes soft before *e, i,* and *y* as in *cell, city,* and *cypress.* Likewise, the *g* in *go* or *gas* is hard, whereas *g* before *e, i,* and *y* is soft as in *gem, ginger,* and *Gypsy.* The letter *s* is usually pronounced as /s/ as in *snake* but sometimes has the /z/ sound as in *dogs.* Note that *x* is omitted from Table 4.2; it represents two possible sounds. The letter *x* at the end of a word makes the sound of /ks/ as in *box* but makes the sound of /z/ at the beginning of some words. These words, such as *xylophone* and *xenophobe,* are usually of Greek origin.

Consonant blends (sometimes called *consonant clusters*), which are made up of two or three adjacent consonants that retain their individual sounds in a syllable, are

Table 4.2. English consonant spelling–sound correspondences with dictionary (phonic) and phonetic symbols

Consonant graphemes	Examples[a]	The American Heritage Dictionary, Fourth Edition (2000)[a]	International Phonetic Alphabet (IPA)
b	bib	b	b
d	deed	d	d
f, ph, gh	fife, phone, laugh	f	f
g	gag	g	g
h	hat	h	h
j, g, dge	jam, ginger, fudge	j	dʒ
k, -ck, c, ch, -que	kick, cat, chorus, unique	k	k
l, -le	lit, needle	l	l, ļ
m	mom	m	m
n	no, sudden	n	n, ņ
p	pop	p	p
r	roar	r	r
s, c, sc	sauce, science	s	s
t	tot	t	t
v	valve	v	v
w	with	w	w
y	yes	y	j
z, -s	zebra, dogs	z	z
-ng	thing	ng	ŋ
ch, -tch	church, pitch	ch	tʃ
sh	ship	sh	ʃ
th	thin	th	θ
th	that	*th*	ð
wh	when	hw	ʍ
si, su, -ge	vision, treasure, garage	zh	ʒ

[a]Copyright © 2010 by Houghton Mifflin Harcourt Publishing Company. Adapted and reproduced by permission from *The American Heritage Dictionary of the English Language, Fourth Edition.*

common (e.g., *bl* and *mp* in *blimp*; *spl* and *nt* in *splint*). In contrast to blends, **consonant digraphs,** which evolved in Middle English times, are two or more adjacent letters that form only one speech sound. Often, one of the letters of a consonant digraph is *h* (e.g., *sh* in *ship*, *ch* in *chump*, *th* in *this*, *wh* in *when*).

Vowel graphemes tend to be more difficult to learn than consonant graphemes because they can represent more than one sound and are often difficult to discriminate. Single vowels are generally either short or long. Words often contain clues, referred to as markers, that indicate whether the **short** or **long** sound should be used. A vowel with a consonant after it in the same syllable carries the short sound (e.g., *cat, let, fit, fox, fun*). In contrast, a vowel at the end of a syllable becomes long or "says its own name" (e.g., *go, baby, pilot*). A silent *e* at the end of a word, as in *shape* and *vote,* also signals that the word has a long vowel sound. A doubled consonant, as in *pinning* and *cutter,* marks that the preceding vowel has a short sound. The doubled consonant cancels the long-vowel signal that would otherwise be given by the *i* in *ing* and the *e* in *er*.

Students will also read words with a vowel plus *r* or *l.* The vowel sounds are often neither short nor long. These patterns are best taught as combinations, such as *ar* in *star, or* in *corn, er* in *fern, ir* in *bird, ur* in *church,* and *al* in *falter.* (See Appendix 4.1 at the end of this chapter for an example of a lesson contrasting *ar* and *or* patterns.)

Table 4.3.   English vowel spelling–sound correspondences with dictionary (phonic) and phonetic symbols

Vowel graphemes	Examples*	*The American Heritage Dictionary, Fourth Edition* (2000)*	International Phonetic Alphabet (IPA)
a	pat	ă	æ
a, a-consonant-e, ai, ay, ei, eigh, ey	baby, made, pail, pay, veil, eight, they	ā	e
e	pet	ĕ	ε
e, e-consonant-e, ee, ea, ie, y, ey, ei	me, scheme, greet, seat, thief, lady, alley, ceiling	ē	i
i	bit	ĭ	ɪ
i, i-consonant-e, igh, ie, y	hi, kite, fight, pie, sky	ī	aj
o	hot	ŏ	ɑ
o, o-consonant-e, oa, ow, oe	go, vote, boat, grow, toe	ō	o
u	cut	ū	ɨ
a	father	ä	ɑ
(schwa)	alone, item, credible, gallop, circus	ə	ə
au, aw	fault, claw	ô	ɔ
ew, oo	chew, room	o͞o	u
oo	book	o͝o	ʊ
oi, oy	coin, toy	oi	ɔj
ou, ow	cloud, clown	ou	æw
ar	car	är	ɑ:r**
are	care	âr	er**
er, ir, ur, or, ear (*stressed*)	fern, bird, burn, word, heard	ûr	ɜr**
er (*unstressed*)	butter	ər	ɚ
ier, eer	pier, deer	îr	ɪr, ir

*Copyright © 2010 by Houghton Mifflin Harcourt Publishing Company. Adapted and reproduced by permission from *The American Heritage Dictionary of the English Language, Fourth Edition.*

**Phonetic notation for the *r*-controlled sounds varies.

Vowel digraphs consist of two adjacent vowel letters that represent one sound (e.g., *oa, ee, oi, ou, au*); these often occur in words of Anglo-Saxon origin. A vowel digraph usually occurs in the middle of a word. Vowel digraphs are often difficult for students to acquire because of their variability and because of interference from previously learned associations. They can be divided into two sets—those that are fairly consistently linked to a single sound (e.g., *ee, oa, oi, oy*) and those that may have either of two pronunciations (e.g., *ea* in *bead* or *bread, ow* in *show* or *cow*). (It should be noted that linguists differentiate between the terms *vowel digraph* and *diphthong*. Both contain two adjacent vowels letters in the same syllable. **Diphthongs** contain two vowels with a slide or a shift in the middle; they include *au/aw, oi/oy,* and *ou/ow.*) Balmuth provided the historical origins of vowel digraphs and diphthongs and noted that during Middle English times diphthongs were "especially varied in spelling because of the confusions that resulted from the separation of the written *i* and *y* and the introduction of the *w* and other French spelling conventions" (2009, p. 102).

By the end of the second grade, children should have mastered all of the common letter–sound correspondences and related spelling patterns (see Chapter 9). For example, children need to learn when to use -*ck* rather than -*k* at the end of a one-sylla-ble word. The appendixes at the end of this chapter provide examples of instruction on reading and writing words containing new target patterns.

Syllable Patterns

Syllables are units of spoken language consisting of a vowel sound or a vowel–consonant combination. Words of Anglo-Saxon origin have a variety of syllable patterns. Students first learn that each syllable must have a vowel. Children generally have less difficulty with hearing syllables in words than with identifying the syllables in written words (Balmuth, 2009; Groff, 1971). Therefore, teachers often begin by hav-ing children say their own names and count the number of syllables. Students also begin to listen for **accent** or stress in words of more than one syllable. Teachers can help students discover that words of Anglo-Saxon origin (e.g., *sleep, like, time*) tend to retain the accent when affixes are added (e.g., *asleep, likely, timeless*).

Groff (1971) emphasized that syllables are not units of writing, grammar, or struc-ture. He noted that the boundaries of syllables rather than the number of syllables in a word cause difficulty in their analysis. He made the distinction between how linguists divide words based on morphemic boundaries and how dictionaries divide syllables based on sounds. For example, some linguists may prefer to divide the word *disruptive* as *dis|rupt|ive* (prefix, root, and suffix), whereas dictionaries usually divide the word as *dis|rup|tive*. Groff wondered whether teaching syllable division is an important part of teaching reading. Although this argument continues, it is useful for teachers to know the six major syllable types and the predominant syllable-division patterns because children will read multisyllabic words in the primary grades and will find syllable divi-sion useful in hyphenating words.

The major types of syllables are 1) closed, 2) vowel-consonant-*e*, 3) open, 4) vowel pair (or vowel team), 5) **consonant-*le*,** and 6) ***r*-controlled** (see Moats, 1995, 2010; Steere, Peck, & Kahn, 1971). Teachers introduce **closed syllables** first. In these sylla-bles, the single vowel has a consonant after it and makes a short vowel sound (e.g., *map, sit, cub, stop, bed*). The **final** *e* in a **vowel-consonant-*e* syllable** makes the vowel long (e.g., *made, time, cute, vote, Pete*). An **open syllable** contains a vowel at the end of the syllable, and the vowel usually has a long sound (e.g., mē and hōbō). Stanback (1992) found that closed syllables alone make up 43% of syllables in English words. Open syllables and closed syllables together account for almost 75% of English syllables. A **vowel pair (or vowel team) syllable** contains two adjacent vowel letters as in *rain, green, coil,* and *pause*. Children learn the long, short, or diphthong sound of each pattern. A syllable ending in -*le* is usually preceded by a consonant that is part of that syllable. For example, *bugle* has a long *u* because the *gle* stays together and makes *bu* a long syllable. *Tumble,* in contrast, contains *tum* and *ble*; with *tum* being a closed sylla-ble. *Little* requires two *t*s to keep the *i* in *lit* short. As discussed previously, vowel sounds in ***r*-controlled syllables** often lose their identity as long or short and are coarticu-lated with the /r/ (as in *star, corn, fern, church,* and *firm*).

Students also need to learn some common rules for syllable division so that multi-syllabic words are easier to read and spell. By understanding and practicing identifica-tion of the various syllable types in one-syllable words first, readers will recognize these common syllable types as they learn to divide words into syllables. Understanding how to spell the vowel sounds in syllables gives readers an advantage and a more productive grasp of syllable-division rules. Readers may recognize syllable-division patterns such as vowel-consonant-consonant-vowel (VC|CV) and others (V|CV as in *hobo* and VC|CCV as in *hundred*). These are useful separations to know when analyzing unfamiliar words (see Chapter 8).

Morpheme Patterns

A morpheme is the smallest meaningful linguistic unit. Prefixes (beginnings), suffixes (endings), and roots are the morphemes that are helpful for students learning to read and write because they appear in literally hundreds of thousands of words (Brown, 1947; Henry, 1993). By knowing the common morphemes, students enhance not only their decoding and spelling skills but also their vocabulary skills. Anglo-Saxon morphemes are found in both compound (e.g., *football, blackboard*) and affixed words (e.g., *lovely, timeless*). These words tend to be simple because they contain regular orthographic features. Compound words generally comprise two short words joined together to form new, **meaning-based words** (e.g., *blackboard* suggests a *black board, football* refers to a *ball* for kicking with one's *foot*). Computer technology has been the impetus for many new compound words, such as *software* and *shareware*.

Words can also be expanded by affixing prefixes and suffixes to the base word. These base words, or free morphemes, can stand alone as words, such as *like* or *hope*. Morpheme affixes have two forms. Inflectional morphemes indicate grammatical features such as number, person, tense, or comparison (e.g., *dog, dogs; wait, waits; walk, walked; small, smaller*). Derivational morphemes, in contrast, change one part of speech to another, chiefly by adding affixes to root words (e.g., *hope, hopeless, hopelessly*; see Chapter 3).

Students begin learning morpheme patterns by adding suffixes to words requiring no change in the base form (e.g., *help, helpless; time, untimely*). Soon after that, they must learn suffix addition rules that affect some base words, such as the rule about when to drop a final *e* or change *y* to *i* (see Chapter 9).

LATIN LAYER OF LANGUAGE

The Latin layer of the English language consists of words used in more formal settings. Latin-based words, including words from the Romance languages, are often found in the literature, social studies, and science texts in upper elementary school and later grades.

Letter–Sound Correspondences

Many students expect Latin-based words to be more complex because they are longer than Anglo-Saxon–based words. Yet, in most cases, the words follow simple letter–sound correspondences. Single consonants are identical to those found in Anglo-Saxon-based words, but words of Latin origin contain fewer vowel digraphs. Most Latin roots contain short vowels as in *dict, rupt, script, struct, tract, tens, pend,* and *duct.* The consonant combination *ct* is a signpost for words of Latin origin as in *contradict, construct,* and *viaduct.*

Latin-based digraphs generally appear in suffixes such as *-ion, -ian, -ient,* and *-ial.* When these vowel digraphs come after the letters *c, s,* and *t,* they combine with those letters as the /sh/ sound as in *nation, politician, partial, social,* and *admission (-sion* is also pronounced as /zhən/ in words such as *erosion* and *invasion.)* The schwa (/ə/), or unstressed vowel sound, is often found in words of Latin origin in the unaccented prefixes and/or suffixes and is discussed next.

Syllable Patterns

Latin word roots tend to be closed (e.g., *rupt, struct, script*), vowel-consonant-*e* (e.g., *scribe, vene*), and *r*-controlled (e.g., *port, form*). Usually, the accent falls on the root, but stress patterns can be fairly complex when adding affixes. The schwa (/ə/) is common in longer words of Latin origin such as *excellent* and *direction*. When one pronounces *excellent,* for example, stress occurs on the first syllable, so the **initial** *e* receives the regular short sound. The following two *e*'s, appearing in unstressed syllables, have the schwa sound (/ə/). Listening for the unstressed vowels in open and closed syllables is an advanced skill that students with reading difficulties need to learn. Students who can discover the base word (e.g., *excel*) often will be able to spell the longer word.

Morpheme Patterns

Although Anglo-Saxon base words can make up compound words (e.g., *houseboat*) and can have affixes added to them (e.g., *hopelessly*) and become affixed, Latin roots usually are affixed but can be compounded (e.g., *aqueduct, manuscript, artifact*). Nist provided another key example: "So great, in fact, was the penetra*tion* of Latin *af*fixing during the *Renais*s*ance* that it quite *un*did the Anglo-Saxon habit of *com*pounding as the leading means of word forma*tion* in English" (1966, p. 11).

Words of Latin origin become affixed by adding a prefix and/or a suffix to a root, which rarely stands alone (e.g., *rupt, interrupt; mit, transmitting; vent, prevent*). For example, the prefix *in-* can be added to the bound morpheme *spect* to get *inspect,* and the suffix *-ion* can be added to get *inspection.* (*Note:* Some sources, such as Barnhart, 1988; Gillingham & Stillman, 1997; and *Webster's New Universal Unabridged Dictionary,* 1983, explain *-tion* and *-cian* as noun suffixes. Others teach only *-ion* and *-ian* as suffixes added to roots such as *invent* and *music,* respectively. Teachers and students need to know that *-ion* and *-ian* are the suffixes but that these are often preceded by *t, s,* or *c.* These may be taught as specific patterns.)

The final consonant of a Latin prefix often changes based on the beginning letter of the root. For example, the prefix *in-* changes to *il-* before roots beginning with *l* (e.g., *illegal, illicit*); to *ir-* before roots beginning with *r* (e.g., *irregular*); and to *im-* before roots beginning with *m, b,* and *p* (e.g., *immobile, imbalance, important*). These **chameleon prefixes** are found in several forms (see Henry, 2010a, 2010b, and Henry & Redding, 1996).

Latin word roots form the basis of hundreds of thousands of words (Brown, 1947; Henry, 1993, 2010a). These roots are useful not only for decoding and spelling words but also for enhancing vocabulary. Students can readily observe the prefixes, roots, and suffixes in such words as *prediction, incredible, extracting,* and *reconstructionist.* Although most words of Latin origin follow regular letter–sound correspondences, some do not. Morphophonemic relations are the conditions in which certain morphemes keep their written spelling when affixes are added, although their phonemic forms change. This concept provides students with a logical reason for many English spellings. For example, in *knowledge,* the morpheme *know* is pronounced differently than the base word *know.* The meaning of *knowledge,* however, is based on the base word *know.* Balmuth noted that

> It can be helpful to readers when the same spelling is kept for the same morpheme, despite variations in pronunciation. Such spellings supply clues to the meanings of words, clues

that would be lost if the words were spelled phonemically, as, for example, if *know* and *knowledge* were spelled *noe* and *nollij* in a hypothetical phonemic system. (2009, p. 199)

GREEK LAYER OF LANGUAGE

Greek words also entered English by the thousands during the Renaissance to meet the needs of scholars and scientists. In addition, Bodmer noted that "the terminology of modern science, especially in aeronautics, biochemistry, chemotherapy, and genetics" (1944, p. 246) is formed from Greek. Greek roots are often called *combining forms* and compound to form words. Words of Greek origin appear largely in science textbooks (e.g., *microscope, hemisphere, physiology*). The following passage from a middle school science text shows not only how short words of Anglo-Saxon origin mix with longer Romance words but also how the scientific terminology is couched in words of Greek origin.

> Suppose you could examine a green part of a plant under the *microscope*. What would you see? Here are some cells from the green part of a plant. The cells have small green bodies shaped like footballs. They give the plant its green color. They are called *chloroplasts*. A single green plant cell looks like this. *Chloroplasts* are very important to a plant. As you know, plants make their own food. This food-making process is called *photosynthesis*. It is in these *chloroplasts* that *photosynthesis* takes place. (Cooper, Blackwood, Boeschen, Giddings, & Carin, 1985, p. 20)

Letter–Sound Correspondences

Greek letter–sound correspondences are similar to those of Anglo-Saxon, but words of Greek origin often use the sounds of /k/, /f/, and /ĭ/ represented by *ch, ph,* and *y,* respectively, such as in *chlorophyll*. These peculiar consonant combinations were introduced by Latin scribes and make words of Greek origin easily recognizable (Bodmer, 1944). Less common Greek letter–sound correspondences, found in only a handful of words, include *mn-* in *mnemonic, rh-* in *rhododendron, pt-* in *pterodactyl, pn-* in *pneumonia,* and the better known *ps-* in *psychology* and *psychiatry.*

Syllable Patterns

Syllable types most prevalent in Greek-based words are closed (CVC, as in *graph*) and open (CV, as in *photo*). In addition, a unique type of syllable can be found, that of adjacent vowels in separate syllables (CV|VC), as in *theater, create,* and *theory.* These vowels appear in distinct syllables and therefore have distinct sounds. Syllable division in words of Greek origin generally follows the rules given for Anglo-Saxon words, especially the rules for open syllables (e.g., *phono, photo, meter, polis*). For example, the letter *y* sounds like short *i* in closed syllables (e.g., *symphony, gymnasium*), and these syllables are divided after the consonant. The letter *y* sounds like long *i* in open syllables (e.g., *cyclone, gyroscope, hyperbole*), and these syllables are divided immediately after the *y.* Combining forms such as *semi, hemi,* and *micro* do not follow traditional V|CV or VC|CV division. CVVC words such as *create* and *theory* divided between the vowels (*cre|ate, the|or|y*). Students rarely need to depend on strategies for syllable division because they learn the patterns as wholes.

Morpheme Patterns

If students recognize relatively few Greek roots (or combining forms), then they can read and spell many words. As students learn the common Greek roots that hold specific meaning, such as *micro, scope, bio, graph, helio, meter, phono, photo, auto,* and *tele,* they begin to read, spell, and understand the meaning of words such as *microscope, telescope, phonoreception, telephoto, telescopic, photoheliograph, heliometer, biography,* and *autobiography.* (*Note:* Suffixes can be added, as in the last two examples.) Many Greek roots are often called prefixes because they appear at the beginning of words (e.g., *auto* in *autograph, hyper* in *hyperbole,* and *hemi* in *hemisphere*). Numeral prefixes such as *mono-* (1), *di-* (2), *tri-* (3), *tetra-* (4), *penta-* (5), *hexa-* (6), *hepta-* (7), *octa-* (8), *nona-* (9), *deca-* (10), *centi-* (100), and *kilo-* (1,000) become useful in the study of mathematics and geometry.

Ehrlich (1972); Fifer and Flowers (1989); Fry, Polk, and Fountoukidis (1996); Henry (2010a, 2010b); and Henry and Redding (1996) provided numerous resources for words containing both Latin- and Greek-based words. Specific instructional activities can be found in the latter three sources. (See Appendixes 4.2 and 4.3 for examples of lessons for Latin and Greek morpheme patterns, respectively.)

CONCLUSION

Perfetti asserted that "only a reader with skilled decoding processes can be expected to have skilled comprehension processes" (1984, p. 43). Children's understanding will be enhanced when they are able to grasp words important to the gist of a story or to the meaning of text.

Teachers who comprehend the origins of the English language along with the primary structural patterns within words can improve their assessment skills, enhance their understanding of reading and spelling curricula, communicate clearly about language issues, and effectively teach useful language strategies to their students. Influences on English orthography stem from the introduction of letters and words from diverse origins. When teachers and their students understand the historical basis and structure of written English, they can better understand the regularities as well as the very few irregularities in English words.

Young students will use these language strategies to decode and spell short, **regular words** as well as Anglo-Saxon compound words and words using common prefixes and suffixes. Older students and adult learners receiving instruction in more advanced language structure will focus on Latin and Greek roots and affixes.

Finally, students of all ages often enjoy learning about the structure and origins of English words. Students who are learning English as a second language find that English is quite regular after all and is not a language of exceptions. Children with or without specific language disabilities benefit as they learn effective and efficient strategies to read and spell numerous words.

REFERENCES

Adams, M.J. (1990). *Beginning to read: Thinking and learning about print.* Cambridge, MA: The MIT Press.

The American heritage dictionary (4th ed.). (2000). Boston: Houghton Mifflin.

Balmuth, M. (2009). *The roots of phonics: A historical introduction.* (Rev. ed.). Baltimore: Paul H. Brookes Publishing Co.

Barnhart, R.K. (1988). *The Barnhart dictionary of etymology.* New York: H.W. Wilson.

Bodmer, F. (1944). *The loom of language.* New York: W.W. Norton.

Brown, J.I. (1947). Reading and vocabulary: 14 master words. In M.J. Herzberg (Ed.), *Word study* (pp. 1–4). Springfield, MA: Merriam-Webster.

Chall, J.S. (1983). *Learning to read: The great debate revisited.* New York: McGraw-Hill.

Chall, J.S., & Popp, H.M. (1996). *Teaching and assessing phonics.* Cambridge, MA: Educators Publishing Service.

Claiborne, R. (1983). *Our marvelous native tongue.* New York: Times Books.

Cooper, E.K., Blackwood, P.E., Boeschen, J.A., Giddings, M.G., & Carin, A.A. (1985). *HBJ science* (Purple ed.). Orlando, FL: Harcourt Brace.

Ehri, L.C. (2005). Learning to read words: Theory,

findings, and issues. *Scientific Studies of Reading, 9*(2), 167–188.

Ehrlich, I. (1972). *Instant vocabulary.* New York: Pocket Books.

Fifer, N., & Flowers, N. (1989). *Vocabulary from classical roots.* Cambridge, MA: Educators Publishing Service.

Fry, E.B., Polk, J.D., & Fountoukidis, D.L. (1996). *The reading teacher's new book of lists* (3rd ed.). Upper Saddle River, NJ: Prentice Hall.

Gillingham, A., & Stillman, B.W. (1997). *Remedial training for children with specific disability in reading, spelling and penmanship* (8th ed.). Cambridge, MA: Educators Publishing Service.

Groff, P. (1971). *The syllable: Its nature and pedagogical usefulness.* Portland, OR: Northwest Regional Educational Laboratory.

Hanna, P.R., Hodges, R.E., & Hanna, J.S. (1971). *Spelling: Structure and strategies.* Boston: Houghton Mifflin.

Henderson, E.H. (1990). *Teaching spelling* (2nd ed.). Boston: Houghton Mifflin.

Henry, M.K. (1988a). Beyond phonics: Integrated decoding and spelling instruction based on word origin and structure. *Annals of Dyslexia, 38,* 259–275.

Henry, M.K. (1988b). Understanding English orthography: Assessment and instruction for decoding and spelling (Doctoral dissertation, Stanford University, 1988). *Dissertation Abstracts International, 48,* 2841-A.

Henry, M.K. (1993). Morphological structure: Latin and Greek roots and affixes as upper grade code strategies. *Reading and Writing, 5*(2), 227–241.

Henry, M.K. (2010a). *Unlocking literacy: Effective decoding and spelling instruction* (2nd ed.). Baltimore: Paul H. Brookes Publishing Co.

Henry, M.K. (2010b). *WORDS: Integrated decoding and spelling instruction based on word origin and word structure.* Austin, TX: PRO-ED.

Henry, M.K., & Redding, N.C. (1996). *Patterns for success in reading and spelling.* Austin, TX: PRO-ED.

Jespersen, O. (1971). *Growth and structure of the English language.* New York: The Free Press.

Liberman, I.Y. (1973). Segmentation of the spoken word and reading acquisition. *Bulletin of the Orton Society, 23,* 65–77.

Liberman, I.Y., & Liberman, A.M. (1990). Whole language vs. code emphasis: Underlying assumptions and their implications for reading instruction. *Annals of Dyslexia, 40,* 51–78.

Liberman, I.Y., & Shankweiler, D. (1985). Phonology and the problems of learning to read and write. *Remedial and Special Education, 7,* 8–17.

Liberman, I.Y., & Shankweiler, D. (1991). Phonology and beginning reading: A tutorial. In L. Rieben & C.A. Perfetti (Eds.), *Learning to read: Basic research and its implications* (pp. 3–17). Mahwah, NJ: Lawrence Erlbaum Associates.

Liberman, I.Y., Shankweiler, D., Fischer, F.W., & Carter, B. (1974). Explicit syllable and phoneme segmentation in the young child. *Journal of Experimental Child Psychology, 18,* 201–212.

Moats, L.C. (1995). *Spelling: Development, disability, and instruction.* Timonium, MD: York Press.

Moats, L.C. (2010). *Speech to print: Language essentials for teachers* (2nd ed.). Baltimore: Paul H. Brookes Publishing Co.

Nist, J. (1966). *A structural history of English.* New York: St. Martin's Press.

Perfetti, C. (1984). Reading acquisition and beyond: Decoding includes cognition. *American Journal of Education, 93,* 40–60.

Pinker, S. (1994). *The language instinct: How the mind creates language.* New York: William Morrow.

Richardson, S.O. (1989). Specific developmental dyslexia: Retrospective and prospective views. *Annals of Dyslexia, 39,* 3–23.

Stanback, M.L. (1992). Syllable and rime patterns for teaching reading: Analysis of a frequency-based vocabulary of 17,602 words. *Annals of Dyslexia, 42,* 196–221.

Steere, A., Peck, C.Z., & Kahn, L. (1971). *Solving language difficulties.* Cambridge, MA: Educators Publishing Service.

Venezky, R.L. (1970). *The structure of English orthography.* The Hague, The Netherlands: Mouton.

Webster's new universal unabridged dictionary (2nd ed.). (1983). New York: Simon & Schuster.

APPENDIX 4.1

Sample Lesson for Anglo-Saxon Letter–Sound Correspondences: *ar* and *or*

OPENING

State that students will review the pattern *ar* and learn a new pattern, *or*.

REVIEW

Have children write the pattern *ar* on their tablets and repeat the sound /är/. Remind them that the letter *r* with a vowel before it often changes the vowel sound from its typical short or long sound. Ask students whether they remember any words that use the pattern /är/ (as in *car*). As children generate words, write them on the chalkboard. Words could include the following:

car	dark	harm	starting	yard	target
par	stark	harming	started	arch	tarnish
jar	shark	harmed	charts	part	harmless
star	sharp	barn	mark	tarts	harmful
scar	march	farm	marking	partly	garden
park	starch	farmer	marked	discard	harvest
lark	harp	start	hard	market	alarm

After you write the words and add some of your own, have children read the words together. You may want to point out prefixes and suffixes if they have been included. Ask children to put their reading papers aside as you dictate a few of the words for spelling.

NEW

Write *or* on the board, and ask children whether they know what it says (/or/ as in *corn*). Have children write *or* on their tablets, first tracing, then copying, then writing while carefully monitoring the letter formation. As children write the pattern four or five times, they repeat the sounds. Have children generate words containing *or*. Words might include the following:

corn	pork	sport	morning	horse	record
for	stork	storm	thorn	order	report
fort	forth	north	shorn	forget	border
port	snort	scorch	short	hornet	
sort	form	morn	porch	sordid	

Again, add words of your own, and have the children read the words. Dictate a few words for spelling.

Now ask children to take a piece of paper and fold it in half, lengthwise. Have them write *ar* in the left-hand column and *or* in the right-hand column. Dictate a number of *ar* and *or* words. Children must listen carefully to the vowel sound and write words in the appropriate column.

Note: Adapted from *Patterns for Success in Reading and Spelling: A Multisensory Approach to Teaching Phonics & Word Analysis* (pp. 59–60, 81–82), by M.K. Henry & N.C. Redding, 2002, Austin, TX: PRO-ED. Copyright 2002 by PRO-ED, Inc. Adapted with permission.

Give students sentences containing *ar* and *or* words to read and spell. For example,

Please sort the cards.

They saw a shark jump in the storm.

He played many sports in the park.

The farmer planted corn on his farm.

She sat on the north side of the porch.

Her horse marched by the cars.

CLOSING

Review the two patterns emphasized in this lesson. Why are they important to learn?

Sample Lesson for Latin Roots

OPENING

After an introduction to common Latin prefixes and suffixes, students are now ready to learn many of the common Latin roots. Ask students whether they know what a *root* is (the main part of the word, to which prefixes and suffixes are added and which usually receives the accent or stress in Latin-based words). Tell students that roots are valuable not only as patterns for decoding and spelling but also as aids for learning new vocabulary to enhance reading, writing, listening, and speaking.

NEW

Begin by writing *rupt* on the chalkboard; students write *rupt* in their word booklets. Ask students to generate a number of words with *rupt* as the root. Write these words on the board. Words might include the following:

rupture	disrupt	corruptly	abruptly	interrupted
erupt	disrupting	bankrupt	interrupt	disruptive
eruption	corrupt	abrupt	interruption	irrupt

After students read all of the words that have been generated, see whether they can figure out the root's meaning (*to break*). Next, dictate some of the words for spelling.

Continue giving new Latin word roots in this manner. For each group of words, have students recognize the common roots. Have them note the placement of the root within the word (the beginning if there is no prefix, the end if there is no suffix, the middle if there are prefixes and suffixes). Show them how the root generally cannot stand alone—it is bound to the prefix and/or suffix.

Following are three Latin roots and only a few of the many words containing these roots. Additional suffixes may be added to most of the following words.

port (to carry)	*form* (to shape)	*tract* (to pull)
import	reform	tractor
export	deform	traction
portable	inform	attract
transport	transform	attraction
porter	transformer	attractive
transported	formula	contract
deport	informal	subtract
report	informative	retract
support	conform	protract
deportation	formal	distract
deportment	formality	distraction

Note: Adapted from *Patterns for Success in Reading and Spelling: A Multisensory Approach to Teaching Phonics & Word Analysis* (pp. 251–252), by M.K. Henry & N.C. Redding, 2002, Austin, TX: PRO-ED. Copyright 2002 by PRO-ED, Inc. Adapted with permission.

Begin dictating sentences that contain the various roots that have been taught. For example,

The contract supported the bankruptcy report.

The exporter interrupted the attractive informant.

Continue teaching common roots such as *spect, scrib/script, stru/struct, dic/dict, flect/flex, mit/miss, cred, duce/duct, vert/vers, pend/pens, jac/jec/ject, tend/tens/tent,* and so forth.

FOLLOW-UP

Have students begin looking for Latin-based affixes and roots in their textbooks and in newspapers.

APPENDIX 4.3

Sample Lesson for Greek Roots (or Combining Forms)

OPENING

Tell students that many of the Latin roots just studied were actually borrowed from the Greeks. The Greek roots are often called *combining forms* because the two roots are of equal stress and importance and compound to form a word. Some of the forms appear only at the beginning of a word (and so may be considered prefixes), others come at the end (sometimes thought of as suffixes), and some forms can be used in either position. A few words contain three combining forms (e.g., *photoheliograph*).

Point out that although Greek-based words contain many of the same letter–sound correspondences found in Anglo-Saxon and Latin-based words, they also have unique letter–sound relationships (e.g., *ph* is pronounced as /f/ as in *photograph*; *ch* is pronounced as /k/ as in *chemist*; *y* is either a short or long *i* sound as in *physician* and *typhoon*).

NEW

As you introduce the combining forms, have students carefully write each form, along with its meaning.

phon, phono (sound)

auto (self)

photo (light)

tele (distant)

graph, gram (written/drawn)

ology (study, from *logos/logue* [speech/word])

Have students generate words containing the combining forms. Have students read long lists of words containing the previous forms, such as the following:

phone	graphite	photogram	automobile
phonics	graphics	telecast	photology
phonogram	autograph	telegram	telephotography
phonology	photograph	telephone	monologue
phonological	photography	telephoto	prologue
phoneme	photographer	telethon	dialogue
phonemic	photocopy	automation	epilogue
phonograph	photoflash	automatic	

Have students spell words from dictation. Have students read and spell sentences containing Latin- and Greek-based word parts. For example,

He collected several autographs from the conductors.

The TelePrompTer gave the television broadcaster visual messages.

Phonics instruction is useful in developing reading and writing skills.

Note: Adapted from *Patterns for Success in Reading and Spelling: A Multisensory Approach to Teaching Phonics & Word Analysis* (pp. 283–284), by M.K. Henry & N.C. Redding, 2002, Austin, TX: PRO-ED. Copyright 2002 by PRO-ED, Inc. Adapted with permission.

Continue adding combining forms, including *micro, meter, therm, bio, scope, hydro, helio, biblio, crat/cracy, geo, metro, polis, dem, derm, hypo, chron, cycl, hyper, chrom,* and so forth.

FOLLOW-UP

Have students look for Greek-based words in science and mathematics textbooks.

5

Teaching Phonemic Awareness

JOANNA K. UHRY

Volumes of research on phonemic awareness indicate the importance of phonemic awareness instruction as a component of the curriculum in the early stages of reading acquisition (National Institute of Child Health and Human Development [NICHD], 2000; Snow, Burns, & Griffin, 1998). What is phonemic awareness, and how does it serve as a foundation for early word reading? How do weaknesses in phonological processing disrupt the acquisition of word reading? What should be included in an effective instructional plan for phonemic awareness? And how do we assess to see if the plan is working?

WHAT IS PHONEMIC AWARENESS?

Phonemic awareness involves sensitivity to the phoneme—the smallest unit of sound that carries meaning (e.g., the sounds /h/ and /b/ differentiate meaning in the words *hug* and *bug*). Toddlers can tell the difference between the spoken forms of "Give me a hug" and "Give me a bug." They can hear this fine distinction in sounds (i.e., **auditory discrimination**) and can correctly interpret the meaning of either sentence. But phonemic awareness is more than auditory discrimination. By the time children are ready to read, they should be able to do more than perceive these differences. They should know that *hug* starts with the /h/ sound and *bug* starts with the /b/ sound. They should know that /h/ and /b/ come at the beginnings of the words and that the ends of the words rhyme.

Phonemic awareness is considered a **metacognitive strategy,** not a skill. It is hard to teach by rote. Stanovich defined *phonemic awareness* as "conscious access to the phonemic level of the speech stream and some ability to cognitively manipulate representations at this level" (1986, p. 362). Phonemes are difficult to distinguish in speech because the sounds in a word are coarticulated or blended together. This conscious access to phonemes is particularly difficult in English. Although it is an alphabetic language, English is not a transparent language; it lacks a one-to-one match between phonemes and graphemes or written letters. It has roughly 98 letter–sound representations for its roughly 44 phonemes. For example, the letter *a* represents multiple sounds as in *cat, Kate, banana, watch,* and *tall.* The long /a/ sound can be spelled in multiple ways as in *apron, sail, say, Kate, weigh,* and *hey.*

Phonemic awareness involves a hierarchy of abilities proposed by Adams (1990), including 1) being sensitive to rhyme, 2) matching spoken words by initial sound, 3) segmenting initial sounds and blending phonemes into spoken words, 4) fully segmenting words into phonemes, and 5) manipulating phonemes in words (e.g., "Say *same* without the /s/ sound"). Phonemic awareness, together with recognizing the names of alphabet letters, are powerful predictors of later reading (e.g., Share, Jorm, Maclean, & Matthews, 1984). These two skills, in combination, prepare emerging readers for the alphabetic principle, the idea—which is often a flash of insight for children—that there is logic to the way a temporal sequence of sounds in the speech stream is mapped onto a left-to-right sequence of letters on a page.

Phonemic awareness is a crucial factor in predicting how easily young children will acquire reading. Furthermore, phonemic awareness can be taught. When children receive instruction in phonemic awareness around the time they begin to learn to read, their reading tends to be more skillful than that of children without this instruction. Children with dyslexia tend to be very poor at phonemic awareness and other forms of phonological processing. Direct instruction in phonological processing strategies is particularly beneficial to them.

PHONEMIC AWARENESS, PHONICS, AND PHONOLOGICAL PROCESSING

There are a number of *ph-* terms that are often confused. All are of Greek origin and all relate to speech sounds.

Phonemic Awareness and Phonics

Phonemic awareness and phonics are often confused. Both are critically important to word reading and both have to do with speech sounds. The difference between these two *ph*-words is that phonemic awareness is about speech sounds alone, and phonics is an instructional method that teaches grapheme–phoneme associations. Phonics is about using this knowledge to turn print into speech. Unlike the other terms that follow here, phonics involves print as well as speech sounds.

Phonological Processing

Phonological processing is an umbrella term for four oral language processing abilities that are related to the sounds in spoken language: phonological awareness, verbal short-term memory, **rapid serial naming,** and speech articulation speed. All four of these phonological processes affect reading (Wagner & Torgesen, 1987). Figure 5.1 presents a diagram of the relationships among these terms.

Phonological Awareness

Phonological awareness is a broader term than phonemic awareness. Phonological awareness involves awareness of units of speech (e.g., **concept of word,** syllable

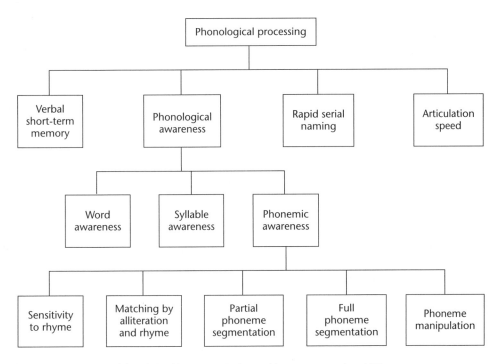

Figure 5.1. Diagram of the relationships among the four oral language processing abilities.

awareness, phonemic awareness) and is important to developing the alphabetic principle in the early stages of word reading. Concept of word can be developed as the teacher reads aloud and runs his or her finger under the print and tags each word under its first letter. Syllabus awareness is often taught through clapping the syllables in the children's names (e.g., one clap for Ann, two for Jaden, three for Emily, and four for Jeremiah). Phonemic awareness is taught through drawing attention to phonemes. More detail about resources for instruction in phonemic awareness is provided toward the end of this chapter.

Rapid Serial Naming

Rapid serial naming is measured by "reading" the names of pictures arranged serially, randomly reading letters presented in rows, and reading **sight words** quickly. Wagner and Torgesen's (1987) term for rapid serial naming is *phonological recoding in lexical access*. It refers to the process of moving from one code to another, and in the case of reading, moving from letter symbols to a phonological code in terms of gaining access to or retrieving names for letters or words. This process can be measured in prereaders by asking them to name, as quickly as possible, a series of printed color swatches or pictured objects, letters, or numerals repeated in random order in a matrix (Denckla & Rudel, 1974). Children who are poor at naming tend to be poor at word reading. Once they learn to read, they read slowly. Wolf (1991) provided a detailed description of this deficit and its effects. The combination of phonemic awareness and rapid serial naming deficits is often called the **double deficit**. Uhry (1997) found that 9-year-old children with poor phonemic awareness made slower progress in reading after 2 years of phonemic awareness training if they were also slow at rapid serial naming in comparison with children who were poor at phonemic awareness alone. Wood and Felton (1994) found that adults with a childhood history of dyslexia often read accurately following remediation, but those who had had rapid serial naming difficulties as children continued to read quite slowly.

Verbal Short-Term Memory

Wagner and Torgesen (1987) called verbal short-term memory *phonetic recoding to maintain information in working memory.* Young readers with this type of phonological processing difficulty can recode letters to sounds but have difficulty remembering the sounds long enough to blend them into words. Older readers can learn to decode words but have difficulty remembering them long enough to put them together in sentences and extract meaning.

Speech Articulation Speed

Catts (1986, 1989, 1993) described speech articulation speed as a fourth phonological processing ability important to reading. To read quickly involves being able to reproduce speech sounds quickly. Some children with dyslexia scramble speech sounds (e.g., saying "aminal" for animal) and produce complex phonological sequences more slowly than children with typically developing reading. Repeating the nonsense syllables "pa-ta-ka" as quickly as possible is one task for measuring articulation speed (Wolff, Michel, & Ovrut, 1990). It may be that slow articulation rate interferes with the ability to maintain phonological models in verbal short-term memory.

PHONEMIC AWARENESS DEVELOPMENT AND EARLY READING

Phonemic awareness is the most critical of all the phonological processing components during the early reading process. Knowing how to isolate, combine, and manipulate phonemes is critical to understanding the relationship between speech and print. That is, in addition to letter knowledge, beginning readers need phonics knowledge—or knowledge of the letters that are used to represent each of the 44 phonemes in English—and they need to know how sounds in speech relate to the letters on a printed page.

Adams's Five Levels of Phonemic Awareness

Phonemic awareness is a precursor to reading and begins to develop during the preschool years. Adams (1990) described phonemic awareness as progressing through five levels of difficulty, which are discussed next. Yopp (1988) carried out a study of the reliability of 10 phonemic awareness tasks and found a similar pattern.

An Ear for Rhymes

The first level in developing phonemic awareness involves a sensitivity to rhyme. British researchers Maclean, Bryant, and Bradley (1987) followed preschoolers from age 3, when differences were found in children's ability to memorize nursery rhymes, through school age, when early rhyming ability was found to be correlated with later reading ability. Children who can perceive rhymes can intuitively recognize that part of the word, the initial phoneme, before the vowel, often called the **onset** by researchers, is exchanged for another phoneme in rhyming words. The word **rime** is a linguistic term for the spoken or written vowel and the final consonant(s) (if any) in a word (e.g., *-o* in *do; -oat* in *boat; -eat* in *meat*). Even though 3-year-olds cannot consciously segment the initial phoneme, they are acquiring what Adams called "an ear" for this structure (1990, p. 80). This ability typically develops before letters are taught. Teachers wishing to draw attention to written rhymes in read-aloud picture books need to be careful to demonstrate with words that are not just sound-alike rhymes but look-alike rimes (e.g., *mean* and *bean* but not *weigh* and *say*). Many rhyming picture books are not sensitive to this point. Although there is agreement in the field that rhyming is the easiest of the phonemic awareness tasks, teaching rhyming is not as directly linked to reading acquisition as the more explicit forms of phonemic awareness that follow. Keeping this in mind, using rhyming books is an ideal way to introduce phonemic awareness to classes or small groups of young children. Just listening to the rhymes can sensitize the ear, and more advanced children in a group can actually provide the rhyme if the teacher pauses as he or she comes to the end of the line. Rereading rhymes and even rereading to the point of memorization seems to help children notice the rhymes.

Matching Words by Rhyme and Alliteration

The second level of phonemic awareness typically develops around 4–5 years of age. It involves being able to match spoken words by either alliteration (i.e., same onsets) or by rhyme. This can be assessed by using a research task designed by Bradley and Bryant (1983, 1985) called the **oddity** or **odd-man-out task.** For example, with alliteration as the focus, a child is asked to listen to the words *ball, bat, tub,* and *bird* and to identify the odd man out (*tub*).

Sorting by sounds is considered an important cognitive operation in developing phonemic awareness. One difficulty, however, is that letter sounds are not exactly alike (e.g., the /b/ in *bag* is different from the /b/ in *but*). Research using functional magnetic resonance imaging (fMRI) technology has identified areas in the brain used for making judgments about categorizing speech sounds (Blumstein, Myers, & Rissman, 2005; Myers, Blumstein, Walsh, & Eliassen, 2009).

Just as exposure to poodles, golden retrievers, and pugs helps toddlers develop a **schema** for the idea of *dog,* games with variations on the initial /b/ sound help sensitize the young child's ear. Just as sorting sounds is easier than actually segmenting a sound, sorting words into /b/ versus /s/ is much easier than sorting /b/ from /p/. This linguistic difference introduces a whole new dimension into curriculum-building decisions about what is harder and what is easier in learning phonemic awareness.

There is evidence that using alphabet letters helps children learn phonemic awareness (e.g., Hohn & Ehri, 1983; NICHD, 2000). Teachers can use sorting and matching tasks to introduce letters. The concept of the sound /b/ is developed first through listening and then through looking at the letter *b*. Shoeboxes of objects for sorting by initial phonemes can be made available and eventually labeled with the initial letter. These materials can be organized at a center for follow-up play after direct instruction in sorting.

Another complication with the sorting task is that children with oral language deficits can have difficulty with instructional language. The direction, "Say the sound that comes at the beginning" or "at the end" can be difficult for some children. See Chapter 3 for more information on teaching children with language disorders.

Partial Phoneme Segmentation

Syllable splitting is the third level of phonemic awareness Adams (1990). By around age 5, phonemes are not merely intuited but are consciously segmented from spoken words. The most common first attempts at segmenting involve the initial phoneme or onset. Researchers have evidence that syllables break apart most easily at the onset-rime division, with the initial phoneme being separated from the middle-vowel/ending-consonant (or coda) unit. That is, there is evidence that it is easier to segment the word *map* into /m/-/ap/ than into /ma/-/p/ or /m/-/a/-/p/ (e.g., Treiman, 1985).

Kindergarten children exhibit this level of phonemic awareness when they segment initial phonemes and represent them with letters in **invented spellings.** Early spellings often involve just the initial sound in a word, represented by a letter whose name makes the same sound (e.g., *p* for *picking*). *Dress* is often spelled with a *j*, the letter name that comes closest to the initial sound in *dress* (Morris & Perney, 1984; Treiman, 1985). Teaching children to listen to sounds for spelling is a form of phonemic awareness training and can actually increase early reading ability (Moats, 2005; Uhry & Shepherd, 1993). Adams (1990) included blending as a task at this level. Many children can blend spoken phonemes into words (e.g., blending /s/-/ă/-/m/ into *Sam*) while still being unable to segment more than an initial phoneme.

This level of phonemic awareness supports what Ehri (2005, 2007; Ehri, & McCormick, 1998) called the partial alphabetic stage of learning to read. Knowing the names of letters and being able to segment the initial—or initial and final—sounds in spoken words allow children to recall words they have seen before (e.g., using *jl* to recall *jail*). Ehri (2007) cited Gough and Hillinger's (1980) claim that this method begins to break down at around 40 words if phonemic awareness is not developed to the point where **medial** sounds can be segmented.

Full Phoneme Segmentation

Full segmentation is difficult because of a phenomenon known as *coarticulation.* Vowel sounds can exist on their own as short words or syllables (e.g., *oh, a, I*), but most consonant sounds are coarticulated with vowels. For example, when the sound of the letter *b* is said alone, it is hard to pronounce it without a following vowel (e.g., "buh," "bah"). As mentioned earlier, what we conceptualize as the /b/ sound is really a series of /b/-like consonant sounds, each a little different depending on the vowel it accompanies. Identifying speech sounds in invented spelling can be conceptualized as a form of categorization.

The medial sounds in words are particularly hard for young children to segment, perhaps because of the coarticulation phenomenon. Medial vowels are coarticulated with both the initial and final consonants. For example, the short vowel sound in *mop* is coarticulated with initial /m/ and final /p/, making it hard to segment. Kindergarten children tend to segment this word as /m/-/p/ or as /m/-/ŏp/, leaving out the vowel or leaving it attached to the final consonant. Although medial vowels are especially difficult to segment in words with a **consonant-vowel-consonant** (**CVC**) structure, they are considerably easier to segment in short words beginning with vowels, such as *age* and *up* (Uhry & Ehri, 1999).

Not until around age 6, or the beginning of formal reading instruction, are children usually able to perform Adams's (1990) fourth level of phonemic awareness, in which all phonemes can be segmented (e.g., the spoken word *map* segmented as the sounds /m/-/a/-/p/). What Ehri (2007) called the full alphabetic stage of reading has a parallel stage in spelling (Frith, 1986). At this point, a child is ready to understand and use the alphabetic principle to figure out how to read unfamiliar words on his or her own.

Manipulation of Phonemes

Children are able to delete or exchange phonemes at the fifth and most complex of Adams's (1990) levels; they can say the word *seat* without the /s/ sound as "eat," and they can reverse the sounds in *cat* to say "tack." Children who cannot carry out these phoneme manipulation activities as easily as their same-age peers are much more apt to have difficulty in reading and writing. This level is rarely reached in nonreaders.

Other Factors Influencing Level of Difficulty

The complexity of task structure is just one factor influencing young children's ability in phonemic awareness. Another factor is the complexity of the words used in these tasks. This includes linguistic structure and location of articulatory gestures.

Linguistic Complexity

The linguistic complexity of the words chosen for assessment and instruction is another factor influencing the level of difficulty in phonemic awareness tasks (Stahl & Murray, 1994). For example, two-phoneme words are easier to segment than three-phoneme words, and CVC words are easier than words beginning with consonant blends (Rosner, 1975, 1999; Uhry & Ehri, 1999).

To examine the issue of task sophistication versus structural complexity, Stahl and Murray (1994) carried out a longitudinal study with 113 kindergarten and first-grade children. The measure they designed for this used four levels of structural complexity: 1) onsets and rimes, as in *map;* 2) vowels and codas within rimes, as in *side;* 3) onset consonant clusters, as in *float;* and 4) consonant clusters within codas, as in *bump.* Each of the word structures was tested on each of the four tasks: 1) blending, 2) beginning and ending phoneme isolation, 3) segmenting all phonemes, and 4) deleting phonemes. Some initial consonants are easier to identify than others; **continuant** consonants (e.g., /m/, /s/) are easier than stop consonants (e.g., /p/, /t/, /k/).[1] To control for this, half the consonants used in the experiment's words were continuants and half were stops. The authors found that task difficulty in their study was similar to Adams's (1990) levels, but deleting/manipulating phonemes was easier than full segmentation. In regard to levels of linguistic complexity within each task type, they found the following progression from easiest to hardest: initial single consonant (CVC), to final single consonant (CVC), to initial consonant cluster (CCVC), to final consonant cluster (CVCC). They also found that mastering linguistic complexity was more important to later reading than differences in task types. Their results are consistent with a model of phonological awareness and reading with reciprocal causation; letter knowledge precedes and supports onset segmentation, which precedes and supports word reading. This mutual causality model is similar to one proposed by Darrell Morris (Morris, Bloodgood, Lomax, & Perney, 2003). In Morris's study, phonemic awareness supports concept of word (pointing at words in memorized text while pretending to read), which, in turn, supports letter–sound knowledge, which supports word reading.

Articulatory Gestures

Articulary gestures—the place in the mouth that is used to produce sound—is another aspect of phonemes that affects the development of their segmentation. Vowels that are

---

[1]See Moats (2010) for information on linguistic characteristics useful for teachers.

articulated in the same part of the mouth are more easily confused (e.g., the short vowel sounds /a/ and /e/ sound more alike than do short /a/ and /i/). When planning a teaching sequence, teach short /a/ first, followed by short /i/, rather than short /e/. Moats (2010) explained that /a/ and /e/ are articulated in similar parts of the mouth, whereas /i/ is formed at a greater distance and easier to differentiate from /e/. The *e* in the word *dress* is often misspelled as *a* (Morris, 2005).

Summary of Phonemic Awareness Development

Phonemic awareness is critical to early reading acquisition. There is a vast set of research articles indicating the important foundational role that phonemic awareness plays in learning to read. Together, phonemic awareness and letter-name knowledge provide predictive information valuable in planning early interventions for children at risk for word-reading failure. Phonemic awareness develops through a series of progressively more difficult tasks, articulatory gestures, and linguistic structures.

DYSLEXIA

All children benefit from phonemic awareness instruction, but it is particularly helpful to children at risk for reading failure or who are already struggling with reading. The term *dyslexia* is used here for children with severe difficulty in learning to read words. There is evidence that children with dyslexia benefit from early intervention and that instruction with phonemic awareness can actually change the way the brain functions during reading (Blachman et al., 2004; Shaywitz et al., 2004).

The Discrepancy Model for Diagnosing Dyslexia

Historically, the term *dyslexia* has been conceptualized as a discrepancy between IQ score (average or above) and reading achievement (low), despite adequate instruction. Vellutino, Scanlon, and Zhang (2007) referred to this model as the psychometric/exclusionary approach because it rests on excluding a number of factors (e.g., low IQ score, sensory impairment) as causing academic difficulty. This definition works for a diagnosis, but it does not work for getting children with dyslexia the help they need right from the start. Fuchs, Fuchs, and Vaughn called the discrepancy model a "wait to fail" model (2008, p. 1). Typically, eligibility for special services using the discrepancy model has not been available until reading is 2 years below grade level. This means that if this model is used, children are left to struggle without services into third grade.

The Phonological Core Deficit Model of Dyslexia

The International Dyslexia Association (IDA) and the NICHD have provided an alternative model. They attributed the reading and spelling difficulties of dyslexia to "a deficit in the phonological component of language" (Lyon, Shaywitz, & Shaywitz, 2003, p. 2). That is, deficits in phonemic awareness and other forms of phonological processing are the characteristic early markers of dyslexia. Although early scientists such as Samuel Orton believed that dyslexia involved a vision problem with perceptual reversals, overwhelming amounts of evidence dating back as far as the 1970s indicate that dyslexia involves a phonological processing difficulty. In a joint statement issued in 2009, the American Academy of Pediatrics Section on Ophthalmology reaffirmed the following:

Most experts believe that dyslexia is a language-based disorder. Vision problems are not the cause of primary dyslexia or learning disabilities. Diagnostic and treatment approaches that lack scientific evidence of efficacy, including eye exercises, behavioral vision therapy, or special tinted filters or lenses, are not endorsed. (2009, p. 44)

Neurological research using fMRI confirms the phonological core deficit model of dyslexia (e.g., Frost et al., 2009; Papanicolaou, Pugh, Simos, & Mencl, 2004). Yale pediatric neurologist Sally Shaywitz stated, "The pattern of under-activation in the back of the brain provides a neural signature for the phonologic difficulties characterizing dyslexia" (2003, p. 82). These difficulties, apparent to trained early childhood classroom teachers through listening attentively to children's oral language, can now be viewed in particular locations in the brain. Studies by Shaywitz and others indicated that children with weak phonemic processing skills compensate by using a part of the brain that is not used by typically developing readers and is not efficient for reading (Shaywitz & Shaywitz, 2004). Early instruction that focuses on phonemic awareness and phonics can actually change the way the brain functions as these children's reading improves (Blachman et al., 2004; Shaywitz et al., 2004).

Adams (1994) estimated that roughly 25% of beginning readers fail to grasp the alphabetic principle without direct instruction in phonics and phonological awareness. The percentage is even higher for children from low socioeconomic areas. Results of a longitudinal study that has now followed kindergarten children for more than 20 years indicated that about 20% of all elementary-age children eventually develop symptoms of dyslexia, or word-level reading disability (Shaywitz, Fletcher, & Shaywitz, 1996).

Children with dyslexia typically memorize individual words but have difficulty generalizing from one word to another because of deficits in phonemic awareness. For example, knowing how to read the word *cat* does not generalize to knowing how to figure out sounds for /c/ in *cup,* /a/ in *map,* or /t/ in *nut.* These children struggle with unfamiliar words, a characteristic that is often assessed by asking them to read **phonetically regular** nonwords. Without direct instruction in phonological processing, children with dyslexia continue to be poorer at reading nonwords than real words relative to proficient readers (Rack, Snowling, & Olson, 1992). Research focused on reading disability and funded by the NICHD (DeFries et al., 1997) indicated that nonword reading disability is associated with a deficit in phonemic awareness. This deficit runs in families and is believed to be inherited through a specific gene. The deficit persists into adulthood for many people with dyslexia (Felton & Wood, 1989), even for those who have received remedial instruction.

Response to Intervention

Response to intervention (RTI) is a third model for diagnosing a reading disability. This model provides a system for diagnosis, intervention, and ongoing assessment. RTI draws on the unexpectedness of a child's reading difficulty, but instead of unexpectedness in the presence of average or above-average IQ, it draws on unexpectedness in the presence of good instruction and good progress by classmates receiving the same instruction. RTI is a complex concept with both assessment and intervention services differentiated across a series of steps or tiers. It involves increasing the intensity of instruction for children who are not responding to classroom instruction (Tier 1) through, for example, small-group instruction (Tier 2), and for those still not responding, referral for additional assessment aimed at planning even more intensive special services (Tier 3).

Primary Intervention: Tier 1

The following describes RTI using kindergarten children as the example because this is the point at which early identification and prevention is most effective in catching children up to peers in this important foundation to early reading. In Tier 1, the whole kindergarten class receives explicit instruction in phonemic awareness (and other early literacy skills such as letter-name knowledge) based on scientifically researched best practices. RTI involves early screening to identify children at risk, followed by explicit whole-class phonemic awareness instruction and careful ongoing observation and classroom-based assessment. Vaughn, Wanzek, Woodruff, and Linan-Thompson (2007) recommended 90 minutes a day of Tier 1 literacy instruction for the whole class. Any of the phonemic awareness programs described at the end of this chapter could be used for this systematic whole-class instruction in phonemic awareness.

The National Reading Panel (NRP) report (NICHD, 2000) stated that phonemic awareness is only one element in initial reading and writing instruction. Most phonemic awareness programs are designed to supplement the picture book read-alouds and writing activities that are typical of meaning-based early literacy programs. In addition to direct phonemic awareness instruction, the 90-minute classroom literacy block needs to integrate phonemic awareness into other components of literacy (e.g., listening for sounds, listening for meaning, writing, spelling). The findings of the NRP report (NICHD, 2000) are mentioned repeatedly in the literature on RTI (e.g., Al Otaiba, & Torgesen, 2007; Fuchs et al., 2008; Haager, Klingner, & Vaughn, 2007).

During this period, many kindergarten children who enter school without experience in playing language games, listening to rhyming books, or learning to name letters respond to effective instruction and begin to catch up. Other children are not as responsive as their peers and do not seem to be making progress.

Secondary Intervention: Tier 2

Assessment to look for evidence of failure to respond to phonemic awareness instruction could take place at any point during mid-to-late fall or early winter of the kindergarten year. Assessment would need to include children who are making progress because the notion of contrast with responders is embedded in RTI. For those children who need extra support, Vaughn et al. (2007) recommended continuing Tier 1 instruction with an additional 20 minutes a day of small-group work for children receiving Tier 2 instruction. The same phonemic awareness program is recommended for this extra work for the sake of consistency. The smaller group size and additional time differentiates Tier 2 from regular classroom instruction.

Tertiary Intervention: Tier 3

Vaughn et al. (2007) reported that most of the children in five studies that they reviewed were responsive to Tier 2 treatment, but despite this effective treatment, there were some nonresponders who were recommended to Tier 3 intervention at the time of a third assessment near the end of the school year. Instruction in Tier 3 involves a longer period of time each day (e.g., 45–60 minutes) beyond the classroom Tier 1 instruction and an even smaller group size—around three children per group (recommended by the NRP report [NICHD, 2000]) or individual instruction. For some children, it may mean moving to an even more intensive program. For example, a child receiving classroom instruction in *Wilson Fundations* (Wilson, 2002) could receive Tier 3 instruction in the Lindamood Phoneme Sequencing (LiPS; 1998) program using the intensive multisensory nature of the program as a rationale for the choice.

Summary of Information on Diagnosing Dyslexia

Diagnosing dyslexia is important for receiving appropriate services. RTI provides a viable option built on the premise that if a classroom provides effective phonemic awareness instruction, then most children will learn from it. Yet, those children who are not responsive need additional phonemic awareness services. This is a fairly widely accepted model because the Individuals with Disabilities Education Improvement Act (IDEA) of 2004 (PL 108-446) permits states to use RTI rather than discrepancy as evidence of need for special services. Rather than waiting 2 years for special services, a child with dyslexia could receive direct instruction in phonemic awareness right from the start, with intensified services as early as midyear and special instruction in literacy before the year is out.

ASSESSING PHONOLOGICAL AWARENESS

The advent of RTI has introduced major changes to the protocols used for assessing school progress, especially in the lower grades and in phonological processing because of the important role it plays as a foundation for reading. The following information on assessing phonological processing is organized into subsections suggested by the structure of RTI.

Classroom teachers are expected to carry out much of the assessment mandated by RTI. Teachers need to practice these tests before using them with children. Two areas need particular attention. First, be sure the child is looking at your mouth as you pronounce words and phonemes. Second, when you administer tests in which you pronounce phonemes, be sure not to add vowel sounds. For example, do not pronounce /t/ as "tuh" or /b/ as "buh." If you are new to teaching phonemic awareness and phonics, review the exercises in Moats (2010).

Early Screening and Periodic Retesting

Classroom assessment at the beginning of the year should focus on phonemic processing in the early grades. The purpose is to establish the early literacy level of all the children in a class in order to plan for instruction as well as identify children who appear to be at risk for difficulty in reading.

ECLAS-2

Many school districts mandate a particular instrument for periodic use for screening and progress monitoring. For example, New York City uses the Early Childhood Language Arts System (ECLAS-2) for K–3 assessment. It includes letter knowledge as well as a phonemic processing strand with rhyme recognition, rhyme generation, syllable clapping, identifying first and final consonants in words, blending , and full segmentation of short words. Each of the ECLAS-2 subtests is administered repeatedly until the strategy has been mastered. Children found to be at risk at school entry can be retested regularly to identify those who are not catching up and may need classroom instruction supplemented with Tier 2 intervention.

PALS

Virginia uses the Phonological Awareness Literacy Screening (PALS), which was designed at the University of Virginia's Curry School of Education. The screening includes forms for pre-K (Invernizzi, Sullivan, Meier, & Swank, 2004), kindergarten (Invernizzi, Juel, Swank, & Meier, 2005), and Grades 1–3 (Invernizzi, Meier, & Juel, 2005), with subtests in letter knowledge and sounds, matching oral words by initial sounds, saying initial sounds, concept of word (pointing at words in memorized text), spelling, and reading words. PALS can be used up to three times a year and is designed to identify children who need extra support in acquiring literacy and track their progress.

DIBELS

Many districts, especially those using Reading First funding, have mandated frequently recurring phonemic awareness assessment in the classroom to ensure that progress is being made and that instruction is based on recent assessment. The Dynamic Indicators of Basic Early Literacy Skills (DIBELS; Good & Kaminski, 2002, 2004; Kaminski & Good, 1996; Riedel, 2007) involve a series of 1-minute measures. The training manual provides directions for four measures for kindergarten and early first grade. Letter Naming Fluency (LNF) involves naming as many letters as can be identified in 1 minute from a page of randomly organized upper- and lowercase letters. The Initial Sound Fluency (ISF) subtest asks children to point to one of four pictures beginning with a designated sound. The Phoneme Segmentation Fluency (PSF) subtest asks children to say phonemic segments in three- and four-phoneme words as quickly as possible. Nonsense Word Reading (NWR) involves responding to "make-believe" words (e.g., *sim*) and either saying the phoneme for each letter or saying the word. Two additional subtests are provided for mid-Grade 1 through Grade 3. Oral Reading Fluency (ORF) measures the number of words read from a passage in 1 minute, and Retell Fluency (RTF) measures the number of words used in an oral retell in 1 minute.

DIBELS can be used to establish mastery of established criteria or identify children who may need more intensive instruction. Because the subtests are short, they can be given more often than longer test batteries such as the ECLAS-2 or PALS. Alternate forms and scores for both benchmark goals and indicators of risk are provided by the DIBELS.

Riedel (2007) carried out a study challenging the assumption that DIBELS measures are valuable because speed is a component of fluency and fluency contributes to comprehension. He found that the ORF subtest administered in mid-first grade predicted comprehension, but that tests of speeded phonological awareness and phonics did not. Keeping Chall's (1983) reading stages in mind, accuracy in phonemic awareness ought to precede speed, but DIBELS folds accuracy into the speed measure. Using the phonemic awareness portion of DIBELS as the only measure is questionable for struggling readers.

Blending

Teachers in districts without mandated measures will want to put together a battery of phonemic awareness tests for periodic classroom use. Wagner et al. (2003) reminded us to remember the cognitive challenges of various phonemic awareness task demands. Roswell and Chall's blending test (1963, 1997) is fairly straightforward. It involves saying parts of words aloud and asking the child to blend them into words. The test moves from the early first-grade level, in which the child blends two-phoneme words (e.g., *a-t*, *s-ay*), to blending onsets and rimes (e.g., f-at, ch-ain) and three sound segments (e.g., *c-a-t, t-oa-st*). This test is still reliable and useful (Chall, Roswell, & Blumenthal, 1963; Roswell & Chall, 1963; Yopp, 1988).

Phonemic Segmenting and Manipulation

The Phonological Awareness Skills Program (PASP; Rosner, 1999) is a set of **deletion,** substitution, and analogy tasks (e.g., "Say *same*. Now say it again but do not say /s/"). Tasks are progressively more difficult, moving from deleting syllables and initial consonants to deleting interior consonants in initial clusters, such as *stale* and *smack* and substituting the /u/ sound for /a/ in *crash* to make *crush*. The test ends with analogy items such as "Dim is to dip as rim is to _____." It is short, fairly easy to administer, and provides norms for ages 5–10.

Developmental Scoring of Invented Spelling

Morris (2005) provided a list of spelling words to dictate as well as a developmental scoring system. Rather than use the usual spelling test scoring (either right or wrong), this developmental system gives progressively higher scores for increments of spelling development representing successive developmental levels.

Spelling samples	Example	Scoring and spelling stage
Random strings of letters	h4ee	0 points (no phonetic representation)
Letter representing initial sound	p	1 point (prephonetic)
Initial and final consonants	bk	2 points (prephonetic)
All sounds represented	bec	3 points (alphabetic)
Some letter units	beck	4 points (transition to orthography)
All letter units	back	5 points (orthographically correct)

Morris's (2005) test works well as a quick screen for an entire kindergarten or early first-grade class. Invented spelling has been shown to be an excellent predictor of later reading skills (e.g., Ehri & Wilce, 1987; Morris & Perney, 1984; Uhry, 1999, 2002a; Uhry & Goodman, 2009). It is also a useful tool in planning instruction. For example, children spelling *back* as *bk* and *feet* as *ft* may benefit from focusing on the segmentation of medial vowels. Although only about 9% of the spelling words administered in Morris and Perney's study were spelled conventionally in September of Grade 1, using their developmental scoring system made spelling a strong predictor of May reading. In this scoring system, spellings were credited based on the degree to which they reflected the sound structure of the spoken word. For example, in the word *dress*, the spelling *j* received 1 point, *js* received 2 points, *das* received 3 points, and *dres* received 4 points, even though none of the children spelled *dress* conventionally. In combination, the Rosner (1999) deletion task, the Roswell-Chall (1963) blending task, and the Morris invented spelling test are all short, reliable, easy to administer, and provide information that is useful in planning instruction.

Observations of Phonemic Awareness Indicators in the Classroom

In addition to gathering phonemic awareness information from ongoing testing, experienced teachers should be able to spot early indicators of difficulty in a natural classroom setting. This can be noticed across multiple activities.

Rhyming

Preschoolers who have difficulty learning rhymes may be at risk for phonemic awareness–based reading difficulty. To follow the RTI model, observe nonrhymers early in the year and teach rhyme explicitly. Exaggerate the first in a pair of end-rhymes and then stop before the second end-rhyme for the children to join in (e.g., "Humpty Dumpty sat on a wall. Humpty Dumpty had a great _____"). Notice who always knows and who never knows. Observe over time to see if the child who never knows begins to catch on. Poem suggestions from teachers include "The Itsy-Bitsy Spider"; "One, Two, Buckle My Shoe"; and "Twinkle, Twinkle Little Star." "Miss Mary Mac, Mac, Mac, all dressed in black, black, black" works for almost everyone; slow responders have a chance to join in on the repetitions in "black, black, black."

Matching Words by Alliteration and Rhyme

Four- and five-year-old children should be able to match classmates' names by initial sounds. Try calling children to line up for lunch with "Line up if your name sounds like *Jaden* at the beginning." They should be able to guess the word that rhymes with the word containing the manipulated phoneme in playful poems such as "Willoughby Wallaby Wemily, the elephant sat on _____ (Emily)." Again, watch the children who perform the lowest to see if they begin to respond to instruction. Try a 3-minute individual lesson during independent work time and see if this makes a difference.

Invented Spelling in Classroom Writing

The inability to invent spellings for words during kindergarten or early first grade is one of the best classroom-based indicators of at-risk status. Spelling samples from classroom writing can be scored using Morris's (2005) system. If most children in the class are using beginning and ending consonants to spell, whereas a few are just drawing the story or using random letters, then it should be clear who needs help. Sit with a child who seems stuck and model spelling of phonemes in the words a child is trying to write. If more structure seems needed, then dictate a short sentence with short words with phonemes that the nonresponder knows.

Concept of Word with Finger-Point Reading

Concept of word or **finger-point reading** (Ehri & Sweet, 1991; Morris, 1983, 1993; Morris et al., 2003; Uhry, 1999, 2002a) is another classroom-based activity that reflects kindergarten and early first-grade phonemic awareness. Following **shared readings** by the teacher, children pretend to read by approximating familiar stories or reciting memorized text. A teacher can point at the initial letter of each word as he or she reads aloud from a big book or from the poems mentioned previously, inviting the class to join in. Children who are strong in phonemic segmentation will be able to identify most initial phonemes in the text they are reciting from memory (e.g., identify the /d/ sound in *dirt*) and match the spoken text with initial consonants (e.g., the letter *d* in printed words) as they follow the teacher's pointing from word to word or recite and point in their own book. There is a strong research base for the role of phonemic awareness in successfully matching voice with print. In a longitudinal study, Morris et al. (2003) found that partial phonemic awareness (ability to segment onsets) facilitated concept of print in finger-point reading, which in turn facilitated full phoneme segmentation and, later, word reading.

Classroom teachers can use rhyming, initial sound matching, invented spellings, and finger-point reading to identify children who do not learn these tasks following systematic, explicit, multisensory instruction. Those who still need support after multiple exposures may benefit from Tier 2 support. Periodic retesting and classroom observations in combination can be used in making decisions about moving children into Tier

2 instruction to supplement classroom instruction. Both are also helpful in making decisions about referring children for the more formal assessment used for eligibility for Tier 3 instruction.

Formal Assessment for Diagnosis

When a child is referred for formal evaluation by an assessment specialist, such as a school psychologist, the process should begin with classroom observations of the child during instruction and a lengthy conversation with the classroom teacher. Reviewing the record of ongoing assessment should be an important part of the agenda; it is the pattern of scores over time that provides the record of failure to respond to instruction. Assessment might include additional use of the previous measures or one or both of the following.

CTOPP

Wagner, Torgesen, and Rashotte's (1999) Comprehensive Test of Phonological Processing (CTOPP) is a **norm-referenced test** based on phonological processing research, much of it carried out by the test authors, and published in peer-reviewed journals. It was normed on 1,656 individuals and has been used for both research and educational decision making. The subtests go beyond phonemic awareness to cover other elements of phonological processing described earlier in this chapter. The CTOPP is individually administered and has separate forms for different ages. The version for ages 5–6 has the following seven subtests: 1) Elision (e.g., "Say *picnic* without the *pic*"; "Say *meat* without the /m/"; "Say *clap* without the /k/"); 2) Rapid Color Naming, 3) Blending Words, 4) Sound Matching, 5) Rapid Object Naming, 6) Memory for Digits, and 7) Nonword Repetition, as well as a supplemental subtest, Blending Nonwords. The version normed for ages 7–24 has six subtests: 1) Elision, 2) Blending Words, 3) Memory for Digits, 4) Rapid Digit Naming, 5) Nonword Repetition, and 6) Rapid Letter Naming. It also has norms for using certain subtests in the 5- to 6-year age version with older individuals (i.e., Color and Object Naming, Blending Nonwords) as well as supplemental phonemic awareness subtests: Phoneme Reversal, Segmenting Words, and Segmenting Nonwords. It comes with a well-organized examiner's manual and with an audio CD for administering subtests in which phonemes need to be pronounced precisely. Standard scores are provided for each subtest and for three composite scores that combine sets of subtests: Phonological Awareness, Phonological Memory, and Rapid Naming. According to the manual, examiners should be highly trained (e.g., educational or psychological evaluators) and familiar with the statistical properties of tests.

LAC-3

The Lindamood-Bell Auditory Conceptualization Test–Third Edition (LAC-3; Lindamood & Lindamood, 2004) focuses in depth on the precursor skills to phonemic awareness. The examiner begins by asking the child to use small wooden cubes to represent sounds in a sequence. For example, the phoneme sequence /d/-/d/-/j/ could be represented by red-red-blue. Next, sounds are analyzed in nonwords (e.g., yellow-blue-red could represent the nonword *vop*). Performance criteria are provided for levels from kindergarten through adult readers. The current edition includes more items in comparison with earlier editions, making it more reliable. The LAC-3 requires expertise on the part of the examiner. See Chapter 14 for additional information on assessment.

RESEARCH ON INSTRUCTION IN PHONEMIC AWARENESS

This section focuses on the effects of phonemic awareness instruction on the acquisition of reading. It includes three sets of studies: 1) early studies linking phonemic awareness and phonemic awareness instruction to early reading, 2) the NRP's meta-analysis of conditions under which phonemic awareness instruction is most effective, and 3) research on using RTI to identify children at risk and provide intervention.

Important Early Studies

Since the 1980s, researchers have found consistent and compelling experimental evidence of the importance of phonemic awareness in predicting reading. These studies, as a group, are important because they strengthen the link between phonemic awareness and early reading and provide early evidence that intervention is needed.

The Link Between Phonemic Awareness and Early Reading

Share et al. (1984) tested 543 Australian children in kindergarten and again in first grade using 39 measures (e.g., teacher predictions, letter copying, syntax comprehension, extent of parent–child reading, hours of television watched, IQ score, preschool attendance). Measures of word reading, spelling, and reading comprehension were administered at the end of first grade, and a reading composite score was developed. The two factors with the highest correlations with this composite were phoneme segmentation ($r = .62$) and letter naming ($r = .58$). **Multiple regression analysis** was then used to see if these measures overlapped at all in their contribution or if they made unique contributions. That is, were the measures examining two manifestations of the same underlying factor or two different factors? Again, phoneme segmentation made the largest unique contribution, far surpassing all other predictors. Screening batteries using a variety of phonological and phonemic awareness tasks as well as letter identification tasks are consistently and strongly correlated with later reading. Screenings incorporating phonemic awareness tasks are quite accurate at identifying those children who are at greatest risk of struggling with first-grade reading.

Three additional early researchers are often cited as providing seminal evidence of the importance and effectiveness of phonemic awareness training. Together, they provide evidence that phonemic awareness and early word reading are strongly correlated and that training in phonemic awareness increases early reading skills. Each of these research studies has provided a phonemic awareness program currently in use and is described in the final portion of this chapter.

Elkonin

Elkonin (1963, 1973), described his Russian colleagues' and his own training studies with young children. The studies are important because the teaching method (known as **"Elkonin boxes"**) has been widely incorporated into training programs in the United States. Children are presented with a picture of an object—or a spoken word—and asked to say the word and then asked to represent its phonemes with small tiles that are moved into a square below the picture as each phoneme is pronounced. For example, providing three squares for three phonemes was believed to help children conceptualize the sound structure of words. Elkonin used letters instead of blank tiles once phonemes were mastered. A number of studies have incorporated Elkonin boxes. In my research, I have used a version of this task called "Mrs. Magic Mouth," in which tiles are pulled out of the mouth of a drawing of a face (Uhry & Goodman, 2009). Blachman called this task Say It and Move It (e.g., Blachman, Ball, Black & Tangel, 1994). Blachman's phonemic awareness program, *Road to the Code,* is described at the end of this chapter.

Bradley and Bryant

In their 1983 training study, Bradley and Bryant used highly directed individual instruction in sorting words by rhyme and alliteration to teach phonemic awareness to British 4- and 5-year-olds who were at risk. The children who had received phonemic awareness training outperformed controls at posttest, with a condition combining phonemic awareness and letters providing the strongest effect. Trained children continued to outperform controls in print-based tasks after the experimental training had been discontinued (Bradley & Bryant, 1983, 1985). Sorting is considered a cognitive task and provides a thoughtful approach to phonemic awareness and phonics instruction. Word sorts are the basis of instruction in *Words Their Way* (Bear, Invernizzi, Templeton, & Johnston, 2008), which is described at the end of this chapter.

Lundberg, Frost, and Petersen

In Denmark, Lundberg, Frost, and Petersen (1988) successfully taught teachers to use games and songs with whole classrooms of preschoolers in order to increase their phonemic awareness before reading instruction. The study is distinguished from the others in that it does not use letters to teach phonemic awareness. An English-language version of this program (Adams, Foorman, Lundberg, & Beeler, 1998) is described in detail at the end of this chapter.

Lundberg et al.'s (1988) study is often used to make the point that phonemic awareness precedes and is causal to reading, as no experiences with print were offered during this preschool training. Bradley and Bryant (1983), however, included two phonemic awareness training conditions, one with and the other without the use of letters. The training with letters had the most dramatic effect on later reading and spelling, indicating that although phonemic awareness may be a necessary precursor to reading, using letters increases the effectiveness of training, and the relationship between the two is reciprocal rather than unidirectional. Some researchers make the point that children may be overwhelmed by both sounds and letters and need to learn to listen selectively to phonemes before letters are used in this training. Hohn and Ehri (1983) found the opposite, that letters can actually help young children conceptualize the sound structure of words. The optimal time for introducing letters in phonemic awareness training continues to be a point of dispute in the reading field, but there is evidence from the NRP (NICHD, 2000) that using letters to teach phonemic awareness is more effective than teaching phonemic awareness through sound alone.

Research on Phonemic Awareness Treatments Reported by the National Reading Panel

By the late 1990s, there were enough studies utilizing peer-reviewed experimental design with control groups and with random assignment to treatment for the NRP (NICHD, 2000) to carry out its meta-analysis of the effectiveness of various phonemic awareness treatments. Both the report itself and a summary journal article written by Ehri et al. (2001) discussed evidence of the effect of phonemic awareness instruction on reading and spelling. The 1990s produced a particularly large number of published studies showing the positive effects of phonemic awareness (NICHD, 2000). Many of the phonemic awareness programs described at the end of this chapter were developed for research carried out during this period (e.g., Blachman et al., 1994; O'Connor, Notari-Syverson, & Vadasy, 1996).

Following is a brief summary of the NRP's findings (NICHD, 2000). Both a short version—*The Summary Report*—as well as the full report—*Reports of the Subgroups*—can be read, downloaded, or ordered through the NRP web site (http://www.national readingpanel.org). There are also print and video materials on this web site for teachers and children.

Is Phonemic Awareness Instruction Effective?

Instruction in phonemic awareness had a positive effect on phonemic awareness itself and on reading and reading comprehension for young children (i.e., pre-K through Grade 1), young children at risk, children speaking English as a second language, and older students with reading disabilities (NICHD, 2000). Effects on spelling were significant for most but not all of these children; older children with reading disabilities did not improve in spelling following phonemic awareness training. This is consistent with what is known about adult dyslexics; spelling can remain a weak area even when reading catches up in response to special instruction. This finding supports the importance of early intervention in phonemic awareness. Using the discrepancy model of identifying children with dyslexia denies them support during this critical period, whereas RTI provides appropriate intervention as soon as the need is clear.

Which Forms of Phonemic Awareness Instruction Are Most Effective?

The NRP (NICHD, 2000) reported that virtually all of the phonemic activities taught (e.g., identifying, segmenting, blending) in these studies produced significant effects on phonemic awareness itself, reading for all children, and spelling for children in pre-K through Grade 1. The most powerful treatments were those focusing on just segmenting and blending rather than on multiple activities. Using letters was another powerful determinate; phonemic awareness instruction involving letters was more effective than instruction using sounds alone. The report noted that phonemic awareness instruction using letters is "the equivalent of invented spelling instruction" (NICHD, 2000, p. 2-41). This integrates the visual and auditory components of reading early in the development of literacy. Although it is possible to develop phonemic awareness on its own, using letters as soon as letter names can be identified moves children toward the alphabetic principle early in phonemic awareness instruction.

How Is Phonemic Awareness Instruction Best Scheduled?

Two factors concerning scheduling phonemic awareness instruction were included in the NRP report (NICHD, 2000): 1) time spent teaching phonemic awareness and 2) instructional grouping. The report suggested that phonemic awareness can be taught to young children in roughly 20 hours or less and in 25- to 30-minute sessions, but recommended that number and length of lessons be planned based on the particular children.

Findings on grouping for phonemic awareness instruction indicated the advantage of small groups over either whole class or one-to-one tutoring (NICHD, 2000). This is surprising considering the long tradition of providing tutoring to children who struggle to read. Another promising finding of the NRP report was that the phonemic awareness instruction provided by classroom teachers was effective. Teachers in these studies averaged 21 hours of professional development in teaching phonemic awareness. Although Moats (1994) and others have found teachers lacking in a solid knowledge base in phonemic awareness, results here indicated that teachers can learn to teach phonemic awareness effectively.

Introducing RTI as a structure for making these decisions supports the NRP's approach to scheduling. It stated that, "Transfer to reading was greatest for studies lasting less than 20 hours" (NICHD, 2000, p. 2-42). In addition:

> Individual children will differ in the amount of training time they need to acquire PA [phonemic awareness]. What is probably most important is to tailor training time to student learning by assessing who has and who has not acquired the skills being taught as training proceeds. Children who are still having trouble should continue PA training whereas those who have learned the skills should move on to other reading and writing instruction (NICHD, 2000, p. 2-42).

Research on Response to Intervention

Much research has focused on RTI. Not all RTI models are the same, and looking for comparison points is complicated. Research issues revolve around the adequacy of classroom instruction, treatment validity, the customized interventions preferred by practitioners versus standardized interventions preferred by policy makers, universal screening, screening cut-point scores, local norms, curriculum-based assessment, progress monitoring, and system outcomes versus student outcomes (Fuchs & Fuchs, 2006; Gersten & Dimino, 2006; Kovaleski, 2007; Kratochwill, Clements, & Kalymon, 2007).

Research dealing with these complex systems is a challenge. Al Otaiba and Torgesen (2007) described a series of seven studies carried out by research teams at Vanderbilt and Florida State Universities that explored the effectiveness of interventions for the lowest 30% of kindergarten and first-grade children. Variables such as adequacy of instruction at each tier plus shifting instructional groups based on response over time make longitudinal research complicated. The seven studies range in intensity from two with low-intensity intervention and implicit classroom instruction to three with high-intensity intervention and implicit classroom instruction, and, finally, to two with high-intensity intervention and explicit classroom instruction. Al Otaiba and Torgesen reported a trend across the seven studies in which the percent of children reading below the 30th percentile decreases as the intensity of instruction increases.

Research on Teachers and Phonemic Awareness

Although there is strong evidence supporting the benefits of direct and intensive phonemic awareness instruction, many teachers are not adept at this sort of language analysis. Teachers are mature, capable readers, and most are not conscious of using the alphabetic principle themselves during reading and do not remember having learned about it in school (Uhry, 2002b; Uhry & Goodman, 2009). Moats (1994, 2010) pointed out that many teacher preparation programs neglect phonemic awareness as a topic for teacher education. Moats stressed the importance of teachers having a firm grasp of the structure of spoken and written language in order to interpret children's **miscues** and present solid examples through which patterns can be taught. For example, even though a teacher may not use terminology with 6-year-olds such as "consonant cluster" for the first two sounds in the word *clip* or "consonant digraph" for the first sound in the word *chin,* these labels will help the teacher conceptualize for him- or herself the idea of listening for two sounds in one case and just one in the other as he or she works with a child trying to sound out and spell a word.

Moats (2010) is highly recommended for anyone teaching phonemic awareness. Research indicates that teachers provided with instruction and supervision in phonemic awareness can increase their own phonemic awareness abilities as well as the phonemic awareness and early reading skills of their students (Spear-Swerling, 2009; Uhry, 2002b; Uhry & Goodman, 2009).

PROGRAMS FOR TEACHING PHONEMIC AWARENESS

There are a number of commercially available curriculum materials for teaching phonemic awareness. Most provide theoretical information as well as a systematic sequence and concrete ideas to use with children. The explicit nature of instruction in many of these materials makes them appropriate for children with dyslexia. Most include activities that could be used in regular classrooms as well.

This section includes programs supported by research in the NRP report (NICHD, 2000) or meeting research standards from the What Works Clearinghouse (http:ies.ed .gov/ncee/wwc/). These programs are all responsive to research in that they tend to move through a common sequence of activities in which the focus moves toward smaller and smaller segments of sound in oral language and in which the sound structure of words is established through oral activities prior to introducing letters.

Wilson Fundations

The *Wilson Reading System* (Wilson, 1988) is an Orton-Gillingham–based, systematic, multisensory remedial reading program that was originally designed for adolescents and adults. *Wilson Fundations* is Wilson's relatively new program (2002) designed with a curriculum for each grade, K–3. *Wilson Fundations* was one of the first commercially available programs structured around RTI. It was designed to be used preventively in whole-class settings for 30-minute lessons that supplement meaning-based reading programs. It is also designed to be used for small-group extension lessons for the 30% of a class that needs extra help and for children who are not responsive to this small-group help and need more intensive individualized instruction. It includes simplified versions of typical Orton-Gillingham lessons (e.g., letter-key-word-sound cards, multisensory tasks such as linking handwriting with **sky writing** and with letter sounds and names). Two particularly appealing materials are Wilson's magnetic letter cards for constructing words on small boards, with one board for each child, and an owl puppet named Echo used for repeating oral material.

Wilson teaches phonemic awareness using letters right from the start. Spelling lessons involve segmenting spoken words into phonemes using a multisensory task in which the word is said aloud and then segmented by tapping. Each phoneme is voiced as the child taps the thumb to one, two, three, or four fingertips and then writes a letter for each tap.

Wilson Fundations is at one extreme in a continuum of programs ranging from fully integrating letters into phonemic awareness instruction to using sound only. Programs such as *Lindamood Phoneme Sequencing Program for Reading, Spelling, and Speech* (Lindamood & Lindamood, 1998) and *Phonemic Awareness in Young Children: A Classroom Curriculum* (Adams et al., 1998) are at the opposite extreme. These programs teach phonemic awareness without letters for an extended period of time and only later begin to link phonemes with letters.

Although *Wilson Fundations* was designed to be used together with meaning-based programs, it includes all five of the literacy components addressed in the NRP report (NICHD, 2000). The program has been reviewed by the Florida Center for Reading Research as having numerous strengths (e.g., systematic, derived from research, flexible regarding grouping) and having no weaknesses.

Ladders to Literacy

Ladders to Literacy: A Preschool Activity Book was designed for young children with special needs but has also been found to be effective for their classmates without disabilities. O'Connor was an early advocate of using phonemic awareness instruction with young children with developmental disabilities, and the effects of her training appear to be particularly long lasting for these children. The materials consist of two activity books, both in their second editions—one for preschool (Notari-Syverson, O'Connor, & Vadasy, 2007) and one for kindergarten (O'Connor, Notari-Syverson, & Vadasy, 2005).

The program was carefully developed based on ongoing research (e.g., O'Connor, Jenkins, & Slocum, 1995; O'Connor et al., 1996, 1998). Program effectiveness is well documented. Several of O'Connor's studies using this instruction are included in the NRP report (NICHD, 2000). Three early experiments reported by O'Connor et al. (1993) meet the What Works Clearinghouse standards.

The program is based on two theoretical constructs: the Vygotskian notion of providing a scaffold or support system to guide children in learning and the notion that cognitive processes such as phonemic awareness play a role in developing reading. *Ladders to Literacy* includes activity books at both the preschool and kindergarten levels. The activity books differ from other idea books in that these provide both a theoretical base and examples of ways in which teachers can support children's learning through questioning and playful materials.

The version for preschool children (Notari-Syverson et al., 2007) is designed to be developmentally appropriate and encourage emergent literacy in a print-rich environment. Activities involve direct instruction, can be used for groups or individuals, and are designed to be integrated into existing curricula. The curriculum begins with representational play and picture books and has sections on print and book awareness, metalinguistic skills (including phonological awareness), and oral language development. Preschool phonemic awareness activities include reciting nursery rhymes and changing the end rhymes, clapping syllables, drawing pictures of multisyllabic words and cutting the pictures apart to reassemble syllable by syllable (e.g., drawing a dinosaur and then cutting the picture into three parts), and listening for onsets in words with target sounds of the week. For each of these and many other activities, low, medium, and high levels of support are outlined as a guide for teachers to meet the needs of all individuals.

Ladders to Literacy: A Kindergarten Activity Book (O'Connor et al., 1998, 2005) follows a similar format, with sections on print awareness, phonemic awareness, and oral language. Phonemic awareness activities overlap with those in the preschool book, but the end of the activity book includes sound matching, blending, and three-phoneme segmentation and incorporates the use of letters associated with sounds. As with the preschool book, teachers are guided through the possible difficulties of various task demands so that instruction can be made appropriate for each child.

Lindamood Phoneme Sequencing Program

Patricia and Charles H. Lindamood's program, *Auditory Discrimination in Depth* (ADD; 1975) is based on the Lindamoods' backgrounds in linguistics and speech-language pathology. The ADD program was revised by Patricia and Phyllis Lindamood, and its third edition was renamed the *Lindamood Phoneme Sequencing Program for Reading, Spelling, and Speech* (LiPS; 1998). The distinguishing characteristic of the program continues to be its early focus on drawing a student's attention to the oral-motor processes used in articulating phonemes.

Special names describe the multisensory aspects of phoneme production. For example, the voiced and unvoiced **labiodental fricatives** /v/ and /f/ are called Lip Coolers, with the former the Noisy Brother, or voiced phoneme, and the latter the Quiet Brother, or **unvoiced** phoneme. Training involves helping students identify phoneme sounds by matching them with photographs of the lips, teeth, and tongue engaged in articulatory gestures. Changes in spoken words are analyzed or tracked as single-phoneme changes occur, first with the mouth pictures and later with colored blocks. For example, the teacher sets up a sequence of colored blocks (blue, red, green) and says, "That's *zab*; show me *zaf*." The student exchanges the green block for a white one and responds, "The Lip Popper is gone and a Lip Cooler took its place" (Lindamood & Lindamood, 1998, p. 12). This involves phoneme manipulation, which is Adams's (1990) highest level of phonemic awareness. Also, letters are not yet associated with instruction at this point in LiPS.

Once complex word structures such as CCVCC words (e.g., *stand*) can be segmented and manipulated, then lettered tiles are introduced for segmenting and spelling real words. Spelling instruction leads to reading instruction using lettered tiles and eventually to printed text, consistent with the Lindamoods' notion that speech should precede written work. Letter–sound associations are introduced in a carefully sequenced plan, and a set of readers is available for practicing reading. Word reading is done through a careful analysis of letter–sound correspondences, in the Orton-Gillingham tradition, with the focus initially on accuracy and later on fluency. DVDs and a CD-ROM provide support for the teacher.

The Lindamood program (1975, 1998) was used by Torgesen, Wagner, Rashotte, Alexander, and Conway (1997) in an NICHD-funded longitudinal intervention study with first-grade children in Florida who were at risk. Another Torgesen study, which met the What Works Clearinghouse research standards (i.e., random assignment, control group), found LiPS to have a positive effect on tasks measured by two CTOPP subtests, phoneme **elision** and phoneme segmentation (Torgesen, Wagner, Rashotte, & Heron, 2003).

Phonemic Awareness in Young Children: A Classroom Curriculum

Lundberg's phonemic awareness program, reported in a study that is considered seminal research (Lundberg et al., 1988), was developed for and used successfully with Danish kindergarten children. An English-language version was used in a Houston, Texas, kindergarten class where Foorman, Francis, Beeler, Winikates, and Fletcher (1997) carried out a successful intervention project funded by the NICHD. Again, there is strong evidence that this program increases phonemic skills.

This phonemic awareness training program, which was subsequently published as *Phonemic Awareness in Young Children: A Classroom Curriculum* (Adams et al., 1998), is designed for kindergarten and first-grade classrooms and consists of a carefully sequenced hierarchy of games and activities. The sequence is arranged by chapters that focus on the following:

1. *Listening games:* Children are encouraged to listen selectively to environmental sounds, including the human voice, and follow directions.

2. *Rhyming:* Children listen to and generate rhymes in order to become sensitive to the sound structure of words.

3. *Sentences and words:* This chapter includes activities for segmenting sentences into words.

4. *Syllables*: Children segment words into syllables and blend syllables into words.

5. *Initial and final sounds:* Initial and final phonemes are segmented and blended in short, linguistically simple words.

6. *Phonemes*: At this level, all phonemes in a word are segmented.

7. *Letters*: Phonemes are represented by letters to provide support for understanding the alphabetic principle.

Unlike many commercially available collections of ideas, there is sufficient theory throughout to enable a teacher to use the guide to plan his or her own program. A sample day-by-day schedule is included for both kindergarten and first grade in order to help teachers select and repeat activities from the suggested sequence. The theoretical material is an exemplary feature of this program guide.

The activities are playful, child centered, and developmentally appropriate (e.g., clapping, dancing, whispering, tossing balls back and forth). Rhythmic dance and movement activities introduce a kinesthetic element to some of the early listening games.

Later, children pull mystery objects from a box and then clap the syllables in the objects' names or guess classmates' names after listening to the teacher say the initial phoneme. Each activity is explained carefully not only in terms of procedures but also in terms of its linguistic features and possible pitfalls. The linguistic features of words have been carefully considered in planning the instructional sequences, and numerous word lists are included for playing the games at each level. Teachers are provided with clear guidelines for deciding when to move on to harder activities. Most of the games have variations so that children needing additional work at a particular level can be provided with extension activities.

Phonological Awareness Training for Reading

Torgesen and Bryant (1994) developed the *Phonological Awareness Training for Reading* program out of several research projects seeking to identify those components of phonological awareness that would most effectively increase reading-related skills in beginning readers. Torgesen and his colleagues at Florida State University carried out a training study using these materials in which they demonstrated that both analytic and synthetic phonological skills were advantageous in learning to read (Torgesen, Morgan, & Davis, 1992). In a second study (Torgesen & Davis, 1993), a revised program was used with minority children at risk for reading difficulty because of low phonemic awareness skills. These children outperformed controls on phonemic awareness tasks immediately after training in kindergarten and on a second testing early in first grade.

The program uses activities from a number of sources, including classroom teachers, and has been validated by research carried out by Torgesen and others in the field. It is designed for use with individuals or with small groups. It can be used during the second semester of kindergarten or for older children who are at risk during first or second grade. The program is planned to last a semester when used in short sessions four times a week. There are four phases to the program:

1. *Warm-up activities: Rhyming*—This short, introductory phase introduces the idea of listening to sounds through rhyming games and activities. The program includes sets of cards to match (e.g., pictures of an egg and a leg). The authors stress that the purpose of the activities should be made clear to the participants.

2. *Phonological training activities: Blending*—Children begin by blending onsets and rimes (e.g., blending the phoneme /k/ with the rime unit /at/) and then later blend all three phonemes in short words (e.g., /k/-/a/-/t/ blended into /kat/). This leads into segmenting the initial phoneme in a word.

3. *Phonological training activities: Segmenting*—Phoneme segmentation activities use a sequence moving from initial to final to middle phonemes in words. Segmentation training also progresses from matching by phoneme to actually segmenting the phoneme in each of the three positions. There is a focus on awareness of the feeling experienced in the mouth as various sounds are produced, and children are asked to listen for differences between voiced and unvoiced consonants.

4. *Phonological training activities: Reading and spelling*—Letters are introduced to represent phonemes in Level 4 activities for both reading and spelling. Letters are used to help children manipulate the sounds in words as in the following example from the manual in which the teacher uses letter cards to spell a word and then asks the children to change the letters to spell a second word. "This is the word *top*, /t/-/o/-/p/. What letter should we change to write the word *mop?*" (Torgesen & Bryant, 1994, p. 25).

Phonological Awareness Training for Reading (Torgesen & Bryant, 1994) includes a teacher's manual, game parts, and an audiotape. The game parts involve small pictures that can be used to play the games described in the manual. For example, a child says "cap" while looking at a picture of a cap, and then the teacher points to one of three blocks in a line and asks which sound it is (e.g., /k/ for the first block in *cap*). The audiotape provides sample pronunciations for words segmented into onsets and rimes and into all phonemic segments.

Reading Readiness

The Neuhaus Education Center in Houston, Texas, is an educational foundation that offers training to teachers in reading instruction. The center uses Alphabetic Phonics (see Uhry & Clark, 2005) as a remedial program and as the basis of beginning reading and spelling instruction in general education classes. In 1992, Benita Blachman presented a workshop at the center on the importance of phonemic awareness, and following this, center staff developed the *Reading Readiness* program for younger children (Carreker, 2002).

Reading Readiness (Carreker, 2002) involves many of the elements of Alphabetic Phonics lessons and includes phonemic awareness activities. The program can be used in the early grades. It begins with daily lessons in letter recognition and sequencing, phonemic awareness, and oral language skills. Once letter recognition and phonemic awareness are mastered, the lesson is extended from 20 to 30 minutes by adding hand-writing and multisensory sound–symbol activities. Phonemic awareness activities, such as the following examples from the program (Carreker, 2002), are presented in a se-quence based on research.

1. Rhyming activities are presented at the initial level (e.g., "Do *go* and *top* rhyme? Find a rhyme for *cat*").

2. Awareness of words in sentences and syllables in compound and multisyllabic words is taught through clapping and counting activities.

3. Initial sound awareness is taught through attention to lip movements (e.g., "As I say *monkey,* what happens to my mouth? When I say the word *many,* what happens to my mouth? Are my lips together when I start to say each word?")

4. Phoneme segmentation is taught through a series of activities based on Ball and Blachman's (1991) Say-It-and-Move-It technique in which markers representing phonemes are moved from a picture down to a line below in left-to-right order.

5. Segmenting and spelling are taught once students have learned sound–symbol as-sociations. The phoneme segmentation activities are extended by segmenting and then using lettered markers to spell pictured words with simple CVC constructions, such as *mop.* This activity is similar to one first introduced by Elkonin (1963, 1973).

Road to the Code: A Phonological Awareness Program for Young Children

Road to the Code: A Phonological Awareness Program for Young Children was written by Blachman et al. (2000) as a teacher's guide for some of the activities used by the au-thors in their research with young readers. It is an 11-week sequence of 44 lessons for small groups or individuals in kindergarten and first grade. Although designed for chil-dren who need extra help in early literacy, the program would be beneficial in any class-room of emergent or beginning readers. Each lesson is constructed around three activities.

1. Say-It-and-Move-It is a phoneme segmentation game in which tiles representing phonemes are moved from a picture down onto an arrow pointing from left to right. The tiles are placed on the arrow in the order in which the children hear the teacher say them. Early in the program, sounds are said in isolation (e.g., /t/-/t/, /a/-/t/). Later, words are said so that children need to segment them into phonemes. Eventually, lettered tiles are used so that segmenting becomes spelling.

2. Letter Name and Sound Instruction involves large cards with letters and pictures (e.g., a vampire playing a violin while lying across the top of a large *v*). The teacher instructs the sound directly, helps the children identify the pictures, and then en-courages them to generate other words with the sound. Later lessons involve re-view through clapping games and chants.

3. Phonological Awareness Practice is carried out through a series of games, songs, and read-alouds designed to focus on sounds in words. For example, a set of sound

categorization cards can be photocopied from the book and used in a singing game to find the card whose sound does not match the others. The words *hat, cat,* and *bat* all rhyme, and *jug* does not. In another game, pictures are "mailed" or sorted by initial sound into paper bags called "mailboxes."

Words Their Way: Word Study for Phonics, Vocabulary, and Spelling Instruction

Bear et al. (2008) developed *Words Their Way: Word Study for Phonics, Vocabulary, and Spelling Instruction* (4th edition) as an outgrowth of their work as students with Edmund Henderson at the University of Virginia. The program is based on the constructivist notion that sorting by attributes is a form of cognitive problem solving. This is the same rationale that was used in the seminal Bradley and Bryant study (1983) in which phonemic odd-man-out tasks were used to teach phonemic awareness. Sounds are represented by letters very early, which is also consistent with the findings of Bradley and Bryant. Two other features of *Words Their Way* have been mentioned earlier in this chapter. One is using developmental spelling levels for grouping emergent readers for instruction (Morris 1983, 1993, 2005). The other is finger-point reading to teach concept of word. Both of these procedures have been researched extensively (Ehri & Sweet, 1991; Morris, 1983, 1993; Morris et al., 2003; Uhry, 1999, 2002a).

Words Their Way is designed for K–8 classrooms with instruction organized around what the authors call, "the braid of literacy," which consists of orthography, reading, writing, oral language, and stories. These components are all instructed from the beginning, but focus on the components shifts over time as children move through five developmental spelling stages (prephonetic, letter name, within word orthographic patterns, syllables and affixes, and derivational spelling). The instructional focus in Stage 2 is alphabet knowledge and phonemic awareness. Sorting games at this level includes sorting pictures by rhymes, initial sounds, and final sounds, with letters used to organize the sorts. The manual includes materials for this. For example, there are pages of pictures to be photocopied and cut out so that each child can be given a plastic bag with cut-out sortables. A CD-ROM that comes with the manual demonstrates variations on word sorts for multiple purposes.

There is a supplementary book of additional sortables for each level of the program, including one titled *Words Their Way: Letter and Picture Sorts for Emergent Spellers* (Bear, Invernizzi, Johnston, & Templeton, 2006), which is suitable for kindergarten and early first grade. The next level, *Words Their Way: Word Sorts for Letter Name—Alphabetic Spellers* (Johnston, Bear, Invernizzi, & Templeton, 2009), includes sorting tasks at Chall's (1983) Stage 1. Each lesson follows a systematic routine: 1) demonstration by the teacher, 2) sort and check by each child using his or her own sort materials, 3) reflection on the lesson guided by teacher questioning (e.g., "Explain why you sorted this way," "What's alike in this category"), and 4) independent practice through extensions such as games. Materials at this stage include pictures for sorting by rhyme, onset, and final consonant. Children's literature is incorporated as a vehicle for oral language development and then integrated into letter and sound study through games and exercises. Familiar books and poems are used for teaching concept of word through modeling, touching each word in a story as the teacher—and later, the student—reads it aloud. Another supplementary text is for children learning English as a second language (Bear, Helman, Invernizzi, Templeton, & Johnston, 2006).

SUMMARY

Research demonstrates a strong link between children's early abilities in phonemic awareness and their later reading skills. Children with dyslexia are apt to have phonological processing deficits that are causal to their word-reading deficits. Extensive research, including meta-analyses, demonstrates the powerful effect of phonemic awareness training on reading and spelling, especially when the prevention or early intervention takes place in pre-K through second grade. A number of phonemic awareness programs are commercially available and share the following principles derived from the research literature and mentioned in the recommendations of the NRP report (NICHD, 2000).

- Teach phonemic awareness systematically and explicitly rather than implicitly and informally.

- Teach phonemic awareness using a sequence from easier to more difficult phonemic awareness tasks as in Adams's (1990) research-based hierarchy.

- Teach with awareness that some phonemes are linguistically easier to identify than others. For example, /m/ is a continuant and easier to identify than stop consonants (e.g., /p/, /t/).

- Once children know letter names, teach letter–sound associations explicitly and phonemic awareness using letters to represent sounds.

- Link phonemic awareness activities to reading and writing.

- Use the principles of RTI in planning for grouping and intensity of instruction.

- Teachers need to continue to develop their own phonemic awareness skills through ongoing professional development.

REFERENCES

Adams, M.J. (1990). *Beginning to read: Thinking and learning about print.* Cambridge, MA: The MIT Press.

Adams, M.J. (1994). Phonics and beginning reading instruction. In R. Lehr & J. Osborn (Eds.), *Reading, language, and literacy* (pp. 1–23). Mahwah, NJ: Lawrence Erlbaum Associates.

Adams, M.J., Foorman, B.R., Lundberg, I., & Beeler, T. (1998). *Phonemic awareness in young children: A classroom curriculum.* Baltimore: Paul H. Brookes Publishing Co.

Al Otaiba, S., & Torgesen, J. (2007). Effects from intensive standardized kindergarten and first-grade interventions for the prevention of reading difficulties. In S.R. Jimerson, M.K. Burns, & A.M. Van Der Heyden (Eds.), *Handbook of response to intervention: The science and practice of assessment and intervention* (pp. 212–222). New York: Springer.

American Academy of Pediatrics, (2009, August). Learning disabilities, dyslexia, and vision. *Pediatrics, 124*(2), 837–844.

Ball, E.W., & Blachman, B.A. (1991). Does phoneme segmentation training in kindergarten make a difference in early word recognition and developmental spelling? *Reading Research Quarterly, 26,* 49–66.

Bear, D.R., Helman, L.R., Invernizzi, M., Templeton, S., & Johnston, F. (2006) *Words their way for English learners: Word study for phonics, vocabulary, and spelling instruction.* Upper Saddle River, NJ: Pearson.

Bear, D.R., Invernizzi, M., Johnston, F., & Templeton, S. (2006). *Words their way: Letter and picture sorts for emergent spellers* (2nd ed.). Upper Saddle River, NJ: Pearson.

Bear, D.R., Invernizzi, M., Templeton, S., & Johnston, F. (2008). *Words their way: Word study for phonics, vocabulary, and spelling instruction* (4th ed.). Upper Saddle River, NJ: Pearson.

Blachman, B.A., Ball, E.W., Black, R.S., & Tangel, D.M. (1994). Kindergarten teachers develop phoneme awareness in low-income, inner-city classrooms: Does it make a difference? *Reading and Writing: An Interdisciplinary Journal, 6,* 1–18.

Blachman, B.A., Ball, E.W., Black, R., & Tangel, D.M. (2000). *Road to the code: A phonological awareness program for young children.* Baltimore: Paul H. Brookes Publishing Co.

Blachman, B., Schatschneider, C., Fletcher, J.M., Francis, D.J., Clonan, S., Shaywitz, B.A., et al. (2004). Effects of intensive reading remediation for second and third graders and a one year follow-up. *Journal of Educational Psychology, 96,* 444–461.

Blumstein, S.E., Myers, E.B., & Rissman, J. (2005). The perception of voice onset time: An fMRI investigation of phonetic category structure. *Journal of Cognitive Neuroscience, 17*(9), 1353–1366.

Bradley, L., & Bryant, P.E. (1983). Categorizing sounds and learning to read: A causal connection. *Nature, 301,* 419–421.

Bradley, L., & Bryant, P.E. (1985). *Rhyme and reason in reading and spelling.* Ann Arbor: University of Michigan Press.

Carreker, S. (2002). *Reading readiness.* Bellaire, TX: Neuhaus Education Center.

Catts, H.W. (1986). Speech production/ phonological deficits in reading disordered children. *Journal of Learning Disabilities, 19,* 504–508.

Catts, H.W. (1989). Defining dyslexia as a developmental language disorder. *Annals of Dyslexia, 39,* 50–64.

Catts, H.W. (1993). The relationship between speech-language impairments and reading disabilities. *Journal of Speech and Hearing Research, 36,* 948–958.

Chall, J.S. (1983). *Stages of reading development.* New York: McGraw-Hill.

Chall, J., Roswell, F.G., & Blumenthal, S.H. (1963). Auditory blending ability: A factor in success in beginning reading. *The Reading Teacher, 17,* 113–118.

DeFries, J.C., Filipek, P.A., Fulker, D.W., Olson, R.K., Pennington, B.F., Smith, S.D., et al. (1997). Colorado learning disabilities center. *Learning Disabilities: A Multidisciplinary Journal, 8,* 7–19.

Denckla, M.B., & Rudel, R.G. (1974). Rapid "automatized" naming of pictured objects, colors, letters, and numbers by normal children. *Cortex, 10,* 186–202.

Ehri, L.C. (2005). Learning to read words: Theories, findings, and issues. *Scientific Studies of Reading, 9,* 165–188.

Ehri, L.C. (2007). Development of sight word reading: Phases and findings. In M.J. Snowling & C. Hulme (Eds.), *The science of reading: A handbook* (pp. 135–154). Maldon, MA: Blackwell Publishing.

Ehri, L.C., & McCormick, S. (1998). Phases of word learning: Implications for instruction with delayed and disabled readers. *Reading and Writing Quarterly, 14,* 135–163.

Ehri, L.C., Nunes, S.R., Willows, D.M., Schuster, B.V., Yaghoub-Zadeh, Z., & Shanahan, T. (2001). Phonemic awareness instruction helps children learn to read: Evidence from the National Reading Panel's meta-analysis. *Reading Research Quarterly, 36,* 250–287.

Ehri, L.C., & Sweet, J. (1991). Fingerpoint-reading of memorized text: What enables beginners to process the print? *Reading Research Quarterly, 26,* 442–462.

Ehri, L.C., & Wilce, L.C. (1987). Does learning to spell help beginners learn to read words? *Reading Research Quarterly, 18,* 47–65.

Elkonin, D.B. (1963). The psychology of mastering the elements of reading. In B. Simon & J. Simon (Eds.), *Educational Psychology in the U.S.S.R.* (pp. 165–179). London: Routledge & Kegan Paul.

Elkonin, D.B. (1973). U.S.S.R. In J. Downing (Ed.), *Comparative reading* (pp. 551–579). New York: Macmillan.

Felton, R.H., & Wood, F.B. (1989). Cognitive deficits in reading disability and attention deficit disorder. *Journal of Learning Disabilities, 22,* 3–13

Foorman, B.R., Francis, D.J., Beeler, T., Winikates, D., & Fletcher, J.M. (1997). Early interventions for children with reading problems: Study designs and preliminary findings. *Learning Disabilities: A Multidisciplinary Journal, 8,* 63–71.

Frith, U. (1986). A developmental framework for developmental dyslexia. *Annals of Dyslexia, 36,* 69–81.

Frost, S.J., Landi, N., Mencl, W.E., Sandak, R., Fulbright, R.K., Tejada, E.T., et al. (2009, March). Phonological awareness predicts activation patterns for print and speech. *Annals of Dyslexia, 59*(1), 78–97.

Fuchs, D., & Fuchs, L. (2006). Introduction to response to intervention: What, why, and how valid is it? *Reading Research Quarterly, 41*(1), 93–99.

Fuchs, D., Fuchs, L.S., & Vaughn, S. (Eds.). (2008). *Response to intervention: A framework for reading educators.* Newark, DE: International Reading Association.

Gersten, R., & Dimino, J. (2006). RTI (response to intervention): Rethinking special education for students with reading difficulties (yet again). *Reading Research Quarterly, 41,* 99–108.

Good, R.H., & Kaminski, R.A. (Eds.). (2002). *Dynamic Indicators of Basic Early Literacy Skills* (6th ed.). Eugene, OR: Institute for the Development of Educational Achievement.

Good, R.H., & Kaminski, R.A. (Eds.). (2004). *DIBELS training manual: Catch them before they fall.* Tallahassee: Florida Center for Reading Research.

Gough, P.B., & Hillinger, M.L. (1980). Learning to read: An unnatural act. *Bulletin of the Orton Society, 20,* 179–196.

Haager, D., Klingner, J., & Vaughn, S. (Eds.). (2007). *Evidence-based reading practices for response to intervention.* Baltimore: Paul H. Brooks Publishing Co.

Hohn, W.E., & Ehri, L.C. (1983). Do alphabet letters help prereaders acquire phonemic segmentation skill? *Journal of Educational Psychology, 75,* 752–762.

Individuals with Disabilities Education Improvement Act (IDEA) of 2004, PL 108-446, 20 U.S.C. §§ 1400 *et seq.*

Invernizzi, M., Juel, C., Swank, L., & Meier, J. (2005). *Phonological Awareness Screening Test (PALS)—Kindergarten.* Charlottesville: University of Virginia Printing Services.

Invernizzi, M., Meier, J., & Juel, C. (2005). *Phonological Awareness Screening Test (PALS)—1–3.* Charlottesville: University of Virginia Printing Services.

Invernizzi, M., Sullivan, A., Meier, J., & Swank, L. (2004). *Phonological Awareness Screening Test (PALS)—Pre-K.* Charlottesville: University of Virginia Printing Services.

Johnston, F., Bear, D.R., Invernizzi, M., & Templeton, S. (2009). *Words their way: Word sorts for letter name-alphabetic spellers* (2nd ed.). Boston: Allyn & Bacon.

Kaminski, R.A., & Good, R.H. (1996). Toward a technology for assessing basic early literacy skills. *School Psychology Review, 25,* 215–227.

Kovaleski, J.F. (2007). Potential pitfalls of response to intervention. In S.R. Jimerson, M.K. Burns, & A.M. Van Der Heyden (Eds.), *Handbook of response to intervention: The science and practice of assessment and intervention* (pp. 80–89). New York: Springer.

Kratochwill, T.R., Clements, M.A., & Kalymon, K.M. (2007). Response to intervention: Conceptual and methodologic issues in implementation. In S.R. Jimerson, M.K. Burns, & A.M. Van Der Heyden (Eds.), *Handbook of response to intervention: The science and practice of assessment and intervention* (pp. 25–52). New York: Springer.

Lindamood, C.H., & Lindamood, P.C. (1975). *The ADD program: Auditory discrimination in depth: Books 1 and 2.* Austin, TX: PRO-ED.

Lindamood, C.H., & Lindamood, P.C. (2004). *Lindamood-Bell Auditory Conceptualization Test–Third Edition (LAC-3).* Austin, TX: PRO-ED.

Lindamood, P., & Lindamood, P. (1998). *The Lindamood phoneme sequencing program for reading, spelling, and speech: Teacher's manual for the classroom and clinic* (3rd ed.). Austin, TX: PRO-ED.

Lundberg, I., Frost, J., & Petersen, O.P. (1988). Effects of an extensive program for stimulating phonological awareness in preschool children. *Reading Research Quarterly, 23,* 263–284.

Lyon, G.R., Shaywitz, S.E., & Shaywitz, B.A. (2003). A definition of dyslexia. *Annals of Dyslexia, 53,* 1–14.

Maclean, M., Bryant, P.E., & Bradley, L. (1987). Rhymes, nursery rhymes, and reading in early childhood. *Merrill-Palmer Quarterly, 33,* 255–281.

Moats, L.C. (1994). The missing foundation in teacher education: Knowledge of the structure of spoken and written language. *Annals of Dyslexia, 44,* 81–102.

Moats, L.C. (2005). How spelling supports reading: And why it is more regular and predictable than you may think. *The American Educator, 12*(22), 12–43.

Moats, L.C. (2010). *Speech to print: Language essentials for teachers* (2nd ed.). Baltimore: Paul H. Brookes Publishing Co.

Morris, D. (1983). Concept of word and phoneme awareness in the beginning reader. *Research in the Teaching of English, 17,* 359–373.

Morris, D. (1993). The relationship between children's concept of word in text and phoneme awareness in learning to read: A longitudinal study. *Research in the Teaching of English, 27,* 133–153.

Morris, D. (2005). *The Howard Street tutoring manual: Teaching at-risk readers in the primary grades* (2nd ed.). New York: Guilford Press.

Morris, D., Bloodgood, J.W., Lomax, R.G., & Perney, J. (2003). Developmental steps in learning to read: A longitudinal study in kindergarten and first grade. *Reading Research Quarterly, 38,* 302–328.

Morris, D., & Perney, J. (1984). Developmental spelling as a predictor of first-grade reading achievement. *The Elementary School Journal, 84,* 441–457.

Myers, E.B., Blumstein, S.E., Walsh, E., & Eliassen, J. (2009). Inferior frontal regions underlie the perception of phonetic category invariance. *Psychological Science, 20*(7) 895–903.

National Institute of Child Health and Human Development. (2000). *Report of the National Reading Panel: Reports of the subgroups. Teaching children to read: An evidence-based assessment of the scientific research literature on reading and its implications for reading instruction* (NIH Publication No. 00-4754). Washington, DC: Government Printing Office.

Notari-Syverson, A., O'Connor, R.E., & Vadasy, P.F. (2007). *Ladders to literacy: A preschool activity book* (2nd ed.). Baltimore: Paul H. Brookes Publishing Co.

O'Connor, R.E., Jenkins, J.R., Leicester, N., & Slocum, T.A. (1993). Teaching phonological awareness to young children with learning disabilities. *Exceptional Children, 59*(6), 532–546.

O'Connor, R., Jenkins, J., & Slocum, T. (1995). Transfer among phonological tasks in kindergarten: Essential instructional content. *Journal of Educational Psychology, 87,* 202–217.

O'Connor, R., Notari-Syverson, A., & Vadasy, P. (1996). Ladders to literacy: The effects of teacher-led phonological activities for kindergarten children with and without disabilities. *Exceptional Children, 63,* 117–130.

O'Connor, R., Notari-Syverson, A., & Vadasy, P. (1998). First-grade effects of teacher-led phonological activities in kindergarten for children with mild disabilities: A follow-up study. *Learning Disabilities Research and Practice, 13,* 43–52.

O'Connor, R.E., Notari-Syverson, A., & Vadasy, P.F. (2005). *Ladders to literacy: A kindergarten activity book* (2nd ed.). Baltimore: Paul H. Brookes Publishing Co.

Papanicolaou, A.C., Pugh, K.R., Simos, P.G., & Mencl, W.E. (2004). Functional brain imaging: An introduction to concepts and application. In P. McCardle & V. Chhabra (Eds.), *The voice of evidence in reading research* (pp. 385–416). Baltimore: Paul H. Brookes Publishing Co.

Rack, J.P., Snowling, M.J., & Olson, R.K. (1992). The nonword reading deficit in developmental dyslexia: A review. *Reading Research Quarterly, 27,* 28–53.

Riedel, B.W. (2007). The relationship between DIBELS, reading comprehension, and vocabulary in urban first-grade students. *Reading Research Quarterly, 42*(4), 546–567.

Rosner, J. (1975). *Helping children overcome learning difficulties.* New York: Walker & Co.

Rosner, J. (1999). *Phonological Awareness Skills Program.* Austin, TX: PRO-ED.

Roswell, F., & Chall, J. (1963). *Roswell-Chall Auditory Blending Test.* Cambridge, MA: Educators Publishing Service.

Roswell, F., & Chall, J. (1997). *Roswell-Chall Auditory Blending Test.* Cambridge, MA: Educators Publishing Service.

Share, D., Jorm, A., Maclean, R., & Matthews, R. (1984). Sources of individual differences in reading acquisition. *Journal of Educational Psychology, 76,* 1309–1324.

Shaywitz, B.A., Shaywitz, S.E., Blachman, B.A., Pugh, K.R., Fulbright, R.K., Skudlarski, P., et al. (2004). Development of left occipitotemporal systems for skilled reading in children after a phonologically-based intervention. *Biological Psychiatry, 55,* 926–933.

Shaywitz, S. (2003). *Overcoming dyslexia: A new and complete science-based program for reading problems at any level.* New York: Alfred A. Knopf.

Shaywitz, S.E., Fletcher, J.M., & Shaywitz, B.A. (1996). A conceptual model and definition of dyslexia: Findings emerging from the Connecticut Longitudinal Study. In J.H. Beitchman, N. Cohen, M.M. Konstantareas, & R. Tannock (Eds.), *Language, learning and behavior disorders* (pp. 199–223). New York: Cambridge University Press.

Shaywitz, S.E., & Shaywitz, B.A. (2004). Neurobiologic basis for reading and reading disability. In P. McCardle & V. Chhabra (Eds.), *The voice of evidence in reading research* (pp. 417–442). Baltimore: Paul H. Brookes Publishing Co.

Snow, C.E., Burns, M.S., & Griffin, P. (Eds.). (1998). *Preventing reading difficulties in young children.* Washington, DC: National Academies Press.

Spear-Swerling, L. (2009). A literacy tutoring experience for prospective special educators. *Journal of Learning Disabilities, 42*(5), 431–443.

Stahl, S.A., & Murray, B.A. (1994). Defining phonological awareness and its relationship to early reading. *Journal of Educational Psychology, 86*(2), 221–234.

Stanovich, K.E. (1986). Matthew effects in reading: Some consequences of individual differences in the acquisition of literacy. *Reading Research Quarterly, 21,* 360–406.

Torgesen, J.K., & Bryant, B.R. (1994). *Phonological awareness training for reading.* Austin, TX: PRO-ED.

Torgesen, J.K., & Davis, C. (1993, April). Individual difference variables that predict response to training in phonological awareness. In R. Wagner (Chair), *Does phonological awareness training enhance children's acquisition of written language skills?* Symposium conducted at the annual meeting of the American Educational Research Association, Atlanta, GA.

Torgesen, J.K., Morgan, S., & Davis, C. (1992). The effects of two types of phonological awareness training on word learning in kindergarten children. *Journal of Educational Psychology, 84,* 364–370.

Torgesen, J.K., Wagner, R.K., Rashotte, C.A., Alexander, A.W., & Conway, T. (1997). Preventive and remedial interventions for children with severe reading disabilities. *Learning Disabilities: A Multidisciplinary Journal, 8,* 51–61.

Torgesen, J.K., Wagner, R.K., Rashotte, C.A., & Herron, J. (2003). Summary of outcomes from first grade study with Read, Write, and Type and Auditory Discrimination In Depth instruction and software with at-risk children (FCRR Tech. Rep. Num. 2).

Treiman, R. (1985). Onsets and rimes as units of spoken syllables: Evidence from children. *Journal of Experimental Child Psychiatry, 39,* 161–181.

Uhry, J.K. (1997). Case studies of dyslexia: Young readers with rapid serial naming deficits. In R.M. Joshi & C.K. Leong (Eds.), *Cross-language studies of learning to read and spell: Phonological and orthographic processing* (pp. 71–88). Dordrecht, Netherlands: Kluwer Academic.

Uhry, J.K. (2002a). Finger-point reading in kindergarten: The role of phonemic awareness, one-to-one correspondence, and rapid serial naming. *Scientific Studies of Reading, 6*(4), 319–342.

Uhry, J.K. (2002b, June). *The relationship between teachers' knowledge of phonology and their grade 1 students' progress in reading and phonemic awareness.* Paper presented at the annual meeting of the Society for the Scientific Study of Reading, Chicago.

Uhry, J.K., & Clark, D.B. (2005). *Dyslexia: Theory and practice of instruction.* Timonium, MD: York Press.

Uhry, J.K., & Ehri, L.C. (1999). Ease of segmenting two- and three-phoneme words in kindergarten: Rime cohesion or vowel salience? *Journal of Educational Psychology, 91,* 594–603.

Uhry, J.K., & Goodman, N.E. (2009). University-school partnerships in urban classrooms: Professional development in applying reading research to practice. In S. Rosenfield & V. Berninger (Eds.), *Implementing evidence-based interventions in school settings* (pp. 627–654). New York: Oxford University Press.

Uhry, J.K., & Shepherd, M.J. (1993). Segmentation/spelling instruction as part of a first grade reading program: Effects on several measures of reading. *Reading Research Quarterly, 28,* 218–233.

Vaughn, S., Wanzek, J., Woodruff, A.L., & Linan-Thompson, S. (2007). Prevention and early identification of students with reading disabilities: A research review of the three-tier model. In D. Haager, J. Klingner, & S. Vaughn (Eds.), *Evidence-based reading practices for response to intervention.* Baltimore: Paul H. Brookes Publishing Co.

Vellutino, F.R., Scanlon, D.M., & Zhang, H. (2007). Identifying reading disability based on response to intervention: Evidence from early intervention research. In S.R. Jimerson, M.K. Burns, & A.M. Van Der Heyden (Eds.), *The handbook of response to intervention: The science and practice of assessment and intervention* (pp. 185–211). New York: Springer Science.

Wagner, R.K., Muse, A.E., Stein, T.L. Cukrowicz, K.C., Harrell, E.R., Rashote, C.A., et al. (2003). How to assess reading-related phonological abilities. In B.R. Foorman (Ed.), *Preventing and remediating reading difficulties: Bringing science to scale.* Baltimore: York Press.

Wagner, R.K., & Torgesen, J.K. (1987). The nature of phonological processing and its causal role in the acquisition of reading skills. *Psychological Bulletin, 101,* 192–212.

Wagner, R.K., Torgesen, J.K., & Rashotte, C. (1999). *Comprehensive Test of Phonological Processing (CTOPP).* Austin, TX: PRO-ED.

Wilson, B.A. (1988). *Wilson Reading System: Teacher's guide and student material.* Oxford, MA: Wilson Language Training. (Available from the publisher http://www.wilsonlanguage.com)

Wilson, B.A. (2002). *Wilson Fundations (Levels K, 1, 2, 3): Teacher's guide and student material.* Oxford, MA: Wilson Language Training. (Available from the publisher. http://www.wilsonlanguage.com)

Wolf, M. (1991). Naming speed and reading: The contribution of the cognitive neurosciences. *Reading Research Quarterly, 26,* 123–141.

Wolff, P.H., Michel, G.F., & Ovrut, M. (1990). The timing of syllable repetitions in developmental dyslexia. *Journal of Speech and Hearing Research, 33,* 281–289.

Wood, F.B., & Felton, R.H. (1994). Separate linguistic and attentional factors in the development of reading. *Topics in Language Disorders, 14,* 42–57.

Yopp, H.K. (1988). The validity and reliability of phonemic awareness tests. *Reading Research Quarterly, 23*(2), 159–177.

6

Alphabet Knowledge

Letter Recognition, Naming, and Sequencing

KAY A. ALLEN with
GRAHAM F. NEUHAUS
AND MARILYN BECKWITH

Letters make reading possible. Letters are those abstract visual symbols that bridge the gap between oral and written alphabetic languages. Awareness of the alphabetic principle, that letters represent sounds of spoken language, is essential for learning to read in any alphabetic language (Chall, 1996; Juel, 1988; Stanovich, 1986). When children can recognize and name the letters of the alphabet, they have the foundation for learning the alphabetic principle and learning to read (Adams, 1990a; Ehri, 1983).

This chapter offers a rationale and pedagogy for teaching letter recognition and alphabet knowledge. Specifically, it describes principles of effective classroom teaching, as well as the instruction, guided practice, and **review** that all students, especially those with dyslexia, require to fully develop their letter-reading skills.

The first section of this chapter discusses the importance of automatic letter recognition within the reading process. The second section provides considerations in teaching these letter recognition skills to all students, and the last section supplies activities known to develop automatic letter reading, accurate alphabet knowledge, and its application to reference materials such as the dictionary.

ROLE OF LETTER RECOGNITION IN THE READING PROCESS

The importance of explicitly teaching letter recognition includes these notable points:

1. Letters are the written symbols that are cognitively processed to make reading possible (Adams, 1990b).

2. Letter names are the only stable property of letters (Cox, 1992), as shapes and sounds of letters vary.

3. Knowing letter names provides a springboard for learning and remembering letter–sound relationships (Ehri, 1983; National Institute of Child Health and Human Development [NICHD], 2000; Treiman, Tincoff, Rodriguez, Mouzaki, & Francis, 1998).

4. Beginning readers who automatically recognize individual letters can begin unitizing orthographic clusters (familiar letter sequences), an essential step in automatic word recognition (Ehri, 1980, 1998; Neuhaus, Roldan, Boulware-Gooden, & Swank, 2006).

5. The rate that a student acquires letter knowledge predicts how quickly the student will learn to read words (Bond & Dykstra, 1967; Chall, 1996).

6. Accurate letter recognition is a complex skill that is only slightly less demanding than word reading (Neuhaus, 2002). More important, it informs and supports the later acquired skill of automatically transforming graphemes into phonemes, which students need to read words. Thus, automatic single-letter recognition is essential if students are to benefit from further reading instruction (Berninger et al., 2002; Vellutino, Scanlon, & Jaccard, 2003)

Letters: Introducing the Reading Code

As unlikely as it may seem, "Skillful readers visually process virtually every individual letter of every word as they read, and this is true whether they are reading isolated words or meaningful, connected text" (Adams, 1990b, p. 18). Although processing is not perceived on a conscious level, studies show that misprints of even familiar words cause our eye-fixation times to increase and slow down our reading (Adams, 1990b).

In a model of word recognition based on work by Seidenberg and McClelland (1989), Adams (1990a) described the vital role of letter recognition and its relationship to the processing of speech sounds, meaning, and context. Print provides the data that the reader recognizes, recodes, and interprets in context (e.g., *rose* as flower or action). If readers have fast, accurate recognition of individual letters, then they can identify and learn familiar letter sequences. Letter sequences within the words are eventually unitized through repeated reading of words (Ehri, 1998).

Ehri suggested that automatic word recognition, or sight word reading, involves recognizing each individual letter within a word because ultimately letters are the "distinctive cues that make one word different from all the others" (1998, p. 13). To illustrate, the *t* and *d* are the only two letters that differentiate the words *time* and *dime*.

Importance of Letter Sounds and Names

Letter recognition is necessary for word reading but alone is not sufficient for good word reading. Automatic word reading cannot occur without a complete understanding of the correspondences between every letter and its phonological reality (Ehri, 1998). This means a reader must understand that the *t* in *time* represents /t/ and that the sound /t/ is different from /d/, the initial sound of *dime*.

Logically, a student must first learn that letters carry sounds and then which sound or sounds are associated with each letter and **letter cluster.** When students have reliable knowledge of the sound or sounds a letter makes, they understand the alphabetic principal—phonemes of language correspond to the letters that represent them. To translate spoken language to the written code, children must acquire the explicit awareness "that all words are specified by an internal phonological structure, the shortest elements of which are the phonemes that the letters of the alphabet represent" (Liberman & Liberman, 1990, p. 60). Even beginning readers must learn that words do not differ "holistically, one from another, but only in the particulars of their internal structure" (Liberman & Liberman, 1990, p. 61).

The names of letters may be learned early, and students who know them have an advantage for learning the alphabetic principle and reading more than those who do not know letter names. Ehri and Wilce (1979) found that preschool children who did not know letter names experienced greater difficulty in learning letter sounds, and Vellutino et al. (2003) discovered that virtually all children who were later classified as poor readers entered kindergarten with poorly developed foundational reading skills such as letter knowledge and phonemic awareness. Clearly, letter-name knowledge helps students learn letter sounds and remember those sounds (Ehri & Wilce, 1979; Treiman et al., 1998).

Letter-name knowledge also helps students read novel or unfamiliar words because the phonemes represented by graphemes (letters or letter clusters) are often embedded within the letters' names (Ehri, 1987). For example, the sound /m/ is found within the letter name *m*. Similarly, all vowels represent sounds that are identical to their names. The spellings of beginning readers (invented or transitional spellings) often reflect their assimilation of this knowledge: *ppl* is *people,* and *km* represents *came.* When writing a word the way it sounds, students begin to use **sound–symbol correspondences** and develop an appreciation of the sequencing of the sounds and letters in words. These skills are essential to learning to read.

Labeling an item helps consolidate information about that item in long-term memory so that its memory can be recalled quickly and accurately (Gibson, 1969, and Murray & Lee, 1977, both cited in Walsh, Price, & Gillingham, 1988). Naturally, having well-developed letter-name knowledge facilitates the recall of letter–sound associations. Letter-name knowledge also facilitates communication about letters among students and their teachers and parents. Teachers can provide clear instruction when the beginning reader understands the common referents used for letters (Walsh et al., 1988). In addition, parental interaction in the reading process is enhanced when children understand the common name of letters that their parents use (Sulzby, 1983).

Most important, a letter's name is its only stable property (Cox, 1992), as the shape may change (e.g., upper- and lowercase forms, cursive and printed forms, differing fonts), and the speech sounds represented by letters may change (e.g., long and short vowel sounds). This means that letter names anchor the other properties of letters. According to Adams, "The provision of a distinctive and uniform label for a concept is especially important—perhaps critically so—for the attainment of concepts whose context and superficial expression varies across occurrences" (1990a, p. 352).

Knowing the different letter names allows children to uniquely label different letter shapes. Gibson, Gibson, Pick, and Osser (1962) described how children learn letter shapes. Children learn first to differentiate letters from other symbols that are not letters and then distinguish one letter from another "by noting distinctive features such as whether lines are curved or slanted, open or closed" (as cited in Gunning, 1996, p. 55). Through many exposures, children compare and contrast letters as they learn to identify and remember their distinctive features.

Some reading programs begin by teaching students to associate a letter shape with the sound it represents rather than with the letter's name. Because students will eventually need to associate symbols with sounds, some educators ask, "Why not go directly to sound–symbol association and bypass letter names?" According to Adams (1990a), there are some drawbacks to teaching only sound–symbol associations without teaching the names of the symbols:

- Several graphemes in English regularly represent more than one phoneme (e.g., *c* can be pronounced as /k/ as in *cat* or /s/ as in *city*).

- When trying to identify unknown words, new readers are limited to the number of letter–sound correspondences that have been taught; however, students with more complete letter-name knowledge may be able to use it to help retrieve the sounds of the letters that they are still learning.

Letter-Name Knowledge Predicts Reading Achievement

Since the late 1960s, research has shown that letter-naming accuracy predicts later reading achievement (Badian, 1994, 1995; Chall, 1996; Share, Jorm, Maclean, & Matthews, 1984). Bond and Dykstra (1967) found that the ability of prereaders to name letters was the single best predictor of end-of-year reading achievement. Badian (1995) followed students from preschool through sixth grade to find that preschool letter-naming accuracy (speed was not a factor in the letter-naming task) significantly predicted reading vocabulary, reading comprehension, and spelling achievement at each grade level.

Preschool letter-naming accuracy predicts word reading because of the similarity of letter and word reading. Reading both letters and words requires the ability to encode, store, and retrieve lexical labels for abstract symbols. Although letter naming has often been assumed to be a prereading skill (Badian, 1995), it has been recognized as a simple form of reading (Neuhaus & Swank, 2002). So, letter naming is really letter reading, or, in the case of the words *I* or *a*, it is single-letter word reading.

Letter-reading success is dependent on the same component skills that are necessary for accurate word reading. This means that automatic letter-reading skill predicts reading comprehension achievement through word-reading or decoding accuracy (Perfetti, 1985). Imperfect knowledge of single letters and letter clusters has been shown to "compromise early reading development for at-risk beginning readers in general, not just the slow responders, especially in application of the alphabetic principal to unfamiliar words" (Berninger et al., 2002, p. 63). Moreover, inaccurate or inconsistent letter recognition prevents the developing reader from unitizing letters into whole words that he or she can recognize within 1 second (Ehri & Wilce, 1983). Succinctly, letter recognition must be accurate to support adequate decoding and reading comprehension.

Letter-Recognition Errors

Letter reversals and letter transpositions are commonly associated with beginning readers and students who continue to struggle to read. These students may read letters such as *b*, *d*, or *p* as though they were reversed or rotated, such as when *bad* becomes *dad*, *dab*, or *pad*. The transposition of letters may also result in novel or different words: *felt* becomes *flet* and *sacred* is *scared*.

Liberman, Shankweiler, Orlando, Harris, and Berti (1971) determined that 1) letter reversals and letter transpositions of low-scoring second-grade readers are independent of each other, and together these two types of errors represented only 25% of misread letters; 2) less-skilled beginning readers make more errors when reading vowels than consonants; and 3) letter reversals are rare when individual letters are presented at rapid exposures but occur more often within the context of a word. Together, these findings seem to suggest that accurate recognition may be compromised by an added cognitive load of coordinating multiple phonological or orthographic representations inherent in letters or words.

Liberman and colleagues' (1971) research, supported by investigations by Shank-weiler and Liberman (1972) and Vellutino (1979, 1980), further suggests that letter-recognition inaccuracies do not often result from deficiencies in the visual-perceptual system (i.e., that students, even dyslexic students, do not perceive letters and words differently). Rather, it has been shown that poor readers often have degraded reading performance on tasks that require associating linguistic labels with letters (Vellutino, Smith, Steger, & Kaman, 1975). Following are some of these labeling tasks:

1. Associating a letter name with the letter (the name *b* with the symbol *b*)

2. Mapping sounds onto symbols (the letter *b* represents the phoneme /b/)

3. Learning to associate orthographic patterns with the sounds they represent (*igh* = /ī/ as in *bright*)

4. Recognizing an orthographic pattern as a whole word (*bright* = /brīt/)

When students misidentify *b* as *d* or *p,* visual perception or visual memory are not typically the sources of the error. The students may not have made a reliable association between the letter name or sound and the shape or spatial orientation of the letter (Vellutino, 1979). In other words, the student has not securely attached a verbal label to the particular letter.

For many students, it is only through extensive practice that secure associations are formed between the visual form and its verbal label. Research has demonstrated that poor readers are significantly more likely to rely on an orthographic (visual) strategy to read words (Neuhaus, 2000; Siegel, Share, & Geva, 1995; Stanovich & Siegel, 1994). Specifically, the overreliance on a visual reading strategy in first-grade children has been found to result in slow and inconsistent letter recognition, which was later associated with inaccurate word recognition (Neuhaus, 2000). Therefore, when students misread *tale* for *teal,* they most likely use a visual or orthographic reading strategy that includes very little phonological mediation that provides an internal verbal affirmation of the appropriateness of the pronunciation (Siegel et al., 1995).

Succinctly, letter recognition often becomes impaired only when linguistic representations must be attached to the visual symbol or when letters are embedded within words. This suggests that increased cognitive demand or inaccurate or incomplete phonological knowledge hampers letter recognition, rather than visual perception.

Letter-Naming Speed Predicts Reading Achievement

Research supports not only that letter naming must be accurate, but it also must be fast. Rapid letter naming is the basis for accurate word reading (Neuhaus, Carlson, Jeng, Post, & Swank, 2001; Neuhaus, Foorman, Francis, & Carlson, 2001; Neuhaus & Swank, 2002; Wolf, 1997; Wolf, Bowers, & Biddle, 2000; Wolf & Obregón, 1992; Wolf et al., 2003). Accurate word reading leads to good reading comprehension. Wolf and Obregón noted succinctly, "the need to develop automatic letter and word recognition skills is critical" (1997, p. 200).

The goal of all letter identification is to be able to recognize each letter automatically. Letters, letter clusters, and words are recognized automatically when they are processed accurately, rapidly, and unconsciously. Automaticity is thought to be achieved when 1) letter identification is effortless, 2) it occurs without willful initiation, and 3) it cannot be willfully stopped. To illustrate, complete this 30-second exercise. Cover the page of this book with your hand, and then move your hand to expose a few words. Now, do *not* read the words. Can you stop the reading process, or do you unconsciously or automatically decode and understand the words you see? For clarity, automaticity is reached when it is literally easier to recognize and read a letter or word than it is *not* to read it.

Automaticity is important because it frees a limited amount of cognitive attention to focus on higher-level reading comprehension (LaBerge & Samuels, 1974). Simply stated, reading comprehension cannot occur when a student's attention is consumed by matching letter symbols with their sounds.

Although the goal of automatic letter recognition sounds easy, it may be the most difficult task for the reading instructor to teach, and likewise, the most formidable goal for beginning students to reach. First, letter automaticity assumes that all 26 letters must become equally automatic. Second, students reach automaticity at different rates.

For readers to become successful, recognizing each of the 26 letters must become automatic. Clearly, there are no unimportant letters. Students are more familiar with some letters than others, however—beginning readers often are familiar with the letters in their names, even if the letters are used infrequently in other words. The goal for the teacher is to identify which individual letters each child is familiar with and which letters are still in need of greater familiarization and more practice. All letters must be read automatically because when an unfamiliar letter appears in a word, it stops the reader from identifying the word readily, and it disrupts the attention needed to comprehend the text. Consequently, all letters, and many letter clusters, must become automatically recognized before fluent reading and reading comprehension can be achieved.

The time and practice needed to reach automatic letter reading varies dramatically among students. Berninger (2000) found that students identified with dyslexia needed more than 20 times the practice than students without dyslexia to learn letter sequences. For example, good readers may learn to rapidly spell a word with 20 repetitions; however, poor readers may be challenged to reach automaticity with 400 repetitions, or 20 times the amount of practice than the good readers require. In addition, Neuhaus, Carlson, et al. (2001) found that even second-, third-, and fourth-grade students still have significant variation in their letter-naming speed, meaning that letter knowledge for many students is not fully automatic by first grade, and secure letter knowledge requires more extensive exposure and practice for some students. Therefore, allowing each student sufficient time and practice to solidify knowledge of letter names, shapes, and sounds is time consuming and challenging, but imperative.

Letter-naming speed has been identified as the single largest predictor of word-reading ability for first-grade students (Neuhaus & Swank, 2002). Letter-naming speed is influenced by a number of learned skills and cognitive abilities; specifically, phonological awareness, orthographic recognition, general naming speed, and visual attention skills. These are the same skills and abilities needed to read words, demonstrating that letter reading, such as word reading, requires multiple sources of knowledge and exact coordination of cognitive systems.

The importance of automatic letter reading cannot be overstated. Fast and accurate letter reading is not the end goal, however; rather, it is the stepping-off point to automatic word reading that allows students to attend to the comprehension demands of the text.

TEACHING LETTER SYMBOLS, NAMES, AND SOUNDS

All students, especially those with dyslexia, can be taught to develop accurate and rapid associations of letter symbols with names and sounds through a variety of instructional activities. Clinical experience has shown that using these activities increases both accuracy and speed in letter identification and naming (Frankiewicz, 1985; Stein, 1987).

Although many students come to school with literally years of exposure to letters, others do not. Simply, students come to school with varying degrees of preexisting letter knowledge. In addition, students have individual differences in their ability to create and store visual and verbal memories. All together, different innate abilities and environmental exposure result in a wide variation in students' letter knowledge.

Ideally, when entering kindergarten, children have the opportunity to develop or consolidate letter identification with uppercase letters before lowercase letters are formally introduced. The same principle is seen in the recommendation that students know letter names well before instruction in sound–symbol association begins (Adams, 1990a; NICHD, 2000). Much confusion among kindergarten and first-grade students can be avoided if letter names are secure.

Writing plays an influential role in the beginning reader's ability to recognize letters. Letter writing practice focuses students' attention on the particular features of letters' shapes and thus reinforces letter recognition.

Although the letter learning process is the same for all students, Foorman and Torgesen (2001) reminded us that some students will only become literate when the instruction is more intense, more explicit, more comprehensive, and more supportive. In other words, the same effective pedagogy for all students is required, but increased repetitions; greater clarification of concepts; and additional reteaching of letters, letter names, and sounds is necessary for some students to reach the same level of proficiency that others reach with less intensity, practice, reteaching, and support.

Implementing response to intervention (RTI) should prevent many students from reaching upper grades without adequate letter knowledge, but a child without adequate letter knowledge may somehow slip through and reach third or fourth grade without well-developed letter knowledge. This means that most students in the class have already been instructed in both upper- and lowercase letters and probably to both **print** and **cursive handwriting.** In order to simplify instruction for students lacking speed and accuracy, letter identification can be taught or improved through the use of only uppercase block capitals because they contain fewer confusing letter shapes and are more graphically distinct. Letter identification is reinforced by using three-dimensional (3-D) letters in alphabetizing activities as part of a comprehensive lesson plan. Alphabet sequencing activities reinforce left-to-right directionality as well, which is an essential element in reading.

Although students are learning to recognize uppercase block letters accurately and speedily during the Alphabet segment of a lesson, they are introduced to lowercase printed letters through the "linking procedure" (see Chapter 8). The names and sounds they represent are reviewed each day during the Reading Deck segment. During the Alphabet segment of the lesson, students progress from working with the uppercase alphabet letter strips and 3-D letters to the lowercase letter strips and 3-D letters.

Principles of Effective Instruction

Pedagogical considerations of effective letter identification instruction include the following.

1. *Multisensory teaching:* The purpose of multisensory teaching is to provide instruction that simultaneously engages and encodes the information in different forms. This provides an opportunity for knowledge to be retained in multiple domain-specific memory stores, especially those associated with visual, verbal, kinesthetic, and tactile experiences. Multisensory instruction is consistent with connectionist theory that suggests that reading ability is optimized when both phonological and orthographic representations are simultaneously engaged and interactive (Harm & Seidenberg, 2004; Plaut, McClelland, Seidenberg, & Patterson, 1996). More important, multisensory reading instruction has been found to be significantly more effective than traditional instruction for teaching phonological awareness, decoding skills, and reading comprehension (Carreker et al., 2005; Carreker, Neuhaus, & Swank, 2007; Foorman, Francis, Shaywitz, Shaywitz, & Fletcher, 1997; Joshi, Dahlgren, & Boulware-Gooden, 2002).

This instruction may be more effective because it allows the storage of information in multiple sensory-specific memory systems (Gardner, 1985) and allows students with limitations in one storage system to gain access to information from other memory modules (Hallahan & Kauffman, 1976). It appears that children's visual attention is focused by their manual tasks (Thorpe & Borden, 1985), so physical manipulation of stimuli such as letter forms increases the likelihood that the letter shapes are remembered.

Students with reading difficulty often have trouble storing and retrieving lexical labels (including letter names) and need the opportunity to learn and practice, especially through simultaneously engaging at least two or three learning modalities: visual, auditory, and tactile/kinesthetic (involving muscle memory). For example, students can say the names of letters as they see and touch 3-D plastic letters and arrange them in alphabetical order. Simply, using multisensory instruction seems to help build visual, verbal, and tactile/kinesthetic memories associated with letters.

2. *Sequential presentation:* Information must be presented in a sequence that builds logically on previously taught material. Letter-name instruction precedes letter-symbol instruction, which is then informed by letter-sound instruction.

3. *Early identification and intervention:* Any reading dysfunction, including slow or inaccurate letter recognition, should be identified as early as possible so that children's reading-related difficulties can be remediated before they experience years of frustration and school failure. Vellutino et al. (1996, 2003) suggested that the majority of students from middle- and upper middle-class families who are ultimately identified with reading difficulties have instructional deprivation rather than basic cognitive deficits. Therefore, deficient achievement levels of letter recognition or any skill known to predict later difficulty with word reading and reading comprehension must be identified and remediated early in a child's academic career. Students do not outgrow reading disability, nor do they learn letter recognition on their own.

4. ***Guided discovery teaching:*** The **Socratic method** leads learners to discover information through carefully guided questioning based on information they already possess. This method builds interest and aids memory. Also, when the teacher reviews by starting a sentence and then pauses for students to complete it, students are encouraged to participate rather than being placed on the defensive by a direct question

(e.g., "The initial letter of the alphabet is _____," rather than, "What is the initial letter of the alphabet?").

5. *Brief instructional segments:* Frequent and brief instructional segments are more effective than less frequent segments lasting longer periods of time. Extensive guided practice is required for letter-reading automaticity, and more intense practice will be needed when a student does not easily make memories of letters and connect them to names and sounds.

6. *Teaching to automaticity:* After presenting the letters through guided discovery, the teacher models and provides ample practice activities, reviews the material on a regular basis, and assesses whether students can accurately name the letters previously taught. The rate at which students will reach letter automaticity will vary according to their ability to store, coordinate, and reconstruct the visual and verbal memories associated with each letter. The teacher should ensure success for all students by reviewing the procedure or concept before asking students to apply it. For example, a quick warm-up of touching and naming the letters on an alphabet strip is strongly encouraged before students work on sequencing or alphabetizing. This review "sets up the student for success," an underlying tenent of all informed instruction.

As noted previously, students learn at different rates. The rate of letter mastery will differ among students and will vary according to a student's ability to consolidate the memories needed to recall the visual and verbal characteristics of each letter. The issue is more complex, however—some letters will be learned more easily than others. First, letters with multiple sound associations (i.e., *a* has five different sounds associated with it) may be more difficult to learn because the letter symbol has multiple associations rather than just one sound and one name to learn. Second, although some letters are easily reinforced because they appear in words outside of the direct instructional period, other letters are infrequently encountered and do not provide extra exposures or reinforcement. More important, the teacher should plan varying amounts of time for each student to reach automaticity of each letter because of 1) variance in the students' innate ability to fully encode letter information, 2) variation in specific cognitive demands of each letter, and 3) frequency of individual letter exposure.

7. *Teach proofreading:* The teacher guides students through the process of proofreading by which they discover and correct their own errors instead of relying on an outside source (teacher or computer). Although proofreading seems old-fashioned, its greatest benefit, "the do over," is current. Inform students that mistakes are a large part of reading and writing, but when they catch their own mistakes, they get a "do over," even if the mistake is just incorrectly reading or writing a single letter.

Activities

The teacher-led activities included in this chapter have been used successfully to teach accurate and efficient letter recognition. These activities have been a part of a multi-sensory, structured, sequential reading instructional program that has been shown to increase reading skills for many students, including general education elementary school students (Day, 1993); minority students from low-income families who changed schools frequently (Post, 1999); and high-achieving elementary school students (Frankiewicz, 1984b). These letter-learning activities also have been included in a first- and second-grade multisensory reading intervention program shown to significantly enhance the third- and fifth-grade reading comprehension performance of both

English-speaking and bilingual Hispanic elementary school students on a high-stakes state-mandated achievement test over traditional instruction offered to the other students in the district (Carreker et al., 2005, 2007).

In addition, the letter and alphabet activities presented in this chapter have been shown to significantly enhance the reading progress of students with learning disabilities in elementary, middle, and high school resource classrooms (Frankiewicz, 1984a; Reed, Selig, Young, & Day, 1995) and when implemented in one-to-one instruction (Frankiewicz, 1985; Stein, 1987). In short, these letter-naming activities have been validated as effective for virtually all students beginning the journey toward literacy.

The following activities and recommended materials are based on the work and writings of Gillingham and Stillman (1960); Cox (1992) and the teaching staff of the Language Laboratory of the Scottish Rite Hospital in Dallas, Texas; Hogan and Smith (1987) of EDMAR Educational Associates in Forney, Texas; and the teaching staff of the Neuhaus Education Center in Bellaire, Texas (1998).

Materials for Instruction

See Appendix B at the end of the book for information on purchasing the materials for instruction.

- A small, round mirror for each student, approximately 2" in diameter with plastic encasing the edges.

- Classroom uppercase alphabet strip, a minimum of 3" × 48", with block letters, without pictures or graphics which can be visually distracting to students, mounted at students' eye level

- Set of 3-D plastic uppercase block letters for each student and for the teacher

- Individual uppercase alphabet strip for each student, made of laminated strip of cardstock, approximately 2" × 17", with block letters

- Class set of instant letter recognition charts, seven with uppercase letters and seven with lowercase letters (see Figure 6.1); each chart has five rows of six letters

- For each student, 8 sets of 10 word cards approximately 1" × 2", with words printed in lowercase, to be used for alphabetization by 1) first letter; 2) second letter; 3) first and second letters; 4) third letters; 5) second and third letters; 6) fourth letter; 7) third and fourth letters; and 8) first, second, third, and fourth letters. The card sets should be identical across the class. Use different colors of cards for the eight sets of cards. Word sets can be stored in small plastic sandwich bags. These card sets are described in further detail in the section on alphabetizing activities.

- For the teacher, 8 sets of word cards approximately 5" × 7" with words printed in lowercase. The words used in the teacher's sets should not be identical to those in the students' sets. The teacher's cards are larger than the students' cards so that all students can see them.

- Container for each student in which to store the individual alphabet strip(s), plastic letters, and word cards to be alphabetized

- Guide-word practice dictionary for each student, purchased or made by the teacher

- Dictionary for each student, appropriate to the students' ability level

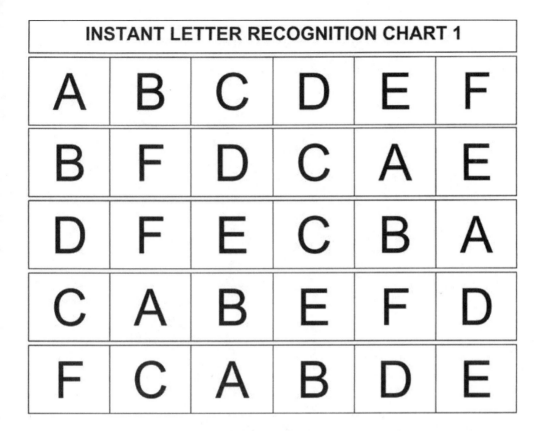

Figure 6.1. Instant letter recognition chart. (From Carreker, S. [2002]. *Reading readiness*. Bellaire, TX: Neuhaus Education Center; reprinted by permission.)

For younger students:

- Alphabet matching mat made of poster board or heavy laminated paper, approximately 24" × 18", with the outlines of uppercase block letter shapes arranged alphabetically in an arc (see Figure 6.2). Students can practice matching by placing plastic letters on the mat.

For students who do not need to start with a matching activity:

- Alphabet sequencing mat made of poster board or heavy laminated paper, approximately 24" × 18", with uppercase block letters in alphabetical order printed across the top and the letters *A, M, N,* and *Z* forming an arc (or rainbow) beneath. *M* and *N* are printed at the top of the arc, *A* and *Z* are in the initial and final positions, and space is left for the missing letters to be placed within the arc (see Figure 6.3).

For students who have learned uppercase letters:

- Individual lowercase alphabet strip for each student, made of a 2" × 17" strip of laminated cardstock

- Classroom lowercase alphabet strip, minimum of 3" × 48", with block letters, without pictures or graphics, mounted at students' eye level

Figure 6.2. Alphabet matching mat.

Activities for Developing Letter Identification, Naming, and Sequencing Skills

Schedule

Allot 5 minutes within a 50- to 60-minute lesson for letter identification, rapid naming, and sequencing activities. Continue using uppercase letters in these activities until students can rapidly and accurately identify all uppercase letters in sequence and at random.

Lowercase letters (and letter clusters) should be taught individually through a multisensory letter-introduction procedure often referred to as *linking* (see Chapter 8) in which the letter's name, shape, and sound(s) it represents are concurrently linked in memory. Lowercase letter names should be reviewed daily by using a reading deck (see Chapter 8).

Students may need to reinforce speed and accuracy of lowercase letter recognition through the same activities and materials discussed for uppercase letters. *Use the lowercase instant letter recognition charts to increase students' speed of letter naming even after accuracy has been established.*

The activities that follow can be rotated within a weekly lesson plan. Students should touch and name letters on an alphabet strip as a warm-up before each activity. The strip remains in place during the activity as a reference.

Matching and Naming

- 3-D uppercase letter sets
- Alphabet matching mats (see Figure 6.2)

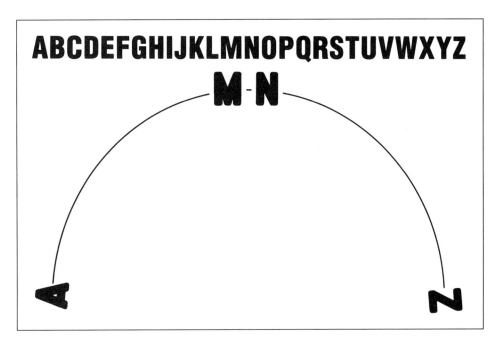

Figure 6.3. Alphabet sequencing mat.

Students who cannot match 3-D uppercase letters with the outlines of uppercase letters printed on paper should begin with this activity. The teacher has students turn the 3-D plastic letters right side up and facing the correct direction inside the arc on the alphabet matching mat. The teacher tells students that these are the letters found in the words we read and write. He or she points out the alphabet on the classroom alphabet strip and leads students to discover that an alphabet contains these same letters in a fixed order. The teacher asks students to name each letter before they place the plastic letter on top of the printed form on their individual alphabet matching mats. If all of the letters are not matched within 5 minutes, then the activity is repeated the next day, starting with the letters matched the day before and continuing with additional letters until students can place all of the letters on the mat. The teacher has students check their work each time by touching and naming the letters they have just placed (e.g., students say "A" and touch the plastic letter sitting on top of the printed letter). The teacher leads students to discover the number of letters in the alphabet by pointing to each letter and counting. The teacher leads students in completing the sentence, "The number of letters in the alphabet is [26]."

Students progress from 1) placing the plastic letters on top of the printed forms on the mat for matching, to 2) placing the letters beneath the printed letters on an alphabet strip, to 3) placing the letters in an arc on the mat for sequencing (see Figure 6.3). When students can accurately place plastic letters beneath the letters on an alphabet strip, they are ready for the following activity.

Naming, Sequencing, and Discovery of Middle

- Classroom uppercase alphabet strip
- Individual uppercase alphabet strips

Students who do not need to start with a matching activity will start here. The teacher leads students to discover the number of letters in the alphabet (see description in Matching and Naming).

The teacher asks students to name each letter as he or she points to it in sequential order on the classroom uppercase alphabet strip. The teacher asks students to touch and name each letter on their individual uppercase alphabet strips as he or she leads them in naming the letters together.

The teacher asks students to discover the middle of the alphabet by putting one index finger on the first letter of the alphabet and one index finger on the last letter and moving in toward the middle. Students discover that the exact middle is between the letters *M* and *N*. The teacher leads students in completing the sentence, "The two middle letters of the alphabet are [*M* and *N*]."

After students can accurately perform this touching and naming activity, any daily alphabet activity should begin with a warm-up in which students touch and name the letters of the alphabet on their strips. This warm-up activity provides the repetition that many students require to develop automaticity.

Discovery of Vowel and Consonant Sounds

*   Mirror for each student

Before students learn that there are two kinds of letters (consonants and vowels) in the alphabet, the teacher introduces the concept of two kinds of sounds. The teacher leads students to discover that we use only two kinds of sounds when we talk: the sounds we form when the mouth is open (vowels) and the sounds we form when the mouth is closed or partially closed (consonants). The teacher illustrates that when we say words, we open and close our mouths. The students try to talk by putting together only closed-mouth sounds, such as /m/, /l/, or /p/. The students try to talk using only open-mouth sounds, such as /ă/, /ĕ/, or /ŭ/. The teacher explains that to form words, we must both open and close our mouths. The teacher illustrates by slowly saying a word, such as *map,* and letting the students see the mouth closing for the consonant, opening for the vowel, and closing for the consonant.

The teacher asks students to look into a mirror as they say /ă/, /ĕ/, /ĭ/, /ŏ/, and /ŭ/ and leads them to discover that their mouths are open when they say these sounds. The shape of the mouth changes, but nothing blocks the air that comes out of the mouth to form these sounds. The teacher explains that vowel sounds open our mouths. Next, the teacher directs students to look in a mirror to see what happens when they say the sound /s/. The teacher explains that their teeth and tongue partially close their mouths. Then the teacher has the students say /l/ and notice that the tongue partially closes their mouths. Students then say /m/ and notice that their lips close their mouths. These are consonant sounds. The teacher says that consonant sounds close or partially close our mouths. The teeth, tongue, and/or lips block the air used in making these sounds. The teacher leads the students in saying, "Vowel sounds open our mouths, and consonant sounds close or partially close our mouths with our teeth, tongue, or lips." The teacher and students use gestures for open (hands open like a crocodile mouth) and closed (palms together) and point to their teeth, tongue, and lips.

The teacher provides practice for the students in differentiating between consonant and vowel sounds by having students look into their mirror, repeat sounds, and discover whether their mouth is open or closed (or partially closed) when they say the sound. The teacher starts with consonant sounds for which the mouth is obviously closed or partially closed, such as /s/, /l/, /m/, or /n/, interspersed with both long and short vowel sounds. After students are aware of the difference between consonant and vowel sounds, they are ready to discover that the letters that represent these sounds are classified as consonant letters and vowel letters.

Discovery of Vowel and Consonant Letters

- Individual uppercase alphabet strips (for reference)
- Mirrors

The teacher tells the students that they are going to discover the two kinds of letters in the alphabet. The teacher explains that just as there are two kinds of sounds (vowels and consonants) in spoken words, there are two kinds of letters in the alphabet. The teacher and students review together, "Vowel sounds open our mouths, and consonant sounds close or partially close our mouths." The names of the letters give clues as to which letters will be called vowels and which will be called consonants. The teacher directs the students to look in a mirror to see what happens to their mouths when they say the names of the letters *a, e, i, o,* and *u.* Their mouths stay open when they say these letter names. The teacher tells students that these letters represent vowel sounds.

Students use their mirror to discover that when they say the name of the letter *s,* the mouth is partially closed by the teeth and tongue. When they say the name of the letter *l,* the mouth is partially closed, with the tongue closing against the roof of the mouth. When they say the name of the letter *m,* the lips close the mouth.

After students are aware that the alphabet is made up of vowel and consonant letters that represent vowel and consonant sounds, the teacher can vary the daily warm-up activity of touching and naming the letters by having students whisper or cheer for the vowel letters.

Discovery of Initial, Medial, and Final

- Classroom uppercase alphabet strip
- Individual uppercase alphabet strips

The alphabet can be used to teach students terminology that will be used in other aspects of written language training. For example, in phonemic awareness training, students will be asked whether they hear a specific sound in the initial, medial, or final position in a word. Students can understand the meaning of the abstract spatial terms *initial, medial,* and *final* by learning them in relation to the alphabet strip. The terms *initial, medial,* and *final* can be introduced by teaching the initial, medial, and final letters of the alphabet.

The teacher writes the initials of his or her name on the board and leads students to discover that these letters are the first letters of his or her name. The teacher writes several students' initials on the board and helps students discover that initials are the first letters of names. The teacher explains that *initial* means first and that the alphabet also has an initial letter, *A.* The teacher points to the *A* on the classroom alphabet strip, asks students to touch the letter *A* on their alphabet strips, and leads them in saying, "*A* is the [initial] letter of the alphabet."

The teacher touches *Z* on the classroom alphabet strip and asks students to touch *Z* on their strips. The teacher tells students that the last letter of the alphabet is *Z* and that another way of saying *last* is *final*. The teacher leads students in saying, "*Z* is the [final] letter of the alphabet." The teacher tells students that all of the letters between *A* and *Z* are medial letters and that there is a difference between medial and middle. The exact middle of the alphabet is found between the letters *M* and *N*. *Medial* means anything between initial or final. A medial letter is any letter occurring between *A* and *Z*. The teacher asks students to name some of the medial alphabet letters (any letter that is not *A* or *Z*) and identify initial, medial, and final letters within other words written on the board, such as their own names or the teacher's name.

The teacher provides kinesthetic reinforcement for this information through gestures. The teacher stands with his or her back to the students, facing the classroom alphabet strip, and raises both arms, fingers pointing above his or her head. The teacher drops his or her left arm horizontally to the left (parallel to the floor) while saying, "Initial means *first*." The teacher drops his or her right arm horizontally to the right while saying, "Final means *last*." The teacher brings both arms back above his or her head and says, "Medial means anything between initial (dropping left arm to horizontal) and final (dropping right arm to horizontal)."

Sequencing with 3-D Letters

- Individual uppercase alphabet strips (for reference)

- 3-D uppercase letter sets

- Alphabet sequencing mats (most older students will place the letters on their desks rather than using mats)

The teacher writes *A, M, N,* and *Z* in an arc on the board with *M* and *N* at the top of the arc. The teacher directs students to name and place the initial letter of the alphabet on their alphabet sequencing mats (or desks). They name and place *A* and say, "*A* is the initial letter of the alphabet." Students name and place *Z* and say, "*Z* is the final letter of the alphabet." Students name and place *M* and *N* and say, "*M* and *N* are the two middle letters of the alphabet." The teacher directs students, "Name it, find it, place it," as they fill in the arc with missing letters in alphabetical order. Students say a letter, find it, and place it in the arc until the alphabet is complete. Students then proofread their work by touching and naming each letter from *A* to *Z*, using the index finger of their writing hand. Soon after beginning this activity, the teacher begins timing the students and charting results. The initial goal is accurate naming and placement of all letters in less than 5 minutes, with an ultimate goal of 2 minutes or less. The reason that students place letters in an arc is that often there is not enough space on a desk or a tabletop to place all of the letters in a straight line.

Note for working with younger students: Some young students may have difficulty crossing the mid-line (moving the right hand and arm into the space to the left of the mid-line of their body or vice versa for left-handed students). These students will want to place the first half of the alphabet letters with their left hand and the second half with their right hand rather than place all of the letters with their writing hand. This is a function of motor skill development; the teacher will encourage them to work toward the time when they can place all of the letters with their writing hand.

Note for working with older students: Older students may enjoy a variation of this activity. For sequencing, have students use plastic poker chips labeled with block capital letters. Older students particularly enjoy the challenge of being timed and having their progress charted.

Other variations:

- Students proofread by returning letters to the storage container in sequence and naming each letter, rather than just touching and naming letters to check.

- After students are able to place the plastic letters in alphabetical order, students may place *A, M, N,* and *Z* as usual and then randomly select letters and place them one by one in the approximate place in the semicircle.

Discovery of Before and After

- Classroom uppercase alphabet strip

- Individual uppercase alphabet strips

Students often have difficulty with abstract spatial terms such as *before* and *after* and may be confused by directions such as, "Look at the consonant after the vowel" or "Listen for the sound before the /k/ sound." To make the abstract terms *before* and *after* more concrete, the teacher directs students to place both hands below their alphabet strips and then models for students with the classroom alphabet strip. The teacher asks students to raise the hand that is closer to *A* and tells them that this is their *before* hand. The teacher asks students to raise the hand closer to *Z,* which is their *after* hand. Next, the teacher names a letter, such as *E,* and places both index fingers under the letter on the classroom alphabet strip. The teacher moves the index finger of the *after* hand to the letter after *E* and says, "*F* is after *E.*" Students then echo and place their index finger under the chosen letter (*E*) on their individual alphabet strips. With the index finger of their *after* hand, students touch and name the letter that comes after the named letter. Students say, "*F* is after *E.*" The teacher names several other letters, and students respond appropriately.

The concept *after* is taught first because it reflects the left-to-right progression of the alphabet. The concept *after* should be practiced in several sessions until it is mastered. Then, the teacher has students work with the concept *before.* The teacher names a letter, such as *T,* and asks students to tell which letter is before it. Students place both index fingers under *T,* point to *S* with the index finger of their *before* hand, and say, "*S* is before *T.*" Finally, the teacher provides practice with both *before* and *after:* "Find *W.* Tell me what is before and after *W.*"

Instant Letter Recognition Charts

- Class set of seven uppercase instant letter recognition charts and seven with lowercase letters (see Figure 6.1)

Each chart is a grid of five rows of six letters. Chart 1 has *A, B, C, D, E,* and *F* in the first row. In Rows 2–5, those letters are randomly distributed with six letters in each row. The teacher displays Chart 1 to the class and names the six letters in the first row. The teacher points to each letter in the first row as students name the letters. Students then name the letters as the teacher points to them in Rows 2–5. Later, students are timed, and the number of letters read in 1 minute is charted and compared with later timed readings. Students progress from Charts 1–7 with all uppercase letters to Charts 8–14 with all lowercase letters. This exercise provides vital practice in developing accuracy and speed in letter naming.

Missing Letter Decks

- Individual uppercase alphabet strips (for reference)

- Missing letter decks (teacher-made uppercase decks and commercially available lowercase deck)

To make a missing letter deck with uppercase block letters, the teacher prints the alphabet on cards, with two letters and a blank on each card. In the first set, the third letter is missing and is represented by a blank line (AB_, BC_). In the second set, the alphabet is printed in groups of three letters with the middle letter missing (A_C, B_D, C_E). In the third set, the first letter is missing (_DE). In the fourth set, the first and third letters are missing. (_B_, _C_, _D_).

After students can place all 26 3-D letters of the alphabet in correct sequence within 3 minutes, the teacher introduces the uppercase missing letter deck. Only after students have been introduced to all lowercase letters should the commercially available missing letter deck with lowercase block letters be used. Students keep their alphabet strips in front of them to refer to if needed. The teacher makes sure the missing letter deck is in alphabetical order and holds up the first card in the first set of cards. Students name the two letters on each card and the missing letter: AB_[C], BC_[D], and so forth. When students can rapidly and accurately name all three letters on each card with the cards in alphabetical sequence (after many practice sessions), the teacher shuffles the cards and presents them in random order. The students then progress to the second, third, and fourth teacher-made sets of the missing letter decks. As with the first set, these are practiced first in sequence, then shuffled. Students should be fluent at each level before progressing to the next level. Students do not need to master all four levels before the teacher introduces the additional activities that follow. The teacher intersperses the missing letter deck activity within a weekly lesson plan with more advanced activities for developing alphabetizing and dictionary skills.

Accent and Rhythm

- Mirrors

Many students have difficulty hearing the rhythm or the accented syllable in a word. This difficulty has consequences for developing reading and spelling skills. The following activity provides practice in hearing accented syllables while also reinforcing alphabetic sequence. The teacher says the names of several students, overemphasizing the accented syllable in their names (*Ja mal´, Sta´ cy, Ta ke´ sha, Ja´ son, Jo sé´*). The teacher asks students whether they hear a difference in the way one part of the name is said. The teacher models "robot talk" in which there is no accent. The students discover that we say some parts of spoken words louder than other parts. The teacher explains that when we accent one part of a word, the mouth opens wider, the voice is louder, and the tone is higher. The teacher reinforces each part of the definition with gestures: Mouth opens wider (hands open like a crocodile mouth), voice is louder (cupped hand behind ear), and tone is higher (flattened hand, palm to floor, is raised above head to designate higher).

Some students can learn to "see" accented syllables by using a mirror to notice when their mouths open wider. For students who find perceiving accent particularly difficult, the teacher models laying both hands along the jaw line so that students can feel the jaw opening wider on the accented syllable. Students may be better able to discern the change in pitch that occurs with accent if they place their hands over their ears and hum a word rather than say it.

The teacher recites the letters of the alphabet in pairs and accents the first letter of each pair: "*A´ B, C´ D, E´ F, G´ H*," and so forth. The teacher asks students whether the first or the second letter is being accented. The teacher encourages students to use a mirror to see their mouths opening wider and to cup their jaws in their hands to feel their mouth opening wider. Using block letters and accenting the first letter in each pair, the teacher writes the first eight letters of the alphabet on the board in pairs: *A B, C D, E F, G H*. Stressing the first letter in each pair, the teacher reads the list. With their alphabet strips in view, students say the alphabet and accent the first letter in each pair. Variations include having students clap on the accented letter. After students are able to accent the first letter of each pair (after many practice sessions), the teacher writes on the board and leads students in accenting the second letter: "*A B´, C D´, E F´, G H´*," and so forth. Eventually, students practice accenting the first of a group of three letters ("*A´ BC, D´ EF*"), then the second letter ("*A B´ C, D E´ F*"), and finally, the third letter ("*AB C´, DE F´*"). Students will need to apply their knowledge of accenting patterns when reading unfamiliar longer words. In English, multisyllabic words are accented more often on the first syllable (e.g., *bas´ ket*), and second most often on the second syllable (*pa rade´, con ven´ tion*),

Naming of Lowercase Letters

- Individual lowercase alphabet strips

Chapter 8 describes introducing lowercase letters through multisensory letter introduction. If students need additional practice in naming the lowercase letters accurately and rapidly, then many of the previous activities for uppercase letters may be used. The daily warm-up of touching and naming letters can be done with an alphabet strip of lowercase letters, as can activities such as the instant letter recognition charts, missing letter decks, accent and rhythm, and the game Don't Say *Z*.

Games to Reinforce Letter Identification, Naming, and Sequencing Skills

Alphabet Battle

- Individual alphabet strip and 3-D letter set for each pair of students

Students are divided into pairs. Simultaneously, both players draw a letter from the set of 3-D letters without looking at the letters. Each player places his or her letter on the desk and says the name of the letter. The player whose letter is closer in alphabetical order to *Z* wins both letters. The student must say, for example, "*U* is after *G*." The winner is the player with the most letters at the end of the game.

Variation: The player whose letter is closer to *A* wins the letters (e.g., "*J* is before *T*").

Alphabet Bingo

- Individual alphabet strip (for reference) and 3-D letter set for each student

- 3-D letter set for the teacher

Each student selects any seven letters from his or her container of letters and places them on the desk in a vertical column on the *before* (left-hand) side. The other letters are put away. The teacher selects one letter from another container, shows it to the students, and names it. Students repeat the name. If they have the letter on their desk, then they move it to the *after* (right-hand) side of the desk to form a second vertical column. The first person to move all seven letters to the *after* side of the desk is the winner. The teacher checks for accuracy by having the winner name the seven letters.

Alphabet Dominoes

- Individual alphabet strip (for reference) and 3-D letter set for each pair of students

Students should be proficient in *before* and *after* activities. Each pair of students places the letters *M* and *N* on the desk. Each student draws five letters without looking. The remaining letters become the "bone yard" and are placed inside the storage container on top of the desk. The teacher designates which student in each pair goes first. That student tries to play a letter immediately before *M* or after *N*. The student must have *L* or *O* to play initially. If not, then he or she draws a letter from the bone yard without looking. The letters are to be played in alphabetical order to the right of *N* and in reverse alphabetical order to the left of *M*. For example, if the letters *JKLMNOPQ* have been placed, then the next player may play *I* or *R*. If a player draws a letter from the bone yard that can be played, then he or she must wait until the next turn to play it. Each player plays only one letter at a time. As each student places a letter, he or she says, "_ is before (or after) _." The winner is the first student to play all of his or her letters (even if there are letters remaining in the bone yard).

Guess What?

- 3-D letter set for each pair of students

A student closes his or her eyes and draws a letter from a container. The student tries to identify the letter by its shape. If successful, the student keeps the letter and his or her opponent takes a turn. If unsuccessful, the student returns the letter to the container and his or her opponent takes a turn. Play continues until all 26 letters have been named or time runs out. The student with the most letters at the end of play is the winner.

Don't Say Z

- Individual alphabet strip for each pair of students

Two players alternate saying letters of the alphabet in sequence. Each player may choose to say two or three letters in one turn. For example, if Player 1 says "*AB*" and Player 2 says "*CDE*," then Player 1 can say "*FG*" or "*FGH*," and so forth. The object is to avoid saying *Z*.

Variation: The game can be changed to Catch the *Z* in which the object is to be the player who says *Z*. An additional challenge is added when an object such as a stuffed animal is tossed between teacher and student while saying two or three letter sequences.

Twenty Questions

The teacher prints the alphabet on the board (or on a sheet of paper, if working with one or two students). The teacher says, "I am thinking of a letter. I want you to try to guess the letter. You can ask me questions about the letter. I can only answer 'yes' or 'no.' See if you can guess the letter in fewer than 20 questions." Students begin to ask questions about the letter. The teacher encourages students to ask questions that eliminate several letters at a time. Questions such as "Is it a vowel?" or "Is it made of only straight lines?" will eliminate several letters at a time. The teacher helps students to rephrase questions that require more than an answer of "yes" or "no."

As students eliminate letters, the teacher crosses the letters off the alphabet. The teacher records the number of questions required for students to guess the letter. The teacher can chart the number of questions. Students can compare the number of questions they ask each time the game is played.

Super Sleuth

- One individual alphabet strip (for reference) and 3-D letter set for each pair of students

- Pencil and paper

The students work together in pairs to arrange the 3-D letters in an arc. Then, the first student closes his or her eyes while the second student removes one letter and closes the gap in the arc. The first student must discover the missing letter. After the missing letter has been identified, it is replaced in the arc and the other student gets the chance to identify a missing letter. Students may keep track of correct guesses to determine the winner. The game continues until time runs out.

Activities for Developing Alphabetizing Skills

The alphabet provides a systematic approach to organizing, classifying, and codifying information in myriad fields, such as science, law, engineering, the social sciences, business, education, communication, and entertainment. The order of the alphabet provides the order of words for every kind of information we seek in libraries, books, newspapers, and on the Internet.

Schedule

Students are ready to learn to alphabetize words when they show competence with letter recognition, naming, and sequencing. They should be able to place the 3-D plastic letters in an arc within 2 minutes, be fluent with at least the first set of the uppercase missing letter deck, and be accurate with random naming of upper- and lowercase letters. Students begin alphabetizing word cards rather than lists of words. Mistakes can be easily corrected by rearranging a card rather than erasing a word in a list. Students move from alphabetizing word cards, to alphabetizing lists of words, and then to locating words in the dictionary and other reference materials. The missing letter decks activity should be interspersed among the following activities within the weekly schedule to provide review for letter sequencing.

Students touch and name letters on an alphabet strip as a warm-up before any sequencing-related activity. The strip remains in place as a reference.

Alphabetizing Word Cards by the First Letter

- Pocket chart

- For the teacher, a set of 10 cards, each of which has a word beginning with a different lowercase letter

- For each student, a set of 10 cards, each of which has a word beginning with a different lowercase letter

- Individual alphabet strips (for warm-up activity and reference)

The teacher places 10 cards in a vertical column on the *before* side of the pocket chart (or desk, if working with one or two students), ensuring that the words are not in alphabetical order. In keeping with the principle of having one focus, the words on these cards are for alphabetizing, not for reading. The teacher asks students whether the first letter of each word is the same as or different from the first letters of the other words. Students respond that they are different. The teacher asks the students which letter will guide them in putting these words into alphabetical order. The teacher explains that the letter used for alphabetizing is called the **guide letter.** The answer to the question is always an ordinal number (e.g., "The first letter is the guide letter").

The teacher points to the first letter of each word as the students recite the alphabet. For example, as students say, "*A*," the teacher points to the first letter of each word. If the students see a word beginning with the letter *A* as they are saying, "*A*," then they say, "Stop!" The teacher forms a second column by placing the word card at the top of the pocket chart on the right side. The teacher points to the first word in the first column as the students say "*B*" and look at the first letter of each of the remaining words. The students continue reciting the alphabet and saying, "Stop!" as the cards are aligned in alphabetical order. The students finish saying the alphabet even after all of the cards are placed. Students proofread by saying the alphabet again, and the teacher touches the first letter of each card when the students say that letter. The teacher taps the space to the left of the words when students say letters not found at the beginning of one of the words.

Students have sets of word cards that are the same as each other for ease in checking. Students line up their set of word cards vertically on the *before* side of their desks. The teacher asks students which letter is their guide letter. The students reply, "The first letter is my guide letter." The students recite the alphabet while pointing to the first letter of each word. If students find a word beginning with *A,* then they place it in a vertical column on the *after* side of the desk. They follow the same procedures for saying the entire alphabet and then proofread. Have several different sets of word cards to be alphabetized by the first letter so that the students work with different sets over a period of time. When students can perform this activity easily and efficiently, they are ready to progress to the next level—alphabetizing word cards by the second letter.

Alphabetizing Word Cards by the Second Letter

- Pocket chart

- For the teacher, a set of 10 cards with words that begin with the same first letter followed by a different letter, such as *set, sun, street, six, sled, sand, scout, show, sip,* and *snake*

- For each student, a set of 10 smaller cards with words that begin with the same first letter but are followed by different second letters

- Individual alphabet strips (for warm-up activity and reference)

The teacher places 10 cards in a vertical column on the *before* side of the pocket chart, ensuring that the words are not in alphabetical order. The students discover that the first letter of each of the words is the same. Students respond to the question "What is your guide letter?" by saying, "The second letter is my guide letter." The teacher points to the second letter of each of the words as students follow the procedures detailed in the previous activity for reciting the alphabet, forming a new column on the *after* side, and proofreading. Students follow the same procedures as they practice with their word cards in columns on their desks.

Alphabetizing Word Cards by the First and Second Letters

- Pocket chart

- For the teacher, a set of 10 cards with words, some of which have the same first letter and some of which have a different first letter

- For each student, a set of 10 cards with words, some of which have the same first letter and some of which have a different first letter

- Individual alphabet strips (for warm-up activity and reference)

The teacher places 10 cards in a vertical column on the *before* side of the pocket chart, ensuring that the words are not in alphabetical order. The students discover that some of the first letters are the same and some are different. Students respond to "What is your guide letter?" by saying, "For most of the words, the first letter is the guide letter; for some, the second letter is the guide letter." Students recite the alphabet, saying "Stop!" when they see a word beginning with the letter they are saying. For example, in a list of words that contains *tent* and *trunk,* when students say "*T,*" they say, "Stop!" The teacher moves both *tent* and *trunk* to the column on the right and aligns them side by side, with a space beneath the two words. Students continue reciting the alphabet through *Z* as the teacher places the words in order in the column to the right. Students then come back to the two words beginning with *T* and say, "*Te* comes before *tr.*" The teacher places *trunk* in the empty space below *tent.* Students recite the alphabet again to proofread their work as usual. After saying, "*T,*" students say, "*Te* comes before *tr, U, V, W, X, Y, Z.*" Students follow the same procedures as they practice with their word cards on their desks.

After students are proficient at this level, the teacher introduces and students practice alphabetizing by the third letter; by the second and third letters; by the fourth letter; by third and fourth letters; and finally, by first, second, third, and fourth letters. In typical classrooms, students can apply this procedure by alphabetizing their spelling or vocabulary words written on index cards. After students can efficiently alphabetize a group of word cards with mixed guide letters, students are ready to alphabetize word lists.

Alphabetizing Words in Lists by the First Letter

- Individual alphabet strips (for warm-up activity and reference)

The teacher writes a list of words on the board to be alphabetized by the first letter. Students discover that the initial letter is their guide letter, and the teacher underlines each initial letter. Students recite the alphabet as the teacher points to the initial letter of each word. Students say, "Stop!" when they say a letter that matches the letter to which the teacher is pointing. The teacher numbers the words to the left of the word list to indicate alphabetical order. The teacher then gives students a list of words on paper to be alphabetized by first letter, and students follow the same procedure in numbering the words. As always, students check their work by reciting the alphabet again.

Alphabetizing a List of Words by the First and Second Letters

- Individual alphabet strips (for warm-up activity and reference)

The teacher writes a list of words on the board to be alphabetized by first and second letters. Some words have the same first letters, and some do not. The teacher draws a column of lines to the right of the list labeled *Letter* and a second column of lines labeled *Number*. An example follows.

Word	Letter	Number
track	_____	_____
den	_____	_____
tag	_____	_____
cube	_____	_____
bland	_____	_____
vote	_____	_____
same	_____	_____
gloss	_____	_____
camp	_____	_____
again	_____	_____

The students discover that the first and sometimes second letters are their guide letters. The teacher asks the students to name the initial letter of each word and writes the letter on the *Letter* line. If a letter is a duplicate, then the students name and the teacher writes the second letter of the word beside the initial letter. An example follows:

Word	Letter	Number
track	*tr*	_____
den	*d*	_____
tag	*ta*	_____

Students then recite the alphabet as the teacher points to the letters in the *Letter* column. The teacher numbers the words when the students say the guide letter(s). When the second letter is the guide letter, as with *track* and *tag*, students say, "*Ta* comes before *tr*." *Tag* is given the next number and *track* the next. The teacher gives students a list of words on paper with *Letter* and *Number* columns to the right of the list. Students follow the same procedures for numbering their list of words and checking their work. Students progress to alphabetizing word lists by the third letter; by the second and third letters; by the fourth letter; by the third and fourth letters; and by the first, second, third, and fourth letters. Eventually, students will number mixed word lists without the *Letter* column.

Activities for Developing Dictionary Skills

Schedule

After students can alphabetize word lists proficiently to the fourth letter, they are ready to develop dictionary skills. The teacher includes the missing letter decks, alphabetizing word cards, and words in lists activities within the weekly lesson plan as review. Students may not need to recite the alphabet as a warm-up activity at this point, but the individual alphabet strips remain in place for reference.

Discovery of Quartiles

- Dictionary for each student

- Three 3" × 5" index cards for each student

- Individual alphabet strips (for reference)

The teacher leads students in dividing the dictionary into two parts and marking the location (in the words beginning with *m*) with a 3" × 5" index card. Dividing the first part into halves again, students place a card in the words beginning with *e*. Dividing the second part into halves, students place a card in the words beginning with *s*. The teacher explains that the four parts of a gallon are called *quarts* and that the four parts of a dollar are called *quarters*. The teacher then tells students that the four parts of a dictionary are called *quartiles*. The letters that begin the four quartiles are *a, e, m,* and *s*.

Students create a sentence to aid memory such as, "All eagles must soar." If students ask why certain quartiles of the dictionary have fewer letters than others, then the teacher can explain that certain letters in the dictionary have more entries (e.g., there are more words starting with *a* than with *x*). Placing the quartiles where they are (rather than having an equal number of letter groups in each quartile) divides the dictionary more evenly.

Quartile Practice with 3-D Letters

- 3-D letter set for each student

- Individual alphabet strips

- Paper clips

The teacher directs students to place the 3-D letters into the four quartiles:

ABCD
EFGHIJKL
MNOPQR
STUVWXYZ

The teacher names a letter, such as *q*. Students echo the letter name and say the letter's quartile ("Q. Q is in the third quartile"). Students practice designating quartiles. After students are proficient, they may mark the quartiles on their alphabet strips with paper clips and designate the quartile of target letters while looking at the strips.

Discovery of Guide Words and Cornering

- Dictionary for each student

- Individual alphabet strips (for reference)

After students have become proficient with designating quartiles, the teacher directs them to a designated page in their dictionaries. Students are told that the two words at the top of each page are called **guide words.** The teacher explains that the guide word on the left is the first **entry word** (in bold print) on the page. The guide word on the right is the last entry word on the page. Just as guide letters are useful when students alphabetize words, guide words at the top of a dictionary page show the first and last entry words that will be on the page according to alphabetical order.

The teacher illustrates the **cornering** technique with the dictionary, an efficient way to focus only on the guide words. When the teacher looks forward in the dictionary (at the right-hand pages), the right hand turns only the corners of the pages while the left hand holds the turned pages. When the teacher looks backward in the dictionary (at the left-hand pages), the teacher's left hand "corners" the pages while the right hand holds those pages. Students practice cornering.

Locating a Letter Group within a Quartile by Cornering

- Dictionary for each student

- Individual alphabet strips (for reference)

The teacher directs students to find any guide word in the dictionary that begins with a designated letter, such as *r*. Students echo and say, "R is in the third quartile" and turn to the third quartile of their dictionaries. Students corner as they say, "R is after *o*. R is after *q*. Here is *r*." Students then name the letters of any guide word beginning with *r*. This activity is practiced several times until students can proficiently use the cornering technique.

Using Guide Words

- 3" × 5" index cards each bearing a target word in lowercase block letters

- Guide-word practice dictionary (contains only guide words and a **column word**)

- Individual alphabet strips (for reference)

The teacher writes two guide words with a target word between them on the board. The teacher explains that the word to be located in the dictionary is called the *target word.*

$$\textit{Example:} \quad \underline{\text{beam} \qquad \text{bet}}$$
$$\text{bend}$$

The teacher reviews the definition and purpose of guide words and target words. The guide word on the left is the first entry on the dictionary page; the guide word on the right is the last entry on the page. If the target word is on a particular page, then the target word will come after the first guide word and before the second guide word alphabetically. The teacher models by spelling the target word, *b-e-n-d,* and comparing it with the guide word on the left, *b-e-a-m.* (By naming the letters rather than the word, the teacher keeps the focus on the alphabetizing task rather than on reading.) The teacher asks, "What are your guide letters?" Students should respond, "The third letters are the guide letters because they are different." The teacher emphasizes the importance of starting with the letters of the target word and says, "*B-e-n* [emphasizing the guide letter] comes after *b-e-a.* I will draw an arrow under *beam* that points to the *after* side. My target word may be on this page because it comes after the first guide word."

Example: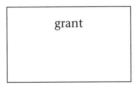

The teacher directs students to compare the target word with the guide word on the right and asks for the guide letters. The teacher leads the students in saying, "The third letters are the guide letters. *Ben* comes before *bet.* I will draw an arrow to the *before* side. The target word is on this page because it comes after the first guide word and before the second guide word. My arrows meet in the middle and show me that my target word is on this page."

Example: beam   bet
———→ bend ←———

The teacher gives each student a 3" × 5" index card on which a target word has been written.

The teacher directs students to a page in their guide-word practice dictionaries that contains only two guide words. A sample practice page follows:

glow | green

The teacher leads students in using guide words as detailed previously to discover whether the target word *grant* would be found on this page. (Students discover that the target word comes after the first guide word and before the second. The arrows meet in the middle, so the word is found on this page.) At first, all target words can be found on the page designated by the teacher. Sample guide words and target words for guide word practice pages follow.

Guide words	*Target words*
bingo bit	biology, biped, bird, bison
tumbling turboprop	tumult, tuna, tune, turbine
sail scout	saint, same, Saturday, scale

After students have had many practice sessions and are proficient at finding the target word when the teacher sends students to a designated page on which the target word is found, the teacher writes two guide words and a target word that comes after the guide words.

Example: <u>tumbling   turboprop</u>
turtle

The teacher directs students to a matching page in their guide-word practice dictionaries. The teacher first models the procedure on the board and then directs students to do the activity in their guide-word dictionaries. Comparing the target word with the guide word on the left, the teacher asks which letters are the guide letters. The teacher leads the students in saying, "The third letters are the guide letters. *Tur* is after *tum.* I will draw an arrow to the *after* side. The target word may be on this page because it is after the first guide word. In the second guide word, the fourth letters are the guide letters. *Turt* is after *turb.* I will draw an arrow to the *after* side. The target word cannot be on this page because it is after the second guide word on this page. The arrow shows that I need to turn to the page after this one to see whether the target word is on that page."

Students practice in their guide-word dictionaries with words found after the designated page occurs first because it reflects the left-to-right progression of the alphabet. After students have had many practice sessions and are proficient at finding out that the target word is after the designated page, the teacher writes two guide words and a target word that comes before the guide words.

Example: <u>glean   gluten</u>
glad

The students discover that the target word given by the teacher comes before that page. Students practice in their guide-word dictionaries and progress to locating a written target word without the teacher designating a page. Students verbalize as they compare the letters of their target word with those of the guide words at the top of the pages of their guide-word practice dictionaries (e.g., "*Ge* is after *ga*").

Using Column Words

- Guide-word practice dictionary for each student
- Individual alphabet strips (for reference)

After students are proficient at locating the correct page in a guide-word dictionary with designated target words, they are ready to discover whether their target word falls within the first or second column of a dictionary page. The teacher writes two guide words and a target word on the board, for example, *tell* and *tent,* and the target word *temper.* Students discover that their target word falls on this page. The teacher draws a line to indicate the two columns found on a dictionary page. At the top of the second column, the teacher writes a word representing the first entry in that column, such as *tend.* The teacher explains that this word is called the *column word* and it can be used to learn if the target word is in the first or second column. Students compare the target word (*temper*) with the column word (*tend*). The guide letter is the third letter. *M* comes before *n,* so the target word *temper* will be found in the first column.

Applying Skills Using a Regular Dictionary

- Dictionary for each student
- Individual alphabet strips (for reference)

After students are proficient at locating the correct page and column for written target words on pages in their guide-word practice dictionaries, the teacher leads them in applying the same skills using a regular dictionary. The dictionary should be appropriate for the level of the students with large print and no tabs. Students work with target words written by the teacher on 3" × 5" cards or on the board. Students locate the quartile, page, column, and word itself in the dictionary. Locating a word in 60 seconds or less is the goal.

Using Alphabetizing Skills with Other Reference Materials

- A variety of print and Internet reference materials
- Individual alphabet strips (for reference)

Students locate target words in a variety of other reference materials: computer listings, telephone directories, encyclopedias, and indexes in books.

Game to Reinforce Dictionary Skills

Dictionary Scavenger Hunt

- Dictionary for each student
- Individual alphabet strips (for reference)

The teacher leads students in discovering **sound pictures** (phonetic respellings for pronunciation), word origins, parts of speech, and examples of usage in the dictionary. After students are familiar with these aspects of the dictionary, they may apply their knowledge in a dictionary scavenger hunt. Students work individually or in teams to complete a page. A sample dictionary scavenger hunt follows.

1. Look up *telepathy*. What is the first entry word on that page?

    _____

2. What is the sound picture for *doubloon?* _____

    Copy a definition of *doubloon* from the dictionary. _____

3. Look up *run*. You may find more than one entry. This word can be used as how many different parts of speech? ____

    Write a sentence that illustrates *run* as a verb and another sentence that illustrates *run* as a noun. _____

4. Give the language of origin of these words or word parts:

    photo _____

    truck _____

    chiro _____

    tomato _____

    biped _____

    bio _____

Variation: Students can complete a reference scavenger hunt using materials such as Internet sites, encyclopedias, telephone books, and indexes in books.

CONCLUSION

Complete letter knowledge is essential for reading success. Knowledge of letters' shapes, names, and the phonemes they represent provides students with a solid foundation for using the alphabetic principle in learning to read. Moreover, this foundation needs to be strongly formed early in a child's academic career because word knowledge is built on letter knowledge. Inaccurate, incomplete, or inconsistent letter knowledge jeopardizes a student's ability to unitize letter sequences that can be automatically recognized by sight.

The ability to learn letter knowledge is dependent on multiple factors. First, some children have an advantage because they come to school with knowledge of letters' shapes, names, and sounds. Still other children begin school without any real letter knowledge and are already at an academic disadvantage when they begin formal schooling (Vellutino et al., 1996, 2003). Moreover, students learn about letters at inherently different rates. Regardless of each child's innate ability or preschool learning history, every child must know the shapes, names, and sounds of all the letters to be a good reader.

This presents a challenge to teachers because they must provide adequate letter-learning experiences for each child regardless of his or her prior letter knowledge or inherent ability to remember letters. Consequently, instruction must be individualized to meet the specific needs of every child in the class. Although some children may need only 10–20 exposures to a letter to recognize it automatically, other children may need 20 times that amount to overlearn the letters to the point of automaticity.

The NRP's meta-analysis (NICHD, 2000) stressed that letter knowledge enhances the effectiveness of both phonemic awareness and systematic phonics instruction for reading and spelling. In other words, students benefit more from instruction when the sound structure of words is linked to letters. Multisensory instruction directly and concretely links sounds and letter names to letter shapes to build a solid foundation of letter knowledge in the beginning reader. This type of instruction introduces letter knowledge and reinforces that knowledge by providing concrete mnemonic strategies and varied exercises designed to provide opportunities for letter mastery. Multisensory instruction is also paced so that prior knowledge is well established before new knowledge is introduced.

Beginning readers must also learn to sequentially process the letters they see in words, as well as the phonemes the letters represent. Repeated exposure to letters in the alphabet and practice in sequencing the alphabet provide reinforcement of sequential processing of letters. Facility in using alphabetical order gives students efficient access to information available through reference materials such as dictionaries, encyclopedias, and the Internet.

In review, good word-reading ability starts with well-established letter reading. Letter reading may seem simple, but learning the alphabet is challenging for many young readers. Vellutino et al. (1996, 2003) have found that dysfunctional readers more often have experiential or instructional deprivation rather than an innate learning disability. Intensive, systematic, and cumulative instruction has been validated as instruction that enhances children's ability to develop well-established letter knowledge by directly and concretely linking the letter symbols with their names and sounds and by providing adequate practice of the **linkages** (Carreker et al., 2005, 2007; Stein, 1987). Over time, teaching practice has shown that multisensory, structured, sequential instruction provides the strong foundation of letter knowledge that is required to support good word reading.

REFERENCES

Adams, M.J. (1990a). *Beginning to read: Thinking and learning about print.* Cambridge, MA: The MIT Press.

Adams, M.J. (1990b). *Beginning to read: Thinking and learning about print* [A summary]. (Prepared by S.A. Stahl, J. Osborn, & F. Lehr). Cambridge, MA: The MIT Press.

Badian, N.A. (1994). Preschool prediction: Orthographic and phonological skills, and reading. *Annals of Dyslexia, 44,* 3–25.

Badian, N.A. (1995). Predicting reading ability over the long term: The changing roles of letter naming, phonological awareness and orthographic processing. *Annals of Dyslexia, 45,* 79–96.

Berninger, V.B. (2000, November). *Language based reading and writing intervention: Findings of the University of Washington Multi-Disciplinary Disability Center.* Paper presented at the meeting of the International Dyslexia Association, Washington, DC.

Berninger, V.B., Abbott, R.D., Vermeulen, K., Ogier, S., Brooksher, L., Zook, D., et al. (2002). The comparison of faster and slower responders to early intervention in reading: Differentiating features of their language profiles. *Learning Disability Quarterly, 25*(1), 59–76.

Bond, G.L., & Dykstra, R. (1967). The cooperative research program in first-grade reading instruction. *Reading Research Quarterly, 2,* 5–142.

Carreker, S.H., Neuhaus, G.F., & Swank, P.R. (2007). Teachers with linguistically-informed knowledge of reading subskills are associated with a Matthew Effect in reading comprehension for monolingual and bilingual students. *Reading Psychology, 28,* 187–212.

Carreker, S.H., Swank, P.R., Neuhaus, G.F., Tillman-Dowdy, L., Monfils, M.J., & Montemayor, M.L., et al. (2005). Language enrichment teacher preparation and practice predicts third grade reading comprehension. *Reading Psychology, 26,* 401–432.

Chall, J.S. (1996). *Learning to read: The great debate* (3rd. ed.). Orlando, FL: Harcourt Brace & Co.

Cox, A.R. (1992). *Foundations for literacy: Structures and techniques for multisensory teaching of basic written English language skills.* Cambridge, MA: Educators Publishing Service.

Day, J.A. (1993). *Effectiveness of the Alphabetic Phonics teacher training course on student spelling ability for predictable and unpredictable words.* Unpublished manuscript.

Ehri, L.C. (1980). The development of orthographic images. In U. Frith (Ed.), *Cognitive processes in spelling* (pp. 311–338). San Diego: Academic Press.

Ehri, L.C. (1983). A critique of five studies related to letter-name knowledge and learning to read. In L.M. Gentile, M.L. Kamil, & J.S. Blanchard (Eds.), *Reading research revisited* (pp. 143–153). Columbus, OH: Charles E. Merrill.

Ehri, L.C. (1987). Learning to read and spell words. *Journal of Reading Behavior, 19,* 5–31.

Ehri, L.C. (1998). Grapheme-phoneme knowledge is essential for learning to read words in English. In J.L. Metsala & L.C. Ehri (Eds.), *Word recognition in beginning literacy* (pp. 3–40). Mahwah, NJ: Lawrence Erlbaum Associates.

Ehri, L.C., & Wilce, L.S. (1979). The mnemonic value of orthography among beginning readers. *Journal of Educational Psychology, 71,* 26–40.

Ehri, L.C., & Wilce, L.S. (1983). Development of word identification speed in skilled and less skilled beginning readers. *Journal of Educational Psychology, 75,* 3–18.

Foorman, B.R., Francis, D.J., Shaywitz, S.E., Shaywitz, B.A., & Fletcher, J.M. (1997). The case for early reading intervention. In B. Blachman (Ed.), *Foundations of reading acquisition and dyslexia* (pp. 243–264). Mahwah, NJ: Lawrence Erlbaum Associates.

Foorman, B.R., & Torgesen, J. (2001). Critical elements of classroom and small-group instruction promote reading success in all children. *Learning Disabilities Research and Practice, 16*(4), 203–212.

Frankiewicz, R.G. (1984a). *An evaluation of the impact of the Alphabetic Phonics program in Cypress Fairbanks Independent School District from 1981 through 1984.* Unpublished manuscript.

Frankiewicz, R.G. (1984b). *An evaluation of the impact of the Alphabetic Phonics program in River Oaks Baptist School from 1983-1984.* Unpublished manuscript.

Frankiewicz, R.G. (1985). *An evaluation of the Alphabetic Phonics program offered in a one-to-one mode.* Unpublished manuscript.

Gardner, H. (1985). *Frames of mind: The theory of multiple intelligences.* New York: Basic Books.

Gibson, E.J., Gibson, J.J., Pick, A., & Osser, H. (1962). A developmental study of the discrimination of letter-like forms. *Journal of Comparative and Physiological Psychology, 55,* 897–906.

Gillingham, A., & Stillman, B.W. (1960). *Remedial training for children with specific disability in reading, spelling, and penmanship* (6th ed.). Cambridge, MA: Educators Publishing Service.

Gunning, T.G. (1996). *Creating reading instruction for all children* (2nd ed.). Boston: Allyn & Bacon.

Hallahan, D.P., & Kauffman, J.M. (1976). *Introduction to learning disabilities: A psychobehavioral approach.* Upper Saddle River, NJ: Prentice Hall.

Harm, M.W., & Seidenberg, M.S. (2004). Computing the meanings of words in reading: Cooperative division of labor between visual and phonological processes. *Psychological Review, 111*(3), 662–720.

Hogan, E.A., & Smith, M.T. (1987). *Alphabet and dictionary skills guide.* Cambridge, MA: Educators Publishing Service.

Joshi, R.M., Dahlgren, M., & Boulware-Gooden, R. (2002). Teaching reading in an inner city school through a multisensory teaching approach. *Annals of Dyslexia, 52,* 229–242.

Juel, C. (1988). Learning to read and write: A longitudinal study of fifty-four children from first through fourth grade. *Journal of Educational Psychology, 80,* 437–447.

LaBerge, D., & Samuels, S.J. (1974). Toward a theory of automatic information processing in reading. *Cognitive Psychology, 6,* 293–323.

Liberman, I.Y., & Liberman, A.M. (1990). Whole language vs. code emphasis: Underlying assumptions and their implications for reading instruction. *Annals of Dyslexia, 40,* 51–76.

Liberman, I.Y., Shankweiler, D., Orlando, C., Harris, H.S., & Berti, F.B. (1971). Letter confusion and reversals of sequence in the beginning reader: Implications for Orton's theory of developmental dyslexia. *Cortex, 7,* 127–142.

National Institute of Child Health and Human Development. (2000). *Report of the National Reading Panel: Reports of the subgroups. Teaching children to read: An evidence-based assessment of the scientific research literature on reading and its implications for reading instruction* (NIH Publication No. 00-4754). Washington, DC: Government Printing Office.

Neuhaus Education Center. (1998). *Basic language skills: Book 1.* Bellaire, TX: Suzanne Carreker.

Neuhaus, G.F. (2000). An investigation of phonological awareness, orthographic recognition, and attention as predictors of Rapid Automatized Naming (RAN) and reading. *Dissertation Abstracts International,* 136–138. (UMI No. 9979233)

Neuhaus, G.F. (2002). What does it take to read a letter? *Perspectives, 28*(1), 6–8.

Neuhaus, G.F., Carlson, C., Jeng, M.W., Post, Y., & Swank, P.R. (2001). The reliability and validity of rapid automatized naming (RAN) scoring software for the determination of pause and articulation component durations. *Educational and Psychological Measurement, 61*(3), 490–504.

Neuhaus, G.F., Foorman, B.R., Francis, D.J., & Carlson, C. (2001). Measures of information processing in rapid automatized naming (RAN) and their relation to reading. *Journal of Experimental Child Psychology, 78*(4), 359–373.

Neuhaus, G.F., Roldan, L.W., Bouware-Gooden, R., & Swank, P.R. (2006). Parsimonious reading models: Identifying teachable subskills. *Reading Psychology, 27*, 37–58.

Neuhaus, G.F., & Swank, P.R. (2002). Understanding the relations between RAN letters subtest components and word reading in first grade students. *Journal of Learning Disabilities, 35*(2), 158–174.

Perfetti, C.A. (1985). *Reading ability.* New York: Oxford University Press.

Plaut, D.C., McClelland, J.L., Seidenberg, M., & Patterson, K.E. (1996). Understanding normal and impaired word reading: Computational principles in quasi-regular domains. *Psychological Review, 103*, 56–115.

Post, Y. (1999). *Building bridges: Literacy instruction links success to low-SES mobile minority population.* Retrieved February 17, 2003, from http://www.neuhaus.org/Research/BuildingBridges-070101.doc

Reed, L., Selig, H., Young, N., & Day, J.A. (1995). A working model for implementing multisensory teaching in the classroom. In C.W. McIntyre & J.S. Pickering (Eds.), *Clinical studies of multisensory language education for students with dyslexia and related disorders* (pp. 23–35). Dallas, TX: International Multisensory Structured Language Education Council.

Seidenberg, M.S., & McClelland, J.L. (1989). A distributed, developmental model of word recognition and naming. *Psychological Review, 96*, 523–568.

Shankweiler, D., & Liberman, I.Y. (1972). Misreading: A search for causes. In J.F. Kavanagh & I.G. Mattingly (Eds.), *Language by ear and by eye* (pp. 293–317). Cambridge, MA: The MIT Press.

Share, D.L., Jorm, A.F., Maclean, R., & Matthews, R. (1984). Sources of individual differences in reading acquisition. *Journal of Educational Psychology, 76*, 1309–1324.

Siegel, L.S., Share, D., & Geva, E. (1995). Evidence for superior orthographic skills in dyslexics, *Psychological Science, 6*(4), 250–254.

Stanovich, K.E. (1986). Matthew effects in reading: Some consequences of individual differences in the acquisition of literacy. *Reading Research Quarterly, 21*, 360–406.

Stanovich, K.E., & Siegel, L. (1994). Phenotypic performance profile of children with reading disabilities: A regression-based test of the phonological-core variable-difference model. *Journal of Educational Psychology, 86*(1), 24–53.

Stein, T. (1987). *An evaluation of the impact of the Alphabetic Phonics program: One-to-one instruction from 1983 through 1986.* Unpublished manuscript.

Sulzby, E. (1983). A commentary on Ehri's critique of five studies related to letter-name knowledge and learning to read: Broadening the question. In L.M. Gentile, M.L. Kamil, & J.S. Blanchard (Eds.), *Reading research revisited* (pp. 155–161). Columbus, OH: Charles E. Merrill.

Thorpe, H.W., & Borden, K.S. (1985). The effect of multisensory instruction upon the on-task behaviors and word reading accuracy of learning disabled children. *Journal of Learning Disabilities, 18*, 279–286.

Treiman, R., Tincoff, R., Rodriguez, K., Mouzaki, A., & Francis, D.J. (1998). The foundations of literacy: Learning the sounds of letters. *Child Development, 69*(6), 1524–1540.

Vellutino, F.R. (1979). *Dyslexia: Theory and research.* Cambridge, MA: The MIT Press.

Vellutino, F.R. (1980). Dyslexia—perceptual deficiency or perceptual inefficiency? In J.F. Kavanagh & R.L. Venezky (Eds.), *Orthography, reading, and dyslexia* (pp. 251–270). Baltimore: University Park Press.

Vellutino, F.R., Scanlon, D.M., & Jaccard, J. (2003). Toward distinguishing between cognitive and experiential deficits as primary sources of difficulty in learning to read: A two year follow-up of difficult to remediate and readily remediated poor readers. In B.R. Foorman (Ed.), *Preventing and remediating reading difficulties: Bringing science to scale* (pp. 73–120). Timonium, MD: York Press.

Vellutino, F.R., Scanlon, D.M., Sipay, E.R., Small, S.G., Pratt, A., Chen, R., et al. (1996). Cognitive profiles of difficult to remediate and readily remediated poor readers: Early intervention as a vehicle for distinguishing between cognitive and experiential deficits as basic causes of specific reading disability. *Journal of Educational Psychology, 88*(4), 601–638.

Vellutino, F.R., Smith, H., Steger, J.A., & Kaman, M. (1975). Reading disability: Age differences and the perceptual deficit hypothesis. *Child Development, 46*, 487–493.

Walsh, D.J., Price, G.G., & Gillingham, M.G. (1988). The critical but transitory importance of letter naming. *Reading Research Quarterly, 23*, 108–122.

Wolf, M. (1997). A provisional, integrative account of phonological and naming-speed deficits in dyslexia: Implications for diagnosis and intervention. In B. Blachman (Ed.), *Foundation of reading acquisition and dyslexia: Implications for early intervention* (pp. 67–92). Mahwah, NJ: Lawrence Erlbaum Associates.

Wolf, M., Bowers, P.G., & Biddle, K. (2000). Naming-speed processes, timing, and reading: A conceptual review. *Journal of Learning Disabilities, 33*, 387–407.

Wolf, M., & Obregón, M. (1992). Early naming

deficits, developmental dyslexia, and a specific deficit hypothesis. *Brain and Language, 42,* 219–247.

Wolf, M., & Obregón, M. (1997). The "double-deficit" hypothesis: Implications for diagnosis and practice in reading disabilities. In L. Putnam (Ed.), *Readings on language and literacy* (pp. 177–209). Cambridge, MA: Brookline Books.

Wolf, M., O'Brien, B., Adams, K.D., Joffe, T., Jeffrey, J., Lovett, M., et al. (2003). "Working for time": Reflections on naming speed, reading fluency, and intervention. In B.R. Foorman (Ed.), *Preventing and remediating reading difficulties: Bringing science to scale* (pp. 355–380). Timonium, MD: York Press.

7
Teaching Handwriting

BEVERLY J. WOLF

In many textbooks on teaching reading, handwriting is classified as one of the mechanics along with spelling, punctuation, and grammar. Rarely is handwriting given the importance it deserves in the overall language arts program for typical students or even in intervention programs for students with learning disabilities, although writing disabilities are often more persistent than reading disabilities. Whether teachers are prepared to teach handwriting to struggling students or even to all students in the general classroom is an important question. This chapter gives the rationale for including handwriting as a vital component of multisensory instruction of literacy skills and a component skill for developing a functional writing system (Berninger, 1999).

This chapter also highlights the importance of handwriting instruction in early education and in remediation, provides a brief history of handwriting instruction, and discusses some of the syndromes related to difficulties with handwriting. Following that are reports of research evidence of the efficacy of direct teaching of handwriting to students with dyslexia, general principles and specific information on how to teach print and cursive handwriting using a multisensory framework that integrates handwriting instruction with reading and spelling, ending with a brief discussion of keyboarding and **assistive technology** alternatives.

THE IMPORTANCE OF HANDWRITING
INSTRUCTION IN EARLY EDUCATION AND REMEDIATION

Writing has added a timeless dimension to oral communication, expanding communicative capabilities the way mathematics did to counting on fingers and toes, and has made our modern world possible (vos Savant, 1988). Despite increasing reliance on electronic communication, legible handwriting is still a necessary communication and educational skill. In times of natural disasters such as Hurricane Katrina, for example, handwritten records and information storage was necessary, emphasizing the importance of legible writing. **Cacography,** bad handwriting or spelling, causes business losses—telephone calls to wrong numbers, incorrect items shipped, sloppy tax returns, undeliverable letters and packages—and costs around $200 million annually (Florey 2009).

Research emphasizes the importance of handwriting in developing the orthographic skills needed for reading. "Research shows that handwriting, spelling, and composition are separable processes but that, when all these component processes are adequately developed, they function in concert in the functional writing system" (Berninger & Richards, 2002). Adams suggested that the activities of letter tracing and copying "may contribute valuably toward the development of those **fine motor skills** that determine the willingness as well as the ability to write" and help in "developing necessary skills for reading as well as writing" (1990, p. 357). Instruction in writing and spelling often comes before instruction in reading during efforts to promote phonemic awareness by teaching letter names and sounds and phonemic segmentation while children are in kindergarten (Rubin & Eberhardt, 1996). At this point, it is important for children to know the names of the letters and to distinguish between upper- and lowercase letters (see Chapter 6). Young children want to learn to write. They see older children and adults writing, and they begin to make their own marks on paper, walls, or furniture. They begin the writing process with motivating and meaningful experiences in preschool and kindergarten. They have opportunities to trace and copy letters using markers, pencils, and crayons. Models of letters on alphabet strips or letter cards showing upper- and lowercase letters are available for the children to observe. They progress from drawing and scribbling, to creating strings of letter-like forms, to generating invented spellings (Snow, Burns, & Griffin, 1998). Although Snow et al.'s recommendations for practice do not suggest that teachers, even professional reading specialists, should be prepared to teach handwriting, they clearly outlined the handwriting demands for kindergarten and first-grade reading accomplishments:

Kindergarten

- Writes own name (first and last) and the first names of some friends or classmates

- Can write most letters and some words when they are dictated

First grade

- Composes fairly readable first drafts using appropriate parts of the writing process (e.g., planning, drafting, rereading for meaning, and self-correcting)

- Produces a variety of compositions (e.g., stories, descriptions, journal entries) showing appropriate relationships between printed text, illustrations, and other graphics.

To meet the demands of these accomplishments, children need direct, explicit instruction in letter formation and much guided practice to become proficient in the task of handwriting.

Berninger emphasized that handwriting is not merely a motor act: "It is a written language act that taps the processes of creating letter representations in memory and then retrieving them" (1998, p. 47). She explained that difficulty with "the ability to code an identified language symbol (letter) in memory" (1998, p. 47) accounts for handwriting problems more than trouble with fine motor skills do. Although motor skills contribute to handwriting (Graham & Weintraub, 1996), orthographic coding has a more direct relationship to handwriting than do fine motor skills (Abbott & Berninger, 1993). When children do not remember the sequence of movement required in speech or letter formation, voluntary motor function cannot be triggered. That lack of kinesthetic recall for speech and/or for letter formation may hinder fluent speech and penmanship (Slingerland, 1976).

Even though the computer is a tool for writers that facilitates the act of writing and increases the volume of written material, it is not always as readily available as the pencil and pen, which are easily carried in the pocket. In addition, the computer is not a substitute for kinesthetic reinforcement provided by manual writing when learning to read. Graham, Berninger, Abbott, Abbott, and Whittaker (1997) found that legible letter writing and automatic letter writing contribute to the amount and quality of written composition in Grades 1–6. Furthermore, the quality and utility of accessible and legible handwriting skills have become more essential with the advent of high-stakes testing. Students with writing difficulties are much more likely to stand out.

Many teachers encourage their students to write journal entries to practice letter formation but do not give students an appropriate model and accept either print or cursive as long as it is legible. These teachers appear to be bypassing the use of formal instructional material (Tabor, 1996).

There are many advantages to formal handwriting instruction. Beginning readers are reinforcing awareness of letter shapes when they learn to write—connecting symbols to letter names and sounds. Louise Spear-Swerling said that writing focuses attention on letter form (as cited in Florey, 2009). Time spent on handwriting practice to improve legibility and develop fluency is a time saver for both the teacher, who spends less effort deciphering the writing, and the pupils, who complete written assignments more quickly (McMenamin & Martin, 1980). Spelling improves when legibility increases (Strickling, 1974). Automaticity and fluency in handwriting are also important because they give individuals the freedom to concentrate on accurate spelling, higher level thought processes, and written expression. The more fluent and automatic handwriting is, the more working memory is available for higher level composing processes. Automaticity is also a strong predictor of the quality of composition in typically developing writers and writers with disabilities (Berninger, 1999). A fluent writer can discover errors more easily with fewer ambiguously formed letters, which interfere with proofreading, and a greater amount of reinforcement of correct word patterns becomes available. College students have difficulty with lecture comprehension when their note-taking is too slow (Blalock, 1985).

Individuals need to be able to write legibly to allow others to read easily. In most school districts, formal training in handwriting appears to be limited to the first three or four grades. Some poor handwriting may be caused by students not having enough training to form letters automatically when rapid writing is needed as a tool to perform assigned writing tasks (Hamstra-Bletz & Blöte, 1990). For most students, motor skills used in handwriting can be improved with guided practice once correct models are demonstrated, and many models are made available. Self-help workbooks for students and adults have been developed to facilitate practice.

Kinesthetic memory, the earliest, strongest, and most reliable form of memory, may aid spellers in remembering orthographic patterns. As a final point, students need to be aware that teachers often judge students' abilities and grade them based on the appearance of their written work.

A BRIEF HISTORY OF HANDWRITING INSTRUCTION

The history of teaching handwriting begins in ancient times. Richardson (1995) noted that Plato (428 B.C.–348 B.C.), and Seneca (4 B.C.–A.D. 65) were specific in their instructions to those who taught handwriting. Plato instructed the master to draw lines (letters) for the student to copy. Seneca had the teacher guide the student's hand as the letters were traced. Quintilian (A.D. 35–A.D. 100) suggested using a board with letters cut into it so that the child could keep the pen within the letters to make the letter forms accurately. Quintilian also recommended that the student learn the sound and shape of a letter simultaneously.

Cursive letters have evolved over time from the highly ornamental and calligraphic forms used by medieval monasteries. Today, the more simplified styles of Palmer, Zaner-Bloser, and the D'Nealian method are taught in the United States (Phelps & Stempel, 1987).

In a comprehensive review of research in reading, writing, and math disorders for the U.S. Interagency Committee on Learning Disabilities, Johnson (1988) described a shift in the teaching of penmanship. In the late 1800s and early 1900s, penmanship was taught as a separate subject, with copying drills that focused on the form of the letter itself and appropriate posture. After the 1940s, curricular changes led to a broader emphasis on language arts that resulted in less time being devoted to handwriting instruction in schools. This reordering of priorities led to a debate about whether teachers should provide direct instruction in skills and processes or allow children to engage in extensive reading, writing, and speaking experiences without explicit input on component language **subskills** such as handwriting. As personal computers have become more common, school systems have placed even less importance on teaching handwriting. Both legible letter writing and automatic letter writing contribute to the amount and quality of written composition in Grades 1–6, however (Graham et al., 1997).

SYNDROMES RELATED TO DIFFICULTIES WITH HANDWRITING

Students with dyslexia are impaired in skills such as decoding, word reading, and spelling. **"Dysgraphia** is unusual difficulty with handwriting and/or spelling that may occur alone or with dyslexia" (Berninger & Wolf, 2009, p. 93). Children with dysgraphia may express their difficulties with slow, nonautomatic letter formation or with illegible handwriting. They may use excessive pressure or have incorrect pencil position.

The discussion of whether individuals with dyslexia produce an increased number of letter reversals and transpositions has continued over the years. Dr. Samuel T. Orton (1937) observed directional confusions in his patients. Vellutino (1979) and Brooks (2003) both found that reversals are not related to visual perception. The importance of reversals in individuals with dyslexia has been minimized because typically developing children make reversals, too. Parents and teachers of individuals with dyslexia, however, continue to express concern about these confusions. A study by Brooks, Berninger, and Abbot (2006) examined incidence of reversals in 182 children ages 6–18. They found that not all students made reversals. Although both groups made reversals, students with dyslexia produced a higher proportion of reversal errors than those without dyslexia. They concluded that errors may be a sign that working memory can experience temporary inefficiencies or momentary breakdowns.

Disruption may occur in the storage system, which is both phonologically and orthographically coded, or in the time-sensitive phonological loop that coordinates orthographic

and phonological codes in working memory, or in the executive system that regulates inhibition of irrelevant processes, switching mental state, and self-monitoring and updating
working memory. (Brooks et al., 2006, p. 2)

It is possible to know how to spell words correctly but not be able to write them by hand.
This condition, in which letter shapes, letter sequences, and motor patterns are impaired,
is called **specific agraphia** (Goodman & Caramazza, 1986). In Samuel T. Orton's research on reading problems (as cited in J.L. Orton, 1966), he considered poor handwriting as both an interrelated and a separate language function. According to Orton, poor
handwriting could result in poor visual reinforcement of word patterns and thus a weakened circuit between visual memory for printed words for writing, reading, and spelling
and poor auditory memory for words in speech, spelling, and writing. He recognized,
too, that slow, messy handwriting could constitute a specific language disability itself.

According to Levine (1994), many children have fine motor problems that affect
only writing. These children's writing is slow and laborious as well as sometimes illegible. There are three common forms of this graphomotor dysfunction. The first is
motor memory dysfunction, in which there is trouble integrating motor output
with memory input. Children with this condition have difficulty in recalling the sequence of **motor engrams** (muscle movements) that are needed to form a specific
letter. The second is **graphomotor production deficit,** in which the larger muscles of the wrist and forearm are used during letter formation because they are under
better control than the small muscles of the fingers. This results in laborious and slow
but legible writing. The third is a **motor feedback problem,** sometimes referred to
as **finger agnosia,** in which an individual has to visually monitor the location of the
pencil point because the fingers do not report their location to the brain (Levine, 1994).
A child with agnosia may use an awkward, fist-like pencil grip in which he or she places
the thumb over the other fingers, preventing the fingers from moving the pencil efficiently. Handwriting for such a child is exhausting and painfully slow, to such an extent that it interferes with fluency.

Improvement can be achieved through formal handwriting programs that provide
practice with appropriate models. School occupational therapists are often involved in
providing the instruction (Reisman, 1991). The bypass strategy of learning keyboarding
and using a computer is usually recommended for older students. When they write by
hand, they are encouraged to use either print or cursive, whichever is their preference
(Black, 1996; see Appendix B at the end of the book for recommended keyboarding and
handwriting programs). Berninger and Amtmann (2003) cautioned, "It is important to
remember that these technological tools bypass handwriting difficulties but create new
tasks with processing requirements that may or may not be a challenge for an individual student." Early handwriting instruction and continued practice may reduce the
number of students needing bypass strategies.

EVIDENCE FOR EFFICACY OF THE DIRECT
TEACHING OF HANDWRITING TO STUDENTS WITH DYSLEXIA

Handwriting instruction is beneficial to both students with dyslexia and dysgraphia
and those without. It establishes standards of performance while letter names and forms
are reinforced. Instruction and practice develop secure motor patterns that make handwriting become an automatic skill. When writing is automatic, the brain is free to recall correct spelling and to develop ideas.

Initial Teaching of Manuscript Print versus Cursive Handwriting

Young children usually become aware of the concept of groups of letters as symbols with meaning (i.e., the alphabetic principle) through their most personal possession—their names. Caregivers or teachers who show children how their names are written with printed letters commonly introduce this concept. Whether a child's name is written in upper- or lowercase letters, it becomes a symbol of self. **Manuscript print** is customarily taught to first- and second-grade students in most public schools, and cursive is introduced at the end of second grade or the beginning of third grade. Most public school districts use manuscript print when introducing handwriting to young children, perhaps because it is most consistent with preschool learning and because it is the writing style encountered in reading texts. Berninger and Wolf reported,

> Children who have not mastered manuscript writing may have extreme difficulty in making the transition to cursive writing instruction, but other children make the transition easily from manuscript handwriting to cursive writing instruction. Whether a student with dyslexia also has dysgraphia may influence how the student responds to either manuscript or cursive handwriting instruction. (2009, p. 95)

Reasons to Teach Manuscript Print Initially

- Print writing introduces children to the letter forms they will need to recognize as they begin to learn to read.

- The typeface used in the basic readers is more like print writing than cursive in appearance.

- The use of print by the teacher allows primary-grade children to see the same symbol forms used for reading, writing, and spelling, thereby reducing confusion.

Proponents of the initial teaching of cursive writing, such as Cox (1992), cited a number of advantages of cursive handwriting, especially for students with dyslexia (Phelps & Stempel, 1987; Texas Scottish Rite Hospital for Children [TSRHC], 1996). Cursive handwriting does the following:

- Eliminates a student's need to decide where each letter should begin because all cursive letter shapes begin on the baseline

- Provides directional movement from left to right

- Provides unique letter shapes that are not mirror images of other letters

- Reduces reversals by eliminating the need to raise the pencil while writing a single letter or a series of letters in a word

- Eliminates the need to learn two different writing skills, allowing the student to avoid confusion

Some school districts have devised their own handwriting curriculum by analyzing letters and developing directions to make it easy and legible (Wessel, 1984). The goal is to provide a legible, automatic means of written expression.

Developmental Stages of Learning Handwriting

Acquiring the skills needed for writing occurs in six stages, with variation in the rate of progress of even typically achieving children (Levine 1987).

1. *Imitation—preschool to first grade:* Children pretend to write by mimicking actual writing while acquiring skill in letter and number formation but lack precise graphomotor skill. Early warning signs of potential problems may be observed in children who have fine motor weaknesses and become frustrated and self-conscious as they notice their peers' proficiency. Hand preference is shown, although it is not fully established in all children.

2. *Graphic presentation—first and second grades:* Children become more aware of spatial planning as they learn to form both lower- and uppercase letters and recognize the need for more space between words than between letters. Letter reversals are common, sometimes because of confusion over directionality and **laterality** and at other times because the need to concentrate and remember the configuration of the letter causes a child to overlook directionality. Fine motor control becomes better developed, and the child relies increasingly on **proprioception** and kinesthetic feedback (an inner sense of where the fingers are on the page). Letters become smaller to fit the lines on the paper.

3. *Progressive incorporation—late second to fourth grades:* Children produce print letters with less conscious effort, are less preoccupied with spatial and aesthetic appearance of their writing, and are ready to accept cursive writing as a more efficient system. Rules of capitalization, punctuation, syntax, and grammar are incorporated.

4. *Automatization—fourth through seventh grades:* Writing rate and efficiency become significant as children are expected to communicate in writing using correct grammar, spelling, punctuation, capitalization, and vocabulary while automatically recalling and producing legible letter forms.

5. *Elaboration—seventh through ninth grades:* Writing is used to establish and express a viewpoint. In proficient writers, written language exceeds everyday speech in complexity.

6. *Personalization-diversification—ninth grade and beyond:* Individual style and talent for writing develops. Students who find writing too difficult may never reach this stage.

Luria (1973) described the process of learning to write as initially depending on memorization of the graphic forms of every letter. It takes place through a chain of isolated motor impulses, each of which is responsible for the performance of only one element of the graphic structure. With practice, this structure of the process is radically altered, and writing is converted into a single kinetic melody.

A child with learning disabilities apparently experiences a breakdown in the developmental continuum described by Luria (1973). Handwriting, according to Hagin (1983), should be taught at a level appropriate to the child's motor mastery and as a task that involves visual, motor, kinesthetic, temporal, and spatial skills. Research cited by Getman (1984) showed that arm and hand movements that produce the least physiological and cognitive stress came from the shoulder with the full arm involved in the movements required for forming letters. Completing the motor patterns eventually allows handwriting to become such a habitual skill that the mind is free to think while the arm and hand automatically produce the words chosen by the mind. A student experiencing a problem with the motor act of handwriting often resists writing anything at all because it is tiring or at best writes as little as possible (Cicci, 1995).

Rationale for Multisensory
Teaching of Print and Cursive Handwriting

Although it is not a handwriting program per se, the Fernald (1943) method is a special remedial approach to teaching reading and spelling that involves handwriting directly (see Table 2.1 for more on the **Fernald method**). The tracing of words to be learned involves all four sensory pathways: visual, auditory, kinesthetic, and tactile. For reading, the student traces the word the teacher has written (a process involving the visual, kinesthetic, and tactile senses) while saying the word (a process using the auditory sense). (See Appendix B at the end of this book for a list of other programs utilizing multisensory approaches for teaching handwriting.)

Cox (1980, 1985, 1992) and Slingerland (1971, 1976, 1981), who adapted systems of teaching for children with dyslexia from the Orton (1937) and Gillingham approach (Gillingham & Stillman, 1960), stressed the multisensory aspects of teaching handwriting. Cox insisted on using cursive, suggesting that "a strong kinesthetic memory may reinforce the visual memory of letter shapes for reading" (1992, p. 19). Naming the letters aloud while tracing or copying them is not just a remedial technique. Adams pointed out that children often say the name or the sound naturally as they write, which helps to "bind the visual, motor, and phonological images of the letter together at once" (1990, p. 355). In the Slingerland approach,

> The process of learning to write is not part of ordinary development and should be taught as a basic skill. As the form of each letter is introduced, review time should be planned for strengthening the Visual-Auditory-Kinesthetic (VAK) associations of *sight- sound* (grapheme-phoneme)-*feel* (hand and mouth) of each letter as it is named. (1981, p. 21)

Some students who have better kinesthetic memory than visual memory learn to write more easily than they learn to read; thus, writing training may take the lead in multisensory language training as these students' strongest pathway to learning (Cox, 1992). Difficulty with retrieving letter symbols from visual memory, which is typically weak in individuals with dyslexia, is a major deterrent to rapid, automatic production of alphabet letters, which is a lower order skill that is most important in the beginning stages of writing (Berninger, Mizokawa, & Bragg, 1991).

Kinesthetic performance using visual symbols and their letter names forms a multisensory association that helps strengthen recall for both reading and writing (Cox, 1992; Slingerland, 1971). One activity that accomplishes this is forming a large letter shape made in the air with a straight arm while naming the letter, a key word that begins with that letter, and the letter sound. The addition of this multisensory component is especially valuable for children who confuse commonly reversed letters such as *b*, *d*, *g*, *p*, *q*, and *s*. Students with weaknesses in one modality area can use their strengths to achieve success in another.

GENERAL PRINCIPLES IN THE
MULTISENSORY TEACHING OF HANDWRITING

Multisensory teaching links listening, speaking, reading, and writing. It is a simultaneous linkage of visual, auditory, and kinesthetic-motor that reinforces the close relationships between letter production and letter perception. When students see the letter and associate the form with its name and its feel while writing, the stronger channels reinforce the weak, thus strengthening performance and recall.

Ready Reference

Alphabet wall cards provide an easy reference for children and may be made by the teacher or purchased. Some teachers prefer to use cards with keyword pictures that also serve to help children recall the sounds of the letters. Prepared materials by Cox (1992), Gillingham (Gillingham & Stillman, 1997), Slingerland (1976; Slingerland & Aho, 1985b), and Wilson Language Training (Wilson, 2002) are available (see Appendix B at the end of the book). The cards should be visible so that children can refer to them easily at any time. Most classroom teachers display them in alphabetical order above the chalkboard so that children have a ready reference to the different letter shapes.

Good Posture

Poor body position can significantly interfere with coordinating the hand movements in writing (Kurtz, 1994). The student should use a chair with a flat back and a seat that allows the feet to rest flat on the floor, with the hips, knees, and ankles all at 90-degree angles. The desk should be 2 inches higher than the child's bent elbows (Benbow, 1988, as cited in Kurtz, 1994). A desk that is too high will cause the student to elevate the shoulders, which is tiring and restricts freedom of movement, whereas a desk that is too low could cause the student to slouch. The nonwriting hand and arm should be on the desk to hold the paper in place.

Proper Pencil Grasp

The child should use a normal tripod pencil grip (see Figure 7.1). The pencil rests on the first joint of the middle finger with the thumb and index fingers holding the pencil in place and the pencil held at a 45-degree angle to the page. An awkward pencil grip can indicate finger agnosia. Using an auxiliary plastic pencil grip or a metal writing frame can aid in changing the fatiguing grip to a normal, less tiring one (Phelps & Stempel, 1985; TSRHC, 1990). Children may need to experiment with pencil grips or a writing frame to determine which one works best for them. Many become frustrated with these implements once the novelty has worn off. The pencil should point toward the shoulder of the writing arm for both left- and right-handed students.

An alert, diligent teacher can help a student change pencil position, but this requires consistency and patience. At any time that the teacher notes incorrect position, he or she can instruct the class as follows:

Teacher: Stop.

Students place their pencils on the desk with the point toward them.

Teacher: Pinch.

With the index finger and thumb in a "pinch" position, students lightly grasp their pencils where the paint begins (approximately 1 inch from the point).

Teacher: Lift.

As the children lift the pencil, it will fall back to correct writing position and rest on the first joint of the middle finger.

After a few practice sessions, students only need to hear, "stop, pinch, lift," to adjust their pencil positions. Teacher perseverance will help students become accustomed

Recognized Correct and Incorrect Writing Grips

Correct

1. The pencil rests on the first joint of the middle finger with the thumb and index fingers holding the pencil in place.

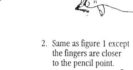

2. Same as figure 1 except the fingers are closer to the pencil point.

3. Same as figure 1 except the pencil is held perpendicular to table.

Incorrect

4. Thumb and index finger holding pencil, with the index finger overlapping the thumb.

5. Pencil held by tips of fingers. Thumb on one side, middle and index finger on the other.

6. Thumb wraps around pencil with the index and middle fingers pressing pencil to ring finger.

7. Index, middle and ring finger tips hold one side of pencil, the thumb holds the other.

8. Pencil is held between the index and middle fingers, pressing pencil to the thumb.

9. Thumb on one side, index and middle fingers on the other, all pressing the pencil to ring finger.

10. Index finger holds pencil to middle finger, with the thumb overlapping the index finger.

11. The thumb holds the pencil along the first joints of the rest of the fingers.

12. The pencil is grasped in the fist, and held up against the thumb.

Thē Pencil Grip

P.O. Box 67096 Los Angeles, CA 90067   (310) 788-9485   Fax (310) 788-0644

Figure 7.1.   Recognized correct and incorrect writing grips. (Reprinted by permission of Thē Pencil Grip. www.the penilgrip.com; The Pencil Group, P.O. Box 67096, Los Angeles, CA 90067)

to the feel of the new position and use it consistently. After a time, only the one or two children who have continued difficulty will need reminders. The older the child, the more difficulty he or she will have with changing the pencil position.

Writing Implement

"The complex motor action of writing is overwhelmingly dependent upon accurate, ongoing kinesthetic [reafferent] feedback" (Levine, 1987, p. 226). While the child is writing, he or she is receiving feedback in the form of pressure and the pull of the pencil against the paper. A No. 2 or softer pencil should be used. Pencils with soft lead require less pressure from the child, thereby reducing fatigue. Children with impaired kinesthetic feedback will benefit from using softer leads, which will not break as the children press firmly in an attempt to receive that feedback when writing (Levine, 1987). It is preferable to use pencils without erasers. Instead, the teacher can instruct children to bracket mistakes: *I [wahsed] washed my dog.* This reduces time spent erasing and allows teachers to see the errors children have made and incorporate reteaching into lesson planning.

Paper

Handwriting instruction begins with activities that involve gross motor movement so that children may feel the movement in the shoulder and arm and improve their kinesthetic memory. Tracing at the chalkboard is the first step. Paper patterns should also be large and gradually become smaller as children become proficient with letter forms. Children of any age should be introduced to folded newsprint or lined paper with the widest spaces available. The space between lines should be reduced as children's form letters automatically.

Initially, letter forms should be taught using a chalkboard or dry erase board, then unlined paper, then wide-lined paper (1" between rows), next primary-grade lined paper (¾", ½", ⅜"), and finally regular lined notebook paper. The size of the spaces between lines is adjusted downward as the child masters the letter forms. The teacher should watch carefully to see that correct posture, full arm movement, and correct form are maintained. Additional practice utilizing other media such as carpet squares; salt or rice trays; sand; tabletops; and varying styles of columned paper, such as newspaper want ads and telephone books, will ensure full arm movement and can vary handwriting practice and make it fun.

Paper Position

As early as the ninth century, scribes discovered that a slight slant seems to be easier than a perpendicular stroke (Florey, 2009). To achieve the consistent slant that is needed in cursive writing, the edge of the paper should be parallel to the writing arm (at about a 45-degree angle to the edge of the desk) and anchored at the top by the nonwriting hand. After the child's writing is small enough to use regular notebook paper, a slant guide (a piece of paper with slanted lines that is positioned beneath the writing paper) can be helpful after the child forms all lowercase letters automatically. Some instructors prefer that a left-handed student write with a backward slant, placing the paper parallel to the left arm; others teach a forward slant to both left- and right-handed students (see Figure 7.2). It has been suggested that left-handed individuals who write with a hook (the "curled wrist" method) were taught by teachers who insisted all students place their papers in the right-handed position. To avoid smudging the paper and to see what they have written, these left-handed individuals curl their wrists while writing. Athènes and Guiard asked, "Is the inverted handwriting posture really so bad for left handers?" By comparing rate of writing of noninverters with that of inverters in left-handed adults and

a   b

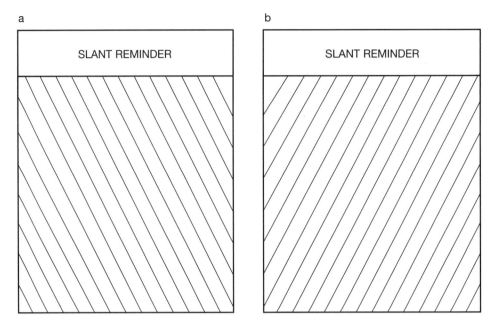

Figure 7.2. Slant reminders for a) left-handers and b) right-handers. (From Texas Scottish Rite Hospital for Children, Child Development Division. [1996]. *Teaching cursive writing* [Brochure]. Dallas, TX: Author; reprinted by permission.)

children, they concluded that "the handwriting performance of inverters was just as good as that of non-inverters" (1991, p. 149). Bertin and Perlman (1997) developed a handwriting program for teaching cursive to left-handed individuals that is available commercially. They also have a handwriting program for numerals. See Figure 7.3 for illustrations of proper posture, pencil grasp, and paper position for both left- and right-handed students.

Slingerland and Aho recommended (1985a) that the paper always be slanted with the upper left corner higher for left-handed students and the upper right corner higher for right-handed students when using cursive. They also suggested that right-handed students keep their papers parallel to the bottom of the desk when using manuscript print. This helps them keep their manuscript letters straight.

Importance of Motivation

Students will be motivated to improve their handwriting if they take part in deciding which areas need help. The teacher can help students analyze the quality of their writing using generally accepted criteria: correct letter forms, rhythm (fluency), consistent slant, good use of space within and between words and lines, and general appearance (copy is free of excessive strikeovers or erasures). The teacher should set daily goals for the student or group. Writing is an acquired skill that requires good training in order to write legibly and rapidly. Although not all individuals have superior handwriting, many can achieve legibility with effort and practice (TSRHC, 1996).

Uppercase letters are introduced only after students write all lowercase letters automatically and legibly because uppercase letters are used in only about 2% of writing. Some teachers prefer to introduce the capitals needed for student names on an individual basis. See Figures 7.4 and 7.5 for a version of simplified uppercase letters in both manuscript and cursive.

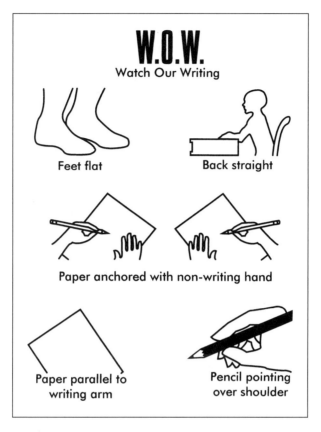

Figure 7.3. Watch Our Writing (W.O.W.) chart. (From Phelps, J., & Stempel, L. [1985]. *CHES's handwriting improvement program* [CHIP]. Dallas, TX: Children's Handwriting Evaluation Scale; reprinted by permission.)

TEACHING LETTER FORMS USING A MULTISENSORY FRAMEWORK

Handwriting instruction and practice are the same for both manuscript and cursive writing and are appropriate for one-to-one therapy, small groups, or general education classrooms at any age. It is neither necessary nor desirable to keep the alphabet in sequence while teaching handwriting. It is preferable to teach the reading, spelling, and writing of sounds and letters that reflect ease of learning and **frequency** in English and similarities of strokes in writing. When planning the presentation of print letters, the following should be considered:

- Ease of production of the letter

- Continuity of stroke

- Similarity of strokes to those letters previously taught

- Ease of perception and production of the sound associated with the letter

Although sounds are not taught during handwriting class, their associations with letter forms are part of the multisensory experience. For example, the manuscript letter *l* is the simplest to write, but its sound is more difficult for young children, so it is a poor choice as the first letter to be introduced. It may be taught more easily after a few letters and their sounds have been presented.

Lowercase Manuscript Letter Forms

All lowercase maunscript letters are made with a
continuous line, except for *f, i, j, k, t,* and *x.*

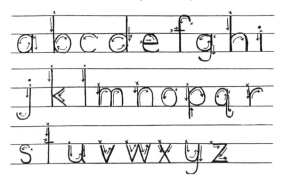

Uppercase Manuscript Letter Forms

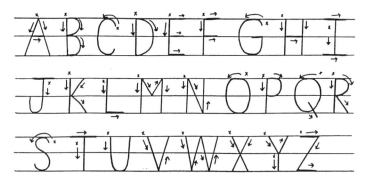

Figure 7.4.   Print letters, using a continuous stroke (when possible). (Developed by the Renton School District, Renton, WA; reprinted by permission; versions taught in other school districts may vary slightly.)

Students appear to recall the sequence of movements of a given letter better if the instructor verbalizes consistent, precise directions for writing each letter shape (see Figures 7.6–7.10). The descriptive phrases should be repeated each time the letter is traced or written to reinforce motor memory until the letter shape is automatic (Slingerland, 1971; TSRHC, 1996). Each time students start to write a letter, it is important for them to name it while writing. This is an adaptation of Gillingham and Stillman's (1960) simultaneous oral spelling, which provides kinesthetic reinforcement in which movements of the speech organs help the memory for letter names, sounds, and shapes.

Manuscript Print Handwriting

Print handwriting introduces primary-grade children to the symbol forms used in printed text. Through multisensory association of sight, sound, and feel, children integrate each letter name with its visual form and the feel of how the letter is written, thus, strengthening intersensory associations. The procedure for instruction for print is the same as cursive writing, which is described later in this chapter, but the pace will be slower for younger children. As much as 1 week or more may be spent on each letter when working with kindergarten or first-grade students.

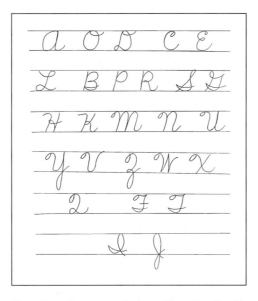

Figure 7.5. Uppercase cursive letters. (From Texas Scottish Rite Hospital for Children, Child Development Division. [1996]. *Teaching cursive writing* [Brochure]. Dallas, TX: Author; reprinted by permission.)

There are many forms of print writing, but the one most often recommended for children with dyslexia is one that utilizes a continuous stroke whenever possible (Beery, 1982; Slingerland, 1971). A continuous stroke letter is most similar to cursive writing in that lines are retraced whenever possible and the pencil is lifted only when necessary (e.g., to cross a *t,* to dot an *i*). This helps prepare the child for a natural transition to cursive writing. Continuous stroke letters also reduce the opportunities for reversals that may occur each time the child lifts the pencil. (Figure 7.4 shows lower- and uppercase print alphabets that use continuous strokes when possible; Figure 7.6 shows descriptions for writing print letters using continuous strokes.)

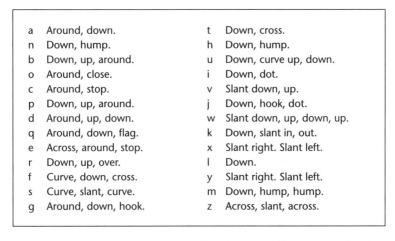

a	Around, down.	t	Down, cross.
n	Down, hump.	h	Down, hump.
b	Down, up, around.	u	Down, curve up, down.
o	Around, close.	i	Down, dot.
c	Around, stop.	v	Slant down, up.
p	Down, up, around.	j	Down, hook, dot.
d	Around, up, down.	w	Slant down, up, down, up.
q	Around, down, flag.	k	Down, slant in, out.
e	Across, around, stop.	x	Slant right. Slant left.
r	Down, up, over.	l	Down.
f	Curve, down, cross.	y	Slant right. Slant left.
s	Curve, slant, curve.	m	Down, hump, hump.
g	Around, down, hook.	z	Across, slant, across.

Figure 7.6. Continuous stroke descriptions of print letters. (Used by permission of Neuhaus Education Center, Bellaire, TX.)

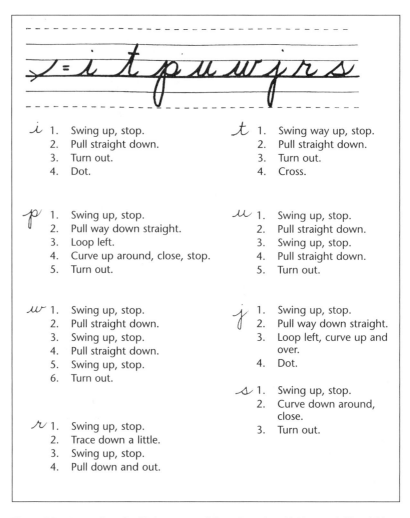

i 1. Swing up, stop.
   2. Pull straight down.
   3. Turn out.
   4. Dot.

t 1. Swing way up, stop.
   2. Pull straight down.
   3. Turn out.
   4. Cross.

p 1. Swing up, stop.
   2. Pull way down straight.
   3. Loop left.
   4. Curve up around, close, stop.
   5. Turn out.

u 1. Swing up, stop.
   2. Pull straight down.
   3. Swing up, stop.
   4. Pull straight down.
   5. Turn out.

w 1. Swing up, stop.
   2. Pull straight down.
   3. Swing up, stop.
   4. Pull straight down.
   5. Swing up, stop.
   6. Turn out.

j 1. Swing up, stop.
   2. Pull way down straight.
   3. Loop left, curve up and over.
   4. Dot.

r 1. Swing up, stop.
   2. Trace down a little.
   3. Swing up, stop.
   4. Pull down and out.

s 1. Swing up, stop.
   2. Curve down around, close.
   3. Turn out.

Figure 7.7.   Approach stroke: "Swing up, stop." (From Texas Scottish Rite Hospital for Children, Child Development Division. [1996]. *Teaching cursive writing* [Brochure]. Dallas, TX: Author; reprinted by permission.)

When a letter such as *h* is taught first, it introduces children to the idea of using a continuous stroke to form a letter because the child starts at the top of the letter, pulls down to the baseline, slides up almost to the midline, curves out and down without lifting the pencil. When a letter such as *t* is taught first, students must lift the pencil to cross the downstroke line; thus, children have more difficulty adjusting to moving their arms without lifting the pencil from the paper when *h* is presented later.

Grouping Printed Letters by Similar Strokes

When a letter is learned and practiced, the child will be prepared to use similar arm movements in new letters with similar strokes. For example, it is easier to teach the letter *b* when students have learned to retrace the downward stroke of an *h* and curve up and around. The movements are the same and help students learn new letters more easily.

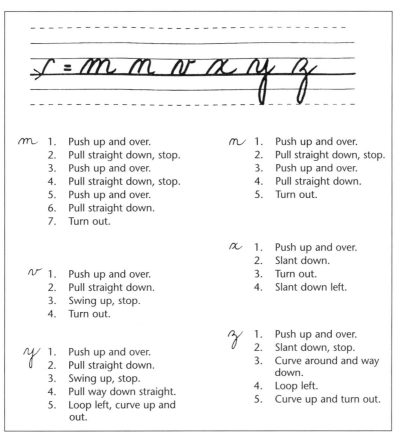

Figure 7.8. Approach stroke: "Push up and over." (From Texas Scottish Rite Hospital for Children, Child Development Division. [1996]. *Teaching cursive writing* [Brochure]. Dallas, TX: Author; reprinted by permission.)

The h Group

The sound of the letter *h* is easy to hear and reproduce. The print letter form introduces the idea of continuous stroke. Its basic arm movement is also used in letters such as *b*, *m*, *n*, *r*, and *p*. Be prepared to spend considerable time on the letter *b* because of the confusion between *b* and *d*. Slingerland (1971) recommended preparing students for writing the letter *b* with an auditory-motor activity in which students stand and hold their writing arms in front of their bodies. The teacher then separates right- and left-handed students and helps them understand that to move in the direction that handwriting should go, right-handed students move their arms away from their bodies, whereas left-handed students move their arms across their bodies. Then, when patterns are introduced at the chalkboard, the teacher verbalizes, "Tall stem down and away from my body (if right-handed)," and, "Tall stem down and across my body (if left-handed)," to help both right- and left-handed students understand and remember the direction of the letter. The students are expected to **subvocalize** the stroke patterns, whispering the same language each time they practice the letter *b*.

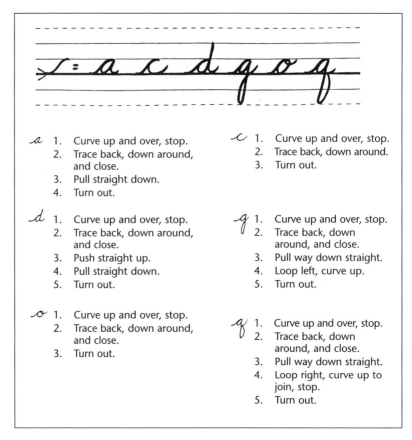

Figure 7.9. Approach stroke: "Curve under, over, stop." (From Texas Scottish Rite Hospital for Children, Child Development Division. [1996]. *Teaching cursive writing* [Brochure]. Dallas, TX: Author; reprinted by permission.)

The a Group

The *a* group consists of letters that start with the same movement as the letter *a* and includes *a, c, d, g, o, q,* and *s.* These letters begin at the 2 o'clock position just below the mid-line. As children begin to form these letters, they should move their pencils at approximately a 45-degree angle toward the mid-line, curving around toward the baseline. The exaggerated slant typical of beginning writers' letters will become more rounded as the children's writing becomes automatic. The angle of the pencil will eliminate a nearly vertical upward stroke and produce a rounded letter.

Other Groups

The letters *i, j, k, l,* and *t* begin with straight downstrokes, whereas the letters *v, w,* and *x* start with slight slants. If the angle of the first slant is exaggerated, then the resulting letter will be sprawled across the page. The letters *e, u, y,* and *z* do not belong to a particular group.

Cursive Handwriting

Lowercase letters are also taught first in cursive handwriting. A new letter is introduced each day, and previously learned letters are reviewed and practiced following the in-

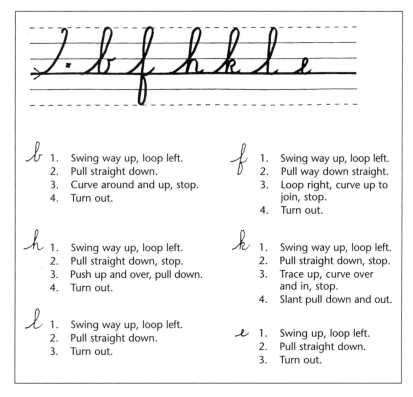

Figure 7.10. Approach stroke: "Curve way up, loop left." (From Texas Scottish Rite Hospital for Children, Child Development Division. [1996]. *Teaching cursive writing* [Brochure]. Dallas, TX: Author; reprinted by permission.)

troduction of the new one. It is beneficial to follow the order and grouping of cursive letters by the four basic approach strokes (see Figures 7.7–7.10). Students learn the four approach strokes as they learn new letters. Each approach stroke always begins on the baseline and moves from left to right. An arrow is provided to establish a baseline when students practice on the chalkboard or on unlined paper. The drop stroke follows the approach stroke and ties the letter to the baseline. The remaining shape is added to form the letter, which is then finished by a release or connecting stroke. The release stroke is an important part of every letter because it allows for uniform spacing between letters and promotes rhythmic, fluent writing.

The Writing Lesson

Classroom teachers should plan to spend 20–30 minutes per day teaching handwriting. When all letter forms are taught, a 5- to 10-minute daily review of difficult letter forms or those that confuse students will maintain standards and automatic performance. The teacher should organize writing instruction with attention to posture, pencil grip, position of the writing surface, and emphasis on naming the letters before writing them. This daily attention to handwriting using a multisensory process helps students learn the letter shapes, increases their automaticity and fluency for writing, and facilitates the connection between the letters and the sounds they represent for reading and spelling. Children should be instructed to write and then trace over each letter rather than writing the same letter repeatedly, as the letters tend to deteriorate and students habituate, writing without attention to task. Berninger (1998) recommended a daily 5-minute handwriting warm-up before starting spelling or written language tasks.

In the Alphabetic Phonics approach (see Appendix B for information on this program), students can practice at different levels during the handwriting part of the daily lesson. Each practice session should establish a single focus. The focus can be practicing a selected approach stroke; exercising rhythm and control when writing by naming letters before writing; copying cursive letters directly on top of print to reinforce a letter shape; regulating letter proportion, especially of tall letters; or repeating individual strokes such as "pull down straight" strokes, circles, release strokes, and lower loops. The Slingerland (1981) format for instruction includes daily practice in moving from one letter to the next smoothly to develop a rhythmic tempo; students form one dictated letter, then trace until the next letter is named. "This automatic recall and rhythmic movement from one letter to the next should precede functional use of letters for writing words. Controlled guidance and practice are essential" (Slingerland, 1981, p. 39).

After all lowercase letters are learned and can be written legibly, students should practice writing the alphabet in sequence in connected cursive, giving extra attention to the bridge strokes used to connect *b, o, v,* and *w* with the next letter. Extra practice should be provided for frequent combinations such as *br, oa, vi,* and *wh* (see Figure 7.11). Henry (2010) pointed out that third-grade students often need practice in these linkages when they are using cursive writing for spelling more complex words. Explicit practice should take place with students tracing and copying these bridge stroke transitions when difficulties arise.

If a student is unable to write a letter satisfactorily, then he or she should return to the tracing step at the board or on a large paper pattern. This procedure should be followed meticulously with each letter until all have been learned and written legibly and automatically. For each activity, the teacher follows a hierarchy of modeling for the students, giving them specific wording to help them monitor their visual-motor responses and having the students air write, trace, copy, and write on their own. In the Slingerland (1981) approach, handwriting practice and review are integrated into the written language lesson to provide success with spelling and written language tasks. For example, if students will be expected to write the word *book,* then they first practice the letter forms and connections necessary to successfully write the word: *bo, ok, oo* before they encode and write *book.*

Handwriting lessons should consist of teaching new letters, practicing letters already learned, and reviewing and practicing with letter connections in cursive writing. The following lesson is an excerpt adapted from the *Slingerland Multisensory Approach: A Practical Guide for Teaching Reading, Writing and Spelling* (Slingerland Institute for Literacy, 2008).

Sample Lesson—Introducing a New Letter and Review

Learning New Letters

Step 1

Teacher: *Shows wall card or class alphabet card. Places hand under the lowercase letter. Names the letter.*

Children: *Each individual child names the letter.*

Figure 7.11.   Lowercase cursive bridge strokes between common letter combinations. (From Texas Scottish Rite Hospital for Children, Child Development Division. [1996]. *Teaching cursive writing* [Brochure]. Dallas, TX: Author; reprinted by permission.)

Step 2

Teacher: *Forms a large letter on the board, naming it as it is formed, stressing difficult parts.*

Children: *Individual children—one at a time—trace and name the letter.*

Step 3

Teacher: *Makes several patterns on the board.*

Children: *Several children trace and name at one time.*

Class: *Children who have traced (for input) form letter with arm swing, naming as it is formed. (The letter is formed with a full arm swing, 1–2 feet high.)*

Step 4

Teacher: *Gives each child a prepared permanent pattern.*

Class: *Children trace and name, using two fingers.*

Step 5

Class: *On the same permanent pattern, children trace and name using the unsharpened end of the pencil.*

Step 6

Teacher: *Provides a three-space expendable pattern for tracing and copying.*

Class: *Traces the pattern, first with two fingers, then with the unsharpened end of the pencil.*

Teacher: *Monitors for full arm swing and correct formation.*

Class: *Children copy, then trace the teacher's pattern until the teacher corrects them as needed.*

Teacher: *Moves about the classroom and corrects students as needed.*

Class: *Children trace and name the pattern. Then, they fold the paper so that only a blank space is visible and they write from memory in the last box of the three-space pattern. When the letter is complete, each child opens the paper to check for correct form and traces the pattern until teacher has checked for correct formation of the letter written from memory.*

Teacher: *Corrects students as needed.*

Steps 2, 3, and 6 are also used for teaching difficult cursive letter connections.

Reviewing Letters

This is a time for practicing the spacing between letters, rhythm, and fluency.

Teacher: *Names a letter.*

Class: *Children form the letter in the air, with arm swing, while naming it. They name the letter while writing on paper.*

Teacher: *Corrects students as needed.*

Class: *Children name and trace the letter.*

When children are more automatic and need less structure, they may move to the next review step.

Teacher: *Names letter or letters to develop rhythm and fluency.*

Class: *Children write, naming and tracing until the next letter is given (about three times). Each time the children write a letter, they should name the letter and, if necessary, remind themselves verbally of the correct formation.*

Teacher: *Corrects very little.*

Teaching Punctuation

The writing lesson provides an opportunity to teach the correct forms of punctuation marks. A period should be a dot, with no circling. Commas and apostrophes begin with a dot followed by a slightly curved tail. As each punctuation mark is taught, students should use them in their writing lessons. Letters may be separated by commas. Sentences using words in the encoding lesson can provide opportunities to practice periods, exclamation marks, and question marks.

Margins and spacing are part of handwriting instruction as well. Students should be taught to attend to margins and spacing, even when practicing individual letters. Daily practice in organizing the writing paper will contribute to clarity and readability of the finished product. "A letter is mostly untouched paper. There is very little ink on a written or printed page" (Reynolds, 1976).

BYPASS TECHNOLOGY

Nearly 20 years of National Institute of Child Health & Human Development (NICHD)-funded research has shown that most students write more, write faster, and express more ideas when composing by hand, but some need support from technology to increase legibility or fluency.

Resources Available

Bypass technology is constantly evolving with new products appearing each year. Keyboarding, **voice recognition software,** and word prediction programs are among the resources available for bypassing handwriting problems. A teacher should use caution and carefully consider the individual strengths and weaknesses of each student before substituting any of these alternatives. Each has distinct advantages and challenges for the student with dyslexia. Continued research is needed to identify the students who will most benefit from using each of these resources as bypass tools.

Keyboarding

Keyboarding should be considered a complement rather than an alternative to handwriting skills. The motor process involved in selecting a key rather than writing a letter may be simpler, but it may require a greater degree of fine motor development. Thought should also be given to the amount of time required to develop fluency on the keyboard. Even students with sufficient dexterity may have difficulty developing automatic use of the keyboard, perhaps because of the difficulties in superimposing the keyboard alphabet (*asdf*) on the known alphabet (*abcd*). If, after careful evaluation, a decision is made to accommodate a student with dysgraphia by providing a keyboard for written assignments, explicit instruction in keyboarding should be provided.

A longitudinal study of manuscript and cursive writing and keyboarding has found that printing manuscript letters, writing cursive letters, and finding letters on a keyboard have different early developmental paths (Berninger et al., 2006). Printing letters in manuscript form and finding the manuscript letters on a keyboard have a statistically significant correlation in typically developing first-grade students. Printing manuscript letters, writing cursive letters, and finding manuscript letters on a keyboard have statistically significant correlations in typically developing third-grade students. Different neurodevelopmental processes uniquely predict automaticity (the ability to produce or find letters accurately, quickly, and effortlessly) of handwriting or keyboarding, however. For printing letters, the unique predictor is storing letter forms in short-term memory while the letter forms are analyzed in working memory. For finding the letters on the keyboard, the same letter-coding and analyzing skill and rapid automatic naming of letters are the unique predictors. For writing cursive letters, the unique predictor is inhibition—an executive function that directs attention to the relevant linguistic information and suppresses the irrelevant linguistic information. Difficulty with inhibition is a nonlinguistic marker of dyslexia (Berninger et al., 2006). Training in cursive writing may help people with dyslexia because it improves their inhibition.

Diana King (2005) developed a multisensory approach to touch-typing that teaches the position of the keys in alphabetic order (see Appendix B). Students learn the position of the keys in as little as 30 minutes, followed by practice based on the Orton-Gillingham Approach to instruction (Gillingham & Stillman 1960, 1997). A document produced on the keyboard may be edited more easily and provides a legible, readable result.

Effective word processing requires integrating multiple operations such as selecting, saving, deleting, cutting, pasting, and formulating (Levine, 2003). When keyboarding and word processing skills become automatic for the student with dyslexia, computers provide excellent support by facilitating written composition, simplifying the editing process, and providing a check for spelling. Berninger (1998) noted that a spell checker is most effective when children have achieved a fifth-grade spelling level so that their spellings can be recognized by the computer. Students must also have adequate reading ability and a sufficient grasp of vocabulary to discriminate between *homographs* (words that have the same spelling but that sound different and have different meanings) and *homonyms* (words that sound the same and that often have the same spelling but have different meanings). Grammar checks can also be an excellent support for emerging writers.

Voice Recognition Software

Some students find that they are able to produce longer and more complex compositions when the chore of handwriting or keyboarding is eliminated by voice recognition software. They are required only to enter simple commands and monitor the text as it is produced on the screen. They are freed of the mechanics of writing and able to focus on content. This tool, however, may not be effective for children with limited working memory because of the demands of simultaneous tasks. Many children with expressive language difficulties are unable to use voice recognition software effectively because of the complexity of monitoring text and the amount of editing required to transfer their thoughts into readable form. Very often it is more frustrating rather than less. A computer-savvy individual with dyslexia now employed in the computer industry said, "I'll just learn to write better; this is too much trouble." Levine recommended that "every effort should be made to enable such individuals to practice their graphomotor function as well" and noted that these individuals "are likely to need manual writing in the future" (2003, p. 189).

Voice recognition technology may be a distraction to the other students in the classroom or may be less effective because of background noise. Each student and learning situation must be individually evaluated to monitor the effectiveness of this or any other adaptive tool. The smart pen is a variation that has proven useful for many students, particularly for notetaking. The Pulse Smartpen by Livescribe records and links the audio to what students write so they do not miss words as they struggle to get them on paper.

Word Prediction Software

Word prediction software allows the child to complete a word, phrase, or sentence with only a few keystrokes. The program is based on the letters typed in the word. It generates words beginning in that particular way. As the writer progresses, the program examines syntax and continues to predict the structure of the sentence. As with voice recognition software, the student is expected to keep a number of tasks in working memory. Editing may be helped by programs that read aloud what the child has written. Headphones may be needed in a classroom environment.

Tablet PC Software

Innovative tablet PC software allows computer users to write directly on the computer screen with a stylus, then manipulate the handwritten text. It offers some of the advantages of keyboarding—manipulating text, checking spell, and editing. It will not be as effective for a student with graphomotor or orthographic weaknesses, however.

As this and other new bypass technologies are developed and existing ones are refined, their effectiveness for individual students will be determined by the students' own individual strengths, weaknesses, and needs. See Chapter 22 for further discussion of assistive technology and students with dyslexia.

CONCLUSION

This chapter presented specific techniques for teaching handwriting using a multisensory framework and integrating the teaching of print and cursive handwriting with reading and spelling. The importance of handwriting instruction in early education and in remediation, a brief history of the teaching of handwriting, techniques used to teach it in schools now, some syndromes related to difficulties with handwriting, research evidence of the efficacy of direct teaching of handwriting to dyslexic students, and the use of assistive technologies have been discussed.

Emphasis is placed on a hierarchy of skills—utilizing large-muscle movements, providing a model of cursive over print to tie the written letter to the printed letter in reading material, practicing individual strokes within letters, and connecting letters. Spacing; proportion of single letter shapes, both individually and in relation to other letters; rhythm; and fluency are emphasized, which leads to instant writing and writing from memory. All is done in a structured way in correct position, with students naming the letters before writing to utilize the visual, auditory, kinesthetic, and tactile senses. The teacher does not hurry students to reduce the size of the letter shapes prematurely but demands automaticity and fluency at each level of **air writing,** tracing, copying, and writing large letters from memory before allowing smaller letters to be practiced.

A number of programs have been specifically developed to emphasize the proper formation of letters, treating handwriting as a basic skill to be taught systematically. All of the programs direct the writer's attention to the distinctive features of each letter. Letters are grouped by beginning strokes; by the number of spaces above and below the lines; and by stopping points, vertical lines, loops, and curves. The main feature of these programs is consistent motor patterns supported by explicit verbalization of the proper order and directions for making the strokes as the letters are learned and practiced. Verbal descriptions have been developed for all 26 lowercase cursive and print letters. Uppercase cursive letters are usually taught later. (See Appendix B for a list of published multisensory structured language programs that deal directly and explicitly with handwriting as a remedial adjunct to reading and spelling.)

Research has shown that students who are unable to take notes and write papers at an efficient level fall behind not only in notation but also in comprehension (Phelps, Stempel, & Browne, 1989). Because the basic skill areas appear closely linked, handwriting should be integrated into curricula designed to help students who have academic difficulties. Very often the focus in language arts education is on spelling and reading to the exclusion of handwriting. This vital omission can lower overall achievement and affect a child's attitude toward all school learning (Askov & Peck, 1982).

Assistive or bypass technologies are available, but careful consideration of a child's strengths and weaknesses is required to determine the degree of assistance that the technologies might provide. Once keyboarding skills are automatic, the keyboard and word processor are useful tools. Students' needs and the limitations of other technologies will influence the effectiveness of these alternatives.

REFERENCES

Abbott, R., & Berninger, V. (1993). Structural equation modeling of relationships among developmental skills and writing skills in primary and intermediate grade writers. *Journal of Educational Psychology, 85,* 478–508.

Adams, M.J. (1990). *Beginning to read: Thinking and learning about print.* Cambridge, MA: The MIT Press.

Askov, E., & Peck, M. (1982). Handwriting. In M.C. Akin (Ed.), *Encyclopedia of educational research* (5th ed., Vol. 2, pp. 764–766). New York: Free Press.

Athènes, S., & Guiard, Y. (1991). The development of handwriting posture: A comparison between left-handers and right-handers. In J. Wann, A.M. Wing, & N. Sovik (Eds.), *Development of graphic skills* (pp. 137–149). London: Academic Press.

Beery, K. (1982). *Administration, scoring, and teaching manual for the Developmental Test of Visual-Motor Integration* (Rev. ed.). Cleveland, OH: Modern Curriculum Press.

Berninger, V. (1998). *Guides for intervention.* San Antonio, TX: Harcourt Assessment.

Berninger, V. (1999). The "write stuff" for preventing and treating writing disabilities. *Perspectives, 25*(2), 20–22.

Berninger, V., Abbot, R., Jones, J., Wolf, B., Gould, L., Anderson-Youngstrom, M., et al. (2006). Early development of language by hand: Composing, reading, listening, and speaking connections; three letter-writing modes; and fast mapping in spelling. *Developmental Neuropsychology, 29*(1), 61–92.

Berninger, V., & Amtmann, D. (2003). Preventing written expression disabilities through early and continuing assessment and intervention for handwriting and/or spelling problems: Research into practice. In H.L. Swanson, K.R. Harris, & S. Graham (Eds.), *Handbook of research on learning disabilities* (pp. 345–363). New York: The Guilford Press.

Berninger, V., Mizokawa, D.T., & Bragg, R. (1991). Theory-based diagnosis and remediation of writing disabilities. *Journal of School Psychology, 29,* 57–79.

Berninger, V., & Richards, T. (2002). *Brain literacy for educators and psychologists.* San Diego: Academic Press.

Berninger, V.W., & Wolf, B. (2009). *Teaching students with dyslexia and dysgraphia: Lessons from teaching and science.* Baltimore: Paul H. Brookes Publishing Co.

Bertin, P., & Perlman, E. (1997). *PAF handwriting book for cursive: Right-handed and left-handed models.* White Plains, NY: Monroe Associates.

Black, J. (1996). *The clumsy child.* Unpublished manuscript. Texas Scottish Rite Hospital for Children, Dallas.

Blalock, J.W. (1985, November 13). *Oral language problems of learning-disabled adolescents and adults.* Paper presented at the 36th annual conference of The Orton Dyslexia Society, Chicago.

Brooks, A. (2003). Neuropsychological processes related to persisting reversal errors in dyslexia and dysgraphia. *Dissertation Abstracts International, 63 (11A),* 3850.

Brooks, A., Berninger, V., & Abbott, R. (2006). *Letter naming and letter writing reversals in children with dyslexia: Reflection of working memory inefficiency.* Unpublished manuscript.

Cicci, R. (1995). *What's wrong with me? Learning disabilities at home and in school.* Timonium, MD: York Press.

Cox, A. (1980). *Structures and techniques: Multisensory teaching of basic language skills.* Cambridge, MA: Educators Publishing Service.

Cox, A. (1985). Alphabet phonics: An organization and expansion of Orton-Gillingham. *Annals of Dyslexia, 35,* 187–198.

Cox, A.R. (1992). *Foundations for oral literacy: Structures and techniques for multisensory teaching of basic written English language skills.* Cambridge, MA: Educators Publishing Service.

Fernald, G. (1943). *Remedial techniques in basic school subjects.* New York: McGraw-Hill.

Florey, K. (2009). *Script and scribble.* Brooklyn, NY: Melville House Publishing.

Getman, G.N. (1984). About handwriting. *Academic Therapy, 19,* 139–140.

Gillingham, A., & Stillman, B.W. (1960). *Remedial training for children with specific disability in reading, spelling, and penmanship* (6th ed.). Cambridge, MA: Educators Publishing Service.

Gillingham, A., & Stillman, B.W. (1997). *The Gillingham manual: Remedial training for children with specific disability in reading, writing, and penmanship* (8th ed.). Cambridge, MA: Educators Publishing Service.

Goodman, R., & Caramazza, A. (1986). Dissociation of spelling errors in written and oral spelling: The role of allographic conversion in writing. *Cognitive Neuropsychology, 3,* 179–206.

Graham, S., Berninger, V., Abbott, R., Abbott, S., & Whittaker, D. (1997). The role of mechanics in composing of elementary school students: A new methodological approach. *Journal of Educational Psychology, 89,* 223–236.

Graham, S., & Weintraub, N. (1996). A review of handwriting research: Progress and prospects from 1980 to 1994. *Educational Psychology Review, 8,* 7–87.

Hagin, R.A. (1983). Write right or left: A practical approach to handwriting. *Journal of Learning Disabilities, 16,* 266–271.

Hamstra-Bletz, L., & Blöte, A. (1990). Development of handwriting in primary school: A longitudinal study. *Perceptual and Motor Skills, 70,* 759–770.

Henry, M.K. (2010). *Unlocking literacy: Effective decoding and spelling instruction* (2nd ed.). Baltimore: Paul H. Brookes Publishing Co.

Johnson, D.J. (1988). Review of research on specific reading, writing, and mathematics disorders. In J.F. Kavanagh & T.J. Truss (Eds.), *Learning disabilities: Proceedings of the national conference* (pp. 79–163). Timonium, MD: York Press.

King, D.H. (2005). *Keyboarding skills* (2nd ed.). Cambridge, MA: Educators Publishing Service.

Kurtz, L. (1994, Fall). Helpful handwriting hints. *Teaching Exceptional Children,* 58–59.

Levine, M. (1987). *Developmental variations and learning disorders.* Cambridge, MA: Educators Publishing Service.

Levine, M. (1994). *Educational care: A system for understanding and helping children with learning problems at home and in school.* Cambridge, MA: Educators Publishing Service.

Levine, M. (2003). *The myth of laziness.* New York: Simon & Schuster.

Luria, A.R. (1973). *The working brain.* London: Penguin Books.

McMenamin, B., & Martin, M. (1980). *Right writing.* Spring Valley, CA: Cursive Writing Associates.

Orton, J.L. (1966). The Orton-Gillingham approach. In J. Money (Ed.), *The disabled reader: Education of the dyslexic child* (pp. 119–145). Baltimore: The Johns Hopkins University Press.

Orton, S.T. (1937). *Reading, writing, and speech problems in children.* New York: W.W. Norton.

Phelps, J., & Stempel, L. (1985). *CHES's handwriting improvement program* (CHIP). Dallas, TX: Children's Handwriting Evaluation Scale.

Phelps, J., & Stempel, L. (1987). Handwriting: Evolution and evaluation. *Annals of Dyslexia, 37,* 228–239.

Phelps, J., Stempel, L., & Browne, R. (1989). *Children's handwriting and school achievement.* Unpublished manuscript, Texas Scottish Rite Hospital for Children, Dallas.

Reisman, J. (1991, September). Poor handwriting: Who is referred? *American Journal of Occupational Therapy, 45*(9), 849–852.

Reynolds, L. (1976). *Italic calligraphy and handwriting: Exercises and text.* New York: Taplinger Publishing.

Richardson, S. (1995). Specific developmental dyslexia: Retrospective and prospective views. In C.W. McIntyre & J.S. Pickering (Eds.), *Clinical studies of multisensory structured language education* (pp. 1–15). Salem, OR: International Multisensory Structured Language Education Council (IMSLEC).

Rubin, H., & Eberhardt, N. (1996). Facilitating invented spelling through language analysis instruction: An integrated model. *Reading and Writing: An Interdisciplinary Journal, 8,* 27–43.

Slingerland, B.H. (1971). *A multisensory approach to language arts: Book I.* Cambridge, MA: Educators Publishing Service.

Slingerland, B. (1976). *Basics in scope and sequence of a multisensory approach to language arts: Book II.* Cambridge, MA: Educators Publishing Service.

Slingerland, B. (1981). *A multisensory approach to language arts for specific language disability children: Book 3. A guide for elementary teachers.* Cambridge, MA: Educators Publishing Service.

Slingerland, B., & Aho, M. (1985a). *Manual for learning to use cursive handwriting.* Cambridge, MA: Educators Publishing Service.

Slingerland, B., & Aho, M. (1985b). *Manual for learning to use manuscript handwriting.* Cambridge, MA: Educators Publishing Service.

Slingerland Institute for Literacy. (2008). *The Slingerland multisensory approach: A practical guide for teaching reading, writing and spelling.* Bellevue, WA: Author.

Snow, C.E., Burns, M.S., & Griffin, P. (Eds.). (1998). *Preventing reading difficulties in young children.* Washington, DC: National Academies Press.

Strickling, C.A. (1974). The effect of handwriting and related skills upon the spelling scores above average and below average readers in the fifth grade. *Dissertation Abstracts International, 34*(07), 3717A.

Tabor, M. (1996, May 8). Penmanship: Fine art to lost art. *The New York Times,* pp. B1, B12.

Texas Scottish Rite Hospital for Children, Child Development Division (TSRHC). (1990). *Dyslexia training program developed in the Dyslexia Laboratory, Texas Scottish Rite Hospital* [Videotape]. Cambridge, MA: Educators Publishing Service.

Texas Scottish Rite Hospital for Children, Child Development Division (TSRHC). (1996). *Teaching cursive writing* [Brochure]. Dallas: Author.

vos Savant, M. (1988, June 5). Ask Marilyn. *Parade,* 8.

Vellutino, F. (1979). *Dyslexia: Theory and research.* Cambridge, MA: The MIT Press.

Wessel, D. (1984, June 27). Pupils are minding their P's and Q's and other letters. *The Wall Street Journal,* p. 1.

Wilson, B.A. (2002). *Fundations.* Oxford, MA: Wilson Language Training.

8

Teaching Reading

Accurate Decoding

SUZANNE CARREKER

Before beginning this chapter, consider a statement by the National Commission on Teaching and America's Future: "What teachers know and can do is one of the most important influences on what students learn" (as cited in Darling-Hammond, 1998, p. 6). Moats's (1994) seminal study on teacher knowledge highlighted what teachers do not know about language structures and teaching reading-related skills, such as decoding. As Moats suggested, "the teacher who understands language will understand why students say and write the puzzling things that they do and will be able to judge what a particular student knows and needs to know about the printed word" (2010, p. 2). Studies have confirmed continuing gaps in teacher knowledge and have documented how teacher knowledge affects student achievement (Joshi et al., 2009; Piasta, Connor, Fishman, & Morrison, 2009; Spear-Swerling, 2009). The goal of this chapter is to inform teachers who provide literacy instruction about the underlying theories and principles, terminology, concepts, and practice of effective decoding instruction.

Here are a few questions to which informed teachers know the answers.

- How many phonemes and graphemes are in the words *sent, fish, split, church,* and *mix?*

- How many syllable types are in English and what are the syllable types?

- How many syllables and morphemes are in the words *darkness, instructor, salamander, phonology,* and *polyglot?*

- Which of these morphemes can be called inflectional endings: *-ing, -ful, -ed, -less, -s, -ment?*

- Which words are accented on the second syllable: *cabin, canteen, pumpkin, bias, extreme, duet, campus, unit, unite?*

- Which words are irregular for reading: *swan, said, plead, hibernate, sword, walk, chlorophyll?*

THE ROLE OF DECODING

The main goal of reading is comprehension. For a person to comprehend written language, symbols on the printed page must be translated into spoken words (i.e., decoding), and meaning must be connected to those words. According to Gough and Tunmer (1986) and Hoover and Gough (1990), reading is the product of decoding and linguistic or language comprehension. These two components work together in a delicate, interdependent balance. Inefficiency in one of the components can lead to overall reading failure. The reader who has difficulty with decoding will not be able to derive meaning from the text; conversely, the reader who has difficulty with specific levels of spoken language will receive little reward for his or her decoding efforts.

A student may have efficient decoding and language comprehension but may demonstrate difficulties in reading comprehension because of a slow processing rate, which results in dysfluent reading (Joshi & Aaron, 2000). Dysfluent reading diverts attention from the meaning of the text and adversely affects comprehension. For students to become fully literate, especially students with dyslexia, decoding, comprehension, fluency, and all other elements of literacy instruction must be explicitly or directly taught in an informed, comprehensive approach (Brady & Moats, 1997; National Institute of Child Health and Human Development [NICHD], 2000). Accurate and automatic decoding supports the development of fluent reading that leads to efficient comprehension and reading achievement.

Decoding facilitates the reader's linkage of the printed word to the spoken word (Beck & Juel, 1995). A reader sees a page full of symbols. The reader's success in making sense of these symbols depends on how well he or she understands that the symbols represent spoken language. Successfully establishing the relationship between the symbols and spoken language is dependent on the reader's sensitivity to the internal sound structure of language (i.e., phonemic awareness; Adams, 1990). The reader must realize that spoken words have constituent sounds. In addition to recognizing that words have sounds, the reader must realize that printed words consist of letters that correspond to those speech sounds. These insights enable the reader to establish the alphabetic principle or code that is necessary for acquiring decoding skills. The importance of phonemic awareness cannot be overemphasized as it provides the foundation for decoding, enabling the reader to unlock the printed word (Adams, 1990; Bradley & Bryant, 1983; Goswami & Bryant, 1990; Liberman, Shankweiler, & Liberman, 1989) (see Chapter 4 for further discussion).

Decoding Strategies

Decoding requires knowledge of the phonemic, **graphophonemic,** syllabic, and morphemic structures of the language. A skilled reader uses a variety of strategies for translating the printed word into its spoken equivalent: sound–symbol correspondences, structural analysis, **instant word recognition,** and contextual clues. Although the primary focuses of this chapter are decoding and fluency, the crucial role of oral language in the reading process must be stressed (see Chapter 3). Not only is oral language the foundation of comprehension, but it also greatly influences and assists the reader's efficient and effective use of the various decoding strategies.

A reader's appreciation of the relationship between sounds and letters develops through phonemic awareness and instant letter recognition (i.e., print awareness; Adams, 1990). This understanding, in turn, develops sound–symbol correspondences (i.e., graphophonemic patterns) that enable the reader to sound out unfamiliar words. Initially, the beginning reader recognizes words by associating a word with some visually distinguishing characteristics (e.g., *dog* has a circle in the middle and a tail at the end; Gough & Hillinger, 1980). As the reader encounters more and more words, the visual characteristics that make words distinguishable diminish. The reader begins to cue recognition by selecting some of the letters in a word, usually the first and last letters (Ehri, 1991). He or she is now better able to distinguish words, but accuracy is limited as many words share the same initial and final letters. When the reader attends to all of the letters, he or she can sound out the correct pronunciation of an unfamiliar word (Gough & Hillinger, 1980).

Both phonological awareness and sound–symbol correspondences are critical corequisites in reading acquisition (Share & Stanovich, 1995). The reader needs an introduction to a few sound–symbol patterns to begin sounding out words. As the reader sounds out words, he or she reinforces the sound–symbol correspondences that have been introduced and establishes new ones (Adams, 1990). New sound–symbol correspondences are then acquired through what Share and Stanovich referred to as the "self-teaching mechanism" (1995, p. 17). By using known sound–symbol correspondences and phonological sensitivity, the reader approximates the pronunciation of the unknown word. This approximate pronunciation combined with available contextual clues enables the reader to determine the correct pronunciation and thereby provides the reader an opportunity to acquire knowledge of the sound–symbol correspondences within the unknown word. With repeated encounters, the reader builds an **orthographic memory** (i.e., memory for patterns of written language) of words so that eventually he or she instantly recognizes the words without having to sound them out (Adams, 1990).

In addition to letters, printed words have syllables (i.e., speech units) and morphemes (i.e., meaning units). Structural analysis, the perception of orthographic syllables and morphemes, enables the reader to decode long, unfamiliar words and fosters a decoding process that is less cumbersome and more efficient than sounding out each letter. Once the reader can recognize different kinds of syllables, he or she can accurately predict the sound of the vowel in a syllable. With knowledge of morphemes, the reader can focus on units of letters that recur in words (e.g., the reader sees *tract* in *tractor, attractive,* and *subtraction*). The reader does not have to sound out every letter in an unknown word, only the letters that he or she does not recognize as part of a morpheme (Henry, 1988). Morphemes also give clues that allow the reader to infer the meanings of words (Henry, 1988, 2010; Moats, 1994).

Orthographic patterns established through graphophonemic, syllabic, and morphemic awareness greatly economize the learning of a reader's lexicon (i.e., spoken and written word knowledge). Every word in the reader's lexicon, which may number more than 50,000 words by the time he or she reaches college, does not have to be stored in memory as separate items. The reader has a way of dealing with the words that he or she has heard and may use in speaking but has never seen in print before (e.g., a young child may not have seen the words *wizard* and *sorcerer* before but is familiar with the words because he or she has seen a Harry Potter movie) (Gough & Hillinger, 1980).

The ease and automaticity with which a skilled reader is able to read individual words is known as instant word recognition. Instant word recognition is achieved by repeated encounters with words and by **overlearning** (i.e., learning to automaticity) the orthographic and phonological patterns of the language. The ultimate goal of decoding instruction is the immediate, facile translation of a printed word into its spoken equivalent. Automaticity with this translation has a significant impact on the reader's attitude toward reading, comprehension, and overall reading success. Word recognition makes reading effortless, and reading becomes enjoyable. When reading is enjoyable, the reader will read more and, thereby, increase his or her word-recognition skills (Beck & Juel, 1995; Juel, 1991). Inadequate word recognition has a negative effect on fluency and comprehension. The reader who does not attain automaticity in word recognition is said to be "glued" to the print (Chall, 1983, p. 17). The reader must focus all of his or her attention on sounding out words and is diverted away from figuring out the meaning (Adams, 1990; Liberman & Liberman, 1990). Evidence suggests that word-recognition accuracy and speed in first-grade students is predictive of later reading comprehension success (Beck & Juel, 1995; Juel, 1991). For example, Juel found that the probability of students who were good readers in first grade remaining good readers in fourth grade was .87; however, students who were poor readers in first grade had a probability of .88 of remaining poor readers in fourth grade.

The skilled reader uses contextual clues to predict unfamiliar words, but evidence suggests that context is not the primary strategy used for word recognition (Juel, 1991; Share & Stanovich, 1995). First, the text may prove to be unreliable in yielding clues for accurate prediction. In most cases, context enables the reader to accurately predict only one out of every four words (Gough & Hillinger, 1980), and the content words that carry meaning are predictable only 10% of the time (Gough, 1983). Therefore, context is not useful when it is needed (Share & Stanovich, 1995). Second, eye-movement research shows that the eyes fixate on a majority of words in a text and do not skip over long words, as a heavy reliance on context as a means for predicting words would suggest.

Only the short, predictable words are skipped. The duration of fixation depends on the length, frequency, and predictability of the word as the reader processes its component letters (Rayner & Pollatsek, 1986). Using context facilitates recognition of an unfamiliar word only when it is coupled with the reader's orthographic knowledge. When context clues are combined with knowledge of sound–symbol correspondences, the skilled reader should be able to identify words that are part of his or her listening vocabulary (Adams, 1990; Perfetti, 1985).

The skilled reader monitors his or her decoding using syntactic (i.e., sentence structure) and semantic (i.e., word meaning) cues (Tunmer, Herriman, & Nesdale, 1988). The reader is able to detect and self-correct a misread word in a sentence using cues and sound–symbol correspondences. Knowing how to detect and self-correct errors also builds sound–symbol correspondences and word recognition as the reader deals with unfamiliar words. It is a particularly beneficial combination with the reader's discovery of more complex sound–symbol relationships.

The reader does not have to learn all of the possible sound–symbol correspondences before learning about and using structural analysis, and word recognition does not occur only after the reader has learned everything about the letter sound and structural patterns of the language. Using a given strategy depends on the reader's available knowledge about language patterns, the length and complexity of the words, the frequency of encounters with the words, and/or the availability of useful contextual clues. These decoding strategies provide the reader a means of translating the printed word into spoken language. Decoding is not an end in itself but is a necessary step in getting to the heart of reading: comprehending meaning.

Dyslexic Readers' Difficulty with Decoding

There is considerable agreement that readers who are at risk and have dyslexia are unable to decode and recognize words accurately and fluently (Adams & Bruck, 1993; Lyon, Shaywitz, & Shaywitz, 2003; Perfetti, 1985; Share & Stanovich, 1995; Stanovich, 1986). Dyslexia stems from a core deficit in phonological processing, not a deficit in visual processing (Adams, 1990; Goswami & Bryant, 1990; Stanovich, 1991; Vellutino, 1980). This difficulty with phonological processing is not a developmental delay. It is a deficit that interferes with reading and spelling development (Foorman, Francis, Shaywitz, Shaywitz, & Fletcher, 1997). Students who have difficulty learning to read have difficulty discovering that spoken words are made up of units of sounds (i.e., phonemic awareness) that relate to letters (Adams, 1990; Adams & Bruck, 1995; Brady & Moats, 1997; Brady & Shankweiler, 1991; Gough, Ehri, & Treiman, 1992). Without this realization, students fail to learn the alphabetic principle and how to decode words accurately. Subsequently, they fail to thrive in reading (Stanovich, 1986).

Evidence suggests that in addition to deficits in phonological processing, students may also exhibit a deficit in naming speed, which can interfere with developing automatic decoding and fluent text reading (Wolf, 1997; Wolf & Bowers, 1999, 2000; Wolf & Obregón, 1992; see also Chapters 4 and 5). This deficit and intervention strategies are discussed later in this chapter.

The student with dyslexia often demonstrates an "unexpected underachievement" (Lyon et al., 2003). The student's difficulty in learning to read is surprising given that the student may have strengths in other areas (e.g., verbal or spatial abilities). The results of a longitudinal study empirically documented unexpected underachievement in readers with reading disabilities (Ferrer, Shaywitz, Holahan, Marchione, & Shaywitz, 2009). In typically developing readers, IQ and reading achievement progress together, with a reciprocal and bidirectional influence of IQ on reading ability and reading ability on IQ. Adults who were identified as at-risk readers in kindergarten and continued to be poor readers to adulthood showed continued growth in IQ without commensurate growth in reading ability. This means that students with reading disabilities, such as dyslexia, have the cognitive resources to learn to read but do not learn; hence, the unexpected underachievement. The conclusion here is that early intervention is essential.

Teaching Decoding Skills

The English language, which has approximately 44 speech sounds and 26 letters, operates on an alphabetic principle or code. The speech sounds are represented in print by letters. About 75% of the school population will deduce the alphabetic principle regardless of how they are taught (Liberman & Liberman, 1990). The other 25% of students, including students with dyslexia, will not intuit this principle and will require explicit, systematic, and sequential instruction. Failure to receive such instruction can intensify these students' reading difficulties (Brady & Moats, 1997; Felton, 1993; Foorman, Francis, Beeler, Winikates, & Fletcher, 1997). A meta-analysis by Wanzek and Vaughn (2007) identified 18 effective or promising early literacy interventions for struggling readers. The beneficial effects of explicit teaching of the alphabetic principle, however, are not limited to students who have difficulty with reading. There is evidence that all students benefit from such instruction (Carreker et al., 2007; Carreker et al., 2005; Joshi, Dahlgren, & Boulware-Gooden, 2002; NICHD, 2000; Ryder, Tunmer, & Greaney, 2007).

Decoding requires knowledge of orthographic patterns of the language that is based on solid phonological processing. Key elements of decoding instruction include the following:

- Phonological awareness training, especially in phonemic awareness

- Instant letter-recognition training

- Introduction of sound–symbol correspondences

- Introduction of the six orthographic types of syllables

- Introduction of morphemes—prefixes, suffixes, roots, and combining forms

- Introduction of common syllable-division patterns

- Training in recognizing and understanding word origins (see Chapter 4)

- Teaching of a procedure for learning to read **irregular words**

- Instruction in the orthographic patterns for encoding (spelling)

- Practice for accuracy and fluency

Teaching decoding is not an incidental part of reading instruction. It is not done through the use of worksheets or rote learning. Successful decoding instruction is a vital part of reading instruction that engages students in active, reflective, and inductive learning. Students learn to be analytic and scientific in their approach to learning the structure of the language. The intensity of instruction will depend on the instructional needs of the students.

MULTISENSORY STRUCTURED LANGUAGE INSTRUCTION

Decoding instruction requires a multisensory structured presentation within a language content. The National Reading Panel (NRP; NICHD, 2000) emphasized that any decoding or phonics instruction should be explicit and incorporated with other reading instruction, such as vocabulary and comprehension instruction, to create a comprehensive reading program. Multisensory instruction implies using multiple senses or modalities—visual, auditory, tactile/kinesthetic—simultaneously or in rapid succession. The concept of multisensory instruction is embraced by many teachers and practitioners for its efficacy, but multisensory instruction has yet to garner support from the research community. As Carreker stated:

> The fundamental question is whether it is engagement of multiple senses, or the teaching of the structure of language, or the combination of the two that makes the instruction effective....It may be some time before research definitively corroborates the value or the role of multisensory instruction. In the meantime, teachers and practitioners can explicitly teach the structure of the language, engage multiple senses, and promote reading success by making sure all the bases are covered. (2006, pp. 24, 28)

Although using multisensory instruction has not been documented empirically by science, the explicit teaching of language structures in this chapter will be accompanied by suggestions for the multisensory teaching of those structures.

In learning to read, students must apprehend phonemes and instantly recognize letters (see Chapters 5 and 6) before they are ready for careful instruction in sound–symbol correspondences, structural analysis, and other concepts. There is no evidence of a best order of concept presentation. Any systematic, sequential order of presentation ensures that all important concepts are taught and maximizes the learning of these concepts.

A logically ordered presentation begins with the most basic concepts and progresses to more difficult concepts, with new learning building on prior knowledge. For example, phonemic segmentation and letter recognition are followed by the concepts of vowel and consonant sounds (i.e., vowel sounds are open; consonant sounds are **blocked** or **partially blocked** by the tongue, teeth, or lips). At first, three or four high-frequency consonants with predictable sounds (see Table 8.1) along with a short vowel (see Table 8.2) are taught.

The concept of blending letter sounds together to form words is introduced, and students begin to read words. Students are taught that a vowel in a syllable that ends in at least one consonant (i.e., closed syllable) is short. After a few more consonants and short vowels are taught, one-syllable words in word lists, phrases, and sentences are presented for students to read.

Table 8.1.   Consonants and consonant clusters

Consonants with one frequent, predictable sound

b = /b/ (*bat*)	j = /j/ (*jam*)	**p** = /p/ (*pig*)	w = /w/ (*wagon*)
d = /d/ (*dog*)	k = /k/ (*kite*)	r = /r/ (*rabbit*)	z = /z/ (*zipper*)
f = /f/ (*fish*)	**l** = /l/ (*leaf*)	**t** = /t/ (*table*)	
h = /h/ (*house*)	**m** = /m/ (*mitten*)	v = /v/ (*valentine*)	

Consonants with more than one sound

c = /k/ (*kite*)—before *a, o, u,* or any consonant
  /s/ (*city*)—before *e, i,* or *y*

g = /g/ (*goat*)—before *a, o, u,* or any consonant
  /j/ (*gem*)—before *e, i,* or *y*

n = /n/ (*nest*)
  /ng/ (*sink* or *finger*)—before any letter that says /k/ or /g/

s = /s/ (*sock*)
  /z/ (*pansy*)

x = /z/ (*xylophone*)—in initial position*
  /ks/ (*excite, box*)—in medial or final position*

Consonant digraphs with one frequent sound

ck = /k/ (*truck*)
ng = /ng/ (*king*)

sh = /sh/ (*ship*)
wh = /hw/** (*whistle*)

Consonant digraphs with more than one sound

ch = /ch/ (*chair*)
  /k/ (*school*)—in words of Greek origin
  /sh/ (*chef*)—in words of French origin

th = /th/ (*thimble*)
  /th/ (*mother*)

Trigraphs with one sound

dge = /j/ (*badge*)

tch = /ch/ (*witch*)

Special situations

y = /y/ in initial or medial position*
  as a consonant

qu = /kw/ (*queen*)—*q* is always followed by *u*

The boldface letters are frequently used consonants that are good to use when beginning to introduce sound–symbol correspondences. When these frequent consonants are combined with short *a, i,* and *o,* many simple words can be presented for reading.

*Initial refers to the first position of a syllable or word; *final* refers to the last position of a syllable or word; and *medial* refers to any position between the first and last positions of a syllable or word.

**This exaggerated pronunciation aids in establishing a strong orthographic memory of words that contain *wh.*

Table 8.2.   Vowels and vowel pairs

Short vowels in closed syllables

a = /ă/ (*apple*)	**i** = /ĭ/ (*it*)	u = /ŭ/ (*up*)
e = /ĕ/ (*echo*)	**o** = /ŏ/ (*octopus*)	

Long vowels in open, accented syllables

a = /ā/ (*apron*)	i = /ī/ (*iris*)	u = /ū/ (*unicorn*)
e = /ē/ (*equal*)	o = /ō/(*open*)	y = /ī/ (*fly*)

Vowels in open, unaccented syllables

a = /ŭ/ (*alike*)	i = /ĭ/ (*divide*)	y = /ē/ (*penny*)

Long vowels in vowel-consonant-e syllables

a-consonant-e = /ā/ (*cake*)	i-consonant-e = /ī/ (*five*)	u-consonant-e = /ū/ (*cube*)
e-consonant-e = /ē/ (*athlete*)	o-consonant-e = /ō/ (*rope*)	y-consonant-e = /ī/ (*type*)

Vowels in vowel-r syllables

ar = /âr/ (*star*)—accented	or = /ôr/ (*fork*)—accented	
/er/ (*dollar*)—unaccented	/er/ (*world*)—after *w*	
er = /êr/ (*fern*)	/er/ (*doctor*)—unaccented	
ir = /êr/ (*bird*)	ur = /êr/ (*turtle*)	

Vowel pairs with one frequent sound

ai = /ā/ (*sail*)	ei = /ē/ (*ceiling*)	oe = /ō/(*toe*)
au = /au/ (*August*)	eu = /ū/ (*Europe*)	oi = /oi/ (*boil*)
aw = /au/ (*saw*)	ew = /ū/ (*few*)	oy = /oi/ (*toy*)
ay = /ā/ (*play*)	ey = /ē/ (*monkey*)	ue = /ū/ (*rescue*)
ee = /ē/ (*feet*)	ie = /ē/ (*chief*)	

Vowel pairs with more than one frequent sound

ea = /ē/ (*eat*)	ou = /ou/ (*out*)	ow = /ou/ (*cow*)
/ĕ/ (*head*)	/o͞o/ (*soup*)	/ō/ (*snow*)
oo = /o͞o/ (*food*)		
/o͝o/ (*book*)		

Special situations

a = /ŏ/ (*watch*)—after *w*	eigh = /ā/ (*eight*)	o = /ŭ/ (*onion*)
a = /au/ (*ball*)—before *l*	igh = /ī/ (*light*)	

The boldface letters are good concepts and letters for beginning reading instruction.

Success with structural analysis is dependent on students' knowledge of syllables, syllable-division patterns, prefixes, suffixes, and roots. Information about structural analysis can be introduced when students can read simple words with affixes. Common suffixes such as -s or -ing are introduced. One-syllable words and derivatives are presented for practice. Once students understand closed syllables, they are taught that two-syllable words with two medial consonants are divided between the consonants (e.g., VC|CV syllable-division pattern as in *mascot* or *napkin*), and, subsequently, one- and two-syllable words and derivatives are presented for practice. After letter clusters such as *ck* and *sh,* along with additional syllable types such as open, consonant-*le,* and vowel-consonant-*e* syllables, are taught, words of various lengths can be read. As each concept is introduced, it is practiced to mastery, first through **homogeneous practice** and then **heterogeneous practice**.

This chapter presents the underlying theories and principles, terminology, concepts, and instructional practices of effective decoding instruction. The intent is not to provide a curriculum. Appendix B at the end of this book has a listing of curricula with systematic orders of presentation that can be used for instruction. If curricula are not available, then the aforementioned concepts and the information from Tables 8.1 and

8.2 could be fashioned into an order of presentation. Once students have practiced with phonemic segmentation and letter recognition, the beginning order might present as follows:

1. Teach definitions of vowels and consonants

2. Introduce *t* = /t/

3. Introduce *i* = /ĭ/

4. Introduce open syllable with word *I*

5. Introduce *p* = /p/ and closed syllable with words *it* and *pit*

6. Introduce *a* = /ă/ and blending

7. Introduce *s* = /s/ (cumulatively students can read words such as *it, at, pit, pat, sit, sat, I, sip, tip, tap, sap*)

8. Introduce suffix *-s*

9. Introduce *n* = /n/

10. Introduce *f* = /f/

11. Introduce *l* = /l/

12. Introduce *g* = /g/

13. Introduce *m* = /m/

14. Introduce *ng* = /ng/

15. Introduce suffix *-ing*

16. Introduce *o* = /ŏ/

17. Introduce *k* = /k/

18. Introduce *c* = /k/ before *a, o, u,* or any consonant (cumulatively students can read words such as *flip, stamps, sang, clasp, claps, lasting, singing*)

19. Introduce VCCV with *mascot* and *napkin*

20. Introduce *ck* = /k/

21. Introduce vowel-consonant-*e* syllable (students can read contrast words such as *not, note, back, bake, rip, ripe, cut, cute*)

22. Introduce vowel pair *ee* = /ē/

23. The introduction of concepts—more letters, letter clusters, syllable types, syllable-division patterns, suffixes, stems, and prefixes—continues, progressing systematically from simple to complex, with each concept building on those previously mastered.

SOUND–SYMBOL CORRESPONDENCES

Generalizations about sound–symbol correspondences are introduced to provide students with a direct link between the printed word and the spoken word and to guide students' attention to the sound–spelling patterns of words. These generalizations are not learned through rote memorization but rather through frequent practice both in and out of context. Once patterns are established, the generalizations are dispensable (Adams, 1990).

Solid Foundation for Sound–Symbol Correspondences

Awareness of the speech sounds of language and print provide the foundation for sound–symbol correspondences. Phonological awareness involves a sensitivity to the sound structure of spoken language, such as rhyming, counting words in sentences, counting syllables in words, and identifying specific sounds in a word. The ability to perceive the constituent sounds of a word (i.e., phonemic awareness) is the key component of phonological awareness (Adams, 1990; Ball & Blachman, 1988; Liberman, 1987; Lundberg, Frost, & Petersen, 1988; Yopp, 1992). Print awareness involves sensitivity to the conventions of the printed page, such as top to bottom, left to right, punctuation, indentations, spaces between words, and the awareness that words consist of letters. The key component of print awareness is the ability to instantly recognize letters (Adams, 1990). A study found little benefit in providing phonemic awareness or letter-recognition training to preschoolers before teaching letter–sound correspondences (Castles, Coltheart, Wilson, Valpied, & Wedgewood, 2009). Given the relatively small sample size (76 children divided among three conditions) of the Castles et al. study and lack of longitudinal data, however, the predominance of evidence continues to support early phonemic awareness and letter-recognition training.

Instant Letter Recognition

A beginning reader's instant letter recognition is a strong predictor of reading success. Knowing the names of the letters can facilitate the learning of the letter sounds as many sounds are embedded in the letter names (e.g., students can hear the /m/ sound in the name of the letter *m*) (Adams, 1990; Gough & Hillinger, 1980). All letters have four properties: name, sound, shape, and feel (i.e., the sensation of muscle movements while writing the letter or while producing the sound). The name is the only property that does not change. The name of the letter is an anchor to which the reader can attach the other properties of the letter. Automatic letter recognition allows the reader to see words as groups of letters instead of as individual letters that must be identified (Adams, 1990). Activities to reinforce letter recognition are easily incorporated into the classroom routine.

- The teacher writes a letter on the board. All students whose names begin with that letter line up.

- The teacher writes a letter on the board and calls on a student who must name the letter before lining up.

- The teacher writes a letter on the board and calls on a student who must name the target letter and the letter that comes after (or before) the target letter before lining up.

Phonemic Awareness

A beginning reader's ability to segment a word into its phonemes (i.e., phoneme segmentation) is one of the best predictors of reading success. A phoneme is the smallest unit of speech that makes a difference in the utterance of a word. Thus, the reader's awareness of individual sounds in a word increases his or her understanding of the role of the individual letters in words and how the written letters can be mapped onto the sounds. Without these insights, the reader will not successfully learn the code of the language (Adams, 1990; Ball & Blachman, 1988; see Chapter 5). Because of the importance of phonemic awareness, activities for reinforcing phonemic awareness should be ongoing and are easily incorporated into the classroom routine.

- The teacher guesses what was for lunch. Students give the teacher rhyming clues so that the teacher can guess what students ate for lunch (e.g., "I had a mapple, a mandwich, and a mookie;" Rubin & Eberhardt, 1996).

- The teacher says a sound. All students whose names begin (or end) with the sound take their place in line (Rubin & Eberhardt, 1996).

- The teacher takes the class roll using blending. The teacher calls out the names slowly. Students guess the name, and the named student indicates his or her presence.

- The teacher says a word with three or four phonemes (e.g., *lap, sit, run, top, dog, jump, stop*). The teacher calls on a student to unblend the word (i.e., say the word slowly) before lining up.

- To hone their attention, students establish a word of the week. The teacher gains students' attention by saying the word. Students respond by **unblending** the word.

- After the teacher reads a book, students apply their phonological awareness skills to play with words from the book (Rubin & Eberhardt, 1996; Yopp, 1995). For example, after reading *The Wind Blew* (Hutchins, 1974), students discover that various items were blown into the air. Students can play with the names of the items. They say words that rhyme with *wig, hat,* and *flag*. They count the syllables in *balloon, letters, umbrella,* and *newspapers*. They segment the words *kite, shirt,* and *scarf* into their component sounds.

Orthographic Patterns

As students acquire basic sound–symbol correspondences, they build their knowledge of orthographic patterns in the language and create a scaffold for refining and expanding their knowledge of the spelling–sound system (Share & Stanovich, 1995).

Some letters have one frequent sound or a one-to-one correspondence with a sound (e.g., letters such as *d, m, p,* and *v* have one sound). Two adjacent letters in a syllable that represent one speech sound are called digraphs. Digraphs that consist of two adjacent consonants are called consonant digraphs (e.g., *sh, ng, ck, th*); digraphs that consist of two adjacent vowels are called vowel digraphs (e.g., *ai, ea, ee, oa*). Some digraphs have one frequent sound (e.g., *sh* as in *ship, ng* as in *king, ck* as in *truck, oa* as in *boat*).

Other digraphs have several sounds (e.g., *th* as in *thimble* and *mother; ea* as in *each, head,* and *steak*). Three adjacent letters in a syllable that represent one speech sound are called **trigraphs** (e.g., *tch, dge*). **Quadrigraphs** consist of four adjacent letters in a syllable that represent one speech sound (e.g., *eigh*). Two adjacent vowels whose sounds blend together are called diphthongs (e.g., *ou, ow, oi, oy*). Considerable attention to orthography is needed for readers to deal with letters that have more than one possible sound. Pronouncing such a letter may depend on its occurrence with other letters (e.g., *c* is pronounced as /k/ before *a, o, u,* or any consonant but as /s/ before *e, i,* or *y*) and/or its position in a word (e.g., *y* is a consonant in initial position pronounced as /y/ but is a vowel in final position pronounced as /ī/ or /ē/). Knowing these patterns of language helps the reader choose the best pronunciation of a letter with more than one possible sound. In addition, there are constraints to the orthography of English. Some letters and letter clusters may not occur in certain positions in a word (e.g., English base words do not end in *j* or *v*). Some letters may or may not occur adjacent to certain letters (e.g., *q* is almost always followed by *u*; *scr* occurs within a syllable, but *skr* does not). Finally, some letters never or rarely double (e.g., *h, j, k, v, w, x, y*) (Moats, 1995; Perfetti, 1985). Careful, reflective study of orthography reinforces information readers need for reading and spelling.

Introduction of a Letter

Sound–symbol correspondences are established thorough instruction of letters and letter clusters. The three major learning modalities or pathways—auditory, visual, and kinesthetic—are engaged in introducing a letter or letter cluster. Students link the look of a letter (visual) with its sound (auditory) and its feel (kinesthetic) to form the letter sound and written shape. The information received through more than one sensory pathway increases the certainty of learning and retrieval. The grouping of the modalities strengthens the weaker pathway(s) as the strongest pathway assumes the lead in learning. The following terms and procedures are helpful in understanding multisensory instruction.

Kinesthetic Awareness

Kinesthetic awareness involves sensitivity to muscle movement. Kinesthetic information heightens students' memory and ability to discriminate speech sounds. Students' awareness of the position of the mouth, tongue, teeth, or lips and the activity of the vocal cords during the production of a sound assists the definitive learning of speech sounds. Kinesthetic information also heightens students' visual memory and ability to discriminate letter shapes. Students' awareness of how a letter feels when written in the air (i.e., sky writing) or on paper connects kinesthetic and visual information so that the letter shapes can be thoroughly learned.

Sounds

The exact individual sounds of letters (i.e., phonemes) are difficult to isolate. Speech sounds do not occur as single units in running speech. In spoken language, sounds in a word are blended together into units with other sounds so that when the speaker says a word, it does not sound as though he or she is spelling the word out loud sound by sound (e.g., *bag* is not pronounced /b/-/ă/-/g/ but rather /bă/-/g/) (Liberman, 1987).

The blending of speech sounds into units is termed coarticulation. For students to learn the sound–symbol correspondences, it is necessary for them to be able to isolate the sounds as close approximations of the actual sounds that will be coarticulated with other sounds. The following terminology helps build the teacher's understanding of sound–symbol relationships.

- A *voiced speech* sound is a sound in which the vocal cords vibrate during its production.

- An *unvoiced speech* sound is a sound in which the vocal cords do not vibrate during its production.

- A *vowel sound* is an open speech sound, produced by the easy passage of air through a relatively open vocal tract. It is unblocked by the tongue, teeth, or lips and is

voiced. (The sound /h/ opens the mouth, but because it is not voiced, it is a consonant sound.)

- A *consonant sound* is a sound that is blocked (e.g., /l/, /s/, /m/) or partially blocked (e.g., /p/, /b/) by the tongue, teeth, or lips and may be voiced (e.g., /m/, /l/, /r/) or unvoiced (e.g., /t/, /s/, /k/).

Note: For decoding instruction, the terms *blocked* and *partially blocked* refer to the kinesthetic feel and visual display of the position of the tongue, teeth, or lips during the production of sounds in isolation. *Blocked* refers to the steady position of the tongue, teeth,
or lips during the entire production of a sound (e.g., the lips stay together in a steady
position as /m/ is pronounced). *Partially blocked* refers to a released position of the
tongue or lips during production (e.g., the tongue is released from the ridge behind the
teeth as /t/ is pronounced). These terms are used in decoding instruction because students can easily and clearly feel or see the characteristics that distinguish consonant
sounds from vowel sounds.

- *Voiced and unvoiced pairs* (see Table 8.3) are sounds with the same visual display (i.e., the same position of the tongue, teeth, and lips) and kinesthetic feel, but the vocal cords vibrate during the production of one (voiced) and not the other (unvoiced).

- A *continuant speech sound* is prolonged in its production (e.g., /m/, /s/, /f/).

- A *stop consonant* is obstructed at its **place of articulation** and not prolonged in its production (e.g., /g/, /p/, /t/, /k/). These sounds must be clipped to prevent the addition of /ŭh/ at the end of the sound (e.g., /p/ not /pŭh/).

Note: The terms *continuant* and *stop consonant* are linguistic terms. In decoding instruction, the term *continuant consonant* is synonymous with *blocked consonant*. The term
stop consonant is synonymous with *partially blocked*.

- A *fricative* is produced by forcing air from the mouth through a narrow opening (e.g., /f/, /v/, /sh/, /s/, /z/).

- A *nasal sound* is produced by forcing air out through the nose (e.g., /n/, /m/, /ng/).

Use of Key Words

Key words serve as a memory device to unlock letter sounds and as a trigger for rapid
elicitation of letter sounds. A key word illustrates the sound of a letter and provides a
connection of that sound to a written symbol (Cox, 1992; Gillingham & Stillman,
1997). A letter–sound deck can be used to systematically review key words and sounds.

Table 8.3.   Voiced and
unvoiced pairs

Unvoiced	Voiced
/p/	/b/
/t/	/d/
/k/	/g/
/f/	/v/
/s/	/z/
/th/	/th/
/ch/	/j/
/sh/	/zh/

When students are shown a letter card, they name the letter, say a key word, and produce the sound (e.g., when shown a card with the letter *a*, students respond, "*a, apple,* /ă/"). Pictures of the key words may be added to the letter cards.

Coding

Using **diacritical markings** for vowels and other code marks provides students with additional visual and kinesthetic information to reinforce the letter sounds. Short vowels are coded with a **breve** (˘). Long vowels are coded with a **macron** (¯). The obscure *a*, found in the word *along* and pronounced /ŭ/, is coded with a dot: *ȧ*. Vowel digraphs (e.g., *ai, ea, ee, oa*), consonant digraphs (e.g., *ch, ng, sh*), and trigraphs (e.g., *tch, dge*) that represent one speech sound are underlined. Vowel diphthongs that represent two speech sounds that are blended together are coded with an arc:

ou   ow   oi   oy

Silent letters are crossed out:

a̶i̶ or t̶ch

Additional codes are introduced later in this chapter.

Sky Writing

Sky writing involves engaging the large "learning" muscles of the upper arm and shoulder. The movement of these muscles produces a strong neurological imprint of letter shapes (Waites & Cox, 1976). For sky writing, the arm of the writing hand is fully extended and tensed. Students use the whole writing arm, with fingers extended, to write large letters in the air, with a large model in front of them, to develop muscle memory. The nonwriting hand is placed on the upper arm or shoulder of the writing arm to create tension and help students feel the individual strokes more discernibly.

Guided Discovery Teaching

Guided discovery teaching is effective in ensuring that students learn sound–symbol correspondences and other patterns of language. The word *education* comes from the Latin word *educere*, which means *to lead out.* Guided discovery teaching uses the Socratic method of asking questions to lead students to discover new information. When students make a discovery, they understand and connect the new learning to prior knowledge.

Students, for example, are led to discover the difference between vowel and consonant sounds. The teacher asks students to repeat each of the following sounds one at a time while looking in a mirror: /ă/, /ĕ/, /ĭ/, /ŏ/, /ŭ/. The teacher asks, "What do you see happening to your mouth as each sound is pronounced?" (The mouth is open.)

The teacher asks students to say the sounds again while placing their fingers on the vocal cords. The teacher asks, "What do you feel?" (The vocal cords are activated, or the throat vibrates.) The teacher explains that these sounds are vowel sounds. Students verbalize what they have learned about vowel sounds through discovery: Vowel sounds are open and voiced (make the throat vibrate).

The teacher can also use guided discovery teaching to help students make discoveries about consonant sounds. When students are asked to repeat consonant sounds such as /l/, /s/, /m/, /b/, and /p/ while looking in a mirror, they discover that these sounds are blocked (/l/, /s/, /m/) or partially blocked (/b/, /p/) by the tongue, teeth, or lips. Consonant sounds can be voiced or unvoiced. Students verbalize what they have learned about consonant sounds through discovery: "Consonant sounds are blocked or partially blocked by the tongue, teeth, or lips. They may be voiced or unvoiced."

A Procedure for Introducing a Letter or Letter Cluster

Letter–sound relationships can be introduced through discovery teaching and a multi-sensory structured procedure, which can be adjusted to meet the specific learning needs of students (Cox, 1992; Gillingham & Stillman, 1997):

1. The teacher reads five or six **discovery words** that contain the new letter sound.

2. Students repeat each word while looking in a mirror and listening for the sound that is the same in all of the words.

3. While looking in the mirror, students repeat the sound and discover the position of the mouth. Is it opened or is it blocked or partially blocked by the tongue, teeth, or lips?

4. While placing their fingers on their vocal cords, students repeat the sound to discover whether the sound is voiced (i.e., the vocal cords vibrate) or unvoiced (i.e., there is no vibration).

5. Students determine whether the new sound is a vowel or a consonant sound. Vowel sounds are open and voiced. Consonant sounds are blocked or partially blocked by the tongue, teeth, or lips. They may be voiced or unvoiced.

6. Students guess the key word for the new sound by listening to a riddle or by feeling an object obscured in a container. The key word holds the new sound in memory.

7. The teacher writes the discovery words on the board.

8. Students determine the letter that is the same in all of the words and that represents the new sound.

9. The teacher shows a card with the new letter on it.

10. Students name the letter, say the key word, and give the sound.

11. The teacher names the new letter just before writing a large model of the letter on the board.

12. The teacher names the letter and then demonstrates sky writing. The teacher describes the letter strokes while sky writing the letter.

13. Students stand and sky write, naming the letter before writing.

14. The teacher distributes papers with a large model of the new letter.

15. Students trace the model three times with the pointer finger of the writing hand and three times with a pencil. Students name the letter each time before writing.

16. Students turn the model over, and the teacher dictates the name of the letter.

17. Students repeat the letter name and write the letter.

18. The teacher shows the letter card again as students name the letter, say the key word, and produce the sound.

During the various steps in this procedure, the four properties of the letter—name, sound, shape, and feel—are being connected through the use of the auditory, visual, and kinesthetic modalities. This multisensory teaching reinforces the discovery information and builds associations in memory.

Blending

Once students have identified the letter–sound relationships of a word, they must meld the sounds to produce a word. Blending sounds in a word is a critical component of learning sound–symbol correspondences. Fluid blending of letter sounds aids students in producing recognizable words. Before students begin reading words, they should have opportunities to blend sounds together orally by using manipulatives (e.g., blocks, buttons, math counters, pennies). Because of the effects of coarticulation on sounds, letter-by-letter blending in reading does not always produce a recognizable word. Several different strategies, best presented one-to-one or in small groups, are used to promote the skill of blending when reading words. When introducing any of the blending activities for reading, it is desirable to begin blending words that have continuant initial sounds (e.g., /f/, /l/, /m/, /n/, /s/). Continuant sounds are easier to blend than the stop consonant sounds (e.g., /d/, /p/, /k/). The continuant sounds allow students to slide into the vowel sound. Blending with initial stop consonants is introduced after students have demonstrated facility with the blending of continuant initial sounds.

Say It Slowly

Using one set of letter cards or lettered tiles, the teacher sets out *m, e,* and *t.* The teacher demonstrates how to say the word *met* by blending the sounds together in units—by saying /m/, then /mě/, then /mět/, not by saying /m/-/ě/-/t/ (Beck & Juel, 1995).

Say It Faster, Move It Closer

Using one set of letter cards or lettered tiles, the teacher sets out *s* and, separated by a wide space, *a.* The teacher points to the first letter. Students say /s/ and hold it until the teacher points to the second letter and students produce /ă/. The letters are moved closer together and the procedure is repeated, with students blending the sounds together faster. The letters are moved closer together and sounds are produced together faster until students can produce the two sounds as a single unit, /să/. A final consonant is added and blended with the unit to produce a word (e.g., *sat, sad, sap;* Blachman, 1987; Englemann, 1969).

Onsets and Rimes

Using letter cards or lettered tiles, the teacher sets out *a* and *t.* Students blend the letter sounds to produce /ăt/. This /ăt/ unit is the rime, the combination of the vowel and the consonant(s) that comes after it in a syllable. The teacher places the letter *m* before the rime. This letter is the onset, the consonant(s) of a syllable before the vowel. Students blend /m/ and /ăt/ to produce /măt/. The teacher changes the onset to create new words that students blend and read (e.g., *sat, rat, fat, bat*). Other rimes for practice include the following: *in, it, an, am, op, ang, ing,* and *ink* (Adams, 1990; Goswami & Bryant, 1990).

Playing with Sounds

Using one set of letter cards or lettered tiles, the teacher sets out *a* and *t.* The student blends the letter sounds to produce /ăt/. The teacher asks the student to change /ăt/ to /săt/. The student adds the card or tile with *s* and reads /săt/. The teacher asks the student to read new words by changing or adding new letter sounds (e.g., change *sat* to *mat, mat to map, map* to *mop, mop* to *top, top* to *stop*) (Beck & Juel, 1995; Blachman, 1987; Blachman, Ball, Black, & Tangel, 2000; Slingerland, 1971).

Tapping Out

The teacher lays out or displays letter cards or lettered tiles to form a word such as *mat*. Using one hand, students quickly tap the pointer finger to the thumb and say the sound of the first letter, /m/. In quick succession, they tap the middle finger to the thumb and say the sound of the second letter, /ă/. Finally, they tap the ring finger to the thumb and say the sound of the final letter, /t/. When all of the letter sounds have been tapped out, students say the word as they drag the thumb across their fingers, beginning with the index finger (Wilson, 1996).

Tapping and Sweeping

The teacher lays out letter cards or lettered tiles to form a word such as *mat*. Each student takes a turn. He or she makes a fist and taps under the *m* as he or she says the sound /m/. Next, he or she taps under the *a* and says /ă/. Finally, he or she taps under the *t* and says /t/. After the student has said each sound, he or she sweeps a fist under the letters and says the word (Greene & Enfield, 1985).

Strategies for Accuracy

Accurately reading words is key to associating pronunciations with correct orthographic patterns as well as facilitating comprehension. The teacher can use the following strategies to guide a student to the accurate decoding of a word or to correct a mistake when he or she is reading:

- *Misreading or skipping letters:* If a student misreads a letter in a word (e.g., *lid* for *lip*) or skips a letter in a word (e.g., *pat* for *past*), then the teacher directs the student to name the letters in the word. Naming the letters focuses the student's attention on the letters and also strengthens the orthographic identity of the word.

- *Misreading a word:* If a student misreads a word (e.g., *pane* for *plant*), the teacher directs the student to use a backing-up procedure. The student identifies the syllable type, determines the vowel sound (short or long), and codes the vowel accordingly (i.e., marks it with a breve or a macron). The student produces the appropriate vowel sound and blends it with the consonant sound immediately after the vowel. He or she blends this unit with any remaining consonant sounds after the vowel, adding sounds one at a time. The reader then blends the vowel and all of the consonant sounds after the vowel with the consonant sound immediately before the vowel. Any remaining consonants that precede the vowel are blended on one at a time. The backing-up procedure with the word *plant* looks like this:

Step 1: The student codes *a* with a breve and says /ă/   plănt

Step 2: The student blends /ă/ with /n/.   plănt

Step 3: The student blends /ăn/ with /t/.   plănt

Step 4: The student blends /l/ with /ănt/.   plănt

Step 5: The student blends whole word.   plănt

STRUCTURAL ANALYSIS

Knowing sound–symbol correspondences enables a reader to successfully read one-syllable base words. Once the reader has established a few sound–symbol correspondences and can blend them together successfully to form words, information about structural analysis is taught concurrently with new sound–symbol correspondences. Structural analysis of the syllabic and morphemic segments of language facilitates the recognition of longer words. *Syllables* are speech units of language that contain one vowel sound and can be represented in written language as words (e.g., *cat, mop, sad*) or parts of words (e.g., *mu, hin, ter*) with a single vowel or pair of vowels denoting the vowel sound. When a syllable is part of a word, it does not necessarily carry meaning (e.g., *mu* in *museum* or *music*). Awareness of syllables helps the reader perceive the natural divisions of words to aid recognition. Six types of syllables are represented in written English (e.g., a closed syllable ends in at least one consonant; an open syllable ends in one vowel). The types of syllables are discussed in detail later in this chapter.

Awareness of syllable types gives the reader a way to determine how to pronounce the vowel sound in a syllable (e.g., the vowel in a closed syllable is short; the vowel in an open, accented syllable is long). Morphemes are meaning-carrying units of written language (Moats, 1994) such as base words (e.g., *cat, number, salamander*), prefixes (e.g., *un-, re-, mis-*), suffixes (e.g., *-ful, -ness, -ment*), combining forms (e.g., *bio, helio, polis*), and roots (e.g., *vis, struct, vert*). Awareness of morphemes aids recognition as well as word meaning.

Syllables

The teacher leads students to discover the concept of a syllable. Students are asked to repeat words of varying lengths (e.g., *mop, robot, fantastic*), one at time, while looking in a mirror and observing how many times their mouths open when each word is pronounced. They are asked to repeat each word again while cupping their jaws in their hands and feeling how many times their jaws drop or their mouths open. This visual information of seeing the mouth open and kinesthetic information of feeling the mouth open reinforces students' understanding of a syllable. The teacher explains that a syllable is a word or a part of a word made with one opening of the mouth. Students are asked to think about which kind of letter sounds open the mouth. (Vowel sounds open the mouth.) The teacher explains that a syllable has one vowel sound. When students say a word, they determine the number of syllables by counting the number of times the mouth opens when pronouncing the word. This concept carries over when students look at a printed word; they determine the number of syllables in the word by counting the number of sounded vowels.

Auditory Awareness of Syllables

The following activities promote awareness of syllables in words:

- Syllable awareness begins early, with students identifying or generating short words (*farm, feet, fat, fork, food*) and long words (*February, firefighter, fisherman*). The chosen words might begin with a certain sound or pertain to a particular unit of study (*plants, animals, ocean, United States;* Rubin & Eberhardt, 1996).

- Students repeat words dictated by the teacher. They clap or tap out the number of syllables. The teacher starts with compound words (*playground, flashlight, cowboy*), then moves on to two-syllable words (*velvet, plastic, mascot*) and then on to words with three or more syllables (*fantastic, investment, invitation*).

- Students repeat words dictated by the teacher and move a counter (e.g., *block, button, penny*) for each syllable they hear. Using counters provides a visual and kinesthetic anchor for the sounds.

- Students repeat a word with two or more syllables dictated by the teacher. Students are asked to repeat the word again, omitting a designated syllable (Rosner, 1975), as illustrated in the following dialogue:

Teacher: Say *transportation.*

Students: Transportation

Teacher: Say *transportation* without *trans.*

Students: Portation

Teacher: Say *transportation* without *tion.*

Students: Transporta

This activity is effective in helping students pronounce words correctly and aids reading and spelling words of more than one syllable.

Awareness of Accent

Correct placement of the accent or stress on a syllable supports students in pronouncing and recognizing words. The mouth opens wider and the voice is louder and higher when the accented syllable is pronounced. The following activities promote awareness of accent:

- Students practice accent by saying the alphabet in pairs, accenting the first letter in the pair: "A´ B, C´ D, E´ F, G´ H, I´ J."

- Students practice flexibility in accenting by saying the alphabet in pairs and shifting the accent to the second letter in the pair: "A B´, C D´, E F´, G H´, I J´."

- Students practice accenting by saying two-syllable words, first placing an exaggerated accent on the first syllable and then placing it on the second. They then choose the correct accent placement (e.g., *bas´|ket*, not *bas|ket´*; *can|teen´*, not *can´|teen*).

Some words have a noun form and a verb form, and the accent may fall on either syllable depending on the form of the word. The nouns are accented on the first syllable, and the verbs are accented on the second (e.g., *con´|duct, con|duct´*; *ob´|ject, ob|ject´*).

Six Types of Syllables

The instability of vowels—they have more than one sound (e.g., short sound, long sound, unexpected sound when followed by *r* or in combination with another vowel)—is a complicating factor in learning the sound–symbol correspondences of written English. Knowledge of syllable types is an important organizing tool for decoding unknown words. Students can group letters into known syllable types that give clues about the sounds of the vowels. There are six orthographic types of syllables: closed, open, vowel-consonant-*e*, vowel pair (vowel team), **vowel-*r*** (*r*-controlled), and consonant-*le* (which is one kind of **final stable syllable**) (see Table 8.4; Steere, Peck, & Kahn, 1984). A high percentage of the more than 600,000 words of English can be categorized as one of these syllable types or as a composite of different syllable types.

Combining this knowledge of syllable types with known morphemes (e.g., suffixes, prefixes) simplifies decoding words with more than one syllable. The closed syllable is the most frequent syllable type in English (Stanback, 1992). Students can be introduced to the closed syllable when they have learned the letter sounds that make up this pattern (e.g., three or four consonants and one short vowel). The remaining sound–symbol correspondences and syllable types are taught sequentially and cumulatively until all have been introduced, and then students practice them until all are mastered.

Guided discovery teaching techniques for the six syllable types are discussed in the following sections. The syllable types are introduced in the order that they might be presented to students. Students are led to discover the salient characteristics of each syllable type and the effect of the syllabic pattern on the vowel sound. The teacher pauses after the questions to solicit answers from students.

Closed Syllable

Teacher: [Writes discovery words on the board and directs students' attention to them.] Look at these words: *hat, got, hip, mend.* How many vowels are in each word?

Students: There is only one vowel in each word.

Teacher: Look at the end of each word. How does each word end?

Students: Each word ends in at least one consonant.

Teacher: Listen as I read the words. How are the vowels pronounced? [Reads the words.]

Students: The vowels are pronounced with their short sounds.

Teacher: Each of these words ends in at least one consonant after one vowel. What happens to the mouth when a consonant sound is made?

Students: The tongue, teeth, or lips close the sound.

Teacher: Yes, a consonant closes the mouth. What would be a good name for a syllable that ends in a consonant?

Students: A good name is *closed syllable.*

Teacher: A closed syllable ends in at least one consonant after one vowel. Therefore, these words are closed syllables. The vowel in a closed syllable is short; the

Table 8.4.   Six syllable types

Closed	Open	Vowel-consonant-*e*	Vowel pair (vowel team)	Vowel-*r*	Consonant-*le*[a]
it	hi	name	each	fern	-dle
bed	no	five	boil	burn	-fle
and	me	slope	sweet	thirst	-gle
lost	she	these	tray	star	-ple

[a]A consonant-*le* syllable is a kind of final stable syllable. Other final stable syllables include *-age, -sion, -tion,* and *-ture.*

vowel is coded with a breve that is written as (ˇ). [Writes a breve over the vowel in each word.] The word *breve* comes from the Latin word *brevis*, which means *short*. What other words might come from the same Latin word?

Students: *Brief, brevity,* and *abbreviate* also come from the same Latin word.

Teacher: Let's review what you have discovered about closed syllables. A closed syllable ends in at least one consonant after one vowel. The vowel is short; code it with a breve.

Note: When reviewing the concept of a closed syllable, or any kind of syllable, a cloze procedure can be used, with students filling in the most salient characteristics of the syllable type. Pausing for students' replies, the teacher says, "A closed syllable ends in at least one [consonant] after one [vowel]. The vowel is [short]; code it with a [breve]."

Students must be sensitive to the fact that accent may affect the sound of a vowel in a syllable. Short vowel sounds in unaccented closed syllables, particularly before *m*, *n*, or *l*, may be distorted. The resultant vowel sound is schwa, which is denoted as /ə/ and is pronounced approximately as /ŭ/. This sound does not build a strong orthographic memory of the words because the schwa sound is not uniquely represented by one letter (Ehri, Wilce, & Taylor, 1987). Students should use an **exaggerated pronunciation,** or spelling-based pronunciation, when decoding these words (e.g., students pronounce *ribbon* as /rĭbŏn/). The teacher helps students match the printed word to a familiar word in running speech.

Short vowels before nasal sounds /m/, /n/, or /ng/ are nasalized and may seem distorted (e.g., *jam, ant, drank, thing*). Awareness of this possibility helps students better match the orthographic representation with a known word in their listening and speaking vocabularies. (See Ehri et al., 1987, for more discussion of short vowels.)

Open Syllable

Teacher: [Writes discovery words on the board and directs students' attention to them.] Look at these words: *he, go, hi, me.* How many vowels are in each word?

Students: There is only one vowel in each word.

Teacher: Look at the end of each word. How does each word end?

Students: Each word ends in one vowel.

Teacher: Could these words be called closed syllables?

Students: No, closed syllables end in at least one consonant after one vowel.

Teacher: When the words are read, how are the vowels pronounced? [Reads the words.]

Students: The vowels are pronounced with their long sounds.

Teacher: Each of these words ends in one vowel. What position is the mouth in when a vowel sound is made?

Students: The mouth is open.

Teacher: What would be a good name for a syllable that ends in one vowel?

Students: A good name is *open syllable.*

Teacher: An open syllable ends in one vowel. The vowel in an open, accented sylla-
             ble is long; the vowel is coded with a macron, which is written as (‾). [Writes
             a macron on the board.] The word *macron* comes from the Greek word
             makros, which means *long.* Let's review what you have discovered about an
             open syllable: An open syllable ends in one vowel. The vowel is long; code
             it with a macron.

Vowel-Consonant-e *Syllable*

Teacher: [Writes discovery words on the board.] Look at these words: *cake, theme, five,
             rope, cube.* How many vowels are in each word?

Students: There are two vowels in each word.

Teacher: Look at the end of each word. How does each word end?

Students: They end with an *e.*

Teacher: What comes between the vowel and the final *e* in each word?

Students: One consonant.

Teacher: When the words are read, what happens to the final *e?* [Reads the words]

Students: The *e* in final position is silent.

Teacher: How are the vowels pronounced?

Students: They are pronounced with their long sounds.

Teacher: Each of these words ends in one vowel, one consonant, and a final *e.* What
             would be a good name for this kind of syllable?

Students: A good name is *vowel-consonant-e* syllable.

Teacher: The vowel in a vowel-consonant-*e* syllable is long. How is a long vowel
             coded?

Students: A macron shows a long vowel.

Teacher: The final *e* in this syllable is silent. How can the *e* be coded?

Students: The silent *e* can be crossed out: *e̸.*

Teacher: Let's review what you have discovered about the vowel-consonant-*e* sylla-
             ble: A vowel-consonant-*e* syllable ends in one vowel, one consonant, and a
             final *e.* The *e* is silent; cross it out. The vowel is long; code it with a macron.

Vowel-Pair (Vowel-Team) *Syllable*

Teacher: [Writes discovery words on the board in two columns.] Look at these words:
             sea, feet, paint, boat, zoo, book, point, head. How many vowels are in each
             word?

Students: There are two vowels in each word.

Teacher: Look at the end of each word. How does each word end?

Students: Some words end with at least one consonant.

Teacher: Are they closed syllables?

Students: No, a closed syllable has only one vowel.

Teacher: How about the other words?

Students: They end in a vowel.

Teacher: Are they open syllables?

Students: No, an open syllable has only one vowel.

Teacher: These words are called *vowel-pair syllables* or *vowel-team syllables* because they have two vowels next to each other. Each vowel pair has a different letter combination and sound. Let's review what you have discovered about the vowel-pair syllable: A vowel-pair (or vowel-team) syllable has two vowels next to each other.

Note: The generalization of "when two vowels go walking, the first one does the talking" is only reliable about 45% of the time (Adams, 1990). The first four discovery words (*see, feet, paint, boat*) in this activity follow this generalization; the last four discovery words (*zoo, book, point, head*) do not. For accuracy, each pair must be explicitly taught.

*Vowel-*r *(*r*-Controlled) Syllable*

Teacher: [Writes discovery words on the board.] Look at these words: *met, red, step, hen, her*. How many vowels are in these words?

Students: There is one vowel in each word.

Teacher: Look at the end of each word. How does each word end?

Students: They end in at least one consonant after one vowel.

Teacher: What kind of syllable ends in at least one consonant after one vowel?

Students: A closed syllable ends in at least one consonant after one vowel.

Teacher: Tell me about the vowel in a closed syllable.

Students: The vowel in a closed syllable is short; code it with a breve.

Teacher: Let's code and read these words. [Students direct the teacher to code each word. Students read each word after it is coded. When students reach the word *her*, they discover they cannot read the word with a short *e* sound.] What happened when you tried to read the word *her?*

Students: The vowel is not short in the word *her.*

Teacher: Something unexpected happens to the vowel in this word. We expect the vowel to be short because it is in a closed syllable. What letter do you see after the vowel?

Students: The letter *r* is after the vowel.

Teacher: In the word *her,* the *r* comes after the vowel. What would be a good name for this syllable?

Students: A good name would be *vowel-r syllable.*

Teacher: What happens to the vowel in a vowel-*r* syllable?

Students: The vowel makes an unexpected sound.

Teacher: When an *r* comes after a vowel, the vowel and the *r* are coded with an arc beneath them:

her

The vowel-*r* combination in an accented syllable is also coded with a circumflex:

hêr

Let's review what you have discovered about a vowel-*r* syllable: A vowel-*r* syllable has an *r* after the vowel. The vowel makes an unexpected sound; in an accented syllable, code the vowel-*r* syllable with an arc and code the vowel with a circumflex.

Note: The vowel before an *r* in an accented syllable is coded with a **circumflex** (ˆ). In an unaccented syllable, the vowel-*r* combination is coded with an arc and the vowel with a tilde (˜). The vowel-*r* combinations *er, ir,* and *ur* in an accented or unaccented syllable are pronounced /er/. The vowel-*r* combination *ar* in an accented syllable is pronounced /ar/ as in *star.* In an unaccented syllable, *ar* is pronounced /er/ as in *dollar.* The vowel-*r* combination *or* in an accented syllable is pronounced /or/ as in *fork.* In an unaccented syllable, *or* is pronounced /er/ as in *doctor.*

The terms *vowel-r syllable* and *r-controlled syllable* are used interchangeably. The term *vowel-r* focuses attention on the orthographic pattern, and the term *r-controlled* focuses attention on the influence of the *r* on the vowel.

Consonant-le (Final Stable) Syllable

Teacher: [Writes discovery words on the board.] Look at these words: *ramble, uncle, candle, simple, table.* What looks the same in all of these words?

Students: They all have a consonant and *l* and *e* at the end.

Teacher: When these words are pronounced, how many syllables do you hear or feel? [Reads the words one at a time as students echo each word.]

Students: There are two syllables.

Teacher: The second syllable in these words is spelled with a consonant, an *l,* and a final *e* and is called a consonant-*le* syllable. Tell me about the sound of the *e* in final position.

Students: It is silent.

Teacher: Because the final syllable in each of these words does not have a sounded vowel, these syllables are rule breakers. The final syllable is coded with a bracket: [. The accent falls on the syllable before the final syllable. Let's code the discovery words. [Students verbalize coding of the final syllable and the syllable before the consonant-*le* syllable. Students read words.] Let's review what you have discovered about a consonant-*le* syllable: A consonant-*le* syllable ends in a consonant, an *l*, and a final *e*. Code the syllable with a bracket, and accent the syllable before.

Note: The consonant-*le* syllable is one of several syllables that are referred to as *final stable syllables* (Cox, 1992). These syllables appear in the final position in words, and their pronunciations are fairly stable. Advanced final stable syllables, which include syllables such as *ture, age, sion,* and *tion,* are also coded with a bracket. Some of the advanced final stable syllables are also identified as suffixes. The advantage of treating these units as final stable syllables is twofold (Cox & Hutcheson, 1988): 1) They serve as an early, interim bridge to reading words of more than one syllable before students know syllable division or advanced morphemes (e.g., *pic´[ture, man´[age, mo´[tion*); and 2) they provide predictable identification of the accent, which usually falls on the syllable before the final stable syllable (e.g., *va|ca´[tion, ex|plo´[sion*).

Morphology

Morphology comes from the Greek *morphe,* meaning *form,* and *ology,* meaning *study of.* Morphemes are the smallest forms or units of language—base words, prefixes, suffixes, roots, and combining forms—that carry meaning. A word may contain several syllables but may represent only one morpheme (e.g., *salamander;* Moats, 1994), or a word may contain several syllables and represent several morphemes (e.g., *instructor* contains three syllables and the morphemes *in-, struct,* and *-or*). Study of morphemes not only facilitates decoding but also provides a springboard for vocabulary development and spelling (Adams, 1990) and bridges the gap between alphabetic reading (i.e., word-level reading) and comprehension (Foorman & Schatschneider, 1997). The following definitions are important to the study of morphemes.

- A *base word* is a plain word with nothing added to it.

- An *affix* is a suffix or a prefix that is added to a base word or a root.

- A root is an essential base of letters to which prefixes and suffixes are added (e.g., *audi, vis, struct*). Roots are primarily of Latin origin. A root that stands alone as a word is called a *free morpheme;* a root that requires the addition of an affix(es) to form a word is called a *bound morpheme* (Moats, 1995).

- A *suffix* is a letter or a group of letters added to the end of a base word or a root to change its meaning, form, or usage. A suffix that begins with a consonant is called a **consonant suffix** (e.g., *-ful, -less, -ness, -ment, -cian*). A suffix that begins with a vowel is called a **vowel suffix** (e.g., *-en, -ist, -ible*). *Derivational suffixes* are added to a base word or root and change the part of speech or the function of the base word or root (e.g., *-ful, -less, -cian, -or;* Moats, 1995, 2010). Some suffixes are grammatical endings called *inflections* or *inflectional endings* (e.g., *-s, -ed, -er, -est, -ing*), which, when added to base words, change their number, tense, voice, mood, or comparison (Moats, 1995, 2010).

For the most part, the spelling of a suffix does not change. The spelling of the base word, however, may change when a vowel suffix is added. In the initial stages of introduction and practice, suffixes are added to base words. The suffix can be coded with a box. This coding visually separates the base word and the suffix, making it easier for students to attend to the base word:

standing

- A *prefix* is a letter or a group of letters added to the beginning of a base word or a root to change its meaning (e.g., *mis-, un-, con-, re-*). A prefix that ends in a consonant is called a **consonant prefix.** The spelling of a consonant prefix may change (e.g., *in-* may be spelled *il-, im-,* or *ir-*). A prefix that ends in a vowel is called a **vowel prefix.** The spelling of a vowel prefix does not change.

- A *derivative* is a base word or root plus an affix.

- *Combining forms* are similar to roots, but they are combined with equal importance in a word (e.g., *auto* and *graph,* which are neither affixes nor base words, combine to make *autograph;* see Henry, 1990). Words that are derived from combining forms can be affixed (e.g., *autobiography, autobiographic*). Combining forms are primarily of Greek origin (see Chapter 4).

Multisensory Introduction of Affixes

Quite often, the means to reading multisyllabic words is identifying affixes (i.e., prefixes and suffixes) that are part of the word. Students may be able to recognize an unfamiliar word simply by identifying the affixes and then the remaining base word or root.

Affixes can be introduced using a multisensory guided discovery teaching approach:

1. The teacher reads a list of five or six derivatives that have a common trait as students repeat each word (e.g., *joyful, careful, helpful, graceful, cheerful*).

2. Students discover what sounds the same in each word.

3. The teacher writes the derivatives on the board.

4. Students discover which letters are the same in each word and where the letters are found.

5. Students discover whether the same letters (the affix) are a suffix or a prefix, and they discover the meaning of the affix.

6. Students verbalize what they have discovered (e.g., *-ful* is a consonant suffix that means *full of*).

7. The teacher writes the new affix on an index card and adds it to an affix deck that is systematically reviewed. During review, students identify and spell the affix, give a key word, give the pronunciation, and give the meaning of the affix (e.g., when looking at the affix card for suffix *-ful,* students say, "Consonant suffix *f-u-l, hopeful,* /fŭl/, *full of*").

Syllable Division

Skilled readers are able to sense where to divide longer words because they have an awareness of syllables and have internalized the orthographic patterns of the language so well (Adams, 1990). The following activities heighten students' visual awareness of syllables and syllable division patterns.

Separated Syllables

Students identify syllable types of separated syllables, join them into words, and read the words aloud (Gillingham & Stillman, 1997):

cac|tus   mas|cot   ban|dit   nut|meg

mag|net   gob|let   prob|lem   nap|kin

Manipulation of Multisyllabic Words

Students identify syllables written on individual cards, arrange them into words, and read the words aloud (Gillingham & Stillman, 1997):

tas	fan	tic
lan	tic	At
pen	tine	tur

| lec | net | e | mag | tro | ic |

Scooping the Syllables

As students read multisyllabic words on a worksheet, they call attention to the syllables in the words by scooping the syllables. Using a pencil, students "scoop" (i.e., draw an arc underneath) the syllables from left to right, identify the syllable type, place a syllable code under each syllable (e.g., *o* for open, *r* for *r*-controlled) and code the vowel (Wilson, 1996):

Common Patterns for Dividing Words into Syllables

There are four major patterns in English (VCCV, VCV, VCCCV, and VV) that indicate that a word will be divided into syllables according to how it is pronounced. For each of these four patterns, there are different choices for division and accent placement. The best choices for dividing and accenting are listed here in order of frequency. Students must learn to be flexible when they make choices about dividing and accenting multisyllabic words. If the first choice of a pattern does not produce a recognizable word, then they need to try a second choice, which usually requires a change in accent placement. If necessary, they may need to try a third choice, which usually requires a change in the division of the word. Familiarity and flexibility with syllable-division patterns help students develop strategies for reading multisyllabic words; students do not have to guess or give up when they encounter unfamiliar long words.

VCCV—Two Consonants Between Two Vowels

- **VC´|CV**—When two consonants stand between two vowels, the word is usually divided between the two consonants. The accent usually falls on the first syllable. Examples include the following: ***nap´**|kin, **vel´**|vet, **can´**|did, **cac´**|tus, **cam´**|pus, **mag´**|net, **bas´**|ket, **in´**|sect, **op´**|tic,* and ***mus´**|lin. Note:* Consonant digraphs such as *ch, ck, sh, ph, th,* and *wh* are treated as single consonants because they represent single speech sounds (***ath´**|lete, **dol´**|phin).*

- VC|**CV**´—The word may be divided between the consonants, with the accent falling on the second syllable. Examples include the following: un|**til**´, pas|**tel**´, dis|**cuss**´, can|**teen**´, in|**sist**´.

- **V**´|CCV—The word may be divided before both consonants with the accent falling on the first syllable. Examples include the following: se´|cret, **fra**´|grant, and **ma**´|cron.

Note: Consonant digraphs, two adjacent consonants that represent one sound (e.g., *sh, th, ck, ng*), are never divided. Some consonant clusters contain two adjacent consonants, commonly known as *consonant blends,* whose sounds flow together. It is not necessary for these clusters to be introduced as separate sound–symbol correspondences because each sound in a consonant cluster is accessible. Consonant blends may divide (e.g., *fab|ric*) or may not divide (e.g., *se|cret*).

VCV—One Consonant Between Two Vowels

- **V**´|CV—When one consonant stands between two vowels, the word is usually divided before the consonant. The accent usually falls on the first syllable. Examples include the following: **i**´|ris, **o**´|pen, **u**´|nit, **o**´|ver, **ro**´|tate, **a**´|corn, **mu**´|sic, **tu**´|lip, **va**´|cate, **si**´|lent, **su**´|per, and **e**´|ven.

- V|**CV**´—The word may be divided before the consonant, with the accent falling on the second syllable. Examples include the following: re|**quest**´, e|**vent**´, o|**mit**´, u|**nite**´, pa|**rade**´, a|**like**´, a|**lone**´, sa|**lute**´, and di|**vine**´.

   Note: The vowels in an open, unaccented syllable require careful attention during syllable division. If students are overly sensitive to sounds in their speech, then they may not make the connection between orthography and speech (Ehri et al., 1987). For example, the *e* in the word *elect* sounds more like /ĭ/ in running speech. If students are too sensitive to the /ĭ/ sound, then they will not build an orthographic memory of *elect* spelled with *e*. The *e* in an open, unaccented syllable should be perceived as having a pronunciation that is long (e.g., e|vent´) but is shorter than an *e* in an open, accented syllable (e.g., ze´|ro). In an open, unaccented syllable, *o* and *u* remain long, but their pronunciations are shortened (e.g., o|mit´, u|nite´). The *e, o,* and *u* are coded with a macron. The *a* in an open, unaccented syllable is obscure and pronounced as /ŭ/ (e.g., a|long´). The *a* is coded with a dot. The *i* in an open, unaccented syllable is short (e.g., di|vide´). The *i* is coded with a breve.

- **VC**´|V—The word may be divided after the consonant, with the accent falling on the first syllable. Examples include the following: **rob**´|in, **riv**´|er, **cab**´|in, **trav**´|el, **mag**´|ic, **tim**´|id, **mod**´|ern, **plan**´|et, **sol**´|id, and **sev**´|en.

   Note: As mentioned previously, consonant digraphs (i.e., two adjacent consonants that represent one sound) are treated as one consonant. Words with consonant digraphs may be divided before the digraph (e.g., go´|pher) or after the digraph (e.g., rath´|er).

VCCCV—Three Consonants Between Two Vowels

- **VC**´|CCV—When three consonants stand between two vowels, the word is usually divided after the first consonant. The first syllable is usually accented. Examples include the following: **pil**´|grim, **chil**´|dren, **pan**´|try, **spec**´|trum, **mon**´|ster, **lob**´|ster, **hun**´|dred, **scoun**´|drel, **ham**´|ster, and **os**´|trich.

- **VC|CCV´**—The word may be divided after the first consonant, with the accent falling on the second syllable. Examples include the following: *im|**ply´**, com|**plete´**, sur|**prise´**, in|**trude´**, en|**twine´**, em|**blaze´***, and *ex|**treme´***.

- **VCC´|CV**—The word may be divided after the second consonant or after a final consonant cluster (e.g., *mp* and *nd* are consonant clusters that often occur in final position in one-syllable words); the accent falls on the first syllable. Examples include the following: ***pump´**|kin, **sand´**|wich, **bank´**|rupt, **part´**|ner, **musk´**|rat*, and ***irk´**|some*.

VV—Two Adjacent Vowels

- **V´|V**—A word with two adjacent vowels that do not form a vowel pair is divided between the vowels, with the accent falling on the first syllable. Examples include the following: ***di´**|al, **cha´**|os, **tru´**|ant, **tri´**|umph*, and ***li´**|on*.

  Note: Because the vowel pairs in these words (i.e., *ia, ao, ua, iu, io*) do not constitute digraphs or diphthongs, a reader knows immediately to divide the words between the two vowels.

- **V´|V**—A word with two adjacent vowels that typically form a vowel pair may be divided between the vowels, with the accent falling on the first syllable. Examples include the following: ***po´**|em, **qui´**|et, **sto´**|ic*, and ***bo´**|a*.

  Note: Adjacent vowels that frequently form digraphs or diphthongs include *ai, ay, au, aw, ea, ee, ei, ey, eu, ew, ie, oa, oe, oi, oo, ou, ow*, and *oy*. Although consonant digraphs are not divided, adjacent vowels that can form digraphs and diphthongs may be divided. A reader first tries reading an unfamiliar word with two adjacent vowels using the pronunciation of the digraph or diphthong that the vowels represent (e.g., reading *poem* as /pōm/). If reading the words in this manner does not produce a recognizable or a correct word, then he or she divides the words between the vowels and reads it.

- **V|V´**—The word may be divided between the vowels, with the accent falling on the second syllable. Examples include the following: *du|**et´**, cre|**ate´***, and *co|**erce´***.

Procedure for Dividing Words

A structured procedure provides readers with a systematic approach for reading long, unfamiliar words and builds an orthographic memory for syllable-division patterns. Students with dyslexia may need additional visual and kinesthetic information to build the memory of these patterns. Information helpful to students at risk and with dyslexia is given in parentheses (Cox & Hutcheson, 1988).

1. *Count the vowels.* To determine the number of syllables in a word, students count the number of sounded vowels from left to right. Vowel pairs count as one sounded vowel. (The vowel pairs can be underlined to call attention to the fact that the two vowels make one sound.) All suffixes are boxed. By boxing suffixes, students may see a base word that requires no further division. Students place brackets before any final stable syllables. By bracketing a final stable syllable, students may see that no further division is needed.

2. *Touch the vowels.* Using the index fingers of both hands, students touch the sounded vowels or vowel pairs and identify them. (A line can be drawn over the word from

sounded vowel to sounded vowel. The vowels can be labeled by writing a small *v* over each vowel.) Example:

v   v
mascot

The word *mascot* has two syllables because it has two sounded vowels. The vowels are *a* and *o*.

3. *Count the consonants.* Students count the number of consonants between the two vowels or vowel pairs and identify the division pattern. (Consonant digraphs can be underlined to call attention to the fact that the two letters are treated as one consonant sound. Each consonant or consonant digraph can be labeled with *c*. Labeling the vowels and consonants expedites the orthographic memory of the syllable-division patterns.) Example:

vcc v
mascot

There are two consonants between the vowels in *mascot.* The syllable-division pattern is VCCV.

4. *Divide.* Students draw a vertical line to divide the word according to the most frequent division of this pattern. *Example:* Because the most common division choice for VCCV is to divide between the consonants, *mascot* is divided between *s* and *c*.

5. *Accent.* Students place an accent mark on the appropriate syllable according to the most frequent accent of the pattern. *Example:* With a VC|CV word, the accent is most frequently placed on the first syllable.

6. *Code.* Students identify each syllable type and code the vowels accordingly. *Example:* The first syllable of *mascot* is closed. The vowel is short; code it with a breve. The second syllable is closed. The vowel is short; code it with a breve.

7. *Read.* Students read each syllable without accenting either syllable.

8. *Read again.* Students read the syllables together with the appropriate accent.

9. *Adjust.* Students adjust the accent or division if the word is not recognizable. Adjusting the accent or the division to produce a recognizable word teaches students to be flexible with language.

See Figure 8.1, which is a pictorial representation of the previously delineated steps and is helpful for students with limited reading skills to use; Figure 8.2 shows the steps when dividing the word *mascot.*

Reading Practice

Reading practice to reinforce a syllable-division pattern or any other decoding concepts must be focused. The teacher reviews all information that is pertinent to reinforcing the concept. For example, before reviewing a syllable-division pattern, the teacher might review the definition of a suffix, the syllable types that are germane to the pattern, the pattern itself, and the procedure for dividing words into syllables. After a review of relevant information, the teacher models the coding of a word while verbalizing the process and then reads the word. The teacher presents three or four additional words.

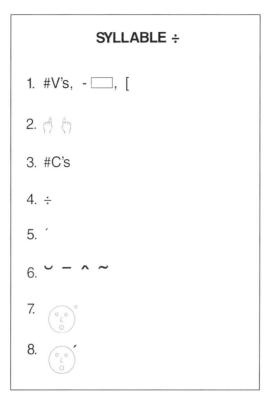

Figure 8.1. The syllable-division procedure provides ready access to multisyllabic words. Students 1) count the vowels, box suffixes, and add a bracket to mark a final stable syllable; 2) touch the vowels; 3) count the consonants; 4) draw a vertical line to divide the word; 5) mark the accent; 6) code the vowels; 7) read without accent; and 8) read with accent.

Students verbalize the coding and/or division of these words and read them. The teacher then presents a list of words that contain the new concept for students to read, silently and then aloud. The teacher provides immediate feedback and leads students to self-correct errors so that students connect the correct orthographic patterns and pronunciations (Foorman, 1994). Students use words orally in complete sentences to ensure they understand the meanings of the words so that comprehension is obtained even at the word level (Foorman & Schatschneider, 1997). Students also read sentences. Spelling practice with the dictation of sounds, words, and sentences follows the reading practice. After the practice of skills, equal time is given to reading from connected text that mirrors what students have recently learned. Comprehension and fluency are addressed using this text. Irregular words that will be encountered in the text are reviewed before students read the text. Composition activities can also be incorporated at this time.

Well-matched reading text extends and reinforces the learning of orthographic patterns and gives relevance to what is being learned (Adams, 1990). When reading in connected text, the reader should be encouraged to pause and study unknown words instead of skipping or guessing an unfamiliar word. Figure 8.3 shows how reading practice can be incorporated into an intensive, therapeutic reading lesson, with extended reading of text.

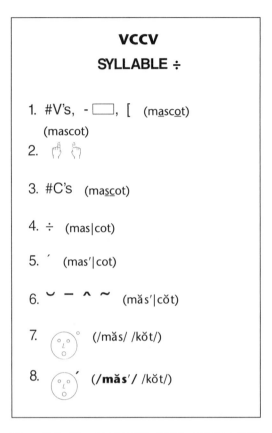

Figure 8.2. The word *mascot* is divided using the syllable-division procedures.

Decodable Text

Decodable text is text that matches the sound–symbol correspondences and irregular words that have been systematically introduced and is a logical choice for fluency practice. Decodable text provides practice of previously introduced sound–symbol correspondences and irregular words, which builds automatic word recognition. The repeated reading of decodable text further secures those concepts in memory. A second benefit of decodable text is that it develops independence in dealing with new words. Students learn that they can sound out most unfamiliar words while reading. When selecting text to read for fluency practice, students should be able to read the text with 95% accuracy. In other words, students misread only 1 of every 20 words of text (NICHD, 2000).

Advanced Morphemes

Students benefit from learning about prefixes, suffixes, roots, and combining forms. These morphemes are predominantly of Latin and Greek origins, respectively. The ability to instantly recognize roots and combining forms gives students a ready strategy for decoding longer words as well as insight into the meanings of the words. Once students have a core knowledge of morphemes, the first step in deciphering longer words is identifying the morphemes. For example, when students encounter as word such as

1. Review with letter–sound deck
2. Introduction of new concept or review of previously introduced concept
3. Reading practice: word lists and sentences
4. Spelling practice: sound dictation, word dictation, and sentence dictation
5. Introduction of irregular words
6. Reading of connected text
7. Listening to books

Figure 8.3.   Daily reading lesson plan.

instructor, they can identify three morphemes that aid the pronunciation of the word: *in, struct,* and *or.*

Common Latin Roots

Words of Latin origin are common in literature and academic writing. Latin words generally are characterized as having a root with affixes. The root carries the base of the meaning.

- *audi* (to hear)—*auditory, audience, audit, auditorium, audible, inaudible, audition*

- *dict* (to say)—*dictate, predict, dictator, edict, contradict, dictation, indict, prediction*

- *ject* (to throw)—*reject, inject, projection, interjection, eject, objection, dejection*

- *port* (to carry)—*transport, transportation, import, export, porter, portable, report, support*

- *rupt* (to break)—*rupture, erupt, eruption, interrupt, interruption, disruption*

- *scrib, script* (to write)—*scribe, describe, manuscript, inscription, transcript, descriptive, prescription*

- *spect* (to watch)—*spectator, inspect, inspector, respect, spectacle, spectacular*

- *struct* (to build)—*structure, construct, construction, instruct, destruction, reconstructionist*

- *tract* (to pull)—*tractor, traction, attract, subtraction, extract, retract, attractive*

- *vis* (to see)—*vision, visual, visit, supervisor, invisible, vista, visualize, visionary*

Common Greek Combining Forms

Words of Greek origin are most often scientific, medical, and technical terms. They are characterized as having combining forms that carry equal importance in the meaning of the word.

- *auto* (self)—*automatic, autograph, autobiography, automobile, autocracy*

- *bio* (life)—*biology, biosphere, biography, biochemistry, biometrics, biophysics*

- *graph* (write, recording)—*graphite, geography, graphic, photograph, phonograph*

- *hydro* (water)—*anhydrous, dehydration, hydrogen, hydrant, hydrostatic, hydrophobia, hydrotherapy, hydroplane*

- *meter* (measure)—*speedometer, odometer, metronome, thermometer, chronometer, perimeter, hydrometer*

- *ology* (study of)—*geology, theology, zoology, meteorology, phonology*
- *photo* (light)—*photography, photocopy, photosynthesis, phototropism, photostat, photogenic*
- *scope* (view)—*periscope, stethoscope, telescope, microscope, microscopic*
- *tele* (at a distance)—*telephone, telepathy, telegraph, television*
- *therm* (heat)—*thermos, thermodynamics, thermostat, thermophysics*

Introduction of Roots and Combining Forms

The teacher writes a root or combining form on the board. Students generate derivatives of the word part. The teacher writes the derivatives on the board so that the new word part in each word is aligned. Students determine the meaning of the word part (Henry, 1990).

struct

*struct*ure

de*struct*ion

in*struct*or

recon*struct*ionist

The teacher writes the new root or combining form on an index card and adds it to a deck that is systematically reviewed. During a review, students read the word part on each card, give the meaning, and generate derivatives of the root (e.g., students say, "*struct; to build; construct, structure, instructor,* and *destruction*").

Dividing Words with Three or More Syllables

As previously mentioned, when students encounter longer words, students should first look for recognizable morphemes. Students may not recognize all morphemes in a longer unfamiliar word, however, or a longer word may not have recognizable morphemes that would give clues to the pronunciation of the word. The same procedure used for dividing two syllables can be used with words of three or more syllables. Students choose the most frequent division of a pattern (e.g., VCCV is usually divided between the consonants; VCV is usually divided before the consonant). Choosing accent requires the following considerations.

- Roots draw the accent; prefixes and suffixes are rarely accented (e.g., in|vest′|ment).
- The syllable before a final stable syllable is usually accented (e.g., im|mi|gra′[tion).
- A final syllable that ends in *-a* or *-ic* is not accented, and the accent usually falls on the syllable before the final syllable (e.g., va|nil′|la, At|lan′|tic).
- If there are no clues for accent, then try accenting the first syllable (e.g., cu′|cum|ber) or the second syllable (e.g., es|tab ′|lish).

Careful attention to vowels in **polysyllabic** words is needed. The *a* in an open, unaccented syllable is obscure and is coded with a dot (e.g., al|fal ′|fa). The *i* in an open, unaccented syllable is short and coded with a breve (e.g., ar ′|ti|choke). The *i* before a final stable syllable is short and is coded with a breve (e.g., *ig|ni´[tion*). The *i* in an open, un-accented syllable before another vowel is pronounced as /ē/ (e.g., *sta´|di|um*).

RECOGNITION OF IRREGULAR WORDS

Knowledge of the orthographic patterns of language and practice with these patterns develop instant word recognition. But how do readers learn those words with irregular orthographic patterns? Despite claims to the contrary, English is a highly reliable language for reading (Gough & Hillinger, 1980). Approximately 87% of the English language is regular and can be predictably decoded using the orthographic patterns described in this chapter; this leaves only 13% of the language as irregular (Hanna, Hanna, Hodges, & Rudorf, 1966). The irregularities of written English are generally limited to the vowels and silent consonants. For most irregular words, the consonants offer sufficient support so that when the reader encounters an irregular word in everyday reading, he or she can determine the correct pronunciation of the word with partial decoding (Share & Stanovich, 1995).

Irregular words, particularly high-frequency irregular words (e.g., *the, said, have*), are learned through repeated encounters in text. Understanding word origins further assists students' orthographic memory of irregular words by giving insight into the spellings of words that do not match their pronunciations. Analyzing irregular words to determine their irregularities reinforces reliable sound–letter relationships, helps students build an orthographic memory of the words, and establishes that the irregularities in English words are not arbitrary (Gough & Hillinger, 1980). Patterns, even if infrequent, can be found in irregular words (e.g., *gh* may be silent as in *taught,* pronounced /g/ in initial position as in *ghost,* or pronounced /f/ as in *laugh*). When students discover an irregularity in a word, a resounding "Good for you! You found a word that doesn't fit the pattern!" from the teacher confirms that the students are thinking about the language and acquiring a flexible understanding of the language.

Procedure for Teaching Irregular Words

A multisensory structured procedure helps students achieve permanent memorization of irregular words (Cox, 1992; Gillingham & Stillman, 1997).

1. The teacher writes an irregular word on the board, such as *said.*

2. Students identify the syllable type and code the word according to the regular patterns of reading. Students read the word and discover it does not follow the reliable patterns of the language: /sād/.

3. The teacher erases the coded word and rewrites the word on the board: *said.* Beside the word, the teacher writes the pronunciation in parentheses: (sĕd).

4. Students compare the word and the pronunciation. They decide which part is irregular.

5. The teacher circles the irregular part:

    s (*ai*) *d*

6. The teacher writes the word on the front of a 4" × 6" index card. On the back of the card, the teacher writes the pronunciation. The teacher cuts off the upper left-hand

corner of the front of the card. The irregular shape of the card cues students that the word printed on it is an irregular word.

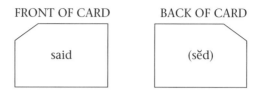

FRONT OF CARD   BACK OF CARD

said   (sĕd)

7. The teacher holds up the card so that students see the front of the card. Students read the word aloud.

8. The teacher turns the card around, and students read the pronunciation aloud.

9. The teacher slowly turns the card from front to back four or five times as students read the word and then read the pronunciation aloud.

10. The new card is added to a deck of irregular words that is reviewed daily.

Review of Irregular Words

Using a rapid word-recognition chart (RWRC; see Figure 8.4) builds instant recognition of high-frequency irregular words. The chart contains five rows of six irregular words. Each row contains the same six words in a different order. The teacher makes an RWRC transparency. After placing the transparency on the overhead projector, the teacher points to 8–10 words at random as a warm-up. After the warm-up, students are timed

RAPID WORD RECOGNITION CHART

pretty	said	who	there	they	what
said	pretty	there	who	what	they
there	who	they	said	pretty	what
who	what	said	they	there	pretty
they	there	pretty	what	who	said

Figure 8.4. The rapid word-recognition chart (RWRC) increases instant word recognition, particularly the recognition of words with phonetically irregular orthography.

for 1 minute. The teacher points to each square in order on the transparency, starting with the top row and working across each row. Students read aloud the word in each of the squares. In the 1-minute time frame, students may read through the chart more than once. At the end of 1 minute, students count and record the number of words they have successfully read. Progress can be graphed. The practice concludes with the teacher pointing at random to any troublesome words to provide further practice and secure the recognition of those words.

Rapid Word Reading

Evidence indicates that practice that involves the rapid reading of single words can result in improved speed and comprehension of text reading (Tan & Nicholson, 1997). Using flashcards or an RWRC to preview words in a passage before reading keeps the words in memory for students to refer to as they read. In addition to using an RWRC for high-frequency, irregular words as shown in Figure 8.4, the chart can be used for repeated exposure to an orthographic pattern found in words in the planned passage (Fisher, 1999). For example, an RWRC could be filled with words that contain trigraph *tch* (e.g., *match, etch, itch, blotch, Dutch, catch*). Using the procedure described previously, students read these words and build a memory of a frequent, reliable orthographic pattern that is found in the planned passage as well as in other text.

Word Origins

A brief overview of word origins helps students develop an understanding of why some words are pronounced in an unexpected way. This understanding allows students to forgive the language for being irregular and, more important, allows them to forgive themselves for having difficulty with the language (Cox, 1992; Gillingham & Stillman, 1997). Words may be pronounced irregularly for four reasons:

1. They are borrowed from another language such as French (*hors d'œuvre*), Dutch (*yacht*), or Greek (*ocean*).

2. They are **eponyms,** or words derived from proper names, such as the German botanist L. Fuchs (*fuchsia*) or the French statesman E. de Silhouette (*silhouette*).

3. They are words from the Anglo-Saxon language whose spellings did not keep pace with their changing pronunciations, such as *laugh, enough, said, through,* and *where.*

4. They are irregular with no easily identifiable reason or "just because," such as *curmudgeon.*

Investigating the irregularities of words raises students' **word consciousness.** Becoming more sensitive to the irregular spellings of these words builds students' memory for instant recognition.

THE SPELLING CONNECTION TO READING

Noah Webster once wrote, "Spelling is the foundation of reading and the greatest ornament of writing" (as cited in Venezky, 1980, p. 12). Spelling, by its nature, is a multisensory skill, involving translating auditory sounds into visual symbols that are reinforced with the kinesthetic act of writing. A beginning reader's use of invented spelling (Read, 1971) provides the teacher with considerable insight as to how well the reader is learning and internalizing information about the language. The beginning reader applies his or her phonological awareness and acquired knowledge of sounds and patterns to the task of spelling an unfamiliar word. Students who have a sense of how the language works become risk takers. They attempt to sound out and spell words for which they may not have a strong visual image but that are, nevertheless, the best, most appropriate words for their writing (e.g., students attempt *tremendous* or *gigantic* instead of using *big*). In their trials of spelling these unfamiliar words, students reinforce and enhance their reading skills. Using these more sophisticated words embellishes their writing and better reflects their oral vocabulary. Although it is important for students to become confident risk takers, it is also imperative for them to learn to spell words correctly because their spelling knowledge has a direct affect on their reading proficiency (Adams, 1990). Chapter 9 provides suggestions for spelling instruction and using spelling practice to reinforce reading.

FLUENCY

Snow referred to fluency as "both an antecedent and a consequence of comprehension" (2002, p. 13). Most successful readers seem to move from word-level reading to the fluency of phrase reading easily. Their development of fluency is due, in part, to the fact that these readers learned the alphabetic code early, had more time to read (Adams & Bruck, 1995; Juel, 1988), and received more encouragement to attend to fluency (Allington, 1983; Chall, 1983). Fluent readers can attend to meaning, which aids the prosodic flow of reading. It cannot be assumed, however, that developing accurate decoding skills guarantees application of those skills to fluency (Torgesen, 1997; Torgesen & Hudson, 2006).

Fluency development requires intentional, well-designed practice. Researchers are currently studying the brain and the time it takes the brain to process written language, and they are investigating sources for speed-related deficits that affect reading fluency. As more becomes known about the sources of speed-related deficits, the best designs for fluency interventions will be ascertained. To date, research suggests the most effective practices for improving fluency are those that involve the repeated reading of letters, words, phrases, and text and are supported by increased knowledge of the systems of oral and written language (Wolf, 2001). Figure 8.3 delineates a daily reading lesson in which activities that improve fluency at the letter, word, phrase or sentence, and text levels are easily incorporated.

Rapid Letter Naming

Neuhaus and Swank (2002) proposed that letter naming is only slightly less complex than word reading and that automatic letter recognition is the key to automatic word recognition. Rapid letter recognition is dependent on the familiarity of the orthographic and phonological properties of letters and directly predicts rapid recognition of words. Therefore, students benefit from overlearning the associations of letter shapes, names, and sounds. The use of a letter–sound deck in a daily reading lesson firmly secures these associations (see Figure 8.3). Chapter 6 outlines many activities that can be used for the rapid naming of letters.

Repeated Reading

The NRP (NICHD, 2000) concluded that guided oral reading, including repeated reading, is the most effective technique for improving word recognition, speed, accuracy, and fluency. Repeated reading involves the oral reading and rereading of the same passage of 50–200 words several times. The rereading of the same text provides the repeated exposures of words needed for the reader to form new or access previously formed orthographic images of letter patterns and words (Torgesen, Rashotte, & Alexander, 2001).

Oral reading fluency is enhanced when repeated readings are proceeded by teacher modeling of fluent reading (Rose, 1984). The modeling provides a positive framework for students to strive for when they read. The teacher should provide guidance and feedback as students read and reread the passage (NICHD, 2000). Background knowledge should be activated before the initial reading of the passage, and comprehension should be assessed, even informally, after the initial reading of the passage because the goal of fluency training is to aid comprehension and comprehending text aids fluency by allowing students to anticipate what is to come in the text (Wood, Flowers, & Grigorenko, 2001). Repeated reading can be incorporated in the daily reading lesson plan during the reading of connected text (see Figure 8.3).

Measuring Oral Reading Rate

Measures of oral reading rate (i.e., the number of words read correctly in 1 minute) should be recorded regularly. These measures need to be assessed on a one-to-one teacher–student basis. There are two methods in which rate can be determined. In one method, a student orally reads a passage from the beginning or from another starting point within the text for 1 minute as the teacher times the student with a stopwatch. While the student reads, the teacher records any errors (e.g., a misread word, a skipped word, a substituted word). At the end of the minute, the teacher stops the stopwatch. He or she counts the total number of words read and subtracts the errors. This number represents the rate and is recorded in *number of words correct per minute* (WCPM).

A second way to establish rate is to mark 100 words at the beginning of or within the passage. When the student begins to orally read the first of the 100 words, the teacher begins timing. Errors are recorded. When the student has finished reading the last of the 100 words, the stopwatch is stopped. The teacher subtracts the errors from 100 and divides the number of words read correctly by the total time. It may be necessary to convert the total time into a decimal. For example, if a student reads 96 of 100 words correctly in 1 minute and 20 seconds (80 seconds), then the teacher converts the time into a decimal to represent the total time in minutes (80 seconds ÷ 60 seconds + 1.33 minutes). The teacher then divides 96 by 1.33. The resultant number is the rate (72) and is recorded as WCPM (72 WCPM). Although the calculations are more cumbersome in this method, it is easier to use this method if the rates of many students are being measured at one time. The teacher does not have to individually count the words each student reads. The difficulty of a text can be assessed quickly because more than 5 errors in 100 words means that the text is too difficult for fluency practice. Because all students read the same 100 words, the teacher can judge overall mastery of concepts and determine if the pace of instruction for the group of students is appropriate.

The NRP (NICHD; 2000) suggested that an appropriate oral reading rate by the end of first grade is 60 WCPM. By the end of second grade, students should read orally at a rate of 90–100 WCPM and approximately 114 WCPM by the end of third grade. A rate of 120–150 WCPM is desired by end of fifth grade and beyond (Meyer & Felton, 1999).

Prosody

Successful decoding requires the reader to translate printed words into their spoken equivalents, whereas successful fluency requires the reader to connect the flow of printed text to the flow of spoken language. Spoken language has intonation, phrasing, and stress, which are not present in written language. Early on, children rely on all of these features to understand speech (see Chapter 3 for more information). When these features are present in oral reading, there is a rhythmic flow (i.e., **prosody**) that makes it sound as if the reader is speaking. Although fluency practice that includes attention to prosodic features does not produce stronger gains (Torgesen et al., 2001), it is prudent to practice such features because lack of prosody results in word-by-word reading and prevents some readers from learning to group words into meaningful units that support comprehension. Oral fluency, which leads to reading fluency, can be taught to readers who do not move from the word level to the phrase level of reading. Phrasing, intonation, and stress can be applied to written language with oral practice, the study of punctuation, and the study of grammar. Chapter 10 provides additional information on fluency instruction.

TEACHER KNOWLEDGE

This chapter has introduced the underlying theories and principles, terminology, concepts, and instructional practices of effective decoding instruction. How important is teacher knowledge of decoding to student achievement? In a study of 42 first-grade teachers, Piasta et al. (2009) examined the literacy-related knowledge of the teachers and the impact of teacher knowledge on student growth in word reading. Teachers with knowledge at the 75th percentile who consistently taught decoding had students with greatest gains in word reading. Teachers with the same knowledge who did not consistently teach decoding had students with word-reading outcomes that were equal to the outcomes made by students of teachers with much lower levels of literacy content knowledge. The students with the weakest gains were consistently taught decoding by teachers with knowledge at the 25th percentile or below. Therefore, student gains were the result of an interaction between teacher knowledge and instructional practices. Even teachers' years of teaching or extensive experience with highly effective scripted curricula did not overcome the lack of literacy-related knowledge.

Knowledge counts, and the knowledgeable teachers know:

- The phoneme/grapheme counts for the following words: *fish* (3/3), *church* (3/3), *sent* (4/4), *split* (5/5), and *mix* (4/3).

- The six syllable types in English are closed, open, vowel-*r* or *r*-controlled, vowel pair or team, vowel-consonant-*e,* and final stable syllables.

- The syllable/morpheme counts for the following words: *darkness* (2/2), *instructor* (3/3), *salamander* (4/1), *phonology* (4/2), and *polyglot* (3/2).

- These are inflectional endings: *-ing, -ed, -s.*

- These words are accented on the second syllable: *canteen, extreme, duet,* and *unite.*

- These words are irregular for reading: *said, sword,* and *walk.*

SUMMARY

Reading is a complex process involving decoding, which enables a reader to translate printed symbols into words, and comprehension, which enables the reader to derive meaning from the printed page. With the insight that spoken words consist of sounds and that printed words consist of letters, the beginning reader is able to connect sounds to letters and to read words. Initially, the reader is focused on sounding out words. Practicing graphophonemic, syllabic, and morphemic patterns using word lists, phrases, sentences, and repeated readings of connected text, the reader's decoding skills become automatic, and he or she is able to give greater attention to the prosodic features of reading such as phrasing and intonation, which further aid fluency. The fluent translation of the flow of print to the flow of spoken language enables the reader to attend to the meaning rather than to the features of the printed text. Fluency is vital to comprehension, which is the main goal of reading. Ultimately, a student's success in reading is predicated on knowledgeable teachers who explicitly and systematically teach reliable language structures using research-based instructional practices.

REFERENCES

Adams, M.J. (1990). *Beginning to read: Thinking and learning about print.* Cambridge, MA: The MIT Press.

Adams, M.J., & Bruck, M. (1993). Word recognition: The interface of educational policies and scientific research. *Reading and Writing: An Interdisciplinary Journal, 5,* 113–139.

Adams, M.J., & Bruck, M. (1995, Summer). Resolving the "great debate." *American Educator, 19,* 7–12.

Allington, R.L. (1983, February). Fluency: The neglected reading goal. *The Reading Teacher,* 556–561.

Ball, E.W., & Blachman, B.A. (1988). Phoneme segmentation training: Effect on reading readiness. *Annals of Dyslexia, 38,* 208–225.

Beck, I., & Juel, C. (1995, Summer). The role of decoding in learning to read. *American Educator, 19,* 8–12.

Blachman, B.A. (1987). An alternative classroom reading program for learning disabled and other low-achieving children. In R. Bowler (Ed.), *Intimacy with language: A forgotten basic in teacher education* (pp. 49–55). Baltimore: International Dyslexia Association.

Blachman, B.A., Ball, E.W., Black, R., & Tangel, D.M. (2000). *Road to the code: A phonological awareness program for young children.* Baltimore: Paul H. Brookes Publishing Co.

Bradley, L., & Bryant, P.E. (1983). Categorizing sounds and learning to read: A causal connection. *Nature, 303,* 419–421.

Brady, S., & Moats, L.C. (Eds.). (1997). *Informed instruction for reading success: Foundations for teacher preparation.* Baltimore: International Dyslexia Association.

Brady, S., & Shankweiler, D. (1991). *Phonological processes in literacy: A tribute to Isabelle Y. Liberman.* Mahwah, NJ: Lawrence Erlbaum Associates.

Carreker, S. (2006, Fall). Teaching the structure of language by seeing, hearing, and doing. *Perspectives, 32*(4), 24–28.

Carreker, S.H., Swank, P., Tillman-Dowdy, L., Neuhaus, G., Monfils, M.J., Montemayor, M.L., et al. (2005). Language enrichment teacher preparation and practice predicts third grade reading comprehension. *Reading Psychology, 26,* 401–432.

Carreker, S.H., Swank, P., Tillman-Dowdy, L., Neuhaus, G., Monfils, M.J., Montemayor, M.L., et al. (2007). Teachers with linguistically informed knowledge of reading subskills are associated with a Matthew effect in reading comprehension for monolingual and bilingual students. *Reading Psychology, 28,* 187–212.

Castles, A., Coltheart, M., Wilson, K., Valpied, J., & Wedgewood, J. (2009). The genesis of reading ability: What helps children learn letter-sound correspondences? *Journal of Experimental Child Psychology, 104,* 68–88.

Chall, J.S. (1983). *Stages of reading development.* New York: McGraw-Hill.

Cox, A.R. (1992). *Foundations for literacy: Structures and techniques for multisensory teaching of basic written English skills.* Cambridge, MA: Educators Publishing Service.

Cox, A.R., & Hutcheson, L.M. (1988). Syllable division: A prerequisite of dyslexics' literacy. *Annals of Dyslexia, 38,* 226–242.

Darling-Hammond, L. (1998). Teachers and teaching: Testing hypotheses from a national commission report. *Educational Research, 27,* 5–15.

Ehri, L.C. (1991). Development of the ability to read words. In R. Barr, M.L. Kamil, P.B. Mosenthal, & P.D. Pearson (Eds.), *Handbook of reading research* (Vol. 2, pp. 383–417). Reading, MA: Addison Wesley Longman.

Ehri, L.C., Wilce, L.S., & Taylor, B.B. (1987). Children's categorization of short vowels in words and the influence of spelling. *Merrill-Palmer Quarterly, 33,* 393–421.

Englemann, S. (1969). *Preventing failure in the primary grades.* Chicago: Science Research Associates.

Felton, R. (1993). Effects of instruction on decoding skills of children with phonological processing problems. *Journal of Learning Disabilities, 26,* 583–589.

Ferrer, E., Shaywitz, B.A., Holahan, J.M., Marchione, K., & Shaywitz, S.E. (2009). Uncoupling of reading and IQ over time: Empirical evidence for a definition of dyslexia. *Association for Psychological Science, 21,* 93–101.

Fisher, P. (1999). Getting up to speed. *Perspectives, 25*(2), 12–13.

Foorman, B.R. (1994). The relevance of a connectionist model for reading for "the great debate." *Educational Psychology Review, 6,* 25–47.

Foorman, B.R., Francis, D.J., Beeler, T., Winikates, D., & Fletcher, J.M. (1997). Early intervention for children with reading problems: Study designs and preliminary findings. *Learning Disabilities: A Multidisciplinary Journal, 8,* 63–71.

Foorman, B.R., Francis, D.J., Shaywitz, S.E., Shaywitz, B.A., & Fletcher, J.M. (1997). The case for early reading intervention. In B. Blachman (Ed.), *Foundations of reading acquisition and dyslexia: Implications for early intervention* (pp. 243–264). Mahwah, NJ: Lawrence Erlbaum Associates.

Foorman, B.R., & Schatschneider, C. (1997). Beyond alphabetic reading: Comments on Torgesen's prevention and intervention studies. *Journal of Academic Language Therapy, 1,* 59–65.

Gillingham, A., & Stillman, B. (1997). *The Gillingham manual: Remedial training for children with specific disability in reading, writing, and penmanship* (8th ed.). Cambridge, MA: Educators Publishing Service.

Goswami, U., & Bryant, P. (1990). *Phonological skills and learning to read.* Mahwah, NJ: Lawrence Erlbaum Associates.

Gough, P.B. (1983). Context, form and interaction. In K. Rayner (Ed.), *Eye movements in reading: Conceptual and language processes* (pp. 203–211). San Diego: Academic Press.

Gough, P.B., Ehri, L., & Treiman, R. (Eds.). (1992). *Reading acquisition.* Mahwah, NJ: Lawrence Erlbaum Associates.

Gough, P.B., & Hillinger, M.L. (1980). Learning to read: An unnatural act. *Bulletin of The Orton Society, 30,* 179–196.

Gough, P.B., & Tunmer, W.E. (1986). Decoding, reading and reading disability. *Remedial and Special Education, 7,* 6–10.

Greene, V.E., & Enfield, M.L. (1985). *Project Read reading guide: Phase I.* Bloomington, MN: Bloomington Public Schools.

Hanna, P.R., Hanna, J.S., Hodges, R.E., & Rudorf, E.H. (1966). *Phoneme-grapheme correspondences as cues to spelling improvement.* Washington, DC: U.S. Government Printing Office.

Henry, M.K. (1988). Beyond phonics: Integrating decoding and spelling instruction based on word origin and structure. *Annals of Dyslexia, 38,* 259–277.

Henry, M.K. (1990). *WORDS: Integrated decoding and spelling instruction based on word origin and word structure.* Austin, TX: PRO-ED.

Henry, M.K. (2010). *Unlocking literacy: Effective decoding and spelling instruction* (2nd ed.). Baltimore: Paul H. Brookes Publishing Co.

Hoover, W.A., & Gough, P.B. (1990). The simple view of reading. *Reading and Writing: An Interdisciplinary Journal, 2,* 127–160.

Hutchins, P. (1974). *The wind blew.* New York: Scholastic.

Joshi, R.M., & Aaron, P.G. (2000). The component model of reading: Simple view of reading made a little more complex. *Reading Psychology, 21,* 85–97.

Joshi, R.M., Binks, E., Hougen, M., Dahlgren, M.E., Ocker, E., & Smith, D. (2009). Why elementary teachers might be inadequately prepared to teach reading. *Journal of Learning Disabilities, 42*(5), 392–402.

Joshi, R.M., Dahlgren, M., & Boulware-Gooden, R. (2002). Teaching reading in an inner city school through a multisensory teaching approach. *Annals of Dyslexia, 52,* 229–242.

Juel, C. (1988). Learning to read and write: A longitudinal study of 54 children from first to fourth grades. *Journal of Educational Psychology, 80,* 437–447.

Juel, C. (1991). Beginning reading. In R. Barr, M.L. Kamil, P.B. Mosenthal, & P.D. Pearson (Eds.), *Handbook of reading research* (Vol. 2, pp. 759–788). Reading, MA: Addison Wesley Longman.

Liberman, I.Y. (1987). Language and literacy: The obligation of the schools of education. In R. Bowler (Ed.), *Intimacy with language: A forgotten basic in teacher education* (pp. 1–9). Baltimore: International Dyslexia Association.

Liberman, I.Y., & Liberman, A.M. (1990). Whole language vs. code emphasis: Underlying assumptions and their implications for reading instruction. *Annals of Dyslexia, 40,* 51–76.

Liberman, I.Y., Shankweiler, D., & Liberman, A.M. (1989). The alphabetic principle and learning to read. In D. Shankweiler & I.Y. Liberman (Eds.), *Phonology and reading disabilities: Solving the reading puzzle* (pp. 1–33). Ann Arbor: University of Michigan Press.

Lundberg, I., Frost, J., & Petersen, O.P. (1988). Effects of an extensive program for stimulating phonological awareness in preschool children. *Reading Research Quarterly, 23,* 264–284.

Lyon, G.R., Shaywitz, S.E., & Shaywitz, B.A. (2003). A definition of dyslexia. *Annals of Dyslexia, 53,* 1–14.

Meyer, M.S., & Felton, R.H. (1999). Repeated reading to enhance fluency: Old approaches and new directions. *Annals of Dyslexia, 49,* 283–306.

Moats, L.C. (1994). The missing foundation in teacher education: Knowledge of the structure of spoken and written language. *Annals of Dyslexia, 44,* 81–102.

Moats, L.C. (1995). *Spelling: Development, disabilities and instruction.* Timonium, MD: York Press.

Moats, L.C. (2010). *Speech to print: Language essentials for teachers* (2nd ed.). Baltimore: Paul H. Brookes Publishing Co.

National Institute of Child Health and Human Development. (2000). *Report of the National Reading Panel: Reports of the subgroups. Teaching children to read: An evidence-based assessment of the scientific research literature on reading and its implications for reading instruction* (NIH Publication No. 00-4754). Washington, DC: Government Printing Office.

Neuhaus, G.F., & Swank, P.R. (2002). Understanding the relations between RAN letters subtest components and word reading in first grade students. *Journal of Learning Disabilities, 35*(2), 158–174.

Perfetti, C.A. (1985). *Reading ability.* New York: Oxford University Press.

Piasta, S.B., Connor, C.M, Fishman, B.J., & Morrison, F.J. (2009). Teachers' knowledge of literacy concepts, classroom practices and student reading growth. *Scientific Studies of Reading, 13,* 224–248.

Rayner, K., & Pollatsek, A. (1986). *The psychology of reading.* Upper Saddle River, NJ: Prentice Hall.

Read, C. (1971). Pre-school children's knowledge of English phonology. *Harvard Educational Review, 41,* 1–34.

Rose, T.L. (1984). The effects of two prepractice procedures on oral reading. *Journal of Learning Disabilities, 17,* 544–548.

Rosner, J. (1975). *Test of auditory analysis skills. Helping children overcome learning difficulties.* New York: Walker and Co.

Rubin, H., & Eberhardt, N.C. (1996). Facilitating invented spelling through language analysis instruction: An integrated model. *Reading and Writing: An Interdisciplinary Journal, 8,* 27–43.

Ryder, J.F., Tunmer, W.E., & Greaney, K.T. (2007). Explicit instruction in phonemic awareness and phonemically based decoding skills as an intervention strategy for struggling readers in whole language classrooms. *Reading and Writing: An Interdisciplinary Journal, 21,* 349–369.

Share, D.L., & Stanovich, K.E. (1995). Cognitive processes in early reading development: Accommodating individual differences into a model of acquisition. *Issues in Education, 1*(1), 1–57.

Slingerland, B.A. (1971). *A multi-sensory approach to language arts for specific language disability children: A guide for primary teachers.* Cambridge, MA: Educators Publishing Service.

Snow, C.E. (2002). *Reading for understanding: Toward an R&D program in reading comprehension.* Santa Monica, CA: RAND Corporation.

Spear-Swerling, L. (2009). A literacy tutoring experience for prospective special educators and struggling second graders? *Journal of Learning Disabilities, 42,* 431–443.

Stanback, M.L. (1992). Analysis of frequency-based vocabulary of 17,602 words. *Annals of Dyslexia, 42,* 196–221.

Stanovich, K.E. (1986). Matthew effects in reading: Some consequences of individual differences in the acquisition of literacy. *Reading Research Quarterly, 21,* 360–407.

Stanovich, K.E. (1991). Cognitive science meets beginning reading. *Psychological Science, 2,* 70–81.

Steere, A., Peck, C.Z., & Kahn, L. (1984). *Solving language difficulties: Remedial routines.* Cambridge, MA: Educators Publishing Service.

Tan, A., & Nicholson, T. (1997). Flashcards revisited: Training poor readers to read words faster improves their comprehension of text. *Journal of Educational Psychology, 89*(2), 276–288.

Torgesen, J.K. (1997). The prevention and remediation of reading disabilities: Evaluating what we know from research. *Journal of Academic Language Therapy, 1,* 11–47.

Torgesen, J.K., & Hudson, R.F. (2006). Reading fluency: Critical issues for struggling readers. In S.J. Samuels & A.E. Farstrup (Eds.), *What research has to say about fluency instruction* (pp. 130–158). Newark, DE: International Reading Association.

Torgesen, J.K., Rashotte, C.A., & Alexander, A.W. (2001). Principles of fluency instruction in reading: Relationships with established empirical outcomes. In M. Wolf (Ed.), *Dyslexia, fluency, and the brain* (pp. 333–355). Timonium, MD: York Press.

Tunmer, W.E., Herriman, M.L., & Nesdale, A.R. (1988). Metalinguistic abilities and beginning reading. *Reading Research Quarterly, 23,* 134–158.

Vellutino, F.R. (1980). Perceptual deficiency or perceptual inefficiency. In J. Kavanagh & R. Venezky (Eds.), *Orthography, reading and dyslexia* (pp. 251–270). Baltimore: University Park Press.

Venezky, R.L. (1980). From Webster to rice to Roosevelt. In U. Frith (Ed.), *Cognitive processes in spelling* (pp. 9–30). London: Academic Press.

Waites, L., & Cox, A.R. (1976). *Remedial training programs for developmental language disabilities.* Cambridge, MA: Educators Publishing Service.

Wanzek, J., & Vaughn, S. (2007). Research-based implications from extensive early reading interventions. *School Psychology Review, 36,* 541–561.

Wilson, B. (1996). *Wilson reading system instructor manual* (3rd ed.). Oxford, MA: Wilson Language Training.

Wolf, M. (1997). A provisional, integrative account of phonological and naming speed deficits in dyslexia: Implications for diagnosis and intervention. In B. Blachman (Ed.), *Foundations of reading acquisition and dyslexia: Implications for early intervention* (pp. 67–92). Mahwah, NJ: Lawrence Erlbaum Associates.

Wolf, M. (Ed.). (2001). *Dyslexia, fluency, and the brain.* Timonium, MD: York Press.

Wolf, M., & Bowers, P. (1999). The "double deficit hypothesis" for the developmental dyslexias. *Journal of Educational Psychology, 91*(3), 1–24.

Wolf, M., & Bowers, P. (2000). The question of naming-speed deficits in the developmental reading disabilities: An introduction of the double-deficit hypothesis. *Journal of Learning Disabilities, 33,* 322–324.

Wolf, M., & Obregón, M. (1992). Early naming deficits, developmental dyslexia, and a specific deficit hypothesis. *Brain and Language, 42,* 219–247.

Wood, F.B., Flowers, L., & Grigorenko, E. (2001). On the functional neuroanatomy of fluency or why walking is just as important to reading as talking is. In M. Wolf (Ed.), *Dyslexia, fluency, and the brain.* Timonium, MD: York Press.

Yopp, H.K. (1992). Developing phonemic awareness in young children. *The Reading Teacher, 45*(9), 696–703.

Yopp, H.K. (1995). Read-aloud books for developing phonemic awareness: An annotated bibliography. *The Reading Teacher, 48,* 538–542.

9

Teaching Spelling

SUZANNE CARREKER

In many classrooms, spelling instruction is treated as an afterthought to or as a byproduct of reading. The assumption is that if students learn to read, they learn to spell; therefore, spelling instruction is given little importance and minimal attention during the instruction day. Frequently, the subject of spelling is relegated to memorization of word lists with little or no instruction (Joshi, Treiman, Carreker, & Moats, 2008/2009). This view fails to recognize the integral role spelling instruction plays in learning to read (Moats, 2005/2006). Spelling instruction enhances reading proficiency by reinforcing sounds and letter patterns (Adams, 1990). In addition, spellings of words facilitate learning word pronunciations and meanings (Ehri & Rosenthal, 2007). Spelling, a cognitive linguistic process, is more difficult to learn than reading (Frith, 1980; Joshi et al., 2008/2009). As Ehri noted, "it is easier to read words accurately in English than to spell them. Failure to remember one or two letters dooms a perfect spelling but not necessarily an accurate reading" (2000, p. 24). Learning to spell requires explicit instruction (Brady & Moats, 1997; Joshi et al., 2008/2009; Moats, 1995). This chapter discusses the explicit and systematic spelling instruction that helps students become skilled and confident spellers.

THE DISTINCTIVENESS OF SPELLING

To decode text, a reader must translate symbols on a printed page that represent spoken words (see Chapter 8). The reader must attach a speech sound to each letter in a printed word. In this manner, the reader can sound out or pronounce the spoken word that is represented by printed symbols. To spell, the speller must translate spoken words into printed symbols. That means a speller must attach a written letter or group of letters to each speech sound in a spoken word. In this manner, the speller can represent spoken words with printed symbols. It would appear from these simple descriptions that decoding and spelling are simply inverse operations that require knowledge of sound–symbol correspondences and are performed in opposite order.

Following this logic, it could be assumed that if a student can read a word, then he or she can also spell the word. Although both decoding and spelling require phonological and orthographic knowledge, the two skills are not simply inverse operations (Frith, 1980). First, sound-to-spelling translations are less dependable than spelling-to-sound translations (Adams, 1990). Second, decoding requires only recognizing words, whereas spelling requires complete, accurate recall of letter patterns and words (Frith & Frith, 1980; Fulk & Stormont-Spurgin, 1995).

Orthography refers to how spoken words are represented in written language. When the reader has mastered the decoding skills discussed in Chapter 8, English orthography becomes 87% reliable (regular) for reading (Hanna, Hanna, Hodges, & Rudorf, 1966). The reader needs to memorize or infer from the context only about 13% of the words he or she will encounter. The rest of the words that are not instantly recognized can be sounded out. To sound out an unfamiliar word, the reader assigns known sounds to known letters in the word. With the assistance of phonological awareness, approximate pronunciations, and contextual clues, the reader can accurately pronounce the unfamiliar word (Share & Stanovich, 1995). When a letter or group of letters has more than one possible pronunciation (e.g., *ea* can be pronounced /ĕ/, /ē/, or /ā/), the reader affirms his or her pronunciation choice by determining whether the chosen word makes sense in the sentence (e.g., one nods one's /hĕd/, not one's /hēd/ or /hād/). The more the reader knows about decoding, the easier it is for him or her to recognize words, but even with partial decoding, a reader can read unfamiliar words.

The 87% reliability of English orthography (Hanna et al., 1966) may make the task of spelling an unfamiliar word that one can read seem deceptively simple. The speller must rely on phonological awareness to segment the unfamiliar word into its constituent sounds and then determine how those sounds are best represented in print; however, because many speech sounds in English are represented by **multiple spellings** (e.g., initial or medial /ā/ in a one-syllable word can be spelled *a*-consonant-*e* as in *cake, ai* as in *rain, ei* as in *vein, eigh* as in *eight*, or *ea* as in *steak*), making the correct choice can be confusing to the speller. Contextual clues do not affirm the speller's choice of spelling (Fulk & Stormont-Spurgin, 1995). After all, the word that is pronounced /tām/ (*tame*), spelled incorrectly as *taim, teim, teighm*, or *team*, would share the same context.

The speller's only confirmation of a correct spelling is to compare the spelled word with a word held in memory. If the word is not held in memory because the speller has not seen it before or because the speller has a poor memory for letters and words (i.e., poor orthographic memory), then it is difficult for him or her to independently confirm that the spelling choice is correct. Spelling requires an awareness of and exact memory for letter patterns and words that reading does not require.

In addition to the need for exact recall and the ambiguities of sound-to-spelling translations, spelling is a complex linguistic skill that demands simultaneous integration of syntactic (cf. Bryant, Nunes, & Bindman, 1997, for a discussion), phonological, morphological, semantic, and orthographic knowledge (Frith, 1980; Moats, 1995; Smith, 1980). This integration can be illustrated as a speller attempts to spell /jŭmpt/. Phonological awareness enables the speller to hear all of the sounds and play with the idea that /jŭmpt/ without /t/ is /jŭmp/. Syntactic awareness alerts the speller that /jŭmp/ can be used as a verb and that verbs have tenses. Morphological awareness helps the speller realize that /jŭmpt/ consists of two meaningful units—base word /jŭmp/ and suffix /t/.

Semantic awareness provides the speller with the understanding that /t/ represents the past tense. Finally, using orthographic knowledge, the speller apprehends that /t/ will be spelled *ed* and not *t*. Spelling obligates the speller to attend to multiple layers of language concurrently. Knowing how to read a word does not guarantee that a person can spell the word correctly. If this were true, then there would be no individuals who read quite well but are poor spellers, and spelling development would not lag behind reading development. Spelling instruction should be intimately integrated with the teaching of reading, but because spelling has its own distinctive characteristics and demands, it also must be distinct from reading and explicitly taught. Spellers must be taught in a manner that will increase their awareness and memory of letter patterns and words. Developing proficiency in spelling is different from developing proficiency in reading, but the English language is not chaotic (Kessler & Treiman, 2003) and hopeless, and sequential, structured instruction of language structures can lead to skilled spelling.

SPELLING DEVELOPMENT

It is important to understand how spelling develops to understand the vital role spelling plays in learning to read and the errors students make. Evidence suggests that spelling is a unitary, interactive process that requires both phonological and orthographic knowledge (Lennox & Siegel, 1998). Beginning spellers take advantage of both phonological and visual strategies (Bryant & Bradley, 1980; Treiman, Cassar, & Zukowski, 1994).

Spelling proficiency tends to develop or unfold in a fairly predictable and gradual sequence, which is often described by stages or phases; however, students will rarely move through any stages or phases in an exact and orderly progression. A young child's first writing experience is usually in the form of drawing. As the child is exposed to print, he or she begins to differentiate writing from drawing and begins to imitate the print he or she has seen, using letter-like or number-like forms (Cassar & Treiman, 1997). In this precommunicative or **prephonetic stage** or phase (Moats, 1995), the child's writing shows a lack of understanding of the concept of a word, the alphabetic principle, or the conventions of print such as spaces between words and the left-to-right progression of writing. Bear, Invernizzi, Templeton, and Johnston suggested that the organization of the child's writing may be described as "willy-nilly" (1996, p. 16). Pollo, Kessler, and Treiman noted, however, "our results speak against the idea that early prephonological spellings are random and unpatterned" (2009, p. 424).

At age 3 or 4, the child may think that the length of the word reflects the size of the object it names instead of the sounds of language (e.g., *cow* should have more letters than *chicken* because a cow is bigger than a chicken) (Treiman, 1997). To the 3- or 4-year-old child, meaning takes precedence over spelling. Only when the child becomes aware that print is related to speech does he or she come to understand that letters represent speech sounds.

A grasp of the alphabetic principle emerges with the child's realization that spoken words are made of sounds that can be represented in print. He or she will first attempt to connect speech to print at the syllable level instead of at the phoneme level and will write a symbol for each syllable (e.g., *b* for *be* or *nf* for *enough*) (Ferreiro & Teberosky,

1982). As the child becomes more aware that individual letters represent individual sounds, he or she enters this **semiphonetic stage** (Moats, 1995) and uses incomplete but reasonable phonetic representations of words. The child usually uses the initial or salient consonants of a word, such as *s, c,* or *sd* for *seed* (Rubin & Eberhardt, 1996), or the child may use letter names, such as *lft* for *elephant* (Adams, 1990; Treiman, 1994). At this semiphonetic stage or phase, the child demonstrates awareness of left-to-right progression, but he or she tends to run letters together with little or no sense of word boundaries (e.g., RUDF for *Are you deaf?*) (Moats, 1995).

Further experiences with print and writing move the child to a stage of complete phonetic representations, or the **phonetic stage** (Moats, 1995). Every sound in a word is represented, but the child does not demonstrate knowledge of conventional spelling patterns. The child may spell *same* as *sam,* thus neglecting the final silent *e* (Treiman, Zukowski, & Richmond-Welty, 1995). The inflection *-ed* may be represented as *t* as in *askt* or *d* as in *hugd* (Read, 1971). At this phonetic stage, the child is aware of not only sounds but also the mouth positions used to make sounds. Moats suggested that the child may seem to be "spelling by mouth" (1995, p. 37). For example, the child may use *y* to spell /w/ because not only does the letter name contain /w/, but also the mouth position to say the letter name *y* is the same as /w/. Other odd but linguistically understandable spelling choices may be observed at this point, such as spelling /t/ before /r/ as *ch* as in *chrie* for *try* or /d/ before /r/ as *j* as in *jragin* for *dragon* (Read, 1971). Phonetically, /t/ or /d/ would not be spelled with *ch* or *j*, but when /t/ or /d/ occur before /r/, the place of articulation (i.e., where the sound is obstructed in the mouth during production) matches the place of articulation for /ch/ and /j/, respectively (Treiman, 1998). Consistent spelling anomalies may occur, such as /r/ overwhelming the vowel as in *hr* for *her* or the omission of nasal (i.e., /m/, /n/, /ng/) and liquid sounds (i.e., /l/, /r/) as in *drik* for *drink, jup* for *jump,* and *od* for *old* (Treiman, 1998; Treiman et al., 1995).

In early spelling development, a child is literal in his or her spelling of words (e.g., /k/ is almost always spelled *k*). As the child begins to read more, he or she becomes more sensitive to the letter patterns in words. Without being taught, he or she may discover an orthographic pattern and sense its constraints. The child may discover that /k/ can be spelled *ck* and may sense that it does not occur in the initial position of a word. He or she is more likely to spell *cake* as *kack* than *ckak* (Treiman, 1997). In this transitional stage or phase of spelling, as the child becomes more aware of letter patterns in words, his or her spelling may seem "off-base" (Moats, 1995, p. 40). From exact phonetic representations of every sound, the child's spelling may become a mixture of phonetic components and salient visual features in words. This change in spelling usually signals a heightened awareness of letter patterns. Through their early spelling experiences, children build a foundation for reading as they begin to establish sound–symbol correspondences and develop a sensitivity to letter patterns. But just as beginning readers need explicit teaching to become good readers, beginning spellers need explicit teaching to become good spellers. Without this formal instruction, beginning spellers will not establish the awareness and memory of letter patterns that will make them good spellers.

GOOD AND POOR SPELLERS

Good spelling ability is contingent on a speller's sensitivity to letter patterns (Adams, 1990). Research has shown that good and poor spellers do not differ greatly in their visual memory abilities (Lennox & Siegel, 1996). What differs in good spellers is that they possess well-developed phonological processing skills that not only make them aware of the sounds in words but also support the learning of letter patterns in words (Lennox & Siegel, 1998; Moats, 1995). Good spellers possess an orthographic memory. This orthographic memory is a more specific memory than visual memory; it is specific to remembering letter patterns and words. Developing this memory is dependent on well-developed phonological processing skills. Good spellers know not only how sounds are represented in language but also how words should look (Adams, 1990). They are able to deal with the ambiguities of orthography (e.g., the multiple spellings of /ā/) by weighting the variable spellings by their frequency or exposure in reading (e.g., the good speller weights *a*-consonant-*e* as a more frequent or stronger connection to /ā/ than *eigh* because he or she sees it more frequently) (Adams, 1990; Foorman, 1994; Seidenberg & McClelland, 1989). In addition to possessing phonological and orthographic knowledge, good spellers are able to simultaneously draw support from their awareness of syntax, morphology, and semantics. Because good spellers possess the very skills that are needed for good decoding, good spellers are good readers (i.e., decoders). It is unusual to find a good speller who is a poor reader (decoder).

The definition of dyslexia endorsed by The International Dyslexia Association (Lyon, Shaywitz, & Shaywitz, 2003) included reading disabilities as well as specific spelling disabilities. As noted in Chapters 5 and 8, students with dyslexia have difficulty learning to decode because of a core deficit in phonological processing (Adams, 1990; Bradley & Bryant, 1983; Goswami & Bryant, 1990). It is rare for students with dyslexia who have difficulty with decoding not to have difficulty with spelling. It is possible, however, for students to be fairly good readers but poor spellers. Moats (1995) made these observations about poor spellers. Good readers who are poor spellers have problems with the exact recall of letter sequences and subtle difficulties with complex spelling patterns and aspects of language structure, but they do not have a deficit in phonological processing. Poor readers who are poor spellers have a deficit in phonological processing that interferes with their mastery of spelling. These readers also have a specific problem with memory of letter patterns, which is rooted in their poor phonological processing. In addition, poor spellers do not possess the ability to deal with several layers of language simultaneously. With proper instruction, poor spellers who are poor readers will improve their decoding skills, but they seldom master spelling (Moats, 1994; Oakland, Black, Stanford, Nussbaum, & Balise, 1998).

Roberts and Mather (1997) characterized poor spelling as the result of difficulties in both phonological and orthographic processing. Difficulties with phonological processing may include poor sequencing of sounds, omission or addition of sounds, confusion with similar-sounding phonemes (e.g., /f/ and /th/, /p/ and /b/), and limited knowledge of spelling rules. Orthographic processing difficulties are manifested as poor sequencing of nonphonetic patterns, confusion with graphemes that look similar (e.g., *b* and *d, n* and *u*), transposition of letters (e.g., *fro* instead of *for*), overgeneralization of rules, and overreliance on auditory features (e.g., *becuz* for *because*).

Poor spellers may be perceived as "free-spirit" spellers who spell words the way they sound without regard to conventional letter patterns. The free-spirit spellers may spell *does* as *duz*, *dress* as *dres*, or *girl* as *gerl*. They may spell the same word several different ways within the same paragraph, such as *thay, tha,* and *thai* for *they*. The spellers with dyslexia may be perceived as "bizarre" spellers. They struggle with the conventional letter patterns of words and use inappropriate letter sequences, such as *oridr* for *order;* transpositions, such as *gril* for *girl;* letter reversals, such as *dady* for *baby;* or incomplete letter patterns, such as *boht* for *bought.* Not only do spellers with dyslexia lack the ability to use conventional letter patterns, but they also are unable to fully or correctly translate the sounds in words. They may have difficulty hearing the word correctly (e.g., hearing *fan* instead of *van*), hearing all of the sounds in a word (e.g., hearing *butful* for *beautiful*), or keeping the sounds in sequence (e.g., using *slpit* for *split*). They may have difficulty discriminating similar sounds as (e.g., hearing *baf* for *bath* or *wint* for *went*).

Problems with spelling persist in adolescents and adults with dyslexia. Moats (1996) found that adolescents with dyslexia showed lingering, subtle signs of phonological difficulty, primarily in segmenting words into their phonemic and morphemic units, as evidenced by their consistent omissions, substitutions, and misrepresentations of inflected morphemes (e.g., *-ed* spelled as *t* or *d*). Their errors in spelling **high-frequency words** suggested that their underdeveloped phonological and linguistic awareness compromised the development of orthographic memory. When comparing the writing samples of adults with and without dyslexia, Sterling, Farmer, Riddick, Morgan, and Matthews (1998) found that the sentences of adults with dyslexia were no shorter or longer than those of their peers but that there was a conspicuous use of **monosyllabic** words and misuse of **homophones.** Spelling errors suggested specific phonological impairment as well as problems with the complexities of English. Adolescents and adults who are poor spellers demonstrate the tenacious nature of the phonological processing deficit and its chronic effect on spelling development. Phonological awareness along with morphemic and orthographic awareness must be considered significant elements of spelling instruction.

It is important to note that spelling ability and IQ scores are not related. Poor spelling does not reflect a lack of intelligence (West, 1991). Take, for example, the spelling errors of neurosurgeon Harvey Cushing: *swoolen* for *swollen, neybour* for *neighbor,* and *quire* for *choir.* Cushing was a brilliant man who was a *"mediocher"* speller.

KNOWLEDGE NECESSARY FOR SPELLING

Traditional spelling instruction that involves the repetitious copying of words or the memorization of word lists does not promote active, reflective thought about language (Joshi et al., 2008/2009). Informal spelling instruction that assumes that spelling will develop through writing experiences does not provide students with the necessary knowledge of language structure they need to become correct spellers. Students must be explicitly taught about language structure for spelling, and they must be actively engaged in thinking about language. The teacher must assume an active role in spelling instruction. As Moats stated, "rather than a developmental progression characterized by distinct stages, learning to spell is more accurately described as a continual amalgamation of phonological, morphological, and orthographic knowledge" (2005, p.14). It is imperative that the teacher have and be able to impart knowledge about the sounds of the language, the most frequent and reliable letter patterns and rules of English orthography, morphology, and word origins to help students consolidate their knowledge of language structures into correct spellings (Brady & Moats, 1997; Joshi & Carreker, 2009; see Chapter 4 for a discussion of English word origins).

Phonetics, Phonology, and Phonics

Phonetics is the study of the characteristics of individual speech sounds (i.e., phonemes) that occur in all languages (see Scarborough & Brady, 2002, for a discussion about related *phon* terms). There are approximately 44 speech sounds in English, with some variants of these sounds (i.e., allophones) that are not considered separate speech sounds (e.g., the /ă/ in the word *sank* is different from the /ă/ in *sack* but is not a separate speech sound). Phonetics involves categorizing or describing the articulation of each speech sound—where the sound is produced, the way in which air stream flows through the mouth and nose, and the activity of the vocal cords during production.

Spoken words are made up of the speech sounds. Every language has its own set of rules that governs the utterance of these sounds and the sound patterns that are allowed. This system of rules that determine how sounds are used in spoken language is called *phonology* (Moats, 1995). There are constraints about sound sequences in spoken language based on what humans are capable of producing easily (e.g., /np/ rarely occurs in spoken English, hence the pronunciation /ĭm|pôrt/ rather than /ĭn|pôrt/).

Pronunciation variations may occur because of a phoneme's position in a word (e.g., /p/ in *pot* is different from the /p/ in *spot* or *top*) or because of surrounding sounds (e.g., the vowel in *sank* may be perceived as a long vowel instead of a short vowel because it is nasalized before nasal /ng/). These perfunctory pronunciation differences do not affect meaning (Treiman et al., 1994). Accent, however, may vary pronunciations as well as the meanings of words (e.g., /ŏb´|jĕkt/ is a noun, and /ŏb|jĕkt´/ is a verb). It is not necessary to teach the rules that govern the use of speech sounds when a child is learning to speak (Read, 1971); the rules are unconscious rules that automatically occur in spoken language.

Phonics is an instructional method that teaches the use of written symbols to represent speech sounds for reading and spelling. Phonics provides a visual representation of the phonology of spoken language (e.g., the /ă/ in *sank* is nasalized before *n*, which is nasalized; the *n* is pronounced /ng/ instead of /n/ before any letter pronounced /k/ or /g/). In order for students to be successful with phonics, they must be aware of the sounds in spoken words.

Brady and Moats (1997) contended that knowledge of phonetics and phonology assists the teacher in understanding the reading and spelling errors of students, increases his or her ability to provide **corrective feedback,** and enables him or her to plan instruction that is linguistically informed. Knowledge of phonetics heightens the teacher's awareness of speech sounds and how they are produced so that he or she can provide correct models for students. Knowing phonology also gives the teacher insight into why students might have difficulty segmenting or spelling words. For example, a nasalized vowel plus a nasal consonant sound is pronounced as a unit. Therefore, students may have difficulty hearing that /jŭmp/ consists of four separate speech sounds. Students may segment it as three sounds: /j/, /ŭm/, and /p/. When spelling, students may hear /t/ before /r/ as /ch/ and spell it accordingly. As mentioned previously, /t/ before /r/ has a place of articulation in the mouth that is similar to /ch/, so using *ch* is not outrageous but instead is "reasonable and well motivated" (Treiman et al., 1994, p. 1336) and worthy of recognition (Read, 1971). The teacher need not be a linguist but rather should possess phonemic awareness skills and a working knowledge of the sound structure of English.

Production of Speech Sounds

Correct pronunciation of speech sounds is encouraged by understanding the descriptions of the individual speech sounds (Moats, 1995). Students are able to distinguish sounds better when they understand the kinesthetic feel and the visual display of the mouth as a sound is pronounced.

In decoding instruction, students learn that vowel sounds are open and voiced. (See Figure 3.3 for the vowel sounds, arranged by mouth position.) The short vowels are most difficult to discriminate. Figure 9.1 (Cox, 1992) illustrates the mouth positions of the short vowel sounds. The teacher should study and share this figure with students. Visual awareness of the mouth positions for producing vowel sounds heightens students' ability to discriminate the vowel sounds. Awareness of the distinctive, kinesthetic feel of sounds as they are produced also assists in discriminating easily confused vowel sounds (e.g., /ĭ/ makes you grin, /ĕ/ drops your chin).

To be able to provide correct models of consonant sounds, the teacher should study the production of consonant sounds according to three properties: the place of articulation, the flow of the air stream, and the activity of the vocal cords. Table 9.1 provides information about the place of articulation of the consonant sounds, using the phonic spellings that often are used in reading and spelling instruction. Table 9.2 provides information on the kinesthetic feel of the mouth and how the air stream flows from the mouth or nose during production of consonant sounds. Table 9.3 presents information about voiced and unvoiced consonant sounds.

Teaching Spelling

Spelling is translating speech sounds into letters or letter patterns. Two critical facets of skilled spelling are the awareness of 1) speech sounds in spoken words (i.e., phonemic awareness) and 2) frequently recurring orthographic patterns in English (i.e., orthography). Successful spelling instruction promotes awareness of these facets.

Phonemic Awareness

The importance of phonemic awareness in learning to read and spell has been well documented (Adams, 1990; Bradley & Bryant, 1983; Goswami & Bryant, 1990; Liberman, Shankweiler, & Liberman, 1989). Spelling begins with the speller's awareness that spoken words are made up of sounds that are represented in print by letters. For the speller to represent those sounds in print accurately, he or she must be able to pronounce them correctly and discriminate them clearly.

Activities that promote phonological awareness, especially phonemic awareness, are outlined in Chapter 5 and must be included in beginning reading and spelling in-

Figure 9.1.   Mouth position for the short vowel sounds. (From Cox, A.R. [1992]. *Foundations for literacy: Structures and techniques for multisensory teaching of basic written English language skills* [p. 129]. Cambridge, MA: Educators Publishing Service. Used by permission of Educators Publishing Service, 625 Mt. Auburn St., Cambridge, MA, [800] 225-5750, www.epsbooks.com)

Table 9.1. Places of articulation of consonant sounds

Both lips	Teeth and lower lip	Between the teeth	Ridge behind teeth	Roof of mouth	Back of mouth	From the throat
/b/	/f/	/th/	/d/	/ch/	/g/	/h/
/m/	/v/	/th̲/	/l/	/j/	/k/	/hw/
/p/			/n/	/sh/	/ks/*	
			/r/	/y/	/kw/*	
			/s/	/zh/	/ng/	
			/t/		/w/	
			/z/			

*These combination sounds represent the most frequent sounds of *x* (/ks/) and *q* (/kw/), which is usually followed by *u.*

struction. As students prepare to spell words, they need to engage in activities that promote the recognition or discrimination of specific sounds in words.

- *To heighten sensitivity to a particular sound in a word:* The teacher says a word and asks students to listen for a certain sound. Students repeat the word, listening for the sound. If they hear the sound, then they say the sound. If they do not hear the sound, then they say, "No."

- *To heighten sensitivity to the position of a particular sound in a word:* The teacher says a word and asks students to listen for the position of a particular sound in the word. Students repeat the word, listening for the position of the sound. Students indicate the position: initial, medial, or final (see Chapter 6 for activities that explore the concepts *initial, medial,* and *final*).

- *To promote spelling by analogy* (Goswami, 1988; Nation & Hulme, 1998): The teacher says a word, and students repeat it. The teacher tells students to change a sound

Table 9.2. Flow of air during production of consonant sounds

Partially blocked and clipped	Blocked and continuous	Unblocked and aspirated	Through the nose, blocked, and continuous
/b/	/f/	/h/	/m/
/ch/	/hw/		/n/
/d/	/ks/		/ng/
/g/	/kw/		
/j/	/l/		
/k/	/r/		
/p/	/s/		
/t/	/sh/		
/y/	/th/		
	/th̲/		
	/v/		
	/w/		
	/z/		
	/zh/		

The terms *blocked, partially blocked,* and *unblocked* are used in spelling instruction to refer to the kinesthetic feel of the position of the tongue, teeth, or lips during the production of sounds in isolation. *Blocked* refers to the steady position of the tongue, teeth, or lips during the entire production of a sound. *Partially blocked* refers to a released position of the tongue or lips during the production of a sound. *Unblocked* refers to no obstruction of the sound by the tongue, teeth, or lips during the production of a sound. These terms are used to aid students in clearly feeling and distinguishing sounds for spelling.

(not a letter name) in the word and to pronounce the new word (e.g., change /s/ in *sat* to /m/ and pronounce the new word, change /t/ in *bat* to /g/ and pronounce the new word).

Orthography

Orthography refers to the rules that govern how words are represented in writing. Chapter 8 contains information that assists the student in managing English orthography for reading. With this information, the reader knows how to translate the orthography into its spoken equivalents. The speller's task is to determine how the phonemes of oral language are transcribed into the graphemes (i.e., letters or letter clusters) of written language. There are constraints in English orthography; for example, certain letters never double (e.g., *j, y, w*), certain letters do not occur in sequence (e.g., *skr* does not occur within a syllable), and words do not end in certain letters (e.g., *v, j*). Formal spelling instruction calls attention to these constraints and helps students manage English orthography for spelling by establishing a sense of the frequency and reliability of letter patterns (Brady & Moats, 1997).

Table 9.3. Unvoiced and voiced consonant sounds

Unvoiced	Voiced
Pairs (read across)	
/p/	/b/
/t/	/d/
/k/	/g/
/f/	/v/
/s/	/z/
/th/	/<u>th</u>/
/ch/	/j/
/sh/	/zh/
Nonpairs (read down)	
/h/	/kw/
/hw/	/l/
/ks/	/m/
	/n/
	/ng/
	/r/
	/w/
	/y/

Twenty-four speech sounds can be established as having a one-to-one correspondence with written letters (see Table 9.4). These sounds have only one spelling (e.g., /m/ is spelled *m*, /p/ is spelled *p*), or they have one spelling that is far more frequent than any other spelling (e.g., /f/ is spelled *f* much more often than *ph* or *gh*, /ĕ/ is spelled *e* much more often than *ea*) (Hanna et al., 1966). This information will enable students to spell more than half of the phonemes of English.

The other speech sounds of English have a more precarious link to orthography (see Table 9.4). The transcription of each of these sounds depends not only on frequency but also on the position of the sound in a word, the length of the word, the accent, or the influence of surrounding sounds. To make sense of spelling choices, students must realize there is a difference between decoding and spelling. When decoding, students look at the printed symbols and translate those graphemes into phonemes. Students have no difficulty reading *gate* because they know that the vowel sound in an *a*-consonant-*e* syllable is pronounced as /ā/. They can read *bait* because they know that *ai* is pronounced /ā/. Knowing that *eigh* is pronounced /ā/ enables readers to pronounce the word *weight*. All of these words follow frequent, reliable patterns for reading.

Spelling a word starts with sounds, not letter sequences. For spelling, students hear /gāt/, /bāt/, and /wāt/. Except for the initial phonemes, these words sound similar. They all are one-syllable words with medial /ā/ that end in /t/. Students will have little trouble spelling the initial or final sounds, but spelling the medial sounds may be problematic. Without the memory of letter patterns, either because of lack of exposure to print or because of poor orthographic memory, spellers have difficulty knowing whether to use *a*-consonant-*e*, *ai*, or *eigh*. They must be taught that when they hear /ā/ before a final consonant sound, it is most frequently represented with *a*-consonant-*e* (e.g., *cake, insane, equivocate*). With this information, students will be able to spell a high percentage of words with initial or medial /ā/ correctly (Hanna et al., 1966). Not only does their spelling accuracy increase, but also the focus on one spelling establishes that pattern well and actually heightens awareness of other possible spellings of /ā/. If

Table 9.4. Sound-to-spelling translations of speech sounds, based on frequency

Vowel sounds with one frequent spelling	Consonant sounds with one frequent spelling	Vowel sounds with more than one frequent spelling	Consonant sounds with more than one frequent spelling
/ă/ = a (apple)	/b/ = b (bat)	/ŏ/ = o (octopus)	/ch/ = ch (cheek)
/ĕ/ = e (echo)	/f/ = f (fish)	a (watch)	ch (lunch, speech)
/ĭ/ = i (itch)	/g/ = g (goat)	/ŭ/ = u (cup)	tch (catch)
/ŏŏ/ = oo (book)	/h/ = h (house)	a (banana)	/d/ = d (dog)
/ōō/ = oo (moon)	/l/ = l (leaf)	/ā/ = a-consonant-e (cake, vacate)	ed (smelled)
/âr/ = ar (star)	/m/ = m (mitten)	a (apron)	/j/ = j (jam)
/ôr/ = or (fork)	/n/ = n (nest)	ay (tray)	g (gentle, giant, biology)
	/p/ = p (pig)	/ē/ = ee (feet)	dge (edge)
	/kw/ = qu (queen)	e-consonant-e (athlete)	ge (hinge)
	/r/ = r (rabbit)	e (equal)	/k/ = c (cat, cot, cut, clam, crab)
	/w/ = w (wish)	ee (three)	k (keep, kite, sky)
	/ks/ = x (box)	y (penny)	ck (pocket)
	/y/ = y (yarn)	/ī/ = i-consonant-e (five, invite)	ck (back)
	/th/ = th (rather)	i (iris)	k (book, milk)
	/th/ = th (thimble)	y (fly)	ke (make)
	/hw/ = wh (whistle)	/ō/ = o-consonant-e (rope, remote)	c (music)
	/sh/ = sh (ship)	o (open)	/ng/ = ng (king)
	/zh/ = si (erosion)	ow (snow)	n (sink, angle)
		/ū/ = u-consonant-e (cube, infuse)	/s/ = s (sock)
		u (unicorn)	c (grocery, icicle)
		ue (statue)	ss (kiss, discuss)
		/er/ = er (fern)	s (cactus)
		or (world)	ce (mice)
		/au/ = au (saucer)	se (horse, mouse)
		aw (saw)	/t/ = t (table)
		a (ball)	ed (jumped)
		/oi/ = oi (boil)	/v/ = v (valentine)
		oy (boy)	ve (have)
		/ou/ = ou (out)	/z/ = z (zipper)
		ow (cow)	s (pansy)
			s (has)
			se (cheese)

all of the possible spellings of /ā/ are taught at one time, however, then beginning spellers and poor spellers in particular will be overwhelmed with choices. Words such as *bait* and *weight,* which contain less frequent spellings of /ā/, are best learned or memorized as whole words.

This problem exists with most published spelling series. The weekly spelling lists confuse students with multiple choices and seldom offer direction in terms of establishing frequency or reliability, as in the following example (Cook, Farnum, Gabrielson, & Temple, 1998, p. 28):

Words with /ū/ and /ōō/

1.	bloom	6.	few	11.	clue	16.	dew
2.	ruler	7.	used	12.	rescue	17.	flute
3.	broom	8.	loose	13.	movie	18.	due
4.	usual	9.	whose	14.	human	19.	tune
5.	roof	10.	glue	15.	avenue	20.	beautiful

This list has two sounds, /ū/ as in *use* and /ōō/ as in *moon*. These two sounds are heard similarly with similar visual displays. The only noticeable difference is in producing the two sounds. The tongue is tensed when pronouncing /ū/, so it sounds like /yōō/. But because /ū/ is often pronounced /ōō/ in running speech, it will be difficult for students to clearly discriminate the two sounds. The other problem with this list is the number of spelling choices (seven) for these two sounds: *u*-consonant-*e, ue, u, oo, o, ew,* and *eau.* Some of the choices are extremely infrequent (see Table 9.5). Few words have the /ū/ or /ōō/ sound spelled with *o* as in *move, ew* as in *dew,* or *eau* as in *beautiful.* Helpful information for students includes the following: /ū/ is best spelled with *u*-consonant-*e* before a final consonant sound as in *cube* or *infuse;* /ū/ at the end of a syllable is spelled *u* as in *human* or, at the end of a word, *ue* as in *statue;* and the /ōō/ sound in initial, medial, or final position is best spelled *oo* (Cox, 1977). It also may be helpful for students to over-pronounce or exaggerate the /ū/ sound in some words as /yōō/ to differentiate it from /ōō/ and to clarify the best spelling choice (e.g., an overpronunciation of *tube* as /tyōōb/ rather than /tōōb/ clarifies the spelling as *u*-consonant-*e* instead of *oo*).

Good spellers, who of course are good readers (decoders), begin to weight the frequency of these spellings as they read (Adams, 1990; Foorman, 1994; Seidenberg & McClelland, 1989) and are better able to deal with a list that has multiple spellings of one sound. Poor spellers who are poor readers do not receive sufficient exposure to these patterns to weight them. Poor spellers who are good readers do not have adequate sensitivity to letter patterns to determine frequency. The goal of effective spelling instruction is to make the reliability of English orthography obvious to all students by teaching the most frequent, reliable orthographic patterns of English (Post & Carreker, 2002; Post, Carreker, & Holland, 2001).

Morphology

Morphology is the study of *morphemes,* the smallest units of language that carry meaning (prefixes, suffixes, roots, and combining forms; see Chapters 4 and 8 for more information on morphemes). Morphemic knowledge advances students from the spelling of one-syllable base words to the spelling of one-syllable base words with suffixes and

Table 9.5.   Infrequent spellings of vowel sounds

/ă/ = pl*ai*d, l*au*gh
/ā/ = r*ai*n, caf*é*, st*ea*k, matin*ee*, v*ei*n, *eigh*t, th*ere*, th*ey*, ball*et*
/au/ = c*augh*t, br*ough*t, br*oa*d
/ĕ/ = h*ea*d, s*ai*d, *a*ny
/ē/ = b*ea*ch, c*ei*ling, vall*ey*, sk*i*, pr*ie*st, pet*ite*
/er/ = doll*ar*, b*ir*d, anch*or*, b*ur*n, s*ear*ch, j*our*nal
/ĭ/ = capt*ai*n, clim*ate*, forf*ei*t, frag*ile*, g*y*m
/ī/ = *ai*sle, kay*ak*, h*eigh*t, t*ie*, l*igh*t, n*y*lon, st*y*le, d*ye*, b*uy*
/ō/ = b*eau*, b*oa*t, t*oe*, d*ough*
/ŏŏ/ = p*u*sh
/ōō/ = s*ou*p, d*o*, sh*oe*, thr*ough*, fr*ui*t
/ou/ = pl*ough*
/ŭ/ = s*o*n, bl*oo*d, t*ou*ch
/ū/ = b*eau*ty, *Eu*rope, n*ew*

eventually to the spelling of other derivatives (i.e., a base word plus one or more affixes) and multisyllabic words. Knowing suffixes and inflectional morphemes signals to students that /pĭnz/ contains two morphemes or meaningful units: the base word /pĭn/ and the suffix /z/, which makes the word plural; therefore, /z/ is spelled *s* not *z*. Without understanding suffixes and inflectional morphemes, students remain literal in their spellings and write /jŭmpt/ as *jumpt* and /băngd/ as *bangd* because that is what they hear. The understanding that a suffix that begins with a consonant is a consonant suffix and a suffix that begins with a vowel is vowel suffix helps students when they add suffixes to base words to spell derivatives. The final letter of a base word may be doubled or dropped, but this is true only when adding a vowel suffix (e.g., *starring* but not *starless, hoping* but not *hopful*).

Knowing prefixes and roots facilitates students' spelling of multisyllabic words (Adams, 1990; Brady & Moats, 1997; Henry, 1988). For example, the word *attraction* contains three morphemes. These morphemes serve not only as meaning-filled units but also as spelling units. The word *attraction* can be spelled in chunks instead of sound by sound. Knowing that some consonant prefixes change their spellings for **euphony** (i.e., to ease pronunciation; see Table 9.6), students know to spell a word such as *attraction* with two *t*'s because the *at-* in *attraction* represents a spelling deviation of the prefix *ad-*. The prefix changes the final letter to match the initial letter of the root *tract*. With knowledge of morphology, students can clarify spelling choices and contend with more complex levels of orthography.

Word Origins

Chapter 4 outlines the Anglo-Saxon, Latin, and Greek layers of language in English (see also Henry, 2010). These languages and others have shaped the orthography of English as evidenced in the spelling of /sh/. Fourteen different spellings have been noted in English (Bryson, 1990): *sh* as in *ship; ch* as in *chef; ti* as in *nation; si* as in *discussion; ci* as in *special; xi* as in *anxious; sci* as in *conscious; sch* as in *schnauzer; ce* as in *ocean; se* as in *nauseous; s* as in *sugar; ss* as in *tissue; psh* as in *pshaw*; and *chsi* as in *fuchsia*. These spellings represent different layers of language within English: *sh* from Anglo-Saxon; *ch* from French; *ti, ci, si, xi*, and *sci* from Latin; *sch* from German; *ce* from Greek; and *chsi* after German botanist Fuchs. The layers of other languages make English a rich tapestry of words, but they create a confusing orthography, thus compounding the difficulties poor spellers have with spelling. It would seem logical to change orthography to make it less confusing and to make words easier to spell.

There have been attempts to reform English orthography but to no avail. Benjamin Franklin proposed a phonetic alphabet with a better one-to-one letter–sound correspondence, which in the end did not gain much favor. Noah Webster, who advocated educational reform and America's own form of spelling to complement its unique form of government, proposed changes such as *bred* for *bread, laf* for *laugh*, and *crum* for *crumb*. Although these changes were

Table 9.6. Prefixes that change spelling for euphony

Prefix	Prefix changed for euphony
ab-	a-, abs-
ad-	a-, ac-, af-, ag-, al-, an-, ap-, ar-, as-, at-
con-	co-, col-, com-, cor-
en-	em-
ex-	e-, ec-, ef-
in-	il-, im-, ir-
ob-	oc-, of-, op-
sub-	suc-, suf-, sup-, sur-, sus-

not accepted, Webster was successful in changing the spellings of words such as *honour* to *honor, centre* to *center,* and *publick* to *public.* The American Philological Association, an organization dedicated to spelling reform, made concerted efforts to change the orthography of English in the late 1800s and early 1900s but had little success. In the 1930s, *The Chicago Tribune,* in an effort to increase readership by making words easier to read, used these spellings in their newspaper: *thru, tho,* and *thoro* (Venezky, 1980). Although it seems reasonable to simplify and unify orthography, such attempts have failed. Perhaps this is because changing the orthography of English would mask its rich, interesting history and the interrelatedness of words (e.g., *muscle* is related to *muscular,* which accounts for the silent *c* in *muscle; sign* is related to *signature,* which accounts for the silent *g;* see Henry, 2010).

Rather than bemoan the inconsistencies of English, students can take advantage of information about word origins to refine their spelling knowledge. Initially, students are taught that the most frequent, though not the only, spelling of /f/ is *f.* This information serves them well for spelling most words. Knowing that long, scientific terms are usually of Greek origin and that Greek words containing /f/ are spelled with *ph,* students have information that will help them to spell words such as *chlorophyll* and *photosynthesis.* Students will also note that words of Greek origin containing /k/ are often spelled with *ch* and those containing /ĭ/ are often spelled with *y.* Students who know word origins come to understand why some words are spelled in unexpected ways, and, more important, students can determine the appropriate spellings for these words. (See Henry, 1988, 2010, for more on spellings according to word origin.)

FORMAL SPELLING INSTRUCTION

Spelling is a skill that must be formally taught. Using invented spelling in preschool and kindergarten should be encouraged and supported with phonological awareness training (Blachman, Ball, Black, & Tangel, 1994, 2000; Castle, Riach, & Nicholson, 1994; Rubin & Eberhardt, 1996). (See Chapter 5 for activities that can be incorporated into the classroom routine; see also Adams, Foorman, Lundberg, & Beeler, 1998.) By using invented spelling, students learn the essence of spelling—translating sounds to symbols. Good spelling, however, requires more than translating sounds to symbols; it also demands a sensitivity to letter patterns in words. Although invented spelling reinforces sound–symbol correspondences, it does not provide the correct models that students need to build orthographic knowledge. Students must be formally taught the patterns and rules of English orthography, beginning in the middle of first grade. Learning the patterns and rules cannot be left to chance. Correct spelling has a direct impact on students' reading proficiency (Adams, 1990). Formal spelling instruction should include the following:

- Phonological awareness training

- Opportunities for kindergarteners and beginning first graders to experiment with writing using invented spelling

- Guided discovery teaching introductions to the sounds, sound–symbol correspondences, patterns, rules, and morphemes of English, beginning in the middle of first grade and using a systematic, sequential, cumulative order of presentation

- Opportunities to analyze and sort words

- Practice using multisensory structured procedures

- A multisensory procedure for learning irregular words

- Opportunities to use the words in writing through dictation and personal writing

Formal spelling instruction extends the spelling information students gain through their invented spellings and teaches the structure of the language for spelling, thus enabling students to move from invented spelling to conventional spelling. Words can be categorized as regular, rule, and irregular (Carreker, 2002). It will be helpful to introduce information for spelling instruction in these same categories.

Regular Words

Regular words are spelled the way they sound. They follow the frequent, reliable sound-to-letter translations or patterns of the language (see Table 9.4). Some regular words are transparent in their spellings, such as *in, rag,* or *help.* There is only one spelling or only one predominant spelling of the sounds; hence, there is no confusion about how to spell the sounds in these words. Not all regular words are as transparent in their spellings. Some regular words contain sounds with indefinite spellings, such as /k/, which can be spelled *k, c,* or *ck.* One spelling is not overwhelmingly apparent as the best choice. Students need to be taught generalizations about the use and frequency of letter patterns in English (Cox, 1977; Post & Carreker, 2002; Post et al., 2001).

Sounds with Multiple Spelling or Letter Patterns

When there is more than one frequent spelling or letter pattern for a sound, the best choice of the pattern is based on the frequency of the pattern and the situation of the sound in a word. The situation (i.e., the particular circumstances of how a sound occurs in a word) of the sound may be based on the position of the sound in a word, the placement of accent (see Chapters 6 and 8 for activities that promote awareness of accent), the length of the word, the influence of surrounding sounds, or a combination of these factors. Awareness of sounds and syllables in words is important in determining the best choice of letters or letter patterns (see Chapter 8 for activities that promote awareness of syllables). The terms that are introduced in decoding to express the positions of letters in words—*initial, medial,* and *final*—are also used to describe the positions of sounds in words. *Initial* refers to the first position in a syllable. *Final* refers to the last position in a syllable. *Medial* refers to any position between the first and last positions.

Students need not guess or give up when dealing with the sounds that have more than one frequent spelling or letter pattern. Instead, they consider the situation of the sound that may be represented by more than one spelling. The situation provides clues that will help students in their decision-making process. For example, in considering the spelling of /măch/, students think about possible, frequent spellings of /ch/ (*ch* or *tch*). To decide which spelling is the best choice, students determine the situation of the sound in the word. The sound is in the final position of a one-syllable word, and it comes after a short vowel. On the basis of this situation, students know that *tch* is the best choice for spelling /ch/ in the word *match.* The following examples of spelling patterns show the best choices for spelling sounds according to their situations. Each pattern should be introduced one at a time and practiced to mastery. A suggested order of introducing these patterns is mentioned later in this chapter.

Spelling Choices with Situations Based on Position

1. When is /oi/ spelled *oi*, and when is it spelled *oy*?

oil	*boy*
ointment	*toy*
boil	*joy*
coin	*enjoy*
joint	*employ*
In initial or medial position, /oi/ is spelled *oi*.	In final position, /oi/ is spelled *oy*. (A less frequent but reliable spelling choice for /oi/ at the end of a syllable is *oy* as in *royal* or *voyage*.)

2. When is /ou/ spelled *ou*, and when is it spelled *ow*?

out	*cow*
ouch	*how*
found	*plow*
shout	*meow*
ground	
In initial or medial position, /ou/ is spelled *ou*.	In final position, /ou/ is spelled *ow*.

(Less frequent but reliable spelling choices that could be introduced later as refinement include the following: /ou/ is spelled *ow* in a one-syllable word before final /l/ or /n/ *owl* or *down*, and /ou/ is spelled *ow* before /er/ as in *shower* or *flower*.)

Spelling Choices with Situations Based on Surrounding Sounds or Letters

1. When is /k/ spelled *k*, and when is it spelled *c*?

keep	*cat*
kit	*cost*
sky	*cup*
Before any sound represented by *e, i*, or *y*, /k/ is spelled *k*.	*clasp*
	cramp
	Before everything else, /k/ is spelled *c*.

2. When is /j/ spelled *g*, and when is it spelled *j*?

gem	*jam*
giant	*jot*
biology	*just*
Before any sound represented by *e, i*, or *y*, /j/ is spelled *g*.	Before everything else, /j/ is spelled *j*.

Spelling Choices with Situations Based on Position, Length, and Surrounding Sounds

1. When is final /ch/ spelled *tch*, and when is it spelled *ch*?

catch	*speech*
sketch	*porch*

pitch
blotch
Dutch
Final /ch/ in a one-syllable base word after a short vowel is spelled *tch*.

pouch
belch
sandwich
Final /ch/ after two vowels or a consonant or in a word of more than one syllable is spelled *ch*.

2. When is final /j/ spelled *dge?*

badge
edge
ridge
dodge
fudge
Final /j/ in a one-syllable base word after a short vowel is spelled *dge*.

3. When is final /k/ spelled *ck,* and when is it spelled *c?*

back
peck
sick
block
stuck
Final /k/ after a short vowel in a one-syllable word is spelled *ck*.

picnic
music
lilac

Final /k/ in a multisyllabic base word after a short vowel is spelled *c*.

Spelling Choices for Vowels

1. What are the best choices for spelling /ŏ/?

odd
hot
top
lost
spot
The sound /ŏ/ is spelled *o*, except after /w/, when /ŏ/ is spelled *a*.

want
wash
wand
wasp
wall

2. What are the best choices for spelling /ŭ/?

up
us
cup
rust
shut
The sound /ŭ/ is spelled *u*, except at the end of an unaccented syllable, when /ŭ/ is spelled *a*.

alike
along
parade
tuba
sofa

3. What are the best choices for spelling /ā/?

ate
ape
made
insane

day
say
play
delay

evaluate
Initial or medial /ā/ before a final consonant sound is spelled *a*-consonant-*e*.

repay
Final /ā/ is spelled *ay*.

table
baby
lady
basic
paper
At the end of a syllable, /ā/ is spelled *a*.

4. What are the best spelling choices for /ē/?

eel
feet
green
need
Initial or medial /ē/ in a one-syllable word is spelled *ee*.

stampede
complete
extreme
intervene
Before a final consonant sound in a word word of two or more syllables, /ē/ is spelled *e*-consonant-*e*.

meter	*bee*	*tardy*
fever	*see*	*sixty*
even	*free*	*ugly*
evil	*three*	*candy*
At the end of a syllable, /ē/ is spelled *e*.	In final position of a one-syllable word, /ē/ is spelled *ee*.	In final position of a word with two or more syllables, /ē/ is spelled *y*.

5. What are the best choices for spelling /ī/?

ice
five
recline
excite
Initial or medial /ī/ before a final consonant sound is spelled *i*-consonant-*e*.

fly
try
deny
reply
At the end of a word, /ī/ is spelled *y*.

iris
fiber
tiger
lilac
At the end of a syllable, /ī/ is spelled *i*.

6. What are the best ways to spell /ō/?

rope
home
explode
trombone
Initial or medial /ō/ before a final consonant sound is spelled *o*-consonant-*e*.

show
slow
window
yellow
Final /ō/ is spelled *ow*.

open
over
robot
polite
At the end of a syllable, /ō/ is spelled *o*.

7.   What is the best way to spell /ū/?

use	*sue*
cube	*cue*
infuse	*rescue*
constitute	*continue*
Initial or medial /ū/ before a final consonant sound is spelled *u*-consonant-*e*.	Final /ū/ is spelled *ue*.

unit
tunic
music
tuna
At the end of a syllable, /ū/is spelled *u*.

Note: When spelling words with /ū/, it may be necessary to overpronounce or to exaggerate the sound as /yo͞o/.

Summary of Sounds with Multiple Spelling or Letter Patterns

These spelling patterns offer students a way to manage English orthography for spelling. There will be exceptions to these patterns. It is exciting when students discover the exceptions. To find an exception, students must understand the pattern when it is introduced and remember it. They must compare that pattern with words they hold in memory and realize that there are words that share the same sound but have different spelling patterns. That is active reflection about language. An enthusiastic "Good for you! You found a word that doesn't fit the pattern!" from the teacher affirms that students are thinking about language.

The patterns are not to be memorized. The patterns are established in memory through guided discovery introductions, practice, and opportunities to write through spelling dictation and personal writing. The teacher should direct students' attention to spelling patterns as they occur in the reading. The teacher should refrain from describing the patterns as rules. The term *rule* should be reserved for situations in which a letter in a base word is doubled, dropped, or changed (**rule words** are discussed later in this chapter).

Order of Presentation of Spelling Patterns

The situation of the sound and the frequency of possible letter patterns are important determiners when students are deciding the best spelling choice for a sound with multiple spellings. Students first learn the letter patterns that occur with greater frequency so that they can spell many words. Less frequent patterns are taught later. For beginning spellers or spellers with dyslexia, introducing multiple spelling patterns of a sound should be separated to allow these students time and practice to master one possible pattern before another is introduced. In considering the sounds with multiple spelling patterns just delineated, which represent a sampling of patterns, the approximate order of introduction based on frequency might be as follows. It is important to note that other spelling patterns not delineated previously (e.g., /ĭ/ = i, /p/ = p, /ă/ = a) will be interspersed in the order of introduction.

1. /ŏ/ = o as in *octopus*

2. /ŭ/ = u as in *up*

3. /k/ = k as in *kit*

4. /k/ = c as in *cup*

5. /k/ = ck as in *truck*

6. /j/ = j as in *just*

7. /ē/ = ee as in *feet* and *three*

8. /ā/ = a-consonant-e as in *cake*

9. /ī/ = i-consonant-e as in *five*

10. /ō/ = o-consonant-e as in *rope*

11. /ū/ = u-consonant-e as in *cube*

12. /ē/ = e-consonant-e as in *athlete*

13. /ī/ = y as in *fly*

14. /ē/ = y as in *penny*

15. /ā/ = ay as in *tray*

16. /ā/ = a as in *apron*

17. /ē/ = e as in *even*

18. /ī/ = i as in *iris*

19. /ō/ = o as in *open*

20. /ū/ = u as in *unit*

21. /k/ = c as in *music*

22. /oi/ = oi as in *oil*

23. /oi/ = oy as in *boy*

24. /ch/ = ch as in *chip*

25. /ch/ = tch as in *witch*

26. /ou/ = ou as in *out*

27. /ou/ = ow as in *cow*

28. /ŭ/ = a as in *along* or *sofa*

29. /ō/ = *ow* as in *snow*

30. /j/ = *g* as in *giant*

31. /j/ = *dge* as in *badge*

32. /ū/ = *ue* as in *statue*

33. /ŏ/ = *a* as in *watch*

Introduction of Spelling Patterns with Guided Discovery Teaching

The patterns of spelling are introduced using a guided discovery teaching procedure, similar to that used in introducing reading concepts. The guided discovery teaching procedure uses a Socratic method in which the teacher asks questions to lead students to discover a new spelling pattern. This procedure heightens students' awareness of sounds in words; encourages students to think about how sounds are represented in words; and gives students the opportunity to notice letters in words, thereby heightening their sensitivity to letter patterns.

1. *Auditory discovery:* The teacher reads five to seven discovery words one by one, which contain the same sound and spelling pattern. Students repeat each word after the teacher. Students discover the sound that is the same in all of the discovery words and the position(s) of the sound. It is helpful for students to look in small mirrors as they repeat the words. The visual display on the mouth helps students discriminate the sound. Attention to the kinesthetic feel of the mouth also helps students discriminate the sound. **Auditory discovery** heightens students' awareness of a particular sound in words.

2. *Prediction:* After students have discovered the sound, they predict how the sound might be spelled. The sound students are discovering has been previously introduced for reading. This step encourages students to reflect on their language knowledge.

3. *Visual discovery:* After students have made their predictions, the teacher writes the discovery words on the board. Students carefully look at all of the words and decide which letter or letters are the same and where the letter or letters are located in the words. They also notice any other common features about the words, such as number of syllables, accent, or surrounding sounds. This step heightens awareness of letter patterns.

4. *Verbalization of the pattern:* With the discovery of the sound and its spelling, students verbalize the pattern (e.g., final /k/ after a short vowel in a one-syllable word is spelled *ck*) in their own words. Students then apply this information by spelling five to seven new words with the pattern.

Introducing a Spelling Pattern

Teacher: Listen as I read some words. I want you to repeat each word after me. Listen for the sound that is the same in all of the words. [The teacher reads the words *pick, sack, luck, clock,* and *peck* one at a time as students repeat.] What sound (not letter name) do you hear in all of the words?

Students: /k/

Teacher: Where do you hear the sound? In what position(s)?

Students: The sound is in the final position.

Teacher: Make a prediction about how this sound might be spelled. Think about what you know about the language. How might this sound be spelled? [Students might predict *c, k,* or *ck.*] Watch carefully as I write the discovery words on the board. What letter or letters are the same?

Students: All of the words have the letters *ck.*

Teacher: In what position(s) do you see the letters?

Students: The letters *ck* are in final position.

Teacher: Is there anything else that is similar about these words?

Students: All of the words have short vowel sounds and have one syllable.

Teacher: What does the pattern seem to be?

Students: Final /k/ after a short vowel in a one-syllable word is spelled *ck.*

Teacher: I want you to apply what you have discovered. I will dictate some words for you to spell. [The teacher dictates five to seven words with the pattern one at a time as students write them on paper. The **simultaneous oral spelling (S.O.S.)** procedure described later in this chapter is a helpful tool in word dictation.]

Practice of Sounds and Patterns

Spelling sounds and patterns are practiced daily using multisensory structured procedures.

Sound Dictation   Daily review with a sound or spelling deck (**sound dictation**) develops automaticity in translating sounds to spellings (Cox, 1992). Each introduced sound is written on a separate index card. The sounds are represented by letters with appropriate diacritical markings that are enclosed in parentheses or slash marks (e.g., (ā) or /ā/). The possible spellings of the sound are written on each card. Key words that unlock the spellings of each sound are also written on the cards. While looking at a card that is not shown to the students, the teacher dictates the sound written on the card. Students repeat the sound and name the letter or letters that spell the sound as they write them. If students hesitate about the spelling of a sound, the teacher cues students with the appropriate key word. (See Appendix B at the end of this book for multisensory structured reading programs with spelling components. Several of these programs have commercially produced spelling decks that provide daily review of sounds that have been taught through a multisensory procedure for reading.)

When students are spelling sounds with multiple spellings, they repeat the sound and name and write the frequent, reliable spelling choices. For example, if the teacher dictates /ā/, students repeat /ā/ and say, "*a*-consonant-*e, a;* final, *ay.*" In this abbreviated response, the best spelling choices for /ā/ are recognized. Students write this information in shorthand: *a-e, a // ay.* The double slash marks (//) define the spellings according to their positions in words. Everything to the left of the slash marks represents possible spellings of a sound in initial or medial position. Everything to the right represents possible spellings of a sound in final position.

The media that students use to write their responses can be varied daily to provide different kinesthetic reinforcement. Students may write responses on unlined paper, on the chalkboard, on their desktops, on carpet squares, or in salt trays.

Word Dictation   As each new spelling pattern is introduced, it is practiced to mastery first by using homogenous practice sessions in which every word contains the new pattern. When students demonstrate success in spelling the new pattern, heterogeneous practice sessions that contain the new pattern and previously introduced patterns are used. The words used for these practice sessions are not words that students have memorized or will need to memorize. At first, the words for heterogeneous practice should be one-syllable words that progress from two to three sounds to five to six sounds. When students are ready, they start with the spelling of one-syllable base words with suffixes, then move on to multisyllabic words, and finally, to multisyllabic derivatives. Word dictation practices provide review of sounds and patterns and instills a thinking process for spelling.

A structured procedure can be used for word dictation practice to establish this thinking process for spelling. S.O.S. was introduced by Gillingham and Stillman (1960) and adapted by Cox (1992; see Figure 9.2). The steps and rationale are as follows:

1. *Look and listen.* Students look at the teacher and focus on his or her mouth as he or she dictates the word. By focusing on the teacher's mouth, students use the visual display to clarify the sounds in the dictated word. For example, /f/ will be visually displayed with the upper teeth resting on the lower lip, whereas /th/ will be displayed with the tip of the tongue protruding between the teeth.

2. *Repeat and segment.* Students repeat the word while looking in a small mirror. Using a mirror provides visual cues such as the position of the mouth or the placement of the tongue, teeth, or lips. Repeating the word affirms that students heard the word

Figure 9.2.   Simultaneous oral spelling (S.O.S.) procedure. 1) Look and listen, 2) repeat (echo) and segment, 3) name the letters, 4) name and write, and 5) read to check. (Used by permission of Neuhaus Education Center, Bellaire, TX. *Sources:* Cox, 1992; Gillingham & Stillman, 1960.)

correctly and gives them additional auditory input and kinesthetic feedback. The kines-thetic feedback clarifies the sounds in the dictated word. For example, with /f/, stu-dents feel the upper teeth resting on the lower lip, and with /th/, they feel the tip of the tongue protruding through the teeth.

The segmenting part of this step depends on the kind of word students are spelling and the needs of students. Initially, students segment monosyllabic words with two to five sounds. Students segment each word into its constituent sounds. They may use their fingers to mark the sounds. They make a fist, and beginning with the thumb of their nonwriting hand (left palm up for right-handers; right palm down for left-handers) and moving in a left-to-right progression, students extend a finger for each sound that they hear as they segment the word. Instead of using their fingers, students may move counters such as blocks, buttons, or pennies for each sound they hear as they segment the word. Students continue spelling monosyllabic words until they can segment words into constituent sounds with ease.

When students can successfully spell monosyllabic words of five sounds, they are ready to spell derivatives and multisyllabic words. A derivative should be orally sepa-rated into morphemic units (e.g., /jŭmpt/ is base word; /jŭmp/ plus suffix /t/). A mul-tisyllabic word should be segmented into its component syllables. Students may use the fingers of their nonwriting hand, blocks, buttons, or pennies to segment the words into morphemic units or syllables.

3. *Name the letters.* Before writing the word on paper, students spell the word aloud. This is a rehearsal step for writing. The teacher can guide students to the correct spelling before they write. Naming letters impresses letter sequences in memory (Gillingham & Stillman, 1997). If students have segmented the word using their fingers or counters, then they may want to touch each finger or counter as they spell, thereby reinforcing the sound–letter connection and sequence.

4. *Name and write.* Students write the word while naming the letters (Cox, 1992; Gillingham & Stillman, 1997). The rationale for this step is that naming letters builds the visual sequence of letters in the word through auditory and kinesthetic input. It is important for students to see the word they have spelled orally. If handwriting is not fluent, then students can use plastic letters or letter cards to spell the words, or the teacher could serve as an **amanuensis** by writing for students on paper or on the board. *Note*: Some students may be more inclined to translate sounds immediately into letters without naming the letters, which is certainly acceptable. The aim is to help stu-dents develop a procedure that will be most useful to them.

5. *Read to check.* After students have written the word, they read the word silently, using their decoding information. Knowing syllable types and syllable-division patterns will aid students' accurate reading of the word and confirmation of the spelling (see Chapter 8). It is permissible, and actually desirable, for a student to write a misspelled word without immediate correction by the teacher. This final step is intended to build independence in determining whether a word is spelled correctly. To monitor a large group in a class environment, the teacher may have students read the word aloud to-gether and then touch and name the letters of this word. The teacher gives appropri-ate corrective feedback as needed.

The S.O.S. procedure provides a structure for teaching students how to think about the process of spelling a word. Instead of impulsively writing a word on paper, students think about the sounds in the word and how those sounds can be spelled. They also im-press the letter sequence in memory by naming the letters, monitor the spelling of the word by naming the letters while writing, and check the spelling by reading the word. In the initial stages of spelling instruction with students with dyslexia, it may be necessary to build an understanding and memory of the five steps gradually by breaking the procedure down into smaller parts. Students may begin with Steps 1 and 2. The teacher says the word, and students repeat the word and segment it into its constituent sounds. Students with recalcitrant spelling deficits may require practice with this abbreviated procedure for several days or weeks.

When students are secure with these two steps, Step 3 may be added, in which students spell the word aloud. When these three steps are secure, students can add Steps 4 and 5, with the teacher serving as the amanuensis. When the teacher writes the word, students can better attend to the letter sequence in the word and do not have to worry about the formation of the letters. Eventually, students will complete all five steps of the S.O.S. procedure independently.

Sentence Dictation   Dictating phrases and sentences can begin when students' handwriting is fluent and students have demonstrated success with word dictation. The dictation practice sessions are designed to review previously introduced spelling patterns and irregular words in context. Only three or four phrases or simple sentences are used for a dictation session. A structured procedure for dictation aids this process (Cox, 1992; Gillingham & Stillman, 1997; see Figure 9.3). The steps and rationale of the procedure are as follows:

1. *Look and listen.* Students look at the teacher and listen as the teacher dictates a sentence. As with S.O.S., students look at the teacher's mouth to clarify the sounds in the words.

Figure 9.3.   Dictation procedure. 1) Look and listen, 2) repeat (echo), 3) write, and 4) proofread. (Used by permission of Neuhaus Education Center, Bellaire, TX. *Sources:* Cox, 1992; Gillingham & Stillman, 1960.)

2. *Repeat.* Students repeat the sentence. Using a nonverbal cue, the teacher signals that students should repeat the sentence. Students continue to repeat the sentence until it is secure.

3. *Write.* When the teacher believes that the sentence is secure, he or she indicates that students should begin writing the sentence. The teacher again uses a nonverbal cue to indicate that students should begin to write. The use of nonverbal cues does not interrupt students' auditory memory of the sentence sequence.

4. *Proofread.* When students have finished writing the sentence, the teacher dictates it three times as students check for missing words, capitalization and punctuation, and spelling errors. As students check each feature, they place a checkmark at the end of the sentence. Three checkmarks after the sentence indicates that all three features have been checked. Students can extend this method of checking to their written composition. After writing a paragraph, they should check it three times for these same features. Three checkmarks in the top margin of a paper indicate that all three features have been checked.

It is suggested that students be given one more opportunity on another day to check the dictation paper for spelling errors. A freshly completed dictation paper is considered "hot" (Cox, 1992). It is difficult to see errors in a "hot" dictation paper. Students are able to see errors better when they have the opportunity to review the dictation sentences at another time. Othography is no longer a conundrum to students when they know the frequently recurring patterns in English. They have a means of organizing and managing the language for spelling.

Rule Words

Rule words are spelled the way they sound, but certain information needs to be considered before the word is written. There are five major rules that indicate when a letter should be doubled, dropped, or changed. Two of these rules are used for doubling consonants within a base word. The other three major rules deal with spelling derivatives. They involve a change to the spelling of a base word (i.e., a letter is doubled, dropped, or changed) when adding a suffix. All of the rules are introduced through guided discovery teaching procedures.

Major Spelling Rules

The five major rules include the Rule for Doubling the Final Consonant (Floss Rule), the Rule for Doubling a Medial Consonant (Rabbit Rule), the Doubling Rule, the Dropping Rule, and the Changing Rule. Each rule has a set of **checkpoints.** These checkpoints signal students that a letter may be doubled, dropped, or changed. All of the salient checkpoints must be present for a letter to be doubled, dropped, or changed.

The Rule for Doubling the Final Consonant (Floss Rule)   Discovery words:

tiff	*tell*	*toss*
puff	*doll*	*pass*
staff	*hill*	*mess*

In a one-syllable base word after a short vowel, final /f/, /l/, and /s/ are spelled *ff, ll,* and *ss,* respectively. When deciding whether to apply this rule, students must think about these checkpoints: 1) one syllable; 2) short vowel; and 3) final /f/, /l/, or /s/. If all three checkpoints are present, then the final consonant is doubled. If any one of the checkpoints is missing, then the final consonant will not be doubled.

Note: The term *floss* is a mnemonic device that reminds students that *f, l,* or *s* will double in a one-syllable base word after a short vowel.

The Rule for Doubling the Medial Consonant (Rabbit Rule)   Discovery words:

sudden

tennis

mitten

pollen

muffin

In a two-syllable base word with one medial consonant sound after a short vowel, the medial consonant is doubled. The three checkpoints for this rule are 1) two syllables, 2) one medial consonant sound, and 3) a short vowel in the first syllable. If all of the checkpoints are present, then the medial consonant is doubled. If any checkpoint is missing, then the medial consonant will not be doubled. When a reader encounters these words in text, the doubled medial consonants indicate to the reader that the first vowel is short.

Note: The term *rabbit* is a mnemonic device that reminds students that a medial consonant doubles in a two-syllable base word after a short vowel.

The Doubling Rule   Discovery words:

hop + *ed* = *hopped*   *star* + *ing* = *starring*

red + *ish* = *reddish*   *begin* + *er* = *beginner*

When a word ends in one vowel and one consonant and the final syllable is accented (all one-syllable words are accented), and a vowel suffix is being added, the final consonant is doubled before the suffix is added. There are four checkpoints for consideration: 1) one vowel in the final syllable, 2) one consonant after that vowel, 3) final syllable accented, and 4) a vowel suffix that is being added. If all four checkpoints are present, then the final consonant is doubled. If one checkpoint is missing, then the suffix is just added on. A doubled final consonant before a vowel suffix indicates to the reader that the vowel before the final consonant is short (e.g., in *hopping,* the final consonant is doubled before the vowel suffix and the vowel is short; in *hoping,* the final consonant is not doubled before the vowel suffix and the vowel is long).

Seven letters in English orthography do not or rarely double. Knowing these seven letters assists students in deciding whether to double a letter. These letters can be taught as a cheer:

h, k

y, j

v, w, x

Never or rarely double in English words.

With this bit of information, students will understand why the *x* in *faxing* or *relaxing* does not double or why the *v* in *river* or *seven* does not double.

The doubling rule is an extremely important rule for students to know for writing, as it is used often in spelling participles and the past tense of verbs. Figure 9.4 (Carreker, 2002) shows a visual aid that students can use to remember the four checkpoints of this rule. The four-leaf clover can be reproduced on green cardstock and cut apart for each student. As students search for the checkpoints in a word, they build the four-leaf clover. If all four leaves of the clover are used, then students are lucky. The stem is added to the clover, and students know they must double the final consonant. If any leaf is missing, then they will not double the final consonant.

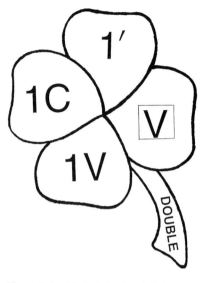

Figure 9.4. Manipulative four-leaf clover indicating checkpoints for the doubling rule: one vowel (1V), one consonant (1C), one accent (1′), and a vowel suffix (a boxed V). When a word has these checkpoints, students add the clover stem, indicating that the final consonant of the base word should be doubled. (From Carreker, S. [2002]. *Scientific spelling* [Rev. ed.; Section 3, p. 7]. Bellaire, TX: Neuhaus Education Center; reprinted by permission).

The Dropping Rule   Discovery words:

bake + er = baker

solve + ed = solved

blue + ish = bluish

house + ing = housing

complete + ed = completed

When a base word ends in *e* and a vowel suffix is being added, the final *e* is dropped before the suffix is added. The two checkpoints are 1) final *e* and 2) a vowel suffix that is being added. If a consonant suffix is being added, then the final *e* is not dropped. As mentioned previously, a single final consonant before a vowel suffix indicates to a reader that the vowel before the final consonant is long.

The Changing Rule   Discovery words:

try + ed = tried

silly + est = silliest

penny + less = penniless

happy + ness = happiness

When a base word ends in a consonant before a final *y* and a suffix that does not begin with *i* is added, the final *y* changes to *i* before the suffix is added. The checkpoints for this rule are 1) a consonant before a final *y*, 2) final *y*, and 3) a suffix that does not begin with *i*. If the base word has a vowel before the final *y*, then the *y* does not change to *i* (e.g., *boys, enjoying, stayed*). If a suffix that begins with *i* is added, then the *y* does not change to *i* (e.g., *crying, babyish, lobbyist*). The teacher can explain to students that the *y* does not change when adding a suffix that begins with *i* because "two *i*'s are unwise." Of course, when students discover the word *skiing*, the teacher will say, "Good for you!"

Introduction of the Spelling Rules

As mentioned previously, introducing spelling patterns begins with an auditory guided discovery procedure to get students to focus on the sound. The goal of teaching the patterns is that when students hear a particular sound in a word, they will know the most frequent, reliable way to spell the sound. Spelling rules are introduced differently. **Visual discovery** is used to introduce the spelling rules because students must learn to recognize and remember not a sound but a distinguishing visual feature of the rule words.

Introducing the Rules with Doubled Consonants (Floss Rule and Rabbit Rule)

Teacher: Watch carefully as I write some words on the board. [When introducing the Rabbit Rule, for example, the teacher writes discovery words such as *rabbit, pollen, tennis, mitten,* and *sudden* on the board in a column as students watch.] What looks the same in all of these words? [Students notice doubled letters and the position of the doubled letters.] Do you notice anything else? [The teacher leads students to discover the other checkpoints of the rule.] Let's review the checkpoints and state the rule. [After students have reviewed the checkpoints and stated the rule, they spell five to seven new words that follow the rule.]

Introducing the Rules for Spelling Derivatives (Doubling Rule, Dropping Rule, and Changing Rule)

Introducing rules for spelling derivatives begins with the teacher writing a list of three to five discovery words on the board in a formula format: a base word + a suffix = the derivative. The teacher then leads students to discover similarities among all the base words, similarities among the suffixes, and similarities among the derivatives. Introducing each of rule would be comparable with this introduction of the Doubling Rule.

Teacher: Watch carefully as I write some words on the board. [The teacher writes the discovery words in a formula format such as *run* + *er* = *runner, shop* + *ing* = *shopping,* and *stop* + *ed* = *stopped*.] The first column of words contains base words. The second column contains suffixes. The third column contains derivatives. Look at the column of base words. How are all the base words the same?

Students: They each have one vowel, one final consonant, and an accented final syllable.

Teacher: Look at the column of suffixes. How are all the suffixes the same?

Students: All of the suffixes are vowel suffixes.

Teacher: Look at the derivatives. How are all of the derivatives the same?

Students: The final consonant of each base word is doubled.

Teacher: Let's review the checkpoints and state the rule. [After students have reviewed the checkpoints and stated the rule, they spell five to seven new derivatives that follow the rule.]

Importance of Awareness of Language Domains

As mentioned previously, spelling requires attention to several domains of language (i.e., phonology, syntax, morphology, semantics, orthography) at once. If these different domains are taught as part of or concurrently with formal spelling instruction, then the necessity of teaching many traditional spelling rules is eliminated. For example, the teacher could state the following spelling rule: "After the **sibilant** sounds /s/, /z/, /sh/, and /ch/, the plural form of a noun is spelled by adding -*es*." This rule would help students spell the word *wishes,* but students might be able to spell the word correctly without knowing the rule. Students could do so with phonemic awareness (the word ends in /ĕz/) supported by awareness of syntax (a plural form is needed), morphology (the word has two meaningful units—/wĭsh/ and /ĕz/), semantics (/ĕz/ means more than one), and orthographic knowledge (suffix /ĕz/ is spelled *es*). Therefore, careful instruction with all language structures is important to support spelling. Learning too many rules is burdensome. Many rules are superfluous when instruction with all language structures is provided. Only the rules that aid in the memory of words by drawing attention to visual features (e.g., doubled letters) need to be introduced. These visual features cannot be accessed through awareness of any other language structure or system and must be taught through spelling rules.

Irregular Words

Irregular words have unexpected spellings. A word may be irregular for one of two reasons: 1) its orthographic representation does not match its pronunciation (e.g., *should, enough, colonel*), or 2) it contains an infrequent orthographic representation of a speech sound (e.g., the spellings of the vowel sounds in *beach, train,* and *soap*; see Table 9.5).

Words whose orthographic representations do not match their pronunciations are usually also irregular for reading. Words with infrequent orthographic representations are usually regular for reading, but because they contain less frequent representations of sounds, they are classified for spelling as irregular. Different procedures can be used to establish irregular words in memory. Various mnemonic strategies help students learn words that contain less frequent patterns. A more structured and multisensory procedure (Cox, 1992; Fernald, 1943; Gillingham & Stillman, 1997) is needed to ensure the learning of some irregular words. Introducing irregular words should be kept to a minimum when working with students with dyslexia. They must establish a sense of the regular, reliable patterns of English before working extensively with irregular words.

Irregular Word Procedure

The following procedure uses visual, auditory, and kinesthetic input to assist in the permanent memorization of those words with truly atypical spellings. It is an involved but effective procedure that must be directed by the teacher. The efficacy of the procedure depends on students' naming the letters. This naming of letters as students trace or write is more effective than writing or copying words repeatedly because it focuses students' attention on the letter sequence in the word. The steps and rationale for each step follow:

1. *Circle the irregular part.* The teacher provides students with a large model of the irregular word on a sheet of paper. Students circle the part of the word that does not conform to the frequent, reliable patterns or rules. Analyzing the irregular part engages students in active reflection of the language. Circling the irregular part draws

their attention to the letter patterns in the word. Because many irregular words are from Anglo-Saxon or are borrowed from other languages, a discussion of **etymology** can provide insight into the unexpected spelling of the word (see Chapter 4 for a discussion of words from Anglo-Saxon, Latin, and Greek). Over time, students may begin to recognize patterns in irregular words (e.g., words from Anglo-Saxon are short, common, everyday words with the sound /f/ occasionally spelled as *gh* as in *enough* or *laugh*).

2. *Trace a model.* Students trace the model word three times, saying the word before they write and naming the letters as they write. Tracing the word while naming the letters provides the consummate multisensory experience. The students reinforce the letter sequence in the word through the visual, auditory, and kinesthetic modalities.

3. *Make copies.* Students make three copies of the word with the model in view, saying the word and naming the letters of the word as they write. This step extends the multisensory impressing of the letter sequence of the word in memory.

4. *Spell the word with eyes closed.* Students close their eyes and spell the word, imagining the word as they spell. They open their eyes and check the model. They close their eyes and spell the word two more times in this manner.

5. *Write from memory.* Students turn their papers over or fold them so that the model does not show. They write the word three times, saying the word before they write and naming the letters of the word as they write. Because students no longer have a model to rely on, they must call on their memory of the letter sequence of the word that was established through the multisensory input.

Other Procedures for Learning Irregular Words

Some irregular words do not require the intensity of the irregular word procedure just outlined. Instead, using exaggerated or spelling-based pronunciation builds a strong orthographic memory of these irregular words (Cox, 1992; Ehri, Wilce, & Taylor, 1987). Silent consonants often mark that a word will be irregular for spelling. When practicing irregular words, students may pronounce the silent *k* in words such as *knee, knife,* and *knock* or the silent *b* in words such as *comb, limb,* and *crumb* so that they will remember to write the silent *k* or *b* when they spell. Students might exaggerate the pronunciation of *i* as /ī/ in *fragile* so that they will remember to spell the word with an *e* at the end.

Schwa is not uniquely represented in English and therefore is difficult to spell. It is best managed by using the exaggerated or spelling-based pronunciation (e.g., students say /rĭbŏn/ instead of /rĭbŭn/) (Ehri et al., 1987). To remember the spellings of certain irregular words, students could use a mnemonic association: "There is *a rat* in se*parate*," "The *capitol* has a *dome*," or "The *principal* is your *pal*" (Moats, 1995). Students could group words in whimsical sentences as a mnemonic device to remember the infrequent spelling patterns that words share: "*Which rich* people have so *much* money and *such* big houses?" or "I am *ready* to s*pread* the *bread*" (Cox, 1992).

Spelling Homophones

Homophones are words that share the same pronunciation but differ in their orthographic representations (e.g., *plane/plain, to/too/two, red/read*). Published spelling series are notorious for presenting lists of homophones for students to learn. Students often find these words difficult to learn. The problem usually is not the spelling of homophones but rather their usage. Students are not sure when to use which spelling. To alleviate this confusion, homophones should not be introduced in pairs. Often, one word in a pair of homophones is regular for spelling (e.g., *plane*) and the other word is not (e.g., *plain*). Students first should be introduced to the homophone with the regular spelling. When students are secure with the spelling of that word and are clear about its usage, the other homophone can be introduced. If both homophones are irregular for spelling (e.g., *there, their*), then the word with the most frequent usage should be introduced first, followed by the other.

SPELLING LESSONS

This section discusses spelling lessons in therapeutic environments (one to one or small group) with students with dyslexia and spelling lessons in general classrooms. In any environment, it is important to remember that spelling is an interactive process that involves phonological and orthographic knowledge. Spelling instruction enhances this knowledge through synthetic and analytic teaching. Synthetic teaching (i.e., sounds to whole words) systematically builds awareness of sound–letter correspondences and provides a foundation for phonological knowledge and reinforcement of orthographic knowledge. Analytic teaching (i.e., whole words to sounds) builds awareness of letter patterns and provides the foundation for orthographic knowledge and reinforcement of phonological knowledge. Effective lesson planning employs both teaching strategies to provide opportunities for students to develop both phonological and orthographic knowledge. Appendix B at the end of this book lists programs for spelling and resources for planning spelling lessons.

Spelling Lessons for Students with Dyslexia

Teaching students with dyslexia to spell is a long, tedious process that requires careful lesson planning. The teacher must plan for success because success builds confidence and confidence builds independence. Students with dyslexia need spelling instruction that is closely integrated with reading instruction. Because of the exacting demands of spelling on complete and accurate recall of letter patterns, students with dyslexia need to spell words with sounds and patterns that have previously been introduced for reading and practiced. Reading words before spelling them heightens students' awareness of orthographic patterns. The number and choices of activities for a spelling lesson will depend on the readiness and needs of the student or students. The teacher will want to plan a rotation of activities that ensures that all areas of spelling are covered regularly. The teacher also will want to discuss the meanings and usages of spelling words to ensure that all of the different layers of language structure are covered in a lesson.

Spelling instruction must be designed to address phonological processing because it is the primary deficit of students with dyslexia. Without phonemic awareness, students with dyslexia will not be able to develop facility in reading or spelling. Initially, spelling instruction for students with dyslexia should build phonemic awareness. Students should engage in activities that require segmenting words into sounds. As students prepare to spell words, they need to engage in activities that heighten the recognition or discrimination of specific sounds, such as listening for a specific sound in a word or listening for the position of a specific sound in a word. After letter–sound correspondences have been introduced for reading, they can be introduced for spelling. These spelling associations are reviewed daily using a sound or spelling deck. Students spell words and derivatives with regular spellings using these sounds. Students can use the S.O.S. procedure when spelling words. New spelling patterns or rules are introduced as needed. As described in previous sections, multisensory structured guided discovery teaching is used to introduce the new pattern or rule.

When students are ready, the lesson plan is extended. Students begin dictation practice, first with phrases and then with sentences. High-frequency irregular words can be introduced as needed, and students can use the irregular word procedure discussed previously. Analyzing and sorting activities focus students' attention on letter patterns in words, reinforce letter–sound correspondences, and help students generalize patterns and rules. Students can analyze and sort words written on individual index cards by sounds or letter patterns. As they gain greater knowledge of letter patterns, they may analyze and sort words as regular words, rule words, or irregular words. Students can compile a spelling notebook in which they record information about spelling. The notebooks could contain a section for spelling patterns, with one page for each speech sound (see Figure 9.5). The reliable patterns for each sound are delineated on the pages. Students write words that follow each pattern as well as exceptions to the patterns on each page as the sound and spelling(s) are taught. Students may also have a section for rule words, with one page for each rule, and a section for irregular words, with one page for each letter of the alphabet so that irregular words can be recorded on the pages by first letter. Students may record information in their spelling notebooks once a week during a spelling lesson. On other days, students may simply read information from the notebooks as a means of reviewing spelling information.

Initial Lesson Plan for Spelling

1. Phonological awareness activities

   The teacher chooses one or two of the following activities:

   - Students repeat words dictated by the teacher and listen for a specific sound.
   - Students repeat words dictated by the teacher and identify the position of a specific sound.
   - Students repeat and segment words dictated by the teacher.
   - Students repeat words dictated by the teacher and change a sound in a word as designated by the teacher to create a new word.

2. Sound dictation

   - The teacher dictates the sounds one at a time.
   - Students echo the sounds, then name and write the letter or letters that spell each sound. (A mirror is available for students who are unable to discriminate the sounds.)
   - The teacher cues students with a key word if they cannot remember the spelling.
   - The teacher varies the media for the response daily (e.g., unlined paper, chalkboard, desktop).

3. Word dictation

   - Before students spell words, the teacher reviews the patterns or rules that are germane to the practice session.

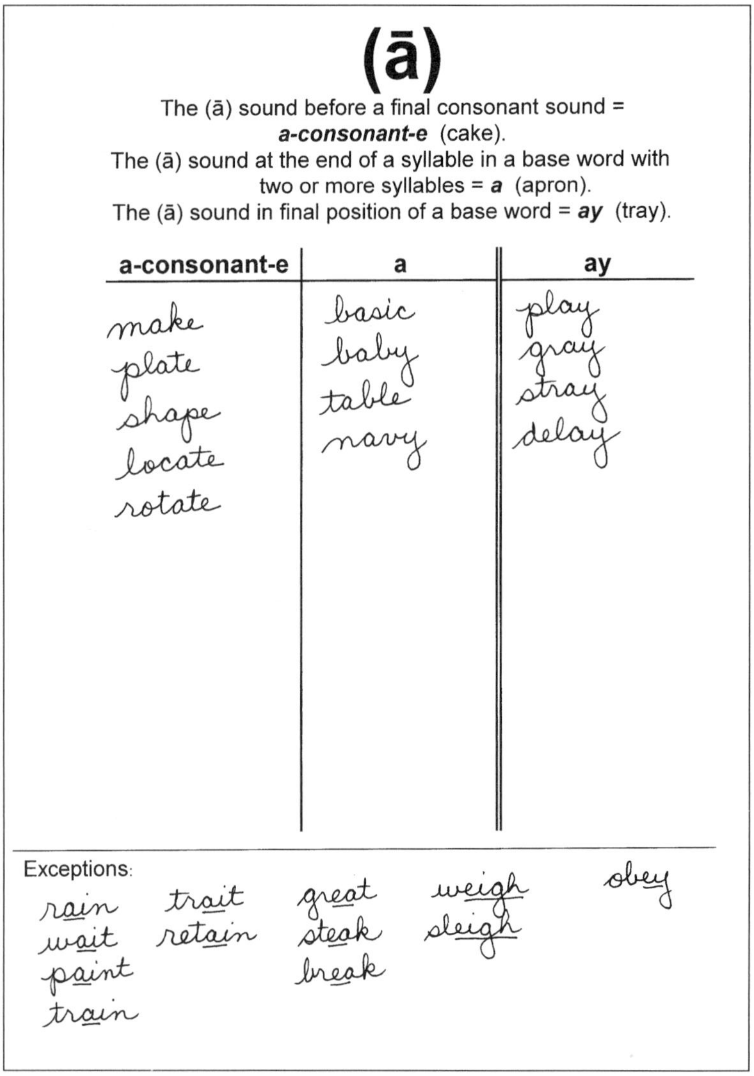

(ā)

The (ā) sound before a final consonant sound =
a-consonant-e (cake).
The (ā) sound at the end of a syllable in a base word with
two or more syllables = ***a*** (apron).
The (ā) sound in final position of a base word = ***ay*** (tray).

a-consonant-e	a	ay
make	basic	play
plate	baby	gray
shape	table	stray
locate	navy	delay
rotate		

Exceptions:

rain   trait   great   weigh   obey
wait   retain   steak   sleigh
paint   break
train

Figure 9.5. Spelling notebook page. This page reviews the most frequent spelling patterns of /ā/. The teacher dictates words that follow these patterns. Students write the words in the correct columns. Words with less frequent patterns that students find as they are reading are written at the bottom of the page. These words are not dictated. (From Carreker, S. [2002]. *Scientific spelling* [Rev. ed.; Student Notebook, p. 2]. Bellaire, TX: Neuhaus Education Center; reprinted by permission.)

- The teacher reviews the appropriate steps of S.O.S.
- The teacher dictates the words (as few as 3–4 and no more than 10–12) as students spell using S.O.S. The words should be homogeneous when students are practicing a new spelling concept and then heterogeneous when students demonstrate mastery of the concept. The teacher should be careful to plan a lesson rotation that includes the spelling of regular words on one day and the spelling of rule words on another day.
- The teacher provides immediate corrective feedback as needed.

4. Introduction of new spelling concept (synthetic teaching)

    • The teacher introduces a new spelling pattern or rule following a sequential, cumulative order that allows time for concepts to be practiced to mastery.
    • The teacher uses guided discovery teaching techniques.
    • After the new pattern or rule has been introduced, students apply the concept by spelling three to five words with the pattern or rule.

Extended Lesson Plan for Spelling

This extended lesson plan for spelling includes the four activities of the initial lesson plan plus three additional activities. The word dictation activity is expanded to include the dictation of phrases and simple sentences. This new lesson plan can be used after students have been introduced to 10–12 spelling patterns and the Floss Rule and are spelling words with these concepts with relative ease and accuracy.

1. Phonological awareness activities

2. Sound dictation

3. Word dictation and/or sentence dictation

4. Introduction of a new spelling concept (synthetic teaching)

5. Introduction of a high-frequency irregular word

6. Analyzing or sorting spelling words (analytic teaching)

7. Use of spelling notebook

Spelling Lessons for the Classroom

Spelling instruction that requires the copying of words or the memorization of lists is dull and uninspiring. Spelling instruction that engages students in active, reflective thought about language is exciting. The goal of spelling instruction is to teach the reliable patterns and rules of English for spelling, thereby creating enthusiasm for language. Effective spelling instruction provides students with meaningful lists of words they will use in their academic work.

Order of Presentation

The order of presentation of spelling concepts could follow the order of presentation of reading concepts (see Chapter 8 for order of presentation of reading concepts). Because of the demands of spelling, introducing spelling concepts will lag behind introducing reading concepts.

Weekly Lesson Plan

The following weekly lesson plan systematically teaches the patterns and rules of English for spelling and provides opportunities for students to generalize and apply this information. The plan allows for modification to meet the needs of students with dyslexia in the general classroom. These activities could also be incorporated into therapy lessons with students with dyslexia.

Monday (15 minutes)   A new spelling pattern (e.g., initial or medial /ou/ is spelled *ou*) or rule is introduced through multisensory guided discovery teaching. Students spell five to seven words with the new pattern or rule, using S.O.S. This synthetic teaching ensures that students are systematically learning information about the structure of language for spelling. The words that students practice on Monday become the first words of the weekly spelling list.

Tuesday (15–20 minutes)   The rest of the words for the weekly spelling list come from the content area (e.g., words from a map skills unit in social studies). The number of words presented depends on the ages or the needs of the students. Because the words are selected from the content area, students will need to know and use them. The need for and use of the words increases the likelihood that students will learn them. Arbitrary lists of words from published spelling series seldom present words commensurate with students' classwork.

Students must analyze the words on the weekly spelling list and decide whether the words are regular words, rule words, or irregular words. To be successful with analyzing, students must disengage what they have learned about decoding. It is true that they will be able to read a word such as *east,* but for spelling purposes, it is considered irregular because *ea* is not the most frequent spelling of /ē/ in initial or medial position of a one-syllable base word. Words such as *eel* or *street* follow the frequent, reliable patterns of the language and would be analyzed as regular words.

The Tuesday lesson provides analytic teaching that ensures that students will look carefully at words to notice how the words are spelled. It helps them generalize the patterns and rules students have learned. It engages students in active reflective thought about language. Students cannot decide the category of a word without thinking about all of the aspects of the word.

When students have finished analyzing and sorting the words, they have strategies for learning them. The regular words are spelled just the way the words sound and can be sounded out. The rule words can be sounded out, but students must remember there is a letter that must be doubled, dropped, or changed before the students write each word. Irregular words have unexpected spellings. The words cannot be sounded out and must be memorized (see Table 9.7). No more than three or four irregular words should be included in the Tuesday lesson.

The weekly spelling list is easily modified for students with dyslexia in the classroom. Rather than require these students to learn all of the words in the list, the teacher may ask them to be responsible for only the discovery words from the Monday lesson (e.g., all of the words with /ou/ that are spelled *ou*), or if students are ready, the teacher may ask them to be responsible for all of the regular words in the weekly list. Adding the daily use of a spelling deck and phonological awareness activities for these students creates a pattern of covering all areas of the spelling curriculum routinely and intensively.

Table 9.7.   Weekly spelling list with five discovery words from the Monday lesson and 10 words from content areas

Regular	Rule	Irregular
found	mapping	ocean
mouth		country
ouch		east
count		
shout		
north		
south		
west		
globe		
river[a]		
continent		

[a]Note that the inclusion of *river* shows an example of how *v* usually is not doubled in English.

Wednesday (15 minutes)   Students practice the irregular words that were sorted in the Tuesday lesson. Students decide the best way to learn them: using the irregular word procedure, a mnemonic device, or a spelling-based pronunciation. If time permits, students use the dictionary to determine why each word is irregular: 1) the words are from Anglo-Saxon; 2) the words are borrowed from another language; 3) the words are slang or an abbreviated form of a word; 4) the words are borrowed from a proper name; or 5) the words are spelled that way "just because," with no apparent reason listed in the dictionary.

Thursday (15 minutes)   The teacher uses the spelling words in various phonological awareness activities segmenting words into sounds, counting syllables, omitting syllables, and changing sounds in words. Students also practice words through word or sentence dictation.

Friday (15 minutes)   Throughout the week students have had the opportunity to analyze, play with, read, and write the spelling words. On Friday, students are tested on the words through word and/or sentence dictation.

Going Beyond Right and Wrong Spellings

Students' spelling errors provide teachers with insights as to the progress of students' understanding of the patterns of the language. Going beyond right and wrong gives teachers an idea of what students know and do not know (Joshi, 1995). As Joshi and Carreker stated,

> The dualist and finite assessment of spelling words as *right* or *wrong* is counter to the nature of spelling development and masks the predictable progression of spelling development. As previously mentioned, spelling proficiency unfolds in a gradual sequence. The progression of the sequence relies on specific underlying phonological and orthographic knowledge that is ultimately consolidated to form conventional spellings. (2009, p. 117)

In addition, scoring spelling words as right or wrong does not give students credit for the spelling patterns they have learned. For example, the spellings of *celebrate* as *selebrate* and *salaprat* are both incorrect and not acceptable as final representations. The student who spells *celebrate* as *selebrate,* however, has greater knowledge of spelling patterns than the student who spells *celebrate* as *salaprat.* Some acknowledgment should be given for what students know about spelling, and the types of spelling errors students make inform instructional decisions. In a study of preservice and in-service teachers, Carreker, Joshi, and Boulware-Gooden (2010) found that teachers with greater knowledge of language structures were better able to identify the underlying causes of student spelling errors and choose the most appropriate instructional activities.

Rubrics can be developed to evaluate students' spelling knowledge qualitatively. What sounds and spelling patterns have students remembered and used correctly even though the spellings are not perfect? Table 9.8 presents a sample rubric, with scores from 0 to 5. The teacher examines students' spelling errors on spelling tests or in daily written work and assigns a score to each word. The teacher looks at the preponderance of errors, determines the underlying difficulties that are causing students' spelling errors, and decides what instructional activities would remediate the difficulties.

For example, using the rubric presented in Table 9.8, a student who scores 0 on several words would benefit from additional training in phonemic awareness. Practicing words using tiles or blocks would help the student detect each individual sound in a word as he or she moves one tile or block for each sound in the word. The student

Table 9.8.   Sample rubric for qualitative evaluation of spelling errors

0 = *Not all sounds are represented* (*tk* or *thk* for *thick*)

1 = *All sounds are marked, but two or more letters are not reasonable representations of the sounds; or extra letters are added* (*tig* or *fek* for *thick*; *tickgt* or *thiegk* for *thick*)

2 = *All sounds are marked, but one letter is not a reasonable representation of a sound; no extra letters are added* (*tik* or *thek* for *thick*)

3 = *All sounds are marked with reasonable representations* (*thik* or *thic* for *thick*)

4 = *The spelling is almost conventional, but a letter is added or doubled* (*thicke* or *thickk* for *thick*)

5 = *Correct spelling*

can then progress to tiles with letters. A student with scores of 1 because of the extraneous addition of letters would also benefit from using letter tiles. Scores of 1 without additional letters or scores of 2 suggest that although the student perceives the individual speech sounds in words, he or she would benefit from activities that would help the student discriminate similar sounds, such as /ĕ/ and /ĭ/ or /f/ and /th/. Using a mirror would help the student see the differences in sounds as well as feel and hear the differences.

A student whose scores are mostly 3s is detecting individual sounds in words accurately and is spelling the words in a reasonable manner. This student would benefit from instruction in specific spelling patterns, such as final /k/ after a short vowel in a one-syllable base word is spelled *ck* as in *thick* and *back*. The student who scores a majority of 4s is aware of spelling patterns, but he or she is overgeneralizing the patterns. Having the student verbalize patterns would focus his or her attention on whether a pattern is needed in a particular word. Of course, scores of 5 mean that the student understands and can use knowledge of language structures to spell the words he or she needs: This is the goal of effective spelling instruction.

SUMMARY

Spelling serves as a foundation for reading; provides a means of communication; and, even if not rightly or fairly, is used by society to judge one's level of literacy and intelligence. Spelling is a valuable skill, yet it receives a modicum of attention and respect in schools. It has been reduced to mindless busywork or has been subjugated by the content in writing. Perhaps this has happened because of the misconception that English orthography is impossibly irregular and that there is no way to teach it or because of the perception that spelling is a rote, mechanical skill that does not promote cognition. The time has come to view spelling instruction in a different light.

The orthography of English is not hopeless (Kessler & Treiman, 2003). There are frequent, reliable patterns and rules that can be taught, which thus equips students with a system for managing the orthography of English for spelling. These patterns and rules are not taught through passive, rote memorization. Spelling instruction is deeply ensconced in a rich study of language structures and takes place in a manner that promotes active, reflective thought. Spelling instruction does not distract from the content of writing but rather enhances it by enabling students to choose the words that best express their thoughts instead of those words that are easy to spell. Effective spelling instruction is engaging, thought provoking, and exciting.

REFERENCES

Adams, M.J. (1990). *Beginning to read: Thinking and learning about print.* Cambridge, MA: The MIT Press.

Adams, M.J., Foorman, B.R., Lundberg, I., & Beeler, T. (1998). *Phonemic awareness in young children: A classroom curriculum.* Baltimore: Paul H. Brookes Publishing Co.

Bear, D.R., Invernizzi, M., Templeton, S., & Johnston, F. (1996). *Words their way: Word study for phonics, vocabulary, and spelling instruction.* Upper Saddle River, NJ: Prentice Hall.

Blachman, B.A., Ball, E.W., Black, R., & Tangel, D.M. (1994). Kindergarten teachers develop phoneme awareness in low-income, inner-city classrooms: Does it make a difference? *Reading and Writing: An Interdisciplinary Journal, 6*(1), 1–18.

Blachman, B.A., Ball, E.W., Black, R., & Tangel, D.M. (2000). *Road to the code: A phonological awareness program for young children.* Baltimore: Paul H. Brookes Publishing Co.

Bradley, L., & Bryant, P.E. (1983). Categorizing sounds and learning to read: A causal connection. *Nature, 303,* 419–421.

Brady, S., & Moats, L.C. (1997). *Informed instruction for reading success: Foundations for teacher preparation.* Baltimore: International Dyslexia Association.

Bryant, P.E., & Bradley, L. (1980). Why children sometimes write words which they do not read. In U. Frith (Ed.), *Cognitive processes in spelling* (pp. 355–370). London: Academic Press.

Bryant, P.E., Nunes, T., & Bindman, M. (1997). Children's understanding of the connection between grammar and spelling. In B. Blachman (Ed.), *Foundations of reading acquisition and dyslexia: Implications for early intervention* (pp. 219–240). Mahwah, NJ: Lawrence Erlbaum Associates.

Bryson, B. (1990). *The mother tongue and how it got that way.* New York: Avon Books.

Carreker, S. (2002). *Scientific spelling* (Rev. ed.). Bellaire, TX: Neuhaus Education Center.

Carreker, S., Joshi, R.M., & Boulware-Gooden, R. (2010). Spelling-related teacher knowledge and the impact of professional development on identifying appropriate instructional activities. *Learning Disabilities Quarterly, 33,* 148–158.

Cassar, M., & Treiman, R. (1997). The beginnings of orthographic knowledge: Children's knowledge of double letters in words. *Journal of Educational Psychology, 89*(4), 631–644.

Castle, J.M., Riach, J., & Nicholson, T. (1994). Getting off to a better start in reading and spelling: The effects of phonemic awareness instruction within a whole language program. *Journal of Educational Psychology, 86*(3), 350–359.

Cook, G.E., Farnum, M., Gabrielson, T., & Temple, C. (1998). *McGraw-Hill spelling.* New York: McGraw-Hill School Division.

Cox, A.R. (1977). *Situation spelling: Formulas and equations for spelling the sounds of spoken English.* Cambridge, MA: Educators Publishing Service.

Cox, A.R. (1992). *Foundations for literacy: Structures and techniques for multisensory teaching of basic written English language skills.* Cambridge, MA: Educators Publishing Service.

Ehri, L.C. (2000). Learning to read and learning to spell: Two sides of a coin. *Topics in Learning Disorders, 20,* 19–49.

Ehri, L.C., & Rosenthal, J. (2007). Spellings of words: A neglected facilitator of vocabulary learning. *Journal of Literacy Research, 39,* 389–409.

Ehri, L.C., Wilce, L.S., & Taylor, B.B. (1987). Children's categorization of short vowels in words and the influence of spelling. *Merrill-Palmer Quarterly, 33,* 393–421.

Fernald, G. (1943). *Remedial techniques in basic school subjects.* New York: McGraw-Hill.

Ferreiro, E., & Teberosky, A. (1982). *Literacy before schooling.* Portsmouth, NH: Heinemann.

Foorman, B.R. (1994). The relevance of a connectionist model for reading for "The Great Debate." *Educational Psychology Review, 6,* 25–47.

Frith, U. (1980). Unexpected spelling problems. In U. Frith (Ed.), *Cognitive processes in spelling* (pp. 495–515). London: Academic Press.

Frith, U., & Frith, C. (1980). Relationships between reading and spelling. In J.P. Kavanagh & R.L. Venezky (Eds.), *Orthography, reading, and dyslexia* (pp. 287–295). Baltimore: University Park Press.

Fulk, B.M., & Stormont-Spurgin, M. (1995). Spelling interventions for students with disabilities: A review. *Journal of Special Education, 28*(4), 488–513.

Gillingham, A., & Stillman, B.W. (1960). *Remedial training for children with specific disability in reading, spelling, and penmanship* (6th ed.). Cambridge, MA: Educators Publishing Service.

Gillingham, A., & Stillman, B.W. (1997). *The Gillingham manual: Remedial training for children with specific disability in reading, writing, and penmanship* (8th ed.). Cambridge, MA: Educators Publishing Service.

Goswami, U. (1988). Children's use of analogy in learning to spell. *British Journal of Developmental Psychology, 6,* 21–23.

Goswami, U., & Bryant, P. (1990). *Phonological skills and learning to read.* Mahwah, NJ: Lawrence Erlbaum Associates.

Hanna, P.R., Hanna, J.S., Hodges, R.E., & Rudorf, E.H. (1966). *Phoneme–grapheme correspondences as cues to spelling improvement.* Washington, DC: U.S. Government Printing Office.

Henry, M. (1988). Beyond phonics: Integrating decoding and spelling instruction based on word origin and structure. *Annals of Dyslexia, 38,* 259–277.

Henry, M.K. (2010). *Unlocking literacy: Effective decoding and spelling instruction* (2nd ed.). Baltimore: Paul H. Brookes Publishing Co.

Joshi, R.M. (1995). Assessing reading and spelling skills. *School Psychology Review, 24,* 361–375.

Joshi, R.M., & Carreker, S. (2009). Spelling: Development, assessment, and instruction. In G. Reid (Ed.), *Routledge companion to dyslexia* (pp. 113–125). London: Routledge.

Joshi, R.M., Treiman, R., Carreker, S., & Moats, L.C. (2008/2009). How words cast their spell: Spelling instruction focused on language, not memory, improves reading and writing. *American Educator, 32*(4), 6–16, 42–43.

Kessler, B., & Treiman, R. (2003). Is English spelling chaotic? Misconceptions concerning its irregularity. *Reading Psychology, 24,* 267–289.

Lennox, C., & Siegel, L.S. (1996). The development of phonological rules and visual strategies in average and poor spellers. *Journal of Experimental Child Psychology, 62,* 60–83.

Lennox, C., & Siegel, L.S. (1998). Phonological and orthographic processes in good and poor spellers. In C. Hulme & R.M. Joshi (Eds.), *Reading and spelling development and disorders* (pp. 395–404). Mahwah, NJ: Lawrence Erlbaum Associates.

Liberman, I.Y., Shankweiler, D., & Liberman, A.M. (1989). The alphabetic principle and learning to read. In D. Shankweiler & I.Y. Liberman (Eds.), *Phonology and reading disabilities: Solving the reading puzzle* (pp. 1–33). Ann Arbor: University of Michigan Press.

Lyon, G.R., Shaywitz, S.E., & Shaywitz, B.A. (2003). A definition of dyslexia. *Annals of Dyslexia, 53,* 1–14.

Moats, L.C. (1994). Assessment of spelling in learning disabilities research. In G.R. Lyon (Ed.), *Frames of reference for the assessment of learning disabilities: New views on measurement issues* (pp. 333–349). Baltimore: Paul H. Brookes Publishing Co.

Moats, L.C. (1995). *Spelling: Development, disabilities, and instruction.* Timonium, MD: York Press.

Moats, L.C. (1996). Phonological spelling errors in the writing of dyslexic adolescents. *Reading and Writing, 8*(1), 105–119.

Moats, L.C. (2005). *Spellography for teachers: How English spelling works (Language essentials for teachers of reading and spelling (LETRS), Module 3).* Longmont, CO: Sopris West Educational Services.

Moats, L.C. (2005/2006). How spelling supports reading: And why it is more regular and predictable than you may think. *American Educator, 29*(4), 12–22, 42–43.

Nation, K., & Hulme, C. (1998). The role of analogy in early spelling development. In C. Hulme

& R.M. Joshi (Eds.), *Reading and spelling development and disorders* (pp. 433–445). Mahwah, NJ: Lawrence Erlbaum Associates.

Oakland, T., Black, J.L., Stanford, G., Nussbaum, N., & Balise, R.R. (1998). An evaluation of the dyslexia training program: A multisensory method for promoting reading in students with reading disabilities. *Journal of Learning Disabilities, 31*(2), 140–147.

Pollo, T., Kessler, B., & Treiman, R. (2009). Statistical patterns in children's early writing. *Journal of Experimental Child Psychology, 104,* 410–426.

Post, Y.V., & Carreker, S. (2002). Orthographic similarities and phonological transparency in spelling. *Reading and Writing: An Interdisciplinary Journal, 15,* 317–340.

Post, Y.V., Carreker, S., & Holland, G. (2001). The spelling of final letter patterns: A comparison of instruction at the level of the phoneme and the rime. *Annals of Dyslexia, 51,* 121–146.

Read, C. (1971). Pre-school children's knowledge of English phonology. *Harvard Educational Review, 41*(1), 1–34.

Roberts, R., & Mather, N. (1997). Orthographic dyslexia: The neglected subtype. *Learning Disabilities Research and Practice, 12*(4), 236–250.

Rubin, H., & Eberhardt, N.C. (1996). Facilitating invented spelling through language analysis instruction: An integrated model. *Reading and Writing: An Interdisciplinary Journal, 8,* 27–43.

Scarborough, H.S., & Brady, S.A. (2002). Toward a common terminology for talking about speech and reading: A glossary of 'phon' words and some related terms. *Journal of Literacy Research, 34,* 299–336.

Seidenberg, M., & McClelland, J. (1989). A distributed developmental model of word recognition and naming. *Psychological Review, 96,* 523–568.

Share, D.L., & Stanovich, K.E. (1995). Cognitive processes in early reading development: Accommodating individual differences into a model of acquisition. *Issues in Education, 1*(1), 1–57.

Smith, P.T. (1980). Linguistic information in spelling. In U. Frith (Ed.), *Cognitive processes in spelling* (pp. 33–49). London: Academic Press.

Sterling, C., Farmer, M., Riddick, B., Morgan, S., & Matthews, C. (1998). Adult dyslexic writing. *Dyslexia: An International Journal of Research and Practice, 4*(1), 1–15.

Treiman, R. (1994). Use of consonant letter names in beginning spelling. *Developmental Psychology, 30*(4), 567–580.

Treiman, R. (1997). Spelling in normal children and dyslexia. In B. Blachman (Ed.), *Foundations of reading acquisition and dyslexia: Implications for early intervention* (pp. 191–218). Mahwah, NJ: Lawrence Erlbaum Associates.

Treiman, R. (1998). Beginning to spell in English. In C. Hulme & R.M. Joshi (Eds.), *Reading and spelling development and disorders.* Mahwah, NJ: Lawrence Erlbaum Associates.

Treiman, R., Cassar, M., & Zukowski, A. (1994). What types of linguistic information do children use in spelling? The case of flaps. *Child Development, 65,* 1318–1337.

Treiman, R., Zukowski, A., & Richmond-Welty, D.A. (1995). What happened to the "n" in sink? Children's spelling of final consonant clusters. *Cognition, 55,* 1–38.

Venezky, R.L. (1980). From Webster to rice to Roosevelt. In U. Frith (Ed.), *Cognitive processes in spelling* (pp. 9–30). London: Academic Press.

West, T.G. (1991). *In the mind's eye.* Buffalo, NY: Prometheus Books.

10

Fluency in Learning to Read

Conceptions, Misconceptions, Learning Disabilities, and Instructional Moves

KATHERINE GARNETT

This chapter traces the evolving concept of reading fluency, considering it from many angles. What is it? How does it affect reading comprehension? What instructional practices develop it? And, what are the outcomes of fluency intervention for students with reading/learning disabilities at different ages? The investigation of these questions draws on cognitive psychology, research and practice, and two major studies of reading fluency among fourth graders nationwide, also offering case studies, instructional pointers, and cautions. This rich grounding is meant to inform instruction, especially crucial instruction for students with significant reading/learning disabilities. The chapter aims to contribute to teachers' serious and skilled work in preventing reading problems, strengthening early reading interventions and addressing advanced fluency-related skills that are critical to proceeding beyond basic reading.

WHAT IS FLUENCY?

Fluency is a critical facet of complex skill development. Reading—like playing the piano, driving a car, or juggling—is a complex skill made of myriad subskills that require much practice to "come naturally." Early stages of piano playing, driving, juggling—and reading—are jerky, slow, and uncoordinated, characterized by inaccuracies and great effort. With practice, clusters of subskills become accurate. As practice proceeds *beyond accuracy*, performance commences to "flow," an indicator that some lower level skills are no longer consuming the mind's conscious attention. This *freeing* of attention allows the emergent musician, driver, juggler, or reader to redeploy attention to other subskills. On the way to becoming fluent, focal attention is literally commandeered by lower level subskills, so little is available for coordination, flow, or higher level processing (LaBerge & Samuels, 1974; Topping, 2006).

Fluent skills are marked by many subskills sinking below awareness—we can simply perform the subskills as needed while our attention focuses on orchestrating their interplay (e.g., braking, steering, gear-shifting, checking in all directions). Most people forget how much time, effort, and repeated experience it took to develop fluent driving (or reading)—and, relatedly, how it felt along the way—because now it just seems natural. Actually, though, to reach just a basic level of fluent skill takes enormous effort and prodigious practice. Getting beyond basic levels demands effortful attention to new subskills, with yet more practice integrating these into more complex performance. As performance becomes more adept at basic and then more advanced skill levels, initial subskills become even speedier and more efficient—they become overpracticed, even faster, or increasingly automatized, which results in more fluent overall performance of the complex skill. So, fluency is not achieved at one point in time but increases with practice over a long span.

The Complex Skill of Reading

Students in the early stages of learning to read cannot modulate tone, tempo, or phrasing; their reading is loud, labored, lurching, and largely monotone because they are expending all available attention on lower level subskills involved in letter, letter–pattern, and word recognition (LaBerge & Samuels, 1974). As word skills become well practiced, they no longer hijack attention, so attention can be deployed to phrasing, tempo, meaning (especially unpredicted meaning), and self-monitoring. That is why smooth, expressive reading—a kind of orchestrating—is virtually impossible below a threshold of basic reading skill. The same holds true for noticing and repairing breakdowns, a central role of self-monitoring; this, too, requires a sufficiently skilled foundation. Self-monitoring, or executive attention, draws on limited mental resources—the mind cannot attend everywhere at once. When commandeered at the word level, attentional resources are unavailable for much else.

With instruction and practice, most students become reliably accurate with a repertoire of word skills; with more practice, most students' skills become more efficient and attention free—that is, students reach a fluent level of basic reading. Some students, on the other hand, require more directed instruction, more intense focus, and more practice to become accurate at the word level; they also need yet more support and practice to become fluent. These very same students tend to read little, if at all; so, while they need more, they get less.

The foregoing concepts have shaped a computational estimate of reading fluency: word accuracy plus reading rate, commonly assessed by the student reading aloud a calibrated passage and the teacher then calculating the number of words read correctly per minute (WCPM).

$$\text{accuracy} + \text{rate} = \text{reading fluency}$$

It is important to remember that fluency is not the endgame; it is a facet, an often overlooked facet, of reading and learning to read. Fluency interacts with word meanings, sentence sense, background experiences, and more; myriad cognitive-linguistic players perform in concert to produce a full orchestration—skilled proficient reading.

Of course, with both music and reading, there are stages of proficiency, from dit-ties to Carnegie Hall—from learning-to-read basics (pre-K to third-grade level), to reading-to-learn consolidation (level of Grades 4–8), to traveling the many branches of the human mind (ninth-grade level to college), to the pursuit of knowledge and plea-sure through written language over a lifetime. Progress along these stages of proficiency involves ongoing accuracy-to-fluency of subskills, always propelled by prodigious prac-tice—lots of reading. Figure 10.1 captures the process of gaining basic reading accuracy to fluency, with a concomitant sense of how the learner feels. As you review this, pause to consider the toll on students with reading/learning disabilities, whose efforts result in little progress month by month and even year by year.

Early Fluency Notions and Current Constructs

While the historical roots of reading fluency (i.e., oral reading, reading rate) stretch to the turn of the prior century (see Rasinski, 2006), reading fluency's modern debut was sponsored by LaBerge and Samuels' (1974) article on automaticity. They proposed that slow, labored, word-by-word reading is symptomatic of a reader's lack of word auto-maticity, reflecting the fact that the mind's limited focal attention is all consumed by processing the written words (or word parts). This is in stark contrast to skilled readers, who process written words largely without conscious attention. The instructional im-plication was clear and groundbreaking: ensure practice well *beyond accuracy*. In other words, make certain that students practice enough to be automatic at word recogni-tion so that attention—that fast-flitting narrow window of consciousness—is freed up for other duties.

The term *fluency* migrated from speech-language pathology and refers to a dimen-sion of spoken language—the flow of sounds, syllables, words, or phrases—which, when impaired, results in slow, blocked, or choppy speech, as in stuttering or cluttering. Be-cause the term came to be applied to reading around the time of LaBerge and Samuels' (1974) influential article, the two terms—fluency and automaticity—have been used somewhat interchangeably. But, as research and conceptualizing have proceeded, flu-ency has emerged as the broader concept, subsuming the idea of automaticity of sub-skills. Current definitions include notions of reading rate, word accuracy and automaticity, phrasing, and positive effects on reading comprehension:

Effortful accuracy → Reliable accuracy → Word automaticity → Basic reading fluency (decoded and sight words)

Labored focus on accuracy	Some reliable accuracy	Automatic with many words
Word by word	Accurate but labored	Flow
Slow processing	Picking up speed	Increasing rate and flexible
Tiring "work"	Some phrasing	Phrasing and expressiveness
Halting, choppy, tone	Mixed choppiness/prosody	Monitors sense—breakdown → repair
Effortful → little progress	Effortful → progress	Sense of effortlessness
Feeling of incompetence	Feeling of work = growth	Feeling of competence (at basic level)

Figure 10.1. Basic reading fluency: The look, the sound, the feel.

- Increases in reading rate and ease of reading, resulting from automaticity of word-level processes (Samuels, 2006)

- Rapidity, smoothness, effortlessness, with little conscious attention to mechanics (Meyer & Felton, 1999)

- The bridge between low-level skills involved in learning-to-read and high-level skills required for reading-to-learn (Chall, 1983; Pearson & Johnson, 1978)

- A critical dimension of learning-to-read, linking word recognition and comprehension, and affecting/intertwining with reading comprehension (Chard, Vaughn, & Tyler, 2002; Kuhn & Stahl, 2000)

- Related to accuracy and rate, but not synonymous with them; characterized by phrasing, natural flow of speech, with intonation, stress, and pauses related to author's syntax; meaningful expressiveness (National Assessment of Educational Progress [NAEP], 2002)

- One of the five pillars of reading (along with phonemic awareness, decoding, vocabulary, and comprehension); rapid accurate reading of **continuous text** with appropriate expression, requiring well-developed word-recognition skills (National Institute of Child Health and Human Development [NICHD], 2000)

- A unique and fundamental component of skilled, proficient reading with close links to comprehension and motivation; ability to read "like you speak," with reasonable accuracy, at a rate appropriate to the task, and with suitable expression (Hasbrouck, 2010)

- Fluent reading is accurate, conversational, flows, is not easily distracted, generalizes across texts, and is maintained over long periods (Torgesen & Hudson, 2006)

- A multidimensional concept related to reading rapidly and modulating the flow of connected text with appropriate prosody (phrasing, stress, juncture, and intonation) (Dowhower, 1987; Rasinski & Lenhart, 2007)

Common across these definitions is a broader conceptualization of reading fluency that incorporates degrees of comprehension as well as phrasing and expressiveness (see Figure 10.2). Other interesting elements offered in a few of these definitions are flexibility or modulation of rate, motivation, and durability over time (like riding a bicycle, reading skill stays with you).

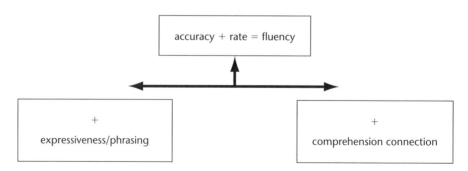

Figure 10.2.   Conceptualization of reading fluency.

EXPRESSIVENESS AND THE COMPREHENSION CONNECTION

An emphasis on expressiveness, or prosody, is understandable given that fluency is measured by sampling *oral* reading which, unlike silent reading, reveals accuracy, speed, and also phrasing and prosody. But there remains controversy over *the role* of prosody (Rasinski, 2004; Torgesen & Hudson, 2006). While expressiveness obviously helps listeners being read to, it is not clear whether it actually facilitates *readers'* understanding or whether it merely reflects that understanding. Furthermore, for some readers and under some circumstance, flowing reading and prosody may actually be a smokescreen of superficial contours, covering the reader's significant *lack* of comprehension. Given such variation in the functioning of oral reading expressiveness, it is crucial neither to assume understanding from flowing expressive reading nor to presume noncomprehension from lackluster oral reading. There are far more potent indicators of reading comprehension (i.e., having students paraphrase, retell, summarize, compare, provide examples, predict, and both answer and formulate questions), all important instructional means to routinely employ in pursuit of comprehension.

Instructionally, it is crucial to underscore that the goal of fluency building is not speeding up per se, but greater understanding—practicing beyond accuracy to become stronger readers. Students need to hear this message regularly so they don't slide into minimizing, or jettisoning, comprehension as they pursue increasing speed with word and phrase drills and in repeated passage reading. It is important to cue students frequently about the purpose of fluency practice—which is to build mental muscles for stronger and more flexible reading *so they understand and recall more* of what they read.

There is, in fact, strong evidence that increased fluency is related to improved comprehension and recall (NAEP, 1992, 2002). In other words, practice that increases fluency positively affects reading comprehension, whether that practice is simply lots and lots of reading or whether it involves specific fluency interventions like word drills, phrase reading, repeated reading of passages, and/or monitoring progress by speed/accuracy charting (NICHD, 2000).

Why? Why should greater fluency (WCPM) improve reading comprehension? How can we understand this influence? First, increased WCPM supports working memory. Slow, word-by-word reading makes it hard for the mind to hold onto what was just read and also process the next chunk. Reading faster and in chunks (phrasing) helps working memory keep track of the connected threads. Second, fluent reading frees attention so the reader can focus on a train of thought, switch to a momentary complexity or, of particular importance, notice a breakdown in sense-making and reread to repair it. When attention is tethered to processing many words slowly and with effort, the mind gets mired and cannot shift quickly or strategically. So, increasing word automaticity, phrasing, and overall reading rate reduces the cognitive work of processing written language. This lightening of the load allows the reader to pause and enjoy, ponder, and interact with the mind of the author. Those with inadequate word automaticity and slow reading find the act of reading laborious, stressful, and truly tiring.

CAN FLUENCY BE DISTINCT AND SEPARATED FROM COMPREHENSION?

Although comprehension is generally enhanced as readers gain fluency, it is worth noting that fluency is a distinct facet of reading that is separable from comprehension, as in the following examples.

- My mother could read the Russian newspaper *Известия (Isvestia)* accurately, and with expression, but she barely understood what she read because her vocabulary in the language of her parents had reached an early plateau.

- **Hyperlexics** read at a very young age with great accuracy and flow, but without comprehension.

- Anyone can detach from the meaning of what he or she is reading under various conditions (e.g., when performing a cold reading before an audience, under high anxiety, when word-decoding skills outstrip a person's lexicon or mental store of word meanings).

Some might say that these counterexamples should be considered pseudofluency because degrees of comprehension are implicit in reading, but that view is worthy of stopping to consider. Fluency—one of several fundamental components of proficient reading—like phonological skill, can and does develop and operate on its own; it also can, and usually does, interact with other linguistic processes that relate to meaning making—semantics and morphology. Reading accuracy and increasing speed are cognitively distinct, or compartmentalized, from comprehension, even though most of the time for most people, they develop in tandem and work in concert.

The fact that meaning *can be* detached from fluent reading has very practical implications, reminding teachers to emphasize meaning making and to actively promote students' *monitoring* of meaning. Whether the mind detaches from meaning or adheres to it is influenced by what teachers say or neglect to say—how teachers frame practice, point to purposes, and respond when students stumble over confusing text. Maintaining meaning awareness is important in all reading-related instruction—having students aim at understanding, dig for it, notice when it derails, and engage actively in dialogue with the author on the page. It is all too easy for many students to "sound like they are reading" and "seem to be fluent" while they are only minimally processing what they read. When teachers don't notice this disconnect, it is reinforced and, over years, can become a debilitating habitual way of approaching reading.

HOW BIG A PROBLEM IS LACK OF FLUENCY?

Lack of fluency is a widespread problem, impeding progress for many students, just at a critical point when their schooling requires new skills to build on a firm foundation (NAEP, 1992, 2002). Slow and labored reading compromises comprehension, especially when students move into denser material requiring that they read and reread to learn. Starting in about fourth grade, students must deploy their mental resources in many directions, such as processing unfamiliar concepts and sentence complexities, following a line of argument, comparing one idea with another, interpreting a metaphor, amassing subject-specific vocabulary, and noticing when the mind derails and is no longer making sense of what's on the page (Nathan & Stanovich, 1991).

Two national initiatives have raised awareness of fluency as a major dimension of reading and as a serious area of need for many students:

1. The NAEP, also known as the Nation's Report Card, undertook two fourth-grade oral reading substudies (NAEP, 1992, 2002).

2. The National Reading Panel (NRP) was convened by Congress to report on the state of reading research and practice. The panel gave prominence to fluency by listing it as one of five major aspects of reading (NICHD, 2000).

National Assessment of Educational Progress

The NAEP (1992) oral reading substudy found that many fourth-grade students across the country had not developed fluent reading on easy fourth-grade material. This large-scale study characterized fluency instruction in schools as the crucial—and neglected—bridge from the basics to broader and more complex reading. NAEP's (2002) subsequent oral reading investigation revealed that the problem had not gone away 10 years later. Results of these two major studies uncovered lack of fluent reading in approximately 40% of fourth-grade students. Thus, at this major demarcation in schools' reading demands, the famed fourth-grade slump (Chall & Jacobs, 1983, 2003), a large number of students are ill-equipped for the oncoming escalation in reading volume and complexity (see Figure 10.3).

National Reading Panel

The NRP reviewed research and practice, framing its report (NICHD, 2000) in terms of five major components of reading and reading instruction: phonemic awareness, decoding, fluency, vocabulary, and comprehension. The panel gave distinction to fluency as one of the top five facets, precipitating long-needed attention from publishers, researchers, teacher educators, and schools.

The NRP reviewed fluency intervention studies that included practices such as repeated reading, paired and assisted reading, radio reading, and neurological impress. They concluded that these variations of guided, repeated, oral reading significantly boosted fluency, word recognition, and comprehension across a range of elementary grades. These findings form the foundation for the panel's strong advocacy of fluency-building practices

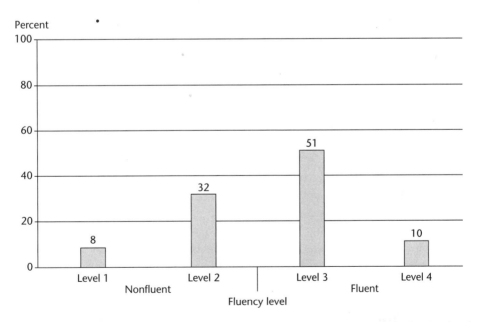

Figure 10.3.   Percentage of fourth-grade students by National Association of Educational Progress (NAEP) oral reading fluency scale level. (*Note:* These results were not from an unpracticed cold reading; students' oral reading was evaluated only after several prior readings of the same fourth-grade passage.) (From U.S. Department of Education, Institute of Education Sciences, National Center for Education Statistics, National Assessment of Educational Progress [NAEP], 2002 Oral Reading Study. Retrieved from http://nces.ed.gov/nationsreportcard/studies/ors/; reprinted by permission.)

throughout the elementary years—and for older students with reading levels in the first-through sixth-grade range.

FLUENCY AND READING/LEARNING DISABILITIES

Children with reading/learning disabilities have difficulty with word-reading accuracy and with the linguistic processes that underlie it—sublexical, phonological, and phonemic skills (Blachman, Tangel, Ball, Black, & McGraw, 1999; O'Connor & Jenkins, 1999). Many of these children also have difficulty accelerating words that they read accurately to faster and less effortful levels. They also are slow on tasks reflecting linguistic processes that underlie this automaticity (e.g., certain "naming" tasks, specifically rapid automatic naming and rapid alternating naming) (Denckla & Rudel, 1976; Wolf, 2001). One or both of the bedrock components in all conceptualizations of fluency—word accuracy and automaticity—are problem areas for most students with reading/learning disabilities. Furthermore, such students display these problems before they start learning to read on nonreading tasks reflecting underlying linguistic weaknesses, sublexical phonemic skills, and automatizing of rapid oral language processes.

Children with reading/learning disabilities have inordinate difficulty developing a basic fund of reading words, associating regularities of common spelling patterns (orthography) with the oral counterparts (phonology), and generalizing such correspondences to new words (Torgesen & Hudson, 2006). Because word recognition, both sight words and decoding, is so hard for them, intervention emphasizes securing accurate word reading through explicit teaching of word analogies and word-part skills (e.g., letter–sound associations, onset-rime, beginning-medial-ending sequencing, sound segmenting and blending, syllable or orthographic patterns). For those with reading scores between the 10th and 25th percentiles, such systematic word work solidly sets their foundation, so their reading is under way. Students at or below the 10th percentile require more to secure basic word recognition, develop phrase reading, and navigate sentence contours; they need more fluency building.

The Good News

Students with a range of reading disabilities who do not establish foundation skills by the end of second or third grade can develop accurate word recognition later and can increase reading accuracy and fluency when provided appropriate intervention that is focused on both areas (Torgesen, Rashotte, Alexander, Alexander, & MacPhee, 2003).

The Bad News

Students who get effective intervention later (after third grade) do not catch up in terms of reading fluency. With intervention, they get close to their grade peers in terms of accuracy, but fluency, even though it improves over time, remains way behind peers' and represents a significant reading impediment (Pressley, Gaskins, & Fingeret, 2006; Torgesen et al., 2003).

The Interesting News

Under the proper teaching conditions, even students at the lower reading percentiles can reach a threshold of reading accuracy and fluency by the end of second or third grade. And *then,* going forward, they remain on par with their peers in accuracy, fluency, and comprehension (Torgesen et al., 2003)! In other words, it is possible to short-circuit the usual year-by-year widening gap between average readers and those with reading disabilities when the "catch-up" occurs within the window of the early school years (Grades 1–3). Over several carefully designed intervention studies, Torgesen and his colleagues delineated the necessary conditions for such effective early reading intervention: sufficient direct focus on word-level accuracy (phonemic skill and orthographic correspondences), systematic sequencing of instructional elements, sufficiently intensive practice of skills, and sufficiently prolonged intervention for students with the severest needs (those at the 10th percentile and below).

This evidence highlights how crucial it is to intervene in the early school years, providing sufficient intensity to have an early effect. Clearly, some students need more than others—more focus, more substeps, more frequent practice, and more support—to propel across a basic reading threshold. When schools undertake this within the early window of opportunity, students reap lifelong benefits.

Longstanding evidence (Reitsma, 1983a, 1983b) reveals a striking difference in the number of practice repetitions different children require to reach a reliable level of word reading accuracy (with basic words whose meaning is already familiar). These startling differences should activate all teachers to differentiate the intensity and frequency of practice to meet students' differing needs:

- Four to fourteen repetitions for average young readers

- More than 40 repetitions for those with reading difficulties (Reitsma, 1983a; 1983b)

Young children who gain just enough skill early on feel drawn to reading, so they readily engage in simple, repetitious practice reading that consolidates the interconnections of their reading mind. They read a lot of easy redundant things because they can. They love it because they can do it. In contrast, those who cannot, do not.

Those students not reading in the first 3 years of schooling are denied the powerful inner voice of confidence: "I am a reader, smart and capable." An alternate inner narrative commences by second grade, as the nonreader attempts to make sense of why "I can't." As important, such students miss out on all that repetitious, imprinting of seemingly simple skills that confident readers practice week-by-week over 3 years. Torgesen and Hudson (2006) estimated that to catch up in fluency, students with reading disabilities not reaching reading-level parity by the third grade would have to read massively more (at their lower reading level) than their peers read over several years! This underscores how crucial it can be to intervene effectively early on.

Torgesen and Hudson's (2006) findings that youngsters with serious reading disabilities can *stay* caught up when provided what they need in the primary years, should fuel all educators' urgency about early intervention. These authors' evidence-based suggestions are concrete, doable, and effective:

1. Screen early for reading difficulties (phonemic skills, underlying naming speed, and attention to early progress).

2. Follow up with intervention that directly focuses on word-level accuracy (phonemic skill and orthographic correspondences), systematic sequencing of instructional elements, and frequent instruction/practice over a sufficient period.

3. Teach through the full cycle: from word accuracy to rapid word recognition and phrased connected text, repeating the cycle with new words, word patterns, word groups, and other linguistic elements.

4. Concurrently, teach attention to meaning (i.e., early comprehending habits of mind; see Pressley et al., 2006).

5. Intensify intervention for those below the 25th percentile.

6. Intensify and increase duration of intervention for those below the 10th percentile.

How Does Fluency Develop?

Educators often consider fluency building appropriate at a certain stage of reading in-struction—after word skills and before comprehension—undertaken when students are reading on a second- to fourth-grade level. While not entirely wrong, this perspective seems an inadequate way to think about fluency. The view was probably fostered by Samuels' (1979) influential work on repeated reading, a procedure that requires stu-dents to read practice passages at least at a basic reading level. As we have come to understand though, students need fluency-related practice both well before and long after that stage. Developing fluency involves ensuring that subskills, from the earliest to the most advanced, progress from accuracy, through practice beyond accuracy, to ready retrieval or automaticity.

Developmental Viewpoint

Wolf and Katzir-Cohen (2001) proposed that fluency is a developmental linguistic pro-cess, originating well before learning to read, proceeding through early reading, and extending to sophisticated linguistic complexities in high school and beyond. This com-prehensive developmental view is a significant shift, with profound implications for practice:

- We must not wait to work on fluency until students acquire basic reading (from sec-ond to fourth grade levels). Instead, fluency building needs to be an aspect of our work on early reading subskills (e.g., letter names, sounds, blending, pattern recog-nition, word recognition)—first establishing accuracy, then practicing beyond ac-curacy and increasing speed so these become automatized.

- We are not finished with fluency after the second- through fourth-grade reading lev-els. Instead, it is important to identify critical linguistic complexities, teach them, practice them sufficiently, and integrate these new subskills into fluency at higher levels of reading (Berninger, Abbott, Billingsly, & Nagy, 2001).

Do Teachers Work on Fluency at the Earliest Reading Levels?

Rarely do teachers appreciate how critical fluency work is during early reading instruc-tion. Early subskills require lots of (fun) practice to become not only accurate but in-creasingly rapid and eventually effortless. Unfortunately, reading instruction often gallops on while foundational skills are still unsteady, outstripping the learner whose word skills are neither fully accurate nor even close to effortless.

Do Teachers Work with More Advanced Readers on Linguistic Complexities?

Unfortunately, schooling rarely treats advanced linguistic complexities as the skills they are. Rather, these are commonly addressed in the English language arts curriculum as elements to learn *about*, rather than skills to be clarified and practiced from accuracy to fluency. For students with reading/learning disabilities, these advanced subskills are often major blockages to developing fluency and reading comprehension at higher levels (Nagy, 2006; Nagy, Berninger, & Abbott, 2006). It is important to note, however, that these complexities are not necessarily hard to master. While they often require instructional attention and practice, they can be learned.

What Are "Linguistic Complexities" and How Do You Teach Them?

A variety of linguistic complexities crop up in reading material starting at a fourth-grade level, causing most students to stumble. Where many falter, those with reading disabilities frequently fall. Teachers—not only English, but science, math, social studies, and special education teachers—can make a critical difference by anticipating such unfamiliar linguistic elements, such as complex terms, unfamiliar phrases, confusing sentence constructions, **transition words,** and discourse devices. Common stumbling spots include multisyllable words (especially morphological transformations), idiomatic expressions, complex sentence contours (especially reversals), cross-sentence signals (e.g., anaphora), within-sentence signal words (or functors), and discourse signals that point the reader toward the author's next move (see Table 10.1). Teachers are often perplexed about how to teach these, commonly resorting to unplanned and intermittent explanations, as though a bit of explaining would yield understanding, accuracy, and then an effortless new skill. While explaining alone is wholly inadequate, teaching these complexities need not be arduous or even very time consuming. In fact, it can be quite straightforward, repaying with huge dividends. What is required is 1) *clarifying, amplifying,* and *practicing* within a potent (and brief) routine and 2) the commitment to *engage* that routine regularly. See the 5-minute routine in Table 10.2 for teaching those text complexities that so often confuse students from fourth grade onward.

Related suggestions include, from the text or class readings, preplan one complexity per lesson (or one per lesson, reviewing that same one in the follow-up lesson). Get in the habit of including such a routine—do not discontinue after a few trials. Once established, you will be able to engage the routine spontaneously as complex elements crop up in readings. Keep track of the complexities you teach so the class (or a subgroup) can circle back and review/repractice them. Examples of tracking include a wall flipchart, class binder, or 3" × 5" card box. In addition, you can have students also keep the complexities in their notebook. Through regular routines and tracking, these linguistic complexities become part of classroom discourse, with focused and efficient teaching that yields effective student learning.

METHODS AND MEANS FOR BUILDING FLUENCY

In this section, instructional methods that have been mentioned throughout this chapter are further detailed. It is important to realize that these remain simply samples. As skilled teachers become alert to the importance of focusing on subskill accuracy and following up with engaging and frequent practice for fluency, they can draw on these or make up their own methods to get there. The various practices are grouped by whether they focus at the word level, focus at the phrase level, or make use of passage reading, also referred to as *continuous text*.

Word Work

As Torgesen (as cited in Hasbrouck, 2010) said, "There is no comprehension strategy that compensates for difficulty reading words accurately and fluently." The implication

Table 10.1.   Examples and notes for a selection of complexities to help propel the more advanced instruction that many weak readers urgently need

Linguistic complexity	Examples	Notes
Sentence forms		
Appositives	The camel, a desert animal, can go for miles without drinking.	Sentence (i.e., thought) complexities are a great human pleasure when one can follow where they lead. For example, "There stood a personage only slightly taller than themselves, but whom they knew at once to be the Great Ta because of a certain unmistakable kingliness about him" (Cameron, 1954, p. 100).
Lists	I won't go unless you clean up your room, get into clean clothes, and find out where little Sue has gone.	
Reversed	Even though you have bad breath, I love you.	
Cohesive ties		
Backward reference (anaphora)	Dorothy and Toto tip-toed out. *They* worried about every step. *This* made *them* tremble something terrible.	Cohesive ties are certain types of words or clauses that tie together ideas within and between sentences.
Forward reference (cataphora)	Perhaps I shouldn't tell you *this*, but it was unzipped all evening.	When the words seem easy, but the reader stumbles, consider whether there is an unfamiliar sentence form or cross-sentence tie that needs teaching and practicing (using multiple examples).
Ellipsis (words omitted, assumes the mind fills in)	The cat [that was] hit yesterday by that car has disappeared.	Cohesive ties are an important aspect of teaching English as a second language.
Cohesive ties		
Introductory	Once upon a time; two important ideas animate; it was the best of times	These cohesive ties are also known as *functors, signal words, noncontent words,* and *connectors.* They operate *within* sentences, as well as *across* sentence boundaries, and also serve as major markers pointing to where the author is going (discourse signals).
Causals	So, because, thus, as a result of, consequently, therefore, furthermore	Mastering these for reading (as well as writing) is important, especially as they are employed extensively in content-area (information) reading.
Reversals	However, nevertheless, even though, although, in spite of, despite, notwithstanding	
Concluding	In conclusion, to summarize, to conclude, in sum	*Writing idea:* A cue card with these signal words grouped by type can trigger their use by older students and make the students' essays sophisticated.
Sequentials	First, second; at the start, by the end; initially, subsequently; to begin with, in conclusion; primarily, secondarily	

Note: "Written language is not just spoken language written down" (Nagy, 2006).

is to take instruction *beyond accuracy* at every step—at the letter, word-part, word, and phrase level. Fluency builds over time, picking up momentum from many sources. When securing letter–sound associations, make sure that these connections are accurate, stable, and then so well-practiced that they feel easy. When working on a word set, or word card stack, focus first on accuracy, then practice to read the stack in less time,

Table 10.2.   Five-Minute Multiple Example Routine

Introduction (30 seconds)

Pluck the complexity (word, phrase, sentence, device) out of its context and present it visibly and vividly for all to focus on. Read it aloud—let the students *hear* it. Acknowledge this as a complicated word, phrase, sentence, or discourse signal. (*Caution:* Do not ask questions.)

Clarify (60 seconds)

Offer a second example of the complexity, one you made up using content closer to the students' frame of reference. Read this one aloud; be sure students take it in. Talk through (or have students join you in talking through) the meaning or purpose—how the complexity works. Then once more, read aloud the initial example from their text so they can *hear* the resonance between the two.

Amplify and practice (90 seconds)

Share a third close-to-home example that you created, again by reading it aloud. Help students make connections. Follow with two or three *more* examples, reading each aloud. (If students show readiness, they can read aloud.) Talk together about how the complexity works. Ask two students, one after the other, to read the initial example and then one of the others, for all to hear yet again.

Amplify (30 seconds)

Suggest or solicit a mascot name for this complexity to make it easier to identify, recall, and talk about (e.g., "butt-ins" for appositives) and use this name going forward. Then, call on students to read the clearest example and to explain in their own words how it works.

Practice (60 seconds)

Have all students read all sentences (preferably more than once). This can be accomplished in any of several fun ways, such as a muttering free-for-all for 30 seconds, partners reading the examples to one another, or a student "conductor" calling on groups of three to read three examples in unison.

Extension (30 seconds)

Seek students' own examples in class, as an exit ticket, or for homework. Be sure to capture all their high-quality examples (with the author's name appended) and add them to the list of examples.

Note: Timings are only suggested but indicate what to aim for in a "brief" routine.

while motivating progress by charting it. Or, conversely, increase the number of WCPM (chart *that*) through practice toward even higher targets. This fluency work adds up over days, weeks, and months, fueling increasingly fluent reading at ever higher levels (see Table 10.3).

There are levels of word reading skill from basic to advanced but, in some sense, word skills are never really complete. Advanced word work (multisyllabic, morphological, etymological) stretches beyond fourth grade, seventh grade, high school, and college. Like with musical proficiency, there are gradations of reading proficiency, with learners attaining varying heights (or depths), as well as varying skill across different genres. For students with reading/learning disabilities, the kind of carefully structured and sequenced word work that anchors their basic reading can also benefit them at higher levels. Said another way, these students commonly need explicit and well-practiced instruction at higher levels.

Hiebert and Fisher (2005) offered a strong case for focusing on morphologically related word sets as a powerful approach to advanced word work. Teaching and practicing words with their morphological siblings creates networks in the reading mind, organizing these by salient aspects of word structure.

Many students require more interconnection between morphological variants (e.g., *comment* and *commentator, sign* and *signature,* and *kindle, rekindle, kindling*). The mind needs to congregate these related words, rather than have them dispersed to all corners of the mental lexicon. It is important that schooling beyond third grade

Table 10.3. Reading: A complex cognitive-linguistic skill set

Level	Broad stage	Accuracy to fluency: Skill by skill
Kindergarten to third grade	Foundation building Long runway Lift off Steep initial climb Early aerodynamics Practice reading is required	Sublexical skills (e.g., letter recognition, sound blending/segmenting, sound–symbol association) Orthographic regularities (spelling patterns) Word recognition: reliable to automatized Simple morphological affixes and derivations Phrasing, expressiveness, breakdown to repair Simple grammar/familiar content Fund of reliably recognized words
Fourth grade: Shift in reading demands	Confident and fluent reader Pilot-in-training permit = Handling and flying maneuvers Extended excursions Unfamiliar destinations Reading regularly is required	Many words recognized at sight Many multisyllabic words read readily Morphological variation (*congress, congressional*) Increased sentence complexity and length Vocabulary (meaning) expansion Increased understanding of idiomatic expressions Passage complexity (cohesive ties) Increasingly unfamiliar content
Seventh grade: Shift in reading demands	Well-developed reader Provisional pilot license A lot of regular reading is required	Many words recognized at sight Morphological sophistication (*ambulance, ambulatory, perambulator*) Content-area sentence complexities Vocabulary expansion and elaboration Increased conceptual load Complex discourse structures Text that is dense with information

repeatedly return to these so that students' repertoires expand while their morphological awareness gets sharpened. This is not merely about studying prefixes, suffixes, roots, and word permutations but about *seeing and hearing* the relatedness among these linguistic siblings, understanding and storing them in a mental network, and then using them appropriately. Morphological variants are not to learn *about*; they represent critical word-linking skills to master for increasing proficiency. Students with weaknesses in underlying linguistic processes need particular help making these linkages. And, like many skills, while not all that hard to learn, they do need to be *taught*.

How do you teach these? Straightforward and simple: through a well-practiced, brief, and frequent *routine*. First, teach the concept (or idea) of morphological word sets (mates, siblings, or cousins) and then ensure practice. Word sets can come from a novel being read in class, subject-matter vocabulary, or common sight words in the process of being learned. The following is a sample instructional routine meant to take 15–20 minutes to set up the first time and from 5 to 10 minutes thereafter. There is good reason to weave such a regular focus into many subject areas across the years from third to twelfth grade—such a brief, frequent routine on morphological connections can have a profound cumulative effect.

Routine for Morphological Awareness and Skill

Teach it:

- Provide several sets of easy examples (e.g., *happy, unhappy, happiness, happily; warm, warmer, warmest, warmth*). Read these to the students. With them, come up with a conceptual name for these kinds of related words (e.g., "morph mates"). *Note*: Don't quiz students during this intro teaching time.

- Provide several more complex examples appropriate to students' age and stage (e.g., *manage, manager, management; sign, signing, signer, signature, signatory*). Again, read these aloud for all. Do not ask students for illustrative sentences—*provide* these. You can also make **semantic maps** with a core word in the center and variants at the ends of the spokes, along with an easy-to-grasp sentence for each morph to make clear how it is used.

Practice it:

- Make drill cards, with a core word on Side 1 (e.g., *amble*) and with morphological variants on Side 2 (e.g., *ambling, ambled, ambulate, ambulance*). On separate cards, provide multiple, helpful sentences with each of the morphological variants (one sentence per card), such as *"The cowboy and his girl were ambling along the path, acting like they had all the time in the world." "After my car accident, ambulating around the apartment was torturous."*

- Create activities (whole class, subgroups, partners) that involve practicing the linking of the core word (Side 1) with the variants (Side 2) and with illustrative sentences with the variants. Be sure students read both the words and the sentences *aloud*—in a sense, they are training their reading "ear" to increase sensitivity to these word structures. Have students match the variant sentences with the core word (Side 1).

  Note: this morphological work is useful for both early readers (*sit, sitting, sat; wonder, wondering, wonderful*) and for advanced readers with morph mates from fiction, as well as subject areas (*virulent, viral, virus; sign, signer, signature, signifying*).

Phrase Work

Once early readers have a store of reliable words, it is worthwhile to focus on phrasing (Rasinski, 2006). Practice connector words (e.g., *the, and, of, in, at, up, but, over, out*) not on their own but rather in common phrases. Phrase work can propel students who are clinging to accurate but very plodding habits to let the words flow as they focus on the phrase. Here are several useful ways bear down at the phrase level:

- Practice reading phrase cards (e.g., *in a pot, up the hill, into the water, he is coming, she is going, we are waiting*).

- Make large phrase cards; hold them up, one at a time, each for 3 seconds. Have students read them (when they are out of sight) from short-term memory.

- Find appropriate practice sentences and passages. Have students practice "scooping" by penciling a "scoop line" beneath phrases. They can also scoop phrases using the eraser (fewer marked-up pages).

- Find or create phrased cued text: Thomas Alva Edison/ invented many things/ that are still in use/ today.// He had/ good ideas.// When Edison had ideas,/ he worked on them.// He would try/ many things.//

Continuous Text

Rereading continuous text is a time-honored practice. We reread deep texts to absorb lifelong nourishment; we reread favorite pieces that repay us with memories, joy, tears, and laughter; we reread to make better sense of a proposition, a metaphor, or a line of argument; we reread in the process of studying to better remember; we reread when we stumble on a complexity that leaves us confused; and we reread in our early reading career as an unconscious means of gaining fluency (see Figure 10.4). A prominent method for rereading, developed specifically to increase the fluency of struggling readers, goes under the name of *repeated reading*.

Repeated Reading

Repeated reading is a simple but powerful set of fluency-building procedures first developed by Samuels (1979). Research has confirmed that repeated reading is effective and has delineated particular procedures that can make it more so.

Meyer and Felton (1999) reviewed repeated reading studies and concluded that the method increases reading speed for a wide variety of readers. From their findings, they recommended that instruction:

- Engage students in multiple readings (three to four times) in short, but frequent, fluency practice sessions.

- Make use of instructional-level text (or decodable text with struggling readers).

- Include concrete measures of progress for all sessions.

- Provide differentiated teacher support (e.g., modeling and practicing words between instructional sessions for students with weak skills).

Chard et al. (2002) highlighted research findings from studies of repeated reading that they considered particularly useful for students with reading/learning disabilities:

- Work on phrasing as part of repeated reading to promote automaticity.

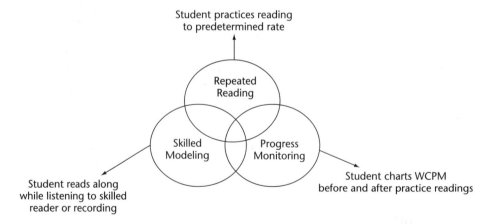

Figure 10.4.   The schematic shows the main interrelated ingredients that are common to many effective fluency-building methods with continuous text. (*Key:* WCPM, words read correctly per minute.)

- Include a skilled model since that enhances the comprehension effects of repeated reading (e.g., live modeling as well as recordings and computer).

- Alert students to stay connected to comprehension, to notice when it breaks down, and to activate repair strategies.

Note: More procedures from effective repeated reading programs are detailed in the appendixes at the end of this chapter.

Repeated Reading Controversy

Controversy continues over whether passages used for repeated reading should be challenging, moderately challenging, or easy. The "right" answer may depend on the age and other characteristics of the learner and the specific level of reading skills. Differing views also persist about how valuable skilled model reading is as part of repeated reading intervention. Some adult modeling is clearly effective, but how much yields what level of benefit is not yet clear.

Other Fluency Methods with Continuous Text

While repeated reading is the most well-known fluency intervention that engages students in rereading continuous text, other methodologies and programs have emerged, employing continuous text and incorporating effective and efficient rereading techniques. Some are "old-time" practices that predate concepts of reading fluency (e.g., **choral reading**); others grew out of early special education traditions of "precision teaching" (e.g., Great Leaps); and still others have emerged from educators' seeking to motivate struggling readers (e.g., **reader's theatre**).

Reader's Theatre   Reader's theatre has a considerable reputation as a real-world reason to reread—the imperative to rehearse in preparation for performance. Reader's theatre has interesting aspects that can spur fluency and be a serious motivator for reading and rereading. It makes use of performance scripts and a rehearsal process but does not culminate in a full-scale production. Students, commonly rehearse sitting on stools with music stands to hold their scripts. They perform in that same format, without costumes, sets, or interactive movement. The teacher/director orchestrates rehearsals (rereadings), urging fluency and expression. Often, readers are taught to scan their line, look up, and then deliver it—a practice that promotes seeing/reading in phrases. An interesting twist is reading *lines* sequentially, rather assigning character *parts* to particular students. In this mode, each reader delivers a line, with the next reading the next line, and so forth down the row of readers on their stools. Not being assigned parts requires that everyone perform with the expression of the character, even though characters' lines are spoken by various readers.

Details and variations of both repeated reading and reader's theatre can be found on the Internet, which offers multiple resources and video demonstrations.

Neurological Impress Method (Plus)   Neurological impress method (NIM) was originally developed by Heckleman (1969) and was the focus of two studies with struggling readers in third through sixth grades that found improvement in fluency and comprehension scores (Flood, Lapp, & Fisher, 2005). The researchers added ("plus") a brief comprehension connection at the end of the original method.

NIM (Plus) is to be used 10 minutes per day, 4 days per week, for 5 or more weeks. General guidelines are as follows:

1. Use instructional-level text (or student selected).

2. Sit next to and slightly behind the student and read into his or her ear (side of handedness).

3. Slide finger along text during reading; student rests finger on top of teacher's finger.

4. Read the text aloud together, with the teacher setting the pace and modeling skilled expressiveness (phrasing, intonation, pauses). The student's voice trails just behind the teacher's.

5. Gradually release the lead to the student, lowering volume and letting the student's pace overtake the teacher's.

6. Gradually have the student take over the finger tracking accompanying the reading.

7. *Plus*: After reading, have the student retell the text. Also, talk together about aspects of interest or confusion (prior knowledge connections, high points, humor, unfamiliar vocabulary).

Notes on NIM (Plus) include the following:

*   The focus of NIM (Plus) is on fluency and making the voice match the print, so do not correct, teach, or question as you go through the passage.

*   The purpose of the extra step is to maintain the comprehension connection, have a brief enjoyable chat, and provide any needed clarification.

*   Keep sessions short and fun, no longer than 10 minutes, and acknowledge the student's good work.

Variations on Choral Reading   NIM (Plus) is a variant of choral reading (reading in concert); other variations include whole-class choral reading, call and response (**echo reading**), and paired and buddy reading. These variants hold promise for building fluency when done at the appropriate stage of students' reading development. The research to date has been positive (NRP, 2002), so these remain valuable adjuncts to a multidimensional reading program or intervention.

Great Leaps   The Great Leaps reading program (Campbell, 1996) consists of 1-minute timings that make use of three stimuli: phonics, sight phrases, and reading short stories. This is a highly motivating, daily 5- to 10-minute intervention that can be carried out by trained nonteachers. Performance is charted so both students and teachers see and evaluate progress. The program has several levels from elementary to high school, with the K–2 version providing a phonological awareness component (Mercer & Campbell, 1998). Study results showed growth in overall reading as well as increased reading rate for middle school students with reading/learning disabilities (Mercer, Campbell, Miller, Mercer, & Lane, 2000).

The Art and Science of Fluency Practice

Fluency work is not a matter of seat-work practicing. It involves teaching (cuing, modeling, explaining, coaching, encouraging, correcting), accompanied by supported and properly framed interactive practice. In the interplay between clear and explicit teaching and interactive, progressive practice, we need also to engage students' understanding of what the fluency work is all about and gain their informed partnership.

The characteristics of practice text matters; not just any reading material facilitates reading fluency (Hiebert & Fisher, 2005; NICHD, 2000). Elfrieda Hiebert has built a powerful case about the effects of text characteristics in facilitating or hindering learning to read and developing reading fluency (http://textproject.org). Hiebert has amassed evidence that most students who are learning to read require material that is engineered for redundancy. She specifically recommends repeated practice with the 930 most frequent words (see the Zeno list on her text project web site), as well as practice with words whose graphophonic patterns are most consistent and most common. The nature of the practice material for developing a reading foundation, most especially, the words—their high frequency and their redundancy—can, and does, make a huge difference in whether and how well many children read.

Active Practice (Drill)

Drill, another name for active practice, is highly motivating and highly effective, especially when done interactively, with progress charted regularly. Focused interactive practice enables subskills to increase in speed and decrease in focal attention, keys to fluent reading. Many classrooms routinely ignore the basics of effective practice, from drill to distributed practice, intermittent review, and cumulative practice. Drill is often demonized, rather than appreciated for its motivating efficiency at providing needed practice. Many students suffer from insufficient securing of skills—lack of sufficient practice. Clearly, students with reading/learning disabilities are among those needing to be well-taught—and then to

Practice enough
on the right stuff,
in the right portion size,
with teacher modeling, guidance, and corrections,
with visible feedback from tracking progress,
while keeping the mind attuned to sense.

How to Self-Monitor for Sense

When targeting speed, prompt the mind to be guided by sense. Share information with students about how all minds get derailed, distracted, or off track and how we all bring our minds back into focus. Self-monitoring is a kind of self-message, triggered by noticing when the mind has derailed. Developing self-monitoring requires considerably more than pep talks or regularly reminding students. Using self-cuing message cards is far more effective in developing self-monitoring habits. By pointing, tapping, or simply winking, teachers can turn students' attention in the direction of the cue card. Effective cuing messages are frequently formulated as self-questions because these slip into the mind as the start of an inner dialogue. When such an external cue is close up and personal, students start to trigger the habit themselves, shifting their eyes to the card independently and, eventually, shifting their mind's eye (see Figure 10.5 and Table 10.4).

CONCLUSION

We do not want students to be fluent; we want them to be active, interacting, sense-seeking readers with accurate, automatic word-recognition skills and fluency to spare. Unfortunately, fluency has been largely neglected in classrooms, which has hobbled many readers. Fluency building needs considerably greater play in the teaching of reading overall and in interventions for students with intensive needs. On the other hand, a common misconception is that fluency work is all about reading faster, fostering with a hurry-up, rush-rush mentality that can throw meaning to the winds. There is much more to developing fluency. There is art, science, and subtlety to the complex skill of teaching students to read. This teaching and learning is both straightforward simple and mind-boggling complex and, with practice, eminently doable.

Figure 10.5. A self-monitoring cue card (3″ x 5″ folded tent on student's desk) can nudge the young reader's mind to be guided by sense.

Table 10.4.   Teacher take-aways about fluency in learning to read

Do not assume. *Find out* the fluency level of your struggling readers. Nonfluent reading is an impairment you can do something about.

Do not trade off speed for accuracy or comprehension; keep the minds tuned to sense.

Practice is an art, a science, and a pleasure that depends on teacher skill. Seeing the fruits of practice and charting student progress is powerful motivation.

Consider making full use of short, intense, and frequent teach-it/practice-it sessions (10 minutes, 3–5 times per week, 5 minutes two times per day).

Caution: Students are different: many respond to speed work with alerted attention and focused effort; others become anxious. Take care with those who become distressed when they feel speed pressure; find ways to reduce that burden.

REFERENCES

Allington, R.L. (2006). Fluency: Still waiting after all these years. In. S. Samuels & A. Farstrup (Eds.), *What research has to say about fluency instruction* (pp. 94–105). Newark, DE: International Reading Association.

Arnbak, E., & Elbro, C. (2000). The effects of morphological awareness training on the reading and spelling skills of young dyslexics. *Scandinavian Journal of Educational Research, 44*(3), 229–251.

Berninger, V.W., Abbott, R.D., Billingsly, F., & Nagy, W. (2001). Processes underlying timing and fluency of reading: Efficiency, automaticity, coordination, and morphological awareness. In M. Wolf (Ed.), *Time, fluency, and dyslexia.* Timonium, MD: York Press.

Blachman, B.A., Tangel, D.M., Ball, E.W., Black, R.S., & McGraw, C. (1999). Developing phonological awareness and word recognition skills: A two-year intervention with low-income, inner-city children. *Reading and Writing: An Interdisciplinary Journal, 11,* 239–273.

Cameron, E. (1954). *The wonderful flight to the mushroom planet.* New York: Little, Brown and Company

Campbell, K. (1996). *Great Leaps reading program.* Gainesville, FL: Diarmuid.

Chall, J. (1983). *Stages of reading development.* New York: McGraw-Hill.

Chall, J.S., & Jacobs, V.A. (1983). Writing and reading in the elementary grades: Developmental trends among low-SES children. *Language Arts, 60*(5), 617–626.

Chall, J.S., & Jacobs, V.A. (2003, Spring). The classic study on poor children's fourth-grade slump. *American Educator.* Retrieved Oct. 24, 2007, from http://www.aft.org/pubs-reports/american _educator/spring2003/chall.html

Chard, D.J., Vaughn, S., & Tyler, B. (2002). A synthesis of research on effective interventions for building fluency with elementary students with learning disabilities. *Journal of Learning Disabilities, 35,* 386–406.

Denckla, M.B., & Rudel, R.G. (1976). Rapid automatized naming (R.A.N.): Dyslexia differentiated from other learning disabilities. *Neuropsychology, 14,* 471–479.

Deno, S.L., & Marston, D. (2006). Curriculum-based measurement of oral reading: An indicator of growth in fluency. In. S. Samuels & A. Farstrup (Eds.), *What research has to say about fluency instruction* (pp. 179–203). Newark, DE: International Reading Association.

Dowhower, S.L. (1987). Effects of repeated reading on second-grade transitional reader's fluency and comprehension. *Reading Research Quarterly, 22,* 389–406.

Flood, J., Lapp, D., & Fisher, D. (2005). Neurological impress method plus. *Reading Psychology, 26*(2), 147–160.

Good, R.H., Simmons, D.S., Kame'enui, E.J., Kaminski, R.A., & Wallin, J. (2002). *Summary of decision rules for intensive, strategic, and benchmark instructional recommendations in kindergarten through third grade* (Technical Report No. 11). Eugene: University of Oregon.

Hasbrouck, J. (2010). *Developing fluent readers white paper.* St. Paul, MN: Read Naturally.

Hasbrouck, J., & Tindal, G.A. (2006). Oral reading fluency norms: A valuable assessment tool for reading teachers. *The Reading Teacher, 59*(7), 636–644.

Heckelman, R.G. (1969). A neurological impress method of remedial reading instruction. *Academic Therapy, 5*(4), 277–282.

Hiebert, E.H., & Fisher, C.W. (2005). A review of the National Reading Panel's studies on fluency: On the role of text. *Elementary School Journal, 105,* 443–460.

Kuhn, M.R., & Stahl, S.A. (2000). *Fluency: A review of developmental and remedial practices* (CIERA Rep. No. 2-008). Ann Arbor, MI: Center for the Improvement of Early Reading Achievement.

LaBerge, D., & Samuels, J. (1974). Towards a theory of automatic information processing in reading. *Cognitive Psychology, 6,* 293–323.

Mercer, C.D., & Campbell, K.U. (1998). *Great Leaps reading K–2 edition.* Gainesville, FL: Diarmuid.

Mercer, C.D., Campbell, K.U., Miller, M.D., Mercer, K.D., & Lane, H.B. (2000). Effects of a reading fluency intervention for middle schoolers with specific learning disabilities. *Learning Disability Research and Practice, 15*(4), 179–189.

Meyer, M.S., & Felton, R.H. (1999). Repeated reading to enhance fluency: Old approaches and new directions. *Annals of Dyslexia, 49,* 283–306.

Nagy, W. (2006). *Morphological contributions to literacy.* Presentation at the New York Branch of the International Dyslexia Association.

Nagy, W., Berninger, V., & Abbott, R. (2006). Contributions of morphology beyond phonology to literacy outcomes of upper elementary and middle school students. *Journal of Educational Psychology, 98,* 134–147.

Nathan, R.G., & Stanovich, K.E. (1991). The causes and consequences of differences in reading fluency. *Theory Into Practice, 30*(3), 176–184.

National Association of Educational Progress (NAEP). (1992). *NAEP oral reading sub study.* Retrieved from http://nces.ed.gov/nationsreportcard /studies/ors/

National Association of Educational Progress (NAEP). (2002). *Nation's report card.* Retrieved from http://nces.ed.gov/pubsearch/getpubcats .asp?sid=031#

National Institute of Child Health and Human Development. (2000). *Report of the National Reading Panel: Reports of the subgroups. Teaching children to read: An evidence-based assessment of the scientific research literature on reading and its implications for reading instruction* (NIH Publication No. 00-4754). Washington, DC: Government Printing Office.

National Reading Panel (NRP). (2000). *Teaching children to read.* Retrieved from http://www. nationalreadingpanel.org/publications/citation _examples.htm

O'Connor, R.E., & Jenkins, J.R. (1999). The prediction of reading disabilities in kindergarten and first grade. *Scientific Studies of Reading, 3,* 159–197.

Partnership for Reading. (2001). *Developing early literacy: Report of the national early literacy panel.* http://www.nifl.gov/

Pearson, P.D., & Johnson, D.D. (1978). *Teaching reading comprehension.* Austin, TX: Holt, Rinehart & Winston.

Pressley, M., Gaskins, I.W., & Fingeret, L. (2006). Instruction and development of reading fluency in struggling readers. In S. Samuels & A. Farstrup (Eds.), *What research has to say about fluency instruction* (pp. 47–69). Newark, DE: International Reading Association.

Rasinski, T.V. (2004). *Assessing reading fluency.* Honolulu, HI: Pacific Resources for Education and Learning.

Rasinski, T.V. (2006). A brief history of reading fluency. In S. Samuels & A. Farstrup (Eds.), *What research has to say about fluency instruction* (pp. 4–23). Newark, DE: International Reading Association.

Rasinski, T., & Lenhart, L. (2007). *Explorations of fluent readers.* Newark, DE: International Reading Association.

Reitsma, P. (1983a). Printed word learning in beginning readers. *Journal of Experimental Child Psychology, 36,* 321–339.

Reitsma, P. (1983b). Word-specific knowledge in beginning reading. *Journal of Research in Reading, 6,* 41–56.

Samuels, S.J. (1979). The method of repeated readings. *The Reading Teacher, 32,* 403–408.

Samuels, S.J. (2006). Toward a model of reading fluency. In S. Samuels & A. Farstrup (Eds.), *What research has to say about fluency instruction* (pp. 24–46). Newark, DE: International Reading Association.

Topping, K.J. (2006). Building reading fluency: Cognitive, behavioral and socioemotional factors and the role of peer mediated learning. In S.J. Samuels & A. Farstrup (Eds.), *What research has to say about fluency instruction* (pp. 24–46). Newark, DE: International Reading Association.

Torgesen, J.K., & Hudson, R. (2006). Reading fluency: Critical issues for struggling readers. In S.J. Samuels & A. Farstrup (Eds.), *Reading fluency: The forgotten dimension of reading success* (pp. 130–158). Newark, DE: International Reading Association Monograph of the British Journal of Educational Psychology.

Torgesen, J.K., Rashotte, C.A., Alexander, A., Alexander, J., & MacPhee, K. (2003). Progress towards understanding the instructional conditions necessary for remediating reading difficulties in older children. In B. Foorman (Ed.), *Preventing and remediating reading difficulties: Bringing science to scale* (pp. 275–298). Timonium, MD: York Press.

Wolf, M. (Ed.). (2001). *Time, fluency, and dyslexia.* Timonium, MD: York Press.

Wolf, M., & Katzir-Cohen, T. (2001). Reading fluency and its interventions. *Scientific Studies of Reading, 5,* 211–239.

APPENDIX 10.1

Case Studies

The following section has four case studies that portray different manifestations of difficulties with fluency. Consider two questions as you read each case study.

1. What do you now understand about this student's problems and needs?

2. What should a skilled teacher do to be most effective with this student?

Read each case and create appropriate plans to ensure increased fluency for each individual.

ANDY

At age 8, Andy could read 13 words, knew many letter names, and knew the sounds of many consonants but no vowels. He could spell five words and print his letters in a scrawl that was either sprawling or cramped. In other words, Andy was a nonreader and nonwriter at the start of third grade. From age 8 to 10, he worked intensively with a skilled tutor, after which he scored at a mid–third-grade level on most measures, but remember, Andy was in fifth grade by now. Happily, he could now read and spell hundreds of words—those that incorporated the orthographic regularities he had been taught (both one- and two-syllable words with digraphs, diphthongs, and most vowel teams), along with a reliable stockpile of 30–40 sight words.

Teaching Andy had been carefully engineered using word elements, patterns, and sequences; multiple examples, learning routines, extensive practice, systematic mixing of each new word pattern into ongoing cumulative review, and practice in phonetically controlled continuous text readers. This work had to be meticulous because Andy had demonstrated that he did not learn reading or writing under less structured, less carefully sequenced, or less intense conditions—understandably so, since he was from a long line of severe dyslexics (grandfather, father, and two older siblings).

Andy was well taught from ages 8 to 10 and had learned what he had been taught directly, systematically, and with sufficient practice. Andy's reading, although now reliably accurate, was plodding, jerky, slow, and largely effortful. Word speed, phrasing, and fluent reading at each step had not been emphasized in his intensively engineered teaching. Unfortunately, neglecting fluency is common; teachers often *proceed* once their students display accurate reading of a set of words or word patterns, failing to shift instructional gears and increase practice *beyond accuracy* to propel students from accuracy to fluency. And some students, such as Andy, require intense teaching efforts and repetitions to make this critical shift.

GEOFFREY

Geoffrey, a wiry 11-year-old, scored mid–second grade on reading measures when he entered our after-school tutoring lab. He was a wild guesser and self-deprecating, full of "No, no, wait…" His early schooling had emphasized rereading leveled trade books of children's literature that schools consider motivating, with the stunning result that near the end of second grade, Geoffrey's teachers found out that could read several books from memory without recognizing their constituent words in any other context. He was referred for special education services.

Geoffrey and his tutor began their work by building his word-recognition foundation: letter sounds (especially vowels), blending, segmenting, word analogies, and syllable patterns. Geoffrey loved the daily word-card practice and charting his increasing
speed. Then, his tutor introduced phrase and sentence practice, which resulted in a totally unexpected slowdown. This slowdown was fascinatingly the opposite of many
other kids, whose reading gets more fluent in context with the support of phrase structure and the flow of sense. Instead, Geoffrey experienced a slowdown when words came
together in the continuous flow of text. When he tried speeding up, he became wildly
inaccurate.

PAULINE

Pauline had experienced reading difficulties all her life but never got special support.
She slid into college on her sheer intelligence and self-developed compensations.
Pauline described herself as a speedy reader who dared not slow down for fear of losing
track of sense and becoming mired in an impossibly slow word-on-word bog. "I'm kind
of racy. I don't stop on the words—that's certain death. I slide through and keep going.
In fifth grade, I started doing multiple flyovers, so I could 'get it.' Like flying over new
territory, the first time, I see the hills and valleys. The second time, I notice roads and
rivers and I feel like I know where I'm going. The third time, I zoom in and out and see
stuff I totally missed before. It's crazy, but I can't even begin taking notes until the third
flyover."

JOCELYN

Jocelyn, identified as having a learning disability in second grade, received services
through her elementary years but not in secondary school. She struggled through college, taking only a few courses at a time. Now, in graduate school, she was running into
familiar problems:

"I start off understanding what I'm reading and by the time I get to the bottom of
the page, I'm lost. I am okay with novels I like, but when I read information for school,
my mind is like a sieve. I can't remember what I'm reading. Even though, you know, in
my *life* I have a better than average memory. It's so confusing. Help!"

Now in my graduate class, Jocelyn brought in her textbook, and together we in-
vestigated our way through three pages. Jocelyn's reading was largely accurate but dis-
tinctly slow. She understood the vocabulary, could process each sentence, and could
paraphrase a sequence of sentences or paragraph, but as the text chapter proceeded,
she lost track of connections, the main thrust, a shift of thought, and what *it* or *that* referred to halfway into a new paragraph. She had the pieces and started connecting them
but, as the working memory load mounted, the glue for all she was reading did not
hold.

APPENDIX 10.2

Assessing Oral Reading Fluency

Schools have long underappreciated the importance of fluency as a focus of reading instruction (Allington, 2006). Assessing fluency can encourage attention to it. In addition, assessing fluency can keep teachers honest by looking directly at the effects of their instruction. Hasbrouck and Tindal (2006) have provided useful norms for assessing oral reading fluency for first- through eighth-grade reading levels (see Appendix 10.3). The following are their guidelines for assessing fluency for three purposes—for screening, as part of diagnosing, and to monitor progress. Basic administration of these 1-minute fluency probes is the same for each of these three purposes. What *differs* is the level of text used, comparison norms, and follow-up.

Basic administration of 1-minute probes for assessing oral reading fluency:

1. Administer individually.

2. Use unpracticed text, with teacher and student having identical text copies.

3. Student reads text aloud while teacher times 1-minute reading sample and marks words read incorrectly.

4. Calculate fluency score (WCPM) by totaling the number of words read in 1 minute, minus the number of words read incorrectly.

5. Use Hasbrouck and Tindal's (2006) norms—differently for different purposes (see Tables 10.5 and 10.6 and Appendix 10.3).

SCREENING

- *Use*: Grade-level text (the grade in which student is enrolled)

- *Compare*: Use the norms for the student's actual grade level (see Appendix 10.3).

- *Follow-up*: Expected oral reading fluency scores for grade level should be at the 50th percentile, plus or minus 10 words. Anything below this indicates reading difficulty, to be followed up with further assessment.

Screenings are brief and easily administered tools used to spot students who *may* be having difficulty with reading, not to confirm or clarify the nature of those difficulties. Although it may seem counterintuitive, this kind of brief 1-minute screening probe has been found not only to reliably reflect fluency but also to predict overall reading

Table 10.5. Grade 1 oral reading fluency general guidelines

Grade level	WCPM on unpracticed passages	Level of risk for reading failure
End of first grade	40 +	Low risk
	< 40 (39–20)	Some risk
	< 20	High risk

Key: WCPM, words read correctly per minute.

Source: Good, Simmons, Kame'enui, Kaminski, & Wallin (2002).

Table 10.6.   Grade 2–8 oral reading fluency guidelines for progress monitoring using 1-minute reading probes

Reading levels	Frequency	Duration	Notes
6–12 months below grade level	1–2 times per month	As long as supplementary instruction is provided	Monitoring effects of interventions, even with students who do not seem far behind, can ensure ongoing progress. The procedures (below) for severe reading difficulties can be used at all levels. Tracking progress is motivating to students, teachers, and other people across many endeavors.
1 or more years below grade level	1 time per week or 1 time per 2 weeks	For duration of intervention or until target goals are achieved	Graph WCPM scores (for grading period, trimester, or another selected time span). Use average weekly improvement (AWI) from Hasbrouck and Tindal's (2006) norms table to set and ambitious and reasonable goal. Set up a graph for each student. Draw an aim-line from the current score to your goal. Add the WCPM score after each assessment. Consider setting a fluency goal with the student, who can also record WCPM on the graph with an aim-line. If three consecutive scores fall below the aim-line, discuss what more and/or different to undertake.

Key: WCPM, words read correctly per minute.
Source: Good, Simmons, Kame'enui, Kaminski, & Wallin (2002).

proficiency with a high degree of accuracy, particularly for students reading at first-through fifth-grade levels (Hasbrouck, 2010; Rasinski, 2006).

DIAGNOSING

- *Use*: Text at student's estimated *instructional*[1] level

- *Compare*: Use the norms for the grade level of the selected passage (not the student's actual grade level) (see Appendix 10.3).

- *Follow-up:* An oral reading fluency score at the 50th percentile indicates that fluency is on par with the student's overall reading level. Below the 40th percentile indicates that fluency is particularly slow, even in relation to lower-than-grade-level material in the reader's instructional zone. Intensive fluency intervention is called for, with progress charted frequently.

The point of diagnosing is to sort out the different aspects of a student's reading difficulties in order to select appropriate emphasis for reading interventions. A brief fluency

---

[1]*Instructional level* is considered challenging but manageable material for a given reader; at least 90% success, meaning substantial comprehension with fewer than 10 out of 100 words the reader finds difficult to read (excluding proper nouns). *Independent level* is 98% success, meaning substantial comprehension with fewer than 2 out of 100 words the reader finds difficult (excluding proper nouns). *Frustration level* is more than 10/100, or less than 90% success (Partnership for Reading, 2001).

probe is *one* diagnostic; others include assessing decoding, sight words, vocabulary, background experience, and comprehension with skill-specific tools and multidimensional diagnostic reading inventories.

MONITORING PROGRESS

- *Use*: Teacher/student–determined *goal-level* text (or, if within reach, grade-level text)

- *Frequency*: Once a week or bimonthly

- *Follow-up:* Graph fluency scores (WCPM) as points on a graph, connecting the points to determine the "slope"—angled up, flat, or down. Consider instructional changes if the slope is flat or not sufficiently angled upward. Also, view progress by comparing the student's weekly improvement (WCPM) over time to the *average* weekly improvement documented for students at the reading level being used (see Hasbrouck & Tindal, 2006).

The point of monitoring progress is to pay attention to the effects of instruction, to motivate efforts, and to adjust teaching when there is little or no sign of learning. Charting progress is important for both student and teacher, providing both with feedback and support for efforts. Frequent, graphed, 1-minute probes (often called *curriculum-based measurements*) have a long history of research demonstrating value as sensitive, reliable, and timely feedback on a student's reading progress (Deno & Marston, 2006).

Hasbrouck and Tindal's (2006) Oral Reading Fluency Data

Grade	Percentile	Fall WCPM	Winter WCPM	Spring WCPM	AWI
1	90		81	111	1.9
	75		47	82	2.2
	50		**23**	**53**	**1.9**
	25		12	28	1.0
	10		6	15	0.6
2	90	106	125	142	1.1
	75	79	100	117	1.2
	50	**51**	**72**	**89**	**1.2**
	25	25	42	61	1.1
	10	11	18	31	0.6
3	90	128	146	162	1.1
	75	99	120	137	1.2
	50	**71**	**92**	**107**	**1.1**
	25	44	62	78	1.1
	10	21	36	48	0.8
4	90	145	166	180	1.1
	75	119	139	152	1.0
	50	**94**	**112**	**123**	**0.9**
	25	68	87	98	0.9
	10	45	61	72	0.8
5	90	166	182	194	0.9
	75	139	156	168	0.9
	50	**110**	**127**	**139**	**0.9**
	25	85	99	109	0.8
	10	61	74	83	0.7
6	90	177	195	204	0.8
	75	153	167	177	0.8
	50	**127**	**140**	**150**	**0.7**
	25	98	111	122	0.8
	10	68	82	93	0.8
7	90	180	195	202	0.7
	75	156	165	177	0.7
	50	**128**	**136**	**150**	**0.7**
	25	102	109	123	0.7
	10	79	88	98	0.6
8	90	185	199	199	0.4
	75	161	177	177	0.5
	50	**133**	**151**	**151**	**0.6**
	25	106	124	124	0.6
	10	77	97	97	0.6

Figure 10.6. Oral reading fluency data. (*Key:* WCPM, words correct per minute; AWI, average weekly improvement or average words per week growth.) (From Hasbrouck, J., & Tindal, G. [2005]. *Oral Reading Fluency: 90 Years of Measurement* [Tech. Rep. No. 33]. Eugene, Oregon: University of Oregon, College of Education, Behavioral Research and Teaching; reprinted by permission.)

11

Word Learning and Vocabulary Instruction

NANCY E. HENNESSY

We are verbivores, a species that lives on words, and the meaning and use of language are bound to be among the major things we ponder, share and dispute.

—Pinker (2007, p. 24)

A student's lexicon expands and deepens over a lifetime through multiple and varied experiences with words that serve both receptive (listening, reading) and expressive (speaking, writing) purposes. Language serves thought, and words come alive within their context. Yet, despite consensus on the pivotal role of vocabulary in our lives and its well-documented contributions to literacy development and academic performance, vocabulary has been the stepchild of reading instruction.

The National Reading Panel (NRP; National Institute of Child Health and Human Development [NICHD], 2000) identified the essential components of reading (instruction) as phonemic awareness, phonics, fluency, vocabulary and comprehension. Although each contributes independently to reading performance, these work in concert to accomplish reading proficiency. The role of vocabulary was described by Hiebert and Kamil as "the bridge between word level processes and the cognitive processes of comprehension" (2005, p. 4). Much remains to be learned about vocabulary instruction, but we do have a sufficient knowledge base to inform and change educational practices now. This chapter addresses what we know about the nature of vocabulary acquisition, with a focus on instructional applications. Topics include vocabulary and reading proficiency, vocabulary acquisition, individual differences, design and delivery of effective instruction, and technology.

VOCABULARY AND READING PROFICIENCY

Proficient reading demands the development, coordination, and interaction of multiple skills that develop over time. Several theoretical models exist that can inform our understanding of the complexity of reading and the critical role of vocabulary. Samuels concluded "that to be considered a fluent reader, the person should be able to decode and comprehend at the same time" (2006, p. 340). His words are reminiscent of the **Simple View of Reading** (Gough & Tunmer, 1986), a model that defines reading comprehension as the product of word recognition (lower order skills) and listening comprehension (higher order thinking processes). Yet, the Simple View of Reading is not all that simple. Questions related to identifying lower and higher order skills and their development and contribution to reading proficiency and the role of vocabulary surface as one considers what lies beneath this formula. A discussion of the Four-Part Processing Model for Word Recognition (Rayner, Foorman, Perfetti, Pesetsky & Seidenberg, 2001; Seidenberg & McClelland, 1989) and Scarborough's (2001) Rope Model of Reading Development will serve to clarify the Simple View of Reading and the development of component skills necessary for reading proficiency, their relationships, and the contribution of vocabulary.

Four-Part Processing Model for Word Recognition

The Four-Part Processing Model for Word Recognition provides a framework for understanding the neural systems involved in reading words. Four unique, complex, yet interrelated systems contribute to word recognition: phonological, orthographic, meaning, and context processing (see Figure 11.1). This model explains how the reader maps sound onto print and uses word meaning to read the printed word. Delving into the function of and interactions between each of these systems can provide clarity

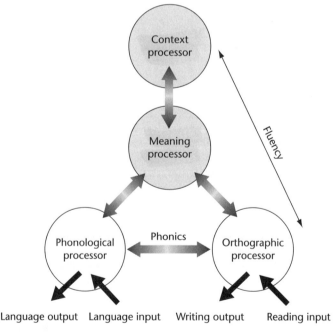

Figure 11.1.   A four-part processing model of word recognition. (Reprinted with permission from Sopris West Educational Services. LETRS for Early Childhood Educators by Lucy Hart Paulson and Louisa C. Moats © 2010.)

about the contributions to reading proficiency when and if each does its job well. Consider how each system contributes to reading the word *catch:*

- Phonological processor: phoneme identification (e.g., /k/ /a/ /ch/)

- Orthographic processor: recognizing letter and letter patterns (graphemes) (e.g., *c a tch*)

- Meaning processor: access to semantic network and varied meanings (e.g., If you *catch* an item moving through the air, then you seize it with your hands; if you *catch* an animal or person, you capture them)

- Context processor: use language experiences and context to confirm word recognition and meaning (e.g., We will *catch* the 6:00 A.M. train into the city)

Although each processor is responsible for its own task, they simultaneously coordinate and support each other to facilitate performance. The bidirectional arrows in Figure 11.1 indicate the interdependence of these systems and the arrow to the side indicates the importance of automaticity and fluency in each of the processors. Although this is a rather simplistic explanation for a complex process, it provides understanding about how different processing systems contribute to and work together for automatic word recognition. It also gives insight into potential sources of difficulty and the importance of instruction that fosters the development of all processing systems.

Vocabulary, Phonological Awareness, and Word Recognition

The relationship between vocabulary and comprehension is somewhat self-evident; however, the role of vocabulary in developing phonological awareness and word recognition is not as evident. Developing the phonological processing system is essential to skilled reading. Phonological awareness knowledge has consistently been described as the best single predictor of reading performance (Liberman, Shankweiler, & Liberman, 1989). Word recognition is dependent on this ability to recognize, manipulate, and use sounds within words. Phonological awareness is a prerequisite to mapping symbols onto sounds and necessary for the phonological system to work in concert with the orthographic system. Children with speech-language difficulties often have delayed phonological awareness, and it is generally accepted that weaknesses in this area are the most common cause of reading difficulties (Lyon & Shaywitz, 2003).

Phonological skills contribute individually to developing early literacy, but they also present as partially dependent on other contributors such as vocabulary. Researchers have theorized that developing phonological awareness is, in part, a product of vocabulary development. It is thought that words are stored holistically in the young child's lexicon and gradually become more segmented during preschool and early school years. As a child's vocabulary grows, he or she becomes more aware of phonological similarities and discovers that it is more efficient to remember and recognize words in terms of their constituent parts rather than as whole entities (Lonigan, 2007). This change in representations of words to segmental units is described in the lexical restructuring model (Walley, Metsala, & Garlock, 2003). Restructuring the phonological representation of words depends on vocabulary growth and is thought necessary for developing explicit phoneme awareness. A review of studies regarding the early development of literacy skills indicates that phonological awareness is correlated both concurrently and longitudinally with oral language skills in preschool and beyond (Lonigan, 2007). It is theorized that spoken words for which children have fully specified phonological representations can be more easily accessed for phonological awareness tasks (Gillon, 2004).

Rope Model of Reading Development

Scarborough's (2001) Rope Model of Reading Development (see Figure 11.2) provides an analogy for understanding how skilled reading—the fluent execution and coordination of word recognition and text comprehension—develops.

The skills represented in the word recognition strands of the rope (phonological awareness, decoding, sight recognition) represent the primary focus of instruction in the early grades and the major contributor, at that point, to reading comprehension. Language comprehension abilities become more influential as students gain competency in word-reading skills and are capable of reading texts independently. Results from the Connecticut Longitudinal Study (Foorman, Francis, Shaywitz, Shaywitz, & Fletcher, 1997) provided evidence of the changing relationship between decoding and reading comprehension, with language comprehension competencies becoming increasingly influential. Vellutino, Tunmer, Jaccard, and Chen concluded that "language comprehension becomes the dominant processing in reading comprehension when the reader has acquired enough facility in word identification to comprehend in written language text that would be normally comprehended in spoken language" (2007, p. 26). The strands that represent language comprehension include not only vocabulary but also literacy knowledge, language structures, background knowledge, and verbal reasoning. This model is particularly informative regarding the specific or independent role of vocabulary in proficient reading but also is a reminder that the strands are interdependent and develop over time. For example, consider the connections between word meaning, background knowledge, and language structures (syntax). Words do not

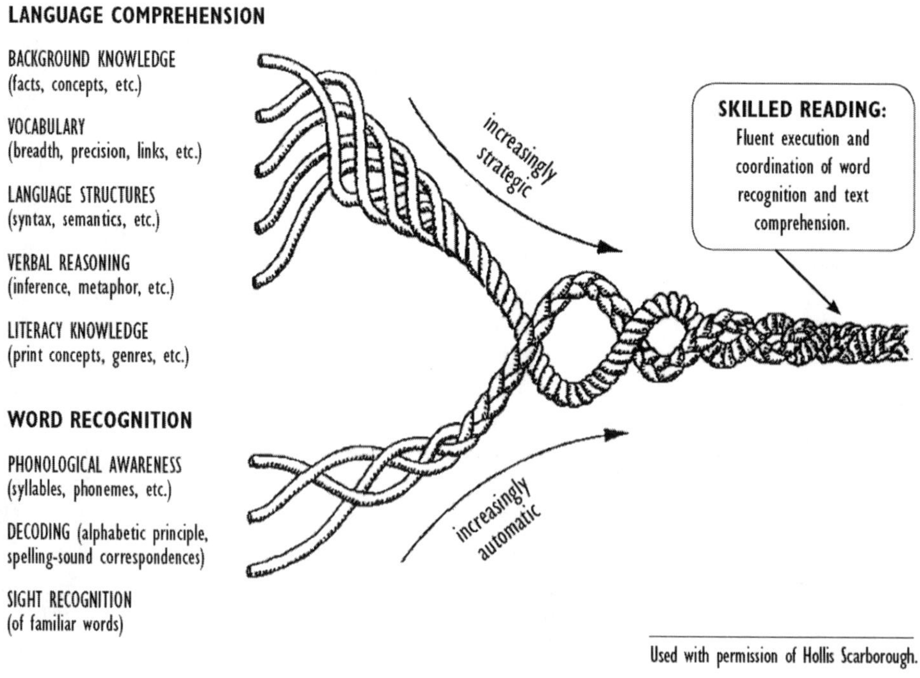

LANGUAGE COMPREHENSION

BACKGROUND KNOWLEDGE
(facts, concepts, etc.)

VOCABULARY
(breadth, precision, links, etc.)

LANGUAGE STRUCTURES
(syntax, semantics, etc.)

VERBAL REASONING
(inference, metaphor, etc.)

LITERACY KNOWLEDGE
(print concepts, genres, etc.)

WORD RECOGNITION

PHONOLOGICAL AWARENESS
(syllables, phonemes, etc.)

DECODING (alphabetic principle, spelling-sound correspondences)

SIGHT RECOGNITION
(of familiar words)

increasingly strategic

SKILLED READING:
Fluent execution and coordination of word recognition and text comprehension.

increasingly automatic

Used with permission of Hollis Scarborough.

Figure 11.2. The reading rope. (Reprinted with permission from Hollis Scarborough, 2010.)

exist in isolation but rather as part of a word schema or a connected network of meaning. Word meanings do not live apart from their syntactic function; it is a dimension of their meaning. This model provides further opportunity for exploring the vocabulary–comprehension connection.

Vocabulary and Comprehension

Although vocabulary facilitates phonological awareness and word recognition in students, its power lies in its relationship to reading comprehension. The strength of vocabulary's contribution to skilled reading has been documented over time. Both causal and correlational links between vocabulary and comprehension reflect the importance and complexity of their relationship. Vocabulary has predictive value for later reading comprehension, and the relationship between kindergarten and first-grade word knowledge and elementary, middle, and secondary grade-level performance has been documented through several studies. Knowing individual word meanings is thought to account for as much as 50% of the variance in reading comprehension (Stahl & Nagy, 2006). It is also estimated that adequate reading comprehension depends on a person already knowing between 90% and 95% of the words in a text (Nagy & Scott, 2000). Tannenbaum, Torgesen, and Wagner (2006) reported the range of correlation between vocabulary and comprehension as .3–.8 dependent on factors such as age, dimension of the words assessed, and test format. In addition, many have studied the reciprocal relationship between vocabulary and comprehension, with reading comprehension influencing the growth of vocabulary knowledge during the school years (Nagy, 2005; Stanovich, 1986). Vocabulary eventually emerges as the single most important thread in the language comprehension strand of the reading rope.

These theoretical models provide a framework for understanding reading proficiency and the individual competencies necessary for word recognition and language comprehension as well as the importance of their relationships. It is essential to acknowledge vocabulary's connections to phonological awareness, word recognition, and comprehension to understand vocabulary development as more than an isolated proficiency and as a component of reading instruction.

Reflect and Respond

1. How has the review of theoretical models contributed to your understanding of vocabulary and its role in skilled reading?

WORD LEARNING AND VOCABULARY ACQUISITION

Although estimates of word meanings learned by the time an individual graduates from high school vary, the numbers are still staggering. Consider that some report that kindergarteners come to school recognizing 4,000–5,000 base words, and the average high school graduate has a lexicon of 40,000–50,000 words (Biemiller, 2005). How are thousands of words acquired and used in speaking, writing, listening, and reading comprehension? The following sections consider two phases of language/vocabulary acquisition: infancy to preschool and school age to adulthood.

Language Acquisition: Infancy to Preschool

Language is an essential characteristic of being human. Language acquisition is complex and complicated beginning in infancy and continuing across a lifetime. Infants come into the world capable of perceiving and producing sounds. Initially, infants use gestures (e.g., waving or lifting up their arms) to communicate. The speech stream of those around them (e.g., parents, caregivers, siblings) is perceived holistically rather than consisting of meaningful units (e.g., sounds, syllables, words). As children grow physically, however, so does their ability to analyze and discern phonemes, syllables, and words. Carlisle and Katz (2005) described this experience as akin to adults learning a foreign language in which it is nearly impossible at first to distinguish words in a seemingly endless stream of sounds, but with experience, patterns emerge that provide clues to phonological units. Infants eventually parse out the sounds of their native language and combine them to repeat and produce words. Words must have some relevance to prompt acquisition (i.e., an understanding that words reference objects, events, and actions). Thus, infants' first words usually relate to things in their environment or to actions related to their needs (e.g., *ba-ba/bottle*). Their understanding of words is greater than their ability to produce them as evidenced by using general terms to identify different objects with similar features (e.g., all animals with four legs are "doggies"). Subsequently, children acquire words at an amazing rate between 18 and 24 months. This "spurt" or "vocabulary burst" period is marked by the ability to make inferences about relationships between words and referents, even after as little as one exposure. This phenomenon is described as **"fast mapping"** (Carey & Bartlett, 1978). Simultaneously, children's labels for objects, people, and actions grow as does their syntactical awareness. In other words, they no longer just imitate or memorize language, they analyze, extract, and even experiment with rules of speech that govern stringing words together for asking and telling. Chomsky (1965) suggested that children are equipped with an innate "universal grammar." Between the ages of 2 and 3, children seem to have a word for almost everything and even invent creative combinations of different parts of speech that reflect this basic understanding of word formation, such as a grandchild requesting that her Nana stand in a particular place by saying, "Stand here. Be a good *stander.*"

Significant numbers of words are acquired by children before they become literate or able to interact with print. Young children typically learn words receptively (through listening) before using them expressively (speaking). McLaughlin (1998) estimated the average number of expressive vocabulary words acquired by age 24 months to be 200–300 (see Table 11.1); an estimate of average receptive vocabulary can be obtained by multiplying the expressive language number four times.

The fast mapping of words that begins at 18–24 months of age is sufficient to promote partial knowledge of word meaning. Building a deeper representation of a word requires multiple exposures in different contexts. It is this extended or slow mapping that prompts elaborating on word meaning and developing semantic networks. The child's everyday language experiences, including oral language interactions and involvement in structured programs, directly influence the number of words known and the richness of understanding.

Table 11.1. Number of expressive vocabulary words.

Age	Number of words
12 months	First word
18 months	50
24 months	200–300
3 years	900–1,000
5 years	2,100–2,200

Reprinted with permission from Sopris West Educational Services. LETRS for Early Childhood Educators by Lucy Hart Paulson and Louisa C. Moats © 2010.

Informed Oral Language Interactions

The critical role of parents, caregivers, and preschool educators in creating and nurturing informed oral language environments is undisputable. Rich and responsive language experiences from infancy to preschool age directly influence oral language acquisition that, in turn, is highly predictive of later reading abilities. How then should these adults shape this environment?

Adult talk that is responsive to beginning and later language attempts influences a young child's language development. Productive parent–child interactions depend on the nature of language input (e.g., word expansion) and using different contexts (e.g., book reading) as well as content of speech (Landry & Smith, 2007). Most parents, educators, or caregivers would assert that they regularly talk with the children in their care. It is the quality of the talk that matters, however; quantity alone is not sufficient. Differences in parent and teacher quality of interaction affect language development. Consider the following sample (*Animals in the Wild* by Mary Hoffman) collected during a study of parent interaction.

Mother: That's a tusk, see? It's white. Know what, Domingo?

Child: Hmmmm?

Mother: Hunters kill elephants for that.

Child: Why?

Mother: Because they want it, um, well they use it for different things. I think that some museums buy them and...I don't know about museums, but I know they kill for this white um...

Child: There's no tusks on those elephants though.

Mother: See? That one is bigger so some of them die because of that. That is sad.

Child: I wish there was no such thing as hunters and guns.

Mother: I know it, me too. Oh, there's a herd. That's a lot of them. See how they walk.

Child: Ma, here's one that's dead.

Mother: I don't think he's dead. We'll find out. "They use their tusks to dig." Oh see, he's digging a hole. "They use their tusks to dig for salt." (DeTemple & Snow, 2003, pp. 23–24)

This parent purposely used the content of story to interact with her child and to expand on word use and elaborate on content.

To promote language acquisition, Moats and Paulson (2009) recommended that adults intentionally use language-stimulation techniques such as parallel talk, self-talk, and expansion while interacting with young children. In other words, describing what the child is doing, talking about what the adult is doing, or expanding on a child's expressive language can prompt increased talk and language development.

The following are some examples of how adults can incorporate purposeful elaboration and questioning related to a typical 2- or 3-year-old child's comment or activity.

• Repeat what your child has said and expand on it. For example, if your child says, "pretty flower," then you can respond by saying, "Yes, that is a pretty flower. The flower is bright red. It smells good too. Do you want to smell the flower?"

• Put objects into a bucket and have your child remove one object at a time, saying its name. Repeat what your child says and expand on it: "Yes, that is a comb. You comb your hair." Take the objects from the bucket and help your child group them into categories (e.g., clothes, food, drawing tools).

Adults can become more aware of everyday opportunities as sources of potentially rich conversation. *Talking on the Go* (Dougherty & Paul, 2007) is chock-full of age-appropriate activities. It uses a framework of common experience (home, outside, on the road, supermarket) and suggests specific activities based on the child's age. Suggestions for a 3- or 4-year-old child's visit to the supermarket include the following:

- Identify hard, soft, rough, and smooth. Let the child feel a hard carrot, soft bread, smooth apples, and rough pineapple.

- Learn how items are used as they are placed in the shopping cart. What do we use to sweep the floor? What do we wash clothes with?

- Name cleaning items that you see in the store and talk about how they are used (e.g., broom, cleansers, soaps, brush, cloth, dish soap).

- Set up a store using real and pretend food and containers. Help the child group by size, shape, color, and name. Pretend to be the shopper and the store clerk. Think of all the possibilities for categorizing items found in a store—the beginning of a semantic map for the supermarket.

Preschool educators have similar countless opportunities. Consider how a walk outside might generate conversation about identifying items that can be collected (e.g., rocks, leaves), and compared (e.g., oak, maple, elm leaves) by describing shapes, textures, colors, and sizes.

Shared storytime can also be a source of productive dialogue between the adult and the child at home or in preschool. Moats and Paulson (2009) reminded adults to be active listeners, ask questions, encourage response, and expand on children's comments and recommended general steps for preparing for reading with young children:

1. Always read the book beforehand.

2. Do most of the talking the first time, highlighting what children may not know.

3. Next time, use general questions to get children to respond with more than one word.

4. Read and talk about the book many times.

The importance of early language development and the critical role that adults, whether parents, caregivers, preschool educators, or clinicians, can play in structuring oral language and instructional environments is obvious. A commitment to creating and sustaining those environments is needed now.

Reflect and Respond

1. How does vocabulary develop in the infancy to preschool years?

2. What are the critical attributes of adult–child oral language interactions?

3. What role can the educational community play in prompting the development of vocabulary?

Language Acquisition: School Age to Adult

Young children who are naturally inquisitive about words appear spongelike in their receptivity to learning new words; however, vocabulary learning extends over a lifetime. Estimates of vocabulary size of school-age students and number of words learned yearly differ, based on the definition of word knowledge and the assessment technique. Most agree that students learn approximately 3,000 words per year, or about 7 words per day (Beck, McKeown, & Kucan, 2002). These are startling statistics, particularly for educators who work with diverse learners such as English language learners (ELLs) or students with language learning disabilities who struggle to attain these averages.

As seen during the infancy to preschool phase, the desire to acquire and deepen word knowledge often reflects an innate curiosity about words and a need to communicate. As students move through school, however, increasing academic demands of content area text and tasks often become a strong motivating factor. Students must know the common everyday words used in conversation as well as the more unique sophisticated words encountered in texts. Stahl (2004) described this academic vocabulary as synonymous with the vocabulary of school. This word knowledge is central to student understanding of the critical concepts of content areas. Throughout school, students are called on to use words with increasing precision and in response to tasks requiring different degrees of complexity.

How do students accrue word meanings during this period? Oral language interactions remain important, but new avenues of acquisition open. As students become skilled at reading, wide reading emerges as a potentially critical source of word learning. In addition, vocabulary becomes an essential component of reading instruction with educators incidentally and explicitly teaching individual word meanings as well as independent word-learning strategies. Vocabulary-savvy teachers know that acquiring word meaning is slow, incremental, and requires multiple exposures for thorough understanding. Thus, they create learning environments to address the nature of vocabulary acquisition.

Recognizing that they cannot teach all word meanings explicitly, informed educators purposefully create rich receptive and expressive language experiences for their students. This understanding is demonstrated through incidental instruction that includes formal and informal activities centered on teacher talk and student interactions (e.g., dialogue, discussion, read-alouds, structured independent reading). Talking teachers literally create talking classrooms that accommodate for differences in student vocabulary needs and provide differentiated opportunities for interacting with more sophisticated words that strengthen the vocabulary strand of the reading rope.

Intentional instruction is explicit and systematic, targeting individual words, developing semantic relationships, and teaching essential independent word-learning strategies, including context, morphology, and using the dictionary. It is this combination of incidental and intentional instruction that allows students to learn new words and deepen their knowledge of previously learned words.

Individual Differences

Consideration must be given to students with individual differences, such as those who are ELLs or those with language-based learning disabilities. Although their needs will be addressed throughout the chapter, it is essential to consider foundational knowledge given the significant role vocabulary plays in their ability to read and write proficiently. A shared understanding of the multiple aspects of vocabulary instruction and coordinated efforts between educators and specialists is necessary to design effective instruction for all students and differentiated instruction for those who need more time, frequency, and small-group settings.

Language Learning Disabilities

Students with language-based learning or reading disabilities often demonstrate significant delays in vocabulary knowledge. Although these students may acquire fewer word meanings than their peers, the reasons differ. Students with reading disabilities, such as dyslexia, often have phonological processing deficits that not only influence the development of word recognition skills but may be responsible for weaknesses in memory, interpretation, and retrieval of language-based information. Students with weak language abilities progress more slowly in learning words directly and from context (Curtis, 1987; Shefelbine, 1990). Their knowledge of word meaning is often more shallow than their peers and lacks conceptual depth. Accurate and automatic word recognition is a necessary condition for interacting independently with text, a major source of incidental word learning. These factors, coupled with an increased sense of inefficacy and waning motivation, contribute to a gap in word and world knowledge that directly affects reading comprehension. Regardless of the cause, increased intensity of instruction, incidentally and intentionally, is necessary. The oral language environment is important as many of these students have stronger listening than reading comprehension abilities. The instructional routines and methods that will be discussed, including semantic mapping, semantic feature analysis, and word-analysis strategies, are effective for these students when instruction is explicit, systematic, and cumulative, providing sufficient opportunity for guided and independent practice. Regular and special educators need to design differentiated, individualized instruction based on students' learning needs. These students will require increased intensity of instruction, practice, and application of new words and word-learning strategies.

English Language Learners

ELLs are one of the fastest growing populations in our schools. They are a diverse group that consists of more than 70% whose first language is Spanish, with the remainder represented by students who speak more than 400 different languages at home (August & Shanahan, 2006; Goldenberg, 2008). Informed educators recognize that ELLs must learn a different phonological, syntactic system and the meanings of new words. These learners need explicit vocabulary instruction that includes the features of English (e.g., syntax, grammar, pronunciation), balanced by social interactions with others who speak English well and multiple opportunities for meaningful use (Fillmore & Snow, 2002; Goldenberg, 2008). Targeted instruction should include academic words; sophisticated, high-utility words (Tier 2); precision words (e.g. synonyms with more precise meaning); multiple meanings; figurative language; and cognates when applicable (see Table 11.2). *Cognates* are words that are spelled similarly and have similar meanings in both languages. Many cognates for English words exist in Spanish. Studies have shown that more proficient Spanish-speaking English readers recognize more cognates than their less-proficient peers and use this knowledge to infer English word meanings (Nagy, Garcia, Durgunoglu, & Hancin-Bhatt, 1993).

Instruction designed for ELLs should build on what they know, including basic understanding or concept development reflected in their own language. These students will require a multiyear intensive program of vocabulary instruction consisting of approaches that benefit all students. Instruction will be more effective if enhanced by using real objects, visual images, graphic organizers, multimedia, and drama to clarify the meanings of unfamiliar words and figurative language.

Reflect and Respond

1. In what ways does vocabulary acquisition differ for school-age children?

2. What instructional practices have you observed in classrooms?

3. In what ways is instruction different for ELLs or students with language-based learning disabilities?

Table 11.2. Examples of Spanish and English cognates

English	Spanish
accident	accidente
accompany	acompañar
admire	admirar
air	aire
announce	anunciar
arithmetic	aritmética
artist	artista
attention	atención
bicycle	bicicleta
biography	biografía
brilliant	brillante
cafeteria	cafetería
cause	causa
center	centro
circle	círculo
class	clase
color	color

DESIGN AND DELIVERY OF EFFECTIVE VOCABULARY INSTRUCTION

The design and delivery of effective vocabulary instruction requires more than formulating a lesson plan; it also requires a comprehensive understanding of goals, word-learning characteristics, stages of word acquisition, and instructional approaches. This discussion should deepen our knowledge base, clarify our thinking, and inform our instructional decision making.

Goals of Instruction

Learning is incredibly dependent on vocabulary because it is a language-based activity. Without adequate vocabulary, learners are consistently being asked to connect ideas and develop novel concepts with insufficient tools (Baker, Simmons, & Kame'enui, 2005). Knowing and using words receptively and expressively requires more than a brief identification of meaning and use in a sentence. Whether instruction is characterized as being incidental or intentional, students need both a breadth and depth of word knowledge that facilitates comprehension and expression of thoughts. In a study of third graders, Tannenbaum et al. (2006) indicated the importance of breadth for performance on reading outcome assessments as well as the relationship between depth and performance on classroom-based academic tasks. Although some might argue that the primary goal of vocabulary instruction should be comprehension, a broader perspective would include developing and gaining access to a lexicon that allows students to not only listen and read with comprehension but also express understanding and thinking orally and in writing.

Nature of Word Learning

Vocabulary acquisition has been described as incremental, interrelated, and multidimensional (Nagy & Scott, 2000). For example, an individual's understanding of a simple word such as *dog* changes as one encounters different types of dogs and notices different characteristics, behaviors, and even varied roles of dogs. A student's semantic network for the word *dog* consists of interrelated information that is semantic, syntactic, and linguistic in nature. This network or word schema for *dog* eventually includes literal and figurative meanings (e.g., dog days of summer), use as a noun or verb (e.g., dogged by worries), synonyms (e.g., mutt) and subcategories such as dog heroes (e.g., Bolt). This multidimensional nature of word learning can be illustrated in a semantic map (see Figure 11.3).

Calfee and Drum described understanding of word meaning as it "involves depth of meaning; precision of meaning; facile access; the ability to articulate one's understanding; flexibility in application of knowledge of a word; the appreciation of word play; the ability to recognize; to define; to use expressively" (1986, pp. 825–826). Others, such as Nation (2001) have identified the facets of word knowledge to include:

- Spoken form

- Written form

- Role in sentences

- Frequency in oral and written language

- Conceptual meaning

- Use of words

- Association with other words

The challenge for educators is to design instruction that recognizes the importance of each dimension and accommodates for development of deep understanding of all interrelated facets of word meaning.

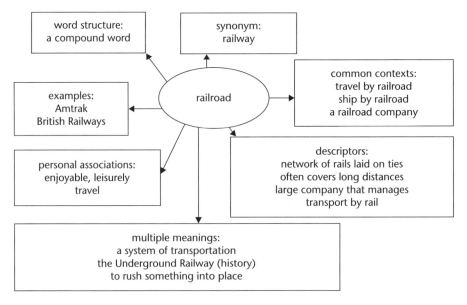

Figure 11.3. Dimensions of word knowledge. (Reprinted with permission from Sopris West Educational Services. LETRS Module 4: The Mighty Word: Building Vocabulary and Oral Language [2nd ed.] by Louisa Moats ©2009.)

Framework for Instruction

Consider Graves's (2006) comprehensive approach to vocabulary instruction when thinking about organizing instruction that is focused on long-term growth:

- Providing rich and varied language experiences

- Teaching individual words

- Teaching word-learning strategies

- Fostering word consciousness

Although terminology may differ, there is consensus for an organizational framework comprised of these four components. Baumann and Kame'enui (2004) described this organizational grammar as a compelling structure for negotiating the research to practice linkage in vocabulary instruction. The NRP (NICHD, 2000) findings regarding vocabulary instruction provided another perspective for instructional decision making. Their meta-analysis of effective practices yielded the following recommendations for vocabulary instruction (Kamil, 2004):

- Repetition and rich support for learning vocabulary items are important.

- Vocabulary tasks and instructions should be restructured when necessary.

- Group learning formats may be helpful for vocabulary instruction.

- Vocabulary learning should entail active engagement in learning tasks.

- Computer technology can be used to help teach vocabulary.

- Vocabulary should be directly taught.

- Vocabulary can be acquired through incidental learning.

Ebbers and Denton (2008) reminded educators to consider approaches to vocabulary instruction that reflect principles of instruction found to be effective for students with reading disabilities, including using

- Explicit instruction

- Application of cognitive and metacognitive strategies

- Questioning approaches

- Collaborative engagement involving verbal interactions

- Many opportunities for practice and with feedback

It is apparent that vocabulary can no longer be banished as the stepchild of reading instruction given all that has been discussed regarding the role of vocabulary, its development, and its considerations related to design and delivery. Using Graves's (2006) organizational approach, in conjunction with other sources, the following sections elaborate on a comprehensive approach to instructional practices under the umbrella terms of *incidental on purpose* and *intentional* instruction.

Incidental on Purpose Instruction

Words are uniquely human. We use them to communicate thought and they literally surround us from birth onward. The oral language environment is a critical contributor to vocabulary acquisition and plays a prominent role particularly for younger children and those in early school grades. Its role in the upper grades, however, should not be overlooked. Many children who do not have access to print, such as students with language learning disabilities, depend on other sources of input, such as classroom discussion, for knowledge building. The problem is that not all language environments are equal or sufficiently robust to create a lexicon adequate to meet academic demand. Consider that most adult conversation is simple and usually consists of the same 5,000–10,000 words; it is not these words but rather the more unique words that constitute an essential academic vocabulary. Educators need to be purposeful in creating rich oral language environments, hence the term *incidental on purpose* instruction. Informed educators recognize that a knowledge base related to sources of academic or less common words should inform choice of words used in classroom dialogue and books chosen for structured read-alouds as well as independent reading. Consider the following study of the frequency of words used in major sources of oral and written language (see Table 11.3) as illustrative of significant differences between adult speech and children's books as a source of richer language.

Students are immersed in words through listening, reading, and speaking activities when oral environments are purposefully rich. Teacher talk, including discussions and dialogue, are elevated to a new level. The goal is to get students to tune in and be more interested in words. After all, words carry the concepts of content regardless of the subject matter. The nature of the student's word environment, coupled with developing a positive disposition, can be a powerful instructional resource. The oral language environment, particularly when purposeful, can provide unlimited and productive opportunities to learn new words. How is this translated into instructional practice? Consider how classroom/school language environments, structured read-alouds, independent reading, and a bit of word consciousness can contribute to word learning.

Table 11.3.   Frequency of rare words in text, television, and speech

Item	Rare words per 1,000
Printed texts	
Abstracts of scientific articles	128.0
Newspapers	68.3
Popular magazines	65.7
Adult books	52.7
Comic books	53.5
Children's books	30.9
Preschool books	16.3
Television texts	
Popular prime-time adult shows	22.7
Popular prime-time children's shows	20.2
Cartoon shows	30.8
Mr. Rogers and *Sesame Street*	2.0
Adult speech	
Expert witness testimony	28.4
College graduates to friends, spouses	17.3

From Hayes, D.P., & Ahrens, M.G. (1998). Vocabulary simplification for children: A special case of "motherese"? *Journal of Child Language, 15*(2), 395–410; reprinted by permission.

Classroom/School Language Environment

A commitment to infusing rich oral language is quickly apparent if we listen to the words educators use in explanations, discussions, directions, and conversations within the classroom. Educators generally view themselves as talkers; however, it is the nature of their talk that makes a difference in expanding their students' vocabulary. The vocabulary-attuned teacher takes responsibility for being more reflective and selective about his or her own oral language. This requires a conscious effort because everyday spoken language is less formal than academic language or the language of texts. This on purpose choice of words can make a difference, and the opportunities abound. Consider a mundane everyday direction such as, "Line up and walk to the cafeteria for lunch." Substitutions for *walk,* coupled with a physical demonstration, could include semantic relatives such as *amble, strut, march, saunter,* or *meander.* When confronted with a consistent loss of recess due to weather, a teacher might describe the situation as *frustrating, annoying,* or *disappointing.* A questioning student could be complimented for being *inquisitive* or *curious;* successfully completing a class project could be labeled as *fulfilling* or *exhilarating.*

Educators also have golden opportunities to intersperse more mature words in classroom discussion or one-to-one exchanges and prompt students to think about and use these words. *50 Nifty Speaking and Listening Activities* (Dodson, 2010) contains multiple activities that can help teachers be more purposeful:

- *The 30-second conversation:* This activity enhances purposeful listening and talking in addition to structuring conversation around a connection shared by the teacher and student. The teacher provides a model of natural, authentic conversation and observes changes in the elaboration of responses in children who may have not had much exposure to conversation.

  The 30-second conversation models and engages students in brief authentic conversations led by the teacher. This brief, one-to-one activity allows teachers to reframe brief, truncated answers and model longer responses in an effort to expose students to good linguistic models of responsive and authentic conversation that they may have missed in their home environment. In addition to the linguistic advantages of this activity, it also builds a student's sense of being, which is an integral and valued part of the class and school community, as they are singled out by their teacher for individual "talk time."

- *Link to literacy:* This experience supports literacy development because exposure to good syntax with appropriately challenging vocabulary will better prepare students when they encounter complex syntax and vocabulary in their reading. The more natural hearing models of good language becomes, the more likely students are to use those forms they have been exposed to in their own speaking and writing. Research shows that children are not always exposed to many words and turn-taking opportunities with language in their home setting (Hart & Risley, 1995). Conversation can be modeled and learned through listening purposefully and responding appropriately.

Materials: 30 seconds of one-to-one time

Activity:

- Choose those children in your class who appear to have low language skills, are shy, or are reluctant to talk.

- Take 30 seconds each day (or several days a week) and meet with the student for a short, responsive conversation.
- Make sure the conversation includes some affirmations.
- Begin and end with appropriate salutations (e.g., "Hi, how are you?" "Thanks so much for talking with me today").

Teachers of older students can also scaffold student participation in discussions by providing prompts such as those suggested by Kate Kinsella (http://www. kinsella.org):

Expressing an opinion

I think/believe that . . .

In my opinion . . .

Based on my experience, I think . . .

Asking for clarification

What do you mean?

Will you explain that again?

I have a question about that.

Soliciting a response

What do you think?

We haven't heard from you yet.

Do you agree?

What answer did you get?

Predicting

I predict/imagine that . . .

Based on . . ., I infer that . . .

I hypothesize that . . .

Paraphrasing

So you are saying that . . .

In other words, you think . . .

What I hear you saying is . . .

Acknowledging ideas

My idea is similar to/related to...

I agree with (a person) that . . .

My idea builds on ____'s idea.

Structured Read-Alouds

Reading aloud to children, particularly in preschool and the early grades, is a common practice and acknowledged as an important source of language development. Less attention has been given to the value of read-alouds for older children; yet, there is evidence that even after children learn to read independently, they benefit from listening to text read aloud. Carlisle and Katz (2005) reported that studies show that kindergarteners and sixth graders learn words by listening to books read aloud and read-alouds can facilitate the understanding of complex texts.

In addition, the benefits of read-alouds have been documented for special populations (e.g., children with limited vocabulary and language delays) (Crain, Thoreson, Dale, & Phillips, 1999; Hargrave & Senechal, 2000). Students who struggle with word recognition and students with dyslexia benefit from hearing text at their listening comprehension level. Although read-alouds are typically considered an incidental instructional technique, there are some on purpose conditions that contribute to effectiveness. Numerous studies indicate that effects vary depending on how words are explained, supports provided, amount of repetition, and how much the language of the books varies from everyday language. Listening for a purpose, discussing what was heard, and connecting to what is known facilitates student engagement. In other words, children will not reap the potential benefits if a text is just read and no response is required. Consequently, read-alouds are most productive when preplanned and structured.

Graves (2006) and others have studied and suggested the following characteristics of effective read-alouds:

1. Use carefully selected books

2. Focus on a relatively small number of words

3. Read text with appropriate intonation and expression

4. Is interactive in nature and involves talk that goes beyond the information in the text to make predictions and inferences

5. Involves rereading

Programs that incorporate these characteristics, such as Dialogue Reading (Zevenberger & Whitehurst, 2003), Text Talk (Beck, McKeown, & Kucan, 2001), and Anchored Instruction (Juel & Deffes, 2004) are useful resources for educators and parents.

The power of the read-aloud cannot be underestimated. Some children may come to school not having had the benefit of interacting with books in a structured way. Teachers can maximize the potential of the read-aloud and address differences in children's oral language experiences using activities found in "The 1,000 Book Kid" (Dodson, 2010). The author suggested that if a kindergarten, then a first-grade teacher read 3 books a day across the school year and into January of first grade, he or she would have students who had heard 1,000 books. Teachers could choose favorites for rereading, including expository text and poetry, thus "washing" their kids in words and building word meaning and background knowledge.

The purpose of the read-aloud drives book selection. Although some are read to foster motivation, practice word-recognition skills, or just for fun, the focus is developing vocabulary. Generally, the text selected should contain novel words that are somewhat more sophisticated than those found in the student's lexicon. Resources, such as *The Read-Aloud Handbook* (Trelease, 2006), provide guidance for designing effective read-alouds and information on recommended books in numerous categories.

Although some students such as those with language learning disabilities or ELLs may not know the basic words of oral language, researchers such as Beck, McKeown, and Kucan (2008) recommended a focus on unique words. They posited that basic words are more likely to be encountered informally in everyday interactions, whereas unique words will not, unless purposefully targeted. Teaching materials that focus on high-frequency words by developing decoding coupled with vocabulary (e.g., Vadasy & Nelson, 2008), however, may be necessary to supplement instruction for these students.

Although much of the research has focused on storybook reading, there is an increasing awareness of the importance of introducing informational text to students in earlier grades. There is an acknowledged scarcity of informational text in primary classrooms and the resulting impact on accruing background knowledge necessary for reading proficiency. Selecting text is critical as students in lower and upper grade levels need to build word meaning and schema related to the academic concepts of content in order to succeed in the language environment of school.

The guidelines remain the same regardless of whether text is narrative or informational. Teachers target unique words, explain meaning in context using supports available (e.g., visuals, text), and ask questions that tap into understanding (why) and application (when). Students can be taught to tune into interesting words while listening; older students can note words for discussion following reading (Paynter, Bodrova, & Doty, 2005). It is reported that it may take as many as 6–12 exposures of a word in context to prompt the extended mapping that is necessary for storage and access for use (Jenkins, Stein, & Wysocki, 1984). Hence, it is important to commit to rereading and using targeted words in other oral/written language interactions.

Independent Reading

Once students acquire automatic word-reading skills, wide reading emerges as the major source of vocabulary development with many indications that the best way to learn words is to read and read widely. While studying the effects of independent reading on reading ability, verbal intelligence, and general knowledge, Cunningham and Stanovich (1991) found that out-of-school reading is a powerful predictor of vocabulary and knowledge. Book reading has been correlated with vocabulary growth and subsequent academic achievement. The work of Anderson, Wilson, and Fielding (1988) was informative in understanding the importance of wide reading while undoubtedly creating some discomfort given what we know about the diminishing reading habits of many children. They studied fifth-grade students' reading habits over several months. Based on daily diary recordings, Anderson and colleagues estimated and extrapolated how many words per year these students read based on the percentage of time spent reading independently. Their data are somewhat alarming given the importance of wide reading as a primary source of word learning after the early grades (see Table 11.4). It is estimated that a child at the 80th percentile (amount of independent reading time) read 14.2 minutes daily or more than 20 times as much as the child at the 20th percentile, and the entire year's out-of-school reading for the child at the 10th percentile amounted to just 2 days of reading for the child at the 90th percentile. In addition, differences in amount and type of reading can have significant consequences for other reading skills, including automatic word recognition, building of semantic–syntactic connections, and conceptual relationships.

Are there other factors besides time that influence word learning during independent reading? Carlisle and Katz (2005) included the number of times a word is repeated in text, nature of clues to word meaning (context), and the difficulty of the text itself. Book choice is a critical consideration for all of these reasons. The NRP (NICHD, 2000) recognized that children need to read for varied purposes and read texts at var-

Table 11.4. Differences in amount of independent reading.

Test percentage	Minutes of reading per day	Words read per year
98	65.1	4,358,000
90	21.1	1,823,000
80	14.2	1,146,000
70	9.6	622,000
60	6.5	432,000
50	4.6	282,000
40	3.2	200,000
30	1.3	106,000
20	0.7	21,000
10	0.1	8,000
2	0.0	0

From Anderson, R.C., Wilson, P.T., & Fielding, L.G. (1988). Growth in reading and how children spend their time outside of school. *Reading Research Quarterly, 23,* 285–303; reprinted by permission.

ied levels of difficulty, with some being read for enjoyment and others for more specific purposes. Although there has been debate about which books will most effectively promote vocabulary acquisition, there is some consensus. It is generally accepted that books that are moderately challenging, rather than those that are too difficult or too easy, are most appropriate for vocabulary acquisition. Biemiller (2004) also stressed the importance of allowing children with below-average vocabularies opportunities to acquire words known by their above-average peers. Of course, availability and access to text are necessary conditions. Teachers need collections that allow for choice but also books that contain the rich language and repetition necessary to grow word and world knowledge. "Book baskets" or "library collections" should contain varied genres linked to developing specific grade-level themes or academic content as well as books that can be taken home and read for enjoyment.

Although many students have their preferences for reading selections, teachers may have to monitor and guide choice depending on its purpose. Understandably, struggling readers read fewer and easier books. Students who have not fully developed the word recognition strand of the reading rope do not have the necessary competencies to engage independently with age-appropriate text. A lack of proficiency, interest, or accessibility to print can have significant negative effects on exposure to word. Cunningham and Stanovich (1998) described the consequences of poor reading skills on vocabulary and language development as the **Matthew effect.** Quoting from the Bible, they explained "that the rich get richer and the poor get poorer." In other words, over time, these students fall further behind their peers and become less likely to engage in reading, which results in a cycle that is difficult to break. Intervention and intensive instruction in word-recognition skills are necessary regardless of the age of the student. The need to provide access to text through assistive technology for these students, however, is imperative as one considers the implications for vocabulary growth and reading proficiency. Students with reading disabilities often have adequate listening comprehension abilities that facilitate acquisition in oral environments. New technologies, as well as some familiar ones (e.g., Learning Ally, Kurzweil 3000, Kindle, Intel Reader), allow them to read with their "ears" and benefit from interaction with text that is appropriate to their abilities, interests, and academic expectations.

Independent reading, particularly in the classroom, should be purposeful and structured. Reading is not a passive activity, whether listening or reading independently. Students need assigned tasks such as searching out intriguing words that can then be recorded on sticky notes, discussed, displayed on word walls, or added to personal dictionaries. Teachers should develop general questions about word meaning and text meaning to guide reading and provide peer time for discussion. A student's independent reading and subsequent discovery of word meaning can be supported by explicit instruction in independent word-learning strategies including using a dictionary (hardcover and online), morphology, and context.

Word Consciousness

Word consciousness is defined as an interest in and awareness of words (Graves & Watts, 2002). Although this instructional approach has not yet been fully researched, it is considered a promising practice. Those who are word conscious might be described as being words attuned or word omnivores. They are attracted to interesting words read or heard, recognize their communicative powers, and are metalingusitically responsive to all aspects of a word including linguistic structure and semantic connections. Teachers and students who are word conscious openly display an excitement and eagerness for learning new words.

Word consciousness can be nurtured in several ways in the educational setting by a thoughtful teacher. Word play includes at least eight categories that are rich sources of student activity (Johnson, Johnson, & Schlicting, 2004):

1. Expressions (proverbs, idioms)

2. Figures of speech (similes, metaphors)

3. Word associations (synonyms, antonyms)

4. Onomastics (story of names)

5. Word formations (affixes, acronyms)

6. Word manipulations (anagrams, palindromes)

7. Word games (alliteration, tongue twisters)

8. Ambiguous words and phrases

Authors of children's and adult's books, such as Dr. Seuss, Shel Silverstein, and Richard Lederer, have recognized the potential of word play, and their works contain multiple examples of the subtleties of language. Consider this excerpt containing an illustration of "mangling modifiers" from Lederer's *Anguished English:*

> Newman, author of two Book-of the Month Club books on the abuse of language, hinted in a speech to nearly 1,300 persons in the Memorial Union Theater that efforts to improve language may be the results of attacks on pompous, weird language such as his. (1987, p. 150)

Exploring figurative language can be intriguing and stimulate interest in words and, at the same time, clarify many of the confusions caused by its abstract nature. Digging into the history of an expression is often enlightening. For instance, how did the expression "face the music" come to mean accepting the consequences of an unpleasant situation? It is reported that long ago, when soldiers were derelict in performing their duties, they were dismissed and required to march slowly between their colleagues as they played drums and other musical instruments to signal their departure (Garrison, 1992). Children are often fascinated by these language forms but confounded by their meanings. In a conversation with a 6-year-old child, he shared that he had learned a saying, "chip off the old block." When asked for an example of the meaning, he replied that he knew he was not a chip off the old block of his father. He explained that his dad is bald and quickly added that he was a chip off his mother because they both have blue eyes. Although his example is somewhat basic, this child is beginning to grasp the more abstract meaning of the expression. By the way, the expression originated in the 1600s and literally meant a chip off a block of wood. It eventually came to mean a person made of the same stuff or the spitting image of someone.

Figurative language can be problematic for many children, particularly students who are ELLs and have language learning disabilities. Teachers need to demystify meaning; hence, the need for on purpose incidental instruction. It is suggested that educators identify more transparent examples of these expressions in speech and print as a starting point and also consider these instructional tips (Moats & Hennessy, 2010):

• Recognize figurative language in text or in conversation—explain it directly.

• Connect it to context and provide an additional example.

- Ask students to explain meaning in their own words.

- Ask students to use the expression and provide more examples.

- Create visuals (posters, picture walls) of meaning.

Students can also tap into multiple resources such as the *Dictionary of Idioms* (Terban, 1996) to support understanding of figurative language and other aspects of word meaning in the home and classroom. *Super Silly Sayings that Are Over Your Head: A Children's Illustrated Book of Idioms* (Snodgrass, 2004) is specifically designed for children who have difficulty with expressions that say one thing and mean another. The author used illustrations to explain the literal and abstract meanings of expressions (e.g., "when something is over your head" is defined as really meaning "something is very hard to understand" and is accompanied by illustrations of both the literal and figurative meaning of the expression). In *More Parts* (Arnold, 2001), the author concluded that adults say the strangest things, such as "give me a hand," "hold your tongue," and "scream your lungs out." *The King Who Rained* (Gwynne, 1970) targeted multiple meanings, and *The Phantom Tollbooth* (Juster, 2001) took students on a journey to the fantasy world of Dictionopolis where they encounter fascinating plays on words from music, mathematics, science, and other fields.

One other activity that may stand alone or be integrated with others (read-alouds or structured independent reading) asks students to become word detectives and search out "fancy" words. Consider how one primary-grade teacher facilitated a discovery and shared words by reading the story of a lone buoy in St. Louis Bay and its adventures as a hurricane roared ashore (Andry, 2005). The teacher discussed essential background information and key word meanings prior to initial reading. During a second reading, children listened for fancy words with the teacher, pausing purposefully and asking for examples. As students identified words (e.g., *swirling, nautical, turbulent*), the teacher briefly provided a student-friendly definition using the context of the story. Students collected favorite words, wrote them on index cards, illustrated with a picture, and provided an example of use. Cards were posted around the room and in the halls outside the classroom. As the collection grew, the teacher periodically scheduled a "walk about" for students to discuss those words that interested them and asked them to add information to the cards (e.g., synonyms, antonyms, related words, figurative expression). There are several ways this could be adapted for older students who can discover and record words independently from texts or discussions and then discuss individual personal dictionaries during scheduled meet-and-greet times.

Teachers have the power and potential to promote word consciousness in their students. They can influence student perception and interest in words through a word use focus during reading, writing, and discussion as exemplified in a 7-year teacher-based project (Scott & Nagy, 2004). Several of the activities are similar to those already described, including focusing students on how authors and students themselves use words and phrases to express thinking orally and in writing.

Reflect and Respond

1. What on purpose incidental instructional practices do you use?

2. What changes might you make to instruction based on your reading?

3. What insights have you gained about incidental instruction?

Intentional Intensive Instruction

Multiple approaches and activities are necessary for school-age individuals to acquire the word meanings necessary to participate in academic tasks. Intentional intensive instruction includes the explicit teaching of individual words and independent word-learning strategies. Teaching individual words brings up questions about instructional guidelines and routines, choice of words, and design of activities that foster breadth as well as depth. Instruction of independent word-learning strategies requires discussing effective approaches including using the dictionary, context, and morphology.

Explicit Teaching of Individual Words

Strong evidence exists for teaching individual words using practices that maximize learning. Research studies, reviews, and reports of groups such as the NRP (NICHD, 2000) point to several factors that contribute to teaching/learning of individual word meanings. Researchers (Biemiller & Slonin, 2001) have noted that differences in vocabulary acquisition emerge early, and the gap only widens as students move through the grades. Hence, the need to teach targeted words early to all students but particularly to those who struggle with reading and, subsequently, are less likely to read independently. Stahl and Fairbanks (1986) identified three principles that remain relevant for teaching individual words and are reflected in the work of others. Stahl (2005) has elaborated on and provided additional examples for these guidelines.

1. Using definitional and contextual information. Definitional information can include synonyms, antonyms, examples, nonexamples, and differences in related words. Contextual information can be provided through discussing meaning in different sentences, scenarios, creation of sentences, and silly questions.

2. Providing multiple exposures to targeted words. Use words orally and in written expression in different contexts individually and collaboratively.

3. Engaging in deep processing of word-generating information that ties the word to known information. Building connections to related words and knowledge through activities such as extended discussion, categorization, and semantic mapping.

Others (e.g., Kame'enui, Carnine, Dixon, Simmons, & Coyne, 2002) have advocated for using validated principles such as conspicuous instruction, which includes direct presentation of word meaning, extensive teacher modeling in multiple contexts, and scheduled practice and review. This type of instruction goes beyond the outdated practice of simply looking up the word in the dictionary and using it in a sentence. The teacher is in control of word choice, context, and the activities necessary to prompt deep understanding necessary for applying knowledge.

Word Choice

The question of word choice is complicated by many factors, beginning with the number of words students encounter in oral and print environments. We already know that dictionaries have close to 300,000 words. Nagy and Anderson (1984) reviewed 5 million words sampled from school texts (third through ninth grade) and estimated there to be 88,500 word families in printed school English. Why so many? Our language is "promiscuous" based primarily in Anglo-Saxon, Romance, and Greek roots. It continues to grow each year, as evidenced by the fact that Oxford tracks how our language changes yearly (http://www.oxford.com). Their researchers discuss newly coined terms yearly and ultimately choose a "word of the year." The 2009 choice was *unfriend,* which is defined as a verb meaning, *"to remove someone as a 'friend' on a social networking site such as Facebook."*

Although the average student accrues 2,500–3,000 word meanings yearly, it is impossible for teachers to directly and explicitly teach that many words. As noted earlier, the majority of word meanings will be acquired incidentally. How many words can a teacher target for instruction? Most in the field agree that optimally 10–15 words per week can be taught directly and in depth (Beck et al., 2002; Biemiller, 2005). This equates to approximately 300–400 words per year. Which words should educators choose to target? The nature of the words themselves, some more common than others, some more reflective of academic texts, others content specific, and some cross content boundaries, has influenced the thinking of researchers in this field. Although the question of selection has not yet been entirely resolved, several researchers have provided a rationale for word choice. Hiebert and Kamil (2005) proposed that word frequency, importance, and utility and instructional potential should guide decisions about choice. Most agree that students must learn academic words that are multifunctional (cut across domains) and that are critical to understanding text.

Beck et al. (2002) provided a teacher-friendly framework that uses a tiered structure and is based on the role words play in language. These tiers provide guidance for selecting words for intentional instruction:

- *Tier One words* are common basic words that are used in everyday conversations and that most children know (e.g., *tell, ask, work*); these are not usually the target of instruction. When students are not familiar with these words, the authors suggested informal and brief ways to prompt encounters with them.

- *Tier Two words* are more sophisticated and are often used by mature language users in speech and writing; found across a variety of texts and domains (e.g., *declare, inquire, product*); and students usually have an understanding of underlying concepts. This tier is the instructional target.

- *Tier Three words* have more narrow and specific roles in language; words that are not necessarily familiar to mature language users. They are more specific to a domain and are more likely to be taught through explanation in context (e.g., *homeostasis*). Although important, they are not the focus of targeted productive instruction.

The lines between the tiers are not crystal clear and teacher judgment will always be a critical variable. Knowing what your students know as well as the academic demand is key to selecting words for instruction. For example, Tier Two words for Spanish-speaking ELLs should include cognates.

Beck et al. (2002) also offered general criteria for selection, including:

- *Importance and utility*: Words that are characteristic of mature language users and appear frequently across a variety of domains

- *Instructional potential*: Words that can be worked within a variety of ways so that students can build deep knowledge of them and of their connections to other words and concepts

- *Conceptual understanding*: Words for which students understand the general concept but provide precision and specificity in describing the concept

Graves (2006) proposed that the answers to the following four questions may be helpful in deciding which words to teach from a reading selection:

1. Is understanding the word important to understanding the selection in which it appears. If the answer is yes, then the word is a good candidate.

2. Are students able to use context, structural word analysis, or dictionary skills to discover the word's meanings? If yes, then this is an opportunity for practice.

3. Can working with this word be useful in furthering student's context, structural analysis, or dictionary skills? If yes, then working with the word will help them learn the word and acquire word-learning strategies.

4. How useful is this word outside of the reading selection currently being read? If it is a word that appears more frequently in text, then the more important it is to know and increased encounters will facilitate learning it.

His questions consider not only the explicit teaching of individual words but also independent learning strategies.

Where do teachers find the words they can choose for instruction? There are several word lists that are important sources of information about word frequency that can provide guidance, but there is no perfect list. Some common recommendations include Fry's *Instant Words* (1985), which consists of 1,000 words that students will frequently encounter in oral and written language. *A General Service List of English Words* (West, 1953) has twice as many words that were selected as those of greatest "general service" to learners of English. Marzano, Kendall, and Paynter (1991) developed *Analysis and Identification of Basic Words in Grades K–6,* which includes a set of almost 7,000 basic words encountered in academic settings. Coxhead's (2000) *A New Academic Word List* has 570 word families consisting of words that occur frequently over a wide range of academic texts that are relevant for students in middle school and beyond. Last, another source that is less accessible is *The Living Word Vocabulary* (Dale & O'Rourke, 1981), which provides a sense of words students are likely to know or not at various grade levels.

Educators have traditionally used their teacher editions/student text as a source of vocabulary words that may or may not identify words based on criteria discussed. Teachers need to be empowered to identify words in student text and from other sources that are most critical for their students' understanding and ability to participate in academic tasks. These may include words from the lists noted and curriculum and standards documents as well as common assessment terms. Just imagine regular and special educators, informed by suggested guidelines and sources, working collaboratively across disciplines and/or grade levels to identify common targeted vocabulary terms that could be addressed throughout a school day.

Instructional Routines

Effective instructional routines acknowledge dimensions of word knowledge and principles of effective instruction. Moats (2009) suggested the following steps for introducing a new word:

1. Pronounce the word, write and read it (discuss linguistic structure).
"Say this word after me: *exotic*. How many syllables do you hear in this word? Let's read, spell, and write this word. What part of speech is this word?"

2. Tell students what the new word means, using a student-friendly definition that includes references that they will understand.

"Something or someone that is *exotic* is interesting or different and often comes from another country."

3. Say more about the word and use it several times in examples of use.

"People who travel to other parts of the world often sample different foods, see unusual sights, and purchase interesting gifts. They might describe their experience as *exotic*."

"I recently visited China and bought unusual gifts, including a hand-woven silk jacket. I also ate food I had never eaten before, such as sea urchins. My purchases and food choices could be described as *exotic*."

"We sometimes describe aspects of a person's appearance that are unusual or different as *exotic*. The model's makeup was reminiscent of traditional Chinese style. It was *exotic* in appearance."

4. Ask students questions about the word's meaning.

"Could something be *exotic* and ordinary at the same time?"

"Could something be *exotic* and unusual at the same time?"

5. Elicit word use by students.

"Can you use the word *exotic* in a sentence? What are some examples of things that are *exotic*?"

This routine reflects the importance of providing definitional and contextual information. It also recognizes the limitations of dictionary definitions, which are based on an Aristotelian view of meaning that sorts words by category and how the word differs from other members of the category or genus (Stahl, 2005). Although it is important for students to understand the relationship of a word to others, category, and distinguishing or different features, the explanation needs to be expressed in language that students can understand and use. Student-friendly definitions explain word meanings in everyday language and in complete sentences. The words *someone* or *something* usually frame the definition (Beck, McKeown, & Kucan, 2008). Context is integral to understanding meaning. Although text may provide that context, teachers may have to create or elaborate by providing additional scenarios or other contexts for word use. Questioning and word use prompt thinking about word meaning and possible connections with other words. Remember, students will need many encounters in varied contexts for the deep processing necessary for understanding.

Paynter et al. (2005) suggested six concrete steps for learning words, including multiple activities for processing word meaning that represent a combined effort of teacher and student. This framework for direct instruction could be enriched by adding pronunciation and discussing linguistic structure.

1. The teacher identifies the new word and elicits students' background knowledge.

2. The teacher explains the meaning of the new word and clears up confusion.

3. Students generate their own examples.

4. Students create a visual representation of the new word.

5. Students engage in experiences that depend on their understanding of the new word.

6. Students engage in vocabulary games and activities to help them remember the word and word meaning.

Many of the elements of instructional routines are incorporated in supplemental programs such as Marzano and Pickering's (2005) *Building Academic Vocabulary* and Ebbers and Carroll's (2009) *Daily Oral Vocabulary Exercises*. The latter program also accommodates for students who are ELLs and those with language learning disabilities. Multiple repetitions of targeted words (minimum 30) and contextualized exposures (maximum 88) across a year's instruction recognizes increased intensity necessary for struggling readers. The pairing of Spanish cognates with targeted words, which is an effective method for teaching ELLs, is included as words are introduced.

Strategies and Activities

There are two general categories of strategies for teaching new words—teach new words for known concepts and teach new words for new concepts (Baumann, Kame'enui, & Ash, 2003). Approaches for teaching new concepts often involve exploring semantic and conceptual relationships and engaging in multiple receptive and expressive processing opportunities. The following strategies and activities will focus on connections and relationships between words by using semantic maps, scaling, concept maps, visual and physical representations, and mnemonics.

Semantic Relationships

Semantic mapping is a broad term for any graphic organizer that focuses on the relationships of words. These maps can serve multiple purposes but usually focus on semantic features of words such as categories, subcategories, synonyms, antonyms, or multiple meanings. They allow students to consider a hierarchy of information as well as connect known and new information to facilitate learning. Semantic mapping contributes to text comprehension and is effective for all students as well as for upper elementary bilingual and secondary students with learning disabilities (Bos & Anders, 1992).

Stahl and Kapinus (2001) provided some useful procedures for developing semantic maps when working with text:

- Brainstorm and discuss words that go with the targeted topic.

- Develop a map with the topic printed in a circle in the middle. Have the students come up with categories for the brainstormed words, add the words to these categories, connect the categories to the topic, and add a blank category circle to use after reading.

- Read the selection and follow up with the map, adding additional terms and categories from the text when appropriate.

For example, if the text topic was storms, then a brainstorming session might initially bring up words such as *northeaster, hurricane, blizzard, wind, heavy rain, snow, flooding, loss of electricity,* and *downed trees* (see Figure 11.4).

Students, particularly those with language learning disabilities or ELLs, may need more **scaffolding** and support creating semantic maps. For example, after introducing a topic word, teachers can create sets of related word cards that include subcategories with more words. Students can work in large or, eventually, small groups to sort and arrange cards. In a large group, each student would receive a card and the class would arrange themselves in a circle. The teacher would model review of each word, the discovery of "relatives" that could cluster, and a label based on shared features (subcategory). Students could arrange themselves physically as a map of the word *storm*.

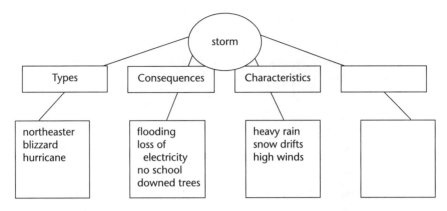

Figure 11.4.   A semantic map. (Reprinted with permission from Sopris West Educational Services. LETRS Module 7: Teaching Phonics, Word Study, and the Alphabetic Principle by Louisa C. Moats © 2005.)

The blank box on the map represents additional information gained from text reading that could be incorporated into the map.

Semantic maps reflect the extent or depth of a student's word knowledge. A more mature learner's map of this word or other words grows with experience and exposure. Sophisticated semantic maps eventually contain other dimensions of word knowledge. Revisit the semantic map for the word dimensions (see Figure 11.4). Although this representation appears complex for most learners, much of the information represented can be elicited by thoughtful questioning. Consider the following activity based on *Anything Goes* (Richele, 2004), which incorporates words from *Henry and Mudge and the Starry Night* (Rylant, 2005), a story in a second-grade basal. The questions can be adapted based on words selected but each taps different aspects of word meaning (see Table 11.5). After introducing and discussing targeted words, the teacher displays the vocabulary words on easel paper, chalkboard, or white board; identifies specific words; and asks students to respond to related questions.

Semantic Feature Analysis   Semantic feature analysis assists students in thinking about what features discriminate one word from another. This technique is particularly helpful in assisting students to understand the relations between concepts, vocabulary words, and ideas in text (Bos & Anders, 1990). Students work with a matrix that identifies words related to a particular topic or concept usually found in the left-hand column of the matrix. Shared or different characteristics are arranged along the top of the chart. Students check off shared features and can indicate uncertainty with a question mark (see Figure 11.5). Topics can range from types of vehicles and descriptions of energy sources to traits of world leaders. Depth of understanding is reflected in the ability to actually identify shared semantic properties or features. Semantic feature analysis is particularly appropriate for use in content areas (Stahl & Kapinus, 2001) and for junior and high school students with learning and reading disabilities (Bos & Anders, 1990). Discussion is critical to deep understanding of the topic and related words.

Semantic Gradients for Synonyms and Antonyms   Definitional information includes semantic information about words, such as category and features. The more semantic features words share, the more synonymous there are, with the reverse being true for antonyms. Using semantic gradients, teachers and students can order or arrange words

Table 11.5.   Anything goes!

Targeted words	Questions
Lantern	Who can pronounce this word?
Snuggled	Who can put this word in a sentence?
Sappy	What part of speech is this word?
Shiver	How many syllables in this word?
Doe	Can you find a compound word?
Fawn	What is the base word in this word?
Tender	What is the past tense of this word?
Tent	Spell it.
Campfire	How are these two words related?
Hike	What is the definition of this word?

by comparing subtle differences in meaning. Authors choose words carefully to convey precise meaning. It is expected that students will understand these subtle differences when they read and when they choose precise words to express themselves in writing. Engaging in semantic gradient exercises can clarify understanding (see Figure 11.6). Although *sad* describes someone who is unhappy, other words such as *pained, down, gloomy, dejected, despondent, heartbroken, miserable, unhappy,* and *depressed* could be used to express this emotion. Likewise, the word *happy* describes someone who is pleased, but words such as *cheerful, content, glad, thrilled, delighted, overjoyed,* and *ecstatic* are usually considered synonymous. Each word is subtly different from the other, even though they are close in connotation. Consider the synonyms provided for *happy* and *sad*. Where might you place them on this continuum that ranges from *really happy* to *really sad?*

Of course, prerequisites to this activity include developing synonyms for targeted words incidentally and intentionally. For example, synonyms are taught as they are encountered in speech or text. Stahl (2004) called this "point of contact" teaching. This activity can be scaffolded through brainstorming, discussing, using word cards (with picture cues), and providing examples of meaning ranging from *a little sad* to *really sad*. Can you visualize students arranging themselves physically from *happiest* to *saddest* and then discussing their placement? Eventually, students can be responsible for brainstorming, scaling, and rationalizing assigned pairs of words.

Categories	Invertebrates	Vertebrates	Wings	Scales	Limbs/legs	Fins	Cold blooded
Birds		✓	✓		✓		
Insects	✓		✓		✓		✓
Fish		✓		✓		✓	✓
Reptiles		✓		✓	*		✓
Crustaceans	✓				✓		
Rodents		✓			✓		
Amphibians		✓			✓		✓

Figure 11.5.   A semantic feature analysis matrix. (*Key:* *some reptiles.)

Really happy _____ Really sad

Using the words provided in the chapter text, where would you place them on the continuum?

Figure 11.6. Semantic gradient scale.

Concept Maps   Concept maps are similar to semantic maps and are generally used to teach new words for new concepts. The procedure for the original Frayer Model (Frayer, Frederick, & Klausmeier, 1969) includes seven steps:

1. Define the new concept, discriminating the attributes relevant to all instances of the concept.

2. Discriminate the relevant from irrelevant properties of instances of the concept.

3. Provide an example of the concept.

4. Provide a nonexample of the concept.

5. Relate the concept to a subordinate concept.

6. Relate the concept to a superordinate concept.

7. Relate the concept to a coordinate term.

The procedure is rather complex and time consuming, even though it is considered effective for teaching new words. It has provided guidance, however, for more streamlined models including the concept map (see Figure 11.7), developed by Schwartz and Raphael (1985), or Four Square, suggested by Lenski, Wham, and Johns (2003). These generally call for a definition, characteristics of the words, and examples and nonexamples.

Variations on this model include changing content, such as substituting personal connection for examples or a picture or synonyms/antonyms for nonexamples. Yet, another model taps into attributes of word meaning using descriptions or clues related to the senses to identify the targeted word. This model also supports understanding context clues. After introducing and discussing the targeted word, the teacher presents and fills in clues step by step as students attempt to identify the word. Eventually, students work individually or with a partner to develop their own maps and can attempt to stump their peers. A map for the word *tenement* is illustrated in Figure 11.8.

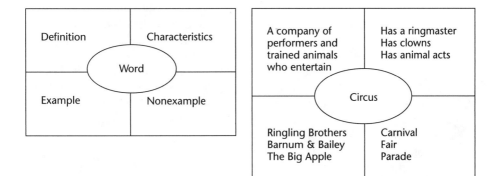

Figure 11.7. Concept map. (From Paynter, D.E., Bodrova, E., & Doty, J.K. [2005]. *For the love of words: Vocabulary instruction that works in grades K–6.* San Francisco: Jossey-Bass; adapted by permission.)

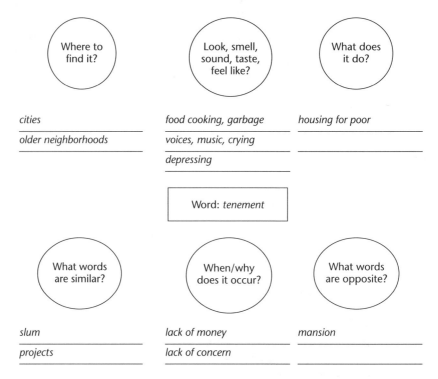

Figure 11.8. Word clues. (From Graves, M.F. [2006]. *The vocabulary book: Learning and instruction.* New York: Teachers College Press; adapted by permission.)

Questions, Examples, and Connections   Beck et al. (2002) developed several extension activities that probe individual word meanings and relationships (see Figure 11.9). These incorporate using questions, examples, and connections to other word meanings so that students have the opportunity to work with definitional and contextual information and engage in deep processing of word meaning.

Visual Representations and Physical Responses   Creating visual representations of word meaning can be effective with younger and older students as well as those with individual needs. Pictures can be accessed electronically (clip art) or drawn by hand. A key consideration is the student's ability to explain why the picture is representative of meaning. Following explicit teaching of word meaning, students write their own definitions of words, create pictures, and generate example sentences. These may be recorded on index cards, in notebooks, in vocabulary logs, or on posters. In one ninth-grade cotaught English class, teachers asked students to create posters representing targeted vocabulary words for each unit of study. These were displayed around the classroom and served as reference, discussion, and review purposes. At quiz time, definitions were covered but pictures were available to prompt recall of meaning. Students' learning of vocabulary words was sufficiently scaffolded to facilitate performance on quizzes and tests.

Movement can also play a role in learning word meaning. Beck and colleagues (1982) designed an activity that grouped specific words from a reading passage by the

Example/nonexample	Questions, reasons, examples
Repeat the description.	Why would someone weep?
If I say something that would be considered traditional, then say "traditional."	Under what circumstances have you had to adapt?
Turkey at Thanksgiving, gifts at Christmas, cake at birthday parties	When might you compensate someone?
	How might you be demanding?
	Can you think of a family tradition?
Applause, applause	**Connections**
Clap how much you would like to be described as adaptable.	Would you be considered responsible if you accepted consequences of misbehaving?
Clap how much you would like to be described as demanding.	In what ways might being traditional be in conflict with being adaptable?
Clap how much you would like to be described as responsible.	
Describe a time when:	**Relationships**
You were responsible	How are these words related?
You celebrated a tradition	Adapt, consequences
You were demanding	Demanding, weep
You wept	Tradition, responsible

Figure 11.9.   Examples of questions, examples, and connections. (*Source:* Beck, McKeown, & Kucan, 2002.)

semantic category "How We Move Our Legs." Students were taught a limited set of movements for each word (e.g., stalk, trudge). As words were encountered during oral reading of the passage, students acted them out. Teachers indicated students were enthusiastic about this activity and researchers reported some success with putting motions to words. Paynter et al. (2005) described a sixth-grade activity involving words associated with parts of a tree such as *crown, trunk, xylem, sapwood, phloem,* and *bark.* After instruction and creating word cards with a definition and picture, students thought about the position their word would occupy in a drawing of a tree. Then, instead of drawing it, students became the tree by placing themselves on the floor to represent each of their words.

Key Word Method   The key word method links an acoustic cue to a pictorial representation associated with the meaning of the word. Carlisle and Katz (2005) reported that this and other mnemonic strategies for teaching vocabulary are prevalent in the learning disabilities literature and have been effective in promoting word recall comprehension in students with learning disabilities (Scruggs & Mastropieri, 1990) and with limited English proficiency (Zhang & Schumm, 2000). Learners identify a part of a word to be learned that sounds like a known word. For example, the word *log* is recognizable in *loggia,* which means balcony. This becomes the key word referent and is represented with a picture and word meaning. The association itself does not need to make a lot of sense; its memorability is more important. This method has been well researched and there have been positive results for different learners and varied words (NICHD, 2000). Despite its effectiveness, this method has not had a significant affect on educational practice, possibly because of the time required for implementation.

Review and Respond

1. Why was it important to discuss explicit teaching, word choice, and instructional routines before considering strategies and activities?

2. What is the common instructional thread in the majority of these strategies and activities?

3. In what ways are they different from traditional vocabulary instruction?

Independent Word-Learning Strategies

Given that independent reading is a primary source of word learning, students need tools to unlock and infer the meanings of unknown words in text. The explicit teaching of independent word-learning strategies will facilitate their ability to work with text. Three effective strategies include using

1. Dictionaries

2. Context

3. Morphology

Although each will be discussed separately, they are often used interdependently by students. Teachers should be careful not to convey that one excludes the use of the other.

Dictionaries

The dictionary can be a valuable resource and reference tool if students understand how and when to use it. Dictionaries are a source of information on linguistic structure, etymology, syntax, and meaning. They should not be viewed as an effective method for explicitly teaching individual word meanings due to inherent limitations, including truncated or shortened definitions, multiple definitions that necessitate identification of relevant meaning, provision of definitional information, and lack of contextual information.

Dictionaries usually work best when the student has some sense of the targeted word's meaning. Carlisle and Katz (2005) reported students with language learning disabilities often have trouble with densely worded and multiple definitions provided for a given word. These students find it difficult to tell which definition is appropriate for a word in a given context and need additional techniques for figuring out the meaning of a word in a specific context. There are also a number of prerequisite skills for independent use, not the least of which are reading and spelling skills that may be problematic for struggling readers. Explicit instruction in the subskills of this independent word-learning strategy, such as alphabetical order (see Chapter 6); use of guide words, symbols, and abbreviations; and overall format is essential. Knowing that definitions typically include category or synonym as well as features or characteristics that differentiate the word from others that are similar can be useful. Blachowicz and Fisher (2010) identified five steps necessary to using a dictionary effectively:

1. Knowing when to use a dictionary

2. Knowing how to locate a word

3. Knowing the parts of a dictionary entry

4. Choosing between multiple meanings

5. Applying the meaning

In addition, not all dictionaries are created equal. There are student-friendly editions such as the *Collin's COBUILD New Students' Dictionary* (2002) or *Longman Dictionary of American English* (4th edition; 2007) that provide contexts for word meanings that help clarify understanding and meaning.

Other sources of word meaning include online dictionaries (e.g., http://www.merriam-webster.com) and online thesauruses (e.g., http://www.visualthesaurus.com) can extend understanding of word meaning by providing distinctions between targeted words, synonyms, and visual representations. The Visual Dictionary (http://www.visual.merriam-webster.com) includes more than 6,000 visual images on 15 different themes (e.g., animal kingdom, human body, energy). These resources often have an audio component that pronounces targeted words and reads entries, which is particularly helpful for struggling readers.

Context

Context can be broadly interpreted as any meaning cues within context, including linguistic (e.g., words, phrases, sentences) and nonlinguistic information (e.g., illustrations, typographic features that surround the unfamiliar word), that can be used to infer the word's meaning (Edwards, Font, Baumann, & Boland, 2004). Generally, research studies have focused on using linguistic cues. Blachowicz and Fisher (2010) suggested that the following are representative of necessary metacognitive processes for using context:

1. Students must know why and when to use context.

2. Students must have a general idea about clues that may be provided by context.

3. Students must know how to look for and use these clues.

Educators need to understand that not all contexts are sufficiently explicit to prompt inference of word meaning. In fact, some contexts may confound understanding. Educators need to sensitize students as to why and when to use context. Beck et al. (2002) studied natural contexts (texts) in which words are encountered and identified four categories that describe characteristics of context for inferring word meaning:

1. Misdirective: Inadequate information leads to incorrect meaning.

2. Nondirective: Insufficient information leads to the inability to infer meaning.

3. Directive: Adequate information leads to specific meaning.

4. General: Adequate information leads to general understanding.

If the context is to be meaningful, then students need to identify and use specific linguistic cues. Baumann, Edwards, Boland, Olejnik, and Kame'enui (2003) explored the effectiveness of teaching middle school students to use word part clues and context clues separately and in conjunction with each other. They directly explained and taught students to use different types of context cues, including:

- Definition: The author explains the meaning of the word in the sentence or selection.

- Synonym: The author uses a word similar in meaning.

- Antonym: The author uses a word nearly opposite in meaning.

- Example: The author provides one or more examples of words or ideas.

- General: The author provides several words or statements that give clues to the word's meanings.

Explicit instruction of context cues included teacher modeling and guided and independent practice on selected passages. Results indicated that students who were taught specific types of context cues could and did use this knowledge to infer meanings of unfamiliar words.

A more basic approach designed by Lubliner (2005) for upper elementary students teaches context cues as one of several strategies for figuring out word meaning while reading. A context cue card prompts students to use the following clues that have been previously taught:

- Consider the context (read the sentence, paragraph, or passage for clues)

- Look for comma clues (meanings sometimes hide within commas [e.g., definition])

- Look for explanation clues (explanation is sometimes provided in adjacent sentences)

- Look for feeling clues (other words that represent a feeling or emotion)

- Look for opposition clues—words such as adversative or conditional conjunctions (e.g., *but, even though, however*)

Students who have language learning disabilities are often less successful inferring meaning from either external (context) or internal (prefixes, roots, suffixes) cues. They may lack the semantic and conceptual knowledge needed to infer meanings of words from context (whether oral or written language is involved). The usefulness of any context clue depends on a reader's linguistic knowledge and ability to see relationships between words. Even when context can yield sufficient information for a specific or general meaning, it cannot be assumed that students will use this resource. According to Carlisle and Katz (2005), teachers should not avoid instruction in using context clues to learn new words; rather, instruction should be carefully planned and scaffolded as needed. More intensive instruction specific to cues and increased amounts of guided practice may be needed for students with language learning disabilities or ELLs.

Morphology

Morphology plays an essential role in reading, spelling, and developing a receptive and expressive vocabulary. Morphemes are the basic units of language learning that carry meaning. Our metalinguistic awareness of language is not limited to an analysis of sound but includes the ability to recognize these meaning units (e.g., base words, prefixes, inflectional and derivational suffixes, roots, Greek forms). The English language is considered morphophonemic with sounds and meaning driving orthographic representation. For example, the spelling of the root *duc* in *deduce, deduct,* and *reduction* is preserved, despite the addition of affixes, to maintain meaning. It might also be considered morphosyntactic in that derivational endings drive part of speech or function of words within sentences. Morphological awareness accounts for unique variance in vocabulary beginning in kindergarten and increases over time (Carlisle, 2000). Students who are better readers tend to be more aware of morphemes and their meanings than students who struggle with reading (Carlisle & Rice, 2002). Those with reading difficulties also exhibit significantly lower recognition and spelling of derived words (Carlisle & Katz, 2005).

A young child's first words are basic, relate to everyday experiences, and are usually Anglo-Saxon in origin (e.g., *mother, food, play, sun*). As children become more inventive and insightful about language, these base words are compounded (e.g., *sunshine, playground*) and inflectional endings are added (e.g., *walked, stopping, boys*). Eventually, children become aware of more complex meaning structures that include bound morphemes such as prefixes, roots, and derivational suffixes (e.g., *instruction*) as well as Greek forms (e.g., *psychology*).

Good readers' minds coordinate the information inherent within words, the phonology, orthography, morphology, and vocabulary, to facilitate the reading of text. Studying meaningful parts of words and their origin assists vocabulary development, word recognition, and spelling. Morphemic analysis allows students to parse words into parts to infer meaning of unknown words. In addition to context cues in text, morphemic analysis is considered a major source of information immediately available to a reader as he or she encounters new words (Nagy & Scott, 2000). Anglin (1993) found that the majority of new words learned by students in first through fifth grade were derivations. This is not surprising when one considers the nature of words encountered in text. The estimated numbers of derived words in text (60% in printed school English; Nagy & Anderson, 1984) and on academic word lists (more than 85% are from Latin and/or Greek origin) confirm the importance of developing student ability to tap into this resource. An examination of social studies, literature, and science texts for later elementary through high school yield multiple examples that affirm this statement.

There is evidence that morphemic cues can assist students with high and low reading proficiency decode words and decipher the meaning of words (Nagy & Scott, 2000). Students with and without learning disabilities can make significant improvement in word learning, reading, and spelling when provided with instruction in structural analysis and etymology (Henry, 2010). Analysis of words with prefixes and suffixes has been found to be helpful for older students with learning disabilities (Elbro & Arnbak, 1996). Although research studies in this area are more limited, researchers recognize the need for additional study, acknowledging that this area is "too valuable a resource to ignore" (Stahl & Nagy, 2006, p. 159).

It is particularly important that morphemes be explicitly and systematically taught. Modeling and guided and independent practice, coupled with discussion, are critical to student learning. An instructional sequence should be logical and based on emergence and frequency of morphemes in spoken and written language. Children generally understand inflectional endings (*-ed, -ing, -s*) and compounds before they understand derivations, which are learned more gradually with instruction usually beginning in third grade. Stahl (1999) suggested that instruction begin with the most common affixes and roots. White, Sowell, and Yanaghihara (1989) identified the most common prefixes and suffixes (see Table 11.6), providing a starting point for instruction.

The literature provides general principles and guidelines for teaching morphemes:

- Teach morphology in the context of rich explicit vocabulary instruction.

- Teach students to use morphology as a cognitive strategy with explicit steps (e.g., decomposition of words into free and bound morphemes).

- Teach the underlying morphological knowledge needed in two ways—explicitly and in context.

- Teach morphology in relation to cognate instruction for students with a developed knowledge of Spanish.

Table 11.6. Common prefixes and suffixes

Frequency rank	Prefix	Suffix
1	*un-*	*-s, -es*
2	*re-*	*-ed*
3	*im-, in-, il-*	*-ing*
4	*dis-*	*-ly*
5	*en-, em-*	*-er, -or* (agent)
6	*non-*	*-ion, -ation, -ition, -tion*
7	*in-, im-*	*-able, -ible*
8	*over-*	*-al, -ial*
9	*mis-*	*-y*
10	*sub-*	*-ness*
11	*pre-*	*-ity, -ty*
12	*inter-*	*-ment*
13	*fore-*	*-ic*
14	*de-*	*-ous, -ious, -eous*
15	*trans-*	*-en*
16	*super-*	*-er* (comparative)
17	*semi-*	*-ive, -tive, -ative*
18	*anti-*	*-ful*
19	*mid-*	*-less*
20	*under-* (too little)	*-est*

From White, T.G., Sowell, J., & Yanagihara, A. (1989). Teaching elementary students to use word part clues. *The Reading Teacher, 42,* 302–308; reprinted by permission.

Edwards et al. (2004) specifically recommended

- Providing explicit instruction in how morpheme analysis works.

- Using word families to promote vocabulary growth (e.g., *cycle, monocycle, bicycle, tricycle*).

- Promoting independent use of morphemic analysis (e.g., create an "affixionary") by alphabetically listing affixes and roots.

- Enhancing student awareness that morphemic analysis does not always work (e.g., inconsistency of prefix meanings: *in* means "into" or "not").

Direct instruction of meaning, examples in context, and working with addition/substitution of affixes can facilitate recognition and understanding of morphemic clues. Multiple activities including manipulating affix and root cards, brainstorming semantic maps (e.g., root words and relatives), sorting (e.g., suffix—part of speech), and word-building activities are effective tools for teaching morphemes. For example, derivational suffixes can signal function and meaning of affixed words. A "suffix sort" uses a set of two-sided suffix cards and a set of headings (e.g., noun, adjective, adverb, verb). Side A has the suffix written on it (see Figure 11.10). Side B identifies the part of speech and additional information about the suffix (see Figure 11.11). Students arrange headings across their desks and work in pairs to categorize suffixes by parts of speech and then flip cards over to check responses.

Baumann, Edwards, and colleagues (2003), in conjunction with their study on context clues, studied the effectiveness of teaching middle school students to use word

Parts of speech *Noun* *Verb* *Adjective* *Adverb*		*-al, -ial*	*-ly*
-able	*-ous, -ious*	*-en*	*-est*
-ment	*-ful*	*-ize*	*-ion, -tion, -sion*
-ance	*-age*	*-ty, -ity*	*-er*
-ture	*-ible, -able*	*-ive*	*-ary*

Figure 11.10. Suffix sort (Side A).

Parts of speech *Noun* *Verb* *Adjective* *Adverb*		*-al, -ial* relating to or characterized by *adjective*	*-ly* like or manner of *adverb*
-able able, can do; usually used with Anglo-Saxon words *adjective*	*-ous, -ious* full of or having; usually used with Latin roots *-cious, -ious, -tious* *adjective*	*-en* made of *verb* usually used with Anglo-Saxon words *adjective*	*-est* superlative degree *adjective*
-ment act of, state of, result *noun*	*-ful* full of or full; usually used with Anglo-Saxon words *adjective*	*-ize* make *verb*	*-ion, -tion, -sion* act of, state of; *-tion* more common; *-sion* after *ss* *noun*
-ance action or state of *noun*	*-age* collection, mass *noun*	*-ty, -ity* state of or quality *noun*	*-er* one who; *noun* comparative degree; usually used with Anglo-Saxon words *adjective*
-ture state of, process, function, or office *noun*	*-ible, -able* can do; usually used with Latin roots; has a corresponding *-tion* or *-sion* word *adjective*	*-ive* causing or making *adjective*	*-ary* relating to person, place, thing *noun* connected with *adjective*

Figure 11.11. Suffix sort (Side B).

parts, including prefixes, suffixes, and root words. High-frequency prefixes and a few suffixes were emphasized in instruction. Affixes were also clustered into families. Word part clues included

- Looking for the root word, which is a single word that cannot be broken into smaller words or word parts. See if you know what it means.

- Looking for a prefix, which is a word part added to the beginning of a word that changes its meaning. See if you know what the prefix means.

- Looking for a suffix, which is a word part added to the end of a word that changes its meaning. See if you know what the suffix means.

- Putting the meanings of the root word, prefix, and suffix together and see if you can build the meaning of the word.

After explicit instruction, students were able to use their knowledge of morphemes and specific context cues to figure out word meaning.

There are several resources that educators can use to design and deliver explicit instruction in morphology, such as *Unlocking Literacy: Effective Decoding and Spelling Instruction, Second Edition* (Henry, 2010) and *Vocabulary Through Morphemes* (Ebbers, 2003), a comprehensive approach to teaching word structure primarily for vocabulary growth.

Reflect and Respond

1. What insights have you gained about independent word-learning strategies?

Technology

Computer and technology-based activities can support acquisition of vocabulary. The NRP (NICHD, 2000) found four studies that indicated computers may be a vehicle for instruction; two of which suggested that animations of target words may support vocabulary learning and the effectiveness of multimedia presentations for ELLs. **Electronic texts** that include animation cues can provide an enriched context for word learning. Electronic books, which provide facilitation for student engagement, can be effective in word learning. Online resources, such as dictionaries and thesauruses with visual and audio components, are particularly useful for struggling readers and ELLs. **Hyperlinks** or software that allows students to highlight words within text and then hear pronunciations and definitions or view additional graphics can accommodate for reading difficulties. Animations of particular concepts and access to content area web sites can also facilitate understanding. WordSift (http://www.wordsift.com) is an online teacher tool developed for use with ELLs that has potential benefit for all students. Teachers can insert text into a text box that quickly identifies academic vocabulary words. This tool is integrated with Visual Thesaurus (http://www.visualthesaurus.com) and Google Images; as a result, the user is provided with a definition, map of related words, and visual image. Other features are available, including online teacher training videos.

Although there are many vocabulary software programs and online activities available, not all are designed based on what we have learned about productive instruction. It appears it is difficult to design something that moves beyond memorization and drill of isolated meanings and focuses on thinking about understanding of words in varied discourse situations. The PBS Kids sites for younger children are notable exceptions.

The Martha Speaks site (http://www.pbskids.org) is part of PBS' Raising Readers program. Martha is a talking dog who eats the letters of the alphabet, which go to her brain; then she speaks. Games, activities, and video assist young children in learning new words. Activities are also provided for parents and teachers. *Word Girl,* also a PBS creation, is a television show and web site that focuses on word learning. One valuable teaching resource for ELLs and students with language learning disabilities is Lexia Learning products (http://www.lexialearning.com), which includes software and web-based programs.

Last, using digital tools and podcasts to reinforce word learning is a novel idea that deserves attention and more research. This has potential, particularly for students struggling with increasing demands of informational texts. Putnam and Kingsley (2009) provided direction and practical applications in this area through a discussion of teacher-created podcasts.

CONCLUSION

Skilled fluent reading requires developing and interacting with multiple skills. Vocabulary facilitates word recognition through its contributions to phonological awareness and decoding. Its real power, however, lies in its role in comprehension. The ability to construct meaning from text and express it precisely in writing depends on breadth, depth, and access of word meanings.

Vocabulary acquisition begins with birth and continues throughout a lifetime. Initially, learning is incidental and primarily depends on oral language environments. The richness of a child's early language environment has a profound effect on vocabulary growth. Other factors, however, such as language learning disabilities or bilingualism, may inhibit acquisition. The adults in the child's early years play a pivotal role in language development and can intervene effectively when they have the necessary tools.

On average, students recognize 2,500–3,000 words when they enter school and at least 40,000–50,000 when they leave high school. How do they come to know so many words? What does productive vocabulary instruction look like? Students learn words through incidental and intentional instruction. Many words are learned through incidental instruction. Read-alouds, discussions, and independent reading are more effective if purposeful. Word consciousness also plays a role in motivating and getting students interested in words. Once students have acquired proficient word-recognition skills, independent reading becomes the primary source of vocabulary acquisition. This is problematic for the struggling reader or student with dyslexia who cannot read independently; they must be provided with access to print. Intensive intentional instruction includes the explicit teaching of individual words and independent word-learning strategies. Traditional vocabulary practices such as looking up a word in the dictionary and using it in a sentence are replaced by instructional routines and activities that provide definitional and contextual information about words, deep processing of meaning, and multiple encounters in varied contexts. Multiple strategies and activities focus on developing all dimensions of word knowledge, including linguistic structure, synonyms, antonyms, multiple meanings, connotations, and denotations. Independent word-learning strategies for using the dictionary, context, and morphology teach students how to use these approaches to unlock the meaning of words encountered in text.

Regular and special education teachers and specialists must consider effective practices for instruction and the individual needs of ELLs and those with language-based learning disabilities. These students may require more time, practice, feedback, and smaller groups as well as some modification in strategy and activity to become proficient in this critical component of skilled reading.

REFERENCES

Anderson, R.C., Wilson, P.T., & Fielding, L.G. (1988). Growth in reading and how children spend their time outside of school. *Reading Research Quarterly, 23*, 285–303.

Andry, A.A. (2005). *Louie the buoy: A hurricane story.* Sandy Hook, CT: Sandy Hook Press.

Anglin, J.M. (1993). Vocabulary development: A morphological analysis. *Monographs of the Society for Research in Child Development, 58*(10, Serial No. 238).

Arnold, T.A. (2001). *More parts.* New York: Penguin Press.

August, D., & Shanahan, T. (Eds.). (2006). *Developing literacy in second-language learners: Report of the national literacy panel on language minority children and youth.* Mahwah, NJ: Lawrence Erlbaum Associates.

Baker, S.K., Simmons, D.C., & Kame'enui, E.J. (2005). *Vocabulary acquisition: Synthesis of the research.* Washington, DC: National Center to Improve the Tools of Educators.

Baumann, J.F., Edwards, E.C., Boland, E., Olejnik, S., & Kame'enui, E.J. (2003). Vocabulary tricks: Effects of instruction on morphology and context on fifth grade students' ability to derive and infer word meaning. *American Educational Research Journal, 40*, 447–494.

Baumann, J.F., & Kame'enui, E.J. (2004). (Eds.). *Vocabulary instruction: Research to practice.* New York: Guilford Press.

Baumann, J.F., Kame'enui, E.J., & Ash, G. (2003). Research on vocabulary instruction. Voltaire redux. In J. Flood, D. Lapp, J.R. Squire, & J. Jensen (Eds.), *Handbook of research on teaching in the English language arts* (pp. 752–785). Mahwah, NJ: Lawrence Erlbaum Associates.

Beck, I.L., McKeown, M.G., & Kucan, L. (2001). Text talk: Capturing the benefits of reading aloud experiences for young children. *The Reading Teacher, 55*, 1–20.

Beck, I.L., McKeown, M.G., & Kucan, L. (2002). *Bringing words to life: Robust vocabulary instruction.* New York: Guilford Press.

Beck, I.L., McKeown, M.G., & Kucan, L. (2008). *Creating robust vocabulary: Frequently asked questions and extended examples.* New York: Guilford Press.

Beck, I.L., Perfetti, C.A., & McKeown, M.G. (1982). Effects of long-term vocabulary instruction on lexical access and reading comprehension. *Journal of Educational Psychology, 74*(4), 506–521.

Biemiller, A. (2004). Teaching vocabulary in the primary grades: Vocabulary instruction needed. In J.F. Baumann & E.J. Kame'enui (Eds.), *Vocabulary instruction: Research in practice* (pp. 28–40). New York: Guilford Press.

Biemiller, A. (2005). Addressing developmental patterns in vocabulary: Implications for choosing words for primary grade vocabulary instruction. In E.H. Hiebert & M.L. Kamil (Eds.), *Teaching and learning vocabulary: Bringing research to practice* (pp. 223–242). Mahwah, NJ: Lawrence Erlbaum Associates.

Biemiller, A., & Slonin, N. (2001). Estimating root word vocabulary growth in normative and advantaged populations. *Journal of Educational Psychology, 93*, 498–510.

Blachowicz, C., & Fisher, P.J. (2010). *Teaching vocabulary in all classrooms.* Boston: Allyn & Bacon.

Bos, C.S., & Anders, P. (1992). A theory driven interactive instructional model for text comprehension and content learning. In B.Y.L. Wong (Ed.), *Contemporary intervention research in learning disabilities: An international perspective* (pp. 81–95). New York: Springer-Verlag.

Bos, C.S., & Anders, P.L. (1990). Effects of interactive vocabulary instruction on the vocabulary learning and reading comprehension of junior high learning disabled students. *Learning Disability Quarterly*, 13, 31–42.

Calfee, R.C., & Drum, PA. (1986). Research on teaching reading. In M.C. Wittrock (Ed.), *Handbook of research on teaching* (3rd ed., pp. 804–849). Mahwah, NJ: Lawrence Erlbaum Associates.

Carey, S., & Bartlett, E. (1978). Acquiring a single word. *Papers and Reports on Child Language Acquisition, 15*, 17–29.

Carlisle, J.F. (2000). Awareness of the structure and meaning of morphologically complex words: Impact on reading. *Reading and Writing: An Interdisciplinary Journal, 12*(3), 169–190.

Carlisle, J.F., & Katz, L.A. (2005). Word learning and vocabulary instruction. In J.R. Birsh (Ed.), *Multisensory teaching of basic language skills* (2nd ed., pp. 345–376). Baltimore: Paul H. Brookes Publishing Co.

Carlisle, J.F., & Rice, M.S. (2002). *Improving reading comprehension.* Timonium, MD: York Press.

Chomsky, N. (1965). *Aspects of a theory of syntax.* Cambridge: MA: The MIT Press.

Collins Co-Build New Student's Dictionary. (2002). Glasgow, Scotland: Harper Collins.

Coxhead, A. (2000). A new academic word list. *TESOL Quarterly, 34*, 213–238.

Crain W., Thoreson, C., Dale, P.S., & Phillips S. (1999). Enhancing linguistic performance: Parents and teachers as book reading partners for children with language delays. *Topics in Early Childhood Special Education, 19*(1), 28–39.

Cunningham, A.E., & Stanovich, K.E. (1991). Tracking the unique effects of print exposure in children: Associations with vocabulary, general knowledge, and spelling. *Journal of Educational Psychology, 83,* 264–274.

Cunningham, A.E., & Stanovich, K.E. (1998). What reading does for the mind. *American Educator, 22,* 8–15.

Curtis, M.E. (1987). Vocabulary testing and instruction. In M.G. McKeown & M.E. Curtis (Eds.), *The nature of vocabulary acquisition* (pp. 37–51). Mahwah, NJ: Lawrence Erlbaum Associates.

Dale, E., & O'Rourke, J.P. (1981). *The living word vocabulary.* Chicago: Worldbook-Childcraft International.

DeTemple, J., & Snow, C. (2003). Learning words from books. In A. van Kleeck, S.A. Stahl, & E.B. Bauer (Eds.), *On reading storybooks to children: Parents and teachers* (pp. 16–26). Mahwah, NJ: Lawrence Erlbaum Associates.

Dodson, J. (2010). *50 nifty speaking and listening activities: Promoting oral language and comprehension.* Longmont, CO: Sopris West Educational Services.

Dougherty, D.P., & Paul, D.R. (2007). *Talking on the go: Everyday activities to enhance speech and language development.* Rockville, MD: American Speech-Language-Hearing Association.

Ebbers, S.M. (2003). *Vocabulary through morphemes.* Longmont, CO: Sopris West Educational Services.

Ebbers, S.M., & Carroll, J. (2009). *Daily oral vocabulary exercises.* Longmont, CO: Sopris West Educational Services.

Ebbers, S.M., & Denton, C.A. (2008). A root awakening: Vocabulary instruction for older students with reading difficulties. *Learning Disabilities Research & Practice, 23*(2) 80–90.

Edwards, E.C., Font, G., Baumann, J.F., & Boland, E. (2004). Unlocking word meanings. In J.F. Baumann & E.J. Kame'enui (Eds.), *Vocabulary instruction: Research to practice* (pp. 159–173). New York: Guilford Press.

Elbro, C., & Arnbak, E. (1996). The role of morpheme recognition and morphological awareness in dyslexia. *Annals of Dyslexia, 46,* 209–240.

Fillmore, L.W., & Snow, C.E. (2002). What teachers need to know about language. In C.T. Adger, C.E. Snow, & D. Christian (Eds.), *What teachers need to know about language* (pp. 7–53). McHenry, IL: Delta Systems.

Foorman, B.R., Francis, D.J., Shaywitz, S.E., Shaywitz, B.A.. & Fletcher, J.M. (1997). The case for early reading intervention. In B. Blachman (Ed.), *Foundations of reading acquisition and dyslexia: Implications for early intervention* (pp. 243–264). Baltimore: Paul H. Brookes Publishing Co.

Frayer, D., Frederick, W.C., & Klausmeier, H. J. (1969). *A schema for testing the level of cognitive mastery.* Madison: Wisconsin Center for Education Research.

Garrison, W. (1992). *Why you say it: The fascinating story behind over 600 everyday words and phrases.* New York: MJF Books.

Gillon, G.T. (2004). *Phonological awareness: From research to practice.* New York: Guilford Press.

Goldenberg, C. (2008). *Teaching English language learners: What research does and does not say. American Educator,* 8–44.

Gough, P.B., & Tunmer, W.E. (1986). Decoding, reading and reading disability. *Remedial and Special Education, 7,* 6–10.

Graves, M.F. (2006). *The vocabulary book: Learning and instruction.* New York: Teachers College Press.

Graves, M.F., & Watts, S.M. (2002). The place of word consciousness in a research-based vocabulary program. In J. Samuels & A.E. Farstrup (Eds.), *What research has to say about reading instruction* (3rd ed., pp. 140–165). Newark, DE: International Reading Association.

Gwynne, F. (1970). *The king who rained.* New York: Simon & Schuster.

Hargrave, A.C., & Senechal. M. (2000). A book reading intervention with preschool children who have limited vocabularies: The benefits of regular reading and dialogic reading. *Early Childhood Research Quarterly, 15*(1), 75–90.

Hart, B., & Risley, T.R. (1995). *Meaningful differences in the everyday experience of young American children.* Baltimore: Paul H. Brookes Publishing Co.

Hayes, D.P., & Ahrens, M.G. (1988). Vocabulary simplification for children: A special case of "motherese?" *Journal of Child Language, 15*(2), 395–410.

Henry, M.K. (2010). *Unlocking literacy: Effective decoding and spelling instruction* (2nd ed.). Baltimore: Paul H. Brookes Publishing Co.

Hiebert, E.H., & Kamil, M.L. (Eds.). (2005). *Teaching and learning vocabulary: Bringing research to practice.* Mahwah, NJ: Lawrence Erlbaum Associates.

Jenkins, J.R., Stein, M.L., & Wysocki, K. (1984). Learning vocabulary through reading. *American Educational Research Journal, 21*(4), 767–787.

Johnson, D.D., Johnson, B.V.H, & Schlicting, K. (2004). Logology: Word and language play. In J.F. Baumann & E.J. Kame'enui (Eds.), *Vocabulary instruction: Research to practice* (pp. 179–200). New York: Guilford Press.

Juel, C., & Deffes, R. (2004). Making words stick. *Educational Leadership, 61*(6), 30–34.

Juster, N. (2001). *The phantom tollbooth.* New York: Random House.

Kame'enui, E.J., Carnine, D.W., Dixon R.C., Simmons, D.C., & Coyne, M.D. (2002). *Effective teaching strategies that accommodate diverse learners* (2nd ed.). Columbus, OH: Charles E. Merrill.

Kamil, M.K. (2004). Vocabulary and comprehension instruction: Summary and implications of the National Reading Panel findings. In P. McCardle & V. Chhabra (Eds.), *The voice of evidence in reading research* (pp. 213–214). Baltimore: Paul H. Brookes Publishing Co.

Landry, S.H., & Smith, K.E. (2007). Parents support of children's language provides support for later reading competence. In R.K. Wagner, A.E. Muse, & K.R. Tannenbaum (Eds.), *Vocabulary acquisition: Implications for reading comprehension* (pp. 32–51). New York: Guilford Press.

Lederer, R. (1987). *Anguished English.* New York: Dell Publishing.

Lenski, D., Wham, M., & Johns, J. (2003). *Reading and learning strategies: Middle grades through high school.* Dubuque, IA: Kendall/Hunt.

Liberman, I.Y., Shankweiler, D., & Liberman, A.M. (1989). The alphabetic principle and learning to read. In D. Shankweiler & I. Y. Liberman (Eds.), *Phonology and reading disability: Solving the reading puzzle* (pp.1–33). Ann Arbor: University of Michigan Press.

Longman dictionary of American English (4th ed.). (2007). Essex, England: Pearson.

Lonigan, C.J. (2007) Vocabulary development and the development of phonological awareness skills in preschool children. In R.K. Wagner, A.E. Muse, & K.R. Tannenbaum (Eds.), *Vocabulary acquisition: Implications for reading comprehension* (pp. 15–31). New York: Guilford Press.

Lubliner, S. (2005). *Getting into words: Vocabulary instruction that strengthens comprehension.* Baltimore: Paul H. Brookes Publishing Co.

Lyon, G.E., & Shaywitz, S.E. (2003). Defining dyslexia, comorbidity, teacher knowledge: A definition of dyslexia. *Annals of Dyslexia, 53,* 1–14.

Marzano, R.J., Kendall, J.S., & Paynter, D.E. (1991). *Analysis and identification of basic words in grades K–6.* Aurora, CO: Mid-Continent Research for Education and Learning.

Marzano, R.J., & Pickering, D.J. (2005). *Building academic vocabulary: Teacher's manual.* Alexandria, VA: Association for Supervision and Curriculum Development.

McLaughlin, S. (1998). *Introduction to language development.* San Diego: Singular Publishing.

Moats, L.C. (2009). *The mighty word: Building vocabulary and oral language* (2nd ed.). Longmont, CO: Sopris West Educational Services.

Moats, L.C., & Hennessy, N. (2010). *Digging for meaning: Teaching text comprehension* (2nd ed.). Longmont, CO: Sopris West Educational Services.

Moats, L.C., & Paulson, L.H. (2009). *Early childhood LETRS.* Longmont, CO: Sopris West Educational Services.

Nagy, W. (2005). Why vocabulary instruction needs to be long-term and comprehensive. In Hiebert, E.H. & Kamil, M.L. (Eds.), *Teaching and learning vocabulary: Bringing research to practice.* Mahwah, NJ: Lawrence Erlbaum Associates

Nagy, W.E., & Anderson, R.C. (1984). How many words are there in printed school English? *Reading Research Quarterly, 19,* 304–330.

Nagy, W., Garcia, G.E., Durgunoglu, A., & Hancin-Bhatt, B. (1993). Spanish-English bilingual student's use of cognates in English reading. *Journal of Reading Behavior, 25,* 169–201.

Nagy, W.E., & Scott, J.A. (2000). Vocabulary processes. In M.L. Kamil, P.B. Mosenthal, P.D. Parson, & R. Barr (Eds.), *Handbook of reading research* (Vol. III, pp. 269–284). Mahwah, NJ: Lawrence Erlbaum Associates.

Nation, I.S.P. (2001). *Learning vocabulary in another language.* Cambridge, England: Cambridge University Press.

National Institute of Child Health and Human Development. (2000). *Report of the National Reading Panel: Reports of the subgroups. Teaching children to read: An evidence-based assessment of the scientific research literature on reading and its implications for reading instruction* (NIH Publication No. 00-4754). Washington, DC: Government Printing Office.

Paynter, D.E., Bodrova, E., & Doty, J.K. (2005). *For the love of words: Vocabulary instruction that works in grades K–6.* San Francisco: Jossey-Bass.

Pinker, S. (2007). *The stuff of thought: Language as a window into human nature.* New York: Viking/Penguin Group.

Putnam, M.S., & Kingsley, T. (2009). The atoms family: Using pod casts to enhance the development of science vocabulary. *The Reading Teacher, 63(2),* 100–108.

Rayner, K., Foorman, B.F., Perfetti, C.A., Pesetsky, D., & Seidenberg, M.S. (2001). How psychological science informs the teaching of reading. *Psychological Science in the Public Interest, 2(2),* 31–74.

Richele, M.A. (2004). Have fun! Increasing vocabulary for at-risk learners. *Perspectives, 30,* 17–23.

Rylant, C. (2005). Henry and Mudge and the starry night. In J.J. Pikulski & D.J. Cooper (Eds.), *Houghton Mifflin Reading, Theme 2, Grade 2.* Boston: Houghton Mifflin.

Samuels, J. (2006). Looking backward: Reflections on a career in reading. *Journal of Literacy Research, 38(3),* 327–344.

Scarborough, H. (2001). Connecting early language and literacy to later reading (dis)abilities: Evidence, theory and practice. In S.B. Neuman & D.K. Dickinson (Eds.), *Handbook of early literacy research* (pp. 97–110). New York: Guilford Press.

Schwartz, R.M., & Raphael, T. (1985). Concept of a definition: A key to improving student's vocabualry. *The Reading Teacher, 39,* 198–203.

Scott, J.A., & Nagy, W.E. (2004). Developing word consciousness. In J.F. Baumann & E.J. Kame'enui (Eds.), *Vocabulary instruction: Research to practice* (pp. 201–217). New York: Guilford Press.

Scruggs, T.E., & Mastropieri, M.A. (1990). Mnemonic instruction for students with learning disabilities: What it is and what it does. *Learning Disabilities Quarterly, 13*, 271–280.

Seidenberg, M.S., & McClelland, J.L. (1989). A distributed, developmental model of word recognition and naming. *Psychological Review, 96*, 523–568.

Shefelbine, J.L. (1990). Student factors related to variability in learning word meanings from context. *Journal of Reading Behavior, 22*, 71–97.

Snodgrass, C.S. (2004). *Super silly sayings that are over your head: A children's illustrated book of idioms.* Higanum CT: Starfish Specialty Press.

Stahl, S.A. (1999). *Vocabulary development.* Cambridge, MA: Brookline Books.

Stahl, S.A. (2004). Scaly? Audacious? Debris? Salubrious? Vocabulary learning and the child with learning disabilities. *Perspectives, 30*, 5–13.

Stahl, S.A. (2005). Four problems with teaching word meanings (and what to do to make vocabulary an integral part of instruction). In E.H. Hiebert & M.L. Kamil (Eds.), *Teaching and learning vocabulary: Bringing research to practice* (pp. 95–114). Mahwah, NJ: Lawrence Erlbaum Associates.

Stahl, S.A., & Fairbanks, M.M. (1986). The effects of vocabulary instruction: A model-based meta-analysis in. *Review of Educational Research, 56*(1), 72–110.

Stahl, S.A., & Kapinus, B.A. (2001). *Word power: What every educator needs to know about teaching vocabulary.* Washington, DC: National Education Association.

Stahl, S.A., & Nagy, W.E. (2006). *Teaching word meanings.* Mahwah, NJ: Lawrence Erlbaum Associates.

Stanovich, K.E. (1986). Matthew effects in reading: Some consequences of individual differences in the acquisition of literacy. *Reading Research Quarterly, 21*, 360–406.

Tannenbaum, K.R., Torgesen, J.T., & Wagner, R.K. (2006). Relationship between word knowledge and reading comprehension in 3rd grade children. *Scientific Studies of Reading, 10*, 381–398.

Terban, M. (1996). *Dictionary of idioms.* New York: Scholastic.

Trelease, J. (2006). *The read-aloud handbook.* New York: Penguin Books.

Vadasy, P., & Nelson, J.R. (2008). *Early vocabulary connections: Important words to know and spell.* Longmont, CO: Sopris West Educational Services.

Vellutino, F.R., Tunmer, W.E., Jaccard, J.J., & Chen, R. (2007). Components of reading ability: Multivariate evidence for a convergent skills model of reading development. *Scientific Studies of Reading, 11*(1), 3–32.

Walley, A.C., Metsala, J.L., & Garlock, V.M. (2003). Spoken vocabulary growth: Its role in the development of phoneme awareness and early reading ability. *Reading and Writing: An Interdisciplinary Journal, 16*, 5–20.

West, M. (1953). *A general service list of English words.* London: Longmans, Green and Company.

White, T.G., Sowell, J., & Yanagihara, A. (1989). Teaching elementary students to use word part clues. *The Reading Teacher, 42*, 302–308.

Zhang, Z., & Schumm, J.S. (2000). Exploring effects of keyword method on limited English proficient students' vocabulary recall and comprehension. *Reading Research and Instruction, 39*, 202–221.

Zevenberger, A.A., & Whitehurst, G.J. (2003). Dialogic reading: A shared picture book reading intervention for preschoolers. In A. van Kleeck, S.A. Stahl, & E.B. Bauer (Eds.), *On reading to children: Parents and teachers* (pp. 177–200). Mahwah, NJ: Lawrence Erlbaum Associates.

12

Strategies to Improve Reading Comprehension in the Multisensory Classroom

EILEEN S. MARZOLA

S ince the last edition of this chapter, the focus on comprehension instruction has broadened and intensified dramatically in this country. An explosion of interest about improving students' comprehension of texts has begun to come to light, offering tantalizing guides to improving reading instruction as well as challenging questions for further study.

The primary factors affecting a skilled reader's comprehension of text have not changed. They include

- Accurate, fluent word reading

- A broad base of vocabulary knowledge

- Access to robust background knowledge

- An awareness of sentence, paragraph, and text structure

- Ongoing monitoring of comprehension

- Application of strategies where appropriate (Carlisle & Rice, 2002)

In addition to these basics, some new areas of concern have arisen. For example, with the growth of response to intervention (RTI) as a framework for evaluating the effectiveness of strategies used with struggling students, educators have been compelled to determine best practices to monitor progress in comprehension (see Chapter 14). Comprehension challenges facing English language learners (ELLs) have taken a more visible place in the field (see Chapter 20). And, finally, the growing call to apply comprehension skills judiciously to the Internet has invigorated discussion among researchers and practitioners.

This chapter explores some of the more pressing challenges educators face related to reading comprehension. How can they best tackle obstacles their students face when they are asked to comprehend a wide range of texts? After a brief history of how comprehension instruction has changed since the 1960s, this chapter presents a developmental framework for comprehension followed by a review of research-supported strategies as well as other promising methods designed to improve this essential reading skill within a multisensory learning environment

HISTORICAL PERSPECTIVE OF COMPREHENSION

Although reading comprehension is viewed as the "essence of reading" (Durkin, 1993) and the "ultimate goal of reading education" (Adams, Treiman, & Pressley, 1998), much of the reading research before 2000 focused more on understanding the development of word reading as well as improving instruction for children who struggle with reading at the word level. During the more limited occasions when instructional strategies for comprehension were proposed, they were rarely validated by controlled studies to see whether their adoption really did improve student performance (for reviews, see Adams et al., 1998).

Comprehension instruction was largely absent from classrooms throughout the 1960s and 1970s (Durkin, 1979; Williams, 1987). Durkin's observational studies of reading instruction in fourth-grade classrooms revealed that of more than 4,000 minutes of reading, only 20 minutes of comprehension instruction were observed. Instead of the focus being on teaching comprehension, the spotlight was on testing it. Research conducted in the late 1990s showed that attention to comprehension in instruction is still woefully underrepresented in classrooms (Pressley, 2000; Taylor, Pearson, Clark, & Walpole, 1999).

For many years, students were required to answer questions included at the end of packaged reading selections as a way of testing comprehension and sometimes stimulating discussion and/or reflection. This was done even though little thought had been given to the steps readers go through to process and understand what they read. Most often, teachers spent no time instructing students about the strategies required to answer those questions (Maria, 1990). At best, if difficulties were noted in responding to questions after reading a text, a quick dip into a specific skill exercise (e.g., finding the main idea, drawing inferences, determining sequence) was a common (and frequently the only) prescription recommended. There was little, if any, transfer to real text reading. Allington (2001) labeled this approach "assign and assess" because no instruction was provided with the materials used. This method rarely met students' needs. Activities were usually completed silently, with no direct instruction. Students were expected to acquire useful comprehension strategies through self-discovery, but many students were not able to discover effective reading strategies without teacher modeling.

Much reading comprehension instruction today is constructivist in nature. It focuses on the distinctive knowledge base each reader brings to the text and results in a unique interpretation of the text for each reader (Williams, 2002). The role of the teacher in this model is one of facilitator. Instruction is organized around discussion, with each student contributing his or her own individual interpretation that can then be expanded and refined as discussion evolves.

STRATEGIES USED BY GOOD READERS

Much of the research conducted in the past about reading comprehension has focused on strategies used by good readers. Table 12.1 outlines the differences between behaviors

Table 12.1. Behaviors of good and poor readers before, during, and after reading

GOOD READERS	POOR READERS
Before reading . . .	
Activate prior knowledge	Begin to read without preparation
Understand what they need to do and set a purpose for reading	Are unaware of their purpose for reading
Are self-motivated to read	Tend to read only because they have to
Make positive self-statements about their progress	Make negative self-statements about their progress
Choose strategies that are appropriate for the task	Begin to read without any specific plan or strategy in mind
During reading . . .	
Are focused	Are distracted easily
Monitor their understanding as it is occurring	Are often unaware of their lack of understanding
Anticipate and predict what is likely to happen next	Read just to get it over with
Are able to use fix-up strategies if their comprehension gets off track	Do not know what to do to help themselves if they begin to lose understanding
Can use context to understand the meaning	Do not recognize which of new vocabulary is important
Recognize and use text structure to support their comprehension	Do not recognize any organization within the text
Organize and integrate new information	Tend to add on rather than integrate new information with what they already know
After reading . . .	
Think about what was read	Stop both reading and thinking
Summarize main ideas in some manner	
Seek more information from other sources	
Affirm that their success is a result of their effort	Believe that any success they experience is a result of luck

Adapted from Deshler, D.D., Ellis, E.S., & Lenz, B.K. (1996). *Teaching adolescents with learning disabilities: Strategies and methods* (2nd ed., p. 68). Denver, CO: Love Publishing. Originally adapted by Deshler et al. (1996) from Grover, H., Cook, D., Benson, J., & Chandler, A. (1991). *Strategic learning in the content areas.* Madison: Wisconsin Department of Public Instruction.

of good and poor readers before, during, and after reading. Good readers have many strengths that prevent them from encountering the pitfalls experienced by less skilled readers. For example, good readers understand the complexities of the reading process. They can identify key ideas from the text they are reading, and they are aware of text structures that can assist their comprehension (e.g., headings, subheadings). Good readers rarely allow themselves to get too lost in the text they are reading. They monitor their comprehension and know how to employ fix-up strategies (often rereading) to get back on track before they have gone too far astray. Good readers tend to have a stronger background knowledge and vocabulary foundation than poor readers. They have knowledge of and use a variety of reading strategies effectively. They are flexible in adjusting their understanding of the topic to fit in new information.

In contrast to the powerful behaviors of good readers, poor readers have a weak understanding of the variables that are part of the reading process. They struggle to separate important from unimportant information in text. They are often unaware of text structures that could aid their understanding. Even if they do not understand what they are reading, they still continue reading until the end. Completing the task, rather than understanding the text, becomes the primary goal. Finally, poor readers do not make adjustments in their background knowledge to accommodate the new information they are acquiring. Instead, they make adjustments in the information they are absorbing so that it fits with their previous understanding (Deshler, Ellis, & Lenz, 1996).

SOURCES OF COMPREHENSION DIFFICULTIES

Individuals who are strong comprehenders bring much to the complexities of the reading task. They carry with them rich experience with literacy and an understanding of text structure; strong oral language ability; breadth of background knowledge (including understanding of both high-utility and content-specific vocabulary); accurate, fluent decoding skills; and efficient, active comprehension strategies, including monitoring their understanding of their interactions with text (Gambrell, Block, & Pressley, 2002; Shaywitz, 2003). People who struggle to comprehend may have deficits in any one of these areas. In addition, the source of difficulty may change as students age (Aaron, Joshi, & Williams, 1999). For example, these researchers reported that weak word-reading skill was the major contributor to poor reading comprehension for third graders, but by fifth and sixth grades, word reading and listening comprehension played equal roles in comprehension performance, with word-reading fluency also playing a crucial role.

Most would agree that two essential tools required for good reading comprehension are strong general language comprehension skills and accurate, fluent word-reading skills (Gough, 1996; Torgesen, 1998). Comprehension cannot occur without them. Discussions of these factors have dominated the literature. For many years, educators believed that when individuals had at least average intelligence and could decode accurately and fluently, good reading comprehension would naturally follow (Allington, 2001; McNeil, 1987). Although few would deny the critical importance of accurate, fluent decoding as a requirement for strong comprehension (Adams, 1990; Ehri, 1998; see Chapter 8 for more on this topic), there has been a growing awareness of other factors that promote successful development of skilled comprehension of text. For example, a robust as well as active prior knowledge base, a rich vocabulary foundation (see Chapter 11), and employing metacognitive strategies are also fundamental components of the reading process.

People with dyslexia, although certainly not the only group who may struggle with comprehension issues, have the most profound difficulty with reading text in general. Dyslexia is a language-based disorder, and some individuals with dyslexia may have more pronounced deficits in language beyond difficulty with written language comprehension. Individual deficits in oral language, syntax, morphology, semantics, pragmatics, and understanding narrative structure will negatively affect reading comprehension for those individuals with more global language impairments (see Chapter 3).

Many times, however, a person with dyslexia's difficulty with language is much more apparent at the word-reading level. People with dyslexia as well as other individuals with poor reading performance may appear to be poor comprehenders when, in reality, their difficulties lie in decoding accuracy and reading fluency (see Chapter 8). If an individual has strong listening comprehension skills but stumbles when asked to demonstrate understanding of something read independently, then it is often because higher order thinking and reasoning skills cannot be accessed until the words on the page can be read accurately and fluently. Individuals who are dyslexic as well as those with general decoding weaknesses must allocate their efforts to sound out words strategically at the expense of using that same effort to monitor comprehension strategically

(Rose & Dalton, 2002). Pressley stated it succinctly: "If the word-level processes are not mastered (i.e., recognition of most words is not automatic), it will be impossible to carry out the higher order processes that are summarized as reading comprehension strategies" (2000, p. 551).

Another group of individuals is not able to maintain the balance between reading fluency and reading comprehension. They focus too much on the word level and fail to derive meaning from what has been read. When asked what is the most important part of reading, getting all of the words right or understanding what has been read, they answer without hesitation, "Getting all of the words right." They miss the point of reading; they are not always aware of when they become lost in the text; and, if they are aware, they lack the active comprehension strategies needed to get themselves back on track. One of the most important benefits of the latest focus on strategy use is that it encourages readers to recognize that the goal of reading is to gain meaning and to monitor their progress toward that goal on a continuous basis (Willingham, 2006/2007).

The Role of Background Knowledge in Reading Comprehension

Gaps in background knowledge and weak vocabulary development can have a significant effect on comprehending text (Hirsch, 2003, 2006; McKeown & Beck, 1990; Stahl, 1991; Willingham, 2007). Unfortunately, most widely used basal reading programs do not offer the strong background knowledge that students need to develop more sophisticated reading skills (Walsh, 2003). In addition, poor readers often struggle to understand how and when to use their background knowledge to generate missing details or bolster weak connections in text (Cain & Oakhill, 1999).

E.D. Hirsch, who founded the Core Knowledge Foundation in 1986, has probably done more to draw attention to the role of background knowledge in facilitating comprehension than anyone. Hirsch draws on the work of Hart and Risley (1995), who documented the extreme gap in vocabulary development between welfare, working class, and professional families. Hirsch proposed that the dramatic drop in scores on national reading tests experienced by students in the fourth grade who come from low-income families arises because of a large language gap between advantaged and disadvantaged students. He also observes that reading tests in earlier grades are heavily focused on testing more basic reading skills such as decoding, and it is not until fourth grade that the differences in vocabulary and background knowledge show their effect (Hirsch, 2003).

Lack of adequate background knowledge can have a particularly negative effect on higher level comprehension skills such as inferencing (Willingham, 2006). Authors frequently use a verbal shorthand to communicate ideas. For example, a story about a character "meeting his Waterloo" is an abbreviated way of communicating his defeat. If the reader has no background knowledge of Bonaparte's defeat at Waterloo, however, then he or she will be hard pressed to make sense of the reference. We can say that students who have a rich fund of background knowledge process new information more deeply, make more significant connections between what is new and what is known, and, in general, will learn more (Willingham, 2006).

Probably the most widely used approach to building background knowledge through the grades has been through teacher read-alouds addressing rich content materials coupled with audiovisual supports and engaging discussion. For a more systematic approach to incorporating specific content into instruction, Hirsch's (2009)

Core Knowledge Sequence for students in kindergarten through Grade 8 has been adopted by many schools, and in 2004, the American Federation of Teachers recommended this program to fill the background knowledge gap for children in these grades.

A CONTINUUM OF COMPREHENSION DEVELOPMENT WITHIN A MULTISENSORY TEACHING ENVIRONMENT

There is a continuum of comprehension development beginning at the word level and progressing through increasingly complex units of text. The more students are actively involved in their learning, the more the retention and application of strategies are apparent. Students with dyslexia as well as others with poor reading skills benefit from multisensory learning that captures their attention. Involving at least two or more modalities in teaching simultaneously helps students to solidify their grasp of the strategies they are being taught (see Chapter 2).

When Adams and her colleagues (1998) reviewed research on reading comprehension instruction, they concluded that silent reading and independent seat work were not nearly as effective as active verbal modeling by the teacher coupled with active, vocal student practice of basic comprehension techniques, including summarizing, questioning, and predicting. This model of active involvement by both student and teacher may begin at the earliest levels of instruction.

Aural activities coupled with opportunities for students to articulate the strategies they are using to comprehend text are good ways to begin comprehension instruction. Creating and using visual representations of the organization as well as the content of the text through graphic organizers add yet another modality. As students gain in skill, they can demonstrate their understanding through drawing or writing. Examples of specific strategies to involve students actively as they create meaning from text are woven throughout the rest of this chapter.

BEGINNING COMPREHENSION INSTRUCTION

Planning for instruction must begin with a good assessment (see Chapter 14). Is a student having difficulty reading the words with accuracy and fluency? How extensive (and accurate) is the student's prior knowledge? Vocabulary? Does the size of the text affect the student's comprehension?

Can the student make sense of what he or she reads when only a sentence or a short paragraph is presented? What happens when the individual is asked to retell what he or she has read? Is the student able to make connections between what is known and what is new? Can the individual answer questions when answers are explicitly stated in the text? Is there evidence of higher level thinking, or is the student bound to the concrete level of understanding? Is there evidence of self-monitoring of comprehension, or is the student merely "word-calling?" Is there any evidence of active repair strategies if something read obviously does not make sense? Is there a difference between the student's silent and oral reading comprehension? What about listening comprehension? All of these are important questions that need to be explored to determine which strategies will be most effective for which students.

Developing Listening Comprehension Skills

Students who are dyslexic and others who have not yet mastered decoding skills need not wait until they become fluent readers to begin addressing comprehension. Instruction can be started early by bypassing reading altogether and focusing instead on an aural level (Williams, 2002). Reading high-quality narratives and rich informational texts can also play an important role in building and expanding important background knowledge and vocabulary.

Kindergarten and even preschool-age children can improve their comprehension performance through experiences that support both oral language and reading skills. If students have adequate listening skills, then stories can be read to them and oral discussion can be the mode of instruction. Students can be encouraged to "read" picture books to hone their comprehension skills. Describing the characters and actions in pictures begins the process of comprehension. It also sets the tone for helping students to focus on what factors come into play in comprehending text. Students can listen to stories read by older students, parents, teachers, and other adults. At this age, students can participate in analytic conversations in which they practice connecting events in stories with their own experiences. They can learn about predictable story structure and use graphic organizers such as story maps to aid their recall and retelling of stories. They can be engaged in drawing inferences, making predictions, analyzing characters, and following sequences of events. They can be exposed to rich vocabulary and background knowledge within meaningful contexts. Teachers can begin modeling their own thinking at this early level.

Visual presentations (e.g., short films or stories on CD-ROMs coupled with conventional text stories) may entice young children's attention and draw them more deeply into stories they hear. A word of caution is necessary here, however. If our ultimate goal is reading comprehension, then we do not want to overemphasize nontext presentation. That would reduce the amount of textual language the children hear, and familiarity with the linguistic features of written language fosters the acquisition of reading comprehension. (Williams, 2002)

Developing Reading Comprehension at the Sentence Level

There are times when decoding and fluency are in place, yet an individual still struggles to gain meaning from the page. Once students have adequate decoding skills to begin to read independently, the unit size of the presentation must be considered. Some students may need to begin at the word level as they develop their understanding of the meanings of single words (see Chapter 11), whereas the sentence level may be the most appropriate starting point for other students. A wide range of studies have shown that there is a strong association between a strong grasp of sentence grammar and reading performance (Fowler, 1988; Siegel & Ryan, 1988; Weaver, 1979). Children with good grammatical awareness may be able to monitor their oral reading accuracy better (Carlisle & Rice, 2002).

Carnine, Silbert, and Kame'enui (1990) described a sequence of sentence comprehension activities designed to teach students how to identify what has happened in a sentence, who was involved, when the event occurred, where the event took place, and why the event happened. Using this strategy can serve as a foundation for comprehension activities using larger chunks of text later.

The question words *who, what, when, where, why,* and *how* are used during this exercise. A prerequisite skill for engaging in this activity is the ability to repeat five- to seven-word statements (e.g., The girl skipped up the street. The boy jumped over the fence). If individuals cannot retain the information in a sentence long enough to repeat it, then they are unlikely to be able to recall the information needed from those sentences to answer simple questions.

Instruction begins with the introduction of *who* and *what* questions and is followed by extensive practice until the students can answer questions independently:

Teacher	**Students**

1. The teacher models:

    a. "Betty went to school."

       Who went to school? Betty."

    b. "What did Betty do? She went to school."

2. The teacher provides practice and tests:

"Listen. The dog ate his food. Say that."	"The dog ate his food."
"Who ate his food?"	"The dog"
"What did the dog do?"	"Ate his food"

3. The teacher repeats Step 2 with more sentences and questions.

A similar procedure follows for *when* and *where* words:

1. The teacher models:

    a. "I'll say phrases that tell *when*. *Tomorrow morning* tells *when*. *Last Friday* tells *when*. *Before the sun rises* tells when. After breakfast tells *when*."

    b. "Now I'll say phrases that tell *where*. *In the backyard* tells *where*. *At the pool* tells *where*. *On the sofa* tells *where*. *Under the bed* tells *where*."

2. The teacher tests. "I'll say a phrase. You say if it tells *when* or *where*."

a.	"In the backyard"	"Where"
b.	"After breakfast"	"When"
c.	"Tomorrow morning"	"When"
d.	"On the sofa"	"Where"
e.	"At the pool"	"Where"
f.	"Last Friday"	"When"

Once students can discriminate between *where* and *when* phrases, they are introduced to *where* and *when* questions. A similar procedure is used for modeling answers to *why* and *how* questions. The teacher gives examples using these question words and then provides discrimination practice.

It is not enough, however, to require students to identify syntactical elements and explain their function. Carlisle and Rice (2002) promoted having students dig deeper into the internal structure of sentences by creating, combining, and expanding sentences. Although they admitted that these strategies have not been evaluated with children with reading or learning disabilities in controlled research studies, they reported that clinical experience of several reading experts including Maria (1990) and McNeil (1987) have suggested that they are helpful for struggling readers.

Helping students to become more familiar with the role of conjunctions in compound and complex sentences may be particularly useful for building sentence comprehension. Carlisle and Rice (2002) advised teaching conjunctions in related groups including those that express "adversative" roles (e.g., *but, however, even though*) with those that play causal roles (e.g., *so, because, as a result*). Among the activities they recommended are highlighting conjunctions in text to draw students' attention to them, rewording sentences using different but similar conjunctions such as *but* and *even though,* and combining sentences using specific conjunctions.

A student's lack of understanding of pronoun referents or cohesive ties is another common obstacle to sentence comprehension (Carlisle & Rice, 2002). Helping students match cohesive ties with their antecedents is helpful in this regard.

Sally ran down the stairs to the parlor on Christmas morning to open her gifts. Her sister, Mary, got there before her.

Whose sister is Mary?

Where did Mary go?

Carlisle and Rice suggested other activities including deleting pronouns from a passage and then having students fill in the blanks, having students substitute pronouns for unnecessarily repeated names, and identifying strategies that they might use when pronoun referents are ambiguous (e.g., reading on in the text for further clues).

A useful series by Joanne Carlisle (1999) also addressed the "anatomy" of the sentence, emphasizing the relationships between sentence parts, including cause and effect, chronology, and comparisons. Once students demonstrate understanding of the application of these important concepts at the simple sentence level, they may be asked to respond to multiple sentences, paragraphs, and eventually longer texts.

GOOD READER STRATEGIES FOR COMPREHENDING LONGER TEXTS

A major goal for teachers of reading is to teach poor readers to use strategies that good readers use spontaneously. Can this be done? Fortunately, the explicit teaching of reading comprehension strategies has been highly effective (Deshler et al., 1996; National Institute of Child Health and Human Development [NICHD], 2000; Sweet & Snow, 2002). It is one thing, however, to be able to demonstrate that a student has mastered the steps to a reading comprehension strategy but quite another to have evidence that using the strategy has been generalized to daily reading experiences. Students need to know not only how to operationalize the strategies but also why they are learning them and under what conditions they should apply them. Mason and Au (1986) outlined six steps to ensure that comprehension strategies will not only be learned, but also applied.

1. Set the stage by discussing how reading activity changes depending on the purpose for reading and the nature of the text.

2. Explain and model the steps in the strategy. Begin with clear, simple examples.

3. Present more than one situation or one kind of text in which the strategy would be useful.

4. Provide many opportunities for practice, starting with easy examples.

5. Encourage students to think out loud when they use the strategy so that they can correct misunderstandings or mistakes.

6. Have students suggest times and conditions when they would use the strategy on their own. When these occasions arise, remind students to use the strategy.

Choosing Research-Validated Strategies for Comprehension Instruction

With the Reading First program, a component of the No Child Left Behind Act of 2001 (PL 107-110), major financial awards have been made available to states that demonstrate that they are using scientifically based reading programs in their schools. The result has been a flood of interest in scientifically validated strategies to improve instruction. A foundation of research has been building that shows what cognitive processes are involved in text comprehension and which comprehension strategies are most effective for improving the skills of students who struggle to understand what they read.

Once we have a good picture of what exactly is working and what is ineffective when a student reads, the next question is how shall we choose which strategies to teach. How do we know which strategies are truly effective? In 1997, an important step was taken in gathering and disseminating information about the effectiveness of different approaches used to teach children to read. At that time, Congress approached the Director of NICHD at the National Institutes of Health, in consultation with the Secretary of Education, to form a national panel to review research-based knowledge on reading instruction. The result of this collaboration was the *Report of the National Reading Panel* (NRP; NICHD, 2000). Evaluating reading comprehension was one of the research areas the panel chose to evaluate.

After identifying almost 500 studies on comprehension published since 1970, the NRP (NICHD, 2000) applied a strict selection process, choosing only those studies that were relevant to instruction of reading or comprehension among typical readers; were published in a scientific journal; had an experiment involving at least one treatment and an appropriate control group; and, if possible, had random assignment of subjects to treatment and control groups. Application of these criteria whittled the number of studies down to about 200. Before conclusions could be drawn about the effectiveness of the strategies selected, the next step for the panel was to select only those studies that had an experimental effect that was "reliable, robust, replicable, and general" (p. 4-42).

The NRP (NICHD, 2000) identified 16 categories of comprehension instruction, 7 of which appear to have a strong scientific basis for concluding that they improve comprehension in typical readers:

1. Comprehension monitoring, in which readers learn how to be aware of their level of understanding as they read

2. Cooperative learning, in which students work together in pairs or small groups as they learn reading strategies

3. Graphic and semantic organizers (including story maps) that help students make graphic representations of the material they are reading in order to bolster comprehension

4. Question answering, in which teachers ask questions and students receive immediate feedback about their responses

5. Question generation, in which students ask themselves questions to clarify understanding

6. Story structure, in which students learn how to use the structure of the text to help them recall content to answer questions about what they have read

7. Summarization, to encapsulate and remember important ideas from the text

Many of these strategies have also been included in an eighth category, multiple strategies. In general, the research suggests that teaching a combination of techniques to bolster comprehension works the best (NICHD, 2000). When these seven strategies are used appropriately, they improve recall, question answering, question generation, summarization of text, and, ultimately, result in improved performance on standardized comprehension tests.

Although not identified as one of the "super seven" strategy categories, the other eight categories (integrating strategies into the normal curriculum, listening actively, mental imagery, mnemonics [including pictorial aids and key words], building prior knowledge, psycholinguistic strategies relating to learning relevant knowledge about language, teacher preparation to learn effective transactional strategies, and the vocabulary–comprehension relationship) should not be dismissed. Many were eliminated because there were simply too few studies in a category to determine the scientific merit of the treatment. Two categories in particular, building prior knowledge (discussed earlier in this chapter) and the vocabulary–comprehension relationship (see Chapter 11) have risen to prominence in the recent literature. The strong research base for the "super seven" strategy categories cannot be denied, however.

Comprehension Monitoring

Comprehension monitoring may be defined as "the active awareness of whether one is understanding or remembering text being processed" (Pressley, Brown, El-Dinary, & Afflerbach, 1995, p. 218). Comprehension monitoring can also be seen as one of the two components of self-regulation as they apply to reading: 1) monitoring and evaluating comprehension and 2) implementing strategies when comprehension breaks down (Klingner, Vaughn, Dimino, Schumm, & Bryant, 2001). The second component may also be looked at as "strategic effort" (RAND Reading Study Group [RRSG], 2002). The temptation to go on automatic pilot and just read on is common for nonstrategic, weak readers. They are much less likely to be tuned in to the need for comprehension monitoring than strong readers (Oakhill & Yuill, 1996).

The goals of comprehension monitoring are to help readers to become aware of whether they are understanding a text as they read and, equally important, to help them identify where their understanding has been blocked. Children as young as first graders can be taught to ask themselves questions as they read and monitor their understanding:

• Does this make sense?

• Do I understand what I am reading?

- What does this have to do with what I already know?

- What will happen next?

Steps readers can take when their comprehension monitoring reveals a roadblock to their understanding include:

- Identifying the difficulty

- Using think-aloud procedures that highlight where and when the difficulty began

- Restating what was read

- Looking back through the text (rereading)

- Looking forward in the text to find information that might help (reading ahead)

When comprehension-monitoring strategies were taught to students in second through sixth grade in the studies reviewed by the NRP (NICHD, 2000), improved detection of text inconsistencies and memory of the text were noted as compared with the performance of control groups. In addition, students also made gains on standardized reading comprehension tests. Transfer and generalization of this strategy were critical outcomes of instruction.

Cooperative Learning

Diversity in classrooms has been increasing dramatically since the 1990s. In addition to rising numbers of children who come from homes where English is not the first language (Hodgkinson, 1991), more children are coming from families below the poverty level (Pallas, Natriello, & McDill, 1989). Also, growing populations of children with disabilities are appearing in general education classrooms. The typical range of academic performance in urban classrooms is 5.4 years (Jenkins, Jewell, Leicester, & Troutner, 1990). Classroom teachers' instructional skills are being challenged as never before as they try to meet the wide range of students' needs. Cooperative or **collaborative learning** is a promising alternative for teaching students with mixed abilities in the same class.

Students are engaged in cooperative learning when involved in clearly defined activities in which they work together to achieve their individual goals. A related approach, collaborative learning, is "learning by working together in small groups, so as to understand new information or to create a common product" (Harris & Hodges, 1995, p. 35). Research has demonstrated growth in elementary school-age children in reading competence when they work collaboratively on structured activities (Greenwood, Delquadri, & Hall, 1989; Rosenshine & Meister, 1994). The benefits of cooperative learning are clear. The creators of the Collaborative Strategic Reading (CSR) program noted that

> Cooperative learning fosters the development of higher-level reasoning and problem solving skills. Cooperative learning is effective in diverse classrooms that include a wide range of achievement levels, and has been recommended by experts in the fields of multicultural education, English as a second language (ESL), special education and general education. (Klingner et al., 2001, p. 6)

In addition, the NRP's summary evaluation of cooperative learning stated, "Having peers instruct or interact over the use of reading strategies leads to an increase in the learning of the strategies, promotes intellectual discussion and increases reading comprehension" (NICHD, 2000, p. 4-45). The panel also cited the social benefits of this approach in addition to students' increased control over their own learning.

Collaborative Strategic Reading

The *From Clunk to Click* program is drawn from original research conducted by Klingner, Vaughn, Hughes, Schumm, and Elbaum (1998). It was designed primarily for students in third through eighth grade who are in mixed-level classrooms and are reading expository or content-area text drawn from textbooks. Although the program was designed with middle school students in mind, adaptations for high school students are also included in the instructional materials (Klingner & Vaughn, 2000).

Students work together to reach five main goals as they read these content-area selections:

1. Discuss the material.

2. Help each other understand it.

3. Encourage each other to do their best.

4. Learn collaborative skills while mastering content.

5. Learn comprehension strategies that are likely to improve reading comprehension.

Each student must participate with a partner or as part of a small group in a cooperative or collaborative learning environment. Students assume specific, meaningful roles within the group as they work on clearly outlined tasks. In some programs, students may exchange roles as part of their activity. All students contribute to the overall success of the group. In this CSR program, at least three roles are essential: leader, "clunk" expert, and "gist" expert. Other roles are included in the program, but they may be shared because they require fewer discrete skills: encourager, announcer, and timekeeper. Roles and responsibilities of each member of the group are clearly outlined on cue cards or sheets that can be referred to as needed:

Leader: Helps the group stay on track and guides members in using the four strategies:

- Preview

- Click and clunk

- Get the gist

- Wrap up

    Announcer: Makes sure that each member of the group participates by sharing his or her good ideas

Clunk expert: Helps the group members figure out words they do not understand and clarify any misunderstandings they may have

    Gist expert: Works with the group to decide on the best gist (main idea to write in their learning logs for each section of the reading assignment)

    Encourager: Watches the group and lets group members know when they are doing something well

    Timekeeper: Helps the group complete the reading assignment in a timely manner

Each member of the group has a cue sheet. These sheets have scripted dialogue to help students know what to say as they assume their roles. Descriptions of extensive practice activities, including question stems, question types (see the description of the Question-Answer Relationships strategy later in this chapter), time allotment sheets, learning logs, and graphic organizers, are included in the manual for the program.

This CSR program's plan for strategic reading includes three phases of activity: before reading, during reading, and after reading. Before reading, students preview by brainstorming what they already know about the topic and predicting what they will learn about the topic when they read the passage.

During reading, students identify and repair "clunks" (parts of text that were hard to understand, including challenging vocabulary). See Figure 12.1 for a sample cue sheet for the clunk expert that includes examples of fix-up strategies. Students also work at getting the gist of the text during reading. They identify the most important person, place, or thing in the section they are reading and then identify the most important idea about that person, place, or thing.

After reading, students wrap up. They identify what questions will check their understanding of the most important information in the passage and then determine whether they can answer those questions. Finally, they review what they have learned.

Clunk Expert's Cue Sheet

1. What is your clunk?

2. Does anyone know the meaning of the clunk?

    YES
    *   Announcer, please call on someone with their hand raised.
    *   Ask them to explain how they figured out the clunk.
    *   Everyone, write the meaning in your Learning Log.

    NO
    *   If NO, follow these steps until you know the meaning of the clunk and are ready to write it in your Learning Log.

        STEP 1: Read the sentence with the clunk and look for key ideas to help you figure out the word. Think about what makes sense.

                 Raise your hand if you can explain the meaning of the clunk.
                 (If NO, go to STEP 2)

        STEP 2: Reread the sentence with the clunk and the sentences before and after the clunk looking for clues.

                 Raise your hand if you can explain the meaning of the clunk.
                 (If NO, go to STEP 3)

        STEP 3: Look for a prefix or suffix in the word that might help.

                 Raise your hand if you can explain the meaning of the clunk.
                 (If NO, go to STEP 4)

        STEP 4: Break the word apart and look for smaller words that you know.

                 Raise your hand if you can explain the meaning of the clunk.
                 (If NO, go to STEP 5.)

        STEP 5: Ask the teacher for help.

Figure 12.1.   Clunk expert's cue sheet. (From Klingner, J.K., Vaughn, S., Dimino, J., Schumm, J.S., & Bryant, D. [2001]. *From clunk to click: Collaborative strategic reading* [p. 91]. Longmont, CO: Sopris West Educational Services; reprinted by permission of Sopris West Educational Services; *Collaborative Strategic Reading,* copyright 2001.)

Research evaluating the effectiveness of CSR, most of which was conducted after the NRP (NICHD, 2000) review, has been promising. For example, when middle school students in fourth and sixth grade engaged in CSR activities were compared with others in a control group, CSR students outperformed the controls on standardized comprehension tests. Even more encouraging was that students who were low achievers showed the greatest gains (Klingner et al., 2001). Another study showed gains in vocabulary knowledge based on text read by ELLs engaged in CSR (Klingner & Vaughn, 2000).

Peer-Assisted Learning Strategies

Peer-Assisted Learning Strategies (PALS) is another popular cooperative learning strategy with a strong research base. Although it was originally designed to work in second-through sixth-grade classrooms, kindergarten and high school versions of the strategy have been added (Fuchs et al., 2001).

In the original model, teachers implement three 35-minute PALS sessions each week. Students are paired by the teacher so that a higher and a lower performing student work together. The teacher splits the class in half and pairs the highest performer in the top half of the class with the highest performer in the bottom of the class and so forth. PALS sessions are quite structured and include frequent verbal interaction and feedback between tutor and tutee.

An exchange of roles within the pairs is built in so that each student has the opportunity to assume the role of both tutor and tutee during each session. It is important to note, however, that the higher performing student in each pair reads first for each activity, serving as a model for the lower performing reader. Material chosen for reading is literature that is appropriate for the lower performing reader. Each 35-minute session is divided into three 10-minute segments for partner reading, paragraph shrinking, and prediction relay, plus an additional 2 minutes are used for a retelling activity that follows partner reading. The remaining time is used for setting up and putting away materials during transitions.

The goal of partner reading is to improve reading accuracy and fluency (Simmons, Fuchs, Fuchs, Hodge, & Mathes, 1994). In paragraph shrinking, students develop comprehension through summarizing and identifying the main idea (Doctorow, Wittrock, & Marks, 1978; Palincsar & Brown, 1984). In prediction relay, students practice formulating expectations about what is likely to follow in their reading. Students who practice making predictions have been shown to improve in reading comprehension (Palincsar & Brown, 1984).

Pairs of students are assigned to one of two teams. They earn points from the teacher for being engaged in their reading activities and helping their partners in a constructive and collaborative manner. Each student acting as the tutor also awards points as activities are completed successfully. Point cards represent joint effort, progress, and achievement. At the end of each week, the points are tallied for each team and the winning team is announced and cheered for. Students are assigned to new pairs and new teams every 4 weeks.

Careful training is required to make PALS work in classrooms. Teachers are expected to model key procedures and allow students to role-play them. It usually takes about seven 45-minute sessions for teachers to train their students. The first session is a general orientation in which students learn how set up materials, be a helpful partner, use a scorecard, and report points. After this first orientation session, each of the three reading activities takes about two 45-minute sessions to teach. Teachers are encouraged to teach one PALS activity at a time, taking at least a week to practice an activity before introducing a new one.

PALS has been approved by the U.S. Department of Education's Program Effectiveness Panel for inclusion in the National Diffusion Network of effective educational practices. Research conducted in second- through sixth-grade classes where PALS has been implemented has shown an enhancement of reading development in low- and typically achieving students as well as students with learning disabilities (Fuchs, Fuchs, Mathes, & Simmons, 1997; Simmons et al., 1994).

Cue cards that may be used by reading partners are found in Figure 12.2. The content of PALS reading activities proceed as follows.

Partner Reading   The partner reading activity is designed to increase students' reading fluency. Beginning with the stronger reader, each student reads connected text aloud for 5 minutes, for a total of 10 minutes. Students are given guidance about how to identify and correct word-recognition errors as they occur.

Retelling   After partner reading by both students, the lower performing reader retells in sequence what has been read. Prompts from the student tutor (the higher performing reader) during this 2-minute retelling include questions such as, "What did you learn first?" and "What did you learn next?" If the weaker reader has difficulty remembering the next piece of information or struggles with sequence, then the tutor can provide help and retelling continues.

Paragraph Shrinking   The paragraph shrinking activity is designed to develop comprehension by identifying and summarizing the main idea. Unlike partner reading, both readers read new text during this activity. Beginning with the stronger reader, the part-

---

Prompt Card 1: Retell

1.   What did you learn first?
2.   What did you learn next?

Prompt Card 2: Paragraph Shrinking

1.   Name the who or what.
2.   Tell the most important thing about the who or what.
3.   Say the main idea in 10 words or less.

Prompt Card 3: Prediction Relay

Predict _____ What do you predict will happen next?
Read _____ Read half a page.
Check _____ Did the prediction come true?

Figure 12.2.   Partner reading question cards from Peer-Assisted Learning Strategy (PALS). (From *Peer-Assisted Learning Strategies: Reading Methods for Grades 2-6,* 2008 Revised Edition. Authors: Douglas Fuchs, Lynn S. Fuchs, Deborah C. Simmons, and Patricia G. Mathes; reprinted by permission.)

ners alternate reading one paragraph at a time for 5 minutes, stopping after each paragraph to identify the main idea in 10 words or fewer. The tutor must make a judgment about whether the main idea is correct as stated. Errors trigger a supportive response by the tutor ("That's not quite right. Skim the paragraph and try again"). If the reader is still incorrect, then the tutor supplies the answer.

Prediction Relay   The prediction relay activity requires students to think ahead because it extends paragraph shrinking to larger chunks of connected text. There are five steps in this activity. In each step, the reader has a specific job:

1. Predict what will be learned on a half-page of text.

2. Read the half-page out loud.

3. Confirm or refute the prediction.

4. Summarize the half-page in 10 words or fewer.

5. Make a new prediction about the next half-page.

Graphic and Semantic Organizers

A graphic or semantic organizer is a visual representation of knowledge. Essentially, it is a diagram or picture that structures information to demonstrate relationships. It has been used effectively for a wide range of purposes, including the following:

*   Generating lists of character traits with supporting evidence within narrative text (see Figure 12.3 for an example of a character map)

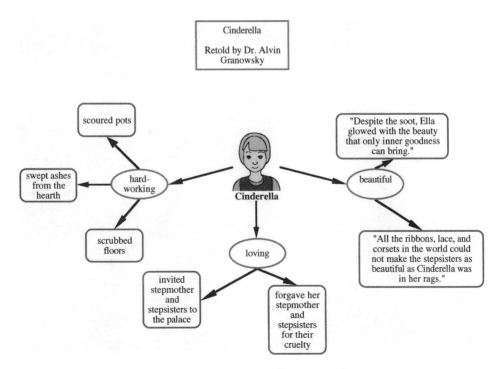

Figure 12.3.   Character map. (Diagram created in Kidspiration® by Inspiration® Software, Inc.) (Text of story from *That Awful Cinderella*, © 1993, Steck-Vaughn. All Rights Reserved. Used with permission of Harcourt Achieve.)

- Deepening understanding of unfamiliar vocabulary (see Figure 12.4 for an example and also Chapter 11 for more on vocabulary word study)

- Depicting relationships in expository texts in social studies or science (see Figure 12.5 for an example of an animal map)

- Activating background knowledge and setting a purpose for reading (see Figure 12.6)

- Helping students to see the text structure of stories, which can enhance students' ability to retell stories they have heard or read themselves (see Figure 12.9 later in the chapter)

The NRP, in its review of research on graphic or semantic organizers, cited three important uses for these visual cues: "(1) help students focus on text structure while reading, (2) provide tools to examine and visually represent textual relationships, and (3) assist in writing well-organized summaries" (NICHD, 2000, p. 4-73).

The most robust finding of the studies reviewed by the NRP (NICHD, 2000) was that using graphic organizers can facilitate memory of the content of what has been read for many students. This may be the result of having a means to retrieve information in a more organized manner because clear relationships between concepts or events are displayed visually. This may also generalize to better comprehension and achievement, particularly in content-area instruction.

Pearson and Johnson talked about comprehension as the process of "building bridges between the new and the known" (1978, p. 24). If a reader has some accurate and appropriate knowledge of the topic, then that building can be accomplished more

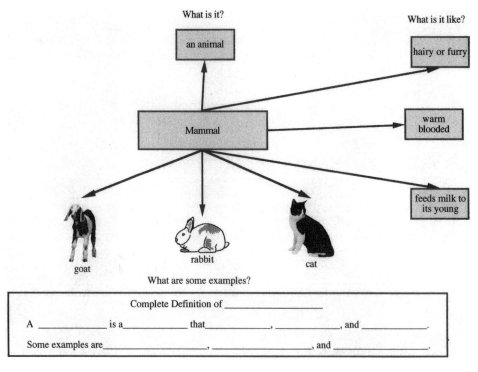

Figure 12.4. Word structure map. (Diagram created in Kidspiration® by Inspiration® Software, Inc.)

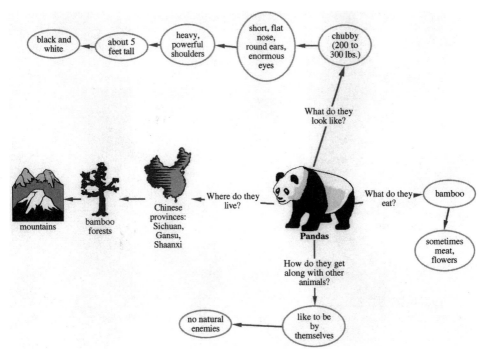

Figure 12.5. Brainstorming map. (Diagram created in Kidspiration® by Inspiration® Software, Inc.)

easily. K-W-L is one comprehension strategy that uses a structured graphic organizer and has facilitated that process for many struggling readers.

K-W-L (Ogle, 1986) and K-W-L Plus (Carr & Ogle, 1987) are procedures that have been used to help both elementary and secondary students to become more active readers of expository text. The two strategies are essentially the same except that in K-W-L Plus, semantic mapping and written summaries have been added to the three basic K-W-L steps.

K-W-L stands for three basic cognitive steps that are often particularly challenging to students with learning disabilities but that are essential to reading comprehension:

K   Accessing what I already **K**now about the topic (activating prior knowledge)

W   Deciding what I **W**ant to learn (setting a purpose for reading, including deciding what categories of information or ideas are likely to be discovered)

L   Recalling what I **L**earned as a result of my reading (including integrating that new information with what I already know)

The teacher plays a critical role in students' mastering this strategy by acting as both a guide and model for the think-aloud strategies that are essential for K-W-L's implementation.

Step K—What I Know

There are two parts to this step. First, the teacher selects a central idea or concept of the text the students are about to read. Next, the students list as many words or phrases as they can associate with the concept. Either the teacher or individual students may

KWL Strategy Sheet

1. K—What we know	W—What we want to find out	L—What we learned and still need to learn

2. Categories of information we expect to use
   A.   E.
   B.   F.
   C.   G.
   D.

Figure 12.6.   K-W-L strategy sheet. (From Ogle, D.M. [1986, February]. K-W-L: A teaching model that develops active reading of expository text. *The Reading Teacher, 39,* 565; reprinted by permission.)

record the results of this brainstorming. In order to deepen the thinking of the students, the teacher may ask, "Where did you learn that?" or "How do you know that?" Students may share information they have learned through personal experience, books they have read or listened to, television, films, videotapes, computer software, or other sources. It is important for students to be aware that they can turn to many resources to broaden their background knowledge.

For the second part of the first step, the teacher cognitively models or thinks aloud the process of classifying pieces of information and then labeling the resulting categories. Figure 12.5 shows an example of a brainstorming map about pandas. The information collected has been categorized by creating a question for each set of grouped facts. For example, *bamboo* and *sometimes meat, flowers* follow the question, "What do they eat?"

Step W—What I Want to Learn

Students set their purpose for reading during this step. They generate questions they want to have answered by reading the text. Sometimes these questions grow out of the brainstorming. Sometimes they arise because of conflicting information supplied by the students that needs to be sorted out or clarified. Questions can also be added as the students begin to read.

Step L—What I Learned

As students read, they record new information in this last step. They and the teacher review the questions generated in Step W to see if they have been answered by their reading. Questions that have not been answered may be highlighted for further study. If there was any disagreement at the beginning over conflicting information supplied by students, then there should be discussion to see whether those conflicts have been resolved by reading. If questions have not been answered, and if conflicts have not been resolved, then teachers and students together should discuss other resources that could be consulted.

The "categories of information we expect to use" section of the K-W-L strategy sheet (Ogle, 1986; see Figure 12.6) is particularly useful for creating written summaries or expanded writing about the topic at hand. For example, when reading a text about an animal, some of the expected categories might be appearance, habitat, food, and behavior. If the topic is a person, then categories might include information about birth, childhood, family influences, education, pivotal life events, important contributions, and death. Each category of information can represent a new paragraph.

Generating these categories early in the K-W-L procedure helps students select and organize information for their writing. Ogle (1986) suggested discussing with students how the results of their brainstorming could help them to generate categories. For example, in the brainstorming graphic organizer about pandas (see Figure 12.5), student attention could be brought to the fact that many of the terms relate to the way pandas look. The name of a category they can expect to use, therefore, might be *appearance*. That category would then be written on the bottom of the K-W-L strategy sheet (Ogle, 1986; see Figure 12.6).

The results of research on K-W-L and K-W-L Plus conducted by Carr and Dewitz (1988) indicated that these strategies are effective in helping students learn new social studies content, develop both literal and inferential comprehension, and improve their summary-writing skills.

The NRPs summary evaluation of graphic and semantic organizer instruction noted students' improvements in remembering what they read after they used this strategy. The panel also suggested that "this may transfer, in general, to better comprehension and achievement in Social Studies and Science content areas" ((NICHD, 2000, p. 4-45).

Question Answering

Good readers ask themselves questions before, during, and after reading. Yet, many students do not self-question spontaneously. They need to have good models of questioning during all three periods of the reading process to have an effect on their comprehension. Results of the NRP's (NICHD, 2000) review of research on questioning confirmed that teaching question-answering strategies can improve student performance in this area. Teaching these strategies before, during, and after reading can have a positive effect on students' comprehension of text.

Before Reading

Teacher questions before reading can help teachers to evaluate (and if necessary supplement and/or modify) students' prior knowledge about a topic. The *K* segment of the K-W-L strategy outlined previously, for example, functions well in this role. Activating prior knowledge and then organizing it into schema can integrate learning more readily into an already existing framework. Asking predictive questions before reading also helps to set readers' purposes for reading and can improve motivation to read. Forming hypotheses about what will happen next has been shown to aid comprehension (Hammond, 1983).

During Reading

Teachers asking questions during reading can help their students to direct their attention to important sections of the text, monitor their comprehension, and serve as a catalyst to get them to activate "fix-up" strategies when comprehension is blocked.

After Reading

Questions asked after reading can encourage students to reprocess what they have read, thereby creating new associations as they review information. If students are to learn to be good self-questioners, then they need to see their teachers as strong models. Although teachers may ask a question or two before reading to motivate students' interest, questioning by the teacher often functions primarily as an evaluative activity following reading (Durkin, 1979). Questions can have a more far-reaching effect, however, if they are used to teach more than to test. Quality of questions asked, feedback given to student responses, and instruction in how to answer challenging questions are critical to the success of this process.

Obviously, attention must be paid to the quality of questions teachers ask. Yet, when researchers have looked at this area, the findings have been dismal. For example, Guszak (1967) observed that about 70% of the questions teachers asked were literal and required only recognition (locating information in the text) or recall (answering from memory) of factual information. Worse yet, the majority of the questions asked neglected literal understanding of essential information presented in stories (e.g., characters, plot, sequence of critical events) in favor of "trivial factual makeup of stories" (p. 233).

Although the need to ask students text-related questions that tap both literal and inferential comprehension is important, questions that extend the discussion beyond the text should also be posed. Unfortunately, however, many struggling readers are unsure of what to do if answers to questions are not immediately obvious. Raphael (1982) found that students did not employ effective strategies when reading and answering questions. Instead of applying specific strategies to meet the demands of different kinds of questions, she found that many readers' approaches to answering questions fell into two broad categories: 1) They overrelied on the content of the text and neglected their own background knowledge, or 2) they ignored the text and answered questions only from their prior experiences. It is obvious that applying either of these approaches exclusively negatively affects question-answering skill.

Questioning the Author:
The Teacher as Facilitator in Talking About Texts

Questioning the author is one of the more popular approaches for engaging children in literature discussion groups (Beck, McKeown, Hamilton, & Kucan, 1997). In this "content" approach, the teacher engages students in open, meaning-based discussion of the text as she or he initiates "queries" rather than questions after a segment of text has been read. Beck et al. described the role of questions as tools to assess student comprehension, in contrast to "queries" that "are designed to assist students in grappling with text ideas as they construct meaning" (p. 23). Questions, in Beck et al.'s view, focus on encouraging students to recall what they have read. Queries support students as they are in the process of building an understanding of what they are reading.

Three types of "initiating queries" begin the process. After a segment of text has been read and summarized the teacher may ask:

1. What is the author trying to say here?

2. What is the author's message?

3. What is the author talking about?

After the entire selection is read, "follow-up queries" commence with the goal of clarifying and elaborating on students' thinking:

1. What does the author mean here?

2. Does the author explain this clearly?

3. Does this make sense with what the author told us before?

4. How does this connect with what the author has told us here?

5. Does the author tell us why?

6. Why do you think the author tells us this now?

In addition to these queries, special queries are designed for narrative text, including:

1. How do things look for this character now?

2. How does the author let you know that something has changed?

3. How has the author settled this for us?

4. Given what the author has already told us about the character, what do you think he or she is up to?

If they do encounter blocks to their understanding, then readers need to be aware of what cognitive processes are involved in their own reading as they employ fix-up strategies to correct their comprehension difficulties. Teacher modeling of the process readers go through when they struggle to understand words, phrases, clauses, sentences, or longer chunks of text is critical to learning this strategy. Students need to know that even good readers encounter obstacles to their understanding as they read; that it is perfectly acceptable to stop when that occurs; and, most important, that there are effective strategies students can use to bypass those blocks (see more about monitoring understanding later in this chapter).

Although this constructivist model has been noted to be effective for many students (Allington, Guice, Michelson, Baker, & Li, 1996), Williams argued, "This constructivist approach would not fully meet the needs of students with learning disabilities, who have been shown to respond well to structured, direct instruction" (2002, p. 129). Weak readers can be taught to improve their thinking and reasoning skills and can be taught interactive reading strategies to bolster their comprehension of text (Simmons, Fuchs, Fuchs, Mathes, & Hodge, 1995). Many of these effective strategies will be discussed next.

Categorizing Questions to Aid Comprehension

Learning how to categorize questions into those that can be answered by referring back to the text and those that require higher level thinking based on personal knowledge can be an effective strategy to improve question-answering performance. Pearson and Johnson (1978) created a model to describe three different types of questions that teachers can ask to help their students to develop both text-related (literal and inferential comprehension) and beyond-text (critical analysis, interpretation, generalization, and extension of ideas from the text) comprehension skills:

1. *Text explicit:* The answer to this type of question can be cleanly lifted verbatim from the text.

2. *Text implicit:* Rather than being explicitly stated, the answers to these questions are suggested in the text. It may be necessary to gather information from several sentences or integrate information from larger sections of text in order to answer this type of question.

3. *Script implicit:* The reader's background knowledge, rather than information from the text, is required to answer this kind of question.

There is a relationship between children's recall of passages they have read and the types of questions they have been asked. If they are asked text-explicit questions, then they recall parts of the text verbatim. If they are asked text-implicit questions, then they tend to draw more inferences from text. If they are asked script-implicit questions, then they make more interpretive and evaluative connections between their own prior knowledge and new information from their readings (Wixson, 1983). If we want children to be able to respond to a variety of question levels, then we must give them opportunities to observe good models and practice extensively.

Question-Answer Relationships

Raphael and her colleagues (1982, 1984, 1986) designed an instructional program called Question-Answer Relationships (QAR), which is based on Pearson and Johnson's (1978) taxonomy. The program was designed to help students label the type of questions being asked and then, as they considered both the text and their prior knowledge before they answered a question, use this information to assist them in formulating answers.

Two major categories of relationships are taught: In the Book and In My Head. Readers must refer back to the text to answer In the Book questions, but in order to respond to In My Head questions correctly, some reference to prior knowledge is required.

Each of these two primary QAR categories is then divided into two subcategories. Two kinds of questions may be found within the In the Book group: Right There and Think and Search (also called Putting It Together). There is one primary difference between Right There and Think and Search questions. Although the answers for both categories of questions may be found in the text, the answers for Right There questions are found in one sentence. In addition, many of the same words used in the question are also in the answer. For example, in a passage about Harriet Tubman, these sentences might be found:

> Harriet Tubman was a nurse and a spy for the Union Army during the Civil War. When the War ended, she continued to help people. Harriet worked to raise money for schools for black children. She also worked for funds to establish a home for old black people. Five years before she died, she established the Harriet Tubman home in Auburn, New York, for poor, elderly black people.

A Right There question about this passage might be, "What kind of work did Harriet Tubman do during the Civil War?" The answer, "Harriet Tubman was a nurse and a spy for the Union Army during the Civil War," can be lifted from one sentence and uses many of the same words as the question. In contrast, a Think and Search question might be, "How did Harriet Tubman help black people before and after the Civil War?" The answer might be, "Harriet Tubman helped black people before the Civil War by being a nurse and a spy for the Union Army. After the war she continued to help by raising money for schools for black children and a home for old black people." The answer, although clearly in the book, requires a bit more work. The reader needs to put together information found in several sentences in order to answer.

Turning to the In My Head broad category, there are also two subcategories: Author and You and On My Own. The main difference between these two is whether the reader must read the text for the questions to make sense (Raphael, 1986). If it is necessary for the reader to connect his or her background knowledge with the information in the text in order to answer the question, then the question fits into the Author and You category. For example, the question "Why was Harriet Tubman a spy for the Union Army even though she was born a Southerner?" requires that readers know at least two things:

1. The fact that Harriet was a black woman who was born a slave in the South (drawn from the text)

2. The conditions black slaves lived under in the South during the Civil War period (drawn from the reader's background knowledge)

Neither piece of information is sufficient alone to answer the question. The reader needs to integrate those two facts in order to formulate a reasonable answer to the question. As a result, this must be categorized as an Author and You question.

Referring once again to the text about Harriet Tubman, two examples of On Your Own questions might be:

1. Why was the Civil War fought?

2. How were black children educated before the Civil War?

In both cases, the author has not given the information needed in order to answer the question. The reader needs to either have the prior knowledge necessary to answer it or has to look to another source to find it.

The general sequence of procedures for teaching the QAR strategy are as follows:

- The teacher introduces the concept of the QAR strategy with the two broad categories (In the Book and In My Head).

- The teacher demonstrates the QAR strategy with several short passages by modeling the thinking behind each label.

- The teacher gives students the text, questions, answers, and the QAR label for each question. The students now supply the reason for the label.

- The teacher gives the text, questions, and answers, and the students provide both the QAR label and the reason for the label.

- The teacher gives students the text and questions, and the students supply the answers, QAR labels, and reasons for the labels.

At the beginning, the teacher needs to provide a lot of modeling and immediate feedback as students begin to assume responsibility for labeling the relationships. Students progress from shorter to longer texts and build independence by moving from group to independent activities. After the two broad QAR categories have been mastered, the teacher repeats the teaching sequence with the two subcategories under each: Right There and Think and Search for In the Book questions, and Author and You and On My Own for In My Head questions. (See Figure 12.7 for an illustration of the cue card used to explain the QAR strategy to students.)

The most important things about the QAR strategy are that students not only learn to identify different categories of questions but they also use this information as a signal to try different strategies to answer those questions. Students become active learners who

In the Book QARs

Right There
The answer is in the text, usually easy to find. The words used to make up the question and words used to answer the question are **Right There** in the same sentence.

In My Head QARs

Author and You
The answer is *not* in the story. You need to think about what you already know, what the author tells you in the text, and how it fits together.

**Think and Search
(Putting It Together)**
The answer is in the story, but you need to put together different story parts to find it. Words for the question and words for the answer are not found in the same sentence. They come from different parts of the text.

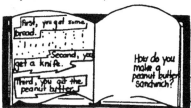

On My Own
The answer is not in the story. You can even answer the question without reading the story. You need to use your own experience.

Figure 12.7. Illustrations to explain Question-Answer Relationships (QARs) to students. (From Raphael, T.E. [1986]. Teaching question answer relationships, revisited. *The Reading Teacher, 39*[6], 519; copyright © 1986 by International Reading Association; reprinted by permission.)

come to value both their own prior knowledge about a topic and the information the author of the text has presented to them.

After reviewing 17 studies on question-answering instruction, the NRP (NICHD, 2000) noted student improvement both in answering questions after reading passages and in strategies of finding answers.

Question Generation

The NRP's review of the research found "the strongest scientific evidence for the effectiveness of asking readers to generate questions during reading" (NICHD, 2000, p. 4-45). It has the strongest evidence for a single reading comprehension strategy among the seven listed. An eighth, which combines several strategies, including self-questioning, is also promising for struggling readers. Self-questioning has been demonstrated to distinguish effective readers and learners from those who have more difficulty with reading (Bransford et al., 1982; Cote & Goldman, 1999).

Strickland, Ganske, and Monroe stated, "Readers who don't think while they read do not generate questions. The most direct and effective way for teachers to help students do this is by demonstrating self-questioning through think-alouds" (2002, p. 162). Opening a window for students onto the kind of self-questioning good readers do as they read can in fact be a powerful strategy. The questioning the author strategy discussed earlier in this chapter is one promising approach to increasing students' awareness about how good readers process (and sometimes struggle with) what they read. There are also other more systematic, explicit methods (e.g., the ReQuest strategy) that can be used to promote students to begin to "interrogate" the text.

As early as 1969, Manzo demonstrated that students could be taught to create their own questions. His technique, ReQuest, was designed to "improve the student's reading comprehension by providing an active learning situation for the development of questioning behaviors" (p. 123). ReQuest can be used with either narrative or expository text and is effective in starting students on the road to active comprehension. It emphasizes modeling, an important feature of cognitive behavior modification. ReQuest has been shown to be particularly effective in helping students focus their attention on the text and pay attention to detail. ReQuest follows a simple sequence:

1. *Silent reading:* The students and the teacher silently read a common segment of text (one to two sentences to one to two paragraphs).

2. *Student questioning:* The teacher closes the book, and students ask him or her as many questions as possible. The teacher models appropriate answers and also provides substantial feedback to students about the questions they generate. Students are asked to "try to ask the kinds of questions a teacher might ask in the way a teacher might ask them" (Manzo, 1969, p. 124).

3. *Teacher questioning:* The students close their books, and the teacher asks the questions. The teacher helps students sharpen their questions by modeling good questioning behavior that includes a range of question types (see the previous discussion of QAR for ideas).

4. *Repetition of sequence:* When questions are exhausted, the students and the teacher read the next segment of text and repeat the procedure. New sections of the text should be integrated with old sections. Questions may relate to new and old sections.

5. *Predictions:* When enough text has been processed for the students to make predictions about the remainder of the text, the exchange of questions stops. The teacher asks predictive questions ("What do you think the rest of the story will be about? Why do you think so?")

6. *Reading:* The teacher and the students read to the end of the passage, verifying and discussing predictions made.

ReQuest was first tested under clinical conditions with students receiving one-to-one remedial instruction, but both Manzo (1969; Manzo & Manzo, 1993) and others (Mason & Au, 1986) have supported its effectiveness when it is used with larger groups. In order to encourage students to generalize questioning to other situations, Bos and Vaughn (1998) advised cuing students to remember to stop while reading and ask themselves questions as they did during ReQuest.

In its summary evaluation of question generation, the NRP (NICHD, 2000) cited significant scientific evidence that instruction on question generation during reading improves reading comprehension in terms of memory and answering questions based on text as well as integrating and identifying main ideas through summarizing. The panel recommended this strategy as part of a multiple-strategy instruction program. (Using multiple strategies is discussed later in this chapter.)

Story Structure

The bulk of texts used in elementary school reading are stories. Story structure pertains to how stories and their plots are organized into a predictable format that includes characters, setting, problem, goal, action, and outcome (or resolution of the problem). When students are taught about story structure, they have an easier time retelling stories within a logical framework. They also show improvements in asking and answering *who, what, when, where, why,* and *how* questions about the story (NICHD, 2000).

Lorna Idol (1987) developed a simple story map with a visual representation of story components and their relationship to one another (see Figure 12.8). She offered one straightforward approach for presenting story mapping in a classroom:

1. *Model:* After introducing the purpose of the strategy, the teacher presents the story elements that are on the story map. The teacher reads a story out loud and stops periodically when story elements are presented in the text. If certain story elements are not presented explicitly, then the teacher needs to model the thinking required to generate the inferences. Students label the parts and write them in the appropriate places on the story map.

2. *Lead:* Students read the story and complete their story maps independently. The teacher gives students feedback about their maps and encourages them to add details they may have omitted.

3. *Test:* Students read a story, generate a story map, and then answer questions that relate to the story elements on the map (e.g., Who are the characters in the story? Where did the story take place? What was the main problem in the story?).

Four optional supports to the story mapping strategy may be helpful for some students. These additions to classic story structure instruction may facilitate recall of story elements for students and spur more active reading of text.

In the first modification, students who have difficulty remembering story elements may use a "five finger retelling" (Stahl, 2004). In this strategy, each finger is used as a reminder or prompt for an element in story structure: characters, setting, problem, plot, and resolution/solution. A chart may serve as an additional reminder of these elements.

For a second modification using the elements from the story map, Bos (1987) proposed a mnemonic, STORE, to help students to retell the story. See Figure 12.9 for a cue card for this story retelling strategy.

For a third option, the Language Circle (see Appendix B at the end of the book) created a set of story elements on sticky notes. Students can use the sticky notes to flag the elements of the story as they read.

According to the NRP (NICHD, 2000) report, instruction in story structure improves students' ability to understand stories, answer questions about them, and remember what was read. The weakest readers benefit the most from this strategy, although even strong readers improve their performance after instruction.

Summarization

In order to summarize, students must orchestrate three important tasks (NICHD, 2000, p. 4-92):

1. Decide what are "the most central and important ideas in the text"

2. "Generalize from examples or from things that are repeated"

3. "Ignore irrelevant details"

Simple Story Map

Name _____   Date _____

```
┌──────────────────────────────────────────────────────────────────────┐
│ The Setting                                                            │
│                                                                        │
│ Characters:              Time:                    Place:               │
│                                                                        │
│                                                                        │
│                                                                        │
└──────────────────────────────────────────────────────────────────────┘
        │
        ▼
┌──────────────────────────────────────────────────────────────────────┐
│ The Problem                                                            │
│                                                                        │
│                                                                        │
│                                                                        │
│                                                                        │
└──────────────────────────────────────────────────────────────────────┘
        │
        ▼
┌──────────────────────────────────────────────────────────────────────┐
│ The Goal                                                               │
│                                                                        │
│                                                                        │
│                                                                        │
└──────────────────────────────────────────────────────────────────────┘
        │
        │        ┌───────────────────────────────────────────────────────┐
        │        │ The Action                                            │
        │        │                                                       │
        │◄──────►│                                                       │
        │        │                                                       │
        │        │                                                       │
        │        └───────────────────────────────────────────────────────┘
        ▼
┌──────────────────────────────────────────────────────────────────────┐
│ The Outcome                                                            │
│                                                                        │
│                                                                        │
│                                                                        │
│                                                                        │
└──────────────────────────────────────────────────────────────────────┘
```

Figure 12.8.   Simple story map. (From Idol, L. [1987]. Group story mapping: A comprehension strategy for both skilled and unskilled readers. *Journal of Learning Disabilities, 20,* 199; copyright © 1987 by PRO-ED, Inc.; reprinted by permission.)

Story-Retelling Strategy

Setting: Who, What, When, Where

Trouble: What is the trouble/problem to be solved?

Order of Action: What happened to solve the problem? (correct/logical order)

Resolution: What was the outcome (resolution) for each action?

End: What happened in the end?

Figure 12.9.   Story retelling strategy. (From Bos, C.S. [1987]. *Promoting story comprehension using a story retelling strategy.* Paper presented at the Teachers Applying Whole Language Conference, Tucson, AZ.)

Researchers who have studied the behaviors of students with learning difficulties have long been aware that these tasks are particularly challenging for these students (Brown & Palincsar, 1982; Graves, 1986; McCormick, 1992; Wong, 1979).

The University of Kansas Center for Research on Learning (Schumaker, Denton, & Deshler, 1984) developed the RAP Paraphrasing Strategy,[1] which helps students bypass these difficulties and improve their ability to recall the main ideas and important facts from expository text they have read. The RAP Paraphrasing Strategy has three specific steps:

1. Read a paragraph.

2. Ask yourself, "What were the main idea and details in this paragraph?"

3. Put the main idea and details into your own words.

The teacher begins by describing the rationale for learning RAP. If students learn to put information into their own words, they will more likely think about what they have read and understand and remember it. Next, the general conditions under which the strategy may be used are noted. Students will be able to use the strategy any time they are reading something in paragraph form that they want to understand and remember. Finally, the teacher shares the positive results that students can expect after learning and applying the strategy.

Next, the teacher describes the three steps of the strategy. As students do Step 1, the teacher reminds them to think about the meaning of the words they are reading. As students do Step 2, they are guided to look back over the paragraph quickly to find the main idea and details. The teacher reminds them that the first or last sentence, key vocabulary, and repetitions of the same word or words in the whole paragraph often give

---

[1]The steps of the remembering system for the RAP Paraphrasing Strategy are part of an instructional program developed and researched at the University of Kansas Center for Research on Learning (Schumaker, Denton, & Deshler, 1984). This system is used to cue strategic thinking. Each step involves a variety of strategic questions and prompts that are described in step-by-step detail in written materials that can only be obtained as part of guided professional development experiences that are offered throughout the nation and are designed to ensure high-quality implementation with students. This program is one of several research-based programs designed for teachers to use as they teach learning strategies to students. Go to http://www.kucrl.org for more information.

hints about the main idea. Important details are related to that main idea. As students prepare for Step 3, the teacher then describes how to locate the main idea. Throughout the description of the strategy, students are reminded of certain requirements of each paraphrased statement (Schumaker et al., 1984):

- It must contain a complete thought, with a subject and a verb.

- It must be totally accurate.

- It must have new information and must not be a repetition of something that was already said.

- It must make sense.

- It must contain useful information.

- It must be in the students' own words.

- Only one general statement per paragraph is permitted.

As students continue to learn the strategy, modeling by the teacher (and by students); verbal practice; controlled practice with short, simple passages; advanced practice; and generalization become integral parts of the instruction.

The NRP's (NICHD, 2000) final evaluation of summarization as a targeted strategy was quite positive. The panel noted that this is a sound method for connecting ideas and making generalizations from text. Other benefits were also listed for summarization, including improving memory of what is read, both for free recall and for answering questions. This strategy has been incorporated successfully into other multiple-strategy interventions, most notably reciprocal teaching (discussed next). In addition, PALS and CSR include a summarization step in their approaches.

Multiple Strategies

Although research on individual reading strategies has yielded many positive results, these strategies may even be more powerful when they are combined into a multiple strategy instructional program. "This method finds considerable scientific support for its effectiveness, and it is the most promising for use in classroom instruction where teachers and readers interact over texts" (NICHD, 2000, p. 4-46).

Reciprocal teaching (Palincsar & Brown, 1984) is probably the most well-known method for teaching multiple comprehension strategies. This approach combines several of the most effective comprehension strategies reviewed by the NRP (NICHD, 2000): prediction, questioning, seeking clarification when comprehension monitoring reveals confusion, and summarization.

As a reciprocal teaching lesson begins, the teacher explains the purpose of the work the students and teacher will do together and describes the four strategies they will be using in the lesson. The teacher models the activity, and the students try to emulate the process. Throughout the lesson, the teacher provides corrective feedback so that students have ample opportunity to be supported in their steps to independence. Students silently read passages that are appropriate to their age and ability. Young children (or very weak readers) may have passages read aloud to them. After a passage has been read, children are asked to state the topic and summarize the important information they have read.

The teacher always models the reciprocal teaching procedure first, but eventually a student is chosen to act as the teacher and asks an important question about the passage that was just read. Next, he or she will summarize, making a prediction and, if necessary, asking for clarification of confusing terms or concepts. The teacher provides support during this process by prompting students to guide them in the right direction, instructing (reminding them about the important steps to the procedure if they have forgotten), modifying the activity for students who appear to be stuck, or asking for other students to step in and help.

Carlisle and Rice (2002) cautioned practitioners to make sure that sufficient time is devoted to the instructional process in reciprocal teaching, that they allow adequate chances for students to practice the strategies, and that they provide continued guidance and support for students to reach independent application of the embedded strategies. Rosenshine and Meister's (1994) review of the research on reciprocal teaching concluded that more time should be spent teaching the individual strategies directly before beginning the more interactive segment of the technique.

Project WebSIGHT, a joint project of the Miami-Dade County Public Schools, the University of Miami, and the Florida Department of Education, has designed a teacher education course incorporating the Internet to bring recommended teaching practices to Florida schools. The project provides support materials for reciprocal teaching lessons on its web site (http://www.miamisci.org/tec). Lesson plans and instructional materials, including student cue cards and bookmarks, may be found on the site.

Reciprocal teaching is similar to CSR. Klingner et al. (2001) acknowledged that CSR is an outgrowth of reciprocal teaching and, in fact, used reciprocal teaching in their earlier work (Klingner & Vaughn, 1996). After adopting many changes to reciprocal teaching over time, they felt that they had created a substantially different approach that deserved its own name (Klingner et al., 2001). An outline of the differences the authors cited between CSR and reciprocal teaching may be found in Table 12.2.

Other Promising Strategies

Experimental research examining various approaches to instruction is relatively new. As a result, there are other reading comprehension strategies that have not yet been confirmed by pre- and posttest control-group studies even though initial, limited research has been promising and reports from practicing teachers suggest that they have merit.

Visualization or Mental Imagery

Visualization or mental imagery is one strategy with tantalizing potential. **Imagery training** has been found to improve students' memory of what they read (Pressley, 1976) as well as improve inferential reasoning about written text (Borduin, Borduin, & Manley, 1994). Depending on the program used, individuals are guided to create visual images to represent a picture or a text as they read it.

Researchers and practitioners in reading have offered several models of visualization strategies. For example, *Visualizing and Verbalizing for Language Comprehension and Thinking,* developed by Nanci Bell (1991) for Lindamood-Bell products, is widely used. This program may be particularly helpful for individuals with weak language skills. The program begins with the picture level, so even individuals who are poor decoders can start to address comprehension.

Beginning at the picture level and gradually moving through word imaging, single sentences, and multiple sentences (in which higher order thinking skills are introduced), single and multiple paragraphs, and eventually whole pages, Visualizing and Verbalizing uses a structured format of modeling, questioning, and helping students to

Table 12.2.   How reciprocal teaching and *Collaborative Strategic Reading (CSR)* differ

Reciprocal teaching	Collaborative Strategic Reading
Designed primarily for use with narrative text	Designed primarily for use with expository text
No **brainstorming** before reading	Students **brainstorm** to activate prior knowledge as part of preview (before reading).
Students predict what they think will happen next before reading each paragraph or segment of text.	Students only **predict** as part of the Preview strategy (before reading), making informed guesses about what they think they will learn.
Students **clarify** words or chunks of text they don't understand by rereading the sentences before and after the sentence they don't understand and/or asking a peer for assistance.	Students use fix-up strategies to clarify **clunks** (words they don't understand). • Reread the sentence. • Reread the sentences before and after. • Break apart the word and look for smaller words they know. • Look for a prefix or suffix they know. • Look at the picture for clues. • Ask for help.
Students **summarize** the paragraph or segment of text they have just read.	Students **get the gist** of the paragraph or segment of text they have just read, identifying "the most important who or what" and the most important thing about the who or what. They then say the gist in ten words or less.
Students **generate questions** after each paragraph or segment of text they have just read.	Students only **generate questions** as part of a **wrap up** after they have read the entire day's selection. Students answer each other's questions.
No **review** after reading	Students **review** what they have learned after reading the day's selection.
8–12 students in the group; the teacher in the group	An entire class is divided into **cooperative groups** of 2–5; the teacher circulates rather than staying with a group.
No learning logs	Students record their previews, clunks, questions, and what they've learned in individual **CSR Learning Logs.**
The leader (a student) facilitates the discussion about a paragraph or section of text; this role rotates after each paragraph.	Every student in the group has a meaningful role; one of these roles is to be the leader. Roles are assigned for an entire lesson (only rotating biweekly in some classes).
No cue cards	Students use **Cue Cards** to help them implement their roles and the comprehension strategies.

From Klingner, J.K., Vaughn, S., Dimino, J., Schumm, J.S. & Bryant, D. (2001). *From clunk to click: Collaborative strategic reading* (p. 7). Longmont, CO: Sopris West; reprinted by permission of Sopris West Educational Services; *Collaborative Strategic Reading*, copyright 2001.

expand descriptions of visual images to improve understanding. Using structure words (e.g., *what, size, color, number, shape*) written on cards, students build their mental images in increasing complexity and depth. Clinical studies conducted at the Lindamood-Bell Learning Processes Center showed highly significant gains in oral and silent reading comprehension measures after individuals received intensive therapy in the Visualization and Verbalizing strategy (Bell, 1991).

Although a promising technique, more research is needed to measure the effectiveness of programs that use visualization strategies. Existing research tends to be limited to experimenter tests tapping recall and ability to answer questions that have short answers. Studies using control groups as well as those identifying transfer of comprehension improvement to **standardized test** performance would be a welcome addition to research.

Computer Technology

Since 1984, the Center for Applied Special Technology (CAST), a research and development group, has been addressing applying computer technology to individualize reading instruction and to improve effective practice of reading strategies in schools. Their work is targeted toward the needs of all individuals, but especially those with disabilities, through **universal design for learning** (UDL). UDL provides a framework to assist teachers in setting goals for diverse learners, choosing or creating flexible materials and media, and assessing students accurately.

One of CAST's programs that was developed from their research—Thinking Reader (Tom Snyder Productions)—presents authentic literature in a supportive environment that embeds prompts, hints, models answers, and gives instant feedbacks to students as they learn to use seven powerful strategies while they read:

1. Summarizing

2. Questioning

3. Clarifying

4. Predicting

5. Visualizing

6. Feeling

7. Reflecting

CAST is currently involved in two research projects that address the comprehension needs of struggling readers. CLIPPS (Custom Learning Interface Production from Pedagogic Semantics) is directed at creating a new technology that will present content that offers adaptations (e.g., graphics, expanded text, supplementary background knowledge, links to vocabulary) for content to meet the needs of different students' learning characteristics. Strategy Tutor is a web-based tool designed to help students read, research, collect, and understand information better and more efficiently within web-based lessons. Students can store all their notes on a personal, sortable electronic worklog that can be accessed from any computer. Research-based learning strategies and vocabulary supports are included in the tool. Go to http://www.cast.org for more information about CAST's projects. See Chapter 22 for more information about technological supports for individuals with dyslexia.

COMPREHENSION CHALLENGES FOR STUDENTS IN THE 21ST CENTURY: NEW LITERACIES

More and more students today use the Internet to locate, understand, and use information online. Current research points to the need for students to develop new comprehension strategies and skills to read and gain meaning from this resource (Biancarosa & Snow, 2004; Coiro, 2003, 2005; Sutherland-Smith, 2002). As the RAND Reading Study

Group (RRSG) noted, "accessing the Internet makes large demands on individuals' literacy skills; in some cases , this new technology requires readers to have novel literacy skills, and little is known how to analyze or teach those skills." (2002, p.4). In addition to understanding how search engines work and how information is organized on web sites, students need to develop higher levels of inferential reasoning as well as comprehension monitoring strategies to effectively use these new literacies (Coiro, 2005).

Members of the New Literacies Research Team at the University of Connecticut have accepted the challenge of identifying the key literacy skills that need to be developed to enable students to use Internet resources effectively during content area lessons. Leu, Kinzer, Coir, and Cammack (2004) have identified five New Literacies for Online Reading Comprehension:

1. Identifying important questions

2. Locating information

3. Critically evaluating that information

4. Synthesizing information

5. Communicating the answers to others

Students need to learn how to formulate a question or define a problem when identifying important questions. Subskills within this topic include understanding the question; narrowing, expanding, and/or refining the question as needed; and knowing when there is a need to shift the question because of new information accessed or lack of information available. In order to locate information on the Internet, students need to know how to use a search engine or other methods to locate an information resource. They must be able to evaluate information they have found, identify any biases, and know how to verify it through alternative or primary sources. In order to synthesize what they have accessed, they need to be able to integrate information from multiple resources including text based, multimedia based, and a combination of text and multimedia. Finally, they need to be able to organize and communicate their findings.

The New Literacies community is asking more questions than providing definitive answers to those questions. Researchers in this community acknowledge that reading comprehension is likely to be the primary focus of investigation because the Internet and other information and communication technologies are focused primarily on information and learning from text (Leu et al., 2004).

NEXT STEPS

We cannot afford to wait to address the needs of students who struggle to gain meaning from text, whether that text is found in a book, a magazine, or on the Internet. As Stanovich noted, "students who do not read well read less and when they read less, they learn less" (1986). As a result, students' comprehension difficulties complicate their learning in all academic areas (Chall, 1996). And although Michael Pressley's observations conflict with common philosophy and practice in many schools today, they must be acknowledged. He noted,

> Despite the improvements in fluency and knowledge permitted by extensive reading, the "read, read, read" approach does not lead to as active meaning construction during reading as occurs when students are taught explicitly to use and articulate comprehension strategies when they read. (2000, p. 554)

There are many powerful, research-supported strategies that hold promise for struggling readers who may be able to decode but who still strive to understand what they read. Although a good amount is known about effective (and ineffective) reading comprehension strategies, there are still many unanswered questions. Concerns about understanding the multiple sources of variance in the reading comprehension process and outcomes, continuing national demand for high literacy skills but stagnant reading test performance, weak teacher preparation, minimal or ineffective reading comprehension instruction in the schools, and a persistent achievement gap between children of different demographic groups continue to be troubling.

In 2000, the RRSG was formed when the U.S. Department of Education's now-defunct Office of Educational Research and Improvement (OERI) asked RAND to look at how OERI could improve the quality and relevance of research that the agency funded (RRSG, 2002). When the final report was released in 2002, the authors recommended that teachers "must teach comprehension explicitly, beginning in the primary grades and continuing through high school" (p. xii). The authors strongly advised that while maintaining methodological rigor, potential research must be "usable" and directed toward improving classroom practices, enhancing curricula, enriching teacher preparation, and producing better and more informative assessments of reading comprehension. As part of this initiative, the RRSG recommended that these questions be addressed:

- What instructional conditions should accompany strategy instruction to encourage students to generalize strategic approaches to learning across texts, tasks, contexts, and different age levels?

- How should teachers of poor comprehenders who are in general education classes prioritize time and instructional emphasis among the many competing calls for their attention to everything from building fluency to teaching vocabulary, using computer technology, and improving reading skills?

- What variations in instructional time and practice optimize opportunities for students who are ELLs to improve their comprehension skills?

The RRSG's research agenda for reading comprehension promises to "build new knowledge that will be helpful to all concerned with reading education—practitioners, teacher educators, policymakers, and parents" (Sweet & Snow, 2002, p. 47). We are being given an opportunity to have a huge effect on the lives of children now and on their futures. The time is ripe to seize that opportunity and build on what we already know to prepare students to be productive, literate adults.

REFERENCES

Aaron, P.G., Joshi, M., & Williams, K.A. (1999). Not all reading disabilities are alike. *Journal of Learning Disabilities, 32,* 120–137.

Adams, M.J. (1990). *Beginning to read: Thinking and learning about print.* Cambridge, MA: The MIT Press.

Adams, M.J., Treiman, R., & Pressley, M. (1998). Reading, writing and literacy. In W. Damon (Series Ed.) & I.E. Sigel & K.A. Renninger (Vol. Eds.), *Handbook of child psychology: Child psychology in practice* (Vol. 4, pp. 275–355). New York: Wiley.

Allington, R.L. (2001). *What really matters for struggling readers: Designing research-based programs.* New York: Longman.

Allington, R., Guice, S., Michelson, N., Baker, R., & Li, S. (1996). Literature-based curricula in high poverty schools. In M.F. Graves, P. van den Broek, & B.M. Taylor (Eds.), *The first R: Every child's right to read* (pp. 73–96). New York: Teachers College Press.

Beck, I.L., McKeown, M.G., Hamilton, R.L., & Kucan, L. (1997). *Questioning the author: An ap-*

proach for enhancing student engagement with text. Newark, DE: International Reading Association.

Bell, N. (1991). *Visualizing and verbalizing for language comprehension and thinking.* Paso Robles, CA: Academy of Reading Publications.

Biancarosa, G., & Snow, C.E. (2004). *Reading next: A vision for action and research in middle and high school literacy.* A report to Carnegie Corporation of New York. Washington, DC: Alliance for Excellent Education.

Borduin, B.J., Borduin, C.M., & Manley, C.M. (1994). The use of imagery training to improve reading comprehension of second graders. *Journal of Genetic Psychology, 155*(1), 115–118.

Bos, C.S. (1987). *Promoting story comprehension using a story retelling strategy.* Paper presented at the Teachers Applying Whole Language Conference, Tucson, AZ.

Bos, C.S., & Vaughn, S. (1998). *Strategies for teaching students with learning and behavior problems* (4th ed.). Boston: Allyn & Bacon.

Bransford, J., Stein, B., Vye, N., Franks, J., Auble, P., Mezynski, K., et al. (1982). Differences in approaches to learning: An overview. *Journal of Experimental Psychology, 111,* 390–398.

Brown, A.L., & Palincsar, A.S. (1982). Including strategic learning from texts by means of informed, self-control training. *Topics in Learning and Learning Disabilities, 2*(1), 1–17.

Cain, K., & Oakhill, J.V. (1999). Inference making ability and its relation to comprehension failure in young children. *Reading and Writing, 11,* 489–503.

Carlisle, J.F. (1999). *Beginning Reasoning and Reading.* Cambridge, MA: Educators Publishing Service.

Carlisle, J.F., & Rice, M.S. (2002). *Improving reading comprehension.* Timonium, MD: York Press.

Carnine, D., Silbert, J., & Kame'enui, E.J. (1990). *Direct instruction reading* (2nd ed.). Columbus, OH: Charles E. Merrill.

Carr, E., & Dewitz, P. (1988). *Teaching comprehension as a student-directed process.* Paper presented at the meeting of the International Reading Association, Toronto.

Carr, E., & Ogle, D. (1987). K-W-L Plus: A strategy for comprehension and summarization. *Journal of Reading, 30,* 626–631.

Chall, J. (1996). *Stages of reading development* (2nd ed.). Orlando, FL: Harcourt.

Coiro, J. (2003). *Reading comprehension on the Internet: Expanding our understanding of reading comprehension to encompass new literacies.* Retrieved September 19, 2009, from http://www.readingonline.org/electronic/elec_index.asp?HREF=/electronic/rt/2-03_Column/index.html

Coiro, J. (2005). Making sense of online text. *Educational Leadership, 63*(2), 30–35.

Cote, N., & Goldman, S. (1999). Building representations of informational text: Evidence from children's think-aloud protocols. In H. Van Oostendorp & S. Goldman (Eds.), *The construction of mental representations during reading* (pp. 169–193). Mahwah, NJ: Lawrence Erlbaum Associates.

Deshler, D.D., Ellis, E.S., & Lenz, B.K. (1996). *Teaching adolescents with learning disabilities: Strategies and methods* (2nd ed.). Denver: Love Publishing.

Doctorow, M., Wittrock, M., & Marks, C. (1978). Generative processes in reading comprehension. *Journal of Educational Psychology, 70,* 109–118.

Durkin, D. (1979). What classroom observations reveal about reading comprehension. *Reading Research Quarterly, 14,* 518–544.

Durkin, D. (1993). *Teaching them to read* (6th ed.). Boston: Allyn & Bacon.

Ehri, L. (1998). Word reading by sight and by analogy in beginning readers. In C. Hulme & R.M. Joshi (Eds.), *Reading and spelling development and disorders* (pp. 87–111). Mahwah, NJ: Lawrence Erlbaum Associates.

Fowler, A.E. (1988). Grammaticality judgments and reading skill in grade 2. *Annals of Dyslexia, 38,* 73–74.

Fuchs, D., Fuchs, L.S., Mathes, P.G., & Simmons, D.C. (1997). Peer assisted learning strategies: Making classrooms more responsive to diversity. *American Educational Research Journal, 34,* 174–206.

Fuchs, D., Fuchs, L.S., Thompson, A., Svenson, E., Yen, L., Al Otaiba, S., et al. (2001). Peer-assisted learning strategies in reading: Extensions for kindergarten, first grade, and high school. *Remedial and Special Education, 22,* 15–21.

Fuchs, D., Mathes, P.G., & Fuchs, L.S. (2001). *Peer-assisted learning strategies: Reading methods for Grades 2–6* [teacher manual]. Nashville: Vanderbilt University.

Gambrell, L.B., Block, C.C., & Pressley, M. (2002). Introduction: Improving comprehension instruction: An urgent priority. In C.C. Block, L.B. Gambrell, & M. Pressley (Eds.), *Improving comprehension instruction* (pp. 3–16). San Francisco: Jossey-Bass.

Gough, P.B. (1996). How children learn to read and why they fail. *Annals of Dyslexia, 46,* 3–20.

Granowsky, A. (n.d.). *Point of view stories series: Cinderella.* Orlando, FL: Harcourt Achieve.

Graves, A.W. (1986). Effects of direct instruction and metacomprehension training on finding main ideas. *Learning Disabilities Research, 1*(2), 90–100.

Greenwood, C.R., Delquadri, J.C., & Hall, R.V. (1989). Longitudinal effects of classwide peer tutoring. *Journal of Educational Psychology, 81,* 371–383.

Guszak, F.J. (1967). Teacher questioning and reading. *The Reading Teacher, 21,* 227–234.

Hammond, D. (1983). How your students can predict their way to reading comprehension. *Learning, 12,* 62–64.

Harris, T.L., & Hodges, R.E. (Eds.). (1995). *The literacy dictionary: The vocabulary of reading and writing.* Newark, DE: International Reading Association.

Hart, B., & Risley, T.R. (1995). *Meaningful differences in the everyday experience of young American children.* Baltimore: Paul H. Brookes Publishing Co.

Hirsch, E.D., Jr. (2003, Spring). Reading comprehension requires knowledge—of words and the world: Scientific insights into the fourth-grade slump and the nation's stagnant comprehension scores. *American Educator, 27,* 10–22, 28–44.

Hirsch, E.D., Jr. (2006). *The case for bringing content into the language arts block and for a knowledge-rich curriculum core for all children.* Retrieved October 25, 2009, from http://www.aft.org/pubs-reports/american_educator/issues/spring06/hirsch.htm

Hirsch, E.D., Jr. (2009). *Core Knowledge Sequence: Content and skill guidelines for grades K–8.* Charlottesville, VA: Core Knowledge Foundation.

Hodgkinson, H. (1991). Reform versus reality. *Phi Delta Kappan, 73,* 9–16.

Idol, L. (1987). Group story mapping: A comprehension strategy for both skilled and unskilled readers. *Journal of Learning Disabilities, 20,* 196–205.

Jenkins, J.R., Jewell, M., Leicester, N., & Troutner, N.M. (1990). *Development of a school building model for educating handicapped and at-risk students in general education classrooms.* Paper presented at the annual meeting of the American Educational Research Association, Boston.

Klingner, J.K., & Vaughn, S. (1996). Reciprocal teaching of reading comprehension strategies for students with learning disabilities who use English as a second language. *Elementary School Journal, 96,* 275–293.

Klingner, J.K., & Vaughn, S. (2000). The helping behaviors of fifth-graders while using collaborative strategic reading (CSR) during ESL content classes. *TESOL Quarterly, 34,* 69–98.

Klingner, J.K., Vaughn, S., Dimino, J., Schumm, J.S., & Bryant, D. (2001). *From clunk to click: Collaborative strategic reading.* Longmont, CO: Sopris West Educational Services.

Klingner, J.K., Vaughn, S., Hughes, M.T., Schumm, J.S., & Elbaum, B. (1998). Academic outcomes for students with and without learning disabilities in inclusive classrooms. *Learning Disabilities Research and Practice, 13,* 153–160.

Leu, D.J., Kinzer, C.I.K., Coiro, J.L., & Cammack, D.W. (2004). Toward a theory of new literacies emerging from the Internet and other information and communication technologies. Retrieved October 18, 2009, from http://www.readingonline.org/newliteracies/leu/

Manzo, A. (1969). The ReQuest procedure. *Journal of Reading, 13,* 123–126.

Manzo, A.V., & Manzo, U.C. (1993). *Literacy disorders: Holistic diagnosis and remediation.* Orlando, FL: Harcourt.

Maria, K. (1990). *Reading comprehension instruction: Issues and strategies.* Timonium, MD: York Press.

Mason, J.M., & Au, K.H. (1986). *Reading instruction for today.* Glenview, IL: Scott Foresman.

McCormick, S. (1992). Disabled readers' erroneous responses to inferential comprehension questions: Description and analysis. *Reading Research Quarterly, 27,* 54–77.

McKeown, M.G., & Beck, I.L. (1990). The assessment and characterization of young learners' knowledge of a topic in history. *American Educational Research Journal, 27,* 688–726.

McNeil, J.D. (1987). *Reading comprehension.* Glenview, IL: Scott Foresman.

National Institute of Child Health and Human Development. (2000). *Report of the National Reading Panel: Reports of the subgroups. Teaching children to read: An evidence-based assessment of the scientific research literature on reading and its implications for reading instruction* (NIH Publication No. 00-4754). Washington, DC: Government Printing Office.

No Child Left Behind Act of 2001, PL 107-110, 115 Stat. 1425, 20 U.S.C. §§ 6301 et seq.

Oakhill, J., & Yuill, N. (1996). Higher order factors in comprehension disability: Processes and remediation. In C. Cornoldi & J. Oakhill (Eds.), *Reading comprehension difficulties: Processes and intervention* (pp. 69–92). Mahwah, NJ: Lawrence Erlbaum Associates.

Ogle, D.M. (1986). K-W-L: A teaching model that develops active reading of expository text. *The Reading Teacher, 39,* 564–570.

Palincsar, A.S., & Brown, A. (1984). Reciprocal teaching of comprehension-fostering and comprehension-monitoring activities. *Cognition and Instruction, 1,* 117–175.

Pallas, A.M., Natriello, G., & McDill, L. (1989). The changing nature of the disadvantaged population: Current dimensions and future trends. *Educational Researcher, 18,* 16–22.

Pearson, P.D., & Johnson, D.D. (1978). *Teaching reading comprehension.* Austin, TX: Holt, Rinehart & Winston.

Pressley, G.M. (1976). Mental imagery helps eight-year-olds remember what they read. *Journal of Educational Psychology, 68,* 355–359.

Pressley, M. (2000). What should comprehension instruction be the instruction of? In M. Kamil, P. Mosenthal, P.D. Pearson, & R. Barr (Eds.), *Handbook of reading research* (Vol. III, pp. 545–562). Mahwah, NJ: Lawrence Erlbaum Associates.

Pressley, M., Brown, R., El-Dinary, P., & Afflerbach, P. (1995). The comprehension instruction that students need: Instruction fostering constructively responsive reading. *Learning Disabilities Research and Practice, 10*, 215–224.

RAND Reading Study Group (RRSG). (2002). *Reading for understanding: Toward an R & D program in reading comprehension*. Retrieved January 25, 2005, from http://www.rand.org/publications/MR/MR1465/MR1465.pdf

Raphael, T.E. (1982). Teaching children question-answering strategies. *Reading Teacher, 36*, 186–191.

Raphael, T.E. (1984). Teaching learners about sources of information for answering comprehension questions. *Journal of Reading, 28*, 303–311.

Raphael, T.E. (1986). Teaching question-answer relationships, revisited. *Reading Teacher, 39*, 516–522.

Rose, D., & Dalton, B. (2002). Using technology to individualize reading instruction. In C.C. Block, L.B. Gambrell, & M. Pressley (Eds.), *Improving comprehension instruction* (pp. 257–274). San Francisco: Jossey-Bass.

Rosenshine, B., & Meister, C. (1994). Reciprocal teaching: A review of the research. *Review of Educational Research, 64*(4), 479–530.

Schumaker, J.B., Denton, P.H., & Deshler, D.D. (1984). *The paraphrasing strategy (learning strategies curriculum)*. Lawrence: University of Kansas.

Shaywitz, S. (2003). *Overcoming dyslexia: A new and complete science-based program for reading problems at any level*. New York: Alfred A. Knopf.

Siegel, L.S., & Ryan, E.B. (1988). Development of grammatical-sensitivity, phonological, and short-term memory skills in normally achieving and learning disabled children. *Developmental Psychology, 24*, 28–37.

Simmons, D.C., Fuchs, D., Fuchs, L.S., Hodge, J.P., & Mathes, P.G. (1994). Importance of instructional complexity and role reciprocity to classwide peer tutoring. *Learning Disabilities Research and Practice, 9*(4), 203–212.

Simmons, D.C., Fuchs, L.S., Fuchs, D., Mathes, P.G., & Hodge, J.P. (1995). Effects of explicit teaching and peer tutoring on the reading achievement of learning-disabled and low-performing students in regular classrooms. *Elementary School Journal, 95*, 387–408.

Stahl, K.A.D. (2004). Proof, practice, and promise: Comprehension strategy instruction in the primary grades. *The Reading Teacher, 57*(1), 598–609.

Stahl, S.A. (1991). Beyond the instrumentalist hypothesis: Some relationships between word meanings and comprehension. In P. Schwa-

nenflugel (Ed.), *The psychology of word meanings* (pp. 157–178). Mahwah, NJ: Lawrence Erlbaum Associates.

Stanovich, K.E. (1986). Matthew effects in reading: Some consequences of individual differences in the acquisition of literacy. *Reading Research Quarterly, 21*, 360–406.

Strickland, D.S., Ganske, K., & Monroe, J.K. (2002). *Supporting struggling readers and writers*. Portland, ME: Stenhouse Publishers.

Sutherland-Smith, W. (2002). Weaving the literacy web: Changes in reading from page to screen. *The Reading Teacher, 55*, 662–669.

Sweet, A.P., & Snow, C. (2002). Reconceptualizing reading comprehension. In C.C. Block, L.B. Gambrell, & M. Pressley (Eds.), *Improving comprehension instruction* (pp. 17–53). San Francisco: Jossey- Bass.

Taylor, B.M., Pearson, P.D., Clark, K.F., & Walpole, S. (1999). Effective schools/accomplished teachers. *The Reading Teacher, 53*(2),156–159.

Torgesen, J.K. (1998, Spring/Summer). Catch them before they fail. *American Educator*, 1–8.

Walsh, K. (2003, Spring). Basal readers: The lost opportunity to build the knowledge that propels comprehension. *The American Educator, 27*, 24–27.

Weaver, P. (1979). Improving reading comprehension: Effects of sentence organization instruction. *Reading Research Quarterly, 15*, 127–146.

Williams, J. (1987). Educational treatments for dyslexia at the elementary and secondary levels. In R. Bowler (Ed.), *Intimacy with language: A forgotten basic in teacher education* (pp. 24–32). Baltimore: International Dyslexia Association.

Williams, J. (2002). Using the theme scheme. In C.C. Block & M. Pressley (Eds.), *Comprehension instruction: Research-based best practices* (pp. 126–139). New York: Guilford Press.

Willingham, D. (2006, Spring). How knowledge helps. *American Educator, 30*, 30–37.

Willingham, D. (2006/2007, Winter). The usefulness of brief instruction in reading comprehension strategies. *American Educator, 30*, 39–45, 50.

Willingham, D. (2007, Summer). Can critical thinking be taught? *American Educator, 30*, 8–19.

Wixson, K. (1983). Questions about a text: What you ask about is what children learn. *The Reading Teacher, 37*, 287–293.

Wong, B.Y.L. (1979). Increasing retention of main ideas through questioning strategies. *Learning Disability Quarterly, 2*(2), 42–47.

13

Composition
Evidence–Based Instruction

JUDITH C. HOCHMAN

Many individuals with excellent reading and speaking skills have problems generating written language. Even for typical learners, mastering the skills associated with good writing is a daunting task, but those students with learning and language problems face formidable obstacles. They have difficulties with decoding, spelling, word retrieval, and syntax, which are often exacerbated by a limited vocabulary and limited background knowledge. These obstacles significantly compromise their capacity for comprehension as well as clear accurate communication. In addition, weak organizational skills often accompany learning and language problems. The inability to distinguish essential from nonessential information and to set forth facts or ideas in logical order can impede students as they try to formulate outlines and generate well-organized paragraphs and compositions.

Written language is considered by many to be the most challenging skill to teach and learn. Its demands on graphomotor skills, cognitive and linguistic abilities, and awareness of text and social conventions pose problems for many students. When writing, there is a need to clarify thoughts and express oneself with far more precision and accuracy than when speaking. Facial expressions, gestures, and prior knowledge provide a speaker with information about his or her audience, but a writer lacks these cues. As a result, writing requires a high level of abstraction, elaboration, and reflection.

The executive functions play an enormous role in writing, especially when completing academic, professional, or business-related assignments (Hochman, 2009). These functions affect a writer's ability to plan, organize, monitor, and revise text (Singer & Bashir, 2004). The writer must

- Strategize (select a topic)

- Initiate a series of actions (gather information)

- Plan approaches (develop an outline)

- Organize approaches (sequence and order material within the outline)

- Inhibit and monitor diversions

- Sustain task and effort

- Monitor and assess outcomes against plans

- Institute needed changes

Each of these steps requires **selective attention,** as well as sustained and divided attention, span of attention, and the ability to shift attention (Singer & Bashir, 2004). In addition, the demands of the writing process on working memory, a manipulative function that allows the management of multiple features and simultaneous processing, are enormous. Writers must think about meaning, purpose, audience, syntax, and semantics. They have to plan ahead, as well as sequence and organize information. These tasks require simultaneous processing at higher cognitive levels than are required in other areas of skills acquisition. Moreover, older students are often required to demonstrate their understanding of subject matter in writing assignments by paraphrasing or summarizing texts that are linguistically complex or densely loaded with factual information.

Writing problems remain a persistent learning disability personally, vocationally, and academically for many adults who were not taught specific strategies as young students (Scott, 1989b). Many students receive little, if any, explicit instruction in written language because writing problems do not receive as much attention as reading disabilities (Scott, 1989a). Too often, it is assumed that mastering the conventions of written language will naturally follow fluent decoding and good reading comprehension. Evidence clearly demonstrates that explicit writing instruction can help students' reading skills (Berninger, Garcia, & Abbott, 2009; Graham & Hebert, 2010).

Developing narrative skills and sound **expository writing** abilities (i.e., discussing ideas, explaining processes) should be the primary aims of a written language curriculum. Given the limited time teachers have to provide instruction in writing, the goal should be to help students develop a solid foundation in those writing skills that are required most often in academic tasks and assignments. Writing and thinking are inextricably linked. Therefore, the most important instructional goals should be to enhance clarity and precision in both process and product. Although mechanics such as spelling and handwriting are important and must not be ignored, they should be addressed separately from composition whenever possible so that students can focus on developing the higher level skills required for written language.

Writing can take many forms. It can serve as a means of transcription, demonstrate knowledge, or communicate and facilitate learning (Scott, 1999, 2005). Ultimately, writing serves two primary functions: It is either knowledge telling, which is often a narrative recounting, or knowledge transforming, which requires many high-level thought processes (Bereiter & Scardamalia, 1987). Knowledge transforming writing enables the student to formulate ideas, synthesize and analyze information, persuade, and solve problems. Every student should have the opportunity to become a writer who can transform knowledge.

Creative writing activities that center on self-expression rather than on communication with the reader are frequently the major focus of elementary school writing programs. Imaginative stories, poems, journal writing, and descriptions involving personal perceptions are assigned in many classes, often with little or no guidance from the teacher. However, direct, explicit instruction is the key to developing good writing skill. Students with and without learning and language disabilities should be given opportunities to experiment with a variety of forms and styles only after they learn how to write sentences and paragraphs competently.

Although writing lessons should take place daily, tasks involving paper and pencil are not always necessary. For example, many sentence and paragraph activities can and should be done orally. This is particularly important in the primary grades. Independent writing should not take place until a great deal of time has been spent on teacher modeling and group lessons. Activities for longer compositions should include carefully orchestrated discussions dealing with identifying the audience, selecting a topic, and describing the purpose of the assignment. The teacher must provide explicit demonstrations of what is expected.

Reinforcement across the curriculum is important whenever possible because many students have difficulty applying the writing principles learned in one class to the subject matter of another. For teachers to achieve the best results, writing instruction should be integrated into every content area and at all grade levels through secondary school. Students with a wide range of abilities will then have a chance of becoming better writers in all academic areas.

This chapter describes strategies for writing sentences, paragraphs, and compositions. Sentence activities are the foundation for revising and editing skills, which are crucial in developing competency in writing. They include working with sentences and **fragments,** unscrambling sentences, identifying sentence types, developing complex sentences, expanding sentences, and generating topic sentences. Most of these activities should take place concurrently. Next come activities for paragraphs and compositions that are necessary to develop the thinking and study skills that students need. Along with detailed descriptions for planning and outlining, there are effective strategies for helping all students learn drafting and then revising and editing their written work. All of the explicit, systematic instruction involved in written expression will also enhance reading comprehension.

SENTENCES

complexity + editing

Sentence activities have two primary purposes. The first goal is to enable students to write compound and complex sentences rather than only simple, active, declarative forms. This will enhance reading comprehension (Maria, 1990). The second goal is to improve revision and editing skills, which benefit critical thinking skills. Students' awareness of grammar and the functions of the parts of speech are enhanced by emphasizing sentence structure and sentence activities (Scott, 2002). The importance of allocating a great deal of time working with sentences cannot be emphasized enough.

Teachers may use many sentence activities, most of which can be performed both orally and in writing. They should provide as many opportunities as possible to practice developing sentence skills. These activities can be adapted to be made more challenging or easier, depending on the age and ability levels of the students.

Sentences and Fragments

Teacher: A sentence is a complete thought. Tell me whether the groups of words you hear (or read) are sentences or not: Jane gave me her book.

Student: *Sentence*

Teacher: into the forest

Student: *Not a sentence*

Teacher: A fragment is part of a sentence. Change this fragment into a sentence: at night.

Student: *The deer ran at night.*

Note: Students often use fragments (incomplete sentences) in spoken language, and they do the same when they write. The teacher must explain that far more precision is necessary in writing than in speaking. Students should be able to identify fragments in a selection that is read aloud before attempting to correct them in their own work. When teachers write fragments they should not be capitalized or punctuated.

Scrambled Sentences

Teacher: Rearrange the words into sentences, and add the correct punctuation and capitalization: live did where tim

Student: *Where did Tim live?*

Rearranging sequences of words into sentences and adding the correct punctuation and capitalization reinforce the concept of a sentence. Younger students may need to be given the first word of the sentence with the first letter capitalized.

Sentence Types: Statements, Questions, Exclamations, and Commands

Teacher: Add the correct punctuation and capitalization to these sentences. Write this as a statement: john stayed at home

Student: *John stayed at home.*

Teacher: Write this as a command: give that to me immediately

Student: *Give that to me immediately!*

Teacher: Write this as a question: where are you going

Student: *Where are you going?*

Teacher: Write this as an exclamation: my father hates cauliflower

Student: *My father hates cauliflower!*

Teacher: [Asks students to write an example of each of the four sentence types, using a particular spelling or vocabulary word.] Write a statement, a command, a question, and an exclamation using the word *retract*.

Student: *The teacher retracted what she said.*

Retract that statement.

Will he retract that remark?

I want you to retract that statement!

Teacher: [Asks students to change statements to questions (and vice versa).] He is the governor.

Student: *Is he the governor?*

Teacher: [Asks students to generate a question from an answer; students can do this orally or in writing.] Albany

Student: *What is the capital of New York?*

Teacher: [Asks students to help develop essay questions for social studies, science, or literature tests.]

Student: *Discuss the events leading up to the War of 1812.*

            Describe the process of photosynthesis.

            Explain the great and continuing public interest in The Diary of Anne Frank.

It is just as important to have students generate questions as it is for them to respond to the questions. For example, the teacher can show primary students a picture and ask them what question(s) the picture suggests. Older students should be asked to anticipate essay questions on upcoming tests or produce questions after assigned reading and reading comprehension exercises. Research indicates that this exercise enhances reading comprehension (Graham & Hebert, 2010).

Conjunctions

Conjunctions are uninflected words that join words, phrases, or clauses. Their purpose is to link or relate parts of a sentence. Figure 13.1 lists conjunctions that the teacher may use as a reference and insert in students' notebooks to aid them in independent writing.

Teacher: [Asks students to use conjunctions to create complete sentences.] The teacher was happy because...

Student: *The teacher was happy because we did our homework.*

Teacher: The teacher was happy, but...

Student: *The teacher was happy, but he still assigned homework over the weekend.*

Teacher: The teacher was happy, so...

Student: *The teacher was happy so he let us have a longer recess.*

This activity is useful in assessing students' understanding of literature, social studies, or current events, as shown in the following examples:

Teacher: Andrew Jackson was a popular president, but...

Student: *Andrew Jackson was a popular president, but there were many critics of his "kitchen cabinet" and the "spoils system."*

Teacher: Andrew Jackson was a popular president because...

Student: *Andrew Jackson was a popular president because he was a champion of the common people.*

Teacher: Andrew Jackson was a popular president, so...

coordinating conjunctions
A coordinating conjunction joins two or more independent clauses.

and, but, or, yet, nor, for, so

Terrell ate quickly, <u>yet</u> he was still late.

correlative conjunctions
A correlative conjunction is a pair of words that joins independent clauses.

both...and	*just as...so*
either...or	*not only...but also*
neither...nor	*whether...or*

<u>Either</u> we go to the game, <u>or</u> we go out for ice cream.

subordinating conjunctions
A subordinating conjunction introduces an adverb clause and signals the relationship between that clause and the main idea.

<u>common subordinating conjunctions:</u>

after	*although*	*as*	*while*
as if	*because*	*before*	*until*
if	*in order that*	*once*	*when*
since	*so that*	*than*	*where*
that	*though*	*unless*	*regardless*

<u>Although</u> the book sold well, it was not very good.

Figure 13.1. Conjunctions for use in independent writing. (From Hochman, J.C. [2009]. *Teaching basic writing skills: Strategies for effective expository writing instruction.* [p. 140]. Longmont, CO: Sopris West Educational Services. Used with permission from Cambium Learning Group Sopris West Educational Services.)

Student: *Andrew Jackson was a popular president, so he won the election of 1828 easily.*

Teacher: Anne Frank and her family were hidden in the attic; however...

Student: *Anne Frank and her family were hidden in the attic; however, they were discovered by the Nazis.*

Students should write sentences starting with subordinating conjunctions to construct linguistically complex sentences. The teacher can consider having students embed spelling or vocabulary words in their sentences or write about their experiences.

Teacher: Use the three following conjunctions, and write one sentence about the ice skating trip for each: *whenever, since, after*

Student: *Whenever we go ice skating, we have a great time.*

Since we are going ice skating, I am going to get my skates sharpened.

After we go ice skating, we will write about it in school.

Teacher: Write three sentences using the words *hydrogen* and *oxygen* using the following conjunctions: *as soon as, unless, if*

Student: *As soon as hydrogen and oxygen form a compound, they are no longer explosive.*

Unless hydrogen and oxygen form a compound, they are explosive and dangerous.

If hydrogen and oxygen form a compound, they lose their original properties of being explosive and supporting combustion.

Sentence Combining

Sentence combining is the most effective way to teach grammar (Graham & Perin, 2007; Shanahan, 2009). Students should have plenty of practice combining short, declarative sentences using pronouns, commas, and conjunctions as needed. More capable writers may also be taught to use colons and semicolons.

Teacher: [Asks students to combine short, active, declarative sentences using conjunctions and explains that repetition can be avoided by using pronouns.] Combine these sentences using a conjunction: John was at the bus stop. John's car was being repaired.

Student: *John was at the bus stop because his car was being repaired.*

Teacher: Combine the following sentences.

The periodic table is a chart of chemical elements.

The chart displays the elements in horizontal rows.

The elements are displayed horizontally in order of increasing atomic number.

The elements are displayed vertically in order of the structured similarity of their atoms.

Student: *The periodic table, a chart of chemical elements, displays them horizontally in order of increasing atomic number and vertically in order of the structural similarity of their atoms.*

Sentence Expansion

The teacher should display the question words *who, what, when, where, why,* and *how* and then give students **sentence kernels** (a simple sentence without modifiers), such as *Jane ran* or *The candidates debated.* The teacher should ask the class to expand the kernels by using one, two, three, or more of the question words. When introducing this strategy, it is best for the teacher to begin with *when, where, or why* because *who, what,* and *how* may confuse the students (see Figure 13.2). Reading comprehension or knowledge in any content area can be assessed using sentence kernels and question words, such as *The colonists fled. Where? Why?* Students often assume that the reader has more prior knowledge than is actually the case; **sentence expansion** enables them to provide information with greater precision. Responses to the question words should be written in key words and phrases, not complete sentences. Older students should use abbreviations and note-taking symbols such as asterisks, slashes, and arrows when appropriate.

Sentence expansion is a useful strategy for teaching students how to summarize. A kernel sentence is not always necessary if the student is summarizing a chapter, unit of study, or an article. Writing summaries is a well-documented method of enhancing reading comprehension (Graham & Hebert, 2010; Shanahan, 2009).

Grammar and Usage

The parts of speech and their usage should be taught within the writing program. Teaching grammar during sentence activities helps students gain an understanding of how parts of speech are used in context, which proves especially useful when students are expected to revise and edit their own work or assigned passages.

```
DIRECTIONS:
Expand the sentence using any three of the question words: who, what, when, where, why, how.
─────────────────────────────────────────────────────────────
The boys ran.
    when              last Tuesday
    how               quickly
    where             in the park

Expanded sentence:
    Last Tuesday, the boys ran quickly in the park.
```

Figure 13.2.   Sentence expansion worksheet. (From Hochman, J.C. [2009]. *Teaching basic writing skills: Strategies for effective expository writing instruction.* [p. 34]. Longmont, CO: Sopris West Educational Services. Used with permission from Cambium Learning Group Sopris West Educational Services.)

Teacher: [Asks students to change nouns to pronouns.] Mary danced.

Student: *She danced.*

Teacher: [Asks students to change tenses from present to past (or from present to future or vice versa).] The car races.

Student: *The car raced.*

The car will race.

Teacher: [Asks students to insert an adjective, an adverb, and a prepositional phrase.] The runner won.

Student: *The amazing runner won easily in spite of keen competition.*

Teacher: [Asks students to use an appositive after a proper noun (an **appositive** is a second noun, placed beside the first noun to explain it more fully; it usually has modifiers).] George Washington was a brilliant general.

Student: *George Washington, our first president, was a brilliant general.*

Topic Sentences

The topic sentence of a paragraph or **thesis statement** of a composition should clearly state the writer's objective, and the product should contain sufficient support for the writer's position. The teacher should show students how to generate topic sentences for given topics. He or she explains to the students that the topic sentence is the leading or controlling sentence of the paragraph (Morgan, 2001). Students brainstorm sentences about a given topic. For example, if the topic is hiking, then a range of topic sentences can emerge: Hiking can be dangerous. My favorite weekend activity is hiking. Hiking is a great way to enjoy nature. Try hiking this summer! The teacher should encourage students to experiment using different sentence types and remind students that topic sentences do not necessarily have to begin with the topic word.

Teacher: Topic: New York City

Student: *Many tourists visit New York City.*

Do you have a favorite place to visit in New York City?

Visit New York City!

New York City is a study in contrasts.

The teacher should make sure that students can distinguish between topic sentences and supporting details. *Visiting the Metropolitan Museum of Art is a wonderful experience* supports but does not convey the main idea—New York City. Selecting the topic sentence from a group of sentences is a beneficial activity.

Teacher: For each topic, write a topic sentence.

                Dogs

Student: *Dogs are great pets!*

Teacher: Computers

Students: *Think about the many ways computers have influenced our lives.*

Teacher: Ancient Egypt

Student: *Ancient Egypt, an advanced civilization, thrived near the Nile River.*

PARAGRAPHS AND COMPOSITIONS

Teachers should spend plenty of time teaching students how to plan and write a single good paragraph before moving on to writing compositions. Many teachers, confusing quantity with quality, encourage their students to write at great length about a topic. If students write too much too soon, then they will drift from the topic and fail to proofread and improve their writing.

Students should practice writing five types of paragraphs: narrative, expository, persuasive, descriptive, and compare and contrast (a type of expository writing).

Narratives setting forth a sequence of events are the form of composition taught most frequently to younger or less skilled writers (Alley & Deshler, 1979). **Narrative writing** relates events in chronological order, and sentences can be sequenced using transition words, such as *first, next, then,* and *finally* (see Table 13.1). Written in the first person (narrator as a participant) or third person (narrator as an observer), this type of composition is most beneficial when it is based on a personal or a class experience. Older students write narratives when describing historical events or a scientific process.

In contrast with narratives, expository writing explains or informs. Typically, students are asked to define, discuss, criticize, list, compare, contrast, explain, justify, and summarize. Teachers should spend the most time on expository writing because it is the kind of writing most frequently required in school in fourth grade and beyond (Alley & Deshler, 1979). Several common types of expository writing are described next.

Persuasive writing presents a point of view to a specific audience, such as parents, fellow students, teachers, or the editor of a newspaper. Facts are gathered in order to convince the reader of the validity of the writer's position. The conclusion usually proposes the action that the writer would like the reader to take. Persuasive writing is often considered the most difficult to master because at its highest level it incorporates and rebuts opposing points of view.

Table 13.1. Transition words and phrases

Group 1 Time and sequence	Group 2 Conclusion	Group 3 Illustration
first	in conclusion	for example
second	consequently	for instance
then	in closing	specifically
next	in summary	as an illustration
also	to conclude	
after	therefore	
later on	as a result	
in addition	thus	
before		
last of all		
finally		

Group 4 Change of direction	Group 5 Emphasis	
but	keep in mind	furthermore
however	remember that	undoubtedly
yet	a major concern	certainly
in contrast	the best thing	above all
otherwise	the biggest advantage	most important
still	it is valuable to note	primarily
on the other hand	obviously	
on the contrary		

Descriptive writing taps the five senses in order to effectively transmit experiences about people, places, things, and thoughts. Varied and vivid vocabulary is especially important when developing a descriptive passage. Brainstorming and generating lists of adjectives and adverbs or more precise nouns and verbs are appropriate activities to use in conjunction with descriptive writing lessons. It is often beneficial to employ spatial and visual terms in descriptive writing such as *beyond, underneath, below, above, to the left,* and so forth.

The **compare-and-contrast composition** highlights the similarities (comparisons) and differences (contrasts) among two or more people, places, things, ideas, or experiences. A conclusion is sometimes developed from the facts presented. When presenting this type of writing assignment, teachers should be aware that organizing compare-and-contrast essays can be particularly challenging for the less skillful writer.

The following four steps are involved in most writing assignments. A lesson can end after any one of them, except that it is not a good idea to have students end an assignment with an uncorrected draft.

1. Planning and outlining
2. Drafting
3. Revising and editing
4. Writing a final copy

The first step, planning and outlining, and the third step, revising and editing, are the most important to master. Therefore, they should be given far more instructional time than drafting or producing final copies, which can be done independently by some students.

Planning and Outlining

The planning or prewriting stage requires more instructional time than is generally given to writing activities and assignments. This is the point at which students begin to organize their assignments and thoughts systematically and sequentially. Class discussions that establish the topic, purpose, audience, and type of the paragraph or composition are extremely important. During the planning phase, information is gathered and shared. Students are guided to distinguish between relevant and nonessential material. Ideas and supporting details are categorized and sequenced in outline form. Topic sentences and thesis statements can be developed at this time. Initially, all of these activities can be done as a class with teacher demonstrations and guidance. When students become more proficient, they can begin to work independently.

Initial lessons in how to develop outlines are done with the teacher guiding the development of a model for the class. By providing an overall view of the finished product, the outline serves as a map that allows students to visualize the project as a cohesive whole that has a beginning, middle, and end. Outlines help students to distinguish essential from nonessential material and to sequence information. As students become more proficient through practice and group work, they can develop their outlines independently. Three useful outline forms are as follows (Hochman, 2009):

1. The Quick Outline is used for developing a single paragraph and is intended to help the students discern the basic structure of the paragraph: topic sentence, supporting details, and concluding sentence.

2. The Transition Outline is used when students are beginning to write compositions of two or three paragraphs.

3. The Multiple Paragraph Outline (MPO) is used for developing compositions of three or more paragraphs.

After students have mastered a particular outlining format, they can be encouraged to proceed to writing drafts. When teaching outlining, teachers should use topics that require no special prior knowledge unless something that has just been taught or experienced by the class is being reviewed or reinforced. The emphasis should be on the skills required to outline, not on the material to be learned or reviewed.

Quick Outline

Students must master several preliminary skills before they can develop a quick outline independently (see Figure 13.3) (Hochman, 2009). Several activities for developing and improving outlines are helpful in providing practice for students. First, the student must be able to produce a topic sentence for a given topic. (e.g., if the topic is the Industrial Revolution, then a topic sentence might be *There were several major causes of the Industrial Revolution*). Second, the student must learn to supply supporting details using key words or phrases (e.g., *Eli Whitney —> cotton gin & interchangeable parts*). This skill is an important one and is a precursor to notetaking. A great deal of practice is needed for students to convert sentences into phrases. Complete sentences should not be used on the outline except for the topic and concluding sentences. Third, the student must understand that the concluding sentence is either a rephrasing of the topic sentence or a

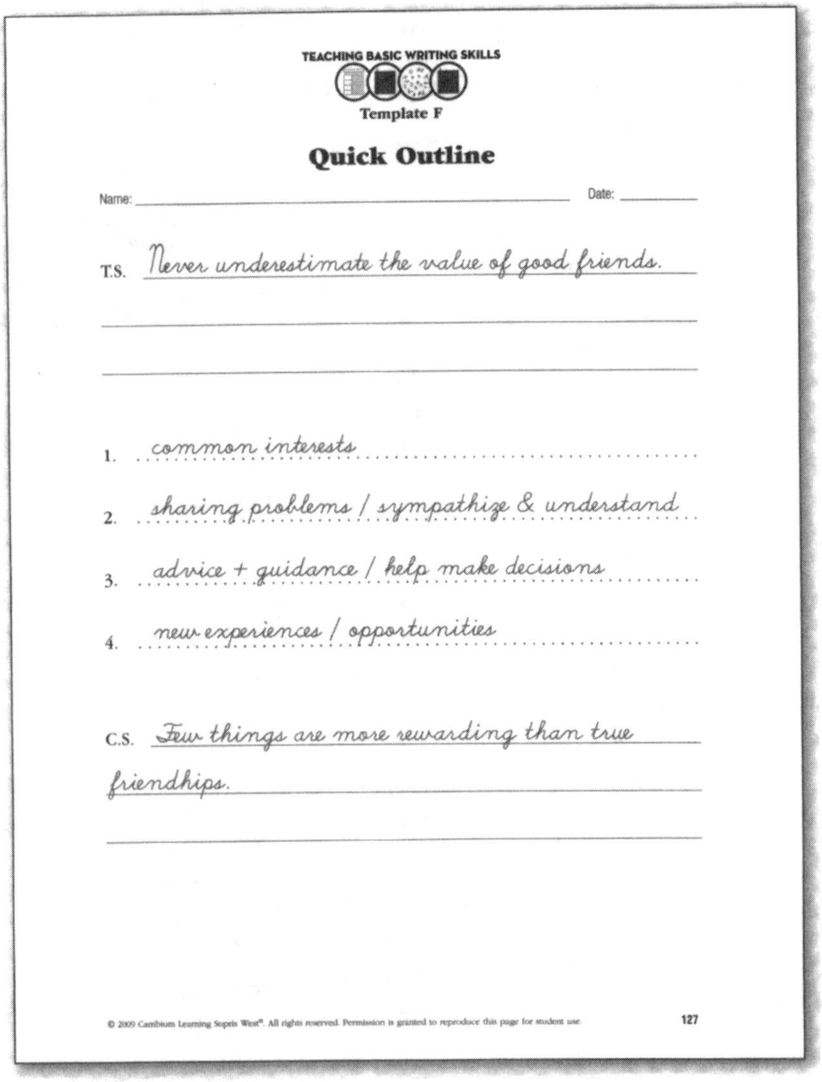

TEACHING BASIC WRITING SKILLS

Template F

Quick Outline

Name: ______ Date: ______

T.S. Never underestimate the value of good friends.

1. common interests
2. sharing problems / sympathize & understand
3. advice + guidance / help make decisions
4. new experiences / opportunities

C.S. Few things are more rewarding than true friendhips.

© 2009 Cambium Learning Sopris West®. All rights reserved. Permission is granted to reproduce this page for student use. 127

Figure 13.3. Quick Outline. (From Hochman, J.C. [2009]. *Teaching basic writing skills: Strategies for effective expository writing instruction.* [p. 85]. Longmont, CO: Sopris West Educational Services. Used with permission from Cambium Learning Group Sopris West Educational Services.)

summary of the paragraph's main point (e.g., *The Industrial Revolution was a time of great change*). Teaching the skills used in creating Quick Outlines requires a great deal of teacher demonstration and group work.

Many activities focus on just one segment of the Quick Outline. These activities can be done before or concurrently with completing a full Quick Outline.

Teacher: Provide the details for this topic sentence: Thanksgiving is a wonderful traditional holiday.

Student: *Pilgrims, Native Americans*

Preparation

Parade

Football

Family reunion

Wonderful food

Teacher: Generate a topic sentence from the following phrases:

Pilgrims and Native Americans

Families and friends

Turkey, trimmings, desserts

Football/parade

Student: *Thanksgiving is a popular American holiday.*

Teacher: Identify the topic sentence and sequence the others.

We ate too much candy. [4]

My sister and I selected our costumes. [2]

Sheila was a princess, and I was a witch. [3]

Last Halloween was great! [Topic sentence]

The next day we were exhausted. [5]

Student: *The topic sentence is* Last Halloween was great! *The others should be in this order:*

My sister and I selected our costumes.

Sheila was a princess, and I was a witch.

We ate too much candy.

The next day we were exhausted.

Teacher: Identify the topic sentence, and write the others in phrases and key words.

Texas was perfect for raising cattle and growing cotton.

There was fertile land in Oregon.

Americans believed in Manifest Destiny.

There were many causes of the westward expansion in the United States.

Mormons wanted a safe haven.

Gold was discovered in California.

Student: *The topic sentence is* There were many causes of the westward expansion in the United States. *Key words are*

Perfect for cattle & cotton

Oregon/fertile

Belief in Manifest Destiny

Mormons/safe haven

California/gold

Teacher: Here is a topic sentence: Autumn is my favorite season. Eliminate irrelevant phrases and those that do not relate directly to the topic sentence.

Go for drive/changing colors

Buy cider/doughnuts/pumpkin

Watch video

Carve jack-o'-lantern

Concluding sentence: Some of my best memories take place in autumn.

Student: *Watch video is the irrelevant phrase.*

Teacher: Convert the following paragraph into a Quick Outline: Label the topic and concluding sentences. Underline the key words and phrases.

(TS) All Americans should recognize the achievements of George Washington and Abraham Lincoln on Presidents' Day. <u>George Washington</u>, the <u>first president</u> of <u>the United States</u>, was one of the most important leaders in the nation's history. Washington <u>helped the colonies gain independence from Great Britain</u> and contributed to <u>the formation of the new government</u>. <u>Abraham Lincoln</u>, the <u>sixteenth president</u>, rose from a <u>modest</u> backwoods <u>upbringing</u> to become <u>one of the greatest political leaders</u>. Lincoln, <u>president during the Civil War, helped to preserve the country</u>. (CS) Presidents' Day honors two of the greatest presidents.

(TS) All Americans should recognize the achievements of George Washington and Abraham Lincoln on Presidents' Day.

1. G.W. 1st U.S. president

2. Helped colonies —> independence from Great Britain/form new govt.

3. A.L./16th president/modest upbringing

4. Civil War —> preserved the country

(CS) Presidents' Day honors two of the greatest presidents.

To develop a complete Quick Outline with the class, the following sequence is suggested:

- Introduce and discuss a topic.

- Identify audience and discuss purpose.

- Present a topic sentence to the students, or have them generate one as a group.

- Elicit as many supporting details as possible from the class, and write them on the chalkboard, a Smartboard, or on a flipchart. If the details are stated as complete sentences, then convert them into phrases or key words. Use abbreviations and outline symbols.

- Depending on the topic and number of details, either select three or four of the most important ones or, whenever possible, group the details in categories for the outline.

- Distribute a blank Quick Outline to each student.

- Ask the students to write their preferred topic sentence (if more than one was generated) and to select details for the outline.

- Generate a concluding sentence as a class. If students are able, then they can do this independently.

Transition Outline

The Transition Outline (see Figure 13.4) is used after the students have had experience writing paragraphs and are ready to attempt to produce longer compositions. Students should be comfortable with the format of the Quick Outline before moving on to the Transition Outline. This outline provides an overview of the whole composition, including topic sentences and details for every paragraph. A concluding sentence is not necessary for any paragraph other than the last one.

Multiple Paragraph Outline

The MPO (see Figure 13.5) is designed for students who are ready to develop unified, coherent compositions of three or more paragraphs. Students must be careful not to be given or to select topics that are either too broad or too narrow. A specific purpose for writing as well as the audience must be identified. The thesis statement should be clear and succinct.

In order to develop an MPO, students must be able to construct a good paragraph. Unlike the Quick Outline, the main idea of each paragraph is not written as a topic sentence but as a category on the left side of the MPO (e.g., pro, con; cause, effect; similarities, differences; first reason, second reason). Supporting details should be written as brief, clear phrases or key words. The MPO helps students learn to construct an introduction; a body, which can consist of several paragraphs; and a conclusion. This kind of outline guides students to stay with a consistent topic, purpose, and point of view by providing a clear visual diagram of the entire work. As with the other outlines, students will need group work and teacher modeling before they can develop an MPO independently.

The teacher does not need to move in sequence from three- to four- to five-paragraph compositions because the number of paragraphs usually depends on the topic. For example, a book report may require three paragraphs, with categories such as introduction, plot summary, and opinion. A topic such as pollution might have four categories: introduction, causes, effects, and possible solutions. A biographical essay about Andrew Jackson may require five categories, such as introduction, early life, military career, presidency, and conclusion.

Depending on the topic, most MPO's require a thesis statement, which can be presented as one of the following:

- A personal judgment on a topic

- Advice or directions

- Consequences

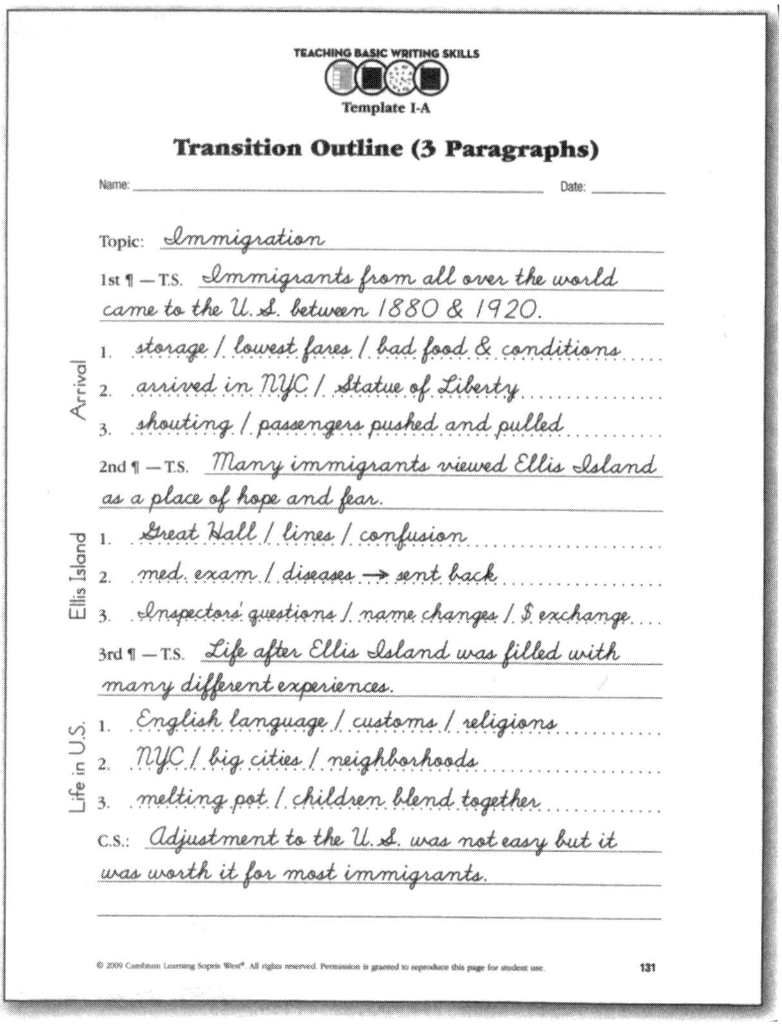
TEACHING BASIC WRITING SKILLS

Template I-A

Transition Outline (3 Paragraphs)

Name: ______ Date: ______

Topic: Immigration

1st ¶ — T.S. Immigrants from all over the world came to the U.S. between 1880 & 1920.

Arrival
1. storage / lowest fares / bad food & conditions
2. arrived in NYC / Statue of Liberty
3. shouting / passengers pushed and pulled

2nd ¶ — T.S. Many immigrants viewed Ellis Island as a place of hope and fear.

Ellis Island
1. Great Hall / lines / confusion
2. med. exam / diseases → sent back
3. Inspectors' questions / name changes / $ exchange

3rd ¶ — T.S. Life after Ellis Island was filled with many different experiences.

Life in U.S.
1. English language / customs / religions
2. NYC / big cities / neighborhoods
3. melting pot / children blend together

C.S.: Adjustment to the U.S. was not easy but it was worth it for most immigrants.

© 2009 Cambium Learning Sopris West®. All rights reserved. Permission is granted to reproduce this page for student use. 131

Figure 13.4. Transition Outline. (From Hochman, J.C. [2009]. *Teaching basic writing skills: Strategies for effective expository writing instruction.* [p. 86]. Longmont, CO: Sopris West Educational Services. Used with permission from Cambium Learning Group Sopris West Educational Services.)

- An argument for or against an issue
- An interpretation (usually when writing about fiction or poetry)

At this point, older or more advanced students can be taught that it is not necessary for the topic sentence to be the first one in a paragraph. The teacher should explain that the last few words in a paragraph or composition have the most effect on the reader, and, therefore, the points the writer wishes to emphasize should be at the end. The last sentence of a selection is as important as the first one.

To develop a complete MPO, the following sequence is suggested:

- Select the topic that will be the basis for the title when writing the draft.
- Discuss purpose and audience.

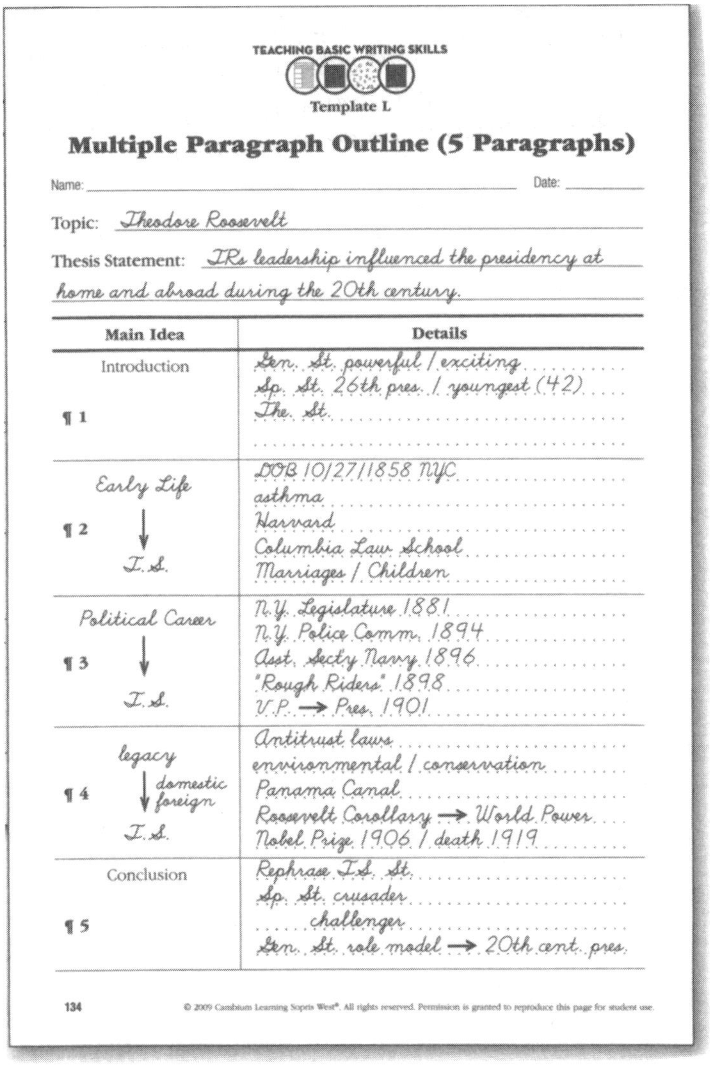

TEACHING BASIC WRITING SKILLS

Template L

Multiple Paragraph Outline (5 Paragraphs)

Name: ____________ Date: ______

Topic: Theodore Roosevelt

Thesis Statement: TR's leadership influenced the presidency at home and abroad during the 20th century.

Main Idea	Details
Introduction ¶ 1	Gen. St. powerful / exciting Sp. St. 26th pres. / youngest (42) The. St.
Early Life ↓ T. S. ¶ 2	DOB 10/27/1858 NYC asthma Harvard Columbia Law School Marriages / Children
Political Career ↓ T. S. ¶ 3	N.Y. Legislature 1881 N.Y. Police Comm. 1894 Asst. Secty Navy 1896 "Rough Riders" 1898 V.P. → Pres. 1901
legacy ↓ domestic / foreign T. S. ¶ 4	Antitrust laws environmental / conservation Panama Canal Roosevelt Corollary → World Power Nobel Prize 1906 / death 1919
Conclusion ¶ 5	Rephrase T.S. St. Sp. St. crusader challenger Gen. St. role model → 20th cent. pres.

134 © 2009 Cambium Learning Sopris West®. All rights reserved. Permission is granted to reproduce this page for student use.

Figure 13.5. Multiple Paragraph Outline. (From Hochman, J.C. [2009]. *Teaching basic writing skills: Strategies for effective expository writing instruction.* [p. 91]. Longmont, CO: Sopris West Educational Services. Used with permission from Cambium Learning Group Sopris West Educational Services.)

- Develop the thesis statement.
- Write the main idea of each paragraph as a phrase or a category in the left-hand column. This prevents repetition and enables the students to plan the entire composition more effectively. Each paragraph must relate to the overall theme.
- After determining the main idea for each paragraph, write the supporting details in the right-hand column. Remind students that each supporting detail should relate directly to the main idea of its paragraph.

Writing the introduction and the conclusion requires the ability to summarize information. Students should be given plenty of oral practice summarizing news stories, chapters, or plots in one or two sentences. The sentence expansion strategy (*who, what, when, where, why*) and conjunctions are helpful aids when summarizing. Because many writers have difficulty with summarizing, it is a good idea to provide lessons that focus exclusively on introductions and conclusions of given topics.

Older and/or more advanced students can be introduced to a strategy that can be helpful when writing introductions and conclusions. Teachers can explain that an introduction can consist of at least three sentences and that the last sentence should be the thesis statement. The first sentence should take the form of a general statement, and the second sentence should be a specific statement (Lunsford & Connors, 1995). Two examples of that strategy are as follows:

1. Many people have a favorite possession. Mine is my photograph album. Each time I look at it, I think of all of the wonderful experiences I have shared with my family and friends.

2. It has often been said that necessity is the mother of invention. After the War of 1812, the United States, a new nation, was forced to rely on its own resources when England blockaded American ports. The resulting acceleration of the Industrial Revolution led to a number of changes in American society.

In contrast, a concluding paragraph can begin with the thesis statement rephrased, then a specific statement, and, finally, a general statement. Examples of conclusions for the previous introductions follow:

1. I will always treasure my photograph album. As time goes by, I hope that the number of photographs in my album will increase. They represent memories I never want to forget.

2. A way of life disappeared when the Industrial Revolution reached the United States. Factories, new inventions, and better transportation affected the way Americans lived and worked. The dramatic changes brought by the Industrial Revolution influenced every aspect of the nation.

Drafting

Drafting begins with writing paragraphs or compositions based on Quick Outlines, Transition Outlines, or MPOs. Inexperienced or less competent writers should limit their writing to one paragraph of five or six sentences because longer papers tend to discourage attempts to revise and edit. The teacher should tell students that a draft can never be left uncorrected or unimproved. Students should always expect to revise and edit their writing. In order to provide room for improving their work, students must skip lines when writing drafts or leave sufficient space when working on a computer. A teacher may decide to end an activity with a corrected draft instead of moving on to a final copy if the objectives of the lesson have been met.

Even after a final copy is produced, drafts should not be discarded because they can be helpful in assessing how much the students have improved and the areas in which students need further work. Drafts also provide students with graphic examples of their progress.

Revising and Editing

It is important to stress revising and editing when teaching writing skills to students. Revision is clarifying or altering the meaning or structure of a draft. This is in contrast to editing, which involves proofreading and correcting errors in grammar, punctuation, syntax, and spelling. Highly competent writers spend the most time on revision, and, consequently, it is the area in which the largest amount of instructional time should be invested. The sentence activities presented previously provide the foundation for developing the skills to improve written work. In order to teach students to refine their own or others' writing, the teacher can show students several ways to improve the quality of written language. The five fundamental techniques for revising and editing are as follows:

1. Add words

2. Delete words

3. Substitute words, phrases, or clauses

4. Rearrange words, phrases, clauses, and sentences

5. Proofread for errors

As noted earlier, all too frequently students are given credit for the quantity of their written work rather than for the quality. Instead, teachers should encourage students to adopt clarity and accuracy as their goals, not length. Brief assignments help to promote this kind of written work.

Often, it is helpful for younger or less advanced students to be given a brief, unelaborated paragraph and then shown how to revise it, first as a class, then independently. For example:

Teacher: Improve this paragraph by following the directions.

I went to my friend's party. I had fun. We had cake and ice cream. We played some games.

Directions:

•   Improve topic sentence

•   Combine two sentences

•   Vary **sentence starters**

•   Add concluding sentence

•   Add descriptive words

•   Expand sentences

•   Give examples

•   Sequence

Student: *Last Sunday, Jim invited eight boys to his birthday party. First, we played touch football outside for almost an hour. Then, we had delicious pizza and made our own sundaes. I put sprinkles, hot fudge, nuts, and whipped cream on mine. Everyone had a terrific time!*

The teacher should provide students with checklists for revising and editing. Typical items include the following, with variations for age and ability:

- Does your draft follow your outline?

- Is your topic sentence clearly stated?

- Are the supporting details clear and in order?

- Do the details support the topic sentence?

- Did you use different types of sentences?

- Do your sentences vary in length?

- Are there sentences that should be combined or expanded?

- Did you use transition words or phrases?

- Are your word choices repetitive? Vivid? Accurate?

- Have you checked for **run-on sentences?** Fragments? Spelling, punctuation, or capitalization errors?

- Have you checked tense and number agreement?

Initially, only a few items should be selected from the checklist to provide a focus for the students as they improve and correct their work. As they become more adept, more checklist items can be added. Students will need reminders to revise style first and then edit the mechanics.

   In addition to listing specific items on the checklist, it is often helpful for the teacher to give younger or less advanced students explicit instructions that will add flair to their compositions, such as "Give an example," "Insert transition words," or "Expand this sentence." At first, the teacher will have to show students exactly where to place the words and phrases. In time, students will be able to see where to insert them independently. Much attention should also be given to selecting strong and varied nouns and verbs as well as modifiers. Time and sequence transitions should be taught first, followed by conclusions, and then illustration transitions. The remaining two groups can be taught in any order (see Table 13.1). The teacher should encourage students to use transitions even at the beginning stages of paragraph development. Applying transitions, sentence starters, and conjunctions will raise the level of linguistic complexity and quality of the students' written work. The teacher should stress that a draft can be reworked at least two or three times and that the better the writer, the more often the draft will be rewritten.

   Students require a great deal of direct instruction, demonstrations, and group participation as they correct and improve their work. They have to understand that their goals should be compositions that flow smoothly, are properly organized, and maintain the reader's interest. Sentences should vary in length and style. Although short, simple, active declarative sentences are useful for emphasis, too often they are the only forms used by less skillful writers. Teachers' comments and feedback should be explicit and plentiful during drafting and during revising and editing.

   Students should routinely read their work aloud as an important component of any writing program. This can take place during sentence activities and the drafting or revising and editing stages. Students can read to a partner, to a small group, or to the entire class. One purpose of oral reading is to sharpen proofreading capabilities. Many students are able to correct their errors more accurately and effectively when they read their written work aloud. Another goal is to enhance critical listening skills. The reader's classmates can contribute suggestions based on the checklist for revision and editing explained previously, which will improve proficiency in these skills.

Writing a Final Copy

It is not advisable for students to spend a great deal of time recopying written work for final copies. Certainly, this type of activity should not be done during instructional time. Therefore, teachers must be selective as to which activities should be developed to this stage. If final copies are produced, then every effort should be made to display them. Students should be given opportunities to see their written work on bulletin boards or published in a class journal, school or local newspaper, or parent bulletin. Writing letters that will accomplish a purpose or elicit a reply can also be rewarding.

CONCLUSION

Explicit instruction of narrative and expository writing skills is given little time in most schools, although students routinely have independent writing assignments. Because writing is the most difficult skill to teach and learn, teachers often need to use a writing program with clear guidelines and goals that will enable students to succeed. Providing the students with the structure and strategies for building acceptable sentences, paragraphs, and compositions is the key to helping all students, but especially those with learning and language disabilities, develop proficiency in written language. Teachers should establish goals carefully but not be overly ambitious. Teaching primary, elementary, or even high school students several strategies for writing better sentences as well as activities for developing outlines in the course of a year can be considered a great accomplishment. If students move more quickly than anticipated, then the activities can easily be made more challenging. Composition skills do not develop automatically. Students need carefully sequenced direct instruction, teacher demonstrations, and a great deal of practice in order to succeed.

REFERENCES

Alley, G.R., & Deshler, D.D. (1979). *Teaching the learning disabled adolescent strategies and methods.* Boulder, CO: Love Publishing Co.

Bereiter, C., & Scardamalia, M. (1987). *The psychology of written composition.* Mahwah, NJ: Lawrence Erlbaum Associates.

Berninger, V.W., Garcia, N.P., & Abbott, R.D. (2009). Multiple processes that matter in writing instruction and assessment. In G.A. Troia (Ed.), *Instruction and assessment for struggling writers: Evidence based practices* (pp. 113–131). New York: Guilford Press.

Graham, S., & Hebert, H. (2010). *Writing to read: Evidence for how writing can improve reading.* A report to Carnegie Corporation of New York. Washington, DC: Alliance for Excellent Education.

Graham, S., & Perin, D. (2007). *Writing next: Effective strategies to improve writing of adolescents in middle and high schools.* A report to Carnegie Corporation of New York. Washington, DC: Alliance for Excellent Education.

Hochman, J.C. (2009). *Teaching basic writing skills: Strategies for effective expository writing instruction.* Longmont, CO: Sopris West Educational Services.

Lunsford, A., & Connors, R. (1995). *St. Martin's handbook* (3rd ed.). New York: St. Martin's Press.

Maria, K. (1990). *Reading comprehension instruction: Issues and strategies.* Timonium, MD: York Press.

Morgan, C.G. (2001). *When they can't write.* Timonium, MD: York Press.

Scott, C.M. (1989a). Learning to write: Context, form, and process. In A.G. Kamhi & H.W. Catts (Eds.), *Reading disabilities: A development language perspective* (pp. 261–392). New York: Little, Brown.

Scott, C.M. (1989b). Problem writers: Nature, assessment, and intervention. In A.G. Kamhi &

H.W. Catts (Eds.), *Reading disabilities: A developmental language perspective* (pp. 303–344). New York: Little, Brown.

Scott, C.M. (1999). Learning to write. In A.G. Kamhi & H.W. Catts (Eds.), *Language and reading disabilities* (pp. 224–258). Boston: Allyn & Bacon.

Scott, C.M. (2002). Sentence comprehension instruction. In J.F. Carlisle & M.S. Rice (Eds.), *Improving reading comprehension: Research-based principles and practices* (pp. 115–127). Timonium, MD: York Press.

Scott, C.M. (2005). Learning to write. In A.G. Kamhi & H.W. Catts (Eds.), *Language and reading disabilities* (pp. 233–273). Boston: Allyn & Bacon.

Shanahan, T. (2009). Connecting reading and writing instruction for struggling learners. In G.A. Troia (Ed.), *Instruction and assessment for struggling writers: Evidence based practices* (pp. 113–131). New York: Guilford Press.

Singer, B.D., & Bashir, A.S. (2004). Developmental variations in written composition skills. In C.A. Stone, E.R. Silliman, B.J. Ehrren, & K. Apel (Eds.), *Handbook of language and literacy: Development and disorders* (pp. 559–582). New York: Guilford Press.

14

Assessment

MARGARET JO SHEPHERD AND EILEEN S. MARZOLA

A *ssessment* is an information gathering process, undertaken to solve a problem, that culminates in decisions and actions that affect an individual's life (Salvia & Ysseldyke, 1998). This chapter is about assessments that take place in schools, clinics, and therapists' offices. The chapter describes three types of assessment undertaken on behalf of individuals who struggle with reading, spelling, and writing: 1) assessment of learning used to guide teaching, 2) assessment to locate individuals "at risk" for reading failure, and 3) assessment to determine the presence (or absence) of reading disability (dyslexia).

The chapter begins with information about sources of assessment data that includes the distinction between *formative* and *summative* assessment. Next, *response to intervention (RTI)*, a continuous (formative) means for assessing learning and using the data to guide instruction, is described. Third, the chapter presents a rationale for early identification of individuals at risk for reading failure and a review of screening tools. Then, procedures for monitoring learning, not included in the earlier discussion of RTI, are described. The chapter concludes with one interpretation of the comprehensive evaluation that federal special education law mandates before an individual can be placed in a special education program. This interpretation includes the role RTI data have in that evaluation.

SOURCES OF ASSESSMENT DATA

Teachers, psychologists, and therapists who conduct assessments with individuals who struggle with reading, spelling, and writing use several sources for data, including the following: 1) family, developmental, medical, and educational histories; 2) school records and examples of schoolwork; 3) interviews; 4) observations; 5) **formal** and **informal**

tests; 6) rating scales; and 7) structured presentations of reading, spelling, and writing tasks. Data collection is comprehensive and may include examinations by physicians and speech-language pathologists as well as neuropsychologists and occupational therapists.

Types of Tests

Different types of tests are used in an assessment. Tests can be classified as *formal* (standardized) or *informal*. Standardized tests must always be administered and scored following procedures that are prescribed in the manual accompanying the test. Unless people who give a standardized test follow the prescribed procedures exactly, the interpretation of the test scores will be compromised. Tests are standardized on the performance of a carefully selected sample of people who are representative of the larger group of people for whom the test was created. Informal tests, in contrast, are structured but not standardized. Typically, informal tests use the format of a standardized test, but the person giving the test can modify the presentation of test items and probe the test taker's responses in ways that are not permissible during the administration of standardized tests.

Tests can be classified as norm referenced, **criterion referenced,** or **curriculum referenced.** Norm-referenced tests produce scores that permit comparisons among people. These tests allow a person's command of the knowledge and/or skill measured by the test to be compared with that of other people of the same age. Standards for judging the performance of the person taking a norm-referenced test have been determined by the performance of the group of people who took the test when it was standardized. The people whose performances created the norms, or standards, against which the test taker's performance is compared were selected to be comparable to all people who might take the test with regard to characteristics that influence test performance (e.g., age, gender, ethnicity, socioeconomic status, geographic region of residence, native language). Norm-referenced tests, then, give information about a child's development relative to the development of other children of the same age. All norm-referenced tests are standardized.

The difference between criterion-referenced tests and norm-referenced tests is the standard used for judging performance. Norm-referenced tests produce an index (score) of one person's development relative to the development of other comparable people, whereas criterion-referenced tests produce descriptions of one person's knowledge and/or skill within the domain represented by the test. Criterion-referenced tests allow the test administrators to generate an item by item description of the knowledge and/or skills attained and those yet to be acquired. Curriculum-referenced tests are a variation on criterion-referenced tests; questions include information taught in the test taker's school and classroom. Curriculum-referenced tests avoid the error of testing a person on content that he or she has not had the opportunity to learn. Thus, curriculum-referenced tests allow for a good match between assessment and instruction; people are only tested on material they have been taught. Criterion- and curriculum-referenced tests can be standardized or informal. The important point about these two types of tests is that they allow comparisons to be made between a person's immediate performance and immediate past performance. The previous performance (rather than other people's performance) is the standard for judging learning. Criterion- and curriculum-referenced tests were designed to guide instruction.

Formative and Summative Assessment

There is another way to classify assessment procedures that is particularly important when the assessment question is about a person's progress (learning). Data collection can be **formative** or **summative.** Torgesen and Miller (2009) neatly distinguished between assessment *for* learning (formative) and assessment *of* learning (summative). Formative assessment applies to immediate or short-term learning goals and yields information about a person's progress acquiring specific skills or knowledge. Summative assessment applies to long-term learning goals and yields information about accumulated and integrated knowledge and/or complex skills. Formative assessments create a detailed record of learning whereas summative assessment is usually a norm-referenced test or a project. In the context of literacy assessments, a formative assessment might evaluate a person's knowledge of the *r*-controlled syllable rule using a list of *r*-controlled words; a summative assessment would evaluate reading comprehension using a norm-referenced test.

Criterion- and curriculum-referenced tests can be used for summative assessment, but norm-referenced tests don't work well for formative assessment. Many norm-referenced tests have one or, at best, two forms and cannot be given repeatedly because the person will learn the test and it will no longer be a reliable indicator of performance. A second limitation is the possibility of a mismatch between the content of the test and the instruction the person has received. Finally, learning should be documented in smaller increments and greater detail than norm-referenced tests provide. Assessment of progress depends on both formative and summative data. The details of progress, however, are provided by formative data.

Testing and assessing are different processes. Tests measure characteristics of a person (knowledge, skills, and traits or dispositions). If the test is standardized and norm-referenced, a person's score can be compared with scores of other people who have taken the test. The ranking (high to low) of this person's score compared with others' scores is used to make decisions about the person. An assessment, although done on behalf of a person, has a broader scope and, as indicated previously, includes records of a person's life experiences as well as tests and data from other sources. Decisions are made about a person based on converging data rather than a single score or ranking. This distinction between giving a test to a person and conducting a broader investigation of that person and his or her experience is particularly important now because tests have increasing influence on educational practice in our schools and people need to be aware of the relatively limited sample of behavior represented by a single test score (Koretz, 2008).

RESPONSE TO INTERVENTION

Children and youth who have cognitive, physical, or emotional disabilities have a protected right to special education and related services at public expense. (See Chapter 22 for descriptions of the federal laws that give these rights to people with disabilities.) If a person's difficulty learning to read and write is so severe that special education is indicated, that person will typically be determined to have a *specific learning disability (SLD)*. The legal definition of SLD posits *"a disorder in one or more of the basic psychological processes* [italics added] in understanding or in using language, written or spoken, which may manifest itself in an *imperfect ability* [italics added] to listen, speak, think, read, write, spell or do mathematical calculations" (Education of the Handicapped Act of 1970, PL 91-230). Unfortunately, the key concepts in this definition (those in italics) are not defined, and the definition alone cannot be used to make the SLD diagnosis. This is a problem because a disability diagnosis has to precede placement in special education. A resolution to the SLD diagnostic problem was reached by 1975 when PL 91-230 was reauthorized as the Education for All Handicapped Children Act (PL 94-142). The definition stayed intact, and two diagnostic criteria were included in the law. SLD was determined by an IQ score that was significantly higher than the score on an achievement test in any one of the seven domains included in the 1970 definition. *Unexpected under-achievement* (the IQ/achievement discrepancy) became the first diagnostic criteria for SLD. Second, the diagnostic team had to rule out sensory and motor disabilities; intellectual disabilities; emotional disturbance; and environmental, cultural, or economic disadvantage as causes of the unexpected underachievement. Criticism of these criteria is legion and has been voiced since the regulations for PL 94-142 were released in 1977. (See Fletcher, Lyon, Fuchs, & Barnes, 2007, pp. 31–45, or Donovan & Cross, 2002, pp. 285–289, for particularly comprehensive critiques.) RTI is one step toward improving procedures for identifying students with an SLD in reading (dyslexia). RTI gives teachers and psychologists tools for separating individuals with a reading disability from individuals whose struggle with reading is caused by inappropriate instruction.

The **Individuals with Disabilities Education Improvement Act (IDEA) of 2004 (PL 108-446)** includes RTI among procedures for identifying SLD. This authorization of the law does not require (nor prohibit) severe discrepancy between IQ and achievement to determine SLD. IDEA 2004 permits school teams to use an individual's response to scientific, research-based intervention as *part* of the evaluation used to determine SLD.

At present, school teams can assess underachievement as the first criteria for determining SLD using either an IQ–achievement discrepancy or RTI (Salvia, Ysseldyke, & Bolt, 2010). IDEA 2004 does require two more exclusionary "tests" in addition to those that have been in the law since 1975. An individual cannot be determined to have SLD if he or she has limited English proficiency and/or has not had research-based reading instruction that includes phonemic awareness, phonics, reading fluency, vocabulary, and comprehension as recommended by the National Reading Panel (NRP, National Institute on Child Health and Human Development [NICHD]) and incorporated into the No Child Left Behind Act of 2001 (NCLB; PL 107-110).

Despite the fact that RTI originated in concerns about the identification of individuals with SLDs, people who conduct RTI research and those who implement RTI in schools tend to describe it in different ways. If you ask a person engaged in early reading research to explain RTI, he or she might describe it as a program designed to prevent reading failure (Gersten et al., 2009). If you ask a school administrator the same question, he or she might say that RTI is a means for controlling the flow of students into special education. As you learn more about it within this frame of reference, you might conclude that it is an effort to improve the prereferral practices that many states require before a teacher can refer a child for a special education evaluation (Batsche et al., 2005). If you ask a school psychologist serving as head of a child study team in a public school, he or she might say that RTI is an alternate and better way to identify students who have a specific learning disability in reading. This is certainly the intent of some RTI researchers (Fuchs, Fuchs, & Compton, 2004; Speece, Case, & Molloy, 2003; Vaughn & Fuchs, 2003).

Joseph Torgesen, known for the clarity he brings to complex topics, noted that RTI is both an instructional delivery system and an assessment methodology (as cited in Kovaleski & Black, 2010). Since this chapter focuses on assessment, we emphasize that component but we realize that we cannot explain RTI assessment without first describing the structure in which it is used.

The RTI Instructional Delivery System

Douglas Fuchs gives a simple and clear start; he described RTI as follows (Fuchs, Mock, Morgan, & Young, 2003):

- Students are provided with "generally effective" instruction by their classroom teacher.

- Their progress is monitored.

- Those who do not respond get something else, or something more, from their teacher or someone else.

- Again, their progress is monitored.

- Those who still do not respond either qualify for special education or for special education evaluation.

This sequence is usually represented as a pyramid divided into three (or four) sections, each described as a tier. Tier 1 is the core reading curriculum delivered in the general education classroom by a qualified teacher who has participated in professional development activities designed to ensure that he or she understands the research base for the curriculum. The curriculum must be evidence based to the extent that it includes the five essential domains (phonemic awareness, phonics, fluency, vocabulary, and comprehension) recommended by the NRP (NICHD, 2000) and incorporated in NCLB. The committee convened by the Institute of Education Sciences to create an evidence-based RTI Practice Guide for use in Grades K–2 added differentiated instruction for all students in the class based on assessment data (Gersten et al., 2009). Differentiated instruction typically means creating small, flexible groups of students with similar skill profiles and including cooperative learning, peer-assisted learning, and computer-assisted instruction in the reading program. The progress of all students in the class is monitored, with more frequent monitoring for those students who show early signs that their progress is discrepant from the norm.

Students whose achievement and rate of learning are significantly below average for the class move to Tier 2, where they receive reading instruction in addition to the classroom instruction in which they still participate. Although there is significant research indicating that Tier 2 instruction is effective for the majority of students who receive it (see Gersten et al., 2009; Reed & Vaughn, 2010; Swanson, Hoskyn, & Lee, 1999; Wanzek & Vaughn, 2010), there is currently a lot of variation in the way Tier 2 instruction is conducted. Although it is small-group instruction, group size varies. Some RTI programs use reading specialists as teachers; others use classroom aides. Instructional time can vary from 30 minutes to 1 hour and from 2 to 5 days per week. Gersten et al. (2009) recommended the use of standard protocols for Tier 2 instruction, which would reduce variation in the instruction students receive. (Standard protocols are described later in this chapter.)

Tiers 1 and 2 belong to general education and fit well into the requirements for reading instruction in NCLB. Currently, most RTI programs have three tiers. Although there may be others, we only found two four-tier programs. One is the Heartland Area Education Agency in Iowa (Ikeda et al., 2007) that Douglas Fuchs reported has been reduced to three tiers (Fuchs, Fuchs, & Strecker, 2010). This speaks to the important issue of how long RTI should be tested before a special education evaluation is initiated. Some critics of RTI (see, e.g., Reynolds, 2008) believe extended time in general education classes before referral for special education is a major flaw in the program. Idaho's Department of Education, Department of Special Education, implements the other four-tier program. If you are interested in a detailed description of an RTI program, including the reading programs used in Tiers 1 and 2, the Idaho program (Callender, 2007) is a good one to study.

Tier 3 is implemented in different ways among school districts with RTI programs (Denton & Vaughn, 2010). In some districts, Tier 3 is special education, and the move between Tiers 2 and 3 is preceded by a comprehensive individual evaluation protected by **due process** procedures. In other districts, Tier 3 remains the responsibility of general education; referral for special education evaluation occurs only if a student fails to make progress with different instruction than was provided in Tier 2. A significant, and as yet unanswered, question about RTI concerns distinctions in instruction between Tiers 2 and 3 (Fuchs et al., 2010).

RTI Assessment Methodology

Although most of the early reading intervention studies that provide the empirical support for the effectiveness of Tier 2 instruction used other assessment tasks (Gersten et al., 2009), formative assessment using curriculum-based measures is central to RTI (Johnson, Mellard, Fuchs, & McKnight, 2006). Fuchs and Deno (1991) organized curriculum-based measures into categories: specific subskill mastery assessments and general outcome measures. Specific subskill mastery assessments are derived from behavioral psychology and are the most familiar (the measurement map looks like a scope and sequence chart). Global curriculum outcomes are disaggregated into component subskills. Test items and mastery criteria are created for each subskill. These criterion-referenced items produce the student performance data that allow a teacher to infer mastery of the subskills from easy to difficult. For example, a teacher (or curriculum specialist) conducts a task analysis of spelling patterns in the 408 words in a third-grade spelling curriculum, ranks the patterns from easy to difficult (the map), and creates assessment items and mastery criteria for each pattern (Fuchs & Deno, 1991).

In contrast, general outcome measures, the curriculum-based measures in RTI, assess increased proficiency over time on the global outcome toward which the entire curriculum is directed. Using the spelling example, 20 word tests are created using randomly selected words across the entire spelling curriculum. These "probes" are given to students as timed dictation tests. The student's score is determined by counting all of the correctly spelled words and letter sequences. These measures have the psychometric properties of academic achievement tests. Procedures for administering and scoring are standardized, and reliability and validity coefficients are determined. The measures are used to index both academic status (e.g., number of words and letter sequences spelled correctly) and learning (e.g., rate at which number of words and letter sequences spelled correctly is increasing).

This conception of curriculum-based measures is credited to Stanley Deno and his colleagues at the University of Minnesota (Deno, 1985). Although there are other similar curriculum-based measures available, the original measures from the Minnesota group include a measure of oral reading fluency (words correct while reading text for 1 minute); a multiple-choice cloze task as a measure of reading comprehension (number of correct choices in 5 minutes); for spelling, dictation of words at 5-, 7-, or 10-second intervals for 2 minutes (as indicated previously, number of correct words and letter sequences); for writing, 3 minutes to write a story prompted by a story starter (number of words written and spelled correctly and/or correct letter sequences); and for math, answer computation problems in 2- to 5-minute probes (number of digits written correctly) (Shinn & Bamonto, 1998). All probes in each subject at each grade level are of equal difficulty, so change in a student's score from one probe to another is attributed to learning rather than to changes in the difficulty of the task. These probes are, in fact, short standardized tests that meet official standards for reliability and criterion validity (Good & Jefferson, 1998).

Curriculum-based measurement combines two approaches to assessment—measures anchored in psychometric science and visual displays of learning data anchored in behavioral psychology and the science of applied behavior analysis (Engelmann, 1968; Lindsley, 1991). The central feature of curriculum-based measurement is the opportunity it gives the teacher to make decisions about what and how to teach based on reliable data from the student. How does this work? Reading instruction can illustrate the process. Imagine a child who is struggling with reading and a teacher who has the tools (reading fluency measures, a monitoring graph, a long-term reading goal, lesson plans, and decision rules for modifying instruction) she needs to make data-based decisions about reading instruction. She establishes the student's baseline performance in oral reading fluency and then draws a diagonal line on the graph indicating how many words the child should be reading in 1 minute at a designated time in the future (the aim line). She starts the lessons, tests twice per week to learn the number of words read correctly, and records those numbers on the graph. In 8 weeks, she will have enough data points to draw a trend line for her student (Burns, Deno, & Jimerson, 2007). If the trend line is a significant distance below the aim line, then she knows that she should change the instruction.

The teacher will draw a vertical line through the graph and label the change in instruction. She will proceed in this fashion until the student reaches the goal or until the student's performance indicates the instruction needs to change in more significant ways than the modifications the teacher has already made. The teacher has achievement data (i.e., the number of words the student reads correctly) and learning data (i.e., the rate at which number of correct words is increasing) for her student, and she can compare it with local or national norms. See Fuchs and Fuchs (2007) and Jenkins, Hudson, and Lee (2007) for more detailed descriptions of curriculum-based measures. A useful table of reading fluency norms for first through eighth grade may be found in Hasbrouck and Tindal (2006) (see Chapter 10, Appendix 10.3).

A Sea Change in the Means for Determining Eligibility for Special Education

In the early 1980s, the National Research Council (NRC) released a remedy for racial/ethnic and gender disproportion in special education referrals and placements. The remedy represented a significant change in assessment practices used to determine eligibility for special education (Heller, Holtzman, & Messick, 1982).

The Office of Civil Rights in the U.S. Department of Education has been documenting overrepresentation of minority students and males in special education programs for students with intellectual disabilities since they began collecting data on students enrolled in special education in 1970. Nine years into that effort, a panel was convened under the auspices of the NRC and given the responsibility to identify factors that account for overrepresentation and identify placement criteria or practices that should not affect minority students and males disproportionately.

Rather than recommend ways to counteract bias in standardized tests, particularly intelligence tests, panel members worked from the premise that the main purpose of assessment in schools is to improve instruction and learning. They concluded that overrepresentation of minority groups and males in special education is not inequitable if special education proves to be the optimal learning environment for the student. That is, if placement in special education is a benefit and not a penalty, then the student's civil rights are not violated. Panel members went one step further and claimed that the only valid assessment procedures in schools are those that have a direct link to instruction and enhance learning. Having established this criterion for selecting assessment procedures and interpreting the results, members of the panel set three validity requirements for determining eligibility for special education: 1) assessment of the learning environment in which the student is currently enrolled proves that it is adequate for the majority of students but inadequate for the student in question and modifications in instruction do not improve outcomes for the student; 2) assessments used to establish disability are valid; and 3) the special education program produces positive outcomes for the student.

Panel members envisioned a two-phase assessment process wherein the first phase is an assessment of the learning environment in which the student is currently enrolled and the second phase is an individual assessment to determine if the student has a disability. Panel members were silent on the assessment of special education outcomes, apparently preferring to review research on effective instruction for students with high-incidence disabilities as a guide for constructing effective instruction in special education programs (Heller et al., 1982).

We call these recommendations "a sea change" because they call for assessing learning environments first and then assessing individual traits and dispositions of the individual in the process of determining whether that individual has a disability. Curriculum-based measures, in development when the NRC report was published, add exponentially to the tools that educators and psychologists can use to assess learning environments. The NRC's recommendations for a remedy to minority and gender over-representation in special education is important to our concerns about students who struggle to become literate because of the claim that special education must produce learning benefits for the student or it is a violation of that student's civil rights. IDEA 2004 endorses a student's response to instruction, a significant part of the learning environment, as one test for SLD. Note, however, that the people who studied psychometric issues with the diagnosis of an intellectual disability recommended assessment of the learning environment as an addition to, not as a substitute for, a comprehensive individual evaluation.

RTI has an assessment methodology that typically operates within a three-tiered structure in which intervention is differentiated across the tiers. Federal law stipulates that intervention must be research based if a student's RTI experience is part of the evaluation used to diagnose SLD. There are two approaches to selecting and delivering interventions that are not mutually exclusive in practice but derive from different psychological orientations (Fuchs et al., 2003). One originates with school psychologists and the other with researchers interested in preventing reading failure. Because most referrals for special education evaluation are a consequence of behavior problems or reading failure (Donovan & Cross, 2002), it is to be expected that school psychologists and early reading researchers would be engaged with effective preventive and remedial interventions in schools.

Evidence-Based Intervention: Problem Solving and Standard Protocols

Problem solving originated with school psychologists in a practice called *behavioral consultation,* which is inductive and empirical (Bergan, 1977; Bergan & Kratchowill, 1990).

Supporters believe that student characteristics do not prescribe *a priori* which learning or behavioral intervention will work, nor is it likely that any intervention will work with all students in a particular group. The only way to determine whether an intervention works is to try it out and interpret the outcome (Fuchs et al., 2003). Several generic problem-solving models exist in practice (Burns et al., 2007). Although actions in a problem-solving model are described with different words depending on the person providing the description, all problem-solving models essentially include the same actions. First, identify the problem through universal screening or teacher referral. Second, analyze the problem by determining the discrepancy between current performance levels and a norm-referenced performance standard. As part of problem analysis, an effort may be made to determine whether the problem is an acquisition or performance deficit and to identify any environmental conditions that might be causing the deficit. Third, explore intervention options. Fourth, select an intervention option and implement it with fidelity. Fifth, interpret outcomes from the intervention (Burns et al., 2007; Gresham, 2007).

Problem-solving actions can be recursive, especially those actions that involve choosing, implementing, and evaluating interventions. Problem solving operates at every level of a multitier intervention structure. Problem-solving approaches rely on curriculum-based measures both to identify problems and to obtain student performance data (Burns et al., 2007). Problem solving is usually collaborative, although the people who collaborate (teachers with parents, teachers with teachers, and teachers with teams responsible for special education evaluations) may be different across locations where RTI is implemented or across tiers in a specific location.

Standard protocols originate in the drive for evidence-based practice in education and from the decades of reading research funded by the NICHD and the U.S. Department of Education (McCardle & Chhabra, 2004; NICHD, 2000). In particular, standard protocols originate with the early reading interventions studies referred to previously. These studies demonstrate that of the 20% of students who typically fail to make normal progress in reading as a result of a research-based core curriculum, approximately 15% achieve normal progress in reading as a result of the instruction they receive in Tier 2 of a multitier intervention program (Batsche et al., 2005). Standard protocols come from the reading programs tested in these intervention studies, some of which are scripted and others partially scripted. By virtue of the fact that they have been empirically validated, the fidelity with which they are implemented is of utmost importance (Fuchs et al., 2003). Consequently, curriculum-based monitoring takes place less frequently in Tier 2 when standard protocols are used because the protocol cannot be modified.

Although problem solving and standard protocols derive from different psychological orientations (one seeks truth from the science of applied behavior analysis, in which the unit of study is the individual, and the other from the science of experimental psychology and experimental medicine, in which the unit of study is a collection of individuals whose performance is aggregated), in practice, the two approaches to intervention can be combined. RTI researchers (Burns et al., 2007; Fuchs et al., 2010; Gersten et al., 2009) typically recommend using standard protocols in Tier 2 and problem solving in Tier 3. This is a logical recommendation. We assume that Tier 3 instruction is individualized instruction and problem solving is a means for individualizing instruction. In summary, if teachers follow the recommendations of the *Institute of Education Science Practice Guide* (Gersten et al., 2009), Tier 1 instruction will be guided by research, whereas Tier 2 instruction is research tested and Tier 3 instruction is determined by individualizing instruction and objectively monitoring student performance. Tier 3 instruction might well be called *single subject research*.

So far, the chapter has presented an approach to assessment for students who struggle with reading that adds assessments of learning environments (instruction) to the more traditional assessments of individual traits and dispositions. RTI relies heavily on curriculum-based measures that generate data about learning and achievement. Curriculum-based measures can be used for screening as well as for monitoring students' progress. NCLB, with its aggressive effort to ensure that all children through Grade 8 are literate by 2014, has generated a great deal of interest in universal screening and in formative assessment of progress. There are other screening and progress monitoring tools that teachers can use either within an RTI framework or independent from RTI. We review these tools next.

RATIONALE FOR EARLY IDENTIFICATION AND TOOLS FOR SCREENING

Screening is a critical component of the RTI model. The National Center for Learning Disabilities (Cortiella, 2006) described how children in general education settings are identified as at risk through implementing universal screening measures within the RTI model. Students who are identified early and provided with appropriate interventions as struggling readers have the best outcomes for success (Biancarosa & Snow, 2006). Not long ago, parents of young children who struggled with beginning reading instruction were frequently advised by professionals in the schools to "sit and wait." It was assumed that these students would catch up to their peers spontaneously when they were "ready" to learn to read.

Consequences of Delaying Intervention

Much more is known about the dangers of waiting to intervene. As Torgesen advised, "The best solution to the problem of reading failure is to allocate resources for early identification and prevention" (1998, p. 1). The research is clear. The majority of young children entering kindergarten and elementary school at risk for reading failure have the potential to learn to read at average or above-average levels if they are identified early and given appropriate "systematic, intensive instruction in phonemic awareness, phonics, reading fluency, vocabulary, and reading comprehension strategies" (Lyon & Chhabra, 2004, p. 16). Torgesen (2002) reported that the number of students who read below basic levels can be reduced to less than 6% if a combination of early identification and appropriate interventions are put in place.

The consequences of delaying identification and intervention are ominous. As Shaywitz (2003) reported, at least 70% of students who do not learn to read by age 9 will never catch up to their typically developing peers.

Even the youngest children who may be at risk for reading problems can be identified. For example, Adams (1990) cited rapid identification of upper- and lowercase letters of the alphabet as the single best predictor of early reading achievement. That, coupled with an assessment of phonemic awareness, which is shown to be directly related to the growth of early word-reading skills (Torgesen, 1998), can be helpful in identifying young children at risk for reading failure.

Although common signs of reading difficulties may be apparent before a child even begins formal schooling, reviews of early identification research (Scarborough, 1998) have revealed substantial levels of false positives (an average of 45% of children identified during kindergarten as at risk for reading problems turn out not to be among the readers with the most serious problems by the end of first grade). Most of these children identified as at risk, however, are likely to be below-average readers (Torgesen & Burgess,

1998). The flip side is that about 22% of children who are later judged to have serious reading difficulties are not identified through kindergarten screenings.

Torgesen (1998) advised that screening begin in the second semester of kindergarten so that children may have some opportunity to learn the prereading skills that will later be evaluated. To increase the efficiency of the screening procedure, Torgesen recommended that two tests be given: 1) a test of knowledge of letter names (most predictive for kindergarten students) and/or letter sounds (most predictive for first graders) and 2) a measure of phonemic awareness. Phonemic awareness is commonly measured through tasks grouped in three broad categories: sound comparison, phoneme segmentation, and phoneme blending (see Chapters 5 and 6).

The Focus of Early Identification

Torgesen (2006) reflected back on the "pillars of reading" when recommending the areas to be focused on in screening students in kindergarten through third grade. It is important to remember, however, that although phonemic awareness, phonics, fluency, vocabulary, and reading comprehension should all be addressed, assessing each area must be conducted in a manner that is appropriate to the grade level of the child. In addition, issues of cultural and linguistic differences in this population must be addressed. The National Early Childhood Technical Assistance Center cautioned that nonbiased assessment instruments and procedures that are appropriate for the child should be used to ensure that discerned patterns of development and behavior are a reason for concern and not simply the result of cultural and linguistic differences. The center's web site (http://www.nectac.org/) provides a minibibliography of articles and guidelines that can help the practitioner employ culturally sensitive practices.

For the kindergarten student, phonemic awareness, phonics skills as reflected by knowing letters and beginning decoding skills, and vocabulary are areas that deserve attention during screenings. Fluency and reading comprehension, however, are rarely developed enough to be assessed at this level. Instead, listening comprehension is often assessed instead of reading comprehension to tap into language processing skills that will be necessary for comprehending text once word reading accuracy and fluency are established.

Although phonemic awareness and decoding skills should continue to be monitored in the first-grade student, oral reading fluency measures on an increased role of significance as soon as the ability to read connected text with reasonable accuracy is apparent. Oral reading measures are much more reliable than silent reading measures for young children. Growth in vocabulary should also be assessed regularly at this age, and reading comprehension can be evaluated by the end of first grade for most children.

As second- and third-grade students progress to decoding multisyllable words, they need continued monitoring of their phonemic decoding ability. Monitoring reading fluency is critical at this stage to determine grade-level reading proficiency. The roles of vocabulary and comprehension assume even greater focus during this time. Listening comprehension should be a must across levels, especially when looking for dyslexia.

Screening Instruments

A substantial number of screening instruments have become available that may be used to identify children as early as kindergarten or even prekindergarten who are at high risk for reading failure and who may require more intense, systematic reading instruction (Smartt & Glaser, 2010). Four short, direct, and simple screening tools hold particular

pals.virginia.edu/activities_PA-BS-1-3.ht

promise: TPRI (Texas Education Agency, 2010b); the Phonological Awareness Literacy Screening (PALS; Invernizzi, Juel, Swank, & Meier, 2003; Invernizzi, Meier, & Juel, 2002; Invernizzi, Sullivan, & Meier, 2001); the Dynamic Indicators of Basic Early Literacy Skills (DIBELS; Good & Kaminski, 2002); and the Developmental Reading Assessment–Second Edition (DRA-2; Beaver, 2006; Beaver & Carter, 2003). (*Note:* DRA-2 is discussed later in the chapter.)

The TPRI is a one-to-one assessment tool designed to be used with students in kindergarten. Assessments for children in first through third grade are also available. The TPRI offers two levels of assessment. In January or February of the kindergarten year, students may take the brief Screening Section, which takes less than 10 minutes. In some states, it is given at the beginning of kindergarten. Students who do not pass this initial screening may then take a more in-depth reading inventory that takes approximately 25–30 minutes to administer. In some schools, the entire Inventory Section is given to all students. This inventory can be used to help teachers identify student strengths and problem areas and also to monitor student progress.

The Screening Section of the TPRI focuses on three areas: graphophonemic knowledge in kindergarten and first grade (recognizing letters of the alphabet and demonstrating understanding of sound–symbol relationships); phonemic awareness in kindergarten and first grade (the ability to identify and manipulate sounds within spoken words); and word reading for first through third grade. The Inventory Section Assessment adds six new components: book and print awareness (general knowledge of the function of print as well as the characteristics of books and other print sources) and listening comprehension to the kindergarten assessment; graphophonemic knowledge in the kindergarten through third grade (recognizing letters of the alphabet and demonstrating understanding of sound–symbol relations for kindergarten and first-grade students, word-building activities for students in first grade, and spelling for students in second and third grade); and reading accuracy, reading fluency, and reading comprehension for first through third grade. An *Intervention Activities Guide* linked to the TPRI is also available to assist plans for instruction (Texas Education Agency, 2010a). A comparable assessment available from the same publisher measures student reading skills and comprehension development in Spanish for students in kindergarten through third grade: Tejas LEE (Texas Education Agency, 2011).

PALS is used three times per year beginning in prekindergarten and kindergarten. Assessments are also available for first through third grade. The first administration is given in the fall of the school year and is used to guide instruction for students who do not meet early literacy benchmarks. A second administration in the spring helps to evaluate progress after targeted interventions have been delivered.

The PALS-PreK (Invernizzi et al., 2001) measures skills such as name-writing ability, upper- and lowercase letter recognition, letter sounds and beginning sound production, print and word awareness, rhyme awareness, and nursery rhyme awareness.

The PALS-K (Invernizzi et al., 2003) focuses on five fundamental literacy skills: phonological awareness (matching rhyming pictures plus beginning sound awareness demonstrated by matching words that begin with the same sound), alphabet recognition (26 lowercase letters), concept of word (touching words in a memorized rhyme, using context to identify individual words, and identifying words outside of the text), knowledge of letter sounds (producing sounds for 23 uppercase letters plus three digraphs), and spelling (five consonant–vowel–consonant words are targeted, and phonetically acceptable substitutions receive credit). PALS-K not only identifies kindergartners who may be at risk for later developing a reading disability but also provides teachers with instructionally useful information about these fundamental components of literacy.

The PALS 1–3 (Invernizzi et al., 2002) for first through third grade is a leveled instrument. Level A is used to identify students at risk of reading difficulties. Levels A, B, and C provide teachers with information that can guide instruction by diagnosing specific skill deficits in students who do not meet the Level A criteria. Spelling, word recognition in isolation, oral reading in context (to assess oral reading accuracy, phrasing, intonation, and expression), reading rate, comprehension, and fluency are all assessed. Students whose entry-level scores do not meet grade-level criteria are assessed with Level B tasks, including alphabet recognition, letter sounds, and concept of word (the latter is explained in the previous PALS-K description). Finally, students who do not meet Level B benchmarks move to Level C for an even more in-depth evaluation of phonemic awareness skills, including blending and segmenting speech sounds.

A Teacher Checklist of Literacy Practices is included in the PALS-PreK Teacher's Set. A videotape that includes demonstrations of instructional strategies for students can be found in both the PALS-K and the PALS 1–3 kits.

DIBELS (Good et al., 2011) is the third screening tool that is widely used in this country. (A Spanish version is available as well as a French version, which is available for research purposes only.) The DIBELS measures are standardized and designed as indicators of the basic early literacy skills of phonemic awareness, the alphabetic principle and phonics, accurate and fluent reading of connected text, and reading comprehension. Benchmark target goals are set for each skill and based on the likelihood of the student reaching later reading outcome goals.

DIBELS universal screening is called *benchmark assessment* and occurs three times per year (typically September, January, and May for schools on a September to June calendar). A set of alternate forms for each of these standardized, 1-minute fluency measures are available to conduct more frequent progress monitoring for students who are not meeting the benchmark goals so that instructional interventions can be adjusted based on progress.

Several data management services are available that allow schools to enter DIBELS data and generate automated reports, including the DIBELS Data System from the University of Oregon (http://dibels.uoregon.edu/) and VPORT from Sopris West (http://www.voyagerlearning.com/vport/).

Which measures are administered varies by grade and time of year. For example, across the year in kindergarten, DIBELS includes first sound fluency and phoneme segmentation fluency (indicators of phonemic awareness), nonsense word fluency (an indicator of the alphabetic principle and basic phonics), and letter naming fluency (a general indicator of risk). In third grade, students are tested on oral reading fluency (an indicator of advanced phonics, accurate and fluent reading of connected text, and reading comprehension) and "daze" (an indicator of reading comprehension constructed similar to maze tasks).

Research conducted on the technical adequacy of the DIBELS measures provided evidence of their reliability and validity as indicators of early literacy development. As with the TPRI and PALS, DIBELS can be used for early identification of students who are not progressing at expected levels and who need targeted intervention strategies. The DIBELS measures may also be used to provide feedback about whether interventions are effective for individual students.

Screening Through the Grades

If early identification and early intervention are carried out carefully with strong, effective tools, then it can be assumed that the numbers of children who will need services after third grade will diminish (Biancarosa & Snow, 2006). Under the best of circumstances, however, it is doubtful that screening to identify struggling readers beyond early elementary grades and into middle and high school grades will be implemented. Typically, students at these levels no longer are being taught how to read. Instead, they are expected to read to learn content. Yet, approximately 8 million students between 4th and 12th grade struggle to read at grade level, and 70% of older readers need some form of remediation (Biancarosa & Snow, 2006).

Torgesen and Miller (2009) called for universal screening as one component of a comprehensive literacy assessment. Although universal screening may seem to be an overwhelming task in secondary school settings, Torgesen and Miller suggested using the data that have already been collected on students to identify those who may need targeted reading interventions. In particular, they advised using general screening information from the previous year's summative assessments to identify which students did not meet grade-level benchmarks. Schools may also use benchmark assessments in the fall that are designed to predict end-of-year state test results. After these data have been analyzed and used to determine an initial pool of students in need, additional assessments should be conducted to determine the nature and severity of their reading problems.

The reasons behind poor performance on these summative assessments are not usually readily apparent. Some students may perform poorly because they simply cannot read the words on the page. Others are not fluent readers even if they are relatively accurate, so they may not be able to complete the test in a timely manner. A substantial number of students at this level have deficient banks of prior knowledge and relevant vocabulary required to comprehend content-area text. Still others have generally weak active comprehension strategies available to them. There is a subgroup that may be classified as students with disabilities who are late-emergent readers. These students may have been relatively successful in school with or without early intervention, but their competence crumbles once the demands imposed on them to master more sophisticated content arise (Compton, Fuchs, Fuchs, Elleman, & Gilbert, 2008).

Torgesen and Miller (2009) suggested that screening tests at this point should be targeted at word-level reading skills, fluency, and comprehension so that interventions can be matched with specific areas of need. Resources are available to fulfill this mission. Johnson and Pool (2009) provided a list of screening measures that work well for students in 4th through 12th grade as well as tools such as informal reading and interest inventories plus decoding, comprehension, and fluency measures to identify specific reading problems of students struggling at this level. Morsy, Kieffer, and Snow (2010) targeted reading comprehension assessments appropriate for adolescents that can be used to inform interventions.

Finally, AIMSweb and the Florida Assessments for Instruction in Reading (FAIR) are computer-assisted screening devices that can be used for screening and formative assessment. Both devices are discussed later in the chapter.

Formative Assessment of Oral Reading Fluency

Oral reading fluency is well regarded as an index of a student's general reading achievement, is sensitive to reading growth, and is well correlated with reading comprehension test performance (Jenkins et al., 2007). In addition to the DIBELS benchmark measures discussed previously, DIBELS also has multiple examples of oral reading fluency measures that can be used for progress monitoring from first to sixth grade. In general, it is suggested that teachers use a student's assigned grade level to decide which reading material will be used for progress monitoring. If a student struggles with grade-level passages, however (less than 90% accuracy), then the student can be monitored with the grade level of text in which he or she can read with 90% accuracy. Three passages are usually administered to establish a baseline at either the median or the mean of the student's scores. Growth goals are set after a baseline of words read correctly within 1 minute is established. For first and second grade, growth goals are about 1.5 words a week. For third through sixth grade, modest goals would be about 0.5 words per week. Students in special learning disabilities programs in which they are receiving more intensive reading instruction usually gain about one word per week but may achieve greater gains (Jenkins et al., 2007). The latest recommendations are for growth measures to be administered about every 3 weeks (Jenkins, 2009). Students' median scores may be plotted on a recording form using a graphing program. The University of Washington offers a free curriculum-based measures growth calculator (http://www.fluent reader.org/calc.html) that automatically charts the weekly growth slope from baseline to successive words-read-correctly results.

Formative Assessment in Multisensory Language Programs

There are still other options for creating progress monitoring tools. Some multisensory programs include information on how to make formative assessments of progress. For example, Alphabetic Phonics (Cox, 1992) uses curriculum-referenced tasks called *benchmark measures* (Cox, 1986) and *progress measurements* (Rumsey, 1992), respectively, to assess progress in letter-knowledge acquisition and alphabetizing skills and to assess reading, spelling, and handwriting. Teachers who use *Road to Reading* (Blachman & Tangel, 2008) administer the levels assessments to each student, which includes a record of regular and high-frequency words the student has learned to read. Notes from the daily lesson plans are put in a folder, dated, and arranged chronologically to facilitate evaluation of progress. The *Basic Language Skills* program (Blachman & Tangel, 2000) has a series of mastery checks given after concepts have been introduced and practiced. The *Wilson Reading System* (Wilson, 1996) and other multisensory structured language education programs include pre- and posttesting along with tests to evaluate mastery of knowledge taught in one curriculum unit before a student moves to the next curriculum unit. Assessing progress in these programs does focus on students' mastery of word-recognition and spelling skills.

WADE

Building on Multisensory Language Instruction Benchmarks

To build on this tradition of assessing progress in multisensory programs, educators can identify the classes of data needed to assess progress and identify some methods of data collection. The following skills should be tracked: phoneme segmentation, letter identification, graphophonemic knowledge (letter–sound associations), word recognition fluency, spelling, oral vocabulary, comprehension, and composition. Although it is useful to assess children's knowledge of letter–sound associations using checklists of phonics knowledge (e.g., Blachowicz, 1980), children's spellings also provide a window on their knowledge of letter–sound relationships. By examining children's spellings, teachers can gain insight into children's phonics knowledge (Treiman, 1998). Using spelling to assess phonics knowledge requires a spelling curriculum that includes a systematic outline of English spelling, knowledge of the developmental sequence for acquiring English spellings, and a method for scoring spellings that evaluates spelling elements within words rather than simply marking words as correct or incorrect. Reading and spelling are usually taught as separate subjects; consequently, teachers might not think to use spelling to assess reading. (See Chapter 9 for a sample spelling rubric that uses qualitative data.)

Although not intended for this purpose, the Spelling Performance Evaluation for Language and Literacy–Second Edition (SPELL-2) assessment tool, which includes a cross-platform CD-ROM and a manual (Masterson, Apel, & Wasowicz, 2006), is a criterion-referenced instrument that is organized to allow the simultaneous assessment of spelling and phonics knowledge. (See Moats, 1995, and Mosely, 1997, for more information about spelling assessment.) SPELL-2 is composed of tests that assess knowledge of phonological awareness and alphabetic letter–sound relationships, letter patterns and vocabulary word parts (prefixes, suffixes, base words), and mental images of words. The Word Identification and Spelling Test (WIST; Wilson & Felton, 2004) is another useful spelling assessment for qualitative data with normative information as well as diagnostic cues for instruction. The spelling subtest assesses a student's ability to spell words correctly from dictation, ability to recall correct letter sequences from familiar words, and ability to apply sound–symbol relationships of English orthography. Regular and irregular words are assessed separately for comparison. Error analysis leads to an appropriate intervention plan to improve spelling.

Informal Reading Inventories

Informal reading inventories (see Leslie & Caldwell, 2010; Woods & Moe, 2010) can be used to obtain the data needed to plan remedial programs. The structure of these inventories is used to establish reading levels for individual students based on accuracy in reading single words, words in text, and answering comprehension questions. These inventories include conventions for marking reading errors (insertions, hesitations, mispronunciations, omissions, regressions, substitutions, self-corrections, pauses, and repetitions) and, more importantly, provide classification systems for word-reading errors, which are commonly called *miscues*.

Mispronounced words (words read incorrectly) are classified as graphically similar, semantically acceptable, or syntactically correct. This classification allows the teacher to make some inferences about the word-recognition strategies students are using. Given the view that word-recognition accuracy and fluency depend on the coordinated use of graphophonemic, semantic, and syntactic cues for word recognition (Ehri & McCormick, 1998), analyzing miscues is important. Some informal reading inventories (e.g., Leslie & Caldwell, 2010) provide procedures for assessing reading rate for words and text and give standards for evaluating a student's fluency with word lists and text. In most informal reading inventories, comprehension is assessed by observing students thinking aloud as they read, retelling stories they have read, and answering questions about the text. Background knowledge is assessed by observing students making predictions about the text before they read based on the title and the first few sentences of the text. Vocabulary is assessed by observing students defining words encountered in the text.

The DRA-2 is another informal reading inventory. It is a criterion-measured assessment used to measure accuracy, fluency, and comprehension for students in kindergarten through third grade (Beaver, 2006). The DRA Word Analysis, which measures phonological awareness and phonics (Beaver, 2005), and the Developmental Reading Assessment 4–8 (Beaver & Carter, 2003) are included in the revised version. The measure categorizes students in a series of levels: emergent (Levels A–3), early (Levels 4–12), transitional (Levels 14–24), extending (Levels 28–38), and intermediate/middle (Levels 40–80). Kindergarten and first-grade students are not timed while reading orally, but students in second through eighth grade complete a timed reading and written responses. Students in kindergarten through third grade choose a book that is neither too hard nor too easy for them to read. Teachers analyze student performance using the student's performance during reading and ability to respond to questions and prompts. Reliability and validity studies have been conducted for this measure and can be found in the technical manual. The test–retest reliability for fluency ranged from .93 to .97, and comprehension from .97 to .95. The DRA-2 measure is widely used as an alternative to the TPRI in Texas.

Most inventories are organized to permit comparisons between a student's skills (e.g., fluency and comprehension) with narrative text and his or her skills with expository text. Comparisons can be made between a student's reading performance (e.g., accuracy and fluency) with word lists and his or her performance with text. Distinctions between reading and listening comprehension may also be drawn. These inventories are criterion-referenced tests, even though the authors may not view the inventories from this perspective. As indicated previously, data obtained from these inventories are used to construct remedial programs. The rules included in these inventories for marking reading errors, classifying miscues, and assessing reading rate can be used to create curriculum-referenced assessments based on the texts used for instruction. These structured observations of reading of texts that students use for reading instruction can also be used to assess comprehension, vocabulary, and use of background knowledge. It is easy to imagine an assessment folder that includes records of such observations made on a regular basis. These records would be similar to the running assessment records recommended by Clay (1995). The text is from the students' reading lessons; the structure for assessing reading is borrowed from informal inventories.

Technology-Enhanced Screening and Progress Monitoring Systems

Since 2000, assessment systems that rely on technology have been developed to help teachers collect and use assessment data to refine instruction. Many of these assessment systems are not tied to a particular curriculum or textbook series (Salvia et al., 2010). Electronic data collection, management, and reporting systems are key to resolving teachers' concerns about the practicality of formative assessment of learning.

AIMSweb (http://www.aimsweb.com), a direct, frequent, and continuous benchmark and progress monitoring system, is one example of a progress monitoring system. AIMSweb has curriculum-based measures probes in reading, math, spelling, writing, and behavior for students in kindergarten through eighth grade. Teachers can have the system generate graphs, tables, and reports that help them manage instruction in their classrooms. The system can also set goals and calculate learning rates for individual students in response to changes in instruction.

FAIR (http://www.fcrr.org/fair/index.shtm), which was developed by the Florida Center for Reading Research in collaboration with Just Read, Florida, is an assessment system that offers teachers screening, diagnostic, and progress monitoring information for students in kindergarten through 12th grade. At this time, the program is offered free to public schools in Florida. The pencil-and-paper version is available for purchase only for K–2, but, at the time of this writing, there is no access to the online Progress

Monitoring and Reporting Network (PMRN) for private schools or schools outside of Florida.

The National Center on Response to Intervention maintains a Progress Monitoring Tools Chart and a Screening Tools Chart on its web site (http://www.rti4success.org). The Progress Monitoring Tools Chart evaluates progress monitoring tools on 10 dimensions, including reliability and validity of performance level scores and of slopes. (See Ysseldyke & McLeod, 2007, for more information about technology tools that support screening and progress monitoring.)

THE COMPREHENSIVE INDIVIDUAL EVALUATION

People who believe that RTI data alone are sufficient for determining if an individual has SLD and placing him or her in a special education program are misinformed. As indicated previously, the definition of SLD and the exclusionary diagnostic criteria have not changed significantly since 1975. Neither have the general (applicable to all handicapping conditions) regulations governing procedures for evaluating individuals and determining their eligibility for special education (Yell, Shriner, & Katsiyannis, 2006). Federal law requires a full (health, sensory, social-emotional status, language, cognitive, academic, and motor abilities) individual evaluation before the initial provision of special education and related services. The evaluation must be conducted by a qualified multidisciplinary team, including a teacher or reading specialist; team members must use technically sound evaluation procedures. Parents must be informed of the purpose of the evaluation and each evaluation procedure and give written consent; parents are also expected to participate. Emphasis is placed on the functional nature of the evaluation, meaning that results from the evaluation will inform instruction and determine if the student needs services in addition to special education, such as speech-language therapy or psychological counseling.

If an individual is determined to have SLD, the evaluation team must prepare a written report that contains, among other data, documentation of the person's profile of strengths and weaknesses and the evidence the team used to exclude sensory deficits; intellectual disability; emotional problems; and cultural, environmental, and economic factors as the cause for persistent difficulty learning academic skills (Donovan & Cross, 2002). Finally, rules and regulations governing IDEA 2004 specify that, despite the fact that the child has not yet been referred for a special education evaluation, parents must be told when their child is in a trial reading intervention. They must know the amount and nature of the performance data that will be collected, the general education services that will be provided, and the strategies chosen for increasing the child's learning rate. They can, if they wish, request a comprehensive individual evaluation before the trial intervention ends (U.S. Department of Education, 2006).

Symptoms in a Research-based Definition of Dyslexia

Unlike the federal definition of SLD, The International Dyslexia Association's (IDA) definition of *dyslexia* specifies symptoms and, therefore, facilitates diagnosis:

> Dyslexia is a specific learning disability that is neurological in origin. It is characterized by difficulties with accurate and/or fluent word recognition and by poor spelling and decoding abilities. These difficulties typically result from a deficit in the phonological component of language that is often unexpected in relation to other cognitive abilities and the provision of effective classroom instruction. Secondary consequences may include problems in

reading comprehension and reduced reading experience, which can impede growth of vo-cabulary and background knowledge. (Lyon, Shaywitz, & Shaywitz, 2003, p. 2)

The definition says that dyslexia is a neurological disorder that affects circum-scribed mental operations, those involved in phonological processing. The consequence of the phonological processing disorder is difficulty learning to decode printed words accurately and rapidly and learning to spell. Slow, laborious reading focused on word recognition limits reading experience and may compromise reading comprehension and vocabulary and general knowledge acquisition. The phonological disorder and re-sultant written language symptoms are unexpected, implying that other mental oper-ations and school performances are intact. Finally, limited or inappropriate instruction must be ruled out as an alternate explanation for difficulty with reading and spelling.

Putting the IDEA 2004 regulations and IDA's definition of dyslexia together suggests an evaluation organized in five domains and conducted in the following sequence:

1. Family, health, developmental, and educational history including data from RTI, if available

2. General academic status looking for significant discrepancies in performance be-tween reading/spelling and other academic domains

3. Reading, spelling, and writing skills with a focus on deficits as specified in the IDA definition of dyslexia and discrepancies among reading skills

4. Cognitive and language development, including phonological processing supple-mented by general cognitive status, if indicated by other assessment data

5. Social-emotional status and attention with an attempt to distinguish between pri-mary disorders, comorbid disorders, and secondary symptoms

Regulations on eligibility evaluations carried into IDEA 2004 from previous authoriza-tions specify that evaluations should be individualized as well as individual. A standard battery of tests is contraindicated (Donovan & Cross, 2002; Yell et al., 2006). The struc-ture of the evaluation is constant, although the tests and other data collection proce-dures will vary with conditions, including age, that are specific to the student.

The evaluation addresses three questions:

1. Does this student have a specific reading disability (dyslexia)?

2. What are the essential features of remedial instruction and a remedial plan for this student?

3. Are services in addition to special education indicated?

Family, Health, Developmental, and Educational History

Although there is substantial evidence that dyslexia is a neurological disorder, the exact biological marker(s) have not been identified (Shaywitz, 2003). Consequently, the di-agnosis is a combination of finding behavioral signs recognized as characteristic of dyslexia and ruling out other known causes for those signs. History is important here. Dyslexia among immediate family members and speech delays are signs of risk and, if present, contribute to the diagnosis. Vision and hearing screening test results and records of pediatric examinations help rule out sensory and health explanations for the reading problem. A student's history with reading instruction helps distinguish between poor reading and reading disability.

If the student is enrolled in a school using RTI, then the instructional history in reading should be documented in detail and examined carefully before planning the rest of the evaluation. Among the data that the evaluation team can expect are scores from screening tests, a description of the core reading curriculum in the student's classroom, data that most (approximately 80%) of the students in the class are making adequate progress in reading, and graphs illustrating the student's level of reading attainment and rate of learning to read words in the core reading curriculum. The classroom teacher will also have information about the student's performance in other school subjects, both past and present, including achievement test scores. If the school uses a standard protocol for Tier 2 instruction, then it will be easy to understand the remedial reading instruction the student received, and graphs constructed during that time period will document limited or no progress in reading. If the Tier 2 teacher used formative assessments in addition to curriculum-based measures, then those data should also be obtained and examined. (Federal special education law has always required classroom observation as one of the components for identifying SLD. RTI formalizes that requirement in a way that should produce records about the student's experience with reading, spelling, and writing that were not imaginable previously.)

General Academic Status

As indicated previously, unexpected underachievement is one of the behavioral signs of dyslexia. An individual general achievement test is one way to document adequate to better progress in academic domains other than reading and spelling. There are several technically sound, individually administered reading achievement tests (see Table 14.1). We have chosen to use the Woodcock-Johnson III Normative Update Tests of Achievement (WJ-III-ACH; Woodcock, Schrank, McGrew, & Mather, 2007) to illustrate the genre because it is comprehensive and includes norms that were constructed in 2007. The following description of the achievement battery was adapted from *Assessment in Special and Inclusive Education* (11th ed.) (Salvia et al., 2010, pp. 263–266).

The WJ-III-ACH has 22 subtests in the Extended Battery, 9 of which constitute the Standard Battery. The difference between the Standard and Extended Battery is labeled as the difference between broad and narrow academic abilities. So, for example, the writing tests in the Standard Battery require producing text under timed and untimed conditions. The Extended Battery adds two more tests, one that requires the student to edit text and one that documents knowledge of rules for using capitals and punctuation. Subtests for both batteries can be clustered into reading/writing, mathematics, and comprehension/knowledge. Given that our purpose is diagnosing dyslexia, three of the reading subtests will be briefly described. Phonemic Awareness (called *Sound Awareness*) requires the student to delete phonemes from spoken words, rhyme spoken words, substitute phonemes in spoken words, and reverse phonemes in spoken words. Word Attack looks at a student's ability to decode without using memory, and Reading Fluency requires reading a sentence (question) quickly and responding to the sentence with "yes" or "no."

Table 14.1 shows three pairs of achievement and intelligence tests. Norms for each pair of tests were created with the same people, making IQ and achievement test score comparisons more reliable. It is wise, therefore, to study both tests in the pair before

Table 14.1. Tests of academic achievement and intelligence

Tests	Publisher/web site	Ages	Grades
Achievement tests			
Diagnostic Achievement Battery–Third Edition (2001)	PRO-ED (http://www.proedinc.com)	6;0 to 14;11 years	—
Peabody Individual Achievement Test–Revised (PIAT-R; 1998)	Pearson Assessments (http://www.pearsonassessments .com)	5;0 to 22;11 years	K–12
Stanford Achievement Test–Tenth Edition (2003)	Pearson Assessments (http://www.pearsonassessments .com)	—	K–12
Terra Nova-III (2008)	McGraw-Hill (http://www.ctb.com)	—	K–12
Wechsler Individual Achievement Test–Third Edition (WIAT-3; 2009)	Pearson Assessments (http://www.pearsonassessments .com)	5–19 years	—
Wide Range Achievement Test–Fourth Edition (WRAT-4; 2006)	PRO-ED (http://www.proedinc.com)	5–95 years	—
Woodcock-Johnson III Normative Update Tests of Achievement (WJ-III-ACH; 2007)	Riverside Publishing (http://www .riverpub.com)	2–90 years	—
Intelligence tests			
Kaufman Assessment Battery for Children–Second Edition (KABC-II; 1983)	Psychcorp/Pearson Assessments (http://psychcorp.pearson assessments.com)	3–18 years	—
Stanford-Binet Intelligence Scales–Fifth Edition (2003)	Riverside Publishing (http://www .riverpub.com)	2–85 years	—
Wechsler Intelligence Scale for Children–Fourth Edition Integrated (WISC-IV Integrated; 2003)	Psychcorp/Pearson Assessments (http://psychcorp.pearson assessments.com)	6–16 years	—
Wechsler Intelligence Scale for Adults–Third Edition (WAIS-III; 1997)	Psychcorp/Pearson Assessments (http://psychcorp.pearson assessments.com)	16–89 years	—
Wechsler Preschool and Primary Scale of Intelligence–Third Edition (WPPSI-3; 2002)	Psychcorp/Pearson Assessments (http://psychcorp.pearson assessments.com)	2;6 to 7;3 years	—
Woodcock-Johnson III NU: Test of Cognitive Abilities (2007)	Riverside Publishing (http://www .riverpub.com)	2–90 years	—

choosing an achievement test in the event the evaluation team decides to use an intelligence test.

Reading, Spelling, and Writing Skills

Evaluating reading, spelling, and writing skills serves to extend the RTI data and inform remedial instruction. It also can provide evidence for dyslexia if the student presents a particular pattern of reading and spelling test scores (Shaywitz, 2003; Uhry & Clark, 2005). Sally Shaywitz suggested that students with dyslexia have particular difficulty decoding nonsense words, and their scores on reading comprehension tests are often superior to their scores when asked to read word lists. Difficulty with function words (*that, is, an, for*); slow, labored oral reading; and poor spelling complete the list of primary reading/spelling symptoms. Joanna Uhry structured a performance pattern that included these symptoms. She contended that the "dyslexic pattern" is characterized by average or higher listening comprehension scores followed in descending order by reading comprehension, decoding words in text, decoding words in lists, and spelling and nonsense word reading. Tests from the WJ-III-ACH (Woodcock et al., 2007) can be used to confirm or disconfirm these behavioral signs of dyslexia.

If the student is in a school using RTI and the classroom teacher and Tier 2 teacher have used curriculum-based measures exclusively to monitor progress, then the evaluation team will have reliable word reading fluency, reading comprehension, spelling, and, in particular, rate of learning data. But there are some limits to these data. The team will know the number of words read correctly in text for 1 minute and the rate at which that number is growing but will not know the phonics knowledge the student has acquired or the word-recognition strategies he or she uses. The team will also know the number of words added successfully to a cloze task and the rate at which that number is increasing but will not necessarily know whether the student is equally skilled at answering literal and inferential comprehension questions or can use knowledge already acquired to make accurate predictions about the content of new text. For this information, we recommend diagnostic reading, writing, and spelling tests, both standardized and informal (see Table 14.2).

Three tests allow us to illustrate standardized, norm-referenced diagnostic reading and writing tests that provide information to supplement curriculum-based measures data. The Gray Oral Reading Test–Fourth Edition (GORT-4; Wiederholt & Bryant, 2001) tests reading rate (time taken by student to read a story); reading accuracy (number of words read correctly); fluency (rate and accuracy scores combined); reading comprehension (five questions about each of the stories read); and overall reading ability (fluency and comprehension scores combined). GORT-4 reading passages are longer than the curriculum-based measures passages, and comprehension is measured by asking questions about the same text used to measure reading fluency. The Nelson-Denny Reading Test (Brown, Fishco, & Hanna, 1993) is considered a screening test by its developers. It can be administered to a group of students and, although it has norms for students as young as 9, is particularly useful for students in 7th through 12th grade. The test has three subtests: Vocabulary (multiple-choice items with five options for each word), Comprehension (read passages and answer multiple-choice questions about the content), and Silent Reading Rate (measured after 1 minute of the comprehension test).

Although the writing test in the WJ-III-ACH can be given to younger students, the Test of Written Language–Fourth Edition (TOWL-4; Hammill & Larsen, 2008) is designed for students between 9;0 and 17;11 years of age. (The following description of TOWL-4 was drawn from Salvia et al., 2010, pp. 228, 231–233.) TOWL-4 uses two writing formats (spontaneous and contrived) to evaluate written language. The first five subtests elicit writing in contrived contexts. Vocabulary requires writing sentences using stimulus words that are provided by the examiner. Spelling requires writing sentences from dictation. Punctuation is assessed by evaluating capitalization and punctuation used in the sentences written from dictation. Logical Sentences requires the student to rewrite illogical sentences to make sense. Sentence Combining requires writing one grammatically correct sentence from several short sentences.

The sixth and seventh subtests are based on spontaneous writing. Contextual Conventions assesses the ability to use grammatical rules, capitalization, punctuation, and

Table 14.2.   Diagnostic assessments of reading, spelling, and writing

Title	Publisher/web site	Ages	Grades
Analytical Reading Inventory— Ninth Edition (2010)	Allyn & Bacon (http://www.allynbaconmerrill.com)	—	K–12
Basic Reading Inventory (BRI; 2008)	Kendall Hunt Publishing (http://www.kendallhunt.com)	—	Preprimer through 12th grade
Blachowicz Phonics Inventory included in Reading Diagnosis for Teachers (2007)	Pearson Higher Education (http://www.pearsonhighered.com)	—	—
Degrees of Reading Power	Questar Assessment (http://www.questarai.com)	—	1–12
Developmental Reading Assessment	Pearson Learning (http://www.pearsonlearning.com)	—	K–8
Early Reading Diagnostic Assessment (ERDA; 2003)	Pearson Assessments (http://www.pearsonassessments.com)	—	K–3
Gates-MacGinitie Reading Tests–Fourth Edition (2006)	Riverside Publishing (http://www.riverpub.com)	—	Kindergarten through adult
Gray Oral Reading Test–Fourth Edition (GORT-4; 2001)	PRO-ED (http://www.proedinc.com)	6;0 to 18; 11 years	—
Group Reading Assessment and Diagnostic Evaluation (2001)	Pearson Assessments (http://www.pearsonassessments.com)	—	Pre-K through 12th grade
Qualitative Reading Inventory– Fifth Edition (QRI-5; 2010)	Allyn & Bacon (http://www.allynbaconmerrill.com)	—	K–12
Slosson Oral Reading Test– Revised Third Edition (SORT-R3)	Slosson Educational (http://www.slosson.com)	—	Preschool through adult
Spelling Performance Evaluation for Language and Literacy– Second Edition (SPELL-2; 2006)	Learning by Design (http://www.learningbydesign.com)	—	—
Standardized Test for the Assessment of Reading (STAR); web based	Renaissance Learning (http://www.renlearn.com/sr/)	—	K–12
Stanford Diagnostic Reading Test–Fourth Edition (SDRT-4; 1995)	Pearson Assessments (http://www.pearsonassessments.com)	—	K–13
Test of Early Reading Ability–Third Edition (TERA-3; 2001)	PRO-ED (http://www.proedinc.com)	3;6 to 8;6 years	—
Test of Reading Comprehension–Fourth Edition (TORC-4; 2009)	PRO-ED (http://www.proedinc.com)	7;0 to 7;11 years	—
Test of Silent Word Reading Fluency (TOSWRF; 2004)	PRO-ED (http://www.proedinc.com)	6;6 to 17; 11 years	—
Test of Word Reading Efficiency (TOWRE; 1999)	PRO-ED (http://www.proedinc.com)	6;0 to 24; 11 years	—
Test of Written Language–Fourth Edition (TOWL-4; 2009)	PRO-ED (http://www.proedinc.com)	9;0 to 17; 11 years	—
Test of Written Spelling–Fourth Edition (TWS-4; 1999)	PRO-ED (http://www.proedinc.com)	—	1–12
Woodcock Diagnostic Reading Battery–Third Edition (2004)	Riverside Publishing (http://www.riverpub.com)	2–90 years	—
Woodcock Reading Mastery Test–Revised (WRMT-R; 1998)	Pearson Assessments (http://www.pearsonassessments.com)	5–75 years	K–16
Word Identification and Spelling Test (WIST; 2004)	PRO-ED (http://www.proedinc.com)	—	2–5; 6–12

correct spelling in a story constructed by the student. In the last subtest, the story written for the sixth subtest is assessed for the features of a good composition (e.g., vocabulary, plot, character development).

As indicated, these tests are illustrative of norm-referenced diagnostic reading and writing tests. Consult Table 14.2 for other tests that can contribute to a rich description of a student's reading, spelling, and writing knowledge and skill and provide the special education teacher with information to guide remedial instruction.

Cognitive and Language Status

Although it is usually classified as a linguistic skill and measured in language tests, phonological processing is considered a cognitive skill and, at present, a causal factor in dyslexia (Fletcher et al., 2007). Although the evaluation team will have some information about phonological processes from the RTI data and the WJ-III-ACH, it is still advisable to test these processes, and the Comprehensive Test of Phonological Processing (CTOPP; Wagner, Torgesen, & Rashotte, 1999) is our choice for illustrating this genre of tests (see Table 14.3). CTOPP has strong psychometric properties and extends over a wider age range than other phonological processing measures listed in Table 14.3. CTOPP tests phonological awareness starting with syllables and moving to phonemes, phonological memory, and rapid naming. The evaluation team will use CTOPP scores to confirm the fact and extent of a phonological processing disorder and, perhaps, make recommendations for reading instruction if the disorder is extensive and severe (Yell et al., 2006).

An intelligence test is indicated if other data suggest that the student might have an intellectual disability and benefit from a more comprehensive special education program than that offered to students with dyslexia. Intelligence tests may be particularly useful in determining that a child with a high IQ score and average performance on reading tests is dyslexic. These are the students who are most likely to be overlooked in schools that have RTI programs and the teacher's attention is directed to low achievement rather than unexpected underachievement. The challenge is to get these students referred by their teachers for evaluation.

Thus far, we have discussed cognitive assessment, deferring to those researchers who classify phonological processing as a cognitive operation. Language assessment has a purpose beyond assessing phonological processing skills when an evaluation team is searching for help for a struggling reader. Documenting strengths or weaknesses in other dimensions of language development (semantics, syntax, pragmatics) influences decisions about the need for speech-language therapy and also influences recommendations for reading instruction focused on comprehension. Language tests are classified as broad or narrow (Wiig, 2001). For struggling readers who do not have a history of speech-language disorders, the evaluation should be broad, followed by narrower testing of particular features of language development as indicated. Of the tests listed in Table 14.3, we have chosen to illustrate a broad language test with the Clinical Evaluation of Language Functions–Fourth Edition (CELF-4; Semel, Wiig, & Secord, 2003) because the evaluation team can proceed from a broad (core) assessment to a narrower focus, if test scores so indicate. Core tests vary depending on the age of the student. For students between 5 and 12 years, core tests that produce a Total Language Score are Concepts and Following Directions, Word Structure (morphology), Recalling Sentences, and Formulated Sentences. If the Total Language Score suggests developmental weakness, eight subtests that further assess receptive and expressive semantics and syntax are used. These subtests

Table 14.3. Language tests

Title	Publisher/web site	Ages	Grades
Clinical Evaluation of Language Functions–Fourth Edition (CELF-4;2003)	Pearson Assessments (http://www .pearsonassessments.com)	5–21 years	—
Comprehensive Assessment of Spoken Language (CASL; 1999)	PRO-ED (http://www.proedinc.com)	3;0 to 21; 11 years	—
Comprehensive Receptive and Expressive Vocabulary Tests–Second Edition (CREVT-2; 2002)	PRO-ED (http://www.proedinc.com)	4;0 to 89; 11 years	—
Comprehensive Test of Phonological Processing (CTOPP; 1999)	PRO-ED (http://www.proedinc.com)	5;0 to 24; 11 years	—
Goldman-Fristoe Test of Articulation–Second Edition (G-FTA-2; 2000)	PRO-ED (http://www.proedinc.com)	2–21 years	—
Lindamood Auditory Conceptualization Test–Third Edition (LAC-3; 2004)	Gander Publications (http://www .ganderpublishing.com)	5;0 to 18; 11 years	—
Oral and Written Language Scales (OWLS; 1995)	PRO-ED (http://www.proedinc.com)	5–21 years	—
Peabody Picture Vocabulary Test–Fourth Edition (PPVT-4; 2007)	Pearson Assessments (http://www .pearsonassessments.com)	2–6 years to more than 90 years	—
Phonological Awareness Test–Second Edition (PAT-2; 2007)	Linguisystems (http://www .Linguisystems.com)	5–9 years	K–4
Test for Auditory Comprehension of Language–Third Edition (TACL-3; 1999)	PRO-ED (http://www.proedinc.com)	3;0 to 9; 11 years	—
Test of Language Competence–Expanded (1989)	Pearson Assessments (http://www .pearsonassessments.com)	L1: 5–9 years; L2: 10–18 years	—
Test of Language Development, Primary–4 (TOLD:P4; 2008)	PRO-ED (http://www.proedinc.com)	4;0 to 8; 11 years	—
Test of Language Development, Intermediate–4 (TOLD:I4; 2007)	PRO-ED (http://www.proedinc.com)	8;0 to 17; 11 years	—
Test of Phonological Awareness–Second Edition: Plus (TOPA-2+; 2004)	PRO-ED (http://www.proedinc.com)	5–8 years	—
Test of Word Knowledge (TOWK; 1992)	Pearson Assessments (http://www .pearsonassessments.com)	5–17 years	—
Yopp-Singer Test of Phoneme Segmentation (informal assessment)	TEAMS Educational Resources (http:// teams.lacoe.edu/reading/assessments/ yopp.html)	—	K–3

produce receptive and expressive language composite scores and four additional composite scores: Language Structure, Language Content, Language Content and Memory, and Working Memory (Digit Span and Repeating Familiar Sequences). CELF-4 also has a group of phonological processing subtests: Phonological Awareness, Rapid Automatic Naming, Digit Span, and Word Associations. Finally, CELF-4 includes Observational Rating Scales for use in school and at home that produce a Pragmatics Profile.

Salvia et al. (2010) gave high ratings to the Test of Language Development: Primary–Fourth Edition (Newcomer & Hammill, 2008) and the Test of Language Development: Intermediate–Fourth Edition (Hammill & Newcomer, 2008). Both tests are included in Table 14.3.

Limited reading practice can have deleterious effects on knowing word meanings. Although achievement tests, reading tests, and general language tests usually include vocabulary measures, a test specifically designed to evaluate vocabulary development may be indicated for some students. The test of choice here is the Test of Word Knowledge (TOWK; Wiig & Secord, 1992), for two reasons. First, it evaluates knowledge of figurative language, conjunctions, and transition words as well as a more general receptive and expressive vocabulary. Students are also asked to give multiple meanings for some words. Second, unlike other popular vocabulary tests that have wide age ranges, TOWK has two levels, one for students between 5 and 8 years and another for students between 8 and 17 years. This means that there are more test items at each age level and, consequently, test scores will be more reliable.

Social-Emotional Status and Attention

With regard to social-emotional status and attention, consider the claim that consequences do not flow directly from the data but from interpretations of the data (Messick, 1984). Data obtained from measures of social-emotional status and attention when evaluating a child struggling to read and spell are particularly difficult to interpret. The point is caution. When you read a diagnostic report that includes assessment in the domains of social-emotional development and attention, be sure to look carefully at the data in the report and study the way members of the evaluation team support their diagnostic conclusions and recommendations with data. The conclusion that a student struggling to read has a primary attention deficit co-occurring with a reading disability leads to different recommendations than the conclusion that the student's documented attention problems are in reaction to a reading disability and will abate as reading improves. Obviously, the way these conclusions are reached is important. (Physicians may have an easier time with distinctions between primary and secondary symptoms, but physicians usually do not participate in evaluations conducted in schools.)

Table 14.4. Assessments of social-emotional status and attention

Title	Publisher/web site	Ages
Manual for the Achenbach System of Empirically Based Assessments (ASEBA) School-Age Form and Profiles (2001)	Burlington: University of Vermont, Department of Psychiatry (http://shop1. mailordercentral.com/aseba/prodinfo .asp?number=505)	6–18 years; self-report component 11–18 years
Behavior Assessment System for Children–Second Edition (BASC-2; 2004)	Pearson Assessments (http://www .pearsonassessments.com)	2–25 years
Brown Attention-Deficit Disorder Scales for Children and Adolescents (2001)	Psychcorp/Pearson Assessments (http:// psychcorp.pearsonassessments.com)	3–7; 8–12; and 12–18 years
Conners' Rating Scales–Revised (2008)	Psychcorp/Pearson Assessments (http:// psychcorp.pearsonassessments.com)	3–17 years; self-report 12–17 years
Attention Deficit Disorders Evaluation Scale–Third Edition (ADDES-3; 1995)	Hawthorne Educational Services (http://www.hawthorne-ed.com)	4–18 years

There are several assessment procedures psychologists and their nonmedical colleagues can use (see Table 14.4). Although some schools use the Connor Rating Scale, we have chosen the Behavior Assessment System for Children–Second Edition (BASC–2; Reynolds & Kamphaus, 2004) because it is comprehensive and includes measures of attention as well as social-emotional status. We have not used this system, nor have we seen reports that include it. We are relying on John Salvia and Jim Ysseldyke's experience and good judgment and base our description on theirs (Salvia et al., 2010).

BASC–2 contains a Teacher Rating Scale, Parent Rating Scale, Self-Report of Personality, Structured Developmental History, and Student Observation System. The Structured Developmental History asks for information about social, psychological, developmental, educational, and medical history and can be used as a questionnaire or in an interview format. The Student Observation System has three components. The first component uses a list of 65 behaviors organized into four categories of positive behavior and nine categories of problem behaviors. Following a 15-minute observation, the observer rates each behavior on a 3-point frequency gradation: *never, sometimes,* or *frequently* observed. The second component asks the observer to decide whether a behavior is present during a 3-second period following a 30-second interval of a 15-minute observation. The third component is completed following the observation of the student. The observer scores the teacher on his or her position in the classroom, use of techniques to change student behavior, and other teacher actions that the observer considered relevant to the assessment of the student.

The Teacher Rating Scale produces three composite scores, two of which represent common clinical categories: Internalizing and Externalizing Problems and School Problems. School Problems are classified as Attention Problems or Learning Problems. Positive behaviors are included in an Adaptive Behavior Composite. The Parent Rating Scale has the same structure as the Teacher Rating Scale. The Self-Report of Personality can be used with students as young as 8 years old. It has four composite scores: Inattention/Hyperactivity, Internalizing Problems, Personal Adjustment, and School Problems.

The Teacher and Parent Rating Scales and the Self-Report of Personality are the only components for which norms have been constructed and, therefore, diagnostic conclusions are confined to these three measures. The psychometric properties of the three components meet the American Psychological Association's standards for tests.

Pulling This Together

Findings from a comprehensive evaluation are organized and interpreted and then presented in a written report, which is used to construct the student's **individualized education program (IEP)** if special education is indicated. Assessment does not stop with placement in special education, however. If the student is in a school using RTI and a standard protocol for Tier 2 instruction, then two instructional programs, one guided by research and one tested through research, have already failed to produce progress learning to read and spell. Recall the NRC panel's claim that special education is not a violation of an individual's civil rights only to the extent that challenging learning goals are set, learning occurs, and learning goals are achieved (Heller et al., 1982; Messick, 1984). Research shows that teachers who incorporate formative assessment into lessons for achieving and struggling readers produce higher scores on reading achievement tests than teachers who do not use formative assessment (Black & Williams, 1998; Strecker, Fuchs, & Fuchs, 2005). If this chapter has a moral message, it is that special education and remedial reading teachers must acquire expertise in the formative assessment of reading, spelling, and writing.

CONCLUDING THOUGHTS

This chapter is about assessments undertaken in educational settings on behalf of individuals who are either not learning to read and write or are at risk for reading failure. The chapter's focus is the interaction between assessment and instruction. To that end, we distinguish between formative and summative assessment and devote more space to formative assessment. Describing RTI within page limits was a challenge. We chose to describe rather than critique. We see RTI as a supplement to, rather than a substitute for, the individual evaluations that, to date, produce the data used to determine eligibility for special education. As a record of learning in well-documented, evidence-based reading programs, RTI is invaluable. We interpret IDEA regulations to allow parents to request a special education evaluation at any time after they have been notified that their child is enrolled in a special reading intervention (RTI).

We are bemused by the fact that a diagnostic practice that was criticized because it wasn't standardized (use of IQ–achievement discrepancy rules) has been superseded by a practice that has many more variables. It is hard to believe that an educational practice as complex as RTI can be standardized to the extent that meaningful hypotheses about diagnostic indicators for any one or more of seven SLDs can emerge and then be tested in well-controlled studies. We juxtaposed the IDEA definition of SLD and the IDA definition of dyslexia for a reason other than giving information to our readers. We hope to show that the SLD definition is the problem and believe that changing diagnostic criteria and procedures without changing the definition will not produce more reliable diagnostic criteria for SLD.

Assessment has so much traction in education in the United States now. When assessment is undertaken to improve instruction, the outcomes are likely to be positive. When tests are used alone to make selection and certification decisions about individuals that cannot easily be reversed, there is reason to be concerned. Because the consequences of assessment can be negative as well as positive, we conclude with two constraints on assessment. People who conduct assessments and give tests strive for objectivity in the data, but data are not necessarily the problem; bias is more likely to occur in interpretations and conclusions drawn from the data (Messick, 1986). Tests produce data but not interpretations. People interpret data, and people, consciously or not, are influenced by their own experiences, values, and opinions. Testing and assessment are not neutral enterprises. Linked to the constraint on the neutrality (objectivity) of interpretations and decisions is the fact that assessment is not a trivial experience. Assessment always carries consequences for the person involved. A single test score can have lifelong consequences, negative or positive. In the same way that special education is valid only if it enhances learning, assessments are valid only to the extent that the consequence for the person is increased opportunity for a productive and satisfying life.

REFERENCES

Adams, M.J. (1990). *Beginning to read: Thinking and learning about print.* Cambridge, MA: The MIT Press.

Batsche, G., Elliott, J., Graden, J.L., Grimes, J., Kovaleski, J.F., Prassee, D. et al. (2005). *Response to intervention: Policy considerations and implementation.* Alexandria, VA: National Association of State Directors of Special Education.

Beaver, J.M. (2005). *Teacher guide: Developmental reading assessment word analysis.* Parsippany, NJ: Pearson Education.

Beaver, J.M. (2006). *Teacher guide: Developmental reading assessment: Grades K–3* (2nd ed.). Parsippany, NJ: Pearson Education.

Beaver, J.M., & Carter, M.A. (2003). *Teacher guide: Developmental reading assessment: Grades 4–8* (2nd ed.). Parsippany, NJ: Pearson Education.

Bergan, J. (1977). *Behavioral consultation.* Columbus, OH: Charles E. Merrill.

Bergan, J., & Kratchowill, T.R. (1990). *Behavioral consultation and therapy.* New York: Plenum Press.

Biancarosa, G., & Snow, C.E. (2006). *Reading next: A vision for action and research in middle and high school literacy. A report to the Carnegie Corporation of New York.* Washington, DC: Alliance for Excellent Education.

Blachman, B.A., & Tangel, D.M. (2000). *Basic language skills.* Bellaire, TX: Neuhaus Education Center.

Blachman, B.A., & Tangel, D.M. (2008). *Road to reading: A program for preventing and remediating reading difficulties.* Baltimore: Paul H. Brookes Publishing Co.

Blachowicz, C.L.Z. (1980). *Blachowicz informal phonics survey.* Unpublished assessment device, National College of Education, Evanston, IL.

Black, P., & Williams, D. (1998). Inside the black box: Raising standards through classroom assessment. *Phi Delta Kappan, 80,* 139–144.

Brown, J.I., Fishco, V.V., & Hanna, G.S. (1993). *The Nelson-Denny Reading Test.* Chicago: Riverside Publishing.

Burns, M.K., Deno, S.L., & Jimerson, S.R. (2007). Toward a unified response-to-intervention model. In S.R. Jimerson, M.K. Burns, & A.M. VanDerHeyden (Eds.), *Handbook of response to intervention: The science and practice of assessment and intervention* (pp. 428–440). New York: Springer.

Callender, W.A. (2007). The Idaho Results-Based Model: Implementing response to intervention statewide. In S.R. Jimerson, M.K. Burns, & A.M. VanDerHeyden (Eds.), *Handbook of response to intervention: The science and practice of assessment and intervention* (pp. 331–342). New York: Springer.

Clay, M.M. (1995). *An observation survey of early literacy attainment* (Rev. ed.). Portsmouth, NH: Heinemann.

Compton, D.L., Fuchs, D., Fuchs, L.S., Elleman, A.M., & Gilbert, J.K. (2008). Tracking children who fly below the radar: Latent transition modeling of students with late-emerging reading disability. *Learning and Individual Differences, 18,* 329–337.

Cortiella, D. (2006). *A parent guide to response to intervention.* Retrieved from http://www.ncld.org/publications-a-more/parent-advocacy-guides/a-parent-guide-to-rti

Cox, A.R. (1986). *Benchmark measures.* Cambridge, MA: Educators Publishing Service.

Cox, A.R. (1992). *Foundations for literacy: Structures and techniques for multisensory teaching of basic written English language skills.* Cambridge, MA: Educators Publishing Service.

Deno, S.L. (1985). Curriculum-based measurement: The emerging alternative. *Exceptional Children, 52,* 219–232.

Denton, C.A., & Vaughn, S. (2010). Preventing and remediating reading difficulties: Perspectives from research. In T.A. Glover & S. Vaughn (Eds.), *The promise of response to intervention: Evaluating current science and practice* (pp. 78–112). New York: Guilford Press.

Donovan, M.S., & Cross, C.T. (2002). *Minority students in special and gifted education.* Washington, DC: National Academies Press.

Education for All Handicapped Children Act of 1975, PL 94-142, 20 U.S.C. §§ 1400 *et seq.*

Education of the Handicapped Act (EHA) of 1970, PL 91-230, 84 Stat. 121-154, 20 U.S.C. §§ 1400 *et seq.*

Ehri, L.C., & McCormick, S. (1998). Phases of word learning: Implications for instruction with delayed and disabled readers. *Reading and Writing Quarterly, 14,* 135–163.

Engelmann, S. (1968). Relating operant techniques to programming and teaching. *Journal of School Psychology, 6*(2), 89–96.

Fletcher, J.M., Lyon, G.R., Fuchs, L.S., & Barnes, M.A. (2007). *Learning disabilities.* New York: Guilford Press.

Fuchs, D., Fuchs L.S., & Compton, D.L. (2004). Identifying reading disabilities by responsiveness-to-instruction: Specifying measures and criteria. *Learning Disability Quarterly, 27,* 216–227.

Fuchs, D., Fuchs, L.S., & Strecker, P.M. (2010, March). The "blurring" of special education in a new continuum of general education placements and services. *Exceptional Children.*

Fuchs, D., Mock, D., Morgan, L.P., & Young, C.L. (2003). Responsiveness-to-intervention: Definitions, evidence, and implications for the learning disabilities construct. *Learning Disabilities Research and Practice, 18,* 157–171.

Fuchs, L.S., & Deno, S.L. (1991). Paradigmatic distinctions between instructionally relevant measurement models. *Exceptional Children, 57,* 488–501.

Fuchs, L.S., & Fuchs, D. (2007). Progress monitoring within a multitiered prevention system. *Perspectives on Language and Literacy, 33*(2), 43–47.

Gersten, R., Compton, D., Connor, C.M., Dimino, J., Santoro, L., Linan-Thompson, S., et al. (2009). *Assisting students struggling with reading: Response to intervention for reading in the primary grades. A practice guide* (NCEE 2009-4043).Washington, DC: U.S. Department of Education, National Center for Educational Evaluation and Regional Assistance, Institute of Educational Sciences. Retrieved August 8, 2010, from http://ies.ed.gov/ncee/wwc/publications/practice guides/

Good, R.H., & Jefferson, G. (1998). Contemporary perspectives on curriculum-based measurement validity. In M.R. Shinn (Ed.), *Advanced applications of curriculum-based measurement* (pp. 61–88). New York: Guilford Press.

Good, R.H., & Kaminski, R.A. (Eds.). (2002). *Dynamic Indicators of Basic Literacy Skills–Sixth Edition.* Eugene, OR: Institute for Development of Educational Achievement.

Good, R.H., Kaminski, R.A., Cummings, K., Dufour-Martel, C., Petersen K., Powell-Smith, K., et al. (2011). *DIBELS Next.* Longmont, CO: Sopris West Educational Services.

Gresham, F.M. (2007). Evolution of the response-to-intervention concept: Foundations and recent developments. In S.E. Jimerson, M.K. Burns, & A.M. VanDerHeyden (Eds.), *Handbook of response to intervention: The science and practice of assessment and intervention* (pp. 10–24). New York: Springer.

Hammill, D.D., & Larsen, S. (2008). *Examiner's manual for the Test of Written Language–Fourth Edition.* Austin, TX: PRO-ED.

Hammill, D.D., & Newcomer, P. L. (2008). *Test of Language Development-Intermediate* (4th ed.). Austin, TX: PRO-ED.

Hasbrouck, J., & Tindal, G. (2006). Oral reading fluency norms: A valuable assessment tool for reading teachers. *The Reading Teacher, 59*(7), 636–644.

Heller, K.A., Holtzman, W.H., & Messick, S. (Eds.). (1982). *Placing children in special education: A strategy for equity.* Washington, DC: National Academies Press.

Individuals with Disabilities Education Improvement Act (IDEA) of 2004, PL 108-446, 20 U.S.C. §§ 1400 *et seq.*

Ikeda, M.J., Rahn-Blakeslee, A., Niebling, B.C., Gustafson, J.K., Allison, R., & Stumme, J. (2007). The Heartland Area Education Agency 11 problem solving approach: An overview and lessons learned. In S.R. Jimerson, M.K. Burns, & A.M. VanDerHeyden (Eds.), *Handbook of response to intervention: The science and practice of assessment and intervention* (pp. 255–268). New York: Springer.

Invernizzi, M., Juel, C., Swank, L., & Meier, C. (2003). *Phonological Awareness Literacy Screening: Kindergarten (PALS-K).* Charlottesville: University of Virginia.

Invernizzi, M., Meier, J., & Juel, C. (2002). *Phonological Awareness Literacy Screening 1-3* (PALS 1-3). Charlottesville: University of Virginia.

Invernizzi, M., Sullivan, A., & Meier, J. (2001). *Phonological Awareness Literacy Screening: Prekindergarten (PALS-PreK).* Charlottesville: University of Virginia.

Jenkins, J.R. (2009). Measuring reading growth: New findings on progress monitoring (PM). *New Times for Division of Learning Disabilities, 27*(1), 1–2.

Jenkins, J.R., Hudson, R.F., & Lee, S.H. (2007). Using CBM-reading assessments to monitor progress. *Perspectives on Language and Literacy, 33*(2), 11–16.

Johnson, E., Mellard, D.F., Fuchs, D., & McKnight, M.A. (2006). *Responsiveness to intervention (RTI): How to do it.* Lawrence, KS: National Center on Learning Disabilities.

Johnson, E.S., & Pool, J.L. (2009). *Screening for reading problems in grades 4–12.* Retrieved January, 24, 2010, from http://www.rtinetwork.org

Koretz, D. (2008). *Measuring up: What educational testing really tells us.* Cambridge, MA: Harvard University Press.

Kovaleski, J.F., & Black, L. (2010). Multi-tier service delivery: Current status and future directions. In T.A. Glover & S. Vaughn (Eds.), *The promise of response to intervention: Evaluating current science and practice* (pp. 23–56). New York: Guilford Press.

Leslie, L., & Caldwell, J. (2010). *Qualitative Reading Inventory–Fifth Edition.* Boston: Allyn & Bacon.

Lindsley, O.R. (1991). Precision teaching's unique legacy from B.F. Skinner. *Journal of Behavioral Education, 1*(2), 253–266.

Lyon, G.R., & Chhabra, V. (2004). The science of reading research. *Educational Leadership, 61*(6), 12–17.

Lyon, G.R., Shaywitz, S.E., & Shaywitz, B.A. (2003). A definition of dyslexia. *Annals of Dyslexia, 53,* 1–14.

Masterson, J.J., Apel, K., & Wasowicz, J. (2006). *Spelling Performance Evaluation for Language and Literacy–Second Edition* [Computer software]. Evanston, IL: Learning By Design.

McCardle, P., & Chhabra, V. (Eds.). (2004). *The voice of evidence in reading research.* Baltimore: Paul H. Brookes Publishing Co.

Messick, S. (1984). Assessment in context: Appraising student performance in relation to instructional quality. *Educational Researcher, 13*(3), 3–8.

Messick, S. (1986). Test validity and the ethics of assessment. *American Psychologist, 35,* 1012–1027.

Moats, L.C. (1995). *Spelling: Development, disability, and instruction.* Timonium, MD: York Press.

Morsy, AL., Kieffer, M., & Snow, C. (2010). *Measure for measure: A critical consumers' guide to reading comprehension assessments for adolescents.* New York: Carnegie Corporation of New York.

Mosely, D.V. (1997). Assessment of spelling and related aspects of written expression. In J.R. Beech & C. Singleton (Eds.), *The psychological assessment of reading* (pp. 204–223). London: Routledge.

National Institute of Child Health and Human Development. (2000). *Report of the National Reading Panel: Reports of the subgroups. Teaching children to read: An evidence-based assessment of the scientific research literature on reading and its implications for reading instruction* (NIH Publication No. 00-4754). Washington, DC: Government Printing Office.

Newcomer, P.L., & Hammill, D.D. (2008). *Test of Language Development–Primary* (4th ed.). Austin, TX: PRO-ED.

No Child Left Behind Act of 2001, PL 107-110, 115 Stat. 1425, 20 U.S.C. §§ 6301 *et seq.*

Reed, D., & Vaughn, S. (2010). Reading interventions for older students. In T.A. Glover & S. Vaughn (Eds.), *The promise of response to intervention: Evaluating current science and practice* (pp. 143–186). New York: Guilford Press.

Reynolds, C.R. (2008). RTI, neuroscience, and sense: Chaos in the diagnosis and treatment of learning disabilities. In E. Fletcher-Janzen & C.R. Reynolds (Eds.), *Neuropsychological perspectives on learning disabilities in the era of RTI: Recommendations for diagnosis and intervention* (pp. 14–27). New York: Wiley.

Reynolds, C.R., & Kamphaus, R.W. (2004). *Behavior Assessment System for Children Manual* (2nd ed.). Circle Pines, MN: American Guidance Service.

Rumsey, M.B. (1992). *Dyslexia training program progress measurements* (Schedules I–III). Cambridge, MA: Educators Publishing Service.

Salvia, J., & Ysseldyke, J. (1998). *Assessment* (7th ed.). Boston: Houghton Mifflin.

Salvia, J., Ysseldyke, J., & Bolt, S. (2010). *Assessment in special and inclusive education* (11th ed.). Belmont, CA: Wadsworth.

Scarborough, H.S. (1998). Early identification of children at risk for reading disabilities: Phonological awareness and some other promising predictors. In B.K. Shapiro, P.J. Accardo, & A.J. Capute (Eds.), *Specific reading disability: A view of the spectrum* (pp. 75–120). Timonium, MD: York Press.

Semel, E., Wiig, E.H., & Secord, W.A. (2003). *Clinical Evaluation of Language Fundamentals–Fourth Edition*. San Antonio, TX: The Psychological Corporation.

Shaywitz, S. (2003). *Overcoming dyslexia: A new and complete science-based program for reading problems at any level*. New York: Alfred A. Knopf.

Shinn, M.R., & Bamonto, S. (1998). Advanced applications of curriculum-based measurement: "Big ideas" and avoiding confusion. In M.R. Shinn (Ed.), *Advanced application of curriculum-based measurement* (pp. 1–31). New York: Guilford Press.

Smartt, S.M., & Glaser, D.R. (2010). *Next STEPS in literacy instruction: Connecting assessments to effective interventions*. Baltimore: Paul H. Brookes Publishing Co.

Speece, D.L., Case, L.P., & Molloy, D.E. (2003). Responsiveness to general education instruction as the first gate to learning disabilities identification. *Learning Disabilities Research to Practice, 18,* 147–156.

Strecker, P.M., Fuchs, L.S., & Fuchs, D. (2005). Using curriculum-based measurement to improve student achievement: Review of research. *Psychology in the Schools, 4*(8), 795–818.

Swanson, H.L., Hoskyn, M., & Lee, C. (1999). *Interventions for students with learning disabilities: A meta-analysis of treatment outcomes*. New York: Guilford Press.

Texas Education Agency. (2010a). *Intervention activities guide*. Baltimore: Paul H. Brookes Publishing Co.

Texas Education Agency. (2010b). *TPRI*. Baltimore: Paul H. Brookes Publishing Co.

Texas Education Agency. (2011). *Tejas LEE*. Baltimore: Paul H. Brookes Publishing Co.

Torgesen, J.K. (1998, Spring/Summer). Catch them before they fall: Identification and assessment to prevent reading failure in young children. *American Educator,* 1–8.

Torgesen, J.K. (2002). The prevention of reading difficulties. *Journal of School Psychology, 40*(1), 7–26.

Torgesen, J.K. (2006). *A comprehensive K–3 reading assessment plan: Guidance for school leaders*. Portsmouth, NH. RMC Research Corporation.

Torgesen, J.K., & Burgess, S.R. (1998). Consistency of reading-related phonological processes throughout early childhood: Evidence from longitudinal-correlational and instructional studies. In J. Metsala & L. Ehri (Eds.), *Word recognition in beginning literacy* (pp. 161–188). Mahwah, NJ: Lawrence Erlbaum Associates.

Torgesen, J.K., & Miller, D.H. (2009). *Assessments to guide adolescent literacy*. Portsmouth, NH: RMC Research Corporation.

Treiman, R. (1998). Why spelling? The benefits of incorporating spelling into beginning reading instruction. In J.L. Metsala & L.C. Ehri (Eds.), *Word recognition in beginning literacy* (pp. 289–313). Mahwah, NJ: Lawrence Erlbaum Associates.

Uhry, J.K., & Clark, D.B. (2005). *Dyslexia: Theory and practice of remedial instruction* (3rd ed.). Timonium, MD: York Press.

U.S. Department of Education. (August 14, 2006). Assistance to states for the education of children with disabilities: Final rule. *Federal Register, Part II, 34 CFR parts 300 and 301, 71*(156). Washington, DC: Author.

Vaughn, S., & Fuchs, L.S. (2003). Redefining learning disabilities as inadequate response to intervention: The promise and potential problems. *Learning Disabilities Research and Practice, 18,* 137–146.

Wagner, R.K., Torgesen, J.K., & Rashotte, C.A. (1999). *Comprehensive Test of Phonological Processing*. Austin, TX: PRO-ED.

Wanzek, J., & Vaughn, S. (2010). Research-based interventions from extensive early reading interventions. In T.A. Glover & S. Vaughn (Eds.), *The promise of responsiveness to intervention: Evaluating current science and practice* (pp. 113–142). New York: Guilford Press.

Wiederholt, J.L., & Bryant, B.R. (2001). *Gray Oral Reading Test–Fourth Edition*. Austin, TX: PRO-ED.

Wiig, E.H. (2001). Multi-perspective, clinical-educational assessments of language disorders. In A.S. Kaufman & N. Kaufman (Eds.), *Specific learning disabilities and difficulties in children and adolescents: Psychological assessment and evaluation* (pp. 247–279). Cambridge, UK: Cambridge University Press.

Wiig, E.H., & Secord, W.A. (1992). *Test of Word Knowledge*. San Antonio, TX: The Psychological Corporation.

Wilson, B. (1996). *Wilson Reading System instructor manual* (3rd ed.). Oxford, MA: Wilson Language Training.

Wilson, B., & Felton, R. (2004). *Word Identification and Spelling Test*. Austin, TX: PRO-ED.

Woodcock, R.W., Schrank, F.A., McGrew, K.S., & Mather, N. (2007). *Woodcock-Johnson- III Normative Update: Tests of Cognitive Abilities and Tests of Achievement*. Itasca, IL: Riverside.

Woods, M.L., & Moe, A. (2010). *Analytic reading inventory: Comprehensive standards-based assessment for all students including gifted and remedial* (9th ed.). Upper Saddle River, NJ: Prentice Hall.

Yell, M., Shriner, J.G., & Katsiyannis, A. (2006). Individuals with Disabilities Education Act of 2005 and IDEA regulations of 2006: Implications for educators, administrators, and teacher trainers. *Focus on Exceptional Children, 39*(1), 1–24.

Ysseldyke, J.E., & McLeod, S. (2007). Using technology tools to monitor response to intervention. In S.R. Jimerson, M.K. Burns, & A.M. VanDerHeyden (Eds.) *Handbook of response to intervention: The science and practice of assessment and intervention* (pp. 397–407). New York: Springer.

15

Planning Multisensory Structured Language Lessons and the Classroom Environment

JUDITH R. BIRSH AND JEAN SCHEDLER

Lesson planning designed for intervention and remediation is at the heart of multisensory structured language education (MSLE). The first section of this chapter describes the steps in planning multisensory structured language lessons for one-to-one instruction and for both small and large groups. Equally essential to students is a classroom environment that is conducive to learning and teachers who are well prepared to implement MSLE instructional goals. The second section of this chapter covers the essentials of creating a good classroom environment—the physical space, ways to organize and maintain materials, and student behavior.

The need to effectively teach literacy is firmly supported by research. In addition, the Individuals with Disabilities Education Improvement Act (IDEA) of 2004 (PL 108-446) makes clear the critical role of instruction for preventing and identifying learning disabilities with the incorporation of response to intervention (RTI). The previous chapters have provided this ample evidence and the literacy content to be taught. The essential content of literacy instruction (cognitive and linguistic) is well established based on converging scientific evidence since the 1980s (National Institute of Child Health and Human Development [NICHD], 2000).

Now the expertise for melding the specific instructional elements and the teaching techniques into lessons that have a lasting effect on accelerating growth in skills and strategies is of the utmost importance. This chapter addresses how to plan and organize lessons that contain all the elements for building literacy, coupled with ongoing monitoring of progress and sensitivity to differentiating instruction to meet the needs of individual students. Here is where research on what to teach, clinical experience, and intensive teacher preparation come together.

The context for MSLE arises from the imperative to provide reading programs for students for whom modifications in regular classroom programs have not worked. Some have been identified through RTI monitoring and others, failing to thrive in Tier 3 or its equivalent, have had comprehensive individual evaluations of cognitive and academic performance with resulting specific recommendations for multisensory language instruction.

We will begin with a brief history of the development of the multisensory structured lesson plan, based on the work of Anna Gillingham and Bessie Stillman in the 1930s and 1940s. Next, planning multisensory structured language lessons shows how to bring together the language concepts with how to teach them according to research-based principles of learning and instruction. Then, research that supports systematic instruction will be considered as it applies to carrying out instruction based on MSLE. Following that, we will describe how both teachers and students benefit from precisely planned lessons. Next, we will explore the advantages of the multisensory structured lesson plan that benefit both teacher and students. There are sample lesson plans in the last part of this section to demonstrate how all of the levels of language can be combined into an integrated whole for introducing new concepts, providing opportunities for guided practice, and reviewing while intensely focusing on students' most essential needs to accelerate their learning. Underpinning these lessons is the positive belief that these students will be successful due to their teachers' relentless dedication and informed instruction.

THE ORTON-GILLINGHAM APPROACH: HISTORY AND EVOLUTION

The plan for an MSLE lesson includes a specific order of activities taught for a pre-arranged period of time so that all components of the structure of language are included each time the teacher meets with students. Conscious multisensory procedures using the student's eyes, ears, hands, and mouth help to link the sound, sight, and feel of the spoken language to the printed language on the page.

The history of lesson planning for MSLE and how it evolved from the original Orton-Gillingham approach provides a solid background for expert teachers (Gillingham & Stillman, 1956, 1997). The Orton-Gillingham approach to remedial instruction began in the 1930s when Anna Gillingham and Bessie Stillman collaborated to develop remedial techniques based on Dr. Samuel T. Orton's neurological explanation for language learning disabilities (Orton, 1937). Dr. Orton's approach was derived from his neuropsychiatric background and his case studies of children whose individual learning differences and instructional needs did not match the sight word method reading curriculum then being used in the traditional classroom (Henry & Brickley, 1999).

In 1932, Dr. Orton appointed Anna Gillingham, an experienced psychologist at the Ethical Culture School in New York, as a research fellow in language disabilities at the Language Research Project of the New York Neurological Institute. Gillingham had recognized and worked with bright children with academic problems for many years.

She and Bessie Stillman, a gifted teacher, researched ways to organize remedial techniques to meet the unique needs of students who were struggling to read and spell. The understanding that "such children present a challenge which customary teacher-training does not enable the teacher to meet" (Gillingham & Stillman, 1956, p. 1) fueled their efforts. What emerged from their meticulous work with students and teachers was a system of teaching language-related skills incorporating letter sounds, syllables, words, sentences, and writing contained within a daily lesson plan in which all aspects of the alphabetic phonetic approach to reading and spelling were detailed.

The instruction was to be direct, explicit, sequenced, systematic, cumulative, and intensive. In contrast to the sight word method prevalent at the time, their technique was based on the close association of visual, auditory, and kinesthetic elements to teach the phonetic units step by step. Teaching was responsive and intensive, with many opportunities for corrective feedback as each element was taught and practiced.

These basic multisensory teaching techniques to remediate reading problems are still used today, with some adaptations (Gillingham & Stillman, 1997; International Dyslexia Association [n.d.]); see the Chapter 1 section in Appendix B). What has evolved over time is the essence of the MSLE lesson, which is now consistent with the effort to implement evidence-based instructional approaches to assist struggling readers (see Chapter 2).

All MSLE programs rely on these important instructional design principles for diverse learners. Some examples of programs developed from the original Orton-Gillingham multisensory approach are: Slingerland, Spalding, Alphabetic Phonics, Multisensory Teaching Approach, Sonday System, LANGUAGE!, and Project Read (see the Chapter 8 section in Appendix B for information on how to obtain these curricula).

PLANNING MULTISENSORY STRUCTURED LANGUAGE LESSONS

Other chapters in this book describe the linguistic components of MSLE, such as phonology and phonological awareness (Chapter 5), alphabet and letter knowledge (Chapter 6), handwriting (Chapter 7), reading (Chapter 8), spelling (Chapter 9), Fluency (Chapter 10), vocabulary (Chapter 11), comprehension (Chapter 12), composition (Chapter 13), and assessment (Chapter 14). Structured lesson planning supports and integrates these components, giving the teacher the framework to deliver the systematic sequence of the individualized curriculum the students need to master. Lesson planning brings together "the content to be taught, the most effective way to teach it and the principles of learning and instruction" (Spalding, 2003, p. 193).

This section first highlights common features of various MSLE curricula. Then, it discusses the rationale and research support for structured lesson planning. The following section enumerates the benefits of planning MSLE lessons for teachers and students. Last, implementing lesson planning through a variety of planning strategies is presented. Through the sample lessons, teachers have the opportunity to examine varied levels of lesson planning for MSLE. Beginning teachers may find the sample lesson plans particularly useful.

Language Concepts and Common Features of MSLE Curricula

Discrete components of language are included in daily MSLE lesson plans to build the associations necessary for successful reading, spelling, and writing. The discrete components of language are modified for each student or group and for different levels of instruction. Not all components appear every day; they are rotated through the weekly lesson plans to help students establish mastery across the linguistic concepts. The list that follows is an amalgam of language lesson components derived from accredited teacher education programs:

- Alphabet sequence and letter recognition and naming
- Phonemic awareness activities

- Reviewing sound–symbol associations learned in previous lessons using letter decks, and reviewing letter clusters, using cards and key words to aid memory

- Spelling these same sounds to integrate reading and spelling

- Introducing new sounds and language concepts and/or reviewing previously introduced concepts for reading and spelling

- Reading phonetically regular words in lists and sentences with letter patterns already taught and developing automatic recognition of high-frequency sight words to build automaticity

- Vocabulary study

- Reading connected, controlled, and/or decodable text to develop fluency

- Spelling and writing words and sentences from dictation using words from reading practice

- Handwriting practice, with explicit instructions in letter formation

- Comprehension and listening strategies for use with connected text

- Oral language practice and written composition

It is necessary for these discrete components of language to be incorporated into lesson planning (see Chapter 1, Figure 1.3).

Research-Based Principles of Learning and Instruction

During 10 years of research on 1,000 students with dyslexia, the Texas Scottish Rite Hospital in Dallas developed a way to integrate these elements in a lesson plan to facilitate learning. From the research, certain elements were shown to be essential to successfully teaching students (Cox, 1984). One element is a daily lesson plan that follows a set format. Cox suggested four types of structure that are essential in the remediation of language-related skills:

1. Ordered daily presentation of activities and materials

2. Precise steps in procedures

3. Rapid rotation of activities

4. Periodic measurement of progress (Cox, 1984, p. 35)

The lesson activities are short and focused, with small steps taken in sequence, at first easy and then more difficult. The principles of instruction include multisensory presentation of each component of the lesson using visual, auditory, and tactile/kinesthetic cues. The simultaneous presentation through these modalities within the daily structure of the lesson plan ensures learning.

Structured lessons allow a systematic presentation of concepts based on the order established by Gillingham and Stillman. Three major components are always present: reviewing what has been learned, introducing new material, and scaffolding practice in a controlled environment. In summary, common features of MSLE curriculum include integration/inclusion of discrete components of language and lesson activities that are short, focused, and sequenced with multisensory presentation and follow a systematic presentation of concepts from simple to complex.

Rationale and Research Support for MSLE Lesson Planning

The rationale for the MSLE lesson plan is based mainly on clinical experience. Since the 1980s, however, research in reading development and reading disabilities has influenced the creation and organization of the content of sequential language programs and materials needed for the variety of activities incorporated in MSLE lessons. For example, many programs include specific activities for developing phonemic awareness (e.g., *Wilson's Fundations*, *Read Naturally*).

Research in general education has shown that effective teachers are those who specify their objectives in detailed lesson plans. In working with students with learning difficulties, it is crucial that students have interventions that are carefully constructed based on known components that influence remediation outcomes. Structured lesson planning is the opposite of incidental learning. It plans for deliberate, conscious attention to all components of language, from phonemes to written text (Tucker, 2003; see Chapter 2).

Research that Supports Systematic Instruction

Until the 2000s, there was neither research that offered evidence on how to teach the most deeply struggling readers nor research on lesson planning for intensive reading intervention incorporating all of the language components in a single lesson. The same common hallmarks of skillful teaching of literacy subskills established by the Orton-Gillingham approach are now supported by research. Instruction for struggling readers must be direct, explicit, sequenced, systematic, cumulative, and intensive (Gersten et al., 2008).

Direct, Explicit, Sequenced

It is important to understand what is meant by direct, explicit, and sequenced when applied to effective teaching, especially for students who continue to struggle with reading at any level. To be *direct* means to say or define what students are going to learn and why. *Explicit* teaching is marked by stating concepts clearly and leaving no room for confusion or doubt. Teaching *sequentially* is learning language concepts in a logical order from the most simple concepts to the more complex and then taking each concept from reading to spelling and then into comprehension and writing.

Systematic, Cumulative, Intensive

Systematic lessons adhere to a fixed plan or method and are easily depended on by the student. The outcome of this kind of instruction is that students gain knowledge of the language and how it works *cumulatively*. Each new piece of information is carefully and successively added over time and reinforced by practice and review. *Intensive* instruction often occurs daily for an extended period of time and focuses on specific components of reading proficiency for students who need extra time to develop them, often on a one-to-one basis including extensive practice and high-quality feedback (Gersten et al., 2008). What is a priority depends on what students need to know based on a good assessment and ongoing progress monitoring (see Chapter 14).

There is a validated reason for everything that is included in each lesson. Researchers have pinpointed components essential for reading instruction—phonemic awareness, alphabetic code, fluency, vocabulary, and comprehension (NICHD, 2000)—

and others include spelling and writing as well (Moats, 2010). The panel in Gersten et al. (2008) recommended in their What Works Clearinghouse practice guide, based on small scale intervention studies, that lessons for the most challenged readers contain a few targeted reading skills, and that the instructional pace reflects a focus on short introductions, with various ways to review and practice. In addition, they recommended extended time for one-on-one instruction, with active learning on the part of the student and high-quality feedback from the teacher. These students require a lot of support and carefully scaffolded instruction based on progress monitoring—going from easy to difficult while also ensuring that the students master the skill or strategy before moving on. Although there is not yet sufficient evidence through rigorous studies, Fletcher, Lyon, Fuchs, and Barnes (2007) suggested that the effectiveness of the multisensory approaches may come from "the intense, systematic approach to instruction, the link with specific types of struggling readers, and possibly the explicit attention to the structure of language" (p. 153).

Pashler et al. (2007) reported that research studies show when students engage in recalling information, it strengthens their memory and allows that information to be retrieved later. In addition, spacing learning over time can help to improve students' ability to keep content material in their memory, especially when it is carefully introduced, revisited with specific assignments, and recalled several weeks or months after the original introduction. Although these recommendations come from research in teaching math, foreign languages, and history, these tenets of review and spacing learning over time have always been embedded in the MSLE lessons described here. This would be an area calling for research specific to MSLE lessons.

Swanson (1999) concluded in an extension of an earlier meta-analysis (Swanson & Hoskyn, 1998) that using nine key instructional components (see Table 15.1) is the most effective treatment outcome for students with learning disabilities (including dyslexia). Structured lesson planning supports and deliberately integrates these components, thus giving the teacher a scaffold on which to build the sequence of the individualized curriculum for the students to master.

Furthermore, after a thorough review of reading remediation studies and programs for deeply struggling readers, Fletcher et al. reported a critical finding, "programs that are explicit, oriented to academic content, teach to mastery, provide scaffolding and emotional support, and monitor progress are particularly effective" (2007, p. 161). Teachers and students both benefit from the explicit systematic approach but for different reasons, which are discussed in the following sections.

TEACHERS BENEFIT FROM PLANNING MSLE LESSONS

Structured lesson planning ensures that teachers include

> All levels of language in the same instructional session: the sub word level (phonological awareness, letter formation and orthographic awareness); the word level (multiple strategies for connecting spoken and written words while spelling); and [the] text level (constructing sentences and discourse). (Berninger, 1999, p. 20)

A typical MSLE lesson follows this pattern:

- Review of sounds and letters previously taught

- Phonemic awareness activities at appropriate levels incorporated

- Systematic review of words for oral reading

Table 15.1.   Effective instructional components for students with learning disabilities

Sequencing

Breaking down the task, fading of prompts or cues, sequencing short activities, and step-by-step prompts

Drill (repetition) and practice (review)

Daily testing of skills (e.g., statements in the lesson plan relating to master criteria, distributed review and practice, redundant materials or texts, repeated practice, sequenced review, daily feedback, and/or weekly review)

Segmentation

Breaking down the targeted skill into smaller, step-by-step sequences and then synthesizing the parts into a whole

Directed questioning and responses

The teacher verbally asking process- and/or content-related questions of students and engaging in dialogue with students

Controlled difficulty of processing demands of a task

Tasks sequenced from easy to difficult, with only necessary hints and probes provided; short activities with the level of difficulty controlled (the teacher provides the necessary assistance and a simplified model; teacher and students discuss task analysis)

Technology

Use of a computer, structured text, flowcharts, a structured curriculum, pictorial representations, specific or structured material, and/or media to facilitate presentation and feedback

Group instruction

Instruction that occurs in a small group, with students and/or the teacher interacting within the group

Supplement to teacher and peer involvement

Homework, parent involvement, or others supplements to assist instruction

Strategy cues

Reminders to use strategies or multiple steps (the teacher verbalizes problem solving with think-aloud models and presents benefits of using strategies or procedures)

Learning Disabilities Research and Practice, Swanson, H.L. 1999 © John Wiley & Sons, Inc. Reproduced with permission of Blackwell Publishing Ltd.

- Words incorporated into separately read sentences and short paragraphs of connected text based on what has been taught

- Spelling words from dictation that reflect the same letter patterns

- New concepts carefully introduced and linked to students' prior knowledge through **discovery learning**

- Handwriting integrated deliberately to help reinforce the memory for letter sounds and forms and to stress automaticity and legibility of writing

- Oral reading of narrative and expository texts using appropriate materials with an emphasis on accuracy and fluency

- Activities for comprehension strategies and composition

- Direct instruction of vocabulary development

Program fidelity can be addressed in this cyclical teaching format. Expert teacher preparation and supportive mentoring ensure that everything is taught cumulatively to build the concepts for reading and spelling one step at a time. In summary, a lesson plan for MSLE ensures a comprehensive presentation in which all components of language are practiced and reviewed systematically in tightly focused, deliberately paced, intensive lessons. See Table 15.2 for a summary of lesson planning benefits for both teachers and students.

Opportunities for Multisensory Learning

The opportunity to incorporate many instances of multisensory instruction is inherent in planning an MSLE lesson (see Chapter 2). During the review sections, teachers use simultaneous visual, auditory, and kinesthetic/tactile activities to reinforce concepts developed earlier in the lesson by doing, which ensures that all pathways to learning are engaged in every lesson. For example, cards with individual letters and letter clusters printed on them are displayed to the students, who say and hear the letter names and sounds. The teacher dictates sounds, and the students say and write the letters, often naming a key word as well. Students trace and copy new letters that they are learning using a variety of materials and surfaces, including writing in the air. During practice activities, students segment spoken words into phonemes for spelling and tap out syllables or divide written words into syllables with markers to aid reading. Students often use special diacritical markings for vowels, consonants, prefixes, and suffixes to highlight their importance. Because of the variety of modalities and media and the consistency of the approach, teachers experience enthusiastic interaction with their students. What emerges are increased interactive opportunities for students' responses in each lesson as they see, hear, say, and trace the letters, syllables, morphemes, and words in lists and decodable texts. Moats observes, "All of these active techniques require the learner to select, classify, and consciously manipulate sounds and letters so that more thorough word learning occurs" (2010, p. 209). Carefully constructed lesson plans for MSLE help teachers establish a high level of communication with their students.

Diagnostic and Prescriptive Instruction for Struggling Readers

For the student who has failed to derive benefit from a research-based core reading program, the professional educator applies **diagnostic and prescriptive instruction** based on formal and informal assessment data (see Chapter 14). The child's progress needs to be monitored on an ongoing basis according to a plan developed by the learning team. A lesson plan is built on a scope and sequence of an MSLE curriculum, as well as prior testing of the students. It outlines or covers the material, concepts, and ideas that the instructor intends to discuss or teach during an instructional period. The format and

Table 15.2. Benefits of lesson planning

For teachers	For students
All levels of language incorporated in same instructional period	Structure and consistency to each lesson
Multisensory learning provides many student responses and teacher feedback opportunities	Active participation within a daily prescribed order helps keep focus on building skills
Diagnostic and prescriptive approach allows adaptation and differentiation for student learning	Charts for visual reminders and manipulatives to prompt strategies using all sensory systems
Use of well-defined scope and sequence of language concepts	Integration of skills learned and connection of new learning to acquired skills
Lesson plans help organize skills, materials, and presentation	Consistency and structure promotes student organization
Appropriate pacing with short intervals of intensive instruction	Time to review and practice what they are learning

content of a lesson plan is as diverse and varied as the administrative requirements, the curriculum, and the individual instructor's judgment of the needs of the student.

In order for a tutor/teacher/professional to develop an effective lesson plan, he or she needs to be familiar with the intervention, the student, and how to develop a lesson plan that is sensitive to the student's needs.

So often, a lesson plan captures merely the curriculum to be imparted. With RTI, teachers are now held accountable for what a student learns, rather than what curriculum has been imparted. Student progress is monitored, sometimes on a weekly basis. If a student is not deriving benefit from the intervention, then the teacher explores what needs to be done differently. The daily intervention lesson plans are the framework on which to record and make changes.

Each daily lesson plan contains the specific areas to be addressed: the discrete skills to be learned, skills to be reviewed, and skills to be linked and integrated are clearly indicated. As each component is interactively delivered, the teacher diagnoses the individual student's level of mastery as well as applying, integrating, and prescribing instruction for the next day.

RTI-related research is beginning to explore the importance of student engagement and student response opportunities (Blackwell & McLaughlin, 2005) related to improved academic performance. An MSLE lesson maximizes a student's response opportunities. A response opportunity is measured or counted by each opportunity a student has to see it, hear it, say it, and touch/trace it.

Very little (if any) teacher training is provided regarding writing effective lesson plans; although writing, implementing, and using lesson plans diagnostically and prescriptively is an assumed core component in the RTI model. Intrinsic to a well-written and appropriately delivered lesson plan are multiple student response opportunities throughout the lesson. It is only through the student responses that a professional is able to diagnose and then prescribe how to proceed.

There is a long and time-tested clinical approach described here, however, for **diagnostic** and **prescriptive** instruction that can be used successfully to answer important questions about your teaching. How do you know when to reteach a rule or model an application of a strategy? MSLE lessons are meant to be flexible and diagnostically attuned to students' needs and learning rate on a daily basis. The diagnostic part of the lessons occurs while the students are engaged in the discrete components of the lesson. The teacher is constantly observing and noting how students are handling the lesson components. When students are having difficulties, teachers can ask themselves whether they have taught the subskills necessary for students to complete the activity, whether it is necessary to reintroduce the concept, or whether the strategy for comprehending text is clear to the student. The prescriptive part of the lessons entails the changes the teacher makes to tailor the lessons for more practice, review, application, integration, and/or multisensory activities. Lesson planning gives the teacher a concrete way to analyze where the students' learning gaps are and what needs to be included in instruction. The lesson plan is sensitive to the ages of the students, their levels of skill, and the time and space allotted for instruction. When planning lessons for each student or group of students, the teacher keeps long-term goals in mind with regard to the scope and sequence of the curriculum. This road map for instruction tells the teacher where he or she is going with the students, but the teacher must decide how to get there and how fast to go (Tucker, 2003).

Two important sources of data influence the planning involved: data from informal curriculum-based probes given frequently to monitor progress and data from formal testing (see Chapter 14). Frequent informal assessment is needed to determine how much review to build into lessons, how often to review material taught in the past, when to introduce the next concepts, and what multisensory components of the lessons are most effective for the students.

To aid planning, the daily lesson plan has a column for notes. At the end of each lesson, the teacher writes down any significant needs for future lessons. When a teacher has a busy schedule, it is easy to forget that the 10:00 a.m. students need more practice on a certain activity or that he or she did not remember to make a certain point about a new concept that was introduced to the 2:00 p.m. group. When the teacher is making plans for the next week, the notes column of the lesson plan serves as a record of concepts that can be built into the lessons. It is helpful to document what was especially effective as well as note details of presentations that did not have the planned impact.

Because the lessons are clearly demarcated into discrete language components, as discussed previously, the teacher can observe where students' strengths and weaknesses are and can monitor and adjust the instruction from day to day. He or she can allow for uneven development of knowledge and skills by offering different levels of practice activities for each component (Tucker, 2003). For example, it is not unusual for a student to master the ability to read closed syllables with short-vowel sounds before mastering the ability to spell them. This is an opportunity to repeat material already presented in the spelling section until students master it. The lesson format also acts as a blueprint for task analysis so that student knowledge and skills can be monitored and built gradually and consistently toward automaticity.

There is another helpful adjunct to lesson planning. By keeping careful records—for example, by charting words and language concepts the student knows—the teacher has a ready reference to report current progress directly to the students themselves, as well as to parents and caregivers. This is a way for the teacher to be accountable and have evidence of gains and areas of weakness to address in ongoing future sessions.

Well-Defined Scope and Sequence of Language Concepts

MSLE is based on teachers using a well-defined scope and sequence so that there is systematic introduction of new information in small steps for the precise teaching of skills. This feature of MSLE programs affords the opportunity for guided discovery through Socratic questioning to learn new language concepts based on what the student already knows. As Carreker noted in Chapter 8, "Guided discovery teaching uses the Socratic method of asking questions to lead students to discover new information. When students make a discovery, they understand and connect the new learning to prior knowledge." Many programs also have students organize this information in language notebooks, categorized into subsections, for ready reference and a record of their learning. In this way, the learning strategies are made conspicuous as each concept is developed.

Scaffolding and feedback continuously occur during the lessons. The choice of new material to introduce and the number and choice of words to spell can be tailored to what students can learn easily. Similarly, the teacher assigns an adequate amount of oral reading that is consistent with material that has been covered so that students read at a comfortable pace with 80%–90% accuracy. The lesson seamlessly encourages integrating the lower level skills into the students' ability to handle multisyllable words and connected decodable text.

While working at the many complex layers of the language, teachers and students develop a consistent language about language that is used along with multisensory techniques to help students attend to language concepts they need taught directly. For example, in the *Wilson Reading System* (Wilson, 1988, 2002), questioning techniques are used throughout the lesson after new material is introduced to ensure that the student has understood. Terminology such as *digraph, blend, syllable,* and *schwa sound* gives students and teachers a common vocabulary to discuss new concepts, review what they have learned, and make corrections. Again, teachers can prompt students to self-correct their errors by using leading questions about what the student already knows, thus "creating a positive, success-oriented lesson" (Wilson, 2002, p. 25).

Pacing of Learning

Structured lesson planning encourages appropriate pacing with specific objectives in each section of the lesson. Berninger and Wolf suggested, "A well-planned lesson will protect both teachers and students from stolen time" (2009, p. 25). Because the lesson ideally runs from 45 minutes to 1 hour, each section is limited to a short interval of intensive instruction. As teachers gain experience through observing lessons and mentoring, they develop the skill of adjusting the pacing of parts of the lesson. Spalding (2003) pointed out the importance of teaching students how to maintain and switch attention so that they can manage the transitions within the lesson easily. This promotes good pacing and helps students to work independently.

HOW STUDENTS BENEFIT FROM MSLE LESSON PLANNING

The strong emphasis on language instruction brings the students face to face with exactly what they are having the most trouble figuring out for themselves. The lively interaction between teacher and students encourages reflection on the language forms they are learning that underlie reading, spelling, and writing.

Provides Structure

Structured lesson planning is essential for successfully teaching students with language learning disabilities and attention issues for a number of important reasons. From the students' point of view, MSLE lessons fit their need for structure, limits, and an anxiety-free atmosphere in which to learn. Students do not like surprises or last-minute changes that can confuse them and affect their performance. They like to know what is coming next to prepare for it (Frank, 2002). MSLE lessons adhere to a daily structure to ensure that students feel secure in knowing that the lesson is stable and predictable and that it is designed for their success. The agenda of the lesson plan is often displayed using words and symbols for the activities listed. The students and teacher refer to this agenda as the lesson progresses. Often, students use a paper clip to mark each step on the daily lesson plan chart as they work through each task in order. They are frequently surprised at the fast pace and amount accomplished at the end of the session.

Promotes Active Participation

Presenting activities in the same order removes students' anxiety over time. Students know what to expect and when. Because the activities rotate rapidly, none lasting more than 10 minutes, students' attentions are better focused. In addition, students' active participation increases through verbalizing, generalizing, and comparing and contrasting language elements while building the structure of the language for themselves.

Uses Visual Reminders

Most MSLE systems have a structured lesson chart that is a visual reminder of the order of the lesson and, incidentally, how they are slowly mastering the components of written language (Smith, 1989). Spelling, handwriting, and composition lessons have procedure charts that prompt the students to use the strategies they are learning. These familiar structured procedures promote readiness for learning (see Chapters 7, 8, and 9).

Integrates All Language Systems

Careful planning guarantees that many layers of language processing are practiced, integrated, and applied systematically based on an organized curriculum. Students experience short, intensive, interactive activities that integrate reading, writing, and spelling. What they read, they write; what they write, they read; what they read, they spell. Students are taught to use all pathways to learn in every lesson as they work on letter sounds, reading words, spelling, handwriting, vocabulary, comprehension, and composition. This seamless presentation ensures that the basic skills needed for students to become skilled readers are not presented in a disjointed and disconnected way. Grasping written language concepts presents difficulties for students, especially when attention is a problem. Therefore, activities are short and focused with small steps taken in sequence, at first easy and then more difficult. The teacher keeps the lesson interesting with the rapid changing of learning modalities (visual, auditory, and tactile/kinesthetic) and media. Students learn to accept and even anticipate variety within the structure (Tucker, 2003). Necessary repetition builds toward mastery while all taught concepts are maintained in the lessons (Wilson, 1988, 2002). New learning and practice with prior learning are well balanced. Review is automatically built in for purposes of fluency and automaticity of the essential components of reading and writing.

Summary of Benefits of Lesson Planning

Clinicians and teachers have often observed that students barely notice the time passing during well-planned MSLE lessons. Teachers often report that when they inadvertently leave out a portion of the lesson, students quickly notice the omission. This may suggest that they value the time to review and practice what they are learning in a protected atmosphere. Emphasizing consistency and structure promotes student organization in a predictable and consistent environment. Students are aware of the forward motion of the daily schedule and depend on it for keeping organized and sequenced in time and space.

Students often feel less anxiety as they understand the expectations within the lesson structure and begin to experience success, often for the first time. The consistent daily review of learned information and guided practice of new concepts gradually leads to students' mastery and independent application of what has been learned. As students gain mastery of the subskills, teachers continue to introduce new content in the curriculum sequence. Some students take longer to reach mastery during remediation. The strong organization of well-planned MSLE lessons, however, often helps students improve their memories over time and thus experience better retrieval of information.

Gersten et al. (2008), clearly stated that since the 1960s, there is no research that offers evidence on how to teach the most deeply struggling readers. The efforts contained in the RTI movement, however, are driving toward remedying that gap in knowledge as educators begin to put in place tiered assessment-driven intensive instruction to identify children at risk and to differentiate instruction for those who are not thriving under classroom and small-group supplementary instruction in reading (see Chapter 14). Smartt and Glaser (2010) is a good source for MSLE lesson planning ideas and activities connecting RTI literacy assessment to instruction.

LESSON PLAN FORMATS

Implementing planning for MSLE lessons requires using several different lesson plan formats: a daily lesson plan; a weekly lesson plan; and a summary worksheet or scope and sequence, which denotes progress. We suggest that teachers begin with formats provided by a certified trainer or coach. Teachers should be encouraged, however, to fine-tune their lessons to match their style of instruction as they become experienced in implementing the steps in the curriculum from basic to complex.

How to Begin

The teacher begins by identifying the individual components of the reading lesson in the suggested daily lesson plan and the sequence of these components. When the teacher begins planning for a new student or group of students, he or she can assume nothing about the students' previous mastery of material.

If prior progress monitoring, educational evaluations, or report cards are available, then the teacher can refer to them to identify the highest level of mastery attained for each component (see Chapter 14). If a student is new to a reading tutorial approach, then a quick probe of all skills beginning with letter names and sounds is recommended. Each student must be evaluated to determine what material has been mastered and what knowledge is yet to be learned or needs to be reviewed. Once lessons have begun, succeeding steps will be driven by assessment data obtained from records of informal curriculum-based probes and later formal testing. It is important for students to know what they know and for the teacher to be aware of the gaps in students' skills. For students struggling with reading, it is a well-accepted axiom that remediation starts at the beginning and goes as slowly as necessary and as quickly as possible.

Daily Lesson Plan

A detailed daily lesson plan is needed to plan and organize skills, materials, and presentation. Lesson planning can be thought of as a concrete way to analyze the needs of each student. When teachers sit down to plan lessons, they need to keep long-term goals in mind according to the scope and sequence of the MSLE curriculum that delineates the discrete components of language and subskills to be mastered. When teachers are new to this kind of instruction, it often takes 2 or even 3 hours while using assessment materials to plan and organize the materials for a 1-hour tutorial. Teachers find the planning process becomes easier after teaching through all of the elements of the curriculum with several different groups of students. It is important that teachers have the ongoing support of administrators and instructional team members, along with parent input, to carry out this kind of expert, dedicated instruction for it to be successful.

The first daily lesson plan is generally a probe of or review of the student's known skills that are to be mastered in each component of the lesson. Every MSLE program has a beginning series of skills to be mastered. For example, the teacher should check new students for knowledge of the following: the alphabet, sequence, letter names, phonemic awareness of beginning sounds of words, writing upper- and lowercase print letters, some consonants sounds and short vowel sounds on cards, spelling individual sounds, and blending sounds into words (Sonday, 1997).

A variety of daily and weekly lesson plan formats are provided here for review. Figure 15.1 is an example of a beginning-level daily lesson plan after several consonants and two short vowels have been introduced. Figure 15.2 is an example of a more advanced daily lesson plan after the students have progressed to two-syllable words for reading and spelling. The students have worked with the dropping rule and spelling derivatives. The students have also been introduced to four syllable types: closed, vowel pair, vowel-*r*, and vowel-consonant-*e*. The daily lesson plan shown in Figure 15.2 introduces the open syllable.

See Chapters 5, 6, 8, 9, and 10 for elementary students and Chapter 16 for older students for a description of the precise steps in a multisensory introduction of letter sounds and concepts. The times given for each lesson component are approximate. It is likely that teachers may or may not have the opportunity to include every component each day; by using the weekly lesson plan, however, all activities will be incorporated consistently over time. Figures 15.1 and 15.2 list chapters from this book that contain information and guidance on what can be included in each step of the daily lesson plan. Figures 15.3 and 15.4 provide guidance for a beginning-level weekly lesson plan.

The explicit and systematic instruction used in MSLE lessons plays an important role in efforts to improve reading instruction and link instruction to how children are identified with learning disabilities. Using the RTI criteria to assess and identify struggling readers calls for a three-tiered system of intervention (see Chapter 14). In this data-based decision-making model, teachers target and plan their lessons according to their students' identified weaknesses.

Tier 1 is screening for reading difficulties in preschool, kindergarten, and first grade and placement in research-based literacy programs emphasizing the five critical components of early reading (phoneme awareness, phonics, fluency, vocabulary, and comprehension; NICHD, 2000) in the general education classroom. Tier 2 is the provision of small-group intervention and progress monitoring to support students with similar needs for effective instruction in reading along with the general education program. For children who do not progress in reading at a reasonable rate, Tier 3 would include special education services using scientifically based programs with progress regularly monitored (Fletcher, Coulter, Reschly, & Vaughn, 2004).

The lesson plan is the very backbone of RTI. It is through the lesson plan that a tutor is able to "adjust the intensity and nature of those intervention depending on a student's responsiveness" (National Center on Response to Intervention Definition of RTI; http://www.rti4success.org). Regarding the three-tier system of intervention programs in U.S. public schools for students struggling with reading, Dickman, Hennessy, Moats, Rooney, and Tomey (2002) noted that MSLE lessons ought to fit into the third-tier intervention in special education for the poorest readers. Merely using direct instruction and strategy instruction, however, is not sufficient. Students engaging in second- and third-tier intervention must have "structured teaching of language systems" (p. 24).

Structured language interventions must be intensive to be effective. As students reach the third grade, up to 2 hours daily are necessary to remediate severe reading disabilities.

Instructional component	Approximate time	Refer to . . .
ALPHABET KNOWLEDGE AND PHONEMIC AWARENESS ***Alphabet Knowledge*** Students touch and name the letters of the alphabet in sequence as warm-up. Students match plastic uppercase letters to grid of alphabet letters on a mat. ***Phonemic Awareness*** Ask students if these words rhyme: *pill/hill, tip/lip, yes/my, run/sun, mice/nice, now/nap.*	5 minutes	Chapters 5 and 6
READING DECKS Show letter cards for students to name for quick drill. Give key words and sounds: *i, t, p, n, s, a, l, d, f, h, g, o.* Use irregular word deck: *said, the, of, one.*	3 minutes	Chapter 8
SPELLING DECK Using a spelling deck (cards bearing letters and sounds introduced for reading), dictate sounds to students, who repeat the sounds, say the letter names, and write them on chalkboard: /ĭ/, /t/, /p/, /n/, /s/, /ă/, /l/, /d/, /f/, /h/, /g/, /ŏ/.	3 minutes	Chapter 9
MULTISENSORY INTRODUCTION OF LETTER OR CONCEPT Provide multisensory introduction of digraph *ng* using guided discovery of sound, letters, key words, and mouth position. Discovery words: *sing, sang, sting, ding* Reinforce with sky writing, handwriting, reading the sound, and spelling the sound.	5 minutes	Chapters 2, 7, 8, and 9
READING PRACTICE FOR ACCURACY AND FLUENCY Students prepare and read orally closed-syllable words: *hint, stand, tint, slap, split, spat, spin, snap, nips, plant.* *Dad lifts the sand in a tin pan.*	5–10 minutes	Chapters 8 and 10
SPELLING Give warm-up, with review of sounds to be spelled: /ĭ/, /t/, /s/, /a/, /l/, /f/, /h/. Review Floss Rule and spell these words: *sniff, tiff, staff, till, hill, spill.*	5–10 minutes	Chapter 9
HANDWRITING Students practice writing *d* on folded newsprint paper. Students trace the letter three times while listening to guided stroke description: "Curve under, over, stop, back around, up, down, release." Students make three copies, saying the letter name each time.	3 minutes	Chapter 7
COMPREHENSION AND LISTENING STRATEGIES Read "The Tortoise and the Hare" to students. Have students retell the fable with a graphic organizer for stories (simple story map).	10 minutes	Chapter 12
ORAL LANGUAGE PRACTICE AND COMPOSITION Introduce vocabulary: *boasted, plodding, patient.* Have students find and discuss meanings for the descriptive words from the story, use words in sentences, and enter words in the vocabulary section of their language notebooks.	10 minutes	Chapters 3, 11, and 12

Figure 15.1.   Beginning-level daily lesson plan. (*Source:* Cox, 1984.)

Instructional component	Approximate time	Refer to . . .
ALPHABET AND DICTIONARY, PHONOLOGICAL AWARENESS, AND MORPHOLOGY STUDY Students review guide words, target words, and first and last entry words on a dictionary page. Students do guide-word practice in the dictionary with alphabet strip as reference (e.g., if guide words are *lop* and *lot*, students determine whether the entry word *loss* would appear on that page).	5 minutes	Chapters 4, 5, and 6
READING DECKS Students say the sounds represented by symbols in the letter card deck. Students also use a deck of word parts: suffixes, prefixes, and roots.	3 minutes	Chapters 8 and 16
MULTISENSORY INTRODUCTION OF LETTER OR CONCEPT Students learn vowels in open syllables through auditory/visual discovery. Discovery words: *able, ogle, idle, bugle* Explain to students, "All words end in final stable syllables; the first syllable is open and accented. A vowel in an open, accented syllable is long. Long vowels say their names." **sta**'|ble **ri**'|fle **no**'|ble	10 minutes	Chapters 2, 8, 9, and 16
READING PRACTICE FOR ACCURACY AND FLUENCY Read words with vowels in open syllables: *table, cradle, trifle, stable, ruble, sable, title, maple, staple.* Read sentences: *The wooden cradle was carved from pinewood.* Read a review list of words and a short story in a controlled reader.	10 minutes	Chapters 8, 10, and 16
SPELLING Students spell on paper from dictation: *maple, stifle, table, noble, bugle, staple, stable.* Students categorize list of words for spelling as regular, irregular, or rule words: *tank, tail, swimming.* Students write sentences from dictation: *The fish nibbles on the worm on the hook.*	10 minutes	Chapters 9 and 16
HANDWRITING *(does not occur every lesson)* Students practice writing capital letters *T, S,* and *I* in cursive.	5 minutes	Chapter 7
EXTENDED READING AND WRITING Goal is accuracy, fluency, and comprehension. Students read from connected decodable text with controlled vocabulary that is geared to the students' levels. Students write sentences using vocabulary they are reading and spelling.	10 minutes	Chapters 8, 12, 13, and 16
COMPREHENSION AND LISTENING STRATEGIES Read students' stories or expository texts that match their ages and interests. Include comprehension strategies (see Chapter 14).	5 minutes	Chapters 12 and 18
ORAL LANGUAGE PRACTICE AND COMPOSITION Begin expanding written sentences using *where* and *when.* Practice orally, starting with basic simple sentences: *The baseball player left his mitt (where?).* *Molly called her best friend Sara (when?).*	5 minutes	Chapters 3, 11, 13, and 18

Figure 15.2.   Immediate-level lesson plan. (*Sources: Basic language skills: Concept manual, book two,* 2000; Cox, 1984.)

Instructional component	Day 2	Day 3
ALPHABET KNOWLEDGE AND PHONEMIC AWARENESS	*Alphabet knowledge* Students touch and name the alphabet on strip. Students practice accent and rhythm, naming the letters in pairs. Students accent the first letter of pairs. (**A'**B, **C'**D, **E'**F). *Phonemic awareness* Students add a sound to a word: Add /p/ to the beginning of these words: *each, in, age, ill, inch.*	*Alphabet knowledge* Students touch and name the alphabet on strip. With model available, students put plastic letters in alphabetical order. *Phonemic awareness* Students identify the sound at the beginning of each word: *beach, ball, bark, boil, bus.* (Students use mirrors to check lips.)
READING DECKS	Show letter cards for students to name and give key words and sounds for quick drill: *i, t, p, n, s, a, l, d, f, h, g, o, a,* and (new card) *ng.* Use irregular word deck: *said, the, of, one.*	Repeat Day 2 activity.
SPELLING DECK	Dictate sounds to students, who repeat the sounds, says the letter names, and write them on rice tray: /ĭ/, /t/, /p/, /n/, /s/, /l/, /d/, /f/, /h/, /g/, /ŏ/, /ă/, /k/, and (new sound) /ng/.	Repeat Day 2 activity, on table top instead of using rice tray.
MULTISENSORY IN-TRODUCTION OR REVIEW OF LETTER OR CONCEPT	*Review of Day 1's new concept* Review /ng/ sound, letters, key word (*king*) and mouth position. Review digraph *ng* final: *sing, hang, long.* Discover /ng/ medial (*link, sank, honk*) where /ng/ is represented by letter *n* (key word: *sink*). Students draw *g*-curve on *n* to mark new sound: ŋ.	*Review of Day 1's new concept* Review /ng/ sound, letters, key words, and mouth positions. Reinforce with sky writing, hand-writing, reading sound, spelling sound (sometimes *n* = /ng/). Students puts /ng/ in student note-book, with spelling examples of digraph *ng* and *n* with key words.
READING PRACTICE	Students prepare and read orally words with *ng* and other short *a* words: *pat, tang, lap, sat, pang, sap, sang, dad, fang.* Read sentences with *ng* words.	Students prepare and read orally words with short *i* words: *sit, hit, tip, dip, tin, pin, lid, did, pig, sis.* Read controlled sentences for fluency.
SPELLING	Give warm-up, with review of sounds to be spelled: /ĭ/, /p/, /n/, /s/, /ŏ/, /t/, /d/, /g/, /l/. Review suffix *s* rule (/z/ and /s/ = s): *pins, pots, tops, digs, dogs, logs, nips.* Students write sentences from dicta-tion: *Dan sits on the logs.*	Give warm-up, with review of sounds to be spelled: /h/, /ĭ/, /l/, /s/, /f/, /p/, /ŏ/. Review Floss Rule and suffix *s* rule, and have students spell words from dictation: *hills, pills, fills, dolls, sills.* (Also discuss word meanings.)
HANDWRITING	Review guided stroke description for letters *d, p,* and *a.* At the chalkboard, students practice *a, p,* and *d,* connecting them in random order: *adp, pda, dpa.*	Review guided stroke description, and have students practice connecting bridge letter *o.* Students trace *op, od,* and *og* on folded newsprint. Students write copies after tracing.
COMPREHENSION AND LISTENING STRATEGIES	Reread fable ("The Tortoise and the Hare") to students. Using a simple story map as a prompt, have students describe the actions of the hare.	Using a simple story map, have students describe the actions of the tortoise.
ORAL LANGUAGE PRACTICE AND COMPOSITION	*Vocabulary* List adjectives used in the fable to describe the hare.	*Vocabulary* List adjectives used in the fable to describe the tortoise.

Figure 15.3. Days 2 and 3 of a 5-day weekly lesson plan, beginning level.

Instructional component	Day 4	Day 5
ALPHABET KNOWLEDGE AND PHONEMIC AWARENESS	***Alphabet knowledge*** Students touch and name the alphabet on strip. Point to a letter on the alphabet strip. Students name what comes after and before the letter. ***Phonemic awareness*** Using letter tiles *p* and *b*, students point to the first sound in dictated words: *pill, bat, pet.*	***Alphabet knowledge*** Students touch and name the alphabet on strip. Students play Alphabet Bingo. ***Phonemic awareness*** Students add /d/ to the beginning of each syllable: *ear, esk, ock, og, ust, oll, ive, ime, itch.*
READING DECKS	Repeat Day 2 activity.	Repeat Day 2 activity.
SPELLING DECK	Repeat Day 2 activity on chalkboard.	Repeat Day 2 activity on lined paper.
MULTISENSORY IN-TRODUCTION OR REVIEW OF LETTER OR CONCEPT	***Introduction of new concept*** New letter *c* = /k/ before *a, o,* and *u* Visual discovery: *can, cop, cup* Students form linkages with key word *cup* and letter *c* pronounced as /k/. Reinforce with sky writing, handwriting, reading sound, and spelling sound. Students add *c* to the /k/ page in their notebooks.	***Review of digraph <u>ng</u> and <u>n</u> before /k/*** Present mixed review of *ng* and *nk* words presented during the week: *sing, sang, song, ding, dong, gong, tank, pink, honk, stink.* Students read sentences and underline *ng*: He sa<u>ng</u> a so<u>ng</u>. The bell went d<u>ing</u>-dong.
READING PRACTICE	Students prepare and read orally non-sense words with *c* read as /k/ before *a* and *o: cass, coll, caff, scad, scop, scap.* Read sentences with review of new sight words *said, of, the,* and *one:* *One of the cops said, "Stop!"* *Pat spills one of the cans of pop.* Students draw boxes around words containing the suffix -*s*, which says /s/ or /z/.	Present mixed review of words read this week, through the use of a deck of word cards or words listed on the board or on chart paper: *tank, gang, tong, sing, king, sting, pink, honk, dank, sink, lank, stink, cast, cod, can, cop, cap.* Students read sentences listed on chart paper or on strips.
SPELLING	Students review suffix *s* rule, referring to their notebooks. Students write sentences from dictation: *Sis fills the gas can.* *Tad pats the cats.* *One of the kids hits the logs.*	Have students explain the Floss Rule and the suffix -*s* rule. Have students give two examples for each. Students write sentence from dictation: *The dog sniffs the pan and spills the fat.*
HANDWRITING	Students write five previously learned letters three times each (to stress size proportion). Each student places a star by one of each letter that he or she feels is best.	Students write five tall letters (*k, h, t, l, d*) three times each (to stress size proportion). Each student places a star by one of each letter that he or she feels is best.
COMPREHENSION AND LISTENING STRATEGIES	With aid of graphic organizer, students identify and explain the turning point of the fable "The Tortoise and the Hare."	Students identify which character they feel they are most like or give a situation when they were most like each character.
ORAL LANGUAGE PRACTICE AND COMPOSITION	***Vocabulary*** Students list adjectives used to describe the turning point of the fable.	Students lay graphic organizers on the table and generate one or two clear, concise sentences for each map.

Figure 15.4.   Days 4 and 5 of a 5-day weekly lesson plan, beginning level.

Remediation programs with demonstrated effectiveness, staffed by teachers with appropriate training in language and remedial instruction, should be available to older poor readers in lieu of other academic requirements. "Accommodations and modifications are never a substitute for intensive remediation" (Dickman et al., 2002, p. 25).

Weekly Lesson Plan

In addition to a daily lesson plan, a weekly lesson plan is also needed. A model is provided in Figures 15.3 and 15.4. This can be in a separate plan book or more often in the same plan book if there is enough space. Some teachers use a lesson planner. If the planner contains a block for each class, then each block is instead used for one component within a lesson. Sometimes a 9" × 12" sketch pad is used to accommodate daily and weekly plans on the same page. When a teacher first begins to organize MSLE lesson plans, each daily plan may require a full sheet of paper, as shown in Figure 15.1. As the teacher becomes more experienced with planning and implementing the lessons, five daily lessons can be recorded on a single sheet of paper or in a teacher's plan book.

The weekly plan enables the instructor to always be looking ahead to focus the direction of the instruction. In that way, the teacher can ensure that the same components are practiced using different multisensory pathways and media. It is easy to fill a lesson with instructional activities; the real expertise is in continuing to move the lessons and the instruction forward. Pacing is the most difficult skill for inexperienced teachers to acquire because it only comes with experience. Working with both a daily and a weekly lesson plan format (under the guidance of a coach and/or instructional team) enables a novice teacher to begin to see when instruction is moving too quickly or too slowly. As mentioned previously, the idea is to move as quickly as possible but as slowly as necessary. By sketching out five lessons and then adjusting the plan on a daily basis, the teacher is able to begin to recognize and pace instruction based on the performance of his or her students. Figures 15.3 and 15.4 provide a model for a weekly lesson plan that shows the interplay of new information, review of concepts, and practice in controlled lists and texts for reinforcement and the variety of multisensory interactions between teacher and students. Unquestionably, as the week unfolds, the teacher adjusts the lesson plan to suit the needs of the students.

CLASSROOM ENVIRONMENT

The current emphasis on RTI draws educators' attention to identifying the most needy students in a classroom. What may often be overlooked is the challenge to first ensure that students receive classroom instruction that reflects sound instructional design principles. A best practice would be that "school districts choose evidence-based curricula and instruction, and provide teachers with relevant and rigorous professional development. Teachers implement the curricula and instruction and their fidelity of implementation is documented" (Fuchs & Fuchs, 2005, p. 58). Simply having teachers "use" a science-based reading research program (product) is necessary but not sufficient to ensure that a solid Tier 1 (core program) is being implemented (process) in the general education classroom.

The palette on which the instruction is being layered is the organization of the classroom (in terms of materials and behavior) as well as the quality of the lesson planning. This next section will assist teachers with organizing their classroom materials and student behaviors to enable teachers to focus their skills and energies on the delivery of a solid core program. An efficiently organized and functioning classroom coupled with effective lesson planning and the delivery of a solid core program expedites identifying those students who may need supplementary services.

Effective teachers manage their classrooms; ineffective teachers discipline their classrooms.
—Wong & Wong (1998, p. 83)

Lesson plans cannot stand alone; the classroom environment is also important to consider. The second section of this chapter explores in detail the classroom environment that best supports intensive intervention from the standpoint of both the teacher and the students. Explicit lesson planning assumes its powerful place when a positive classroom environment is in place for effective teaching and learning for students struggling with academic subjects.

When considering the classroom environment, the first question teachers need to ask is, "Am I spending most of my time disciplining my students?" If your answer is yes, then this chapter is for you. It is designed to change your approach from one of responding to students' actions to an approach of reinforcing students' positive performance. In order to be effective and successful, you will need to step back and take a broad survey of the entire environment in which you and your students are interacting. It is important to structure every component of the learning environment for success.

Space for Teaching

The classroom is defined here as the space that you have been assigned to instruct your students. This space might be a room with four walls and a door, a space marked off by bookcases, an alcove in a hallway, or a space no bigger than a broom closet. However big or small or permanent or temporary the space may be, it is the space in which you are assigned to teach. Organizing that space must be carefully thought out and arranged. There is no one right plan or organization to any given space. Rather, the space must work for you as the teacher and for the specific students assigned to that space. Often, this means doing the best you can with few resources in terms of physical space, desks, and chalkboards.

The main teaching space is the first space to plan. Begin by standing in the space and mentally listing what you have for classroom furniture (e.g., desks, file cabinets, tables, chalkboards, bulletin boards, shelves, cubbies). Ask yourself these questions:

- Where will you stand (or sit if it is a small-group tutorial setting) during the major portion of classroom instruction?

- Where are the chalkboards or magnetic whiteboards located in relation to the instructional position? Sometimes boards can be moved or added if necessary.

- Where will the other teaching equipment (e.g., easels, overhead projectors) that are used during daily instruction be placed?

- How best can the student desks be arranged so that all students can see you during instruction? What works best for you and your students—desks in rows, desks touching, or desks in a four-square pattern?

- Are the desks the correct size for your students? Students should be able to sit comfortably with feet flat on the floor and knees not hitting the bottom of the desk. Take the time at the beginning of the year to adjust the desks to fit the size of each student. It may be necessary for you to trade desks with other teachers or to add wooden boxes to the bases of desks for your shorter students.

- Where will students keep their books and supplies? What works best for you and your students should be the deciding factor. Do you want them to keep their materials in their desks? If lockers are available, what will be kept in them and what will be kept in students' desks? Even if there is space in the desks for supplies, you may still want to have students keep supplies and books in an assigned tote located elsewhere in the classroom. This will enable students to have only the needed materials at their desks during instruction. It may take several attempts to get the board(s), easels, overhead projector, digital equipment, and student desks to fit and work in the teaching space.

The next decision is where to locate the teacher's desk(s). Decide where to place and how to situate the teacher desk(s), filing cabinets, and bookcases that are to be used exclusively by you and/or classroom assistants. It is often a good idea to locate the teacher desk(s) and confidential materials away from the student traffic pattern. If you plan to have students sit with you at your desk for individualized instruction, then you will need to plan how that area will work as well. Planning the teacher's space may require slight changes to the instructional space. Organizing the teacher's space is discussed more in the following section.

The small-group instructional area or study center is the third important space to plan. This could be a reading corner and/or a learning center based on a topic of study. Once the areas of use for a classroom have been identified and the furniture is placed in its respective area, you will need to check the traffic pattern that results from the current placement of furniture:

- Are the students able to enter and exit the classroom without bumping into desks, bookcases, and tables stacked with papers?

- Is the teacher's desk still situated so as to be undisturbed by students?

- Is there still a place to easily store and gain access to confidential information, such as tests and progress reports, away from students?

- Where will papers be placed that are to be handed in for grading?

- Where will sets of workbooks, teacher's manuals, card decks, reading lists, dictation materials, and alphabet letters and other manipulatives be stored?

- Where are the pencil sharpener, other classroom supplies, and trash can located?

- Is there a space or desk set off as a quiet corner if needed?

- How will the bulletin boards and countertops (if any) be used?

- How will computer time be assigned for practice and review activities?

Every need and movement of students from the time they enter until they exit the classroom must be arranged for what will be most efficient given the classroom size and furniture. The classroom setup may not be perfect; however, it needs to be well thought through for what works best for your teaching style, the students assigned to your class, and the furniture and space available. After your classroom has been set up, take a critical look around the room with an eye toward limiting classroom distractions.

Finding what works best for you may take several attempts, extending over several years. But you will be fine tuning the physical surroundings of the instructional environment with a heightened awareness of your needs as the teacher and your students' needs for logical, systematic order in the classroom's physical environment.

TEACHER ORGANIZATION

Teacher organization encompasses organizing 1) the space used exclusively by the teacher, 2) teaching materials, and 3) teacher transitions. There has been research consensus that the proportion of time in which students are actively and productively engaged in learning best predicts academic achievement and the overall quality of the classroom (Mather & Goldstein, 2008). The teacher must be efficient in having available the materials necessary for a lesson to be successful in keeping students actively and productively engaged in learning.

The Teacher's Personal Space

Organizing a teacher's personal space is often overlooked, yet is so critical for effective, efficient instruction. Begin by thinking of all of the requests made of you as a teacher. Requests come from students, administrators, colleagues, student teachers, and parents. There is the need to communicate with school personnel and supervisors requiring documentation. Students request materials such as paper, tape, scissors, passes, and forms. If these items are going to be stored on your desk, then consider how to make them readily accessible without students accidentally having access to confidential materials. Next, take time to set up folders or files (on a computer if possible) for confidential student information, information for parents, routine memos from the administration, and committee information. This organization is done prior to the arrival of students. Organizing your desk, drawer space, and desktop supplies, as well as setting up any filing cabinets, bookcases, and storage closets, needs to be well thought out for accessibility and keeping daily clutter to a minimum. Make your personal space efficient so that you do not dread sitting down to a disheveled desk at the end of a productive day. By having everything organized, the items are readily accessible and do not become distractions or disruptions to implementing the lesson.

At the start of a school year, teaching materials are usually neatly stacked and ready for use. As the school year progresses, however, the stacks become untidy, materials are lost or damaged, and needed supplies get depleted. At the beginning of the year, set up labeled shelves or containers to accommodate materials that are critical to the success of your lessons. Each group or individual student should have the core daily lesson materials in a clearly marked bin. The bin could contain card decks for review and teaching new concepts, current reading lists, workbooks, manipulatives, extra pencils, and index cards. Student notebooks used in the lesson should be nearby. For older students, it is helpful to number handheld spellcheckers and assign each student a specific spellchecker. Provide a labeled storage box that can hold the entire set of spellcheckers at the end of the lesson. Store the spellcheckers in the same place on the shelf for the entire year. Setting up computers and scheduling time for your students for practice and review becomes part of the learning process. This thoughtful attention to detail will enable the lessons to move efficiently and smoothly.

Teachers, as well as their students, have transitions in their academic day. Teachers may make transitions from subject to subject or from instructional group to instructional group, including from one discrete instructional component to the next within a lesson. Teachers are usually thoughtful about making sure they have all the necessary materials needed for implementing a lesson. Time also needs to be spent planning what to do with teacher and student materials at the end of a specific lesson or component so that the next subject or instructional group can be initiated efficiently. Furthermore, keeping track of teaching and student materials during each component of the lesson leads to better planning and scaffolding of instruction for the next day. For example, enclosed plastic folders with multiple sections are ideal for students for holding letter tiles, writing boards, and student composition books.

An effective teacher organizes and maintains the classroom learning environment to maximize the time spent engaged in productive activity and minimize the time lost during transitions or disruptions due to disciplinary action (Mather & Goldstein, 2008). Taking the time to get one's personal space organized; setting up a system for storage of instructional materials; and being able to efficiently access teaching materials before, during, and after instruction contributes to a productive classroom environment.

Classroom Environment and Student Behavior

So far this chapter has considered structuring the physical space and organizing oneself for success, all prior to students' arrival in the classroom or tutorial space. The effect of the classroom environment on student behavior begins the second the students step through the doorway into the room. First of all, some students actively seek and draw attention to themselves more than others. Teachers should structure the environment so that attention directed to students is positive, while keeping negative attention to the absolute minimum. Often, teachers are so focused on the curriculum to be taught that not enough time is allocated to developing positive student behavior.

One way to visualize the importance of positive student interactions is to think of each student as an individual drinking glass. The size of this glass varies according to the amount of attention that each student requires. A student will strive to keep his or her glass full of attention. It often does not matter to some students whether the attention is positive or negative, rather that attention is given. Your objective is to keep each glass filled to the brim with positive attention. False praise does not work. If students know the expectations for a classroom in terms of behavior, participation, or routine, then there will be many naturally occurring opportunities for giving praise. Use these opportunities to compliment students who require a lot of attention. It will take concerted and conscientious efforts on your part not to criticize an attention-seeking student for what he or she is doing wrong. Rather, you should keep an eagle eye out for ways to sincerely and appropriately compliment such a student for specific actions that merit praise. Beware of false praise, however, which is often more general and less tangible. For example, praising a student for better behavior after she or he has repeatedly been disruptive is false praise. A sincere praise is to compliment the student for the specific appropriate behavior of entering the classroom quietly. The goal is to drain the negative attention from the glass and fill the glass to the brim with positive attention.

The way to build a positive environment begins with thinking through expected student behavior and classroom procedures from the moment students enter the classroom. These expectations need to be explained to the students, clearly understood by the students, and reinforced by you in a positive manner. The next key piece is to maintain consistent rules and expectations from one day to the next. It is important to take the time (even if it reduces the amount of instruction) to reinforce the established rules and expectations. It is better to do this at the beginning of the year than to have the students repeatedly disrupt instruction throughout the rest of the year. When reinforcing classroom expectations, explain these in a patient, nonjudgmental tone. Use a tone that firmly repeats what the students may already know but have yet to internalize. Once classroom rules and expectations have been established, the key is to be consistent and follow through on those rules and expectations. Students are more successful in environments in which they know what to expect. They need to be held accountable for classroom rules and expectations on the days when everything is going well, as well as on the days when nothing is going right. For example, one middle school special education teacher successfully used only one rule in her classroom: "You are responsible" (E.F. Bitler, personal communication, 2004). Her focus was to keep the rule simple and applicable to the real world. Whatever the difficulty (lost homework, broken pencil, inappropriate behavior), the student is held responsible for the action as well as determining an appropriate solution. Teachers may need to model how one determines or problem solves an appropriate solution.

Along with using clear classroom expectations, there are many ways for teachers to reduce student anxiety starting in the first days of school. Wong and Wong (1998) identified questions students have as they begin the school year:

- *Am I in the right room?* Have your room number clearly visible.

- *Where am I supposed to sit?* Assign seats or display a sign indicating that students may select their own seats.

- *What are the rules in this classroom?* Have rules clearly visible, and take time to discuss the rules and reasons and to follow through on them.

- *What will I be doing this year?* Make a syllabus or lesson plan chart available.

- *How will I be graded?* Furnish a record keeper for grades.

- *Who is the teacher as a person?* Introduce yourself and tell something about your experience, hobbies, and interests.

- *Will the teacher treat me as a human being?* Your actions will speak louder than your words.

In the face of such uncertainties, teachers need to ensure that the classroom is a safe environment for students to be able to take academic risks, explore friendships, learn to negotiate a classroom setting, and learn appropriate expectations and behaviors that are transferable to the outside world. Students must know that the classroom is where unexpected negative things are not going to happen. It is okay to be incorrect; it is not okay to not try. There will be time and opportunity to develop social skills. Students will learn how to be students. They will be explicitly guided toward learning appropriate expectations and behaviors. A well-managed classroom is task oriented and predictable. This kind of environment has

- A high level of student involvement with work

- Clear student expectations

- Relatively little wasted time, confusion, or disruption

- A relaxed and pleasant climate

BUILDING THE STUDENT–TEACHER CONNECTION

It is important to bond and connect with all students, but especially with students who have experienced limited academic success. A key behavior is to establish eye contact during teaching and while conversing with a student. When you first meet, shake hands and look the student in the eye. It may feel corny, but this is a powerful first tool for establishing a unique, caring connection. Using students' names is critical, especially when working with adolescents. Eye contact and addressing a student by name are powerful constructive tools in providing positive attention.

Once students begin to feel that you are an approachable teacher, it is critical that you practice active listening. Active listening involves maintaining attention to the students by simultaneously looking at the students while they are talking and keeping focused on what is being said. It is important not to interrupt the student. Acknowledge that you have listened by neutrally responding to what the student has said, even though you might disagree with what he or she has said. This will often require momentarily setting aside the agenda you have for a student so that you can hear and understand what information or request the student wishes to convey.

Assuring students that you will not ask them to do what you know they have not learned yet and what you have not already taught them is another important way to gain their confidence. This helps to eliminate guessing and encourages them instead to practice the strategies you are instructing them to use to master the intricacies of the language. Being successful on a daily basis builds trust and confidence so much that students are quick to recognize your inadvertent use of something in a lesson they have not yet learned.

Using less teacher talk is another key strategy to improve student–teacher interactions. By using active listening and structuring lessons to engage learners by using Socratic questioning, a skillful teacher is able to use what students already know to further their understanding and to help them integrate their knowledge of the components of reading. Concentrating on asking content- or process-related questions of students and then engaging in dialogue with students creates respect for what they are learning and helps them verbalize their understandings (Swanson, 1999). Very often, it is possible to use only quick prompts such as verbal cues, gestures, and visual reminders to keep students on track. There are many ways to build relationships with students, including those just described. Effective teachers know that it is important to acknowledge each student, engage in meaningful feedback dialogues during teachable moments, and recognize individual student successes. Other ways to engage students positively are to establish classroom traditions to celebrate successes and possibly even to disclose something meaningful about yourself. During student–teacher interactions, it is important to genuinely convey an attitude of respect, make oneself available for individual questions, and care enough to make a difference by doing what is needed to assist the student.

Appendix 15.1 at the end of this chapter provides the Building Block Checklist for Effective Classroom Management (Schedler & Bitler, 2004). Teachers can use this checklist to review what they are already doing and to evaluate what further actions need to be taken to build a good classroom environment.

CONCLUSION

Change done to you is debilitating; change done by you is exhilarating.
—Anonymous

Be exhilarated by making needed changes to your classroom—your space, your interactions with your students, and your lesson planning. The aim of this chapter is to provide you with fresh ideas and a new perspective on your instruction of students with specific language learning disabilities. Use the Building Block Checklist for Effective Classroom Management in the appendix at the end of this chapter to reflect on what you are presently doing and what you want to do differently.

A lesson plan for MSLE instruction is the framework for interaction between the teacher and the student. It is designed to support teachers in their efforts to teach the linguistic content to be mastered, using the most effective ways to teach according to informed principles of learning and instruction. An MSLE lesson highlights the progression of time-intensive activities, which include reviews of previously taught information, practice in all levels of language, and introducing new concepts based on a systematic curriculum. Careful planning of MSLE lessons builds the foundation for discovery learning and enables both the teacher and the students to work within a framework designed for explicit individualized instruction. Time spent ensuring that each part of the lesson includes multisensory components provides students with multiple opportunities to be active participants in the learning process.

As mentioned at the beginning of this chapter, although lesson planning is at the heart of MSLE, it cannot stand alone. It is important that teaching and learning take place in a positive environment. Multisensory structured language lesson planning assumes its powerful place when the teacher creates a positive classroom environment. A primary consideration is organizing the physical space for both the students and the teacher. The next priority is teacher organization and organizing and maintaining materials for instruction and record keeping in order to maximize the time spent engaged in productive activity and minimize the time lost during transitions or disruptions. The third focus is student expectations and behavior, with a strong emphasis on building a positive learning environment. Once the learning environment has been addressed, the teacher can create and implement detailed daily and weekly MSLE lesson plans. Students benefit when the environment is conducive to learning and when teachers are well prepared to implement instructional goals.

REFERENCES

Berninger, V.W. (1999). The "write stuff" for preventing and treating writing disabilities. *Perspectives, 25*(2), 20–22.

Berninger, V.W., & Wolf, B.J. (2009). *Teaching students with dyslexia and dysgraphia: Lessons from teaching and science.* Baltimore: Paul H. Brookes Publishing Co.

Blackwell, A.J., & McLaughlin, T.F. (2005). Using guided notes, choral responding, and response cards to increase student performance. *International Journal of Special Education, 20*(2), 1–5.

Cox, A.R. (1984). *Structures and techniques: Multisensory teaching of basic language skills.* Cambridge, MA: Educators Publishing Service.

Dickman, G.E., Hennessy, N.L., Moats, L.C., Rooney, K.J., & Tomey, H.A., III. (2002). *Response to OSEP Summit on Learning Disabilities.* Baltimore: International Dyslexia Association.

Fletcher, J.M., Coulter, W.A., Reschly, D.J., & Vaughn, S. (2004). Alternative approaches to the definition and identification of learning disabilities: Some questions and answers. *Annals of Dyslexia, 54*(2), 304–331.

Fletcher, J.M., Lyon, G.R., Fuchs, L.S., & Barnes, M.A. (2007). *Learning disabilities: From identification to intervention.* New York: Guilford Press.

Frank, R. (with Livingston, K.E.). (2002). *The secret life of the dyslexic child: How she thinks, how he feels, how they can succeed.* Emmaus, PA: Rodale Press.

Fuchs, D., & Fuchs, L.S. (2005). Responsiveness-to-intervention: A blueprint for practitioners, policymakers, and parents. *Teaching Exceptional Children, 38*(1), 57–61.

Gersten, R., Compton, D., Connor, C.M., Dimino, J., Santoro, L., Linan-Thompson, S., et al. (2008). *Assisting students struggling with reading: Response to intervention and multi-tier intervention for reading in the primary grades. A practice guide.* (NCEE 2009-4045). Washington, DC: National Center for Education Evaluation and Regional Assistance.

Gillingham, A., & Stillman, B.W. (1956). *Remedial training for children with specific disability in reading, spelling and penmanship* (5th ed.). Cambridge, MA: Educators Publishing Service.

Gillingham, A., & Stillman, B.W. (1997). *The Gillingham manual: Remedial training for children with specific disability in reading, spelling, and penmanship* (8th ed.). Cambridge, MA: Educators Publishing Service.

Henry, M.K., & Brickley, S.G. (1999). *Dyslexia: Samuel T. Orton and his legacy.* Baltimore: International Dyslexia Association.

Individuals with Disabilities Education Improvement Act (IDEA) of 2004, PL 108-446, 20 U.S.C. §§ 1400 *et seq.*

International Dyslexia Association. (n.d.). *Framework for informed reading and language instruction: Matrix of multisensory structured language programs.* Retrieved December 27, 2010, from http://www.interdys.org

Mather, N., & Goldstein, S. (2008). *Learning disabilities and challenging behaviors: A guide to intervention and classroom management* (2nd ed.). Baltimore: Paul H. Brookes Publishing Co.

Moats, L.C. (2010). *Speech to print: Language essentials for teachers* (2nd ed.). Baltimore: Paul H. Brookes Publishing Co.

National Institute of Child Health and Human Development. (2000). *Report of the National Reading Panel: Reports of the subgroups. Teaching children to read: An evidence-based assessment of the scientific research literature on reading and its implications for reading instruction* (NIH Publication No. 00-4754). Washington, DC: Government Printing Office.

Orton, S.T. (1937). *Reading, writing and speech problems in children.* New York: W.W. Norton.

Pashler, H., Bain, P., Bottge, B., Graesser, A., Koedinger, K., McDaniel, M., et al. (2007). *Organizing instruction and study to improve student learning* (NCER 2007-2004). Washington, DC: National Center for Education Research.

Schedler, J.F., & Bitler, E.F. (2004). *A classroom management secret: Keep the glasses full.* Workshop presented at the annual conference of the New York Branch of the International Dyslexia Association, New York.

Smartt, S.M., & Glaser, D.R. (2010). *Next STEPS in literacy instruction: Connecting assessments to effective intervention.* Baltimore: Paul H. Brookes Publishing Co.

Smith, M.T. (1989). *MTA classroom charts.* Cambridge, MA: Educators Publishing Service.

Sonday, A. (1997). *The Sonday System: Learning to read.* St. Paul, MN: Winsor Corporation.

Spalding, R.B. (2003). *The writing road to reading: The Spalding method for teaching speech, spelling, writing, and reading* (5th rev. ed.). New York: HarperCollins.

Swanson, H.L. (1999). Instructional components that predict treatment outcomes for students with learning disabilities: Support for a combined strategy and direct instruction model. *Learning Disabilities Research and Practice, 14*(3), 129–140.

Swanson, H.L., & Hoskyn, M. (1998). A synthesis of experimental intervention literature for students with learning disabilities: A meta-analysis of treatment outcomes. *Review of Educational Research, 68,* 277–321.

Tucker, V. (2003). *Planning multisensory structured language lessons.* Manuscript in preparation.

Wilson, B.A. (1988). *Wilson Reading System: Teacher's guide and student material.* Oxford, MA: Wilson Language Training. (Available from the publisher http://www.wilsonlanguage.com)

Wilson, B. (2002). *Wilson Reading System instructor manual* (3rd ed.). Oxford, MA: Wilson Language Training.

Wong, H.K., & Wong, R.T. (1998). *The first days of school: How to be an effective teacher.* Mountain View, CA: Harry K. Wong Publications.

Building Block Checklist for Effective Classroom Management

Things I *am* doing	Aspect of planning	Things I want to do differently
	Classroom environment	
	Bulletin boards	
	Furniture	
	Student desks	
	Traffic pattern(s)	
	Teacher organization	
	Teacher(s) desk(s)	
	Organization of teaching materials	
	Plan for instructional transitions	
	Student behavior	
	Establishment of classroom rules and expectations	
	Reduction of student anxiety	
	Bonding and connecting with all students	
	Connecting with individual students	
	Active listening to students	
	Self-evaluation of classroom needs	
	Is it a safe environment?	
	Can students take academic risks?	
	Are students exploring friendships?	
	Are students negotiating the classroom setting?	
	Are students learning appropriate expectations and behaviors?	
	Are students' behaviors transferable to the outside world?	

Directions:

1. Read through all items in the Building Block Checklist.

2. In the left column, place a check mark next to each item currently being addressed.

3. In the right column, place a check mark next to each item that needs to change to improve classroom management.

From Schedler, J.F. & Bitler, E.F. (2004). *A classroom management secret: Keep the glasses full.* Workshop presented at the annual conference of the New York Branch of The International Dyslexia Association, New York; adapted by permission.

16

Instruction for Older Students with a Word-Level Reading Disability

BARBARA A. WILSON

For students in fourth grade and beyond to be successful readers, they must be able to decode and read text fluently, understand advanced vocabulary, draw on substantial background knowledge, and comprehend diverse text structures (Biancarosa & Snow, 2006; Snow, 2002). Today, far too many adolescents cannot achieve this reading success and are thus considered struggling adolescent readers. This group includes students in 4th through 12th grade who are reading 2 or more years below grade level (Torgesen, 2005). Many states have also defined this population as students reading at or below the 40th percentile.

The statistics about reading failure in the United States are astounding. The 2009 National Assessment of Educational Progress (NAEP) reported that 33% of fourth-grade students and 25% of eighth-grade students scored below the basic level in overall reading skill and that 34% of fourth-grade students and 43% of eighth-grade students scored at the basic level (National Center for Education Statistics, 2009). Clearly, this confirms that millions of students in middle and high schools across the nation struggle to read in school every day.

Children in primary grades with reading difficulty usually have decoding deficits at the phoneme or word level. Children beyond third grade who have reading difficulty may have word-level deficits, comprehension deficits, or both (Hock et al., 2009; Leach, Scarborough, & Rescorla, 2003). This chapter focuses on instruction for those students beyond third grade who have word-level reading difficulty with or without an accompanying comprehension deficit. This accounts for up to 67% of students who have late-identified reading disabilities (Leach et al., 2003).

In urban settings, the percentages of adolescents with basic literacy levels are especially pronounced (Hock et al., 2009; Snow & Biancarosa, 2003). Many of these students have difficulty at the word level. A study of 320 struggling high school freshmen in a large urban district found that 74% of all ninth-grade students scored at the "unsatisfactory" or "basic" levels on the state assessment test in reading. Those in the "unsatisfactory" level were at the third percentile in decoding and word recognition and the first percentile in reading comprehension. Those at the "basic" level were reading at the ninth percentile in decoding and word recognition and at the eighth percentile in reading comprehension (Hock, Deshler, Marquis, & Brasseur, 2005).

In another adolescent study in urban school settings, the domains of word level, fluency, vocabulary, and comprehension were assessed, and an analysis of the results found that 61% of the struggling adolescent readers had significant deficits in all of these reading components, including word-level skills (Hock et al., 2009).

These data inform us that a significant percentage of students beyond the elementary grades lack decoding and fluency skills and cannot read grade-level text with ease. Jeanne S. Chall (1983) explained it well: First, students learn to read, and then students read to learn. Students are expected to read to learn beginning in the upper elementary grades. If students in 4th through 12th grade lack sufficient reading skills, then this expectation places extraordinary demands on them.

STUDENTS BEYOND GRADE 3 WITH A WORD-LEVEL READING DISABILITY

An adolescent struggling reader faces many academic challenges that must be addressed. Students beyond Grade 3 are expected to decode with ease. When this is not possible, the student struggles with all aspects of the school day. There is a persistent belief that it is inappropriate to provide word-level instruction to older students who cannot yet do this; however, "for older students struggling at the word level, word-study intervention is an appropriate response" (Scammacca et al., 2007, p. 13).

Academic Challenges

Although it is obvious that fluent decoding alone will not result in proficient reading, it is necessary. Older students who do not yet have automatic single-word reading skills have difficulty at the beginning levels of reading. But these older students also likely have underlying phonological awareness deficits and persistent difficulty mapping the alphabetic symbols to sounds (Bruck, 1990, 1992; Spreen, 1989). As a result, they stumble over words, often even monosyllabic words, which are unfamiliar to them. The words *depth, gene, nerve,* and *source* are just a few such examples that they will encounter in their content-area courses that might cause difficulty without sufficient sound–symbol knowledge.

Adolescent students with word-level deficits have well-established guessing habits. Lacking knowledge about the patterns that make up longer words, they demonstrate limited orthographic awareness (Bruck, 1990). Subsequently, they misread multisyllabic words, guessing at words using clues such as the first or last letters in the word, the length of the word, or other features.

Academic problems go well beyond decoding. If a student cannot adequately map alphabetic symbols to sounds and lacks orthographic awareness, then he or she will have a corresponding spelling deficit (Banks, Guyer, & Guyer, 1993; Bruck, 1993; Ehri, 2000). This, in turn, significantly limits their written output. Students find themselves unable to transfer their thoughts into written words, even when answers are known.

An older student with basic decoding problems has limited experience with text, despite several years of schooling. His or her peers who can read with ease have so much more exposure to the written word. Unlike them, struggling adolescent readers tend to avoid reading so that many benefits associated with this practice elude them. The problem increases exponentially over the years. Clearly, daily academic challenges face these students. Without fluent decoding and limitations in reading rate, the adolescent students are unable to negotiate the demands of content areas of study. The struggling reader's lack of experience with print results in lower levels of vocabulary and significantly less background knowledge so that the deficits in word-level decoding, vocabulary, and content knowledge compound each other, resulting in significant academic challenges and, all too often, failure.

Not Too Late

Adolescent students with word-level deficits require instruction that targets their deficits (Deschler & Hock, 2006; Hock et al., 2009). Students beyond elementary grades (including high school students) with significant deficits can benefit from intensive word-level instruction (Curtis & Longo, 1999; Deschler et al., 2001; Lovett, Barron, & Benson, 2003; O'Connor & Wilson, 1995; Penney, 2002).

A meta-analysis of research by the Center on Instruction (Scammacca et al., 2007) determined that word-level interventions are appropriate for older students struggling at the word level. Word-level intervention is not too late even if students are beyond the third grade. Typically, learners at the initial stages of reading can benefit from intervention targeted at word-reading strategies. They require word study instruction including phonemic awareness, word analysis, and sight word recognition as well as vocabulary, fluency, and comprehension. They may require between 50 and 100 minutes per day of reading instruction. Typically, however, most middle and high schools have not addressed these basic skills even in classes for struggling readers who cannot yet efficiently decode.

> It is often assumed that by adolescence, readers have acquired adult-like decoding and word recognition abilities. However, recent work suggests that many struggling adolescent readers lack sufficient fluency in word recognition and can benefit from intervention targeted at word reading strategies. (Hock et al., 2009)

Word-study interventions, then, are appropriate for older students struggling at the word level. In order to properly address the needs of this student population, literacy planning will require identifying these students and placing them into intervention classes that are appropriate for their needs.

STRUGGLING ADOLESCENT READERS: ASSESSMENT AND INSTRUCTIONAL RESPONSE

> Older students with reading difficulties benefit from interventions focused both at the word level and the text level. Identifying need and intervening accordingly in the appropriate areas (e.g., vocabulary, word reading, comprehension strategies, and so on) is associated with improved outcomes for older students with reading difficulties. (Scammacca et al., 2007, p. 12)

Assessment to Determine Needs

Students beyond third grade vary in reading in more ways than younger students. For one thing, the range of overall reading levels in a given grade is much greater in the later grades. An eighth-grade class, for example, might include some students who are nonreaders as well as some who read at a high school level. This poses many challenges for instruction. It also requires schools to do more than simply identify their struggling readers through annual testing.

There is an important variable that must be considered when designing the intervention plan for older students with reading difficulty—the specific area of deficit. As we have discussed, the struggling reader is an individual who is unsuccessful in school literacy tasks. This label, however, gives little information about the reader's specific areas of difficulty (Alvermann, 2001). Student performance data are central to literacy improvement efforts in middle and high school settings (Irvin, Meltzer, & Dukes, 2007) because students with late-identified reading disabilities may have word-level deficits or comprehension deficits or both (Hock et al., 2009; Leach et al., 2003).

The *Reading Next* report (Biancarosa & Snow) summarized the varying needs of adolescent struggling readers:

> Part of what makes it so difficult to meet the needs of struggling readers and writers in middle and high school is that these students experience a wide range of challenges that require an equally wide range of interventions. Some young people still have difficulty simply reading words accurately. Most older struggling readers can *read* words accurately, but they do not *comprehend* what they read for a variety of reasons. For some, the problem is that they do not yet read words with enough fluency to facilitate comprehension. Others can read accurately and quickly enough for comprehension to take place, but they lack the strategies to help them comprehend what they read. In addition, problems faced by struggling readers are exacerbated when they are ESL or have learning disabilities. (2006, p. 8)

Beyond third grade, an effective assessment plan must be put into place in order to develop a responsive literacy plan. State- and districtwide English language arts and reading tests provide general reading scores and can identify struggling readers. More comprehensive assessments will determine subskills, however, so that instruction can be properly planned and executed. Deficits in the following subskills indicate weaknesses that need to be addressed: phonological awareness, sound–symbol relationships, word attack (decoding), word identification, fluency, and spelling. Assessing these subskills will identify students who require an intervention that targets their specific needs.

A general screening will assist in determining the students' needs. State literacy tests provide an overall reading score that can be combined with a quick universal screening of key word-level subskills. School districts completing this process in late spring or at the end of the school year will be prepared to schedule appropriate intervention classes for these struggling students for the following school year.

One such screening process uses two tests: the Test of Silent Word Reading Fluency–Second Edition (TOSWRF-2; Mather, Hammill, Allen, & Roberts, in press) and the spelling subtest of the Word Identification and Spelling Test (WIST; Felton & Wilson, 2004). Both tests can be quickly administered in a group setting within one class period. The TOSWRF-2 provides students with a single page of words that are presented with no spaces between them. The students are timed for 3 minutes as they put slashes between the words (see Figure 16.1). Students who can adequately decode are able to discern the division between words, whereas those who cannot decode randomly divide the letters on the page. The spelling subtest of the WIST takes approximately 20–25 minutes in a group setting. Students with poor decoding also have poor spelling. The WIST subtest, a nationally normed spelling assessment for older students, provides information on the knowledge of specific syllable patterns.

Results from this screening will help to identify struggling students with word-level deficits. To assist with instructional planning, the additional WIST subtests can be ad-

bigtwolookhegreenmylikebblueupwecar/
toinfunisflyauntnestwhystayoldallout/
unclecouldbirdnightfivebagwouldlaugh/
pigpullbyarebutprizeammuchunderour/
anveryguessbuyflewtakeletgiveduckif/
peoplefoundsunbackhurryicegirldress/
yardtryroomlostcakelunchhurtloudnut/
armgrewbothsignwildemptyfewablecut/

Figure 16.1. Sample page showing the Test of Silent Word Reading Fluency–Second Edition (TOSWRF-2). (*Note:* From *Test of Silent Word Reading Fluency–Second Edition,* by N. Mather, D. Hammill, E.A. Allen, and R. Roberts, in press, Austin, TX: PRO-ED, Inc. Copyright by PRO-ED, Inc. Reprinted with permission.) (The TOSWRF-2 includes four equivalent forms, a practice form, and normative data up to age 24.)

ministered subsequently to those students with poor decoding and spelling to further determine which skills are lacking. Furthermore, an oral reading fluency assessment that includes a prosody measure can provide valuable information for the intervention plan.

Other similar screening tests can be utilized; however, it is essential to select testing that will separately examine the two different areas of reading difficulty—lack of basic decoding skills versus difficulty with comprehension. You want to be able to distinguish between older struggling readers who have trouble reading due to a lack of basic reading skills and those who are struggling with understanding but can decode (see Chapters 12, 14, and 17). It is important to conduct a comprehensive evaluation for students with significant reading and writing deficits (see Chapter 14).

Multitiered intervention classes can then be scheduled to address the actual identified needs of the students, rather than assigning them to a generic reading class that does not provide the differentiated instruction that they need. Adolescents who cannot yet decode efficiently require specific and skillful word-level instruction (Hock et al., 2009). Adolescents who decode fluently but have poor comprehension can benefit from interventions that focus on comprehension and strategy instruction (Deschler et al., 2001; Moore, Bean, Birdyshaw, & Rycik, 1999; Scruggs, Mastropieri, Berkeley, & Graetz, 2010). Furthermore, students with a diagnosed reading disability need more intensive instruction than other students (Lyon et al., 2001; see Figure 16.2 and Chapter 17 for information on planning for differentiated instruction for varying student needs across content areas.)

Clearly, school policies and structures need to be in place to support an action plan. In particular, effective scheduling is needed to allow for the literacy interventions to be delivered. Leadership at the building and district level is necessary to assure success. School leaders must make it a priority to support literacy across the content areas and provide professional development for teachers to succeed with students who bring varied literacy skills into the classroom (Irvin et al., 2007). Furthermore, in a summary of their work, Deschler et al. (2001) concluded that students with severe difficulties will

Example of Literacy Planning Beyond Grade 3

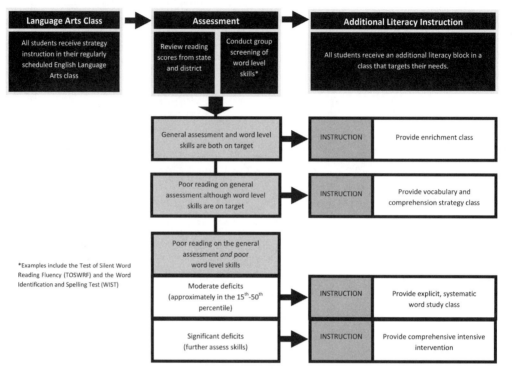

Figure 16.2.   Example of literacy planning beyond third grade. (From Wilson, B.A. [2009]. *Example of literacy planning beyond grade 3* [p. 1]. Wilson Academy Resources, http://www.wilsonacademy.com; reprinted by permission. Copyright © 2009 Wilson Language Training. All rights reserved.)

need a more intensive level of instruction from someone other than the content-area classroom teacher.

Teacher Preparation for Word-Level Instruction

One of the most important conclusions from research is that learning is hard work for children with learning problems. A corollary to this finding is that instruction is hard work and requires an enormous amount of training and support for their teachers.

"Children who have difficulty learning to read will likely not benefit from 'more of the same' but require an alternative method of teaching to assist their learning" (Semrud-Clikeman, 2005, p. 567). Teachers who work with struggling readers beyond elementary grades are generally not familiar with word-level instruction. Most teachers are uncomfortable presenting older students with phonics—they may resist or avoid this instruction. Their discomfort comes partly from expecting that older students will not want to work on basic skills, but mostly it comes from their inexperience with teaching basic skills and their lack of preparation. Unfortunately, all too often, teachers do not know how to teach word structure in depth. Furthermore, they lack core information about phonology, orthography, and morphology (American Federation of Teachers, 1999; McCutchen et al., 2002). This makes basic skills instruction challenging for a teacher working with elementary school students, but it makes it even more difficult for a teacher working with older students.

For adolescents at the initial stages of reading, teachers who teach intensive interventions in alphabetics must be trained specifically in those methods (Curtis, 2004). Because older students will be hesitant to work on basic skills, precise, experienced teaching is necessary. Teachers must overcome their discomfort in order to achieve success. To begin with, they should be skilled and proficient with multisensory structured language teaching methods. It is also important for the teacher to present the systematic language instruction with confidence and with absolutely no hint of apology. In order to do this, the teacher must believe strongly that this teaching is appropriate and necessary. Thus, teachers cannot be expected to implement a program for struggling readers without substantial targeted professional development and ongoing support.

INSTRUCTION FOR STUDENTS WITH WORD-LEVEL DEFICITS

A student who has difficulty decoding words should receive instruction in word study whether he is in first grade, fourth grade, or 12th grade. The instructional materials used may vary depending on age and grade level, but the learning objectives remain the same. (Boardman, et al., 2008, p. 5)

Instruction in advanced word study teaches the letter patterns and structural features of predictable speech sounds. Students learn how to identify syllable patterns and break difficult words into manageable parts. Students also learn the recognition and meanings of prefixes, suffixes, inflectional endings, and roots. Vocabulary instruction must be interwoven into the word-study work (Boardman et al., 2008; Murray et al., 2010).

Older students with decoding deficits need much practice applying newfound decoding strategies. Word-level instruction provides a critical base; however, supported practice with connected text is essential to the students' development as skilled readers. Instruction must include fluency work beyond speed, including oral reading prosody with an emphasis on comprehension (Kuhn, Schwanenflugel, & Meisinger, 2010; Samuels & Farstrup, 2006; Wilson, 1989).

For both word study and fluency instruction, students progress to more advanced work only when mastery is achieved. This principle requires demonstration of learning by applying skills and content and is a core element of competency-based instruction (Sturgis & Patrick, 2010).

Components of a lesson plan include the following:

- Phoneme/grapheme instruction

- Study of word structure for decoding

- Word reading (accuracy/automaticity focus)

- Connected text reading (prosody/automaticity focus)

- Study of word structure for spelling

- Word/sentence dictation

Accuracy and Automaticity of Single-Word Reading

The difficulty of mapping alphabetic symbols to sounds can persist in older students, resulting in lingering problems with reading and spelling (Bruck, 1990, 1993; Spreen,

1989). Adolescents with decoding deficits have not fully internalized the sound system of the language, and they do not understand the structure of English words. As a result, they cannot accurately or fluently read text, and they are poor spellers. Although it may seem awkward to present basic skills to older students, this is not a good reason to let problems go unaddressed. If students who need basic skills are taught in a multi-sensory, systematic way, then they will make substantial progress (Curtis & Longo, 1999; O'Connor & Wilson, 1995; Penney, 2002). This instruction needs to focus on developing the students' phonemic awareness, sound–symbol knowledge, understanding of word structure (syllable patterns and affixes), and high-frequency irregular words.

Teaching Sounds

Phonemic awareness instruction is most effective when students are taught to manipulate phonemes by using the letters of the alphabet (National Institute of Child Health and Human Development [NICHD], 2000). Thus, phonemic awareness training is closely linked with the direct teaching of letter–sound (grapheme-phoneme) correspondences. Accuracy with sounds is a crucial first step for students. The teacher begins instruction by teaching letter names and sounds for consonants, short vowels, and consonant digraphs.

An assessment such as WIST (Felton & Wilson, 2004) can help the teacher determine a baseline of sound knowledge. Many older students know most of the consonant sounds. They often add a vowel sound to each consonant, however, for example, saying /muh/ rather than /m/. It is more natural to say /muh/, and therefore /m/ must be carefully taught and practiced. Teach students how to clip consonant sounds, explaining that it is important to clip sounds in order to blend them into words. It helps to explain that one should minimize the dropping of the chin when pronouncing consonant sounds. Say /tuh/, then /t/. When the sound is clipped, the chin does not drop.

Illustrate the importance of clipping sounds using sound or phoneme cards. Make the word *mat*. If the sounds are said /muh/ /ă/ /tuh/, then the word will not blend to make the word *mat*. The sounds /m/ /ă/ /t/, however, do blend to say *mat*.

Unlike younger children, older students only need key words for consonant sounds that are either unknown or are not well established. Use key words for any troublesome consonants, always linking the key word to the letter(s) and the sound—*qu, queen*, /kw/. Key words aid memory and provide a reference to help students gain access to the sound. The same key word should be consistently used to represent a sound. For example, many students say that the sound for *y* is /w/ because the name of the letter *y* starts with a /w/ sound. The key word *yellow* can help students remember that the sound for *y* is /y/, not /w/.

Typical consonants needing key words include *qu, w, x,* and *y*. Key words are also useful for the consonants *g* and *c* to emphasize the primary sound (*g, game,* /g/; *c, cat,* /k/). Students who have not mastered the sound system often say the secondary sound for these letters—/j/ for the letter *g*— when trying to decode unfamiliar words. Also, teach students the basic consonant digraphs: *sh, th, wh, ch,* and *ck*. Using a sound card with two letters on one card, show students that digraphs are two letters that have only one sound (*sh, ship,* /sh/).

Use key words for all of the short vowels regardless of baseline assessments because these sounds are critical and are easily confused. The key word helps students isolate and gain access to the sound; they learn to extend the vowel sound that begins the key word. The key word *apple* is used for short *a*. Say "aaaaaaaapple" and have students repeat it. Ask students to say the sound until they run out of breath or to extend the sound at the beginning of the key word until you hold up your hand. Have them repeat the letter, key word, and sound after you: "Say *a, apple, /ă/.*"

Each student can develop a notebook divided into several sections to record information about the word structure of the English language. The first section of the notebook, labeled "sounds," is used for reference. Have students enter the short vowel sounds on one page, the consonants on another page, and basic digraphs on a third page. See the student notebook sample in Figure 16.3 and note that the consonant page only has three key word pictures—for the three consonant sounds that were unknown or insecure for this particular student. The rest of the notebook is devoted to recording word/syllable structure, spelling rules, vocabulary, and high-frequency nonphonetic irregular words (Wilson, 1989).

Do not teach all of the sounds at once; instead, present them incrementally and cumulatively in a sequence that reflects frequency in the language and ease of learning. Carefully teach all sounds to mastery. Initially, model the sounds and have students repeat after you until they can accurately pronounce each sound independently. As each sound is introduced, practice it in two directions: first for decoding (students look at the letter and name the sound) and second for spelling (students hear the sound and identify the letter). For spelling practice, dictate a sound, such as /m/, and have students (individually or as a group) repeat it. Then have them name the letter (*m*) that makes that sound.

Teach Blending and Segmenting

Mastering sounds of the English language is critical; however, this skill is not sufficient for successful decoding or spelling. Students must also be able to blend and segment

			Consonants				
a	apple /ă/	b	c	d	f		
e	Ed /ĕ/	bat /b/	cat /k/ /s/ after e, i, y	dog /d/	fun /f/		
i	itch /ĭ/	g	h	j	k	l	
		game /g/ /j/ after e, i, y	hat /h/	jog /j/	kite /k/	lamp /l/	
o	octopus /ŏ/	m	n	p	qu	r	s
		man /m/	nut /n/	pan /p/	queen /kw/	red /r/	snake /s/ bags, wise /z/
u	up /ŭ/	t	v	w	f	y	z
		tap /t/	van /v/	wind /w/	fox /ks/	yellow /y/	zebra /z/

Figure 16.3.   Pages from a student notebook for noting key words and pictures for short vowel and consonant sounds.

sounds. Phoneme segmentation, the ability to pull apart the sounds in a given word, is a critical skill for reading and spelling success. Poor readers often need direct teaching of this skill. Students can learn how to blend and segment three sounds, then four, five, and six sounds, using one-syllable short-vowel words. One multisensory method for phoneme blending and segmentation training utilizes a combination of phoneme cards, blank cards (for segmenting), and a finger-tapping procedure (Wilson, 1989).

This method begins with teaching students how to segment and blend familiar three-sound words such as *map*. Put three phoneme cards (*m a p*) on a table surface or in a pocket chart. The card with the vowel should be represented by a different color. Teach students how to say each sound as they tap a finger to their thumb: As they say /m/, they tap their index finger to their thumb; as they say /ă/, they tap their middle finger to their thumb; and as they say /p/, they tap their ring finger to their thumb. Then have students say the sounds as they drag their thumb across their fingers, starting with their index finger for /m/. This multisensory approach has been successful in getting students to blend sounds.

The tactile input to the fingertips appears to aid in the blending process. With a word such as *math*, the *th* digraph should be one card to represent one sound. The student also taps only three times because the digraph *th* stays together to make only one sound. Some students prefer to tap on the table surface rather than the thumb. This still provides tactile feedback. To tap out the word *map* on the table, a student says /m/ while tapping the index finger on the table, /ă/ while tapping the middle finger, and /p/ while tapping the ring finger. The student then taps all fingers to the table while saying the word *map*.

With older students, you should immediately show them that they can decode a word that they have never seen before. They will usually read three-sound words such as *map* without a problem, but there are many words that have three sounds that are unfamiliar. Tell the students that the tapping-out method works with these unfamiliar words as well. Examples of three-sound words that are often unknown by sight are *vat, shod, posh, thud, yen,* and *sod*. Form these words, one at a time, with cards. Be sure students say the sounds accurately with each tap, clipping the consonant sounds.

Model the blending as needed. When you make a three-sound word that the students do not know, help them decode it with tapping. Students often have an "aha" moment the first time they successfully decode an unfamiliar word—take advantage of this moment by explaining that you will be showing them ways to determine hundreds of words that they have never seen before without memorizing them. Students often feel encouraged when they are successful with some of these words that they do not know by sight. Be sure to take the time to talk about this with them and give them hope. They have tried to memorize so many words. Tell them, "See, you don't need to memorize. I'm going to show you how to figure words out."

Gradually build short-vowel words with three sounds (e.g., *cap, cash*), then four (e.g., *step, stash*), then five (e.g., *stump, shrimp*) and six sounds (e.g., *script*). This teaching of sounds, phoneme segmentation, and blending sets the essential groundwork for successful and fluent decoding. Students should not progress to words with four sounds until they can read and spell any unfamiliar three-sound words without tapping. Tapping is a useful tool, but the goal is for students to read fluently without tapping. For some students this might take several lessons.

Also teach students how to identify closed syllables during this initial phase of word study. The English language uses six kinds of syllables; closed syllables are the most common. Students must learn to visually recognize when a syllable is closed, which tells them that the vowel in that syllable has a short sound. (See Chapter 8, Table 8.4 for six syllable types.)

Students must easily blend and segment the sounds in a single syllable before progressing to multisyllabic work. In addition to the methods already described, give students a lot of application practice with short-vowel words on flashcards, on word lists, and within connected text (Wilson, 1989). This is just the beginning stage for decoding and encoding, but it is a crucial one.

Help students become metacognitive thinkers about word structure to develop accurate reading of words. They should be aware of what they know and understand how it helps them determine an unknown word. Use questioning techniques to facilitate this. For example, if a student reads the word *shop* instead of *chop,* ask, "What is the digraph in that word?" and "What sound does the digraph make?" to lead to the correction. When the student determines the correct word, say, "That is the word! What did you do to figure it out?" Use questioning to emphasize word structure and to correct errors, but do not overuse it. Reduce questioning as a student becomes more accurate so that you can then work on quick and automatic word recognition. When students become accurate, you can do timed drills to increase their automaticity.

Introduce Multisyllabic Words

Students need to learn the sounds of the language, but they must also learn total word structure. Teaching the students more detail about word structure helps them accurately apply the sounds in longer words. Syllable patterns are an important part of that instruction because the type of syllable regulates the vowel sound. Also, spelling instruction that emphasizes syllable types assists older students with word-analysis skills (Bhattacharya & Ehri, 2004; Curtis & Longo, 1999; Wilson, 1989). What is unclear from research, however, is the amount of explicit multisyllabic word instruction necessary for struggling readers beyond third grade (Torgesen et al., 2007).

It is important to give older students a feeling of accomplishment with longer words as soon as possible. Teach them how to combine closed syllables so that they succeed with multisyllabic words. The word *combat,* for example, combines two closed syllables. The word *Wisconsin* combines three closed syllables. When students master one type of syllable, teach them the next type, manipulating sound cards to teach the concept. When you introduce a new syllable type, use words combining the new and previously learned syllable types (Wilson, 1989). For example, after students learn closed and vowel-consonant-*e* syllables, have them read and spell words such as *reptile, inflate,* and *compensate*. The word *compensate,* for example, has two closed syllables (with short vowels) and a vowel-consonant-*e* syllable. With older students, present long words containing only one or two types of syllables as soon as possible. By reading and spelling longer words, they gain confidence and a sense of success they would not achieve by only decoding short words. Students should practice reading and spelling these words in isolation as well as within sentences and passages.

Teaching basic syllable patterns should be done gradually and cumulatively. As students learn each syllable type, they add the definition of each pattern, word examples, and corresponding rules of syllable division to their student notebooks.

Teach Rules of Orthography

Students with a language learning disability actually can learn rules, although they might have difficulty with the language of the rules. Words get in their way. For students with a language learning difficulty, instruction that includes demonstration and practice with manipulatives helps to clarify verbal explanations (Banks et al., 1993; Janney & Snell, 2000; Wilson, 1989). When students add a rule to their notebooks for reference, they also need to learn all about word structure in detail by means other than memorizing the wording of the rule. Manipulating word parts helps them see and feel the structure. For example, the silent *e* spelling rule can be taught with sound cards and suffix cards. Present suffixes to students on individual cards. First, have the students categorize suffixes into two columns, putting the suffixes that begin with a vowel in one column and the suffixes that begin with a consonant in another column.

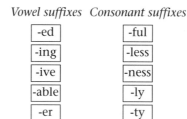

Make the word *hope* with the sound cards:

h   o   p   e

Tell the students that words ending in a silent *e* follow a rule when a vowel suffix is added. Put the *-ing* suffix card to the right of the word *hope*. Explain that whenever a vowel suffix (point to the column of vowel suffixes) is added to a word with a silent *e*, the *e* must drop from the end. Pull down the silent *e* card and move the *-ing* suffix card over to form *hoping*. Put the *e* back and make *hope* again. Tell the students that whenever a consonant suffix is added to a silent *e* word (point to the column of consonant suffixes), the suffix is simply added and the *e* does not drop. Add the suffixes *-ful* and *-less* to demonstrate. Next, explain that this rule applies no matter when there is a silent *e*. Add suffixes to several words and again explain the addition of the vowel versus consonant suffixes. Help students to understand the dropping of the *e* because the *e* is literally dropped whenever a vowel suffix is added. Some word examples include the following:

Word	*Reason for silent e*	*Addition of suffixes*
shape	Vowel-consonant-*e* syllable	shaped, shaping, shapeless
give	No English word ends in *v*	giving, giver, gives
settle	Consonant-*le* syllable	settling, settler, settlement
infringe	Letter *g* with a /j/ sound	infringing, infringement
nice	Two jobs: vowel-consonant-*e* and *c* with an /s/ sound	nicest, nicer, nicely

Demonstrate word structure for this and other rules of orthography with sound cards and suffix cards. This is usually necessary for students to process the information, understand it, and thus succeed in the learning and application. Teach and thoroughly practice each rule. Provide multiple opportunities to read words in isolation on flashcards and on word lists. Also, dictate the words for spelling. When students demonstrate mastery, introduce another rule, but continue to practice and review all rules previously taught. Students must overlearn the application of the rule as opposed to the wording of the rule. The wording is added to their notebooks for reference only.

Teaching Morphology

When you teach students about syllables and suffix rules (as previously discussed), you are changing their focus from individual sounds to word parts. Older students have difficulty with the word patterns of roots, prefixes, and suffixes that increasingly appear in more challenging content-area textbooks. Between fourth grade and high school, knowing common English roots, prefixes, and suffixes is increasingly important to word-level reading success (Nagy, Diakidoy, & Anderson, 1993).

The direct teaching of morphology, then, is another effective means to help older students understand and apply word structure for decoding and spelling (Carlisle, 2010; National Institute for Literacy, 2007). A morpheme is the smallest unit of meaning. The word *predict,* for example, has two morphemes: the prefix, *pre-,* and the root, *dict.* This instruction has the added benefit of teaching vocabulary as well. Use flashcards to gradually teach the recognition, spelling, and meaning of roots, prefixes, and suffixes (Henry, 1993).

Explicit instruction in the most frequently used prefixes helps students decode, spell, and figure out the meaning of many longer words. There are 20 prefixes that represent 97% of prefixed words in English, and only 4 of these (*un, re, in,* and *dis*) account for 58% of prefixed words (White, Sowell, & Yanagihara, 1989). Build related words by adding prefixes and suffixes to root words such as *nation, national, international, multinational,* and *nationality.* You can also introduce the Anglo-Saxon roots and then the Latin and Greek structures to provide a more in-depth word study (see Chapter 4).

Application of Skills and Fluency Instruction

From the early grades, poor readers are exposed to much less text than students who read well. Although this is true in the primary grades, the gap increases dramatically as students progress into higher grades. A landmark study of fifth-grade students conducted by Anderson, Wilson, and Fielding (1988) clearly showed an enormous gap in independent reading practices. Students at the 98th percentile of reading read approximately 4,358,000 words per year; students at the 10th percentile read 8,000 words per year; and students at the 2nd percentile read 0 words per year.

A 10-year longitudinal study conducted by Cunningham and Stanovich (1997) showed that the very act of reading can help children build their vocabulary, general knowledge, and cognitive structures. This is true even for children with poor comprehension skills. The amount or volume that a student reads makes a difference because reading builds comprehension and fluency. Students need to practice reading in order to become fluent (NICHD, 2000). The Partnership for Reading explained,

> Fluency develops as a result of many opportunities to practice reading with a high degree of success. Therefore, your students should practice orally rereading text that is reasonably easy for them—that is, text containing mostly words that they know or can decode easily.

> In other words, the texts should be at the students' independent reading level. If the text is more difficult, students will focus so much on word recognition that they will not have an opportunity to develop fluency. (2003, p. 27)

Although reading develops reading skills (Cunningham & Stanovich, 1997), the National Reading Panel (NRP; NICHD, 2000) suggested that sustained silent reading does not demonstrate benefits with students who have not yet developed the critical alphabetic and word-reading skills. Thus, initially, most reading opportunities for these students must be with direct teacher instruction. Interactively work with the students as they read in order to help them integrate their decoding skills and model both fluent reading and thinking.

Using curriculum-based measurement to assess oral reading fluency on a regular basis can help identify a student's instructional level and progress for the instruction he or she is receiving (Hosp, Hosp, & Howell, 2007; see Chapters 8, 10, and 14). Fluency proficiency goals for students in 4th and 5th grade are 120–140 words correct per minute (WCPM) and 150 WCPM for students in 6th through 12th grade (Hasbrouck & Tindal, 2006). Students must practice to achieve these goals. Increasing evidence indicates that any assessment of fluency should also include a prosody measure. Otherwise, fluency instruction might simply address correct words per minute, which is inadequate and incomplete (Kuhn et al., 2010; Samuels & Farstrup, 2006). Prosody is the rhythmic or tonal aspects of spoken language, and prosodic reading involves chunking groups of words into meaningful phrases according to syntax (Kuhn & Stahl, 2003). The National Assessment of Educational Progress (NAEP) uses a rubric to rate prosody that can help guide instruction.

Motivation to read is an important factor in getting students to practice. Students respond best when their work is challenging yet at a level where students can be successful (Christiensen, Horn, & Johnson, 2010). Students report that having the right materials motivates them to read (Ivey & Broaddus, 2001). If the material used with students is too difficult, then it is discouraging and frustrating. If the material is too juvenile, then it is demeaning. Thus, the challenge is to find decodable text passages for a reading class on subjects that interest the students written at an appropriate readability level. (See Appendix B at the end of this book for list of decodable texts.)

The proportion of words that a student recognizes instantly and the student's decoding speed and accuracy are two of the variables that influence a student's fluent reading of a text (Torgesen & Hudson, 2006). As the student's skill level for single-word decoding increases with instruction, then the level of text difficulty should gradually be increased as well.

Application of Skills and Fluency Work: Controlled Decodable Text

Figure 16.4 outlines the concurrent uses of **controlled decodable text,** noncontrolled decodable text, and enriched text instruction for students. According to the NRP (NICHD, 2000), decodable text, which is text written at the independent reading level of a student, is necessary to develop fluency. For text to be decodable, the student should be able to read 95%–100% of the words independently, with no more than 1 error per 20 words. If a student is able to read a given passage with ease and accuracy, then it is decodable to that student. In other words, readability depends on the student, not the text. Thus, to be decodable a text does not necessarily need to be controlled (limited to studied word structures). Initially, however, if a student has severe dyslexia or very limited word-attack skills, then the text will likely need to be controlled to achieve 95% accuracy for independent reading.

Controlled decodable text (see Figure 16.5) is limited to text with words that contain only the sounds and structures that have been taught. If students have been

Use of Differentiated Texts & Their Interrelationships for Students with Primary Decoding Deficits

FOCUS: ACCURACY & AUTOMATICITY OF SINGLE WORD READING	+	FOCUS: FLUENCY	+	FOCUS: VOCABULARY AND COMPREHENSION

Goals of Instruction: To develop the student's basic skills for both reading and spelling, including phonemic awareness, phonics, understanding of word structure (syllable patterns and affixes) and high frequency irregular words.

Goals of Instruction: To develop the student's fluent and rate-appropriate independent reading of connected text for meaning and to develop a student's oral reading with ease and expression.

Goals of Instruction: To develop the student's vocabulary and understanding of both narrative and expository text and to increase a student's background knowledge and schema.

⇩ ⇩ ⇩

CONTROLLED TEXT	DECODABLE TEXT	ENRICHED TEXT

Controlled Text Flashcards, Pseudo-words, Wordlists, Phrases, Sentences

Text is determined by the word structure that has been directly taught.

It is 95–100% controlled to have graphemes, pseudo words, syllables, phonetically regular and irregular words with high potential for accuracy measured against curriculum.

Controlled Decodable Text Passages

Text is determined by the word structure that has been directly taught.

It is 95–100% controlled to have graphemes, pseudo words, syllables, phonetically regular and irregular words with high "potential for accuracy" measured against curriculum.

Non-Controlled Decodable Text Passages

Text determined by a student's decoding response to a given passage. Student must read 95–100% of the words independently.

Important considerations are student interest and/or background schema.

Enriched Text Passages

Narrative and Expository Text determined by highest appropriate instructional listening comprehension level of student.

Passage is read to the students with interactive dialogue so that they can develop comprehension skills at a higher level than their decoding ability.

EXAMPLE OF CONTROLLED TEXT

sh

shop | from

from the shop

Jack will get the subs from the shop.

Use for application of skills and to buid automaticity ⇨

EXAMPLES

Subs in the Mud

The men on the job got subs from the sub shop. They set the bag of subs on the top of Ben's van. Then Ben had to dash off. He had to pick up a set of hubcaps for his van...

Monkey Face

A study shows that a monkey knows what another monkey's face is saying. A Rhesus monkey has one look on its face when it makes a happy sound. When it makes a sound because it is afraid, its face looks different...

EXAMPLE OF ENRICHED TEXT

Rhesus Monkeys Demonstrate Language Skill

Research conducted at the Max Planck Institute for Biological Cybernetics in Germany suggests that human's capacity to read facial expressions may have evolved from monkeys. Asif Ghazanfar, who studied the monkeys, reports that rhesus monkeys can combine visual and auditory information to perceive vocal signals...

⇦ *Use to build schema for non-controlled decodable text reading.*

Focus On:

Phoneme-grapheme and grapheme-phoneme correspondence

Blending and segmenting with letter manipulation

Six syllable types in English

Orthographic rules and affixes

High frequency irregular words

Phrasing

Focus On:

Application and mastery of specific decoding skills

Breaking an established guessing habit

Helping students see the structure of words in English

Reading for meaning

Prosody

Focus On:

Application and generalization of decoding skills in a non-controlled environment

Use of context clues in conjunction with decoding strategies, as appropriate

Reading for meaning

Prosody

Focus On:

Vocabulary

Comprehension of narrative text

Comprehension of expository text

Mental Imagery and retelling

Instruction:

Cumulative building of skills

Manipulation of word parts (letter cards, syllables, affixes)

Concurrent teaching of decoding-spelling

Repetition and practice

Timed drills

Instruction:

Teacher-assisted silent and oral reading with retelling

Teacher modeling of phrasing and expression

Repeated reading

Echo, choral and shared reading

Tape-assisted reading

Instruction:

Teacher modeling of fluent reading (passage read by teacher – students do not track)

Teacher modeling of thinking

Pictorial representations of content

Retelling

Graphic organizers

Increase Difficulty of Text:

Difficulty increases in relation to taught patterns of word structure: mash > script > contract > compensate > compensation > illustrious

Increase Difficulty of Text:

Difficulty increases in relation to size of font, length of passage, decoding level of text and complexity of content, themes and ideas

Difficulty increases in relation to taught patterns of word structure: mash > script > contract > compensate > compensation >illustrious

Difficulty increases in relation to increase of a student's overall ability to apply decoding and context clues

Increase Difficulty of Text:

Difficulty increases in relation to complexity of content, themes and ideas.

⇩ ⇩ ⇩ ⇩

Goal: The convergence of the skills that enable the student to independently read high-level text with ease, expression and comprehension.

From Wilson, B. (2003) Wilson Academy Resources, www.wilsonacdemy.com, Oxford, MA: Wilson Language Training Corp.; reprinted by permission.

Figure 16.4. Use of differentiated texts and their interrelationships for students with primary decoding deficits. (From Wilson, B.A. [2003]. *Use of differentiated texts and their interrelationships for students with primary decoding deficits.* Retrieved December 23, 2009, from http://www.wilsonacademy.com; reprinted by permission. Copyright © 2003 Wilson Language Training. All rights reserved.)

Subs in the Mud	**Flipping Pancakes**
The men on the job got subs from the sub shop. They set the bag of subs on the top of Ben's van. Then Ben had to dash off. He had to pick up a set of hubcaps for his van. But the subs sat on the top of the van. On his run to the shop, a big log fell in the path of his van. Ben hit the log with a thud, and the subs fell off in the mud...	Jim has a job at the Esquire Pancake Shop. His boss is Mr. Musgrave, but they call him "Bigtime." Bigtime has the shop as a franchise. On the front of the shop, in big print, is HANDMADE PANCAKES Jim, Helene, and a kid they call "Wishbone" run the shop. Jim and Wishbone make pancakes. Jim gets up at sunrise and commutes to the shop on his bike. He has to compete with the traffic stampede, inhale its fumes...

Figure 16.5.   Two samples of controlled decodable text. *Subs in the Mud:* Use after introducing short vowels, consonants, and basic consonant digraphs in three-sound words. *Flipping Pancakes:* Use after introducing multisyllabic words with closed syllables and vowel-consonant-*e* syllables. (From Brown, J. [1998]. Flipping pancakes. In *Stories for older students* [Book 2, Steps 4–6, p. 9] and Subs in the mud. In *Stories for older students* [Book 1, Steps 1–3, p. 1]. Oxford, MA: Wilson Language Training; reprinted by permission. Copyright © 1998 Wilson Language Training. All rights reserved.)

introduced to the sounds of the short vowels, consonants, and basic consonant digraphs in three-sound words, then a controlled text such as "Subs in the Mud" could be used. The passage "Flipping Pancakes" is a sample of controlled text that can be presented when students have learned multisyllabic words combining closed syllables and vowel-consonant-*e* syllables.

Controlled text for older students should be written specifically for them to provide them with substantial practice within context. This kind of text is key for students with emerging decoding skills, offering the following benefits:

- To give students practice applying specific word-attack skills, to develop accuracy, and to break the habit of guessing

- To give students repeated practice for mastery of skills

- To demonstrate word structure so that they "see" the system of the language

- To provide them with text to develop fluency

Application of Skills and Fluency Work: Noncontrolled Decodable Text

Adequate progress in learning to read beyond the initial level depends on...sufficient practice in reading to achieve fluency with different kinds of texts written for different purposes.
—Snow, Burns, and Griffin (1998, p. 223)

Noncontrolled decodable passages (containing patterns and sounds not already taught) should be used with students as skills allow them to read a given text with 95% accuracy or better. Interest-driven content is preferred because the subject is familiar and therefore the student will know the vocabulary. It will also be more motivating to students to read something of interest when decoding skills are just emerging (Fink, 1998).

The term **high interest–low level readers** has been used to describe text written at a basic decoding level with older students in mind. These are intended to provide older students with text written at the level at which they scored on reading assessments. The level of text difficulty might be reported by grade level.

A variety of methods have been used to determine the difficulty level of written text, such as readability formulas, the lexile system, and text leveling (Hiebert, 2002). With each of these systems, there is an attempt to determine the difficulty of text using various factors, including print features (e.g., length of passage, layout, font), text structure (e.g., narrative, expository), vocabulary, predictability (e.g., repeated patterns, familiar concepts), syntactic difficulty (e.g., sentence length and structure), and semantic difficulty. Ways of measuring text difficulty are not consistent. To date, there is not one clear way to measure the real difficulty level of text, although it may be assigned a grade level or a lexile by a particular rating system. Student assessment scores will not necessarily match a text's assigned difficulty level. Although a student's reading assessment may indicate a reading grade-level score of 5.0, a text assigned a grade 5.0 level of difficulty may not be decodable text for that student. The student may struggle to read too many words despite the text's seeming appropriateness based on the student's test score and the assignment of text difficulty. Thus, text cannot truly be determined decodable for a student by lexiles, readability formulas, or grade-leveling systems. These can simply be used as guides. Text can be determined as decodable only by a student's response to the given passage. Again, in order for text to be decodable, a student must read 95%–100% of the words independently.

You need a way to find suitable passages because high interest–low level readers require substantial practice applying their developing skills with noncontrolled decodable text. Although imperfect, various measures of text difficulty can be useful as a guide when searching for appropriate reading material for emergent older readers. Use test scores and text difficulty guidelines to help select reading material. Also, use student interest and student background knowledge because the more a student knows about a topic, the more likely he or she will be able to successfully determine the words. When you initially work with students with noncontrolled text, it will help if you read to them on the subject that they will subsequently read on their own. Match the content of an enriched text to a decodable text passage provided to students. First, read the enriched text to the students while at the same time structuring their comprehension. Then, present the same topic with similar information but written at an easier level. Because you have provided the schema, or background information, you will have the opportunity to teach the students how to use context clues in combination with their emerging decoding strategies to determine unfamiliar words (see Figures 16.6 and 16.7).

Increasing students' independent ability to decode a passage and comprehending it at the same time is the primary aim of your instruction with decodable text. Once identified, this text should be used for guided reading instruction. Help the students with applying and generalizing decoding skills in the noncontrolled text environment. Encourage them to use context clues in conjunction with their decoding strategies, as appropriate. Work with your students, showing them how to apply the decoding skills (e.g., tapping) if they struggle with a word that contains elements that have been taught. Students are usually accustomed to teachers telling them the unknown words. Instead, use questioning techniques to guide students whenever words correspond to the structures (e.g., syllable types, affixes) you have taught. If students struggle with a word with untaught elements, then direct them to use the context and/or the word's structure if these will be helpful, and if not, tell them the word. Be sure that passages are read for meaning, helping the students to focus on comprehension as they successfully decode.

> Fluency combines accuracy, automaticity, and oral reading prosody, which taken together, facilitate the readers' construction of meaning. It is demonstrated during oral reading through ease of word recognition, appropriate pacing, phrasing, and intonation. It is a factor in both oral and silent reading that can limit or support comprehension. (Kuhn et al., 2010, p. 240)

A Hidden World in New Guinea

During an *expedition* in December of 2005 to the Foja Mountains located on the western side of New Guinea Island, a team of American, Indonesian and Australian scientists uncovered dozens of *exotic* plants, new *species* of frogs, birds, and butterflies.

The team was dropped by helicopter to the *isolated* mountainous tropical forest that is about the size of the state of Rhode Island. It is said to be one of the largest *pristine* forests in Asia and remains free of hunting, logging, and human *impact* because of its *remote* location and *restricted access*. No one has ever built *dwellings* there.

Many new *species* were discovered in their *natural habitat* during the month-long *expedition*. At least 20 new *species* of frog, several butterfly *species* and 5 new palm plants were found...

Figure 16.6. Sample enriched text passage to be read to students. (From Wilson, B.A. [2006]. A hidden world in New Guinea [enriched version]. *Wilson Fluency/Basic, Basic Reader* [p. 32]. Oxford, MA: Wilson Language Training; reprinted by permission. Copyright © 2006 Wilson Language Training. All rights reserved.)

Decodable text should be used to practice fluent reading with an emphasis on prosody and comprehension. For fluency practice, select a decodable passage and provide oral models of phrasing and expression. Scoop the passage into phrases to model fluent reading with prosody (Wilson, 2006). You read a paragraph, and then a student reads the next paragraph, with you assisting with words as needed.

You can draw scooped lines under the text to illustrate appropriate phrasing in accordance with the syntactic structure of the text:

Next Monday, our class will visit the New England Aquarium.

or

Next Monday, our class will visit the New England Aquarium.

Initially, you can read the text to the students and have them echo your phrasing and expression. Do this in a manner that emphasizes the meaning of the passage. Model this for a paragraph, and have the students read a paragraph silently to practice phrasing and expression before reading it aloud.

Research indicates that fluency aids comprehension and comprehension aids fluency (Chard, Vaughn, & Tyler, 2002). Be sure that students understand the text's meaning. Again, comprehension is the aim of reading and must always be presented as the foremost purpose. If a student understands what he or she is reading, then he or she will likely read more fluently.

A Hidden World in New Guinea

In 2005, people visited New **Guinea** to find many hidden

things. There were a lot of plants and insects that **no** one

had **ever** been **able** to see before this visit to this land.

People have not travel**ed** to this spot because it is very

remote with big **mountains** that are **difficult** to cross.

People do not inhabit the land there. Plus, the **government**

is not fond of **visitors**. People have not hunt**ed**, fish**ed**, or

put dwellings there. There has been **no** logging. This land

has not had people there for all **these** years...

Figure 16.7.   Sample decodable text passage to be read by students with guidance from the teacher. (From Wilson, B.A. [2006]. A hidden world in New Guinea [decodable version]. *Wilson Fluency/Basic, Basic Reader* [p. 30]. Oxford, MA: Wilson Language Training; reprinted by permission. Copyright © 2006 Wilson Language Training. All rights reserved.)

The text your students practice rereading orally should be relatively short—approximately 50–200 words—with many words repeated. If using repeated reading methods, then students can read passage orally two or three more times with a focus on ease of reading and expression. Read the same passage up to four times because it appears that most of the benefit of multiple readings is achieved by then (O'Shea, Sindelar, & O'Shea, 1985).

Repeated reading does improve fluency, but too much attention to it may detract from reading comprehension (Anderson, Wilkinson, & Mason, 1991). Findings from a synthesis of fluency research suggest that interventions that involve repeated reading for students with learning disabilities are associated with improvements in reading rate, accuracy, and comprehension (Chard et al., 2002). There is also some evidence that nonrepetitive reading with a wide variety of decodable text can be equally helpful to older students in increasing reading speed (Homan, Klesius, & Hite, 1993; Rashotte & Torgesen, 1985). The wide reading has the added benefit of exposing students to more vocabulary and additional background knowledge.

Wide reading with varied text is the essential component for reading practice. Students with emerging reading ability must read, read, read. As students demonstrate sufficient success with more challenging text, gradually increase the level of text difficulty in relation to length of passages, size of font, complexity of content, and overall level of difficulty, being careful to present text that is decodable.

In addition to the decodable nonfiction passages, use high-interest fiction at a decodable level to provide reading practice. Do not use fiction for repeated reading and fluency work because this will likely destroy the story and reduce the students' interest in reading it. In addition, vocabulary is not repeated as often in fiction and is less predictable (Hiebert, 2002). Thus, it is better to use relatively short nonfiction passages for the repeated reading and fluency work. There are limited sources for controlled text for older students, but there are many sources of potential decodable fiction and nonfiction text passages for older students (see Appendix B). See Chapters 10 and 14 for more information about oral reading fluency instruction and assessment.

Development of Vocabulary, Background Knowledge, and Comprehension

Reading develops general language skills, vocabulary, background knowledge, and familiarity with complex syntax structures (Cunningham & Stanovich, 1997). Good readers may read up to 10 times as many words as poor readers (Nagy & Anderson, 1984). Students who do not learn to read fluently in elementary school are at a major disadvantage in background knowledge and vocabulary development. Vocabulary depends more on exposure to written text than oral language because it is developed largely through print (Nagy & Anderson, 1984; Stanovich, 1986). Students who are unable to gain access to print will have limited exposure to vocabulary. Students at the bottom percentiles of reading ability cannot read independently. Thus, they do not read, which limits their exposure to vocabulary. Over time, they exhibit what has become widely known as the Matthew effect (Stanovich, 1986). Students who are behind become even further behind.

Older students who are just entering a multisensory structured language education (MSLE) program have a lot of catching up to do. True, they need to learn how to decode and read text fluently in a multisensory, sequential manner. This will not happen overnight, however. In the meantime, these students need as much exposure to enriched text as possible in order to develop their background knowledge, vocabulary, and comprehension.

Access to Curriculum and Other Enriched Text: Reading to Students

Students who are not yet able to sufficiently read their grade-level text must have the printed word read to them, either by an individual or through technological means. Too often, reading to students ends in the primary grades. As older students are being taught with structured phonics to develop their decoding, enriched text at a higher level than they can independently decode should be read to them. Controlled and noncontrolled decodable text is rarely enriched with vocabulary and content. Reading more sophisticated text to students who cannot do so independently will expose them to more advanced vocabulary, substantially more background knowledge, more complex syntax structure, and higher level thinking. Include both narrative and expository selections in your choices. An important part of instruction, then, is to read to the students at a much higher level than they could decode and comprehend on their own.

Students can track the words when you read decodable text to them because they are working on applying decoding skills. When reading enriched text to students, however, do not have them follow along while you read. They can simply listen and visualize or create a mental image of the text. Because you are reading text at a much higher level than students can independently decode, they will likely lose their place if they try to follow along, hindering their word-level understanding. You do not want to distract them from the meaning by having them try to stay on track and attempt to decipher the words. Help students focus on meaning through periodic discussion, modeling of thinking, and retelling of the story using mental imagery as a guide for words (Beck, Kucan, & McKeown, 2002; Wilson, 1989). Help them with challenging vocabulary, providing student-friendly explanations using everyday language. Draw simple picture representations of the concepts to aid students' understanding of the content. Literally pull apart the text with them to create understanding by using comprehension strategies such as retelling and making graphic organizers (see Chapters 11 and 12).

Access to Curriculum and Other Enriched Text: Exposure to Print Through Technology

Electronic text with screen-reading software and e-books (including downloadable and CD/ROM) can also provide students with the essential access to enriched text. Technology can provide reading assistance that allows students who are unable to decode to gain access to the standard curriculum. Public libraries have some novels on CD/DVD, but students will need access to their classroom reading materials. For students with a language learning disability or dyslexia, taped versions of their classroom textbooks can be attained from Learning Ally. (For more information on assistive technology, see Chapter 22.)

Studies have found that adding speech synthesis to the print material presented on computers was an effective practice for reading instruction (NICHD, 2000). If the text is on a computer screen, then it can be enlarged; enlarged font size is helpful to students who are just learning to read. More important, this **digital text** can be read aloud by screen-reading software. **Speech synthesis software** (also called **text-to-speech software**) may therefore be an effective component of instruction for older students. Digital or electronic text can be extremely useful in assisting students who struggle with reading (Higgins, Boone, & Lovitt, 1996; Raskind, Goldberg, Higgins, & Herman, 1999).

The Intel Reader provides access to a variety of printed materials by converting text to digital form and then reading it aloud. Because it is a mobile device, it gives students great flexibility and can be used within their classrooms. Kurzweil 3000 (http://www.kurzweiledu.com) is another software program that reads printed text aloud, highlighting the sentence and words being read in color. For writing assistance, the software provides **templates,** word prediction, spellcheck, and graphic organizers. Students with word-level deficits will also benefit from spelling assistance. Electronic spellcheckers with speaking dictionaries are useful when students have a basic level of phonetic and orthographic spelling skill (see http://www.franklin.com).

Screen-reading software and e-books are appropriate for students who have poor decoding but who have adequate listening comprehension, giving them access to curricular materials in a form that they can use. This has exciting potential for all students, allowing them to participate more fully in their academic classes. Caution must be used with students who have poor decoding and poor comprehension, however. These tools might be helpful only if these students are closely monitored and given much assistance with comprehension.

Students with decoding challenges have difficulty with spelling and cannot easily keep up with notetaking in the classroom. A new assistive technology product is designed to synchronize an audio recording with written notes. A Livescribe Pulse Smartpen device (http://www.livescribe.com/en-us/smartpen/pulse/) is used in conjunction with special paper so that the student can simultaneously make an audio recording and take notes. The student can then go back to a specific word or doodle in their LiveScribe notebook to hear the full recording of what the speaker was saying at the time the notes were made.

Technology can provide struggling readers with application and practice opportunities, but they cannot replace a skilled teacher (Fisher & Ivey, 2006). Teachers provide interactive dialogue and essential strategy instruction for comprehension. Furthermore, it is critical that these tools not supplant the creation of classes that provide the direct, systematic instruction that will yield decoding and spelling independence.

OTHER CONSIDERATIONS

There are many factors involved in properly addressing the literacy needs of all students beyond the elementary grades. The challenges of students who cannot yet decode are great. With guidance, schools can create a successful literacy environment in middle and high school settings (Irvin et al., 2007). This includes addressing reading instruction in content-area classes, determining of the needs of struggling readers, and scheduling necessary interventions.

English language learners (ELLs) with decoding deficits present increased instructional needs. ELLs need intensive and intentional vocabulary instruction—even more so than other native-speaking struggling readers. Their literacy instruction should provide cultural schema and provide substantial background information to the students (Short & Fitzsimmons, 2007).

Provide Successful Classroom Practices

It is hard to imagine the daily challenges faced by older students who are unable to read grade-level text. Throughout the entire day, they must rely on others for information. These students should have access to the content in all classes, but they need a tremendous amount of support in order to succeed. Content-area teachers need professional development to assist them with these challenges.

As discussed throughout this chapter, students in fourth grade and beyond should have reading classes to develop their independent skills as indicated by testing. In addition, students should participate in content-area classes with the supported inclusion of differentiated instruction necessary to succeed. If a student's reading level is below the text level, then the student cannot independently gain access to the information from textbooks and other printed material presented in class. He or she requires instruction that integrates reading with subject-area content.

The following four-step process can assist teachers with a systematic approach to integrating reading and vocabulary instruction with content (Wilson, 1987). For students who cannot decode, the process assists them because the text is read to them. For students who can decode but lack comprehension, the process supports them through discussion and the modeling of the thinking processes used to understand text.

1. *Advance organization*: This first step requires some kind of discussion to direct the focus of the students' attention. The teacher might provide background informa-

tion, or the class might discuss previously taught material that is related to the new information. The teacher might also state the reason for reading the text or the objective of the instruction. Advance organization was one of two instructional components found to consistently enhance outcomes with adolescents in a study looking at the challenges faced by adolescents with learning disabilities (Swanson, Hoskyn, & Lee, 1999).

2. *Picture concepts:* This step involves the teacher quickly sketching the concepts as they are explained in his or her own words. The teacher dramatizes and draws out the information without getting bogged down by the specific vocabulary words, substituting easy words as necessary to develop understanding. The vocabulary labels are then attached to concepts by writing the words into the picture.

3. *Reading aloud and thinking aloud from text:* This step involves a teacher reading and periodically stopping to discuss the text and describe his or her own thinking process to help the students create a visual image of the text in their minds. The teacher can refer back to the drawing and label it with more specific vocabulary as appropriate.

4. *Study cards and retelling:* In this step, students develop study cards to help them learn the vocabulary and integrate the information. The teacher provides the list of vocabulary words, divided into syllables. Students write each word, divided into syllables, on one side of a card. On the other side, students draw a picture and/or write a user-friendly definition of the word. The cards are then spread out to display their relationships. This can be done with the pictures face up or with words face up. Students then retell the information with the cards as a guide. This retelling can be done in pairs, in small groups, and/or with the whole class.

Last, it is important to note that content-area vocabulary words present a significant challenge to students with poor decoding and spelling. When assessing their knowledge of content, it is best to avoid word-retrieval questions and instead ask students about the content. If students must come up with the labels, then provide a **word bank** to select from (see Chapter 12).

All students can benefit from integrating reading comprehension instruction specific to content, but content-area teachers have resisted an integrated approach over the years (O'Brien, Dillon, Wellinski, Springs, & Stith, 1997; Ratekin, Simpson, Alvermann, & Dishner, 1985). Long ago, Anderson, Hiebert, Scott, and Wilkinson (1985) noted that reading should be part of content-area instruction but that the integration does not occur in practice. Sadly, that is still the case even today (see Chapter 15).

Instructing English Language Learners

ELLs are a population defined as national-origin-minority students who are limited-English proficient (U.S. Department of Education, 2000). National and state assessment scores reveal a significant discrepancy in reading proficiency levels between ELLs and native English speakers, which only widens as students progress through school (National Center for Educational Statistics, 2007).

Research with struggling ELLs suggests that the most effective interventions correspond to the skills that are the basis of difficulty, utilizing developmentally appropriate instruction that builds on students' current abilities in the particular skill area (Gerber et al., 2004; Leafstedt, Richards, & Gerber, 2004). Explicit and scaffolded teaching in targeted skill areas is necessary for instruction of ELLs with reading difficulties (Pollard-Durodola, Mathes, Vaughn, Cardenas-Hagan, & Linan-Thompson, 2006). This research indicates that word-level instruction should be available for ELLs with decoding deficits.

In addition, Francis, Rivera, Lesaux, Kieffer, and Rivera (2006) recommended the following research-based practices for interventions for ELLs:

- Provide explicit phonological awareness and phonics to build decoding skills. (Delay in providing intervention until students gain proficiency in English is discouraged.)

- Increase instruction and opportunities to develop vocabulary, including academic vocabulary.

- Teach strategies to comprehend and monitor understanding because many ELLs passively read text.

- Provide exposure to print and fluency work with repeated oral readings, emphasizing vocabulary.

- Engage students in academic talk and structured opportunities.

- Provide independent reading with structure and a careful selection of text to match reading ability (90% accuracy), with follow-up discussion.

Furthermore, classroom demonstrations of concepts can be particularly effective for ELLs (Janney & Snell, 2004). Classroom demonstrations occur when a teacher's verbal explanation for concepts is enhanced by visual, physical, and kinesthetic involvement. Thus, the multisensory instruction described in this chapter provides multiple examples of these demonstrations that can benefit ELLs.

Spanish is by far the most prevalent language of the ELL population. Spanish-speaking ELLs can benefit from direct instruction about the similarities and differences between the sound and spelling systems of the two languages; clearly teach key words to assist with any differences. For example, a key word for the consonant *h* is important (*h, hat,* /h/) because it is silent in Spanish. Also, identify cognates such as *accident* and *accidente* (see Chapter 20).

The lack of English vocabulary and background knowledge presents additional challenges to comprehension for ELLs (August, Carlo, Dressler, & Snow, 2005; Bernhardt, 2005). Teachers can interactively dialogue in the student's native language to relate the material to the student's experience and discuss background information and vocabulary. Although research is inconclusive, several studies suggest that students who receive instruction in both their native language and in English outperform students in English-only programs on English reading proficiency measures (August & Shanahan, 2006; Genesee, Lindholm-Leary, Saunders, & Christian, 2006).

Develop Students' Belief in Their Potential

Students with significant word-level deficits cannot achieve the literacy levels expected of them on a daily basis. This problem is often accompanied by heightened stress, behavior and social problems, a lack of motivation, and low self-esteem (Alexander-Passe, 2008; Daniel et al., 2006). The teacher must help establish clear goals, provide relevant and timely feedback, and find a balance between the right level of challenge and the students' abilities to meet that challenge. Students must not become either overwhelmed by expectations beyond their reach or bored by a slow introduction of concepts (VanDeWeghe, 2009).

Older students who are struggling with reading have likely met with much failure throughout the years. Students in middle school have a high interest in learning to read, regardless of their failure and varied reasons for it (McCray, 2001). It is hard to imagine the feelings these students have when facing undecodable words on a page. Most do not believe they can improve, so they do not want to show their interest. Expect this. Students protect their self-esteem by resisting instruction. It has failed them in the past; why should this be different? For this reason, teachers must not feel thwarted in the beginning, as this is a likely response. Instead, the teacher can respond sympathetically and help the student understand that it is the beginning of a detailed and sophisticated study of the English language. The teacher can explain that abundant research now indicates that many people share the difficulty of mastering the sound system and that systematic, sequential instruction has been proven to make mastery of it possible.

Explain to the students that they will be studying the structure of the English language in depth and that English is based on a sound system in which 44 sounds are put together to make thousands and thousands of words. Most people think of English as a jumbled mix of words, formed without rhyme or reason. A study conducted by Hanna, Hanna, Hodges, and Rudorf (1966), however, determined that the spellings of a majority of words in English follow a system. Explain that English is logical if one carefully studies sound–symbol correspondence as related to syllable patterns; orthographic (spelling) rules; and prefixes, roots, and suffixes. You can tell the students that they will learn more about English than most people know and that this will help them tremendously with both reading and spelling.

Older students who have had a history of academic failure need help to motivate them and program them for success. Today's adolescents may be motivated to master reading and writing basics for different reasons than students in the past. Some students may want to read text on the Internet as well as various interactive communications. Access to the written word in technology environments can increase students' motivation to become independent readers and writers (Kamil, Intrator, & Kim, 2000). Several studies have demonstrated that students with learning disabilities who possess certain personal attitudes and behaviors have more successful life outcomes. Specifically, the attributes of self-awareness, perseverance, proactivity, emotional stability, goal setting, and the use of support systems are powerful predictors of success (Raskind et al., 1999; Reiff, Gerber, & Ginsberg, 1997; Wehmeyer, 1996; Werner & Smith, 1992). Help students become aware of their strengths as you work with them to overcome their difficulties. Many students with phonological weaknesses have strengths in areas other than phonological coding (Geschwind, 1982; Shaywitz, 2003; West, 1997).

The writing sample and drawing shown in Figure 16.8 demonstrate the strengths of a sixth-grade student diagnosed with dyslexia. Clearly, he has difficulty with the basics of written language. Yet, his creativity shines through with his choice of words, such as "I scream and the echo fades into the dark void in my heart." The same student quickly copied the illustration by freehand within minutes.

The goal of your instruction should include an increased understanding of your students' strengths so that they can have a clearer direction for their future. Combined with the skills that will develop with sufficient multisensory structured language instruction, students can begin to believe in themselves. Given appropriate instruction and time, you can help them set goals and develop support systems for success.

I'm walking throug the besert Sand I jift my head, and sp abnd of trees and rivers and water falls, and that not at I see a camal ona rope and oh I be camaflashd from the writer of the bag but then I realyzed it was just a marash the camle fads the river weeks and turns into a sandy creek my arms are sprax my chest stuck out I screem an the ecoe fades into the dark void in my hart my head is light my dones are week I've been here for 50 week

Figure 16.8.   Writing and illustration created by a sixth-grade student with dyslexia.

Effect on Individual and Society

The effect of inadequate reading skill on the lives of individuals and on society is great. These students are much more likely to drop out of school, have trouble finding employment, and experience ongoing challenges in society (National Association of State Boards of Education [NASBE], 2006; RAND Reading Study Group, 2002).

Shockingly, some 30% of students drop out of school (Greene & Winters, 2005). When adolescents have low-level literacy skills and cannot adequately decode, it may become impossible for them to sustain participation. Students entering ninth grade in the lowest 25% of achievement are 20 times more likely to drop out than their higher performing peers (Carnevale, 2001).

> The fact that so many individuals lack basic literacy skills has serious economic consequences for individuals and society. Of the individuals who graduate from high school approximately 40% lack the literacy skills employers seek (Achieve, 2005). Deficits in basic skills cost the nation's businesses, universities, and underprepared high school graduates as much as $16 billion annually in lost productivity and remedial costs. (Greene, 2000; National Governors Association [NGA], 2005, p. 4)

The cost on human suffering has not been measured. It is all too clear that middle and high schools need to respond. Failure must not be the continued path. Students must be provided with the instruction that they require in order to develop proficient reading and writing skills for success in school and beyond. Given appropriate MSLE instruction and sufficient time, you can help students set goals and develop skills for their success.

REFERENCES

Achieve. (2005). *Rising to the challenge: Are high school graduates prepared for college and work?* Washington, DC: Author.

Alexander-Passe, N. (2008). Sources and manifestations of stress amongst school-aged dyslexics, compared with sibling controls. *Dyslexia, 14*(4), 291–313.

Alvermann, D.E. (2001). *Effective literacy instruction for adolescents.* Chicago: National Reading Conference.

American Federation of Teachers. (1999). *Teaching reading is rocket science: What expert teachers of reading should know and be able to do*. Washington, DC: Author.

Anderson, R.C., Hiebert, E.H., Scott, J.A., & Wilkinson, I.A.G. (1985). *Becoming a nation of readers: The report of the Commission on Reading*. Washington, DC: National Academy of Education, Commission on Education and Public Policy.

Anderson, R.C., Wilkinson, I.A.G., & Mason, J.M. (1991). A microanalysis of the small-group, guided reading lesson: Effects of an emphasis on global story meaning. *Reading Research Quarterly, 26*, 417–441.

Anderson, R.C., Wilson, P.T., & Fielding, L.G. (1988). Growth in reading and how children spend their time outside of school. *Reading Research Quarterly, 23*, 285–303, 611–626.

August, D., Carlo, M., Dressler, C., & Snow, C. (2005). The critical role of vocabulary development for English language learners. *Learning Disabilities: Research and Practice, 20*(1), 50–57.

August, D., & Shanahan, T. (Eds.). (2006). *Developing literacy in second-language learners: Report of the National Literacy Panel on Language-Minority Children and Youth*. Mahwah, NJ: Lawrence Erlbaum Associates.

Banks, S.R., Guyer, B.P., & Guyer, K.E. (1993). Spelling improvement by college students who are dyslexic. *Annals of Dyslexia, 43*, 186–193.

Beck, I.L., Kucan, L., & McKeown, M.G. (2002). *Bringing words to life: Robust vocabulary instruction*. New York: Guilford Press.

Bernhardt, E. (2005). Progress and procrastination in second language reading. *Annual Review of Applied Linguistics, 25*, 133–150.

Bhattacharya, A., & Ehri, L.C. (2004). Graphosyllabic analysis helps adolescent struggling readers read and spell words. *Journal of Learning Disabilities, 37*(4), 331–348.

Biancarosa, C., & Snow, C.E. (2006). *Reading next: A vision for action and research in middle and high school literacy. A report to Carnegie Corporation of New York*. Washington, DC: Alliance for Excellent Education.

Boardman, A.G., Roberts, G., Vaughn, S., Wexler, J., Murray, C.S., & Kosanovich, M. (2008). *Effective instruction for adolescent struggling readers: A practice brief*. Portsmouth, NH: RMC Research Corporation, Center on Instruction. Retrieved December 23, 2009, from http://www.centeroninstruction.org/files/Practice%20Brief-Struggling%20Readers.pdf

Brown, J. (1998a). Flipping pancakes. In *Stories for older students* (Book 2, Steps 4–6, p. 9). Oxford, MA: Wilson Language Training.

Brown, J. (1998b). Subs in the mud. In *Stories for older students* (Book 1, Steps 1–3, p. 1). Oxford, MA: Wilson Language Training.

Bruck, M. (1990). Word recognition skill of adults with childhood diagnoses of dyslexia. *Developmental Psychology, 26*, 439–454.

Bruck, M. (1992). Persistence of dyslexics' phonological awareness deficits. *Developmental Psychology, 28*, 874–886.

Bruck, M. (1993). Component spelling skills of college students with childhood diagnoses of dyslexia. *Developmental Psychology, 16*, 171–184.

Carlisle, J.F. (October/November/December 2010). Review of research: Effects of instruction in morphological awareness on literacy achievement: An integrative review. *Reading Research Quarterly, 45*(4), 464–487.

Carnevale, A.P. (2001). *Help wanted: College required*. Washington, DC: Educational Testing Service, Office for Public Leadership.

Chall, J.S. (1983). *Stages of reading development*. New York: McGraw-Hill.

Chard, D.J., Vaughn, S., & Tyler, B.J. (2002). A synthesis of research on effective interventions for building reading fluency with elementary students with learning disabilities. *Journal of Learning Disabilities, 35*, 386–406.

Christensen, C.M., Horn, M.B., & Johnson, C.W. (2010). Rethinking student motivation: Why understanding the "job" is crucial for improving education. Retrieved January 24, 2011, from the Innosight Institute web site: http://www.innosightinstitute.org/innosight/wp-content/uploads/2010/09/Rethinking-Student-Motivation.pdf

Cunningham, A.E., & Stanovich, K.E. (1997). Early reading acquisition and its relation to reading experience and ability 10 years later. *Developmental Psychology, 33*, 934–935.

Curtis, M.E. (2004). Adolescents who struggle with word identification: Research and practice. In T.L. Jesson & J.A. Dole (Eds.), *Adolescent literacy research and practice* (pp. 119–134). New York: The Guilford Press.

Curtis, M.E., & Longo, A.M. (1999). *When adolescents can't read: Methods and materials that work*. Cambridge, MA: Brookline Books.

Daniel, S.S., Walsh, A.K., Goldston, D.B., Arnold, E.M., Reboussin, B.A., & Wood, F.B. (2006). Suicidality, school dropout and reading problems amongst adolescents. *Journal of Learning Disabilities, 39*(6), 507–514.

Deschler, D.D., & Hock, M.F. (2006). *Shaping literacy achievement*. New York: The Guilford Press.

Deshler, D.D., Schumaker, J.B., Lenz, B.K., Bulgren, J.A., Hock, M.F., Knight, J., et al. (2001). Ensuring content-area learning by secondary students with learning disabilities. *Learning Disabilities Research and Practice, 16*(2), 96–108.

Ehri, L.C., (2000). Learning to read and learning to spell: Two sides of a coin. *Topics in Language Disorders, 20*(3), 19–36.

Felton, R., & Wilson, B.A. (2004). *Word Identification and Spelling Test (WIST)*. Austin, TX: PRO-ED.

Fink, R. (1998). Literacy development in successful men and woman with dyslexia. *Annals of Dyslexia, 48,* 311–346.

Fisher, D., & Ivey, G. (2006). Evaluating the interventions for struggling adolescent readers. *Journal of Adolescent and Adult Literacy, 50,* 180–189.

Francis, D.J., Rivera, M., Lesaux, N., Kieffer, M., & Rivera, H. (2006). *Practical guidelines for the education of English language learners: Research-based recommendations for instruction and academic interventions.* Retrieved January 10, 2007, from http ://www.centeroninstruction.org/resources.cfm ?category=ell&subcategory=research&grade_start =0&grade_end=12

Genesee, F., Lindholm-Leary, K., Saunders, W., & Christian, D. (Eds.). (2006). *Educating English language learners: A synthesis of research evidence.* New York: Cambridge University Press.

Gerber, M., Jimenez, T., Leafstedt, J.M., Villaruz, J., Richards, C., & English, J. (2004). English reading effects of small-group intensive intervention in Spanish for K–1 English learners. *Learning Disabilities Research Practice, 19*(4), 239–251.

Geschwind, N. (1982). Why Orton was right. *Annals of Dyslexia, 32,* 13–20.

Greene, J. (2000). *The cost of remedial education: How much Michigan pays when students fail to learn basic skills.* Midland, MI: Mackinac Center for Public Policy.

Greene, J.F., & Winters, M. (2005). *The effect of school choice on public high school graduation rates.* New York: Manhattan Institute for Public Policy.

Hanna, P.R., Hanna, J.S., Hodges, R.E., & Rudorf, E.H., Jr. (1966). *Phoneme-grapheme correspondences as cues to spelling improvement* (USOE Publication No. 32008). Washington, DC: U.S. Government Printing Office.

Hasbrouck, J.E., & Tindal, G.A. (2006). Oral reading fluency norms: A valuable assessment tool for reading teachers. *The Reading Teacher, 59*(7), 636–644.

Henry, M.K. (1993). Morphological structure: Latin and Greek roots and affixes as upper grade code strategies. *Reading and Writing: An Interdisciplinary Journal, 5*(2), 227–241.

Hiebert, E.H. (2002). Standards, assessment, and text difficulty. In A.E. Farstrup & S.J. Samuels (Eds.), *What research has to say about reading instruction* (pp. 337–369). Newark, DE: International Reading Association.

Higgins, K., Boone, R., & Lovitt, T. (1996). Hypertext support for remedial students and students with learning disabilities. *Journal of Learning Disabilities, 29*(4), 402–412.

Hock, M.F., Brasseur, I.F., Deshler, D.D., Catts, H.W., Marquis, J.G., Mark, C.A., et al. (2009). What is the reading component skill profile of adolescent struggling readers in urban schools. *Learning Disability Quarterly, 32*(1), 21–38.

Hock, M.F., Deshler, D.D., Marquis, J.G., & Brasseur, I.F. (2005). *Reading component skills of adolescents attending urban schools.* Lawrence: University of Kansas, Center for Research on Learning.

Homan, S.P., Klesius, J.P., & Hite, C. (1993). Effects of repeated readings and nonrepetitive strategies on students' fluency and comprehension. *Journal of Educational Research, 87,* 94–99.

Hosp, M.K., Hosp, J.L., & Howell, K.W. (2007). *The ABC's of CBM: A practical guide to curriculum-based measurement.* New York: Guilford Press.

Irvin, J.L., Meltzer, J., & Dukes, M. (2007). *Taking action on adolescent literacy: An implementation guide for school leaders.* Alexandria, VA: Association for Supervision and Curriculum Development.

Ivey, G., & Broaddus, K. (2001). Just plain reading: A survey of what makes students want to read in middle school classrooms. *Reading Research Quarterly, 36,* 350–377.

Janney, R., & Snell, M.E. (2004). *Teachers' guides to inclusive practices: Modifying schoolwork* (2nd ed.). Baltimore: Paul H. Brookes Publishing Co.

Kamil, M.L., Intrator, S.M., & Kim, H.S. (2000). The effects of other technologies on literacy and literacy learning. In M.L. Kamil, P.B. Mosenthal, P.D. Pearson, & R. Barr (Eds.), *Handbook of reading research* (Vol. 3, pp. 771–788). Mahwah, NJ: Lawrence Erlbaum Associates.

Kuhn, M.R., Schwanenflugel, P.J., & Meisinger, E.B. (2010, April/May/June). Review of research: Aligning theory and assessment of reading fluency: Automaticity, prosody, and definitions of fluency. *Reading Research Quarterly, 45*(2), 230–251.

Kuhn, M.R., & Stahl, S.A. (2003). Fluency: A review of developmental and remedial practices. *Journal of Educational Psychology, 95*(1), 3–21.

Leach, J., Scarborough, H., & Rescorla, L. (2003). Late-emerging reading disabilities. *Journal of Educational Psychology, 95,* 211–224.

Leafstedt, J.M., Richards, C.R., & Gerber, M.M. (2004). Effectiveness of explicit phonological-awareness instruction for at-risk English learners. *Learning Disabilities Research and Practice, 19,* 252–261.

Lovett, M.W., Barron, R.W., & Benson, N.J. (2003). Effective remediation of word identification and decoding difficulties in school-age children with reading disabilities. In H.L. Swanson, K.R. Harris, & S. Graham (Eds.), *Handbook of learning disabilities* (pp. 273–292). New York: Guilford Press.

Lyon, G.R., Fletcher, J.M., Shaywitz, S.E., Shaywitz, B.A., Torgesen, J.K., Wood, F.B., et al. (2001). Rethinking learning disabilities. In C.E. Finn, Jr.,

A.J. Rotherham, & C.R. Hokanson, Jr. (Eds.), *Rethinking special education for a new century* (pp. 259–287). Washington, DC: Thomas B. Fordham Foundation and Progressive Policy Institute.

Mather, N., Hammill, D., Allen, E., & Roberts, R. (in press). *Test of Silent Word Reading Fluency–Second Edition* (TOSWRF-2). Austin, TX: PRO-ED.

McCray, A.D. (2001, November). Middle school students with learning disabilities. *Reading Teacher, 55*(3), 298–310.

McCutchen, D., Harry, D.R., Cunningham, A.E., Cox, S., Sidman, S., & Covill, A.E. (2002). Reading teachers' knowledge of children's literature and English phonology. *Annals of Dyslexia, 52,* 207–228.

Moore, D.W., Bean, T.W., Birdyshaw, D., & Rycik, J.A. (1999). *Adolescent literacy: A position statement for the Commission on Adolescent Literacy of the International Reading Association.* Newark, DE: International Reading Association.

Murray, C.S., Wexler, J., Vaughn, S., Boardman, A.G., Roberts, G., Tackett, K.K., et al. (2010). *Effective instruction for adolescent struggling readers: Professional development module facilitator's guide* (2nd ed.). Portsmouth, NH: RMC Research Corporation, Center on Instruction. Retrieved January 24, 2011, http://www.centeroninstruction.org/files/EIASR%20FG%202nd%20Ed.pdf

Nagy, W.E., & Anderson, R.C. (1984). How many words are there in printed school English? *Reading Research Quarterly, 19,* 304–330.

Nagy, W.E., Diakidoy, I.N., & Anderson, R.C. (1993). The acquisition of morphology: Learning the contribution of suffixes to the meanings of derivatives. *Journal of Reading Behavior, 25,* 155–170.

National Assessment of Educational Progress. (2007). *The nation's report card: Reading 2002.* Available at http://nces.ed.gov/nationsreportcard/pdf/main2002/2003521.pdf

National Association of State Boards of Education. (2006). *Reading at risk: The state response to the crisis in adolescent literacy.* Arlington, VA: Author.

National Center for Education Statistics. (2007). *National assessment of educational progress/Nation's report card.* Retrieved January 25, 2008, from http://nces.ed.gov/nationsreportcard/nde/viewresults.asp

National Center for Education Statistics. (2009). *National assessment of educational progress/Nation's report card.* Washington, DC: U.S. Department of Education, Institute of Education Sciences. Retrieved January 24, 2011, from http://nationsreportcard.gov/reading_2009

National Governors Association Center for Best Practices. (2005). *Reading to achieve: A governor's guide to adolescent literacy.* Washington, DC: Author.

National Institute of Child Health and Human Development. (2000). *Report of the National Reading Panel: Reports of the subgroups. Teaching children to read: An evidence-based assessment of the scientific research literature on reading and its implications for reading instruction* (NIH Publication No. 00-4769). Washington, DC: Government Printing Office.

National Institute for Literacy. (2007). *Adapted from what content-area teachers should know about adolescent literacy.* Retrieved from http://www.nifl.gov/nifl/publications/adolescent_literacy07.pdf

O'Brien, D.G., Dillon, D.R., Wellinski, S.A., Springs, R., & Stith, D. (1997). *Engaging "at-risk" high school students.* Athens, GA: National Reading Research Center.

O'Connor, J., & Wilson, B. (1995). Effectiveness of the Wilson Reading System used in public school training. In C. McIntyre & J. Pickering (Eds.), *Clinical studies of multisensory structured language education for students with dyslexia and related disorders* (pp. 247–254). Salem, OR: International Multisensory Structured Language Education Council.

O'Shea, L.J., Sindelar, P.T., & O'Shea, D.J. (1985). The effects of repeated readings and attentional cues on reading fluency and comprehension. *Journal of Reading Behavior, 17,* 129–142.

Partnership for Reading. (2003, June). *Put reading first: The research building blocks for teaching children to read: Kindergarten through grade 3* (2nd ed.). Washington, DC: Author.

Penney, C. (2002). Teaching decoding skills to poor readers in high school. *Journal of Literacy Research, 34,* 99–118.

Pollard-Durodola, S.D., Mathes, P.G., Vaughn, S., Cardenas-Hagan, E., & Linan-Thompson, S. (2006). The role of oracy in developing comprehension in Spanish-speaking English language learners. *Topics in Language Disorders, 26*(4), 365–384.

RAND Reading Study Group. (2002). *Reading for understanding: Toward a research and development program in reading comprehension.* Santa Monica, CA: RAND Corporation.

Rashotte, C.A., & Torgesen, J.K. (1985). Repeated reading and reading fluency in learning disabled children. *Reading Research Quarterly, 20,* 180–188.

Raskind, M.H., Goldberg, R.J., Higgins, E.L., & Herman, K.L. (1999). Patterns of change and predictors of success in individuals with learning disabilities: Results from a twenty-year longitudinal study. *Learning Disabilities Research and Practice, 14*(1), 35–49.

Ratekin, N., Simpson, M., Alvermann, D., & Dishner, E. (1985). Why teachers resist content reading instruction. *Journal of Reading, 28,* 432–437.

Reiff, H.B., Gerber, P.J., & Ginsberg, R. (1997). *Exceeding expectations: Successful adults with learning disabilities.* Austin, TX: PRO-ED.

Samuels, S.J., & Farstrup, A.E. (Eds.). (2006). *What research has to say about fluency instruction.* Newark, DE: International Reading Association.

Scammacca, N., Roberts, G., Vaughn, S., Edmonds, M., Wexler, J., Reutebuch, C.K., et al. (2007). *Intervention for adolescent struggling readers: A meta-analysis with implications for practice.* Portsmouth, NH: RMC Research Corporation, Center on Instruction.

Scruggs, T.E., Mastropieri, M.A., Berkeley, S., & Graetz, J. (2010). Do special education interventions improve learning of secondary content? A meta-analysis. *Remedial and Special Education, 31*(6).

Semrud-Clikeman, M. (2005). Neuropsychological aspects for evaluating learning disabilities. *Journal of Learning Disabilities, 38,* 563–568.

Shaywitz, S. (2003). *Overcoming dyslexia: A new and complete science-based program for reading problems at any level.* New York: Alfred A. Knopf.

Short, D., & Fitzsimmons, S. (2007). *Double the work: Challenges and solutions to acquiring language and academic literacy for adolescent English language learners—A report to Carnegie Corporation of New York.* Washington, DC: Alliance for Excellent Education.

Snow, C.E. (2002). *Reading for understanding: Toward an R & D program in reading comprehension.* Santa Monica, CA: Science and Technology Policy Institute.

Snow, C., & Biancarosa, G. (2003). *Adolescent literacy and the achievement gap: What do we know and where do we go from here?* New York: Carnegie Corporation.

Snow, C.E., Burns, M.S., & Griffin, P. (Eds.). (1998). *Preventing reading difficulties in young children.* Washington, DC: National Academies Press.

Spreen, O. (1989). Learning disability, neurology, and long-term outcome: Some implications for the individual and for society. *Journal of Clinical and Experimental Neuropsychology, 11*(3), 389–408.

Stanovich, K.E. (1986). Matthew effects in reading: Some consequences of individual differences in the acquisition of literacy. *Reading Research Quarterly, 21,* 369–407.

Sturgis, C., & Patrick, S. (2010). *When success is the only option: Designing competency-based pathways for next generation learning.* Vienna, VA: International Association for K–12 Online Learning (iNACOL).

Swanson, H.L., Hoskyn, M., & Lee, C. (1999). *Intervention for students with learning disabilities: A meta-analysis of treatment outcomes.* New York: Guilford Press.

Torgesen, J.K. (2005). *Essential features of effective reading instruction for struggling readers in grades 4–12.* Presented at meetings of the Utah Branch of the International Dyslexia Association, Salt Lake City. PowerPoint available online at http://www.fcrr.org/science/pdf/torgesen/Utah_remediation.pdf

Torgesen, J.K., Houston, D.D., Rissman, L.M., Decker, S.M., Roberts, G., Vaughn, S., et al. (2007). *Academic literacy instruction for adolescents: A guidance document from the Center on Instruction.* Portsmouth, NH: RMC Research Corporation, Center on Instruction.

Torgesen, J.K., & Hudson, R.R. (2006). Reading fluency: Critical issues for struggling readers. In S.J. Samuels & A.E. Parstrup (Eds.), *What research has to say about fluency instruction* (pp. 130–158). Newark, DE: International Reading Association.

U.S. Department of Education Office for Civil Rights. (2000). *The provision of an equal education opportunity to limited-English proficient students.* Washington, DC: U.S. Department of Education. Retrieved December 23, 2009 from http://www.education.com/reference/article/Ref_Provision_Equal/

VanDeWeghe, R. (2009). *Engaged learning.* Thousand Oaks, CA: Corwin Press.

Wehmeyer, M.L. (1996). Self-determination as an educational outcome: Why is it important to children, youth, and adults with disabilities? In D.J. Sands & M.L. Wehmeyer (Eds.), *Self-determination across the lifespan: Independence and choice for people with disabilities* (pp. 17–36). Baltimore: Paul H. Brookes Publishing Co.

Werner, E.E., & Smith, R.S. (1992). *Overcoming the odds: High risk children from birth to adulthood.* Ithaca, NY: Cornell University Press.

West, T. (1997). *In the mind's eye: Visual thinkers, gifted people with dyslexia and other learning difficulties: Computer images and the ironies of creativity.* New York: Prometheus Books.

White, T.G., Sowell, J., & Yanagihara, A. (1989) Teaching elementary students to use word-part clues. *Reading Teacher, 42,* 302–308.

Wilson, B.A. (1987). *Wilson study and writing skills.* Oxford, MA: Wilson Language Training.

Wilson, B.A. (1989). *Wilson Reading System instructor manual.* Oxford, MA: Wilson Language Training.

Wilson, B. (1996). *Wilson Reading System instructor manual* (3rd ed.). Oxford, MA: Wilson Language Training.

Wilson, B.A. (2003). *Uses of differentiated texts and their interrelationships for students with primary decoding deficits.* Retrieved December 23, 2009, from http://www.wilsonacademy.com

Wilson, B.A. (2006). *Wilson fluency: Basic.* Oxford, MA: Wilson Language Training.

17

Adolescent Literacy

Addressing the Needs of Students in Grades 4–12

JOAN SEDITA

Reading is the key. Without it, the instructions for playing Monopoly, the recipe for Grandma's lasagna, The Cat in the Hat, *the directions to the job interview, the* Psalms, *the lyrics to* Stairway to Heaven—*all these and a lifetime of other mysteries large and small may never be known.*

—Kansas City Star newspaper

The quote above reminds us that literacy skills in the 21st century are more essential than ever for success in education, work, citizenship, and our personal lives. However, far too many older students and adults do not have the necessary reading and writing skills to succeed in postsecondary education or the ever-increasing number of jobs that require strong literacy skills.

During the 1990s and through 2008, significant emphasis was placed on the use of research to determine how children learn to read and why some students struggle with reading. Seminal meta-analyses of research and subsequent summary reports such as *Preventing Reading Difficulties in Young Children* (Snow & Burns, 1998) and the report of the National Reading Panel (2000) began to connect that research to implications for instruction. A number of state initiatives, but especially the Reading First initiative, part of the No Child Left Behind Act of 2001 (PL 107-110), contributed significantly to the practical application of science-based literacy instruction in Grades K–3 throughout the country.

Early literacy achievement, however, is not necessarily a guarantee that literacy skills will continue to grow as students move beyond Grade 3. In *Reading Next*, it is noted that

> Recent National Assessment of Educational Progress (NAEP) reading results indicate that efforts to improve K–3 literacy are paying off at the 4th-grade level, but these improvements do not necessarily translate into better achievement among adolescents... Comparing the

most recent NAEP results for all three grade levels (i.e., 4, 8, and 12) to those from 1992, the percentage of students scoring proficient has significantly improved among 4th graders, but not among 8th and 12th graders. (Biancarosa & Snow, 2006, pp. 7–8)

Scores at the secondary level, where there has been relatively little investment, have remained flat since the 1970s (Heller & Greenleaf, 2007). The following observation from *Time to Act: An Agenda for Advancing Adolescent Literacy for College and Career Success* sums up the challenges faced after Grade 3:

> The truth is that good early literacy instruction does not inoculate students against struggle or failure later on. Beyond grade 3 adolescent learners in our schools must decipher more complex passages, synthesize information at a higher level, and learn to form independent conclusions based on evidence. They must also develop special skills and strategies for reading text in each of the differing content areas—meaning that a student who "naturally" does well in one area may struggle in another. (Carnegie Council on Advancing Adolescent Literacy, 2010)

This chapter offers an overview of literacy as it specifically relates to students in Grades 4–12 and how it has evolved as a separate issue from early literacy. While the research base is nascent, a growing body of work is developing about how students in these grades learn to increase their reading and writing skills, why some struggle, and what effective instruction looks like. This chapter will define adolescent literacy, summarize evidence from major research reports concerning adolescent literacy instruction and interventions, and present a multicomponent model for literacy planning at the intermediate, middle, and high school grades.

WHAT IS ADOLESCENT LITERACY?

The term *adolescent* can be misleading—adolescent literacy is not limited to teenagers. This label is used to describe literacy skills for students in Grades 4–12. The axiom that through Grade 3, students are learning to read, but beginning in Grade 4 they shift to reading to learn (Chall, 1983) sums up why Grade 4 is a logical place to make the jump from early literacy to adolescent literacy. The publication of the widely cited reports *Reading Next* (Biancarosa & Snow, 2004) and *Writing Next* (Graham & Perin, 2007), which identified adolescent literacy as beginning in Grade 4, helped solidify this definition of *adolescent literacy*.

The National Reading Panel (2000) identified five components that are essential for learning to read successfully: phonemic awareness, phonics, fluency, vocabulary, and comprehension. There is an assumption that the basic components of reading that have to do with decoding and encoding the words on the page (i.e., phonemic awareness, phonics, and fluency) are in place for grade-level readers by Grade 4. While the components of reading that address making meaning (vocabulary and comprehension) must also be addressed in the early grades, the emphasis on these components becomes paramount in the upper grades.

This does not mean that students in intermediate grades do not need to continue to improve basic literacy skills. Students must increasingly raise their fluency rates, moving from an average benchmark rate of 123 words correct per minute (WCPM) at the end of Grade 4 to 151 WCPM at the end of Grade 8 (Hasbrouck & Tindel, 2005). Advanced phonics and word study skills must also be taught beyond Grade 3. For example, many students may not be developmentally ready to learn some advanced phonics concepts until at least Grade 4 (e.g., digraph *ch* as in *chorus*, *y* as short *i* as in *system*, multisyllable words with prefixes and suffixes added to Latin or Greek roots) (Moats, 1995). These skills should be addressed during intermediate-grade reading instruction that is typically provided during an English-language arts (ELA) period. We also know that for many struggling adolescent readers, deficits in phonics and fluency skills contribute to poor comprehension (Moats, 2001), and these must be addressed through intervention (see Chapter 16).

Adolescent literacy encompasses the skills that must be taught to all students so they can meet increasingly challenging reading and writing demands as they move through the upper grades, as well as what needs to be done for those students who fall behind. In the model provided later in this chapter for literacy planning, a framework is presented that addresses literacy instruction at two levels:

- Instruction for all students embedded in all subject areas that focuses on vocabulary, comprehension, and content writing

- Supplemental and intervention instruction for struggling students delivered in an intervention setting that focuses on decoding, fluency, and language structure as well as vocabulary, comprehension, and content writing

WHAT DO WE KNOW ABOUT THE LITERACY SKILLS OF AMERICAN ADOLESCENTS AND ADULTS?

While the increased focus on adolescent literacy is a natural extension of efforts to improve literacy skills for students in Grades K–3, the National Adolescent Literacy Coalition (NALC) maintains that this focus has a lot to do with Americans' increasing sense of anxiety about the economic and civic health of the nation (NALC, 2007). Graham and Perin (2007) pointed out that reading comprehension and writing skills are predictors of academic success and a basic requirement for participation in civic life and in the global economy. The statistics about the lack of literacy skills among American middle and high school students and adults are alarming. For example,

- Data from the 2007 NAEP in reading show that 69% of eighth-grade students fall below proficient level in their ability to comprehend the meaning of text at their grade level, and 26% read below the basic level (Lee, Griggs, & Donahue, 2007).

- As measured by the NAEP, roughly two thirds of 12th graders read and write below a proficient level, and half of those students lack even the most basic literacy skills needed to succeed in school. Those figures did not change between 1974 and 2005 (NALC, 2007).

- The 2002 NAEP writing report noted that only 22%–26% of 4th, 8th, and 12th graders scored at the proficient level, and alarmingly high proportions of students were found to be at or below the basic level (Graham & Perin, 2007).

- Achievement gaps in upper grades have not narrowed. In 2005, only 12% of African American and 15% of Hispanic eighth graders read at or above a proficient level, compared to 39% of Caucasian eighth graders. In a typical high-poverty urban school, approximately half of incoming ninth-grade students read at a sixth- or seventh-grade level or below (Heller & Greenleaf, 2007; Perie, Grigg, & Donahue, 2005).

- Among the 30 Organization for Economic Cooperation and Development (OECD) free-market countries, the United States is the only nation where young adults are less educated than the previous generation. The United States is also losing ground in international comparisons in terms of high school diplomas and college degrees awarded. Furthermore, while the United States scores as one of the highest countries in numbers of well-educated people, it also scores near the top in the largest number of people at the lowest education levels—about 55% of adults at the lowest literacy levels did not graduate from high school and have no Tests of Educational Development (general equivalency diploma, or GED) or high school equivalency diploma (Council for Advancement of Adult Literacy, 2008).

- Every year, 1 in 3 young adults drops out of high school (Council for Advancement of Adult Literacy, 2008), and one of the most commonly cited reasons for this is that students simply do not have the literacy skills to keep up with the high school curriculum, which has become increasingly complex (Biancarosa & Snow, 2006; Kamil, 2003).

- Almost 40% of high school graduates lack the reading and writing skills that employers seek, and almost one third of high school graduates who enroll in college require remediation (National Governors' Association, 2005).

- Deficits in basic skills cost the nation's businesses, universities, and underprepared high school graduates as much as $16 billion annually in lost productivity and remedial costs (Greene, 2000).

- On average, college graduates earn 70% more than their high school graduate counterparts, while high school dropouts are 4 times more likely than college graduates to be unemployed (Sum, Taggart, & McLaughlin, 2001). Regardless of educational attainment, higher levels of literacy translate into higher earnings (National Governors' Association, 2005).

- The 25 fastest-growing professions have far greater than average literacy demands, while the fastest-declining professions have lower-than-average literacy demands (Barton, 2000).

- One in every 100 U.S. adults 16 years and older is in prison or jail. About 43% do not have a high school diploma or equivalent, and 56% have very low literacy skills. Ninety-five percent of incarcerated people return to their communities, where it is hard to find jobs because of a prison record but even harder without the necessary literacy skills (Council for Advancement of Adult Literacy, 2008).

While the statistics noted above may be overwhelming, the growing acknowledgment that we need to provide better literacy instruction for adolescent students is being matched by increasing federal and state efforts to support schools in this endeavor. More importantly, it is also becoming clear that schools can provide better instruction if they put into practice what is already known about effective reading and writing instruction in the upper grades (NALC, 2007). States that have invested in adolescent literacy initiatives are already seeing positive benefits for their efforts such as Florida's *Just Read!* initiative that mandated K–12 district literacy plans, increased building-based reading coaches in middle grades, and significantly increased professional development for teachers in upper grades. Massachusetts is another example. An adolescent literacy task force was convened in 2006 that developed a 5-year strategic plan to improve literacy in Grades 4–12 across the state, including revision of state standards, enhancing the state testing system, and increasing professional development for teachers in these grades (Carnegie Council on Advancing Adolescent Literacy, 2010).

AN INCREASE IN ATTENTION TO ADOLESCENT LITERACY

There has been a significant increase in attention to adolescent literacy since the start of the new millennium, partly from the national standards movement and the urgency from demands for accountability among the state and federal education officials. The good news is that there is more research available on effective practice for adolescent literacy than ever before. Evidence of the increase in attention and availability of resources can be seen in new initiatives such as those noted below.

AdLit.org

AdLit.org is a national multimedia project offering information and resources specifically related to adolescent readers and writers. It is one of several literacy sites administered by WETA, the public television and radio station in Washington, D.C., including *Reading Rockets* and *LDOnline*. The site provides information and lists resources on adolescent literacy for educators, parents, and students.

Alliance for Excellent Education

The Alliance for Excellent Education (http://www.all4ed.org) was founded in 2001. It is a national policy and advocacy organization that focuses on at-risk secondary students and serves as a national clearinghouse on policies that support effective high-school reform. In 2003, it established an Adolescent Literacy Advisory Group, which resulted in the publication of a series of adolescent literacy reports, white papers, and research meta-analyses. In addition, the Alliance has hosted a number of conferences and symposiums focused on adolescent literacy.

Center on Instruction

The Center on Instruction (http://centeroninstruction.org) provides information about scientifically based research and information on reading and serves as a resource for the 16 regional U.S. Department of Education Comprehensive Centers. Beginning in 2006, the Center began publishing a number of adolescent literacy guidance documents and practice briefs aimed at connecting current research to practice.

Institute of Education Sciences

The Institute of Education Sciences (IES; http://ies.ed.gov), National Center for Education Evaluation and Regional Assistance, focused its attention on adolescent literacy in 2008 with its publication of *Improving Adolescent Literacy: Effective Classroom and Intervention Practices*. This practice guide offers specific evidence-based recommendations that educators can use to improve literacy levels for students in Grades 4–12.

National Governors' Association, Center for Best Practices

In 2005, the National Governors' Association (http://www.nga.org), through its Center for Best Practices, signaled its desire to focus on adolescent literacy when it published the report *Reading to Achieve: A Governor's Guide to Adolescent Literacy*. In 2006, the association funded the *Reading to Achieve: State Policies to Promote Adolescent Literacy* initiative. This initiative provided assistance and funding to develop state literacy plans and policies to improve adolescent literacy to Arizona, Delaware, Florida, Idaho, Massachusetts, Mississippi, New Jersey, and North Carolina.

National Institute for Literacy

The National Institute for Literacy (a federal agency established in 1991; http://www.nifl .gov) now has a specific initiative to address adolescent literacy. Its 2007 report *What Content-Area Teachers Should Know About Adolescent Literacy* summarizes the literature on adolescent literacy and recommends methods for building adolescent reading and writing skills in the classroom, with an emphasis on what content-area teachers can do.

A REVIEW OF MAJOR ADOLESCENT LITERACY REPORTS

As noted previously, in just the past few years a number of resources have become available that provide information about research to date regarding adolescent literacy. In 2002, the Carnegie Corporation of New York commissioned the RAND Corporation (a nonprofit research and analysis institution) to convene a small group of scholars and policy analysts to discuss the relatively small research base that existed at the time on adolescent literacy. While there was a significant body of knowledge about effective literacy instruction in primary grades, adolescent literacy research had been comparatively ignored (Carnegie Council on Advancing Adolescent Literacy, 2010). Beginning in 2004, supported in part through funding from the Carnegie Corporation, a more substantial knowledge base for understanding adolescent literacy and what it takes to implement this knowledge in schools has accumulated. This section summarizes the findings from nine seminal reports and research meta-analyses that address adolescent literacy (see the list of reports in Table 17.1). The summary addresses instruction, assessment, professional development, and literacy planning and policy issues.

Instruction

The findings related to literacy instruction are organized into four categories: content literacy instruction for all students, interventions for struggling readers and writers, literacy motivation and engagement, and English language learners (ELLs).

Table 17.1.   List of adolescent literacy reports

Reading Next: A Vision for Action and Research in Middle and High School Literacy (Biancarosa & Snow, 2004)

Writing Next: Effective Strategies to Improve Writing of Adolescents in Middle and High Schools (Graham & Perin, 2007)

Literacy Instruction in the Content Areas: Getting to the Core of Middle and High School Improvement (Heller & Greenleaf, 2007)

Academic Literacy Instruction for Adolescents: A Guidance Document from the Center on Instruction (Torgesen, Houston, Rissman, Decker, Roberts, Vaughn, et al., 2007)

What Content-Area Teachers Should Know About Adolescent Literacy (National Institute for Literacy, 2007)

Interventions for Adolescent Struggling Readers: A Meta-Analysis with Implications for Practice (Scammacca, Roberts, Vaughn, Edmonds, Wexler, Reutebuch, et al., 2007)

Double the Work: Challenges and Solutions to Acquiring Language and Academic Literacy for Adolescent English Language Learners—A report to Carnegie Corporation of New York (Short & Fitzsimmons, 2007)

Improving Adolescent Literacy: Effective Classroom and Intervention Practices (Kamil, Borman, Dole, Kral, Salinger, & Torgesen, 2008)

Time to Act: An Agenda for Advancing Adolescent Literacy for College and Career Success (Carnegie Council on Advancing Literacy, 2010)

Content Literacy Instruction for All Students

A major and consistent recommendation found in all of the reports is that content literacy skills, taught by content-area teachers, using subject-specific reading materials, and embedded in content-area instruction, are essential for improving adolescent achievement.

Literacy Instruction in the Content Areas (Heller & Greenleaf, 2007) focused specifically on reading and writing instruction in the content areas, including math, science, English, and history. This report maintained that because content instruction comprises the heart of a secondary school curriculum, content literacy instruction must be the cornerstone of any movement to build high-quality secondary schools. While the report applauded efforts to provide support for adolescents who struggle with literacy, it reminded us of the equally important goal of addressing the achievement of the higher literacy levels all students will need in order to succeed in postsecondary training programs, college, and the growing number of jobs that require high-level literacy skills.

Heller and Greenleaf (2007) noted that very few American students, including many who test at grade level, develop sophisticated literacy skills. Reading and writing are more than just basic skills that students use to learn subject matter. Literacy is the very stuff from which the academic content areas are made, and students must learn how to read and write for specific kinds of content learning in order to make progress in learning those subjects.

In the report *Academic Literacy Instruction for Adolescents,* Torgesen and colleagues (2007) made the same point and noted that in order to meet adolescent literacy goals all teachers must be involved, especially since most middle and high school students spend most of their time in content-area classes and must learn to read expository, informational, content-area texts with greater proficiency. The report said, "Although reading strategies might be taught explicitly in a designated reading support class, students are unlikely to generalize them broadly to content areas unless teachers also explicitly support and elaborate the strategies' use with content-area texts" (p. 12).

Beginning in the middle grades, reading in content areas becomes longer, more complex, and more full of content. It also becomes increasingly more varied in vocabulary, text structure, purpose, and style (Heller & Greenleaf, 2007). Every academic subject has different ways of using written materials to communicate information, which means being literate may mean different things in differing contexts and content areas. One of the main conclusions of *Literacy Instruction in the Content Areas* is that comprehension (including before, during, and after routines), word-level, and writing strategies are best taught in the content area classes using challenging, content-rich texts.

Reading Next (Biancarosa & Snow, 2004) identifies 15 elements of successful programs designed to improve adolescent literacy achievement in middle and high schools. Six of these elements directly address content literacy instruction:

- *Direct, explicit comprehension instruction*—in the strategies and processes that proficient readers use to understand what they read, including summarizing, keeping track of one's own understanding, and a host of other practices

- *Effective instructional principles embedded in content*—language arts teachers using content-area texts and content-area teachers providing instruction and practice in reading and writing skills specific to their subject area

- *Extended time for literacy*—including 2 to 4 hours of literacy instruction and practice that takes place in language arts and content-area classes

- *Text-based collaborative learning*—involves students interacting with one another around a variety of texts

- *Diverse texts*—texts at a variety of difficulty levels and on a variety of topics

- *Intensive writing*—instruction connected to the kinds of writing tasks students will have to perform well in high school and beyond (Biancarosa & Snow, 2004, p. 4)

In 2008, the Institute of Education Sciences (IES) published the practice guide *Improving Adolescent Literacy: Effective Classroom and Intervention Practices* (Kamil et al., 2008). The goal of the guide was to present specific and coherent evidence-based recommendations that educators can use to improve literacy levels among students in Grades 4–12. The report made five recommendations about improving practice, provided a review of the evidence supporting each recommendation, and offered suggestions for how to carry out the recommendation. Of the five recommendations, the first three directly addressed content literacy instruction:

> *Provide explicit vocabulary instruction:* Teachers should provide students with explicit vocabulary instruction, both as part of reading and language arts classes and content classes such as science and social studies. By giving students explicit instruction in vocabulary, teachers help them learn the meaning of new words and strengthen their independent skills of constructing the meaning of text. (Kamil et al., 2008, p. 11)

To carry out the recommendation, the report suggests that teachers dedicate a portion of the regular classroom lesson to explicit vocabulary instruction, use repeated exposure to new words in multiple oral and written contexts to allow sufficient practice sessions, and give sufficient opportunities to use new vocabulary in a variety of contexts through activities such as discussion, writing, and extended reading.

> *Provide direct and explicit comprehension strategy instruction:* Teachers should provide adolescents with direct and explicit instruction in comprehension strategies to improve students' reading comprehension. Comprehension strategies are routines and procedures that readers use to help them make sense of texts. These strategies include, but are not limited to, summarizing, asking and answering questions, paraphrasing, and finding the main idea. (Kamil et al., 2008, p. 16)

To carry out the recommendation, the report suggests that teachers select carefully the text to use when teaching a given strategy, show students how to apply the strategies to different texts, use direct and explicit instruction for how to use comprehension strategies, provide the appropriate amount of guided practice, and make sure students understand that the goal is to understand the content of the text.

> *Provide opportunities for extended discussion of text meaning and interpretation:* Teachers should provide opportunities for students to engage in high-quality discussions of the meaning and interpretation of texts in various content areas. These discussions can occur in whole classroom groups or in small student groups under the general guidance of the teacher. (Kamil et al., 2008, p. 21)

To carry out the recommendation, the report suggests that teachers carefully prepare for the discussion, ask follow-up questions that help provide continuity and extend the discussion, provide a task that students can follow when they discuss texts together in small groups, and develop and practice the use of a specific discussion protocol.

What Content-Area Teachers Should Know About Adolescent Literacy (National Institute of Literacy, 2007) also addressed vocabulary and comprehension instruction in the content classroom but added morphology as well. The report pointed out that difficulty with decoding may be the cause for why some students struggle to read. It noted that while it is important for content-area teachers to understand the role of decoding and fluency, they should not be expected to provide intervention instruction in these components. The report defined content reading components and suggested implications for content classroom instruction:

- *Morphology*—Morphology describes how words are formed from morphemes, the smallest units of meaning in a word (e.g., roots, suffixes, prefixes). Students who understand words at the morphemic level are better able to get the meaning of words and use their knowledge of morphological structure to recognize complex words. When students learn frequently used morphemes, this knowledge improves their spelling, decoding, and vocabulary. Content-area teachers should focus on teaching base words, prefixes and suffixes, and compound words relevant to the new content-area vocabulary being introduced.

- *Vocabulary*—Vocabulary refers to words that are used in speech and print to communicate. Vocabulary knowledge is important to reading because the oral and written use of words promotes comprehension and communication. Good readers know a wide range of vocabulary. Preteaching new vocabulary facilitates reading comprehension by giving the students the meanings of the words before they encounter them. Content-area teachers should also use direct and explicit instruction to teach specific key content vocabulary and provide opportunities for students to make connections to related words and background knowledge (see Chapter 11).

- *Text Comprehension*—Comprehension is the process of extracting or constructing meaning from words once they have been identified. Comprehension varies depending on the text being read. Good readers are purposeful, strategic, and critical readers who understand the content presented in various types of texts. Content-area teachers should incorporate the following comprehension strategies into their content-area instruction: generate questions, answer questions, monitor comprehension, summarize text, use text structure, and use graphic and semantic organizers.

Three of the reports summarized in this chapter address writing skills. In addition to the three reading components noted previously, *What Content-Area Teachers Should Know About Adolescent Literacy* (National Institute of Literacy, 2007) provided recommendations for teaching writing in the content classroom. Writing is the ability to compose text for various purposes and audiences and is a tool for communicating, learning, and expressing oneself to persuade others. Along with reading, writing improves one's capacity to learn. Good writers employ different strategies to write across various genres and disciplines. They are self-directed, goal oriented, and employ self-regulation strategies to help them plan, organize, and revise their writing. Content-area teachers should teach the steps of the writing process (planning, drafting, revising, editing). They should provide a supportive environment for writing, including making writing a regular part of content classroom activities, conveying the ways in which writing is useful in school and outside of school, and giving students opportunities to engage in extended writing.

Torgesen et al. (2007) also addressed the importance of including writing as part of literacy instruction for adolescents. There is a close connection between reading and writing across the curriculum, and writing can be used to improve reading comprehension. "Writing activities are often used as a way for students to express their understanding of what they read, and discussing these written products can be an important way for students to receive feedback on their responses to text" (2007, p. 16). The report recommended making close connections between reading and writing activities as one important vehicle for improving middle and high school literacy.

Writing Next (Graham & Perin, 2007) focused exclusively on writing and summarized the results of a large-scale statistical review of research into the effects of specific types of writing instruction on adolescents' writing proficiency. The report identified the following 11 elements of writing instruction found to be effective for helping adolescent students learn to write well and to use writing as a tool for learning. All 11 elements represent instruction that can be embedded in content classroom instruction for all students:

1. *Writing strategies,* which involve teaching students strategies for planning, revising, and editing their compositions

2. *Summarizing,* which involves explicitly and systematically teaching students how to summarize texts

3. *Collaborative writing,* which uses instructional arrangements in which adolescents work together to plan, draft, revise, and edit their compositions

4. *Specific product goals,* which assigns students specific, reachable goals for the writing they are to complete

5. *Word processing,* which uses computers and word processors as instructional supports for writing assignments

6. *Sentence combining,* which involves teaching students to construct more complex, sophisticated sentences

7. *Prewriting,* which engages students in activities designed to help them generate or organize ideas for their composition

8. *Inquiry activities,* which engage students in analyzing immediate, concrete data to help them develop ideas and content for a particular writing task

9. *Process writing approach,* which interweaves a number of writing instructional activities in a workshop environment that stresses extended writing opportunities, writing for authentic audiences, personalized instruction, and cycles of writing

10. *Study of models,* which provides students with opportunities to read, analyze, and emulate models of good writing

11. *Writing for content learning,* which uses writing as a tool for learning content material

See Chapter 13 for additional information about teaching writing.

Interventions for Struggling Readers and Writers

Many of the adolescent literacy reports and numerous district and statewide initiatives focus on providing more effective literacy instruction to the approximately 8 million students in America in Grades 4–12 who read far below grade level. Heller and Greenleaf (2007) concluded that it is possible to help students make significant gains in literacy and perhaps even catch up to their higher performing peers:

> Schools can make a point of assessing students' reading skills when they enter school, in order to identify those who read below grade level and discern their specific learning needs. They can provide intensive support for low-level readers, helping them make rapid progress in reading fluency, basic comprehension, and other skills. They can make special efforts to

motivate those students and engage them in reading and writing assignments that tap into their individual interests. And they can offer teachers high-quality professional development in various aspects of secondary literacy instruction. If state and federal policymakers follow through on current efforts and fund and support these strategies, the effects will be profound, giving millions of youngsters a real opportunity to build on the rudimentary mechanics of reading that were taught in primary school. (2007, p. 4)

Who should provide intervention instruction? *Reading Next* (Biancarosa & Snow, 2004) was one of the first reports to address the need for interventions beyond content classroom instruction and identified *strategic tutoring* as an essential element of successful adolescent literacy programs. Some students, especially those who struggle with decoding and fluency skills, require intense, individualized instruction. *Reading Next* recommends the availability of strategic tutoring sessions during or after the school day to provide literacy intervention instruction as well as skills for how to learn content information.

Torgesen et al. (2007) suggested that it is not reasonable to expect content-area teachers to teach basic reading skills to students who are reading significantly below grade level. Teaching word-analysis strategies to older students requires special knowledge and skills that are far removed from the training and interests of content-area teachers, and these students require more explicit, individualized, and intensive instruction, as well as extended practice to master new reading strategies or improve word level skills. The IES report (Kamil et al., 2008) supported this conclusion. Specifically, the last of its five recommendations was, "make available intensive and individualized interventions for struggling readers that can be provided by trained specialists" (p. 7). This does not mean that content-area teachers should not play a role in helping struggling readers and writers. A combination of word analysis and reading comprehension skills taught by a skilled reading teacher and reinforcement and elaboration of these skills by content-area teachers is the best way to improve adolescent literacy (Torgesen et al., 2007). Biancarosa and Snow pointed out that when content-area teachers have struggling readers in their classes, "instruction in general education classes should be differentiated to allow students access to important content" (2004, p. 18).

What have we learned about the kind of instruction older struggling readers need? Kamil et al. (2008) noted that failure to read at grade level may be caused by several factors, including deficiencies in decoding (including phonemic awareness, phonemic decoding, and other word analysis skills), fluency, vocabulary, background knowledge, and inefficient use of comprehension strategies.

The report *Interventions for Adolescent Struggling Readers* (Scammacca et al., 2007) specifically addressed the research on reading instruction for adolescent struggling readers and offered research-based guidance for intervening with these students. Based on a meta-analysis of the research, the authors offered the following implications for practice:

- Adolescence is not too late to intervene. Interventions do benefit older students.

- Older students with reading difficulties benefit from interventions focused at both the word and the text level.

- Older students with reading difficulties benefit from improved knowledge of word meanings and concepts.

- Word-study interventions are appropriate for older students struggling at the word level.

- Teachers can provide interventions that are associated with positive effects.

- Teaching comprehension strategies to older students with reading difficulties is beneficial.

- Older readers' average gains in reading comprehension are somewhat smaller than those in other reading and reading-related areas studied.

- Older students with learning disabilities (LD) benefit from reading intervention when it is appropriately focused.

- To learn more about instructional conditions that could close the reading gap for struggling readers, we will need studies that provide instruction over longer periods of time and assess outcomes with measures more like those schools use to monitor reading progress of all students. (Scammacca et al., 2007, p. 1)

The report *What Content-Area Teachers Should Know About Adolescent Literacy* (National Institute for Literacy, 2007) identified decoding and fluency as two basic reading components that are deficit areas for some struggling readers. It described each component, explained what good readers do and the challenges facing struggling readers, and presented implications for instruction.

Decoding, or *word identification*, refers to the ability to correctly decipher a particular word out of a group of letters. Two of the skills involved in decoding are phonemic awareness (understanding that spoken words are made up of individual sounds and the ability to identify and manipulate units of sound) and phonics (understanding the relationship between the letters in written words and their sounds when spoken).

What good readers do: Good readers have a conscious understanding of the individual sounds within spoken words and how they are manipulated to form words. With strong phonics skills they are able to use their knowledge of letters and their sounds to pronounce unknown words. They can rely on these skills to quickly decode unknown words that they encounter while reading.

Challenges for struggling readers: It is estimated that 10% of adolescents struggle with word identification skills. Some of these students may struggle with poor phonemic awareness skills, especially those students with dyslexia. Without sufficient awareness of the sounds in words, they are unable to develop phonics or fluency skills. Students who struggle with phonics lack effective strategies for decoding unknown multisyllabic words. This results in poor vocabulary growth and weakened comprehension.

Implications for intervention instruction: Students with decoding difficulties need intensive practice and instructional time to develop their phonics skills. Instruction should be direct, explicit, and systematic. It should emphasize sound–letter correspondence, syllable patterns, and morphology. This instruction should be provided by intervention specialists who have been trained to deliver decoding skills.

Fluency is the ability to read text accurately and smoothly with little conscious attention to the mechanics of reading.

What good readers do: Fluent readers read text with appropriate speed, accuracy, proper intonation, and proper expression. Some researchers have found a relationship between fluency and text comprehension.

Challenges facing struggling readers: Struggling readers read slowly and often stop to sound out words. They may reread sections of texts to identify words and try to gain comprehension.

Implications for intervention instruction: Practice is an essential component of improving fluency. The following promote frequent and regular practice: provide models of fluent reading by reading aloud to students, engage students in repeated oral reading of texts, and engage students in guided oral reading and partner reading.

Academic Literacy Instruction for Adolescents (Torgesen et al., 2007) and the IES report (Kamil et al., 2008) also identified decoding as a possible area for intervention but added comprehension and text structure as possible areas for intervention for struggling readers:

- *Decoding skills*—Inadequate ability to decode printed text accurately and fluently may be one reason for poor comprehension. Interventions focused at the word level result in both improved reading accuracy and reading comprehension (Torgesen et al., 2007).

- *Content literacy skills*—With the exception of instruction in decoding and fluency, the content of effective literacy instruction for struggling readers is very similar to that recommended for students at or above grade level (i.e., comprehension strategies, vocabulary knowledge, instruction tied to improving content-area knowledge, and assignments that are motivating and engaging) (Kamil et al., 2008).

- *Comprehension strategies*—Educators can use multiple approaches to help struggling readers become more active and strategic readers. Strategy instruction should be explicit and include modeling, guided practice, feedback, and scaffolding. Student collaboration in comprehension strategies has also been shown to be helpful (Torgesen et al., 2007).

- *Text structure*—Helping students organize the information through the use of graphic organizers and providing direct instruction on text structures and organizational patterns is helpful (Torgesen et al., 2007).

Finally, it has been suggested that a technology component should be part of instructional plans for adolescent students. Biancarosa and Snow pointed out that technology should be used as both an instructional tool and an instructional topic:

> As a tool, technology can help teachers provide needed supports for struggling readers, including instructional reinforcement and opportunities for guided practice. For example, there are computer programs that help students improve decoding, spelling, fluency, and vocabulary and more programs are quickly being developed to address comprehension and writing. (2004, p. 19)

See Chapter 22 for additional information about ways that technology can support reading and writing skills.

English Language Learners

Two of the major adolescent literacy reports specifically address literacy instruction for ELLs: *Academic Literacy Instruction for Adolescents* (Torgesen et al., 2007) and *Double the Work* (Short & Fitzsimmons, 2007). Torgesen et al. (2007) noted that literacy instruction for these students must consider the unique needs of this group and the individual differences among them. The variation in their learning needs is due to differences in age of arrival to the United States, educational history, native language ability and literacy, placement and instructional context in school, and sociocultural background. They identified three important principles to consider regarding literacy instruction for ELLs:

- Research-based practices that have been identified to ensure the development of successful reading skills in monolingual students may also benefit ELLs.

- ELLs draw on a host of linguistic, metacognitive, and experiential resources from their first language according to their proficiency level.

- Curricular design and delivery for adolescent ELLs must follow the principles of differentiated instruction. (Torgesen et al., 2007, pp. 91–93)

Torgesen et al. (2007) also pointed out that although there have been few empirical evaluations of instructional approaches specifically for adolescent ELLs, there is relevant research that can offer recommendations about effective instruction for ELLs:

- *Content-based language and literacy instruction:* Preparing all students, and especially ELLs, for academic reading tasks requires embedding literacy instruction in content-area classes.

- *Academic oral language and vocabulary:* Effective vocabulary instruction for adolescent ELL's should be explicit, systematic, extensive, and intensive. Teachers should provide both direct teaching of word meanings in meaningful contexts and teaching of word-learning strategies such as using context and word parts. In addition, depending on their native language and reading proficiency, some ELLs may benefit from strategies that draw on cognate knowledge (i.e., words with similar spellings in English as their native language).

- *Direct, explicit comprehension instruction:* As with native English speakers, research indicates that ELLs benefit from direct, explicit instruction in reading comprehension strategies. Because of limited vocabularies and background knowledge, adolescent ELLs tend to be in even greater need of strategies.

- *Targeted interventions for ELLs with very limited literacy skills:* Effective interventions for adolescent ELLs who struggle with decoding words are similar to those found to be effective with younger children and native English speakers with decoding difficulties (i.e., systematic and explicit instruction in phonics). (See also Chapter 20.)

Short and Fitzsimmons (2007) reiterated that many strategies for supporting literacy in native English speakers are applicable to adolescent ELLs. However, they emphasize that there are significant differences in the way that these interventions should be designed and implemented for ELLs. They refer to the title of their report, *Double the Work*, when they summarize the challenges facing ELLs:

> It should be understood that adolescent ELLs are second language learners who are still developing their proficiency in academic English. Moreover, they are learning English at the same time they are studying core content areas through English. Thus, ELLs must perform double the work of native English speakers in the country's middle and high schools. And, at the same time, they are being held to the same accountability standards as their native English-speaking peers. (2007, p. 1).

For *Double the Work*, researchers were asked to review the literature on adolescent literacy and conduct site visits to three promising programs. In addition, researchers collected and analyzed information on the demographic trends and academic achievement of ELLs. A panel of researchers, policy makers, and practitioners reviewed the information and developed the following list of challenges to improving the literacy of ELLs, as well as potential solutions:

- Lack of common criteria for identifying ELLs and tracking their academic performance

- Lack of appropriate assessments

- Inadequate educator capacity for improving literacy in ELLs

- Lack of appropriate and flexible program options

- Inadequate use of research-based instructional practices

- Lack of a strong and coherent research agenda about adolescent ELL literacy

See Chapter 20 for additional information.

Literacy Motivation and Engagement

"Motivation and self-directed learning" was one of the instructional elements identified by *Reading Next* (Biancarosa & Snow, 2004). The report noted that students become increasingly tuned out as they progress through upper grades, and it is therefore important to build student choices about the materials they read into the school day to keep them engaged. Providing relevancy to students' lives in what they read is another way to better engage them.

There is strong evidence that motivation and interest in reading decline after the elementary grades, especially for struggling readers (Torgesen et al., 2007; Kamil et al., 2008). The decline in motivation has two consequences that directly impact the growth of reading proficiency in adolescents. First, students with low interest in reading do not read as much as students with higher motivation, which affects the growth of vocabulary, background knowledge, and reading strategies. Second, these students tend to be less engaged when they do read, which also results in less use and growth of reading strategies (Torgesen et al., 2007).

What Content-Area Teachers Should Know About Adolescent Literacy (National Institute for Literacy, 2007) addressed the role that motivation plays in developing successful adolescent readers and writers. The report noted, "An individual's goals, values, and beliefs regarding the topics, processes, and outcomes of reading affect students' motivation for reading.... Motivation also involves self-efficacy, or the belief that one is capable of success" (p. 34). Motivation contributes to reading engagement, and engaged readers tend to enjoy reading and read more often. Motivated adolescent readers are self-determined (i.e., they feel they have control over their reading); they self-regulate (i.e., they recognize whether they are on task and employ strategies to achieve their goal); and they are engaged. The report also addressed factors that influence adolescents' motivation, including a change in their beliefs, values, and goals regarding school, and for struggling students, the effects of grading and grouping practices.

This report, as well as *Academic Literacy Instruction for Adolescents* (Torgesen et al., 2007), summarized the findings regarding motivational strategies used by teachers who successfully promote literacy in their students. Both reports supported the suggestion of Guthrie and Humenick (2004) to use three to five motivational enhancements, used in concert with one another. They noted that while there is no systematic research to determine which motivational elements are most powerful for specific students, teachers should follow Guthrie and Humenick's (2004) recommendation to first try to

- Focus students by setting clear goals and expectations for performance

- Guide students to focus on their own improvement

- Provide variety and choice in reading materials and assignments

- Provide opportunities for students to interact through reading

The fourth of five recommendations in the IES report is "increase student motivation and engagement in literacy learning" (Kamil et al., 2008, p. 7), and the report offered this advice:

> To foster improvement in adolescent literacy, teachers should use strategies to enhance students' motivation to read and engagement in the learning process. Teachers should help students build confidence in their ability to comprehend and learn from content-area texts. They should provide a supportive environment that views mistakes as growth opportunities, encourages self-determination, and provides informational feedback about the usefulness of

reading strategies and how the strategies can be modified to fit various tasks. Teachers should also make literacy experiences more relevant to students' interests, everyday life, or important current events. (p. 26)

The report explained that although the words *motivation* and *engagement* are often used interchangeably, they are not always synonymous. Motivation refers to the desire to become involved in a reading task, and engagement refers to the degree to which a student processes text deeply through the use of active learning strategies.

The conclusion reached by almost all of the adolescent literacy reports can be summed up by the following statement from *Academic Literacy Instruction for Adolescents*: "Even technically sound instructional techniques are unlikely to succeed unless we can ensure that, most of the time, students are engaged and motivated to understand what they read" (Torgesen et al., 2007, p. 11).

Assessment

Reading Next (Biancarosa & Snow, 2004) identified ongoing formative assessment of students and ongoing summative assessment of students and programs as the most foundational of all 15 elements it identified as essential to successful adolescent programs. The National Institute of Literacy made this point about the need for assessment that guides instruction for adolescents:

Effective instruction depends on sound instructional decision-making, which, in turn, depends on reliable data regarding students' strengths and weakness, and progress in learning content and developing literacy. Adolescent reading difficulties may involve one or more literacy components... without assessments that are sensitive to the contributions of each component to overall reading ability, teachers will not be able to target their instruction to the skills and strategies most in need of improvement. (2007, p. 27)

What is the difference between different types of assessment? *Formative assessment,* which is often informal, assesses how students are progressing under current instructional practices. *Summative assessment* is more formal and provides data that are reported for accountability and research purposes. Screening and diagnostic assessments are also essential, particularly as tools to guide instructional decisions and intervention placement decisions for struggling readers and writers (Biancarosa & Snow, 2004).

The National Institute for Literacy (2007) report described summative assessments as those that provide important information about reading and subject-area achievements. They may include quizzes, chapter tests, district- and statewide tests, and standardized measures of reading. While summative assessments provide important data to assess overall academic achievement, formative and diagnostic assessments are needed to provide data for more informed decisions about literacy instruction. Formative assessments track students' literacy development and can include teacher questioning, observation of reading strategies, classroom discussion, and the reading of students' work. Diagnostic assessments provide a more precise understanding of individual students' strengths and weaknesses. Diagnostic assessment is typically administered, scored, and interpreted by specialists, and these assessments are used to identify which specific reading and writing skills are weak.

The IES report (Kamil et al., 2008) noted that struggling readers can be identified by initial screening measures or consistently low scores on yearly reading tests. The report made the case that a second round of diagnostic assessment should be administered to determine a student's specific needs. When this is not done, students may be assigned to an intervention class with students who may have different intervention instructional needs. The report recommended that a reliable method for identifying strug-gling readers should include, "an initial screening test or a threshold score on a required reading test and subsequent use of a diagnostic reading test that must be administered, scored, and interpreted by a specialist" (p. 34). Once the learning needs are identified, an intervention that provides an explicit instructional focus should be selected that tar-gets the needs of the student. (See Chapter 14 for more detail about literacy assessment.)

Professional Development

Time to Act identified teacher preparation and professional development as one of the major keys to successful adolescent literacy reform:

> Determining what secondary school teachers need to know, ensuring they learn it, and sup-porting them in implementing that knowledge in classrooms is basic to achieving our goal of literacy for all.... Good teachers of adolescent students not only understand their own content-areas deeply, they also understand the specific literacy challenges created by the texts they assign. Such teachers are prepared to address the content learning needs of strug-gling readers as well as on-grade level readers in their classes. (Carnegie Council on Ad-vancing Adolescent Literacy, 2010, p. 18)

Literacy Instruction in the Content Areas (Heller & Greenleaf, 2007) concluded the following about middle and high school content-area teachers:

- Their roles and responsibilities regarding literacy instruction should be clearly de-fined; it should be stated explicitly that they are not expected to provide basic in-tervention literacy instruction to struggling readers.

- They should identify the literacy skills that are essential to their content area, which they should be responsible for teaching.

- They must receive initial and ongoing professional development in teaching read-ing and writing skills that are essential to their content areas.

The report noted that at the secondary level, the responsibility for teaching reading and writing often seems to belong to no one in particular. More often than not, content-area teachers see themselves first as specialists in their content area such as math, sci-ence, or history. While it is sometimes assumed that English teachers should be the ones to address reading skills, many of these teachers see themselves as experts in lit-erature that requires reading and writing skills that are already in place.

If, as Heller and Greenleaf concluded, content literacy instruction must be a cor-nerstone of any comprehensive movement to build high-quality secondary schools, what kind of professional development is needed? The Carnegie Council on Advancing Adolescent Literacy (2010) suggested that improvements need to be made at both the preservice level (i.e., preparation of content-area teachers at the college level) and in-service professional development level (i.e., ongoing, quality training for new and ex-perienced content-area teachers). It recommended that as a bare minimum, all middle and high school teachers should possess a working knowledge of

- How literacy demands change with age and grade
- How students vary in literacy strengths and needs
- How texts in a given content area raise specific literacy challenges
- How to recognize and address literacy difficulties
- How to adapt and develop teaching skills over time (Carnegie Council on Advancing Adolescent Literacy, 2010, p. 20)

Reading Next (Biancarosa & Snow, 2004) identified professional development that is both long term and ongoing as an essential element of successful adolescent literacy programs. The report noted that professional development must be delivered as part of a systematic, long-term effort that supports everyone in a school building: classroom teachers, administrators, reading and intervention specialists, paraprofessionals, and librarians.

Literacy Planning and Policy Issues

All of the adolescent literacy reports reviewed in this chapter concluded that literacy instruction does not end with the teaching of basic reading and writing skills in elementary schools and that all students need literacy instruction that is tied to content learning through high school. They also concluded that secondary school is not too late to help struggling readers and writers, but to ensure that students have the sophisticated literacy skills to succeed in college and the work force, concerted literacy planning efforts must take place at the school, district, state, and national levels.

Reading Next (Biancarosa & Snow, 2004) noted that while instructional improvements can have a tremendous impact, they are more effective if they are implemented in conjunction with infrastructure supports. The report recommended the following infrastructure elements:

- *A comprehensive and coordinated literacy program*—interdisciplinary and interdepartmental that may even coordinate with out-of-school organizations and the local community

- *Leadership*—from principals and teachers who have a solid understanding of how to teach reading and writing to the full array of students present in schools

- *Teacher teams*—interdisciplinary teams that meet regularly to discuss students and align instruction (Biancarosa & Snow, 2004, pp. 4–5)

Literacy Instruction in the Content Areas (Heller & Greenleaf, 2007) also presented several key considerations that education leaders and policy makers should keep in mind as they make policy decisions:

- The roles and responsibilities of content area teachers must be clear and consistent.

- Every academic discipline should define its own essential literacy skills.

- All secondary school teachers should receive initial and ongoing professional development in the literacy of their own content areas.

- Content area teachers need positive incentives and appropriate tools to provide reading and writing instruction. (Heller & Greenleaf, 2007, pp. 25–29)

Time to Act (The Carnegie Council on Advancing Literacy, 2010) stressed the vital role that policy makers at the school, district, state, and federal levels must play in reengineering the nation's schools to support adolescent literacy. The report made recommendations for reengineering for change at the school, district, and state levels (see Table 17.2).

LITERACY PLANNING MODEL FOR GRADES 4–12

Given the information presented thus far in this chapter, the establishment of school and districtwide literacy plans is an obvious first step toward meeting the literacy needs of all students in Grades 4–12. In order to deliver appropriate content and intervention literacy instruction, an assessment plan must be in place to determine the specific needs of individual students. Solutions to scheduling and grouping issues must be addressed

Table 17.2. Recommendations for reengineering for change

At the school level

The school culture is organized for learning

Assessment information drives decisions

Resources are allocated wisely

Instructional leadership is strong

Professional faculty is committed to student success

Targeted interventions are provided for struggling readers and writers

All content-area classes are permeated by a strong literacy focus

At the district level

Organize to promote a culture of learning

Use information to drive decisions

Allocate resources to support learning priorities

Build human capacity

Ensure the provision of targeted interventions for struggling readers and writers

At the state level

Institutionalize adolescent literacy

Revise standards

Develop and revise assessments

Improve data collection and use

Align instruction with standards and assessments

Support targeted interventions for struggling readers and writers

Improve human capacity across the state

Source: Carnegie Council on Advancing Adolescent Literacy (2010).

in order to find time in the daily schedule to deliver intervention instruction. Finally, a long-term plan for professional development is also necessary to provide classroom teachers, specialists, and administrators with the essential information they need in order to play their role in the literacy plan.

The last section of this chapter reviews the Keys to Literacy Planning Model for Grades 4–12 (Sedita, 2004, 2009). The model has been used with a number of schools in New England to develop upper elementary, middle, and high school literacy plans. The Keys to Literacy Planning Model is organized around six essential planning components, each of which is addressed in Table 17.3.

It is important to note that these components are interrelated; plans that are made for one component will affect the other components. Likewise, a plan for one component will not be successful if the other components are not simultaneously addressed. For example, if an assessment plan is developed and used to group students on the basis of instructional need but scheduling and grouping issues are not addressed, the assessment data cannot be acted on. A plan to incorporate content literacy instruction will not be successful if the professional development needs of content-area teachers are not also addressed.

Included in the model is a three-tiered framework for delivering literacy instruction that is guided by assessment data (Sedita, 2008), represented by the graphic organizer in Figure 17.1. This three-tiered framework is similar to those used in the implementation of response to intervention models (Aaron & Joshi, 2009; Burns, 2008). As noted in the adolescent literacy reports summarized previously, content-area teachers must play a role in improving the literacy skills of all adolescent students, but struggling readers and

Table 17.3. *Keys to Literacy Planning*: A model for Grades 4–12

Establishment of a literacy planning team
Assessment planning for screening, guiding instruction, and progress monitoring
Literacy instruction in the content classroom
Interventions for struggling readers that address phonics, word study, fluency, vocabulary, and
    comprehension skills
Flexible scheduling to allow for grouping based on instructional needs
Professional development planning

Sources: Sedita (2004, 2009).

writers will also need intervention instruction. The framework begins with screening assessments to determine which students are at or above grade level with reading and writing skills. A second round of diagnostic assessment is given to those students not at grade level to determine how severe their needs are and which skills require remediation. Based on individual needs, students receive literacy instruction across these three tiers:

- *Tier I—Content Literacy:* Instruction for all students that addresses background knowledge, content vocabulary, comprehension strategies, goals for reading, and the reading/writing connection using classroom materials taught by content-area teachers in content classrooms.

- *Tier II—Supplemental:* Instruction for weak readers with slightly below grade-level reading skills (up to 1 year below grade level) that addresses general vocabulary growth, additional practice of comprehension strategies, advanced word study, or fluency using supplemental materials taught by ELA teachers or trained specialists in extra literacy classes or extended ELA blocks.

- *Tier III—Intervention:* Intensive instruction for struggling students who are more than 1 year below grade level in literacy skills that addresses decoding, spelling, language structures, significant vocabulary growth, or comprehension strategies using intervention materials taught by trained specialists in small-group or individual settings.

The Six Components of the Keys to Literacy Planning Model

This section discusses the six components of the Keys to Literacy Planning Model in more detail.

Establishment of a Literacy Planning Team

In order to develop a schoolwide literacy plan, a literacy planning team must be assembled. There are several ingredients to a successful team: strong leadership, literacy expertise, representation from all stakeholders, good organization, communication, and team-building skills. The involvement of all stakeholders is essential, including administrators, classroom teachers, and specialists. Because content-area teachers will be asked to play a large role in literacy instruction, there should be representation from content-area teachers. Sarason reinforced the importance of having content-area teachers as part of the team:

> When a process makes people feel that they have a voice in matters that affect them, they will have a greater commitment to the overall enterprise and will take greater responsibility for what happens to the enterprise. The absence of such a process insures that no one

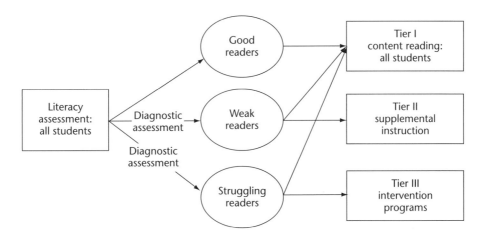

Figure 17.1. Three-tiered framework.

feels responsible, that blame will always be directed externally, and adversarialism will be a notable feature of school life. (1990, p. 61)

It is also important to recognize that literacy planning is a process, not an event. Like most schoolwide initiatives, developing and executing a literacy plan will take time and sustained effort; literacy planning teams should be prepared for the process to take 1–3 years. Fullan (2007) identified three phases of planning that are necessary to ensure long-term success of a school reform such as literacy planning.

Initiation is the period in which a plan is developed and a decision to move forward is made. During this phase, educators develop a set of ideals, goals, and policies that will promote unity of purpose around what students should learn, how they should learn it, and how the school and personnel must be organized to meet the needs of the students for the initiative.

Implementation is the process of putting the literacy plan into practice, typically spanning 1–3 years. Because parts of the initiative may be new to the people expected to participate in it, it is unrealistic to assume that all implementers will wholeheartedly embrace the initiative, but, with support, practice, and accountability, belief systems begin to change. Administrators, teachers, and students eventually begin to see progress and the positive effects of the initiative. This phase requires time, effort, and clarity of purpose. Sometimes there can be an implementation dip: Things get worse before they get better as people grapple with the meaning and skills of change. Even with the best initiation planning, implementers will experience bumps in the road.

Continuance is the process of institutionalizing the literacy initiative. The infrastructure, policies, and mutual accountability developed in the initiation and implementation phases will determine whether the initiative is sustained beyond the initial implementation. Careful planning up to this stage helps the initiative survive budget cuts and changes in personnel. The major challenge at this stage is for administration to continue overt support. As implementation moves toward continuance, it is easy to assume the initiative does not need attention. Teachers may drift and come and go, and the gains made begin to diminish.

The Keys to Literacy Planning Model draws on Fullan's school reform planning model by organizing the literacy planning and implementation process into five phases.

The first three steps occur in the first year. The last two take place in the second year and beyond.

1. *Initiation Stage (1–2 months):* Assemble a representative literacy planning team, learn about literacy.

2. *Self-Assessment Stage (1–3 months):* Gather data and information to determine the current status related to assessment, content and intervention literacy instruction, professional development, scheduling and grouping, and school resources. Identify gaps and needs.

3. *Planning Stage (1–3 months):* Develop a literacy plan that sets goals for the areas noted above and includes action steps to be taken to reach those goals.

4. *Implementation Stage (2–3 years):* Create an ongoing literacy implementation team. Follow through on each action step of the plan. Adjust the details of the plan if needed.

5. *Continuance Stage (ongoing):* Institutionalize the plan to ensure sustainability. Revisit the plan on an annual basis.

Assessment Planning for Screening, Guiding Instruction, and Progress Monitoring

One of the most important components of a schoolwide literacy plan is the development of a complete and efficient assessment plan. As noted earlier in this chapter, literacy assessments play an important role in instruction decision-making. In *Creating a Culture of Literacy: A Guide for Middle and High School Principals,* the National Association of Secondary School Principals noted the following about the purpose of assessment for literacy planning:

> The goal of a school's assessment efforts should be to provide a clear picture of student strengths and weaknesses, teacher professional development needs, and the school's capacity to support a school literacy program. To meet this goal, the school will need to develop a balanced assessment program that uses both formal and informal measures of achievement in gathering data to determine the success of the program. (2005, p. 19)

Torgesen and Miller made this point about different types of assessment:

> Assessments *of* learning, frequently referred to as summative assessments, indicate how well students have learned, or how well they can meet the performance standards in a subject area such as reading or math.... Assessments *for* learning, in contrast, are designed to help teachers provide more effective instruction so that individual students can improve their learning, or so that more students can reach acceptable performance standards. (2009, p. 5)

Assessments *for* learning, also described as *formative assessments,* should be the focus for literacy planning. Formative assessments include screening (to determine which students are having reading and writing difficulty), diagnostic (to determine why students are having difficulty), and progress monitoring assessments (to determine whether students are making progress with the instructional practices that are being used).

By the time students reach upper elementary grades and beyond, assumptions are often made that students have the literacy skills necessary to learn. It is therefore essential to screen all students at least once a year to determine whether their literacy skills are keeping up with grade-level requirements. Many schools rely solely on high-stakes state assessments, but these are not the best screening tools. Although they offer a broad picture of who may be struggling to read, they do not provide sufficient data to determine which students are reading at grade level, which are not, and why. Figure 17.2 illustrates a recommended model for assessment planning that begins with the assessment of all students but progressively assesses fewer students at each stage.

In Step 1, use a screening assessment with all students to determine who is reading at or above grade level and who is not. Use a standardized, group-administered, and norm-referenced assessment that measures reading comprehension as well as vocabulary, if possible. Students who perform at or above grade level on this measure do not require additional assessment unless there is something that would indicate a student may have weak reading skills despite performing well on the standardized measure (e.g., the student has received special education services for a number of years because of a reading disability). Literacy instruction for these students should be provided in the content areas in vocabulary and comprehension by all teachers.

In Step 2, for those students who are not reading on grade level or for whom there are some questions as noted previously, use a series of diagnostic assessments to determine which reading components are contributing to difficulty with comprehension of grade-level material. This might include underlying difficulty with decoding skills (phonics, fluency), background knowledge, insufficient vocabulary knowledge, or a lack of metacognitive comprehension strategies. Start with an assessment that measures oral reading fluency rates. If students are hitting grade-level benchmarks for fluency, further diagnostic assessment to determine whether there are phonics weaknesses is not necessary. Literacy instruction for these students should be provided in the content areas as noted in Step 1 and may also need to include supplemental instruction that provides more explicit instruction and guided practice in vocabulary and comprehension.

In Step 3, for those students who are not reading on grade level and who do not meet fluency benchmarks, use diagnostic assessments to determine whether there is an underlying weakness in phonics skills. Formal and informal phonics screeners and diagnostic spelling assessments can be used for this purpose. If students do not have weaknesses in phonics skills, they do not require additional diagnostic assessments. In addition to receiving literacy instruction in the content areas as noted in Step 1, these students should also receive fluency intervention instruction, and they may also need supplemental instruction that provides more explicit instruction and guided practice in vocabulary and comprehension.

In Step 4, for those students who are not reading at grade level, who do not meet fluency benchmarks, and who show weaknesses in phonics skills, use diagnostic assessments to determine exactly where the breakdown in the phonics scope and sequence occurs. In addition to receiving literacy instruction in the content areas as noted in Step 1, these students will also require significant intervention in the areas of phonics, fluency, and most likely vocabulary and comprehension.

When developing an assessment plan, be sure to prepare for the following:

- Sufficient professional development regarding the importance of using assessment to guide instruction and how to interpret data

- Adequate time and resources to administer assessments

- Sufficient personnel to administer assessments

- A procedure to review the data to guide instructional decisions

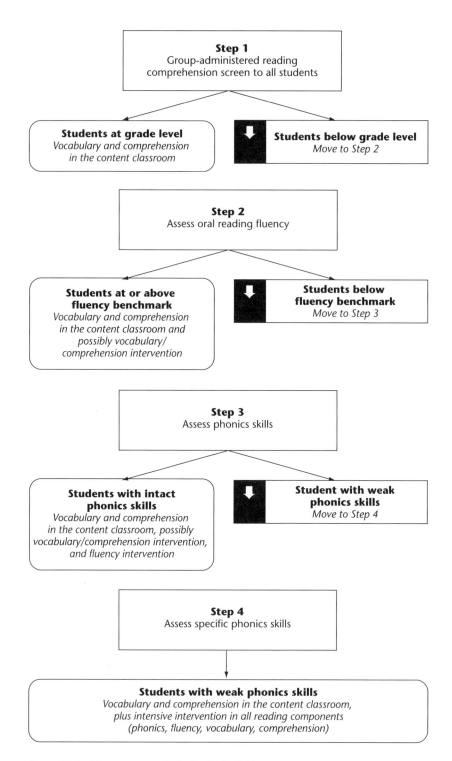

Figure 17.2.   Literacy assessment plan for Grades 4–12.

Literacy Instruction in the Content Classroom

The third component of the literacy plan should be the establishment of goals for content literacy instruction. As students progress from intermediate through high school grades, they must continue to build on their basic reading skills to meet ever-increasing literacy demands. Compared to earlier grades, they must learn from texts that are significantly longer and more complex at the word, sentence, and structural levels; require greater fluency; and demand much greater ability to synthesize information. However, content-area teachers often expect that once students have learned basic reading skills, they will be able to readily apply them as they move through the grades (Carnegie Council on Advancing Adolescent Literacy, 2010).

Vocabulary   Content vocabulary instruction is necessary because of the vast number of words students must acquire each year in order to read and understand grade-level text. If students do not adequately and steadily build their vocabulary knowledge, reading comprehension will be affected (Chall & Jacobs, 2003). Estimates vary of how many words students must learn every year, ranging from 2,000 to 3,500 words per year after Grade 3 (Anderson & Nagy, 1992; Beck & McKeown, 1991).

Explicit instruction in specialized content vocabulary such as in science or social studies has been identified as an important way to contribute to successful reading comprehension among adolescent students, and it enhances their ability to acquire textbook vocabulary (Kamil et al., 2008). In addition, Pressley, Disney, and Anderson (2007) found that students comprehend more when they are taught vocabulary taken from text they are reading. Direct and indirect methods for teaching vocabulary were presented earlier in this chapter; see Chapter 11 for more detail about effective vocabulary instruction.

Comprehension   Research indicates that teachers who provide comprehension strategy instruction that is deeply connected within the context of subject matter learning, such as history and science, foster comprehension development (Biancarosa & Snow, 2004; Snow, 2002). If students learn that strategies are tools for understanding the conceptual context of text, then the strategies become more purposeful and integral to reading activities. Unless the strategies are closely linked with knowledge and understanding in a content area, students are unlikely to learn the strategies fully, may not perceive the strategies as valuable tools, and are less likely to use them in new learning situations with new text. In their summary of the research on secondary school teaching specific to reading, Alvermann and Moore (1991) concluded that the use of strategies such as taking notes, mapping, and paraphrasing should be built into the curriculum of all content areas and that it is a program outcome for which all educators are responsible.

The National Reading Panel (2000) identified the following comprehension strategies as being most effective for improving comprehension:

- *Comprehension monitoring*—Readers approach text with a sense of purpose and adjust how they read.

- *Use of graphic semantic organizers (including story maps)*—Readers create or complete graphic or spatial representations of the topics and main ideas in text.

- *Question answering and generation*—Readers ask and answer questions before, during, and after reading. They learn to consider what type of question is being asked according to a framework and to anticipate test questions they may be asked.

- *Summarization*—Readers select and paraphrase the main ideas of expository text and integrate those ideas into a brief paragraph or several paragraphs that capture the most important propositions or ideas in the reading.

- *Cooperative learning*—Students learn strategies together through peer interaction, dialogue with each other, and with the teacher in whole-group activities.

Suggestions for comprehension strategy instruction were presented earlier in this chapter; see Chapter 12 for more detail about effective comprehension instruction.

Other Content Literacy Skills   In addition to vocabulary and comprehension strategies, morphology, extended discussion of text meaning, and writing skills were addressed previously in this chapter. There is another aspect of content literacy that also supports the case for making content-area teachers part of the solution to improving literacy achievement. After the elementary years, reading assignments become increasingly varied in their style, vocabulary, text structure, purpose, and intended audience (Heller & Greenleaf, 2007). Science textbooks differ from math textbooks. Reading in history can range from a textbook, to a primary source, to an editorial in the newspaper. Reading literature can include multiple genres such as poetry, short story, and fable. Content-area teachers are in the best position to teach students how to read and write in their subject areas (Jetton & Alexander, 2004; Stahl & Shanahan, 2004).

Interventions for Struggling Readers that Address Phonics, Word Study, Fluency, Vocabulary, and Comprehension Skills

One of the most important components of a literacy plan is the development of a plan for assigning students to supplemental and intervention instruction settings and identifying research-based intervention programs and highly trained specialists to take on the tasks of intensive literacy instruction for students with severe difficulties.

As noted previously, failure to read at grade level may be caused by several factors or combinations of factors, including skill deficiency in the following: phonemic awareness, phonetic decoding and word analysis skills that support word reading accuracy, text reading fluency, strategies for building vocabulary, strategies for understanding and using the specific textual features that distinguish different genres, and self-regulated use of reading comprehension (Kamil et al., 2008). As a result, some students may need word-level interventions, including systematic training in decoding skills (see Chapter 16). Other students may require an intervention targeting the development of fluency skills (see Chapter 10). For comprehension and vocabulary, the level of instruction struggling students receive in their content-area classes may not be intense enough. They may require more direct and explicit instruction in these areas with significantly more guided practice.

There are several obstacles to providing appropriate interventions. First, it may be difficult to find the resources to administer diagnostic assessments. Second, schools often do not have the funds to hire specialists who are trained to deliver intervention instruction or to purchase research-based intervention programs. However, assuming the resources are available, older struggling readers can often learn to read if "the teacher is well prepared and supported, and the students are given time, sufficiently intensive instruction, and incentives to overcome their reading and language challenges" (Moats, 2001, p. 11). Development of a schoolwide literacy plan often results in the identification and reallocation of existing resources to support intervention instruction.

Flexible Scheduling to Allow for Grouping Based on Instructional Needs

A challenge of secondary literacy planning is finding the time to schedule supplemental and intervention literacy instruction and how to group students based on their individual needs for that instruction. In early elementary grades, when students are with the same teacher throughout the day and a significant block of time is devoted to reading instruction for all students, it is much easier to apply flexible grouping techniques to deliver targeted supplemental and intervention literacy instruction. There is also a greater chance that the classroom teacher will have a paraprofessional or specialist available for part of the day to assist with flexible grouping. This is often not the case at the middle and high school levels.

Time for Intervention   McEwan (2001) noted that in order to raise student achievement schools must allocate sufficient instructional time to reading, particularly for those students who are well below grade level, and then use every minute of that time wisely. However, the typical scheduling patterns at middle and high schools create significant obstacles to identifying time in the school day for literacy instruction beyond that which can be embedded in content-area instruction. By the middle grades, it is assumed that students will have basic reading skills, so there is often no class period designed to specifically teach reading. It is sometimes assumed that ELA classes should be used for supplemental reading instruction, but teachers of these classes understandably note that the literature content that they must cover does not provide time to teach basic reading.

What is the solution? Every school has a unique set of circumstances that may enable it to consider certain options for intervention time. The following list contains possible options to include in a schoolwide literacy plan:

- Extend the period of time allocated for ELA class to devote some class instruction to specific literacy skills.

- Develop teacher schedules to include opportunities for teachers to work collaboratively to plan and assess teaching strategies based on student assessment data (National Association of Secondary School Principals, 2005).

- Consider reorganizing the schedule and class offerings (e.g., move to alternate or block scheduling, change the length of class time by reducing or increasing number of classes in the day).

- Provide literacy electives for struggling learners that replace other electives or foreign language.

- Standardize curriculum frameworks for which literacy skills will be taught in various subject areas.

- Consider organizing time under a block schedule so all teachers can devote additional time to basic reading skills in addition to delivering content.

- For intervention classes, consider developing a parallel schedule when these classes are taught at the same time of day so students can flexibly move from one group to another based on their progress (Allain, 2008).

- Use after school or Saturdays to conduct tutoring to small groups (McEwan, 2001).

Grouping for Intervention   Balancing various course requirements and myriad complexities during the typical secondary scheduling process makes it difficult to group struggling readers together who have similar instructional needs. As a result, when students are assigned to intervention periods, they often find themselves grouped with students who are at different levels or who need different types of literacy interventions. Added to this is a tendency for teachers, students, and their parents to want to use intervention time to help students with homework or study for tests instead of focusing on improving literacy skills. This hinders the ability to target intervention instruction to the individual needs of each student plus be diligent about monitoring progress.

Another factor that results in inappropriate grouping for intervention is that assessment data are not available or used to determine which students need literacy intervention, which literacy skills are areas of need, or how to best group students with similar areas of need. The report of the Carnegie Council on Advancing Adolescent Literacy pointed out that

> In very few secondary schools is student assessment data used as a basis for assignment to classes—sometimes because such data is not available, but more often because convenience-based scheduling defeats the effort. Many schools that do use assessment data as a basis for assigning classes simply assign students to lower and higher tracks, rather than offering targeted instruction to meet struggling students' needs while making sure that all students receive the same instruction in core academic areas. (2010, p. 4)

Regarding mixed-ability grouping versus similar-ability grouping, McEwan (2001) said that students need specialized instruction, and they need the opportunity to work in groups that reflect the heterogeneity of their school campus. "By the time students reach high school, they may differ by as many as six grade levels in their academic abilities" (p. 27). McEwan further noted that a review of the literature on grouping and student achievement reveals no valid research studies supporting the position that mixed-ability groups are always more effective.

Another issue that needs to be addressed is the provision of common and fair accommodations for students identified with learning disabilities. This includes extra time on tests, shortened reading assignments, the use of digitized materials for reading, universal design technology and software, and even someone to read aloud to students. These are all parts of interventions that should be available for struggling readers along with intensified instruction outlined previously (see also Chapter 22).

Professional Development Planning

The final essential component to a successful literacy plan is a long-term plan for the provision of literacy professional development to classroom teachers, intervention teachers, and administrators. Without appropriate professional development, plans for delivering literacy instruction to both good and struggling readers are unlikely to be sustained or even initially implemented effectively (Biancarosa & Snow, 2004). A major finding of the National Reading Panel (2000) was that professional development is essential for teachers to develop knowledge of comprehension strategies and to learn how to teach and model strategy use. The findings of the RAND Reading Study Group (Snow, 2002) underscored the importance of teacher preparation to delivering effective instruction in reading comprehension strategies, especially when the students are low performing.

Heller and Greenleaf (2007) concluded that the greatest challenge to addressing adolescent literacy has to do with the scarcity of ongoing, high-quality professional development for teachers. This lack of literacy professional development begins at the preservice level, where preparation for middle and high school teaching typically prioritizes content knowledge and gives insufficient attention to the role literacy plays within a content area. Teachers often enter the classroom assuming their students already possess all of the reading and writing skills they need to learn (Carnegie Council on Advancing Adolescent Literacy, 2010).

A lack of quality, meaningful literacy professional development continues at the inservice level. Although there are many workshops and textbooks dedicated to content literacy, relatively few of the nation's secondary school teachers have had meaningful opportunities to learn about the reading and writing practices that go on in their own content area (Heller & Greenleaf, 2007). The National Association of Secondary School Principals made this observation:

> Much of the professional development in U.S. schools is of the one-off variety—popular speakers are invited to provide motivational jolts, or publishers are invited to provide curriculum overviews. Taking student data as the basis for professional work, linking the achievement data to proposed instructional activities, discussing ways to provide instruction across content areas and across years in a manner that is coherent and leads to cumulative results, and engaging in peer observation and evaluation of instruction are relatively rare activities in the nation's schools, yet these activities constitute the most effective approach to instructional improvement." (2005, pp. 4–5)

More optimistically, though, Heller and Greenleaf (2007) pointed out that when content-area teachers receive intensive and ongoing professional support, many of them find a way to emphasize reading and writing in their classes. This chapter's author has experienced this first-hand through her work with the delivery of literacy professional development to teachers in Grades 4–12. A survey of teachers participating in long-term, building-based professional development in the areas of comprehension, vocabulary, and writing found that more than 90% report integrating at least two content literacy strategies on a consistent basis in their classroom teaching as a result of the training (Keys to Literacy, 2009).

Closing Thoughts About Literacy Planning for Grades 4–12

There is no simple, one-size-fits-all model for improving literacy achievement in intermediate through high school grades. Each school has a unique combination of administrators, teachers, students, community support, and resources that must be considered when developing a schoolwide literacy plan. The time, effort, and expertise needed to develop effective, sustainable literacy plans that meet the needs of both good and struggling adolescent readers are significant and present a challenge. The good news is that more attention than ever before is beginning to focus on the literacy needs of these students, including the possibility of increased funding to support adolescent literacy planning and instruction. The time is right, and the challenge is worth accepting.

FINAL THOUGHTS ABOUT ADOLESCENT LITERACY

In just 10 years, we have learned significantly more about effective teaching of reading and writing skills beyond Grade 3. We have also identified the toll that having significant numbers of adolescent students with below grade-level literacy skills takes on high school graduation rates, success in college, and preparedness for the work force. There are numerous web sites and organizations such as the Alliance for Excellent Education and the Center on Instruction that educators can turn to for information about adolescent literacy. There are also a number of research reviews and reports available such as those made possible by funding from sources such as the Carnegie Corporation and the federal government (e.g., Institute of Education Science, the National Institute for Literacy). There is still more we have to learn about how to support content-area teachers to embed literacy instruction in their classrooms, which intervention programs are most effective for struggling readers, and what we can do to address the needs of ELLs. However, research since 2000 has produced enough knowledge about what works so that there should be no delay in applying this knowledge at the classroom, school, and district levels. The following quote from the report of the Carnegie Council on Advancing Adolescent Literacy provides a challenging but attainable goal: "To reach the goal of providing quality literacy instruction for all our nation's adolescents, we must systematically link instruction to the growing knowledge base on literacy and inform it with up-to-date data relating to outcomes and best practices" (2010, p. x). This chapter has attempted to provide readers with the knowledge base necessary to inform their instructional practices.

REFERENCES

Aaron, P.G., & Joshi, R.M. (2009). Why a component model of reading should drive instruction. *Perspectives on Language and Literacy, 35*(4), 35–40.

Allain, J. (2008). *The logistics of literacy intervention.* Longmont, CO: Sopris West.

Alvermann, D.E., & Moore, D. (1991). Secondary school reading. In R. Barr, M.L. Kamil, P. Mosenthal, & P.D. Pearson (Eds.), *Handbook of reading research* (Vol. 2, pp. 951–983). White Plains, NY: Longman.

Anderson, R.C., & Nagy, W.E. (1992). The vocabulary conundrum. *American Educator, 16*(4), 14–18, 44–47.

Barton, P.E. (2000). *What jobs require: Literacy, education, and training, 1940–2006.* Washington, DC: Educational Testing Service.

Beck, I.L., & McKeown, M.G. (1991). Conditions of vocabulary acquisition. In R. Barr, M.L Kamil, P. Mosenthal, & P.D. Pearson (Eds.), *Handbook of reading research* (Vol. 2, pp. 789–814). White Plains, NY: Longman.

Biancarosa, C., & Snow, C.E. (2004). *Reading next—A vision for action and research in middle and high school literacy: A report to Carnegie Corporation of New York.* Washington, DC: Alliance for Excellent Education.

Biancarosa, C., & Snow, C.E. (2006). *Reading next—A vision for action and research in middle and high school literacy: A report to Carnegie Corporation of New York* (2nd ed.). Washington, DC: Alliance for Excellent Education.

Burns, M.K. (2008, March). Response to intervention at the secondary level. *Principal Leadership.* Reston, VA: National Association of Secondary School Principals.

Carnegie Council on Advancing Adolescent Literacy. (2010). *Time to act: An agenda for advancing adolescent literacy for college and career success.* New York: Carnegie Corporation of New York.

Chall, J.S. (1983). *Stages of reading development.* New York: McGraw Hill.

Chall, J.S., & Jacobs, V.A. (2003, Spring). Poor children's 4th-grade slump. *American Educator.* Available online at http://www.aft.org/newspubs/periodicals/ae/spring2003/hirschsbclassic.cfm

Council for Advancement of Adult Literacy. (2008). *Report of the National Commission on Adult Literacy.* New York: Author.

Fullan, M. (2007). *The new meaning of educational change* (4th ed.). New York: Teachers College Press.

Graham, S., & Perin, D. (2007). *Writing next: Effective strategies to improve writing of adolescents in middle and high schools—A report to Carnegie Corporation of New York.* Washington, DC: Alliance for Excellent Education.

Greene, J. (2000). *The cost of remedial education: How much Michigan pays when students fail to learn basic skills.* Midland, MI: Mackinac Center for Public Policy.

Guthrie, J.T., & Humenick, N.M. (2004). Motivating students to read: Evidence for classroom practices that increase reading motivation and achievement. In P. McCardle & V. Chhabra (Eds.), *The voice of evidence in reading* (pp. 329–354). Baltimore: Paul H. Brookes Publishing Co.

Hasbrouck, J.E., & Tindel, G.A. (2005). *Oral reading fluency: 90 years of measurement.* Eugene: University of Oregon, College of Education, Behavioral Research and Teaching. Retrieved October 15, 2009, from http://www.brtprojects.org/tech_reports.php

Heller, R., & Greenleaf, C. (2007). *Literacy instruction in the content areas: Getting to the core of middle and high school improvement.* Washington, DC: Alliance for Excellent Education.

Jetton, T.L., & Alexander, P.A. (2004). Domains, teaching, and literacy. In T.L. Jetton & J.A. Dole

(Eds.). *Adolescent literacy research and practice*. New York: Guilford Press.

Kamil, M. (2003). *Adolescents and literacy: Reading for the 21st century*. Washington, DC: Alliance for Excellent Education.

Kamil, M.L., Borman, G.D., Dole, J., Kral, C.C., Salinger, T., & Torgesen, J. (2008). *Improving adolescent literacy: Effective classroom and intervention practices: A practice guide* (NCEE# 2008-4027). Washington, DC: U.S. Department of Education, Institute of Education Sciences, National Center for Education Evaluation and Regional Assistance.

Keys to Literacy. (2009). *Survey of June '09 Key Three Routine survey results*. Retrieved February 18, 2010, from:http://www.keystoliteracy.com/reading-comprehension/professional-development/consulting-services.htm

Lee, J., Griggs, W.S., & Donahue, P.L. (2007). *Nation's report card: Reading* (NCES 2007-496). Washington, DC: U.S. Department of Education, Institute of Education Sciences, National Center for Education Statistics.

McEwan, E.K. (2001). *Raising reading achievement in middle and high schools: 5 simple-to-follow strategies for principals*. Thousand Oaks, CA: Corwin Press.

Moats, L.C. (1995). *Spelling: Developmental disability and instruction*. Baltimore: York Press.

Moats, L.C. (2001). *When older kids can't read*. Retrieved October 1, 2009, from: http://www.cdl.org/resource-library/articles/older_read.php

National Adolescent Literacy Coalition (NALC). (2007). *Foundational and emergent questions: Smart people talk about adolescent literacy. A report by the steering committee of the National Adolescent Literacy Coalition*. Washington, DC: Author.

National Association of Secondary School Principals. (2005). *Creating a culture of literacy: A guide for middle and high school principals*. Reston, VA: Author.

National Governors' Association, Center for Best Practices. (2005). *Reading to achieve: A governor's guide to adolescent literacy*. Washington, DC: Author.

National Institute for Literacy. (2007). *What content-area teachers should know about adolescent literacy*. Washington DC: National Institute of Child Health and Human Development, National Institute for Literacy.

National Reading Panel. (2000). *Teaching children to read: An evidence-based assessment of the scientific research literature on reading and its implications for reading instruction*. Washington, DC: National Institute of Child Health and Human Development.

No Child Left Behind Act of 2001, PL 107-110, 115 Stat. 1425, 20 U.S.C. §§ 6301 *et seq*.

Perie, M., Grigg, W., & Donahue, P. (2005). *The nation's report card: Reading 2005*. (NCES 2006-451). Washington, DC: U.S. Department of Education.

Pressley, M., Disney, L., & Anderson, K. (2007). Landmark vocabulary instructional research and the vocabulary instructional research that makes sense now. In R.K. Wagner, A.E. Muse, & K.R. Tannenbaum (Eds.), *Vocabulary acquisition: Implications for reading comprehension* (pp. 205–232). New York: Guilford Press.

Sarason, A. (1990). *The predictable future of educational reform: Can we change course before it's too late?* San Francisco: Jossey-Bass.

Scammacca, N., Roberts, G., Vaughn, S., Edmonds, M., Wexler, J., Reutebuch, C.K., et al. (2007). *Interventions for adolescent struggling readers: A meta-analysis with implications for practice*. Portsmouth, NH: RMC Research Corporation, Center on Instruction.

Sedita, J. (2004). *Middle and high school reading achievement: A school-wide approach*. Retrieved October 1, 2009, from: http://www.keystoliteracy.com/reading-comprehension/reading-comprehension-instruction.htm

Sedita, J. (2008). *Three-tiered framework*. Self-published.

Sedita, J. (2009, Winter). Adolescent literacy: A schoolwide approach. *Seen Magazine*, 58–59.

Short, D., & Fitzsimmons, S. (2007). *Double the work: Challenges and solutions to acquiring language and academic literacy for adolescent English language learners—A report to Carnegie Corporation of New York*. Washington, DC: Alliance for Excellent Education.

Snow, C. (2002). *RAND reading study group: Reading for understanding: Toward an R&D program in reading comprehension*. Santa Monica, CA: RAND.

Snow, C., & Burns, M.S. (1998). *Preventing reading difficulties in young children*. Washington, DC: National Academies Press.

Stahl, A.S., & Shanahan, C. (2004). Learning to think like a historian. In T.L. Jetton & J.A. Dole (Eds.), *Adolescent literacy research and practice*. New York: Guilford Press.

Sum, A., Taggart, R., & McLaughlin, J. (2001). *The national economic downturn and deteriorating youth employment prospects: The case for a young adult jobs stimulus program*. Chicago: Alternative Schools Network.

Torgesen, J.K., Houston, D.D., Rissman, L.M., Decker, S.M., Roberts, G., Vaughn, S., et al. (2007). *Academic literacy instruction for adolescents: A guidance document from the Center on Instruction*. Portsmouth, NH: RMC Research Corporation, Center on Instruction.

Torgesen, J.K., & Miller, D.J. (2009). *Assessments to guide adolescent literacy instruction*. Portsmouth, NH: RMC Research Corporation, Center on Instruction.

18

Learning Strategies and Study Skills

The SkORE System

CLAIRE NISSENBAUM AND ANTHONY HENLEY

It is not necessarily the smartest students who get the highest marks; it is the students who know how to study. The most intellectually able students may be among the lowest-performing students in the class. Too often, these are students struggling with unrecognized and untreated language-based learning differences (dyslexia[1]). These differences affect performance in every area of the curriculum, especially for students who have not had effective training in learning strategies and study skills (Deshler, Ellis, & Lenz, 1996; Strichart & Mangrum, 1993; Wiig & Semel, 1990).

Instructors who work with students with specific language-based learning difficulties should be highly trained in methods for addressing the learning problems typical of these students. Excellent training is widely available from accredited programs across the country (see Appendix B at the end of the book).

A significant number of dyslexic students are considered also to have executive function disorder—impaired performance coming from presumed frontal lobe deficits. The emerging understanding of the primacy of executive functioning on academic achievement is an important and complex issue in the field of education for students with learning differences. A comprehensive review of the literature on executive functioning is beyond the scope of this chapter. Presenting a consensus view of executive functioning is even more problematic, given the widely varying views of experts in the field. The very definition of executive functioning is controversial. A review of the lit-

---

[1]The term *dyslexia* is used herein to refer to language-based specific learning differences in receptive and expressive language skills, including conceptualization with verbalisms, phonemics, phonics (decoding), fluency, prosody, comprehension, grammar, syntax, vocabulary, memory (storage and retrieval), and, even in students who are math-talented, difficulties with math concepts, memorizing facts, word problems, and operations. Students with dyslexia may also have difficulties in social skills (Deshler, Ellis, & Lenz, 1996; Wiig & Semel, 1990).

At least 80% of students with learning disabilities have verifiable and diagnosable reading disorders, primarily dyslexia (Lerner, 1989).

erature, however, suggests commonalities in the descriptions of the core components of executive functioning, including goal setting, planning, organizing behaviors over time, flexibility, attention and memory systems, and self-regulation (Meltzer, 2007).

Executive functioning is believed to have a developmental arc, with indications of some executive skills emerging as early as 9 months, accelerating in adolescence, and continuing to develop well into adulthood. Historically, executive functioning skills have been linked to the frontal lobes of the brain. The term *frontal lobe dysfunction* has been used to describe deficits in executive functioning that frequently occur following injury to the frontal lobes of the brain.

As with other areas of cognitive functioning, research suggests a more diffuse, interconnected neurological involvement in executive skills. Different models have been suggested to characterize the relationship among executive functioning and other cognitive skills. Traditionally, executive functioning skills have been considered higher-order cognitive skills, often called *metacognitive skills* (a term now used in academic circles to refer to the application of executive function skills to academics). Others suggest that executive function skills are part of a group of cognitive skills (e.g., language, motor coordination) interconnected with others but not innately of a higher order.

The frontal lobe functions are typically described as higher-level cognitive skills (a description convincingly disputed by neurologist Dr. Martha Denckla). Information-processing models of human behavior often use computer analogies to elucidate cognitive functioning and cognitive deficits. The computer analogy nicely illustrates three different views of the nature of executive functions in the brain: 1) executive function is one of many software programs the brain runs, 2) executive function is a master software program that coordinates and facilitates the performance of other software programs, and 3) executive function is part of the core operating system necessary for other software to function properly.

There is a similar lack of consensus concerning the effect of executive dysfunction on students who experience learning difficulties. Deficits in executive functioning have been identified in students with both attention-deficit/hyperactivity disorder (ADHD) and learning differences. The nature of the relationships among executive function, ADHD, and learning differences has been a continuing source of interest and disagreement among researchers and clinicians. ADHD and learning differences have a high **comorbidity**; the presence of difficulties with executive function in each has been used to explain that comorbidity (Denckla, 2007). The emergence of the theory that ADHD is primarily a disorder of disinhibition (Barkley, 1997) contributed to belief in the primacy of executive function in ADHD and suggested that the core view of ADHD as a disorder of attention may need to be revisited.

Others go further, suggesting that difficulties with executive function actually are the core deficits within both ADHD and learning differences (Brown, 2009). This perspective views the primary academic impairments of students with learning differences (e.g., who have difficulties with task completion, reading comprehension, and written language) as resulting from the highly executive nature of these core academic tasks and the inability to perform those executive tasks efficiently. Another perspective suggests that executive functions and self-regulation are mediated by underlying (usually internalized) language, which suggests the possible primacy of language deficits in executive function, ADHD, and learning differences (Singer & Bashir, 1999). Although it is not possible to reconcile these divergent positions, professionals working with these populations must consider the effects of all these areas on the possible functioning of individual students (see Chapter 19).

With respect to study skills, the most relevant executive function issues are time management; organization, including problems with recognizing and creating structure; prioritizing; self-monitoring; and the ability to change strategies, when necessary. Attention and memory deficits are also issues, but are often present in dyslexia without executive function disorder.

In this chapter, the terms *strategy* and *study skills* are used as follows: An individual's approach to a task is called a *strategy*. Strategies include how a person thinks and acts when planning, executing, and evaluating performance on a task and its subsequent outcomes (Deshler et al., 1996).

Study skills are those competencies associated with acquiring, recording, organizing, synthesizing, remembering, and using information and ideas found in school—the ones more or less indispensable for academic success (Devine, 1981).

Systematic instruction in learning strategies and study skills may or may not be offered to middle or secondary school students. Even when available, the instructor may be inadequately trained to teach the course (Tonjes & Zintz, 1981). The time allotted may be insufficient for students to develop mastery of the strategies and skills (Deshler et al., 1996). Practice in transferring the skills to the classroom, a critical factor in their successful use, may receive little or no attention.

The lack of efficient, effective training in strategies and skills affects all students but is extremely handicapping to students with dyslexia, especially where they are included in general education classes. The conclusion that the effect of executive function deficits on the academic achievement of students is profound does not seem controversial. The daily life of students is fraught with tasks requiring executive function skills, and there can be marked deficits in the ability to perform those tasks adequately. Even the seemingly simple task of getting up in the morning requires complex executive functioning: planning (knowing how much time is required to prepare to leave the house in the morning, having planned time to complete homework the night before), self-regulation (inhibiting pleasurable activities the night before in order to get to sleep at an adequate hour), self-monitoring (knowing how much sleep is needed to perform adequately, being aware of the effect of not getting enough sleep), and goal direction (keeping in mind the desired long-term positive results that depend on adequate sleep, such as good grades and eligibility to play sports). As a result, students are left to a demeaning and unrewarding struggle to survive academically, to narrowly limited college and vocational choices, and to the possibility of physical and mental health problems (Kamhi & Catts, 1989). A few individuals develop self-destructive or antisocial behaviors (Levine, 1987).

Training in learning strategies and study skills must be as efficacious as possible and accomplished in the shortest possible time without sacrificing mastery. The strategies should be applicable in all content classes with minimal teacher involvement. Training in such skills facilitates dramatic change in the student, from passive involvement in learning to proactive and productive participation (Deshler et al., 1996). It also effectively addresses such executive function issues as attention, concentration (sustained focus), memory, time management, organization, planning, and self-monitoring.

OVERVIEW

This chapter discusses unconventional techniques that improve the academic performance of all students, but that make the critical difference between failing and passing for students with dyslexia. The techniques are effective in middle and high school, college, graduate school, and beyond. They may be used with students beginning in fourth grade. After discussing the academic achievement of students with dyslexia, organization, time management, and self-management, this chapter describes the Skills for Organizing and Reading Efficiently (SkORE)[2] system, designed to help students achieve the goals of self-awareness, self-management, and self-advocacy. In addition, strategies for improving memory, comprehension, and test-taking are discussed. SkORE begins by teaching students fast-working "Quick Tricks" to

- Engage their attention and cooperation

- Reduce high-frequency errors and common teacher irritants in written work

- Begin systematic memory training

- Provide emergency strategies for handling long reading assignments

Simultaneously, students are coached in organization and time-management skills.

This introductory step usually has positive effects on students' motivation. Following this, the first phase of SkORE presents strategies for preparing to read a passage of text. The second phase presents strategies and techniques for mastering subject content and rapid improvement in vocabulary, including nonliteral language, comprehension, conceptual and critical thinking, writing skills, and self-confidence. There is strong emphasis on concept formation and explication of abstract terms.

Written language skills are taught incrementally, beginning with the mechanics of English, accurate spelling, sentence and paragraph structure, and, in the third phase of SkORE, summarizing, writing **précis,** outlining, and notetaking. More extensive training in writing skills is neither possible nor defensible in a study skills course due to time limitations. Bringing students to mastery in the strategies and skills is crucial. To attempt to do both is to do an inadequate job of both (Deshler et al., 1996) (see Chapter 13).

ACADEMIC ACHIEVEMENT OF STUDENTS WITH DYSLEXIA: CONVENTION, PERCEPTION, AND REALITY

The problem with conventional courses in study skills is that there is too much study (usually in the form of memorization without true mastery) and not enough skills because teachers cannot teach what they themselves have not been taught (Askov & Kamm, 1982). College and university education courses for teacher preparation do not include methods in teaching study skills (Deshler et al., 1996). Notwithstanding, many elementary and secondary teachers are required to teach them. Teachers often lecture, provide worksheets in discrete skills (e.g., identifying the main idea), and test students' knowledge. Students are expected to pay attention, listen, understand, take notes, remember, and apply the skills to content subjects, which are areas of the greatest difficulty for most students with dyslexia.

Academic achievement is not the only prerequisite to success in adult life as attested to by successful adults with dyslexia who did poorly in school. Since 2000, however, there have been many studies and reports outlining the necessity for high literacy

---

[2]SkORE is a study skills approach developed in the late 1970s at the TRI-Services Center for Children and Adults with Learning Disabilities, Rockville, Maryland. The author gratefully acknowledges the writings of S.T. Orton (1937), Gillingham and Stillman (1956), Cruickshank (1967), Alley and Deshler (1979) and the modeling and direct training of TRI-Services, Rockville, Maryland, founder the late Betty S. Levinson, Ph.D., and the late Alice A. Koontz, M.A., Jemicy School, Owings Mills, Maryland.

rates in order to graduate from high school and college for all students (see Chapter 17). Parents typically believe that academic achievement is directly related to the time and effort spent on homework. Teachers may view parents of students who are low achieving as unable or unwilling to make their children work harder. Both parents and teachers tend to view students who are low achieving as unmotivated, lazy, and not invested in their work.

The effect of executive skills continues throughout the day at school. Often, the focus of the impact of executive function in school is depicted in terms of task completion (both in the classroom and at home), which is certainly an issue for many students. The impact of executive function deficits, however, is far more pervasive. The typical tasks encountered in school, such as oral notetaking, reading comprehension, and written language, are complex activities requiring efficient integration of academic skills (decoding, encoding, grammar, punctuation) and cognitive skills (graphomotor, attention, memory, language processing). Each of these tasks individually depends heavily on executive function skills. The ability to utilize them effectively to obtain the ultimate goals of acquiring knowledge and getting good grades depends even more on efficient executive functioning.

Many students face their greatest challenges with executive functioning after leaving the structure of the school day behind. Without the structure and feedback provided in school, students with executive functioning deficits are often at a loss when confronted with the night's homework. Difficulties with core executive function skills make it hard to know where or how to start tasks and, in many cases, even what needs to be done. The myriad distractions around the house often tax the student's ability to self-regulate and inhibit desires to engage in other, more stimulating activities, which makes sustaining effort on a task difficult. Even when a student completes his or her homework, planning and organizing skills may be so weak that it is not turned in on time. Long-term projects often prove particularly troublesome because the impact of difficulties with planning and organizing are multiplied.

A major stumbling block is met when students with **executive function difficulties** are required to study for a test. The ability to translate the vague admonition "study" into a concrete set of efficient and effective tasks requires applying all the core executive functions.

It is at home that students often experience the most detrimental effects of executive function deficits, the erosion of parent–child relationships when students do not complete academic tasks and household routines that others think they are able to perform. The result is one of the most pernicious aspects of executive function deficits, the routine misattribution of those deficits to characterological flaws by parents, teachers, and even clinicians. The neurologist Martha Denckla wrote: "Dysexecutive children in middle school are in danger of being emotionally traumatized by being called lazy, unmotivated, irresponsible, and other such words implying moral turpitude instead of neurodevelopmental disability or immaturity" (2007, p. 15). In clinical work, it is still common to see students with executive function deficits referred for evaluation because of "lack of motivation" or "not applying" themselves academically.

The reality is that students with learning disorders do poorly because of deficits in cognitive processing resulting from underlying differences in brain anatomy and function (Cruickshank, 1967; Gaddes & Edgell, 1994). These deficits may include one or more of the following:

- Concrete thinking results in difficulty with verbal abstractions, multiple word meanings, and nonliteral language (idioms, metaphors, and proverbs), significantly affecting comprehension due to understanding only the here and now (Cruickshank, 1967; Wiig & Semel, 1990).

- Rigidity, or inability to shift the frame of reference, manifests as difficulty with transitions, changing a routine, and perseveration (Cruickshank, 1967; Wiig & Semel, 1990).

- Difficulties with spatial and temporal sequence as evidenced in poor orientation in space, poor sense of direction, problems with telling time, sensing duration, estimating time, habitual tardiness, vocabulary of time and space (day after tomorrow, second from the last), and sequencing. These difficulties affect comprehension, spelling, arithmetic, and interpersonal relationships.

- Unstable **figure–ground perception,** resulting in difficulty with recognizing whole–part relationships (e.g., forest and trees) and the ability to analyze and synthesize. This affects handwriting, reading, arithmetic, outlining and summarizing, and comprehending complex subject matter (Cruickshank, 1967; Tomatis, 1969) because, as Johnson and Myklebust noted, "A perceptual disorder by reciprocation *disturbs all levels of experience that fall above it"* (1967, p. 33, emphasis added).

- Difficulty with focusing and sustaining attention affects all aspects of intellectual and social functioning, including comprehension.

- Poor and variable memory affects a person's ability to understand, store, retrieve, and use information (Neisser, 1976), therefore affecting comprehension.

- Difficulty with symbolization leads to problems understanding, learning, and using verbal symbols and symbol systems (Orton, 1937; Wiig & Semel, 1990). This difficulty affects speaking, reading, comprehension, arithmetic, and writing skills.

- Deficits in receptive and expressive language affect vocabulary, grammar, comprehension, all communication, and interpersonal relationships (Tomatis, 1969).

- Deficits in simultaneous integration of verbal symbolic data with motor output affect attention, memory, spelling, writing, and notetaking.

- Difficulty processing rapidly spoken information (e.g., a lecture) can include problems with discriminating discrete verbal sound units in words and sentences. This affects listening skills, vocabulary, following directions, notetaking, memory, and comprehension.

- Anxiety may appear as generalized, nonspecific anxiousness and is compounded by stress (e.g., during classroom recitations, oral reading, tests, social introductions). Anxiety affects all areas of thought and learning, especially memory.

- Problems with abstraction include difficulties with classifying, categorizing, generalizing, and making analogies. These problems affect concept development, abstract thought (Lakoff & Johnson, 1980), comprehension, and understanding logical relations (Wiig & Semel, 1990). But, "categorization is the main way we make sense of experience" (Tomatis, 1969, p. 32) (i.e., understand, comprehend).

- Risk aversion, which is the result of repeated failure, can affect class participation, selection of courses, schools, jobs, and friendships, thus the quality of life.

Most important, students with language-based learning differences—with or without executive function disorders—have multiple and serious obstacles to comprehending spoken and print language. SkORE is specifically designed to give them ways to overcome these obstacles.

WORKING WITH STUDENTS WITH DYSLEXIA

The need to prevent early failure is the strongest argument for aggressive intervention in the early school years. Students who have experienced continual failure inevitably have low self-esteem. Once eroded, self-esteem is difficult to restore. Adult achievement does not appear to compensate for early traumas. Professor Seymour Martin Lipset, a fellow of the Hoover Institution at Stanford University and a member of the American Academy of Arts and Sciences, described himself sadly as "the man whose wife had to write his thank-you notes for him" (personal communication, 1986). Katrina de Hirsch (1984) stated that the teacher of a student with language deficits must be the student's ego until he or she begins to experience success. Cruickshank held that a student with a learning disability "needs every stable external support possible to assist him in developing a strong ego" (1967, p. 9).

To provide this support, the study skills instructor functions as mentor, coach, and cheerleader, with unflagging faith in the students' ability to overcome or compensate for the difficulties. The instructor must make learning a process of communication, hope, and trust for students (Tonjes & Zintz, 1981), which requires good organization and thorough preparation, working as "manager, and instructional leader, and a mediator of learning who demonstrates how to think about a task, apply strategies, and problem-solve in novel situations" (Deshler et al., 1996, pp. 463–464).

Experience has shown that having students use the techniques consistently in subject classes is a challenge for everyone involved. The obstacles are the persistent skills deficits, lack of sufficient time for practice in the transfer and application to content subjects, and lack of coordination with content teachers. Therefore, the instructor must be willing and able to work cooperatively with subject teachers. Teachers and students need to know that it takes time to establish effective study skills. "The full benefits of effective programming are realized only over a period of years" (Deshler et al., 1996, p. iii).

The study skills instructor is not a homework aide. Aspects of assignments in subject classes can serve as a vehicle for applying and practicing the techniques, but helping with classwork and test preparation is not part of the coaching process. In the best case, subject teachers work closely with the study skills instructor to reinforce the skills by requiring their use, cuing, and monitoring the students' use of the strategies and techniques in the their classes. These include full use of the binder (described later), systematic and intensive vocabulary work, consistent attention to spelling, notetaking, mnemonics, cue cards, and procedures for homework assignments.

Students need to know that study skills training is a cooperative effort with the instructor, one in which the instructor has the expertise to teach the student the skills for success and to train him or her in the discipline needed. Giving the student the right to set his or her own priorities and goals is essential; it is not necessary for students to get an *A* in every subject.

Catch Them Early

Dr. Helen Hall, an expert in working with adolescents who are failing, noted that "if you are going to catch them, you have 6 weeks to do it" (personal communication, 1977).

Students with dyslexia must experience change for the better very quickly. They need to know that it is really possible to improve performance and get better grades fairly soon after beginning the study skills course. This is the rationale for Quick Tricks, the introductory step in SkORE, described next.

ORGANIZATION, TIME MANAGEMENT, AND SELF-MANAGEMENT

The importance of structure and organization when working with students with dyslexia cannot be overemphasized. One of the primary goals of this chapter is to offer instructors concrete, systematic, structured procedures that give students with both executive function and language-based learning differences a strategic and effective approach to mastering academic work. The suggested interventions for students with language-based learning differences share core commonalities with the academic interventions developed for students with executive function and other deficits. Using simultaneous multisensory structured techniques to aid retention and achieve mastery of content material is incorporated into many of the techniques that follow. Direct, explicit teaching of skills is a key component in teaching study skills to students with executive function problems. As with language skills, many students with executive function problems do not internalize concepts, patterns, and skills that other students pick up implicitly. Similarly, as with other areas of academic work with these students, it is necessary to make explicit whatever is only implied.

The student has to be emotionally and mentally available for learning to benefit from the training. Students with significant nutritional deficiencies, debilitating emotional problems, sleep deficits, or poor oral language skills (including low vocabulary) need direct intervention by health professionals and school personnel simultaneously to mitigate and ultimately eliminate these problems at the same time that the academic issues are being addressed. Strichart and Mangrum (1993) noted that students with learning disabilities typically experience disorganization. It is often overwhelming, even threatening, to students to have to function in an unstructured environment (Cruickshank, 1967). A good study skills instructor imposes and requires maximum structure in every aspect of students' work. The SkORE process accomplishes this by using structured procedures in an orderly sequence of steps in a process for acquiring and applying specific strategies and skills. Deshler et al. noted, "Structured teaching unites the teacher and student in a learning partnership by providing informed, *explicit,* and interactive instruction" (1996, p. 459, emphasis added).

The SkORE strategies and structured procedures described next are designed to address difficulties in the following areas of executive functioning:

- Planning, prioritizing, scheduling

- Focusing, attention, *sustained* focus and attention (concentration)

- Self-monitoring, self-regulating, self-advocacy

- Recognizing and correcting habitual errors

- Identifying and addressing cognitive weaknesses

- Active and interactive learning strategies

- Closure (completing tasks—e.g., letter forms, homework, long-range projects)

- Memory (storage, recall, and retrieval)

- Discernment, based on recognition of saliency

In the section in Appendix B for this chapter and in Chapter 22, on technology supports for literacy and learning, there are recommendations for electronic tools and devices that are compatible with direct personal instruction in SkORE. They have been designed to circumvent common problems in students with dyslexia—decoding, reading fluency, organizing, comprehension, memory, and low vocabulary. Used for reinforcement and repeated practice, they can have a powerful multiplier effect on the impact of the SkORE training. They are not, however, a substitute for direct instruction.

Some interventions for executive functioning are addressed elsewhere in this book. For example, reading comprehension and expressive writing are highly complex tasks requiring executive functioning (see Chapters 12 and 13).

The Binder as a Central Organizing System   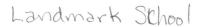 Landmark School

At the first session, students receive basic equipment for the study skills course: a set of two 3-inch sturdy three-ring binders, one for study skills and the other for all other classes. The study skills binder remains with the instructor for the duration of training. Using a single binder for all other subjects requires the prior agreement of subject teachers. (If a teacher requires a spiral notebook, then it should be bound into the school binder in the appropriate class section.) Using a single binder eliminates many of the organization and maintenance problems otherwise sure to occur. The study skills binder serves as a model for the all-subjects school binder.

Furnishings for Each Binder

Each binder should be outfitted with a large plastic zipper case, preferably 7" × 11", containing the following:

- Two pens and two pencils
- Set of colored felt-tipped pens (nontoxic, nonbleeding)
- Gum (art) eraser
- Wedge-shaped metal pencil sharpener (flat and small, such as the one made by Staedtler)
- Paper clips
- Rubber bands
- Index cards: four sets of eight cards, each set a different color
- Several double-fold three-panel industrial-quality paper towels
- Banker's size manila envelopes (2½" × 3½")
- Hole punch that can be clipped into the middle of the binder
- Two sturdy double pocket dividers
- Self-tabbed medium-weight dividers for each subject
- Two or more sheet protectors
- Wide-ruled notebook paper

The plastic pouch, with its contents, is inserted at the front of the binder. The hole punch is inserted in the middle of the binder (to prevent breakage). One two-pocket divider is inserted at the front, and one at the back of the binder. The pocket dividers are labeled as follows:

- *Front side of first divider:* Handouts/Homework Sheets/Assignments

- *Back side:* Work in Progress

- *Front side of back divider:* For Consultation and Reworking

- *Back side:* Completed Assignments to Hand In

Behind the pocket divider in the front of the binder, a copy of the school calendar, the student's class schedule, exam schedules, and a table of contents are inserted into sheet protectors. The contents of the binder may be arranged alphabetically or chronologically according to the daily schedule of classes.

All other papers from the day's work should be filed into the pocket on the inside back cover of the binder, to be filed as soon as possible in the appropriate section. The instructor checks the binder weekly to see that all papers are filed by the end of the week.

Organizing Space

The instructor has to work with students to organize two different areas—the locker and the backpack. The locker is reorganized with specific arrangements for books, clothing, gym bag, and other items. Extraneous items should be eliminated. The locker is inspected weekly and cleaned out once a month. The backpack must be even more organized, with specific places for the binder, textbooks, and reference books. No loose papers should be permitted in the backpack.

The home study area, though ordinarily impossible for the instructor to monitor, also needs to be organized and furnished with all books and supplies the students will need, including the following: (Items listed are for older students; versions for younger students can be downloaded. All sources may be found on Amazon.com.)

- A good collegiate dictionary (hardback), such as the *Merriam Webster's Collegiate Dictionary*

- *Roget's Thesaurus* (original version)

- An etymological dictionary, such as *The Oxford Dictionary of English Etymology*

- Handbook of essential idioms, such as *A Dictionary of American Idioms* (Makkai, Boatner, & Gates, 1995)

- Dictionaries of literary and historical allusions, such as *Brewer's Dictionary of Phrase and Fable* (Rockwood, 2009)

- Reference book of English composition and grammar, such as *English Composition and Grammar: Complete Course* (Warriner, 1988)

- A handbook on English usage, such as *A Dictionary of Modern English Usage* (rev. 3rd ed.; Fowler, 1998) or *Minimum Essentials of English* (2nd ed.; Obrecht, 1999)

- General reference books, such as *The New York Public Library Desk Reference*

- Optional items such as an atlas and books of historical time lines

Time Management

Many people with dyslexia have difficulty with aspects of time, such as learning the language of time, learning to tell time, estimating the duration or passage of time, projecting time budgets, planning and carrying out projects on time, and being punctual. No other aspect of study skills training is more critical to success than time management because individuals with dyslexia must be more organized and efficient than other students to achieve mastery. Being organized alleviates the characteristic free-floating anxiety in students with dyslexia that impairs memory and impedes progress. The study skills instructor has the responsibility to help students understand that they must spend more time on assignments than other students to achieve good grades. The initial training focuses on planning and scheduling.

The first section of the binder contains a set of coordinated calendars, schedules, and time sheets that the student fills out and uses daily, weekly, and monthly:

- Monthly calendar (for secondary students, 60-day calendar)
- Weekly calendar
- Daily time log/class schedule
- Long-range assignments calendar and/or time logs
- Daily assignment sheet (optional)
- Exam schedule(s)

Monthly Calendar

The instructor guides students to note holidays, half-days, special events, and vacations on a blank calendar form. Next, standing commitments are filled in, such as daily classes, sports, or other practices, regular meetings and appointments, volunteer work, and family commitments. Nonroutine commitments are then added, such as medical appointments and sports matches. Finally, deadlines for long-range assignments are added.

Each entry is made as a block of time, posted according to the time of day. Recording entries in this way provides a visual representation of the duration of each event. For example, an afternoon commitment is blocked in below the middle of the square, ending at the expected time of day. Initially, the instructor guides the students. Later, when students can do this independently, the instructor should monitor updates to the calendar weekly.

Long-range assignments require special attention. Students should be trained to build in extra time in case of unexpected events, such as illness or difficulty with an assignment. Ideally, the subject teacher is consulted to approve the schedule. The study skills instructor has a special responsibility to see that students keep to the schedule and the work is appropriate and meets the teacher's standards. Some students work best with a separate planning worksheet for each long-range project on which the separate components can be checked off as completed.

Weekly Calendar

With the monthly calendar as reference, the student blocks out (colors in) the time for each commitment during the week on a blank weekly calendar. If Saturday morning is committed to soccer practice, for example, then the time for the practice, as well as the time for travel, should be blocked out. Deadlines for short- and long-range assignments are noted, as are quizzes and tests. The white space remaining on the weekly calendar graphically displays the time available to study and to complete assignments. It is important that students see clearly when time is available and how much time is available in each instance.

To complete the weekly calendar, the student estimates and schedules in the times needed for studying, completing homework, and working on long-range assignments. Students may lack adequate time sense to plan and schedule realistically or may have only a vague notion of the actual time needed. Students invariably underestimate the time needed to complete an assignment. The instructor must help them break down every task incrementally to make a realistic time budget.

Daily Schedule

On Friday, the student fills out daily schedules for each day of the following week. If homework is due on a certain day, then the student can place an asterisk in red after the name of the class on that day on the daily schedule. A double asterisk can be used to indicate a quiz or test. Figure 18.1 shows a sample daily schedule. In addition, on Friday, the instructor and the students should review and assess the students' ability to schedule appropriately by comparing the estimated and actual time spent on assignments (using the past week's schedule).

Self-Management

Many students with dyslexia actually do not perceive the connection between their academic behavior and their grades. For this reason, it is also useful to create a form to

---

Wednesday, September 28	**RETURN LIBRARY BOOKS**
7:00	Review notes for math test.
7:15	Leave. Take LIBRARY BOOKS.
7:30	Spanish
8:40	*Social Studies
9:30	Math
10:20	Free. RETURN LIBRARY BOOKS. Work on math.
11:30	Lunch—Sit with Guy; discuss science project.
12:00	*Science
12:50	Phys. Ed. SEE MR. HASKINS ABOUT EQUIPMENT ROOM.
1:45	**English—Make appointment with Mrs. G to go over book report draft.
2:45	Meet Reshad to get math book.
3:00	Soccer practice
5:30	Nap
6:00	Dinner
6:45	Science project—Work with Guy, my house.
8:15	Read novel for book report, due 10/5, Chaps 6, 7 (30 pages; 67 to go).
9:00	Spanish assignment
9:20	Math assignment
9:45	Pack backpack; check off assignments.

Figure 18.1.   Sample daily schedule sheet. An asterisk indicates that homework is due; double asterisks indicate a quiz.

compare the time spent studying each subject weekly with the grades received in that class. The form should also note the number of assignments completed and handed in and the number of incomplete and/or not handed in or handed in late. This record keeping is an important step in training the student to develop a more objective view of him- or herself as a student.

QUICK TRICKS: STRATEGIES FOR CHANGING ATTITUDES AND REVIVING HOPE

At the second study skills session, students are coached to use techniques known as Quick Tricks. These are presented as ways to change teachers' attitudes and grading practices to the student's advantage. (Students will need to be cautioned against discussing this with other teachers.) Seemingly simplistic, Quick Tricks almost always result in perceptible changes that students themselves report with obvious satisfaction. Quick Tricks are designed to help the individual student begin using a more intentional, proactive, and responsible mode of behavior and foster better relationships with teachers, thereby gradually reducing whatever tensions may exist. Instructor and students should role-play each set of Quick Tricks before the student implements them in his or her classes.

With the right sell by the instructor—enthusiasm mixed with confident assurances—the Quick Tricks produce results in a short time. After a few weeks, students generally report more positive responses from teachers ("My teacher smiled at me today!"). These changes increase students' motivation to use the Quick Tricks more consistently. Because teachers see a student using Quick Tricks as making greater effort and having a better attitude, they may even give slightly better grades as encouragement. A student using Quick Tricks often assumes that the teacher has changed; it is the student, of course, who is changing, but at this point, the student does not make this connection—nor should the study skills instructor point it out.

Level One (no extra time required, minimal effort required)

1. Look directly at the teacher when he or she is speaking. Look at his or her forehead, ear, or nose if you are uncomfortable making eye contact.

2. Use the teacher's name when speaking to him or her in class at least every other day.

3. In every class, speak at least once. Ask a question, make a comment, or ask to have something repeated.

4. Arrive on time; better yet, be a minute or two early.

5. Avoid watching the clock or glancing at your watch. Move out of your desk when the bell rings.

6. Leave only after the bell has finished ringing. Pack up only if the teacher has finished speaking. Never slam a book shut, slam it on the desk, or slam the chair against the desk.

7. Say "thank you" at least once a week as you leave. (This can be combined with Step 2.)

After the student is comfortable using the Level One Quick Tricks, the instructor presents the Level Two Quick Tricks. Do not present them together.

Level Two (no extra time required, slightly more effort required, bigger payoff)

1. Hand in assignments on time no matter what you think of your work or whether the assignments have been completed. Ask for the opportunity to complete unfinished assignments even if they have already been graded. Return them to the teacher for a better grade, if possible.

2. Always use the heading and format the teacher requires. Be sure every paper is dated.

3. Draw only one line through an error. Never erase (unless instructed by the teacher); never cross out by scribbling.

4. Ask the teacher to explain anything you do not understand by using different words and examples than he or she used the first time.

5. Type or have someone type your papers.

6. Proofread your work for capitalization and end punctuation.

Level Three (some time and effort required at first, with savings on both in the long run)

1. Make an appointment with the teacher to go over any difficulties you are having.

2. Trade with a classmate who is good in a subject in which you need help. Help him or her with computer skills, show him or her how to repair a bike, or coach the classmate in basketball in exchange for assistance in a subject in which you need help.

3. Do not give up. Find someone who is able to help you.

Advanced Quick Tricks

Thus far, working on organizing the binder and presenting the Quick Tricks may have taken two or three sessions, time well invested. The rationale for presenting the binder in advance, fully indexed, organized, and equipped is to make it attractive to students and adults.

With this beginning, the instructor has gained the students' attention and dawning respect. To capitalize on these gains, the instructor must move the students beyond the first three levels of the Quick Tricks to the next phase, which can be presented as advanced Quick Tricks. New gains must be more tangible and must come quickly. Otherwise, earlier gains will be lost, the student will revert to his or her old ways, and it will be difficult to regain his or her attention. Although still preliminary to actual study skills training, training in and using these advanced Quick Tricks soon result in better grades. Askov and Kamm noted that "early success can have a very positive effect on students' attitudes about learning" (1982, p. 3).

The advanced Quick Tricks involve training in the following:

• Structured procedures for completing homework assignments

• Emergency techniques for handling long reading assignments that have been postponed to the last minute

- Structured procedures to reduce spelling errors

- Structured procedures to reduce errors in mechanics

- Spelling by "geometric progression"

Structured Procedures for Completing Homework Assignments

Students who do well in class and on tests may, nevertheless, receive poor grades because of missing homework assignments. Homework represents one of the most frustrating, contentious, and divisive issues for teachers and for students with dyslexia and their parents. The impact on family life can be extreme. As part of the Quick Tricks, students have been trained to hand assignments in on time, even if the assignments are unfinished and to be completed later. As quickly as possible, the study skills instructor must train the students to complete assignments before handing them in. This is done through structured procedures for managing time, managing papers, and self-monitoring and **tracking.**

   Techniques for handling assignments are part of the structured procedures for using the binder. It is critical that students observe these procedures faithfully. The procedure is the same for every class.

- All handouts relevant to assignments are filed in the front side of the pocket divider inside the front cover of the general subject binder (labeled Handouts/Homework Sheets/Assignments). This ensures that students can locate them quickly and easily.

- All assignments that have been started but not completed are filed in the reverse side of the same pocket folder (labeled Work in Progress).

- Completed assignments are filed in the reverse side of the pocket divider at the back of the binder (labeled Completed Assignments to Hand In).

- Homework that has been graded and returned by the teacher is filed in the front side of the same divider for further processing (labeled For Consultation and Reworking). At the first available opportunity, the student takes assignments returned with errors marked to the subject teacher to discuss the errors and ask for the chance to correct them for a better grade. This practice is important to ensure continual improvement in grades. Discussing assignments with the teacher further improves relationships with the teacher and parents. It prompts the subject teacher to go the extra mile to give the student extra assistance. Most important, it is a major step in developing a student's ability to assess his or her own learning style, characteristic errors, strengths, and deficits. Asking for the chance to discuss and correct errors continues the process of self-monitoring; self-evaluation; and, ultimately, self-advocacy.

- Papers free of errors are clipped to the inside front cover of the binder with a large spring clip, to be filed in the appropriate subject section as soon as possible, preferably the same day.

The study skills instructor should work out a consistent system for middle or secondary school students for recording assignments with subject teachers. When this is a problem, then the student should not leave class before the subject teacher has checked to see that the assignments have been recorded correctly and that the student has the books or materials needed to complete the assignment. Assignments can be recorded on a specially designed form filed in the front side of the first pocket divider atop the day's worksheets or filed at the beginning of each subject section in the binder. Younger students should have a single form for listing all daily assignments. (Small assignment pads are easily misplaced or lost. If used, they should be kept in the zipper case.)

Students with dyslexia typically have difficulty remembering to take home what they need to do their homework. They also have difficulty remembering to bring books and homework back to school. When this is a problem, the study skills instructor, subject teacher, student, and parents need to work out a structured routine whereby the student's backpack is checked by an adult before leaving home and school. A careful record should be kept of the student's ability to come to school and go home fully prepared. It is best that student and parent organize the backpack together the night before, using a checklist to make sure that nothing is forgotten. A few students may need to have two sets of textbooks, one for home and one for school.

Emergency Techniques for Postponed Long Reading Assignments

A long reading assignment, such as a social studies chapter, can be quite overwhelming for students with dyslexia. Students typically put off this kind of assignment until the last minute, when they have too little time and too little energy to do the job well. This procrastination becomes habitual. The anxiety and stress generated by the delay compound the problem. While coaching a student in scheduling, the study skills instructor can present techniques to compensate for reading at the last minute.

First, the student should get "psyched up" to be as focused and attentive as possible and to form the intention to hold as much in memory as possible. Then, he or she should complete these steps:

1. Read the introduction, the advance organizer, or the first three paragraphs; the summary; and questions, if any, at the end of the selection.

2. Read the text headings (boldface type) and subheadings in order from first to last.

3. Read all uppercase, boldface, and italic type embedded in the text.

4. Return to the beginning and read the first and last sentence of every paragraph.

5. Read the captions under all graphics, charts, or tables.

6. Copy all definitions set apart in the text onto index cards.

7. If time permits, read through the text rapidly without attempting to remember it, or scan it rapidly without stopping. (Note: Most students with dyslexia do not know how to scan and may not be able to scan.)

8. Discuss the highlights of the selection with a friend before class.

This strategy lays the groundwork for later structured procedures for mastering course content. When it works, it has the advantage of increasing students' trust in the study skills instructor, bolstering self-confidence, and strengthening their motivation.

Structured Procedures to Reduce Spelling Errors: Multisensory Solutions

Misspellings account for the most frequent errors made by college freshmen (Deshler et al., 1996). When students with dyslexia have poor memories for auditory or visual sequential patterns, spelling is "the last skill acquired" (Tomkins, 1963, p. 127). Memory training is facilitated in the initial stages by working on organizing, scheduling,

and managing time; organizing the binder; and introducing certain structured procedures, such as proofreading (described next).

Systematic memory training begins with the structured procedures for improving
spelling. Success with these techniques fosters confidence and a new awareness in students that success in academics does not depend on the ability to memorize information. At this stage, training to correct spelling weaknesses is physical and mechanical,
relying principally on overlearning by frequent repetition and by kinesthetic (muscle)
memory—the most enduring sense memory. This does not involve memorizing or
learning rules. Structured procedures and simultaneous multisensory techniques are
employed, for internalizing orthographic (spelling) patterns. These techniques involve
simultaneously seeing, saying, hearing, and tracing or writing (see Chapter 9). Students
should use cursive handwriting, except where printing is specified (see Chapter 7). The
several techniques for internalizing spelling patterns can be used simultaneously or rotated. When used daily, they result in rapid and significant improvement in spelling and
can, in the best case, eliminate up to 50% or more of a student's habitual errors.

Copying on Wide-Ruled Paper   The instructor writes a model of the word in cursive for the
student to copy. The student copies below the model, keeping the letters aligned under
those above. The copy must be checked to be sure that the student has not made an
error. The student finger-proofs each copy, saying the name of the letter aloud while
touching the index finger of each hand to the same letter in the model and the copy
(one above, one below). Experimenting will determine how many times the student
must copy in order to retain the word. Making about 7–10 copies at a time is usually
effective. If not, the cloze technique may be effective.

Cloze Technique   A series of underlines are made, equal to the number of letters in the word.

t a u g h t	The complete word
_ a u g h t	Easiest letter/sound to remember omitted
_ a u g h _	Next easiest to remember omitted
_ a u _ _ _	Digraph *gh* omitted
_ _ _ _ _ _	Digraph *au* omitted

After the word is prepared as shown, the student begins to fill in the missing letters, covering the word above and the word below at each step, and naming the letters as he or
she prints them. Finally, the student fills in all of the blanks. Then, the student covers
all of the words and writes the word from memory. At each step, the student checks the
newly filled-in line with the line above for accuracy by finger-proofing before moving
to the next line.

It is important for the student to maintain vigilant attention while practicing this
technique. To achieve the best results, he or she should actively intend to attend closely
to spelling aloud, printing the letters neatly, and checking for accuracy. Being on automatic pilot will not do the trick. (Occasionally, a student will display great agitation
and resistance while doing the cloze procedure. In this case, it should be dropped for
the time being and may need to be dropped permanently.)

Tracing   All students with dyslexia should use tracing to learn irregularly spelled words,
such as *their, above,* and *rough.* A medium felt-tip pen and double-fold industrial-
strength paper towels are needed. Work can be done starting with three words per session, working up to five. No more than five words should be attempted in a single

session. With the paper towel folded and open at the top, the tracing procedure is as follows:

1. The student or instructor writes the model in large, evenly spaced cursive letters, with the word centered on the upper front panel.

2. Using the fleshy ends of the index and middle fingers of the writing hand, the student traces the word three times, naming each letter or saying each sound as the fingers trace over it, naming the full word after each tracing.

3. If the student does the second step correctly, then the top panel is dropped behind, and the bottom panel is lifted, exposing the center panel. The word is written again on the center panel and compared with the model. If the student has written the word correctly, then the bottom panel is folded up over the center panel, the top panel is dropped behind, and the word is written again and compared again to the original model on the top panel.

4. If correct, the procedure is repeated for 3 days, then once a week for 3 weeks, and finally once a month for 3 months.

Repeat Step 1 if the student makes a mistake at any point. Three tracings are made each time. Only two retries of the same target word may be made on the same day. If the student has not mastered the word after 3 days, then that should indicate the word is too difficult for him or her at this time.

Syllable Spelling   A student with fairly good phonics skills, at least with closed (e.g., *cat*) and open (e.g., *he, go*) syllables, should use the simultaneous oral spelling (S.O.S.) procedure (Gillingham & Stillman, 1997): Focus on the instructor's lips, listen to the dictated word, echo the word, tap out each sound while saying it (/k/ /à/ /t/), then write it in cursive letters. Words of two, three, and four syllables combining the closed and open syllable patterns can be spelled this way (e.g., *open, event, remit, intended, discontented*) (see Chapters 8 and 9).

Structured Procedures to Reduce Errors in Mechanics

The habit of proofreading written work must become automatic. Teachers view errors in the mechanics of English—capitalization, punctuation, spelling—as carelessness and evidence of indifference, at best, or low ability, at worst. Spotting errors is problematic for students with dyslexia because of their difficulties with attention, memory, and systematic scanning. It is important to prevent the student from surveying his or her work for all possible errors at the same time (Askov & Kamm, 1982). Instead the student searches systematically for possible errors, beginning with the first sentence and moving sentence by sentence.

*   Capitalization of the first word in a sentence

*   Punctuation mark at the end of the sentence

*   Capitalization of proper nouns

*   Apostrophes in contractions

Spelling by Geometric Progression

Students with dyslexia are often at a disadvantage when required to make inferences; these students often do not discern what is obvious to others. They do not perceive or translate patterns from one situation to another, unless these are highlighted, explicated, dramatized, or clearly delineated. This is true even for the spelling of inflected (e.g., *baby/babies*) and derived (e.g., *happy/happiness*) forms of a base word.

The student should practice extending and creating arrays to bring orthographic patterns into sharp focus (see Figure 18.2). Students should not be asked to memorize the spellings. The point is to get students to recognize—to see/discern—the related patterns of roots and affixes. Arrayed in columns, one entry under another, each column of prefixes, roots, and suffixes is coded with a different color. This practice aids decoding as well as spelling.

Further gains in spelling as well as gains in reading speed, fluency, and comprehension can be realized by mastering the meanings of roots and affixes, beginning with J.I. Brown's (1976) Fourteen Master Words: *detain, nonextended, indisposed, oversufficient, intermittent, offer, precept, uncomplicated, aspect, reproduction, mistranscribe, monograph, insist,* and *epilogue.* See Chapter 9 for further discussion of spelling instruction.

MEMORY TRAINING

The student is now ready to begin to learn the specific SkORE techniques for mastering content subject material. Teachers need to be mindful of the student with dyslexia's neuropsychological differences and the resultant problems with association, classification, organization, storage, and recall of verbal information (in addition to decoding, fluency, and comprehension). Memory is inseparable from learning and is related to productivity and "severe problems in memory equate to severe problems in school" (Brown, 1975). Consequently, students with dyslexia need techniques that enable them to internalize and remember information without memorizing; that is, these students need mnemonics (from *mnemon,* Greek for *mindful*) and structured procedures for processing text.

In the process of developing mnemonic devices, the student must work at forming associations that do not exist naturally in the content, a necessary condition for remembering (Trudeau, 1995). Using mnemonics helps students to transform, store, and retrieve information in long-term memory by creating connections in otherwise unconnected data.

Mnemonic Devices

Most students are aware of simple mnemonic devices such as acronyms, words made up of the initial letters in a series of words (HOMES, for remembering the Great Lakes),

Anglo-Saxon			Latin
stand	**sew**	**friend**	**human**
stand s	**sew** s	**friend** s	**human** ness
stand ing	**sew** ed	**friend** ly	in **human** ness
un der **stand** ing	**sew** ing	**friend** ship	in **human** ity
un der **stand** ing s	**sew** er	be **friend**	**human** ize
mis un der **stand** ing	**sew** n	be **friend** ed	**human** iz ed
up **stand** ing	un **sew** n		**human** iz ing
out **stand** ing			

Figure 18.2. Spelling by geometric progression.

and acrostics, groups of words that start with the specific letters of words to be recalled (*every good boy does fine* for the lines of the music staff). Other devices include the following:

- *The key word strategy:* Using a similar familiar word to cue the meaning of an unfamiliar word (*aberrant:* Abner is odd).

- *Chaining:* Linking the words to be recalled in a sentence or story (for a shopping list of bread, milk, party food, and fabric softener sheets: *Brad milked the company dry*).

- *Chunking:* Separating the information into manageable sets to be worked on one at a time (the 50 states, by region; e.g., *New England*).

- *Creating rhymes:* Using rhyming lines to remember factual information (*Columbus sailed the ocean blue in 14 hundred and 92*).

- *Visualizing:* Calling up or forming a mental image (e.g., of the White House, of the numeral 8).

- *Illustrations:* Using drawings to illustrate material.

STRUCTURED PROCEDURES FOR MASTERING CONTENT SUBJECTS: SKORE

Students with dyslexia are at a particular disadvantage when the text (or the teacher) is not organized or well structured. This is especially true when the students come to the subject with inadequate background knowledge, which is often the case because they have read less than other students who are good readers or because they are unable to remember what they have read. Organization, however, "plays an important role in memory and concentration" (Devine, 1981, p. 287).

Unless students process the information to be learned at a deep cognitive level, it is not stored in working or long-term (permanent) memory. Students with dyslexia, however, are rarely taught strategies and techniques for deep processing (Deshler et al., 1996; Levine, 1987; Maria, 1990; McNeil, 1992). They typically resort to rereading every word, from the beginning to the end, a very ineffective way to learn content material.

The study skills instructor can offer students with dyslexia faster, more reliable, and more effective alternatives. Storage in long-term memory can be secured by using SkORE procedures for organizing material, elaborating, deep processing, mind mapping, summarizing, writing précis, and notetaking. A high level of repetition and kinesthetic reinforcement is key to success. SkORE can also be referred to as a CRAP system because it is *c*ognitive, *r*epetitive, *a*ctive, and *p*hysical. The strategies and techniques comprise an integrated system of multisensory structured procedures that facilitate memory, comprehension, reasoning, and written expression. Closely articulated and cumulative skills are built systematically through explicit, direct instruction (especially for extracting meaning); modeling; demonstration; rehearsal; guided practice; transfer; and application to content subjects. The SkORE approach is one example of a teaching device, a construct that Deshler et al. noted "helps make abstract information more concrete, connect new knowledge with familiar knowledge, enable students who cannot spell well to take useful notes, highlight relationships and organizational structures within the information to be presented, and draw unmotivated learners' attention to the information" (1996, p. 445)

SkORE is designed to produce significant improvement in academic performance over the course of one school year. Students need at least 1 year to fully master the strategies and techniques and transfer and apply them. The first two phases of the process, preparing and organizing the material, are critical to the student's mastery of the material to be learned.

The first two phases of SkORE help students understand what and how they need to study. Ellis and Colvert (as cited in Deshler et al., 1996) criticized instruction in which the student with learning disabilities is left alone to make discoveries because such teaching is not usually effective. Conversely, research has shown the effectiveness of explicit, direct teaching strategies with techniques continually demonstrated and modeled for the student.

SkORE strategies and techniques help students compensate for difficulties with attention, scanning, memory, vocabulary, reading comprehension, abstract and nonliteral language, association and categorization, outlining, summarizing, paraphrasing, and critical thinking. The strategies require the following student involvement:

- Frequent consultation with subject teachers

- Continual self-generated questions

- Habitual use of reference books, especially the dictionary and *Roget's Thesaurus* (original version); many students do not have adequate skills in alphabetizing (see Chapter 6)

- Systematic expansion of vocabulary

- Systematic explication of abstract and nonliteral language

- Systematic use of mnemonic devices

- Routine conversion of text to graphic displays

- Ongoing self-evaluation

There is little similarity between SkORE and **Survey, Question, Read, Recite, Review (SQ3R;** Robinson, 1970). SQ3R relies primarily on reading, mental rehearsal, and rote memory—weak areas for most students with dyslexia. With SkORE, the student is trained to deal with text in five progressive sequences:

1. Preparing the text and setting up a skeleton web (mind map)

2. Selecting and organizing salient information

3. Generating graphic displays

4. Extending vocabulary and understanding of concepts

5. Summarizing, composing précis, making conventional outlines, and taking notes

Materials Needed

The following materials should be on hand before beginning: binders with all furnishings (as described previously in this chapter), colored index cards, a banker's size manila envelope, 11" × 17" unlined paper, wide-ruled loose-leaf paper, dictionary, and a thesaurus.

The Instructor's Role

The study skills instructor demonstrates the SkORE procedures for students, beginning with short samples of text and proceeding to longer, more complex text. When the student has understood the structured procedures, the instructor and student together work through several rehearsals until the student reaches a comfort level with the process. Then, under supervision and with guidance, the student practices on new material. Concurrently, systematic instruction in using the dictionary (see Chapter 6) and thesaurus is provided, along with techniques for abstracting, taking notes, creating cue cards and mnemonics, mind mapping (webbing), and writing a précis.

Phase One: Preparing the Text

The first phase of SkORE training is designed to train the student to familiarize him- or herself in advance with the information, vocabulary, and important concepts of the text to be read and to begin the process of organizing and structuring the material. Specific tasks involve 1) surveying and scanning the text; 2) setting up the basic framework of the mind map; and 3) preparing rehearsal or cue cards for learning and reviewing vocabulary, definitions, major concepts, and spelling.

Surveying and Scanning

Beginning with the title and subtitle, if any, the student goes through the text and reads only what "sticks up, stands out," or in some other way is different from the body of the text. This survey includes boldface and italic type, headings, marginal glosses (printed commentary in the margins), boxed text, diagrams, photographs, drawings, charts, and other graphics with captions. (Footnotes should be omitted.) Some students will gain from reading aloud or subvocalizing, but others may lose comprehension; a student should try both at first to determine what works best. Before going on, the student should formulate what he or she believes is the important information or theme of the text in one to three sentences.

Then, the student does a cursory reading of the text (scanning), beginning with the introductory questions, concepts, and/or summary (or the first three paragraphs); the first sentence of each subsequent paragraph; and the concluding summary and questions, if any.

Setting Up the Mind Map

After this cursory reading, the student sets up a mind map, using one to three words printed in block capital letters to designate the topic. A word or a brief phrase to correspond with the headings in the text serve as the main branches of the map. (To build skill in mapping, the student can start with brainstorming familiar topics.)

Preparing Cue Cards

Next, the student reads through the entire text rapidly but at a comfortable rate, making no effort to memorize or remember as he or she goes. During the reading, the student uses code symbols to mark the following in the text: unfamiliar vocabulary, definitions, important concepts, and, separately, vocabulary words that he or she does not know how to spell. The code symbols are arbitrary.

- Underline unfamiliar words for vocabulary study.

- Circle unknown or difficult words for spelling practice.

- Place a single asterisk in the margin next to definitions.

- Place double asterisks in the margin for important concepts and abstract terms.

After the student has marked the text, vocabulary words are written on cue cards using the following procedure (the colors of the cards are arbitrary):

- Print each vocabulary word in the upper left-hand corner of a white index card.

- Using a medium-point black felt-tip pen, write the spelling words *in cursive,* centered on yellow index cards. Write as large as possible in the space. Double-check accuracy by finger proofing, or have someone check the spelling for accuracy. (Tracing the spelling words is useful for acquiring cursive handwriting skill if the model is a good model of cursive writing.)

- Copy the definitions exactly as they appear in the text on gold index cards. Start with the term being defined, and print it in block capital letters. Print the definitions in upper- and lowercase letters, as appropriate.

- Write the concept words or phrases on one side of an orange index card. (It may be necessary to use 4" × 6" cards for concepts. Fold these cards to place them in the manila envelope.)

Next, the student adds definitions to the cue cards:

- From the most recent edition of *Webster's New World Dictionary,* copy the first two definitions given onto the reverse side of the white vocabulary cards, and number the definitions. Younger students should begin with just one definition. On the side of the cards containing the definitions, write a sentence that makes the meaning of the word clear. If the target word is *planet,* then the sentence *Earth is a planet* will do.

- On the front of each white vocabulary card, right next to the word, copy the part of speech from the dictionary (e.g., *n, adj*). In the upper right-hand corner, place an abbreviation for the language of origin—Anglo-Saxon (A.S.), Latin (L), or Greek (G). Later, the student can add inflected forms and extensions of the word on this side of the card—*planet-s, planet-ary, planet-ari-um, planet-oid*—that show the base word and affixes separately.

- The student should trace each spelling word daily by using the fleshy ends of the index and middle fingers, naming aloud each letter as the fingers trace over it, and finally saying the whole word. Each word should be traced three or more times at each rehearsal.

- Print the detailed aspects of the concept according to the related features semantic map (described later) or in a similar manner on the reverse side of the orange concept cards (see Chapter 9 in Deshler et al., 1996, and Chapter 5 in Maria, 1990).

After the cards are prepared, they are banded together by color and kept in the manila envelope in the plastic zipper case at the front of the student's general subject notebook. Students are encouraged to review the cards daily at odd moments, such as in class, during lunch, while on the bus, while waiting for class to begin, and so forth.

Phase Two: Selecting and Organizing the Information

As an adjunct to the SkORE process, separate but concurrent systematic training in related subskills, such as cursive handwriting, abstracting, mind mapping, and précis writing, is necessary for the student to gain facility in these component techniques. To self-monitor attention and concentration—or the extent of his or her distractibility—

the student can be asked to complete a brief reading or exercise and check a form or ring a bell each time his or her attention wanders. Exercises in abstracting information from text should be given, beginning with underlining the most salient information in simple sentences and paragraphs and working up to doing this with a selection of several paragraphs and brief chapters (see Lehmann, 1960a, 1960b). The student should create a mind map or web first by filling in major details under the topic lines, then create topic words and phrases for subsections with details filled in (see Buzan, 1983; Wycoff, 1991). The student with dyslexia needs practice in categorizing and classifying as well as detecting and verbalizing relationships between and among concepts and terms.

The instructor should encourage the student to verbalize his or her thinking as he or she works. This gives the instructor the opportunity to help the student clarify his or her thinking and the chance to model spoken English by repeating what the student says in complete, grammatically correct, coherent sentences. More important, students' verbalizations give the instructor a window on their thought processes.

In Phase Two of SkORE, the student must make the conscious decision to maintain attention and concentration to the best of his or her ability throughout each step. The tasks involve 1) abstracting the text, 2) taking notes on the mind map, 3) consulting with the instructor to correct and complete the mind map, 4) completing and enhancing the mind map by color coding and creating graphics, and 5) creating mnemonics.

Abstracting the Text

The process of abstracting (condensing) text forces the student to determine the essential information in the text. The abstract extracts the most important information from the paragraph or text to reduce the text at least by half and later by as much as two thirds. To do this, the student must ask him- or herself questions. The technique of questioning should be taught concurrently, with the teacher using both Socratic questioning (to get the correct answer) (see Murdoch, 1987) and open-ended questioning (to provoke the student to think) (see Maria, 1990). For lengthy text, such as a chapter in a social studies, history, or science textbook, structured group discussion is a useful tool; in this type of discussion, the questions originate from the students (see Chapter 6 of Christensen, Garvin, & Sweet, 1991). An example of a text marked (underlined) for abstracting follows:

> The student returns to the beginning of the text and, reading paragraph by paragraph, abstracts the text by underlining only the salient parts. (This will be quite difficult because students with dyslexia have significant difficulty determining saliency.) The finished abstract should be in complete, grammatically correct sentences, keeping the author's own words. Paraphrasing is not permitted. Minor changes are permitted for smooth transitions and correct syntax, including transitional words and changes in tense or number. The instructor must approve the final product.

The previous paragraph (92 words) has been abstracted (42 words) to read as follows:

> The student returns to the beginning and abstracts the text. This will be difficult. The finished abstract should be in grammatically correct sentences [in] the author's words. Paraphrasing is not permitted; minor changes are permitted. The instructor must approve the final product.

It is vital that the text be reduced in this manner for the student with dyslexia because he or she has difficulty processing large volumes of language (Deshler et al., 1996). The advantages of abstracting are as follows: The student is not so overwhelmed by the reading task, his or her storage capacity is less taxed by the task (students with dyslexia often think it is necessary to memorize everything), comprehension is improved because the essential information is laid bare, and the student can see the focus of the lesson more clearly. Maria (1990) stated that "in many texts the real point of the lesson is often obscured." Once the abstract is approved by the instructor, the original text is put aside and is never referred to again.

Taking Notes on the Mind Map

Working from the abstract only, the student fills in the details on the mind map, beginning at 12 o'clock and working clockwise. It is best to use unlined 11" × 17" paper. Single words or brief phrases should be printed in block capital letters (Buzan, 1983) to serve as cues for retrieving information. The student must not be permitted to print long phrases, clauses, or sentences or to write in cursive. Unless the headings of the text provide a clear structure for the web, the student usually must reorganize the map by grouping related details in narrower categories. With the instructor's guidance, the student should reexamine each cluster to determine whether details belong under that subtopic label, whether the heading should be reworded, and whether one cluster should be merged with another or, conversely, be made into two clusters.

It is expected that full mastery of the mapping technique will take time and much practice. Both instructor and student should regard the time invested as normal and productive in the learning curve. See Buzan (1983) and Wycoff (1991) for a full treatment of mind mapping. (*Note:* Buzan's system of notetaking is not recommended for students with dyslexia.)

Reexamining the details of the web, the student should try to identify concepts and details that are grouped separately but somehow related. Connections can be shown by dotted lines ending in arrows. The relationships—the basis of the associations—should be verbalized by the student.

Consulting with the Instructor

When a student has finished the mind map, he or she should ask the study skills instructor to review the map with him or her to determine whether important information has been omitted and whether unimportant information has been included. (Later, the student will ask the subject teacher to review the map.) Appropriate corrections are made. This is an important step in facilitating the student's ability to assess his or her own work and monitor the outcomes.

Color Coding and Creating Graphics

After consulting with the instructor, the student color codes the web by lightly shading each module with a different pastel color, circling the modules in different colors, or underlining the branches and subbranches of separate modules with different colors. (Students must not be permitted to print the words in each block using different colors; this is time consuming, and the visual result is disorganizing.) Color differentiation further structures the material by establishing boundaries and enhances the graphic display by helping the student focus on modules of information. Also, it adds to the sensorially pleasing quality of the mind map, which should not be underestimated as an additional reinforcer. In addition, the student creates cartoons, graphs, sketches, diagrams, maps, and other visual aids to illustrate the material to be learned. Students often produce maps that are beautiful and creative enough to display as graphic art.

Creating Mnemonics

After details have been filled in on the mind map, the student devises mnemonics as aids to remember specific data on the map, such as lists. These mnemonics are added to the map. All material is written on the same (front) side of the paper. (*Note:* Students with dyslexia do better with mnemonics that are provided by the instructor, rather than ones they make up themselves, according to Deshler et al., 1996.)

Working with the Mind Map

Students often are amazed and shocked when they are asked to recreate the map without referring to the original. Invariably, they find that they already know 60%–80% of the material without having memorized it. This outcome has a dramatic effect because students typically protest throughout the mind-mapping process that they do not have time to "do all this" because they need the time to memorize the material. After recreating the mind map without referring to it, however, they know what they know and what they do not know. Instead of having to memorize the whole map, they have to review only the portion that has not already gone into memory.

The colored mind map and cue cards should be reviewed and redrawn daily during the first week until the student can complete the entire map accurately without referring to the original. Thereafter, the mind map should be reviewed weekly and then monthly to maintain it in long-term memory. The mind map should be reviewed together with the summary and précis of the material, which are described in the next section.

Phase Three: Summarizing, Writing Précis, Outlining, and Notetaking

In the final phase of the SkORE process, the students use the mind map to write a summary of the information on the map; write a précis of the abstract; and, if teachers insist, create an outline. The student also learns to taken notes from various sources.

Summarizing

After having converted the text into a visual display, the student now converts the visual display back to English discourse. At first, this transformation is a mechanical process. Beginning at 12 o'clock on the map and moving clockwise, the student labels each main branch with a Roman numeral to set up the order of the paragraphs in the summary.

The first branch should be introductory. The details noted on subbranches under each main branch can be assigned letters. If the subbranches are further modified by subbranches, then the details are numbered with Arabic numerals.

When the students have labeled all branches and subbranches of the mind map, they return to the branch labeled with the Roman numeral I and begin to create the summary, using the notation on the main branch as the topic sentence of the first paragraph. The word or phrase that appears at the center of the mind map, which states the general topic to be discussed, should be included in the topic sentence of the first paragraph. Students then make the details on the subbranches into grammatically complete and syntactically correct sentences; these are the supporting detail sentences. This procedure is followed for each main branch around the clock. Then, a closing paragraph is created, either by stressing the main point or by reemphasizing the import of the author's point(s). The précis (described later) can be used as a final paragraph. Finally, the students proofread the summary for errors. The habit of proofreading has been established as an automatic practice long before this, beginning at Level 2 Quick Tricks, and reinforced during the abstracting procedure.

Writing Skills   To prepare for writing the summary, the study skills instructor should inform students that teachers require at least five sentences in a paragraph and at least five paragraphs in a theme or composition. If students follow this recipe, then their work will be accepted. This formulaic approach to devising summaries gives students an initial approach to expository writing that appears to reduce their characteristic resistance to writing by eliminating what they perceive as a vague, indeterminate process. Students need instruction in English sentence patterns to go beyond the mechanical, formulaic method of summarizing (see Helson, 1971). They need practice in elaborating sentences, first with adjectives and adjective phrases, next with adverbs and adverb phrases, and then with clauses. Subjunctive clauses present a particular difficulty for students with dyslexia (see Chapter 13).

Automaticity in handwriting skills is an absolute prerequisite for facility in written English. Students will be far less apt to want to write if they have not mastered automatic letter formation and connected writing; if their inappropriate grip causes fatigue; or if they write with an uncorrected, obstructive hook of the writing hand (see King, 1985; Chapter 7).

There is no good substitute for reading widely and deeply; it is the best way to improve writing skills. The study skills instructor can entice students in two ways into reading for information as well as for pleasure. After determining a student's interest or ambition (e.g., soccer, gymnastics, inventing, computers, space travel, dance), the instructor can get good, well-illustrated trade books, including biographies, in large, clear type from the public library. The first group of books should be written many years below the student's reading ability. For example, when working with a seventh-grade student, books written for fourth-grade students can be useful for this stage. More difficult texts can be used as the student gains facility in reading because of study skills training. The books should never be used for instruction; they are sources of information and pleasure. The instructor should also take a few minutes of every period to read aloud from works of fiction, biographies, essays, and poems of literary worth. These can be tied to classwork in English, science, history, mathematics, and even physical education.

Some students with dyslexia have a talent for writing and aspire to be journalists or authors despite their difficulties with written language. Notable authors who have experienced such difficulties include Agatha Christie, Winston Churchill, W. Somerset Maugham, Beatrix Potter, and John Updike. These people, along with media men Fred Friendly (former CBS News president), Richard Cohen of *The Washington Post,* Robert Scheer of *The Los Angeles Times,* and others have demonstrated that individuals with dyslexia can be successful writers. Students who desire to be writers should be encouraged.

Writing Précis

Unlike the abstract, which must keep to the author's words, the précis is a condensation of the text in the student's own words. The goal is to state the author's essential message, the main thrust of the selection, and the author's underlying thesis or a combination of these in a highly condensed form. A précis of a chapter or even a book might consist of a few sentences or paragraphs. As an example, the moral that follows one of Aesop's fables can be considered a précis (e.g., *Slow and steady wins the race*); a proverb also can serve as a précis (e.g., *Pride goeth before a fall*). The practice of précis writing is an invaluable aid to comprehension. The précis should be no more than one third to one fourth as long as the abstract and may be much shorter. The best technique for formulating a good précis is a group discussion of the essence of the abstract. (See Christensen et al., 1991, for discussion techniques focused on problem solving. See Lehmann, 1960a, for the subskills prerequisite to précis writing.)

Outlining

Ideally, subject teachers will agree to accept the mind map in lieu of traditional, linear outlines from students with dyslexia. Nevertheless, some teachers will not. In this case, it is a simple matter to convert the mind map to outline form. Using the numbers assigned for developing the summary, the student simply copies the Roman numerals, letters, and Arabic numerals onto a template provided by the study skills instructor. The words and phrases on the main branches and subbranches can be copied next to the appropriate number or letter. The outline should be checked by both the study skills instructor and the subject teacher before being put into final form. The study skills instructor should exert every effort, however, to have the mind map accepted by classroom teachers because there is nothing to be gained from the redundant activity of creating an outline from the mind map, and—more important for the student—having to do so needlessly uses valuable time.

Notetaking from Works of Fiction

To retain information about works of fiction, the student should take notes on 3" × 5" index cards, using the following structured procedure. Information is entered onto the cards according to a preset pattern. When completed, the cards are arranged in vertical columns of one, two, or three cards, with each column representing one paragraph. Students may need 20 or more cards when taking notes on one work of fiction. The information is written on the front side of the cards only.

   Data relevant to one topic, such as characters, may require more than one card. The information should be added to the cards in the order shown, and the cards should be numbered. When writing paragraphs, the students should keep the five-sentence rule in mind.

1. Title, author, illustrator (if any), publisher, date of publication

2. Setting: time (or times), place

3a. Major characters

3b. Traits of major characters

4. Story type (e.g., action, romance, historical account, fable)

5a. Content: theme or main idea

5b. The point at which the theme is expressed most clearly*

    How often the theme is expressed*

    Through which characters it is most clearly expressed*

5c. Conflict(s)

6. The author's purpose

7. Actions that take place

8a. Technique: how the text is organized*

8b. Kinds of characters, incidents, or images used

    Why these were used instead of others*

8c. Style of writing used (e.g., realistic, formal, informal)

(Items marked by an asterisk are for use with older students.)

Notetaking from Lectures

Taking notes from lectures is difficult for students with dyslexia because it requires good ability in attention and concentration, processing and remembering rapid speech, rapid and accurate handwriting, good vocabulary, determining saliency, prioritizing, and proficiency in written English, among other skills. Instruction in notetaking must be the most direct, explicit, supported, monitored, and practiced of all of the study skills to be learned. This training should not be attempted unless the student has gained proficiency in handwriting (see Chapter 7) and notetaking from text. These skills are prerequisites to taking notes from lectures because, as Deshler and colleagues explained,

> Note-taking skills and subskills must be applied at the same time and at a rapid rate if the lecture is fast. The student must attend to a lecture idea, process the meaning of the idea by associating or integrating it with prior learning, extract the important information from the lecture idea, retain the meaning in memory, use a framework for recording notes, and write the idea using sufficient speed and abbreviations *while simultaneously listening to additional lecture information.* (1996, p. 271; emphasis added)

These are formidable obstacles for students with dyslexia; nevertheless, many of these challenges have been addressed during the previous phases of SkORE training.

The study skills instructor should begin by arranging for a student to receive lecture notes or a study guide from the subject teacher or from a fellow student by means of carbonless reproduction paper. According to federal, state, and local regulations (e.g., regulations governing implementing the Individuals with Disabilities Education Improvement Act [IDEA] of 2004 [PL 108-446]), students with language and learning disabilities have a legal right to this accommodation. The subject teacher(s), working cooperatively with the study skills instructor, can be kept informed of the student's progress in the subskills for notetaking, such as processing, retaining information in working memory, and using shorthand symbols and abbreviations. It is important for subject teacher(s) to know that the accommodation is temporary but may extend throughout the school year.

The study skills instructor can read aloud brief passages of three or four sentences to assess processing and memory; then the instructor should ask students to orally repeat as much of the information as possible in his or her own words. If a student performs reasonably well, then the instructor can use other passages and ask the student to record only a word or a phrase on a simple web to cue memory of important information. This cuing system of simple webbing should be used without concern for classification or organization. The branches should simply be spokes radiating from the topic word or phrase in the center. It is critical to work at this level until the student has mastered the cuing system—recording a word or a phrase to call up the data—with about 80% accuracy. The length of the passage can be increased gradually as the student gains mastery.

The instructor can also offer direct, systematic instruction in simple shorthand symbols for common words:

(for *the*

• for *a*

) for *if*

Other symbols can be taught: & for *and,* w/ for *with,* % for *percent,* and @ for *at.* Some students will do better with vowel-less writing: *Sm stdnts wll do bttr w/vwllss wrtng;* the instructor must check carefully, however, to determine whether the student can re-translate the notes accurately.

When the student is ready, the study skills instructor and the classroom teacher can monitor the notes that the student takes in class. As with notes taken during train-ing, notes should be merely single words or phrases on spokes radiating from a wheel, recorded without regard to organization or classification. The student should be mon-itored for accuracy, completeness, and the ability to read back and translate the notes.

Once the radial web has been approved by the study skills instructor (later, by the classroom teacher), the student proceeds in the same fashion as with taking notes from the mind map by reordering and reorganizing the web according to classification, cat-egorization, and associated ideas. Cue cards, semantic and concept maps (explained later in this chapter), mnemonics, and graphics are included, just as when working with text. Two advantages of taking notes from lectures this way is that lecture and reading notes can be merged into a single web, and webs made on large paper can be amended and extended for later review.

Key Words   The cue words on the simple webs developed by the student while taking notes from lectures are like the key words that are used in more conventional two- or three-column note-taking systems. Therefore, once a student has mastered the note-taking process just described, he or she will be able to use conventional systems well with a little guided practice (see Deshler et al., 1996).

COMPREHENSION

Good groundwork for improved comprehension has been laid by training in the me-chanics, such as the work on spelling and vocabulary development that occurs through the Quick Tricks, and by training in the SkORE processes for mastering content course information, especially the techniques for abstracting, mind mapping, and précis writ-ing. Some of the benefits of this instruction in terms of comprehension are as follows:

• The improvement in spelling results in improved decoding and, therefore, greater speed and accuracy in reading, which facilitates memory.

• The practice of having the student identify and define unfamiliar words and expli-cate concepts and abstractions before reading the text improves comprehension.

• The process of abstracting forces the student to weigh and consider ideas by asking questions about the relevance and relative importance of every part of the text. Ab-stracting also clarifies the structure of the text and development of the information, thereby greatly increasing comprehension.

• The process of mind mapping—which involves notetaking, categorizing, identifying related concepts and details, and creating graphics and mnemonics—requires the deep processing and manipulation of language that is requisite to deriving meaning and storing information in long-term memory.

As this list demonstrates, students can significantly improve comprehension just by using SkORE strategies and techniques. To further improve comprehension, however, additional techniques are required, such as semantic mapping; concept mapping; creating lexicons by geometric progression; and systematically studying nonliteral language, especially idioms and metaphors. For students with dyslexia, these collateral activities are critical to improvement in comprehension, writing, and higher order thinking skills (see Chapter 12).

See Wiig and Semel (1990) for a discussion of the specific comprehension problems of students with dyslexia. They noted that students with learning disabilities have problems with syntax, semantics, and memory that may cause difficulty with comprehending complex texts. Kamhi and Catts (1989) commented that such problems with reading means reduced exposure to new vocabulary words, and Maria stated that "the reader's level of vocabulary is the best predictor of his or her ability to understand the text" (1990, p. 111). Therefore, as stated previously, extensive discussion is the best tool to rapidly improve the reading comprehension of students with dyslexia.

Semantic Mapping

In addition to vocabulary limitations that result from a combination of language problems, the student with dyslexia typically has poor decoding ability (and thus tends to skip unknown words); limited reading experience (and may hate to read); and a general distaste for multisyllabic words, specific terms, and Greek-derived words (e.g., pneumonia).

Three kinds of semantic maps are recommended to aid in comprehension: synonym-antonym maps, related features maps, and multiple meanings maps. These maps are best developed through group discussion, with Socratic-type questioning from the teacher as the stimulus. By this process, the teacher asks questions designed to elicit the desired answers, such as "What is the missing word in 'Jack fell down and broke his _____'?"

Creating synonym-antonym maps (see Figure 18.3) benefits students' oral and written language ability by expanding vocabulary, offering the opportunity to discuss nuances of meaning (see Hayakawa, 1994), and facilitating the mastery of classification of parts of speech. Resources to use include synonym-antonym dictionaries, *Roget's*

JOY, L. n.

Synonyms	**Antonyms**
(*name for same*)	(*name for what is opposite*)
delight	sorrow
gladness	sadness
elation	depression
lightheartedness	downheartedness
ecstasy	despair
happiness	joylessness

Figure 18.3.   Synonym–antonym map. (*Key:* L., Latin; n., noun.)

Thesaurus (1992, original version), and *The Oxford Dictionary and Thesaurus* (1996). In order to understand the words on the map, students must have extensive practice in using the words correctly in sentences, both orally and in writing.

The related features map (see Figure 18.4) is a simple version of the concept map (explained in the next section) and is a good place to start with younger students. The related features map can be organized to show different categories as the main entry, such as weather, animals, or plants.

Multiple meanings for the same word is a characteristic of English that makes it difficult for nonnative speakers to learn the language. Similarly, the concept of multiple meanings causes great problems for students with dyslexia in both oral and reading comprehension. This is all the more true of words that have metaphorical meanings, such as *foot, head, place, arm,* and *bloom* and words that are part of an idiomatic expression (e.g., I'm burning up). It is important for the student to have practice with the different meanings of such words from the beginning of study skills training. This practice begins when more than one definition is written on a vocabulary cue card created in preparation for mind mapping. That step is a good introduction, but it is an inadequate way to teach the numerous English words that have multiple meanings. Creating multiple meaning maps similar to the one shown in Figure 18.5 is a good second stage. For further development, see the section called Creating Lexicons by Geometric Progression.

These semantic maps are not to be memorized; students achieve better command by discussing the words on the maps and debating the nuances of meaning (e.g., "What is the same about seeing to a guest, seeing the waiter [tipping], and seeing someone home?") and by illustrating the meanings (see McNeil, 1992).

Concept Mapping

Students with dyslexia may have significant difficulty understanding abstract terms; this difficulty can be a major barrier to comprehension for secondary and postsecondary students. Noting that their understanding of words is too concrete and literal, Levine (1987) pointed out that bright students with dyslexia are able to get by with a partial understanding (a corner) of an abstract concept (e.g., democracy, latitude, empathy). This literal understanding of the language, however, results in an imperfect, perhaps distorted, grasp of meanings and implications. Levine stressed that

> The ability to derive concepts is crucial. Several steps are involved: recognizing the salient properties of objects, actions, or events; categorizing those objects, actions, or events by identifying their common properties; forming a superordinate concept to other instances or settings. *The entire process can be viewed as a system of testing hypotheses by making careful decisions to accept or reject formulated hypotheses about problems.* (1987, p. 177, emphasis added)

	DESERT, L. n.	
sand		lizards
dry		tents
oasis		no rain
camel		palm trees
cactus		mirages
sun		sandstorms

Figure 18.4.   Related features map. (*Key:* L., Latin; n., noun.)

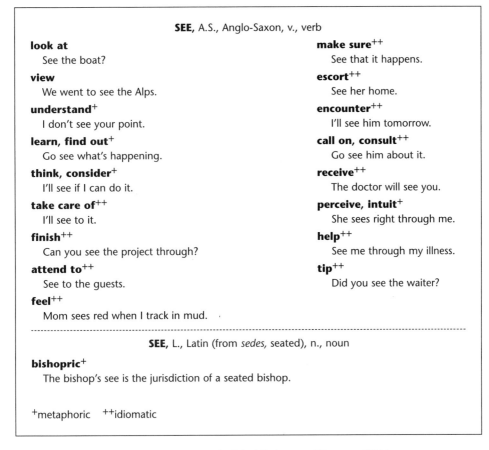

Figure 18.5.   Multiple meanings map. (*Source: The Oxford Dictionary and Thesaurus,* 1996.)

This is deep processing of language that is critical to comprehension.

The study skills instructor must enable students to understand concepts and abstract terms through systematically creating concept maps similar to the one in Figure 18.6 to accompany the cue cards for vocabulary (see Deshler et al., 1996; Maria, 1990; McNeil, 1992).

Creating Lexicons by Geometric Progression

Students with dyslexia must enlarge their vocabulary quickly and efficiently without memorization because they come to the task of comprehension with a smaller personal lexicon than other students. Also, students with dyslexia need explicit instruction in which patterns are highlighted, extensions (e.g., affixes) are easy, and meaning is revealed in a logical and dramatic fashion because of difficulties with recognizing patterns, making associations, seeing relationships, and memorizing. This training is best done using graphic arrays, or lexicons by geometric progression, that expose the morphological structure (the shape or form of units of meaning) of the language, such as roots and affixes. Bywaters (1998) and Murray and Munro (1989) are good resources for lexicons by geometric progression. Partridge (1966) is the best reference for study skills instructors.

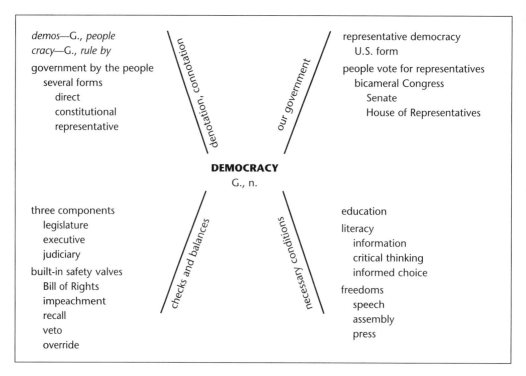

demos—G., people
cracy—G., rule by

government by the people
   several forms
     direct
     constitutional
     representative

denotation, connotation

our government

representative democracy
   U.S. form
people vote for representatives
   bicameral Congress
     Senate
     House of Representatives

DEMOCRACY
G., n.

three components
   legislature
   executive
   judiciary
built-in safety valves
   Bill of Rights
   impeachment
   recall
   veto
   override

checks and balances

necessary conditions

education
literacy
   information
   critical thinking
   informed choice
freedoms
   speech
   assembly
   press

Figure 18.6. Concept map. (*Key:* G., Greek; n., noun.)

The lexicon work should begin with short, easy exercises, such as the one shown in Figure 18.7. It is important to observe the spacing as indicated, highlight the root in color (shown as dark shading in Figure 18.7), include idioms, and ask the student to generate short paragraphs using both literal and nonliteral words from the array.

Studying Nonliteral Language: Idioms, Metaphors, Proverbs, Puns, and Jargon

Individuals with dyslexia commonly have difficulty with nonliteral language (Kamhi & Catts, 1989; Maria, 1990; Wiig & Semel, 1990), which uses words in an atypical way to convey meaning that is different from the standard usage, such as *a raging torrent, out of the mouths of babes, he got the axe, she's a peach, his crimes caught up with him, get off my back,* and *an ounce of prevention is worth a pound of cure.* It is important for the study skills instructor to appreciate the vast amount of figurative language, especially idioms and metaphors, used in reading materials for even the youngest children. Moreover, metaphor is prolific every day in conversations and print media (Lakoff & Johnson, 1980). Although children with dyslexia may not voice their difficulties, these students are often confused by figurative language.

A student with dyslexia does not comprehend nonliteral language incidentally. He or she needs direct, systematic presentation and explication of the language. Makkai and colleagues (1995) is a good resource to begin with, but the instructor must simultaneously search out, list, and teach all nonliteral language in the student's required reading. Students enjoy acting out some of the expressions (e.g., *His eyes are bigger than his stomach*) and creating stories and scenarios to illustrate meaning (e.g., *He did that to*

```
┌─────────────────────────────────────────────────────────────────────────────┐
│         Root    dict (from Latin, dicere, dictus—to show, point out, tell, say, proclaim) │
│   dic tate                    dic tion ar y                    pre dict        │
│   dic tate s                  dic tion ar ies                  pre dic tive    │
│   dic tat ed                                                   pre dic tion    │
│   dic tat (t) ion                                              contra dict     │
│   dic tat or                                                   contra dic tory │
│   dic tat or s                                                 contra dic tion │
│   dic tat or ship                                                              │
│   dit (from Italian, the same as [was said] before)                            │
│         Idiomatic: He can't dictate what I do.    Metaphor: He's a little dictator. │
└─────────────────────────────────────────────────────────────────────────────┘
```

Figure 18.7.   A lexicon by geometric progression.

save face). These exercises can take just a few minutes and can provide pleasant relief in the midst of hard work. All lexical arrays should include figurative uses of some of the words developed (see Figure 18.7).

TAKING TESTS

The goal of teaching study strategies and skills is for students to solve problems. Although study skills instruction focuses on learning how to learn—not on learning how to cram for tests—tests cannot be avoided in the academic setting. Study skills instruction should address test-taking issues in the following ways:

- Training in organizing and scheduling time, given at the outset of training, deals with the issue of time in preparing for tests and final exams.

- Training in semantics should include the distinctions in the vocabulary of testing: *define, discuss, detail, compare, contrast, list, explain, justify,* and so forth.

- The abstracts, mind maps, and summaries developed by the student in the SkORE process are the materials used for study; the student should refer back to these, never to the original text.

- The daily, weekly, and monthly periodic reviews are what constitute studying for tests and exams. This ongoing process is designed to retain and strengthen the information in the student's long-term memory. In this way, the student comes to know the material; he or she does not need to struggle to remember and recall it. Thus, the stress and anxiety typically accompanying cramming and taking tests are much abated, and the negative effect of stress on retrieval (memory) is avoided. In short, the student has a far better chance of doing his or her best on the test.

- Training in self-monitoring for attention should enable the student to sustain concentration during tests better than he or she could before the start of study skills training.

At this point in training, the instructor gives the student test-taking savvy by coaching him or her on how to apportion time for each section; read directions carefully and highlight critical words or phrases; avoid guessing unless only correct answers are scored (i.e., points are not deducted for wrong answers); eliminate answers in multiple-choice tests; and proofread carefully at the conclusion, not only to catch the usual errors in writing but also to ensure that no question was overlooked.

Students with dyslexia need to learn specific strategies for tracking during tests (following along with the text of the test). For example, when doing matching exercises, students may need to number the items on the left, letter those on the right, and cross out the words they have already matched as they work. Other specific strategies for taking tests can be found in Deshler et al. (1996), Millman and Pauk (1969), and Strichart and Mangrum (1993).

CONCLUSION: STUDY SKILLS TRAINING AND METACOGNITION

Metacognition has been described as the individual's conscious awareness of his or her functioning and the ability to verbalize that awareness. Wiig and Semel (1990) and others have called metacognition the ability to use language as a tool. Deshler and colleagues wrote that the term "convey[s] the idea that the learner uses processes to provide [him- or herself] with feedback on learning" (1996, p. 13). *Meta,* from Greek, means *beyond, above,* or *higher.* For the student with dyslexia, the objective of study skills training is to develop higher level thinking, objective judgment, and serious reflection, all of which the student can use to assess him- or herself as a learner.

The strategies and techniques discussed in this chapter build from the beginning techniques for self-monitoring and self-evaluation to the methods for taking notes from texts and lectures and call for frequent interaction with supportive adults who offer feedback and guidance. During study skills training, the student emerges from randomness and confusion to deliberate and focused behavior and develops the capacity to relate his or her habits and actions to achievements. All of the study skills activities contribute to metacognition. They demand more from the student, not less. The procedures take time, discipline, and the will to win. The study skills instructor is the mentor and supporter of the student while he or she acquires the necessary skills. Instructor and student have a formidable task, which was well articulated by Dr. Baruj Benacerraf, recipient of the 1980 Nobel Prize in Physiology or Medicine and former president of Harvard's Dana-Farber Cancer Research Center:

> Dyslexia is a challenge to overcome, rather than a deficiency to be sorry about. To achieve excellence, I found that I needed to always examine my own work with a merciless, critical eye. It is far better to be more severe and demanding of oneself than others can be. (personal communication, 1988)

Teachers, however, should also keep in mind Torgesen's Law: "Know your stuff. Know who you are stuffing. Stuff them as explicitly, as systematically, and as supportively as you possibly can" (personal communication, June 19, 1998).

REFERENCES

Alley, G.R., & Deshler, D.D. (1979). *Teaching the learning disabled adolescent: Strategies and methods.* Denver, CO: Love Publishing.

Askov, E.N., & Kamm, K. (1982). *Study skills in the content areas.* Boston: Allyn & Bacon.

Barkley, R.A. (1997). Behavioral inhibition, sustained attention, and executive functions: Constructing a unifying theory of ADHD. *Psychological Bulletin, 121*(1), 65–94.

Brown, A.L. (1975) The development of memory: Knowing, knowing about knowing, and knowing how to know: In H.W. Reese (Ed.), *Advances in child development and behavior* (Vol. 10, pp. 103–152). New York: Academic Press.

Brown, J.I. (1976). *Efficient reading: Revised form.* Boston: Houghton Mifflin.

Brown, T.E. (2009, August). *Advanced assessment and treatment of attention-deficit disorders (ADD).*

Workshop conducted at the annual convention of the American Psychological Association, Toronto.

Buzan, T. (1983). *Use both sides of your brain.* New York: Dutton/Plume.

Bywaters, D. (1998). *Affix and root cards.* Cambridge, MA: Educators Publishing Service.

Christensen, C.R., Garvin, D.A., & Sweet, A. (1991). *Education for judgment: The artistry of discussion leadership.* Boston: Harvard Business School Press.

Cruickshank, W.M. (1967). *The brain-injured child in home, school, and community.* Syracuse, NY: Syracuse University Press.

de Hirsch, K. (1984). Language and the developing child. *The Orton Society Monographs, 4.* Timonium, MD: York Press.

Denckla, M. (2007). Executive function: Binding together the definitions of attention-deficit/hyperactivity disorder and learning disabilities. In L. Meltzer (Ed.), *Executive function in education: from theory to practice.* New York: Guilford Press.

Deshler, D.D., Ellis, E., & Lenz, B.K. (1996). *Teaching adolescents with learning disabilities: Strategies and methods* (2nd ed.). Denver, CO: Love Publishing.

Devine, T.G. (1981). *Teaching study skills: A guide for teachers.* Boston: Allyn & Bacon.

Fowler, H. (1998). *A dictionary of modern English usage* (3rd ed.). New York: Oxford University Press.

Gaddes, W.H., & Edgell, D. (1994). *Learning disabilities and brain function: A neuropsychological approach* (3rd ed.). New York: Springer Verlag.

Gillingham, A., & Stillman, B.W. (1956). *Remedial training for students with specific disability in reading, spelling and penmanship* (5th ed.). Cambridge, MA: Educators Publishing Service.

Gillingham, A., & Stillman, B.W. (1997). *Remedial training for children with specific disability in reading, spelling and penmanship* (8th ed.). Cambridge, MA: Educators Publishing Service.

Helson, L.G. (1971). *Basic English sentence patterns.* Cambridge, MA: Educators Publishing Service.

Hayakawa, S.I. (1994). *Choose the right word: A contemporary guide to selecting the prcise word for every situation.* New York: HarperPerennial.

Individuals with Disabilities Education Improvement Act (IDEA) of 2004, PL 108-446, 20 U.S.C. §§ 1400 *et seq.*

Johnson, D.J. & Myklebust, H.R. (1967). *Learning disabilities: Educational principles and practices.* New York: Grune & Stratton.

Kamhi, A.G., & Catts, H.W. (1989). *Reading disabilities: A developmental perspective.* New York: Little, Brown.

King, D.H. (1985). *Writing skills for the adolescent.* Cambridge, MA: Educators Publishing Service.

Lakoff, G., & Johnson, M. (1980). *Metaphors we live by.* Chicago: University of Chicago Press.

Lehmann, P.W. (1960a). *The junior précis practice pad.* Cambridge, MA: Educators Publishing Service.

Lehmann, P.W. (1960b). *The senior précis practice pad.* Cambridge, MA: Educators Publishing Service.

Lerner, J. (1989). Educational interventions in learning disabilities. *Journal of the American Academy of Child and Adolescent Psychiatry, 28,* 326–331.

Levine, M. (1987). *Developmental variation and learning disorders* (2nd ed.). Cambridge, MA: Educators Publishing Service.

Makkai, A., Boatner, M.T., & Gates, J.E. (1995). *A dictionary of American idioms.* Hauppauge, NY: Barron's Educational Series.

Maria, K. (1990). *Reading comprehension instruction, issues, and strategies.* Timonium, MD: York Press.

McNeil, J.D. (1992). *Reading comprehension: New directions for classroom practice.* New York: HarperCollins.

Meltzer, L. (2007). Executive function in education: from theory to practice. New York: Guilford Press.

Millman, J., & Pauk, W. (1969). *How to take tests.* New York: McGraw-Hill.

Murdoch, I. (1987). *Acastos.* New York: Viking Penguin.

Murray, C., & Munro, J. (1989). *30 roots to grow on.* Cambridge, MA: Educators Publishing Service.

Neisser, U. (1976). *Cognition and reality: Principles and implications of cognitive psychology.* New York: W.H. Freeman.

Obrecht, F. (1999). *Minimum essentials of English* (2nd ed.). Hauppauge, NY: Barron's Educational Series.

Orton, S.T. (1937). *Reading, writing and speech problems in children: A presentation of certain types of disorders in the development of the language faculty.* New York: W.W. Norton.

The Oxford Dictionary and Thesaurus. (1996). New York: Oxford University Press.

Partridge, E. (1966). *Origins: A short etymological dictionary of modern English.* New York: Greenwich House.

Robinson, F.P. (1970) *Effective study* (4th ed.). New York: Harper & Row.

Rockwood, C. (Ed.). (2009). *Brewer's dictionary of phrase and fable* (18th ed.). Edinburgh, Scotland: Chambers Harrap Publishers.

Roget's thesaurus (5th ed.). (1992). New York: HarperCollins.

Singer, B.D., & Bashir, A.S. (1999). What are executive functions and self-regulation and what do they have to do with language-learning disorders? *Language, Speech, and Hearing Services in Schools, 30,* 265–273.

Strichart, S.S., & Mangrum, C.T., II. (1993). *Teaching study strategies to students with learning disabilities*. Boston: Allyn & Bacon.

Tomatis, A. (1969). *Dyslexia*. Ontario, Canada: University of Ottawa Press.

Tomkins, C. (1963, September 14). The last skill acquired. *The New Yorker*, 127–133.

Tonjes, M.J., & Zintz, M.V. (1981). *Teaching reading, thinking, study skills in content classrooms*. Dubuque, IA: William C. Brown.

Trudeau, K. (1995). *Megamemory*. New York: William Morrow.

Warriner, J.E. (1988). *English composition and grammar: Complete course*. Orlando, FL: Harcourt Brace.

Wiig, E.H., & Semel, E. (1990). *Language assessment and intervention for the learning disabled*. Columbus, OH: Charles E. Merrill.

Wycoff, J. (1991). *Mindmapping: Your personal guide to exploring creativity and problem-solving*. New York: Berkley Books.

19

Working with High-Functioning Adults with Dyslexia and Other Academic Challenges

SUSAN H. BLUMENTHAL

The population of high-functioning dyslexic adults is a specific but quite diverse group of individuals. They are studying and working in a variety of fields and include college students, graduate students, physicians, lawyers, and members of the clergy. Some adults, especially those in graduate school, are required to do tremendous amounts of reading each week. Other graduate students conduct experiments in science research, which may require less reading than is necessary in liberal arts programs. In science settings, however, graduate students need to perform sequential, multistep experiments with relative independence over a period of several days. Frequent shifting from abstract conceptualization to sequenced detail and back again requires a high degree of organization, which can be troublesome for some dyslexics.

Not all high-functioning dyslexics are in a school environment. Some dyslexic adults have already completed school and are working in a business setting. Whether a person runs his or her own business or is in a corporate setting, he or she usually has to do background reading in trade or professional journals to keep abreast of developments in the field. In addition, individuals in professional positions often have to write memos and reports on a regular basis as part of their job.

Virtually all high-functioning dyslexic adults are ambitious and highly motivated, but they also suffer from chronic feelings of inadequacy, stress, and low self-esteem regarding their ability to learn. Almost all of them had a difficult beginning in the early grades of elementary school and continued to function quite unevenly during their school years.

EMOTIONAL REPERCUSSIONS

Despite being above average or quite superior in general ability, nearly all of the high-functioning dyslexic adults who seek help with reading and writing skills experience anxiety about some aspects of their work and learning. They often do not know why they have so much difficulty with written language. Through the years, they have tried to both compensate for and hide the problem. They may have never read a book all of the way through but will rarely miss class so that they can pick up the necessary information from discussion. They may have to write multiple drafts of a term paper but often will ask and be allowed to give an oral presentation or work in tandem with another student. So many of these students have been told to "try harder" throughout their school careers. Nearly every dyslexic adult who goes for a psychoeducational consultation or evaluation thinks that he or she is "lazy," that everyone else is smarter, or that there is something wrong with his or her brain. It does not matter whether these individuals graduated from a state school or an ivy league school, nor does it matter whether they were inducted into Phi Beta Kappa. They almost always are plagued by varying degrees of self-doubt.

There are important differences between children and adults who have learning difficulties that can affect intervention. First, their basic attitudes are generally different. When children are referred for language intervention, they often are resistant at first. They have been identified as not doing well in school, and both the children and the parents may be upset with the children's school performance and/or with the school staff. In contrast, adults usually are highly motivated to improve their language skills. Many are self-referred or are referred by other professionals, such as psychotherapists or college teachers. Consequently, adults with learning difficulties often have definite goals. In addition, they often are relieved when they realize that they can get help.

A sense of awareness is the second difference between children and adults with learning difficulties. Children's awareness of their learning needs and difficulties usually is unformulated. In some way, the children sense that there is something wrong. They say, "Reading is not hard for me—I just don't like it." Adults are much more aware of how learning difficulties, especially reading difficulties, have affected their lives. They may feel self-conscious in a social group—not because they lack social skills but because they do not make the same kind of contributions as others. They may not make the same mental associations because they lack the underlying foundation of knowledge, which is often derived from reading. For example, a 35-year-old physician with a persistent reading problem who came for help had this comment: "I feel I am shallow, compared with all my friends. They read all of the time."

Coping is another difference between children and adults with learning disabilities. Children are part of an established support system; they are evaluated, tested, promoted to or held back from the next grade, and are often the focus of parent–teacher conferences. The responsibility of learning or not learning is shared. Adults with learning disabilities invariably seem to have a secret life. They do not have the same support system as children. Adults have to work in an increasingly independent manner, and they worry about being "found out." Many adults with learning disabilities have learned to hide their problems and compensate as much as possible. Often, they focus on avoidance in order to escape potential humiliation.

Finally, the beginning of the referral process is also different for adults and children. Children are usually referred or evaluated because they are failing or not doing well in school. Adults are referred for a variety of reasons. Some adults experience a change in their work requirements or in their educational setting, and they find that they cannot meet the expected level of the new requirements. For example, a member of the Coast Guard with severe dyslexia was promoted to petty officer. Instead of working on machines, at which he was an expert, he now had to do considerable paperwork and report writing. His performance ratings, which were formerly consistently high, fell below average. In another instance, an ambitious 31-year-old account executive who had a history of dyslexia was quite successful on her job. She had excellent verbal skills and was effective at meetings. Her new boss, however, insisted that there be more memos and outlines of marketing goals and fewer face-to-face meetings. The account executive knew that if she wanted to be promoted, then she would have to get her ideas down in writing.

Some adults who return to school for a higher degree refer themselves for a psychoeducational evaluation. For example, a successful 47-year-old businesswoman with a bachelor of arts degree decided to apply for a master of business administration program. She referred herself for evaluation because she suspected that she had a previously undiagnosed learning problem. When her son was diagnosed with dyslexia, she recognized similar patterns in her own academic life.

More adults are being referred by mental health workers, personnel in the workplace, and college and university faculty to explore whether there is an undetected learning problem. As awareness increases about the different forms that learning problems can take, psychotherapists, job supervisors, and professors have begun to notice areas of discrepancy in people who otherwise are functioning well. For example, an administrator at a university was referred for a psychoeducational evaluation after his boss wrote, "The communication area is of great concern and an obstacle to Mr. K's career development. He exceeds expectations in personal skills and in commitment to all aspects of his job. I recommend that he get help for problems in writing and other communications skills."

EVALUATION AND ASSESSMENT

Gathering information about the individual's early developmental, educational, and medical histories and, if appropriate, employment history is the first component of a comprehensive assessment for an adult. The individual's own perception of the problem is particularly helpful. The latter information can be obtained from a writing sample called Educational Memories (Blumenthal, 1981a), which is described later in this section.

The purpose of the assessment is to try to understand and evaluate the client's presenting problems in order to develop a treatment plan. The assessor tries to determine why the person is having difficulty functioning in an academic or a work setting and explores the client's capabilities and learning patterns to see what interferes with learning. Current information is as important as the individual's history. If the individual is in school, then it is important to read several recent term papers as well as look over class notes from lectures. Individuals with jobs can bring in reports, memos, or letters that are representative of work demands.

There is no specific test battery for diagnosing learning disabilities. Psychologists who specialize in working with people who have dyslexia or other types of learning disabilities use many of the same tests in their evaluation as are used in traditional psychological evaluations, but they view the results in a particular way (see Chapter 14). That is, during assessment of learning disabilities, qualitative information is always an important supplement to the quantitative results. The evaluator wants to know exactly what the client said and how he or she responded to each task. A trained diagnostician always administers tests in a standardized manner according to the test manual, but views each test as a vehicle for deriving other important, perhaps subtle currents of information. By listening carefully and recording precisely what the client says, an evaluator can pick up clues about receptive and expressive language problems, confusion in using prepositions, word substitutions, and so forth. Although this ancillary information may not directly affect the overall test results, it is important because it helps show vulnerabilities in the client's learning and performance and often illuminates why his or her performance in school or on the job has been uneven.

A typical test battery to identify learning disabilities in adults includes the Wechsler Adult Intelligence Scale–Third Edition (Wechsler, 1991); a silent reading test such as the Nelson-Denny Reading Test (Brown, Bennett, & Hanna, 1981) or the Gates-MacGinitie Reading Tests–Third Edition (MacGinitie & MacGinitie, 1989); the Wide-Range Achievement Test–Third Edition (Wilkinson, 1993), which has Word Recognition, Spelling, and Math Computation subtests; a test of oral reading such as the Gray Oral Reading Test–Third Edition (Wiederholt & Bryant, 1992) or the Diagnostic Assessments of Reading with Trial Teaching Strategies (Roswell & Chall, 1992); a design copying test such as the Bender Visual Motor Gestalt Test (Bender, 1938); and several writing samples (usually one written during the session and two written at home between testing sessions), including Educational Memories (Blumenthal, 1981a). Other tests may be included, depending on the client's presenting problems, such as House-Tree-Person Drawing (Buck, 1978), selected cards from the Thematic Apperception Test (Murray & Bellak, 1973), and a sentence completion test such as the Rotter Incomplete Sentences Blank–Second Edition (Rotter, Lah, & Rafferty, 1992). Sometimes a client has had a prior psychological examination but has not undergone reading tests or a writing evaluation. Although it is not necessary to redo what has been done already, a reading and writing assessment should be done before the specialist begins to work with the client.

After the testing is completed, the evaluator interprets the findings and explains them to the client. It is important for the evaluator as well as the remedial specialist (if the specialist is different from the evaluator) to present the results in as constructive a manner as possible. When the evaluator uses trial teaching techniques and judiciously chosen teaching materials, the client can begin to sense how he or she can make progress. After test findings were explained to one young physician and he had begun working on his problems, he wrote the following:

My diagnosis as dyslexic, i.e., reading more slowly in order to understand, was both difficult and refreshing. At first I had attached a stigma to it, yet it was also refreshing, because it validated my life experience. I now feel in control. Adequate time to read translates into adequate time to process and understand.

Educational Memories

The Educational Memories writing sample measure provides information that cannot be obtained through typical diagnostic tests. Between the initial telephone call and the time of the first testing appointment, clients receive a writing assignment that focuses on their school memories. Clients are asked to relate their own version of their educational experience, including both positive and negative memories. They are to write a first draft only, by hand, on 8.5" × 11" paper. They are to avoid talking to family members or using a dictionary or any other reference source. Educational Memories allows evaluators to get to know more about a client and at the same time obtain a writing sample for close examination. Most individuals write seven to nine handwritten pages.

Educational Memories serves as a valuable part of the diagnostic examination for a number of reasons. First, it is possible to find out what insights the client has about his or her own difficulties. Second, the writing sample reveals information about the individual's tendency to blame him- or herself or others for any difficulties faced. Third, the sample gives a sense of the emotional impact of years of struggling with school and/or work. Finally, the writing sample offers an initial view of the person's ability to organize information. This sample also allows an examination of handwriting, grammar, syntax, vocabulary, and spelling. The Educational Memories sample also is a useful part of the diagnostic process because it helps diagnosticians differentiate between people who have learning difficulties and people who do not. People with learning problems rarely report positive memories about school. Their negative memories always center around problems of mastery. In contrast, people with no learning difficulties have many more positive memories of school, and their negative memories relate not to mastery but instead to specific social problems (e.g., I was never popular. I didn't get invited to parties) or to the harshness of particular teachers.

Following are excerpts from the Educational Memories samples of four individuals that illustrate how painful the introduction to school can be, particularly in the beginning years when children are especially vulnerable.

Bobbie

Bobbie, a 45-year-old woman with learning and memory problems, admitted during her first session that she has never read a book all of the way through. She is now in a graduate program with approximately 1,000 pages per week of assigned reading, such as Freud, D.W. Winnicott, and Melanie Klein. Bobbie wrote,

I always have difficulty remembering what I read, and also I have trouble with facts and names. The memory of my education goes back to my very first day at school. I sat there and they debated whether or not I was retarded, because I did not know my name. I had been called Bobbie all my life, and had no idea my given name was Roberta.

Lana

Lana, a 30-year-old woman studying for her bachelor of science degree in physical therapy, wrote the following:

From the time I was around 8 years old, I have had this underlying feeling of inadequacy and inferiority, which is very tied into my feelings about school. The two are almost synonymous. My driving force to get my B.S. is to rid myself of this burden.

Derek

Derek, a 27-year-old law student, recalled the following in his write-up:

I attended private school from nursery through third grade, and it was there where I encountered the most academic difficulty. The school told my parents that I was "unteachable." This attitude is reflected in a progress report from the third grade in which it was stated they no longer measured my advancement on a scale with other students: "His grades reflect individual progress rather than third-grade expectations." These are particularly painful years to remember as my self-esteem was significantly diminished.

Mark

Mark, a 22-year-old dental student, wrote the following:

My earliest academic memories are filled with anxiety—feeling the inability to master all of the spelling words for the Monday morning quiz. As I grew older, reading quickly and accurately became more important. I always had to work longer and concentrate more intently than

my peers. Finally, my compensatory mechanisms of using extra time were inadequate because I was confronted with timed exams, and no matter how much I prepared I was faced with my nemesis, only a limited amount of time to read. This forced me to skim over material rather than master it, and I therefore could not answer questions on topics I was familiar with.

THE MOST COMMON NEEDS OF HIGH-FUNCTIONING DYSLEXICS AND OTHER STUDENTS WITH ACADEMIC CHALLENGES

Individuals with learning difficulties or dyslexia usually need help in one or more of the following areas: silent reading comprehension skills, vocabulary development, expressive language (writing) skills, spelling, study skills, and managing or allocating time in a constructive manner. Each person may have a greater or lesser degree of difficulty with any one of these areas and may not have difficulty with all of them. It is particularly important to remember that each person presents a unique combination of strengths as well as weaknesses. The remediation plan has to be tailored to that person's specific needs. Often, the client manifests competence in unexpected areas as well as surprising gaps in background knowledge. Information gathered from the individual's history, diagnostic study, and examination of current work as well as trial teaching will help to pinpoint areas that need attention.

There are several important goals in treatment. The first goal is to change the individual's perception of him- or herself from someone who cannot learn to one who can learn by helping the person become an active learner. Many readers who have learning and reading problems are too passive in relation to the material they read. As a result, their retention, understanding, and even appreciation are affected. Being an active learner means thinking about and evaluating the material being read. Active learning involves bringing prior information to the discussion of the subject at hand. The active reader tries to discern the author's point of view. Encouraging making the transition from a passive to a more active approach to reading requires guidance from the remedial specialist. The remedial specialist needs to know when to pose evocative questions, how to elicit information, and when to prepare the client to develop insights about the material.

For example, Evelyn, an ambitious college graduate, was running a successful business and wanted to go to graduate school for her master of business administration degree. The evaluation showed that she had a slow reading rate and had difficulty retaining what she read. Evelyn thought that she often missed main ideas, which undermined her confidence in general. An intelligent woman, she was quite interested in world affairs. She was encouraged to read the editorial columns in the daily newspaper to improve her reading comprehension and retention of information. Instead of skimming articles and retaining a minimal amount, as she had done formerly, Evelyn was asked to approach the reading material differently, using a four-step approach.

1. First, she should read the headline and subhead and before reading further, ask herself, "What do I think this article is about?" By posing this question, she immediately became more active and focused on the article's topic.

2. Next, she should read the article and then ask herself, "What did the author say?"

3. Then she should ask, "What did I learn that was new?"

4. Finally, she should ask, "What is my opinion about this subject? Do I agree or disagree?"

After using this approach with one newspaper article, Evelyn wrote a one-page essay about the article, which she brought to the next session. The entire assignment took her about 1 hour at home. This active approach stimulated her ability to concentrate, fostered her retention, and improved her writing skills. After approximately 2 months of remediation, Evelyn commented, "At first it seemed like I was taking baby steps, but the way I read is really changing. When we went out to dinner with friends, it was amazing, I found I had facts and opinions and held my own in the discussion." Evelyn also worked with a variety of other standardized reading comprehension materials, such as Six-Way Paragraphs (Advanced) by Pauk (1983), and in doing so improved her concentration, reading comprehension, and writing skills. At the end of the year, she took the Graduate Management Admissions Test with extended time and was accepted into business school, where she did well.

Progress can be made when the therapeutic alliance is optimal and the demands of the remedial work are challenging but not overwhelming. The client often will report a sense of excitement about his or her own potential being realized. For example, one graduate student declared, "I looked at this assignment and said, 'I know you, you sucker! I can do it.'" Another client said, "I know that what is coming next will be hard, but now I think there is nothing I can't handle."

Helping the individual develop an awareness of his or her own thinking process is the second goal of remediation. Positive changes occur as individuals become aware of their own thinking, and thinking, reading, and writing become more efficient. It is possible to stimulate and activate cognitive processes such as reasoning, organizing, generalizing, and planning so that they are enhanced across a broad range of content areas. One way to encourage this kind of awareness of how one thinks is through the use of Process Notes (Blumenthal, 1981b).

When the clients are disturbed about their reactions to their pattern of work habits or ability to sustain attention, they can be taught to be more aware of how they think, what interrupts their reasoning, and what helps them to continue their work. When a client faces obstacles in doing his or her work, the remedial specialist can encourage the client to write process notes; that is, to evaluate in writing his or her own reactions to the assignment. This often helps the client to develop organizing principles, which facilitates his or her work.

For example, process notes were eventually used by Ted, a dyslexic doctoral student who referred himself for evaluation after he failed his written comprehensive exams. The members of the examining committee had harsh comments and remarked on how "poorly written" and how "disorganized" Ted's written effort was. They raised questions about Ted's suitability in a doctoral program, perhaps forgetting that he had completed all of the coursework up to that point with excellent grades. None of the committee members thought about the discrepancy between Ted's record and his performance on the comprehensives, yet unevenness in performance is the hallmark of almost all learning disabilities.

Reading Ted's comprehensive exam was one of the first steps the remedial specialist took in helping Ted. Although the exam was more than 35 handwritten pages long, it was necessary to read it carefully to understand how Ted performed under pressure, evaluate exactly where he needed help, and develop a treatment plan. Although Ted experienced both anger and mild depression in reaction to his failure, his drive to improve his writing was prodigious. He responded well to the varied writing assignments that the remedial specialist gave him, most of which he completed in the library between sessions. During sessions, all completed work was read aloud, sentence by sentence, and discussed in relation to clarity, organization, and effectiveness. Although the remedial specialist made no marks on Ted's paper, every unclear sentence was discussed. In essence, the remedial specialist modeled an active approach for Ted by questioning unclear areas rather than by writing correct answers. After the 20th session, the specialist encouraged Ted to write process notes. Ted wrote the following passage after the 21st session of work:

I began writing this time before I began typing—I began to frame this essay in my mind ahead of time. I asked a main question, and then made myself ask, "What does another person reading this have to know in order to understand both the question and the answer?" I asked myself, "Does the piece follow a logical and easily understood order?" and "Does each paragraph contain a logical order too? Do all the paragraphs fit together?" Although there were a good many spelling lapses, the general ordering of the ideas seem okay to me—and this is encouraging to me. I would have to say a guarded yes to my questions.

The working relationship between the remedial specialist and the client is never a static one. It draws its strength from the balance between necessary support and the increasing autonomy of the student as he or she becomes more able to compensate for his or her difficulties. In this particular case, we see that Ted has developed an awareness of the specific elements of effective and communicative writing. The revelation that one's writing always needs to be understood by others continued to transform Ted's efforts, and Ted eventually integrated this principle into most of his writing. By the end of the year, he retook the comprehensive exams and passed with high commendations.

Finally, reducing anxiety related to learning is the third goal of treatment. A client can decrease anxiety while working on the area of his or her greatest vulnerability if a positive therapeutic alliance has been established, materials appropriate to the client's intellectual level are used, and each defined goal or task is broken down into manageable parts. Achieving all three goals of treatment—helping the individual to change his or her self-perception, develop an awareness of his or her thought processes, and reduce anxiety—can help the individual to achieve a degree of mastery. The following three case examples illustrate these points.

Janet

The emotional repercussions of learning disabilities can interfere with a sense of positive self-worth and cause a person to feel intense shame. Janet, a friendly 30-year-old who works for a large corporation, graduated from a small liberal arts college with a degree in marketing.

Early History

Janet had difficulty learning to read in the early grades. During reading instruction, she was placed in a corrective reading group that met 5 times per week for 1 hour each time. Janet recalls that reading was always difficult for her. In high school, her parents helped her with assignments. They helped her review before tests and made editorial and spelling changes on her papers. She graduated from high school with a *C* average. Janet's anxiety heightened in college, and she often stayed up all night before an exam. She made it a point to find a study group. Her friends read her papers and made corrections before she handed them in. She did well enough so that no professor ever identified her as someone who needed to be referred for psychoeducational evaluation. After passing all of her courses, she graduated in 4 years.

Work History

After college, Janet worked in sales. Her organizational ability was praised, but she decided to change jobs because she wanted a position that included some travel. She took a job with the large corporation for whom she currently works. Her new job required interpersonal and organizational skills and also involved some travel. After 1 year, she had her first job review. She was rated outstanding in interpersonal skills and in working as a member of a team. In fact, she was rated well above average in every category except writing and communication skills. The job review noted, "Written work is dramatically inadequate for her level of responsibility." Janet was told that the quality of her written work would keep her from being promoted. Janet's boss told her that she thought that Janet had some kind of learning disability and strongly urged her to get help if she wanted to advance on the job.

Testing and Remediation

Janet was extremely anxious when she first consulted the psychoeducational diagnostician and wept helplessly when she talked about her learning problems. Confronting her problems with learning was so traumatic that a month passed after the first interview before she called to begin work. Her parents were supportive both emotionally and financially. Janet asked her parents not to tell anyone else in her family that she was getting help for her learning problems. She told her boss but did not tell any of her close friends. She felt stigmatized and very ashamed.

An intelligence test showed that Janet had average ability, but the unevenness of her subtest scores showed that she had higher potential ability. For example, her general knowledge clearly had been inhibited by lack of background reading. She also experienced considerable anxiety when asked to answer questions and do specific tasks; this anxiety had a definite negative impact on the intelligence test results.

On the Word Recognition subtest of the Wide Range Achievement Test–Third Edition (Wilkinson, 1993), Janet scored at the sixth percentile, which is equivalent to approximately an eighth-grade skill level. Her oral and silent reading were approximately at the 10th-grade level. When answering questions about the silent reading passages, Janet read the passages and had to look back at them to find every answer.

She was asked to write several short summaries. Although it was evident that she could express herself verbally, she was uncertain about how to put what she wanted to say in writing. Her fear about making spelling errors made her choose a simple vocabulary that made her writing seem less mature.

The evaluation was stressful. The findings were interpreted and explained to her in as positive a manner as possible, but Janet felt despair about making progress. It seemed likely that Janet had experienced severe reading problems when she was a child. There was no indication in her history or in the current evaluation, however, that suggested that she would be unable to make progress during remediation, and the evaluator conveyed this positive outlook to her.

The Work

The first goal of treatment was to change Janet's perception of herself from someone who could not learn to someone who could learn by having Janet work on appropriate materials within the context of a supportive relationship. It was also necessary to reduce Janet's anxiety and despair related to learning.

Because of Janet's intense anxiety in relation to reading, writing, and words in general, it was particularly important for the remedial specialist to be supportive and non-pressuring and at the same time choose materials that were mature in format and content and appropriate to Janet's reading level. Janet and the remedial specialist met once per week, before Janet was due at work. Remediation focused on oral reading, vocabulary development, silent reading comprehension, and expressive language skills, including letter and memo writing, spelling, and word analysis. Janet reviewed expressive writing and vocabulary activities during the week at home.

Janet's first writing assignments were to write about members of her family. These assignments required no advance reading. Writing impressions about family and friends usually tends to be less stressful than a more formal assignment. The remedial specialist made no corrections on these first few writing assignments. After a few weeks, the specialist asked Janet to summarize an article of her choice from a newspaper. Janet was able to find articles she could read in *USA Today*. Because she rarely had looked at a newspaper, she and the specialist looked at one together to see how to locate news articles, the weather section, and human interest stories. The specialist asked her to choose a newspaper article that appealed to her, read the article at home, and then summarize it in writing. Janet underlined any words in the article that she did not know or words that she thought she would have trouble defining. She read the summary aloud each week at her remedial session. Again, the specialist made no corrections at the time of the reading. Instead, the specialist chose one aspect of the writing—usually grammar, spelling, or general usage—for teaching during the next session. In this way, Janet felt less threatened because she was not corrected during her presentation and because skills were taught separately from the presentation. She began incorporating the grammar and usage lessons into her writing. After approximately 8 months, Janet started reading *The New York Times* instead of *USA Today*. This change boosted her self-esteem because her family and friends also read *The New York Times*. She generally found at least one article of interest to write about.

The newspaper reading was important to remediation because Janet avoided reading in general and never read the newspaper at all. After she had been attending remediation sessions for a while, Janet started to read the newspaper once per week and, consequently, had more to contribute when she socialized with her co-workers. Each week she added new words to her vocabulary by underlining new words at home. During remediation sessions, she and the specialist discussed and defined each word with the aid of a dictionary. By herself, Janet felt intimidated by the dictionary, but she did use it during sessions. She wrote each new word on a 3" × 5" index card with the definition on the reverse side. She also added a sentence using the word to help her to retain the word. The specialist also encouraged Janet to keep and bring to her sessions a list of any unknown words that she might hear at work. In this way, all of the new words studied were ones that Janet herself had selected rather than words from a list in a vocabulary book.

During each session Janet read a short selection silently and answered accompanying comprehension questions. She and the remedial specialist discussed any incorrect responses. The questions that posed the most problems for Janet were questions that required inferential thinking, a skill that is essential for advanced reading comprehension. Inferential thinking involves making accurate judgments and drawing conclusions about what is read. It was necessary for Janet to approach the text in a more interactive manner than she was accustomed to. She also tended to make literal interpretations that limited her understanding of subtleties. The remedial specialist helped her make more accurate inferences in the following way. Through guided discussion, Janet was encouraged to identify relationships between events in a passage as she and the specialist returned to the text for additional analysis of the content. The specialist helped Janet recognize that she often could use some prior knowledge to figure out an answer. Increased self-monitoring of her own thought processes was also encouraged. In this way, Janet began to derive more meaning from what she read.

Misspelled words were identified in Janet's weekly writing assignments and in the memos or reports that she wrote for her job so that she could improve her spelling skills. When the words were common and likely to be used frequently, she copied them in a small, alphabetized notebook that she could carry in her pocketbook. The remedial specialist reviewed the words with Janet during the weekly sessions and added to the list each week so that Janet became familiar with the words. When she needed to use a word in her writing, she referred to her personal dictionary. As time went on, she memorized many of the words, and they were dropped from the list. New words were added as Janet began to expand her vocabulary. In this way, her spelling skills improved steadily and so did her confidence in including a more varied vocabulary in her writing.

Although Janet was reading at the high school level, she was not confident about applying word analysis skills or syllabication skills to figure out new multisyllabic words. Because review of basic word analysis skills was a painful reminder of early school failures, word analysis was taught in conjunction with the words from newspaper articles that Janet mispronounced. For example, when she was not able to pronounce *mirth,* an opportunity arose for the remedial specialist to introduce the pronunciation of the special letter combinations *ir, ur,* and *er* and select different words for teaching and practice at the following session. Teaching was thus tied to use and did not take on the qualities of drills. Eventually, all of the necessary word analysis skills were reviewed.

Although Janet was motivated and conscientiously completed her writing and vocabulary review at home, she continued to hide her efforts from her friends and close family members. After approximately 8 months of remediation, Janet received a promotion and a pay bonus. Her boss no longer criticized her writing and communication skills. Janet was more confident and handled pressure and stress on her job with greater equanimity. She still tended to procrastinate when she had to write memos and letters, but brought them to the remedial sessions more readily to work on them with her remedial specialist. Janet still found reading to be a struggle, but she was more willing to try to get information from books and began to read some self-help books related to career advancement.

After 1½ years of remedial sessions, Janet had less anxiety and had increased confidence about reading and writing. As a result, she was able to learn and retain information more easily. She became more willing to write memos and letters at work and did not automatically think that whatever she wrote was of poor quality. Her vocabulary expanded, and she realized that she was aware of words in a way that she had not been before. She made an effort to retain what she knew by reviewing and trying to use the words in conversation.

Roy

Many individuals with learning disabilities or symptoms of mild dyslexia who have struggled for years in school tend to become discouraged and take an increasingly passive approach to academic work. This was the case with Roy, an articulate 24-year-old college graduate who was distressed about his future. He wanted to decide on a career but did not think he could do anything well.

Early History

Roy's earliest memory of school was of feeling frightened. In the first and second grade, he did not make sufficient progress in reading and was assigned to remedial reading classes. In addition, he went to tutors periodically throughout elementary school. He never read for pleasure and read only what was assigned. Roy described elementary school as frustrating. Roy chose to attend an alternative high school that offered smaller classes and more individual attention to each student. He became a student government leader but never excelled in his studies. In college, he graduated with a *B*-minus average and felt he had not learned as much as he would have liked. Roy stated that he never put his full effort into schoolwork. He told himself that if he did not do well, then he could also comfort himself with the fact that he had not tried very hard.

Testing and Remediation

After college, Roy was evaluated by a neuropsychologist who administered a comprehensive testing battery. Roy had done mediocre academic work throughout college, and the testing showed Roy to have uneven abilities. He had above-average ability in verbal and math areas, but read very slowly and had a relatively limited vocabulary. He had extensive word retrieval problems and also had difficulty interpreting visual or pictorial material. The neuropsychologist discouraged Roy from attempting graduate school. No silent reading test was administered at the evaluation. Instead of choosing a career, Roy, with the encouragement of his family, decided to seek remediation for his learning difficulties.

Roy was interested in learning more about his problem and wanted to improve his reading skills, but he was ambivalent about working on anything academic. The remedial specialist needed a baseline measure because there was no current information about how well Roy could read textbook-like material. The Nelson-Denny Reading Test (Brown et al., 1981) was administered. The specialist made a mark on Roy's answer sheet when the standard time had passed but then allowed Roy to complete the test to find out his accuracy if he had sufficient time to finish the test. The results (relative to the results of typical college seniors) were as follows:

Area tested	Standard time percentile	Extended time percentile
Vocabulary	12	82
Reading comprehension	31	85

The results indicated that although Roy had a slow rate of reading, he definitely could understand difficult material when he had sufficient time. At this point, Roy was quite discouraged and did not see himself as capable of doing well in school because he had never done so.

Many students who read slowly and struggle constantly to keep up with their work also never learn how to study effectively or sustain effort in order to master material for a difficult course of study. Roy had shown very uneven ability on the intelligence test, but he had average ability, and the pattern of scores suggested that he had higher potential ability. The silent reading test helped confirm his good basic ability. When devising a plan of treatment, the remedial specialist took into account Roy's statement that he had never put in full effort. The specialist interpreted and explained the results of the reading test to Roy in as positive a manner as possible; that is, she told him that the results showed that he had good basic ability and that although he had a slow rate of reading, he definitely could improve. She also told him that he expressed his ideas well in writing.

It is possible to help an individual change from being a passive reader to being an active one if appropriate materials are chosen and if assignments are presented both supportively and incrementally. It was important that Roy not be overwhelmed. The plan was to help him gradually to perceive himself as a learner, as someone who could sustain effort even with difficult material. The plan also incorporated Roy's enjoyment of expressing his ideas in writing.

Roy came to weekly 1-hour remedial sessions and spent approximately 2 hours per week working at home. Each week he was assigned a short story by a writer such as Raymond Carver, Ernest Hemingway, George Orwell, Eudora Welty, or Italo Calvino. Roy was always able to complete each assignment because the stories were short. He felt positive about being able to do the assignments and, at the same time, learned about many new authors. After reading the week's story at home, he wrote a one- or two-page summary that included a discussion about the story's main theme. After a few weeks, he was also assigned to read an editorial essay in *The New York Times* by a regular editorial writer. Roy read and summarized these point-of-view articles at home. He was encouraged to agree or disagree with the columnist at the end of his summary. Roy was slowly but systematically beginning to acquire information both from literature and from current events. Roy liked to write, and the act of writing required him to become more interactive with the text. He began to discuss the new information with his family and his friends and engage more actively in discussion about politics.

Each week, Roy brought in a list of new words from the reading selection. Roy had an excellent speaking vocabulary but had a much more limited reading vocabulary because of his limited reading experience. He, therefore, had many new words to discuss each week. He and the remedial specialist chose 10 words per week to write on 3" × 5" cards and wrote the definitions on the reverse sides along with sentences from the article or book that included the new words. Roy and the remedial specialist discussed the meanings in the sessions, and Roy reviewed the words at home. Roy's vocabulary gradually improved. Other topical articles were introduced, for example, essays by Elisabeth Kübler-Ross and Betty Friedan, to broaden both his interests and his knowledge base. Finally, the remedial specialist asked Roy to get a book by a professional photographer. Every other week he wrote an essay about a photograph of his choice. He had to discern the story the photographer appeared to convey. The book contained no explanatory text, so Roy's entire essay had to be rooted in what he saw in the photograph. He got practice in interpreting visual and pictorial material, which had been identified as a problem area in his neuropsychological testing. His observations became more acute, and with practice, he began producing integrated essays that incorporated most of the visual details as well as the underlying drama in the photographs.

Roy's anxiety about learning and reading gradually lessened. All of Roy's written assignments were read aloud and discussed at the remedial sessions. He received general positive feedback as well as specific suggestions for improving his essays. At the end of 3 months, Roy began to think of himself as both well informed and well read. He saw that he had learned a great deal and had developed his own opinions about world events. He felt so energized by all of the information that he was absorbing and learning that he declared, "This has been the most exciting 3 months of my life!"

At this point, Roy began to have hope for his future. He decided that he might like to go to medical school. First, he had to prove to himself that he could put forth the effort in a sustained way. He and his remedial specialist found an undergraduate science course that he could take on a noncredit basis. He attended each week, did the reading and assignments, took the exams, and saw that he could master the material.

Next, as part of this new long-range plan, Roy had to apply for a program in which he could take all of his premed requirements because he had not been a science major in college. He took these background science courses over a 2-year period so that he and his remedial specialist could concentrate on effective study skills. It was necessary for him not only to become an active learner but also to begin to work in an increasingly independent manner. The remedial specialist encouraged him to sit near the front of the lecture room, prepare for class before going to the lecture, take complete notes, and review the notes after the lecture, underlining important points in red pencil. He learned to apply these study skills as the first term progressed. Before the midterm exams, the specialist encouraged Roy to go to his professors during office hours to ask questions about anything that was not clear. He first wrote out a list of the questions and left space for the answers. Roy was surprised to find that he was the only student who visited during office hours, so each professor spent the entire hour with him. In addition, Roy and the remedial specialist looked over the questions together to see whether his questions were based on insufficient information, misreading the text, or topics that were not covered in lectures. He could then focus on any vulnerable area when he studied.

During his first term, Roy definitely became a more active learner. He was introduced to the Survey, Question, Read, Recite, Review (SQ3R) method of study (Robinson, 1946), which helped him to be less overwhelmed by the science texts. These texts were difficult, but it was particularly helpful for Roy to find out that most of the information in each paragraph is represented in the first sentence of the paragraph and that the remaining sentences in the paragraph support the first sentence with details.

Roy remained motivated throughout the 2 years, even though the premed courses were difficult and demanding. At the end of the 2 years, he had earned seven *A*s and one *B*. He took the Medical College Admissions Test (MCAT) with extended time because he had a diagnosis of dyslexia. His score on the MCAT was above average, and Roy was accepted to medical school. Although Roy's reading rate had improved, it still was slower than that of the average student. Consequently, he requested and was granted extended time on examinations in medical school. Roy continued to do well in medical school.

Evan

A student's reading comprehension, expressive writing, and mathematical skills can be above average, and the student still may not do well in college. Puzzled parents and teachers often call these students "underachievers." Positive changes can occur when these students are helped to become more attentive to their own thinking processes, however. These cognitive processes are usually related to organizational, attentional, and strategy issues. Executive function, a concept from clinical **neuropsychology,** has been useful in understanding and working with these students. Often included under the rubric, executive function are activities such as planning, prioritizing, sequencing, organizing, being able to shift focus, and following a project through to completion (Denckla, 1996). These students may not have actual deficits, but they seem unaware of what they need to do in order to be successful. First, they tend to be passive learners and are overly dependent on their teachers or professors to provide them with information. They do not seem conscious of the fact that it is up to them to initiate ideas, create outlines, and organize their time so that all of the work can get done. They have trouble prioritizing the steps of a task, and they are not flexible in shifting their focus when the task demands it. These issues become increasingly important as the students advance through school. Evan is an example of a student with a mild learning disability combined with problems in executive functioning.

Early History

Evan, a well-spoken 20-year-old, reported that he always had difficulty concentrating in school and was easily distracted. He did not enjoy reading and tended to read only what was assigned for a class. In elementary school, he had been diagnosed as mildly dyslexic, but he did not receive any specialized help, probably because his grades were consistently above average. He did not excel in high school, but graduated with a *B*-minus average and high SAT scores (Verbal, 680; Math, 710). When Evan was accepted at a competitive liberal arts college, he did not anticipate any difficulty with coursework. Not particularly self-reflective, Evan did not give much thought as to how to plan his time or how to study effectively when he began college. To his dismay, he did not do well in his academic subjects. The required reading was much more complex and dense than in high school, and the amount of new information to be absorbed and integrated was considerably higher. He found he could not sustain his concentration long enough to study and retain material at a satisfactory level. He was not used to organizing his time, and often he did not leave sufficient time to complete long assignments, much less do a first draft and revisions. He had trouble working independently, something that is increasingly necessary as a student advances through college. Notetaking was not easy for him. If his attention wavered in class, then he often could not get back on track again for that class period. Sensing he might be in academic trouble, he began to put extra time into studying in the library and in doing his schoolwork, but much to his disappointment, the results were not commensurate with his effort. He began to experience anxiety about his ability to do well in college, and his confidence plummeted. By the end of his sophomore year, Evan had achieved a *C*-plus average. He decided to take an official leave of absence and be evaluated for learning disabilities.

Testing and Remediation

The results of the neuropsychological evaluation showed Evan to be a cooperative and motivated student who was above average in general intelligence. He expressed a wish to do well in school, and he did not understand why his efforts did not result in better grades. He scored higher than the 85th percentile on a reading comprehension test and seemed to have good overall ability in reading. He could solve mental arithmetic problems quickly and accurately, was higher than average in abstract thinking, and had an excellent vocabulary. He was found to have mild organizational weaknesses, however. When a lot of unfamiliar information was presented, Evan seemed rattled and had difficulty deciding where to begin the task. Also, it was noted that, when encountering any degree of challenge in a task, Evan tended to give up easily, rather than plan an approach and then generate strategies to solve the problem. Finally, although Evan did well on reading the relatively short reading comprehension passages, he was slow to apply phonic principles to multisyllabic, unfamiliar words that he had to read. This suggested that there was a lack of automaticity in his reading ability that might account, in part, for some of his problems with assignments. In college, reading material is usually much more difficult than in high school and requires reading original sources as well as the ability to sustain attention over time.

According to the evaluation, Evan was both puzzled and demoralized by his college performance. He pictured himself as a good student, but, at this point, his confidence was quite low. He had put in effort but the results did not bear him out. He had tried studying by himself and with a small group of fellow students. Neither method led to success. A recurring comment by professors was that his papers were superficial and did not go deep enough.

After the results of the evaluation were interpreted to Evan, it was recommended that he begin work with a remedial specialist. Evan first found a part-time job, and then he began remediation. He had a wry, self-deprecating sense of humor, and from the start, it was clear that he was eager to collaborate in finding ways to be a more effective student. The remedial specialist's first goal was to help Evan see himself as someone who could learn and succeed in an academic setting. As part of the remediation plan, Evan was asked to summarize and comment on one chapter per week from *Into Thin Air* by Jon Krakauer, a true adventure account of climbing Mt. Everest. He also was given a newspaper essay on a stimulating topic, which he was asked to summarize and critique. In the past, he had tended to procrastinate, and now he was urged to complete his assignments during the week, not at the last minute, so that he could improve and revise his writing if he wanted to. Evan and the remedial specialist particularly discussed the consequences of the themes included in both the essay and in the book. By starting his work in advance and looking for the ramifications and consequences in the essays, Evan began to spend more time on his own interpretations. As the weeks went on, he became more committed to the work.

During the session, Evan and the remedial specialist worked on improving inferential reading skills, expanding vocabulary, and focusing on writing as a way to communicate ideas. Evan began to care more about the words he chose to express himself and to reread to decide if he had communicated effectively.

After 15 sessions, Evan had to decide whether to reenroll at his college or transfer to a nearby university. Instead of making an impulsive decision, Evan was persuaded to write two essays: one to support reenrollment at his college and the other about whether to transfer to the nearby university. He wrote two detailed essays for and against reenrollment. Evan and the remedial specialist talked about the pros and cons, and he discussed the options with his family. In the end, he decided to enroll as a nonmatriculated student at a nearby university, with the understanding that if he did well he would apply as a matriculated student.

Evan registered for three courses, which he chose himself. All of the courses required a term paper, plus a good deal of reading. To Evan's surprise, he found the lectures, the reading, and the assignments much more stimulating and compelling than he had ever experienced before. Together, he and the remedial specialist worked on planning a study schedule that he agreed he could adhere to. They discussed the topics for the assigned papers, and he chose his topic early in the term. He was encouraged to keep up with the required reading, to participate in class discussions, and begin the research for his assigned papers early in the semester. The therapeutic alliance was positive, and he liked talking over the ideas from his courses. He was receptive to suggestions regarding to how to study effectively. He began to function increasingly as an organized student. Procrastination ceased to be a major problem, and he started to set priorities among the demands of his schedule. After two semesters as a nonmatriculated student, Evan had maintained a GPA of 3.5 and was able to matriculate as a regular student.

Evan was feeling much more confident in general, and he began to look to the future and consider law as a career. In preparation, he decided on political science as a major area of study. By this time, Evan's approach toward mastering his coursework was much more organized. He set aside blocks of time for writing papers. Occasionally, he would procrastinate, but that became much less of a problem. He found his courses interesting, and his attitude toward schoolwork continued to be positive. His written assignments and term papers were no longer criticized for being superficial. Instead his professors tended to write "Good point" and "You write well." After 2 years, Evan graduated with a GPA of 3.5. Instead of going immediately to graduate school, Evan decided to work for 2 years as a paralegal. He found legal work interesting and was given increased responsibility and an opportunity to do legal research. At the end of 2 years he began law school. Law school demands a student's full attention because of the sheer quantity of reading material and the special requirements of detailed written briefs and notes. Evan experienced the academic work as challenging but manageable. He was conscious of allocating his time so that he could complete his work in a timely manner. He was particularly satisfied with the praise he received for his analytic reasoning ability and for the clarity of his writing.

SUMMARY

Although the three individuals described in these case studies are quite different, they made a lot of progress and developed a greater sense of self-confidence. Although learning differences in high-functioning adults with dyslexia and other academic challenges vary greatly, all individuals have the potential to make progress. It is important for each client to have a thorough and competent evaluation (which is interpreted to the client in the most positive manner possible), from which an effective treatment plan can be developed. When a treatment plan is successfully implemented, the clients take an active role in their own learning. Often, when clients understand their strengths and weaknesses, they can advocate for the necessary accommodations in school or on the job. When these accommodations are made, clients can show the extent of their knowledge better. They perform better, receive recognition for their improved performance, can sustain hope about the future, and often achieve their goals.

REFERENCES

Bender, L. (1938). *Bender Visual Motor Gestalt Test.* San Antonio, TX: The Psychological Corporation.

Blumenthal, S. (1981a). *Educational Memories.* Unpublished manuscript.

Blumenthal, S. (1981b). *Process notes.* Unpublished manuscript.

Brown, J.I., Bennett, J.M., & Hanna, G.S. (1981). *The Nelson-Denny Reading Test.* Chicago: Riverside.

Buck, J.N. (1978). *The House-Tree-Person Technique* (Rev. manual). Los Angeles: Western Psychological Services.

Denckla, M.B. (1996). A theory and model of executive function: A neuropsychological perspective. In G.R. Lyon & N.A. Krasnegor (Eds.), *Attention, memory, and executive function* (pp. 263–278). Baltimore: Paul H. Brookes Publishing Co.

MacGinitie, W.H., & MacGinitie, R.H. (1989). *Gates-MacGinitie Reading Tests–Third Edition.* Chicago: Riverside.

Murray, H.A., & Bellak, L. (1973). *Thematic Apperception Test (TAT).* San Antonio, TX: The Psychological Corporation.

Pauk, W. (1983). *Six-way paragraphs (Advanced).* Providence, RI: Jamestown Publishers.

Robinson, F.P. (1946). *Effective study.* New York: HarperCollins.

Roswell, F.G., & Chall, J.S. (1992). *Diagnostic Assessments of Reading with Trial Teaching Strategies (DARTTS).* Chicago: Riverside.

Rotter, J.B., Lah, M.I., & Rafferty, J.E. (1992). *Rotter Incomplete Sentences Blank–Second Edition.* San Antonio, TX: The Psychological Corporation.

Wechsler, D. (1991). *Wechsler Adult Intelligence Scale–III.* San Antonio, TX: Harcourt Assessment.

Wiederholt, J.L., & Bryant, B.R. (1992). *Gray Oral Reading Test–Third Edition (GORT–3).* Austin, TX: PRO-ED.

Wilkinson, G.S. (1993). *Wide Range Achievement Test–Third Edition: Manual.* Wilmington, DE: Jastak Associates.

20

Language and Literacy Development Among English Language Learners

ELSA CÁRDENAS-HAGAN

The number of English language learners (ELLs) in the United States has increased and will continue to increase in the future. At the present time, there has been some research to determine effective practices for this population of students. As the number of language-minority students living in the United States increases, the necessity for instructors to understand how to best develop academic language and literacy skills has increased. In fact, Spanish speakers are the largest language minority group in the country. The first section of this chapter reviews the changing demographics in the United States and the need for understanding how to best instruct this population. In addition, the response to intervention (RTI) model and its implication for ELLs will be discussed. For the purpose of extending the knowledge base of most teachers, the next section briefly reviews the structure of the Spanish language, its phonology, morphology, and syntax. The fourth section discusses multisensory techniques for literacy development in students' native language. The fifth section describes the transfer of language and literacy skills from the native language to the second language using a well-designed, evidence-based instructional approach. The final section describes how to serve adolescent ELLs and the future directions for research.

DEMOGRAPHICS

An estimated 10.9 million school-age children speak a language other than English at home (National Center for Education Statistics [NCES], 2009a). Approximately 80% of these students speak Spanish in the home. It is projected that 1 out of every 5 students will be an ELL by the year 2050 (Fry & Gonzalez, 2008). The dropout rate for Hispanic youths is 21% because Hispanic youth in the United States are more likely to drop out of school than other youth (Fry, 2003). Literacy outcomes among this population have been unsatisfactory (August & Hakuta, 1997). In addition, dropout rates of Hispanic immigrants are 46% (U.S. Census Bureau, 2000). This booming population speaks Spanish and faces the necessity of learning English as a second language. It is clear that we must concentrate on the educational achievement of our nation's Hispanic youth (Fry, 2003).

One of the main concerns for the United States is the fact that many of the children in state-supported schools speak Spanish as their primary language. Many of these students enter school with limited world knowledge and limited exposure to reading and literature even in their first language. There is no doubt that we need to concentrate on increasing the educational achievement of our nation's language-minority students. Historically, ELLs' academic achievements have been below their monolingual English-speaking peers. Results from the National Assessment of Educational Progress (NAEP), conducted in 2009, describe 73% of ELLs as scoring below basic level in reading when compared with non-Hispanic Caucasians (NCES, 2009b). These results are not statistically different from the results obtained in 1992 or 2005. How can an ELL acquire a second language and become literate in that language when his or her first language and literacy skills are not fully established? We must understand the oral language proficiency levels and the literacy skills of ELLs and thus prescribe effective instructional techniques to meet their individual needs.

Today, there are federal laws that describe how schools should serve ELLs in public institutions. For example, the No Child Left Behind (NCLB) Act of 2001 (PL 107-110) holds schools accountable for serving all students, including those who speak English as a second language. The Individuals with Disabilities Education Improvement Act (IDEA) of 2004 (PL 108-446) also recommends RTI for identifying students with learning difficulties. These laws protect all students in public schools but especially those who are ELLs.

RESPONSE TO INTERVENTION MODEL

The RTI model is a commitment to address individual students' needs. In doing so, the outcomes of students who struggle with learning to read will have improved. Subsequently, the needs of ELLs will be more closely considered, and the overrepresentation of language-minority youth in special education programs will be reduced. This is made possible because an RTI model requires universal screening and high-quality instruction for all students in the general education classroom, which is considered the first tier of instruction. An analysis of classroom instruction and the modifications necessary are implemented before it is recommended for certain students to receive more intensive instruction. Progress monitoring tools are also necessary and help educators to make data-driven decisions regarding differentiated instruction. Supplemental interventions should be provided to struggling readers in a small-group setting with no more than five students in the group, which is the second tier of instruction. If students make adequate progress, then they only receive classroom instruction. If they need more assistance, then a minimum of 30 minutes of intervention per day should be provided in a small-group setting. If necessary, even more intense instruction is provided (third tier) before making a referral to special education services (Vaughn & Fuchs, 2003). All students' progress is monitored, including ELLs.

There have been numerous studies that describe the positive outcomes of ELLs in intervention groups (Linan-Thompson, Vaughn, Prater, & Cirino, 2006; Vaughn, Cirino, et al., 2006; Vaughn, Mathes et al., 2006). These studies focus on developing language and literacy skills that are necessary for successful reading abilities. Therefore, a thorough understanding of language and literacy development within and across languages should be understood in order to provide effective instruction.

LANGUAGE COMPONENTS AND LEARNING A SECOND LANGUAGE

Research demonstrates that learning a second language is much easier for a child than an adolescent or adult (August & Hakuta, 1997). Therefore, timing is crucial if the student is to become bilingual and biliterate. Early training in kindergarten through third grade can make a difference.

It is also well known that cognitive skills transfer. Understanding the structure of one's native language is beneficial for learning a second language. Moreover, exploring the common "ties" of languages is extremely beneficial for **biliteracy,** especially for the Spanish language. The Spanish language has many similarities to the English language. Both languages are based on the alphabetic principle, share common sounds, and share common words and word parts that are derived from Latin. There are linguistic elements that can transfer from one language to the other. Focusing on the similarities of Spanish and English can promote biliteracy. ELLs' understanding of concepts in the second language can be facilitated by explicit instruction in the commonalities between the two languages.

Spanish is considered a romance language. Like English, it is based on an alphabetic system. Language has four distinct systems: phonology, morphology, syntax, and pragmatics. In addition, orthography is the written system of a language and relies on phonology and morphology. Phonology includes the study of the sounds of a language. It incorporates the rules that determine how sounds can be combined. Morphology includes the study of word meanings and the structure of the language. Morphemes are the smallest units of meaning in a language and include word parts such as roots, prefixes, and suffixes. Syntax, another system of language, includes the rules for word usage and word order. One might describe pragmatics as the social rules of a language necessary for language usage (Bloom & Lahey, 1978). Rules of conversation, turn-taking, and initiating a topic appropriately are all considered pragmatic language skills. Bloom and Lahey defined language as the integration of content (semantics and morphology), form (syntax and phonology), and use (pragmatics). This model can be applied to all languages. A strong foundation in language is necessary for literacy development. Finally, orthography incorporates the rules for how sounds can be represented in print. Knowing sound–symbol relationships assists students with spelling development. In addition, there are spelling and morphological patterns in Spanish that transfer to English.

LANGUAGE AND LITERACY CONNECTIONS

Language is a natural system. Humans have the ability to understand and communicate. Reading is also a language-based process. Reading is not a natural process, however. It is a skill that must be taught. Thus, in order to read, one's language system should be developed or developing. Language skills are necessary for successful reading skills. For example, phonology is necessary for phonological awareness, phonics, and orthography development. Morphology is necessary for understanding the structure of text, thus contributing to comprehension. Semantics is necessary for understanding the meaning of the words that are read. Pragmatics is necessary for composing and creating written language that is comprehensible. Biliteracy, therefore, requires knowing phonology, morphology, syntax, and pragmatics in both Spanish and English. Working with students in small groups is helpful for engaging students in using their pragmatic language skills. These skills can be facilitated through role playing, giving a topic and determining how students maintain the topic and take turns. Often, there are differences across cultures and language in the social use of language (see Chapter 3).

Spanish and English can serve mutually as resources for second language acquisition. Understanding the structure of one language facilitates the acquisition of the second language. Children who are provided with explicit instruction in all components of language and literacy are more likely to achieve biliteracy.

According to Bialystok (2002), when children learn literacy skills in a weak language at the same time as they learn to read in their strong language, the transfer of skills from the dominant language facilitates the literacy attainment in the weaker language. Individual differences in reading ability account for the variance in performance. Bialystok also reported that intact language proficiency skills increase the probability for literacy acquisition. Chiappe, Siegel, and Wade-Woolley (2002) determined that acquiring basic literacy skills for children with different backgrounds and cultures developed in a similar manner. Alphabetic knowledge and phonological processing were important contributors to children's early literacy performance. Phonological awareness is the ability to process, segment, and manipulate the sounds and syllables of a language. Phonological awareness includes skills such as rhyming, identifying sounds and syllables, and adding or deleting sounds and syllables within words. Phonemic awareness is the ability to process and manipulate the smallest unit of sound known as a phoneme. Phonological awareness was correlated with literacy skills by the end of kindergarten. In Spanish, phonemic awareness tended to be more highly related to literacy than rhyme identification and syllable identification. Other researchers reported similar results (Francis & Carlson 2003).

The importance of early development of strong second language skills is indicated by the fact that Hispanic 16- to 19-year-olds who have poor English language skills have dropout rates as high as 60% (Fry, 2003). Preventing reading disabilities is possible when individuals have the opportunity to learn in an explicit, systematic manner (National Institute for Child Health and Human Development [NICHD], 2000).

SPANISH PHONOLOGY AND ORTHOGRAPHY

Phonology is the system of rules that determine how sounds exist and can be combined in a language. Processing and understanding sounds of a language are necessary skills for reading English (Adams, 1990). Proficient Spanish readers also transfer phonological awareness skills to their reading (Quiroga, Lemons-Britton, Mostafapour, Abbott, & Berninger, 2000). Although Spanish is a syllabic language, in that it has reliable syllable patterns, knowing sounds (phonemes) at the beginning of reading instruction can assist with predicting future reading ability (Francis & Carlson, 2003). There are 23 phonemes in the Spanish language (Barrutia & Schwegler, 1994). Spanish has 5 vowel sounds and 18 consonant sounds. In addition, variations in Castillian Spanish include /th/, /zh/, and /v/.

The structure of the Spanish language consists of common syllable patterns. Some of the most common syllable patterns in Spanish are also common syllable patterns in English. The Spanish consonant–vowel (CV) pattern, as in *ma, pa, la,* and *sa,* is a basic syllable pattern and can be combined to form a CV-CV pattern, as in the words *mala, pala, sala, masa,* and *pasa.* Thousands of words can be formed from this common syllable pattern, which is regular in Spanish. The CV-CV pattern is divided after the first vowel. The vowel-consonant-vowel (VCV) syllable pattern is also common in the Spanish language. It can be divided after the first vowel. Spanish words such as *uno, oso,* and *ala* represent this syllable pattern. The English language also has the vowel-consonant-vowel (VCV) syllable type. It can be divided after the first vowel as in the words *pilot, token,* and *paper.* It can also be divided after the consonant as in the words *visit, exit,* and *valid.* Another common syllable pattern is the VC/CV pattern, as in the Spanish words *lista, isla, esta, hasta,* and *norte.* This syllable pattern is also common in the English language. In Spanish and English, the VC/CV pattern is divided between the two consonants. Reading teachers will utilize these common syllable patterns to practice reading multisyllabic words. In Spanish, the CVC syllable pattern is present, but fewer words in Spanish than in English utilize this pattern. Words in Spanish with this pattern include *mes, dos, las, gis,* and *luz.* Words in English using this pattern include *pat, met, his, cot,* and *cut* (see Chapter 9).

There are syllable types in English that will need to be explicitly taught. Those include the open, closed, vowel-pair, vowel-*r*, vowel-consonant-*e*, and final stable syllables. Some of these letter combinations or syllable patterns exist in the Spanish language. For example, the open and closed syllables are present in the Spanish language but are not taught in this manner because the vowel sounds in Spanish do not change. Spanish-speaking ELLs will have difficulty with the vowel-consonant-*e* pattern as they will tend to produce the final *e.* In Spanish, the pattern of a vowel and the letter *r* exists but is not taught in this manner because vowel sounds are regular and do not change.

ELLs will need to understand when vowel sounds are pronounced as short or long sounds in the English language. They will need to learn vowel-*r* syllables and unfamiliar vowel pairs, such as *ea, ei,* and *ou.* Vowel pairs such as *oi, ai,* and *eu* exist across the two languages; however, the pronunciation is not the same. Letter patterns that look similar to those in English, such as final stable syllable patterns, exist in Spanish. For example, the words *palacial* and *edición* are similar to the English final stable syllables *-cial* and *-tion.* Patterns in English with final *-le* will need to be explicitly taught as Spanish speakers will tend to produce the final silent letter *e.* Knowing English syllable types and the similarities and differences among the two languages will assist students with learning to read. Table 20.1 compares the syllable types across the English and Spanish languages.

Table 20.2 categorizes vowel sounds by three mouth positions. The vowel sounds produced in the back of the mouth are /o͞o/ and /ō/. When /o͞o/ and /ō/ are uttered as in *uno* and *hola,* they produce high and middle tones, respectively. The vowel /ä/ is produced in the central position of the mouth and has a low tone as in the Spanish word *amigo.* The long and short vowels /ē/ and /ĕ/ are produced toward the front of the mouth and have high and middle tones as in the Spanish words *iguana* and *elefante.*

Spanish consonant sounds can be characterized by the placement of the tongue and the **manner** of production (see Table 20.3) The sounds /b/ and /p/ are made with the two lips and are considered **bilabial** sounds (e.g., *bate, beso, piano, peso*) The manner in which they are produced is considered a stop because the air is abruptly stopped by the lips when the sound is produced.

The consonant sound /f/, a labiodental sound, is produced with the upper teeth placed on the lower lip. It is a fricative sound because it is produced by the friction of the teeth on the lower lip. The Spanish word *fiesta* begins with this sound. Speakers of

Table 20.1.   English and Spanish syllable types

English syllable type	Spanish syllable type
Closed syllable *těn*	Closed syllable—vowel sounds do not change *těn*
Open syllable *no*	Open syllable—vowel sounds do not change *no*
Vowel-consonant-*e* *base*	Vowel-consonant-*e* (*e* is pronounced) in Spanish *base*
Vowel-*r* syllable *arc*	Vowel-*r* syllable *arco*
Vowel-pair syllable *automobile*	Vowel-pair syllable *automóvil*
Final stable syllable *emotion*	Final stable syllable *emoción*

Castillian Spanish produce the fricative sound /th/, which is produced like the English /th/ sound as in the English word *bath*. This sound may also be produced as a dialectal variant for the /s/ sound in Spanish. The ridge behind the front teeth is known as the **alveolar ridge.** Sounds such as /n/ and /s/, which are produced with the tongue touching this ridge, are categorized as **alveolar** sounds. The Spanish words *sol* and *noche* begin with alveolar sounds. **Palatal** sounds are produced by the tongue touching the palate in the medial position. The Spanish words *yoyo* and *llanta* begin with the palatal sound /y/.

Speakers of Castillian Spanish produce this sound as /zh/. Sounds such as /k/ and /g/ are produced close to the structure in the back of the mouth known as the **velum.** These two particular **velar** sounds are categorized as stops because the air is stopped abruptly by the tongue (e.g., *kilo, gusano*).

By comparing the placement of the tongue and the manner of production of Spanish consonant sounds in Table 20.3 with those of English consonant sounds in Table 20.4, the well-informed teacher can understand the commonalities and possible sources of difficulty in learning the sounds in a second language. For example, the /ng/ sound can be difficult to produce for ELLs; however, it does exist in Spanish, as represented by the letter *n* before the /k/ sound as in *nunca*. In English, the letter *n* before the /k/ sound is produced as /ng/ as in the word *sink*. The Spanish sound represented by the letter *ñ* is not represented in English. Although the letter *r* transfers from Spanish to English, the sound is mostly trilled in Spanish and is not as trilled in English. It is also important to understand the medial *r* in Spanish when placed between two vowels is soft and not trilled; rather, it is pronounced as a **flap** sound. (A flap sound is produced when the

Table 20.2.   Spanish vowel sounds, by tone and mouth position

Tone	Mouth position		
	Front	Central	Back
Low	/ē/		/o͞o/
Middle		/ě/	/ō/
High		/ä/*	

*This is the obscure *a* sound as in the Spanish word *mañana*.

le 20.3. Spanish consonant sounds, by manner and place of articulation

nner of ‍culation	Place of articulation							
	Bilabial	Labiodental	Interdental	Dental	Alveolar	Palatal	Velar	Glottal
ɔ	/p/, /b/[a]			/t/, /d/			/k/, /g/	
‍al	/m/				/n/	/ñ/[b]		
‍ative		/f/, /v/[a]	/th/[c]		/s/	/zh/[c]	/h/[d]	/x/[e]
‍icate						/ch/		
‍uid					/r/, /l/, /rr/	/y/		
‍de	/w/							

Some dialects of Spanish do not use the /v/ sound and use the bilabial /b/ sound in its place. English language learners would benefit n learning these two sounds, as they correlate with the English sounds and thus facilitate the transfer to English.

The /ñ/ sound in Spanish can be an alveolar-palatal nasal sound.

The unvoiced /th/ sound and the /zh/ sound exist in Castilian Spanish.

The /h/ sound exists in Spanish and is spelled with the letter *j* or the letter *g* before *e* or *i*.

The /x/ sound is a glottal fricative as in the words *Xavier* and *Oaxaca*.

tongue strikes against another articulator, such as the palate, and then returns to its rest position.) The flapping of medial Spanish *r* is similar to the flap sounds of medial *d* and *t* in English as in the words *battle* and *ladder*. *Cara* and *pera* are examples of Spanish words with a medial flap. Therefore, medial *r* between two vowels transfers to medial *t* and *d* in English.

There are a total of 44 phonemes in English that are represented by 26 alphabetic symbols. Many sounds in Spanish and English directly transfer from one language to the other. The place, manner, and production are directly related in English and Spanish. As noted before, this facilitates the acquisition of phonology in the two languages. Table 20.5 illustrates the common consonant sounds between the two languages.

Although Spanish and English have some sounds in common, the orthographic representations of some of these sounds may differ. For example, /h/ is spelled with the letter *h* in English but with the letters *j* or *g* (before *e* or *i*) in Spanish. The /w/ exists in Spanish. In English, the /w/ sound is spelled with the letter *w*. In Spanish, the /w/ sound can be heard in words such as *guante* pronounced /gwanteh/ in English. This sound is produced in Spanish when the letter *g* or *c* is followed by *u*.

Spanish consists of a transparent orthographic system in that the correlations between the sounds and the symbol are regular and reliable. The English orthographic system is more complex as there are more rules and irregularities in the English language. It appears that the development of spelling is similar in English and Spanish;

Table 20.4. English consonant sounds, by manner and place of articulation

Manner of articulation	Place of articulation					
	Bilabial	Labiodental	Interdental	Alveolar	Palatal	Velar
Stop	/p/, /b/			/t/, /d/		/k/, /g/
Nasal	/m/			/n/		
Fricative		/f/, /v/	/th/ (unvoiced), /<u>th</u>/ (voiced)	/s/, /z/	/sh/,/zh/	/h/
Affricate					/ch/, /j/	
Liquid				/l/, /r/		
Glide	/hw/, /w/				/y/	

Table 20.5.   Common consonant sounds of Spanish and English

Manner of articulation	Placement						
	Bilabial	Labiodental	Interdental	Alveolar	Palatal	Velar	Glottal
Stop	/p/, /b/			[a]		/k/, /g/	
Nasal	/m/			/n/			
Fricative		/f/, /v/	/th/[b]	/s/	/zh/[b]	/h/	
Affricate					/ch/		
Liquid				/l/, /r/[c]			
Glide	/w/				/y/		

[a]The /t/ and /d/ sounds in Spanish are dental as they are produced in a slightly more forward position of the mouth than the English /t/ and /d/ sounds.

[b]The unvoiced /th/ sound and the /zh/ sound exist in Castilian Spanish and in English.

[c]This symbol represents the flap sound, which occurs as a medial sound in the American English pronunciation of the words *ladder* and *bottle* and in the Spanish words *cara* and *pera*.

however, students begin by understanding the sounds of a language and the representation of these sounds by symbols. Next, they then learn the patterns and morphological influences on spelling. Arteagoitia, Howard, Louguit, Malabonga, and Kenyon (2005) noted that Spanish spelling knowledge can transfer to English spelling abilities. Cárdenas-Hagan and Carlson (2009) suggested Spanish spelling can influence English spelling, and errors can result from overgeneralization of Spanish to English. One example would be using the Spanish letter *i* for the English long *e* sound. Errors may also be a result of Spanish sound approximations for English phonemes not present in Spanish. One example would be digraph *ch* for the English letter *j*. The difference between these two sounds is voicing, and these students can benefit from working with voiced and voiceless pairs of sounds, including /s/ and /z/, /f/ and /v/, and /sh/ and /zh/. Finally, as students transfer to the English language, they may overgeneralize English spelling for English words as do monolingual English speakers. Knowing the Spanish orthographic system does not negatively influence English spelling; instead, it is a more natural progression for developing spelling among bilingual students (Arteagoitia et al., 2005). Therefore, it is important for teachers to understand that spelling patterns transfer from one language to another. For example, in Spanish as well as English, the letter *c* before *a, o, u,* or consonants is produced as /k/. The letter *c* before *e* or *i* changes to the /s/ sounds as in words *mice* and *cinema* in English. In Spanish, words such as *centavo* and *cinco* are examples of the pattern. The spelling of the letter *g* before *a, o, u,* and consonants is produced as /g/ in English and Spanish. When the letter *g* is immediately before *e* or *i*, however, the sound changes to /j/ in English (e.g., *gem, gin*) and /h/ in Spanish (e.g., *gente, gigante*). Instructors must understand the language and spelling development levels of their bilingual students in order to better design spelling instruction.

SPANISH MORPHOLOGY

Morphology, the study of morphemes, assists students in decoding and also provides a foundation for vocabulary development and spelling in both Spanish and English (see Chapters 4 and 8). For example, the Spanish word *xilófono* has the morpheme *fono,* which means *sound.* Another example is the word *incompleto,* which contains the morpheme *in-,* meaning *not.* The Spanish word *adorable* includes the morpheme *-able,* which means *able to do.* Teachers can take advantage of the fact that Spanish has morphemes whose meanings are similar in English. These morphemes can take the form of base words, roots, prefixes, and suffixes that carry meaning (see Chapter 4). Studying morphemes can assist children in developing reading as well as increase vocabulary skills. Approximately 60% of English is derived from Latin (Lindzey, 2003). Spanish cognates, therefore, are extremely useful for ELLs. One study showed that Spanish cognates and word knowledge facilitated English vocabulary and reading comprehension (Durgunoglu, Nagy, & Hancin-Bhatt, 1993). Studying word families as groups of words helps readers infer meaning, especially when encountering words in context (Anderson & Nagy, 1992). Corson (1998) reported marked improvement for children who have studied the etymology of words and word relationships. Hancin-Bhatt and Nagy (1994) reported that Spanish-speaking elementary students are not likely to recognize cognates spontaneously. They will need explicit attention to the cognates in a systematic manner. Morphology is helpful for learning words and word meanings in a first and second language.

SPANISH SYNTAX

The Spanish language has its unique grammatical rules. In Spanish, as well as English, children learn the concept of nouns, which name a person, animal, place, thing, or idea. Verbs are considered action words. Adjectives and adverbs have a primary job and that is to describe. Adjectives describe nouns and adverbs describe verbs. The order of a grammatically correct sentence is what often causes the most difficulty when learning a language. In Spanish, for example, the adjective typically follows the noun. In order to describe pretty hair, one would say *pelo bonito,* with the noun placed before the adjective.

Nouns in Spanish have either a masculine or feminine gender. To learn the grammatical rules, an ELL may learn the rules in his or her native language and then apply or compare them with the rules of English syntax. For example, if a teacher is male, then he is referred to as *maestro* in Spanish. Nouns denoting males or animals that are males end in the letter *o.* Nouns denoting females or animals that are generally feminine must end with the letter *a.* A female teacher therefore is referred to as *maestra.* Spanish speakers must not only learn nouns but must also learn how to apply the rules of gender. Therefore, ELLs should be able to understand the concept of nouns because they do not have to learn the rules of gender for English.

The Spanish language has three regular classes of verbs, with infinitives ending in *-ar, -er,* and *-ir.* The regular tenses of verbs are formed by dropping the *-ar, -er,* and *-ir* and adding the endings shown in Table 20.6.

Table 20.6.   Regular Spanish verb endings

Person	Verb ending		
	-ar	-er	-ir
yo	-o	-o	-o
tú	-as	-es	-es
él, ella, usted	-a	-e	-e
nosotros	-amos	-emos	-imos
vosotros	-amaís	-eis	-is
ellos, ellas, ustedes	-an	-en	-en

Spanish adjectives ending in *o* change the *o* to *a* in the feminine gender. Adjectives ending in a vowel other than *o* have the same form for masculine or feminine. Adverbs related to manner are often formed in Spanish by adding the suffix *–mente* to the feminine form of the adjective.

Adjectives		
Masculine	Feminine	Adverbs
rápido	rápida	rápidamente
lento	lenta	lentamente
correcto	correcta	correctamente
triste	triste	tristemente
alegre	alegre	alegremente

COMMON TIES BETWEEN SPANISH AND ENGLISH

Instructors can facilitate English language literacy development by providing instruction that builds on native language and literacy knowledge.

Alphabets

There are 30 letters and digraphs that are regarded as individual letters in the Spanish alphabet and 26 letters in the English alphabet.

Spanish: a b c ch d e f g h i j k l ll m n ñ o p q r rr s t u v w x y z

English: a b c d e f g h i j k l m n o p q r s t u v w x y z

Although there is movement to remove *ch, ll, ñ,* and *rr* from the alphabet system, students at risk for reading difficulty benefit from one-to-one correspondence that is regular and stable. Each language has five letters to represent the vowels. Spanish vowels have consistent sounds and consistent spellings. They can also be combined to form diphthongs (two adjacent vowels in a syllable that blend together to make a new sound). English vowels can be short or long, form digraphs and diphthongs, or have unaccented sounds. English vowel sounds can have more than one frequent spelling. The sequential order of the English and Spanish alphabet is similar. In some cases it is useful for teachers to remove the digraphs from the Spanish alphabet; however, doing so can cause a decrease in the one-to-one letter–sound correspondence within the Spanish alphabet during early reading instruction. Struggling readers require regularity of the language and literacy system.

As noted previously, many sounds and symbols transfer from the Spanish language to English. There are 23 phonemes in Spanish compared with English, which contains 44 sounds. Phonemes that directly transfer from English to Spanish include: /b/, /ch/,/e/, /f/, /g/, /k/, /l/, /m/, /n/, /o/, /p/, /s/, /t/, /w/, and /y/ (see Figure 20.1). English and Spanish sound systems can be described by their articulatory manner of production. These concepts are useful for literacy in the two languages.

Diphthongs

Table 20.7 depicts the Spanish–English consonant and diphthong correlations, respectively. Notice that the Spanish vowels can combine to form diphthongs. Diphthong spellings such as *oy* and *au* directly transfer to the English language. If a Spanish vowel

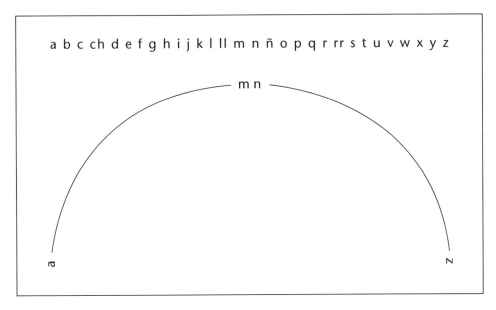

Figure 20.1. Alphabet sequencing mat for the Spanish alphabet.

pair is accented, then the two vowels are produced separately and are not combined (e.g., *oído, tía*).

MULTISENSORY INSTRUCTION OF LANGUAGE COMPONENTS IN SPANISH

Reading in two languages is possible when students' strengths and knowledge base are considered. The National Reading Panel (NRP; NICHD, 2000) reported important findings regarding the development of English reading skills. The results acknowledged the importance of direct, systematic instruction in phonological awareness, letter knowledge, phonics, vocabulary, reading fluency, and reading comprehension as skills im-

Table 20.7.   Spanish–English diphthong correlations

Spanish	English
ai (*bailarina*)	i (*light, like*)
au (*autobús*)	ou (*out*)
ey (*rey*)	ey (*they*)
ei (*peine*)	a (*pay*)
oi, oy (*oigan, voy*)	oi, oy (*oil, joy*)
ia (*media*)	ya (*yarn*)
ua (*cuando*)	wa (*wand*)
ie (*hielo*)	ye (*yet*)
ue (*cuete*)	we (*went*)
io (*radio*)	yo (*yoke*)
uo (*cuota*)	uo (*quote*)
iu (*ciudad*)	yu (*Yule*)
ui (*cuidar*)	wee (*week*)

portant for successful reading development. Considering the challenge of biliteracy, learning to read in two languages can be facilitated by transferring these same skills from one language to the other. The following exercises, which are similar to English reading instruction, were developed to facilitate teaching reading in Spanish. The first groups of activities presented are several levels of phonological awareness in a developmental progression of difficulty.

Phonological Awareness

The first activities under the category of phonological awareness begin with rhyming. Alliteration and syllable-level activities are described. Finally, phoneme blending and segmenting activities are presented.

Rhyme Identification

Children are manipulating an initial sound or cluster of sounds when they rhyme. This is sound manipulation and is necessary as a step toward achieving a higher level of phonological awareness, such as phoneme manipulation. Students and the teacher can utilize mirrors and observe that only the initial sound is substituted when rhyming words.

Teacher	Students	Teacher	Students	Teacher
(Digan = Say)		(¿Riman? = Do they rhyme?)		(Cambiamos . . . por . . . = We change . . . for . . .)
Digan *mía tía.*	mía tía	¿Riman?	Sí	Cambiamos /m/ por /t/.
Digan *sol gol.*	sol gol	¿Riman?	Sí	Cambiamos /s/ por /g/.
Digan *las mas.*	las mas	¿Riman?	Sí	Cambiamos /l/ por /m/.
Digan *sí no.*	sí no	¿Riman?	No	Cambiamos todos los sonidos. (We change all of the sounds.)
Digan *luna cuna.*	luna cuna	¿Riman?	Sí	Cambiamos /l/ por /k/.

Rhyme Generation

Rhyme generation is the ability to produce rhyming words. The teacher can scaffold this skill by using flashcards of Spanish letters. The ultimate goal is for student to perform this skill by listening. Therefore, the teacher dictates words that end in the same VCV pattern and asks the students to change the initial sound. One example is the ending *-asa.* Children can change the initial sound and generate rhyming words: *asa, casa, masa, pasa, taza.* Other endings include *-eso, -ano, -ala, -elo, -una.*

Rhyming

Teacher: Digan *mía.* (Say *mía.*)

Students: Mía

Teacher: Digan una palabra que rime con *mía.* (Say a word that rhymes with *mía.*)

Students: Tía

The teacher continues the activity with the following Spanish words: *sol, las, mes, gato, casa, luna, pino, nido, mal, pala,* and *usa.*

Alliteration Repetition and Identification

Alliterations are called *trabalenguas* in Spanish. It is important to initially have students repeat the alliteration and identify the common initial sound. Later, students can sing and generate Spanish alliterations.

1. Mí mamá me mima.

2. ¿Cómo Como? Como, como, como.

3. Tres tristes tigres tragan tres tragos.

4. Pepe Pecas pica papas con un pico pica papas Pepe Pecas.

Alliteration Generation

The teacher can scaffold the ability to produce alliterations by providing the first two words of the alliteration and asking the students to extend the alliteration with words that begin with the same initial sounds. As students progress, they can generate their own alliterations.

Teacher	Students
Manuel mira _____.	mangos, muebles, mariposas
Consuelo come _____.	carne, caldo, cacahuates
Triana toca _____.	tomates, tamales, timbres
Daniel debe _____.	dinero, donas, dulces

Syllable Blending

Children are asked to listen, repeat, and blend syllables to form words. They can use counters or their fingers to blend syllables and form words.

Teacher	Students	Teacher	Students
(Digan = Say)		(La palabra es = The word is)	
Digan /mä/ /sä/.	/mä/ /sä/	La palabra es	masa
Digan /lo͞o/ /nä/.	/lo͞o/ /nä/	La palabra es	luna
Digan /säl/ /gō/.	/säl/ /gō/	La palabra es	salgo
Digan /bä/ /tĕ/.	/bä/ /tĕ/	La palabra es	bate
Digan /mĕ/ /sä/.	/mĕ/ /sä/	La palabra es	mesa

Syllable Omission

Students can clap their hands, use counters, or use their fingers to practice syllable omission activities. They can also use their bodies and move from left to right as they repeat the syllables and then omit the movement when they delete a syllable. Total physical body response is a technique that will assist ELLs. Deleting an initial or a final syllable is easier than deleting a medial syllable, so the teacher should first ask students to delete initial and final syllables before moving on to deleting medial syllables.

Teacher	Students	Teacher	Students
(Digan = Say)		(Ahora digan . . . sin . . . = Now say . . . . .)	
Digan *mango*.	mango	Ahora digan *mango* sin *man*.	go
Digan *asiento*.	asiento	Ahora digan *asiento* sin *a*.	siento
Digan *silla*.	silla	Ahora digan *silla* sin *lla*.	si
Digan *rápido*.	rápido	Ahora digan *rápido* sin *rá*.	pido
Digan *abajo*.	abajo	Ahora digan *abajo* sin *ba*.	ajo

Phoneme Blending

Students can listen, repeat, and blend sounds to form words. They can use counters or their fingers to illustrate the concept of blending phonemes.

Teacher	Students	Teacher	Students
(Digan = Say)		(La palabra es = The word is)	
Digan /s/ /ä/ /l/.	/s/ / ä / /l/	La palabra es	sal
Digan /m/ /ĕ/ /s/.	/m/ /ĕ/ /s/	La palabra es	mes
Digan /g/ /ō/ /l/.	/g/ /ō/ /l/	La palabra es	gol
Digan /g/ /ä/ /t/ /ō/.	/g/ /ä/ /t/ /ō/	La palabra es	gato
Digan /b/ /ä/ /t/ /ĕ/.	/b/ /ä/ /t/ /ĕ/	La palabra es	bate

Phoneme Substitution

Students can use their mirrors to view the position of the mouth as they substitute the initial sounds.

Teacher	Students	Teacher	Students
(Digan = Say)		(Cambia . . . por . . . = Substitute/change . . . for . . .)	
Digan *mesa*.	mesa	Cambia /m/ por /p/.	pesa
Digan *luna*.	luna	Cambia /l/ por /t/.	tuna
Digan *sal*.	sal	Cambia /s/ por /m/.	mal
Digan *gato*.	gato	Cambia /g/ por /p/.	pato
Digan *cena*.	cena	Cambia /s/ por /p/.	pena

Alphabet Knowledge

Alphabet knowledge can be taught using manipulatives. Activities such as singing the alphabet, placing letters in order, and identifying missing letters can be performed in Spanish as well as English. The alphabet activities described in Chapter 6 can be incorporated into reading instruction in Spanish. One example is sequencing and manipulating plastic letters into an arc and teaching the sequential order of the alphabet (see Figure 20.1). The same procedures incorporated for acquiring alphabet knowledge in English can be utilized in Spanish. In addition, games that focus on a missing letter or a game of alphabet bingo can be used (see Chapter 6). As students begin to master phonological awareness and letter knowledge, they are prepared to learn letter–sound correspondences.

Letter–Sound Correspondences

Children learn new sounds by listening to words with common initial sounds, looking at the letter that represents the sound, and feeling their mouth and throat as they produce the sounds. They discover the letter, a key word, and a sound to facilitate the letter and sound correlation. Using flashcards depicting each letter, key word, and sound is helpful as students learn the letter–sound correspondences.

Teacher: Digan *pala, pesa, punto.* (Say *pala, pesa, punto.*)

Students: *pala, pesa, punto*

Teacher: ¿Cuál sonido oyeron ? (What sound did you hear in the beginning of the words?)

Students: /p/

Teacher: Miren su boca ¿Está abierta o cerrada? (Look at your mouth. Is it open or closed?)

Students: Cerrado por los labios. (Closed by the lips.)

Teacher: ¿Es vocal o consonante? (Is it a vowel or consonant?)

Students: Es consonante. (It is a consonant.)

Teacher: La palabra clave es *piano.* (The key word is *piano.*)

Students: Piano

Teacher: Letra *p,* piano, /p/. (Letter *p,* piano, /p/.)

Students: Letra *p,* piano, /p/. (Letter *p,* piano, /p/.)

It is important for Spanish speakers to learn the letter–sound correspondences in order to learn to decode. In one program, Spanish speakers are exposed to sounds, symbols, and words that directly transfer to the English language (Cárdenas-Hagan, 1998). For example, when learning the short *e* vowel sound, students learns the key word *elefante* (elephant). This letter, sound, and word can directly transfer to English, therefore facilitating the knowledge of letter–sound correlations from one language to the next. Letters, sounds, and key words in Spanish and English are illustrated in Table 20.8. Figure 20.2 shows key word pictures and letters.

Table 20.8. Key words and sounds in Spanish and English

Letter	Sound(s)	Spanish key word	English key word
b	/b/	bate	bat
c	/k/	cámara	camera
d	/d/	doctor	doctor
e	/e/	elefante	elephant
f	/f/	fuego	fire
g	/g/	ganso	goose
i	/i/	iguana	iguana
k	/k/	kilo	kilo
l	/l/	limón	lemon
m	/m/	mamá	mother
n	/n/	nido	nest
p	/p/	piano	piano
r	/r/	rosa	rose
s	/s/	sol	sun
t	/t/	tomate	tomato
y	/y/	yoyo	yoyo
x	/ks/	saxofón	saxophone

From Cárdenas-Hagan, E. (2000). *Esperanza training manual* (p. 18). Brownsville, TX: Valley Speech, Language, and Learning Center; reprinted by permission.

Auditory Discovery

Teacher: Estudiantes saquen sus espejos y miren su boca mientras que repiten estas palabras que tienen la misma raíz: *teléfono, micrófono xilófono*. (Students, take out your mirrors and look at your mouth as you repeat these words that have the same root: *telephone, microphone, xylophone*.)

Students: *Telefóno, micrófono, xilófono*

Visual Discovery

Teacher: Miren el pizarrón mientras que yo escribo las palabras *teléfono, micrófono, xilófono*. Cada palabra tiene la misma raíz. La raíz es ____. (Look at the board as I write the words *telephone, microphone,* and *xylophone*. Every word has the same root. The root is _____.)

Students: Fono (phone)

Tactile/Kinesthetic Discovery

Teacher: Miren y toquen mi teléfono. Yo uso el teléfono para oír los sonidos de la voz de otra persona. Miren y toquen mi xilófono. Ustedes pueden escuchar el sonido de este instrumento. Miren el micrófono. Ustedes pueden escuchar los sonidos de mi voz muy recio. Entonces el significado es _____. (Look at and touch my telephone. I use the telephone to listen to the sounds of another person's voice. Look and touch my xylophone. You can listen to the sounds of this instrument. Look at the

Figure 20.2.   Key word pictures and letters. (From Cárdenas-Hagan, E. [1998]. *Esperanza: A multisensory Spanish language program* [Reading deck cards]. Brownsville, TX: Valley Speech, Language, and Learning Center; adapted by permission.)

microphone. You can hear the sounds of my voice. It is loud. Therefore, the meaning of *phone* is _____.)

Students: Sonidos (sounds)

Teacher: Miren la tarjeta de la raíz *fono*. La palabra clave es *micrófono*.

Conocen otras palabras con la raíz *fono?* (Look at this card with the root *phone*. The key word is *microphone*. Do you know other words with this root?)

Students: Audífonos, fonología, megáfono (audiophones, phonology, megaphone)

Teacher: Muy bien. Ahora pueden usar estas palabras con la raíz *fono*. (Very good. Now you can use these words with the root *phone*.)

Ahora pueden crea oraciones con las palabras *audífonos, fonología, y megáfono*. (Now you can create sentences with the words *audiophones, phonology,* and *megaphone*.)

Tables 20.9–20.12 are helpful to teachers working with ELLs. These tables display the correlations between Spanish and English prefixes, suffixes, and roots and their meanings in both languages. Reaching beyond phonics and basic orthographic patterns, these comparisons can lead to a wider understanding of the similarities and differences in the meaning units of Spanish and English. Students can write the affixes and roots on index cards with their meanings and examples on the back to form a deck for review and practice during reading lessons. Teachers may use the graphic organizer shown in Table 20.12 as a tool for multisensory introduction of base words and affixes.

In addition, there are words that are cognates between languages. Some words are similar in orthography and meaning (true cognates). Other cognates have different orthography and meanings (false cognates). For example the word *largo* in Spanish means *long*. The English word *large* looks similar, but the meaning is different. Teachers will need to be aware of *true* and *false* cognates.

True cognates		False cognates	
English	Spanish	English	Spanish
animal	animal	pie	pie
doctor	doctor	large	largo
kilo	kilo	embarrassed	embarazada
capital	capital	ten	ten
natural	natural	red	red
jaguar	jaguar	sin	sin
cereal	cereal	son	son
zebra	zebra	fin	fin

Syntax

The Spanish language has the same parts of speech with the same functions as English: nouns, verbs, articles, adjectives, adverbs, conjunctions, and prepositions. Knowing the rules of one language and the similarities and differences with the second language is helpful for learning to read and write. Students can be taught the similarities between Spanish and English.

Similarities of Rules to Learn

- Nouns name a person, place, thing, or idea.

- Verbs are used for depicting action.

- Articles come before a noun.

- Adverbs describe verbs.

- Adjectives describe nouns.

- Conjunctions connect thoughts.

- Prepositions are words that relate to other words.

Table 20.9. Spanish prefixes and their English correlations

Spanish		English	
Prefix	Meaning	Prefix	Meaning
ante-	antes	ante-	before
anti-	contra	anti-	against
con-	unión	con-	with
contra-	contra	contra-	against
des-	negación	dis-	not
dis-	oposición	dis-	not
ex-	afuera de-	ex-	outside of
extra-	más	extra-	above
in-	no	in-	not
inter-	entre	inter-	between
intro-	dentro	intro-	within
multi-	mucho	multi-	many
pre-	antes	pre-	before
pro-	por	pro-	for
re-	repetir	re-	again
sin-	con	syn-	with
sub-	debajo	sub-	under
super-	sobre	super-	above
trans-	al otro lado	trans-	across
tri-	tres	tri-	three
uni-	uno	uni-	one

From Cárdenas-Hagan, E. (2000). *Esperanza training manual* (p. 19). Brownsville, TX: Valley Speech, Language, and Learning Center; reprinted by permission.

Activities for Learning Syntax in Spanish

Teacher: Miren, yo hablo español. Miren, ahora yo camino. Miren, ahora yo brinco. (Look, I speak Spanish. Look, I walk. Look, I jump.)

Digan *hablo, camino, brinco.* (Say *hablo, camino, brinco.*)

Estas palabras son verbos. Cada palabra termina en la letra *o.* El verbo es *hablar.* En el presente indicativo pongo la letra *o* al final de cada palabra. Ahora pueden usar el verbo *apagar.* (These words are verbs. Each word ends in the letter *o.* The verb is *hablar.* In the present indicative I place the letter *o* at the end of each word. Now you can use the verb *apagar.*)

Students: Yo apago.

Teacher: Muy bien usaron la leta *o* al final del verbo *apagar.* (Very good. You used the letter *o* at the end of the verb.)

Sigue con los verbos. (Continue with the following verbs.)

- hallar
- lavar

Table 20.10.   Spanish suffixes and their English correlations

Spanish		English	
Suffix	Meaning	Suffix	Meaning
-able	capaz de	-able	able to
-ancia	forma de ser	-ance	state of being
-ano	nativo	-an	native of
-ante	alguien que	-ant	one who
-cial	en relación con	-cial	related to
-ción	estado de	-tion	state of being
-encia	estado de	-ence	state of being
-idad	calidad de	-ity	quality of
-ido	en relación con	-id	related to
-ista	alguien que	-ist	one who
-itis	inflamación	-itis	inflammation
-ito	diminutivo	-ite	related to
-ivo	causa de	-ive	causing
-lento	en relación con	-lent	relating to
-osis	enfermedad	-osis	disease
-oso	lleno de	-ous	full of
-sión	estado de	-sion	state of being
-tad	forma de ser	-ty	state of being
-undo	en relación con	-und	related to
-ura	estado de	-ness	state of being

From Cárdenas-Hagan, E. (2000). *Esperanza training manual* (p. 20). Brownsville, TX: Valley Speech, Language, and Learning Center; reprinted by permission.

- llamar
- llevar
- recomendar
- sacar
- tirar
- trabajar
- pintar
- visitor

Adolescent English Language Learners

It is necessary to describe the needs of our adolescent ELLs. It is reported that there is a 24-point score gap between Hispanic and Caucasian eighth-grade students' reading achievement, which was not significantly different from the gaps in 2007 and 1992 (NCES, 2009b). In addition, the percentage of Hispanic students grew from 8% to 20%. The ability to read is a necessary skill for success in school. When ELLs enter the public educational system in middle school or high school, these students will have to mas-

Table 20.11. Spanish roots and their English correlations

Spanish		English	
Root	Meaning	Root	Meaning
audi	oír	audi	to hear
auto	solo	auto	by itself
cent	cien	cent	one hundred
ducto	guiar	duct	to lead
fam	fama	fam	famous
fin	final	fin	final
fono	sonido	phono	sound
graf	escribir	graph	written
gram	peso	gram	weight
kilo	mil	kilo	one thousand
liber	libre	liber	free
lingua	lengua	lingua	tongue
logía	estudio de	ology	study of
luna	lunar	luna	moon
metro	medida	meter	measure
novel	nuevo	novel	new
port	cargar	port	carry
semi	mitad	semi	half
tract	estirar	tract	to pull
trans	cruzar	trans	across
vis	ver	vis	to see
voc	voz	voc	voice

From Cárdenas-Hagan, E. (2000). *Esperanza training manual* (p. 21). Brownsville, TX: Valley Speech, Language, and Learning Center; reprinted by permission.

ter complex coursework. They will need further language development because they have had limited exposure to the English language. Therefore, these students will need to develop academic literacy that involves reading, writing, listening, and speaking. The Adolescent English Language Learner Literacy Advisory Panel (Short & Fitzsimmons, 2007) suggested that adolescent ELLs will need much more time developing vocabulary and background knowledge when compared with their monolingual English peers. ELLs will need integration of reading, writing, speaking, and listening across the curriculum (Genesee, Lindholm-Leary, Saunders, & Christian, 2006). It will be important to teach students who do not read or write the foundation skills of phonemic awareness and phonics and work on vocabulary comprehension and fluency (August & Shanahan, 2006). Once the basic skills of literacy are attained, then adolescent ELLs will need to use reading and writing processes such as previewing, making predictions, paraphrasing, brainstorming, drafting, editing, and publishing. Adolescent ELL literacy is enhanced when students are taught using a process-based approach (Garcia & Godina, 2004). It is important for all teachers to integrate reading comprehension strategies during their instruction. ELLs will also benefit from learning basic and academic vocabulary throughout the school day. Using visual graphic organizers and demonstrations can help these students better understand the new concepts and the new

Table 20.12. Enseñanza de prefijos, sufijos o raíces (in Spanish and English)

Descubrimiento auditivo	Nombra tres palabras con el prefijo, sufijo o raíz. Los estudiantes repitan la palabra. Los estudiantes nombren el prefijo, sufijo o raíz gue oyeron.
Visual	La maestra escribe tres palabras en el pizarrón. Los estudiantes pueden ver el prefijo, sufijo o raíz.
Significado kinestético	La maestra usa cada palabra en una oración. La maestra puede demostrar el significado de la palabra. La maestra usa las tarjetas de prefijos, sufijos o raíces. Los estudiantes escriben una oración para cada palabra. Los estudiantes usan y escriben los palabras en sus cuadernos de vocabulario.
Auditory discovery	Name three words with the prefix, suffix, or root. The students repeat the words. The students name the prefix, suffix, or root that they heard.
Visual discovery	The teacher writes three words on the board. The students can see the prefix, suffix, or root.
Kinesthetic discovery	The teacher uses each word in a sentence. The teacher can demonstrate the meaning of the word. The teacher uses prefix, suffix, or root cards. The students write a sentence for each word. The students use the words and write them in their vocabulary notebooks for further reference.

vocabulary words (August & Shanahan, 2006). Once again, using native language as a resource for words that are cognates is helpful in developing English vocabulary.

Adolescent ELLs also benefit from reciprocal teaching whereby teachers and students share responsibility for a dialogue centered on understanding the meaning of text (Rivera, Moughamian, Lesaux, & Francis, 2008). Reciprocal teaching has been described as successful in improving the reading and oral language proficiency outcomes for middle school ELLs who had learning difficulties (Klinger & Vaughn, 1996). More research is needed in the area of adolescent literacy. Instructors will need to continue to address language development as well as content knowledge. ELLs are doing twice the cognitive work—developing language and content. This is possible when instructors have an understanding of their language proficiency skills, literacy skills, and content-area knowledge (see Chapter 17).

Biliteracy Education Model

A biliteracy model was implemented in a small city along the Texas–Mexico border. Indeed, the citizens shared the necessity to speak in two languages. The community also shared a vision with the local public school district that it was important to become bicultural and biliterate. A 5-year strategic plan was developed that included intensive professional development for all kindergarten through third-grade teachers in two programs, *Esperanza* (Cárdenas-Hagan, 1998) for Spanish literacy and *Language Enrichment* (Carreker, 1992) for English literacy. Bilingual classrooms were provided on-site training with the *Esperanza* program. The school district considered these two programs as the core reading programs. Its strategic plan was approved by the local school board, which demonstrated a commitment to the reading reform effort from the classroom to the top administrators of the school district to the school board and to the community.

The students in bilingual classrooms participated in the *Esperanza* program (Cárdenas-Hagan, 1998) on a daily basis during the 90-minute language arts block. The students were therefore exposed to phonological awareness, phonics, vocabulary, reading fluency, and reading comprehension in their native language. In January of the first-grade year, students continued with their Spanish literacy instruction but were also introduced to the *Language Enrichment* (Carreker, 1992) program during their English as a second language period. Both of these programs are multisensory, systematic, and structured language approaches for language and literacy instruction. Parallel activities were conducted in the two languages. Each lesson incorporated systematic and structured reviews of previous lessons. Students were exposed to auditory, visual, tactile, and kinesthetic modalities in order to learn new reading, language, or writing concepts. As the students learned a new concept, they immediately applied it to reading, writing, and spelling.

From second grade to the end of third grade, the students in the bilingual classrooms continued with vocabulary and comprehension instruction in Spanish and focused on reading English utilizing the *Language Enrichment* (Carreker, 1992) program until the end of third grade.

Teachers were provided with monthly updates and at least two *Esperanza* (Cárdenas-Hagan, 1998) coaching sessions during the school year. The program included instruction in phonological awareness, letter–sound correspondences, decoding, reading fluency, alphabet knowledge, writing, spelling, vocabulary, oral language, syntax, and comprehension. The *Language Enrichment* (Carreker, 1992) program was implemented once students demonstrated grade-level literacy in Spanish. This program involved a 5-day training for teachers with at least one mentoring session. Instructional facilitators were trained to provide staff support at the campus level. The school district reported an 84% reduction in referrals for special education services such as dyslexia by year 3 of the project. Figure 20.3 shows the percentage of students requiring intervention (the students in the remediate group) in the school district dropped from 26% to 13%. The school district continued to implement an RTI model and was awarded the Broad Prize for Urban Education in 2008 for outperforming similar districts in the country who had similar demographics and challenges. A monetary award was then utilized for scholarships for graduating seniors. The future will look hopeful for these first generation college-bound seniors.

CONCLUSION

Reading in two languages is possible when students' strengths and knowledge base are considered. The NRP (NICHD, 2000) reported important findings regarding the development of English reading skills. The results acknowledged the importance of phonemic awareness, phonics, vocabulary, reading fluency, and reading comprehension as skills important for successful reading development. Now consider the challenge of biliteracy. Learning to read in two languages can be facilitated by incorporating similar skills from one language to the next in a systematic, direct, and comprehensive instructional program that focuses on the structure of each language using instruction to facilitate learning. Implementing an RTI model will enhance the understanding of the language and literacy needs of ELLs. Differentiated instruction benefits all students, including those who are learning English as a second language.

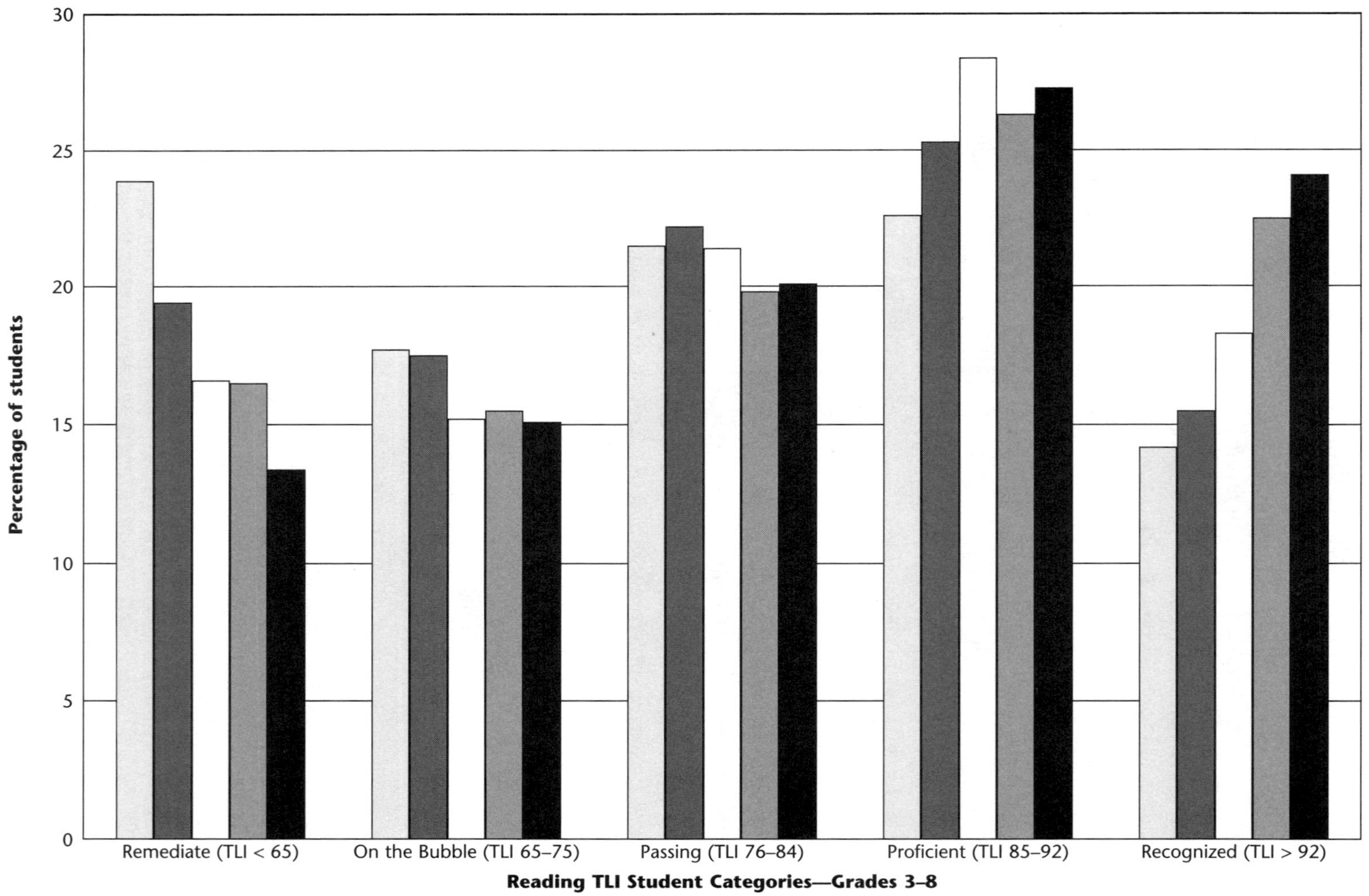
Percentage of students
30
25
20
15
10
5
0
Remediate (TLI < 65)
On the Bubble (TLI 65–75)
Passing (TLI 76–84)
Proficient (TLI 85–92)
Recognized (TLI > 92)
Reading TLI Student Categories—Grades 3–8

Figure 20.3. Texas Learning Index 5-year progress report for students in a biliteracy program. (*Key:* 1996–1997, 1997–1998, 1998–1999, 1999–2000, 2000–2001.)

REFERENCES

Adams, M.J. (1990). *Beginning to read: Thinking and learning about print.* Cambridge, MA: The MIT Press.

Anderson, R.C. , & Nagy, W.I. (1992). The vocabulary conundrum. *American Educator, 16*(4), 14–18, 44–47.

Arteagoitia, I., Howard, E.R., Louguit, M., Malabonga, V., & Kenyon, D. (2005). Spanish developmental contrastive spelling test: An instrument for investigating intra-linguistic and crosslinguistic influences on Spanish-spelling development. *Bilingual Research Journal, 29*(1), 541–560.

August A., & Hakuta, K. (Eds.). (1997). *Improving school for language-minority children: A research agenda.* Washington, DC: National Academies Press.

August, D.L., & Shanahan, T. (2006). Introduction and methodology. In D.L. August & T. Shanahan (Eds.), *Developing literacy in a second language: Report of the National Literacy Panel.* Mahwah, NJ: Lawrence Erlbaum Associates.

Barrutia, R., & Schwegler, A. (1994). *Fonética y fonología españolas* (2nd ed.). New York: Wiley.

Bialystok, E. (2002). Acquisition of literacy in bilingual children: A framework for research. *Language learning, 52*(1), 159–199

Bloom, L., & Lahey, M. (1978). *Language development and language disorders.* New York: Wiley.

Cárdenas-Hagan, E. (1998). *Esperanza: A multisensory Spanish language program.* Brownsville, TX: Valley Speech, Language, and Learning Center.

Cárdenas-Hagan, E. (2000). *Esperanza training manual.* Brownsville, TX: Valley Speech, Language, and Learning Center.

Cárdenas-Hagan, E., & Carlson, C.D. (2009). *Orthography and ELLs.* Paper presented at Tejas Lee Reading Conference, San Antonio, Texas.

Carreker, S. (1992). *Language enrichment: Reading concepts manual.* Houston, TX: Neuhaus Education Center.

Chiappe, P., Siegel, L., & Wade-Woolley, L. (2002). Linguistic diversity and the development of reading skills. *Scientific Studies of Reading, 6*(4), 369–400.

Corson, D. (1998). *Language policy in schools: A resource for teachers and administrators.* Mahwah, NJ: Lawrence Erlbaum Associates.

Durgunoglu, A.Y., Nagy, W.E., & Hacin-Bhatt, B.J. (1993). Cross-language transfer of phonological awareness. *Journal of Education Psychology, 85,* 453–465.

Francis, D., & Carlson, C. (2003). Tejas Lee Early Spanish Reading Symposium, Houston, Texas.

Fry, R. (2003, June). *Hispanic youth dropping out of U.S. Schools: Measuring the challenge.* Washington, DC: Pew Hispanic Center.

Fry, R., & Gonzales, F. (2008). *One-in-five and growing fast: A profile of Hispanic public school students.* Retrieved January 18, 2010, from http://pewhispanic.org/files/reports/89.pdf

Garcia, G.E., & Godina, H. (2004). Addressing the literacy needs of adolescent English language learners. In T. Jetton & J. Dole (Eds.), *Adolescent literacy: Research and practice* (pp. 304–320). New York: Guilford Press.

Genesee, F., Lindholm-Leary, K., Saunders, W., & Christian, D. (2006). *Educating English language learners: A synthesis of research evidence.* New York: Cambridge University Press.

Hancin-Bhatt, B.J., & Nagy, W.E. (1994). Lexical transfer and second language morphological development. *Applied Psycholinguistics, 15*(3), 289–310.

Individuals with Disabilities Education Improvement Act (IDEA) of 2004, PL 108-446, 20 U.S.C. 1400 §§ *et seq.*

Klingner, J.K., & Vaughn, S. (1996). Reciprocal teaching of reading strategies for students with learning disabilities who use English as a second language. *The Elementary School Journal, 96,* 275–293.

Linan-Thompson, S., Vaughn, S., Prater, K., & Cirino, P. (2006). The response to intervention of English language learners at risk for reading problems. *Journal of Learning Disabilities, 39,* 390–398.

Lindzey, G. (2003). *Why study Latin?* [Brochure]. Retrieved December 23, 2004, from http://www.promotelatin.org/latin.htm

National Center for Education Statistics. (2009a). *Fast facts.* Retrieved January 24, 2011, from http://nces.ed.gov/fastfacts/display.asp

National Center for Education Statistics. (2009b). *National assessment of educational progress/nation's report card.* Retrieved April 21, 2010, from http://nces.ed.gov/nationsreportcard/nde/viewresults.asp

National Institute of Child Health and Human Development. (2000). *Report of the National Reading Panel: Reports of the subgroups. Teaching children to read: An evidence-based assessment of the scientific research literature on reading and its implications for reading instruction* (NIH Publication No. 00-4754). Washington, DC: Government Printing Office.

No Child Left Behind Act of 2001, PL 107-110, 115 Stat. 1425, 20 U.S.C. §§ 6301 *et seq.*

Quiroga, T., Lemons-Britton, Z., Mostafapour, E., Abbott R.D., & Berninger, V.W. (2000). Phonological awareness and beginning reading in Spanish-speaking ESL first grade: Research into practice. *Journal of School Psychology, 40*(1), 85–111.

Rivera, M.O., Moughamian, A.C., Lesaux, N.K., & Francis, D.J. (2008). *Language and reading interventions for English language learners and English language learners with disabilities.* Portsmouth, NH: RMC Research Corporation, Center on Instruction.

Short, D., & Fitzsimmons, S. (2007). *Double the work: Challenges and solutions to acquiring language and academic literacy for adolescents English language learners.* A report to Carnegie Corporation. Washington, DC: Alliance for Excellent Education.

U.S. Census Bureau. (2000). *Population.* Retrieved from http://www.census.gov/population

Vaughn, S., Cirino, P.T., Thompson, L., et al. (2006, Autumn). Effective of a Spanish intervention and an English intervention for English language learners at risk for reading problems. *American Educational Research Journal, 43*(3), 449–487.

Vaughn, S., & Fuchs, L.S. (2003). Redefining learning disabilities as inadequate response to treatment: The promise and potential problems. *Learning Disabilities Research and Practice, 18*(3), 137–146.

Vaughn, S., Mathes, P., Linan-Thompson, S., et al. (2006). Effectiveness of and English intervention for first-grade English language learners at risk for reading problems. *The Elementary School Journal, 107*(2), 153–180.

21

Multisensory Mathematics Instruction

MARGARET B. STERN

This chapter is devoted to describing the Structural Arithmetic (Stern & Stern, 1971) method of teaching mathematical concepts, in which multisensory materials are used. Over much of her lifetime, Catherine Stern, working with her daughter-in-law, Margaret Stern (author of this chapter), and her daughter, Toni Gould, crafted instructional tools and systematic methods to develop children's visual, spatial, and kinesthetic sense of mathematical relationships as the foundation for higher level mathematics. For more than 60 years the Structural Arithmetic approach has been used both as a foundation for young children and as a robust remedial program for students of all ages. Rooted in spatial-mathematical relationships and the ways they intersect with the number line, the Stern approach develops fundamental understandings that have come to be called "number sense."

When taught with this method, children achieve mastery of arithmetic without being forced to learn by memorizing and parroting. These materials provide children with the opportunity to gain insight into mathematical ideas and to enjoy the effectiveness of their own minds. For example, if a child makes a "mistake" by selecting a block that is too big to fit into a groove, the mistake has meaning and the child corrects himself, adding to his number sense of bigger and smaller. After giving the Structural Arithmetic materials to her students, one first-grade teacher cried, "They teach themselves!"

The author would like to acknowledge and thank Temple Ary, Math Chair, Ramaz Lower School, New York; Kate Garnett, Professor, Hunter College Graduate Program in Learning Disabilities; and Frederick Stern, Clinical Psychologist. All three made essential contributions to the introduction by locating the ideas of this chapter in the context of current research. I am immeasurably grateful for their hard work and for their enduring confidence in this approach to teaching arithmetic.

Researchers have pushed for a greater emphasis on the critical need of understanding math (Campione, Brown, & Connell, 1988; Gersten, Jordan, & Flojo, 2005). The National Council of Teachers of Mathematics' (NCTM) *Curriculum Focal Points for Prekindergarten Through Grade 8 Mathematics: A Quest for Coherence* called for a sharpened focus on the most critical aspects of pre-K–8 mathematics (2006, p. 5). Despite these nationally endorsed guidelines, instructional tools that actually develop and secure robust math understandings have remained elusive in much classroom practice, especially for students with significant learning disabilities affecting math performance.

A structured, multisensory teaching approach is of special importance to children with learning disabilities. These students are struggling with a combination of deficits that includes difficulty with language concepts and memory associations and difficulties with attention. These students often have trouble "getting things" from books and need to receive and integrate information from as many different senses as possible. Structural Arithmetic guides students through a careful sequence of activities with crafted materials designed to make mathematical concepts explicit and memorable.

The materials described in this chapter convey concepts through structures that are true to the mathematical relationships being taught. To understand these relationships, children pick up the materials and measure and compare them. A concept or a quantity is presented in context rather than in isolation so that children can explore and discover the different mathematical relationships that are possible. Good multisensory materials not only stimulate such activities but also present concepts so vividly and clearly that children can visualize them later. As you read this chapter, try the activities and games, experiencing how clear mathematical concepts become with structured, graspable, mentally anchoring materials employed systematically.

More than 100 sequenced activities and games have been gathered together in the teacher's guides titled *Experimenting with Numbers: A Guide for Preschool, Kindergarten, and First Grade Teachers* (Stern, 1988) and *Structural Arithmetic Workbooks 1–3 and Teachers' Guides* (Stern & Gould, 1988–1992). They are the result of the further development of the original work published in *Children Discover Arithmetic: An Introduction to Structural Arithmetic* (Stern & Stern, 1971), which provides illustrated directions that make teaching with multisensory structured materials much easier. (For more information on the Structural Arithmetic approach go to http://www.SternMath.com.)

What is involved in the formation of concepts? Current neuropsychological and educational research points to spatial understanding as central to mathematical understanding (Butterworth, 2005; Dehaene, 1997). Mathematical concepts are rooted in spatial concepts, and children seem to reason with mental pictures (Krasa & Shunkwiler, 2009). Therefore, when teaching children to think, we must develop their ability to form images. This ability is emphasized in a report published by the Institute of Education Sciences (Gersten et al., 2009) titled *Assisting Students Struggling with Mathematics: Response to Intervention (RtI) for Elementary and Middle Schools.*

> In the view of the panel, the ability to express mathematical ideas using visual representations and to convert visual representations into symbols is critical for success in mathematics. A major goal of interventions should be to systematically teach students how to develop visual representations and how to transition these representations to standard symbolic representations used in problem solving. (2009, p. 30)

Math learners must build mental representation of spatial-math relations (i.e., concepts) and link these to an evolving mental number line. Furthermore, they need to learn the precise ways we talk, and teach, about these spatial/math relational concepts (e.g., more/less, equal, fewer, same as, difference, before/after, between, near/far, larger/smaller, etc.). "Spatial thinking is at the heart of almost all mathematical thought...being able to translate freely between conventional verbal or symbolic formats and spatial images can facilitate the solving of many types of mathematical problems" (Krasa & Shunkwiler, 2009, p. 33).

Instruction using such concrete representations in systematic and sufficiently practiced ways—and talked about in clear, consistent language—lays a mathematical bedrock for a range of learners, from young children to elementary students with "glitches" of language or attention and to individuals with serious spatial processing deficits.

Multisensory materials will have fulfilled their purpose when the children can visualize the concepts presented. It is not sufficient, however, for the children to visualize a quantity in isolation; they must be able to visualize it in relation to other numbers and turn it around in their minds, and they must understand the actions that can be performed on it. For example, a teacher turned a pattern board with blanks for eight cubes face down and asked Sean to build the cube pattern he thinks will fit into it. When Sean built the eight pattern correctly, he explained, "I imagined it in my brain, then I built it, then I turned the board over, and the cubes all fit!"

In addition to mental pictures, language plays a crucial role in forming concepts. The best way to teach children the meaning of spoken language is to give them the opportunity to see and touch what the words describe and, thus, work out for themselves what the words mean. In many of the math games in this chapter, children are asked to follow spoken directions, which develops both their receptive language and their auditory memory. It is especially important for children with language deficits to develop these abilities.

In mathematics, as in any other subject, language is a vehicle for thought; therefore, students need many opportunities to put newly discovered concepts into their own words. Parroting the words of the teacher is not a sign of true learning. Instead, the teacher should often encourage students to talk about concepts by asking them, "How did you figure out your answer?"

In the Structural Arithmetic approach, the children progress from activities and games with concrete materials that help them form basic concepts to the final steps of recording addition and subtraction facts with number symbols, or numerals. Here are the steps of Structural Arithmetic, stated as goals and objectives, to be followed in the first years of mathematics instruction:

- *Level I:* To discover size relationships between amounts from 1 to 10, to know where each comes in the sequence from 1 to 10, to recognize odd and even numbers built as cube patterns, and to form number combinations with sums ranging from 1 to 10 using number blocks

- *Level II:* To learn number names and how to count from 1 to 10, to understand terms such as *bigger than* and *smaller than,* and to recite the addition facts with sums of 10 or less that have been discovered with the materials

- *Level III:* To identify and write the numerals 1–10 and 0, to understand the amount each numeral stands for, to understand the meaning of addition or subtraction equations, to write the answers to addition facts with sums of 10 or less and the answers to their related subtraction facts, and to demonstrate the solution of a word problem with materials and then record the addition or subtraction equation used to solve it

At Levels I and II, the amounts from 1 to 10 are introduced in two different ways: with groups of cubes to be counted and with number blocks. For example, the amount of 4 is introduced both with four single cubes and by a number block called a *4-block,* which looks like four cubes glued together in a straight line. Number symbols or numerals are introduced later on. Children realize that they can name a small number block of two or three units at a glance but that they need to verify the name of a longer number block of eight or nine units by counting its units. They soon realize that each number block is easily recognized by its relative size, its position in the sequence from 1 to 10, and its color (a peripheral characteristic that is not mathematical). For example, children learn that the 10-block is the biggest number block, stands last in the sequence from 1 to 10, and is blue. The 9-block, thus, is recognized as the next-to-biggest number block, comes just before the last number block, and is black. These characteristics enable children to identify each number and study its changing role in different situations.

FIRST EXPERIMENTS: THE COUNTING BOARD

Children begin exploring number concepts by fitting cubes or number blocks into grooves of the counting board (see Figure 21.1). Using the board, the children carry out many experiments on their own. Concrete materials alone, however, do not lead to developing mathematical thinking. The number blocks or cubes must be looked at, picked up, compared, and fit into activities that have been fashioned to clearly show the structure of our base-10 number system. The teacher as well as children must put discoveries and relationships into words. Once the students understand these concepts, the teacher introduces the symbols that stand for them (see the section called Number Symbols and Signs: Level III).

Number Concepts and Language: Levels I and II

Children discover the many things they can do with numbers by experimenting with materials. Soon they are impatient to tell each other about their discoveries. Once they

Figure 21.1. The counting board: Matching number markers to numerals on the number guide.

have learned the number names of the blocks, they begin to express their thoughts in language that comes to them naturally. For example, Sumi might point to a 5-block and a 3-block and say, "I am 5, but my brother is only 3." When children express ideas about numbers in their own words, they will have a more secure understanding of the language of mathematics when they hear it later. Teachers who listen to their students' words are often alerted to difficulties in comprehension and are able to give help before the problems cause even more trouble. In more formal environments, teachers give children orders to carry out. In doing so, children show whether they understand new vocabulary. For instance, a teacher might say, "Add 3 and 2, and tell me what 3 plus 2 equals." Students respond by adding together a 3-block and a 2-block and placing them alongside a 5-block. The students see that 3 and 2 are "the same size as 5," which they learn is expressed by the words "equals 5." The relationship among the blocks enables the children to gain this insight. In contrast, the piecemeal act of counting single cubes often camouflages the meaning of the word *equal*.

Number Symbols and Signs: Level III

The teacher should introduce number symbols (numerals) after number concepts have been explored. The teacher fits the number guide into the slot at the top of the counting board (see Figure 21.1). When attached, the number guide shows where each numeral comes in the sequence from 1 to 10. Each numeral appears above the groove that holds the number of cubes or the number block for which it stands (e.g., the 10 on the number guide appears above the groove that can hold 10 cubes or a 10-block). Empty spaces for number markers or tiles bearing the numerals 1–10 are between the number guide and the grooves. A line beneath the numeral on each number marker indicates the correct orientation of that numeral (e.g., 6 indicates the marker is for 6, not 9). Having children match the numerals on the markers to the numerals on the number guide is an excellent check of the children's ability to perceive symbols and position them correctly. This step prevents errors that might arise when the children try to read or write numerals.

The teacher then lets the numerals "call back" the number blocks, which is an activity that the children enjoy. The teacher says, "Pick a number. Where does it go?" A child selects a number marker such as 3, matches it to the 3 on the number guide, then finds the 3-block and fits it into the 3-groove.

Building Basic Concepts

Children who do not know math facts (e.g., 4 + 4 = 8) will have had difficulty learning them by rote and will resort to counting them out repeatedly because they have become rigidly attached to the "counting song." Such children profit from remedial work with basic math concepts. When they realize they can learn basic concepts by playing exciting games with the counting board, they respond with improved concentration, which helps them retain the new knowledge better. One such game follows.

The Snake Game

The object of the Snake Game is to build the longest snake of number blocks. The teacher fills a counting board with number blocks and divides students into two teams of six to eight players. The teams take turns selecting a number marker from the ones that are scattered on the table. Each number marker indicates which number block the team may add to their snake of blocks. Children give up counting individual units on the number blocks when they realize it is quicker to name and select the number block below the number on the guide that matches the marker drawn. The winning team is the one that has the longer snake of blocks after the counting board has been emptied.

The Snake Game prepares students to see and remember number combinations that they will discover when they later fill a number box with blocks (discussed later in this chapter). It is more impressive to note that working with counting board materials will enable children to move easily from addition to subtraction. But first they must be able to name the numbers and understand the concepts for which the number symbols stand.

DEVELOPING A NUMBER SENSE: PATTERN BOARDS

Each pattern board provides between 1 and 10 empty blanks in a set pattern into which cubes may be inserted (see Figure 21.2). Children show that they recognize a number pattern by building it with cubes. They then check the pattern they have built by placing the cubes into the blanks of the correct pattern board. Children count the cubes to learn the name of each number pattern.

Even and Odd Numbers

The characteristics of evenness and oddness cannot be taught with number blocks, but they can be taught with cubes and pattern boards. Even numbers are formed by pairs of cube partners so that the pattern ends evenly. They are named 2, 4, 6, and 8. Children see that even numbers are made with $1 + 1$, $2 + 2$, $3 + 3$, $4 + 4$, and $5 + 5$ (math facts that are taught later). When one cube is added to an even number pattern, it becomes odd. Children learn that "one cube all alone" distinguishes an odd number and that odd numbers are named 1, 3, 5, 7, and 9. A stick or a pencil can be used to split an odd number pattern down the center to yield the two consecutive numbers that form it. These odd number patterns are $1 + 0$, $2 + 1$, $3 + 2$, $4 + 3$, and $5 + 4$. When building the sequence from 1 to 10, the odd number patterns are positioned between the even patterns. These facts are studied later under the name Doubles and Neighbors (dis-

Figure 21.2.   Pattern boards: Matching cube patterns.

cussed later in this chapter). The structure of these patterns makes the relationships visible and easy to recall later as addition facts.

Introduction to Word Problems

Acting out word problems with multisensory materials will prepare children to analyze complex word problems later. It is important for children to learn how to demonstrate word problems of their own creation. Pattern boards and cubes are excellent materials with which to begin. Each child in the group selects a different pattern board. For example, Laura selected the pattern board for the number 6, filled it with cubes, and then acted out her problem, saying, "My dog had six puppies. I gave four away. How many are left?" Even though she had subtracted four cubes, the children could still see the original number she started with because she chose a pattern board with six blanks. The pattern board allowed Laura's classmates to see at the same time the four subtracted cubes, the remaining two cubes, and their relationship to the original total of six cubes. Teachers know that some children, when taking four loose cubes away from six loose cubes, cannot visualize the original amount and wonder just how much they began with. These children lose any sense of the relationship of 4 to 6 and of the remaining 2 to the 6 they began with. Well-planned lessons in which children act out word problems with multisensory materials such as pattern boards will help build strong foundations for later learning.

ADDITION AND SUBTRACTION WITH THE 10-BOX

Many children are taught to rely on counting to solve problems of addition and subtraction. When two sets of objects are added together, children are taught to count the objects in the first set and then, without stopping, to continue counting the objects in the second set to arrive at the total. In the absence of objects, children rely on their fingers to solve problems. This is an inefficient and error prone method. The Structural Arithmetic approach gives the children the experience of combining two parts (blocks) to make the whole. Children understand the relationship of the parts to the whole from the start and easily come to understand the relationship between addition and subtraction.

Discovering Combinations that Make 10

The 10-box, a square measuring 10 units by 10 units, has a frame around the edge that tells children when the total units of the block partners is 10 (see Figure 21.3). In the beginning, children fill the 10-box with pairs of number blocks in any sequence, as though they were working on a puzzle. Kindergartners often know which blocks go together in the 10-box before they can name or designate them with number symbols. Each time these children put a number block in the 10-box, they measure with their eyes to judge the size of the block that will fit with it. Thus, they systematically study the relationship between each separate number block and the total, which is 10 units long. When they make a mistake, they can see and feel how the block does not fit. The teacher does not need to say, "Wrong!" The emphasis is on experimenting.

Children feel a satisfaction that is unforgettable when they find pairs of blocks that fit. This success with filling the 10-box helps them remember the block combinations that total 10 units. Once the children have learned the names of the blocks, they will find it easy to name the block partners that make 10 (see Figure 21.3).

Figure 21.3. Filling the 10-box with number blocks.

When the combinations making 10 are placed in sequence, the combination in the middle is a double, a 5-block and a 5-block. A double, children will discover, can be found in the center of every even number. In addition, students will understand the zero fact even before it is recorded; they can put the 10-block in the 10-box and say, "10 needs no other block to make 10." The children can show that they understand the concept of equality when they place two number blocks next to the 10-block and say, for example, "8 and 2 are just as big as 10." This concept will be recorded later with the equal sign.

Building the Stair from 1 to 10 in the 10-Box

The teacher scatters number blocks 1–10 next to the 10-box and begins to build the stair in the lower left corner with the 1-, 2-, and 3-blocks. The teacher asks the children to complete the stair. When the children put in a block that is too long (e.g., placing the 5-block after the 3-block), they realize that the structure is wrong and they look for the correct block (e.g., the 4-block). The choices they make are guided by how the stair looks. The teacher can also challenge the children by removing one step of the completed stair while they are not looking and asking them to name the missing step.

Recording the Story of 10: Writing Equations

The goal is for students to record from memory the "Story of 10," the pairs of numbers that equal 10, but first, students must learn how to record an equation after they fill a column in the 10-box. The teacher places the empty 10-box and two sets of number blocks before the children and sets the number markers 1–10 and the plus and equal signs to one side. The children put two number blocks (**addends**) into the 10-box and name them, for example, "6 and 4." The teacher records this by arranging the symbols 6 + 4 next to the 10-box. The students continue by saying, "equal 10," and the teacher records this by putting the appropriate symbols last, yielding 6 + 4 = 10. When the children write equations later, they understand the process from having recorded the combinations of blocks as they placed them in the box. Using the 10-box while recording equations also enables students to understand an equation when they read it.

The **missing addend** form of an equation (e.g., 6 + __ = 10) is difficult for many children because they do not understand what it means. When the children put a 10-block in the box and place a 6-block next to it, however, they find it natural to ask, "6 needs what to make 10?" They then record what they have just said with the number markers and symbols: 6 + __ = 10. Students discover that the missing symbol is the numeral that stands for the missing block, which they know is the 4-block. Teachers often find that using the 10-box is the first time they have had an easy way of teaching equations with missing addends.

Subtraction and Its Relation to Addition

An addition example contains two or more addends, and students are asked for the sum or total; subtraction can easily be shown to have the opposite character. The children place a 6-block and a 4-block into the first column of the 10-box and note that they measure 10. The teacher states the addition fact 6 + 4 = 10. The teacher's next step is to explain how this addition fact will yield two subtraction facts. To demonstrate the first fact, the children realize that they begin with the total, 10, from which they subtract the 4-block; the 6-block remains. This demonstration gives meaning to the words, "10 take away 4 leaves 6," which students record as 10 − 4 = 6. The teacher then asks someone to demonstrate the other subtraction fact, 10 − 6 = 4, and to record it below the first. The structure of the materials makes it obvious that the smaller number is always subtracted from the larger number.

Combinations that Make 10

Playing the Hiding Game (described next) gives children more than practice in remembering the combinations that make 10. To discover which part (block) of the combination has been hidden, the children must first figure out how the block combinations have been organized; then they find a strategy for identifying the missing combination. Afterward, it is interesting to ask students, "How did you do that?"

The Hiding Game

The teacher displays the 10-box filled with number block combinations in sequence from 1 + 9, 2 + 8, 3 + 7, and so forth up to 10 + 0. When the children's eyes are closed, the teacher removes one combination, such as 4 + 6, and says, "Open your eyes. What did I hide?" A child answers, "4 + 6," and says while pointing to the blocks in the lower stair, "I counted each step, 1, 2, 3, and found 4 was missing, so I knew 4 and 6 were missing."

ADDITION AND SUBTRACTION: OTHER NUMBER BOXES

Children are delighted to find there are more number boxes smaller than the 10-box and enjoy fitting them inside one another to form a pyramid. On finding that the peak of the pyramid would be the 1-box, a precocious kindergartner called out, "I have the pièce de résistance!"

When asking the children to fill one of the smaller boxes, such as the 8-box, the teacher presents two sets of blocks as well as the box to be filled. Students respond by rejecting the blocks that are too big (the 9- and 10-blocks) and finding the block combinations that exactly fit the 8-box. They realize that this task has the same features as filling the 10-box and adjust their performance accordingly. This adjustment comes about as a result of learning through insight, not by rote. Students enjoy playing the same addition and subtraction games with each box as they played with the 10-box. They later write the number story for each box and give each a title, such as the "Story of 8."

Different Roles a Number Can Play

Students will be excited when they become aware that a number plays a different role in each number box. Each number block's distinctive size and color enables children to observe how a number changes its role as it comprises the total of each different box. For example, consider the changes in the role of the 5-block. When filling the 5-box, a kindergarten child said, "5 is the control of this box!" When discovering the combinations while filling the 6-box, another child ran to his teacher and said, "Look! 5 is the 9 of this box." He had noticed that the 5-block plays the same role in the 6-box as the 9-block does in the 10-box: Both are the next-to-biggest block and thus join with a 1-block to fill a column in the box.

In addition, when putting together the combinations to make 9, an odd number, children find that there are two sets of consecutive numbers that make 9; they see that a 5-block joins a 4-block to make 9 and that next to these blocks, a 4-block joins a 5-block to make 9. Finally, they discover that doubles are found only in the even-number boxes. Thus, when filling the 8-box, they find a pair of 4-blocks in the center.

SOLVING WORD PROBLEMS

It is easy for children to understand when to solve a word problem by addition: There are two or more addends and the total is being asked for. Children have greater difficulty identifying problems that are to be solved by subtraction. It is relatively easy for children to decide to solve the problem by subtraction when a total is stated and a smaller amount is lost. Children, however, are more confused when trying to solve problems that say nothing about an amount being lost or taken away. A total and one amount are given in this type of problem, and children must figure out the other amount (e.g., "The book costs $10. Tobias has $3. How much does he need to earn in order to buy it?"). The children have to learn that the way to solve this type of word problem, a missing addend problem, is to subtract. Teachers usually start with problems in which the numbers are small, as in the previous example. Unfortunately, using small numbers makes it difficult for children to understand why they must subtract because they can so easily solve this kind of problem in their heads: "3 needs what to make 10? 7." This type of problem is especially difficult for children to solve later when the problems deal with big numbers (e.g., "The television set costs $225. Tobias has $37. How much does he need to earn?"). Children cannot solve $37 + \_\_ = 225$ in their heads. The teacher must show the children how to think about this type of problem by setting up a model so that when the numbers are big, it will make sense to subtract. For example, the teacher can put 10 cubes in a number track (a grooved track with numerals on one side that holds cubes or number blocks in sections of 10 units or decades; see Figure 21.4) and say, "The book costs $10. Tobias doesn't need to earn all $10; he already has $3." The teacher covers 3 cubes with a scarf and says, "I covered 3 cubes to show that Tobias doesn't need to earn those $3; he already has them. I've taken 3 away from 10." The teacher writes $10 - 3 = \_\_$ and says, "Tobias needs to earn the rest." The

Figure 21.4. Building 14 in the number track.

children conclude in a full sentence, "Tobias needs to earn $7." The children now have a model of how to solve missing addend problems. Later, they will be able to substitute big numbers in this model. For example, "Ted wants $225. He has $37. He doesn't need to earn it all, so I'll take $37 away! He needs to earn the rest!" The students will understand that missing addend problems are solved by subtraction and will set them up correctly.

TEEN NUMBERS

It is important for the teacher to show mathematical concepts such as teen numbers in more than one way. The teen numbers are the numbers above 10 through 19, composed of a 10-block and a number of ones (the rest of the number). They will be shown first in the 20-tray (a square tray, similar to a 10-box, that measures 20 units by 20 units), then in the number track (see Figure 21.4), and also in the dual board (see Figure 21.5).

Building the Stair from 1 to 20

In the 20-tray, children begin by building the familiar stair from 1 to 10. On reaching 10, they discover they must piece together the next numbers using a 10-block and another number block (e.g., 1 ten and a 1-block to make 11, 1 ten and a 2-block to make 12, 1 ten and a 3-block to make 13). Students will be surprised when they see that the stair from 1 to 10 repeats itself in the teen numbers on a base of 10-blocks. They name each number in the 20-tray by naming the steps from 1 to 20. To make certain that the

Figure 21.5. A dual board. The example 30 − 6 is worked out by carrying back 1 ten to the ones compartment, exchanging it for 10 ones, and subtracting 6.

students understand the structure of teen numbers, the teacher says, "Close your eyes" and hides the blocks composing a teen number such as 14. When the children look at the stair of teen numbers, they see which step is missing and cry, "14!" As the teacher replaces the number blocks in the missing step, the students name them: "10 and 4." After this activity they will think of the number 14 as the teacher has built it, with 1 ten and 4 ones (a 4-block). Visualizing the structure and naming the blocks enables students from the start to write the digits in the correct order as 14, not as the number is pronounced, "four-teen."

Measuring Teen Numbers in a Number Track

The numerals on the side of the number track record the total created by the number blocks that are placed in the track. Children need to be familiar with the structure of a teen number in the number track. Operating from this base, they will easily understand the next step, that of adding to 9, in which they first add a number block, such as a 3-block, to a 10-block and then to a 9-block. They can see that the 10-block and the 3-block reach 13 but that the 9-block and the 3-block only reach 12.

Building Teen Numbers in the Dual Board

The dual board has two compartments, a large tens compartment the same size as a 10-box, and a small ones compartment that holds a column of 10 1-blocks or several unit blocks from 1 to 9. It is important for children to construct the teen numbers in the dual board before using it for purposes such as subtracting from 2-place numbers (see Figure 21.5).

When children first look at a written number such as 12, they see two numerals that seem to stand for numbers of about the same size. By building a number in the dual board, the children gain insight into the important role that the place, or the position, of each numeral plays. The teacher builds a number, such as 12, in the dual board by placing 1 ten in the tens compartment and a 2-block in the ones compartment. To record this number, the number marker 1 is put below the tens compartment and the number marker 2 is put below the ones compartment. This shows the meaning of each symbol in the written number 12. To make the term **place value** clear, the teacher can change the places of the number markers 2 and 1 and have children show the new value of each symbol, that is, 2 tens and a 1-block.

ADDITION FACTS WITH ANSWERS IN THE TEENS

There are 36 addition facts with answers in the teens (e.g., $9 + 2 = 11$ to $9 + 9 = 18$). These facts can be categorized into different groups of structurally related facts: Adding 9, Adding to 9, Combinations that Make 11 and 12, and Doubles and Neighbors. Children master them by understanding the general rules for each group.

Adding 9

There are 8 facts in the Adding 9 group ($2 + 9$, $3 + 9$, $4 + 9$, $5 + 9$, $6 + 9$, $7 + 9$, $8 + 9$, $9 + 9$). Children can master these 8 facts at once by learning only one general rule. First, they add a 10-block to any block, such as the 3-block, in the number track and realize that the digit in the ones place of the total, 13, is the same as the unit block that was added to the 10-block (e.g., $3 + 10 = 13$). Students then add a 9-block to the 3-block and discover that they only reach 12, a number that is 1 less than if they had added a 10-block to the unit block they started with (e.g., 3 + 10 = 13, but 3 + 9 = 12). Students demonstrate that they understand these facts by adding a 9-block to each number block from 2 to 9.

Adding to 9

Eight addition facts result from adding a number to 9 (9 + 2, 9 + 3, 9 + 4, 9 + 5, 9 + 6, 9 + 7, 9 + 8, 9 + 9). To learn these Adding to 9 facts, which are the reverse of the Adding 9 facts, children add blocks to a 9-block. This time, the teacher places a 9-block in the number track, holds a 3-block above the track, and asks, "What do you think 9 + 3 equals?" The children have time to answer before the teacher places the 3-block after the 9-block in the number track. When the blocks are joined end to end, the children can see that the 3-block had to move down one unit to fill the gap between 9 and 10; thus, adding 3 to 9 reaches the number 12 (i.e., 10 + 3 = 13, but 9 + 3 = 12). They figure out all of the Adding to 9 facts adding the numbers 2 through 8 to 9.

Combinations that Make 11 and 12

The children begin working with the facts for Combinations that Make 11 and 12 by building a stair from 1 to 10 in the 10-box. They then fill the 10-box by adding the reverse stair of blocks (9, 8, 7, 6, 5, 4, 3, 2, 1) to this stair. Thus, each column in the 10-box is filled. Now the children move the whole top stair up and over one step. This move results in the combinations that make 11, by adding 1 to 10, 2, to 9, 3 to 8, and so forth. The children know the combinations that make 10, so when making combinations that total 11, they realize that one of the component parts will be 1 unit bigger. For example, 5 + 5 = 10, but 5 needs 6 to make 11; 7 + 3 = 10, but 7 needs 4 to make 11.

To build combinations that make 12, students again move the blocks of the top stair up one step. This time 2 units must be added to one of the component parts that totaled 10; for example, 5 + 5 = 10, but 5 needs 7 to make 12. The teacher can now use the clock on the wall as an unforgettable way to show the combinations making 12. The numbers that stand across from each other on the clock face add up to 12. For example, 9 is across from 3, and 9 + 3 = 12; 8 is across from 4, and 8 + 4 = 12; and 7 is across from 5, and 7 + 5 = 12. Once the children have learned Adding 9, Adding to 9, and Combinations that Make 11 and 12, they have studied two thirds of the addition facts with sums that are teen numbers.

Doubles and Neighbors in the Teens

The next group of structurally related addition facts is called Doubles and Neighbors in the Teens and consists of six new facts. Children usually find the doubles easy to learn (6 + 6 = 12; 7 + 7 = 14; 8 + 8 = 16; 9 + 9 = 18; 10 + 10 = 20). To illustrate the doubles, the teacher places pairs of like blocks side by side and explains that the sum of each pair is an even number. Children should play a game such as Stop and Go (described later in this chapter) to practice learning doubles. To illustrate the facts that are neighbors of the doubles (5 + 6 = 11, 6 + 7 = 13, 7 + 8 = 15, 8 + 9 = 17, 9 + 10 = 19), the teacher places the pair of 6-blocks (12) next to the pair of 7-blocks (14) and leaves a space between the pairs. The teacher points to this empty space. To make the neighbor between 12 and 14, a child takes a 6-block from the pair that totals 12 and a 7-block from the pair that totals 14. This produces the number 13, built from the consecutive numbers 6 and 7. The teacher demonstrates how each odd teen number can be formed from two consecutive numbers. Once students have mastered Doubles and Neighbors in the Teens, there are only four final addition facts with answers in the teens to be learned: 8 + 5 and 8 + 6 and the reverse facts, 5 − 8 and 6 − 8.

Addition and Subtraction Facts in the Teens

Teachers often must work with children who find math especially difficult to comprehend. A teacher must first discover which concepts these students do not understand. Looking at students' final answers to math problems does not indicate students' level of understanding. For example, if the teacher sees that a student wrote 15 + 9 = 6, then the teacher still does not know how the student figured out the answer. If the teacher, however, sees that the student made 15 dashes, crossed off 9 of them, and counted the remaining dashes, then the teacher has gained valuable information. Students who have difficulty with math concepts need to work with materials structured so as to give them the foundation they never had to understand computation with answers that are teen numbers.

First, students must build the stair of teen numbers in the 20-tray using 10-blocks and unit blocks to construct the numbers 11–20. Second, they must build a teen number such as 15 in the number track using a 10-block and a 5-block. Then, by substituting the 9-block and the 1-block for the 10-block, they should conclude that the result of taking 9 from a teen number such as 15 is easy to figure out. When the 9-block is removed, the 1-block remains in the number track with the 5-block to yield the answer, 6. Children find it easy to demonstrate similar examples with the same structure: 17 − 9 = 8 or 16 − 9 = 7. This kind of insight gives children confidence in their ability to answer difficult math problems without the endless counting of dots or dashes. In particular, children with learning disabilities profit most from such experiences. They need to realize that they can think and that they can do arithmetic.

Games with Teen Numbers

It is important for all children to learn the concepts about teen numbers and to practice them by playing games that they find challenging.

The Hard Snake Game

The Hard Snake Game may be played by two teams or two children. The teacher writes a different teen number on 10 cards and turns them face down. One member of Team A selects a card and announces the number written on it. The player must form this total by adding two blocks, one of which must be a 9-block. Thus, if the card says 15, then the player must build 15 using a 9-block and a 6-block. If the player forms the correct total, the blocks are then added to Team A's snake of blocks. The winner is the team with the longest snake of blocks. This game reinforces the students' learning of these difficult teen number facts.

The Probe Game

To prepare for the Probe Game, the teacher displays the number track from 1 to 20 and covers the numbers 1–10 with a cardboard box. The teacher has the children close their eyes and then hides a number block, perhaps the 5-block, under the cardboard box. The teacher lets the students open their eyes and asks a child to discover the size of the hidden block by using the 9-block as a probe. As he or she pushes the 9-block down the track and under the box, the children wait expectantly until it stops and shows that the sum is 14. The child must reason, "If this were the 10-block, then the hidden block would be the 4-block, but it is only the 9-block, so the hidden block has to be one bigger than 4; it must be the 5-block." At this point the teacher verifies the answer by lifting the cardboard box to reveal that the hidden block is indeed the 5-block.

PLACE VALUE OR POSITIONAL NOTATION

Giving up dealing with ones and grouping them into tens as a new unit of measure is one of the most ingenious ideas of humankind. Here is an experiment that will show the children how the use of place value, or positional notation, helps us deal with big numbers. The teacher throws only a few cubes on the table and explains that it is easy to say how many are in a small group of cubes. Next, the teacher throws more than 50 cubes onto the table and writes down a few of the children's estimates of the amount. To determine the exact number, the teacher arranges the cubes in rows of 10 in the tens compartment of the dual board and places any leftover cubes in the ones compartment. Students can see at a glance that the amount of cubes is 5 tens plus the 4 leftover cubes in the ones compartment (i.e., 54). The teacher can explain that grouping objects in tens and ones is one advantage of the structure of our number system.

Recording Teen Numbers and Understanding the Numeral 0

When students built the teen numbers, they discovered that the composition of each number corresponded exactly with its numerals: 1 ten and 1 one were recorded as 11, 1 ten and 2 as 12, and so forth, up to 1 ten and 9 as 19. The teacher asks the children to put two 10-blocks in the dual board and record it by placing the number marker for 2 below the tens compartment. The teacher then places the number marker for 0 below the empty ones compartment and explains why 0 is called a place holder: "If we write the numeral 2 and let it stand alone, it would mean 2 ones. So we write 0 in the ones place to tell us that this time the digit 2 stands for 2 tens and that there isn't anything in the ones place. Moreover, in 20, the 0 is also holding a place for another numeral. If we replace 0 with 1, then we must also put 1 cube in the ones compartment." The teacher explains that the numeral is now 21, records the amount in the dual board, and says, "2 tens, 1 one."

Building 2-Place Numbers in the Dual Board and the Number Track

Children are now ready to discover the meaning behind the structure of the 2-place, or 2-digit, numerals between 10 and 100. The children first build a number such as 25 with 2 tens and 5 ones, then they reverse the digits and build 52, using 5 tens and 2 ones. They are now ready to play an interesting game.

Build Your Guess

The Build Your Guess game gives children practice building 2-place numbers in the dual board and then measuring them in the long number track to note where they come in the sequence of 1 to 100. To begin, the teacher writes a 2-place number on a piece of paper and hides it. The student who comes closest to guessing the teacher's number is the winner. Each child should guess a different number and must then build his or her guess in the dual board. For example, Erin decides to guess 39, so she puts 3 tens in the tens compartment and a 9-block in the ones compartment and records it with number markers for 3 and 9. She then measures her blocks in the number track; they reach 39. She places her number markers, 39, next to the track to show her guess. Then the teacher shows the hidden number, 36. Erin finds that her guess, 39, is 3 units bigger than 36, whereas Toshi's guess, 32, is 4 units smaller than 36. The others were even further away. Erin concludes she is the winner.

In this game and the other Structural Arithmetic activities, children express their ideas by building numbers with blocks and recording them with numerals. This solid foundation in understanding two-digit numbers will make regrouping in addition and subtraction (i.e., **carrying** and **borrowing**) easier to understand.

REGROUPING IN ADDITION

The procedure called **regrouping** is known to previous generations as *carrying and borrowing*. The teacher explains that in our system of positional notation, when the amount in one column exceeds 9, it can only be expressed by a two-digit numeral that has a tens digit and a ones digit; therefore, the amount must be regrouped. For example, when dealing with an amount in the ones column such as 12 ones, 10 ones must be exchanged for or regrouped as 1 ten and carried to the tens column. That leaves 2 in the ones place. The numeral that records 1 ten and 2 ones is 12. These procedures will have meaning from the very start when children work with the blocks in the dual board.

Students learn addition with regrouping step by step using the dual board. The first step in adding two numbers, such as 39 and 1, is to build the 2-place number in the dual board. The children place 3 tens in the tens compartment and 9 ones in the ones compartment and say the name of the number: "thirty-nine." The teacher adds 1 cube to the 9 cubes that are already in the ones compartment and explains, "We cannot record the 10 cubes in the ones compartment with a single numeral; we must regroup!" Students exchange the 10 cubes for 1 ten, carry it to the tens compartment, and add it to the 3 tens already there, resulting in a total of 4 tens.

Once the children have understood regrouping, they record each step on paper; writing on paper lined in half-inch squares is a great help. The children write 39, then they write + 1 below the 9 in the ones column, draw a horizontal line beneath it, and say, "9 plus 1 equals 10. I must regroup." They reenact the carrying of 1 ten to the tens compartment and record this move by writing a small figure 1 above the 3 in the tens column of their example. They write 0 in the ones place below the horizontal line (because there are no ones left). Next, they add the digits in the tens column and say, "3 plus 1 equals 4." They write 4 in the tens place in their answer. The sum is written as 40 and named "forty," which accurately records the 4 tens in the dual board.

Next, the students add a bigger number, perhaps 3, to 39. When they add three cubes to the 9 that are already in the ones compartment, they see that they have twelve cubes and must regroup. They exchange ten cubes for 1 ten and carry it to the tens compartment to join the 3 tens. That move leaves 2 cubes in the ones compartment. The students record each step on paper and get the answer, 42, which they see accurately records the 4 tens and 2 ones in the dual board.

Money and Regrouping

To make clear the value of different coins, the teacher tapes a dime to each of several 10-blocks, a nickel to each of several 5-blocks, and a penny to each of about 20 cubes.

Children are now able to see the relationship among the values of the different coins. The nickels are taped to blocks that are half the size of the blocks to which the dimes are taped. Students can see that nickels, which are larger in size than dimes, are worth less than dimes and that it takes 10 pennies (also larger in size than dimes) to equal a dime, or 10 cents. The children will enjoy using the money on blocks in a store game. They can also use the money on blocks in other games.

Score 1 if You Carry

This game is played with the dual board, money on blocks, and a die. The teams take turns tossing the die and placing pennies in the ones compartment of the dual board. For example, Team A tosses the die, gets 3, and places 3 pennies in the ones compartment. Team B tosses a 4 and adds 4 pennies, bringing the total to 7. Team A tosses the die and gets 5, which, when added to 7, yields 12 pennies. Team A must regroup; it exchanges 10 pennies for 1 dime and carries it to the tens compartment. The team puts the 2 remaining cents in the ones column. Team A "scores 1" because it got the chance to regroup, or "carry 1." The game continues. The game could end when one team's score is 5.

REGROUPING IN SUBTRACTION

The process of regrouping in subtraction has also been known as *borrowing*. The children again work in the dual board. They write 30 on their papers and build it with 3 tens. The teacher dictates, "Subtract 6." The children write − 6 below the 0 in 30 and draw a horizontal line below the subtraction example. The teacher explains that the students cannot take 6 cubes away from the ones compartment of the dual board because there are no cubes there and that they must regroup. They carry back 1 ten from the tens compartment and exchange it for 10 ones. On their papers they cross out the 3 and write a small 2 above it to indicate that there are only 2 tens left. The students write a small figure 1 above and to the left of the 0 in the ones place to indicate they now have 10 cubes in the ones column (see Figure 21.5). Now they can subtract 6 cubes, which leaves 4 cubes. The final amount is 2 tens and 4 ones, which matches the written answer, 24.

Regrouping with the Dual Board

After working with the blocks in the dual board, the children need to practice regrouping in a more exciting situation, such as a game.

Your Answer Is Your Score

During each turn in the Your Answer Is Your Score game, one player selects two face-down number markers and uses them to build a two-digit number with number blocks in the dual board. He or she must then subtract an amount that is large enough to require regrouping. The player's score is the number that remains after this subtraction operation; the player with the highest score wins. For example, Robert, who has selected the markers 6 and 3, understands that the goal is to get a big score, so he explains, "I don't want to build 36; I'll build 63, of course!" The teacher asks, "How much will you subtract from 63 so that you must regroup?" Robert reasons, "I have only 3 cubes in the ones compartment, so I think I'll subtract 4 from 63." He exchanges 1 ten for 10 ones and puts them into the ones compartment; he now has a total of 13 single cubes. He subtracts 4 cubes from the 13, and this leaves 9 cubes. Robert sees that there are now 5 tens and 9 ones in the dual board and exclaims, "My score is 59!" He writes 59 on the chalkboard. The rest of the players will try to beat his score.

MULTIPLICATION

To most people, multiplication still means memorizing 100 facts, such as $7 \times 6 = 42$, which are repeated until they have been learned by heart. Actually, multiplication and division are fascinating operations that, when studied with the Structural Arithmetic materials, allow children to discover new relationships among numbers. The children come to realize that they are viewing the same facts from opposite sides when they discover that the relationship between multiplication and division is one of doing and undoing, just as it is between addition and subtraction. Students will not only grasp this relationship but also understand, through their experiments with the materials, just how division is the opposite of multiplication.

The operation of multiplication can, of course, be taught by the addition of equal addends. For example, the answer to 5×2 can be figured out by addition: $2 + 2 = 4$, $4 + 2 = 6$, $6 + 2 = 8$, and $8 + 2 = 10$. In Structural Arithmetic, however, children produce an amount a given number of times, and they discover how this total is expressed in our base-10 system (i.e., tens and ones) by measuring it in the number track.

Discovery of What a Multiplication Table Is

The children will discover that multiplication is a new way of expressing number relationships. The essence of multiplication is that an amount is taken not once but several times. Therefore, to find the answer to 5×2, the children take a 2-block five times. The number 5 is not represented by a block but is the **operator** and plays a different role from the 2; it indicates how many times 2 is to be produced.

Multiplication tables are often recited by saying, for example, "5 times 1 equals 5, 5 times 2 equals 10, 5 times 3 equals 15," and so forth. To represent these facts with materials would mean changing the size of the number blocks used each time: five 1-blocks, then five 2-blocks, then five 3-blocks, and so forth. It makes more sense to demonstrate the multiplication table using the same size number block each time: one 5-block, then two 5-blocks, then three 5-blocks, and so forth (see Figure 21.6). Children will be able to discover the products of any multiplication table by themselves by following this procedure. They can take a block a certain number of times and measure the total in the number track. They can find, for example, the way that 3 fives are expressed in our base-10 number system: 1 ten and 5 ones, or 15 (see Figure 21.6). Students discover not only the interrelationship among the facts within one multiplication table (e.g., 1×5, 2×5, 3×5, and so forth up to 10×5) but also the interrelationship among the facts of different tables, such as the multiples that two or three tables have in common.

Drawing circles and stars is one approach used to teach children to represent a multiplication fact. To demonstrate 3×4, they make three circles and put four stars in each circle. This arrangement shows the role of the operator, or **multiplier,** 3, and the size, 4, but does not show how the total is expressed in the denominations of our number system, tens and ones. There is no visible connection between the fact 3×4 and the product 12, which can only be found by counting. The same is true when children create arrays, such as 4 rows of 5 dots each.

Figure 21.6. Discovering what 3 times 5 equals.

Sequence of Teaching the Multiplication Tables

Children begin by studying the 10-table because our number system is built on base 10. When the **multiplicand** is 10, each product can be expressed immediately. The product of 3 × 10, 30, does not have to be calculated but can be shown by writing 3 in the tens place of the numeral and adding a 0 as a placeholder; the multiple is already expressed in tens and ones. The need for multiplication tables arises because the products must be expressed in tens and ones for any multiplicand other than 10.

The multiplication facts in the 1-table can be shown by producing the 1-block a certain number of times (5 × 1) or each number block one time (e.g., to show 1 × 5, a student produces a 5-block); the answer is the quantity the number block itself represents. The 2-table is studied next because its characteristic feature is that a given number of 2s is the same as the double of that given number (e.g., 6 × 2 = 12 and the double of 6 is 12). Because the children know the doubles, they easily master the 2-table. The 5-table is studied next because of the special relationship of 5 to 10 (5 is half of 10), followed by the 9-table because of the closeness of 9 to 10 (9 is 1 less than 10).

To teach the 9-table, the teacher puts one 10-block in the number track and writes 1 × 10 = 10. The 10-block is then replaced by a 9-block and a 1-block. The teacher then subtracts the 1-block and writes 1 × 9 = 10 − 1; beneath that he or she writes, 1 × 9 = 9. To show the second multiple of 9, the teacher places two 10-blocks in the track and writes 2 × 10 = 20. Next, the teacher replaces the 10-blocks with two sets of 9-blocks and 1-blocks. Both 1-blocks are subtracted, and the two 9-blocks are shoved together; they reach 18. The teacher writes 2 × 9 = 20 − 2. Below that he or she writes 2 × 9 = __; the children copy the fact and write 18 in the blank. By following this procedure the teacher and the children continue to demonstrate and record the 9-table and finish with 10 × 9 = 100 − 10; 10 × 9 = 90.

Multiplication Games

As you have seen throughout, I encourage the use of games. Children have fun both through the pleasure of insight and the excitement of participating in a game. They are spared the tedium of memorization and consequently retain a lively interest in learning math.

Stop and Go

Stop and Go is one of several exciting games that children can play to reinforce their understanding of a multiplication table. To play Stop and Go with the 5-table, the teacher fills the number track with 10 of the 5-blocks. He or she assigns a red cube to the Red Team and a blue cube to the Blue Team and places them at the beginning of the track. The stop-and-go cube has two red "Stop" sides and four green "Go" sides. The Red Team drops the stop-and-go cube and gets Go. The Red Team places its cube on the end of the first 5-block above the number 5 on the track, and one of the Red Team's players says, "1 times 5 equals 5." The Blue Team also gets Go, so it places its blue cube piggyback on top of the red cube. Here are the two possible moves for the Red Team: If Red gets Go, then it must carry the Blue Team's cube, move both cubes up to the end of the number 10 on the number track, and say, "2 times 5 equals 10." If the Red Team gets Stop, however, then both teams' cubes remain on 5. If the Blue Team gets Go at the next turn, then it will move off of the red cube. In this way, they race each other up the track landing on each multiple of 5 until one team reaches the 10th multiple, 50.

The children discover while playing the game that each decade in the number track holds 2 fives. Therefore, when the multiplier is even, the product ends in 0 because it equals a number of 10s; when the multiplier is an odd number, the product has 5 in the ones place because an odd number of 5s reaches the middle of a decade: $1 \times 5 = 5$, $3 \times 5 = 15$, $5 \times 5 = 25$, $7 \times 5 = 35$, $9 \times 5 = 45$.

Capture Peaks

Capture Peaks is another favorite game. First, the children choose a multiplication table and place 10 of the appropriate blocks in the number track. For example, the children decide on the 4-table and place 10 4-blocks successively in the number track. Then they dictate each fact for the teacher to write on the chalkboard. On each of 10 dominoes a fact is printed in this form: $1 \times 4 = \underline{\quad}$. The Red and Blue Teams each get 10 cubes of their respective color, which thus limits each team to 10 turns. A member of the Red Team turns up one of the dominoes and reads it aloud: "3 times 4 equals 12." Then the team places its red cube on 12 in the number track. The domino is then returned to the pool so that each multiple in the number track can have more than one cube on it. After several more turns a member of the Blue Team might get $3 \times 4 = \underline{\quad}$ and say, "3 times 4 equals 12! I'm on top of the Red Team!" At the end of the game, the color cube on top of each peak or multiple determines which team claims the entire tower of cubes beneath it. The team with the most cubes wins.

The Screen Game

The Screen Game, which focuses on using words in math, builds a foundation that will enable students to understand similar wording when they encounter it later in algebra problems. Children who have had difficulty understanding the meaning of words sometimes mistake the words *3 times as big as* to mean *3 times bigger than* and thus produce an amount *3 times as big as* the original and then add this tripled amount to the original amount. The result is an amount that is four times as big as the original. The Screen Game is an important activity for children who make similar mistakes.

To begin, the teacher suggests that the children watch the Screen Game carefully so that they can invent similar problems of their own. Then the teacher writes a few math expressions on the chalkboard, such as *times as big as, times as long as, times as much as, times as heavy as,* and *times as old as.* The children then invent their own problems in which they use one of the expressions.

The teacher gives the children a pile of number blocks and stands a screen on a table. He or she places a 6-block in front of the screen and says, "This represents a stick 6 feet long. In back of the screen is a stick 3 times as long. Show me with the blocks how long the hidden stick is." If the children have understood the words *3 times as long,* then they will build a stick with 3 of the 6-blocks. The hidden stick is then revealed for comparison. The children write their equations on paper ($3 \times 6 = 18$) and say, "The stick is 18 feet long." The teacher then asks several children to demonstrate a problem of their own.

For example, Chan invented this problem: "My dog weighs 20 pounds. I weigh 3 times as much. How much do I weigh?" The teacher had to help another student come up with the wording of his problem: "My father is 4 times as old as I am. I am 10 years old. How old is my father?" After having students come up with their own problems, teachers often reflect that they have been too interested in leading every activity themselves. They realize that they must learn to stand back and encourage the children to develop and use their own powers of creation.

THE RELATIONSHIP BETWEEN MULTIPLICATION AND DIVISION

Students who have learned multiplication with the Structural Arithmetic materials have experienced for themselves how different the role is that each number in an equation plays. For instance, in a multiplication example, such as $3 \times 5 = \_\_$, the multiplier, 3, and the multiplicand, 5, are given; the product is to be found. In one of the related division examples, the total, called the **dividend,** is given and has to be divided into a given number of parts. The question is "What is the size of each part?" ($15 \div 3 = \_\_$). This is the partition aspect of division. In contrast, when the total and the size of the part are given, the question is "How many times is the size, or part [5], contained in the dividend?"

$$5\overline{)15}$$

The answer, 3, is called the **quotient.** This is the containing aspect of division. Students can take the idea that three 5s make 15, turn it around to answer the new question, "How many 5s are in 15?" and immediately answer, "3." By contrast, children who learn the 100 multiplication facts by rote acquire a habit of absent-minded mechanical activity that does not allow them to see the relationship between multiplication and division.

The Partition Aspect of Division

Most children experience the partition aspect of division at home whenever food or toys are divided among a few children. For example, a total, such as 15 cookies, is divided among 3 children; the answer to the question, "How many cookies will each child receive?" (5) is the answer to the division problem $15 \div 3$. The children can carry out many such problems and record them (e.g., $15 \div 3 = 5$).

The Containing Aspect of Division

When considering the partition aspect of division, the total and the number of shares are stated, and the question is to find the size of the share. In contrast, when considering the containing aspect of division, the total and the size of the part are given. The question is to find the number of shares (e.g., "How many times is the part contained in the total?"). For example, the previous problem changed to demonstrate the containing aspect of division would be stated like this: "Mother has 15 cookies. She wants to give 5 cookies to each child. How many children can she give cookies to?"

The containing aspect of division is taught first because it makes the structure of the division algorithm so clear. Children find they can solve a division example as soon as they understand multiplication.

The **division radical** looks like this: $\overline{)}$ and can be presented so as to make sense to students. The teacher places a small paper division radical on the number track over a multiple, such as 15. By doing this the teacher shows how the number 15 changes roles from being the product in a multiplication example to being the dividend in a division example. When the children see a division example, such as

$$5\overline{)15}$$

the teacher explains that this asks, "How many 5s are in 15?" To answer this question, students lay their pencils across 15 on the number track and find it takes 3 of the 5-blocks to reach 15, thus 3 tells them "how many times" the **divisor** (5) is contained in the dividend (15) (see Figure 21.6). The children then place the number marker for 3 on top of the number track above the number 15. This placement reminds them to write the quotient above the division radical when they record the answer to a division example (see Figure 21.7). By working with examples such as this one, the children begin to understand the relationship between multiplication and division.

Under the Box

The Under the Box game helps children remember which number in a division example is written "under the box" (under the division radical). When children hear words such

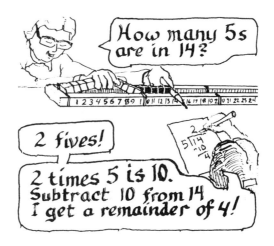

Figure 21.7. Division with remainder.

as "24 divided by 4," they often write the numbers in the order in which they hear them, like this:

$$24 \overline{)4}$$

The teacher hides several number blocks of the same size under a box, such as four 5-blocks, writes the total on a card, and says, "The blocks under the box make 20." The children write 20 under the box on their papers, like this:

$$\overline{)20}$$

The teacher continues, "The blocks under the box are 5-blocks. How many 5s are there?" The students ask themselves, "How many 5s are in 20?" and write

$$5 \overline{)20}$$

They answer "4" and lift the box, which reveals the four 5-blocks. They write 4 above the division radical:

$$5 \overline{)20}^{\quad 4}$$

Division with Remainder

Children can see that each step of the process makes sense when long division is presented with the Structural Arithmetic materials. The teacher dictates a division example that will have an answer with a remainder, such as "How many 5s are in 14?" (see Figure 21.7). The children place two 5-blocks in the number track plus 4 cubes to reach 14, and write

$$5 \overline{)14}$$

on their papers. The children see that there are two 5s in 14, so they write 2 above the division radical, but they know that 2×5 is only 10. The teacher explains that now the students should find the number of cubes left, so he or she takes the two 5s out of the track. The children say, "Subtract 10 from 14," and they write -10 below 14 in their examples:

$$\begin{array}{r} 2 \\ 5 \overline{)14} \\ -10 \end{array}$$

Because 10 has been subtracted from 14, 4 cubes remain in the number track. Thus, the expression "remainder of 4" makes sense to the students. They complete their work by writing the remainder in their answers:

$$\begin{array}{r} 2R4 \\ 5 \overline{)14} \\ -10 \\ \hline 4 \end{array}$$

Division Word Problems

It is important to provide children with word problems that require both the containing aspect and the partition aspect of division. By helping children to represent the problem with the manipulatives, teachers help children understand the differences between the two aspects of division.

Division (Containing Aspect)

Fifteen children want to go on boat rides (total). One boat holds 5 children (size of part).

Question: How many boats will the children need? We want to find how many 5s are contained in 15, so we write

$$5\overline{)15}$$

They will need 3 boats. We can check this: $3 \times 5 = 15$.

Division (Partition Aspect)

Fifteen children want to go on boat rides (total). There are only 3 boats. Question: If there are an equal number of children in each boat, then how many children are in each boat? We want to know the size of the part or the number of children in each boat. [To show that the students are finding the size of the part this time, the teacher can use a different way of writing the example, such as $15 \div 3 = 5$.] There will be 5 children in each boat. They can state that 3 boats containing 5 children in each will carry 15 children.

CONCLUSION

This chapter shows how the multisensory Structural Arithmetic materials enable children to discover mathematical concepts and relationships that they could not have discovered through counting procedures and memorization alone. Children often respond appreciatively when a demonstration gives them insight into a new concept. Such enthusiasm is quickly responded to by the other children and gives the teacher special pleasure in working with these materials.

Today, educators and parents are concerned about children using computers. What effect will their use have on the ability of children to develop intellectual competence and to learn effectively? Jane Healy made extensive studies of children working with computers at different ages. She wrote,

> It is no accident that formal schooling in most countries begins at the time when the brain is sufficiently organized to grasp abstract symbols. Prior to that time, young children are "concrete learners:" They need to "mess around," experiment, and create meaning with their own symbol systems. Preschoolers don't learn language and concepts from two-dimensional flash cards, but from multidimensional experience. (1999, p. 221)

Premature reliance on abstractions, visual images, and mouse movements and clicks without sufficient exposure to three-dimensional experience is likely to diminish the density of meaning children associate with symbols. To the extent that computers may deprive young children of such experience, or cut dramatically into the time they spend interacting with the concrete world, the symbols may come to hold less tangible associations.

Piaget (1952) explained that children develop an understanding of mathematical concepts as a result of the actions they perform with objects, not as a result of the objects themselves. This makes clear why pictures in workbooks do not teach children. The Structural Arithmetic blocks invite children to handle them and perform actions at every step. By the time students reach the level of writing in workbooks, they are free to focus on how to write numbers and equations; they have already worked out the concepts with the multisensory materials and are ready to record them.

By using these structured materials, children, especially children with learning disabilities, learn to trust their intelligence; they come to feel pleased with themselves and proud of their ability to think. This feeling of self-confidence increases their self-esteem and often spreads to their work in other fields. Furthermore, they have developed a reliable understanding of number concepts from the beginning. They will not have to discard these early formulations as deceptively simple but can carry them forward as the building blocks of algebra.

When we teach children mathematical truths and facts by rote, we take away not only the joy of using their minds but also their sense of independence. They feel manipulated, and the result is unimaginative mechanical work. In some cases, this causes students to be bored; in other cases, this leads students to turn off their minds, withdraw, or fail. Children crave freedom to carry out their own experiments and draw their own conclusions. Their work will be fulfilling when they are permitted to do this to the degree that they can.

REFERENCES

Butterworth, B. (2005). The development of arithmetical abilities. *Journal of Child Psychology and Psychiatry, 46*(1), 3–18.

Campione, J.C., Brown, A.L., & Connell, M.L. (1988). Metacognition: On the importance of understanding what you are doing. In R.I. Charles & E.A. Silver (Eds.), *Research agenda for mathematics education: The teaching and assessing of mathematical problem solving* (pp. 93–114). Mahwah, NJ: Lawrence Erlbaum Associates.

Dehaene, S. (1997). *The number sense.* New York: Oxford University Press.

Gersten, R., Beckmann, S., Clarke, B., Foegen, A., Marsh, L., Star, J.R., et al.. (2009). *Assisting students struggling with mathematics: Response to intervention (RtI) for elementary and middle schools* (NCEE 2009-4060). Washington, DC: U.S. Department of Education, Institute of Education Sciences, National Center for Education Evaluation and Regional Assistance. Retrieved from http://www.rti4success.org/images/stories/tiered Instruction/rti_math_pg_042109.pdf

Gersten, R., Jordan, N.C., & Flojo, J.R. (2005). Early identification and intervention for students with mathematical difficulties. *Journal of Learning Disabilities, 38*(4), 293–304.

Healy, J. (1999). *Failure to connect.* New York: Simon & Schuster.

Krasa, N., & Shunkwiler, S. (2009) *Number sense and number nonsense: Understanding the challenges of learning math.* Baltimore: Paul H. Brookes Publishing Co.

National Council of Teachers of Mathematics. (2006). *Curriculum focal points for prekindergarten through grade 8 mathematics: A quest for coherence.* Reston, VA: Author.

Piaget, J. (1952). *The child's concept of number.* London: Routledge & Kegan Paul.

Stern, M. (1988). *Experimenting with numbers: A guide for preschool, kindergarten, and first grade teachers.* Cambridge, MA: Educators Publishing Service.

Stern, M., & Gould, T. (1988–1992). *Structural arithmetic workbooks 1–3 and teachers' guides.* Cambridge, MA: Educators Publishing Service.

Stern, C., & Stern, M. (1971). *Children discover arithmetic: An introduction to structural arithmetic.* New York: HarperCollins.

22

Technology that Supports Literacy Instruction and Learning

LINDA HECKER AND ELLEN URQUHART ENGSTROM

The influence of technology and digital media on educational practice has grown exponentially since the latter part of the 20th century. The Internet offers a myriad of engaging and interactive experiences for expanding students' knowledge of the world beyond their classrooms. This explosion of technological capability has paved the way for new ways of thinking about how to support students with diverse learning profiles in their classrooms. Universal design for learning and instruction has emerged as a theoretical framework that addresses the challenge of making learning more accessible to diverse groups of students. Universal design comes to education from the field of architecture, which informs the design of buildings that are accessible to people with disabilities, but has features that are beneficial to everyone. Universal design for learning emphasizes designing educational environments to accommodate the needs of diverse learners while providing high-quality learning experiences for all students. The Center for Applied Special Technology (CAST) ties universal design for learning to the learning principles articulated by Vygotsky (1978) and defines it by three key components: multiple means of representation, multiple means of expression, and multiple means of engagement (Rose & Meyer, 2002).

Assistive technology fits well into a universal design framework because of its ability to lower or even eliminate the barriers to academic achievement for so many students. Schools must no longer rely exclusively on expensive reading or writing software for their students with reading and writing difficulties. The availability of low-cost or no-cost text readers and voice recognition software make these accommodations far more accessible to students than in the past. Text readers and voice recognition are now standard features in computer operating systems. These features are utilized by popular software applications to provide support and access to students who struggle with reading and writing. Beyond their ability to accommodate students with print disabilities, technology tools provide more options for all learners. For example, books can be digitized with supports embedded for students who have trouble with decoding or comprehension. Students with decoding difficulties can listen to the text while reading along. Students with comprehension difficulties can respond to prompts that ask them to question, predict, or summarize. Hyperlinks can give students immediate access to vocabulary definitions and background knowledge (Anderson-Inman & Horney, 2007). An Inspiration template for follow-up work allows students to use a flexible graphic organizer that can engage students while enhancing their comprehension. Dave Edyburn (2009) highlighted the benefit of making traditional assistive technology devices available to all students in a general classroom setting. He suggested that the technology is no longer "assistive" but has become a universal design support.

The federal education laws that have been passed since 2000 raise the likelihood that technology supports will be integrated into the standard school curriculum. The No Child Left Behind Act (NCLB) of 2001 (PL 107-110) recommended integrating technology into students' opportunities to learn to read (Title I, Part B, Subpart 1). The Individuals with Disabilities Education Improvement Act (IDEA) of 2004 (PL 108-446) allowed response to intervention (RTI) to emerge as the predominant educational model to prevent school failure. RTI is a model for quickly identifying students who are struggling and responding to them with appropriate interventions, rather than waiting for them to fall far behind their peers (see Chapter 14). The RTI model includes three tiered interventions that become progressively more intensive. Universal design, which emphasizes valuing differences and flexible instruction, is by nature a Tier 1 strategy, and using technology tools is integral to it. Educators can determine which students need more intensive and specialized interventions through progress monitoring. Assistive technology could be considered a Tier 1 strategy within an RTI setting (Edyburn, 2009) because it is a universal design support to advance the achievement of a diverse group of students within a mainstream educational setting. Assistive technology has the potential to offer more intensive performance supports for students at Tier 2 or 3. Because of the sophistication of dedicated reading and writing software programs, students with severe print disabilities can function well in a challenging educational setting. The assumption that only remedial interventions can be used within Tier 2 or 3 settings, however, limits the use of assistive technology as a viable intervention. Edyburn (2007) argued that educators must take into account how much remediation should be provided while also considering how much compensation is appropriate. He suggested that a mix of remediation and compensation is desirable, but the amount of each will vary depending on the student's age and academic level. Edyburn also contended that a student's inability to satisfactorily perform at his or her level will limit the student's ability to advance within the educational hierarchy.

Assistive technology has reached an unprecedented level of sophistication since this chapter was originally published. There is an abundance of assistive technology to help students with language-based learning disabilities overcome the barriers they face in reading and writing (Rose & Rose, 2008). Increasingly, school districts provide digitized versions of textbooks along with software applications that automatically translate text into speech. Software to support writing includes voice recognition of spoken words, speak-as-you-write features, word prediction, homophone detection, as well as the more common spelling and grammar check features of word processing software. Using assistive technology in conjunction with learning strategies and remedial reading instruction is particularly effective (Engstrom, 2005). For example, an active comprehension strategy lends itself particularly well to use with a text reader. A student can engage in prereading activities with the help of a text reader by quickly scanning headings and selected vocabulary. A student can use electronic sticky notes and highlighters during reading to reflect on the material and annotate its text. The following sections review the current research on assistive technology, as well as discuss the state-of-the-art technology tools for supporting reading, writing, and studying skills for students.

WHAT RESEARCH SAYS ABOUT ASSISTIVE TECHNOLOGY

Although assistive technology is a relatively recent addition to the educational toolbox, there is a small but growing research literature that examines its benefits to students with learning disabilities in a variety of academic tasks. Research shows that assistive technology can provide a bridge between students' current skills and the tasks they must perform by supporting them in skills they have not yet acquired. Emerging evidence suggests that assistive technology can also contribute to strengthening students' skills in decoding, comprehending, and spelling and in reading and writing fluency. Assistive technology, however, is generally not effective for students with learning disabilities unless it is combined with instructional and learning strategies that prepare students to take advantage of the technology. Furthermore, assistive technology is often abandoned by the very students who could benefit most when they are not adequately supported while learning to use the technology tools efficiently.

Research on Assistive Technology as a Support for Writing

Assistive technology alone is unlikely to improve students' writing. "The positive effects of technology depend on instruction that is designed to help students take advantage of the power of technology" (MacArthur, 2009, p. 31). MacArthur (2006) made this point strongly in his research involving word processing, the most studied assistive technology that supports writing. Word processing alone does not change the revising behavior or overall writing quality of students with learning disabilities (MacArthur & Graham, 1987). Word processing in combination with instruction in a revising strategy, however, was found to improve the amount and quality of revision and the overall quality of students' writing in three studies (reviewed in MacArthur, 2006). As MacArthur pointed out, word processing does make revising easier and may contribute to motivation, but students' writing does not improve just from access to computers without instruction in revising techniques such as diagnosing problems and applying fix-it strategies. Similarly, students need instruction in spell-checking strategies, such as recognizing homophone substitutions, and keyboarding fluency to fully reap the advantages of word processing (MacArthur, 2009). A 2-year study by the Washington Technology for Learning Disabilities Project (http://www.cwu.edu/~setc/tld/) employed a comprehensive reading-writing assistive technology tool (Read and Write 9 Gold) with 6th- to 12th-grade students with learning disabilities in a program that provided extensive professional development training and support for teachers. Students in the experimental group significantly improved the quantity and quality of their writing at the end of the second year, and teachers reported that students increased their motivation and confidence as they were able to complete more of their assignments. Of special note, teachers reported they needed 2 years of sustained support to effectively integrate the technology into their teaching routines.

In addition to word processing, a number of studies have examined other assistive technology tools for writing, notably the transcription tools of word prediction and voice recognition. Word prediction, especially when supported by text-to-speech pronunciation of the listed words, can improve the transcription accuracy of students with severe spelling difficulties, although it generally reduces the transcription speed for all except the slowest writers by hand (MacArthur, 1999, 2000). Although word prediction reduces the number of keystrokes required to accurately transcribe a word, students' output rate is slowed by having to scan and select the appropriate word from a list of presented choices (Koester & Levine, 1996). Word prediction can also increase the number of appropriate vocabulary items students use in their writing by offering them choices of words that are specific to the genre or content studied (Lewis, Graves, Ashton, & Kieley, 1998). Significantly, students who had ample time to learn and practice using word prediction increased the accuracy of their transcriptions the most (MacArthur, 1998).

Voice recognition has the potential to circumvent transcription difficulties posed by poor spelling and inefficient handwriting, but presents challenges of its own, such as need for training the software to transcribe accurately as well as training the individual to recognize and correct transcription errors (Hartley, Sotto, & Pennebaker, 2003; Honeycutt, 2003; Sanderson, 1999). The technology has been evolving rapidly, so it is difficult to compare results from studies using different versions of the software, but overall, research suggests voice recognition can improve accuracy and speed of transcription as well as composition length and quality (Quinlan, 2004; Roberts & Stodden, 2005). MacArthur (2006) also reported on the validity of using voice recognition as a test accommodation for high school students with learning disabilities. As with other assistive technology, "sufficient systematic instruction, using strategies adapted to the learner" (Peterson-Karlan & Parette, 2007, p. 13) is critical to help students overcome the challenges that lead them to abandon the software before they experience its full benefits.

Finally, there are a few studies on the efficacy of digital outlining and concept-mapping programs (such as Inspiration) to support the prewriting stages of writing—generating and organizing ideas. Although preliminary in nature, work by Anderson-Inman at the University of Oregon (Anderson-Inman & Horney, 1998), Haynes and McMurdo (2001), and MacArthur and colleagues (Karchmer-Klein, MacArthur, & Najera, 2008) reported promising results when students are taught to use digital concept mapping to take notes, plan, and produce academic writing. As reported in other research, these tools are effective in the context of pedagogically sound instruction that promotes student self-understanding and self-regulation around the challenging tasks of writing. In sum, "technologies are not meant to replace good writing-as-process instruction. Instead, they provide scaffolding" (Peterson-Karlan & Parette, 2007, p. 4).

Research on Assistive Technology as a Support for Reading

Assistive technology can benefit students with learning disabilities in the area of reading, provided it is combined with instruction in learning strategies and processes. For example, Wise, Olson, Ring, and Johnson (1998) found that **synthesized speech** feedback during oral reading practice supported the development of students' reading skills and phonemic awareness. This technology support was more effective, however, when combined with instruction in phonemic awareness. Studies of the effects of text-to-speech software by students with learning disabilities have found positive effects on fluency but not on comprehension without integrated instruction in comprehension and study strategies (MacArthur, Ferreti, Okolo, & Cavalier, 2001). Preliminary studies by Engstrom (2005) at Landmark College and researchers at the CAST (Pisha & O'Neill, 2003) have explored the benefits of combining instruction in traditional comprehension strategies such as reciprocal teaching with text-to-speech software and electronic texts with built-in scaffolding such as maps, illustrations, dictionaries, and cues to employ those strategies at appropriate times.

According to the literature review conducted by Strangman and Dalton, "digital technologies (**computer-mediated text,** text-to-speech, voice recognition) have the potential to support struggling readers in both compensatory fashion, providing access to text, and remedial fashion, helping students learn how to read with understanding" (2005, p. 545). The research, however, has focused more on computer-mediated text than on assistive technology interventions. The Strangman and Dalton review suggested that technology shows mixed results in improving phonemic awareness, phonics, and vocabulary, with computer-mediated approaches having no clear advantage over traditional ones. Assistive technology, however, shows promise in promoting fluency and comprehension, with studies by Elkind (1998); Gehrmann and Kinas (2002); Montali and Lewandowski (1996); and Wise, Ring, and Olson (2000) that confirm the benefits of using text-to-speech software to support students' reading rate, fluency, and comprehension. In particular,

> For older students who have already experienced debilitating effects of poor reading on academic achievement, motivation and self-efficacy, it is important to provide, at minimum, digital versions of core curriculum and literature with text-to-speech support so that they have access to, and are able to participate in the general education curriculum. (Strangman & Dalton, 2005, p. 559)

Although there is evidence that students do not always use the supports that are available in computer-mediated texts (such as linked glossaries or prompts to apply strategies, answer questions, or take notes), Strangman and Dalton (2005) suggested that these **hypertexts** promote student motivation and engagement and may encourage students to read more actively and independently. In addition, a study by Hecker, Burns, Elkind, Elkind, and Katz (2002) established the benefits of text-to-speech software for improving reading stamina and concentration in students with attention disorders.

In conclusion, research on assistive technology and learning strategies provides strong evidence for the potential of programs that integrate the two methods.

Resources to Keep up with Research

Because research and development of assistive technology is constantly evolving, it is helpful to know where to gain access to current information. One of the most useful sources is David Edyburn's annual reviews of top articles in the area of special education technology (http://www.uwm.edu/~edyburn/what.html) and his daily online journal Special Education Technology Practice (http://www.setp.net/index.html). The Connecticut State Education Resource Center library (http://ctserc.org/s/index.php ?option=com_content&view=article&id=522&Itemid=179) is a comprehensive source for bibliographies, including specialized bibliographies on assistive technology, computers, and special education. There are numerous web sites that will be listed in Appendix B, but three national research centers are of special note:

1. National Assistive Technology Institute (http://natri.uky.edu)

2. Assistive Technology Outcomes Measurement System project (ATOMS; http:///www.atoms.uwm.edu)

3. Consortium for Assistive Technology Outcomes Research (CATOR; http://www.atoutcomes.org)

Print journals that focus on issues in assistive technology and special education include *Assistive Technology, Closing the Gap, Journal of Special Education Technology,* and *Technology and Disability,* whereas online journals include *AT Benefits and Outcomes* (http://www.atia.org/atob/ATOBV1N1) and *Journal of Special Education Technology* (http://jset.unlv.edu).

SELECTING AND INTRODUCTING ASSISTIVE TECHNOLOGY

Too often schools purchase assistive technology that winds up sitting on a shelf, sometimes in its original packaging, because educators are unclear about how to actually use it with their students. Other times the technology is abandoned after a few frustrating sessions because the tools are not a good match for the intended students. Educators need a thoughtful process for selecting the best technology for their students and for introducing it in a way that promotes success from the start.

Principles for Matching Assistive Technology to Student Need

Because the goal of assistive technology use is to enhance the performance of an individual with a disability, the selection process should start with assessing the individual's learning needs, including academic strengths, difficulties, and preferences, as well as the learning tasks and environments. For students with documented disabilities in a public school setting, this assessment may be part of the individualized education program (IEP) process, which directs the school to "consider whether the child requires assistive technology devices and services" (Section 300[324][a][2][v]) as part of IDEA 2004).

There are several frameworks offering guidance on matching assistive technology to students' needs. The SETT framework (Zabala, 1995) considers the *Student, Environment, Tasks,* and *Tools,* in that order, by gathering information about each of the four areas through a series of straightforward questions such as, "What does the student need to do?" The framework explanation and worksheets are available online at http://plone.rockyview.ab.ca/ss/a-t-l/atl-decision-making/sett-framework.

The Matching Person and Technology model (MPT; Scherer, 1998) provides a comprehensive set of inventories that suggest appropriate technology for individuals and evaluate their success. The assessments were developed from a validated research study (Scherer, 2002; Scherer & Craddock, 2002) and are based on the belief that technologies must be adjusted to the needs of the user just as users must adapt or adjust to the technologies (http://matchingpersonandtechnology.com/).

Both SETT and MPT outline a process of gathering information to inform decisions about selecting and using assistive technology. These steps involve users and professionals working collaboratively, and include

1. Identifying user's strengths and needs, goals and preferences, motivation and readiness, and expectations

2. Identifying the educational task demands and environment

3. Identifying technology used in the past and the user's level of satisfaction and comfort, as well as potential new technology

4. Anticipating problems that may interfere with effective use of the technology

5. Setting strategies and an action plan to deal with potential problems

6. Reviewing user's performance and progress, with opportunities to modify the technology to improve the user's effectiveness and achievement of academic goals

Resources for Selecting Assistive Technology

With the proliferation of technology tools since 2000, the task of selecting from among many alternatives has become increasingly daunting. Yet, there are resources that help identify and sort technology by use, function, features, age/grade range, and cost.

The TechMatrix (http://www.techmatrix.org) is the most comprehensive resource for matching user needs with assistive technology. It is sponsored by the Center for Implementing Technology in Education and the National Center for Technology Innovation. Resource guides suggest questions to ask and provide guidance on how to make informed assistive technology decisions. Users can search for technology by subject, such as math, reading, and writing, or by learning supports, such as reinforcement and practice or opportunities to learn concepts. The search yields a matrix of available products sorted by features, with links to product descriptions with information about costs, grade levels, hardware requirements, and support of practices recommended by the National Reading Panel, Writing Next, or the National Council of Teachers of Mathematics.

Using Assistive Technology Effectively

The research is clear about how to maximize the effectiveness of assistive technology—students need sufficient training and practice, and the tools work best in the context of pedagogically sound learning strategies. "Technologies provide scaffolding for a process-based approach and instruction, especially for struggling students" (Peterson-Karlan & Parette, 2007, p. 4). Many of these process-based approaches will be explained in the reading, study skills, and writing sections of this chapter. This section considers how to use technology in relation to student skills and needs. It also suggests how to introduce students to technology in a way that anticipates difficulties and helps them persist to the level of confidence they need to reap the benefits technology can offer.

David Edyburn's publications on remediation versus compensation offer an excellent guide for considering how to use technology with students with mild disabilities. His premise is "assistive technology is a means for enhancing functional performance when a person with a disability is unable to perform an activity that can normally be completed by other people" (2005, p. 244). Edyburn (2006) urged educators to consider both remediation (such as additional and more intensive instructional approaches) and compensation as valid approaches, with assistive technology often providing the means for compensation, when considering the needs of students with disabilities. Remediation and compensation are not mutually exclusive; instead, educators should design a balance of these approaches that meets the needs of individuals. Edyburn (2007) suggested a high ratio of compensation to remediation, on the order of 60%–70% compensation versus 30%–40% remediation, for students who have already experienced failure despite remedial efforts. For example, for a high school student who is decoding at a fourth-grade level but has to keep up with content reading in his or her academic subjects, the school should provide remedial instruction in decoding accuracy and fluency as well as compensatory assistive technology in the form of screen readers and digital texts. "Technological scaffolding provides a compensatory function in that it permits students to perform at higher levels of proficiency" (Peterson-Karlan & Parette, 2007, p. 4). Edyburn made the compelling point that assistive technology promotes the kind of sustained engagement that leads to "high levels of expertise" by providing access to increasingly challenging tasks over time and positive experiences of success (2006, p. 26).

Sometimes, students with learning differences reject using educational technologies out of fear that they will once again be labeled as different. Following are suggestions to help students adjust to and embrace technology:

- Give students a clear understanding of their learning strengths and weaknesses.

- Be clear about the rationale for using the technology. If a student fears that using a text reader will prevent him or her from learning to read independently, then discuss the need for developing vocabulary and background knowledge to be an independent learner.

- Support students in learning the technology and individualizing its use to become independent and automatic with it.

- Help students make adjustments to their computers that simplify their use (e.g., shortcuts on the desktop, changes in tracking pad settings to make laptops easier to manipulate, using an external mouse or keyboard).

- Encourage students to pursue remedial strategies to achieve their goal of independence.

The power of digital media has expanded higher education beyond the text- and teacher-centered curriculum of the past. Technology offers the ability to adjust learning environments by making classroom materials more flexible and the ability to expand access to the curriculum to a greater range of students.

USING TECHNOLOGY TO ASSIST WITH READING

Although research on the causes and effects of students' failure to read well has provided educators with greater knowledge and understanding of this phenomenon, vast numbers of children continue to move through school without gaining the literacy knowledge and reading skills they need to allow them to successfully engage in higher level problem solving. Poor reading skills are a result of multiple factors:

- Insufficient instruction in decoding and comprehension strategies

- Slow processing of text, leading to poor fluency

- Lack of exposure to written text, leading to background knowledge deficits

- Poor comprehension

Although the need for effective code-based reading instruction remains great, assistive technology can help students bridge the gap between their poor reading skills and their ability to comprehend higher level concepts. Text-to-speech software removes the burden of decoding text. Readers can focus all of their attention on understanding the text and making connections to background knowledge. Without the burden of decoding, readers are free to think about and gain control over reading while using active reading strategies and concept mapping to support comprehension.

A text-to-speech screen reader can convert computer-based text into spoken words. It also allows readers to engage with text-based information aurally and visually and enables slow readers to process text more quickly and efficiently. Screen readers vary widely from the most bare-bones versions with no features other than the ability to read the text, to the most sophisticated, which may include features for scanning text, unlocking text, highlighting, notetaking, writing, and range from little or no cost to a thousand dollars or more. These more sophisticated software programs fall under the category of reading systems. Student needs must be carefully evaluated in order to choose the appropriate software program. What can reading software programs do?

- Read digital text out loud
- Highlight text as it reads
- Allow the reading rate to be adjusted
- Provide options for voice type
- Read text files
- Read text on the Internet
- Allow text to be edited and altered
- Alter the text color
- Alter the background color
- Include options for writing
- Spellchecking
- Word prediction
- Homophone detection
- Provide reference tools: thesaurus and dictionary
- Provide a means for digitizing text or unlocking digital text files
- Provide tools for highlighting and notetaking

Students who need to read textbooks are likely to need a program that has note-taking and highlighting features to support their study skills. Students who need to hear what they have written in order to revise and proofread their work need a program that includes a writing feature with spellchecking and word prediction. Students who use the Internet for research need a program that is designed to read text blocks and the special formatting characteristic of web sites on the Internet. Students who need the screen reader to read articles and textbooks need a program with reliable optical character recognition (OCR) that can convert the document file into a format that is recognizable to the text reader. Choosing an appropriate software program for a student with reading difficulties requires careful consideration of the tasks the student is required to complete, the cost of the software, the availability of tech support, and the ease of use.

Reading Software and Digital Text

The text must be in digital form in order for a text reader to convert text to speech. The simplest form of digitized text is a rich text file, which all screen readers can read. The problem with rich text files is that they do not retain the original formatting of the text. Sophisticated screen readers such as Kurzweil 3000 or Read and Write 9 Gold can read text that has been scanned and converted into a graphic file, such as a .tiff or portable document format (PDF), for a permanent document file. The advantage of this type of file is that it retains its original formatting, so a scanned textbook looks the same on the computer screen as it does in its original form. Scanning entire texts to make them accessible to students with print disabilities, however, is time consuming and labor intensive.

Until recently, digital file formats were not standardized. Print materials had to be physically scanned to convert the print to digital text. Software programs had their own proprietary OCR capability, which meant that they could only read text that had been scanned using their own OCR. Scanning text is a labor and time intensive activity, and it requires special equipment. Publishers were reluctant to produce textbooks in digital format because of their concerns about copyright protection as well as some confusion over which file format to use. As a result, digital text files were not readily accessible to students who could benefit most from them. IDEA 2004 established the National Instructional Materials Accessibility Standard (NIMAS; http://nimas.cast.org/about/idea2004 .index.html) in order to promote production of digitally accessible materials for students with disabilities. Additional federal support was given to the CAST (http://nimas .cast.org) and Bookshare (http://www.bookshare.org) so that they can work more closely with publishers and school districts to make accessible instructional materials more prevalent.

A consensus has emerged that favors using PDF files as a standard digital text format. PDF files are created to retain all the color, layout, and graphic features of a document as intended by its author. PDF files have varying levels of security from unsecure, which allows editing, to fully secure, which allows no editing. PDF files are accessed with a simple version of Adobe Acrobat, which can be downloaded for free: Adobe Reader is a text reader embedded in the Adobe Acrobat software. Documents are easily converted to PDF format with Adobe Acrobat Pro, a more sophisticated and costly version. Increasingly, publishers are producing digital versions of their textbooks in PDF format, making educational materials more accessible to students with print or vision disabilities.

The availability of digital text has increased along with the increased use of text reading. Bookshare and the National Instructional Materials Instructional Center are two sources for books and texts that are available to students with print disabilities for no cost.

Software Focus: Commonly Used Reading Software Programs

Kurzweil 3000 (http://www.kurzweiledu.com) is a software program that includes reading and reference tools; study skills and test taking; writing supports; Internet access; and OCR to convert textbooks, articles, PDFs, and .tiff and .html files into image documents that retain their original layout. The voices are high quality, the reading rate is adjustable, and many options exist to customize the tasks that students perform most often. Text is highlighted as it is spoken aloud. The professional version of Kurzweil 3000 can read PDF files without conversion, whereas the less expensive Read Station lacks that capability.

Read and Write 9 Gold (http://www.texthelp.com) is designed as an integrated text reader that works in conjunction with Windows. It features a floating toolbar that includes a screen reader, study skills tools, word prediction, a spellchecker, and a homophone checker. Read and Write 9 Gold highlights text as it is spoken aloud, and it reads text directly on the Internet. Read and Write 9 Gold integrates with Adobe Acrobat 9 Pro. When used together, the study skills features include note-taking capability in addition to highlighting.

Adobe Acrobat 9 Pro (http://www.adobe.com/acrobat) is a program designed to convert documents to PDF files. Once a document is converted to a PDF file, its access can be controlled and the document retains its integrity. Adobe Acrobat 9 Pro includes the Adobe Reader, as well as well as text marking features to support reading comprehension.

USING TECHNOLOGY TO SUPPORT STUDY SKILLS

Study skills are practices that offer a concrete way to represent how the brain processes and retains information. Working memory, which is the part of the brain that stores information for short periods of time and retrieves information from long-term memory, manipulates information, and focuses attention, is crucial to that process. The working memory is not equipped to retain all the information contained in a textbook or a lecture, so good study skills strategies are necessary to foster information processing and its transfer into long-term memory (see Chapter 18). Effective reading comprehension strategies involve the reader actively engaging the text in three stages: before reading, during reading, and after reading. Active reading is one strategy that fosters interaction between the reader and the text and provides a process for comprehending and retaining information in written text. The **active reading process** offers the reader an effective system for processing the meaning of the text in progressively deeper stages. The steps of the active reading process are

Preread

- Read the title, note pictures, and diagrams; read any headings or questions posed

Read

- Read the text carefully
- Highlight main ideas and supporting details

Margin note

- Paraphrase the most important ideas in the text and write them in the margins

Chunk

- Reflect on the text as a whole and note where topics change within the text

Summarize

- Create a written summary, an outline, or a concept map that reflects the main ideas in the text

There are many barriers to using an active reading strategy for those with reading difficulties. Poor decoding skills, a slow reading rate, or inconsistent attention can interfere with a student's ability to gain knowledge from textbooks or other academic reading. Strategic use of software programs can bridge the gap between reading deficits and successful active reading. Students who use a text-to-speech program (e.g., Kurzweil 3000) have the capability not only to read a text fluently, but also to annotate it. In Figure 22.1, the student highlighted headings in magenta, key words and phrases in yellow, and vocabulary in green (color not shown in figure). In addition, the student wrote a margin note (not captured in Figure 22.1) that paraphrases the information provided in the paragraph and text notes that define vocabulary.

If the student extracts the highlights, then he or she has a rudimentary outline from the text that the Kurzweil 3000 will read aloud (see Figure 22.2). If the student extracts the margin notes, then he or she has paraphrased notes that the Kurzweil 3000 will read aloud (see Figure 22.3). Students can create study guides for test taking and/or a summary of the text's content with these text marking and annotation features.

The act of summarizing a text offers students the opportunity to make and explain connections among the concepts expressed in the reading. Traditionally, summaries are created in essay form. Summaries can reflect the concepts of a reading in a visual format with the assistance of visual mapping software. Figure 22.4 illustrates a concept map that summarizes the memory process using symbols and notes that can be hidden to avoid visual clutter.

Using a two- or three-column note-taking format is a more traditional way to organize information from a text. The Kurzweil 3000 Version 11 has the ability to extract highlights into a two-column note template (see Figure 22.5), which provides an additional level of support for students who may not be able to use standard two-column notetaking effectively.

Using the outline side of Inspiration to capture headings, vocabulary, and key ideas in a digital outline format is another approach to textbook notetaking that makes note revision simple and clear. Students can use the Inspiration text reader to listen to their notes while they review them. For students who prefer to organize information in a visual spatial format, Inspiration has premade templates for language arts, social science, science, patterns of thinking, and planning.

HOW PEOPLE LEARN AND REMEMBER

Three stages are involved in the memory process: encoding, storage, and retrieval. First, information enters the brain from a variety of sources. This process is known as *encoding.* In reading and study situations, information is entered primarily through reading or listening. This information lingers briefly in what is known as *sensory storage* and is then either *stored* or discarded. Momentary or brief storage is called *short-term memory.* Next, information in short-term memory is either forgotten or transferred into more lasting storage called *long-term memory.* Anything that is to be remembered for more than a few seconds must be stored in long-term memory. To place information in long-term memory, one must learn it in some way. Finally, information can be brought back, or remembered, through a process known as *retrieval.* Figure 3.2 is a visual model of the learning and memory processes. Refer to it frequently as you read the sections that explain each stage.

Figure 22.1. A student has highlighted headings, key words and phrases, and vocabulary to make the text easier to understand. (Excerpts, pp. 41–43 from COLLEGE READING & STUDY SKILLS, 7th by Kathleen T. McWhorter. Copyright © 1998 by Kathleen T. McWhorter. Reprinted by permission of Pearson Education, Inc.)

FORGETTING

forgetting occurs right after learning

levels off over time.

    retention curve,

recall drops to below 50 percent within an hour

25 percent within two days.

taking notes during class lectures helps you learn and remember

HOW PEOPLE LEARN AND REMEMBER

Three stages

in the memory process: encoding, storage, and retrieval

information enters the brain

Figure 22.2. A rudimentary outline that the Kurzweil 3000 will read aloud. (Excerpts, pp. 41–43 from COLLEGE READING & STUDY SKILLS, 7th by Kathleen T. McWhorter. Copyright © 1998 by Kathleen T. McWhorter. Reprinted by permission of Pearson Education, Inc.)

The ability to take notes on a lecture is another key study skill. The two-column note-taking strategy provides students with a system for capturing important concepts from a lecture and processing those concepts in a format that becomes an effective study tool. Like other effective study skills strategies, the two-column note-taking strat-

Footnote 1
The retention curve is how much you are able to remember over time.

Footnote 2
Encoding means where information is brought into the brain

Footnote 3
Encoding: where information is stored for no more than 2 minutes

Footnote 4
Short term memory: information is stored for no more than 2 minutes

Footnote 5
Long term memory: Information is stored for a long time and can be recalled.

Footnote 6
Retrieval is your ability to remember what you have learned.

Footnote 7
Schema is organized information in your long-term memory

Sticky Note 2
Add a footnote that
tells the meaning

Figure 22.3. Paraphrased notes that the Kurzweil 3000 will read aloud. (Excerpts, pp. 41–43 from COLLEGE READING & STUDY SKILLS, 7th by Kathleen T. McWhorter. Copyright © 1998 by Kathleen T. McWhorter. Reprinted by permission of Pearson Education, Inc.)

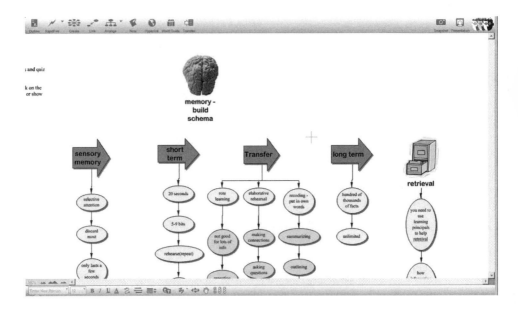

Figure 22.4. Concept map that summarizes the memory process using symbols and notes that can be hidden to avoid visual clutter. (Copyright 2010. Concept map created in Inspiration® by Inspiration® Software. Used with permission.)

egy mirrors the memory process in the brain by separating notetaking into discrete stages of perceiving, recording, reviewing, and summarizing (Pauk, 2008). A two-column note template is easily created in Microsoft Word (see Figure 22.6), which makes this highly effective system more accessible for students who have graphomotor and language-based difficulties. The portability of laptop computers allows students to bring them to lectures or use them in a library. The template can be used in combination with voice-recognition software, making notetaking accessible to students with severe dysgraphia.

Capturing information from lectures and classroom discussions is one of the greatest problems faced by students with language-based learning difficulties. Voice-recognition software does not provide much help in this setting because students will disrupt the classroom when they speak into their microphones. Many students have difficulty simultaneously listening to the lecture and capturing notes. Students can record lectures,

Main Ideas	Supporting Ideas	Other
HOW PEOPLE LEARN AND REMEMBER	- Three stages - in the memory process: encoding, storage, and retrieval. - information enters the brain - information lingers briefly - brief storage is called - short-term memory - more lasting storage - Anything that - remembered for more than a few seconds - stored in long-term memory. - information can be brought back, - process known as	- encoding. - sensory storage - stored - short-term memory. - long-term memory. - retrieval.

Figure 22.5. The Kurzweil 3000 Version 11 has the ability to extract highlights into a two- or three-column note template, which provides an additional level of support for students who may not be able to use standard two-column notetaking effectively. (Excerpts, pp. 41–43 from COLLEGE READING & STUDY SKILLS, 7th by Kathleen T. McWhorter. Copyright © 1998 by Kathleen T. McWhorter. Reprinted by permission of Pearson Education, Inc.)

Title	
Main Ideas	***Notes From Text or Lecture***
• •	
Vocabulary	
Words	***Definitions***
Questions (possible test questions for self study or questions for the instructor)	
Questions?	***Answers***

Figure 22.6. A two-column note template created in Microsoft Word. (Copyright Landmark College, 2003. Used with permission.)

but they must replay the whole lecture in order to extract relevant information. The Pulse Smartpen by Livescribe offers a solution for students who want a complete set of notes without having to write everything on paper. The Pulse Smartpen is a digital pen that has a camera and a recorder in it. Students can write or draw on specialized paper and record what is being said at the same time. Therefore, a student does not have to reproduce the lecture or discussion in writing. Key words or pictures combined with a recording result in notes that can be uploaded to a computer and saved. Note revision can be accomplished electronically.

USING TECHNOLOGY TO ASSIST THE WRITING PROCESS

We no longer think of word processing as a form of specialized technology, but anyone who grew up writing in the days of typewriters and correction tape can fully appreciate the way computers assist in creating error-free academic papers or business documents. However, the full value of computer-based technology for writing will be realized only when it is used within a sound pedagogical approach, such as using a systematic writing process.

Rationale for Using a Writing Process

Most successful writing instruction for students with learning disabilities begins with the writing process—a methodical sequence of strategic activities that break the task of writing into discrete steps. Generating and organizing ideas, drafting, revising, and proofreading are the steps that lead to successful writing outcomes. Teaching the writing process involves acquainting students with a variety of strategies for each stage of the process and helping them learn to use the strategies flexibly in response to the varying demands of different kinds of writing (see Chapter 13).

Writing is an extraordinarily complex act, heavily influenced by cognitive and affective factors. Teaching writing explicitly as a process encourages students to see writing as a task that involves a series of mental activities and promotes the self-regulation needed to complete tasks independently over time. It also helps students to gain awareness of their strengths and weaknesses throughout the various stages of written composition. Students can evaluate their own composing habits, choosing those strategies that work best for them.

What Are the Barriers to Writing?

Barriers to successful writing fall into three categories:

1. Language-based difficulties, which include persistent problems with generating ideas fluently, spelling, handwriting, word choice and retrieval, sentence structure, paragraphing, and punctuation

2. Attention and working memory difficulties, which include random errors in spelling, punctuation, and syntax and difficulty maintaining focus and coherence throughout the writing task

3. Executive function difficulties, which include poor planning, disorganization of time and materials, difficulty sustaining effort throughout the writing task, and procrastination and anxiety that result in writer's block (see Chapter 18)

How Can Technology Improve Writing Outcomes?

Most modern writers use word processing software without even thinking of it as assistive technology. Word processors offer flexibility, spelling and grammatical help, and time efficiency. Inexpensive portable word processors and **netbooks** can provide immediate access to these tools in classrooms or other environments where desktop or more expensive laptop computers are not available. Visual mapping software offers enhanced opportunities for generating and organizing ideas. Word prediction, synthesized speech feedback, and voice recognition provide alternatives to handwriting or keyboarding while drafting text. Strategically using software programs can bridge the gap between the varied needs of writers and their abilities. Technology offers the chance for students whose potential was overlooked in the past to become successful writers.

Tools and Strategies for Teaching Writing

It is useful to look at each stage of the writing process in terms of barriers to success and assistive technology tools that address those barriers. This section treats each stage of the writing process in turn, using the following format:

• A summary chart of barriers to success and assistive technology tools

• A more detailed discussion of assistive technology tools appropriate for that stage

Keep in mind that many assistive technology tools assist students at multiple stages of the writing process, as indicated on the summary charts, even if they are discussed in detail under one particular stage (see Table 22.1).

Table 22.1.   Brainstorming or generating ideas

Barriers to success	Assistive technology tools
Poor spelling	*Word processing software*
This barrier causes the writer to be so focused on spelling individual words that writing fluency is lost and the writer's ideas are blocked. It may also limit word choice to words the writer can spell reliably.	This tool provides spelling support through spellchecker.
	Word prediction software
	This tool accurately completes words.
Difficulty expressing concepts in writing	*Word prediction software*
This barrier results in frustration and writer's block when the writer fails to produce the words to express his or her ideas.	This tool predicts words that the writer is most likely trying to write.
	Software can be trained to predict words based on the writer's style of writing.
Difficulty with working memory	*Voice-recognition software*
This barrier prevents the writer from managing more than one aspect of the writing task at a time.	This tool allows the writer to use oral language to express ideas, which are recorded and saved in a word processing file.
The writing task takes a long time to complete.	Spelling concerns are reduced.
	Fluency is greatly improved when concepts can be expressed and recorded orally.
	Visual mapping software
	This tool allows the writer to generate ideas in a visual map, which can be converted to an outline and exported to a word processing file.
	Less writing is required at the brainstorming stage.
	This tool reduces some of the burden on working memory so that the writer is able to focus on the primary task of generating ideas.
	Visual images provide stimulation and reinforcement, which may reduce boredom and increase motivation.

Software Focus: Visual Mapping Software

Brainstorming is the process of associative thinking that leads to the generation of ideas. Many students who have difficulty expressing thoughts in writing find that visually mapping concepts frees them from the limitations of their working memory and syntax and capitalizes on strengths in visual-spatial thinking. **Visual mapping** is often used as a strategy for prewriting, but it is also an effective strategy for activating prior knowledge before a lesson, a reading, or a research project.

Visual mapping software allows for visual representation of ideas and reduces the need for writing because concepts can be expressed in brief phrases while the visual array represents relationships among concepts, which is more taxing cognitively and linguistically. Coupled with technology, visual mapping offers an intuitive and effective way to generate ideas and represent them visually.

Visual mapping software is readily available, easy to use, and relatively inexpensive. The most commonly used versions in school settings are Inspiration and Kidspiration, a version for younger students. These allow writers to brainstorm ideas in a visual format, supported by an enormous choice of colors, symbols, and easy-to-insert graphics. One feature of Inspiration and Kidspiration that makes them especially useful in the writing process is that graphic displays can be automatically converted to outlines with the click of one button (see Figure 22.7). This helps students move from brainstorming and organizing into drafting because it transforms the visually organized ideas into a linear sequence that can be used to guide writing, sentence by sentence. Although Inspiration and Kidspiration are the best-known products in this category, most graphics programs can be used for creating visual maps (see Table 22.2).

Software Focus: Programs that Extend Visual Mapping with Templates

Inspiration and Kidspiration are excellent tools for the organizing stage of the writing process because it is easy to add, delete, and organize topics and enhance them with graphics. Much of the academic writing, however, needs to follow a specific organizational scheme, sometimes called a rhetorical pattern. For instance, students may be required to write a persuasive essay, a compare/contrast paper, or an analysis of a process, each of which has a distinctive organization and flow of ideas. Software that reminds students of these patterns can be invaluable in developing their ability to produce higher level writing.

Inspiration and Kidspiration both come with numerous templates. A template is a blank pattern that can be filled in by the student that defines the structure of essential elements for writing. For instance, a template for a generic paragraph would include blank boxes for a title, a topic sentence, several supporting sentences, details for each supporting sentence, and a concluding sentence. Some of the writing templates available in Inspiration include comparative analysis, persuasive essay, definition, and au-

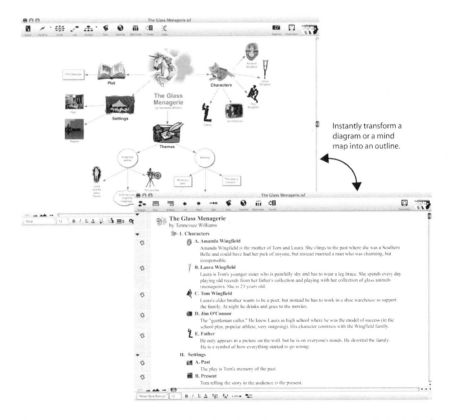

Instantly transform a diagram or a mind map into an outline.

Figure 22.7.   Inspiration diagram and outline views. (Copyright 2010. Diagram created in Inspiration® by Inspiration® Software. Used with permission.)

Table 22.2   Organizing ideas

Barriers to success	Assistive technology tools
Difficulty identifying relationships between concepts This barrier results in writing that lacks a logical connection between the ideas expressed. Thesis is unclear because ideas are not prioritized in terms of importance to the topic.	*Visual mapping software* This tool allows concepts generated in the brainstorming stage to be moved and reordered within an outline or a map. Visual templates for rhetorical patterns can be created to assist in structuring essays. Visual maps make the relationships between concepts clear and explicit.
Difficulty with time order and sequencing Topics and subtopics are not distinguished. Paragraph structure is weak.	*Word processing software* Templates provide structure for beginning writers who prefer not to work with visual maps to help them organize ideas. Outlines are easily generated using outlining tools, and topics can be moved and sorted within the outline.
Poor planning strategies The writer may avoid the organizing stage of writing altogether.	*Integrated writing software* This tool prompts writers to follow stages of writing process. It provides graphic cues to planning steps.

tobiographical event. The templates scaffold the process with embedded notes that prompt the student about how to complete each box or section of the template. For example, the template for comparing historical events shown in Figure 22.8 directs students to explain the significance of the event.

Haynes and McMurdo (2001) developed a manual and accompanying CD-ROM that capitalize on the power of Inspiration-based templates. They designed a sequence

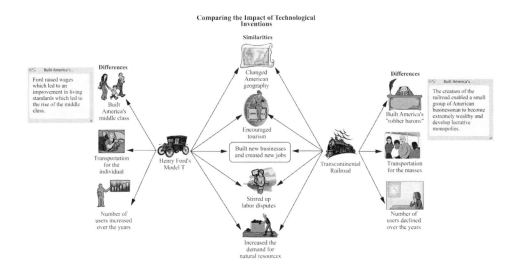

Figure 22.8.   Inspiration template for comparing/contrasting historical events. (Copyright 2010. Diagram created in Inspiration® by Inspiration® Software. Used with permission.)

of lessons that move students from mastering basic paragraphs through increasingly complex rhetorical patterns such as reasons, examples, process, classification, and compare/contrast. They use recurring visual and color patterns to identify key elements of paragraph structure.

Draft:Builder (Don Johnston) is another promising software that builds on visual mapping strategies. It models the sequential, recursive nature of the writing process and uses split screens, prompts, cues, and visual maps to help students move seamlessly through the stages. Draft:Builder offers three different screen views, which mirror the steps of creating a draft: Outline/Map view for generating and organizing ideas, Notes view for adding details and elaborating ideas, and a Draft view (see Figure 22.9) for converting the map or outline into connected text.

One of the strengths of this program is that the Outline/Map and Notes Views are integrated and remain on the screen during the drafting stage and can even be dragged and dropped verbatim into the draft, eliminating the need for rewriting information that has already been created. Students have the option of hearing text as they enter it or checking their progress and accuracy at any point during drafting. Draft:Builder includes a number of templates, such as compare/contrast, three- and five-paragraph essays, and specific types of common reports (animals, food groups, states), and a spellchecker (see Table 22.3).

Figure 22.9.   Draft:Builder offers three different screen views, which mirror the steps of creating a draft: Outline/Map, Notes, and Draft. (Reprinted by permission from Don Johnston, Inc.)

Table 22.3.   Drafting

Barriers to success	Assistive technology tools
Reading difficulties	*Text-to-speech software*
This barrier interferes with a writer's ability to read and reflect on his or her writing.	This tool reads the essay, allowing the writer to hear it and reflect on its content.
Poor spelling	*Word prediction software*
This barrier interferes with language production.	This tool (often included in writing software programs) predicts the words that the writer is trying to spell.
	This kind of software is good for poor spellers who can spell enough sounds in words to allow the prediction of likely words.
Poor sentence structure	*Voice-recognition software*
Students may struggle at the sentence level, impeding their ability to express complex ideas in writing.	This tool improves sentence structure for writers whose oral language is clearer than their written language.
Writing may be so garbled that the writer may not remember what he or she was trying to express.	This kind of software improves writing fluency and results in more language production.
Graphomotor difficulty	*Word processing software*
This barrier interferes with writing, typing speed, and accuracy.	Keyboarding assists with handwriting difficulties.
	Spellcheckers and grammar checkers assist with some spelling and sentence structure problems.
Poor word retrieval or limited vocabulary	*Word prediction software*
This barrier limits diction and the ability to express concepts.	This tool (often included in writing software programs) aids word retrieval and vocabulary expansion.
Poor working memory	*All of the above technologies*
This barrier makes it difficult for the writer to manage the multiple tasks necessary to produce writing.	These tools support drafting by reducing the burden of language production and accurate transcription, allowing the writer to focus on the content.

Drafting represents the Waterloo stage of the writing process for many students with learning disabilities. Students may be adept at generating ideas and organizing them using visual mapping tools, but the difficulties begin when they have to convert images or discrete concepts into coherent, grammatically correct sentences that are logically sequenced, with clear transitions, correctly spelled vocabulary choices, and accurate punctuation and paragraphing conventions. The mechanics of transcription—whether by pencil and paper or by keyboarding—are an insurmountable hurdle for many students. For these students, word prediction and voice-recognition software may be the means to the previously unattainable goal of effective composition.

Software Focus: Word Prediction

Word prediction software uses spelling knowledge, grammar rules, and context clues to predict what word a student is thinking of as he or she enters the first few letters. Students who struggle with keyboarding, spelling, and retrieving words may increase writing fluency using a word prediction program. Most of these programs can be used in standard word processing applications; the writer opens a word processing document and then opens the word prediction program. Many word prediction programs can also speak aloud the offered word choices so that writers are not hampered by poor decoding in selecting among visually similar words. Some word prediction software programs, such as Don Johnston's Co:Writer (see Figure 22.10), also offer grammar support, checking for subject–verb agreement, capitalization, punctuation, word usage, and correct word forms. Dictionaries can be customized according to the level of the writer from beginner to advanced and also by topic, such as sports, school subjects, or holidays, so that the word choices generated are appropriate to the writer and the subject. Users can create their own specialized dictionaries. Good word prediction programs adjust to the writer's style and diction so that the word choices grow increasingly accurate with use.

Although word prediction can be helpful for some students, others are frustrated by the number of decisions required to complete words as they are entered. Word prediction may seem like an interruption or more of a hindrance than a help for a student who has adequate keyboarding skills and is only a moderately poor speller. Many word prediction programs allow the writer to turn off the program altogether or to use it only on demand for particular words. If the software will be used by a variety of students, then this flexibility is important.

Word prediction is a feature of some integrated writing software packages such as Read and Write 9 Gold and Co:Writer, which combine word prediction with text-to-speech software that reads back what has been written so students can check their work aurally. These programs also have spellcheckers specialized for students with learning, which recognize a wider range of phonetically misspelled words than typical spellcheckers.

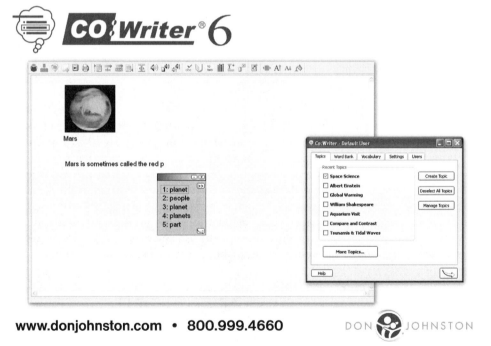

Figure 22.10.   Some word prediction software programs, such as Don Johnston's Co:Writer, also offer grammar support, checking for subject–verb agreement, capitalization, punctuation, word usage, and correct word forms. (Reprinted by permission from Don Johnston, Inc.)

Software Focus: Voice Recognition

Although voice recognition (or voice synthesis) has been a life-changing tool for some students (one college student claimed that he "never would have wound up in jail if he had had access to voice-recognition software in high school"), other students have stopped using it in frustration. The technology can perform remarkably well, but only under some conditions with some profiles of writers. Students who use voice-recognition software do not automatically improve the quality of their writing, but they can usually produce more writing with less effort, which allows them to focus more on ideas and organization than on the mechanics of handwriting, keyboarding, or spelling.

It is important to recognize the limitations of voice recognition and also the time and effort required to train the software to accurately recognize an individual's voice and diction. According to Follansbee (2003), an expert on voice recognition, students who may be good candidates for using voice recognition

- Have strong oral composing skills and a level of ease and fluency dictating their thoughts

- Have relatively clear articulation and speak in a manner that is not heavily inflected (students with speech impediments or strong, nonstandard accents may have trouble training the software)

- Are able to analyze and then modify their speech patterns and articulation for higher accuracy

- Show patience and persistence in training and correcting the software

- Recognize the purposes of literacy

Follansbee concluded that most successful users are at least 10 years old. We would add that students who are good candidates for using voice recognition software

- Understand that voice recognition accomplishes only one stage of the writing process—drafting—and realize that producing acceptable writing still requires planning, organizing, revising, and proofreading

Teachers and parents need to be committed to providing a supportive environment, graduated practice, and a sophisticated level of technical expertise as students strive to achieve accuracy because students are likely to give up in the early stages of using voice recognition without adequate training, guidance, and encouragement. Voice recognition never misspells words, but it may misrecognize them, sometimes producing gibberish that must be diligently corrected and trained out. The latest versions of voice recognition include Dragon NaturallySpeaking (Scansoft) and IBM ViaVoice, which come in versions for Windows and Macintosh. (ViaVoice products are available through ScanSoft at http://www.scansoft.com/viavoice.) There is also a Macintosh-only software product, iListen (MacSpeech). These recent versions use continuous speech recognition, which allows speakers to talk fluently at a regular conversational pace. Older versions used discrete speech recognition, which required a pause between each word. Although many users objected to the unnatural pace of discrete speech recognition, there is evidence that this version of voice recognition promotes improved spelling and word recognition as students watch the words they speak get transcribed, word by word, on the monitor (see Table 22.4).

Table 22.4. Revising and proofreading

Barriers to success	Assistive technology tools
Difficulty with decoding text Students cannot accurately read back their work. Once revisions are made, students cannot effectively read and evaluate their revisions.	*Text-to-speech software* This tool allows students to listen to drafts to improve their logic and fluency.
Trouble with attention to visual detail Students have difficulty reading handwritten comments by teachers. Students have trouble tracking which corrections have been made and which corrections remain to be made.	*Word processing software: The reviewing toolbar on Microsoft Word* Using the reviewing toolbar eliminates problems with reading teacher handwriting. Comments can be read with text-to-speech software. Graphic nature of working from teacher or peer comments in the revision process simplifies the task of tracking corrections (highlights and comments can be deleted after changes are made).
Poor working memory Students have trouble tracking and utilizing teacher oral comments while revising drafts.	*Word processing software: The reviewing toolbar on Microsoft Word* Students do not have to rely on memory to revise their drafts.
Executive function problems If corrected drafts are lost, then students have no record of teacher comments.	*Word processing software: The reviewing toolbar on Microsoft Word* Teacher comments are recorded electronically and are available if student draft is lost.

Software Focus: Word Processing

Word processing is so commonplace that people scarcely recognize it as a form of assistive technology. Before the computer era, however, which made digital cut and paste functions available, revision literally entailed rewriting large blocks of text, either by hand or typewriter. Correcting even small errors in spelling or punctuation was laborious. Today, the capacity of word processors to easily add, delete, and move limitless amounts of text, as well as insert tables, graphics, and symbols, has brought revision within the reach of most students. Most word processing programs include spellcheckers and grammar checkers of varying degrees of usefulness, and a variety of talking word processors, such as Read and Write 9 Gold and Don Johnston's Write: OutLoud, give immediate speech feedback as students type so they can hear what they have written. Macintosh computers and recent versions of PCs have built-in speech feedback.

The reviewing toolbar, which lets multiple readers add comments and suggestions to a draft, is one feature of Microsoft Word that is especially useful in the revision process. Teachers can encourage students to rethink the organization of a paper, elaborate on certain points, or change wording or sentence clarity simply by inserting comments or highlighting portions of a student's writing. It is easy to establish an electronic dialogue between the student and teacher, and as students systematically review their text from start to end, responding to teachers' comments, they have the added incentive of deleting those comments while creating a finished paper.

Software Focus: Portable Keyboards and Netbooks

Laptops are expensive and fragile; not every classroom has a computer available for every student at all times; and students often need to take notes or write in class, while riding on a bus, or while sprawled in bed. Portable keyboards are the solution to these challenges. They are relatively inexpensive (several hundred dollars compared with $1,200–$1,500 for a laptop), durable, lightweight tools that do simple word processing and not much more. Thus, they do not offer the array of distractions and options found on fully functioning computers: no games, Internet connections, or multiple pathways for performing functions such as saving and opening. In the past, portable keyboards were not able to support word prediction and voice recognition, but that is changing. Don Johnston offers Co:Writer SmartApplet, which adds word prediction and a choice of topic dictionaries to the AlphaSmart 3000 (AlphaSmart), and Write:OutLoud To Go, which adds text-to-speech. Other versions of portable keyboards include the Laser PC6 from Perfect Solutions, which also offers a text-to-speech add-on. Netbooks, including Apple's iPad, are the fastest growing sector of the personal computing market. They are small, lightweight, scaled down versions of computers designed mostly for Internet connectivity. They range in cost from $250–$800. They lack the durability of a well-designed portable keyboard and the high-powered memory of a full-size laptop, but make up for it in their portability and low cost. They can support a range of assistive technology add-ons such as text-to-speech and word prediction.

Software Focus: Text-to-Speech Software

Listening to an essay is an effective strategy for editing and proofreading. Because text-to-speech software programs can read documents aloud, students can easily use them to check for missing words, sentence structure errors, garbled syntax, and other writing problems that may be hard to spot without auditory input. Text-to-speech software is discussed at length in the Using Technology to Support Study Skills section of this chapter.

CONCLUSION

This chapter provides an overview of the current assistive technology applications and their role in providing universal access to learning. The choices are numerous and are likely to increase. The goal of this chapter is to frame an approach to using assistive technology by focusing on the following principles:

- Assistive technology provides academic support for all students, and it is an integral part of a universally designed educational environment.

- Assistive technology is a tool that should support and be integrated into a well-designed educational curriculum.

- Assistive technology has a place in remediation and accommodation. Struggling students need both in order to achieve their learning potential.

- Assistive technology best supports students when we assess their learning profile before selecting specific assistive technology tools.

- Assistive technology is constantly evolving; educators must stay current with its changes in order to provide students with the best technology tools.

As the second decade of the 21st century begins, these principles should serve as a guide to evaluating the myriad of assistive technology tools that will be available to educators and students.

REFERENCES

Anderson-Inman, L., & Horney, M. (1998). Transforming text for at-risk readers. In D. Reinking, L. Labbo, M. McKenna, & R. Kieffer (Eds.), *Handbook of literacy and technology: Technological transformations in a post-typographic world* (pp. 15–43). Mahwah, NJ: Lawrence Erlbaum Associates.

Anderson-Inman, L., & Horney, M. (2007). Supported e-text: Assistive technology through text transformations. *Reading Research Quarterly, 42*(1) 153–160.

Edyburn, D.L. (2005). Assistive technology and students with mild disabilities: From consideration to outcome measurement. In D. Edyburn, K. Higgins, & R. Boone (Eds.), *Handbook of special education technology research and practice* (pp. 239–270). Whitefish Bay, WI: Knowledge by Design.

Edyburn, D.L. (2006). Assistive technology and mild disabilities. *Special Education Technology Practice, 8*(4), 18–28.

Edyburn, D.L. (2007). Re-examining the role of assistive technology in learning. *Closing the Gap, 25*(5), 14–18. Retrieved September 24, 2009, from http://www.closingthegap.com/solutions/articles/1372

Edyburn, D.L. (2009, January/February). Response to intervention (RTI): Is there a role for assistive technology? *Special Education Technology Practice,* 15–19.

Elkind, J. (1998). Computer reading machines for poor readers. *Perspectives, 24,* 238–259.

Engstrom, E.U. (2005). Reading, writing, and assistive technology: An integrated developmental curriculum for college-bound students. *Journal of Adolescent and Adult Literacy, 49*(1), 30–39.

Follansbee, B. (2003). Speaking to write/word for word: An overview of speech recognition. *Perspectives, 29*(4), 10–13.

Gehrmann, M., & Kinas, J.M. (2002). *Assistive technology for students with mild disabilities.* ERIC Clearinghouse.

Hartley, J., Sotto, E., & Pennebaker, J. (2003). Speaking versus typing: A case-study of the effects of using voice-recognition software on academic correspondence. *British Journal of Educational technology, 34*(1), 5–16.

Haynes, C., & McMurdo, K. (2001). *Structured writing: Using Inspiration Software to teach paragraph development.* Eugene, OR: International Society for Technology in Education.

Hecker, L., Burns, L., Elkind, J., Elkind, K., & Katz, L. (2002). Benefits of assistive reading software for students with attention disorders. *Annals of Dyslexia, 52,* 243–272.

Honeycutt, L. (2003). Researching the use of voice recognition writing software. *Computers and Composition, 20*(1), 77–95.

Individuals with Disabilities Education Improvement Act (IDEA) of 2004, PL 108-446, 20 U.S.C. §§ 1400 *et seq.*

Karchmer-Klein, R., MacArthur, C.A., & Najera, K. (2008, December). *The effects of concept mapping software on fifth grade students' writing.* Paper presented at the annual meeting of the National Reading Conference, Orlando, FL.

Koester, H.H., & Levine, S.P. (1996). Effect of a word prediction feature on user performance. *AAC: Augmentative and Alternative Communication, 12*(3), 155–168.

Lewis, R.B., Graves, A.W., Ashton, T.M., & Kieley, C.L. (1998). Word processing tools for students with learning disabilities: A comparison of strategies to increase text entry speed. *Learning Disabilities Research and Practice, 13*(2), 95–108.

MacArthur, C.A. (1998). Word processing with speech synthesis and word prediction: Effects on the dialogue journal writing of students with learning disabilities. *Learning Disabilities Quarterly, 21,* 1–16.

MacArthur, C.A. (1999). Overcoming barriers to writing: Computer support for basic writing skills. *Reading and Writing Quarterly, 15,* 169–192.

MacArthur, C.A. (2000). New tools for writing: Assistive technology for students with writing difficulties. *Topics in Language Disorders, 20,* 85–100.

MacArthur, C.A. (2006). The effects of new technologies on writing and writing processes. In C.A. MacArthur, S. Graham, & J. Fitzgerald (Eds.), *Handbook of Writing Research* (pp. 248–262). New York: Guilford Press.

MacArthur, C.A. (2009). Assistive technology for struggling writers. *Perspectives on Language and Literacy, 35*(3), 31–33.

MacArthur, C.A., Ferretti, R.P., Okolo, C.M., & Cavalier, A.R. (2001). Technology applications for students with literacy problems: A critical review. *Elementary School Journal, 101,* 273–301.

MacArthur, C.A., & Graham, S. (1987). Learning disabled students composing under three methods of text production: Handwriting, word processing, and dictation. *Journal of Special Education, 21,* 22–42.

Montali, J., & Lewandowski, L. (1996). Bimodal reading: Benefits of a talking computer for average and less skilled reading. *Journal of Learning Disabilities, 29*(3), 271–279.

No Child Left Behind Act of 2001, PL 107-110, 115 Stat. 1425, 20 U.S.C. §§ 6301 *et seq.*

Pauk, W. (2008). *How to study in college* (9th ed.). Boston: Houghton Mifflin.

Peterson-Karlan, G.R., & Parette, H.P. (2007, November). *Supporting struggling writers with technology: Evidence-based instruction and decision-making.*

Retrieved November 8, 2010, from http://www.cited.org/library/resourcedocs/TechnologyToSupportWritingSummary.pdf

Pisha, B., & O'Neill, L. (2003). When they learn to read, can they read to learn? *Perspectives, 29*(4), 14–18.

Quinlan, T. (2004). Speech recognition technology and students with writing difficulties: Improving fluency. *Journal of Educational Psychology, 96*(2), 337–346.

Roberts, K.D., & Stodden, R.A. (2005). The use of voice recognition software as a compensatory strategy for postsecondary education students receiving services under the category of learning disabled. *Journal of Vocational Rehabilitation, 22*(1), 49–64.

Rose, D., & Meyer, A. (2002). *Teaching every student in the digital age: Universal design for learning.* Alexandria VA: Association for Supervision and Curriculum Development.

Rose, D., & Rose, K. (2008). Deficits in executive function processes: a curriculum-based intervention. In L. Meltzer (Ed.), *Executive function in education: From theory to practice* (pp. 287–308). New York: Guilford Press.

Sanderson, A. (1999). Voice recognition software: A panacea for dyslexic learners or a frustrating hindrance? *Dyslexia: An International Journal of Research and Practice, 5*(2), 114–118.

Scherer, M.J. (1998). *The Matching Person and Technology (MPT) Model manual and accompanying assessment instruments* (3rd ed.). Webster, NY: Institute for Matching Person and Technology.

Scherer, M.J. (Ed.). (2002). *Assistive technology: Matching device and consumer for successful rehabilitation.* Washington, DC: APA Books.

Scherer, M.J., & Craddock, G. (2002). Matching Person and Technology (MPT) assessment process. *Technology and Disability [Special Issue]: The Assessment of Assistive Technology Outcomes, Effects and Costs, 14,* 125–131.

Strangman, N., & Dalton, B. (2005). Using technology to support struggling readers: A review of the research. In D. Edyburn, K. Higgins, & R. Boone (Eds.), *Handbook of special education technology research and practice* (pp. 545–570). Whitefish Bay, WI: Knowledge by Design.

Wise, B.W., Olson, R.K., Ring, J., & Johnson, M. (1998). Interactive computer support for improving phonological skills. In J.L. Metsala & L.C. Ehri (Eds.), *Word recognition in beginning literacy* (pp. 189–208). Mahwah, NJ: Lawrence Erlbaum Associates.

Wise, B.W., Ring, J., & Olson, R.K. (2000). Individual differences in gains from computer-assisted remedial reading with more emphasis on phonological analysis or accurate reading in context. *Journal of Experimental Child Psychology, 77,* 197–235.

Vygotsky, L. (1978). *Mind in society.* Cambridge, MA: Harvard University Press.

Zabala, J. (1995). *The SETT Framework: Critical areas to consider when making informed assistive technology decisions.* Retrieved September 17, 2009, from http://plone.rockyview.ab.ca/ss/a-t-l/atl-decision-making/sett-framework

23

Rights of Individuals with Dyslexia and Other Disabilities

JO ANNE SIMON AND MICHELE KULE-KORGOOD

This chapter presents basic information about special education law. It is important to understand the massive changes in education for children with disabilities that took place in the 1970s. With this background in mind, federal
legislation and its impact on special education are discussed, along with landmark cases
that led to changes in how children who have disabilities are served. Procedural safeguards within the laws are described. Next, the Individuals with Disabilities Education
Act (IDEA) of 1990 (PL 101-476) and its amendments and who is eligible for funding for
special education are discussed, along with two other important civil rights laws that
protect children with disabilities. How children are identified, referred, evaluated, and
receive services under their individualized education programs (IEPs) under the law is
also explained. This chapter focuses on changes in the law that affect individuals with
learning disabilities.

REVOLUTION IN EDUCATION

The early 1970s brought a revolution in education. Like most revolutions, it had been
brewing for some time, aided by the emergence of certain issues in the public. The
failure to educate children with disabilities had been swept under the rug for many
years. The landmark decision in *Brown v. Board of Education of Topeka* (1954), however,
brought national attention to education as a civil rights issue for the first time. When
President John F. Kennedy was elected, his family's involvement with intellectual disability[1] became more widely known. Eunice Kennedy Shriver created the Special

---

[1]In 2010, Rosa's Law was enacted, changing previous terminology in federal legislation from
"mentally retarded individuals" to "individuals with intellectual disability" (PL 111-256, § 2781).

Olympics. Hubert Humphrey, Vice President during the Lyndon B. Johnson administration, had a granddaughter who was born with Down syndrome. Awareness of the discrimination against, and the exclusion of individuals with disabilities, is frequently traced back to the exposure of the horrid living conditions and treatment of the individuals with disabilities residing at Willowbrook, a state institution located in Staten Island, New York, in 1972. The media coverage of Willowbrook's conditions galvanized public awareness and outrage. Widespread class action lawsuits led to the institution's closure and the deinstitutionalization of individuals with disabilities. The attention brought a new focus to the needs of children with intellectual disabilities, which, when combined with a growing, post–*Brown v. Board of Education* recognition of education as a civil right, gave rise to key disability education cases, which touched off the revolutionary changes.

Previously, children with obvious disabilities were often provided with substandard, if any, education, and it was almost always segregated. Still other children with disabilities, such as children with learning disabilities that often went undetected, languished in classrooms without needed interventions. Education for children with disabilities was viewed as a privilege, not a right. But by the mid-1970s, federal legislation demanded that if states wanted federal funding for education, then they would have to educate their children with disabilities as well.

Pennsylvania Association for Retarded Children (PARC) v. Commonwealth of Pennsylvania (1972) and *Mills v. District of Columbia Board of Education* (1972) were landmark cases that became major influences in bringing about federal special education laws. *PARC* involved children with intellectual disabilities, whereas *Mills* involved children with various disabilities. In both cases, the children also had behavior problems. Proceeding under the equal protection clause of the 14th Amendment to the U.S. Constitution, the courts in both cases required the public school defendants to provide access to the public schools for children with disabilities. The courts also addressed issues of due process, establishing the requirement that basic procedural protections—the right to notice and a hearing—were required before a school system could separate children with disabilities from those in general education. *Mills* relied on a line of precedents dating to *Brown v. Board of Education*. Specifically, the court in *Mills* reasoned that if segregation in public schools on the basis of race was unconstitutional and if using culturally biased measures to place poor children in inferior public school education tracks was unconstitutional, then the District of Columbia's total exclusion of children with disabilities from any kind of education was similarly unconstitutional.

PARC and *Mills* came on the heels of the first federal efforts in funding education—the Elementary and Secondary Education Act (ESEA) of 1965 (PL 89-10), which for the first time provided direct federal aid to the states to support their efforts in educating general education students who were economically disadvantaged.[2] These are what we commonly refer to as Title I funds. That same year, an amendment to Title I also provided federal funds to the states to operate special programs for individuals with disabilities, such as state schools for the deaf, the blind, and individuals with intellectual disabilities. The following year, the Bureau of Education for the Handicapped was created within the U.S. Department of Health, Education, and Welfare, followed 2 years later by the creation of discretionary grant programs to serve handicapped students. (This office is now known as the Office of Special Education Programs [OSEP], which is within the U.S. Department of Education.)

---

[2]Prior to that, the National Defense Education Act was spurred by Sputnik and Cold War fears that the USSR beat the United States into space and created a federal push for funds to strengthen science and math education. This was the beginning of federal funds for education.

These legal decisions and this legislation set the tone for the Education of the Handicapped Act Amendments (EHA) of 1974 (PL 93-380), which amended the ESEA and expanded the funding base for basic state grants and codified the rights established in the *PARC* and *Mills* decisions. The following year, the Education for All Handicapped Children Act of 1975 (PL 94-142) was passed. This law extensively amended the EHA in the following ways:

- It provided direct federal aid to children with one of the enumerated categories of disability.

- It elaborated on the rights established by the EHA.

- It expanded the procedural safeguards first established in *PARC* and *Mills*.

- It created the requirement of an IEP for each qualified child with a disability.

This law has been amended often, most significantly in IDEA 1990 and in the Individuals with Disabilities Education Improvement Act (IDEA) of 2004 (PL 108-446). At its core, this law is a mechanism to help fund special education. States receiving federal monies must guarantee every child with a disability a free appropriate public education (FAPE) by providing special education service or risk the loss of these dollars. This law and its amendments protect basic educational rights for individuals with disabilities from birth through age 21. Although no state has fully complied, case-by-case enforcement by parents and attorneys has protected individual students and encouraged systemic improvements.[3] (For a list of special education acronyms, see Table 23.1.)

WHAT SPECIAL EDUCATION LAW PROVIDES

The procedural safeguards established in the Education for All Handicapped Children Act of 1975 and IDEA 2004 protect a child's right to a FAPE[4] in the **least restrictive environment** (**LRE**). Children are covered if they require special education services in order to benefit from an education. Special education services must ensure a meaningful

Table 23.1. Special education abbreviations

ADA	Americans with Disabilities Act of 1990	IDEA	Individuals with Disabilities Education Act
ADHD	Attention-deficit/hyperactivity disorder	IEP	Individualized education program
EHA	Education of the Handicapped Act	LD	Learning disability
ESEA	Elementary and Secondary Education Act	LEA	Local educational agency
FAPE	Free appropriate public education	LRE	Least restrictive environment
504	Section 504 of the Rehabilitation Act of 1973	SEA	State educational agency

---

[3]"The fee provision of the IDEA allows parents to act as private attorneys general to exercise their rights" (*Park v. Anaheim Union High School District,* 444 F3d 1149 [9th Cir., 2006]).

"IDEA relies upon the central role played by parents in assuring that their child with a disability received a free and appropriate public education" (S. Rep. No. 108-185 [2003]).

"Based on the current statutory language and on the rich legislative history emphasizing the importance of parental involvement, the committee believes that parents have a right to represent their child in court, without a lawyer for purposes of IDEA law, regardless of whether their claims involve procedural or substantive issues" (S. Rep. No. 108-185 [2003]).

[4]FAPE is defined as "special education and related services" that are 1) provided at public expense; 2) meet the standards of the state educational agency (SEA); 3) include an appropriate education at the preschool, elementary, and secondary level school levels; and 4) are delivered in accordance with the child's IEP (20 U.S.C. § 1401 [8][1998]).

Table 23.2.   Individuals with Disabilities Education Improvement Act (IDEA) of 2004 classifications of children with disabilities

Autism	Orthopedic impairment
Deafblindness	Other health impairment
Emotional disturbance	Specific learning disability
Hearing impairment, including deafness	Speech-language impairment
Intellectual disability	Traumatic brain injury
Multiple disabilities	Visual impairment, including blindness

Approximately 90% of the children served under IDEA 2004 are classified within four groups: specific learning disability, speech-language impairments, intellectual disability, and emotional disturbance (U.S. Department of Education, 1998). The other disability categories are lower incidence impairments and thus account for a lower percentage of classified children.

educational benefit. IDEA 2004 protects children whose impairments meet the criteria listed in the 12 classifications set out in the Code of Federal Regulations (see Table 23.2):

> Mental retardation, a hearing impairment (including deafness), a speech or language impairment, a visual impairment (including blindness), a serious emotional disturbance (referred to in this part as "emotional disturbance"), an orthopedic impairment, autism, traumatic brain injury, an other health impairment, a specific learning disability, deaf-blindness, or multiple disabilities. (34 C.F.R. 300.8[a][1])

In addition, schools may also provide special education services to children ages 3 through 9 based on "developmental delay" rather than on a specific disability classification (34 C.F.R. 300.8[b]). The classifications and the state implementing regulations make the categories of children with disabilities covered by IDEA 2004 narrower than those covered by two other important statutes protecting children with disabilities—Section 504 of the Rehabilitation Act of 1973 (PL 93-112) and the Americans with Disabilities Act (ADA) of 1990 (PL 101-336).

Section 504 and the ADA are civil rights laws that provide that qualified individuals with disabilities cannot be excluded from participation in, denied the benefits of, or be subjected to discrimination by any service, program, or activity of an educational institution and further stipulate that services must be provided in the most integrated setting (*Coleman v. Zatcheka,* 1993; *Olmstead v. Zimring, 1999*). Section 504 and the ADA are designed to provide only equivalent access to educational and extracurricular programs and opportunities, not specialized education, such as individualized tutoring, smaller classes, or specialized instructional methods. Most teachers will come into contact with either IDEA 2004 (special education) or Section 504 or the ADA (equal access) in one way or another. Sometimes these laws overlap, which may cause confusion. Therefore, it is important that teachers and administrators have a basic understanding of these laws.

WHO IS PROTECTED?

Both IDEA 2004 and Section 504 provide protection to students with disabilities. However, the definition of a disability contained within Section 504 is much broader than the definition of disability under IDEA 2004. For example, all IDEA students are covered by Section 504, and compliance with the IDEA will, in many cases, meet the requirements of Section 504. The converse, however, is not necessarily true—not all Section 504 students are eligible for services under the IDEA. Under Section 504, individuals with a disability who have a physical or mental impairment that substantially limits one or more major life activities, have a record of such impairment, or are regarded as having such an impairment, are protected. IDEA 2004 protects students with specific disabilities, who require special education/related services due to the adverse effect of their disability (20 U.S.C. 1401[3]).

Individuals with Disabilities Education Act and Its Amendments

IDEA 2004 protects children who fall into the 12 categories listed in Table 23.2 and who require special education services to benefit from an education. Children with disabilities are entitled to the protections of IDEA 2004 from birth through 21 years of age or the attainment of a high school diploma, whichever comes first. No child is considered too "disabled" to be educated, and IDEA 2004 provides that special education can take place in environments that range from inclusive environments, such as general education classes (i.e., **inclusion**), to restrictive special classes, including institutional settings.[5] *Special education* is defined by the statute as

> Specially designed instruction at no cost to the parents, to meet the unique needs of a child with a disability, including (A) instruction conducted in the classroom, in the home, in hospitals and institutions, and in other settings; and (B) instruction in physical education. (20 U.S.C. § 1401[29])

Under IDEA 2004, a team of qualified professionals and the parent of the child determines whether a child is eligible for special education and if so, which special educational services and supplemental (access) services are appropriate for the student. Different states have different names for these teams, but their function is the same. Once the team has determined that a child has a disability, it must also develop an IEP, which will become the road map to be followed in making special education services available to that child. An IEP sets out a baseline of the child's current functioning levels, long-term goals, short-term objectives, and benchmarks for measuring progress toward those goals and objectives each year, as well as the placement and services that will allow the child to reach those goals and must include the opportunity for meaningful participation by the parents. Under IDEA 2004, parents are considered equal participants in developing their child's IEP, and the process should not be one of a majority vote but one of consensus building. IDEA 2004 requires that all students with a disability be educated in the LRE, an environment in which students with disabilities are educated with students without disabilities with the assistance of supplementary aids and services. Students should be educated in this environment to the maximum extent appropriate and should only be removed to a more restrictive environment when the nature and severity of the disability is such that education in a regular class with the use of supplementary aids and services cannot be achieved satisfactorily. Schools must also take intermediate steps where appropriate, such as placing the child in regular education for some academic classes and special education classes for others, mainstreaming the child for nonacademic classes only, or providing interaction with children without disabilities for children during lunch and recess.

IDEA 2004 is federal enabling legislation (legislation that gives appropriate officials the authority to implement or enforce the law). The accompanying regulations put flesh on the bones of the statute (law). Each state, however, must have their own statutes and regulations (promulgated by the SEA) that provide at least as much pro-

---

[5]IDEA 2004 has a **zero-reject principle,** which means that no child is considered too "disabled" to learn and to be provided with educational services. Thus, children with very low intellectual capacity who live in institutions and students who have been placed in juvenile detention facilities are entitled to a FAPE.

tection as the federal law for children with disabilities.[6] State statutes and regulations also cover the curriculum requirements and standards that are called for in the federal legislation.

Unfortunately, placement decisions often depend on available resources and local politics. The level of service provided, therefore, may not be an accurate reflection of a child's educational needs. There has been a rising concern among advocates and enforcement agencies regarding the incidence of harassment and retaliation in kindergarten through 12th grade when parents and caregivers seek services for their children (U.S. Department of Education, 2000). Lawmakers considered the topic of retaliation by public agencies while they were amending IDEA, but decided against including any regulation on the matter. Instead, they determined that Section 504 and Title II of the ADA adequately protected individual's rights.

The definitions or identification methods of several disability categories are also subject to ongoing political debate; particularly *specific learning disabilities* and *emotional disturbance,* but also *autism, traumatic brain injury,* and *other health impairments* to a lesser extent. Some students may not fit neatly into one of the disability categories but still should receive protection and services under the law. For example, attention-deficit/ hyperactivity disorder (ADHD) is not a classification covered by IDEA 2004, but the U.S. Department of Education (1991) indicated that children with ADHD may sometimes be classified as having specific learning disabilities, emotional disturbance, or other health impairment. What is important is that the child has a disability and needs special education services because of that disability. Similarly, IDEA 2004 dealt with the identification issue for specific learning disabilities when it changed the law from requiring a discrepancy model to permitting a response to intervention (RTI) model. The U.S. Department of Education indicated that this change allows earlier intervention for children, rather than a "wait to fail" approach necessary with a discrepancy model approach. This modification in identification technique may ultimately affect both the definition of specific learning disability and the number of students eligible for services or protection under special education law.

In addition to providing specially designed instruction, IDEA 2004 calls for providing various supplemental aids and services without charge, including diagnostic testing and evaluation; occupational and physical therapy; speech-language pathology; specialized tutoring and resource room services; using audio books; counseling; paraprofessional assistance; and using notetaking, testing modifications, and adaptive equipment. Thus, IDEA 2004 is quite broad in the scope of services it provides to students with disabilities but narrow in its criteria as to who is an eligible student with a disability.

Referrals

A child may be referred for evaluation for special education services by a parent or guardian, a teacher, or a school administrator. If the school refers the child for evaluation, then the school must have the parent or guardian's permission before the child

---

[6]See, for example, Texas's statute requiring screening and treatment for dyslexia and related learning disorders. Texas defines *dyslexia* as "a disorder of constitutional origin manifested by a difficulty in learning to read, write, or spell, despite conventional instruction, adequate intelligence, and sociocultural opportunity" (Texas Educational Code § 38.003[d]). See also Louisiana's statute, LA R.S. § 17:7(11).

can be evaluated, except in special circumstances.[7] The school district must provide the evaluation free of charge and within 60 days of receiving parental consent. The "child find" provision of the IDEA 2004 obligates schools to identify, locate, and evaluate children for the presence of a disability and the need for special education and related services (20 U.S.C. §1412[a][3][A]).

No IEP can be developed and no special education placement can occur without a complete, individualized evaluation of the child (20 U.S.C. § 1414 [a][1][A]). Many states have specific requirements as to who must be at the meeting that is initially held to determine whether a child is eligible for special education services. If the child is currently in general education or is being considered for possible placement in a general education setting, then the general education classroom teacher must provide input and share observations of the child's functioning within the general education classroom and curriculum (Assistance to States, 2007, § 300.321 [a][2]). Parents must be given a meaningful opportunity to participate (Assistance to States, 2007, § 300.501[b]). Interpreters are required when the parents speak a language other than English (Assistance to States, 2007, § 300.322[e]).

Procedural Safeguards

If the parents and the rest of the IEP team cannot come to an agreement on the child's educational placement, then the parents may seek due process by requesting an impartial hearing. Such hearings are conducted by an impartial hearing officer, not a judge. Either the parents or the school district may appeal an unfavorable decision, in most states to a state review board and, if unsuccessful, may appeal further to federal district court or a state court. (In some states, there is no secondary level of appellate administrative review, and parties may appeal an unfavorable decision directly to the courts.) The federal district court is the forum chosen most often, although in some states, special education cases are brought in state court, where they get a more favorable review than in the federal courts.

The child must remain in the current educational placement while a judicial or administrative proceeding is pending. This is sometimes referred to as the "stay put" or "pendency" provision of IDEA 2004 and ensures stability—that a child is not bounced back and forth between placements before the matter is finally resolved. A child's placement, therefore, will not be modified unless the parties agree to do so.

A Leading Case

Florence Country School District Four v. Shannon Carter (1993) is one of the leading cases in the field that sets out many of the parameters of the prevailing law. Many teachers and administrators have heard about "*Carter* cases" (cases that raise similar issues as the *Carter* case). Shannon Carter was a ninth-grade student with dyslexia who lived in South Carolina. Her school district proposed placing her in a general education setting and providing three individual instructional periods a week. It proposed specific goals for reading and math, which amounted to 4 months' progress for each year of schooling.

---

[7]See C.F.R. 300.300(a) explaining initial consent is not necessary if a parent cannot be located despite reasonable efforts by the school district; if parental rights have been terminated; or the parental rights to make educational decisions have been subrogated and consent has been granted by an individual appointed to make educational decisions.

Dissatisfied with this plan, Shannon's parents requested an impartial hearing and unilaterally placed Shannon in a special school for children with disabilities. That school, however, was not on the state of South Carolina's list of approved schools. The impartial hearing and state review officers found in favor of the school district, and the parents sued in federal court, claiming that the school district had failed to provide a FAPE for their daughter. They sought reimbursement of the tuition they had paid to the private school. The federal district court ruled in the parents' favor, finding that the proposed IEP was "wholly inadequate" and that the private school "provided Shannon an excellent education in substantial compliance with all the substantive requirements" of the law, in that it evaluated her progress regularly and developed a plan that allowed Shannon to progress from grade to grade (17 EHLR 452). The court further found that Shannon's parents were entitled to reimbursement of tuition and costs. The Fourth Circuit Court of Appeals affirmed the district court's ruling (950 F.2d 156 [1991]). The Fourth Circuit agreed that the public school's IEP for Shannon was inadequate and rejected the public school district's argument that reimbursement was not proper because the parents had chosen a school that had not been approved by the state or that did not comply with all of the requirements of IDEA.

The Supreme Court agreed to hear the case and unanimously affirmed the lower courts' decisions. It relied on its earlier decision in *School Committee of Burlington v. Department of Education of Massachusetts* (1985), which provided for reimbursement of tuition when a parent unilaterally places a child and a court subsequently agrees that the parents' placement decision was proper under IDEA. *Burlington,* however, dealt with state-approved schools.[8] *Carter* made the law clear: Tuition will be reimbursed by a school district if a court concludes that the public school placement violated IDEA *and* the private school placement provided an appropriate education. Shannon Carter's case is a success story in many ways. Today, she is an adult managing her own business—a success by anyone's standards (Staples, 2002). Although *Carter* is still good law, IDEA 2004 also clarifies funding for a unilaterally placed child with a disability. As the Supreme Court explains, parents who unilaterally decide to place their child with a disability in a private school, without obtaining the consent of local school officials, "do so at their own financial risk" (*Burlington,* 471 U.S. 359, 374, p. 15). IDEA 2004 does not require a **local education agency** (**LEA**) to pay for the cost of education, including special education and related services, of a child with a disability at a private school or facility if that agency made FAPE available to the child but parents elected to place the child in such private school anyway (20 U.S.C. § 1412[a][10][C][i]). The threshold question, therefore, must be—was the IEP inadequate? Furthermore, if a parent is eligible for tuition reimbursement, a court may still reduce or deny that reimbursement when parents fail to inform the IEP team of their rejection of a proposed placement to provide FAPE or state their concerns and intent to enroll their child in a private school at public expense; parents do not make their child available for an evaluation by the LEA; or, there is a judicial finding of unreasonableness with respect to actions taken by the parents (20 U.S.C. § 1412[a][10][C][iii]). In *Forest Grove School District v. T. A.,* the Supreme Court refined the law even more when it ruled that private school tuition may

---

[8]Though most of these cases involve tuition reimbursement, recently a federal court in New York held that the right to funding for a nonpublic school, when the district failed to offer a free appropriate public education, cannot be made contingent on the family's financial status. If the hearing officer finds for the parent on all three of the "Burlington/Carter factors," and the family is not in a financial position to "front" the tuition, a hearing officer can order direct funding to the nonpublic school (*Mr. & Mrs. A. o/b/o D.A. v. New York City Department of Education,* 2011).

be reimbursed even if the student never received special education services from a public school.

Reauthorization of the Individuals with Disabilities Education Improvement Act

IDEA 2004 and its predecessors should be reauthorized every 5 years; often, these revisions only involve funding. As mentioned previously, however, the reauthorization from IDEA in 1997 to IDEA 2004 contained several substantial revisions with federal regulations by the U.S. Department of Education further defining the statutes. This section highlights some of the more dramatic changes created by IDEA 2004 and recent federal regulations, but is not intended as a comprehensive analysis of all details. Some highlights from IDEA 2004 include alignment with the No Child Left Behind Act (NCLB) of 2001 (PL 107-110); disproportionality; changes to the section on student discipline; altering the model of identifying students with specific learning disabilities; and changes to the due process rights, evaluation, monitoring, and enforcement sections.

The revision of eligibility for special educational services is one key provision of IDEA 2004, primarily in connection with classifying children with learning disabilities. For example, IDEA 2004 prohibits a child from being classified as having a disability and thus eligible for special educational services if "the determining factor for such a determination is either a lack of appropriate instruction in reading, including the essential components of reading instruction as defined in NCLB; or a lack of instruction in math; or limited English proficiency" (20 U.S.C. § 1414[b][5]). Thus, under IDEA 2004, an LEA will "not be required to take into consideration whether a child has a severe discrepancy between achievement and intellectual ability" and may instead use a process that evaluates whether the child "responds to scientific, research-based interventions" such as those described in NCLB (20 U.S.C. § 1414[b][6]). This is what is commonly referred to as RTI. RTI proved to be one of the more contentious issues during IDEA 2004 reauthorization. It enjoyed much theoretical support, but some advocates also expressed a great deal of concern and confusion regarding implementing its principles in accordance with either the letter or spirit of IDEA 2004.

Proponents argue that the RTI method is an appropriate replacement for a number of reasons. First, the IQ-discrepancy model does not account for students who are subject to bad instruction. Second, the discrepancy model also delays intervention until a student's achievement is low enough to create a discrepancy. Related to this second point, many experts believe remediation is more difficult after the second grade. Finally, many supporters view RTI as a path to limit the number of students gaining access to special education services, with the students remaining without IEPs receiving interventions outside of the formal process. However, the U.S. Department of Education, Office of Special Education and Rehabilitative Services, recently issued a Memorandum to State Directors of Special Education strongly warning states that the IDEA 2004 "provision mandating that States allow, as part of their criteria for determining whether a child has a specific learning disability (SLD), the use of a process based on the child's response to scientific, research-based intervention" (see 34 C.F.R. § 300.307[a][2]) may not "be used to delay or deny the provision of a full and individual evaluation" to "a child suspected of having a disability" under IDEA (U.S. Department of Education, 2011).

Critics counter that the proposed regulations are unclear as to what precisely is meant by RTI, making it unlikely to be successfully implemented and, regardless of intent, lead to the denial or delay of needed services. This is further hampered by a lack of evidence-based reading programs, inadequate numbers of appropriately trained teachers, and confusion as to what methods and/or criteria should be used to evaluate a child's failure to respond to intervention. Because the requirement of short-term goals and objectives was largely eliminated by IDEA 2004, teachers may have more difficulty measuring a child's RTI with sufficient frequency so as to know whether educational interventions are working.

Disproportionality is a second key provision of IDEA 2004. Responding to earlier findings that children classified as having disabilities were disproportionately African American children, IDEA 2004 requires that states modify their policies, practices, and procedures "to prevent the inappropriate over-identification or disproportionate representation by race and ethnicity of children as children with disabilities, including children with disabilities with a particular impairment" (20 U.S.C. §1412 [a][24]). One way states are required to do this is by disaggregating data on suspension and expulsion rates by race and ethnicity (34 C.F.R. 300.170[a]).

Furthermore, IDEA 2004 provided for increased flexibility in parental participation in the educational planning for their children with disabilities. 34 C.F.R. § 300.321 permitted a lessening of the required IEP team members:

- Any special education teacher, instead of one with expertise in the child's disability, may be on a child's IEP team (§ 300.321[a][3]).

- Required team members may not be required to attend if the parent and district agree in writing that the team member's area of service is not being modified or discussed (§ 300.321[e][1]).

- In addition, parents may waive the attendance of a required team member, even when the member's area of service is being modified or discussed, if the parent and district agree in writing and the team member submits a written report.

Of course, the danger in allowing these waivers is the lack of protections to ensure that parents are not put between the proverbial rock and a hard place in terms of scheduling and notice practices.

IDEA 2004 also updates due process procedural safeguards. For instance, 34 C.F.R. §§ 300.507 mandates that a due process complaint must be filed within 2 years of when the parent or LEA would have known of the alleged violation. Furthermore, the LEA must either challenge the sufficiency of the complaint within 15 days of receipt or respond to the subject matter of the due process complaint within 10 days (34 C.F.R. §§ 300.508). If the LEA challenges the sufficiency of the complaint, then the opportunity to amend complaints are limited (34 C.F.R. §§ 300.508[d][3]). In addition, 34 C.F.R. §§ 300.510 allows a 30-day period for the LEA to resolve the dispute. This prevents the due process from occurring for at least 30 days unless both the parent and LEA agree in writing to waive the resolution period. For the thousands of parents who file their due process complaint notices without the assistance of an attorney or advocate, it is essential that these requirements do not undermine their access to due process.

IDEA 2004 also contains significant provisions modifying procedures for student discipline. For example, 34 C.F.R. § 300.530(a) added new authority for school personnel to consider unique circumstances in change of placement cases for a child with a disability who violates a code of student conduct. Thus, if a student violates a code of student conduct, then school officials may suspend the student for up to 10 days. IDEA 2004 also expands removal authority for students causing serious bodily injury. 34 C.F.R. § 300.530(g) allows school personnel to remove a student to an interim alternative educational setting for up to 45 school days without regard to whether the behavior is determined to be a manifestation of the child's disability when the student has inflicted serious bodily injury on another person while at school. In addition, 34 C.F.R. § 300.530(d)(3) clarified that public agencies are only required to provide services if they would provide services to a child without disabilities who is similarly removed. Furthermore, IDEA 2004 established a new standard for manifestation determinations. Within 10 school days of any decision to change the placement of a child with a disability because of a violation of a code of student conduct, the LEA, the parent, and members of the child's IEP team must review all relevant information in the student's file to determine:

- Whether the conduct in question was caused by, or had a direct and substantial relationship to, the child's disability

- Whether the conduct in question was the direct result of the LEA's failure to implement the IEP

If the LEA, the parent, and the IEP team determine that the conduct was a manifestation of the child's disability, then the team must either conduct a functional behavioral assessment or update the behavioral intervention plan for the child. The district must also return the child to the original placement (34 C.F.R. 300.530[f]).

Moving beyond the major revisions, IDEA 2004 continues to be reauthorized every 5 years, and the next major reauthorization is forthcoming. Typically, this involves reauthorization of funding. The Education for All Handicapped Children Act of 1975 established a maximum funding level for special education students at an additional 40% of the average per pupil expenditure. This number was an estimate of the cost states would incur to provide FAPE in the LRE to all students with disabilities. Despite this estimate, Congress has never funded to this maximum level, resulting in school district complaints that the Education for All Handicapped Children Act of 1975 and IDEA 2004 result in an unfunded mandates. The American Recovery and Reinvestment Act of 2009 addressed this complaint by providing a $12.2 billion increase in IDEA 2004 funding, the majority ($11.3 billion) provided to Part B, serving children with disabilities between the ages of 3 and 21. This substantial funding bill was delivered in a lump sum to states for distribution to LEAs and designed to provide 2 years of funding. Critics argued that this massive infusion of money could have been more effective if it was allocated to districts with the greatest need—those districts with a high concentration of special education services.

Section 504 of the Rehabilitation Act of 1973 and the ADA of 1990

Section 504 and the ADA protect individuals with disabilities from discrimination. An "individual with a disability" is a person who 1) has a physical or mental impairment which substantially limits one or more of such person's major life activities, 2) has a record of such impairment, or 3) is regarded as having such an impairment (42 U.S.C. § 12102[2]; 29 U.S.C. § 706[8]). Specific changes to the ADA in 2008 affect the interpretation of the above so as to ensure broader coverage of affected students. Those changes will be discussed in greater detail next.

Most often, the students served under Section 504 and/or the ADA are those who meet the first part of the definition—having an impairment that substantially limits a major life activity. This definition, however, is a less-restrictive definition of *disability* than that required for special education purposes by IDEA 2004. School systems often declassify students with disabilities who are performing well and who no longer need special classes but instead need only reasonable accommodations (academic adjustments or auxiliary aids and services), thus taking these students out of special education and providing them with services under Section 504. The types of students most often served under Section 504 are those with ADHD, allergies, arthritis, asthma, diabetes, epilepsy, heart disease, HIV/AIDS, learning disabilities, Tourette syndrome, or vision impairments who may not need special education classes but who may need large print, additional time to read assignments, or other adjustments to succeed in a general education classroom.

Public schools often develop 504 Plans for such students in a manner similar to developing IEPs for children covered under IDEA 2004, to set out the services that will be provided to each such student. This is because schools and teachers are more likely to carry out a plan that is in writing and because the 504 regulations for kindergarten through 12th grade provide that implementing an IEP is one means of complying with the requirements for children covered under Section 504 (Nondiscrimination on the Basis of Handicap, 2002).

Case law has required that ADA cases involving students from kindergarten through 12th grade also pursue IDEA 2004 administrative remedies to the extent they involve overlapping services (*Hope v. Cortines,* 1995). In other words, if a child is eligible for services under IDEA 2004, then the parents must pursue IDEA 2004 procedures (impartial hearing) for services available under all three laws. Parents cannot bypass these procedures and go directly to court by asserting claims under Section 504 and the ADA only. Examples in which this would not be true are cases involving purely physical access because IDEA 2004 does not require the physical alteration of school buildings in order to accommodate students with physical disabilities—only Section 504 and the ADA do.

The ADA Amendments Act of 2008

The ADA Amendments of 2008 (PL 110-325) effectuated modifications of the law to conform to Congressional findings that the holdings of the Supreme Court in certain decisions in 1999 and 2002 "narrowed the broad scope of protection intended to be afforded by the ADA, thus eliminating protection for many individuals whom Congress intended to protect" leading the lower courts to find that in order to be protected by the ADA, individuals needed to demonstrate a greater degree of limitation across a wide range of substantially limiting impairments than was intended by Congress (42 U.S.C. § 12101). Congress also found that the federal regulations that had defined the term *substantially limits* as *significantly restricted* were inconsistent with congressional intent because they expressed too high a standard of impairment than Congress had intended. Congress, therefore, changed the ADA in certain key ways:

- It eliminated the U.S. Supreme Court's requirement that the ameliorative effects of "mitigating measures," such as medication, prosthetic devices, or learned compensatory methods, must be considered in assessing whether one has a disability (except for ordinary eyeglasses or contact lenses)

- It specifically provided rules of construction requiring that the ADA amendments should be applied in favor of broad coverage of individuals

Congress made clear that the amendments:

- Shifted focus from whether discrimination occurred, not whether the individual's impairment qualified as a disability

- Do not require a student to be severely impaired in order to be protected by the law

- Rejected the assumption implicit in many cases that an individual who has performed well academically cannot be substantially limited in activities such as learning, reading, writing, thinking, or speaking. Specifically, it rejected court holdings that academic success is inconsistent with a student's being substantially limited in major life activities such as learning, reading, or concentrating (*Gonzalez v. National Board of Medical Examiners*, 2000; *Price v. National Board of Medical Examiners*, 1997; *Wong v. Regents of the University of California*, 2005)

- Confirmed that it supported the holding in *Bartlett v. New York State Board of Law Examiners* (1998), stating that a student with learning disabilities would be considered disabled under the law even if he or she managed his or her own adaptive strategies or received informal or undocumented accommodations that lessened the deleterious affects of his or her disability

Thus, Congress made clear that students may be talented and gifted *and* disabled and entitled to accommodations for their disabilities under the ADA and Section 504. During congressional hearings, one witness testifying in opposition to the amendments suggested that a 15-year-old with learning and attention difficulties who got *B*s and *C*s in school should not be protected by the law, but Congress disagreed. As one member of Congress stated,

> For example, people with dyslexia are diagnosed based on an unexpected difficulty in reading. This requires a careful analysis of the method and manner in which this impairment substantially limits an individual's ability to read, which may mean taking more time—but may not result in a less capable reader. *(Id. at H8296)*

Final ADA Amendments Act regulations are forthcoming, but it is clear from the statements of members of Congress that some students who may not have been served by schools in the past will now be entitled to exam accommodations and other modifications for their disabilities.

SUMMARY

Special education and civil rights protections for children with disabilities can seem enormously complicated, but they are also incredibly important to achieving the twin social and educational goals of an educated and productive citizenry. Few would challenge the worthiness of these goals, yet the devil, as they say, is in the details. Each reauthorization of IDEA and Section 504 brings new opportunities for amendments to these laws, with expansions or contractions of these rights. Unlike Section 504 or the IDEA, the ADA is not regularly reauthorized; thus, the 2008 amendments to the ADA will remain in force.

Teachers and administrators are key players in the scheme of federal protections for students with disabilities and are better able to play their respective roles armed with information. Most educators will not find themselves in need of in-depth information regarding the rights of students with disabilities, but knowing where to go for additional information is always helpful (see Appendix B for a list of resources). When children with disabilities are appropriately educated, they become educated adults and an integral part of the fabric of society, in the workplace and the professions, enhancing and enriching our lives and theirs.

REFERENCES

American Recovery and Reinvestment Act of 2009, PL 111-5, 123 Stat. 115.

Americans with Disabilities Act (ADA) of 1990, PL 101-336, 42 U.S.C. §§ 12101 *et seq.*

Americans with Disabilities Amendments Act of 2008, PL 110-325, 42 U.S.C. §§ 12101 *et seq.*

Assistance to States for the Education of Children with Disabilities. (2007). 34 C.F.R. § 300

Bartlett v. New York State Board of Law Examiners, 970 F. Supp. 1094 (S.D.N.Y. 1997) (Bartlett I); aff'd 2 F. Supp. 2d 388 (S.D.N.Y. 1997) (Bartlett II); aff'd in part, rev'd & remanded in part, 156 F. 3d 321 (2d Cir. 1998) (Bartlett III); vacated and remanded, 119 S.Ct. 2388 (1999) (Bartlett IV); aff'd in part & remanded, 226 F. 3d 69 (2d Cir. 2000) (Bartlett V); 2001 WL 930792 (S.D.N.Y. Aug. 15, 2001) (Bartlett VI).

Brown v. Board of Education of Topeka, 347 U.S. 483 (1954).

Carter v. Florence County School District Four, 17 EHLR 452 (1991).

Carter v. Florence County School District Four, 950 F.2d 156 (4th Cir. 1991).

Coleman v. Zatcheka, 824 F. Supp. 1360 (D.Ne. 1993).

Education for All Handicapped Children Act of 1975, PL 94-142, 20 U.S.C. §§ 1400 *et seq.*

Education of the Handicapped Act Amendments of 1974, PL 93-380, 88 Stat. 576.

Elementary and Secondary Education Act of 1965, PL 89-10, 20 U.S.C. §§ 241 *et seq.*

Florence Country School District Four v. Shannon Carter, 510 U.S. 7 (1993).

Forest Grove School District v. T. A., 129 S.Ct. 2484 (2009).

Gonzalez v. National Board of Medical Examiners, 225 F.Ed 620 (6th Cir. 2000).

Hope v. Cortines, 872 F. Supp. 14, aff'd, 69 F.3d 687 (2d Cir 1995).

Individuals with Disabilities Education Act (IDEA) of 1990, PL 101-476, 20 U.S.C. §§ 1400 *et seq.*

Individuals with Disabilities Education Improvement Act (IDEA) of 2004, PL 108-446, 20 U.S.C. §§ 1400 *et seq.*

Mills v. District of Columbia Board of Education, 348 F. Supp. 866 (D.D.C. 1972).

Mr. & Mrs. A. o/b/o D.A. v. New York City Department of Education, 09-CV-5097 (S.D.N.Y. 2011)

No Child Left Behind Act of 2001, PL 107-110, 115 Stat. 1425, 20 U.S.C. §§ 6301 *et seq.*

Nondiscrimination on the Basis of Handicap in Programs or Activities Receiving Federal Financial Assistance. (2002). 34 C.F.R. §104.33 (b)(2).

Olmstead v. Zimring, 119 S. Ct. 2176 (1999).

Park v. Anaheim Union High School District, 444 F3d 1149 (9th Cir., 2006).

Pennsylvania Association for Retarded Children (PARC) v. Commonwealth of Pennsylvania, 343 F. Supp. 279 (E.D.Pa. 1972).

Price v. National Board of Medical Examiners, 966 F.Supp. 419 (S.D.W.Va. 1997).

Rehabilitation Act of 1973, PL 93-112, 29 U.S.C. §§ 701 *et seq.*

School Committee of Burlington v. Department of Education of Massachusetts, 471 U.S. 359 (1985).

Staples, B. (2002, January 5). How the Clip 'N Snip's owner changed special education. *The New York Times,* p. A10.

U.S. Department of Education. (1991). *U.S. Department of Education joint policy memorandum.* Washington, DC: Author.

U.S. Department of Education. (1998). *To assure the free appropriate public education of all children with disabilities: Twentieth annual report to Congress on the implementation of the Individuals with Disabilities Education Act.* Retrieved February 7, 2011, from http://www.ed.gov/about/reports/annual /osep/1998/20thar.pdf

U.S. Department of Education. (2000, July 25). *Department of Education joint policy letter.* Washington, DC: Author.

U.S. Department of Education. (2011). *U.S. Department of Education, Office of Special Education and Rehabilitative Services policy memorandum.* Washington, DC: Author.

Wong v. Regents of University of California, 410 F.3d 1052 (9th Cir. 2005).

Glossary

MARILYN MARTIN

accent   Stress or emphasis on one syllable in a word or on one or more words in a phrase or sentence. The accented part is spoken louder, longer, and/or in a higher tone. The speaker's mouth opens wider while saying an accented syllable. *See also* suprasegmental.

accommodations   Changes within the general classroom to enable students to keep up with the education program, such as intensive instruction; reduced assignments; adapted test procedures; and use of computers, calculators, and tape recorders. The term *accommodations* is not used in the Individuals with Disabilities Education Improvement Act (IDEA) of 2004 (PL 108-446). That law, however, generally refers to supplemental services that are, for the most part, what Section 504 of the Rehabilitation Act Amendments of 1998 (PL 105-220) and the Americans with Disabilities Act (ADA) of 1990 (PL 101-336) call reasonable accommodations.

active learning   Learning in which the learner mentally searches for connections between new and already known information.

active reading process   A reading method that offers the reader an effective system for processing the meaning of text in progressively deeper stages (e.g., preread, read, make margin notes, chunk, summarize).

addend   A number to be added to another. The numbers 1 and 2 are addends in $1 + 2 = 3$.

ADHD   *See* attention-deficit/hyperactivity disorder.

affix   A letter or a group of letters attached to the beginning or ending of a base word or root that creates a derivative with a meaning or grammatical form that is different than the base word or root. *See also* prefix; suffix.

affricate   A consonant speech sound that is articulated with the tongue touching the roof of the mouth (e.g., /ch/ in *chair,* /j/ in *judge*) (Henry, 2003; Moats, 2010).

agnosia   *See* finger agnosia.

agraphia   *See* specific agraphia.

air writing   *See* sky writing.

alliteration   The repetition of the initial sound in two or more words such as "laughing llamas."

allophones   Slight variations in production of vowels or consonants that are predictable variants of a phoneme (e.g., /p/ in *pot* and *spot,* /ă/ in *fast* and *tank*).

alphabet   A series of letters or signs arranged in a fixed sequence, each of which represents a spoken sound of that language. Knowing the 26 letters of the English alphabet is essential to the language skills—phonics, reading, writing, and spelling.

alphabetic language   A language, such as English, in which letters are used systematically to represent speech sounds, or phonemes.

alphabetic principle   The concept, understood by readers, that the letters on the page represent or map onto the sounds in spoken words.

alveolar   Pertaining to sounds produced with the tongue placed against the alveolar ridge behind the upper front teeth (e.g., /n/, /s/).

alveolar ridge   The gum ridge behind the upper front teeth.

amanuensis   A person, such as a teacher, who writes while another person, such as a student, dictates words, sentences, or stories.

analytic   Pertaining to instruction or a process that separates the whole into its constituent parts to reveal the relationships of the parts. Analytic phonics separates the whole word into its constituent parts so that students can deduce the phonic relationships of the separate orthographic patterns. *See also* synthetic.

anaphora   Using a pronoun or a definite article to refer to something already mentioned (e.g., The turtle moved slowly. *It* crept along the road).

Anglo-Saxon   The language of the Germanic peoples (Angles, Saxons, and Jutes) who settled in Britain in the 5th and 6th centuries A.D. Anglo-Saxon was the dominant language in Britain until the Norman Conquest in 1066 and is a major contributor to the English language.

antonyms   Words of opposite meaning.

appositive   A noun or noun phrase that is placed after a noun to explain it more fully; it usually contains modifiers (e.g., Susan B. Anthony, an influential suffragist, appears on the silver dollar).

articulation   The vocal production of speech in which the mouth, tongue, lips, teeth, and other parts of the vocal tract are used in specific ways.

aspiration   The push of air that accompanies the production of some stop consonants (e.g., /t/ in *top*) (Moats, 2010).

assessment   Collection of information to make decisions about learning and instruction.

assistive technology   Any item, piece of equipment, or product that is used to increase, maintain, or improve the functional capabilities of individuals with disabilities.

attention-deficit/hyperactivity disorder (ADHD)   Disorder characterized by difficulty with attending to and completing tasks, impulsivity, and/or hyperactivity that frequently co-occurs with but is not a learning disability. *See also* learning disability.

auditory discovery   Listening and responding to guided questions to discover new information, such as when students echo words dictated by the teacher to discover a new common sound.

auditory discrimination   *See* discrimination.

automaticity   Ability to respond or react without attention or conscious effort. Automaticity in word recognition permits full energy to be focused on comprehension.

background knowledge   The prior knowledge a student brings to a reading task. For example, if a student is reading a passage about the American Revolution, then his or her prior knowledge about the war will bolster comprehension.

base word   A word to which affixes are added (e.g., *whole* in *unwholesome*). A base word can stand alone. *See also* free morpheme.

bilabial   Pertaining to consonant sounds produced with the two lips contacting each other.

biliteracy   The ability to speak, read, and write in two languages.

blend   Two or more adjacent consonants (a consonant blend) or two or more adjacent vowels (a vowel blend) whose sounds flow smoothly together. *See also* blending.

blending   Fusing individual sounds, syllables, or words to produce meaningful units or to sound out (e.g., saying /m/ /ă/ /p/ as "map;" saying "tooth" and "brush" as "toothbrush").

blocked   *See* continuant.

borrowing   *See* regrouping.

bound morpheme   A morpheme that must be attached to other morphemes (e.g., *-ed* in *spotted, -s* in *boys, pre-* in *preview*). *See also* free morpheme.

breve   The curved diacritical mark (˘) above a vowel in a sound picture or phonic/dictionary symbol notation that indicates a short sound in a closed syllable, in which at least one consonant comes after the vowel in the same syllable (e.g., ĭt, căt, blĕnd; exception: dĭvide).

cacography   Poor spelling or handwriting.

carrying   *See* regrouping

chameleon prefix   A prefix whose final consonant changes based on the initial letter of the base word or root (e.g., *in-* changes to *ir-* before base words and roots beginning with *r*, such as *responsible*). *See also* euphony.

checkpoint   *See* marker.

choral reading   Reading in which the instructor and the student(s) read the passage aloud together. *See also* echo reading; shared reading.

circumflex   A diacritical mark (ˆ) placed over certain vowels when coding or when writing a sound picture to indicate an unexpected pronunciation. The circumflex is used in the Alphabetic Phonics (Cox, 1992) code to indicate when a vowel-*r* combination is accented (e.g., âr, êr, îr, ôr, ûr). The circumflex is also used over the circled *a* to indicate the /aw/ pronunciation before /l/ in a monosyllabic word (e.g., b â ll).

closed syllable   A syllable ending with one or more consonants (e.g., *mat, hand*). The vowel is usually short. *See also* open syllable.

cloze technique   Any of several ways of measuring a student's ability to restore omitted portions of an oral or written message from its remaining context. Also called *fill-in-the blank technique*.

clue   *See* context clue; *see also* marker.

coarticulation   The phenomenon of word pronunciation in which adjacent sounds often are spoken in such a way that one phoneme seems to overlap, is changed by, and/or modifies another.

cognates   *See* voiced–voiceless cognates.

cognitive strategies   Self-regulating mechanisms, including planning, testing, checking, revising, and evaluating, during an attempt to learn or to problem solve. Using cognitive strategies is a higher order cognitive skill that influences and directs the use of lower order skills.

collaborative learning   Learning by working together in small groups to understand new information or to create a common product.

column word   The first word in the second column of a dictionary page. This word assists in determining whether a target word will be found in the first or second column of the page.

combination   *See* letter cluster.

combining form   A morpheme to which other roots and/or affixes may be combined to form compound words or derivatives (e.g., *auto, hemi, bio*). Combining forms are usually of Greek origin and are sometimes referred to as roots instead of combining forms.

comorbidity   The presence of two or more learning disorders in an individual at a given time. For example, a student may be diagnosed with dyslexia and ADHD.

compare-and-contrast composition   Writing that explores the similarities and differences between related or unrelated objects, concepts, or categories. For example, writing that describes how dogs and foxes are the same and different.

computer-mediated text   Computer text that is linked to other electronic resources such as online dictionaries, glossaries, and graphic organizers.

compound word   A word composed of two or more smaller words (e.g., *doghouse*). A compound word may or may not be hyphenated depending on its part of speech and conventions of usage (e.g., in modern usage, *football* is not hyphenated). *See also* meaning-based word.

comprehension   Making sense of what we read. Comprehension depends on good word recognition, fluency, vocabulary, worldly knowledge, and language ability.

comprehension monitoring   The active awareness of whether one is understanding or remembering text being processed.

concept of a word   Understanding that sentences are made up of strings of words; the ability to count words in oral sentences and to match spoken words to printed words as demonstrated by pointing to the words of a text while reading. *See also* finger-point reading.

conjunction   A part of speech that serves to connect words, phrases, clauses, or sentences (e.g., *and, but, as, because*). Also called *connectives*.

consonant   One of a class of speech sounds in which sound moving through the vocal tract is constricted or obstructed by the lips, tongue, or teeth during articulation.

consonant blend   *See* blend.

consonant digraph   *See* digraph.

consonant prefix   A prefix with a consonant as the final letter. The spelling of a consonant prefix may change for euphony (e.g., *ad-* becomes *at-* in *attraction, in-* becomes *ir-* in *irresponsible*). *See also* euphony.

consonant suffix   A suffix beginning with a consonant (e.g., *-ful, -ness*).

consonant-*le* syllable   A syllable in final position of a word that ends in a consonant, an *l*, and final silent *e* (e.g., *middle, rifle*). *See also* final stable syllable.

consonant-vowel-consonant (CVC)   Pertaining to a word or syllable composed of letters with a consonant-vowel-consonant pattern. Short words or syllables with this pattern are a common starting point for reading phonetically regular words.

context clue   Information from the immediate setting in which a word occurs, such as surrounding words, phrases, sentences, illustrations, syntax, or typography, that might be used to help determine the meaning and/or pronunciation of the word. Also called *contextual clue, visual hint*.

continuant   Pertaining to speech sounds that are sustained in their production (e.g., /f/, /m/, /s/)

continuous text   Linked words such as the wording found in sentences, phrases, and paragraphs. Also known as connected text.

controlled decodable text   Text that is written using only sound–symbol relationships already taught to provide practice with specific decoding skills; used to apply phonics in reading of text. Also called *controlled text*.

convergence of evidence   Evidence from the identical replication of a study in a similar population by other researchers. Convergence of evidence is important in drawing conclusion from research because the outcomes from a single study are not sufficient to generalize across all populations.

cooperative learning   Instructional approach in which students work together rather than compete to solve a problem or to complete a task.

cornering   Using the thumb, index finger, and middle finger to expose only the guide words in the corners of dictionary pages in rapid succession to find the page on which the targeted entry word is defined.

corrective feedback   Teacher responses during and following performance of a skill that is sensitive to the student's level and that guides him or her closer to mastery.

criterion-referenced test   Test in which performance is assessed in terms of the kind of behavior expected of a person with a given score. A criterion-referenced test permits descriptions of a child's domain of knowledge represented in the test, allows an item-by-item description of knowledge attained and knowledge yet to be acquired, and may be standardized or informal. *See also* informal test; standardized test.

cross-modal integration   Combination of information received as visual, auditory, kinesthetic, and tactile input.

curriculum-referenced test   Test in which items are taken from the curriculum used in the child's classroom so that he or she is not tested on material that has not been taught. A curriculum-referenced test provides a good match between assessment and instruction and may be standardized or informal. *See also* informal test; standardized test.

cursive handwriting   Handwriting with the slanted strokes of successive characters joined and the angles rounded.

CVC   *See* consonant-vowel-consonant.

decodable text   Text that is written at the independent reading level of a student; for the text to be decodable the student should be able to read 95%–100% of the words independently, with no more than 1 error per 20 words.

decode   To break the phonic code (to recognize a word); to determine the pronunciation of a word by noting the position of the vowels and consonants.

deictic term   A word whose use and meaning changes based on context (e.g., *I, you, tomorrow, here, there*).

deletion   *See* elision; *see also* sound deletion.

derivation   The process of building a new word from another word by adding affixes. For example, *deconstructing* is a derivative of *deconstruct,* which in turn is derived from *construct. See also* etymology.

derivational morpheme   Morpheme added to a base word that creates a new word that is a different part of speech from that of the base word (e.g., *-ness* changes adjective *careless* into noun *carelessness*).

derivative   A word made from a base word by adding one or more affixes.

descriptive writing   Writing that describes a person, place, object, or event, often using sensory or figurative language. For example, a description of someone's pet.

diacritical marking   A distinguishing mark used in dictionaries and phonics programs to indicate the pronunciation of a letter or combination of letters. *See also* breve; circumflex; macron.

diagnostic   Pertaining to instruction in which the teacher is constantly taking notice of how students are handling the lesson concepts. Diagnostic instruction is sometimes used in conjunction with prescriptive instruction. *See also* prescriptive instruction.

diagnostic and prescriptive instruction   Instruction in which students are engaged in components of the lesson while the teacher observes how students are handling the discrete components (diagnostic instruction) so that the teacher may plan instruction. The prescriptive part of the lesson may involve changes to permit additional practice, review, and/or multisensory activities.

differentiated instruction   An approach to instruction in which the teacher adapts content in response to student readiness, ability, and learning profile.

digital texts   *See* electronic texts.

digraph   Two adjacent consonants (a consonant digraph) or two adjacent vowels (a vowel digraph) in the same syllable representing a single speech sound (e.g., *sh* in *wish, ee* in *feet*). *See also* diphthong; quadrigraph; trigraph.

diphthong   Two adjacent vowels in the same syllable whose sounds blend together with a slide or shift during the production of the syllable (e.g., *oy* in *toy, ow* in *cow*). *See also* digraph.

directionality   The direction used in a language for reading and writing. English is governed by left-to-right directionality.

discovery learning   *See* Socratic method.

discovery words   Group of related words used during guided discovery teaching to help students perceive a principle, pattern, or feature of the language. *See also* guided discovery teaching.

discrepancy model   A means of identifying a learning disability by using a combination of cognitive and achievement tests. A student is diagnosed with a learning disability and therefore eligible for special education services when he or she exhibits a severe discrepancy between intellectual ability and academic achievement.

discrimination   The process of noting differences between stimuli. Auditory discrimination involves listening for the position of a particular sound in a word.

dividend   In division, the total amount that is to be divided into a given number of parts (divisor) (e.g., 15 is the dividend in 15 ÷ 3 = 5). *See also* divisor.

division radical   Mathematical symbol ($\sqrt{}$) used when writing long division facts.

divisor   In division, the number that the total (dividend) is divided by (e.g., 3 is the divisor in 15 ÷ 3 = 5).

double deficit   Deficit in phonological awareness and rapid serial naming.

due process   A requirement that basic procedural protections be provided before a school system can separate children with disabilities from those in general education; includes the parents' right to receive notice of changes in their child's educational plan and a hearing if they disagree with the changes.

dysarthria   Neurological oral–motor dysfunction including weaknesses of the musculature necessary for making the coordinated movements of speech production.

dysgraphia   Extremely poor handwriting or the inability to perform the motor movements required for handwriting. The condition is associated with neurological dysfunction.

dyslexia   "Dyslexia is a specific learning disability that is neurobiological in origin. It is characterized by difficulties with accurate and/or fluent word recognition and by poor spelling and decoding abilities. These difficulties typically result from a deficit in the phonological component of language that is often unexpected in relation to other cognitive abilities and the provision of effective classroom instruction. Secondary consequences may include problems in reading comprehension and reduced reading experience that can impede growth of vocabulary and background knowledge" (Lyon, Shaywitz, & Shaywitz, 2003, p. 2).

dyspraxia   Sensorimotor disruption in which the motor signals to the muscles, such as those necessary for speech production, are not consistently or efficiently received.

echo reading   Reading in which the instructor reads a paragraph aloud and has the student(s) read it aloud after the instructor has finished reading. *See also* choral reading; shared reading.

effect size   The degree to which a form of instruction is found through research to be more effective than another form.

electronic text   Text material that has been converted to a digital format on a computer. Also called *e-text*.

elision   A language task in which a part is taken away. Also called *deletion*.

Elkonin boxes   An instructional technique to build phonemic awareness in which the teacher draws a series of squares, repeats a word, and then asks the student to place a token in the appropriate number of boxes to indicate how many phonemes in the target word. For example for the target word *wish,* the student would select three tokens and place each of them in three different boxes.

ELL   *see* English language learner.

ellipsis   The omission of one or more words in a statement that must be supplied by the reader so the construction makes sense. (e.g., "Do you like tortillas? I do").

embedded clause   A clause enclosed within a sentence (e.g., The hummingbird, whose wings beat very rapidly, has brilliant plumage).

embedded phonics   Phonological awareness and phonics taught implicitly through reading real words in text.

emergent literacy   A level of cognitive maturation characterized by well-developed oral language ability, exposure to written language, and metalinguistic awareness.

English language learner (ELL)   A student who is learning English, who comes from a language background other than English, and whose English proficiency is not fully developed.

entry word   Word that is defined in a dictionary or glossary; may be divided into syllables.

eponym   A word for a place, an object, or an action that is named after an individual (e.g., *sandwich, Fahrenheit, diesel*).

ethnographic observation   A type of qualitative research in which researchers observe, listen, and ask questions to collect descriptive data in order to understand the content, context, and dynamics of an environment. *See also* qualitative research.

etymology   The study of the origins and historical development of words.

euphony   Beautiful or pleasing sound (from Greek). A desire for euphony may explain why, in the development of the English language, the last letters of certain prefixes have changed to match the first letter of the base words or stems. The result is easier to say and often results in a double consonant (e.g., *irregular,* not *inregular*). Knowing this phenomenon is an aid to spelling.

evidence-based research   *See* scientifically based research.

exaggerated pronunciation   Overpronunciation of a word as an aid to spelling. Students with dyslexia are encouraged to develop and practice exaggerated pronunciation at first as needed to strengthen auditory memory. Thus, vowel sounds in unaccented syllables are not reduced to the indistinguishable schwa sound but are pronounced phonetically (e.g., the closed syllable in *vital* is exaggerated as /tal/ to emphasize the *a*). Also called *spelling-based pronunciation, spelling pronunciation,* or *spelling voice.*

executive function difficulties   Difficulties with certain cognitive skills such as poor planning, disorganization of time and materials, difficulty narrowing a topic in writing, and procrastination.

experimental design   Experimental educational research raises a question based on a theory, which determines the experimental design for directly investigating the question using scientific methods of collecting data using rigorously applied methods of instruction, with detailed descriptions of the participants and measures used. In this kind of experimental research, the data are interpreted to yield results of the impact of the manipulation and control of the conditions of observation. Studies thus designed can be analyzed for knowledge gained and can be replicated.

expository writing   Writing that explains or informs, including persuasive or descriptive writing and compare-and-contrast compositions.

fast mapping   Picking up from context an initial impression of the meaning of a word.

Fernald method   Technique for learning words that involves the visual, auditory, kinesthetic, and tactile (VAKT) modalities. The student looks at a word while saying and tracing it.

figurative language   *See* nonliteral language.

figure–ground perception   The ability to attend to one aspect of a visual field while perceiving it in relation to the rest of the field; ability to identify and focus on salient information.

fill-in-the-blank technique   *See* cloze technique.

final   Pertaining to or occurring at the exact end; pertaining to the very last letter or sound in a word or syllable. *Z* is the final letter of the alphabet.

final stable syllable   A syllable with nonphonetic spelling and relatively stable pronunciation that occurs frequently in final position in English words (e.g., *-tle, -sion, -cial*).

fine motor skills   The strategic control of small sets of voluntary muscles such as in writing, grasping small objects, controlling eye movements, or producing speech.

finger agnosia   A kinesthetic feedback disorder in which the fingers do not report their location to the brain.

finger-point reading   A form of pretend reading in which prereaders point their fingers at the words on a page as they recite the story from memory and synchronize spoken words with words in print. Finger-point reading is facilitated by the ability to segment phonemes and match them with written letters. *See also* concept of a word.

flap   The reduction of /t/ and /d/, such as in the American English pronunciations of *ladder* and *latter,* formed by the tongue flapping on the alveolar ridge.

fluency   In reading, the ability to translate print to speech with rapidity and automaticity that allows the reader to focus on meaning.

formal test   *See* standardized test.

formative data collection   Procedure to gather information about a child's progress in acquiring particular skills or knowledge to be applied to short-term instructional goals; usually collected using criterion- and curriculum-referenced tests. *See also* criterion-referenced test; curriculum-referenced test; summative data.

fragment   A phrase or subordinate clause that is not a sentence (e.g., The girl who was standing).

free morpheme   A morpheme that can stand alone as a whole word (e.g., *box, plant, tame*). Also called *unbound morpheme. See also* bound morpheme.

frequency   The number of times an event occurs in a given category (e.g., frequency in English of multiple spellings of the long /ū / sound as in *cube, human,* and *statue*) that guides the order of introduction for reading and spelling.

fricative   A consonant produced by a partial obstruction of the airflow, which creates friction and slight hissing noise (e.g., /s/, /f/).

functional neuroimaging   Pictures of brain activity of awake subjects performing specific tasks that allow researchers to investigate which brain areas are used during certain tasks. *See also* neuroimaging.

gerund   An English word ending in *-ing* when used as a noun (e.g., She loves dancing and singing).

glide   A vowel-like consonant (i.e., /w/ and /y/) produced with little or no obstruction of the air stream in the mouth. Also called *semivowel.*

glottal sound   A sound produced by using the most posterior part of the mouth, known as the glottis. The sound is produced by complete or partial constriction of the glottis.

grapheme   A written letter or letter cluster representing a single speech sound (e.g., *i, igh*). *See also* digraph; quadrigraph; trigraph.

graphic organizers   Visual displays of information to help a student bolster comprehension and compose written material or study for tests (e.g., outlines, semantic maps, story grammars/diagrams).

graphomotor   Pertaining to the skillful coordination of the muscle groups involved in handwriting.

graphomotor production deficit   Difficulty writing in which the larger muscles of the wrist and forearm are used during letter formation because they are under better control than the small muscles of the fingers.

graphophonemic   Pertaining to letter–sound patterns.

guide letter   The letter in a word that guides the reader in alphabetizing a word or finding it in the dictionary (e.g., when determining if *plow* appears on a dictionary page with the guide words *please* and *prison,* the second letter is the guide word).

guide words   The two words usually found in the upper corner of each dictionary page indicating the first and last words on the page.

guided discovery teaching   Manner of presenting new material or concepts so that they can be deduced or discovered by the students. Only material that relates logically to their previous learning or that evolves through reason or sequence will lend itself to the students' discovery. Students will remember more readily that which they have been allowed to discover. Successful discovery teaching requires careful preparation. *See also* Socratic method.

guided oral reading   An instructional strategy in which an adult or peer reads a passage out loud to model fluent reading and then asks the student to reread the same passage while providing feedback. Also called *repeated reading.*

heterogeneous practice   A spelling or reading practice session with more than one focus that is used only after the student has mastered each of the concepts contained in the practice.

high interest–low level readers   Used to describe text written at a basic decoding level with the subject interests of older students in mind. Also called *high-interest text.*

high-frequency word   A word that is encountered numerous times in text and is important to know.

Hispanic   Relating to people descended from Spanish or Latin American people or their culture.

homogeneous practice   A spelling or reading practice in which every word contains the same pattern or rule that is the single focus of the practice.

homophones   Words that sound like another but have different spellings and meaning (e.g., *bare* and *bear; fourth* and *forth*).

hyperlexic   Learner who exhibits precocious and accurate decoding but who fails to understand the meaning of written words.

hyperlink   A word, phrase, or picture on a web page that a user can click on to jump to a new document or section.

hypertext   Text that appears on a computer or other electronic device that has links to other texts.

IDEA   *See* Individuals with Disabilities Education Improvement Act of 2004 (PL 108-446).

IEP   *See* individualized education program.

imagery training   Training in using language to create sensory impressions and in forming imaginative mental images while reading or listening.

incidental learning   Learning that takes place without any intent to learn. Informal learning.

inclusion   The opportunity for all students with disabilities to have access to and participate in all activities of the neighborhood school environment. An educational placement in which a qualified student with disabilities receives special education and related services in the least restrictive environment, which may involve (to the extent possible) placement in the general education classroom.

Individuals with Disabilities Education Improvement Act (IDEA) of 2004 (PL 108-446)   Special education legislation, originally passed in 1975 (PL 94-142) and amended in 1990 (PL 101-476) and 1997 (PL 105-17), that serves as a mechanism to help fund special education. This legislation mandates that states receiving federal monies must provide special education and other services to qualified children (from birth through age

21) with disabilities or risk the loss of these dollars. IDEA 2004 protects a child's right to a free appropriate public education (FAPE) in the least restrictive environment (LRE).

individualized education program (IEP)   A document that sets out the child's placement in special education as well as the specific goals, short-term objectives, and benchmarks for measuring progress each year. Creating and implementing the IEP must include the opportunity for meaningful participation by the parents.

Indo-European   A family of languages consisting of most of the languages of Europe, as well as those of Iran, the Indian subcontinent, and other parts of Asia. Most English words are ultimately of Indo-European origin.

inflectional morpheme   A morpheme added to the end of a word that shows tense, number, or person of a verb; plural or possessive of a noun; or comparative or superlative form of an adjective (e.g., -ed in *floated*, -s in *tales*, -er in *thinner*).

informal test   A test that is structured but not standardized; it typically follows the format of a standardized test, but presentation can be modified to probe the students' responses in ways that are not permissible with standardized tests. *See also* standardized test.

initial   The first or beginning sound or letter in a word or syllable. *A* is the initial letter of the alphabet.

instant word recognition   The ease and automaticity with which a skilled reader is able to read individual words.

intonation   The pattern or melody of pitch changes revealed in connected speech.

invented spelling   Spelling that is not the same as conventional orthography and that may be encouraged from preschool to first grade to help students develop phonemic awareness and apply their knowledge of sounds, symbols, and letter patterns. Using invented spelling is temporary until regular orthography is learned.

irregular word   A word that has an unexpected spelling either because its orthographic representation does not match its pronunciation (e.g., *colonel, Wednesday*) or because it contains an infrequent orthographic representation of a sound (e.g., *soap*).

juncture   The transition or mode of transition from one sound to another in speech; a pause that contributes to meaning of words (e.g., to make a *name* distinguishable from an *aim*) or rising intonation, as in a question.

key word   A word emphasizing a particular letter–sound association that serves as the key to unlock the student's memory for that association (e.g., *apple* for /ă/, *itch* for /ĭ/).

kinesthetic   Pertaining to the sensory experience stimulated by bodily movements and tensions; often pertaining to the student's feeling of letter shapes while moving parts of the body through space.

kinesthetic memory   A voluntary motor sequence that is recalled by the student after repeated practice and training, such as daily writing of cursive letter shapes while associating them with the name and sounds represented by each.

labiodental fricative   A sound in which the lower lip and the upper teeth touch and partially obstruct the air flow (e.g., /f/, /v/).

language content   Knowing the vast array of objects, events, and relationships and the way they are represented in language.

laterality   The tendency to use either the left or the right side of the body; handedness.

lax vowel   *See* short vowel.

LEA   *See* local education agency.

learning disability   "A generic term that refers to a heterogeneous group of disorders manifested by significant difficulties in the acquisition and use of listening, speaking, reading, writing, reasoning, and mathematics abilities, or of social skills. These disorders are intrinsic to the individual and presumed to be due to central nervous system dysfunction. Even though a learning disability may occur with other handicapping conditions (e.g., sensory impairment, mental retardation, social and emotional disturbance), with socioenvironmental influences (e.g., cultural factors), and especially with attention deficit disorder, all of which may cause learning problems, a learning disability is not the direct result of those conditions or influences." (The Interagency Committee, 1985, as cited in Kavanagh & Truss, 1988, pp. 550–551)

least restrictive environment (LRE)   Public schools are legally required to include learners with disabilities in regular classrooms and educate them as much as possible alongside students without disabilities.

left angular gyrus   Part of the left hemisphere of brain that is the primary location for translating visual-orthographic information into phonological representations (linking symbol to sound).

letter cluster   Group of two or more letters that regularly appear adjacent in a single syllable (e.g., *oo, ng, th, sh, oi, igh*). In spelling instruction, a pattern of letters in a single syllable that occurs frequently together. The pronunciation of at least one of the component parts may be unexpected, or the letters may stand in an unexpected sequence (e.g., *ar, er, ir, or, qu, wh*). A cluster may be a blend (two or more letters that represent more than one sound) or a digraph (two letters that represent one sound). Also called *combination*. *See also* blend; digraph; diphthong; quadrigraph; trigraph.

letter–sound correspondences   *See* phonics.

lexical   Relating to words or the vocabulary of a language or the meaning of the base word in inflected and derived forms.

lexical cohesion   The planning and organizing of the content of a message before it is communicated.

lexicon   A body of word knowledge in linguistic memory, either spoken or written.

linguadental   A sound produced with the tongue contacting the teeth.

linguistic   Denoting language processing and language structure.

linguistics   Study of the production, properties, structure, meaning, and/or use of language.

linkages   The associations developed in language training between students' visual, auditory, kinesthetic, and tactile perceptions by seeing the letter, naming it, saying its sound, and writing it in the air and on paper. Connections between cursive letters. Students may need extra practice with the more difficult linkages such as the bridge stroke after the letters *b, o, v,* and *w*.

liquid   A class of consonant sounds that contains /l/ and /r/ of American English.

literacy socialization   As a result of being read to, the development of the sense that marks on a page relate to the words being said, that there is a correct way to manipulate books, and that there is a positive connection between reading and nurturing experiences (Snow & Dickinson, 1991).

local education agency (LEA)   A public school board of education, school district, or other public authority that responds to local education issues.

long vowel   A vowel sound that is produced by a slightly higher tongue position than the short vowels. The long sounds represented by the written vowels (i.e., *a, e, i, o, u*) are usually the same as their names. When coding or writing a sound picture, any long vowel is marked by a macron. Also called *tense vowel*.

long-term memory   Permanent storage of information by means of primarily semantic links, associations, and general organizational plans; includes experiential, semantic, procedural, and automatic habit memories.

LRE   *See* least restrictive environment.

macron   The flat diacritical mark (‾) above a vowel in a sound picture or phonic/dictionary notation that indicates a long sound (e.g., /fāvor/).

manner   In phonology, the articulation and perceptual character of speech sounds.

manuscript print   *See* print handwriting.

marker   A distinguishing feature of a word that signals the need to apply a spelling rule or a coding for reading. The student may literally place a mark at each crucial point as a reminder. Also called *checkpoint, clue.*

mastery   Proficiency in specific subskills of a new task. Based on the bottom-up notion of gaining automatic recall of basic information or learning to automaticity. Also called *overlearning.*

Matthew effect   A term coined by Stanovich (1986) to describe a phenomenon observed in findings of cumulative advantage for children who read well and have good vocabularies and cumulative disadvantage for those who have inadequate vocabularies and read less and thus have lower rates of achievement. The term is named after a passage from the New Testament: "For unto everyone that hath shall be given, and he shall have abundance: but for him that hath not shall be taken away even that which he hath" (Matthew 25:29).

meaning-based word   As a result of compounding, a word whose meaning may not always be inferred from the meaning of its components (e.g., *greenhouse, flyleaf*). *See also* compound word.

medial   The letters or sounds that occur in the interior of a word or syllable. All of the letters in the sequential alphabet are medial except *a* and *z*. Medial is not a synonym for middle. *See also* middle.

meta-analysis   A statistical technique that allows comparisons of results across many studies.

metacognition   The deliberate rearrangement, regrouping, or transfer of information; the conscious choice of the strategies used to accomplish a task and processes to provide feedback on learning and performance.

metacognitive strategies   Strategies that students may use to think about what they are reading and the factors that influence their thinking.

metalinguistic   Pertaining to an awareness of language as an entity that can be contemplated; crucial to early reading ability, to understanding discourse patterns in the classroom, and to analyzing the language being used to teach the language that must be learned. Metalinguistics is one kind of metacognition.

metaphor   A word or phrase that means one thing and that is used, through implication, to mean something else (e.g., "His remark created a blizzard of controversy"). *See also* simile.

middle   Equidistant from two extremes. Middle and medial are not synonymous. The middle letters of the alphabet are *m* and *n*. *See also* medial.

miscue   Used by reading specialists to refer to inaccurate reading responses to written text during oral reading.

missing addend equation   Addition equation in which only one addend and the sum are given (e.g., 5 + _ = 10); the student must provide the missing addend.

mnemonic strategies   Formal schemes designed to improve memory, including using key words, chunking, rhyming, and visualizing. Arbitrary learning is more difficult for the student with dyslexia than learning that is related and logical, so devices such as mnemonic strategies for grouping needed facts are essential.

modality   A specific sensory pathway. Multisensory instruction simultaneously engages the student's visual, auditory, and kinesthetic/tactile senses.

model   A standard or example provided by the teacher for imitation or comparison (e.g., a model of syllable division procedure before a reading practice); a structure or design to show how something is formed (e.g., teacher skywrites a cursive letter).

modifications   A term used to refer to changes in how an alternate assessment is administered.

monosyllabic   Pertaining to a one-syllable word containing one vowel sound.

morpheme   The smallest meaningful linguistic unit. A morpheme may be a whole word (e.g., *child*), a base word (e.g., *child* in *childhood*), a suffix (e.g., *-hood* in *childhood*), or a prefix (e.g., *un-* in *untie*). *See also* derivational morpheme; inflectional morpheme.

morphological   In linguistic terms, pertaining to the meaningful units of speech; for example, a suffix is a morphological ending.

morphology   The internal structure of the meaningful units within words and the relationships among words in a language. The study of word formation patterns.

morphophonemic relationships   The conditions in which certain morphemes keep their written spelling when affixes are added, although their phonemic forms change.

motor engrams   A set of memorized instructions stored in the brain that lets the body know how to perform a specific motor movement or task, such as how to form a letter.

motor feedback problem   *See* finger agnosia.

motor memory dysfunction   A disorder affecting handwriting in which a person has difficulty recalling the movements needed to form specific letters.

MSLE   *See* multisensory structured language education.

multiple meanings   Different meanings for the same word; characteristic of English language. Students with learning disabilities often have difficulty with multiple meanings of words.

multiple regression analysis   A statistical method that relates a dependent (or criterion) variable (y) to a set of independent (or predictor) variables (x) by a linear equation for the purposes of prediction, controlling confounding variables, evaluating sets of variables, accounting for multivariate interrelationships, and analyzing variance and covariance on levels of independent variables (Fruchter, as cited in Corsini & Auerbach, 1996).

multiple spellings   The various ways in which a sound may be spelled (e.g., long /ā/ may be spelled *a, ay, ei, eigh, ey, or ai*).

multiplicand   The number in a multiplication equation that states the size or amount that is to be multiplied (e.g., 5 is the multiplicand in $3 \times 5 = 15$).

multiplier   The number in a multiplication equation that states how many times a certain size is to be produced (e.g., 3 is the multiplier in $3 \times 5 = 15$). Also called *operator*.

multisensory   Referring to any learning activity that includes using two or more sensory modalities simultaneously for taking in or expressing information.

multisensory strategy   A procedure used most often for novice or poor readers that involves an auditory, visual, tactile-kinesthetic, and/or an articulatory-motor component in the carefully sequenced teaching of language structure.

multisensory structured language education (MSLE)   Instructional approach that incorporates the simultaneous use of visual, auditory, kinesthetic, and tactile sensory modalities to link listening, speaking, reading, and writing together.

multisyllabic   Pertaining to a word of more than one syllable (e.g., *fantastic*). Also called *polysyllabic*.

narrative   Composition containing a sequence of events, usually in chronological order.

narrative writing   Writing that describes an experience or event from a personal perspective, often in story form.

nasal   A sound produced in which air is blocked in the oral cavity but escapes through the nose. The consonants in *mom* and *no* are nasal sounds.

netbook   An inexpensive notebook computer typically with a small screen and limited computing power.

neuroimaging   Diagnostic and research method of viewing brain structures and activity through the use of advanced medical technology, such as magnetic resonance imaging, in which the patient's body is placed in a magnetic field and resulting images are processed by computer to produce an image of contrasting adjacent tissues. *See also* functional neuroimaging.

neuropsychology   The study of areas of the brain and their connecting networks involved in learning and behavior.

nonliteral language   Language that avoids using the exact meanings of words and uses exaggeration, metaphors, and embellishments. Also called *figurative language.*

nonsense word   A word having no meaning by itself, the spelling of which is usually phonetic (e.g., *vop*). Reading and spelling nonsense words are phonic reinforcement for students who have already memorized a large number of words. Nonsense words can be used for teaching older students to apply phonetic decoding. Also called *nonsense syllable, nonword, pseudoword.*

norm-referenced test   Assessment of performance in relation to that of the norm group (cohort) used in the standardization of the test. Norm-referenced tests produce scores that permit comparisons between a student and other children of the same age. All norm-referenced tests are standardized. *See also* standardized test.

oddity task   Task or question in which a student is presented with several items and must select the one that does not fit with the rest (e.g., *"Ball, call, tall, hop*. Which of these words doesn't belong?"). Also called *odd-one-out task, odd-man-out task.*

onset   The initial written or spoken single consonant or consonant cluster before the first vowel in a syllable (e.g., /s/ in *sit*, /str/ in *strip*). Some syllables do not have an onset (e.g., *on, ask*). *See also* rime.

open syllable   A syllable ending with a long vowel sound (e.g., the first syllables in *labor* and *freedom*). *See also* closed syllable.

operator   *See* multiplier.

orthographic memory   Memory of letter patterns and word spellings.

orthography   The writing system of a language. Correct or standardized spelling according to established usage.

Orton-Gillingham approach   Multisensory method of teaching language-related academic skills that focuses on the structure and use of sounds, syllables, words, sentences, and written discourse. Instruction is explicit, systematic, cumulative, direct, and sequential.

outcomes   In assessment, the measured results of an educational program.

overlearning   *See* mastery.

palatal   Pertaining to sounds produced by the tongue touching the hard palate.

paralinguistic   *See* suprasegmental.

partially blocked   *See* stop.

pause   A break, stop, or rest in spoken language; one of the suprasegmental aspects of language. *See also* juncture; suprasegmental.

peer review   Scrutiny and evaluation of the results of a research study by a group of independent researchers with expertise and credentials in that field of study before the research findings are publicly reported.

persuasive writing   Writing whose purpose is to give an opinion by supplying supporting evidence in order to influence the reader's way of thinking. For example, an essay about whether students should be required to wear school uniforms.

phoneme   An individual sound unit in spoken words; the smallest unit of speech that makes one word distinguishable from another in a phonetic language such as English (e.g., /f/ makes *fat* distinguishable from *vat*; /j/ makes *jump* distinguishable from *chump*).

phoneme awareness   *See* phonemic awareness.

phoneme deletion   *See* sound deletion.

phonemic awareness   Awareness of the smallest units of sound in the speech stream and the ability to isolate or manipulate the individual sounds in words. Phonemic awareness is one aspect of the larger category of phonological awareness. Also called *phoneme awareness*. *See also* phonological awareness.

phonetic   Pertaining to speech sounds and their relation to graphic or written symbols.

phonetic stage   Stage in spelling development in which every sound is represented, but the complete knowledge of conventional orthography is not. *See also* prephonetic stage; semiphonetic stage.

phonetically regular word   *See* regular word.

phonetics   The system of speech sounds in any specific language.

phonics   Paired association between letters and letter sounds; an approach to teaching of reading and spelling that emphasizes sound–symbol relationships, especially in early instruction.

phonological   Pertaining to a speaker's knowledge about sound patterns in a language.

phonological awareness   Both the knowledge of and sensitivity to the phonological structure of words in a language. Phonological awareness involves a sophisticated ability to notice, think about, or manipulate sound segments in words. It can progress from rhyming; to syllable counting; to detecting first, last, and middle sounds; to segmenting, adding, deleting, and substituting sounds in words. Phonemic awareness is one component of phonological awareness. *See also* phonemic awareness.

phonological processing   An umbrella term for a large category of oral language processing abilities that are related to the sounds in words and are associated with the ability to read well.

phonological rules   Implicit rules governing speech sound production and the sequence in which sounds can be produced in a language.

phonology   The science of speech sounds, including the study of the development of speech sounds in one language or the comparison of speech sound development across different languages.

PL 108-446   *See* Individuals with Disabilities Education Improvement Act (IDEA) of 2004.

place of articulation   The place in the oral cavity where the stream of air is obstructed or changed during the production of a sound.

place value   The position of a digit in a numeral or series (e.g., the ones place, the tens place, the hundreds place).

polyglot   A language that is made up of words from several languages; English is a polyglot.

polysyllabic   *See* multisyllabic.

pragmatics   The set of rules that dictates behavior for communicative intentions in a particular context and the rules of conversation or discourse.

précis   Condensation in the student's own words of an author's essential message, thesis, moral, or purpose.

prefix   An affix attached to the beginning of a word that changes the meaning of that word (e.g., *tri-* in *tricycle*). *See also* consonant prefix; vowel prefix.

prephonetic stage   Stage in spelling development in which not all of the sounds of the word are represented by letters (e.g., *JS* for *dress*). *See also* phonetic stage; semiphonetic stage.

prescriptive   When used in the context of instruction, entailing the changes made to a lesson to tailor it for more practice, review, and/or multisensory activities.

print awareness   Children's appreciation and understanding of the purposes and functions of written language.

print handwriting   Unconnected letters formed using arcs and straight lines. Also called *manuscript handwriting, manuscript print*.

prosody   Features of spoken language, such as intonation and stress, that fluent readers use for appropriate phrasing of text into meaningful units.

proprioception   An individual's subconscious perception of movement and spatial orientation coming from stimuli within the body.

pseudoword   *See* nonsense word.

quadrigraph   Four adjacent letters in a syllable that represent one speech sound (e.g., *eigh*). *See also* digraph; trigraph.

qualitative research   Research that involves observing individuals and settings and relies on observation and description of events in the immediate context.

quantitative research   Research using experimental or quasi-experimental design methods to gather data. *See also* quasi-experimental research.

quasi-experimental research   Research that determines cause and effect without strict randomized controlled trials and is valid but less reliable than randomized controlled trials.

quotient   In division, the number of shares contained in a total (dividend) (e.g., 5 is the quotient in $15 \div 3 = 5$).

randomized controlled trial   An intervention study in which subjects are randomly assigned to experimental and control groups; all variables are held constant except the one variable that is hypothesized to cause a change.

rapid serial naming   A speed naming task, most often administered to prereaders, in which the individual is asked to quickly name a series of printed letters, numbers, or blocks of color repeated in random order. Also called *rapid automatized naming, rapid automatic naming*.

r-controlled   Pertaining to the phenomenon in English in which the letter *r* affects the way a preceding vowel is pronounced. For example, the *a* in *bar* is influenced by the *r* and sounds different from the *a* in *bad*.

r-controlled syllable   A syllable containing the combination of a vowel followed by *r*. The sound of the vowel often is not short but instead may represent an unexpected sound (e.g., *dollar, star, her*). This kind of syllable is also called a *vowel-r syllable*, a term which focuses on the orthographic pattern (whereas the term *r-controlled syllable* focuses on the sound pattern).

reader's theatre   Fluency-building activity in which students read literature presented in a dramatic form without sets, costumes, or the need to memorize lines.

reading disability   *See* dyslexia.

reading fluency   *See* fluency.

recognition   The act of identifying a stimulus as the same as something previously experienced (e.g., auditory recognition is involved in listening for a particular sound).

regrouping   New mathematical term for carrying (in addition) and borrowing (in subtraction); necessary in the base-10 positional notation system.

regular word   A word that is spelled the way it sounds. Also called *phonetically regular word*.

relative clause   A dependent clause introduced by a relative pronoun such as *who, that, which, or whom* (e.g., We bought ice cream from the man who was standing on the corner). A relative clause is not a complete sentence on its own.

response to intervention (RTI)   An integrated model of assessment and intervention with a multilevel prevention system to identify students at risk as well as monitor their progress, supply evidence-based interventions, and allow for appropriate adjustments based on student responsiveness. An alternative way to identify students with learning disabilities. Also called *response to instruction*.

review   Look over again; bring back to awareness. Used twice in a multisensory lesson to increase automatic reaction to symbols for reading and spelling and to make a brief reference to the day's new material.

rime   The written or spoken vowel and the final consonant(s) in a syllable (e.g., *at* in *cat*, *itch* in *switch*). *See also* onset.

root   A content word (noun, verb, adjective, adverb) or word part to which affixes can be added (e.g., *hat, group, green, fast*). Some roots, usually of Greek or Latin origin, are morphemes that generally cannot stand alone as a word in English (e.g., *cred, dict, struct, tele*). *See also* base word; bound morpheme; free morpheme.

root   The form of a word after removing all the affixes. Also known as a root word.

RTI   *See* response to intervention.

rule word   A word that carries information indicating when a letter should be dropped, doubled, or changed (e.g., *shiny, rabbit, bountiful*).

run-on sentence   Two main clauses incorrectly run together without any punctuation or conjunction separating them (e.g., It began raining they parked the car).

scaffolding   An educational strategy in which the teacher controls the complexity of the lesson and gradually increases the lesson's difficulty as students gain knowledge, skills, and confidence.

schema   A student's prior knowledge and experience relevant to a new topic insofar as it contributes to a frame of reference, factual or attitudinal, for the new information, thus creating links or structures through which the new information can be assimilated. Also called *schemata*.

schwa   An unaccented vowel (ə) whose pronunciation approximates the short /u/ sounds, such as the sound that corresponds to the first and last *a* in *America* or the second *a* in *sandal*.

scientifically based research   A process that gathers evidence to answer questions and bring new knowledge to a field so that effective practices can be determined and implemented. Also called *evidence-based research*.

segmental   Pertaining to a feature of language that can be divided or organized into a class (e.g., place of articulation, voicing).

segmentation   Separating a word into units, such as syllables, onsets, and rimes, or individual phonemes for the purpose of reading or spelling. Also called *unblending*. Breaking down a targeted skill into smaller step-by-step sequenced units and then synthesizing the parts into a whole.

selective attention   The ability to attend to certain stimuli while ignoring other stimuli; in working memory, putting ideas on hold while working on other ideas.

semantics   The meaning of words and the relationships among words as they are used to represent knowledge of the world.

semantic map   A graphic organizer that focuses on the relationship of words.

semiphonetic stage   Stage in spelling development in which a child usually strings consonants together to represent speech sounds in words and syllables (e.g., NTR for *enter*). *See also* phonetic stage; prephonetic stage.

sentence expansion   Addition of details explaining who, what, where, when, and/or how to a sentence kernel (e.g., *Yesterday when I was at the store, I saw the woman with the brown dog* is an expansion of *I saw the woman*).

sentence kernel   A simple sentence without modifiers.

sentence starter   Words used specifically to begin a sentence or complete thought (e.g., *whenever, since, after*).

sequencing   In multisensory structured language education, the orderly presentation of linguistic concepts based on frequency and ease of learning in a continuous series of connected lessons.

shared reading   Reading in which the instructor reads a paragraph aloud and then the student reads a paragraph aloud, with the instructor assisting with words as needed. *See also* choral reading; echo reading.

short vowel   A vowel that is pronounced with a short sound, which is unrelated to the name of the letter. A short vowel usually occurs in a closed syllable and is marked with a breve. Also called *lax vowel.*

short-term memory   Memory that lasts only briefly, has rapid input and output, is limited in capacity, and depends directly on stimulation for its form. Short-term memory enables the reader to keep parts of the reading material in mind until enough material has been processed for it to make sense. Also called *working memory.*

sibilant   A speech sound that is uttered with or accompanied by a hissing sound (i.e., /s/, /z/, /ch/, /j/, /sh/, /zh/).

sight word   A word that is immediately recognized as a whole and does not require decoding to identify. A sight word may or may not be phonetically regular, such as *can, would,* and *the.*

simile   An explicit comparison of two unlike things, usually with the word *like* or *as* (e.g., Her tousled hair was like an explosion in a spaghetti factory). *See also* metaphor.

Simple View of Reading   Model that defines reading comprehension as a product of lower level skills such as word recognition and higher level thinking processes such as listening comprehension.

simultaneous oral spelling (S.O.S.)   A structured sequence of procedures to teach the student how to think about the process of spelling. The student looks and listens to the word, unblends it, spells it aloud, writes it while naming each letter, codes it, and reads it aloud for proofreading (Cox, 1992).

situational   In reading and spelling instruction, a feature in a word that provides clues about how to spell or read a word. The situation refers to the position of letters or sounds, placement of accent, and the influence of surrounding sounds or letters.

sky writing   Technique of "writing" a letter or word in the air using the arm and writing hand. Use of upper arm muscles during sky writing helps the student retain kinesthetic memory of the shape of letters. Also called *air writing.*

Socratic method   A teaching method that leads learners to discover information through carefully guided questioning based on information they already possess. Also called *discovery learning*; *Socratic questioning*. *See also* guided discovery teaching.

S.O.S.   *See* simultaneous oral spelling.

sound deletion   Early literacy task in which the student is presented with a word and is asked to say all of the sounds in the word except one (e.g., "Say *bat* without /b/"). Ability to delete sounds is an important component of phonemic awareness. Also called *phoneme deletion.*

sound dictation   Procedure in which the teacher dictates individual phonemes, words, or sentences, and the student repeats and responds by writing them down. Sound dictation may involve oral and/or written review with a sound or spelling deck to develop automaticity in translating sounds to spellings.

sound picture   Letter or word written with diacritical markings indicating pronunciation. Sound pictures are often enclosed in slashes or parentheses (e.g., /kup/ for *cup*).

sound–symbol associations; sound–symbol correspondences   *See* phonics.

special education A federally defined type of education for a qualified child with a disability that is specially designed instruction, at no cost to the parents, to meet the unique needs of the child with a disability, including—(A) instruction conducted in the classroom, in the home, in hospitals and institutions, and in other settings; and (B) instruction in physical education (PL 108-446, 20 U.S.C. § 1401 [29][a–b]).

specific agraphia Acquired disorder in which ability to form letter shapes, letter sequences, and motor patterns is impaired.

specific learning disability *See* learning disability.

speech synthesis software Software in which synthetic speech is added to the printed material presented on computers or other electronic devices. *See also* text-to-speech software.

SQ3R *See* Survey, Question, Read, Recite, Review.

standardized test A test that is standardized using a carefully selected sample of people representative of the larger group of people for whom the test was created; such a test must be administered and scored following procedures prescribed in the manual accompanying the test. *See also* informal test.

stop In terms of speech sounds, a consonant that is produced with a complete obstruction of air (e.g., /p/, /t/, /k/).

strategy An individual's approach to a task, including how the person thinks and acts when planning, executing, and evaluating performance on a task and its subsequent outcomes.

stress *See* accent.

structural analysis The perception and examination of syllables and morphemes. Structural analysis enables the reader to recognize different kinds of syllables and decode long, unfamiliar words.

study skills Those competencies associated with acquiring, recording, organizing, synthesizing, remembering, and using information and ideas learned in school or other instructional arenas.

subskill A skill that is part of a more complex skill or group of skills. Subskills of reading include phonological awareness and knowledge of letter–sound correspondences.

subvocalize To move the lips without audible vocalization.

suffix A morpheme attached to the end of a word that creates a word with a different form or use (e.g., *-s* in *cats, -ing* in *lettering*). Suffixes include inflected forms indicating tense, number, person, and comparatives. *See also* consonant suffix; vowel suffix.

summative data collection Procedure to gather information about the accumulation and integration of knowledge to be applied to long-term comprehensive teaching goals; typically collected using norm-referenced measures but sometimes collected with curriculum- and criterion-referenced tests. *See also* criterion-referenced test; curriculum-referenced test; formative data; norm-referenced test.

suprasegmental Pertaining to the singular musical qualities of language, including intonation, expression, accent, pitch, juncture, and rhythm, which are significant in our ability to communicate and comprehend emotions and attitudes. Also called *paralinguistic*.

Survey, Question, Read, Recite, Review (SQ3R) Study method in which student surveys the assignment, poses a question, reads to answer the question, recites the answer to the question, and reviews the material read (Robinson, 1946).

syllable A spoken or written unit that must have a vowel sound and that may include consonants that precede or follow that vowel. Syllables are units of sound made by one impulse of the voice.

syllable division   The process of breaking down multisyllabic words into separate syllables for greater ease in learning, pronunciation, or spelling.

syllable division patterns   Patterns for dividing words into syllables. There are four major syllable division patterns in English: VCCV, VCV, VCCCV, and VV.

syllable types   Orthographic classifications for syllables. There are six syllable types in English: closed, open, vowel-consonant-*e,* vowel pair (vowel team), vowel-*r* (*r*-controlled), and consonant-*le. See also* specific syllable types.

synonyms   Words having similar meaning.

syntax   The system by which words may be ordered in phrases and sentences; sentence structure; grammar.

synthesized speech   Computer-generated sounds that simulate human speech.

synthetic   Pertaining to instruction or a process that begins with the parts and builds to the whole. Synthetic phonics starts with individual letter sounds that are blended together to form a word. *See also* analytic.

tactile   Relating to the sense of touch.

target word   A word that is being looked for in a dictionary or other reference source. A word that is the focus of reading, spelling, vocabulary, handwriting, or other instruction.

template   A blank pattern that can be used as a guide to be filled in by the student.

tense vowel   *See* long vowel.

text-to-speech software   Software that can convert computer-based text into spoken words.

thesis statement   A short statement, usually appearing in an essay's opening paragraph in which the writer expresses the main idea, purpose, and intent of a piece of writing.

tracking   The ability to finger point while reading a text, demonstrating the concept of a word. *See also* concept of a word; finger-point reading.

transition words   Words that aid in changing a thought within a sentence or paragraph (e.g., *first, next, then, finally*).

trigraph   Three adjacent letters in a syllable that represent one speech sound (e.g., *tch, dge*). *See also* digraph; quadrigraph.

typography   The physical appearance of written letters such as whether they are upper- or lowercase or formed in cursive or manuscript.

unblending   *See* segmentation.

universal design for learning   An educational approach that concentrates on designing instructional practices, teaching materials, and educational environments that meet the needs and maximize the learning of all students, including those with disabilities.

unbound morpheme   *See* free morpheme.

unvoiced   *See* voiceless.

VAKT (visual, auditory, kinesthetic, tactile)   *See* Fernald method; see also multisensory structured language education (MSLE).

VCE   *See* vowel-consonant-*e* syllable.

velar   Pertaining to sounds produced when the tongue and roof of the mouth contact near the soft palate.

velum   The soft palate.

verbalization   The saying aloud of a pattern or rule for reading or spelling or strokes of a letter shape after that pattern or rule or letter shape has been discovered or learned.

visual, auditory, kinesthetic, tactile (VAKT)   *See* Fernald method; *see also* multisensory structured language education (MSLE).

visual discovery   Information gained by sight. Guided discovery of a reading or spelling rule through looking at written examples of the language concept.

visual mapping software   Software that allows for visual representation of ideas and reduces the need for writing because concepts can be expressed in brief phrases while the visual array does the cognitively and linguistically taxing work of representing relationships among concepts. This software offers enhanced opportunities for brainstorming and organizing on the computer.

vocabulary   A large store of words that a person recognizes and/or uses in his or her oral and written language for communication and comprehension.

voice recognition software   Computer software recognizes the user's voice and provides an alternative to handwriting or keyboarding while drafting text.

voiced   Pertaining to a consonant articulated with vocal vibration (e.g., /z/).

voiced-voiceless cognates   Phonemes produced in the same place of the mouth and in the same manner, but that vary in the voicing characteristic (e.g., /k/, /g/).

voiceless   Pertaining to a consonant articulated with no vocal vibration (e.g., /s/). Also called *unvoiced*.

vowel   A class of open speech sounds produced by the easy passage of air through a relatively open vocal tract. English vowels include *a, e, i, o, u,* and sometimes *y*.

vowel blend   *See* blend.

vowel digraph   *See* digraph.

vowel pair syllable   A syllable containing two adjacent vowels that have a long, short, or diphthong sound (e.g., *meet, head, loud*). Also called *vowel team syllable*.

vowel prefix   A prefix with a vowel as the final letter. The spelling of a vowel prefix does not change when it is added to a base word, a root, or a combining form.

vowel suffix   A suffix beginning with a vowel, such as *-ing* and *-ed*.

vowel team syllable   *See* vowel pair syllable.

vowel-consonant-*e* syllable (VCE)   A one-syllable word or a final syllable of a longer word in which a final silent *e* signals that the vowel before the consonant is long (e.g., *cake, rope, cube, five, athlete*).

vowel-*r* syllable   See *r*-controlled syllable.

Watch Our Writing (W.O.W.)   A checklist designed to help students write accurately, comfortably, and legibly: Place feet flat on the floor, sit up straight, slant the paper at a 45-degree angle, rest arms on the desk, and hold the pencil lightly while pointing its upper end toward the shoulder of writing arm (Phelps & Stempel, 1985).

whole language approach   A perspective on teaching literacy based on beliefs about teaching and learning that include the following: Reading can be learned as naturally as speaking; reading is focused on constructing meaning from text using children's books rather than basal or controlled readers; reading is best learned in the context of the group; phonics is taught indirectly during integration of reading, writing, listening, and speaking; teaching is child centered and emphasizes motivation and interest; and instruction is offered on the basis of need.

word bank   A list of vocabulary words that can be used as answer choices on a vocabulary test.

word blindness   Term used in the late 19th and early 20th centuries for dyslexia. Word blindness now refers to acquired alexia, "the loss or diminution of ability of reading ability resulting from of brain trauma, a tumor, or a stroke" (Shaywitz, 2003, p. 140).

word consciousness   An interest in and awareness of words.

word prediction software   Software that uses spelling knowledge, grammar rules, and context clues to predict what word a student wants to type as he or she enters the first few letters into the computer.

working memory   *See* short-term memory.

W.O.W.   *See* Watch Our Writing.

zero-reject principle   The principle infused in special education legislation that no child's disabilities are too severe for him or her to learn or to be provided with educational services.

REFERENCES

Americans with Disabilities Act (ADA) of 1990, PL 101-336, 42 U.S.C. §§ 12101 *et seq.*

Corsini, R.J., & Auerbach, A.J. (Eds.). (1996). *Concise encyclopedia of psychology* (2nd ed.). New York: Wiley.

Cox, A.R. (1992). *Foundations for literacy: Structures and techniques for multisensory teaching of basic written English language skills.* Cambridge, MA: Educators Publishing Service.

Education for All Handicapped Children Act of 1975, PL 94-142, 20 U.S.C. §§ 1400 *et seq.*

Fromkin, V., Rodman, R., & Hyams, N. (2003). *An introduction to language* (7th ed.). Boston: Thomson/Heinle.

Harris, T.L., & Hodges, R.E. (Eds.). (1995). *The literacy dictionary: The vocabulary of reading and writing.* Newark, DE: International Reading Association.

Henry, M.K. (2003). *Unlocking literacy: Effective decoding and spelling instruction.* Baltimore: Paul H. Brookes Publishing Co.

Individuals with Disabilities Education Act Amendments (IDEA) of 1997, PL 105-17, 20 U.S.C. §§ 1400 *et seq.*

Individuals with Disabilities Education Act (IDEA) of 1990, PL 101-476, 20 U.S.C. §§ 1400 *et seq.*

Individuals with Disabilities Education Improvement Act (IDEA) of 2004, PL 108-446, 20 U.S.C. §§ 1400 *et seq.*

Kavanagh, J.F., & Truss, T.J. (Eds.). (1988). *Learning disabilities: Proceedings of the national conference.* Timonium, MD: York Press.

Lerner, J.W. (1997). *Learning disabilities: Theories, diagnosis, and teaching strategies* (7th ed.). Boston: Houghton Mifflin.

Lyon, G.R., Shaywitz, S.E., & Shaywitz, B.A. (2003). A definition of dyslexia. *Annals of Dyslexia, 53,* 1–14.

Moats, L.C. (1995). *Spelling: Development, disabilities, and instruction.* Timonium, MD: York Press.

Moats, L.C. (2010). *Speech to print: Language essentials for teachers* (2nd ed.). Baltimore: Paul H. Brookes Publishing Co.

Phelps, J., & Stempel, L. (1985). *CHES's handwriting improvement program* (CHIP). Dallas, TX: Children's Handwriting Evaluation Scale.

Rehabilitation Act Amendments of 1998, PL 105-220, 29 U.S.C. §§ 701 *et seq.*

Robinson, F.P. (1946). *Effective study.* New York: HarperCollins.

Shaywitz, S. (2003). *Overcoming dyslexia: A new and complete science-based program for reading problems at any level.* New York: Alfred A. Knopf.

Snow, C., & Dickinson, D. (1991). Skills that aren't basic in a new conception of literacy. In A. Purves & E. Jennings (Eds.), *Literate systems and individual lives: Perspectives on literacy and schooling* (pp. 175–213). Albany, New York: SUNY Press.

Stanovich, K.E. (1986). Matthew effects in reading: Some consequences of individual differences in the acquisition of literacy. *Reading Research Quarterly, 21,* 360–407.

Stedman's Medical Dictionary (27th ed.). (2000). Philadelphia: Lippincott, Williams & Wilkins.

Materials and Sources

MARILYN MARTIN

CHAPTER 1 Connecting Research and Practice

Organizations

The Alliance for Technology Access (ATA)
2175 East Francisco Boulevard
Suite L
San Rafael, CA 94901
415-455-4575
http://www.ataccess.org

American Speech-Language-Hearing Association
2200 Research Boulevard
Rockville, MD 20850-3289
301-296-5700
http://www.asha.org

Association of Educational Therapists
11300 W. Olympic Boulevard
Los Angeles, CA 90064
310-909-1490
http://www.aetonline.org/

Attention Deficit Disorder Association
Post Office Box 7557
Wilmington, DE 19803-9997
800-939-1019
http://www.add.org

British Dyslexia Association
Unit 8 Bracknell Beeches
Old Bracknell Lane
Bracknell, RG12 7BW
0845 251 9003
http://www.bdadyslexia.org.uk/

The Center for Accessible Technology
2547 Eighth Street 12A
Berkeley, CA 94710

510-841-3224
http://www.cforat.org

Center for Advanced Study of Teaching and Learning (CASTL)
Curry School of Education
University of Virginia
350 Old Ivy Way
Charlottesville, VA 22903
434-982-4760
http://curry.virginia.edu/research/centers/castl

Children and Adults with Attention/Deficit Hyperactivity Disorder (CHADD)
818 Professional Place
Suite 150
Landover, MD 20785
301-306-7070
http://www.chadd.org

Division for Learning Disabilities (DLD)
The Council for Exceptional Children (CEC)
1110 North Glebe Road
Suite 300
Arlington, VA 22201
888-CEC-SPED
E-mail: cec@cec.sped.org
http://www.teachingld.org

Dyslexia Foundation
Post Office Box P-22
4 Narragansett Street
South Dartmouth, MA 02748
941-807-0499
http://www.thedyslexiafoundation.org

Dyslexia Research Institute
5746 Centerville Road
Tallahassee, FL 32309
850-893-2216
http://www.dyslexia-add.org/

Florida Center for Reading Research
2010 Levy Avenue
Suite 100
Tallahassee, FL 32310
850-644-9352
http://www.fcrr.org

HEATH Resource Center
American Council on Education
1 Dupont Circle NW
Suite 800
Washington, DC 20036
800-544-3284
202-939-9300
http://www.heath.gwu.edu/

The Institute for Literacy and Learning
Post Office Box 2301
Whitehall, PA 18052-0230
888-955-READ (7323)
http://www.theinstituteforliteracyandlearning.org

The International Dyslexia Association (IDA)
40 York Road
4th Floor
Baltimore, MD 21204-5202
410-296-0232
E-mail: info@interdys.org
http://www.interdys.org

International Reading Association (IRA)
Public Information Office
800 Barksdale Road
Post Office Box 8139
Newark, DE 19714
302-731-1600
http://www.reading.org

Learning Disabilities Association of America (LDA)
4156 Library Road
Pittsburgh, PA 15234
412-341-1515
http://www.ldanatl.org

National Association for the Education of African American Children with Learning Disabilities (NAEAACLD)
Post Office Box 09521
Columbus, OH 43209
614-237-6021
http://www.aacld.org

National Center for Learning Disabilities (NCLD)
381 Park Avenue South
Suite 1401
New York, NY 10016
888-575-7373
http://www.ncld.org

National Dissemination Center for Children with Disabilities (NICHCY)
1825 Connecticut Avenue NW
Suite 700
Washington, DC 20009
800-695-0285
E-mail: nichcy@aed.org
http://www.nichcy.org

Schwab Learning
Charles and Helen Schwab Foundation
1650 South Amphlett Boulevard
Suite 200
San Mateo, CA 94402
650-655-2410
http://www.schwablearning.org

The Yale Center for Dyslexia & Creativity
Yale School of Medicine
333 Cedar Street
New Haven, CT 06510
203-432-4771
http://www.dyslexia.yale.edu

Web Sites

95% Group Inc.
http://www.95percentgroup.com

All About Adolescent Literacy
http://www.adlit.org

Best Evidence Encyclopedia
http://www.bestevidence.org

Big Ideas in Beginning Reading
http://reading.uoregon.edu

Colorin Colorado
http://www.colorincolorado.org

Education Week
http://www.edweek.org/ew/index.html

ERIC Clearinghouse on Disabilities and Gifted
Education
http://ericec.org

The Faculty Room
http://www.washington.edu/doit/faculty/Resources

Florida Center for Reading Research
http://www.fcrr.org/

Great Schools
http://www.greatschools.org/special-
education.topic?content=1541

Helpful Links for Learning Disabilities
http://www.ldaofky.org/helpful_links.htm

Ideas that Work
http://www.osepideasthatwork.org/

The Instant Access Treasure Chest
http://www.fin.vcu.edu/ld/ld.html

iTune U, IRA Radio
Literacy 2.0 The New Frontier of Literacy in the
Digital Age
http://www.apple.com/education/itunes-u/

LD Online
http://www.ldonline.org

National Center on Response to Intervention
http://www.rti4success.org

National Institute for Literacy: LINCS
http://novel.nifl.gov/

National Clearinghouse for Professions in Special
Education (NCPSE)
http://www.specialedcareers.org

No Child Left Behind: A Toolkit for Teachers
http://www.ed.gov/teachers/nclbguide/index2.html

Reading Rockets
http://www.readingrockets.org

ReadWriteThink
http://www.readwritethink.org

What Works Clearinghouse
http://ies.ed.gov/ncee/wwc/

Wrightslaw
http://www.wrightslaw.com/nclb/4defs.reading.htm

Book Publishers

Academic Communication Associates
Publication Center
Department 698
Post Office Box 4279
Oceanside, CA 92058
888-758-9558
E-mail: acom@acadcom.com
http://www.acadcom.com

Academic Therapy Publications
20 Commercial Boulevard
Novato, CA 94949
800-422-7249
http://www.academictherapy.com

Brookline Books
Post Office Box 1047
Cambridge, MA 02238
800-666-BOOK
http://brooklinebooks.com/

CEC Publications
The Council for Exceptional Children
1110 North Glebe Road
Suite 300
Arlington, VA 22201

888-CEC-SPED
http://www.cec.sped.org/bk/catalog2/index.html

Center for Applied Research in Education
Book Distribution Center
Route 59 at Brook Hill Drive
West Nyack, NY 10995
http://isbndb.com/d/publisher/center_for_applied
_research_in.html

Continental Press
520 East Bainbridge Street
Elizabethtown, PA 17022
800-233-0759
http://www.continentalpress.com

Corwin Press
2455 Teller Road
Thousand Oaks, CA 91320
805-499-9734
http://www.corwinpress.com

Educators Publishing Service
Post Office Box 9031
Cambridge, MA 02139-9031
800-225-5750
http://www.epsbooks.com

Guilford Press
72 Spring Street
New York, NY 10012
800-365-7006
http://www.guilford.com

Heinemann
Post Office Box 6926
Portsmouth, NH 03802-6926
800-225-5800
http://www.heinemann.com

Language Circle Enterprises
Post Office Box 20631
Bloomington, MN 55420
800-450-0343
E-mail: projreqdd@mn.uswest.net
http://www.projectread.com

Lawrence Erlbaum Associates
10 Industrial Avenue
Mahwah, NJ 07430
800-926-6579
http://www.taylorandfrancis.com/

LinguiSystems
3100 4th Avenue
East Moline, IL 61244
800-776-4332
E-mail: service@linguisystems.com
http://www.linguisystems.com

Paul H. Brookes Publishing Co.
Post Office Box 10624
Baltimore, MD 21285-0624
800-638-3775

E-mail: custserv@brookespublishing.com
http://www.brookespublishing.com

PRO-ED
8700 Shoal Creek Boulevard
Austin, TX 78757
800-897-3202
http://www.proedinc.com

Research Press Publishers
Department IOW
Post Office Box 9177
Champaign, Il 61826
800-519-2702
http://www.researchpress.com

Routledge Teachers
270 Madison Avenue
New York, NY 10016
212-216-7800
http://www.routledge.com/teachers/

Sopris West
4185 Salazar Way
Frederick, CO 80504
800-547-6747
http://www.sopriswest.com

Walker & Co.
175 5th Avenue
New York, NY 10010
800-AT-WALKER
http://www.walkerbooks.com

York Press
Books available through PRO-ED
800-897-3202

Teacher References

Moats, L. (2010). *Speech to print: Language essentials for teachers* (2nd ed.). Baltimore: Paul H. Brookes Publishing Co.

Snow, C., Burns, M., & Griffin, P. (Eds.). (1998). *Preventing reading difficulties in young children.* Washington, DC: National Academies Press.

Wolf, M. (2007). *Proust and the squid.* New York: HarperCollins.

Parent References

Hall, S. (2002). *Parenting a struggling reader.* New York: Broadway Books.

Healy, J. (2010). *Different learners: Identifying, preventing, and treating your child's learning problems.* New York: Simon & Schuster.

Shaywitz, S. (2003). *Overcoming dyslexia: A new and complete science-based program for reading problems at any level.* New York: Alfred A. Knopf.

Vail, P. (1987). *Smart kids with school problems.* New York: Dutton Signet.

Professional Journals

American Educator
Annals of Dyslexia
Annals of Neurology
Brain
Brain and Language
Child Development
Cognition and Instruction
Developmental Psychology
Dyslexia: An International Journal of Research and Practice
Educational Psychology
Exceptional Children
JAMA: The Journal of the American Medical Association
Journal of Child Neurology
Journal of Child Psychology and Psychiatry and Allied Disciplines
Journal of Consulting and Clinical Psychology
Journal of Educational Psychology
Journal of Educational Research
Journal of Experimental Child Psychology
Journal of Experimental Psychology: Learning, Memory, and Cognition
Journal of General Psychology

Journal of Learning Disabilities
Journal of Literacy Research
Journal of Psycholinguistic Research
Journal of Psychology
Journal of Special Education
Journal of Speech, Language, and Hearing Disorders
Learning Disabilities Quarterly
Learning Disabilities: A Multidisciplinary Journal
Learning Disabilities: Research and Practice
Nature
Neurology
New England Journal of Medicine
Perspectives
Reading and Writing: An Interdisciplinary Journal
Reading Research Quarterly
The Reading Teacher
Remedial and Special Education
Science
Scientific Studies of Reading
Teaching Exceptional Children
Topics in Language Disorders
Trends in Neurosciences

DVDs

Children and ADD by Edward Hallowell, M.D. (Available from Hallowell Center, http://www.drhallowell.com)

Dyslexics Talk About Attaining Success (Available from Joan Kelly, 326 North Cove Road, Hudson, WI 54016; 715-386-2762)

Einstein and Me: Talking About Learning Disabilities (Available from The British Dyslexia Association, 98 London Road, Reading, Berkshire, RG1 5AU, United Kingdom; e-mail: admin@bda-dyslexia-help-bda.demon.co.uk)

Ennis' Gift (Available from the Hello Friend/Ennis William Cosby Foundation, Post Office Box 4061, Santa Monica, CA 90411; 800-343-5540; http://www.hellofriend.org)

Finding the Answers (Available from The International Dyslexia Association, 8600 LaSalle Road, Chester Building, Suite 382, Baltimore, MD 21286; 800-ABC-D123; e-mail: info@interdys.org; http://www.interdys.org)

Fundamentals of Reading Success: An Introduction to the Orton-Gillingham Approach to Teaching Reading (video series, work booklet, and language kit) (Available from Educators Publishing Service, 31 Smith Place, Cambridge, MA 02138; 800-225-5750; http://www.epsbooks.com/dynamic/catalog/series.asp?seriesonly=7250M)

Gifts of Greatness, written and directed by Joyce Bulifant (Available from the National Dyslexia Research Foundation, Post Office Box 393, Boca Grande, FL 33921; 941-964-0999)

Homework and Learning Disabilities: A Common Sense Approach (Available from Altschul Group Corporation Educational Media, 1560 Sherman Avenue, Suite 100, Evanston, IL 60201; 800-421-2363; e-mail: agcmedia@starnetinc.com)

How Difficult Can This Be? The F.A.T. City Workshop (Available from LD Online; http://ldonline.learningstore.org/products/LD1001.html)

Last One Picked, First One Picked On (Available from LD Online; http://ldonline.learningstore.org/products/LD1002.html)

LD/LA: Learning Disabilities/Learning Abilities (video series) (Available from Vineyard Video Productions, Post Office Box 806, West Tisbury, MA 02575; 800-664-6119; e-mail: mpotts@vineyardvideo.org; http://www.vineyardvideo.org)

Learning Disabilities: A Family Crisis (Available from Altschul Group Corporation Educational Media, 1560 Sherman Avenue, Suite 100, Evanston, IL 60201; 800-421-2363; e-mail: agcmedia@starnetinc.com)

Learning Disabilities: The Orton-Gillingham Approach (Available from San Jose State University, 1 Washington Square, San Jose, CA 95192; contact: Paula Galvin at 408-924-3676)

Learning for Life: Kids and Learning Differences (Available from Disney Educational Productions; 800-295-5010; http://www.Edustation.Disney.com)

Look What You've Done! (Available from LD Online; http://ldonline.learningstore.org/products/LD1005.html)

Slingerland Institute Information Video (Available from the Slingerland Institute for Literacy, 411 108th Avenue N.E., Bellevue, WA 98004; 425-453-1190; e-mail: mail@slingerland.org; http ://www.slingerland.org)

Unlocking the Written Word: Reading Assist (Available from Reading ASSIST Institute, 100 West 10th Street, #910, Wilmington, DE 19801; 888-311-1156)

We Can Learn: Understanding and Helping Children with Learning Disabilities (Available from Na-tional Center for Learning Disabilities, 381 Park Avenue South, Suite 1420, New York, NY 10016; 888-575-7373; http://www.ncld.org)

When the Chips Are Down: Strategies for Improving Children's Behavior (Available from LD Online; http://ldonline.learningstore.org/products/LD1004.html)

Wilson Language Training Group Lesson: Step 6 (Available from Wilson Language Training, 47 Old Webster Road, Oxford, MA 01540; 888-899-8454; http://www.wilsonlanguage.com)

CHAPTER 2   Multisensory Structured Language Education

MSLE Teacher Training Programs and Accrediting Organizations

Accrediting and Certifying Organizations

Alliance for Accreditation and Certification of Structured Language Education, Inc.
The Alliance, Inc.
14070 Proton Road
Suite 100, LB 9
Dallas, TX 75244
972-233-9107, x 213
http://www.allianceaccreditation.org

The Alliance is composed of two organizations, one for the accreditation of multisensory structured language education training courses (the International Multisensory Structured Language Education Council) and the other for certification of graduates of these courses (the Academic Language Therapy Association). Graduates are eligible to take the Alliance National Registration Exam.

Academic Language Therapy Association (ALTA) [*Certification*]
14070 Proton Road
Suite 100, LB9
Dallas, TX 75244
972-233-9107, x208
http://www.ALTAread.org (click on "resources" to find academic language therapists and associate academic language teachers listed by state)

International Multisensory Structured Language Education Council (IMSLEC) [Accreditation]
c/o Shelton School
15720 Hillcrest Road
Dallas, TX 75248
972-774-1772
http://www.imslec.org/index.html (click on "membership" to find IMSLEC accredited courses listed by state)

Academy of Orton-Gillingham Practitioners and Educators [Accreditation/Certification]
East Main Street
Post Office Box 234
Amenia, NY 12501
845-373-8919
http://www.ortonacademy.org/

Other MSLE Training Programs

The Stern Center
135 Allen Brook Lane
Williston, VT 05495
802-878-2332
E-mail: educator@sterncenter.org
http://www.sterncenter.org

Wilson Language Training
47 Old Webster Road
Oxford, MA 01540
800-899-8454
http://www.wilsonlanguge.com

Teacher Reference

International Dyslexia Association. (n.d.). *Framework for informed reading and language instruction: Matrix of multisensory structured language pro-*grams. Retrieved November 26, 2010, from http://www.interdys.org/ewebeditpro5/upload/MSL2007finalR1.pdf

Instructional Materials

Avrit, K., Allen, C., Carlsen, K., Gross, M., Pierce, D., & Rumsey, M. (2006). *Take flight: A comprehensive intervention for students with dyslexia.* Dallas, TX: Texas Scottish Rite Hospital for Children.

Avrit, K., Allen, C., Carlsen, K., Pierce, D., Gross, M., & Rumsey, M. (2006). *Rite flight: A classroom reading rate program.* Dallas, TX: Texas Scottish Rite Hospital for Children.

CHAPTER 3   Development of Oral Language and Its Relationship to Literacy

Organizations

American Speech-Language-Hearing Association
2200 Research Boulevard
Rockville, MD 20850
301-296-5700
http://www.asha.org

National Association for the Education of Young Children
1313 L Street N.W.
Washington, DC 20005
800-424-2460
http://www.naeyc.org

Web Sites

Colorin Colorado
http://www.colorincolorado.org/educators/content/oral

Reading Rockets
http://www.readingrockets.org/webcasts/1002

Instructional Materials

Dandy Lion Publications
3563 Sueldo Street
Suite L
San Luis Obispo, CA 93401
805-543-332
E-mail: dandy@dandylionbooks.com
http://www.dandylionbooks.com

Janelle Publications
Post Office Box 811
DeKalb, IL 60115
800-888-8834
E-mail: info@janellepublications.com

http://www.janellepublications.com

LinguiSystems
3100 4th Avenue
East Moline, IL 61244
800-776-4332
E-mail: service@linguisystems.com
http://www.linguisystems.com

Remedia Publications
15887 North 76th Street #120
Scottsdale, AZ 85260
800-826-4740
http://www.rempub.com

The Speech Bin
1965 25th Avenue
Vero Beach, FL 32960
800-4-SPEECH
https://store.schoolspecialtyonline.net

Super Duper Publications
Department SD 2004
Post Office Box 24997

Greenville, NC 29616
800-277-8737
http://www.superduperinc.com

Thinking Publications
8700 Shoal Creek Boulevard
Austin, TX 78757
800-897-3202
http://www.proedinc.com

Teacher References

Agin, M.C., Geng, L.F., & Nicholl, M.J. (2003). *The late talker: What to do if your child isn't talking yet.* New York: St. Martin's Press.

Allen, J. (1999). *Words, words, words: Teaching vocabulary in Grades 4–12.* Portland, ME: Stenhouse Publishers.

Apel, K., & Masterson, J. (2001). *Beyond baby talk: From sounds to sentences.* Roseville, CA: Prima Publishing.

Baron, N. (1992). *Growing up with language.* Boston: Addison Wesley.

Beck, I., McKeown, M., & Kucan, L. (2002). *Bringing words to life.* New York: Guilford Press.

Bielmiller, A. (1999). *Language and reading success.* Cambridge, MA: Brookline Books.

Butler, K.G., & Silliman, E.R. (2002). *Speaking, reading, and writing in children with language learning disabilities.* Mahwah, NJ: Lawrence Erlbaum Associates.

Cain, K., & Oakhill, J. (2007). *Children's comprehension problems in oral and written language: A cognitive perspective.* New York: Guilford Press.

Catts, H.W., & Kamhi, A.G. (Eds.). (2005). *Language and reading disabilities* (2nd ed.). Boston: Allyn & Bacon.

Gopnik, A., Meltzoff, A., & Kuhl, P. (1999). *The scientist in the crib.* New York: HarperCollins.

Hamaguchi, P. (1995). *Childhood speech, language and listening problems.* New York: Wiley.

Hulit, L., & Howard, M. (1993). *Born to talk: An introduction to speech and language development.* New York: Macmillan.

Meltzer, L. (Ed.). (1993). *Strategy assessment and instruction for students with learning disabilities.* Austin, TX: PRO-ED.

Menyuk, P. (1999). *Reading and linguistic development.* Cambridge, MA: Brookline Books.

Merritt, D., & Culatta, B. (1998). *Language intervention in the classroom.* San Diego: Singular Publishing Group.

Owens, R. (1996). *Language development: An introduction* (3rd ed.). Columbus, OH: Charles E. Merrill.

Roberts, J.E., & Burchinal, M.R. (2001). The complex interplay between biology and environment: Otitis media and mediating effects on early literacy development. In S.B. Neuman & D.K. Dickinson (Eds.), *Handbook of early literacy research* (pp. 232–244). New York: Guilford Press.

Stahl, S. (1999). *Vocabulary development.* Cambridge, MA: Brookline Books.

Wallach, G., & Butler, K. (1994). *Language learning disabilities in school-age children and adolescents.* Boston: Allyn & Bacon.

Professional Journals

American Journal of Speech-Language Pathology
Journal of Speech, Language, and Hearing Disorders

Language, Speech, and Hearing Services in the Schools
Topics in Language Disorders

CHAPTER 4   The History and Structure of Written English

Web Sites

American Speech-Language-Hearing Association
http://www.asha.org

Collins Cobuild Dictionary
http://www.collinslanguage.com/

Dictionary.com app
http://dictionary.reference.com/apps/iphone

Explore English Words Derived from Latin-Greek Origins
http://www.wordexplorations.com

Merriam-Webster
http://www.merriam-webster.com/help/faq/history.htm

Reading Rockets
http://www.readingrockets.org

Vocabulary University
http://www.vocabulary.com

A Word A Day
http://wordsmith.org/awad

Instructional Materials

Bebko, A.R., Alexander, J., & Doucet, R. (2001). *LANGUAGE! Roots* (2nd ed.). Longmont, CO: Sopris West Educational Services.

Blanchard, C. (2005). *Word roots series* (Level A, Grades 4–12; Level B, Grade 7–12). Pacific Grove, CA: Critical Thinking Books and Software.

Ehrlich, I. (1972). *Instant vocabulary.* New York: Pocket Books.

Fifer, N., & Flowers, N. (1990). *Vocabulary from classical roots.* Cambridge, MA: Educators Publishing Service.

Henry, M.K. (1990). *WORDS: Integrated decoding and spelling instruction based on word origin and word structure.* Austin, TX: PRO-ED.

Henry, M.K. (2010). *Unlocking literacy: Effective decoding and spelling instruction* (2nd ed.). Baltimore: Paul H. Brookes Publishing Co.

Henry, M.K., & Redding, N.C. (1996). *Patterns for success in reading and spelling.* Austin, TX: PRO-ED.

Johnson, K., & Bayrd, P. (1998). *Megawords series.* Cambridge, MA: Educators Publishing Service.

Johnson, P.F. (1999). *Word scramble 2.* East Moline, IL: LinguiSystems.

Jones, T.B. (1997). *Decoding and encoding English words.* Timonium, MD: York Press. (Available from PRO-ED; 800-897-3202)

Kleiber, M.H. (1990–2004). *Specific language training: An Orton-Gillingham curriculum for adolescents.* Yonkers, NY: Decatur Enterprises. (Available from the publisher; 26 Birch Road, Yonkers, NY 10705)

Marcellaro, E.G., & Ostrovsky, G.R. (1988). *Verbal vibes series.* Sacramento, CA: Lumen Publications.

Moats, L.C. (2010). *Speech to print: Language essentials for teachers* (2nd ed.). Baltimore: Paul H. Brookes Publishing Co.

Morgan, K. (2002). *Dynamic roots.* Albuquerque, NM: Morgan Dynamic Phonics.

Pinnell, G.S., & Fountas, I.C. (1998). *Word matters.* Portsmouth, NH: Heinemann.

Rome, P.D., & Osman, J.S. (1993). *Language tool kit.* Cambridge, MA: Educators Publishing Service.

Rome, P.D., & Osman, J.S. (2000). *Advanced language tool kit.* Cambridge, MA: Educators Publishing Service.

Slingerland, B.H. (1982). *Phonetic word lists for children's use.* Cambridge, MA: Educators Publishing Service.

Steere, A., Peck, C.Z., & Kahn, L. (1971). *Solving language difficulties.* Cambridge, MA: Educators Publishing Service.

UpWords. (1999). East Longmeadow, MA: Milton Bradley (a division of Hasbro).

Wimer, D.B. (1994). *Word studies: A classical perspective: Prefixes, roots, suffixes* (Vol. 1). Richmond, VA: Author. (Available from the author; Post Office Box 5362, Richmond, VA 23220)

Dictionaries

Agnes, M.E. (Ed.). (1999). *Webster's new world children's dictionary* (2nd ed.) [For ages 7–12]. New York: Wiley.

American Heritage student dictionary [For Grades 6–9]. (1998). Boston: Houghton Mifflin.

American Heritage student thesaurus [For Grades 7–10]. (1999). Boston: Houghton Mifflin.

Barnhart, R.K. (Ed.). (1988). *The Barnhart dictionary of etymology.* New York: The H.W. Wilson Co.

Bollard, J.K. (1988). *Scholastic children's thesaurus.* New York: Scholastic.

Collins COBUILD Dictionary. (2010). London: HarperCollins UK.

Crutchfield, R.S. (1997). *English vocabulary quick reference: A comprehensive dictionary arranged by word roots.* Leesburg, VA: LexaDyne Publishing.

Halsey, W.D. (Ed.). (2001). *MacMillan dictionary for children.* New York: Simon & Schuster.

Latimer, J.P., & Nolting, K.S. (2001). *Simon and Schuster thesaurus for children* [For ages 9–12]. New York: Simon & Schuster.

Levey, J.S. (Ed.). (1990). *Macmillan first dictionary* [For ages 4–8]. New York: Simon & Schuster.

Levey, J.S. (Ed.). (2002). *Scholastic children's dictionary* [For ages 8–12]. New York: Scholastic Reference.

Teacher References

Ayto, J. (1999). *Twentieth century words.* New York: Oxford University Press.

Balmuth, M. (2009). *The roots of phonics: A historical introduction* (Rev. ed.). Baltimore: Paul H.

Brookes Publishing Co.

Barnett, L. (1964). *The treasure of our tongue*. New York: Alfred A. Knopf.

Bryson, B. (1990). *The mother tongue: English and how it got that way*. New York: William Morrow.

Claiborne, R. (1983). *Our marvelous native tongue. The life and times of the English language*. New York: Times Books.

Fry, E.B., Kress, J.E., & Fountoukidis, D. (2000). *The reading teacher's book of lists* (4th ed.). Upper Saddle River, NJ: Prentice Hall.

King, D. (2000). *Engish isn't crazy*. Timonium, MD: York Press.

Lederer, R. (1991). *The miracle of language*. New York: Pocket Books.

Logan, R.K. (1986). *The alphabet effect*. New York:

St. Martins Press.

Manguel, A. (1996). *A history of reading*. New York: Viking.

Martin, H.J. (1994). *The history and power of writing*. Chicago: University of Chicago Press.

McCrum, R., Cran, S., & MacNeil, R. (1986). *The story of English*. New York: Viking.

Nist, J. (1966). *A structural history of English*. New York: St. Martin's Press.

Pei, M. (1965). *The story of language*. New York: J.B. Lippincott. (Original work published 1949)

Pinker, S. (1994). *The language instinct*. New York: William Morrow.

Soukhanov, A.H. (1995). *Word watch*. New York: Henry Holt.

Parent References

Beal, G. (1992). *Book of words: A–Z guide to quotations, proverbs, origins, usage, and idioms*. New York: Kingfisher Books.

Brook, D., & Zallinger, J.D. (Illustrator). (1998). *The journey of English*. New York: Clarion Books.

Klausner, J. (1990). *Talk about English: How words travel and change*. New York: Thomas Y. Crowell.

Krensky, S. (1996). *Breaking into print: Before and after the invention of the printing press*. New York: Little, Brown.

Samoyault, T. (1996). *Alphabetical order: How the alphabet began*. New York: Penguin Books.

CHAPTER 5   Teaching Phonemic Awareness

Web Sites

Current Practice Alerts
http://www.dldcec.org/pdf/alert10.pdf

Get Ready to Read!
http://www.getreadytoread.org

Literacy Information and Communication System
http://novel.nifl.gov/

Reading Rockets
http://www.readingrockets.org

Assessment Tools

Lindamood, P., & Lindamood, P. (2004). *Lindamood Auditory Conceptualization Test–Third Edition (LAC–3)*. Austin, TX: PRO-ED.

Robertson, C., & Salter, W. (1997). *The Phonological Awareness Test*. East Moline, IL: LinguiSystems.

Rosner, J. (1999). *Test of Auditory Analysis (TAAS)*. Ann Arbor, MI: Academic Therapy Publications.

Sawyer, D.J. (1987). *Test of Awareness of Language Segments*. Austin, TX: PRO-ED.

Seymour, H.N., Roeper, T.W., & de Villiers, J. (with de Villiers, P.A.). (2003). *Diagnostic Evaluation of Language Variance (DELV-Criterion Referenced)*. San Antonio, TX: Harcourt Assessment.

Torgesen, J.K., & Bryant, B. (2004). *Test of Phonological Awareness—2nd Edition: PLUS (TOPA-2+)* [Complete kit]. Austin, TX: PRO-ED.

Uhry, J.K. (1993). Predicting reading from phonological awareness and classroom print: An early reading screening. *Educational Assessment, 1,* 349–368.

Wagner, R., Torgesen, J.K., & Rashotte, C. (1999). *Comprehensive Test of Phonological Processing (CTOPP)*. Austin, TX: PRO-ED.

Yopp, H.K. (1995). A test for assessing phonemic awareness in young children. *The Reading Teacher, 49,* 20–29.

Instructional Materials

Adams, M.J., Foorman, B.R., Lundberg, I., & Beeler, T. (1998). *Phonemic awareness in young children: A classroom curriculum*. Baltimore: Paul H. Brookes Publishing Co.

Blachman, B.A., Ball, E.W., Black, R., & Tangel, D.M. (2000). *Road to the code: A phonological awareness program for young children*. Baltimore: Paul H. Brookes Publishing Co.

Carreker, S. (1992). *Reading readiness (manual, kit 1 & 2)*. Bellaire, TX: Neuhaus Education Center.

Catts, H.W., & Vartiainen, T. (1993). *Sounds abound: Listening, rhyming, and reading*. East Moline, IL: LinguiSystems.

Fitzpatrick, J. (1997). *Phonemic awareness: Playing with sounds to strengthen beginning reading skills*. Huntington Beach, CA: Creative Teaching Press.

Fredericks, A.D. (2001). *The complete phonemic awareness handbook*. Greenville, SC: Super Duper Publications.

Goldsworthy, C.L. (1998). *Sourcebook of phonological awareness activities: Children's classic literature*. San Diego: Singular Publishing Group.

Lindamood, P., & Lindamood, P. (1998). *Lindamood phoneme sequencing program for reading, spelling, and speech (LiPS): Teacher's manual for the classroom and clinic* (3rd ed.). Austin, TX: PRO-ED.

Notari-Syverson, A., O'Connor, R.E., & Vadasy, P.F. (2007). *Ladders to literacy: A preschool activity book* (2nd ed.). Baltimore: Paul H. Brookes Publishing Co.

O'Connor, R.E., Notari-Syverson, A., & Vadasy, P.F. (2005). *Ladders to literacy: A kindergarten activity book* (2nd ed.). Baltimore: Paul H. Brookes Publishing Co.

Opitz, M.F. (1998). Children's books to develop phonemic awareness—for you and parents too! *The Reading Teacher, 51*, 526–528.

Rosner, J. (1999). *Phonological awareness skills program*. Austin, TX: PRO-ED.

Rowland, P.T. (2007). *Happily ever after*. Madison, WI: The Rowland Reading Foundation.

Smith, M.T. (1999). *Phoneme awareness: Assessment, instruction, practice*. Forney, TX: MTS Publications.

Telian, N. (1993). *Lively letters*. Stoughton: MA: Telian Learning Concepts. (Card sets available through http://www.readingwithtlc.com/)

Torgesen, J.K., & Bryant, B. (1993). *Phonological awareness training for reading* [Kit]. Austin, TX: PRO-ED.

Wilson, B.A. (2002). *Wilson Fundations (Levels K, 1, 2, 3): Teacher's guide and student material*. Oxford, MA: Wilson Language Training. (Available from the publisher; http://www.wilsonlanguage.com)

Yopp, H.K. (1992). Developing phonological awareness in young children. *The Reading Teacher, 45*, 696–703.

Yopp, H.K. (1995). Read-aloud books for developing phonemic awareness: An annotated bibliography. *The Reading Teacher, 48*, 538–542.

Teacher References

Adams, M.J., Bereiter, C., Hirshberg, J., Anderson, V., & Case, R. (1995). *Framework for effective teaching: Sounds and letters* (Teacher's guide). New York: McGraw-Hill.

Bear, D.R., Invernizzi, M., Templeton, S.R., & Johnston, F. (2007). *Words their way*. Upper Saddle River, NJ: Prentice Hall.

Blachman, B.A., Ball, E.W., Black, R., & Tangel, D.M. (1994). Kindergarten teachers develop phoneme awareness in low income inner-city classrooms: Does it make a difference? *Reading and Writing: An Interdisciplinary Journal, 6*, 1–18.

Blevins, W. (1999). *Phonemic awareness activities: For early reading success*. New York: Scholastic.

Blevins, W. (2006). *Phonics from A to Z: A practical guide*. New York: Scholastic.

Byrne, B., & Fielding-Barnsley, R. (1991). *Sound foundations*. Artamon, New South Wales, Australia: Leyden Educational Publishers. (Available from the publisher; 36 Whiting Street, Artamon, New South Wales 2064, Australia)

Clark, D.B., & Uhry, J.K. (1995). *Dyslexia: Theory and practice of remedial instruction* (2nd ed.). Timonium, MD: York Press. (Available from PRO-ED; 800-897-3202)

Conocimiento fonémico [Trans. and adapted by Sánchez Hart Consultants from *Phoneme awareness* by M.T. Smith, 1997]. Forney, TX: MTS Publications.

Cunningham, A.E. (1990). Explicit instruction in phonemic awareness. *Journal of Experimental Child Psychology, 50*, 429–444.

Griffith, P.L., & Olson, M.W. (1992). Phonemic awareness helps beginning readers break the code. *The Reading Teacher, 45*, 516–523.

Honig, B., Diamond, L., & Gutlon, L. (2008). *CORE: Teaching reading sourcebook for kindergarten through eighth grade*. Novato, CA: Academic Therapy Publications.

Hults, A. (2003). *Reading first: Unlock the secrets to reading success with research-based strategies*. New York: Scholastic Publishing.

O'Connor, R.E. (2007). *Teaching word recognition: Effective strategies for students with learning difficulties*. New York: Guilford Press.

Smartt, S.M., & Glaser, D.R. (2010). *Next STEPS in literary instruction: Connecting assessments to effective interventions*. Baltimore: Paul H. Brookes Publishing Co.

Stanovich, K.E., Cunningham, A.E., & Cramer, B. (1984). Assessing phonological awareness in kindergarten children: Issues of task comparability. *Journal of Experimental Child Psychology, 38*, 175–190.

Torgesen, J.K. (1995). *Orton Emeritus series: Phonological awareness. A critical factor in dyslexia*. Baltimore: International Dyslexia Association.

Yopp, H.K. (1992). Developing phonological awareness in young children. *The Reading Teacher, 45*, 696–703.

Resources

Adams, M.J., Foorman, B.R., Lundberg, I., & Beeler, T. (1997). Annotated bibliography of rhyming stories. In *Phonemic awareness in young children: A classroom curriculum* (pp. 159–169). Baltimore: Paul H. Brookes Publishing Co.

Adams, M.J., Foorman, B.R., Lundberg, I., & Beeler, T. (1997). Poems, fingerplays, jingles, and chants. In *Phonemic awareness in young children: A classroom curriculum* (pp. 171–175). Baltimore: Paul H. Brookes Publishing Co.

Blevins, W. (1997). *Phonemic awareness activities for early reading success.* New York: Scholastic.

Launching young readers series: Play with letters, words and sounds (http://www.readingrockets.org/shows/launching%20sounds)

Predictable Books (http://www.monroe.lib.in.us/childrens/predict.html)

Reading Rockets (2008). *Tips for parents of kindergartners.* (http://www.readingrockets.org/article/7834)

Yopp, H.K. (1995). Read-aloud books for developing phonemic awareness: An annotated bibliography. *The Reading Teacher, 48*(6), 538–542.

Software

Earobics. (2007). Boston: Houghton Mifflin Hartcourt Learning Technology.

Erickson, G.C., Foster, K.C., Forster, D.F., Torgesen, J.K., & Packer, S. (1992). *Daisyquest.* Scotts Valley, CA: Great Wave Software.

Erickson, G.C., Foster, K.C., Forster, D.F., Torgesen, J.K., & Packer, S. (1993). *Daisy's castle.* Scotts Valley, CA: Great Wave Software.

CHAPTER 6   Alphabet Knowledge

Web Sites

Literacy Center.NET
http://www.literacycenter.net/lessonview_en.php

Reading Rockets
http://www.readingrockets.org/strategies/alphabet_matching

Starfall
http://www.starfall.com/

Instructional Materials

Beck, R., Anderson, P., & Conrad, D. (2009). *Practicing basic skills in reading: One-minute fluency builders series.* Longmont, CO: Sopris West Educational Services.

Blevins, W. (2006). *Phonics from A to Z: A practical guide.* New York: Scholastic.

Carreker, S. (1992). *Reading readiness (manual, kit 1 & 2).* Bellaire, TX: Neuhaus Education Center.

Letter Land. (n.d.). London: Collins Educational. (Alphabet book, CDs, and workbooks available from http://www.letterland.com/)

Moveable Alphabets and Letters

Abecedarian
Post Office Box 92843
Austin, TX 78709
800-342-1165
E-mail: info@alphabetletter.com
http://alphabetletter.com

Educators Publishing Service
Post Office Box 9031
Cambridge, MA 02139-9031
800-225-5750
E-mail: epsbooks@epsbooks.com
http://www.eps.schoolspecialty.com

Teacher References

Balmuth, M. (2009). *The roots of phonics: A historical introduction* (Rev. ed.). Baltimore: Paul H. Brookes Publishing Co.

Cox, A.R. (1992). *Foundations for literacy: Structures and techniques for multisensory teaching of basic written language skills.* Cambridge, MA: Educators Publishing Service.

Dowdell, D. (1965). *Secrets of the ABC's*. Fayetteville, GA: Oddo Publishing.

Fisher, L.E. (1978). *Alphabet art: Thirteen ABC's from around the world*. New York: Macmillan.

Gillingham, A., & Stillman, B.W. (1997). *The Gillingham manual: Remedial training for children with specific disability in reading, spelling, and penmanship* (8th ed.). Cambridge, MA: Educators Publishing Service.

Hogan, E.A., & Smith, M.T. (1987). *Alphabet and dictionary skills guide*. Cambridge, MA: Educators Publishing Service.

Hughes, V. (2001). *English language skills*. London: Greenwich Exchange.

Logan, R.K. (1986). *The alphabetic effect*. New York: William Morrow.

Museum of the Alphabet. (1990). *The alphabet makers*. Huntington Beach, CA: Summer Institute of Linguistics.

Ogg, O. (1971). *The 26 letters*. New York: Thomas Y. Crowell.

Patton, S.J. (1989). *Alphabetic: A history of our alphabet*. Tucson, AZ: Zephyr Press.

Phonics in a box. Block Island, RI: Emsbro Consulting. Available at http://www.phonicsinabox.com

Smartt, S.M., & Glaser, D.R. (2010). *Next STEPS in literary instruction: Connecting assessments to effective interventions*. Baltimore: Paul H. Brookes Publishing Co.

Alphabet Books

Hennepin County Library. *List of 40 alphabet books for young readers*. Retrieved November 8, 2010, from http://www.hclib.org/BirthTo6/booklistaction.cfm?list_num=202

CanTeach. *List of alphabet books*. Retrieved November 9, 2010, from http://www.canteach

.ca/elementary/theme1.html

ReadWriteThink. *List of alphabet books*. Retrieved November 9, 2010, from http://www.readwritethink.org/files/resources/lesson_images/lesson844/AlphabetBooks.pdf

Software

Bailey's Book House (Edmark; available from Riverdeep; 800-825-4420; http://www.riverdeep.net)

Letter Machine (Edmark; available as a free download from Riverdeep; 800-825-4420; http://www.riverdeep.net)

Lexia Phonics Based Reading (Lexia Learning Systems, 2 Lewis Street, Post Office Box 466, Lincoln, MA 01773; 800-435-3942; http://www.lexialearning.com)

CHAPTER 7   Teaching Handwriting

Web Sites

BBC Typing
http://www.bbc.co.uk/schools/typing/

Handwriting Without Tears
http://www.hwtears.com/

LD online
http://www.ldonline.org/indepth/writing

Teacher References

Bounds, G. (2010, October 5). *How handwriting trains the brain*. Retrieved November 24, 2010, from http://online.wsj.com/article/SB10001424052748704631504575531932754922518.html

Cavey, D.W. (1993). *Dysgraphia: Why Johnny can't write: A guide for teachers and parents* (2nd ed.). Austin, TX: PRO-ED.

Cox, A.R. (1992). *Foundations for literacy: Structures and techniques for multisensory teaching of basic written English language skills*. Cambridge, MA: Educators Publishing Service.

Gillingham, A., & Stillman, B.W. (1997). *The Gillingham manual: Remedial training for children with specific disability in reading, spelling and penmanship* (8th ed.). Cambridge, MA: Educators Publishing Service.

Milsom, L. (2008). *Your left-handed child: Making things easy for left-handers in a right-handed world*. London: Hamlyn.

Richards, R. (1999). *The source for dyslexia and dysgraphia*. East Moline, IL: LinguiSystems.

Rosner, J. (1993). *Helping children overcome learning difficulties*. New York: Walker.

Handwriting Instructional Materials

Barchowsky, N. (2006). *Fix it...write*. Available from http://www.bfhhandwriting.com

Benbow, M. (1999). *Loops and other groups: A kinesthetic writing system*. San Antonio, TX: Psychological Corporation.

Bertin, P., & Perlman, E. (1980). *Preventing academic failure handwriting program*. Cambridge, MA: Educators Publishing Service.

D'Nealian handwriting student edition. (Available from http://www.pearsonschool.com)

Duffy, J. (1974). *Type it*. Cambridge, MA: Educators Publishing Service.

King, D.H. (1987). *Cursive writing skills*. Cambridge, MA: Educators Publishing Service.

Olsen, J.Z. (1998). *Handwriting without tears*. (Kits, training, and materials available through http://www.hwtears.com)

PAF handwriting program for cursive. (1997). Cambridge, MA: Educators Publishing Service.

PAF handwriting program for numerals. (1999). Cambridge, MA: Educators Publishing Service.

PAF handwriting program for print. (1995). Cambridge, MA: Educators Publishing Service.

Palmer, A. (2007). *The Palmer method of business writing*. Whitefish, MT: Kessinger Publishing.

Phelps, J., & Stempel, L. (1985). *CHES's handwriting improvement program (CHIP)*. Dallas: CHES. (Available from the publisher; Post Office Box 25254, Dallas, TX 75225)

Slingerland, B.H., & Aho, M.S. (1971). *Manual for learning to use cursive handwriting*. Cambridge, MA: Educators Publishing Service.

Slingerland, B.H., & Aho, M.S. (1971). *Manual for learning to use manuscript handwriting*. Cambridge, MA: Educators Publishing Service.

Smith, M.T. (2007). *Easing into cursive*. Forney, TX: MTS Publications.

Keyboarding Instructional Materials

Duffy, J. (1974). *Type it*. Cambridge, MA: Educators Publishing Service.

King, D.H. (1986). *Keyboarding skills*. Cambridge, MA: Educators Publishing Service.

Mavis Beacon teaches typing for kids. Novato, CA: Mindscape. (Available from the publisher; 88 Rowland Way, Novato, CA 94945; 415-897-9900)

Read, write & type! (2000). (Kit available from http://www.talkingfingers.com/)

Texas Scottish Rite Hospital for Children. (n.d.). *Keyboarding for written expression*. Dallas, TX: Author. (Available from SofDesign International, 1303 Columbia Drive, Suite 209 Richardson, TX 75081; 800-755-7344)

Grips and Aids

Grotto grip (available from http://www.pathwaysforlearning.com/).

Hub key sensors (fits over computer keyboard to ensure correct finger positioning; available through Herzog; http://www.herzogkeyboarding.com/index.html).

Writing frame (#C1590011; metal frame to help writer's grip and shaping of letters). Columbus, OH: Zaner-Bloser.

Software

abcPocketPhonics (downloadable iPhone app that instructs students to draw letters using correct movements with finger or stylus; http://itunes.apple.com/us/app/abc-pocketphonics-letter-sounds/id299342927?mt=8).

CHAPTER 8   Teaching Reading

Organizations

British Dyslexia Association
Unit 8 Bracknell Beeches
Old Bracknell Lane
Bracknell, RG12 7BW
0845 251 9003
http://www.bdadyslexia.org.uk/

Florida Center for Reading Research
2010 Levy Avenue
Suite 100
Tallahassee, FL 32310
850-644-9352
http://www.fcrr.org

The International Dyslexia Association (IDA)
40 York Road, 4th Floor
Baltimore, MD 21204
410-296-0232
E-mail: info@interdys.org
http://www.interdys.org

International Reading Association (IRA)
Public Information Office
800 Barksdale Road
Post Office Box 8139
Newark, DE 19714
302-731-1600
http://www.reading.org

Web Sites

All About Adolescent Literacy
http://www.adlit.org

Big Ideas in Beginning Reading
http://reading.uoregon.edu

Center for the Improvement of Early Reading
   Achievement
http://www.ciera.org

Colorin Colorado
http://www.colorincolorado.org

Junior Great Books
http://www.greatbooks.org

LD online
http://www.ldonline.org

Reading Rockets
http://www.readingrockets.org

Reading Teachers Network
http://www.readingteachersnetwork.org

Starfall
http://www.starfall.com/

U.S. Department of Education
http://www.ed.gov

Instructional Materials

Bebko, A.R., Alexander, J., & Doucet, R. (2001). *LANGUAGE! Roots* (2nd ed.). Longmont, CO: Sopris West Educational Services.

Bertin, P., & Perlman, E. (2007). *Preventing academic failure: A multisensory curriculum for teaching reading, spelling and handwriting in the elementary classroom.* Cambridge, MA: Educators Publishing Service.

Biddle, M.L., & Raines, B.J. (1980). *Situation learning: Teacher guides and student workbooks* (Vols. 1–3). Cambridge, MA: Educators Publishing Service.

Bloom, F., & Traub, N. (2002). *Recipe for reading* (New century ed.). Cambridge, MA: Educators Publishing Service.

Carreker, S. (1992). *Language enrichment.* Bellaire, TX: Neuhaus Education Center.

Carreker, S. (1998). *Basic language skills* (Books 1–3). Bellaire, TX: Neuhaus Education Center.

Clark-Edmunds, S. (2005). *S.P.I.R.E.* Cambridge, MA: Educators Publishing Service.

Cox, A.R. (1992). *Foundations for literacy: Structures and techniques for multisensory teaching of basic written English language skills.* Cambridge, MA: Educators Publishing Service.

Dillon, S. (1987). *Sounds in syllables.* Albuquerque, NM: S.I.S. Publishing Co.

duBard, N.E., & Martin, M.K. (1994). *Teaching language deficient children: Theory and application of the Association Method for multisensory teaching* (Rev. ed.). Cambridge, MA: Educators Publishing Service.

Edwards, A. (2001). *Bumpy books.* New York: Bumpy Books http://www.bumpybooks.com/index.php

Enfield, M.L., & Greene, V. (1991). *Project read.* Bloomington, MN: Language Circle Enterprise.

Engelmann, S. (2002). *Reading mastery.* Blacklick, OH: SRA/McGraw-Hill. (Available from the publisher; http://www.MHEonline.com)

Gillingham, A., & Stillman, B.W. (1997). *The Gillingham manual: Remedial training for students with specific disability in reading, spelling, and penmanship* (8th ed.). Cambridge, MA: Educators Publishing Service.

Greene, J.F. (1995). *LANGUAGE! A reading, writing, and spelling curriculum for at-risk and ESL students* (Grades 4–12). Longmont, CO: Sopris West Educational Services.

Hall, N., & Price, R. (1993). *Explode the code.* Cambridge, MA: Educators Publishing Service.

Henry, M.K. (1990). *WORDS: Integrated decoding and spelling instruction based on word origin and structure.* Austin, TX: PRO-ED.

Henry, M.K. (2010). *Unlocking literacy: Effective decoding and spelling instruction* (2nd ed.). Baltimore: Paul H. Brookes Publishing Co.

Henry, M.K., & Redding, N.C. (1996). *Patterns for success in reading and spelling: A multisensory approach to teaching phonics and word analysis.* Austin, TX: PRO-ED.

Herman, R.D. (2006). *The Herman Method for reversing reading failure.* (Available at http://www.soprislearning.com)

Jolly phonics. Chigwell, Essex, United Kingdom: Jolly Learning. (Available from the publisher; 50 Winter Sport Lane, Williston, VT 05495-0020; 800-488-2665; e-mail: jolly.orders@aidcvt.com)

Johnson, K., & Bayrd, P. (1988). *Megawords: Multisyllabic words for reading, spelling and vocabulary.* Cambridge, MA: Educators Publishing Service.

Knight, J.R. (1986). *Starting over: A combined teaching manual and student textbook for reading, writing, spelling, vocabulary, and handwriting.* Cambridge, MA: Educators Publishing Service.

LEAD Educational Resources. (n.d.). *LEAD program: Logical encoding and decoding.* Bridgewater, CT: Author. (Available from the author; 144 Main Street North, Bridgewater, CT 06752; 860-355-1516)

Lindamood, P., & Lindamood, P. (1998). *Lindamood phoneme sequencing program for reading, spelling, and speech (LiPS): Teacher's manual for the classroom and clinic* (3rd ed.). Austin, TX: PRO-ED.

McGuiness, C (1999). *Reading reflex: The foolproof Phono-Graphix Method.* New York: Free Press. (Available at http://www.readamerica.net)

Montgomery, D.B. (1975). *Angling for words: The teacher's line.* Novato, CA: Academic Therapy Publications.

Pickering, J.S. (n.d.). *Sequential English education (SEE).* Dallas, TX: The June Shelton School.

Redding, N.C., & Henry, M.K. (2004). *Patterns for success in reading and spelling activity book.* Austin, TX: PRO-ED.

Rome, P.D., & Osman, J.S. (1993). *Language tool kit.* Cambridge, MA: Educators Publishing Service.

Rome, P.D., & Osman, J.S. (2000). *Advanced language tool kit.* Cambridge, MA: Educators Publishing Service.

Slingerland, B.H., & Aho, M. (1994-1996). *A multisensory approach to language arts for specific language disability children* (Rev. ed., Vols. 1–3). Cambridge, MA: Educators Publishing Service.

Smith, M.T. (1996). *MTA reading and spelling program* (Kits 1–7). Cambridge, MA: Educators Publishing Service.

Smith, M.T. (1996). *Multisensory teaching system for reading (MTS).* Forney, TX: MTS Publications.

Sonday, A. (1997). *The Sonday system: Learning to read* [Learning plan and word books]. St. Paul, MN: Winsor Learning (Available at http://www.winsorlearning.com)

Spalding, R.B. (with Spalding, W.T.). (1990). *The writing road to reading: The Spalding Method of phonics for teaching speech, writing, and reading* (4th rev. ed.). New York: Quill.

Steere, A., Peck, C.Z., & Kahn, L. (1971). *Solving language difficulties.* Cambridge, MA: Educators Publishing Service.

Wendon, L. (2004). *Letterland.* Enfield, NH: Enfield Distribution Company. (Available at http://www.letterland.com)

Wickerham, C.W., & Allen, K.A. (1993). *Multisensory reading and spelling* (Books 1-4). Bellaire, TX: Neuhaus Education Center.

Wilson, B.A. (1988). *Wilson Reading System: Teacher's guide and student material.* Oxford, MA: Wilson Language Training. (Available from the publisher; http://www.wilsonlanguage.com)

Wimer, D.B. (1994). *Word studies: A classical perspective. Prefixes, roots, suffixes* (Vol. 1). Richmond, VA: Author. (Available from the author; Post Office Box 5362, Richmond, VA 23220)

Card Sets and Decodable Readers

Abecedarian (Plastic letters in English and Spanish and alphabet strips available at http://www.alphabetletter.com)

Catagnozzi, P. (1996). *Sight words you can see* (card sets available from the publisher; http://readingwithtlc.com/).

Erwin, P. (1992). *Winston grammar cards.* San Diego: Farnsworth Books.

Flyleaf Publishing. *Books to remember.* Manchester, NH: Author. (Available from the publisher; 800-449-7006; http://www.FlyleafPublishing.com)

Gillingham, A., & Stillman, B.W. (1959). *Phonetic word cards: Remedial training for children with specific disability in reading, spelling, and penmanship.* Cambridge, MA: Educators Publishing Service.

Greene, J.F., & Woods, J.F. (1992). *J & J language readers for reading/language delayed and ESL/EFL students* (Levels I–III). Longmont, CO: Sopris West Educational Services.

Luria, A. (2009). *Snap and friends.* Kingston, NY: Lilypod Media. (Available from the publisher; 845-657-9638; http://www.gr8reader.com)

McCracken pocket charts. Seattle, WA: School Art Materials. (Available from the publisher; Post Office Box 94082, Seattle, WA 98124; 800-752-4359)

Neuhaus Education Center. *Procedure charts: LLP, WOW, SOS, Dict, Demo, Copy.* Bellaire, TX: Author (Available at http://www.readingteachers network.org)

Sands, E.M. (n.d.). *SANDS reading cards* [Picture sound cards, letter sound cards, audiocassette]. New York: Davick House. (Available from the publisher; Post Office Box 150136, Kew Gardens, NY 11415)

Smith, L. (2003). *Reading series* (decodable picture books available from http://www.flyleaf publishing. com/).

Smith, M.T. (1987–1993). *MTA reader series.* Cambridge, MA: Educators Publishing Service.

Subway Stamp (Pocket charts and sound cards available from http://www.subwaystamp.com)

The following bookstore also carries instructional materials: BurnsBooks, 50 Joe's Hill Road, Danbury, CT 08811; 203-744-0232.

Teacher References

Adams, M.J. (1990). *Beginning to read: Thinking and learning about print.* Cambridge, MA: The MIT Press.

Adams, M.J. (1994). Phonics and beginning reading instruction. In F. Lehr & S. Osborn (Eds.), *Reading, language, and literacy* (pp. 3–23). Mahwah, NJ: Lawrence Erlbaum Associates.

Adams, M.J. (1995, Summer). Resolving the "great debate." *American Educator,* 7–20.

Balmuth, M. (2009). *The roots of phonics: A historical introduction* (Rev. ed.). Baltimore: Paul H. Brookes Publishing Co.

Bear, D.R., Invernizzi, M., Templeton, S., & Johnston, F. (1996). *Words their way: Word study for phonics, vocabulary, and spelling instruction.* Upper Saddle River, NJ: Prentice Hall.

Beck, I.L., & Juel, C. (1995, Summer). The role of decoding in learning to read. *American Educator,* 8–42.

Blachman, B.A. (1991). Getting ready to read: Learning how to print maps to speech. In J.F. Kavanagh (Ed.), *The language continuum: From infancy to literacy* (pp. 41–62). Timonium, MD: York Press. (Available from PRO-ED; 800-897-3202)

Butler, K.G., & Silliman, E.R. (2002). *Speaking, reading and writing in children with learning disabilities.* Mahwah, NJ: Lawrence Erlbaum Associates.

Calfee, R. (1998). Phonics and phonemes: Learning to decode and spell in a literature-based program. In J.L. Metsala & L.C. Ehri (Eds.), *Word recognition in beginning literacy* (pp. 285–308). Mahwah, NJ: Lawrence Erlbaum Associates.

Calfee, R.C., & Patrick, C.P. (1995). *The portable Stanford book series: Teach our children well.* Stanford, CA: Stanford Alumni Association.

Chall, J.S. (1983). *Stages of reading development.* New York: McGraw-Hill.

Chall, J.S. (1992). The new reading debates: Evidence from science, art, and ideology. *Teachers College Record, 94,* 315–328.

Chall, J.S., & Popp, H.M. (1996). *Teaching and assessing phonics.* Cambridge, MA: Educators Publishing Service.

Cox, A.R. (1992). *Foundations for literacy: Structures and techniques for multisensory teaching of basic written English language skills.* Cambridge, MA: Educators Publishing Service.

Dickinson, D.K., & Tabors, P.O. (Eds.). (2001). *Beginning literacy with language: Young children learning at home and school.* Baltimore: Paul H. Brookes Publishing Co.

Ehri, L. (1998). Research on learning to read and spell: A personal-historical perspective. *Scientific Studies in Reading, 2*(2), 97–114.

Ehri, L. (2000). Learning to read and learning to spell: Two sides of a coin. *Topics in Language Disorders, 20,* 19–36.

Ehri, L.C. (2005). Learning to read words: Theories, findings and issues. *Scientific Studies of Reading, 9,* 167–188.

Felton, R.H. (1993). Effects of instruction on the decoding skills of children with phonological-processing problems. *Journal of Learning Disabilities, 26*(9), 583–589.

Ferrer, E., Shaywitz, B.A., Holahan, J.M., Marchione, K., & Shaywitz, S.E. (2009). Uncoupling of reading and IQ over time: Empirical evidence for a definition of dyslexia. *Association for Psychological Science, 21,* 93–101.

Fry, E.B., Polk, J.K., & Fountoukidis, D.L. (1996). *The reading teacher's new book of lists* (3rd ed.). Upper Saddle River, NJ: Prentice Hall.

Henry, M.K. (1989). Children's word structure knowledge: Implications for decoding and spelling instruction. *Reading and Writing: An Interdisciplinary Journal, 2,* 135–152.

Honig, B. (1996). *Teaching our children to read: The role of skills in a comprehensive reading program.* Thousand Oaks, CA: Corwin Press.

Honig, B., Diamond, L., & Nathan, R. (2001). *Reading research anthology* (2nd ed.). Novato, CA: Academic Therapy Publications.

Honig, B., Diamond, L., & Nathan, R. (2008). *Teaching reading sourcebook* (2nd ed.). Novato, CA: Academic Therapy Publications.

Kendeou, P., Savage, R., & van den Broek, P. (2009). Revisiting the simple view of reading. *British Journal of Educational Psychology, 79,* 353–370.

Liberman, I.Y., & Liberman, A.M. (1990). Whole language vs. code emphasis: Underlying assumptions and their implications for reading instruction. *Annals of Dyslexia, 40,* 51–76.

Mather, N. (1992). Whole language reading instruction for students with learning disabilities: Caught in the crossfire. *Learning Disabilities Research and Practice, 7,* 87–95.

Mathes, P.G., Denton, C.A., Fletcher, J.M., Anthony, J.L., Francis, D.J., & Schatschneider, C. (2005). The effects of theoretically different instruction and student characteristics on the skills of struggling readers. *Reading Research Quarterly, 40*, 148–182.

Moats, L.C. (2010). *Speech to print: Language essentials for teachers* (2nd ed.). Baltimore: Paul H. Brookes Publishing Co.

National Institute of Child Health and Human Development. (2000). *Report of the National Reading Panel: Reports of the subgroups. Teaching children to read: An evidence-based assessment of the scientific research literature on reading and its implications for reading instruction* (NIH Publication No. 00-4754). Washington, DC: Government Printing Office.

O'Connor, R. (2007). *Teaching word recognition: Ef-fective strategies for students with learning difficulties.* New York: Guilford Press.

Pressley, M. (2002). *Reading instruction that works: The case for balanced teaching* (2nd ed.). New York: Guilford Press.

Smartt, S.M., & Glaser, D.R. (2010). *Next STEPS in literary instruction: Connecting assessments to effective interventions.* Baltimore: Paul H. Brookes Publishing Co.

Snow, C.E., Burns, M.S., & Griffin, P. (Eds.). (1998). *Preventing reading difficulties in young children.* Washington, DC: National Academies Press.

Wolf, M., & Katzer-Cohen, T. (2001). Reading fluency and its intervention. *Scientific Studies in Reading, 5*(3), 211–239.

DVDs

Beckham, P.B., & Biddle, M.L. (1988). *Dyslexia training program* [DVD]. Dallas: Texas Scottish Rite Hospital, Child Development Division.

Birsh, J.R. (Consulting Ed.), & Potts, M., & Potts, R. (Producers). (1997). *LD/LA: Learning disabilities/learning abilities: Videotape II. The teaching: What students need. Videotape III. Reading is not a natural skill: Teaching children the code to unlock language.* West Tisbury, MA: Vineyard Video Productions. (Available from the publisher; Post Office Box 806, West Tisbury, MA 02575; 800-664-6119; E-mail: mpotts@vineyardvideo .org; http://www.vineyardvideo.org)

Software and Hardware

Texthelp Systems Ltd. (provides software to help struggling readers and writers). (Available from the publisher; http://www.texthelp.com/)

Kurzweil 3000 (provides visual and auditory feedback with printed material). Waltham, MA: Kurzweil Educational Systems. (Available from the publisher; Cambium Learning Technologies, 24 Prime Parkway, Suite 303, Natick, MA 01760; 800-547-6747)

Lexia Primary Phonics. (n.d.). Lincoln, MA: Lexia Learning Systems. (Available from the publisher; 200 Baker Avenue, Concord, MA 01742 73; 800-435-3942; http://www.lexialearning.com)

Lexia Reading SOS (Strategies for Older Students). (n.d.). Lincoln, MA: Lexia Learning Systems. (Available from the publisher; 200 Baker Avenue, Concord, MA 01742; 800-435-3942; http:// www.lexialearning.com)

ULTimate Reader (speaks back electronic printed matter). Wauconda, IL: Don Johnston. (Available from the publisher; 26799 West Commerce Drive, Volo, IL 60073; 800-999-4660; e-mail: info@donjohnston.com; http://www.donjohnston.com)

V. Reader (hand-held animated storytelling device available from http://www.vtechkids.com/).

CHAPTER 9   Teaching Spelling

Web Sites

BBC: Sand Castle Quiz
http://www.bbc.co.uk/schools/wordsandpictures /phonics/sandcastle/

Reading Rockets: Spelling and Word Study
http://www.readingrockets.org/atoz/spelling_ word_study

Reading Teachers Network
http://www.readingteachersnetwork.org

SpellingCity.com
http://www.spellingcity.com/

Instructional Materials

Bear, D.R., Invernizzi, M., Templeton, S., & Johnston, F. (1996). *Words their way: Word study for phonics, vocabulary, and spelling instruction.* Upper Saddle River, NJ: Prentice Hall.

Bell, N. (1997). *Seeing stars: Symbol imagery for phonemic awareness, sight words, and spelling.* San Luis Obispo, CA: Gander Publishing.

Carreker, S. (1998). *Basic language skills* (Books 1-3). Bellaire, TX: Neuhaus Education Center.

Carreker, S. (2002). *Scientific spelling* (Rev. ed.; Grades 1–8). Bellaire, TX: Neuhaus Education Center.

Cox, A.R. (1992). *Alphabetic phonics.* Cambridge, MA: Educators Publishing Service.

Enfield, M.L., & Greene, V. (1991). *Project read.* Bloomington, MN: Language Circle Enterprise.

Gillingham, A., & Stillman, B.W. (1997). *The Gillingham manual: Remedial training for children with specific disability in reading, spelling, and penmanship* (8th ed.). Cambridge, MA: Educators Publishing Service.

Hall, N.M. (2001). *Spellwell.* Cambridge, MA: Educators Publishing Service.

Henry, M.K. (1990). *WORDS: Integrated decoding and spelling instruction based on word origin and structure.* Austin, TX: PRO-ED.

McCracken pocket charts. (1999). Seattle, WA: School Art Materials. (Available from the publisher; Post Office Box 94082, Seattle, WA 98124; 800-752-4359)

Moats, L.C., & Rostow, B. (2003). *Spellography: Teacher's resource guide.* Longmont, CO: Sopris West Educational Services.

Rak, E.T. (1989). *The spell of the word* (Grade 7-Adult). Cambridge, MA: Educators Publishing Service.

Rome, P.D., & Osman, J.S. (1993). *Language tool kit.* Cambridge, MA: Educators Publishing Service.

Rudginsky, L.T., & Haskell, E.C. (1985). *How to spell* (Grades 1–12). Cambridge, MA: Educators Publishing Service.

Simmons, L. (1997). *Saxon phonics.* Norman, OK: Saxon Publishers.

Slingerland, B.H., & Aho, M. (1994–1996). *A multisensory approach to language arts for specific language disability children* (Rev. ed., Vols. 1–3). Cambridge, MA: Educators Publishing Service.

Smith, M.T. (1996). *MTA reading and spelling program* (Kits 1–7). Cambridge, MA: Educators Publishing Service.

Texas Scottish Rite Hospital for Children. (1992). *Dyslexia training program: Teacher's guides and student's books* (Vols. 1–4). Cambridge, MA: Educators Publishing Service.

Wickerham, C.W., & Allen, K.A. (1993). *Multisensory reading and spelling* (Books 1–4). Bellaire, TX: Neuhaus Education Center.

Wilson, B.A. (1988). *Wilson reading system: Teacher's guide and student material.* Oxford, MA: Wilson Language Training. (Available from the publisher; http://www.wilsonlanguage.com)

Teacher References

Cox, A.R. (1992). *Foundations for literacy: Structures and techniques for multisensory teaching of basic written language skills.* Cambridge, MA: Educators Publishing Service.

Joshi, R.M., Treiman, R., Carreker, S., & Moats, L. C. (2008/2009). How words cast their spell: Spelling instruction focused on language, not memory, improves reading and writing. *American Educator, 32*(4), 6–16, 42–43.

Moats, L.C. (1995). *Spelling: Development, disability, and instruction.* Timonium, MD: York Press. (Available from PRO-ED; 800-897-3202)

Moats, L.C. (2005–2006, Winter) How spelling supports reading: And why it's more regular and predictable than you may think. *American Educator,* 12–22, 42–43.

Smartt, S.M., & Glaser, D.R. (2010). *Next STEPS in literary instruction: Connecting assessments to effective interventions.* Baltimore: Paul H. Brookes Publishing Co.

Software and Hardware Devices

Electronic spellers. (n.d.). Burlington, NJ: Franklin Electronic Publishers.

Ginger (a spellcheck program designed specifically for learners with dyslexia; available at http://www.gingersoftware.com/).

DVDs

Birsh, J.R. (Consulting Ed.), & Potts, M., & Potts, R. (Producers). (1997). *LD/LA: Learning disabilities/learning abilities: Videotape II. The teaching: What students need.* West Tisbury, MA: Vineyard Video Productions. (Available from the publisher; Post Office Box 806, West Tisbury, MA

02575; 800-664-6119; e-mail: mpotts@vineyard video.org; http://www.vineyardvideo.org)

Birsh, J.R. (Consulting Ed.), & Potts, M., & Potts, R. (Producers). (1997). *LD/LA: Learning disabilities/learning abilities: Videotape III. Reading is not a natural skill: Teaching children the code to unlock* *language*. West Tisbury, MA: Vineyard Video Productions. (Available from the publisher; Post Office Box 806, West Tisbury, MA 02575; 800-664-6119; e-mail: mpotts@vineyardvideo.org; http://www.vineyardvideo.org)

CHAPTER 10   Fluency in Learning to Read

Web Sites

All About Adolescent Literacy
http://www.adlit.org/article/3416

Florida Center for Reading Research
Reading Diagnostic Measures
http://www.fcrr.org

Giggle Poetry
http://www.gigglepoetry.com/

Intervention Central
http://www.interventioncentral.org

LD online
http://www.ldonline.org/article/6354

Literary Connections
http://www.literacyconnections.com
/readerstheater.php

National Center on Student Progress Monitoring
http://www.studentprogress.org

Neurological Impress Method YouTube video
http://www.youtube.com/watch?v=7DhpeyI2_2s

Reader's Theater Editions
http://www.aaronshep.com/rt/RTE.html

Reading Rockets
http://www.readingrockets.org/teaching/reading1
01/fluency

Text Project
http://www.textproject.org/

Assessment Tools

Dibels. (2002). (Free downloadable materials, tutorials at https://dibels.uoregon.edu/. $1 charge per student to use their data system.)

Hasbrouck, J., & Tindal, G. (2005). Oral reading fluency norms Grades 1-8. Table summarized from *Behavioral Research & Teaching* (2005, January).

Oral reading fluency: 90 years of assessment. (BRT Technical Report No. 33). (2005). Eugene, OR: BRT. (Available at http://www.brtprojects.org)

Reading fluency benchmark assessor. (2007). St. Paul, MN: Read Naturally.

Instructional Materials

Adams, G., & Brown, S. (2005). *Six minute readers.* Longmont, CO: Sopris West Educational Services.

Adams, M., & Hiebert, E. (2005). *QuickReads.* Lebanon: IN: Pearson. (Available in print and CD-ROM from the publisher; 1-800-848-9500)

Blevins, W. (2001). *Building fluency: Lessons and strategies for reading success.* New York: Scholastic.

Fischer, P. (1995). *Speed drills from concept phonics.* Farmington, ME: Oxton House.

Great leaps. (1998). Gainesville, FL: Diarmuid. (Available from the publisher; http://www .greatleaps.com/index.php)

Hasbrouck, J., & Denton, C. (2005). *The reading coach: A how-to manual for success.* Longmont, CO: Sopris West Educational Services.

Hasbrouck, J., & Denton, C. (2009). *The reading coach 2: More tools and strategies for student focused* *coaches.* Longmont, CO: Sopris West Educational Services.

Hiebert, E. (2002). *QuickReads.* Parsippany, NJ: Pearson Education.

One minute readers. (2006). Read Naturally. (Order individual graded books and CDs at http://www .oneminutereader.com/)

Read naturally. (2007). Read Naturally. (Available from the publisher; http://www.readnaturally .com/)

Reading speed drills. (2006). Farmington, ME: Oxton House Publishers. (Available from the publisher; http://www.oxtonhouse.com/reading_speed_dril ls.html)

Wolf, M. (2010). *Rave-O.* Longmont, CO: Sopris West Educational Services.

Teacher References

A Focus on Fluency is a free publication available through the Pacific Resources for Education and Learning (http://www.prel.org)

Bowers, P.G., Sunseth, K., & Golden, J. (1999). The route between rapid naming and reading progress. *Scientific Studies in Reading, 3*(1), 31–53.

Carreker, S. (1999). *Practices for developing accuracy and fluency.* Bellaire, TX: Neuhaus Education Center.

Chard, D., Vaugh, S., & Tyler, B. (2002). The synthesis of research on effective interventions for reading fluency with elementary students with learning disabilities. *Journal of Learning Disabilites, 35,* 386–406.

Denkla, M. (1999). History and significance of rapid automatized rapid naming. *Annals of Dyslexia, 49,* 29–42.

Dowhower, S. (1999). Speaking of prosody: Fluency's unattended bedfellow. *Theory into Practice, 30,* 165–175.

Dowrick, P., Kim-Rupnow, W., & Power, T. (2006). Video feedforward for reading. *Journal of Special Education, 39,* 197–207.

Foutas, I.C., & Pinnell, G.S. (2001). *Guiding readers and writers: Grades 3–6.* Portsmouth, NH: Heinemann.

Fuchs, L., Fuchs, D., & Hosp, M. (2001). Oral reading fluency as an indicator of reading competence: A theoretical, empirical, and historical analysis. *Scientific Studies of Reading, 5,* 239–256.

Hasbrouck, N., & Tindal, G. (2006). Oral reading fluency norms: A valuable assessment tool for reading researchers. *The Reading Teacher, 59,* 636–644.

Honig, B., Diamond, L., & Gutlon, L. (2008). *CORE: Teaching reading sourcebook for kindergarten through eight grade.* Berkeley, CA: Consortium on Reading Excellence.

Meyer, M.S., & Felton, R.H. (1999). Repeated reading to enhance fluency: Old approaches and new direction. *Annals of Dyslexia, 49,* 283–306.

O'Connor, R., White, A., & Swanson, H.L. (2007). Repeated reading versus continuous reading: Influences on reading fluency and comprehension. *Exceptional Children, 74,* 31–46.

Rasinski, T. (2003). *The fluent reader: Oral reading strategies for building word recognition and comprehension.* New York: Scholastic.

Samuels, S.J. (2002). Reading fluency: Its development and assessment. In A.E. Farstrup & S.J. Samuels (Eds.), *What research has to say about reading instruction* (3rd ed., pp. 166–183). Newark, DE: International Reading Association.

Samuels, S.J., Miller, N., & Eisenberg, P. (1979). Practice effects on the unit of word recognition. *Journal of Educational Psychology, 71,* 514–520.

Smartt, S.M., & Glaser, D.R. (2010). *Next STEPS in literary instruction: Connecting assessments to effective interventions.* Baltimore: Paul H. Brookes Publishing Co.

Wolf, M., & Katzer-Cohen, T. (2001). Reading fluency and its intervention. *Scientific Studies in Reading, 5*(3), 211–239.

CHAPTER 11   Word Learning and Vocabulary Instruction

Web Sites

Collins Cobuild Dictionary
http://www.collinslanguage.com/

Dictionary.com app
http://dictionary.reference.com/apps/iphone

Free Rice
http://www.freerice.com/index.php?&s=English
%20Vocabulary

Quizlet
http://quizlet.com/

Vocabulary University
http://www.vocabulary.com

Wordnik
http://www.wordnik.com/

Teacher References

Allen, J. (1999). *Words, words, words: Teaching vocabulary in grades 4–12.* York, ME: Stenhouse Publishers.

Baumann, J.F., & Kame'enui, E.J. (2004). *Vocabulary instruction: Research to practice.* New York: Guilford Press.

Beck, I., McKeown, M., & Kucan, L. (2002). *Bringing words to life.* New York: Guilford Press.

Bell, N. (1986). *Visualizing/Verbalizing for language comprehension and thinking.* Paso Robles, CA: Academy of Reading Publications.

Bell, N., & Lindamood, P. (1993). *Vanilla vocabulary.* Paso Robles, CA: Academy of Reading Publications.

Biemiller, A. (1999). *Language and reading success.* Newton, MA: Brookline Books.

Fry, E.B., Kress, J.E., & Fountoukidis, D. (2000). *The reading teacher's book of lists* (4th ed.). Upper Saddle River, NJ: Prentice Hall.

Greenwood, S.C. (2004). *Words count: Effective vocabulary instruction in action.* Portsmouth, NH: Heinemann.

Henry, M.K. (2010). *Unlocking literacy: Effective decoding and spelling instruction* (2nd ed.). Baltimore: Paul H. Brookes Publishing Co.

Henry, M.K., & Redding, N.C. (1996). *Patterns for success in reading and spelling: A multisensory approach to teaching phonics and word analysis.* Austin, TX: PRO-ED.

Nagy, W. (1988). *Teaching vocabulary to improve reading comprehension.* Urbana, IL: ERIC Clearinghouse on Reading and Communication Skills.

Rasinski, T.V., Padak, N.D., Church, B.W., Fawcett, G., Hendershot, J., Henry J.M., et al. (2000). *Teaching word recognition, spelling, and vocabulary: Strategies from the reading teacher.* Newark, DE: International Reading Association.

Smartt, S.M., & Glaser, D.R. (2010). *Next STEPS in literary instruction: Connecting assessments to effective interventions.* Baltimore: Paul H. Brookes Publishing Co.

Stahl, S. (1999). *Vocabulary development.* Newton, MA: Brookline Books.

Stahl, S., & Kapinus, B. (2001). *Word power: What every educator needs to know about teaching vocabulary.* Washington, DC: National Education Association.

Parent Readings and Resources

Teachers First: 100 Best Books
http://www.teachersfirst.com/100books.cfm

CHAPTER 12 Strategies to Improve Reading Comprehension in the Multisensory Classroom

Web Sites

All About Adolescent Literacy
http://www.adlit.org/

Association for Library Service to Children
http://www.ala.org/ala/mgrps/divs/alsc/
awardsgrants/bookmedia/newberymedal/
newberymedal.cfm

Book Adventure
http://www.bookadventure.com

Center for the Improvement of Early Reading Achievement
http://www.ciera.org

Center on Accelerating Student Learning
http://kc.vanderbilt.edu/casl/

Computer-Based Study Strategies
http://education.uoregon.edu/degree.htm?id=76

Content Literacy Information Consortium
http://curry.virginia.edu/go/clic/

Dade-Monroe Teacher Education Center
http://www.miamisci.org/tec

Division for Learning Disabilities (DLD)
http://www.teachingld.org

Early Reading Success
http://www.haskins.yale.edu/ers/

Florida Center for Reading Research
http://www.fcrr.org

International Reading Association Article Archive
http://www.reading.org/general/publications/jour
nals/RT/ArchivesRT.aspx

LD online
http://ldonline.org

Learning Strategies Database, Muskingum College Center for Advancement of Learning
http://www.muskingum.edu/~cal/database

Learning Toolbox
http://coe.jmu.edu/LearningToolbox

National Reading Panel
http://www.nationalreadingpanel.org

Peer-Assisted Learning Strategies (PALS)
http://kc.vanderbilt.edu/kennedy/pals

Read Works
http://www.readworks.org/

Read Across America
http://www.nea.org/readacross

Reading ASSIST Institute: Free Downloads
http://www.readingassist.org/downloads.htm

Reading Comprehension
http://www.literacy.uconn.edu/compre.htm

Reading Online
http://www.readingonline.org

Reading Rockets
http://www.readingrockets.org

ReadingQuest
http://www.readingquest.org/links.html

Resource Room
http://www.resourceroom.net/index.asp

SparkNotes
http://www.sparknotes.com

University of Texas at Austin, Vaughn Gross
    Center for Reading and Language Arts
http://www.texasreading.org

Instructional Materials

Auslin, M.S. (2003). *The idioms workbook* (2nd ed.). Austin, TX: PRO-ED.

Bell, N. (2007). *Visualizing and verbalizing kit.* San Luis Obispo, CA: Gander Publishing.

Carlisle, J. (1999). *Reasoning and reading* (various levels). Cambridge, MA: Educators Publishing Service.

Carreker, S. (2005). *Developing metacognitive skills: Vocabulary and comprehension.* Bellaire, TX: Neuhaus Education Center.

Curriculum Associates. (2000). *Strategies to achieve reading success.* North Billerica, MA: Author.

Evans, A.J. (1979). *Reading and thinking: Exercises for developing reading comprehension and critical thinking skills* (Books I & II). New York: Teachers College Press.

Fry, E.B., Kress, J.E., & Fountoukidis, D.L. (2000). *The reading teacher's book of lists* (4th ed.). San Francisco: Jossey-Bass.

Greene, J.F. (1995). *LANGUAGE! A reading, writing, and spelling curriculum for at-risk and ESL students* (Grades 4–12). Longmont, CO: Sopris West Educational Services.

Greene, V., & Enfield, M.L. (1999). *Report form kit.* Bloomington, MN: Language Circle Enterprises.

Greene, V., & Enfield, M.L. (1999). *Story form comprehension kit.* Bloomington, MN: Language Circle Enterprises.

Greene, V., & Enfield, M.L. (1999). *Story form literature kit.* Bloomington, MN: Language Circle Enterprises.

Klingner, J.K., Vaughn, S., Dimino, J., Schumm, J.S., & Bryant, D. (2001). *From clunk to click: Collaborative strategic reading.* Longmont, CO: Sopris West Educational Services.

Kratoville, B.L. (1990). *Listen my children and you shall hear* (3rd ed.). Austin, TX: PRO-ED.

LinguiSystems staff. (2002). *Strategic learning: Reading comprehension.* East Moline, IL: LinguiSystems.

Neuhaus Education Center. (2008). *Colors and shapes of language.* Bellaire, TX: Neuhaus Education Center.

Schumaker, J.B., Denton, P.H., & Deshler, D.D. (1984). *The paraphrasing strategy* (Learning Strategies Curriculum). Lawrence: University of Kansas.

Schumaker, J.B., Denton, P.H., & Deshler, D.D. (1994). *The self-questioning strategy* (Learning Strategies Curriculum). Lawrence: University of Kansas.

Schumaker, J.B., Denton, P.H., & Deshler, D.D. (1993). *The visual imagery strategy* (Learning Strategies Curriculum). Lawrence: University of Kansas.

Smith, M.T., & Hogan, E.A. (1991). *MTA: Teaching a process for comprehension and composition.* Forney, TX: EDMAR Educational Associates.

Staman, A.L. (2000). *Starting comprehension: Stories to advance reading and thinking.* Cambridge, MA: Educators Publishing Service.

Weber, S.G. (1999). *Idioms fun deck.* Greenville, SC: Super Duper Publications.

Reading Comprehension Passages

Boning, R. (1997). *Specific skills series* (Grades pre-k–8). New York: Barnell Loft. (Available through SRA reading; 800-565-5758)

Einstein, C. (2002). *Einstein's who, what, and where* (Grades 4–7). Cambridge, MA: Educators Publishing Service.

Einstein, C. (2000). *Claims to fame* (Grades 2–5). Cambridge, MA: Educators Publishing Service.

Einstein, C. (2006). *Reading for content* (Grades 3–6). Cambridge, MA: Educators Publishing Service.

Ervin, J. (1993). *Early reading comprehension in varied subject area and reading comprehension in varied subject matter* (Books A & B for Grades 2–4). Cambridge, MA: Educators Publishing Service.

Ervin, J. (1997). *More reading comprehension in varied subject matter* (Middle school and up). Cambridge, MA: Educators Publishing Service.

Ervin, J. (2000). *Reading comprehension in varied subject matter* (Grades 3–8). Cambridge, MA: Educators Publishing Service.

Hall, K.L. (1996). *Reading stories for comprehension success: 45 high-interest lessons that make kids think* (Grades 1–3 and 4–6). West Nyack, NY: Center for Applied Research in Education.

Pauk, W. (1999). *Six-way paragraphs*. Providence, RI: Jamestown. (Available from Glencoe/McGraw-Hill; 1-800-334-7344)

Teacher References

Bell, N. (1992). *Visualizing and verbalizing for language comprehension and thinking* (Rev. ed.). San Luis Obispo, CA: Gander Publishing.

Cain, K., & Oakhill, J. (2007). *Children's comprehension problems in oral and written language: A cognitive perspective*. New York: Guilford Press.

Carlisle, J.F., & Rice, M.S. (2002). *Improving reading comprehension*. Timonium, MD: York Press. (Available from PRO-ED; 800-897-3202)

Carnine, D.W., Silbert, J., Kame'enui, E., Trarver, S., & Jungjohann, K. (2004). *Teaching struggling and at-risk readers a direct instruction approach*. Glenview, IL: Pearson Scott Foresman.

Ciborowski, J. (1999). *Textbooks and the students who can't read them*. Brookline, MA: Brookline Books.

Deshler, D.D., Ellis, E.S., & Lenz, B.K. (1996). *Teaching adolescents with learning disabilities: Strategies and methods* (2nd ed.). Denver, CO: Love Publishing.

Harvey, S., & Goudvis, A. (2000). *Strategies that work: Teaching comprehension to enhance understanding*. York, ME: Stenhouse Publications.

Honig, B., Diamond, L., & Gutlon, L. (2008). *CORE: Teaching reading sourcebook for kindergarten through eighth grade*. Novato, CA: Arena Press.

Hults, A. (2004). *Reading first: Unlock the secrets to reading success with research-based strategies*. Huntington Beach, CA: Creative Teaching Press.

IRA Literacy Study Groups. (2003). *Reading comprehension module*. Newark, DE: International Reading Association.

Klingner, J., Vaughn, S., & Boardman, A. (2007). *Teaching reading comprehension to students with learning difficulties*. New York: Guilford Press.

Maria, K. (1990). *Reading comprehension instruction: Issues and strategies*. Timonium, MD: York Press.

(Available from PRO-ED; 800-897-3202)

McLaughlin, M. (2003). *Guided comprehension in the primary grades*. Newark, DE: International Reading Association.

National Institute of Child Health and Human Development. (2000). *Report of the National Reading Panel: Reports of the subgroups. Teaching children to read: An evidence-based assessment of the scientific research literature on reading and its implications for reading instruction* (NIH Publication No. 00-4754). Washington, DC: Government Printing Office.

RAND Reading Study Group. (2002). *Reading for understanding: Toward an R & D program in reading comprehension*. Washington, DC: U.S. Office of Educational Research and Improvement.

Rasinski, T.V., Padak, N.D., Church, B.W., Fawcet, G., Hendersbot, J., et al. (2000). *Teaching comprehension and exploring multiple literacies: Strategies from the reading teacher*. Newark, DE: International Reading Association.

Smartt, S.M., & Glaser, D.R. (2010). *Next STEPS in literary instruction: Connecting assessments to effective interventions*. Baltimore: Paul H. Brookes Publishing Co.

Smith, M.T., & Hogan, E.A. (1991). *MTA: Teaching a process for comprehension and composition*. Forney, TX: MTS Publications.

Strickland, D.S., Ganske, K., & Monroe, J.K. (2002). *Supporting struggling readers and writers: Strategies for classroom intervention 3–6*. Portland, ME: Stenhouse Publisher.

Vaughn, S., & Linan-Thompson, S. (2004). *Research-based methods of reading instruction: Grades K–3*. Alexandria, VA: Association for Supervision and Curriculum Development Deve.

Parent Resources

Gwynne, F. (1987). *A chocolate moose for dinner*. Upper Saddle River, NJ: Prentice Hall.

Gwynne, F. (1987). *The king who rained*. Upper Saddle River, NJ: Prentice Hall.

Gwynne, F. (1987). *The sixteen hand horse*. Upper Saddle River, NJ: Prentice Hall.

Ross, E. (2000). *Parent's guide to the best books for children*. New York: Three Rivers Press.

Treaslease, J. (2006). *Readaloud handbook* (6th ed.). New York: Penguin Books.

CHAPTER 13 Composition

Web Sites

Reading Rockets
http://www.readingrockets.org/webcasts/3001

ReadWriteThink
http://www.readwritethink.org/

Instructional Materials

Composition in the English language arts curriculum K–12. (1986). Boston: McDougal, Littell.

Biddle, M.L. (1998). *Written basic English for dyslexic students.* Cambridge, MA: Educators Publishing Service.

King, D.H. (2004). *Writing skills books A, 1, 2 and 3* (Grades 2–12). Cambridge, MA: Educators Publishing Service.

Jennings, T., & Haynes, C. (2002). *From talking to writing: Strategies for scaffolding expository expres-*

sion. Prides Crossing, MA: Landmark School.

Muschla, G.R. (1991). *The writing teacher's book of lists.* Upper Saddle River, NJ: Prentice Hall.

Region XIII TAAS/Education Service Center. *Reading activities supporting the Texas reading initiative.* Austin, TX: Author.

Schuster, E. (1989). *Sentence mastery: A sentence-combining approach.* New York: Phoenix Learning Resources.

Teacher References

Bereiter, C., & Scardamalia, M. (1987). *The psychology of written composition.* Mahwah, NJ: Lawrence Erlbaum Associates.

Berrninger, V. (1996). *Reading and writing acquisition: A developmental neuropsychological perspective.* Boulder, CO: Westview Press.

Carlisle, J.F. (1998). *Models for writing.* Novato, CA: Academic Therapy Publications.

Catts, H.W., & Kamhi, A.G. (Eds.). (1999). *Language and reading disabilities.* Boston: Allyn & Bacon.

Cheney, T.A.R. (1983). *Getting the words right: How to rewrite, edit, and revise.* Cincinnati, OH: Writer's Digest Books.

Collins, K.M., & Collins, J.L. (1996, October). Strategic instruction for struggling writers. *English Journal, 5*(6), 54–61.

Deshler, D.D., Ellis, E., & Lenz, B.K. (1996). *Teaching adolescents with learning disabilities: Strategies and methods* (2nd ed.). Denver, CO: Love Publishing.

Elbow, P. (1998). *Writing with power.* Oxford, England: Oxford University Press.

Goldberg, A., Russell, M., & Cook, A. (2003). *The effect of computers on student writing: A meta-analysis of studies from 1992 to 2002.* Retrieved Oct. 8, 2010, from http://escholarship.bc.edu/jtla/vol2/1/

Graham, S., & Harris, K. (2005). *Writing better: Effective strategies for teaching students with learning difficulties.* Baltimore: Paul H. Brookes Publishing Co.

Graham, S., & Perrin, D. (2007). *Writing next: Effective strategies to improve writing of adolescent, middle and high school.* Washington, DC: Alliance for Excellence in Education.

Perrin, G.P. (1972). *Handbook of grammar and usage.* New York: William Morrow & Co.

Kamhi, A.G., & Catts, H.W. (1999). *Language and reading: Convergence and divergence.* In H.W. Catts & A.G. Kamhi (Eds.), *Language and reading disabilities* (pp. 1–24). Boston: Allyn & Bacon.

King, D.H. (1985). *Writing skills for the adolescent.* Cambridge, MA: Educators Publishing Service.

Kirby, D., Kirby, D.L., & Liner, T. (2004). *Inside out: Strategies for teaching writing.* Portsmouth, NH: Heinemann.

Johnson, D.J., & Grant, J.O. (1989). Written narratives of normal and learning disabled children. *Annals of Dyslexia, 39,* 140–158.

Levy, N.R. (1996, November). Teaching analytical writing: Help for general education middle school teachers. *Intervention, 32*(2), 95–96.

Scott, C.M. (1999). Learning to write. In H.W. Catts & A.G. Kamhi (Eds.), *Language and reading disabilities* (pp. 224–258). Boston: Allyn & Bacon.

Scott, C.M. (2002). Sentence comprehension instruction. In J.F. Carlisle & M.S. Rice (Eds.), *Improving reading comprehension: Research-based principles and practices* (pp. 115–138). Timonium, MD: York Press. (Available from PRO-ED; 800-897-3202)

State University of New York & New York State Education Department. (1987). *The arts and learning: The write way on.* Albany: Authors.

State University of New York & New York State Education Department. (1988). *English language arts syllabus K–12.* Albany: Authors.

State University of New York & New York State Education Department. (1988). *Helping student writers.* Albany: Authors.

Strunk, W., & White, E.B. (1979). *The elements of style* (3rd ed.). New York: Macmillan.

Westby, C.E., & Clauser, P.S. (1999). The right stuff for writing: Assessing and facilitating written language. In H.W. Catts & A.G. Kamhi (Eds.), *Language and reading disabilities* (pp. 259–324). Boston: Allyn & Bacon.

Software

Co-Writer (a word prediction program available from Don Johnston; 800-999-4660).

Ginger (a spelling and grammar checking tool designed specifically for learners with dyslexia; available at http://www.gingersoftware.com/).

Inspiration (a visual mapping and outlining program; available at http://www.inspiration.com/)

NoodleBib (a bibliography and citation composer for research papers; available at http://www.noodletools.com/)

DVD

Getting ahead: Reading and writing (K–4): Disc 4. Creative Reading and Writing. (Available from LD online; http://ldonline.learningstore.org/).

CHAPTER 14   Assessment

Web Sites

American Institutes for Research's National Center on Response to Intervention
http://www.rti4success.org

Big Ideas in Beginning Reading
http://reading.uoregon.edu

Dibels Data System
https://dibels.uoregon.edu/

Division for Learning Disabilities (DLD) and the Division for Research of The Council for Exceptional Children (CEC)
Current Practice Alerts
http://www.teachingld.org/ld_resources/alerts/default.htm

National Center on Response to Intervention
http://www.rti4success.org

National Center on Student Progress Monitoring
http://www.studentprogress.org

Reading ASSIST Institute: Free Downloads
http://www.readingassist.org/downloads.htm

Reading Rockets
http://www.readingrockets.org

Resource Room
http://www.resourceroom.net/index.asp

Response to Intervention
http://www.sraonline.com/intervention_resources/additional.html

RTI Action Network
http://www.rtinetwork.org

Vaughn Gross Center for Reading and Language Arts
http://www.meadowscenter.org/vgc/

Wilson Academy
http://www.wilsonacademy.com

Instructional Materials

Bear, D.R., Invernizzi, M., Templeton, S., & Johnston, F. (2008). *Words their way: Word study for phonics, vocabulary, and spelling* (3rd ed.). New York: Pearson Education.

Minsky, M. (2003). *Greenwood word lists: One syllable words*. Longmont, CO: Sopris West Educational Services.

Murray, C. (2002). *Scope and sequence for literacy instruction* (2nd ed.). Los Altos, CA: Lexia Institute.

(Available from PRO-ED; 800-897-3202)

Royal, N.S. (2003). *Preparing children for success in reading; A multisensory guide for teachers and parents.* Timonium, MD: York Press. (Available from PRO-ED; 800-897-3202)

Smith, M.T. (1996). *Multisensory teaching system for reading.* Forney, TX: MTS Publications.

Smith, M.T. (n.d.). *MTA lesson planner and record keeping CD.* Forney, TX: MTS Publications.

Teacher References

Allington, R.L. (2009). *What really matters in Response to Intervention: Research-based designs.* New York: Pearson Learning.

Barr, R., Kaufman, B., Katz, C., Blachowicz, C.L., & Blachowicz, C. (2001). *Reading diagnosis for teachers: An instructional approach* (4th ed.). Upper Saddle River, NJ: Pearson Education.

Beaver, J. (2001). *Developmental reading assessment.* New York: Pearson Learning.

Brown-Chidsey, R., & Steege, M. R. (2005). *Response to intervention: Principles and strategies for effective practice.* New York: Guilford Press.

Chall, J.S. (1994). Testing linked to teaching. In N.C. Jordan & J. Goldsmith-Phillips (Eds.), *Learning disabilities: New directions for assessment and intervention* (pp. 163–176). Boston: Allyn & Bacon.

Choate, J.S., Enright, B.E., Miller, L.J., Poteet, J.A., & Rakes, T.A. (1995). *Curriculum-based assessment and programming.* Boston: Allyn & Bacon.

Clay, M.M. (1995). *An observation of early literacy attainment.* Portsmouth, NH: Heinemann.

Cohen, L., & Spenciner, L. (1998). *Assessment of children and youth.* Boston: Addison Wesley.

Darling-Hammond, L., Ancess, J., & Falk, B. (1995). *Authentic assessment in action.* New York: Teachers College Press.

Dehn, M. J (2008). *Working memory and academic learning: Assessment and intervention.* Hoboken, NJ: Wiley.

Fuchs L.S., & Fuchs, D. (2008). The role of assessment within the RTI framework. In D. Fuchs, L.S. Fuchs, & S. Vaughn (Eds.), *Response to intervention: A framework for educators* (pp. 105–122). Newark, DE: International Reading Association.

Gallistel-Ellis Test of Coding Skills (GE Test). Arlington, VA: Montage Press at IBI. Available at http://www.montagepressatibi.com

Ganske, K. (2000). *Word journeys: Assessment-guided phonics, spelling, and vocabulary instruction.* New York: Guilford Press.

Glazer, S.M., & Brown, C.S. (1993). *Portfolios and beyond: Collaborative assessment in reading and writing.* Norwood, MA: Christopher Gordon.

Gresham, F.M., & Vellutino, F.R. (2010). What is the role of intelligence in the identification of specific learning disabilities? Issues and clarifications. *Learning Disabilities: Research and Practice, 25*(4), 194–206.

Hasbrouck, J.E., & Tindal, G. (2006). Oral reading fluency norms: A valuable assessment tool for reading teachers. *The Reading Teacher, 59,* 636–644.

Hewett, G. (1995). *A portfolio primer: Teaching, collecting, and assessing student writing.* Portsmouth, NH: Heinemann.

Hulme, C., & Joshi, R.M. (Eds.). (1998). *Reading and spelling: Development and disorders.* Mahwah, NJ: Lawrence Erlbaum Associates.

Idol, L.A., Nevin, A., & Paolucci-Whitcomb, P. (1996). *Models of curriculum-based assessment.* Austin, TX: PRO-ED.

Jenkins, J.R, Hudson, R.F. & Lee, S.H. (2007). Using CBM reading assessments to monitor reading progress. *Perspectives on Language and Literacy, 33*(2), 11–18.

Johnston, P.H. (2000). *Running records: A self-tutoring guide.* Portland, ME: Stenhouse.

Kibby, M.W. (1995). *Practical steps for informing literacy instruction: A diagnostic decision-making model.* Newark, DE: International Reading Association.

Kubiszyn, T., & Borich, G. (1993). *Educational testing and measurement: Classroom application and practice* (5th ed.). Boston: Houghton Mifflin.

Learning Disabilities Association of America. (February, 2010). *The Learning Disabilities Association of America's white paper on evaluation, identification, and eligibility criteria for students with specific learning disabilities.* Pittsburgh, PA: Author.

Mckenna, M.C., & Stahl, K.A.D. (2009). *Assessment for reading instruction* (2nd ed.). New York: Guilford Press.

Mellard, D.F., & Johnson, E. (2008). *RTI: A practitioner's guide to implementing response to intervention.* Thousand Oaks, CA: Corwin Press.

Miller, D.C. (2007). *Essentials of school neuropsychological assessment.* Hoboken, NJ: John Wiley & Sons.

Miller, W.H. (1995). *Alternative assessment techniques for reading and writing.* West Nyack, NY: Center for Applied Research in Education.

Nilsson, N.L. (2008). A critical analysis of eight informal reading inventories. *The Reading Teacher, 61*(7), 526–536.

Nitkop, A.J. (1996). *Educational assessment of students.* Upper Saddle River, NJ: Prentice Hall.

Pennington, B.F., Gilger, J.W., Olson, R.K., & DeFries, J.C. (1992). The external validity of age- versus IQ- discrepancy definitions of reading disability: Lessons from a twin study. *Journal of Learning Disabilities, 25,* 562–573.

Reutzel, D.R., & Cooter, R.B. (2011). *Strategies for reading assessment and instruction: Helping every child succeed* (4th ed.). Boston: Allyn & Bacon.

Reynolds, C.R., & Shaywitz, S.E. (2009a). Response to intervention: Prevention and remediation, perhaps, diagnosis, no. *Child Development Perspectives, 3*(1) 44.

Reynolds, C.R., & Shaywitz, S.E. (2009b). Response to intervention: Ready or not? Or, from wait-to-fail to watch-them-fail. *School Psychology Quarterly, 24*(2) 130.

Rhodes, L.K., & Shanklin, N.L. (1993). *Windows into literacy.* Portsmouth, NH: Heinemann.

Roskos, K., & Walter, B.J. (1994). *Interactive hand-book for understanding reading diagnosis.* Upper Saddle River, NJ: Prentice Hall.

Sachs, P. (1999). *Standardized minds: The high price of America's testing culture and what we can do to change it.* New York: Da Capo Press.

Shaywitz, S.E. (1996). Dyslexia. *Scientific American, 275,* 98–104.

Shaywitz, S.E. (1998). Dyslexia. *New England Journal of Medicine, 338,* 207–312.

Smartt, S.M., & Glaser, D.R. (2010). *Next STEPS in literary instruction: Connecting assessments to effective interventions.* Baltimore: Paul H. Brookes Publishing Co.

Snowling, M., & Hulme, C. (1989). A longitudinal case study of developmental phonological dyslexia. *Cognitive Neuropsychology, 6,* 379–401.

Spenciner, L.J. (2002). *Assessment of children and youth with special needs.* Upper Saddle River, NJ: Pearson Education.

Texas Scottish Rite Hospital for Children. (1992). *Dyslexia training program (Schedules I–III progress measurements: Teacher's guide and student's books).* Cambridge, MA: Educators Publishing Service.

Torgesen, J.K., & Mathes, P. (2000). *A basic guide to understanding, assessing, and teaching phonological awareness.* Austin, TX: PRO-ED.

Valencia, S.W., Hiebert, E.H., & Afflerbach, P.P. (Eds.). (1994). *Authentic reading assessment: Practice and possibilities.* Newark, DE: International Reading Association.

Walker, B.J. (1996). *Diagnostic teaching of reading: Techniques for instruction and assessment* (3rd ed.). Upper Saddle River, NJ: Prentice Hall.

Parent Resources

Greene, J.F., & Moats, L.C. (2001). *The "T" book. Testing: Critical components in the clinical identification of dyslexia* (3rd ed.). Baltimore: International Dyslexia Association. (Available at http ://www.springtides.org/Bookstore%20Pages/Dyslexia%20and%20Orton%20Emeritus%20Books%20Home.html)

Software

LessonPlanner (This software complements *Scope and Sequence for Literacy Instruction* [Murray, 2002] and is available from Lexia Institute, 766 Raymundo Avenue, Los Altos, CA; 650-964-3666; http://www.lexianet.org/).

DVDs

Beckham, P.B., & Biddle, M.L. (1988). *Dyslexia training program videotapes.* Dallas: Texas Scottish Rite Hospital, Child Development Division.

Informal Reading and Spelling Assessments on the Internet

Elementary Spelling Inventory (may be used as early as first grade; covers more stages than PSI)
http://www.tc.edu/rwp/assessment/2008/materials/documents/spellingele.pdf

Los Angeles County Office of Education (K–3 assessments)
Recognizing Rhyme Assessment, Isolating Beginning Sounds, Isolating Final Sounds, Phoneme Blending, Yopp-Singer Test of Phoneme Segmentation, Concepts About Print, Alphabet Assessment, Phonics Inventory, Learning Records [Reading Scale 1 K–3 Becoming a Reader; Writing Scale 1 K–3 Becoming a Writer] and Spelling Development [primary and elementary levels]

http://teams.lacoe.edu/reading/assessments/assessments.html

Preventing Academic Failure Test of Single Word Reading
http://www.pafprogram.com/downloads/

Primary Spelling Inventory for K–3
http://www.tc.edu/rwp/assessment/2008/materials/documents/spelling_pri.pdf

Upper Level Spelling Inventory (upper elementary, middle, high school, and postsecondary)
http://khup.com/keywor/words-their-way.htm (#17)

CHAPTER 15   Planning Multisensory Structured Language Lessons and the Classroom Environment

Web Sites for Lesson Planning ─────────────────

Big Ideas in Beginning Reading
http://reading.uoregon.edu

Dade-Monroe Teacher Education Center
http://www.miamisci.org/tec

Division for Learning Disabilities (DLD) and the
   Division for Research of The Council for
   Exceptional Children (CEC)
Current Practice Alerts
http://www.teachingld.org/ld_resources/alerts
   /default.htm

Dr. Mac's Behavior Management Site
http://www.behavioradvisor.com

Florida Center for Reading Research
http://www.fcrr.org

National Center on Response to Intervention
http://www.rti4success.org

Neuhaus Education Center
http://www.readingteachersnetwork.org

Reading ASSIST Institute: Free Downloads
http://www.readingassist.org/downloads.htm

Reading Rockets
http://www.readingrockets.org

Resource Room
http://www.resourceroom.net/index.asp

The Sonday System
http://www.winsorlearning.com

Vaughn Gross Center for Reading and Language Arts
http://www.texasreading.org/utcrla/default.asp

Vocabulary University
http://www.vocabulary.com

Wilson Academy
http://www.wilsonacademy.com

Web Sites for Classroom Management ─────────────────

CPI—Educating, Empowering, and Enriching
http://www.CrisisPrevention.com

The Teacher's Guide—Classroom Management
http://www.theteachersguide.com/Class
   Management.htm

National Education Association (NEA)
http://www.nea.org/tools/ClassroomManagement
   .html

Instructional Materials for Lesson Planning ─────────────────

Blachman, B.A., & Tangel, D.M. (2008). *Road to reading: A program for preventing and remediating reading difficulties.* Baltimore: Paul H. Brookes Publishing Co.

Clark-Edmonds. S. (2005). *S.P.I.R.E. and sounds sensible.* Cambridge, MA: Educators Publishing Service.

Fry, E. (1994). *1000 instant words.* Westminster, CA: Teacher Created Materials.

Hochman, J.C. (2009). *Teaching basic writing skills: Strategies for effective expository writing instruction.* Longmont, CO: Sopris West Educational Services.

Honig, B., Diamond, L., & Gutlon, L. (2008). *CORE: Teaching reading sourcebook for kindergarten through eighth grade.* Novato, CA: Academic Therapy Publications.

Mathes, P.G., Allor, J.H., Torgesen, J.K., & Allen, S.H. (2001). *PALS: First-grade peer-assisted literacy strategies.* Longmont, CO: Sopris West Educational Services.

McGuinness, C., & McGuiness, G. (1999). *Phono-Graphix.* Available at http://www.readamerica.net

Smartt, S.M., & Glaser, D.R. (2010). *Next STEPS in literacy instruction: Connecting assessments to effective interventions.* Baltimore: Paul H. Brookes Publishing Co.

Traub, N., & Bloom, F. (2000). *Recipe for reading* (3rd ed.). Cambridge, MA: Educators Publishing Services.

Teacher References

American Federation of Teachers. (1999, June). *Teaching reading is rocket science: What expert teachers of reading should know and be able to do* (Item No. 372 6/99). Washington, DC: Author.

Fay, J., & Funk, D. (1995). Teaching with love & logic: Taking control of the classroom. Golden, CO: The Love and Logic Press. (Available at http://www.loveandlogic.com)

Foorman, B.R., Francis, D.J., Fletcher, J.M., Schatschneider, C., & Mehta, P. (1998). The role of instruction in learning: Preventing reading failure in at-risk children. *Journal of Educational Psychology, 90*, 1–15.

Gersten, R., Compton, D., Connor, C.M., Dimino, J., Santoro, L., Linan-Thompson, S., et al. (2008). *Assisting students struggling with reading: Response to Intervention and multi-tier intervention for reading in the primary grades. A practice guide.* (NCEE 2009-4045). Washington, DC: National Center for Education Evaluation and Regional Assistance, Institute of Education Sciences, U.S. Department of Education.

Grace, K. (2006). *Phonics and spelling through phoneme-grapheme mapping.* Longmont, CO: Sopris West Educational Services.

Henry, M.K. (2010). *Unlocking literacy: Effective decoding and spelling instruction* (2nd ed.). Baltimore: Paul H. Brookes Publishing Co.

Joshi, M.R., Dahlgren, M., & Boulware-Gooden, R. (2002). Teaching reading in an inner city school through a multisensory teaching approach. *Annals of Dyslexia, 52*, 229–242.

MacKenzie, R. (2003) *Setting limits in the classroom: How to move beyond the dance of discipline in today's classrooms* (Rev. ed.). (Available at http://www.crownpublishing.com)

MacKenzie, R.J., & Stanzioine, L. (2010). *Setting limits in the classroom: A complete guide to effective classroom management with a wchool-wide discipline plan* (3rd ed.). (Available at http://www.crownpublishing.com)

Marzano, R.J., Marzano, J.S., & Pickering, D.J. (2003). *Classroom management that works: Research-based strategies for every teacher.* Alexandria, VA: Association for Supervision and Curriculum Development.

Mather, N., & Goldstein, S. (2008). *Learning disabilities and challenging behaviors: A guide to intervention and classroom management* (2nd ed.). Baltimore: Paul H. Brookes Publishing Co.

McCardle, P., & Chhabra, V. (Eds.). (2004). *The voice of evidence in reading research.* Baltimore: Paul H. Brookes Publishing Co.

McIntyre, C.W., & Pickering, J.S. (1995). *Clinical studies of multisensory structured language education for students with dyslexia and related disorders.* Salem, OR: IMSLEC.

McLeod, J., Fisher, J., & Hoover, G. (2003). *The key elements of classroom management: Managing time and space, student behavior, and instructional strategies.* Alexandria, VA: Association for Supervision and Curriculum Development.

Moats, L.C. (1998, Spring/Summer). Teaching decoding. *American Educator, 42*–29, 95–96.

Moats, L.C. (2005). *Language essentials for teachers of reading and spelling (LETRS).* Longmont, CO: Sopris West Educational Services.

Moats, L.C. (2010). *Speech to print: Language essential for teachers* (2nd ed.). Baltimore: Paul H. Brookes Publishing Co.

Paine, S.C., Radicchi, J., Roselini, L.C., Deutchman, L., & Darch, C.B. (1983). *Structuring your classroom for academic success.* Champaign, IL: Research Press.

Pierangelo, R., & Guilani, G.A. (2001). *What every teacher should know about students with special needs.* Champaign, IL: Research Press.

Pierangelo, R., & Guilani, G.A. (2002). *Creating confident children: Using positive restructuring in your classroom.* Champaign, IL: Research Press.

Samuels, S.J., & Flor, R.F. (1997). The importance of automaticity for developing expertise in reading. *Reading and Writing Quarterly: Overcoming Learning Difficulties, 13*, 107–121.

Shaywitz, S. (2003). *Overcoming dyslexia: A new and complete science-based program for reading problems at any level.* New York: Alfred A. Knopf.

Snow, C.E., Burns, M.S., & Griffin, P. (Eds.). (1998). *Preventing reading difficulties in young children.* Washington, DC: National Academies Press.

Sprick, R.S. (2008). *Discipline in the secondary classroom: A positive approach to behavior management* (2nd ed.). San Francisco: Jossey-Bass/Wiley Imprints.

Springer, S., & Alexander, B. (2005). *The organized teacher: A hands-on guide to setting up and running a terrific classroom.* New York: McGraw-Hill.

Torgesen, J.K., Alexander, A.W., Wagner, R.K., Rashotte, C.A., Voeller, K., Conway, T., et al. (2001). Intensive remedial instruction for children with severe reading disabilities: Immediate and long-term outcomes from two instructional approaches. *Journal of Learning Disabilities, 34*, 33–58.

Vadasy, P.F., Sanders, E.A., Peyton, J.A., & Jenkins, J.R. (2002). Timing and intensity of tutoring: A closer look in the conditions for effective early literacy tutoring. *Learning Disabilities Research and Practice, 17*, 227–241.

Vail, P.L. (1993). *Emotion: The on/off switch to learning.* Rosemont, NJ: Modern Learning Press.

Wootan, F., & Mulligan, C. (2007). *Not in my classroom!: A teacher's guide to effective classroom management.* (Available at http://www.adamsmedia.com)

Instructional Materials

Mamchak, P.S., & Mamchak, S.R. (1993). *Teacher's time management survival kit: Ready-to-use techniques and materials*. Upper Saddle River, NJ: Prentice Hall.

Minsky, M. (2003). *Greenwood word lists: One syllable words*. Longmont, CO: Sopris West Educational Services.

Murray, C. (2002). *Scope and sequence for literacy instruction* (2nd ed.). Los Altos, CA: Lexia Institute.

(Available from PRO-ED; 800-897-3202)

Royal, N.S. (2003). *Preparing children for success in reading: A multisensory guide for teachers and parents*. Timonium, MD: York Press. (Available from PRO-ED; 800-897-3202)

Smith, M.T. (1996). *Multisensory teaching system for reading*. Forney, TX: MTS Publications.

Smith, M.T. (n.d.). *MTA lesson planner and record keeping CD*. Forney, TX: MTS Publications.

DVDs

Beckham, P.B., & Biddle, M.L. (1988). *Dyslexia training program videotapes*. Dallas: Texas Scottish Rite Hospital, Child Development Division.

Birsh, J.R. (Consulting Ed.), & Potts, M., & Potts, R. (Producers). (1997). *LD/LA: Learning disabilities/learning abilities: Videotape II. The teaching: What students need*. West Tisbury, MA: Vineyard Video Productions. (Available from the pub-

lisher; Post Office Box 806, West Tisbury, MA 02575; 800-664-6119; e-mail: mpotts@vineyard video.org; http://www.vineyardvideo.org)

Lavoie, R. (1997). *When the chips are down: Strategies for improving children's behavior*. Washington, DC: WETA, The Learning Disabilities Project. (Available at http://ldonline.learningstore.org /products/LD1004.html)

Software for Lesson Planning

LessonPlanner (This software complements *Scope and Sequence for Literacy Instruction* [Murray, 2002] and is available from Lexia Institute, 766 Raymundo Avenue, Los Altos, CA; 650-964-

3666; http://www.lexialearning.com/)

Tutronics EZ-Prep Orton-Gillingham (available at http://www.tutronics.com/overview.htm)

CHAPTER 16   Instruction for Older Students with a Word-Level Reading Disability

Web Sites

AdLit.org
http://www.adlit.org

Alliance for Excellent Education
http://www.all4ed.org/

Book Share
http://www.bookshare.org/

Carnegie
http://www.carnegie.org/literacy/index.html

Center on Instruction
http://www.centeroninstruction.org/index.cfm

International Reading Association:
http://www.reading.org/Resources/ResourcesByTo pic/Adolescent/Resources.aspx

Learning Ally
http://www.learningally.org

National Institute on the Education of At-Risk Students
http://www.ed.gov/offices/OERI/At-Risk

Project ACCESS: Accessing Curriculum Content for Special Education Students
http://web.utk.edu/~access/etexts.htm

Decodable Text Publishers

Academic Therapy Publications
20 Commercial Boulevard
Novato, CA 94949

800-422-7249
http://www.academictherapy.com
High Noon: Sound Out Series

Don Johnston
26799 West Commerce Drive
Volo, IL 60073
800-999-4660
http://www.donjohnston.com
Start to Finish Series (classic stories available at two levels and in three formats—book, audiotape, and CD-ROM with text-to-speech features)

Educators Publishing Service
Post Office Box 9031
Cambridge, MA 02139-9031
800-225-5750
http://www.eps.schoolspecialty.com
MTA Readers

4Mation Educational Resources
Post Office Box 282
Barnstaple, Devon
EX32 2BA United Kingdom
44 (0)1271 325353
http://www.4mation.co.uk/contact.html
Spinout Stories (CD-ROMs, each story with three levels)

Jamestown Education Press
800-USA-READ
http://www.glencoe.com/gln/jamestown
American Portraits (reading levels Grades 5–8)
Best Series
Contemporary Reader (reading levels Grades 2–5)
Five-Star Stories
Six-Way Paragraphs (reading levels Grades 4–8)

Phoenix Learning Resources
2349 Chaffee Drive
St. Louis, MO 63146
800-221-1274
http://www.phoenixlearninggroup.com

New Practice Readers (reading levels Grades 2–6)
Reading for Concepts (reading levels Grades 1–6)
Reading About Science (reading levels Grades 2–6)
Building Reading Skills (reading levels Grades 2–7)

Sopris West Educational Services
4185 Salazar Way
Longmont, CO 80504
800-547-6747
http://www.sopriswest.com
J & J Language Readers
Power Readers

Wilson Language Training
47 Old Webster Road
Oxford, MA 01540
800-899-8454 (ordering materials)
http://www.wilsonlanguage.com
Student Readers: Steps 1–12 (by B. Wilson)
Stories for Older Students (by J. Brown)
Wilson Fluency/Basic Kit (by B. Wilson)
Basic Readers 1–3

Wilson Academy
http://www.wilsonacademy.com (A membership site that provides nonfiction passages with text for teachers to read to students, matched with same content text written at an easier, more decodable level.)

Wieser Educational
30281 Esperanza Rancho
Santa Margarita, CA 92688
800-880-4433
http://www.wiesereducational.com
Cover to Cover Novels (reading level Grades 2–4)
Passages Reading Program (reading level Grades 3–6)

Instructional Materials

Archer, A., Gleason, M., & Vachon, V. (2000). *Rewards*. Longmont, CO: Sopris West Educational Services.

Greene, J.F. (1995). *LANGUAGE! A reading, writing, and spelling curriculum for at-risk and ESL students*. Longmont, CO: Sopris West Educational Services.

Kleiber, M.H. (1990-2004). *Specific language training: An Orton-Gillingham curriculum for adolescents*. Yonkers, NY: Decatur Enterprises. (Available from the publisher; 26 Birch Road, Yonkers, NY 10705, 914-375-1923)

Knight, J.R. (1986). *Starting over: A combined teaching manual and student textbook for reading, writing, spelling, vocabulary, and handwriting*. Cambridge, MA: Educators Publishing Service.

Moats, L. (2010). *Speech to print: Language essentials for teachers* (2nd ed.). Baltimore: Paul H. Brookes Publishing Co.

Tuley, A.C. (1998). *Never too late to read: Language skills for the adolescent dyslexic* (based on the work of Alice Ansara). Timonium, MD: York Press. (Available from PRO-ED; 800-897-3202)

Wilson, B.A. (1988). *Wilson Reading System: Teacher's guide and student material*. Millbury, MA: Wilson Language Training. (Available from the publisher; http://www.wilsonlanguage.com)

Teacher References

Adams, M.J. (1990). *Beginning to read: Thinking and learning about print.* Cambridge, MA: The MIT Press.

Barry, A.L. (1997). High school reading programs revisited. *Journal of Adolescent and Adult Literacy, 40*(7), 524–531.

Brady, S.A., & Skankweiler, D. (1991). *Phonological processes in literacy: A tribute to Isabelle Y. Liberman.* Upper Saddle River, NJ: Lawrence Erlbaum Associates.

Catts, H., Adlof, S., & Ellis-Weismer, S. (2006). Language deficits in poor comprehenders: A case for the simple view of reading. *Journal of Speech-Language-Hearing Research, 49,* 278–293.

Carr, S.C., & Thompson, B. (1996). The effects of prior knowledge and schema activation strategies on the inferential reading comprehension of children with and without learning disabilities. *Learning Disabilities Quarterly, 19*(1), 48–61.

Dehaene, S. (2009). *Reading in the brain: The science and evolution of a human invention.* New York, NY: Penguin Viking.

Graham, S., & Harris, K. (2005). *Writing better: Effective strategies for teaching students with learning difficulties.* Baltimore: Paul H. Brookes Publishing Co.

Haager, D., Klingner, J., & Vaughn, S. (Eds.). (2007). *Evidence-based reading practices for response to intervention.* Baltimore: Paul H. Brookes Publishing Co.

Hall, S., & Moats, L. (1999). *Straight talk about reading: How parents can make a difference during the early years.* Chicago: Contemporary Press.

Henry, M.K. (2003). *Unlocking literacy: Effective decoding and spelling instruction.* Baltimore: Paul H. Brookes Publishing Co.

Henry, M.K., & Brickley, S.G. (Eds.). (1999). *Dyslexia: Samuel T. Orton and his legacy.* Baltimore: International Dyslexia Association.

Hock, M.F., & Brasseur-Hock, I.F. (2009). Literacy interventions for adolescent struggling readers. In S.R. Parris, D. Fisher, & K. Headley (Eds.), *Adolescent literacy, field tested* (pp. 129–142). Newark, DE: International Reading Association.

Houge, T.T., Geier, C., & Peyton, D. (2008, May). Targeting adolescents' literacy skills using one-to-one instruction with research-based practices. *Journal of Adolescent & Adult Literacy, 51*(8), 640–650.

Juel, C. (1996). Beginning reading. In R. Barr, M.L. Kamil, P. Mosenthal, & P.D. Pearson (Eds.), *Handbook of reading research* (Vol. II, pp. 749–788). New York: Longman.

Kamil, M.L. (2003). *Adolescents and literacy: Reading for the 21st century.* Washington, DC: Alliance for Excellent Education.

Mather, N., & Goldstein, S. (2008). *Learning disabilities and challenging behaviors: A guide to intervention and classroom management* (2nd ed.). Baltimore: Paul H. Brookes Publishing Co.

McCardle, P., & Chhabra, V. (Eds.). (2004). *The voice of evidence in reading research.* Baltimore: Paul H. Brookes Publishing Co.

Moats, L.C. (2001). When older kids can't read. *Educational Leadership, 58*(6), 36–40.

Orton, J.L. (1964). *A guide to teaching phonics.* Winston-Salem, NC: Orton Reading Center and Salem College Book Store.

Orton, J. (1966). *The Orton Gillingham approach in the disabled reader.* Baltimore: The John Hopkins University Press.

Panagos, R., & DuBois, D. (1999). Career self-efficacy development and students with learning disabilities. *Learning Disabilities Research and Practice, 14*(1), 25–34.

Piasta, S.B., & Wagner, R.K. (2010, January/February/March). Developing early literacy skills: A meta-analysis of alphabet learning and instruction. *Reading Research Quarterly, 45*(1), 8–38.

Richards, R. (2002). *When writing's a problem: Understanding dysgraphia and helpful hints for reluctant writers.* Riverside, CA: RET Center Press.

Samuels, S.J. (2002). Reading fluency: Its development and assessment. In A.E. Farstrup & S.J. Samuels (Eds.), *What research has to say about reading instruction* (3rd ed., pp. 166–183). Newark, DE: International Reading Association.

Scarborough, H.S. (1998). Predicting the future achievement of second graders with reading disabilities: Contributions of phonemic awareness, verbal memory, rapid naming, and IQ. *Annals of Dyslexia, 68,* 115–136.

Scarborough, H.S., & Parker, J.D. (2003). Matthew effects in children with learning disabilities: Development of reading, IQ, and psychosocial problems from grade 2 to grade 8. *Annals of Dyslexia, 53,* 47–71.

Shaywitz, S.E., et al. (1999). Persistence of dyslexia: The Connecticut longitudinal study at adolescence. *Pediatrics, 104,* 1351–1359.

Torgesen, J. (2004). Lessons learned from research on interventions for students who have difficulty learning to read. In P. McCardle & V. Chhabra (Eds.), *The voice of evidence in reading research.* Baltimore: Paul H. Brookes Publishing Co.

Wilson, B.A. (1998). Matching student needs to instruction: Teaching reading and spelling using the Wilson Reading System. In S.A. Vogel & S. Reder (Eds.), *Learning disabilities, literacy, and adult education* (pp. 213–234). Baltimore: Paul H. Brookes Publishing Co.

Wolf, M. (Ed.). (2001). *Dyslexia, fluency and the brain.* Timonium, MD: York Press.

Software and Hardware Devices

EzDaisy and *Scholar*, Digital Talking Book Players
http://www.sterlingadaptives.com/services.html

Franklin Electronic Publishers, handheld
speaking electronic spellcheckers
http://www.franklin.com

Intel Reader
http://www.intel.com/about/companyinfo/
healthcare/products/reader/index.htm

Kurzweil 3000
http://www.kurzweiledu.com

Literacy Productivity Package
http://www.premier-programming.com/
LPP_packs.htm

Read & Write Gold
http://www.texthelp.com/default.asp?pg_id=

WYNN
http://www.freedomscientific.com/LSG/products/
wynn.asp

CHAPTER 17   Adolescent Literacy

Web Sites

Adolescent Literacy
http://www.literacy.uconn.edu/adolit.htm

All About Adolescent Literacy
http://www.adlit.org/

Alliance for Excellent Education
http://www.all4ed.org/about_the_crisis/Students/
Literacy

Internet4Classrooms
www.internet4classrooms.com/ (Click "links for
teachers," then click "language arts" under the
subject heading)

Learning Point Associates
http://www.learningpt.org/literacy/adolescent/ins
truction.php

National Council of Teachers of English (NCTE)
http://www.ncte.org/adlit

Instructional Materials

Archer, A., Gleason, M., & Vachon, V. (2000). *Rewards* (for grades 4–12). Longmont, CO: Sopris West.

Greene, J.F. (1995). *LANGUAGE! A reading, writing, and spelling curriculum for at-risk and ESL students* (Grades 4–12). Longmont, CO: Sopris West.

Kleiber, M.H. (1990–2004). *Specific language training: An Orton-Gillingham curriculum for adolescents.* Yonkers, NY: Decatur Enterprises. (Available from the publisher, 26 Birch Road, Yonkers, NY 10705)

Knight, J.R. (1986). *Starting over: A combined teach-ing manual and student textbook for reading, writing, spelling, vocabulary, and handwriting.* Cambridge, MA: Educators Publishing Service.

Tuley, A.C. (1998). *Never too late to read: Language skills for the adolescent dyslexic* (based on the work of Alice Ansara). Timonium, MD: York Press. (Available from PRO-ED; 800-897-3202)

Wilson, B.A. (1988). *Wilson Reading System: Teacher's guide and student material.* Oxford, MA: Wilson Language Training. (Available from the publisher; http://www.wilsonlanguage.com)

Teacher References

Alvermann, D., & Strickland, D. (Eds.). (2004). *Bridging the literary achievement gaps: Grades 4–12.* New York: Teachers College Press.

Bell, N. (1992). *Visualizing and verbalizing for language comprehension and thinking* (Rev. ed.). San Luis Obispo, CA: Gander Publishing.

Carlisle, J.F., & Rice, M.S. (2002). *Improving reading comprehension.* Timonium, MD: York Press. (Available from PRO-ED; 800-897-3202)

Carreker, S. (1993). *Multisensory grammar and written composition.* Houston, TX: S.S. Systems. (Available from the publisher; 5434 Darnell Street, Houston, TX 77096)

Ciborowski, J. (1999). *Textbooks and the students who can't read them.* Brookline, MA: Brookline Books.

Deshler, D.D., Ellis, E.S., & Lenz, B.K. (1996). *Teaching adolescents with learning disabilities: Strategies and methods* (2nd ed.). Denver, CO: Love Publishing.

Guthrie, J. (2008). *Engaging adolescents in reading.* Thousand Oaks, CA: Corwin Press.

Harvey, S., & Goudvis, A. (2000). *Strategies that work: Teaching comprehension to enhance understanding.* York, ME: Stenhouse Publications.

IRA Literacy Study Groups. (2003). *Reading comprehension module.* Newark, DE: International Reading Association.

Maria, K. (1990). *Reading comprehension instruction: Issues and strategies.* Timonium, MD: York Press.

(Available from PRO-ED; 800-897-3202)

McEwan-Atkins, E. (2007). *40 ways to support struggling readers in content classrooms: Grades 4–12.* Thousand Oaks, CA: Corwin Press.

McLaughlin, M. (2003). *Guided comprehension in the primary grades.* Newark, DE: International Reading Association.

Smartt, S.M., & Glaser, D.R. (2010). *Next STEPS in literary instruction: Connecting assessments to effective interventions.* Baltimore: Paul H. Brookes Publishing Co.

Software and Hardware Devices

EzDaisy and *Scholar*, Digital Talking Book Players
http://www.sterlingadaptives.com/services.html

Franklin Electronic Publishers, handheld electronic speaking spellcheckers
http://www.franklin.com

Inspiration—outlining and graphic organizer software
http://www.inspiration.com.

Intel Reader
http://www.intel.com/about/companyinfo/healthcare/products/reader/index.htm

Kurzweil 3000—reads and highlights written text
http://www.kurzweiledu.com

Literacy Productivity Package
http://www.premier-programming.com/LPP_packs.htm

Pulse Smartpen, records audio and organizes note taking
http://www.livescribe.com/en-us/

Read & Write Gold
http://www.texthelp.com/default.asp?pg_id=

WYNN
http://www.freedomscientific.com/LSG/products/wynn.asp

CHAPTER 18   Learning Strategies and Study Skills

Free and Low-Cost Tools

"The new definition of literacy is based on a different assumption: that digital technology is rapidly becoming a primary carrier of information and that the broader means of expression this technology makes possible are now critical for education. Text literacy is necessary and valuable, but no longer sufficient" (Meyer & Rose, 2000). There can be no quarreling with this statement. Students today live in a pervasively electronic world; they revel in it and are far more comfortable and proficient in it as a group than most of their floundering elders. More to the point, common sense dictates that anything that will expedite learning and improve performance for all students, but especially for those with language-based learning difficulties, is a boon, and should routinely be incorporated into their bag of tricks. The same common sense dictates that these tools be used to support, intensify, practice, reinforce, and enhance—but not replace, at least at this time, effective personal instruction in print literacy skills—phonology, reading, spelling, writing, and grammar.

The special value of these learning tools is that they require the student to be interactive, to make choices, to use trial and error as essential to learning, to build a personal tool kit, to become the agent of his or her own learning. The tools cannot fail to lead the learner to higher levels of mastery learning, to instill a sense of accomplishment, to restore self-confidence, and to renewed enthusiasm for learning.

Such tools now readily available on the web and free or low cost. Many are excellent complements to Study Skills training and can solidify the skills learned The following is based on the work of Kathleen McClaskey, M.Ed. (see below for link).

Web-based tools are available for

- Learning and expanding vocabulary

- Accessing online encyclopedias

- Accessing textbooks and other print materials on the web (very low cost)

- Converting print into speech

- Replacing electronic voices with the student's own voice

- Organizing, analyzing, and structuring text to improve comprehension

- Highlighting text

- Notetaking from text

- Creating and using graphic organizers

- Using visuals, including photographs, to enhance comprehension

- Creating tables

  Desktop tools (readily available) include the following:

- *MSWord* or *Open Office*

- *Inspiration 8.0*

- *Kidspiration 3.0*

  No-cost tools on the web include the following:

- Text-to-speech tools to read digital text aloud

- *ReadPlease 2003* (PC; http://www.readplease.com)

- Natural Reader (PC; http://www.naturalreaders.com)

- Mac Speech Tool

- Word Web (PC; http://wordweb.info/free)

  Low-cost tools include the following:

- *Bookshare*

- *READ:Outloud*

- *Bookshare Edition*

For additional information, contact Kathleen McClaskey at http://www.edtech-associates.com.

Web Sites

Computer-Based Study Strategies
http://education.uorgeon.edu/feature.htm?id=1588

Homework NYC
http://homeworknycbeta.org

Learning Strategies Database
http://www.muskingum.edu/~cal/database

Learning Toolbox
http://coe.jmu.edu/LearningToolbox

Online Academic Success Videos
http://www.dartmouth.edu/~acskills/videos/index.html

ProQuest K–12
http://www.researchpaper.com

Quizlet
http://quizlet.com/

Instructional Materials

Abbamont, G.W., & Brescher, A. (1997). *Test smart: Ready-to-use test-taking strategies and activities for grades 5–12.* West Nyack, NY: Center for Applied Research in Education.

Askov, E.N., & Kamm, K. (1982). *Study skills in the content areas.* Boston: Allyn & Bacon.

Benne, B. (1988). *WASPLEG and other mnemonics: Easy ways to remember hard things.* Dallas, TX: Taylor Publishing Co.

Bragstad, B.J., & Stumpf, S.M. (1987). *Study skills and motivation: A guidebook for teaching.* Boston: Allyn & Bacon.

Budworth, J. (1991). *Instant recall: Tapping your hidden memory power.* Holbrook, MA: Bob Adams.

Buzan, T. (1991). *Use both sides of your brain* (3rd ed.). New York: E.P. Dutton. [*Note:* Buzan's note-taking system is not recommended for dyslexic students; this source is recommended for mind map design and enhancement only.]

Cherry, R.L. (1989). *Words under construction.* Tucson: University of Arizona Press.

Coffman, N.W. (2002). *Shelton School study skills curriculum.* Dallas, TX: June Shelton School and Evaluation Center.

Coffman, N. (2002). *Shelton School study skills student resource binder.* Dallas, TX: June Shelton School and Evaluation Center.

D'Angelo Bromley, K. (1996). *Webbing with literature: Creating story maps with children's books.* Boston: Allyn & Bacon.

Danner, H.G., & Noël, R. (1996). *Discover it!: A better vocabulary the better way.* Occoquan, VA: Imprimus Books.

Dillon, S. (2000). *Structure of the English language for reading and spelling.* Albuquerque, NM: S.I.S. Publishing Co.

Erwin, P. (1992). *The Winston grammar program.* Battleground, WA: Precious Memories Educational Resources.

Frender, G. (1990). *Learning to learn.* Nashville: Incentive Press.

Gilbert, S. (1990). *Go for it: Get organized. The perfect time-management system for busy teens.* New York: Morrow Junior Books.

Goldberg, D. (2005). *The organized student.* New York: Fireside.

Joseph, L. (2009). *Study skill organizers.* Prides Crossing, MA: Landmark.

Kesselman-Turkel, J., & Peterson, F. (1982). *Note-taking made easy.* Chicago: Contemporary Books.

Meltzer, L., Roditi, B., & Steinberg, J. (2006). *Strategies for success.* Austin, TX: PRO-ED.

Moore, B., & Moore, M. (1997). *NTC's dictionary of Latin and Greek origins.* Lincolnwood, IL: NTC Publishing Group.

Newhall, P. (2008). *Study skills: Research based strategies.* Prides Crossing, MA: Landmark.

Strichart, S.S., & Mangrum, C.T., II. (1993). *Teaching study strategies to students with learning disabilities.* Boston: Allyn & Bacon.

Tonjes, M.J., & Zintz, M.V. (1992). *Teaching reading, thinking, study skills in content classrooms* (3rd ed.). Dubuque, IA: William C. Brown.

Trudeau, K. (1995). *Megamemory.* New York: William Morrow & Co.

Vurnakes, C. (1995). *The organized student: Teaching time management.* Torrance, CA: Frank Schaffer Publications.

Wycoff, J. (1991). *Mindmapping: Your personal guide to exploring creativity and problem-solving.* New York: Berkley Books.

Teacher References

Christensen, C.R., Garvin, D.A., & Sweet, A. (1991). *Education for judgment: The artistry of discussion leadership.* Boston: Harvard Business School Press.

Dawson, P., & Guare, R. (2008). *Smart but scattered: The revolutionary "executive" approach to helping kids reach their potential.* New York: Guilford Press.

Deshler, D.D., Ellis, E., & Lenz, B.K. (1996). *Teaching adolescents with learning disabilities: Strategies and methods* (2nd ed.). Denver, CO: Love Publishing.

Devine, T.G. (1987). *Teaching study skills: A guide for teachers* (2nd ed.). Boston: Allyn & Bacon.

Foorman, B.R. (Ed.). (2003). *Preventing and remediating reading difficulties: Bringing science to scale.* Timonium, MD: York Press. (Available from PRO-ED; 800-897-3202)

Gaddes, W.H., & Edgell, D. (1994). *Learning disabilities and brain function: A neuropsychological approach* (3rd ed.). New York: Springer-Verlag.

Galaburda, A. (Ed.). (1993). *Dyslexia and development: Neurobiological aspects of extraordinary brains.* Cambridge, MA: Harvard University Press.

Levine, M. (1987). *Developmental variation and learning disorders* (2nd ed.). Cambridge, MA: Educators Publishing Service.

Lyon, G.R., & Krasnegor, N.A. (Eds.). (1996). *Attention, memory, and executive function.* Baltimore: Paul H. Brookes Publishing Co.

Martin, M. (2007). *Helping children with nonverbal learning disabilities to flourish.* London: Jessica Kingsley Publishers.

McCardle, P., & Chhabra, V. (Eds.). (2004). *The voice of evidence in reading research.* Baltimore: Paul H. Brookes Publishing Co.

McNeil, J.D. (1992). *Reading comprehension: New directions for classroom practice.* New York: HarperCollins.

Meltzer, L. (Ed.). (2007). *Executive function in education.* New York: Guilford Press.

Shaywitz, S.E. (1998). Current concepts in dyslexia. *New England Journal of Medicine, 338,* 307–312.

Steeves, K.J. (1983). Memory as a factor in the computational efficiency of dyslexic children with high abstract reasoning ability. *Annals of Dyslexia, 33,* 141–152.

Tuley, A.C. (1998). *Never too late to read: Language skills for the adolescent dyslexic* (based on the work of Alice Ansara). Timonium, MD: York Press. (Available from PRO-ED; 800-897-3202)

Wiig, E.H., & Semel, E. (1990). *Language assessment and intervention for the learning disabled.* Columbus, OH: Charles E. Merrill.

Software and Hardware Devices

Inspiration
http://www.inspiration.com

Kurzweil 3000
http://www.kurzweiledu.com/

Pulse Smartpen
http://www.livescribe.com/en-us/

DVDs

Birsh, J.R. (Consulting Ed.), & Potts, M., & Potts, R. (Producers). (1991). *Teaching the learning disabled: Study skills and learning strategies: Videotape III. Organizing time, materials, and information.* West Tisbury, MA: Vineyard Video Productions. (Available from the publisher; Post Office Box 806, West Tisbury, MA 02575; 800-664-6119; e-mail: mpotts@ vineyardvideo.org; http://www.vineyardvideo.org)

The University of Kansas Center for Research on Learning, Institute for Effective Instruction
http://www.kucrl.org/kucrl/

CHAPTER 19   Working with High-Functioning Adults with Dyslexia and Other Academic Challenges

Organizations

The International Dyslexia Association (IDA)
40 York Road, 4th Floor
Baltimore, MD 21204
410-296-0232
http://www.interdys.org

Learning Ally
20 Roszel Road
Princeton, NJ 08540
866-732-3582
http://www.learningally.org

Learning Disabilities Association of America (LDA)
4156 Library Road
Pittsburgh, PA 15234
412-341-1515
http://www.ldanatl.org

National Center for Learning Disabilities (NCLD)
381 Park Avenue South
Suite 1401

New York, NY 10016
888-575-7373
http://www.ncld.org

Yale Center for Dyslexia and Creativity
School of Medicine
Department of Pediatrics, LMP 3089
Post Office Box 208064
New Haven, CT 06520
203-785-4641
http://www.dyslexia.yale.edu

Web Sites

Cyberwink
http://cyberwink.com

Schwab Learning
http://schwablearning.org

Instructional Materials

Cooley, T. (1993). *The Norton sampler: Short essays for composition* (4th ed.). New York: W.W. Norton.
Milan, D. (1991). *Developing reading skills* (3rd ed.). New York: McGraw-Hill.
Milan, D. (1992). *Improving reading skills* (2nd ed.). New York: McGraw-Hill.
Pauk, W. (1983). *Six-way paragraphs: Advanced level* (Rev. ed.). Providence, RI: Jamestown Publishing.
Pauk, W. (1983). *Six-way paragraphs: Middle level* (Rev. ed.). Providence, RI: Jamestown Publishing.

Teacher References

Blumenthal, S.H. (1981). *Educational memories as a diagnostic measure.* Unpublished manuscript. (Available from the author; shb280@aol.com)
Blumenthal, S.H. (1981). *Process notes as a cognitive mediator.* Unpublished manuscript. (Available from the author; shb280@aol.com)
Fink, R.P. (1998). Literacy development in successful men and women with dyslexia. *Annals of Dyslexia, 48,* 311–346.
Gerber, P.J., Ginsberg, R., & Reiff, H.B. (1992). Identifying alterable patterns in employment success for highly successful adults with learning disabilities. *Journal of Learning Disabilities, 25*(8), 475–487.
Gerber, P.J., Ginsberg, R., & Reiff, H.B. (1996). Reframing the learning disabilities experience. *Journal of Learning Disabilities, 29*(1), 98–101.
Levine, M.D. (2002). *A mind at a time.* New York: Simon & Schuster.
Morris, B. (2002, May 13). Overcoming dyslexia. *Fortune,* 54–70.
Reiff, H.B., Gerber, P.J., & Ginsberg, R. (1994). Instructional strategies for long term success. *Annals of Dyslexia, 44,* 270–288.
Reiff, H.B., Gerber, P.J., & Ginsberg, R. (1997). *Exceeding expectations: Successful adults with learning disabilities.* Austin, TX: PRO-ED.
Roswell, F., & Chall, J. (1994). *Creating successful readers.* Chicago: Riverside.
Shaywitz, S.E. (1996). Dyslexia. *Scientific American, 275*(5), 98–104.

Memoirs

Hampshire, S. (1982). *Susan's story.* New York: St. Martin's Press.
Mooney, J., & Cole, D. (2000). *Learning outside the lines.* New York: Fireside.
Simpson, E.M. (1998). *Reversals: A personal account of victory over dyslexia* (Reissue ed.). New York: Noonday Press.
West, T.G. (1991). *In the mind's eye.* Buffalo, NY: Prometheus Books.

Podcast

Philip Schultz, The Poet & His Dyslexia   http://www.writersvoice.net/2010/07/philip-schultz/

CHAPTER 20   Language and Literacy Development Among English Language Learners

Organizations

National Association for Bilingual Education (NABE)
1313 L Street, NW
Suite 210
Washington, DC 20005
202-898-1829
E-mail: nabe@nabe.org
http://www.nabe.org

National Clearinghouse for English Language Acquisition and Language Instructional Educational Programs
2011 Eye Street, NW
Suite 300
Washington, DC 20006
800-321-6223
http://www.ncela.gwu.edu

Web Sites

Colorin Colorado
http://www.colorincolorado.org

ELL Assessment for Linguistic Differences vs. Learning Disabilities
http://www.ldldproject.net/about/index.html

Schwab Learning
http://www.schwablearning.org

The White House Initiative on Educational Excellence for Hispanic Americans
http://www.yesican.gov

Assessment Tools

Muñoz-Sandoval, A.F., & Woodcock, R.W. (1996). *Batería Woodcock-Muñoz: Pruebas de aprovechamiento-revisada.* Itasca, IL: Riverside Publishing.

Office of Bilingual Education, University of Texas, & the Texas Center for Reading and Language Arts. (2003). *El Inventario de Lectura en Español de Tejas: Tejas LEE. A Spanish early reading assessment.* Austin, TX: CSI.

Riccio, C.A., Imhoff, B., Hasbrouck, J.E., & Davis, G.N. (2004). *Test of Phonological Awareness in Spanish (TPAS).* Austin, TX: PRO-ED.

Semel, E., Wiig, E.H., & Secord, W.A. (1995). *Clinical Evaluation of Language Fundamentals–Third Edition* (CELF–3, Spanish ed.). San Antonio, TX: Harcourt Assessment.

Zimmerman, I.L., Steiner, V.G., & Pond, R.E. (2002). *Preschool Language Scale–Fourth Edition.* San Antonio, TX: Harcourt Assessment.

Instructional Materials

Devney, D.M. (1992). *Guide to Spanish suffixes.* Lincolnwood, IL: Passport Books.

Esperanza: A multisensory structured Spanish language program (Materials and training available through Valley Speech Language & Learning Center, Brownsville, TX; http://www.valleyspeech.org/programs.html)

Kendris, C. (1982). *501 Spanish verbs* (2nd ed.). New York: Barron's Educational Series.

Moore, B., & Moore, M. (1997). *NTC's dictionary of Latin and Greek origin.* Lincolnwood, IL: NTC Publishing Group.

Pierson, R.H. (1996). *A practical guide to 2,500 commonly used Spanish idioms: Guide to Spanish idioms/ Gaia de monism's Español es.* Lincolnwood, IL: Passport Books.

Prado, M. (1993). *NTC's dictionary of Spanish false cognates.* Lincolnwood, IL: NTC Publishing Group.

TrabaLenguas: Educational materials for Spanish speech language therapy (Materials available at http://www.spanishspeech.com)

Teacher References

Fitzgerald, J. (1995). English as a second language reading instruction in the United States: A research review. *Journal of Reading Behavior, 27*(2), 115–152.

Gottlieb, M. (2006). *Assessing English language learners.* Thousand Oaks, CA: Corwin Press.

Gunning, T. (2008). *Creating literary instruction for all students.* Columbus, OH: Allyn & Bacon/Merrill.

Harrison-Harris, O.L. (2002, November 5). *AAC, lit-*

eracy, and bilingualism. Retrieved March 8, 2005, from http://www.asha.org/Publications/leader /2002/021105/f021105.htm

Honig, B., Diamond, L., & Gutlon, L. (2008). *CORE: Teaching reading sourcebook for kindergarten through eighth grade.* Novato, CA: Academic Therapy Publications.

International Dyslexia Association. (2000). *Sólo los hechos . . . Información de La Asociación Internacional de Dislexia.* Retrieved January 13, 2011, from http://www.interdys.org/ewebeditpro5 /upload/Acad_Ther_FS_Spanish.pdf

Learning two languages [Brochure]. Rockville, MD: American Speech-Language-Hearing Association (ASHA). (Available from ASHA product sales; 888-498-6699; Product #0112544 [English], Product #0112545 [Spanish])

Sánchez, M.T., Parker, C., Akbayin, B., & McTigue, A. (2010). Processes and challenges in identifying learning disabilities among students who are English language learners in three New York State districts (*Issues & Answers Report, REL 2010–No. 085*). Washington, DC: U.S. Department of Education.

Slavin, R.E., & Cheung, A. (2004). How do English language learners learn to read? *Educational Leadership, 61*(6), 52–57.

Stone, C.A., & Carlisle, J.F. (2005). Learning disabilities in English language learners: Research issues and future directions [Special issue]. *Learning Disabilities Research and Practice, 20*(4), 199.

Tabors, P.O., & Snow, C.E. (2001). Young bilingual children and early literacy development. In S.B. Neuman & D.K. Dickinson (Eds.), *Handbook of early literacy research* (pp. 159–178). New York: Guilford Press.

CHAPTER 21   Multisensory Mathematics Instruction

Organizations

Association of Mathematics Teacher Educators
Center for Research in Mathematics and Science
 Education
San Diego, CA 92120
619-594-3971
https://www.amte.net/home

National Council of Teachers of Mathematics
1906 Association Drive
Reston, VA 20191
800-235-7566
http://www.nctm.org

Web Sites

AAA Math
http://www.aaamath.com

AplusMath
http://www.aplusmath.com

AMTE: Online Teacher Educator Resources
https://www.amte.net/resources/professional

Centre for Innovation in Mathematics Teaching,
 University of Exeter, United Kingdom
http://www.cimt.plymouth.ac.uk

Cool Math
http://www.coolmath.com

Cool Math 4 Kids
http://www.coolmath4kids.com

Khan Academy
http://www.khanacademy.org/

Math Manipulatives
http://www.MathUSee.com

Math Open Reference
http://www.mathopenref.com

Math Parent Handbook: A Guide to Helping Your
 Child Understand Mathematics
http://mathforum.org/library/view/8379.html

Math Playground
http://www.mathplayground.com

Mathematics Learning Forum, Bank Street College
http://www.bnkst.edu/mlf

Stern Structural Arithmetic
http://sternmath.com/index.php

Assessment Tools

Ginsburg, H. (1987). *Assessing the arithmetic abilities and instructional needs of students.* Austin, TX: PRO-ED.

National Council of Teachers of Mathematics. (1995). *Assessment standards for school mathematics.* Reston, VA: Author.

Instructional Materials

Saxon math. (2010). Boston: Houghton Mifflin Harcourt. (Available at http://saxonpublishers.hmhco.com/en/saxonpublishers.htm)

Semple math. (2010). Attleboro, MA: Semple Math Inc. (Available at http://www.semplemath.com/)

Stern, M., & Gould, T. (1988-1992). *Stern Structural Arithmetic materials.* Cambridge, MA: Educators Publishing Service.

Touch math. (2010). Colorado Springs, CO: Innovative Learning Concepts. (Available at http://www.touchmath.com)

Tuley, K., & Bell, N. (1998). *On cloud nine: Visualizing and verbalizing for math.* San Luis Obispo, CA: Gander Publishing.

Manipulatives

Base-10 blocks [Plastic blocks with units marked, used to demonstrate place value: tens, hundreds, and thousands]. White Plains, NY: Cuisinaire Dale Seymour Publications.

Cuisinaire rods [Colored plastic rods with sizes in centimeters, units not marked]. White Plains, NY: Cuisinaire Dale Seymour Publications.

Unifix cubes [Set of colored interlocking plastic cubes and devices into which they fit]. White Plains, NY: Cuisinaire Dale Seymour Publications.

Teacher References

Bley, N., & Thorton, C. (2001). *Teaching mathematics to students with learning disabilities.* Austin, TX: PRO-ED.

Burns, M. (1987). *50 problem solving lessons.* White Plains, NY: Cuisinaire Dale Seymour Publications. (Available from Pearson Education, Parsippany, NJ, http://www.pearsoned.com/)

Burns, M. (1992). *About teaching mathematics: A K-8 resource.* Sausalito, CA: Math Solutions Publications.

Fennema, E., Carpenter, T.P., & Lamon, S. (Eds.). (1991). *Integrating research and teaching and learning mathematics.* Albany: State University of New York Press.

Gardener, H. (1991). *The unschooled mind: How children think and how schools should teach.* New York: Basic Books.

Grouws, D. (1992). *Handbook of research on mathematics teaching and learning.* New York: Macmillan.

Healy, J. (1999). *Failure to connect.* New York: Simon & Schuster.

Jordon, N., & Montani, T.O. (1996). Mathematics difficulties in young children: Cognitive and developmental perspectives. *Advances in Learning and Behavioral Disabilities, 10A,* 101–134.

Kamii, C. (1985). *Young children reinvent arithmetic: Implications of Piaget's theory.* New York: Teachers College Press.

MacNeal, E. (1994). *Mathematics: Making numbers talk sense.* New York: Viking Penguin.

Montessori, M. (1964). *The Montessori method.* Cambridge, MA: Robert Bentley.

National Council of Teachers of Mathematics. (1991). *Professional standards for teaching mathematics.* Reston, VA: Author.

Piaget, J. (1952). *The child's concept of number.* London: Routledge & Kegan Paul.

Pimm, D. (1990). *Speaking mathematically: Communication in mathematics classrooms.* New York: Routledge.

Sawyer, W.W. (1964). *Introducing mathematics: Vision in elementary mathematics.* London: Penguin Books Ltd.

Steen, L.A. (1997). *Why numbers count: Quantitative literacy for tomorrow's America.* Reston, VA: National Council of Teachers of Mathematics.

Stern, M. (2009). *Experimenting with numbers: Developing number skills with Structural Arithmetic. A multi-sensory approach to the first years of mathematics instruction* (Book 1, 3–6 years). Rochester, VT: Stern Math, LLC, (Available at http://sternmath.com/order.html)

Stern, M., & Gould, T. (1988-1992). *Structural Arithmetic workbooks and teacher's guides 1–3.* Cambridge, MA: Educators Publishing Service.

Thiessen, D., Matthias, M., & Smith, J. (1998). *The wonderful world of mathematics: A critically annotated list of children's books in mathematics.* Reston, VA: National Council of Teachers of Mathematics.

Trafton, P.R. (Ed.). (1989). *New directions for elementary school mathematics.* Reston, VA: National Council of Teachers of Mathematics.

Parent Readings and Resources

Cossey, R., Stenmark, J., & Thompson, V. (1986). *Family math.* Berkeley: University of California.

Helping your child learn mathematics. (2005). Retrieved October 1, 2010, from http://www2.ed.gov/parents/academic/help/math/index.html

Kaye, P. (1987). *Games for math.* New York: Random House.

DVD

Birsh, J.R. (Consulting Ed.), & Potts, M., & Potts, R. (Producers). (1997). *LD/LA: Learning disabilities/learning abilities: Videotape VI. Teaching math: A systematic approach for children with learning disabilities.* West Tisbury, MA: Vineyard Video Pro-

ductions. (Available from the publisher; Post Office Box 806, West Tisbury, MA 02575; 800-664-6119; e-mail: mpotts@vineyardvideo.org; http://www.vineyardvideo.org)

CHAPTER 22   Technology that Supports Literacy Instruction and Learning

Web Sites

AbleData
http://www.abledata.com

Adaptive Technology Center, Indiana University
http://www.indiana.edu/~iuadapts

The Alliance for Technology Access (ATA)
http://www.ataccess.org

Assistive Technology for the Classroom, Landmark College
http://www.landmark.edu/institute/assistive_technology/index.html

Assistive Technology Outcomes Measurement System Project (ATOMS)
http://www.atoms.uwm.edu

Center for Applied Special Technology (CAST)
http://www.cast.org

Center for Assistive Technology and Environmental Access (CATEA)
http://www.catea.org

Center for Implementing Technology in Education
http://www.cited.org/index.aspx

Closing the Gap
http://www.closingthegap.com

Community Technology Centers' Network
http://www.ctcnet.org

Connecticut State Education Resource Center (SERC) library of bibliographies
http://ctserc.org/s/index.php?option=com_content&view=article&id=522&itemid=179

Consortium for Assistive Technology Outcomes Research (CATOR)
http://www.atoutcomes.com/

Dave Edyburn's annual reviews of best special education technology articles
https://pantherfile.uwm.edu/edyburn/www/

Digital Directions
http://www.digitaldirections.org/go/topsites
http://www.digitaldirections.org/go/newssletters

eduScapes
http://www.eduscapes.com

The Family Center on Technology and Disability
http://www.fctd.info

Great Schools
http://www.greatschools.org/articles/?topics=188&language=EN

International Society for Technology in Education
http://www.iste.org/welcome.aspx

Johns Hopkins University Center for Technology in Education
http://www.cte.jhu.edu

LD Online's Technology section
http://ldonline.org/ld_indepth/technology/technology.html

LD Resources
http://www.ldresources.com

Learning Aids, Washington Assistive Technology Alliance
http://www.wata.org/resource/learning

Matching Person & Technology
http://matchingpersonandtechnology.com/

National Assistive Technology Research Institute
http://natri.uky.edu

National Center to Improve Practice in Special Education through Technology, Media and Materials
http://www2.edc.org/NCIP

Next Generation Technologies, Inc.
http://www.ngtvoice.com/

Quizinator
http://www.quizinator.com

Schwab Learning
http://www.schwablearning.org

Trace Center
http://trace.wisc.edu/

University of Toronto, Inclusive Design Research
  Centre
http://www.utoronto.ca/atrc/index_E.html

Listservs and Discussion Boards

Kurzweil
http://www.kurzweiledu.com/support_listserv.asp

TechMatrix
http://www.techmatrix.org

Print Journals

Assistive Technology
http://69.89.27.238/~resnaorg/ProfResources
  /Publications/ATJournal/Subscribe.php

Closing the Gap
http://www.closingthegap.com/

Closing the Gap Forums

http://www.closingthegap.org/forums/ubbthreads
  .php

Journal of Special Education Technology
http://www.tamcec.org/jset/

Journal of Technology and Disability
http://resna.org/journal/technology-disability

Online Journals

Assistive Technology Outcomes and Benefits (ATOB)
http://www.atia.org/i4a/pages/index.cfm?
  pageid=3305

Journal of Science and Education Technology

http://www.springerlink.com/content/102587/

Special Education Technology Practice
http://www.setp.net/index.html

Teacher Reference

Friedlander, B. (2010). *Technology: What every educator needs to know.* Wauconda, IL: Don Johnston.

Software and Hardware

This list of software and hardware resources is not exhaustive but surveys the field and offers some leading products in each category. Listing here does not imply endorsement of a particular product. (*Source:* Pisha, B., Hitchcock, C., & Stahl, S. [2003, Fall]. Assistive technologies resource list. *Perspectives, 29*[4], 14–18.)

Text-to-Speech Software

Although some text-to-speech software is available as a free download or as shareware, the features vary greatly among products, and not all digital text can be read by all products.

Freeware

Freeware can be downloaded from the Internet without charge.

HearIt!
http://trace.wisc.edu/world/computer_access
  /mac/macshare.html

HELP Read
http://helpread.net/

Microsoft Reader
http://www.microsoft.com/reader

Text Talkster v1.0
http://yippee.i4free.co.nz/html/win/desktop
  enhancements/title10699.htm

Shareware

Shareware can be downloaded from the Internet and used without cost for a trial period. After the trial ends, users should pay a shareware fee, which is usually relatively inexpensive.

TextAloudMP3
http://www.nextup.com/TextAloud/download.html

Commercial Software

Following are more expensive choices that offer integrated scanning, improved voices, and maintain original page layout.

CAST eReader
http://www.cast.org/research/faq/#q6

Kurzweil 3000
http://www.kurzweiledu.com/

Read & Write Gold and Screenreader v4
http://www.texthelp.com/default.asp?pg_id=

Reading Assistant
http://www.scilearn.com

WordQ Writing Aid Software
http://www.wordq.com

WYNN
http://www.freedomscientific.com

Voice-Recognition Software

Dragon NaturallySpeaking
http://www.scansoft.com/naturallyspeaking

MacSpeech iListen (Macintosh only)
http://www.macspeech.com/products/ilisten

Via Voice
http://download.cnet.com/IBM-ViaVoice/3000-7239_4-19113.html

Graphic Organizer Software

Inspiration and Kidspiration
http://www.inspiration.com

Inexpensive Portable Word Processors

AlphaSmart 3000
AlphaSmart
973 University Avenue
Los Gatos, CA 95032

408-355-1000
http://www.neo-direct.com/intro.aspx

LaserPC6 (with text-to-speech option)
http://www.perfectsolutions.com/pc6f.asp

Other Technology Tools

Draft:Builder, Write:OutLoud, Co:Writer 4000, Co:Writer SmartApplet
http://www.donjohnston.com

Reading Pen
Boston Post Road West 33 Suite 320
   Marlborough, MA 01752
888-777-0552

http://www.wizcomtech.com/usaeng/catalog/a/readingpen/default2.asp?type=0

Pulse Smartpen
http://www.livescribe.com/en-us/

V.Reader
http://www.vtechkids.com/v.reader/

Sources for Digital Text

Abacci Books
http://www.e-book.com.au/freebooks.htm

Accessible Book Collection
http://accessiblebookcollection.org

Alex Catalogue of Electronic Texts
http://infomotions.com/alex/

Audible
http://www.audible.com

Bookshare.org
http://www.bookshare.org

The Children's Literature Web Guide
http://www.acs.ucalgary.ca/~dkbrown

Cinderella Stories
http://www.ucalgary.ca/~dkbrown/cinderella.html

EBooks
http://www.eBooks.com

Elibrary
http://www.elibrary.com

The eText Archive
http://www.archive.org

Fairrisa Cyber Library
http://www.fairrosa.info/

Internet Public Library
http://www.ipl.org

KidSpace at the Internet Public Library
http://www.ipl.org/youth

Learning Ally
http://www.learningally.org

Literature Online from Chadwyck
http://lion.chadwyck.com

The Online Books Page
http://onlinebooks.library.upenn.edu

The Princess and the Pea by Hans Christian
  Andersen
http://hca.gilead.org.il/princess.html

Project Gutenberg
http://www.searcheBooks.com

SearchGov.com
http://www.SearchGov.com

Stories, Folklore, and Fairy Tales Theme Page
http://www.cln.org/themes/fairytales.html

The Texas Text Exchange
http://tte.tamu.edu

Academic Texts, Secondary Level and Above

American Literary Classics
http://www.americanliterature.com

Bartleby.com
http://www.bartleby.com/

Bookshare
http//www.bookshare.org

Camera Obscura
http://www.hicom.net/~oedipus/etext.html

The Cooperative Children's Book Center (CCBC)
http://www.education.wisc.edu/ccbc/

Electronic Text Center, The University of Virginia
http://www2.lib.virginia.edu/etext/index.html

English Language Resources, The University of
  Virginia
http://etext.lib.virginia.edu/collections/languages
  /english/

Gutenberg.org
http://www.gutenberg.org/wiki/Main_Pa

Hypertexts: Electronic Texts for the Study of
  American Culture
http://xroads.virginia.edu/~HYPER/hypertex.html

Internet Archive of Texts and Documents,
  Hanover College History Department
http://history.hanover.edu/texts.html

Literature Project Sites
http://www.literatureproject.com/site-map.htm

The Universal Digital Library
http://www.ulib.org/

University of Toronto English Library, Authors
  Database
http://www.library.utoronto.ca/utel/indexauthors
  .html

DVD

Assistive Technology: Powerful Solutions for Success. Available from Don Johnston;
  http://www.donjohnston.com/

CHAPTER 23   Rights of Individuals with Dyslexia and Other Disabilities

Organizations

Council of Parent Attorneys and Advocates
Post Office Box 6767
Towson, MD 21285
410-372-0208
http://www.copaa.org

Division for Learning Disabilities (DLD)
The Council for Exceptional Children (CEC)
1110 North Glebe Road
Suite 300
Arlington, VA 22201-5704
888-CEC-SPED
http://www.teachingld.org

The International Dyslexia Association (IDA)
40 York Road, 4th Floor
Baltimore, MD 21204

410-296-0232
http://www.interdys.org

Learning Disabilities Association of America (LDA)
4156 Library Road
Pittsburgh, PA 15234
412-341-1515
http://www.ldanatl.org

National Dissemination Center for Children with Disabilities (NICHCY)
1825 Connecticut Avenue, NW
Suite 700
Washington, DC 20009
800-695-0285
http://www.nichcy.org

Web Sites

Great Schools
http://www.greatschools.org/articles/?topics=190&language=EN

LD online
http://www.ldonline.org

Special Ed e-News
http://www.specialedconnection.com/LrpSecStoryTool/enews.jsp

U.S. Department of Justice, ADA home page
http://www.ada.gov/

Wrightslaw
http://www.wrightslaw.com

Parent Resources

Bateman, B., & Herr, C. (2006). *Writing measurable IEP goals and objectives*. Verona, WI: Attainment.

U.S. Department of Education. (2000). *A guide to the individualized education program*. Retrieved October 19, 2010, from, http://www2.ed.gov/parents/needs/speced/iepguide/index.html

Wright, P., & Wright, P. (2006). *From emotions to advocacy: The special education survival guide*. Hartfield, VA: Harbor House Law Press.

Index

Page numbers followed by *t* indicate tables; those followed by *f* indicate figures.

Abstract concepts
  in the academic setting, 77, 78
  dyslexia and, 580–581
  figurative language, 340–341
  letters, 145, 148
  mapping, 580–581
  reflected in writing, 80–81
  spatial terms, 159, 161
Abstracting text, 568, 569, 572–573, 578
Academic achievement
  adult, 555
  federal legislation on, 697
  phonemic awareness and, 6
  students with dyslexia and, 552–555
  teacher knowledge and, 207–208, 246
  tests of, 447*t*
  unexpected lack of, 211, 430, 446–447
  in urban settings, 376
  see also IQ scores
Accent
  activities in, 225
  awareness of, 101, 225
  choosing placement of, 233–235, 240
  coding, 230, 236
  effect on vowels, 227
  Latin words, 103
  syllable division and, 162–163, 236
  voice recognition technology and, 679
  word meaning and, 257
  see also Syllable patterns
Accommodations, 15
  see also Assistive technology
Accuracy
  case study (Geoffrey), 315–316
  as component of reading, 9*t*, 210
  development of, 306*t*
  multisensory structured language education
    (MSLE) lesson sample, 473*f*–476*f*
  older students and, 300
  proceeding beyond, 293, 295, 304
  process of, 295*f*
  reading/learning disabilities and, 300
  strategies of, 223
Active learning processes
  case sample, 600
  instruction in metacognition and, 31
  overcoming barriers to, 665, 667–668
  questioning for, 592
  through active listening, 375, 483
  through active participation, 469
  through active practice, 311
  see also Comprehension
Activities
  alphabet, 26*f*, 153–163, 165–169
  blending, 217, 222–223
  consonants, 158–159

conversational, 328
dictionary skills, 169–173
letter, 153–165, 155*f*, 162, 163–165, 216
phonemic awareness, 217, 259
phonological awareness, 283
rhymes, 217
semantics, 346–349
sentences, 407–413
sequencing, 151, 156–158, 157*f*, 163–165
spelling, 272, 283–284
syllables, 162–163, 224–225, 227–228, 233
vocabulary, 335–336, 337
vowels, 228
ADA, *see* Americans with Disabilities Act of 1990
  (PL 101-336)
Addition, *see* Mathematics instruction
ADHD, *see* Attention-deficit/hyperactivity
  disorder
Adolescent literacy instruction
  assessment for, 489–493, 492*f*
  content literacy, 508–509, 523–526
  defined, 518–519
  English language learners (ELL) reports, 508,
    529–530
  in fluency, 499–506
  increased attention to, 521–522
  integrating with content, 508–509
  intensity of, 15
  interventions in, 526–529, 542
  literature on, 522*t*
  motivation in, 500, 531–532
  planning model for, 534–545
  policy issues, 534, 535*t*
  professional development and, 533–534
  word-level, 493–499
  see also Literacy
Adolescents
  applying skills, 499–506
  conversational styles, 76–79
  current literacy skills of, 519–520
  development of general language skills,
    506–508
  English language learners (ELL), 624–626
  hesitant to work on basic skills, 493
  self-esteem in, 510–511
  with word-level reading disability, 488–489
  see also High school; Middle school
Adults with dyslexia
  case sample (Evan), 600–603
  case sample (Janet), 594–597
  case sample (Roy), 597–600
  Educational Memories writing sample,
    590–592
  emotional repercussions, 555, 587–589
  evaluation and assessment of, 589–590
  identifying strengths in, 592

Adults with dyslexia—*continued*
  indications of, 14
  literacy skills of, 519–520
  reading interventions and, 15
  treatment goals, 592–594
  see also College students; Dyslexia
Affixes
  Anglo-Saxon morphemes in, 102
  defined, 64, 231
  direct instruction in, 65, 355–356, 567
  Latin words, 95, 103
  multisensory instruction in, 232
  Spanish language, 621
African Americans, 62, 519, 694
Alliteration
  to increase word consciousness, 340
  phonemic awareness and, 117, 126, 129
  phonological processing difficulties and, 61
  in Spanish, 617
Alphabet knowledge
  activities in, 153–163, 165–169
  alphabetizing skills, 175
  biliteracy and, 608
  as component of reading, 9t
  effective instruction in, 151–155
  history of the alphabet, 94
  multisensory structured language education
    (MSLE) lesson sample, 473f–476f
  Spanish and English similarities in, 614, 615f,
    619
  see also Letter identification/recognition
Alphabet mats, 155, 156f, 157, 157f, 160, 615f
Alphabetic principle
  awareness of, 114, 145
  defined, 211
  direct instruction in, 121
  importance of, 9t, 208, 211
  Spanish language and, 607
  spelling development and, 253
Alveolar sounds, 610, 611t–612t
Americans with Disabilities Act of 1990
  (PL 101-336), 688, 695–696
Americans with Disabilities Amendments of 2008
  (PL 110-325), 696–697
Anglo-Saxon language/words
  characteristics of, 97–98, 263
  history of, 94–96
  letter-sound correspondences, 98–101
  morpheme patterns, 102
  sample lesson for, 107–108
  structure of, 97f
  syllable patterns of, 101–102
Anxiety
  adults with dyslexia and, 588, 591, 594
  causing detachment, 298
  reducing, 469, 470, 482, 559
  students with learning disabilities and, 554
  test taking, 583
Arm movement/position, 189–190, 191f, 195f,
  220
Articulation
  consonants, 258, 259t
  diagnostic measures of, 451t
  neural functions for, 11f
  place of, 219

relationship to literacy, 56, 60–61
Spanish language, 611t–612t, 614
speed of, 115f, 116
see also Speech production
Assessment
  of adolescents, 489–493, 492f
  of adults with dyslexia, 589–590
  background knowledge, 388–390, 442
  building on multisensory instruction
    benchmarks, 441–442
  commercial programs, 449t
  comprehension, 442, 447–448, 449t
  consequences of, 454
  defined, 427
  of dyslexia, 12
  fluency, 317–320
  of general academic status, 446–447
  informal reading inventories, 442–443
  literacy planning and, 538–540, 540f
  phonemic awareness, 494
  phonological awareness, 123–125, 127
  response to intervention (RTI) and, 432–433,
    434
  resulting in inappropriate grouping, 544
  sources of data for, 427–429
  for special education eligibility, 433–434
  standardized, 449t
  technology and, 443–444
  types of, 428–429, 532–533
  see also Early intervention; Evaluation;
    Screening
Assistive technology
  decoding, 680f
  executive function, 608f
  handwriting, 201–203
  journals in, 662
  matching to student, 662–663
  principles in using, 681
  reading, 339, 507–508, 660–661, 664–667, 677t
  rejection of by student, 664
  remediation and compensation with,
    663–664
  research on, 659–662
  resources for, 661–662
  response to intervention (RTI) and, 658
  sophistication of, 658
  study skills, 667–671
  in the universal design framework, 657
  using effectively, 663–664
  writing process, 659, 671–681, 673t
  see also Accommodations
Attention-deficit/hyperactivity disorder (ADHD)
  dyslexia and, 13
  evaluation of, 452–453, 452t
  executive function and, 550
  explicit instruction and, 39–40
Automaticity
  fluency and, 295–296, 503
  handwriting skills and, 181, 197, 575
  in keyboarding, 201–202
  in letter identification, 150, 153, 174
  process of, 295f
  reading/learning disabilities and, 300
  teaching to, 18, 18f, 19t, 153
  in word recognition, 210, 493–494

Background knowledge
  assessment in, 388–390, 442
  development of, 506–508
  English language learners (ELL), 510, 625
  reading comprehension and, 369–370
  student interests and, 503
Bilabial sounds, 609, 611t–612t
Bilingualism, 62, 607
Biliteracy, 607, 608, 626–627, 628f
Blending
  activities in, 217, 222–223
  assessment in, 124
  instruction for older students, 495–497
  introduction to, 213
  phonemic awareness and, 118
Blocked sounds, 26f, 213, 219, 221, 259t
Brain
  activation patterns in, 34, 35, 121
  executive function and, 550
  injuries to, 27–28, 29t
  learning processes in, 31
  multisensory design of, 35–36
  processing reading, 33–34
  see also Neural systems

Caucasians, 519, 606, 624
Chunking, 568, 667
Classroom management
  checklist for, 486
  environment and behavior, 481–482
  for older students, 508–509
  physical space, 478–479
  rules in, 481–482
  teacher space in, 480–481
Closed syllables
  instruction in, 101, 214t, 226–227, 226t, 497
  Spanish language, 609, 610t
  see also Syllables
Cloze technique, 69, 227, 565
Coarticulation, 57, 118, 218, 222
Coding, 220, 226–231, 236, 573
Cognates, 330, 331t, 343, 510, 613, 622
Cognition, 31–33, 450–452, 607
College students
  dyslexia and, 61
  note-taking skills, 181
  success of, 519–520, 523, 545
  see also Adults with dyslexia
Combining forms, 104, 111–112, 232, 239–240
Composition
  drafting, 422
  instruction in, 405–407
  multisensory structured language education
    (MSLE) lesson sample, 473f–476f
  need for explicit instruction in, 425
  planning and outlining activities, 415–422
  revising and editing, 423–425
  sentence activities for, 407–413
  types of, 413–414
  see also Paragraphs; Writing
Comprehension
  assessment of, 442, 447–448, 449t
  assistive technology for, 507–508, 660–661,
    664–667, 677t

  background knowledge and, 369–370
  checklist for, 63f–64f
  as component of reading, 8, 9t
  decoding and, 20
  detaching from, 298
  dyslexia and, 368, 370
  executive function and, 83–84
  exposure to text and, 506–508
  factors affecting, 365
  fluency and, 7, 244–245, 297–298
  impairment of, 33, 52
  monitoring for, 374, 375–376
  morphological awareness and, 67
  of online information, 399
  prosody and, 297–298
  semantic disabilities and, 73–75
  sources of difficulties in, 368–369
  strategies for, 366–368, 373–374
  syntax knowledge and, 69
  upcoming challenges in, 398–399
  vocabulary and, 7–8, 72–73, 325
  see also Active learning processes
Comprehension instruction
  in the content class, 524–525, 541–542
  for English language learners (ELL), 530
  experimental, 396–398
  graphic and semantic organizers for, 381–385
  history of, 366
  importance of, 400
  listening skills for, 370–371
  multisensory structured language education
    (MSLE) lesson sample, 473f–476f
  planning for, 370
  questioning for, 385–392
  rapid word naming and, 243
  repeated reading and, 505
  research on, 31–32, 374–375
  at sentence level, 371–373
  Skills for Organizing and Reading Efficiently
    (SkORE) system and, 578–579
  story structure in, 375, 392, 393f, 394f
  students goal of, 78–79, 369
  summarization in, 392, 394–395
  systematic phonics and, 7
  technology and, 398
  through cooperative learning in, 376–381
  using multiple strategies in, 395–396
  see also Instruction
Concept mapping
  example of, 349f, 582f
  Inspiration text reader, 670f
  for new words, 349, 350f
  Skills for Organizing and Reading Efficiently
    (SkORE) system and, 580–581
  technology in, 660
  see also Mapping
Consonant blends/clusters, 98–99, 213t, 234
Consonant digraphs
  coding of, 220
  defined, 98–99, 213t, 217
  syllable division and, 233, 234
Consonant prefix/suffix, 231–232
Consonants
  activities, 158–159
  Anglo-Saxon forms of, 98

Consonants—*continued*
    articulation of, 57, 59*t*, 258, 259*t*
    defined, 98–99, 99*t*, 213*t*
    doubling rules for, 276–277, 279
    Greek words, 104
    phonemic awareness and, 119
    sounds of, 219, 494, 495*f*
    sound-to-spelling translations, 261*t*
    Spanish language, 608, 611*t*–612*t*
    syllable division and, 236
    using in the decoding process, 213*t*
Consonant–vowel patterns, 233–236
Contextual clues, 209, 210, 252, 342, 353–354
Controlled decodable text, 500–502, 502*f*
Counting boards activities, 634–636, 634*f*
Criterion-referenced tests, 428, 429, 443
Cue cards, 311, 312*f*, 570–571
Curriculum-referenced tests, 428, 429
Curriculum-based measures, 432–433, 434
Cursive handwriting
    approach strokes, 194*f*, 195*f*, 196*f*, 197*f*
    history of, 182
    letter forms, 193*f*
    multisensory instruction in, 186, 196–197
    see also Handwriting instruction

Daily lesson plans, 471–477
Data collection, 428–429
Decodable text, 238, 502–506, 505*f*
Decoding
    assistive technology for, 680*f*
    compared to spelling, 252, 260
    as component of reading, 9*t*, 73
    dyslexia and, 211
    impairment of, 11, 33
    individual letters, 146
    instruction in, 211–212
    language comprehension, 208
    morphological awareness and, 65
    multisensory instruction in, 212–215
    National Institute for Literacy on, 528
    older students and, 488
    reading comprehension and, 20
    strategies of, 208–211
    teacher knowledge of, 246
    word origin/structure and, 96–97
    see also Comprehension; Reading;
        Sound–symbol correspondences
Development
    fluency, 302–303, 306*t*
    influence of caregivers on, 327
    keyboarding and, 201
    metalinguistics, 81–82
    morphological, 65–66
    phonemic awareness, 116–119
    phonological, 60
    pragmatics, 76–78
    semantics, 71–73
    syntactic, 67–70
    vocabulary, 325–329
    working memory vital to, 83
Diagnostic assessment, *see* Assessment
Dictation, 272–276, 275*f*, 283–284
Dictionaries

electronic, 507
    in independent reading, 352–353
    number of words in, 342
    online, 353
    recommended, 558
    in word prediction software, 678
Dictionary skills instruction
    activities for, 169–173
    games for, 173–174
    multisensory structured language education
        (MSLE) lesson sample, 473*f*–476*f*
    pronunciation symbols, 99*t*, 100*t*
Digraphs, *see* Consonant digraphs; Vowel
    digraphs
Diphthongs, 100, 220, 234, 614–615, 615*t*
Direct instruction
    defined, 19*t*, 463
    figurative language, 582–583
    handwriting, 183
    individual words, 342
    reading components, 17–19
Dysarthia, 60
Dysfluent reading, 208
Dysgraphia, 182–183
Dyslexia
    academic achievement and, 552–555
    in adults, 14, 61
    anxiety and, 588, 591, 594
    attention disorders and, 13
    automatic letter reading, 150
    case study (Andy), 315
    common signs of, 10–12, 444–445
    comprehension and, 368, 370
    decoding and, 211
    defined, 10, 12, 255, 444–445
    diagnosis of, 120–123
    English language learners (ELL) with, 10
    under federal law, 697
    fluency and, 300–302
    handwriting and, 182–183, 202
    instruction for students with, 15–19, 19*t*, 464,
        465*t*
    issues in defining, 454, 690
    memory training and, 567–568
    morphological awareness training and, 67
    neural systems and, 11, 11*f*, 20–21, 567
    patterns in, 448
    phonemic awareness and, 6, 120
    phonological awareness and, 61, 120–121, 211
    Quick Tricks strategies, 561–567
    read-alouds and, 336
    research on, 9, 11–14
    risk factors for, 10, 20
    speech production and, 61
    spelling and, 12, 255, 275, 280, 282–286
    strengths of students with, 511, 512*f*
    structure for students with, 556–557
    successful writers with, 575
    working with students with, 555–556
    see also Adults with dyslexia
Dyspraxia, 61

Early intervention
    changing the way the brain learns, 20–21

checklist for, 63f–64f
  for dyslexia, 15
  for fluency and accuracy, 301–302
  importance of, 20
  in letter recognition, 152
  rationale for, 436–437
  screening instruments for, 437–440
  see also Assessment
Editing, 423–425
Education
  historical perspective of, 686
  multisensory approach to, 28
  in multisensory strategies, 26–27, 44–47
  neuroscience research in, 37
  principles from research in, 38–39
  statistics in, 519–520
  see also Professional development; Teacher
    knowledge
Education for All Handicapped Children Act
    (PL 94-142), 429, 687, 695
Education of the Handicapped Act Amendments
    (EHA) of 1974 (PL 93-380), 687, 688–689
Education of the Handicapped Act Amendments
    of 1990 (PL 101-476), 687
Education of the Handicapped Act of 1970
    (PL 91-230), 429
EHA, *see* Education of the Handicapped Act
    Amendments of 1974 (PL 93-380)
Elementary and Secondary Education Act (ESEA)
    of 1965 (PL 89-10), 686
Elkonin boxes, 128–129
ELL, *see* English language learners
Engagement, *see* Motivation
English language
  growth of, 342–343
  history of, 94–96, 95t
  layers of, 263, 354–355
  regularity of, 241, 252, 288
  rules in, 260
  similarities to Spanish, 607, 614–615
  see also Orthography
English language learners (ELL)
  adolescent, 508, 529–530, 624–626
  background knowledge of, 510, 625
  comprehension instruction for, 530
  cooperative learning and, 376
  demographics of, 605–606
  dyslexia and, 10
  figurative language and, 340–341
  instruction of, 509–510
  literacy instruction for, 62, 529–530
  response to intervention (RTI) and, 606–607
  vocabulary instruction for, 330–331, 343, 346,
    625–626
Enriched texts, 500, 503, 504f, 506–507
Environment, classroom, 433–434, 481–482, 484,
    486
ESEA, *see* Elementary and Secondary Education
    Act of 1965 (PL 89-10)
Etymology, 281, 352, 355, 613
  see also Word origins
Evaluation
  based on dyslexia definition, 444–445
  in cognitive and language status, 450–452,
    452t

comprehensive individual, 444–445
  family, health and development history for,
    445–446
  general academic status for, 446–447, 447t
  in reading, spelling and writing skills, 447–448,
    449t, 450
  in social-emotional status and attention,
    452–453
  using findings of, 453
  see also Assessment; Screening
Evidence-based intervention, *see* Interventions
Evidence-based research, *see* Research
Executive function
  addressed by Skills for Organizing and Reading
    Efficiently (SkORE), 556
  assistive technology for, 680f
  deficits in, 553–554
  disorders in, 549–551
  literacy and, 82–84
  tasks dependent on, 551, 553, 600–601
  writing and, 405–406, 672
Explicit instruction
  in context clues, 354
  defined, 463
  for English language learners (ELL), 509–510,
    530
  in frequently used prefixes, 499
  in letter recognition, 145–146
  in morphology, 65–66, 355–356
  in multisensory structured language education
    (MSLE) lessons, 472
  in reading components, 17–19, 18f, 19t, 20
  in study skills, 556
  in vocabulary, 343
Expressiveness, *see* Prosody

Federal legislation
  abbreviations in, 687t
  on academic achievement, 697
  on funding for education, 686
  history of, 686–687
  protections under, 688–689
  provisions under, 687–688
  regulations on special education eligibility, 444
Figurative language, 61, 71, 340–341, 582–583
Final sounds, 159–160, 265
Final stable syllables, 230, 609, 610t
Finger agnosia, 183, 187
Finger-point reading, 126–127, 274
Finger-tapping, 223, 496–497
First grade
  development of fluency, 306t
  dyslexia risk factors seen in, 20
  handwriting in, 180, 192
  letter naming speed in, 150–151
  oral reading rate in, 245, 317t, 437
  phonics instruction in, 6–7
  reading demands in, 306t
  reading disabilities checklist for, 63f
  spelling in, 125, 126, 264
  vocabulary in, 6–7, 72
  word knowledge in, 325
  word recognition in, 201
  writing in, 185

Floss rule, 276–277, 279
Fluency
    assessment of, 317–320
    assistive technology and, 661
    as component of reading, 9t
    comprehension and, 297–298
    defined, 7, 293–296, 296f
    development of, 295, 302–303, 306t
    estimating rate of, 245, 294, 317t, 441
    history of, 295–296
    importance of, 296
    instruction in, 300–310
    lack of, 298–300, 299f
    learning disabilities and, 300–302
    morphological awareness and, 65
    see also Linguistic complexity
Fluency instruction
    active practice for, 311, 312f
    benchmark scores in, 518
    case studies in, 315–316
    continuous text, 308–310
    goals of, 297, 500
    instruction in, 308f
    in linguistic complexities, 303, 304t
    morphological awareness, 307
    multisensory structured language education
        (MSLE) lesson sample, 473f–476f
    National Institute for Literacy on, 528
    for older students, 499–506
    overview of, 312t
    phrase work, 307
    process of, 295f
    reading comprehension and, 244–246
    sample lesson for, 305t
    syntax knowledge and, 69
    word work, 303
    see also Instruction
FMRI, see Functional magnetic resonance imaging
Formative assessment, 440-442, 532, 538
Formative data collection, 428–429
Four-Part Processing Model for Word
    Recognition, 322–324
Fourth-grade
    comprehension instruction in, 366
    increased reading demands in, 73, 96, 298–299,
        303, 306t
    National Assessment of Educational Progress
        (NAEP) reading scores, 5, 299, 299f, 487
    slump, 299
Fricatives, 57, 59t, 219, 609–610, 611t–612t
Functional magnetic resonance imaging (fMRI),
    15, 21, 33, 34, 121
Funding, 37, 124, 521, 545–546, 695

Games
    alphabet knowledge, 163–165
    dictionary skills, 173–174
    to increase phonemic awareness, 129
    letters, 163–165
    mathematics, 635–636, 639, 644–645, 649–651
Geometric progression, 566–567, 567f, 581–582,
    583f
Glides, 57, 59t, 611t–612t

Glottal sounds, 611t–612t
Grammar
    comprehension skills and, 371
    computers and, 202
    explicit instruction in, 10t
    sentence activities for, 411–412
    Spanish language, 613–614
    teaching with sentence combining, 411
Graphemes, 98–99, 99t, 100t
Graphic organizers, 375, 381–385, 658
    see also Organization
Graphomotor skills, 54, 677t
Greek language/words
    characteristics of, 263
    combining forms, 239–240
    history of, 94–96
    letter-sound correspondences in, 104
    morpheme patterns in, 104–105
    overview of, 104
    sample lesson for, 111–112
    scientific terms of, 104, 264
    structure of, 97f
    syllable patterns in, 104
Grouping, see Small groups
Guided discovery teaching, 152–153, 220–222,
    271–276, 468

Handwriting instruction
    automaticity in older students, 181, 197, 575
    bypass technology, 201–203
    as component of reading, 9t
    development of, 180, 184–185
    dyslexia and, 182–183, 202
    history of, 182
    implements for, 189–190
    importance of, 179–181, 204
    multisensory structured language education
        (MSLE) lesson sample, 473f–476f
    multisensory, 186, 191–192
    pencil grip, 187–188, 188f
    posture, 187
    punctuation, 200–201
    research on, 180
    sample lesson for, 197–200
    syndromes related to, 182–183
    Watch Our Writing (W.O.W.), 191f
    see also Cursive handwriting; Instruction; Letter
        formation; Manuscript print
High school
    differing academic abilities in, 544
    English language learners (ELL) entering system
        in, 624–625
    graduation rates, 519–520
    importance of morphological awareness in, 65,
        355, 499
    importance of syntax knowledge in, 68
    lexicon size of graduates, 325, 360
    literacy skills of students in, 519, 522t
    in urban settings, 487–488
    see also Adolescents
High-functioning dyslexic adults, see Adults with
    dyslexia
Hispanics, 62, 519, 605, 608, 624

IDEA, *see* Individuals with Disabilities Education Act Amendments of 1997 (PL 105-17); Individuals with Disabilities Education Improvement Act of 2004 (PL 108-446)
Idioms
    exploring, 340, 341, 582–583
    linguistic complexity of, 303
    semantic knowledge for, 74, 80, 580
IEP, *see* Individualized education program
Independent reading, 338–339, 370, 499
Individualized education program (IEP), 453, 662, 689, 692
Individuals with Disabilities Education Act (IDEA) Amendments of 1997 (PL 105-17), 693
Individuals with Disabilities Education Improvement Act (IDEA) of 2004 (PL 108-446)
    classifications of children with disabilities, 688t
    determining eligibility under, 444
    dyslexia diagnosis under, 122
    as an enabling legislation, 689–690
    on English language learners (ELL), 606
    notetaking under, 577
    overview of, 687, 689–690
    procedural safeguards under, 691
    reauthorizations of, 693–695
    referrals under, 690–691
    on the role of instruction, 459
    specific learning disability under, 430
    technology and, 658
Initial sounds, 159–160, 265
Instruction
    brain patterns and, 35
    elements of effective, 17
    evidence-based, 14–19
    importance of, 12, 13f
    improving, 1–2
    individualization of, 174–175
    intensity of, 17–19, 463
    principles of, 18, 19t
    reports on, 522–526
    style of discourse in, 76–79
    systematic, 463–464
    unsubstantiated practices in, 38
    see also Comprehension instruction; Fluency instruction; Handwriting instruction; Spelling instruction; Vocabulary instruction
Intelligence, *see* IQ scores
Intent, author
    comprehension and, 79, 80
    linguistic complexity of, 303
    "queries," 386–387, 390–391
    vocabulary selection, 348
Interactions
    language learning and, 326–328
    student–teacher, 481, 482–483, 484, 486
International Phonetic Alphabet, 98, 99t, 100t
Interventions
    consequences of delaying, 436–437
    for English language learners (ELL), 530, 606–607
    evidence-based, 36–39, 434–435
    literacy planning and, 542
    for older students, 489

problem-solving, 435
    for struggling adolescents, 526–529, 542
    see also Early intervention; Response to intervention (RTI)
Intonation, 54, 55, 56, 80, 246, 528
Invented spelling, 118, 125, 126, 243, 264
IQ scores
    achievement and, 20
    dyslexia and, 14, 120, 211
    spelling ability and, 256
    tests for, 447t
    see also Academic achievement
Irregular words, 241–243, 280–282

Key words
    defined, 219–220
    as a memory device, 568
    in note taking, 578
    Spanish language, 620t, 621f
    in vocabulary acquisition, 351
    see also Learning strategies
Keys to Literacy Planning Model (Sedita, 2004, 2009)
    assessment planning, 538–539, 540f
    establishing a planning team, 536–538
    instruction in the content class, 541–542
    interventions for struggling readers, 542
    overview of, 535–536, 537f
    professional development planning, 544–545
    scheduling, 543–544
    see also Literacy
Kindergarten
    development of fluency, 306t
    handwriting instruction in, 180
    invented spelling, 125, 126
    phonics instruction in, 6–7
    reading demands in, 306t
    reading disabilities checklist for, 63f
    response to intervention (RTI) assessment in, 122
    risk factors seen in, 20
    screening in, 437, 438–439
    vocabulary acquisition and, 72
    word knowledge in as predictor, 325
    writing development in, 185
Kinesthetic awareness, 192, 218, 620, 626t
Kinesthetic memory, 26, 181, 186, 565

Language
    acquisition of, 67, 325–331
    biliteracy and, 607–608
    defined, 50–51
    diagnostic measures of, 450–452, 451t
    number concepts and, 634–635
    origins of, 94–96
    reciprocity of with literacy, 51–52
    role in forming concepts, 633
Language arts curriculum, 302, 490, 492f, 519, 523, 543
Language components
    learning a second language and, 607–608
    metalinguistics, 81–82
    morphology, 64–67

Language components—*continued*
  overview of, 55*f*
  phonology, 55–64
  pragmatics, 75–81
  semantics, 70–75
  syntax, 67–70
Language comprehension, 208, 324, 324*f*
Language content, *see* Semantics
Language development, *see* Development
Language disabilities
  as barrier to writing, 672
  dictionary use and, 352
  English language learners (ELL) and, 62
  figurative language and, 340–341
  morphological disorders and, 66–67
  phonological disorders and, 60–62
  pragmatic disorders and, 80–81
  syntactic disorders and, 69–70
  using context clues and, 354
  vocabulary instruction for, 346
Latin language/words
  characteristics of, 102, 263
  common roots, 239
  history of, 94–96
  letter–sound correspondences, 102–103
  morpheme patterns in, 103–104
  sample lesson for, 109–110
  structure of, 97*f*
  syllable patterns in, 103
Learning disabilities
  defined, 10
  fluency and, 300–302
  handwriting and, 185
  key instructional components for, 464, 465*t*
  mathematics instruction and, 632
  perceived stigma behind, 595
  vocabulary and, 330
Learning environments, 433–434, 436, 478, 664
Learning strategies
  active, 31–32
  cognitive, 8
  comprehension monitoring, 375–376
  cooperative learning, 376–379
  decoding, 208–211
  developing listening skills, 370–371
  graphic and semantic organizers, 381–385
  for longer texts, 373–374
  multiple, 395–398
  multisensory, 370
  peer-assisted, 379–381
  questioning, 385–391
  RAP Paraphrasing Strategy, 394
  research-based, 374–375
  sentence level, 371–373
  STORE strategy, 392, 394*f*
  story structure, 392
  summarization, 392–395
  training in, 551
  used by good readers, 367–368, 367*t*
  using with assistive technology, 658, 661, 663
  see also Key words; Mnemonic devices; Skills
    for Organizing and Reading Efficiently
    (SkORE)
Least restrictive environment (LRE), 687, 688,
  689
Lesson plans

  daily reading, 239*f*
  multisensory structured language education
    (MSLE) sample, 464–465, 473*f*–475*f*
  pacing of, 469, 477
  sample in handwriting instruction, 198–200
  spelling for the classroom, 285–287
Letter clusters, 146, 221–222
Letter formation
  cursive, 193*f*
  dysgraphia and, 182
  instruction in, 191–201
  lack of recall of, 181
  manuscript print, 192*f*
  reducing size of, 189, 203
  see also Handwriting instruction
Letter identification/recognition
  activities/games in, 155*f*, 156–165
  automaticity in, 150, 153, 174
  challenges of, 175
  as component of reading, 9*t*
  errors in, 148–149, 223
  importance of, 209, 216
  instruction in, 151–153, 218–222
  matching mat for, 156*f*
  for phonemic awareness, 117
  role of in reading process, 145–146
  see also Alphabet knowledge
Letter patterns
  acknowledging student progress in, 287
  child awareness of, 254
  exceptions to, 269
  guided discovery teaching and, 271–276
  importance of, 260
  instruction in, 269–272
  multiple, 265–270
  sensitivity to, 254–255, 264
Letter shapes
  cursive, 184
  impairment in knowledge of, 183
  importance of, 9*t*
  instruction in, 152, 155, 175, 186
  kinesthetic awareness of, 218
  learning of, 147
  printing, 192, 192*f*
  ready reference to, 187
  reinforced through writing, 181, 192, 197
  size of, 189, 203
  upper-case, 151
  see also Sky writing
Letter-name knowledge
  activities for, 156–158, 163–165
  challenges of, 147, 175
  importance of, 9*t*, 146–148, 216
  instruction in, 151
  for irregular words, 280
  multiple factors in, 174
  predicting reading achievement, 148, 149–151
  simultaneous oral spelling (S.O.S.) approach,
    274
  speed in, 149–151, 211, 244
Letters
  introduction of, 473*f*–476*f*
  procedure for introducing, 221–222
  rarely doubled, 277
  reversals in, 148–149, 182, 185, 255
  transpositions of, 148–149, 255

Letter–sound correspondences
  Anglo-Saxon, 98–101, 99*t*, 100*t*
  awareness of, 146–148
  coding for, 220
  dyslexia and, 11
  Greek, 104
  handwriting skills and, 197
  importance of understanding, 146–148
  instruction in, 147, 221–222
  Latin, 102–103
  for older students, 494–495
  origins of, 97*f*
  sample lesson for, 107–108
  Spanish, 619–620, 620*t*
Lexicons
  geometric progression, 581–582, 583*f*
  importance of, 331
  memory storage of, 209
  personal, 71
  size of, 325
  in the written language, 54
Linguistic complexity, 119, 302–303, 304*t*, 305*t*,
    306*t*
  see also Fluency
Linguistic processes, 49, 251, 298, 300, 306
Lip position
  awareness of, 218
  in decoding instruction, 219
  simultaneous oral spelling (S.O.S.) approach,
    273
  Spanish language, 609
  vowel and consonant sounds, 158, 259*t*
Liquids, 57, 59*t*, 611*t*–612*t*
Listening skills
  compared to written language skills, 49
  comprehension and, 368, 370–371
  learning disabilities and, 330, 339
  multisensory structured language education
    (MSLE) lesson sample, 473*f*–476*f*
  natural development of, 50
  screen readers and, 507–508
Literacy
  adult and adolescent skills in, 519–520
  drop-out rates and, 512
  importance of early activities in, 20
  importance of morphology to, 65
  Internet skills and, 399
  learning a second language and, 607–608
  morphological disorders and, 66–67
  phonological disorders and, 60–62, 63*f*–64*f*
  planning for with older students, 492*f*
  pragmatic disorders and, 78–81
  reciprocity of with language learning, 51–52
  semantic disorders and, 73–75
  spotlight on, 1–2
  statistics, 519–520
  supporting interventions in, 491
  syntactic disorders and, 69–70
  working memory vital to, 83
  see also Adolescent literacy instruction; Keys to
    Literacy Planning Model (Sedita, 2004, 2009)
Lowercase letters
  activities, 156–158, 162, 163
  approach strokes, 197*f*
  cursive, 194*f*, 195*f*, 196*f*
  handwriting and, 190
  instruction in, 151
  manuscript print, 192*f*
LRE, *see* Least restrictive environment

Manuscript print, 184, 186, 192–196, 192*f*, 193*f*
  see also Handwriting instruction
Mapping
  abstract concepts, 580–581
  character, 381*f*
  fast, 326
  mind maps, 570, 573, 574
  multiple meanings, 580, 581*f*
  related features, 580, 581*f*
  story, 392, 393*f*
  visual, 673–677, 673*t*, 675*f*
  word structure, 382*f*
  see also Concept mapping; Semantic mapping
Mathematics instruction
  addition and subtraction, 637–640
  computers and, 654
  developing number sense, 636–637
  division, 651–654
  exploring number concepts, 634–636
  games in, 635, 639, 644–645, 649–651
  introduction to word problems, 637
  multiplication, 648–651
  number boxes, 637–640
  teen numbers, 641–648
  word problems, 640–641
  see also Structural Arithmetic method
Maturation
  comprehension difficulties and, 368
  dyslexia and, 14, 15
  fluency and, 306*t*
  semantics and, 71
  sentence complexity and, 68
  in use of pragmatics, 77
  writing and, 185
Medial sounds, 118, 159–160, 265
Memory
  deficits in, 554
  establishing spelling patterns in, 269
  graphic organizers and, 382
  importance of to literacy, 82–84
  kinesthetic, 26, 181, 186, 565
  long-term, 82
  multisensory teaching and, 39–40, 152, 464
  neural systems and, 39–40
  orthographic, 209, 227, 241, 255
  spelling unfamiliar words and, 252
  training in, 567–568
  verbal short-term, 63*f*–64*f*, 115*t*, 116
  visual, 186
  see also Working memory
Memory devices, *see* Key words; Mnemonic
    devices
Meta-analysis, *see* National Reading Panel (NRP)
Metacognition
  defined, 8, 584
  executive function and, 82–84, 550
  helping students use, 497
  instruction in, 31
Metacognitive strategy, 113, 368
Metalinguistics, 49, 52–53, 81–82
Metaphors, 74, 80, 340, 580, 582–583

Middle school
  collaborative strategic reading in, 377
  English language learners (ELL) entering,
    624–625, 626
  executive function deficits in, 553
  importance of morphological awareness in, 65,
    66
  interests in reading, 511
  literacy skills of students in, 519, 522t
  word lists for, 344
  see also Adolescents
Mnemonic devices
  comprehension and, 375
  creating own, 31
  floss rule, 277
  key words, 351
  overview of, 567–568
  rabbit rule, 277
  Skills for Organizing and Reading Efficiently
    (SkORE) system, 574
  STORE strategy, 392, 394f
  see also Learning strategies
Modeling
  comprehension skills, 370
  for fluency, 308f
  peer, 379
  questioning, 386
  reading comprehension and, 8
  ReQuest technique, 391
Morpheme patterns, 96, 102, 103–105, 209
Morphemes
  derivational, 64, 66, 102, 231
  free, 64, 231
  grammatical, 64
  inflectional, 64, 102, 263
  instruction in, 355–356
  lexical, 64
  origins of, 97f
  Spanish language, 612–613
  structural analysis and, 238–241
Morphological awareness, 65, 67, 307, 355, 499
Morphology
  biliteracy and, 607–608
  in the content class, 525
  development of, 65–66
  for independent reading, 354–359
  instruction in, 18f, 499
  literacy and, 66–67
  multisensory structured language education
    (MSLE) lesson sample, 473f–476f
  overview of, 19t, 64–65, 231–232
  Spanish, 612–613
  spelling and, 262–263
  teacher knowledge of, 45–46
  word work in, 305–306
Motivation
  adolescent, 500, 531–532
  assistive technology and, 661
  executive function and, 553
  for handwriting instruction, 190–191
  noncontrolled decodable text and, 502
  reading failure and, 510–511
Motor skills
  in handwriting, 9t, 180–181, 183, 185
  in keyboarding, 201
  tactile/kinesthetic methods, 28

Mouth position
  accented syllables, 162–163
  awareness of, 218, 254, 258
  in decoding instruction, 219
  pictures of, 134
  simultaneous oral spelling (S.O.S.) approach,
    273–274, 273f
  Spanish language, 609, 610t
  visual display of, 271
  vowel and consonant sounds, 158–159, 258f,
    259t
Multiplication, 648–651
Multisensory structured language education
    (MSLE)
  of affixes, 232
  assessing progress of, 441–442
  checklist for, 486
  classroom environment, 477–479, 484
  comprehension, 370
  content of, 27
  context for, 460
  daily lesson plans, 473f–476f
  decoding, 212–215
  features of, 461–462
  finding opportunities for, 466
  formats for, 471–477
  handwriting, 186–191, 196–197
  history of, 27–28, 460–461
  in the language components of Spanish,
    615–624
  learning teaching strategies for, 26–27, 44–47
  letters, 152, 175, 191–201
  mathematics, 632–633
  neuroscience insights into, 33–39
  overview of, 17, 18f, 25–26
  principles behind, 462
  programs for, 17, 27, 29t–30t
  research and rationale of, 463–464
  strategies of, 26–27, 44–47
  student benefits from, 466t, 469–471
  student–teacher connection in, 482–483
  as support for teachers, 484
  teacher benefits from, 464–469, 466t
  teacher organization, 480–481
Multisyllabic words, 60t, 303, 497

NAEP, see National Assessment of Educational
    Progress
Nasal consonants, 57, 59t, 219, 227, 259t,
    611t–612t
National Assessment of Educational Progress
    (NAEP) on
  English language learners (ELL), 606
  fluency, 298–299, 299f
  older students, 487
  prosody, 500
  reading scores, 5
National Reading Panel (NRP)
  on components of reading, 5–8, 518
  on comprehension instruction, 374–375,
    390–392, 395, 541–542
  on decoding, 212
  on fluency, 299–300, 500
  meta-analysis by, 3
  on phonemic awareness, 122

on professional development, 544
recommendations of, 139
research by, 4–5, 129–131, 298, 299–300
on silent reading, 500
on technology, 359
on vocabulary, 321, 333
see also Research
Neural systems
dyslexia and, 11, 11*f*, 20–21, 567
executive function and, 550
Four-Part Processing Model for Word
    Recognition and, 322–324, 322*f*
memory and, 39–40
multisensory instruction and, 33–39
plasticity of, 15, 20
see also Brain
No Child Left Behind Act of 2001 (PL 107-110)
challenges of, 62
English language learners (ELL), 606
financial awards from, 374
Reading First initiative, 5
results of, 1
science-based literacy instruction, 517
on technology, 658
Norm-referenced tests, 428, 429, 448
Notetaking
assistive technology for, 508
in fiction, 576–577
from lectures, 577–578
smart pens, 202
in text-to-speech programs, 665, 668–670, 669*f*,
    670*f*
NRP, *see* National Reading Panel
Number boxes, 637–640, 638*f*, 641–645, 641*f*
Number concepts, 631, 634–635, 636–637

Older students, *see* Adolescents; Adults with
    dyslexia
Open syllables
activities, 227–228
defined, 101
division of, 234
examples, 214*t*, 226*t*
rules, 104
Spanish language, 609, 610*t*
see also Syllables
Oral language
compared with instructional language, 79*t*
as component of reading, 9*t*
diagnostic measures of, 451*t*
early activities in, 20
multisensory structured language education
    (MSLE) lesson sample, 473*f*–476*f*
natural learning of, 50, 56
parallels to reading, 80
parents providing for child, 326–328
play in, 9*t*
processing functions of, 115*f*
relationship to reading, 49–50, 208–209
requirements to understanding, 52
syntactic difficulties and, 70
vocabulary acquisition and, 329, 333–334
written language and, 51–54
Oral reading
assessment of, 317–320

diagnostic measures of, 449*t*
to enhance fluency, 245
formative assessment in, 440–441
measuring rate of, 245, 294, 317*t*, 441
progress monitoring in, 318*t*
prosody and, 245–246
of student writing, 424–425
Organization
assistive technology for, 675*f*
binders, 557–558
of classroom space, 478–479, 486
dyslexia and, 556–557
space, 558–559
teacher, 480–481, 486
time management, 559–560
see also Graphic organizers
Orthographic knowledge, 217–218
Orthographic memory, 209, 227, 241, 255
Orthographic patterns, 209, 212, 217–218, 254
Orthography
accuracy of English, 9*t*
attempts at changes to, 264
defined, 93
history of, 94–96
instruction for older students, 498–499
processing difficulties in, 255
relationship to handwriting, 181
of Spanish, 608–612
Spanish language, 611
spelling and, 252, 260–262
see also English language
Orton-Gillingham approaches, 27, 202, 460–461
Outlines, 415–422, 576, 669*f*

Paragraphs, 379, 380–381, 380*f*, 413–415, 593
see also Composition
Pencil grip, 183, 187–188, 188*f*
Percentiles
independent reading and, 338, 338*t*, 499
intensity of instruction and, 131, 302
older students, 487
oral reading fluency, 317, 318, 320*f*
of teacher knowledge, 246
urban school settings and, 487–488
Phonemes
defined, 113
phonology and, 56–57
segmentation of, 20, 216–217, 451*t*, 496
Spanish language, 608, 611, 614, 618
Phonemic awareness
acquisition age for, 60*t*
assessment of, 494
assistive technology and, 661
biliteracy and, 608
as component of reading, 5–6, 9*t*
defined, 113–114, 216–217
difficulties in, 11
dyslexia and, 6, 120
early reading and, 116–119
factors influencing, 119–120
importance of, 208, 209
instruction in, 129–138
multisensory structured language education
    (MSLE) lesson sample, 473*f*–476*f*
for older students, 494–495

Phonemic awareness—*continued*
  overview of, 5–6
  processing abilities and, 115*f*
  research on, 128–130
  spelling and, 258–260, 282
Phonetics, 256–257
Phonics
  assistive technology and, 661
  as component of reading, 6–7, 9*t*
  instruction in, 32–33
  older students and, 492
  overview of, 6–7
  phonemic awareness and, 114
  spelling and, 257
Phonological awareness
  activities for, 283
  assessment in, 123–125
  biliteracy and, 608
  checklist for, 63*f*–64*f*
  defined, 19*t*, 114–115, 216
  difficulties in, 11, 255–256
  dyslexia and, 61, 120–121, 211
  formal assessment, 127
  importance of, 61–62, 209
  instruction in, 18*f*
  literacy and, 60–61
  metalinguistic development and, 81–82
  morphological awareness and, 67
  multisensory structured language education
    (MSLE) lesson sample, 473*f*–476*f*
  observing classroom indicators, 125–127
  as predictor for later reading performance, 323
  processing difficulties in, 255–256
  relationship to processing abilities, 115*f*
  in Spanish, 616–617
  spelling and, 255
  vocabulary and, 323–324
Phonological processing, 114–115, 115*f*, 445,
    451*t*
Phonology
  biliteracy and, 607–608
  defined, 19*t*
  development of, 60, 60*t*
  instruction in, 18*f*
  literacy and, 56, 60–62, 63*f*–64*f*
  overview of, 55–59
  rules of, 58–59
  of Spanish, 608–612
  for spelling, 257
  teacher knowledge of, 44
PL 89-10, *see* Elementary and Secondary
    Education Act
PL 91-230, *see* Education of the Handicapped Act
    of 1970
PL 93-112, *see* Rehabilitation Act of 1973
PL 93-380, *see* Education of the Handicapped Act
    Amendments of 1974
PL 94-142, *see* Education for All Handicapped
    Children Act
PL 101-336, *see* Americans with Disabilities Act of
    1990
PL 101-476, *see* Education of the Handicapped
    Act Amendments of 1990
PL 105-17, *see* Individuals with Disabilities
    Education Act Amendments of 1997

PL 107-110, *see* No Child Left Behind Act of 2001
PL 108-446, *see* Individuals with Disabilities
    Education Improvement Act of 2004
PL 110-325, *see* ADA Amendments of 2008
Prefixes, 103, 232, 263, 356*t*, 623*t*
Prekindergarten, *see* Preschool
Preschool, 185, 325–329, 437, 438
Preservice teacher education, 16, 21, 544–545
Print awareness, 52, 216, 253
Print writing, *see* Manuscript print
Professional development
  in adolescent literacy, 533–534
  biliteracy education model, 626–627
  planning for, 544–545
  in reading instruction, 16, 21, 136
  reciprocal teaching, 396
  see also Education; Teacher knowledge
Progress monitoring, 317–320, 443–444, 538
Pronunciation
  exaggerated, 227, 281
  Spanish language, 609
  spelling and, 258
  ways of marking, 98
  word meaning and, 257
Proofreading, 153, 274, 276, 424–425, 566
Prosody
  comprehension and, 297–298
  in fluency, 296, 296*f*, 297, 500, 528
  overview of, 245–246

Read-alouds, 336–337, 369–370, 506–507, 509
Reading
  adolescents struggling in, 526–529
  assistive technology for, 660–661, 664–667,
    677*t*
  behaviors of good and poor readers, 8, 32, 78,
    366–367, 367*t*, 373–374
  benefits of act of, 499–500
  complexities of, 294–295
  components of, 4–8, 9*t*
  diagnostic measures of, 447–448, 449*t*
  direct instruction in, 17–18, 18*t*, 19*t*, 20
  dyslexia and, 12, 13*f*, 18
  errors in, 223
  finger-point, 126–127, 274
  goal of, 369
  improved by effective instruction, 15
  to learn, 298–299, 518
  neuroscience insights into, 33–36
  older student scores in, 487
  online, 399
  with partners, 379, 380, 380*f*
  phonemic awareness and, 116–119
  predictor of achievement in, 148, 149–151,
    210, 323, 325
  risk factors in, 317*t*
  role of letter recognition in, 145–151
  spelling connections, 243–244
  teacher knowledge and, 16, 246
  unnatural process of, 1, 50, 607
  vocabulary and, 321–322
  see also Decoding; Language comprehension
Reading disabilities
  checklist for, 63*f*–64*f*

content and delivery of instruction for, 15–19, 19*t*
fluency and, 300–302
morphological disorders and, 66–67
phonological disorders and, 60–62
pragmatics and, 78–81
semantic disorders and, 73–75
syntactic disorders and, 69–70
Reading First initiative, 1, 5, 374, 517
Reading Next (Biancarosa & Snow, 2004) on
adolescent achievement, 517–518
adolescent assessment, 532
adolescent literacy, 518, 522*t*
adolescent literacy intervention, 527
adolescent literacy planning, 534
elements of successful programs, 523–524
motivation, 531
needs of adolescent readers, 490
professional development, 534
Reading rate, 245, 297, 442–443, 448, 661
Rehabilitation Act of 1973 (PL 93-112), 688–689, 695–696
Research
on assistive technology, 659–662
on components of reading, 9*t*–10*t*
current, 31–36
on dyslexia, 9, 11–14
evidence-based, 2–4
explaining components of reading, 5–9
future implications for, 36–39
handwriting, 180
impact on teaching practices, 20–21
improving instruction, 1–2
in multisensory structured language education, 463–464
phonemic awareness, 128–130
on response to intervention, 131
see also National Reading Panel (NRP)
Response to intervention (RTI)
assessment methodology in, 432–433, 434
for diagnosing dyslexia, 121–123
English language learners (ELL) and, 606–607
growth of, 365
as an identification tool, 14
instructional delivery method, 431–433
issues in, 454, 693–694
letter knowledge and, 151
overview of, 429–430
research on, 131
as result of federal legislation, 1
technology and, 658
using in multisensory structured language education (MSLE) lessons, 472
see also Interventions; Tiered service delivery
Rhymes
activities for, 217
as a memory device, 568
phonemic awareness and, 116–117, 125–126, 129
phonological processing difficulties and, 61
in Spanish, 616
Root words
common Latin, 239
defined, 231
direct instruction in, 65, 355–356, 597

Greek, 104–105
Latin, 103, 239
sample lesson for, 109–110, 111–112
Spanish language, 625*t*
spelling instruction and, 263
RTI, *see* Response to intervention
Rules
child experimentation with, 326
of the classroom, 481–482
difficulties with language of, 498
English orthography, 260
morphology, 64–65
phonology, 58–59
pragmatics, 75–76
Spanish language, 622
spelling, 9*t*, 269, 276–280
syllable division, 101–102
syntax, 67–70

Scaffolding
for adolescent English language learners (ELL), 509–510
for challenged readers, 464
for literacy, 133
orthographic patterns and, 217
for semantic mapping, 346
student participation in discussion, 336
technology as, 660, 663
Schoolwide literacy plans, *see* Keys to Literacy Planning Model (Sedita, 2004, 2009)
Screening
adolescent literacy, 532–533
consequences of delaying, 436–437
to determine student needs, 490–491
for dyslexia, 14
in fluency, 317–320
focus of, 437
instruments for, 437–439
literacy planning and, 538–539, 540*f*
technology-enhanced, 443–444
through the grades, 439–440
see also Assessment; Evaluation
Section 504 of the Rehabilitation Act of 1973 (PL 93-112), 687, 688–689, 695–696
Segmentation strategies
dyslexia and, 465*t*
instruction for older students, 495–497
phonemic awareness and, 118
phonological processing difficulties and, 61
simultaneous oral spelling (S.O.S.) approach, 274
Self-monitoring, 294, 311–312, 312*f*, 375, 385–387
Self-questioning, 375–376, 390
Semantic mapping
beginnings of, 328
Skills for Organizing and Reading Efficiently (SkORE) system and, 579–580
vocabulary acquisition and, 332, 332*f*, 346–347, 347*f*
see also Mapping
Semantics
activities for, 346–349
defined, 19*t*

Semantics—*continued*
  development of, 71–73
  instruction in, 18*f*
  literacy and, 73–75
  overview of, 70–71
  teacher knowledge of, 46–47
  using cues of to self-correct, 210
Sentences
  activities in, 407–413
  assistive technology for, 677*t*
  with complex contours, 303
  comprehension difficulties, 69–70
  comprehension of complex, 68
  development of use of, 67
  expansion of, 411, 412*f*
  linguistically complex forms of, 304*t*
  reading comprehension skills and, 371–373
  simultaneous oral spelling (S.O.S.) approach
    and, 275–276
  types of, 408–409
Sequencing
  activities for, 151, 156–158, 157*f*, 163–165
  assistive technology for, 675*f*
  dyslexia and, 465*t*
  impairment in ability to, 183
  importance of, 175
Simultaneous oral spelling (S.O.S.), 273–274,
    273*f*, 284
Skills for Organizing and Reading Efficiently
    (SkORE)
  areas addressed, 556–557
  comprehension and, 578–579
  concept mapping, 580–581
  geometric progression and, 581–582
  homework assignments, 563–564
  mastering content subjects, 568–574
  memory training, 567–568
  nonliteral language and, 582–583
  organization under, 557–558
  overview of, 552, 568–570
  phase one, 570–571
  phase three, 574–578
  phase two, 571–574
  Quick Tricks strategies, 561–563
  reducing errors, 564–567
  self-management, 560–561
  semantic mapping, 579–580
  test taking, 583–584
  time management and scheduling, 559–560,
    560*f*
  see also Learning strategies
Sky writing, 132, 186, 203, 220
  see also Letter shapes
SLD, *see* Specific learning disability
Small groups
  area for, 479
  collaborative reading in, 377
  for English language learners (ELL), 329
  inappropriate, 544
  intensity of instruction, 18
  intensity of instruction in, 18, 28
  literacy planning and, 536
  response to intervention (RTI) tiers and, 122,
    431, 472, 606
  for revising and editing, 424
  for students with learning disabilities, 464*t*

  teacher planning for, 478, 479
Socratic method/questioning, 152, 220–221, 271,
    468, 572
Software
  portable keyboards and netbooks, 680–681
  reading assistive technology, 666–667
  text-to-speech software, 681
  visual mapping, 673–674
  visual mapping with templates, 674–677
  voice recognition technology, 679
  word prediction technology, 677–678
  word processing, 680
  writing assistance, 658, 673–681
S.O.S., *see* Simultaneous oral spelling
Sound dictation, *see* Dictation
Sound–symbol correspondences
  activities for, 158–159
  activities in, 26*f*
  blending, 222–223
  consonants, 213*t*
  decoding strategies and, 210–211
  defined, 19*t*
  foundations of, 215–217
  importance of, 209
  instruction in, 18*f*, 151
  letter recognition, 218–222
  orthographic patterns and, 217–218
  spelling and, 252
  strategies for accuracy in, 223
  structural analysis and, 224
  teacher knowledge of, 44–45
  see also Decoding
Spanish language
  alphabet knowledge, 619
  Castillian, 608, 610
  cognates, 330, 331*t*, 343, 510, 613, 622
  demographics, 605–606
  letter–sound correspondences, 619–620, 620*t*
  morphology, 612–613
  phonological awareness, 615–618
  phonology and orthography of, 608–612
  similarities to English, 607, 614–615
  syntax in, 613–614, 622–624
Special education
  biliteracy model and, 627
  determining eligibility for, 433–434, 693
  history of, 685–686
  response to intervention (RTI) and, 14
  tiered service delivery and, 430–432
Specific learning disability (SLD), 10, 429–430,
    454, 690
Speech production, 56, 60, 60–61, 63*f*–64*f*, 258
  see also Articulation
Speech sounds
  checklist for, 63*f*–64*f*
  effects of difficulties in, 60–61
  English compared to Spanish, 610, 610*f*
  in the English language, 260
  instruction in, 494, 495*f*
  sound-to-spelling translations of, 261*t*
  spelling and, 257–258, 266–267
Speech-language impairments, 6, 10, 323
Speed
  articulation, 115*f*, 116
  case study (Pauline), 316
  comprehension and, 9*t*, 297–298

increasing, 302, 308, 311
letter naming, 149–151, 211, 244
neglecting for sense, 311, 312*t*
as predictor for reading achievement, 210
rapid serial naming, 114
rapid word naming and, 243
repeated reading and, 244
Spelling
alphabetic principle and, 153
base words, 231–232
as component of reading, 9*t*, 243–244
development of, 253–254
diagnostic measures of, 447–448, 449*t*
difference to decoding, 260
dyslexia and, 12, 255, 275, 280, 282–283, 286
factors in ability in, 254–256
invented, 118, 125, 126, 243, 264
knowledge necessary for, 256–258
morphology and, 66–67
overview of, 251–253
predictability of, 93–94
reform attempts, 263–264
rules in, 276–279
Spelling instruction
assistive technology for, 673*t*, 677*t*
concurrently with other language domains, 280
for dyslexic students, 282–285
formal, 264–265
importance of, 251, 260–261, 288
on irregular words, 280–282
morphology in, 262–263
multisensory structured language education (MSLE) lesson sample, 473*f*–476*f*
orthography in, 260–262
overview of, 264–265
phonemic awareness for, 258–260
Quick Tricks strategies, 564–565
on regular words, 265–276
rules of, 276–280
sample lesson for, 269–270
Skills for Organizing and Reading Efficiently (SkORE) system and, 564–566, 571
Spanish language, 611–612
through word origin/structure, 96–97, 263–264
translation of speech sounds in, 261*t*
vowels, 262*t*
weekly lesson plan sample, 285–287
weekly spelling lists, 261–262
see also Instruction
SQ3R, *see* Survey, Question, Read, Recite, Review
Stop consonants, 57, 59*t*, 119, 219, 609, 611*t*–612*t*
Strategies, *see* Learning strategies
Stress, *see* Accent; Anxiety
Strokes, handwriting
approach strokes, 197*f*
continuous, 193–194, 193*f*
cursive approach strokes, 194*f*, 195*f*, 196*f*
grouping by similar, 194–196
Structural analysis
advanced morphemes, 238–241
irregular words, 241–243
knowledge necessary for, 214
morphology, 231–232
syllables, 224–231, 232–238

Structural Arithmetic method
addition and subtraction, 637–640
building basic concepts in, 635–636
developing number sense, 636–637
division, 651–654
multiplication, 648–651
number concepts in, 634–635
number symbols in, 635
overview of, 631–633
regrouping, 646–648
steps of, 633–634
teen numbers, 641–646
word problems in, 640–641
see also Mathematics instruction
Struggling readers, *see* Dyslexia; Language disabilities; Specific learning disability (SLD)
Students
assistive technology for, 662–663, 664
connecting with teachers, 481, 482–483
developing belief in selves, 510–511
with disabilities, 376, 687–688, 688*t*
identifying strengths of, 511, 512*f*
need for structure, 469
using interests of, 503
Subtraction, *see* Mathematics instruction
Suffixes
Anglo-Saxon, 102
common, 356*t*
defined, 231
Latin, 103
sorting, 356, 357*f*–358*f*
Spanish, 624*t*
spelling instruction and, 263
syllable division and, 235
Summarization, 370, 375, 574–575, 667, 668
Summative assessment, 440, 532
Summative data collection, 428–429
Survey, Question, Read, Recite, Review (SQ3R, 1970), 569, 600
Syllable patterns
activities in, 162–163, 225
Anglo-Saxon, 101–102
common, 233–235
Greek, 104
Latin, 103
Spanish, 608–609, 610*t*
see also Accent
Syllables
awareness of, 115, 115*f*, 224–225
boundaries of, 101
in decoding, 209
defined, 19*t*
division of, 232–238, 237*f*, 238*f*
instruction in, 18*f*, 96
longer words, 240
morphemes and, 231
origins of, 97*f*
Spanish, 617–618
splitting, 117–118
structural analysis and, 224
teacher knowledge of, 45
types of, 225–231, 226*t*
see also Closed syllables; Open syllables
Syntax
awareness of, 326
biliteracy and, 607–608

Syntax—*continued*
  defined, 19*t*
  development of, 67–69
  instruction in, 18*f*
  literacy and, 69–70
  overview of, 67
  self-correction, 210
  Spanish, 613–614
  teacher knowledge of, 46

Teacher knowledge
  decoding skills, 211–212, 246
  effective instruction and, 14–19
  lack of, 21
  language components, 53, 131–132, 246, 287
  lesson planning, 467, 471
  in linguistic tasks, 1–2
  modeling good questioning, 386
  in multisensory structured language education
    (MSLE) strategies, 26–27, 44–47
  novice, 477
  struggling students and, 492–493
  student achievement and, 9*t*, 10*t*, 16–17,
    207–208
  on student strategies, 551, 552
  see also Education; Professional development
Teachers
  connecting with students, 481, 482–483
  organization of, 480–481
  organizing personal space, 480–481
  usage of different sensory modalities, 44–47
Technology
  assessment, 443–444
  concept mapping, 660
  for handwriting, 183, 201–203, 204
  increasing motivation to read, 511
  influence of, 657
  Internet and comprehension, 398–399
  new words for, 102
  reading comprehension and, 398
  for screening and progress monitoring,
    443–444
  for students with learning disabilities, 465*t*
  vocabulary building, 359
  word-level disabilities and, 507–508
  writing and, 672
Teeth position for articulation, 158, 218, 259*t*,
    273, 609–610
Texts
  choosing appropriate, 339
  comprehending longer, 373–374
  controlled, 500–502, 502*f*
  decodable, 500
  determining difficulty level, 502–503
  electronic, 507–508
  enriched, 500, 503, 504*f*, 506–507
  noncontrolled, 502–506
  for practice, 311
  preparing with Skills for Organizing and
    Reading Efficiently (SkORE), 570–571
  rare words in, 334*t*
Text-to-speech software
  annotating, 668, 668*f*
  outlines and notes in, 669*f*

  overview of, 681
  for reading difficulties, 507, 677*t*, 680*f*
  removing decoding burden, 664–665
  research on, 660–661
Tiered service delivery
  for adolescent readers, 491
  for literacy instruction, 535, 537*f*
  multisensory structured language education
    (MSLE) lessons and, 472
  technology and, 658
  see also Response to intervention (RTI)
Tongue position
  awareness of, 218
  in decoding instruction, 219
  simultaneous oral spelling (S.O.S.) approach,
    273
  Spanish language, 609, 610
  vowel and consonant sounds, 158–159
Tracing, 186, 197–198, 203, 281, 565–566

Universal design for learning (UDL), 398, 657
Uppercase letters
  activities, 156–158, 162
  cursive, 193*f*
  handwriting and, 190
  instruction in, 151
  manuscript print, 192*f*

Visual, auditory, kinesthetic, tactile (VAKT), 19,
    19*t*, 186
Visual cues, 273–274, 273*f*, 382
Visual discovery, 271, 279, 620, 626*t*
Visual mapping, 673–677, 673*t*, 675*f*
Vocabulary
  academic, 329, 334
  acquisition of, 72, 73–74
  as component of reading, 7–8, 9*t*, 322–325
  comprehension and, 325
  early acquisition of, 325–328
  importance of, 321–322, 325
  learning/reading disabilities and, 330
  rare words, 334*t*
  reading comprehension and, 72–73
  school age acquisition of, 329–331
  size of, 325, 326*t*, 329, 360
  word meanings and, 70–71
  see also Word meanings
Vocabulary instruction
  assessment, 442, 451*t*
  assistive technology for, 661, 677*t*
  in the content class, 524, 525
  English language learners (ELL), 330–331, 343,
    346, 530, 625–626
  framework for, 333–341
  goals of, 331–332
  guidelines for, 342
  independent word-learning strategies, 352–359
  literacy planning and, 541
  morphology and, 354–359
  older students and, 506–508
  routines in, 344–346
  Skills for Organizing and Reading Efficiently
    (SkORE) system and, 571

strategies and activities, 346–352
systematic, 329
technology to support, 359
using multiple strategies in, 360
word choice, 342–344
see also Instruction
Voice recognition technology
accents and, 679
for handwriting instruction, 202
research on, 660
sentence structure difficulties and, 677t
software for, 679–680
as standard feature, 657
for working memory issues, 673t
Vowel digraphs, 100, 102–103, 217, 220, 234
Vowel prefix/suffix, 231, 232
Vowel–consonant patterns, 233–236
Vowel-consonant-*e* syllable
activities, 228
defined, 101
examples, 214t, 226t
patterns of, 103
Spanish language, 609, 610t
Vowel-pair syllable
activities for, 228–229
defined, 101
division of, 235
examples, 214t, 226t
Spanish, 609, 610t
Vowels
accent and, 227
activities, 158–159
Anglo-Saxon forms of, 98
articulatory gestures and, 119–120
graphemes, 99, 100t
history of shift in, 96
infrequent spellings of, 262t
mouth position for, 58f, 59f, 258, 258f
oral production of, 57
phonic symbols for, 59f
in polysyllabic words, 240–241
sound-to-spelling translations, 261t
Spanish language, 608, 610t, 614
spelling, 58t, 267–269
teaching sounds of, 494, 495f
using in the decoding process, 214t

Watch Our Writing (W.O.W.), 191f
Weekly spelling lists, 261–262, 281–282, 286, 286t
Word meanings
accent and, 257
defined, 332
instruction in, 329
learning disabilities and, 330
reading comprehension and, 74
strategies in, 352–359
using context to discover, 353
see also Vocabulary
Word origins
discussing for irregular words, 281
early English, 94–96
instruction through, 96–97
matrix, 97f
spelling and, 263–264

student overview in, 243
see also Etymology
Word prediction technology
to assist with spelling, 673t, 677t
to assist with word retrieval and vocabulary, 677t
for handwriting instruction, 203
overview of, 677–678
research on, 660
Word processing
to assist with graphomotor difficulties, 677t
to assist with sequencing, 675f
to assist with working memory, 680f
software, 680
to support writing, 659, 671, 672
Word recognition
automaticity in, 201, 493–494
as component of reading, 9t
deficits in, 11
role in reading, 9t
in the Rope Model for Reading, 324f
vocabulary and, 323–324
Word-level disabilities
adolescents, 488–489
application of skills in, 499–506
assessment in, 489–493
classroom management and, 508–509
development of language skills and, 506–508
English language learners (ELL) and, 509–510
instruction for, 493–499
society and, 512
student self-confidence and, 510–511
technology and, 507–508
Word-level instruction
blending and segmenting, 495–497
morphology, 499
multisyllabic words, 497–498
for older students, 489
orthography, 498–499
overview of, 493
sounds, 494–495, 495f
teacher preparation for, 492–493
Working memory
assistive technology for, 673t, 677t, 680f
barriers to writing and, 672
case study (Jocelyn), 316
importance of to literacy, 82–83
letter reversals and, 182–183
morphological knowledge and, 66
multisensory instruction and, 39–40
Skills for Organizing and Reading Efficiently (SkORE) system and, 568
study skills and, 667
see also Memory
W.O.W., *see* Watch Our Writing (W.O.W.)
Writing
adolescents struggling in, 526–529
assistive technology for, 659, 671–681, 673t
barriers to, 672, 673t
as component of reading, 10t
considering needs of reader in, 81
in the content class, 525–526
diagnostic measures of, 447–448, 449t
difficulties with, 406
functions of, 406
instruction in, 406, 407–413

Writing—*continued*
  to learn letter names, 151
  mathematics equations, 638
  process of, 671–672
  skills required for, 405–406
  as a sophisticated language act, 54
  templates for, 674–677, 675*f*
  types of, 413–414
  see also Composition

Written language
  curriculum and instruction in, 96–97
  diagnostic measures of, 451*t*
  history of, 95–96, 95*t*
  instruction in, 50
  invented spelling in, 118, 125, 126, 243, 264
  oral language and, 49–54
  requirements to understanding, 52